MICROSOFT®

Office 2003

Essential Concepts and Techniques

SECOND EDITION

WORD 2003 EXCEL 2003 ACCESS 2003 POWERPOINT 2003

Gary B. Shelly
Thomas J. Cashman
Misty E. Vermaat

Contributing Authors
Steven G. Forsythe
Mary Z. Last
Philip J. Pratt
James S. Quasney
Susan L. Sebok

THOMSON COURSE TECHNOLOGY™

THOMSON COURSE TECHNOLOGY
25 THOMSON PLACE
BOSTON MA 02210

SHELLY CASHMAN SERIES®

Australia • Canada • Denmark • Japan • Mexico • New Zealand • Philippines • Puerto Rico • Singapore • South Africa
Spain • United Kingdom • United States

THOMSON
COURSE TECHNOLOGY

Microsoft Office 2003
Essential Concepts and Techniques, Second Edition

Gary B. Shelly
Thomas J. Cashman
Misty E. Vermaat

Executive Editor:
Alexandra Arnold

Product Manager:
Reed Cotter

Associate Product Manager:
Heather Hawkins

Editorial Assistant:
Klenda Martinez

Product Marketing Manager:
Dana Merk

Marketing Coordinator/ Copywriter:
Melissa Marcoux

Print Buyer:
Justin Palmeiro

Series Consulting Editor:
Jim Quasney

Director of Production:
Patty Stephan

Production Editor:
Pamela Elizian

Production Assistant:
Erin Dowler

Development Editor:
Ginny Harvey

Copy Editors/Proofreaders:
Ginny Harvey
Nancy Lamm
Lyn Markowicz
Lori Silfen
Lisa Jedlicka
Kim Kosmatka
Marilyn Martin

Interior Design:
Becky Herrington

Cover Design:
Richard Herrera

Illustrators:
Richard Herrera
Andrew Bartel
Ken Russo

Compositors:
Jeanne Black
Andrew Bartel
Kellee LaVars
Kenny Tran
Michelle French

Indexer:
Cristina Haley

Printer:
Banta Menasha

Printed in the United States of America

1 2 3 4 5 6 7 8 9 10
BM 09 08 07 06

For more information, contact Thomson Course Technology
25 Thomson Place
Boston, Massachusetts 02210

Or find us on the World Wide Web at:
www.course.com

ISBN 1-4188-5947-8

PHOTO CREDITS: Microsoft Windows XP *Project 1, page WIN 5* Dell computer, monitor, and printer, Courtesy of Dell, Inc.; *page WIN 6* Dell computer and monitor, Courtesy of Dell, Inc.; Microsoft PowerPoint 2003 *Project 1, page PPT 6* notebook computer, Courtesy of PhotoDisc, Inc.

Contents

Preface vii
To the Student xiv

MICROSOFT Windows XP and Office 2003

Project One

Introduction to Microsoft Windows XP and Office 2003

Objectives WIN 4
Introduction WIN 4
Microsoft Windows XP Operating Systems WIN 4
Microsoft Windows XP Professional WIN 6
What Is a User Interface? WIN 6
Launching Microsoft Windows XP WIN 7
The Windows XP User Interface WIN 8
Logging On to the Computer WIN 9
The Windows XP Desktop WIN 11
Displaying the Start Menu WIN 11
Adding an Icon to the Desktop WIN 15
Opening a Window Using a Desktop Icon WIN 17
The My Computer Window WIN 18
Minimizing a Window WIN 19
Maximizing and Restoring a Window WIN 21
Closing a Window WIN 24
Opening a Window Using the Start Menu WIN 25
The My Documents Window WIN 27
Moving a Window by Dragging WIN 27
Expanding an Area WIN 28
Scrolling in a Window WIN 30
Sizing a Window by Dragging WIN 32
Collapsing an Area WIN 33
Resizing a Window WIN 34
Closing a Window WIN 34
Deleting a Desktop Icon by Right-Dragging WIN 35
Summary of Mouse and Windows Operations WIN 36
The Keyboard and Keyboard Shortcuts WIN 37
Launching an Application Program WIN 37
Launching an Application Using the Start Menu WIN 38
Windows Explorer WIN 40
Launching Windows Explorer WIN 40
Expanding a Folder WIN 42
Expanding a Drive WIN 43
Displaying Files and Folders in Windows Explorer WIN 45
Displaying Drive and Folder Contents WIN 45
Launching an Application Program from Windows Explorer WIN 46
Closing Folder Expansions WIN 49
Copying, Moving, Renaming, and Deleting Files in Windows Explorer WIN 50
Copying Files in Windows Explorer WIN 51
Displaying the Contents of the My Pictures Folder WIN 52
Renaming Files and Folders WIN 53
Deleting Files in Windows Explorer WIN 55
Removing the Status Bar WIN 56
Quitting Windows Explorer WIN 57
Using Help and Support WIN 57
Launching Help and Support WIN 57
Browsing for Help Topics in the Table of Contents WIN 59
Using the Help and Support Center Index WIN 61
Logging Off and Turning Off the Computer WIN 63
What Is Microsoft Office 2003? WIN 67
The Internet, World Wide Web, and Intranets WIN 68
Office and the Internet WIN 68
Microsoft Office Word 2003 WIN 69
Word and the Internet WIN 70
Microsoft Office Excel 2003 WIN 71
Excel and the Internet WIN 71
Microsoft Office Access 2003 WIN 73
Access and the Internet WIN 73
Microsoft Office PowerPoint 2003 WIN 75
PowerPoint and the Internet WIN 76
The Web Toolbar WIN 77
Microsoft Office Publisher 2003 WIN 77
Publisher and the Internet WIN 78
Microsoft Office FrontPage 2003 WIN 78
Microsoft Office Outlook 2003 WIN 79
The Microsoft Office 2003 Help System WIN 81
Project Summary WIN 82
What You Should Know WIN 82
Learn It Online WIN 83
In the Lab WIN 84

MICROSOFT® OFFICE Word 2003

Project One

Creating and Editing a Word Document

Objectives WD 4
What Is Microsoft Office Word 2003? WD 4
Project One — Grand Prix Announcement WD 5
Starting and Customizing Word WD 6

The Word Window WD 10
Document Window WD 10
Menu Bar and Toolbars WD 12
Resetting Menus and Toolbars WD 15
Speech Recognition WD 16
Entering Text WD 16
Typing Text WD 17
Entering Blank Lines in a Document WD 20
Displaying Formatting Marks WD 20
Entering More Text WD 22
Using Wordwrap WD 22
Entering Text that Scrolls the Document Window WD 23
Checking Spelling and Grammar as You Type WD 25
Saving a Document WD 28
Formatting Paragraphs and Characters in a Document WD 31
Selecting and Formatting Paragraphs and Characters WD 33
Selecting Multiple Paragraphs WD 33
Changing the Font Size of Text WD 34
Changing the Font of Text WD 36
Right-Align a Paragraph WD 36
Center a Paragraph WD 38
Undoing, Redoing, and Repeating Commands or Actions WD 39
Selecting a Line and Formatting It WD 40
Italicizing Text WD 41
Underlining Text WD 42
Scrolling WD 43
Selecting a Group of Words WD 43
Bolding Text WD 44
Inserting Clip Art in a Word Document WD 45
Inserting Clip Art WD 46
Resizing a Graphic WD 49
Saving an Existing Document with the Same File Name WD 51
Printing a Document WD 53
Quitting Word WD 54
Starting Word and Opening a Document WD 55
Correcting Errors WD 56
Types of Changes Made to Documents WD 56
Inserting Text in an Existing Document WD 57
Deleting Text from an Existing Document WD 58
Closing the Entire Document WD 59
Word Help System WD 60
Using the Type a Question for Help Box WD 60
Quitting Word WD 62
Project Summary WD 62
What You Should Know WD 63
Learn It Online WD 64
Apply Your Knowledge WD 65
In the Lab WD 67
Cases and Places WD 71

MICROSOFT® OFFICE

Excel 2003

Project One

Creating a Worksheet and an Embedded Chart

Objectives EX 4
What Is Microsoft Office Excel 2003? EX 4
Project One — Extreme Blading Second Quarter Sales EX 5
Starting and Customizing Excel EX 6
The Excel Worksheet EX 9
The Worksheet EX 10
Worksheet Window EX 11
Menu Bar EX 11
Standard Toolbar and Formatting Toolbar EX 13
Formula Bar EX 14
Status Bar EX 14
Speech Recognition and Speech Playback EX 15
Selecting a Cell EX 16
Entering Text EX 16
Entering the Worksheet Titles EX 17
Correcting a Mistake while Typing EX 18
AutoCorrect EX 18
Entering Column Titles EX 19
Entering Row Titles EX 20
Entering Numbers EX 21
Calculating a Sum EX 23
Using the Fill Handle to Copy a Cell to Adjacent Cells EX 24
Determining Multiple Totals at the Same Time EX 26
Formatting the Worksheet EX 28
Font Type, Style, Size, and Color EX 28
Changing the Font Type EX 29
Bolding a Cell EX 30
Increasing the Font Size EX 30
Changing the Font Color of a Cell Entry EX 31
Centering a Cell Entry across Columns by Merging Cells EX 32
Formatting the Worksheet Subtitle EX 33
Using AutoFormat to Format the Body of a Worksheet EX 34
Using the Name Box to Select a Cell EX 36
Adding a 3-D Clustered Column Chart to the Worksheet EX 38
Saving a Workbook EX 42
Printing a Worksheet EX 44
Quitting Excel EX 46
Starting Excel and Opening a Workbook EX 47
AutoCalculate EX 48
Correcting Errors EX 50
Correcting Errors While You Are Typing Data into a Cell EX 50
Correcting Errors After Entering Data into a Cell EX 50
Undoing the Last Cell Entry EX 51
Clearing a Cell or Range of Cells EX 52
Clearing the Entire Worksheet EX 52
Excel Help System EX 53
Obtaining Help Using the Type a Question for Help Box on the Menu Bar EX 53
Quitting Excel EX 54
Project Summary EX 55
What You Should Know EX 55
Learn It Online EX 56

Apply Your Knowledge **EX 57**
In the Lab **EX 58**
Cases and Places **EX 63**

Project One

Creating and Using a Database

Objectives **AC 4**
What Is Microsoft Office Access 2003? **AC 4**
What Is New in Access? **AC 4**
Project One — Ashton James College Database **AC 5**
Starting Access **AC 7**
Speech Recognition **AC 9**
Creating a New Database **AC 10**
The Access Window **AC 12**
Title Bar AC 12
Menu Bar AC 12
Toolbars AC 13
Taskbar AC 13
Status Bar AC 13
Database Window AC 13
Shortcut Menus AC 13
AutoCorrect AC 15
Creating a Table **AC 15**
Defining the Fields AC 18
Correcting Errors in the Structure AC 21
Closing and Saving a Table **AC 21**
Adding Records to a Table **AC 22**
Correcting Errors in the Data AC 25
Closing a Table and Database and Quitting Access **AC 25**
Opening a Database **AC 26**
Adding Additional Records **AC 27**
Previewing and Printing the Contents of a Table **AC 29**
Creating Additional Tables **AC 32**
Adding Records to the Additional Table AC 33
Using Queries **AC 34**
Using a Query AC 36
Using a Form to View Data **AC 38**
Creating a Form AC 38
Closing and Saving the Form AC 39
Opening the Saved Form AC 40
Using the Form AC 41
Switching Between Form View and Datasheet View AC 41
Creating a Report **AC 42**
Printing the Report AC 46
Closing the Database **AC 47**
Access Help System **AC 47**
Obtaining Help Using the Type a Question for Help Box on the Menu Bar AC 48
Quitting Access **AC 50**
Designing a Database **AC 50**
Project Summary **AC 52**
What You Should Know **AC 52**
Learn It Online **AC 53**
Apply Your Knowledge **AC 54**
In the Lab **AC 56**
Cases and Places **AC 63**

MICROSOFT® OFFICE
PowerPoint 2003

Project One

Using a Design Template and Text Slide Layout to Create a Presentation

Objectives **PPT 4**
What Is Microsoft Office PowerPoint 2003? **PPT 7**
Project One — Strategies for College Success **PPT 7**
Starting and Customizing PowerPoint **PPT 8**
The PowerPoint Window **PPT 11**
PowerPoint Views PPT 12
Placeholders, Text Areas, Mouse Pointer, and Scroll Bars PPT 13
Status Bar, Menu Bar, Standard Toolbar, Formatting Toolbar, and Drawing Toolbar PPT 14
Speech Recognition **PPT 18**
Choosing a Design Template **PPT 18**
Creating a Title Slide **PPT 21**
Entering the Presentation Title PPT 21
Correcting a Mistake When Typing PPT 22
Entering the Presentation Subtitle PPT 23
Text Attributes **PPT 24**
Changing the Style of Text to Italic PPT 25
Changing the Font Size PPT 26
Saving the Presentation on a Floppy Disk **PPT 27**
Adding a New Slide to a Presentation **PPT 30**
Creating a Text Slide with a Single-Level Bulleted List **PPT 32**
Entering a Slide Title PPT 32
Selecting a Text Placeholder PPT 33
Typing a Single-Level Bulleted List PPT 33
Creating a Text Slide with a Multi-Level Bulleted List **PPT 35**
Adding New Slides and Entering Slide Titles PPT 35
Typing a Multi-Level Bulleted List PPT 36
Creating a Third-Level Paragraph PPT 40
Ending a Slide Show with a Black Slide **PPT 42**
Saving a Presentation with the Same File Name **PPT 43**
Moving to Another Slide in Normal View **PPT 44**
Using the Scroll Box on the Slide Pane to Move to Another Slide PPT 44
Viewing the Presentation in Slide Show View **PPT 46**
Starting Slide Show View PPT 46
Advancing Through a Slide Show Manually PPT 47
Using the Popup Menu to Go to a Specific Slide PPT 48
Using the Popup Menu to End a Slide Show PPT 49
Quitting PowerPoint **PPT 50**
Starting PowerPoint and Opening a Presentation **PPT 51**
Checking a Presentation for Spelling and Consistency **PPT 53**
Checking a Presentation for Spelling Errors PPT 53
Starting the Spelling Checker PPT 54
Correcting Errors **PPT 56**
Types of Corrections Made to Presentations PPT 56
Deleting Text PPT 56
Replacing Text in an Existing Slide PPT 56
Displaying a Presentation in Black and White **PPT 56**
Printing a Presentation **PPT 59**
Saving Before Printing PPT 59
Printing the Presentation PPT 60
Making a Transparency PPT 61

PowerPoint Help System **PPT 62**
Obtaining Help Using the Type a Question for Help Box on the Menu Bar PPT 62
Quitting PowerPoint PPT 64
Project Summary **PPT 65**
What You Should Know **PPT 66**
Learn It Online **PPT 67**
Apply Your Knowledge **PPT 68**
In the Lab **PPT 69**
Cases and Places **PPT 79**

Appendix A

Microsoft Office Help System

Using the Microsoft Office Help System **APP 1**
Navigating the Word Help System **APP 2**
The Office Assistant APP 6
Question Mark Button in Dialog Boxes and Help Icon in Task Panes APP 7
Other Help Commands on the Help Menu **APP 8**
Use Help **APP 10**

Appendix B

Speech and Handwriting Recognition and Speech Playback

Introduction **APP 11**
The Language Bar APP 11
Buttons on the Language Bar APP 12
Customizing the Language Bar APP 12
Speech Recognition **APP 15**
Getting Started with Speech Recognition APP 16
Using Speech Recognition APP 18
Handwriting Recognition **APP 19**
Writing Pad APP 19
Write Anywhere APP 21
Drawing Pad APP 21
On-Screen Keyboard APP 22
Speech Playback **APP 22**
Customizing Speech Playback APP 23

Appendix C

Publishing Office Web Pages to a Web Server

Using Web Folders to Publish Office Web Pages APP 24
Using FTP to Publish Office Web Pages APP 24

Appendix D

Changing Screen Resolution and Resetting the Word Toolbars and Menus

Changing Screen Resolution **APP 25**
Resetting the Word Toolbars and Menus **APP 27**
Resetting the Standard and Formatting Toolbars APP 27
Resetting the Word Menus APP 29

Appendix E

Microsoft Office Specialist Certification

What Is Microsoft Office Specialist Certification? **APP 31**
Why Should You Be Certified? **APP 31**
The Microsoft Office Specialist Certification Exams **APP 32**
How to Prepare for the Microsoft Office Specialist Certification Exams **APP 32**
How to Find an Authorized Testing Center **APP 32**
Shelly Cashman Series Microsoft Office Specialist Center **APP 32**

Index **IND 1**

Quick Reference Summary **QR 1**

Microsoft Office 2003 CourseCard

Preface

The Shelly Cashman Series® offers the finest textbooks in computer education. We are proud of the fact that our series of Microsoft Office 4.3, Microsoft Office 95, Microsoft Office 97, Microsoft Office 2000, and Microsoft Office XP textbooks have been the most widely used books in education. With each new edition of our Office books, we have made significant improvements based on the software and comments made by the instructors and students. This *Microsoft Office 2003: Essential Concepts and Techniques, Second Edition* continues with the innovation, quality, and reliability that you have come to expect from the Shelly Cashman Series. This edition includes the following enhancements:

- Updated Introduction to Windows XP and Office 2003 project that covers both file management and Windows XP Service Pack 2
- All new In the Lab exercises for each Project
- Tear-off quick reference Office 2003 CourseCard, providing Office skills at your fingertips

In this *Microsoft Office 2003* book, you will find an educationally sound, highly visual, and easy-to-follow pedagogy that combines a vastly improved step-by-step approach with corresponding screens. All projects and exercises in this book are designed to take full advantage of the Office 2003 enhancements. The popular Other Ways and More About features offer in-depth knowledge of the Office applications. The new Q&A feature offers students a way to solidify important application concepts. The Learn It Online page presents a wealth of additional exercises to ensure your students have all the reinforcement they need. The project material is developed to ensure that students will see the importance of learning how to use the Office applications for future coursework.

Objectives of This Textbook

Microsoft Office 2003: Essential Concepts and Techniques, Second Edition is intended for a one-credit hour course or a regular semester course that includes a five-to-six-week introduction to Office 2003. No experience with a computer is assumed, and no mathematics beyond the high school freshman level is required. The objectives of this book are:

- To teach the fundamentals of Microsoft Office Word 2003, Microsoft Office Excel 2003, Microsoft Office Access 2003, Microsoft Office PowerPoint 2003, and Microsoft Windows XP
- To expose students to practical examples of the computer as a useful tool
- To acquaint students with the proper procedures to create documents, worksheets, databases, and presentations suitable for coursework, professional purposes, and personal use
- To help students discover the underlying functionality of Office 2003 so they can become more productive
- To develop an exercise-oriented approach that allows learning by doing
- To introduce students to new input technologies
- To encourage independent study, and help those who are working alone

The Shelly Cashman Approach

Features of the Shelly Cashman Series *Microsoft Office 2003* books include:

- **Project Orientation:** Each project in the book presents a practical problem and complete solution in an easy-to-understand approach.

Other Ways

1. On Tools menu click Options, click View tab, click All check box, click OK button
2. Press CTRL+SHIFT+ASTERISK (*)
3. In Voice Command mode, say "Show Hide

More About

Zooming

If text is too small to read on the screen, you can zoom the document by clicking View on the menu bar, clicking Zoom, selecting the desired percentage, and then clicking the OK button. Changing the zoom percent has no effect on the printed document.

Q&A

Q: Can I change the bullet characters?

A: Yes. While default bullets are part of the design templates, they can be modified or deleted. You can use symbols, numbers, and picture files as revised bullets. You also can change their size

- **Step-by-Step, Screen-by-Screen Instructions:** Each of the tasks required to complete a project is identified throughout the project. Full-color screens with call outs accompany the steps.
- **Thoroughly Tested Projects:** Unparalleled quality is ensured because every screen in the book is produced by the author only after performing a step, and then each project must pass Course Technology's award-winning Quality Assurance program.
- **Other Ways Boxes and Quick Reference Summary:** The Other Ways boxes displayed at the end of most of the step-by-step sequences specify the other ways to do the task completed in the steps. Thus, the steps and the Other Ways box make a comprehensive reference unit.
- **More About and Q&A Features:** These marginal annotations provide background information, tips, and answers to common questions that complement the topics covered, adding depth and perspective to the learning process.
- **Integration of the World Wide Web:** The World Wide Web is integrated into the Office 2003 learning experience by (1) More About annotations that send students to Web sites for up-to-date information and alternative approaches to tasks; (2) a Microsoft Office Specialist Certification Web page so students can prepare for the certification examinations; (3) a Quick Reference Summary Web page that summarizes the ways to complete tasks (mouse, menu, shortcut menu, and keyboard); and (4) the Learn It Online page at the end of each project, which has project reinforcement exercises, learning games, and other types of student activities.

Organization of This Textbook

Microsoft Office 2003: Essential Concepts and Techniques, Second Edition provides basic instruction on how to use the Office 2003 applications. The material is divided into five projects, five appendices, and a Quick Reference Summary.

Microsoft Windows XP and Office 2003 – Introduction to Microsoft Windows XP and Office 2003 In this project, students learn about user interfaces, Windows XP, Windows Explorer, and each Office 2003 application. Topics include using the mouse; minimizing, maximizing, and restoring windows; closing and reopening windows; sizing and scrolling windows; launching and quitting an application; displaying the contents of a folder; expanding and collapsing a folder; creating a folder; selecting and copying a group of files; renaming and deleting a file and a folder; using Windows XP Help; and shutting down Windows XP. Topics pertaining to Office 2003 include a brief explanation of Microsoft Office Word 2003; Microsoft Office Excel 2003; Microsoft Office Access 2003; Microsoft Office PowerPoint 2003; Microsoft Office Publisher 2003; Microsoft Office FrontPage 2003; and Microsoft Office Outlook 2003 and examples of how these applications take advantage of the Internet and World Wide Web.

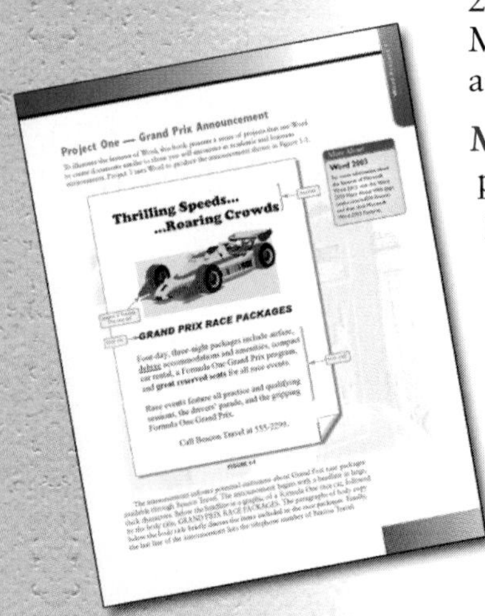

Microsoft Office Word 2003 – Creating and Editing a Word Document In this project, students are introduced to Word terminology and the Word window by preparing an announcement. Topics include starting and quitting Word; entering text; checking spelling while typing; saving a document; selecting characters, words, lines, and paragraphs; changing the font and font size of text; centering, right-aligning, bolding, and italicizing text; undoing commands and actions; inserting clip art in a document; resizing a graphic; printing a document; opening a document; correcting errors; and using the Word Help system.

Microsoft Office Excel 2003 – Creating a Worksheet and Embedded Chart In this project, students are introduced to Excel terminology, the Excel window, speech recognition and speech playback, and the basic characteristics of a worksheet and workbook. Topics include starting and quitting Excel; customizing Excel; entering text and numbers; selecting a range; using the AutoSum button; copying using the fill handle; changing font size and color; formatting in bold; centering across columns; using the AutoFormat command; charting using the ChartWizard; saving and opening a workbook; editing a worksheet; using the AutoCalculate area; and using the Excel Help system.

Microsoft Office Access 2003 – Creating and Using a Database In this project, students are introduced to the concept of a database and shown how to use Access 2003 to create a database. Topics include creating a database; creating a table; defining the fields in a table; opening a table; adding records to a table; closing a table; and previewing and printing the contents of a table. Other topics in this project include creating a query using the Simple Query Wizard; using a form to view data; using the Report Wizard to create a report; and using the Access Help system. Students also learn how to design a database to eliminate redundancy.

Microsoft Office PowerPoint 2003 – Using a Design Template and Text Slide Layout to Create a Presentation In this project, students are introduced to PowerPoint terminology, the PowerPoint window, and the basics of creating a bulleted list presentation. Topics include choosing a design template by using a task pane; creating a title slide and text slides with single and multi-level bulleted lists; changing the font size and font style; ending a slide show with a black slide; saving a presentation; viewing the slides in a presentation; checking a presentation for spelling errors; printing copies of the slides; and using the PowerPoint Help system.

Appendices The book includes five appendices. Appendix A presents an introduction to the Microsoft Office Help system. Appendix B describes how to use the Office speech and handwriting recognition and speech playback capabilities. Appendix C explains how to publish Web pages to a Web server. Appendix D shows how to change the screen resolution and reset the menus and toolbars. Appendix E introduces students to Microsoft Office Specialist certification.

Quick Reference Summary In Office 2003, you can accomplish a task in a number of ways, such as using the mouse, menu, shortcut menu, and keyboard. The Quick Reference Summary at the back of the book provides a quick reference to each task presented.

Microsoft Office 2003 CourseCard Keep your Office skills fresh with this quick reference tool! The Microsoft Office 2003 CourseCard allows you to quickly learn the basics of Office 2003 and access tips and tricks long after your class is complete. This highly visual, 4-color, six-sided CourseCard enables you to effectively utilize key content, reinforces key subject matter and provides solutions to common situations, helps you navigate through the most important menu tools using a simple table of contents model, improves productivity and saves time, effectively shows what you see on your monitor, and provides advanced users with a clear reference guide to more challenging content.

End-of-Project Student Activities

A notable strength of the Shelly Cashman Series *Microsoft Office 2003* books is the extensive student activities at the end of each project. Well-structured student activities can make the difference between students merely participating in a class and students retaining the information they learn. The activities in the Shelly Cashman Series *Office* books include the following.

- **What You Should Know** A listing of the tasks completed within a project together with the pages on which the step-by-step, screen-by-screen explanations appear.

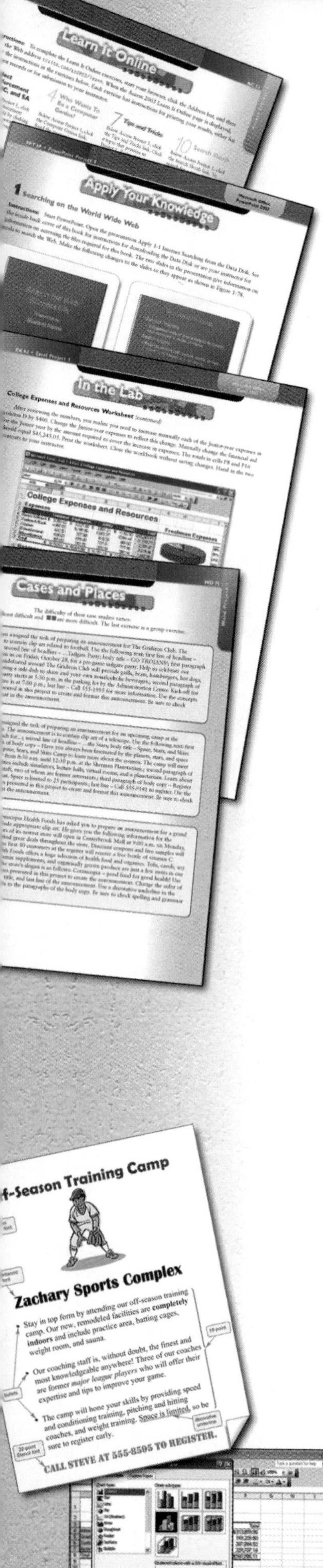

- **Learn It Online** Every project features a Learn It Online page that comprises twelve exercises. These exercises include True/False, Multiple Choice, Short Answer, Flash Cards, Practice Test, Learning Games, Tips and Tricks, Newsgroup usage, Expanding Your Horizons, Search Sleuth, Office Online Training, and Office Marketplace.
- **Apply Your Knowledge** This exercise usually requires students to open and manipulate a file on the Data Disk that parallels the activities learned in the project. To obtain a copy of the Data Disk, follow the instructions on the inside back cover of this textbook.
- **In the Lab** Three in-depth assignments per project require students to utilize the project concepts and techniques to solve problems on a computer.
- **Cases and Places** Five unique real-world case-study situations, including one small-group activity.

Instructor Resources CD-ROM

The Shelly Cashman Series is dedicated to providing you with all of the tools you need to make your class a success. Information on all supplementary materials is available through your Course Technology representative or by calling one of the following telephone numbers: Colleges and Universities, 1-800-648-7450; High Schools, 1-800-824-5179; Private Career Colleges, 1-800-477-3692; Canada, 1-800-268-2222; Corporations with IT Training Centers, 1-800-477-3692; and Government Agencies, Health-Care Organizations, and Correctional Facilities, 1-800-477-3692.

The Instructor Resources for this textbook include both teaching and testing aids. The contents of each item on the Instructor Resources CD-ROM (ISBN 0-619-25479-3) are described below.

INSTRUCTOR'S MANUAL The Instructor's Manual is made up of Microsoft Word files, which include detailed lesson plans with page number references, lecture notes, teaching tips, classroom activities, discussion topics, projects to assign, and transparency references. The transparencies are available through the Figure Files described below.

LECTURE SUCCESS SYSTEM The Lecture Success System consists of intermediate files that correspond to certain figures in the book, allowing you to step through the creation of an application in a project during a lecture without entering large amounts of data.

SYLLABUS Sample syllabi, which can be customized easily to a course, are included. The syllabi cover policies, class and lab assignments and exams, and procedural information.

FIGURE FILES Illustrations for every figure in the textbook are available in electronic form. Use this ancillary to present a slide show in lecture or to print transparencies for use in lecture with an overhead projector. If you have a personal computer and LCD device, this ancillary can be an effective tool for presenting lectures.

POWERPOINT PRESENTATIONS PowerPoint Presentations is a multimedia lecture presentation system that provides slides for each project. Presentations are based on project objectives. Use this presentation system to present well-organized lectures that are both interesting and knowledge based. PowerPoint Presentations provides consistent coverage at schools that use multiple lecturers.

SOLUTIONS TO EXERCISES Solutions are included for the end-of-project exercises, as well as the Project Reinforcement exercises.

RUBRICS AND ANNOTATED SOLUTION FILES The grading rubrics provide a customizable framework for assigning point values to the laboratory exercises. Annotated solution files that correspond to the grading rubrics make it easy for you to compare students' results with the correct solutions whether you receive their homework as hard copy or via e-mail.

TEST BANK & TEST ENGINE The ExamView test bank includes 110 questions for every project (25 multiple-choice, 50 true/false, and 35 completion) with page number references, and when appropriate, figure references. A version of the test bank you can print also is included. The test bank comes with a copy of the test engine, ExamView, the ultimate tool for your objective-based testing needs. ExamView is a state-of-the-art test builder that is easy to use. ExamView enables you to create paper-, LAN-, or Web-based tests from test banks designed specifically for your Course Technology textbook. Utilize the ultra-efficient QuickTest Wizard to create tests in less than five minutes by taking advantage of Course Technology's question banks, or customize your own exams from scratch.

LAB TESTS/TEST OUT The Lab Tests/Test Out exercises parallel the In the Lab assignments and are supplied for the purpose of testing students in the laboratory on the material covered in the project or testing students out of the course.

DATA FILES FOR STUDENTS All the files that are required by students to complete the exercises are included. You can distribute the files on the Instructor Resources CD-ROM to your students over a network, or you can have them follow the instructions on the last page of this Preface to obtain a copy of the data files.

ADDITIONAL ACTIVITIES FOR STUDENTS These additional activities consist of Project Reinforcement Exercises, which are true/false, multiple choice, and short answer questions that help students gain confidence in the material learned.

ADDITIONAL FACULTY FILES In the Lab assignments, solutions, rubrics, and annotated solution files are included from the first edition of *Microsoft Office 2003: Essential Concepts and Techniques*.

SAM 2003: Assessment and Training Software

SAM 2003 helps you energize your class exams and training assignments by allowing students to learn and test important computer skills in an active, hands-on environment.

SAM 2003 ASSESSMENT With SAM 2003 Assessment, you create powerful interactive exams on critical applications such as Word, Excel, Access, PowerPoint, Windows, and the Internet. The exams simulate the application environment, allowing your students to demonstrate their knowledge and think through the skill by performing real-world tasks. Build hands-on exams that allow students to work in the simulated application environment.

SAM 2003 TRAINING Invigorate your lesson plan with SAM 2003 Training. Using highly interactive text, graphics, and audio, SAM 2003 Training gives your students the flexibility to learn computer applications by choosing the training method that fits them best. Create customized training units that employ various approaches to teaching computer skills.

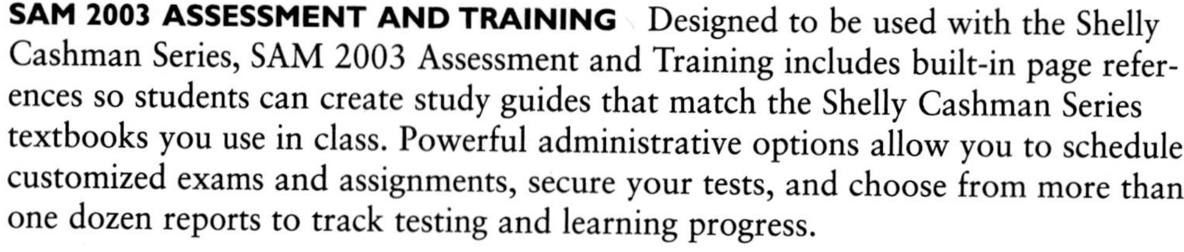

SAM 2003 ASSESSMENT AND TRAINING Designed to be used with the Shelly Cashman Series, SAM 2003 Assessment and Training includes built-in page references so students can create study guides that match the Shelly Cashman Series textbooks you use in class. Powerful administrative options allow you to schedule customized exams and assignments, secure your tests, and choose from more than one dozen reports to track testing and learning progress.

Online Content

Course Technology offers textbook-based content for Blackboard, WebCT, and MyCourse 2.1

BLACKBOARD AND WEBCT As the leading provider of IT content for the Blackboard and WebCT platforms, Course Technology delivers rich content that enhances your textbook to give your students a unique learning experience. Course Technology has partnered with WebCT and Blackboard to deliver our market-leading content through these state-of-the-art online learning platforms. Course Technology offers customizable content in every subject area, from computer concepts to PC repair.

MYCOURSE 2.1 MyCourse 2.1 is Course Technology's powerful online course management and content delivery system. Completely maintained and hosted by Thomson, MyCourse 2.1 delivers an online learning environment that is completely secure and provides superior performance. MyCourse 2.1 allows nontechnical users to create, customize, and deliver World Wide Web-based courses; post content and assignments; manage student enrollment; administer exams; track results in the online gradebook; and more. With MyCourse 2.1, you easily can create a customized course that will enhance every learning experience.

Workbook for Microsoft Office 2003

This highly popular supplement (ISBN 0-619-20028-6) includes a variety of activities that help students recall, review, and master the concepts presented. The *Workbook* complements the end-of-project material with a guided project outline; a self-test consisting of true/false, multiple-choice, short answer, and matching questions; and activities calculated to help students develop a deeper understanding of the information presented.

Shelly Cashman Series Microsoft Office Specialist Center

The Shelly Cashman Series Microsoft Office Specialist Center (Figure 1) has more links to Web pages you can visit to obtain additional information on the Microsoft Office Specialist certification. The Web page (scsite.com/winoff2003/cert) includes links to general information about certification, choosing an application for certification, preparing for the certification exam, and taking and passing the certification exam.

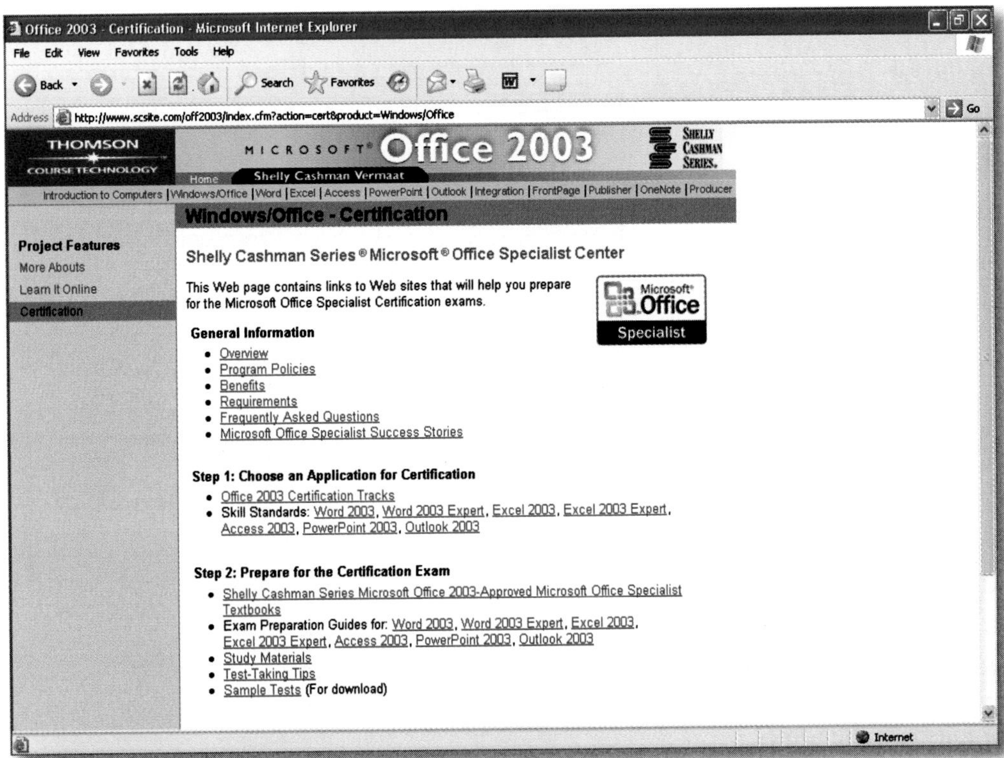

FIGURE 1

To the Student... Getting the Most Out of Your Book

Welcome to *Microsoft Office 2003: Essential Concepts and Techniques, Second Edition.* You can save yourself a lot of time and gain a better understanding of the Office 2003 applications if you spend a few minutes reviewing the figures and callouts in this section.

1 Project Orientation

Each project presents a practical problem and shows the solution in the first figure of the project. The project orientation lets you see firsthand how problems are solved from start to finish using application software and computers.

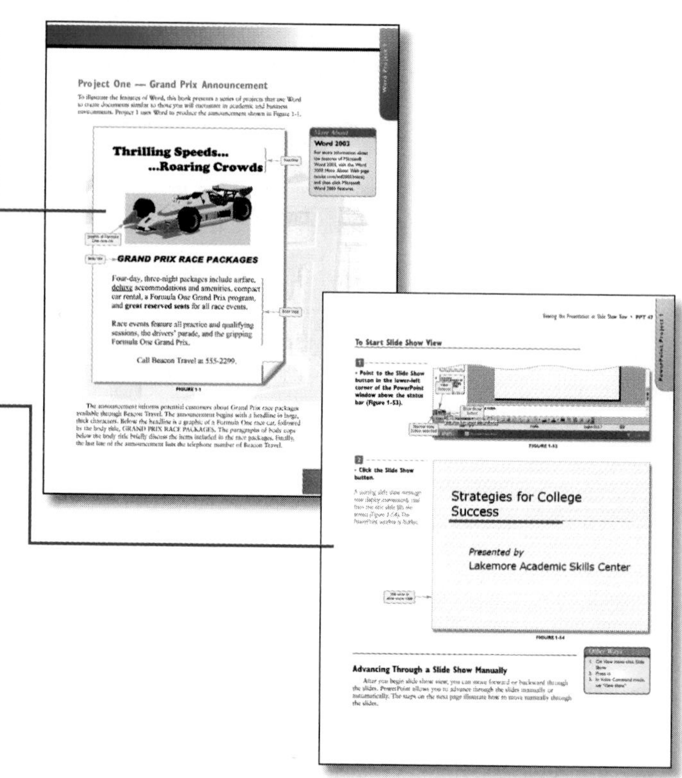

2 Consistent Step-by-Step, Screen-by-Screen Presentation

Project solutions are built using a step-by-step, screen-by-screen approach. This pedagogy allows you to build the solution on a computer as you read through the project. Generally, each step is followed by an italic explanation that indicates the result of the step.

3 More Than Just Step-by-Step

More About and Q&A annotations in the margins of the book and substantive text in the paragraphs provide background information, tips, and answers to common questions that complement the topics covered, adding depth and perspective. When you finish with this book, you will be ready to use the Office applications to solve problems on your own.

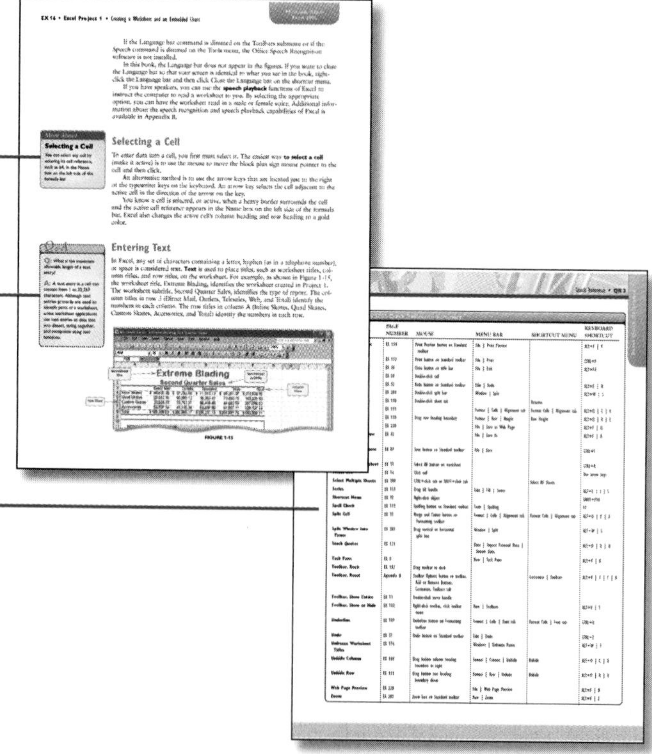

4 Other Ways Boxes and Quick Reference Summary

Other Ways boxes that follow many of the step sequences and a Quick Reference Summary at the back of the book explain the other ways to complete the task presented, such as using the mouse, menu, shortcut menu, and keyboard.

5 Emphasis on Getting Help When You Need It

The first project of each application and Appendix A show you how to use all the elements of the Office Help system. Being able to answer your own questions will increase your productivity and reduce your frustrations by minimizing the time it takes to learn how to complete a task.

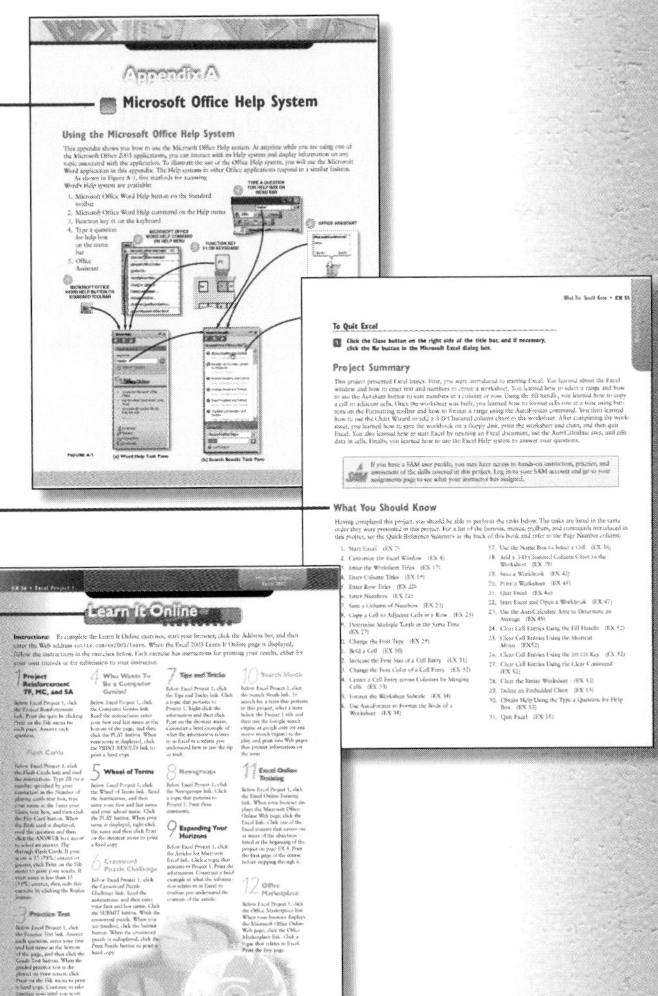

6 Review

After you successfully step through a project, a section titled What You Should Know summarizes the project tasks with which you should be familiar. Terms you should know for test purposes are bold in the text.

7 Reinforcement and Extension

The Learn It Online page at the end of each project offers reinforcement in the form of review questions, learning games, and practice tests. Also included are Web-based exercises that require you to extend your learning beyond the book.

8 Laboratory Exercises

If you really want to learn how to use the applications, then you must design and implement solutions to problems on your own. Every project concludes with several carefully developed laboratory assignments that increase in complexity.

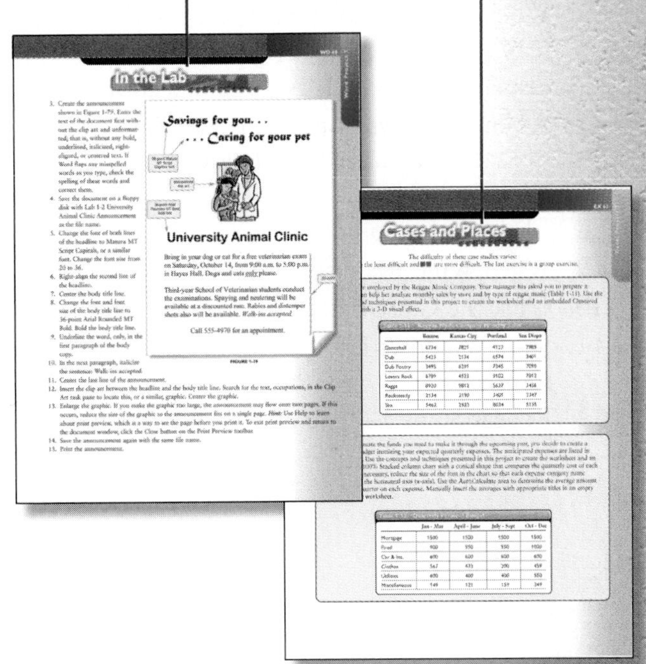

Obtaining the Data Files for Students

A few of the exercises in this book require that you begin by opening a data file. Choose one of the following methods to obtain a copy of the Data Files for Students.

Instructors

- A copy of the Data Files for Students is on the Instructor Resources CD-ROM below the category Data Files for Students, which you can copy to your school's network for student use.
- Download the Data Files for Students via the World Wide Web by following the instructions below.

Students

- Check with your instructor to determine the best way to obtain a copy of the Data Files for Students.
- Download the Data Files for Students via the World Wide Web by following the instructions below.

Instructions for Downloading the Data Files for Students from the World Wide Web

1. Insert your removable media (USB flash drive, floppy disk, or Zip disk) into your computer.
2. Start your browser. Enter scsite.com in the Address box and then click Go.
3. When the scsite.com home page displays, locate your book using one of the methods below.
   - Browse: Using the Browse by Subject navigation bar on the left side of the screen, click the subject category and then sub-category to which your book belongs. For example, click Office Suites, and then Microsoft Office 2003.
   - Search: Using the Find Your Book feature at the top of the screen, enter the title of your book, or other identifying information, and then click Go.
   - Quick Link: If your book is featured in the Quick Link area on the right side of the screen, you may click your book title and proceed directly to your material. Skip to Step 5 below.
4. In the center of the screen, locate your book and click the title. For example, click Microsoft Office 2003: Introductory Concepts and Techniques, Premium Edition. Note: You may need to scroll down or navigate to the next Results Page.
5. When the page for your textbook displays, click the appropriate data files link.
6. If Windows displays a File Download – Security Warning dialog box, click the Run button. If Windows displays an Internet Explorer – Security Warning dialog box, click the Run button.
7. When Windows displays the WinZip Self-Extractor dialog box, type in the Unzip to folder box the portable storage media drive letter followed by a colon, backslash, and a sub-folder name of your choice (for example, f:\Office 2003).
8. Click the Unzip button.
9. When Windows displays the WinZip Self-Extractor dialog box, click the OK button.
10. Click the Close button on the right side of the title bar in the WinZip Self-Extractor dialog box.
11. Start Windows Explorer and display the contents of the folder that you specified in Step 7 to view the results.
12. Repeat Steps 5–11 to download another set of files.

Microsoft Windows XP and Office 2003

MICROSOFT

Windows XP and Office 2003

MICROSOFT
Windows XP and Office 2003

Introduction to Microsoft Windows XP and Office 2003

PROJECT 1

CASE PERSPECTIVE

After weeks of planning, your organization finally installed Microsoft Windows XP Professional on all workstations. As the computer trainer for the upcoming in-house seminar, you realize you should know more about Microsoft Windows XP Professional but have had little time to learn. Since installing Windows XP Professional, many employees have come to you with questions. You have taken the time to answer their questions by sitting down with them at their computers and searching for the answers using the Help and Support feature.

From their questions, you determine that you should customize the seminar to cover the basics of Windows XP Professional, including basic mouse operations, working with windows, starting an application, and searching for answers using Help and Support. Your goal is to become familiar with Microsoft Windows XP Professional in order to teach the seminar more effectively to the participants.

As you read through this project, you will learn how to use the Windows XP operating system to perform basic operating system tasks and become familiar with the Microsoft Office 2003 applications.

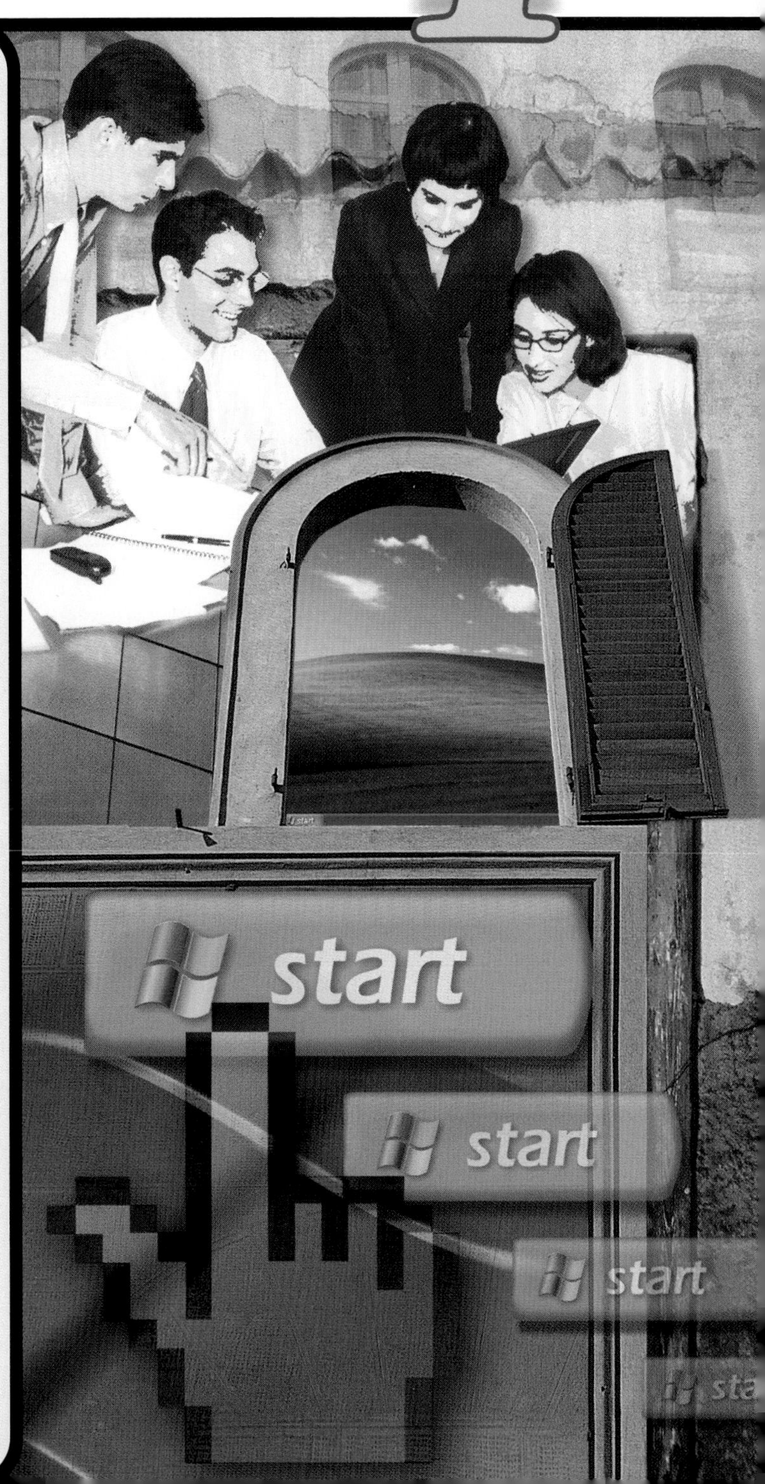

MICROSOFT
Windows XP and Office 2003

Introduction to Microsoft Windows XP and Office 2003

PROJECT

Objectives

You will have mastered the material in this project when you can:

- Launch Microsoft Windows XP, log on to the computer, and identify the objects on the desktop
- Perform the basic mouse operations: point, click, right-click, double-click, drag, and right-drag
- Display the Start menu and start an application program
- Open, minimize, maximize, restore, move, size, scroll, and close a window
- Display drive and folder contents
- Create a folder in Windows Explorer and Microsoft Word
- Type, name, and save a Word document
- Download folders from scsite.com
- Copy, move, rename, and delete files
- Search for files using a word or phrase in the file or by name
- Use Help and Support
- Log off from the computer and turn it off

Introduction

An **operating system** is the set of computer instructions, called a computer program, that controls the allocation of computer hardware such as memory, disk devices, printers, and CD and DVD drives, and provides the capability for you to communicate with the computer. The most popular and widely used operating system is **Microsoft Windows. Microsoft Windows XP**, the newest version of Microsoft Windows, allows you to easily communicate with and control your computer.

Microsoft Office 2003, the latest edition of the world's best-selling office suite, is a collection of the more popular Microsoft application software products that work similarly and together as if they were one program. Microsoft Office 2003 integrates these applications and combines them with the power of the Internet so you can move quickly among applications, transfer text and graphics easily, and interact seamlessly with the World Wide Web. The **Internet** is a worldwide group of connected computer networks that allows public access to information on thousands of subjects and give users the means to use this information, send messages, and obtain products and services. An explanation of each of the application software programs in Microsoft Office 2003 is given at the end of this project.

Microsoft Windows XP Operating Systems

The Microsoft Windows XP operating systems consist of Microsoft Windows XP Professional, Microsoft Windows XP Home Edition, Microsoft Windows XP Media Center Edition, Microsoft Windows XP Tablet PC Edition, and Microsoft Windows XP 64-Bit Edition. **Microsoft Windows XP Professional** is the operating system designed for businesses of all sizes and for advanced home computing. Windows XP is called a **32-bit operating system** because it uses 32 bits for addressing and other purposes, which means the operating system can address more than four gigabytes of RAM (random-access memory) and perform tasks faster than older operating systems.

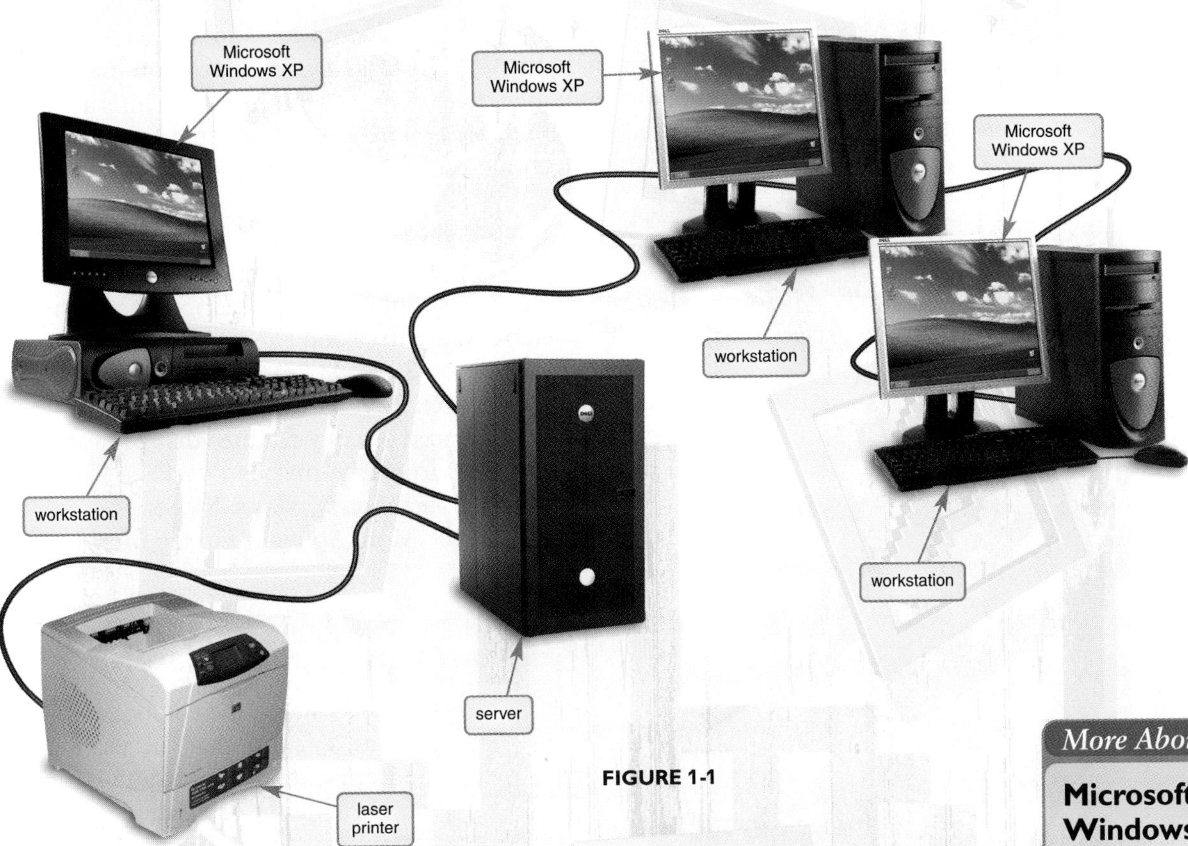

FIGURE 1-1

In business, Windows XP Professional is commonly used on computer workstations and portable computers. A **workstation** is a computer connected to a server. A **server** is a computer that controls access to the hardware and software on a network and provides a centralized storage area for programs, data, and information. Figure 1-1 illustrates a simple computer network consisting of a server and three computers (called workstations) and a laser printer connected to the server.

Microsoft Windows XP Home Edition is designed for entertainment and home use. Home Edition allows you to establish in the home a network of computers that share a single Internet connection, share a device such as a printer or a scanner, share files and folders, and play multicomputer games.

Microsoft Windows XP Media Center Edition is designed for use with a Media Center PC. A **Media Center PC** is a home entertainment desktop personal computer that includes a mid- to high-end processor, large-capacity hard disk, CD and DVD drives, a remote control, and advanced graphics and audio capabilities. **Microsoft Windows XP Tablet PC Edition** is designed for use on a special type of notebook

More About

Microsoft Windows XP

Microsoft Windows XP combines the best features of Microsoft Windows 98 with the power and reliability of Microsoft Windows 2000. Windows 98, which was designed for use on personal computers, was the most popular operating system for PCs. Windows 2000, designed for use on a computer network, was the most widely used business version of Windows.

More About

Microsoft Windows XP

A vast amount of information about Microsoft Windows XP is available on the Internet. For additional information about Microsoft Windows XP, visit the Windows XP More About Web Page (scsite.com/winoff20032e/more) and then click Microsoft Windows XP.

computer, called a Tablet PC. A **Tablet PC** allows you to write on the device's screen using a digital pen and convert the handwriting into characters the Tablet PC can process. A **Windows XP 64-Bit Edition** is also available for individuals solving complex scientific problems, developing high-performance design and engineering applications, or creating 3-D animations.

Microsoft Windows XP Professional

Microsoft Windows XP Professional (called **Windows XP** for the rest of the book) is an operating system that performs every function necessary for you to communicate with and use the computer.

Windows XP is easy to use and can be customized to fit individual needs. Windows XP simplifies the process of working with documents and applications by transferring data between documents, organizing the manner in which you interact with the computer, and using the computer to access information on the Internet or an intranet. Windows XP is used to run **application programs**, which are programs that perform an application-related function such as word processing.

Windows XP Service Pack 2

Periodically, Microsoft releases a free update to the Windows XP operating system. These updates, referred to as **service packs**, contain fixes and enhancements to the operating system. In August 2004, Microsoft released the Windows XP Service Pack 2. **Windows XP Service Pack 2** (**SP2**) contains advanced security features that protect a computer against viruses, worms, and hackers. For more information about Windows XP Service Pack 2, see the More About at the top of page WIN 7.

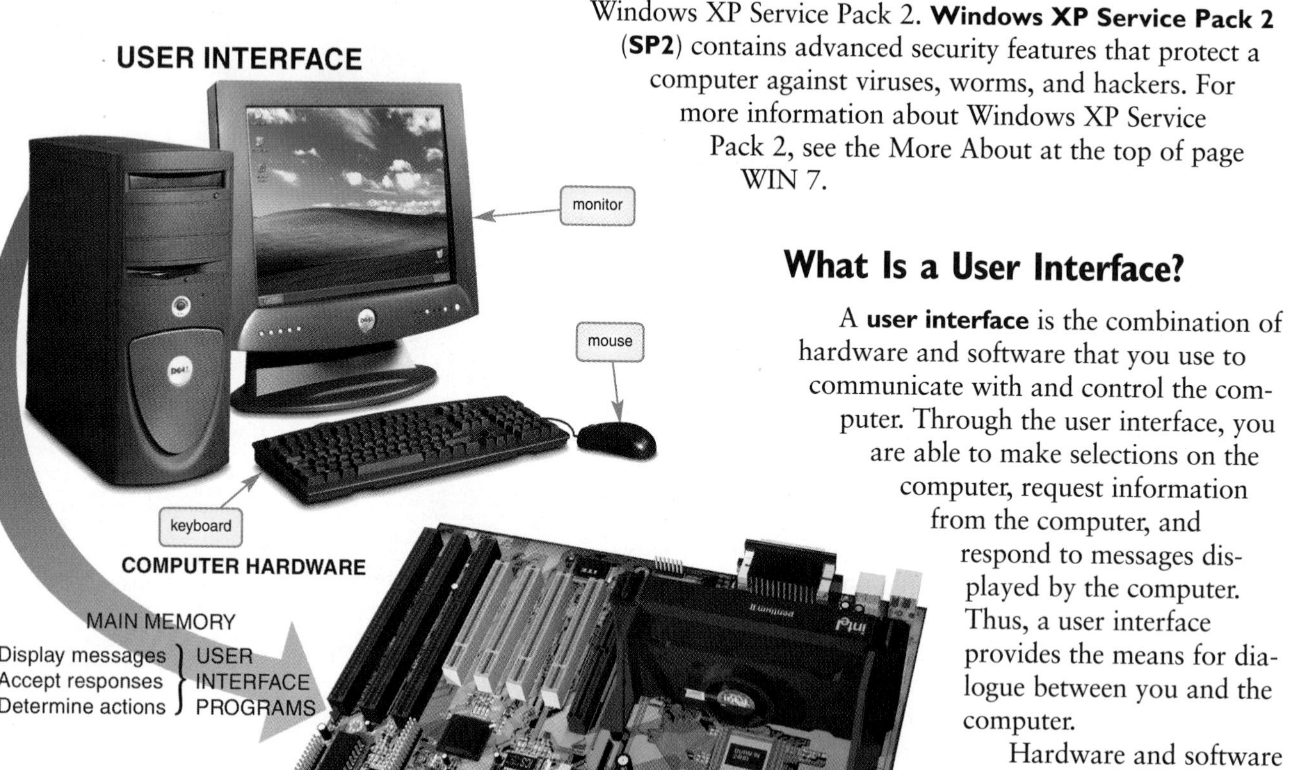

FIGURE 1-2

What Is a User Interface?

A **user interface** is the combination of hardware and software that you use to communicate with and control the computer. Through the user interface, you are able to make selections on the computer, request information from the computer, and respond to messages displayed by the computer. Thus, a user interface provides the means for dialogue between you and the computer.

Hardware and software together form the user interface. Among the hardware devices associated with a user interface are the monitor, keyboard, and mouse (Figure 1-2). The **monitor** displays messages and provides information. You respond by entering data in the form of a command or other response using the **keyboard** or **mouse**. Among the responses available to you are ones that specify which application program to run, what document to open, when to print, and where to store data for future use.

The computer software associated with the user interface consists of the programs that engage you in dialogue (Figure 1-2). The computer software determines the messages you receive, the manner in which you should respond, and the actions that occur, based on your responses.

The goal of an effective user interface is to be **user-friendly**, which means the software can be used easily by individuals with limited training. Research studies have indicated that the use of graphics can play an important role in aiding users to interact effectively with a computer. A **graphical user interface**, or **GUI** (pronounced gooey), is a user interface that displays graphics in addition to text when it communicates with the user.

The Windows XP graphical user interface was designed carefully to be easier to set up, simpler to learn, faster, more powerful, and better integrated with the Internet.

More About

Windows XP Service Pack 2

A table summarizing the new features contained in the Windows XP Service Pack 2 is available on the Internet. For additional information about Windows XP Service Pack 2, visit the Windows XP More About Web Page (scsite.com/winoff20032e/more) and then click Windows XP Service Pack 2.

Launching Microsoft Windows XP

When you turn on the computer, an introductory black screen consisting of the Microsoft Windows XP logo, progress bar, copyright messages (Copyright © Microsoft Corporation), and the word, Microsoft, are displayed. The progress bar indicates the progress of the Windows XP operating system launch. After approximately one minute, the Welcome screen displays (Figure 1-3).

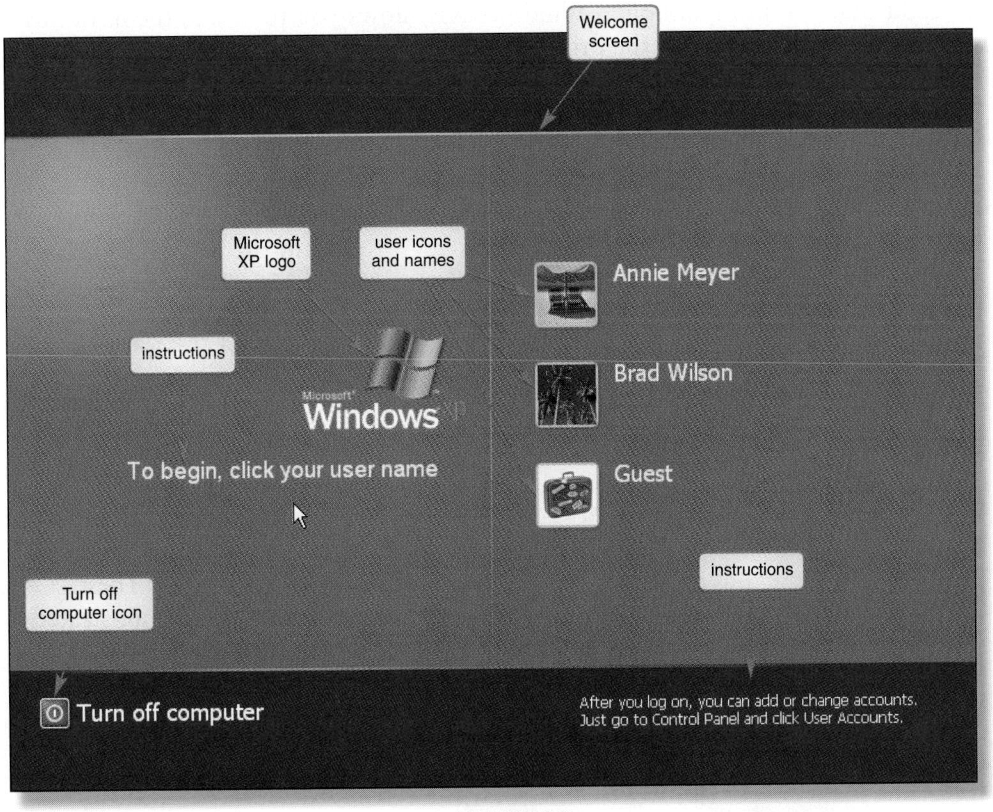

FIGURE 1-3

More About

The Windows XP Interface

Some older interfaces, called command-line interfaces, required you to type keywords (special words, phrases, or codes the computer understood) or press special keys on the keyboard to communicate with the interface. Today, graphical-user interfaces incorporate colorful graphics, use of the mouse, and Web browser-like features, which make them more user friendly.

More About

User Names and Passwords

A unique user name identifies each computer user. In the past, users often entered a variation of their name as the user name. For example, Brad Wilson might have chosen bradwilson or bwilson. Today, most Windows XP users use their first and last names without variation as the user name. A password is a combination of characters that allows a user access to certain computer resources on the network. Passwords should be kept confidential.

The **Welcome screen** on the previous page shows the names of every computer user on the computer. On the left side of the Welcome screen, the Microsoft XP logo and the instructions, To begin, click your user name, appear. On the right side of the Welcome screen is a list of the **user icons** and **user names** for all authorized computer users (Annie Meyer, Brad Wilson, and Guest). Clicking the user icon or user name begins the process of logging on to the computer. The list of user icons and names on the Welcome screen on your computer may be different.

At the bottom of the Welcome screen are the Turn off computer icon and the instructions, After you log on, you can add or change accounts. Just go to Control Panel and click User Accounts. Clicking the Turn off computer icon initiates the process of shutting down the computer. The **Control Panel** allows you to create a new user, change or remove an existing user, and change user information. The user information that can be changed consists of the user icon and user name, user password, and account type (Administrator, Limited, and Guest).

The Windows XP User Interface

The Windows XP interface provides the means for dialogue between you and the computer. Part of this dialogue involves requesting information from the computer and responding to messages displayed by the computer. You can request information and respond to messages by using either the mouse or the keyboard.

More About

Microsoft Mice

For additional information about Microsoft Mice, visit the Microsoft Windows XP More About Web Page (scsite.com/winoff20032e/more) and then click Microsoft Mice.

A **mouse** is a pointing device used with Windows XP that may be attached to the computer by a cable. Although it is not required to use Windows XP, Windows XP supports the use of the **Microsoft IntelliMouse** (Figure 1-4). The IntelliMouse contains three buttons: the primary mouse button, the secondary mouse button, and the wheel button between the primary and secondary mouse buttons. Typically, the **primary mouse button** is the left mouse button and the **secondary mouse button** is the right mouse button, although Windows XP allows you to switch them. In this book, the left mouse button is the primary mouse button and the right mouse button is the secondary mouse button. The functions the **wheel button** and wheel perform depend on the software application being used. If the mouse is not an IntelliMouse, it will not have a wheel button between the primary and secondary mouse buttons.

Using the mouse, you can perform the following operations: (1) point; (2) click; (3) right-click; (4) double-click; (5) drag; and (6) right-drag. These operations are demonstrated on the following pages.

More About

The Mouse

The mouse, although invented in the 1960s, was not used widely until the Apple Macintosh computer became available in 1984. Even then, some highbrows called mouse users wimps. Today, the mouse is an indispensable tool for every computer user.

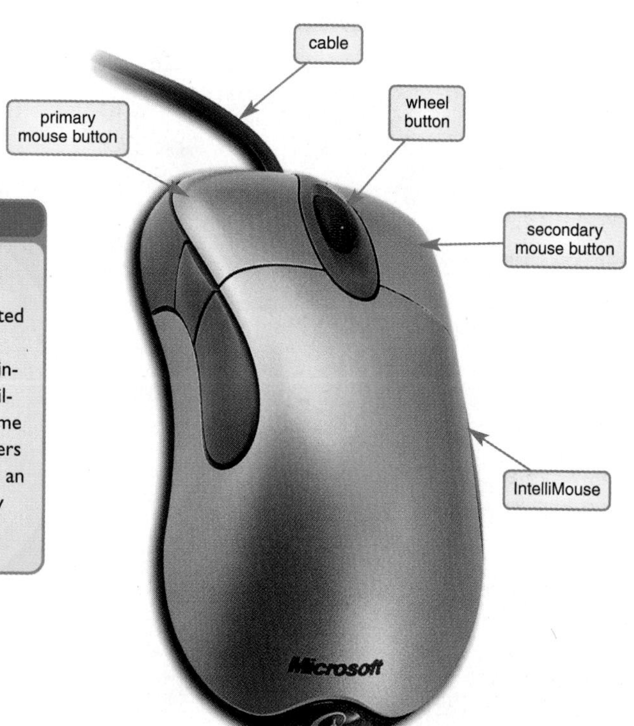

FIGURE 1-4

Many common tasks, such as logging on to the computer or logging off, are performed by pointing to an item and then clicking the item. **Point** means you move the mouse across a flat surface until the mouse pointer rests on the item of choice. As you move the mouse across a flat surface, the IntelliEye optical sensor on the underside of the mouse senses the movement of the mouse (Figure 1-5), and the mouse pointer moves across the desktop in the same direction. If the mouse is not an IntelliMouse, it may have a ball on the underside of the mouse.

Click means you press and release the primary mouse button, which in this book is the left mouse button. In most cases, you must point to an item before you click.

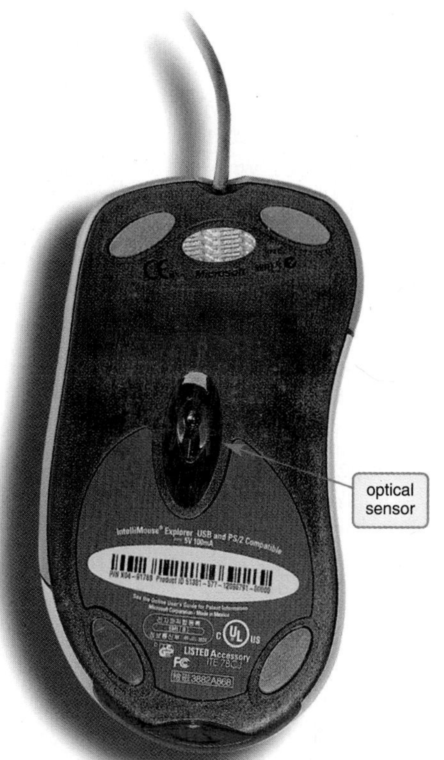

FIGURE 1-5

Logging On to the Computer

After launching Windows XP but before working with Windows XP, you must log on to the computer. **Logging on** to the computer opens your user account and makes the computer available for use. In the following steps, the Brad Wilson icon and the Next button are used to log on to the computer.

Note: In a school environment, you will want to log on to the computer by pointing to and clicking *your user icon* on the Welcome screen and typing *your password* in the text box instead of the password shown in the following steps.

The following steps illustrate how to log on to the computer by pointing to and clicking an icon on the Welcome screen, typing a password, and then pointing to and clicking the Next button.

To Log On to the Computer

1

- **Point to the Brad Wilson icon (or your icon) on the Welcome screen by moving the mouse across a flat surface until the mouse pointer rests on the icon.**

Pointing to the Brad Wilson icon displays a yellow border on the icon and dims the other user icons and names (Figure 1-6).

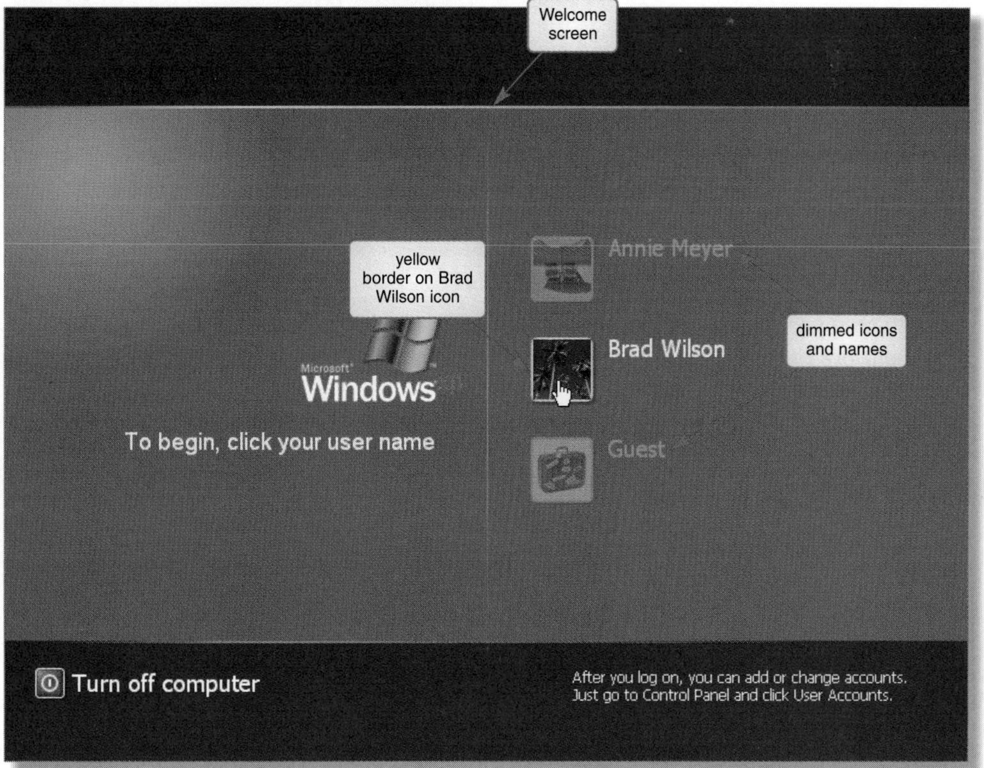

FIGURE 1-6

2

• **Click the icon by pressing and releasing the left mouse button, type** `lakers` **(or your password) in the Type your password text box, and then point to the Next button.**

*Windows XP highlights the Brad Wilson icon and name, displays the Type your password text box containing a series of bullets (••••••) and an insertion point, and the Next and Help buttons (Figure 1-7). A **text box** is a rectangular area in which you can enter text. The bullets in the text box hide the password entered by the user.*

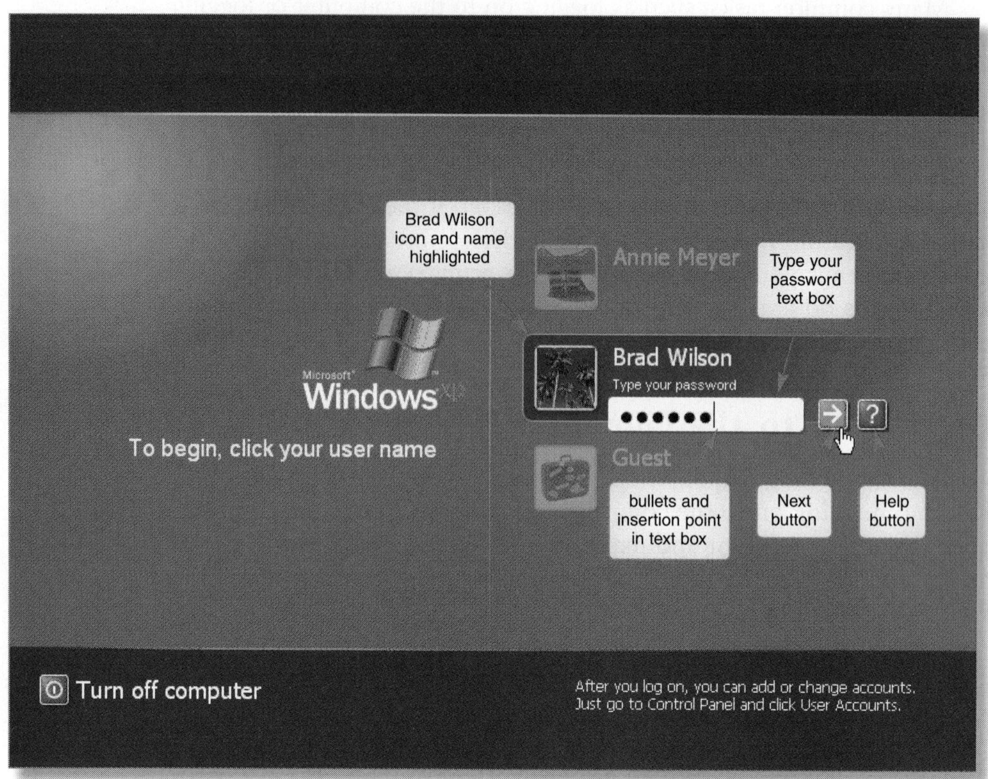

FIGURE 1-7

3

• **Click the Next button.**

The contents of the Welcome screen change to contain the word, Welcome, on the left side of the screen and the user name, user icon, and message, Loading your personal settings..., on the right side. This screen appears momentarily while the user is logged on to the computer and then several items appear on a background called the desktop (Figure 1-8). The background design of the desktop is Bliss, but your computer may display a different design.

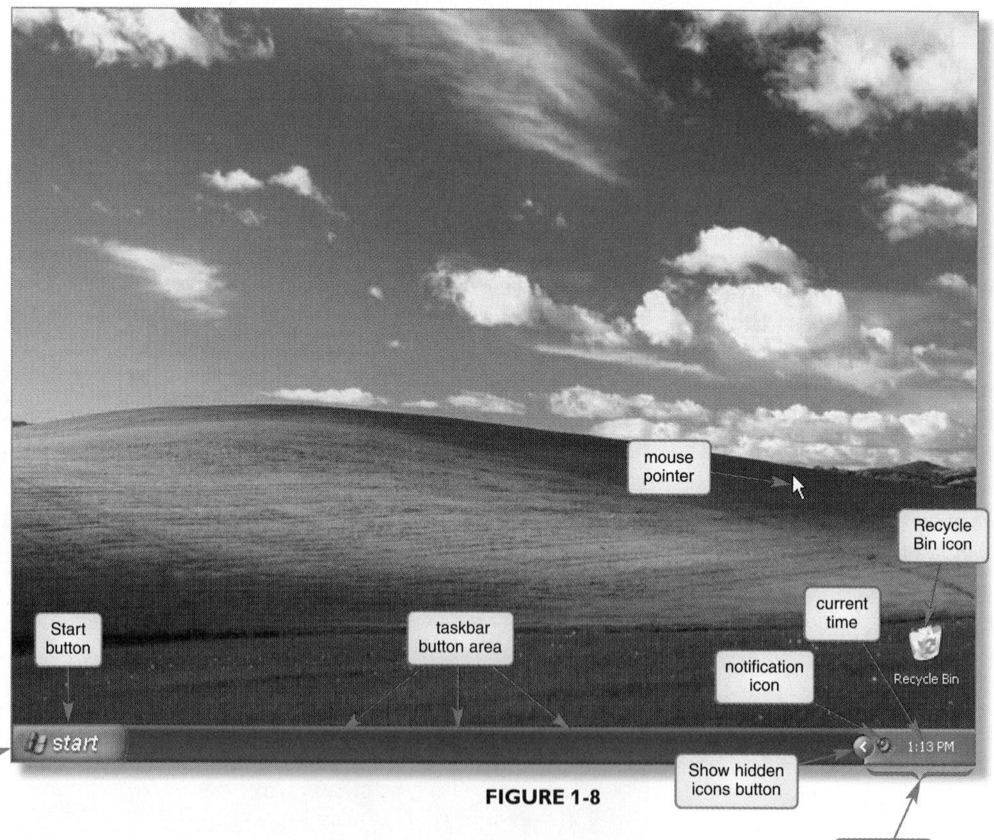

FIGURE 1-8

The items on the desktop in Figure 1-8 include the Recycle Bin icon and its name in the lower-right corner of the desktop and the taskbar across the bottom of the desktop. The Recycle Bin icon (Recycle Bin) allows you to discard unneeded objects. Your computer's desktop may contain more, fewer, or different icons because you can customize the desktop of the computer.

The **taskbar** shown at the bottom of the screen in Figure 1-8 contains the Start button, taskbar button area, and notification area. The **Start button** allows you to start a program quickly, find or open a document, change the computer's settings, obtain Help, shut down the computer, and perform many more tasks. The **taskbar button area** contains buttons to indicate which windows are open on the desktop. In Figure 1-8, no windows are displayed on the desktop and no buttons appear in the taskbar button area.

The **notification area** contains the Show hidden icons button, one notification icon, and the current time. The **Show hidden icons button** indicates that one or more inactive icons are hidden from view in the notification area. The **notification icon** in the notification area provides quick access to programs on the computer. Other icons that provide information about the status of the computer appear temporarily in the notification area. For example, the Printer icon appears when a document is sent to the printer and is removed when printing is complete. The notification area on your desktop may contain more, fewer, or different icons because the contents of the notification area can change.

The mouse pointer appears on the desktop. On the desktop, the **mouse pointer** is the shape of a block arrow. The mouse pointer allows you to point to objects on the desktop and may change shape when it points to different objects. A shadow may be displayed behind the mouse pointer to make the mouse pointer appear in a three-dimensional form.

When you click an object, such as the Brad Wilson icon or the Next button shown in Figure 1-7, you must point to the object before you click. In the steps that follow, the instruction that directs you to point to a particular item and then click is, Click the particular item. For example, Click the Next button means point to the Next button and then click.

More About

Logging on to the Computer

If, after logging on to the computer, you leave the computer unattended for twelve or more minutes, the Welcome screen will appear, and you will have to log on to the computer again to gain access to your account.

More About

The Notification Area

The Show hidden icons button is displayed on the left edge of the notification area if one or more inactive icons are hidden from view in the notification area. Clicking the Show hidden icons button returns the hidden icons to the notification area and replaces the Show hidden icons button with the Hide button. Moving the mouse pointer off the Hide button removes, or hides, the inactive icons in the notification area and displays the Show hidden icons button again.

The Windows XP Desktop

Nearly every item on the Windows XP desktop is considered an object. Even the desktop itself is an object. Every **object** has properties. The **properties** of an object are unique to that specific object and may affect what can be done to the object or what the object does. For example, a property of an object may be the color of the object, such as the color of the desktop.

The Windows XP desktop and the objects on the desktop emulate a work area in an office. You may think of the Windows desktop as an electronic version of the top of your desk. You can place objects on the desktop, move the objects around on the desktop, look at them, and then put them aside, and so on. In this project, you will learn how to interact and communicate with the Windows XP desktop.

Displaying the Start Menu

A **menu** is a list of related commands and each **command** on a menu performs a specific action, such as searching for files or obtaining Help. The **Start menu** allows you to access easily the most useful items on the computer. The Start menu contains commands that allow you to connect to and browse the Internet, start an e-mail program, start application programs, store and search for documents, customize the computer, and obtain Help on thousands of topics.

The steps on the following pages show how to display the Start menu.

Q&A

Q: Can you change the appearance of the desktop?

A: Yes. You may use a different background design and icons on the desktop and in the notification area, and you may display additional toolbars on the taskbar. To change the background design, right-click an open area of the desktop and click Properties on the shortcut menu. To change the contents of the taskbar and notification area, right-click the Start button or taskbar and then click Properties on the shortcut menu.

To Display the Start Menu

1

- **Point to the Start button on the taskbar.**

The mouse pointer on the Start button causes the color of the Start button to change to light green and displays a ToolTip (Click here to begin) (Figure 1-9). The ToolTip provides instructions for using the Start button.

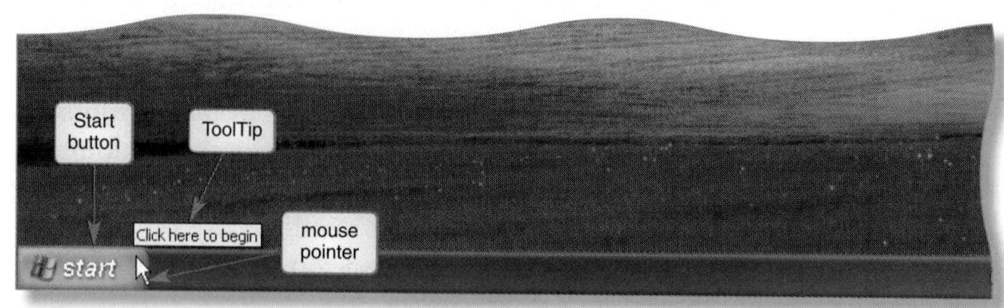

FIGURE 1-9

2

- **Click the Start button.**

The Start menu appears, the color of the Start button changes to dark green, and the Start button becomes recessed (Figure 1-10). The top section of the Start menu contains the user icon and name, the middle section contains two columns of commands, and the bottom section contains two icons (Log Off and Turn Off Computer).

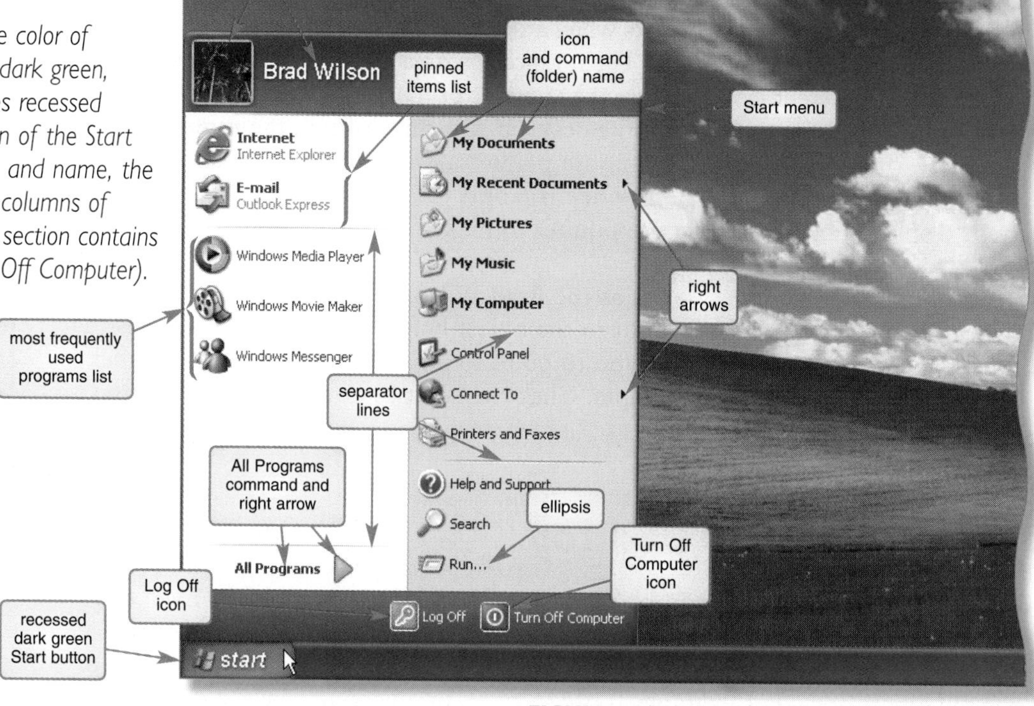

FIGURE 1-10

3

- **Point to All Programs on the Start menu.**

When you point to All Programs, Windows XP highlights the All Programs command on the Start menu by displaying the All Programs command name in white text on a blue background and displays the All Programs submenu (Figure 1-11). A submenu is a menu that appears when you point to a command followed by a right arrow. Whenever you point to a command on a menu or submenu, the command name is highlighted.

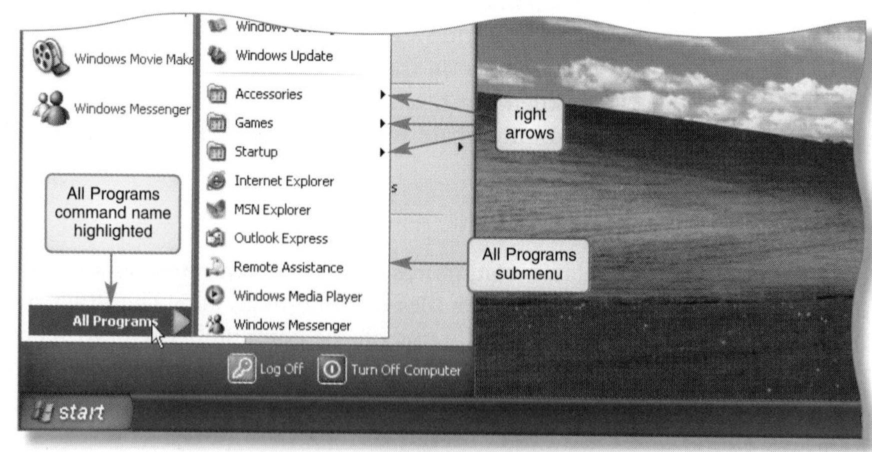

FIGURE 1-11

4

• **Point to Accessories on the All Programs submenu.**

When you point to Accessories, Windows XP highlights the Accessories command on the All Programs submenu and displays the Accessories submenu (Figure 1-12). Clicking a command on the Accessories submenu that contains an application name starts that application. For example, to start Notepad, you would click the Notepad command on the Accessories submenu.

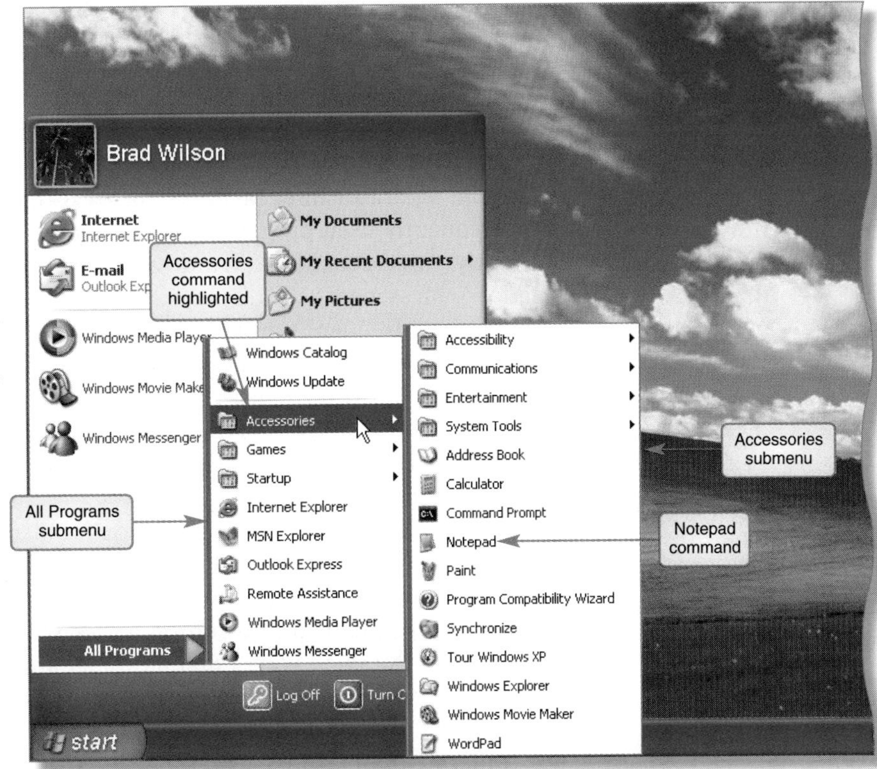

FIGURE 1-12

5

• **Point to an open area of the desktop and then click the open area to close the Start menu, Accessories submenu, and All Programs submenu.**

The Start menu, Accessories submenu, and All Programs submenu close, and the recessed dark green Start button changes to its original light green color (Figure 1-13). The mouse pointer points to the desktop. To close a menu, click any area of the desktop except the menu itself.

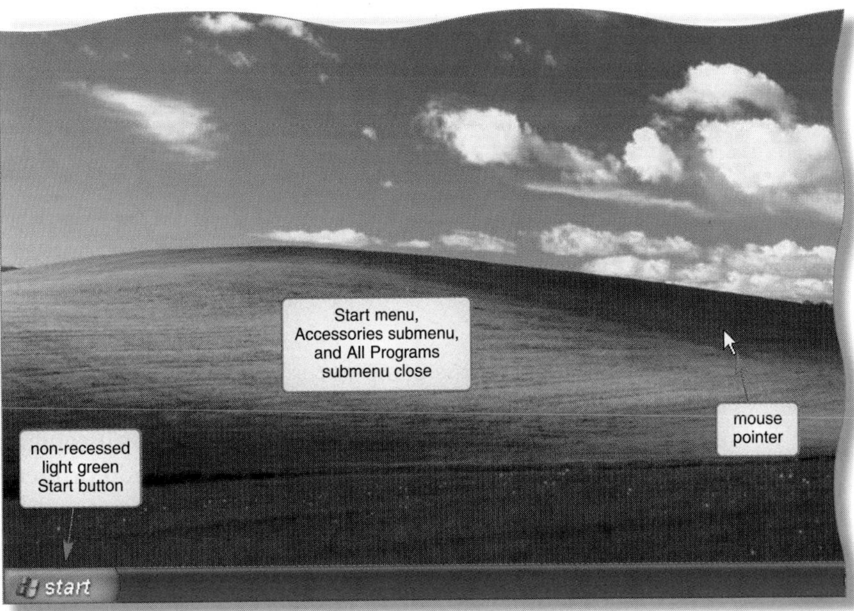

FIGURE 1-13

Other Ways

1. Press CTRL+ESC
2. Press WINDOWS

The middle section of the Start menu shown in Figure 1-10 on page WIN 12 consists of two columns of commands. Each command is identified by a unique icon and name. Commands may represent an application program, folder, or operation.

The list of commands above the separator line at the top of the left column, called the **pinned items list**, consists of the default Web browser program (Internet Explorer) and default e-mail program (Outlook Express). The list of commands below the separator line, called the **most frequently used programs list**, contains the most frequently used programs. Programs are added to the list when you use them. Currently, three programs (Windows Media Player, Windows Movie Maker, and Windows Messenger) are displayed in the list.

The most frequently used program list can contain up to six programs. If the list contains fewer than six programs when you start a new program, the program name is added to the list. If the list contains six names when you start a program that is not on the list, Windows XP replaces a less frequently used program with the new application. The All Programs command appears below the separator line at the bottom of the left column.

A list of commands to access various folders appears above the separator line at the top of the right column (My Documents, My Recent Documents, My Pictures, My Music, and My Computer).

A **folder** is a named location on a disk where files are stored. A folder contains files in much the same way a manila folder stores important documents, such as a class schedule or syllabus. Each folder is identified by a folder icon and folder name. Some folders include a symbol. In Figure 1-14, the Freshman folder consists of a yellow folder icon and folder name (Freshman) and the My Music folder consists of a yellow folder icon, folder name (My Music), and symbol (musical note).

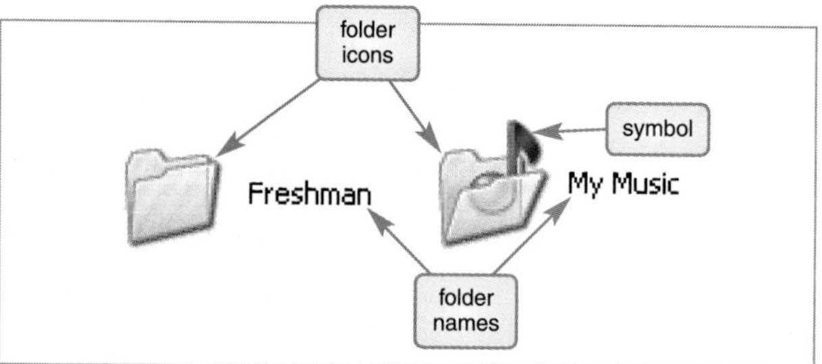

FIGURE 1-14

If the computer is connected to a network, the My Network Places command may appear below the My Computer command. Below the separator line are other commands. They are commands to customize the computer (Control Panel), connect to the Internet (Connect To), and add printers and fax printers to the computer (Printers and Faxes). Below the separator line at the bottom of the right column are commands to obtain Help (Help and Support), search for documents and folders (Search), and start programs (Run). The commands on your Start menu may be different.

A **right arrow** following a command on the Start menu indicates that pointing to the command will display a submenu. The All Programs command is followed by a green right arrow, and the My Recent Documents and Connect To commands are followed by smaller black arrows. One command (Run) is followed by an **ellipsis** (...) to indicate more information is required to execute the command.

Windows XP provides a number of ways in which to accomplish a particular task. In the remainder of this book, a specific set of steps will illustrate how to accomplish each task. These steps may not be the only way in which the task can be completed. If you can perform the same task using other means, the Other Ways box specifies the methods. In each case, the method shown in the steps is the preferred method, but it is important for you to be aware of all the techniques you can use.

More About

The Right Mouse Button

The earliest versions of Microsoft Windows made little use of the right mouse button. In Windows XP, the right mouse button makes it easy to display a list of commands for an object (called a shortcut menu) and to copy and move objects on the desktop.

Adding an Icon to the Desktop

Although the Windows XP desktop may contain only the Recycle Bin icon (see Figure 1-8 on page WIN 10), you may want to add additional icons to the desktop. For example, you may want to add the My Computer icon to the desktop so you can view the contents of the computer easily. One method of viewing the contents of the computer is to click the My Computer command on the Start menu to open the My Computer window. If you use My Computer frequently, you may want to place the My Computer icon on the desktop where it is easier to find.

One method of adding the My Computer icon to the desktop is to right-click the My Computer command on the Start menu. **Right-click** means you press and release the secondary mouse button, which in this book is the right mouse button. As directed when using the primary mouse button to click an object, normally you will point to the object before you right-click it. The following steps illustrate how to add the My Computer icon to the desktop.

To Add an Icon to the Desktop

1

- **Click the Start button, point to My Computer on the Start menu, and then press and release the right mouse button.**

Windows XP highlights the My Computer command and displays a shortcut menu containing nine commands (Figure 1-15). Right-clicking an object, such as the My Computer command, displays a shortcut menu that contains commands specifically for use with that object.

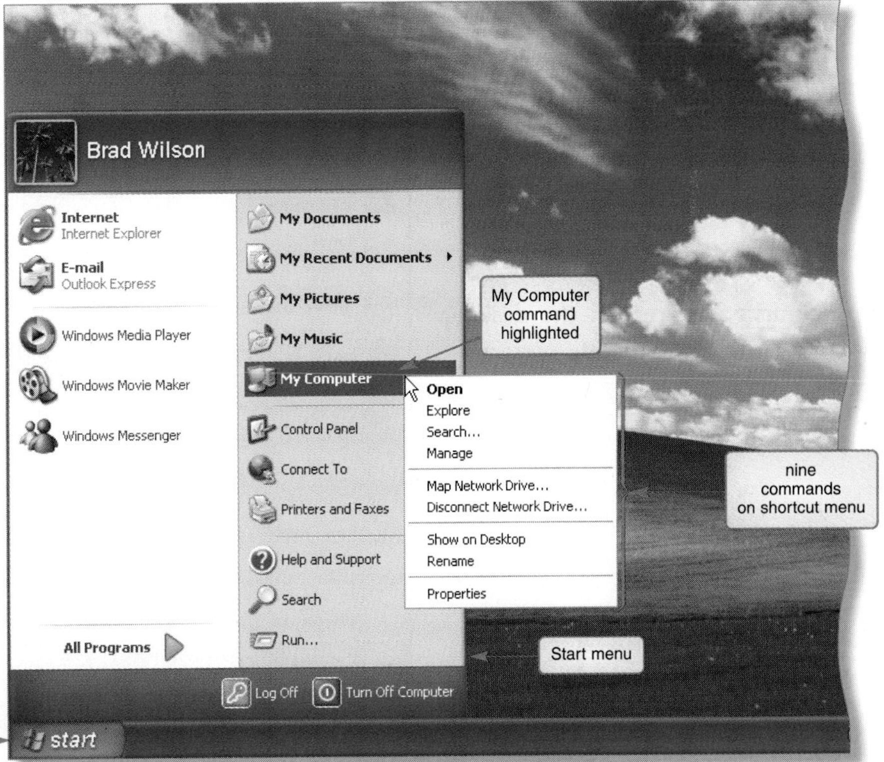

FIGURE 1-15

2

- **Point to Show on Desktop on the shortcut menu.**

When you point to Show on Desktop, Windows XP highlights the Show on Desktop command (Figure 1-16).

FIGURE 1-16

3

- **Click Show on Desktop.**

The shortcut menu closes and the My Computer icon is displayed on the desktop (Figure 1-17). The Start menu remains on the desktop.

4

- **Click an open area on the desktop to close the Start menu.**

The Start menu closes.

Other Ways

1. Right-click desktop, click Properties on shortcut menu, click Desktop tab, click Customize Desktop, click icon title, click OK button, click OK button

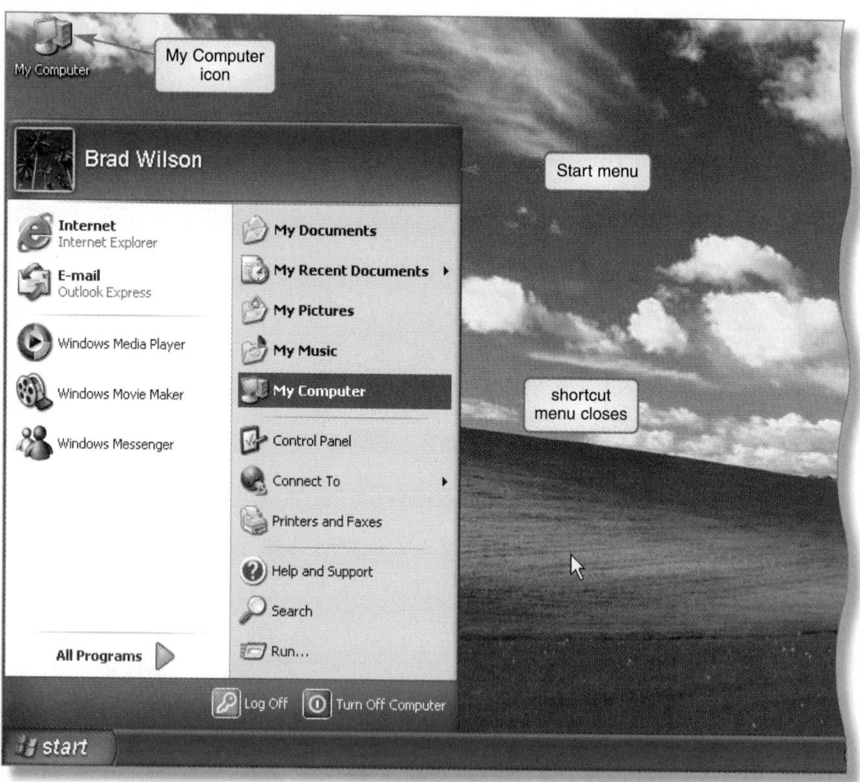

FIGURE 1-17

Whenever you right-click an object, a shortcut menu is displayed. As you will see, the use of shortcut menus speeds up your work and adds flexibility to your interaction with the computer.

Opening a Window Using a Desktop Icon

Double-click means you quickly press and release the left mouse button twice without moving the mouse. In most cases, you must point to an item before you double-click. The following step shows how to open the My Computer window on the desktop by double-clicking the My Computer icon on the desktop.

To Open a Window Using a Desktop Icon

1

- **Point to the My Computer icon on the desktop and then double-click by quickly pressing and releasing the left mouse button twice without moving the mouse.**

The My Computer window opens and the recessed dark blue My Computer button is displayed in the taskbar button area (Figure 1-18). The My Computer window allows you to view the contents of the computer.

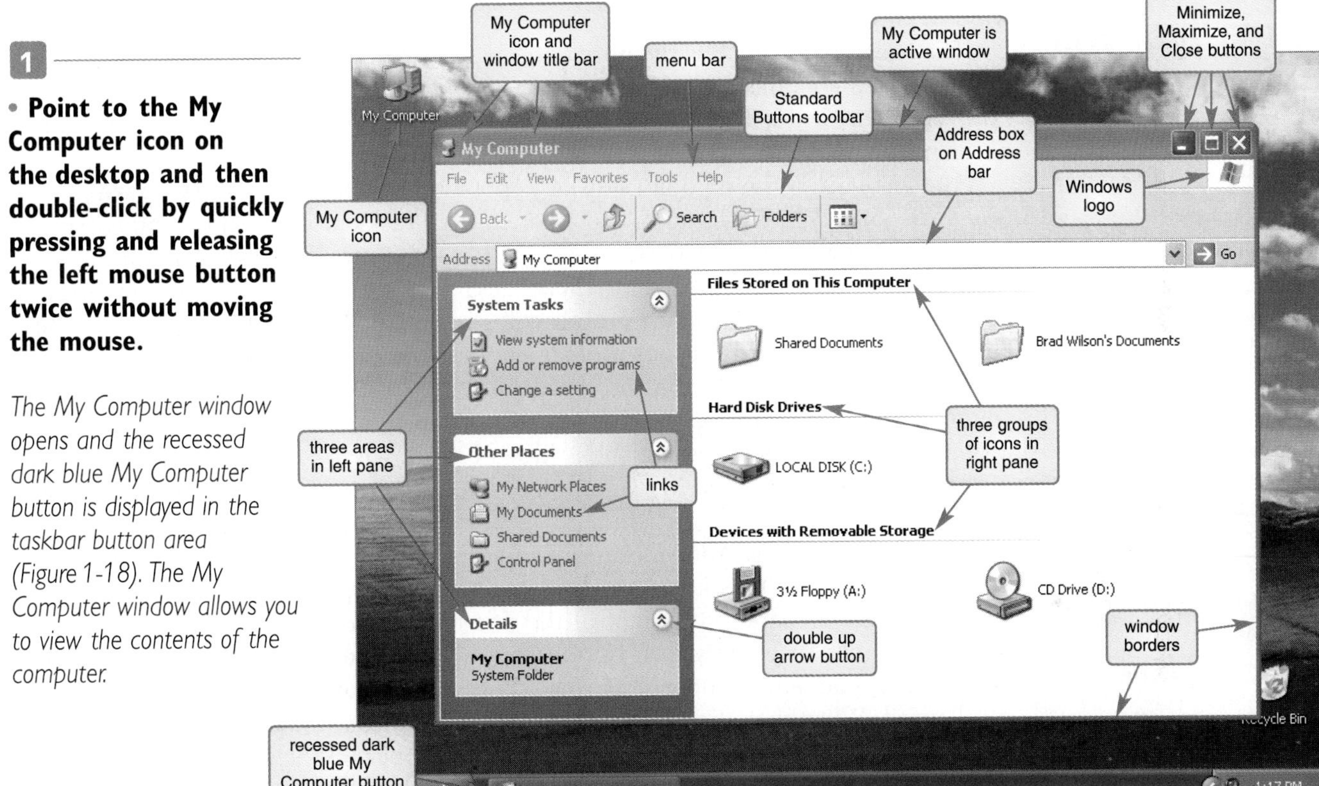

FIGURE 1-18

Other Ways

1. Right-click desktop icon, click Open on shortcut menu
2. Press WINDOWS+E, click Folders

The My Computer window, the only open window, is the active window. The **active window** is the window you currently are using or that currently is selected. Whenever you click an object that opens a window, such as the My Computer icon, Windows XP will open the window and a recessed dark blue button in the taskbar button area will identify the open window. The recessed dark blue button identifies the active window. The contents of the My Computer window on your computer may be different from the contents of the My Computer window shown in Figure 1-18.

More About

Double-Clicking

Double-clicking is the most difficult mouse skill to learn. Many people have a tendency to move the mouse before they click a second time, even when they do not want to move the mouse. With a little practice, you should find double-clicking without moving the mouse becomes quite natural.

More About

The Contents of the My Computer Window

Because windows can be easily customized, your My Computer window may not resemble the window shown in Figure 1-18. For example, different toolbars may appear below the menu bar, icons may appear smaller, icons may not be grouped, and different areas may be displayed in the left pane of the window.

More About

My Computer

While the trade press and media once poked fun at the My Computer name, Microsoft continues to expand the concept. Windows XP now showcases the My Computer, My Documents, My Pictures, and My Music names by placing them on the Start menu. In addition, the new My Videos folder was added to the operating system. Microsoft contends that beginners find these names easier to understand.

The My Computer Window

The thin blue line, or **window border**, surrounding the My Computer window shown in Figure 1-18 on the previous page determines its shape and size. The **title bar** at the top of the window contains a small icon that is similar to the icon on the desktop, and the **window title** (My Computer) identifies the window. The color of the title bar (dark blue) and the recessed dark blue My Computer button in the taskbar button area indicate that the My Computer window is the active window. The color of the active window on your computer may be different from the color shown in Figure 1-18.

Clicking the icon at the left on the title bar will display the **System menu**, which contains commands to carry out the actions associated with the My Computer window. At the right on the title bar are three buttons (the Minimize button, the Maximize button, and the Close button) that can be used to specify the size of the window or close the window.

The **menu bar**, which is the horizontal bar below the title bar of a window, in Figure 1-18 contains a list of menu names for the My Computer window: File, Edit, View, Favorites, Tools, and Help. The Windows logo appears on the far right of the menu bar.

The Standard buttons toolbar displays below the menu bar. The **Standard Buttons toolbar** allows you to perform often-used tasks more quickly than when you use the menu bar. Each button on the Standard Buttons toolbar contains an icon. Three buttons contain a **text label** (Back, Search, and Folders) that identifies the function of the button. Each button will be explained in detail as it is used. The buttons on the Standard Buttons toolbar on your computer may be different.

Below the Standard Buttons toolbar is the Address bar. The **Address bar** allows you to start an application, display a document, open another window, and search for information on the Internet. The Address bar shown in Figure 1-18 displays the Address box containing the My Computer icon, window title, down arrow, and the Go button.

The area below the Address bar is divided into two panes. The System Tasks, Other Places, and Details areas are displayed in the left pane. A title identifies each area. A button appears to the right of the title in each area to indicate whether the area is expanded or collapsed. A button identified by a **double up arrow** indicates the area is expanded. A button identified by a **double down arrow** indicates the area is collapsed. When you click the double up arrow button, the area collapses and only the title and the double down arrow button appear. When you click the double down arrow button, the area expands and the entire contents of the area are visible.

All three areas in the left pane are expanded. The **System Tasks area** contains a title (System Tasks) and three tasks (View system information, Add or remove programs, and Change a setting) associated with the My Computer window. The **Other Places area** contains a title (Other Places) and links to four folders (My Network Places, My Documents, Shared Documents, and Control Panel) associated with the My Computer folder. The **Details area** contains a title (Details), the window title (My Computer), and the folder type (System Folder) of the My Computer window. Clicking the double up arrow collapses the area and leaves only the title and arrow button.

Pointing to a task in the System Tasks area or a folder name in the Other Places area underlines the task or folder name and displays the task or folder name in light blue. Underlined text, such as the task and folder names, is referred to as a **hyperlink**, or simply a **link**. Pointing to a link changes the mouse pointer to a hand icon, and clicking a link displays information associated with the link. For example, clicking the Add or remove programs task in the System Tasks area allows you to install or remove application programs, and clicking the My Documents link in the Other Places area opens the My Documents window.

The right pane of the My Computer window in Figure 1-18 on page WIN 17 contains three groups of icons. The top group, Files Stored on This Computer, contains Shared Documents and Brad Wilson's Documents icons. The **Shared Documents folder** contains documents and folders that are available (shared) to other computer users on the network, and the Brad Wilson's Documents folder contains his personal documents. On your computer, your name will replace the Brad Wilson name in the Brad Wilson's Documents icon.

The middle group, Hard Disk Drives, contains the LOCAL DISK (C:) drive icon. A title to the right of the icon identifies the drive name, LOCAL DISK (C:). The bottom group, Devices with Removable Storage, contains the 3½ Floppy (A:) and CD Drive (D:) icons and labels. The three icons in the Hard Disk Drives and Devices with Removable Storage sections, called **drive icons**, represent a hard disk drive, 3½ floppy disk drive, and a Compact Disc drive. The number of groups in the right pane and the icons in the groups on your computer may be different.

Clicking a drive or folder icon selects the icon in the right pane and displays details about the drive or folder in the areas in the left pane. Double-clicking a drive or folder icon allows you to display the contents of the corresponding drive or folder in the right pane and details about the drive or folder in the areas in the left pane. You may find more, fewer, or different drive and folder icons in the My Computer window on your computer.

Minimizing a Window

Two buttons on the title bar of a window, the Minimize button and the Maximize button, allow you to control the way a window is displayed or is not displayed on the desktop. When you click the **Minimize button** (see Figure 1-19 on the next page), the My Computer window no longer is displayed on the desktop and the recessed dark blue My Computer button in the taskbar button area changes to a non-recessed medium blue button. A minimized window still is open but is not displayed on the screen. To minimize and then redisplay the My Computer window, complete the steps on the next page.

More About

Minimizing Windows

Windows management on the Windows XP desktop is important in order to keep the desktop uncluttered. You will find yourself frequently minimizing windows and then later reopening them with a click of a button in the taskbar button area.

To Minimize and Redisplay a Window

1

• **Point to the Minimize button on the title bar of the My Computer window.**

The mouse pointer points to the Minimize button on the My Computer window title bar, the color of the Minimize button changes to light blue, a ToolTip is displayed below the Minimize button, and the recessed dark blue My Computer button appears on the taskbar (Figure 1-19).

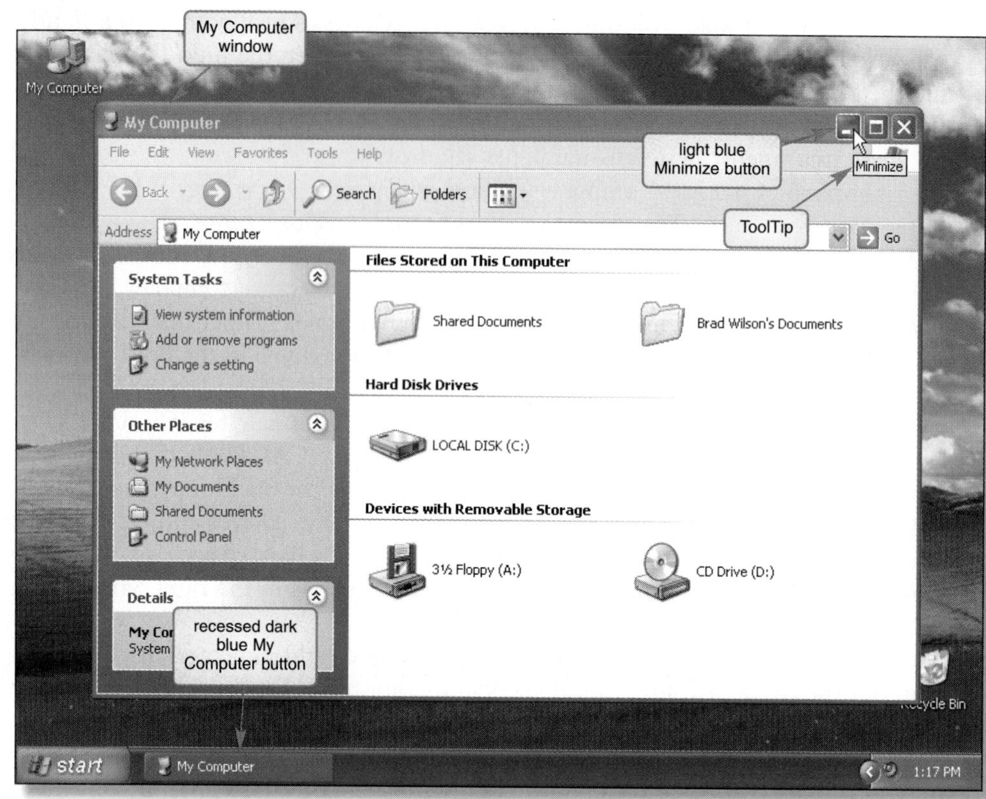

FIGURE 1-19

2

• **Click the Minimize button.**

When you minimize the My Computer window, Windows XP removes the My Computer window from the desktop, the My Computer button changes to a non-recessed button, and the color of the button changes to medium blue (Figure 1-20).

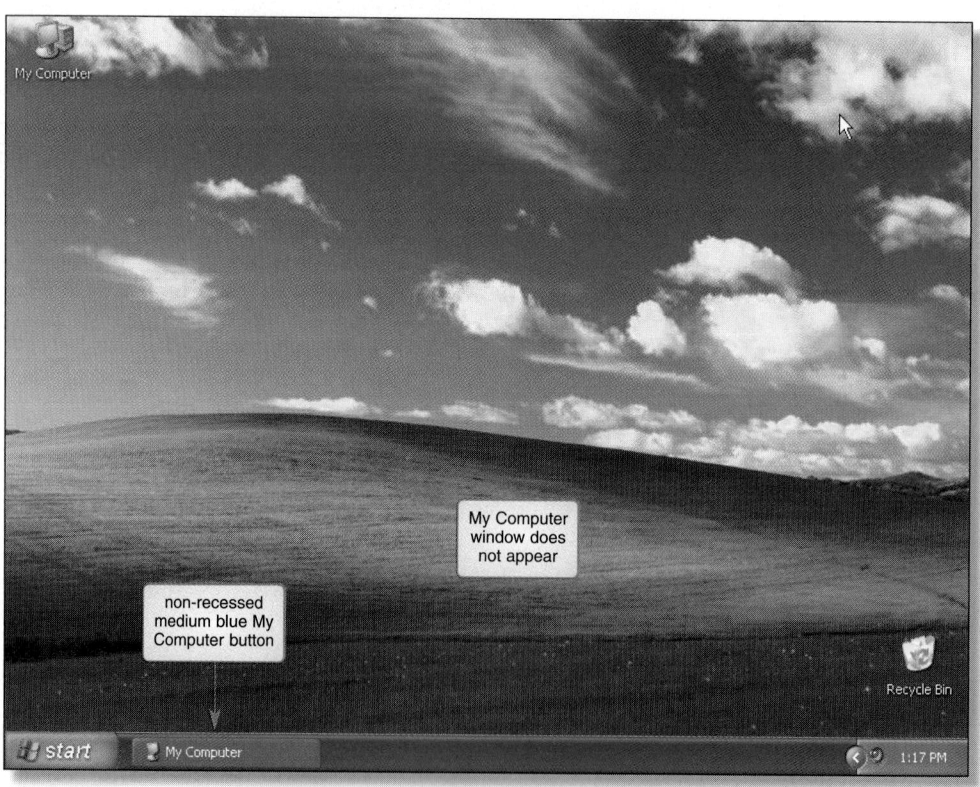

FIGURE 1-20

3

• **Click the My Computer button in the taskbar button area.**

The My Computer window is displayed in the same place with the same size as it was before being minimized, and the My Computer button on the taskbar is recessed (Figure 1-21). With the mouse pointer pointing to the My Computer button, the color of the button is medium blue. Moving the mouse pointer off the button changes its color to dark blue. The My Computer window is the active window because it contains the dark blue title bar.

FIGURE 1-21

Whenever a window is minimized, it is not displayed on the desktop, but a non-recessed dark blue button for the window is displayed in the taskbar button area. Whenever you want a minimized window to display and be the active window, click its button in the taskbar button area.

As you point to many objects, such as a button or command, when you work with Windows XP, Windows XP displays a ToolTip. A **ToolTip** is a short on-screen note associated with the object to which you are pointing. ToolTips display on the desktop for approximately five seconds. Examples of ToolTips are shown in Figure 1-9 on page WIN 12, Figure 1-19, Figures 1-22 and 1-24 on the next page, and Figure 1-26 on page WIN 23. To reduce clutter on the screen, the ToolTips will not be shown on the remaining screens in this book.

Other Ways

1. Click icon on left side of title bar, click Minimize, in taskbar button area click taskbar button
2. Right-click title bar, click Minimize, in taskbar button area click taskbar button
3. Press WINDOWS+M

Maximizing and Restoring a Window

Sometimes when information is displayed in a window, the information is not completely visible. One method of displaying the entire contents of a window is to enlarge the window using the **Maximize button**. The Maximize button maximizes a window so the window fills the entire screen, making it easier to see the contents of the window. When a window is maximized, the **Restore Down button** replaces the Maximize button on the title bar. Clicking the Restore Down button will return the window to its size before maximizing. To maximize and restore the My Computer window, complete the steps on the next page.

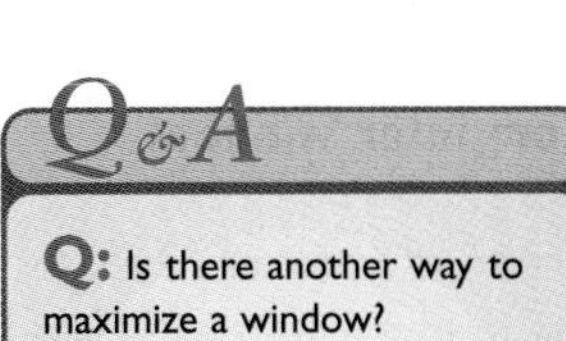

Q: Is there another way to maximize a window?

A: Yes. If the window appears on the desktop, double-click its title bar. If the window is not displayed on the desktop, right-click the window's button on the taskbar and then click Maximize on the shortcut menu.

To Maximize and Restore a Window

1

• **Point to the Maximize button on the title bar of the My Computer window.**

The mouse pointer points to the Maximize button on the My Computer window title bar and the color of the Maximize button changes to light blue (Figure 1-22). A ToolTip identifying the button name is displayed below the Maximize button.

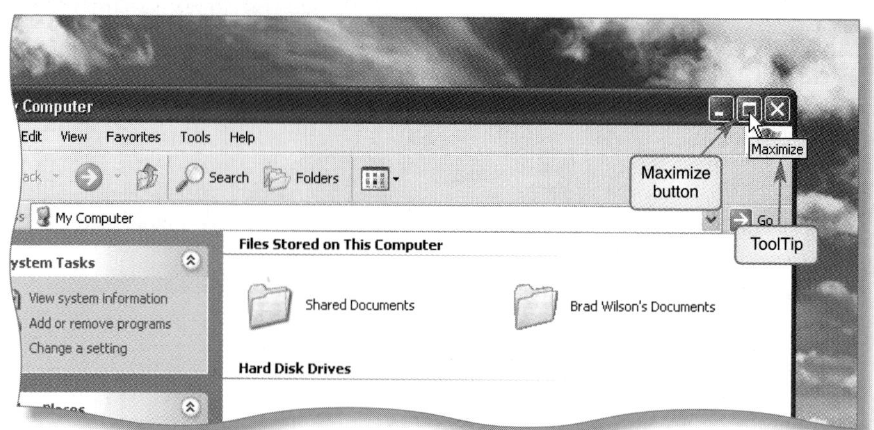

FIGURE 1-22

2

• **Click the Maximize button.**

The My Computer window expands so it and the taskbar fill the desktop (Figure 1-23). The Restore Down button replaces the Maximize button, the My Computer button in the taskbar button area does not change, and the My Computer window still is the active window.

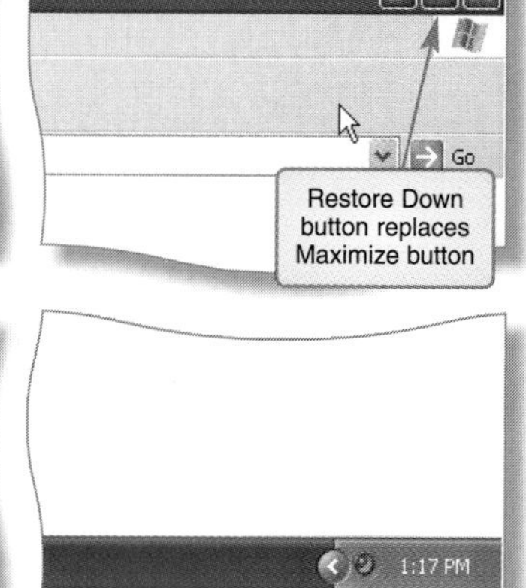

FIGURE 1-23

3

• **Point to the Restore Down button on the title bar of the My Computer window.**

The mouse pointer points to the Restore Down button on the My Computer window title bar and the color of the Restore Down button changes to light blue (Figure 1-24). A ToolTip is displayed below the Restore Down button identifying it.

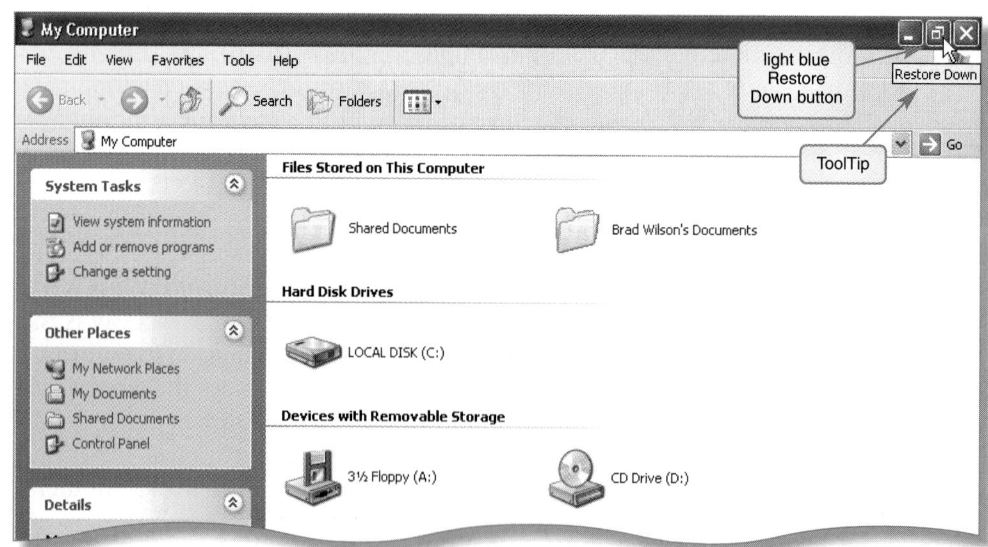

FIGURE 1-24

4

• **Click the Restore Down button.**

The My Computer window returns to the size and position it occupied before being maximized (Figure 1-25). The My Computer button does not change. The Maximize button replaces the Restore Down button.

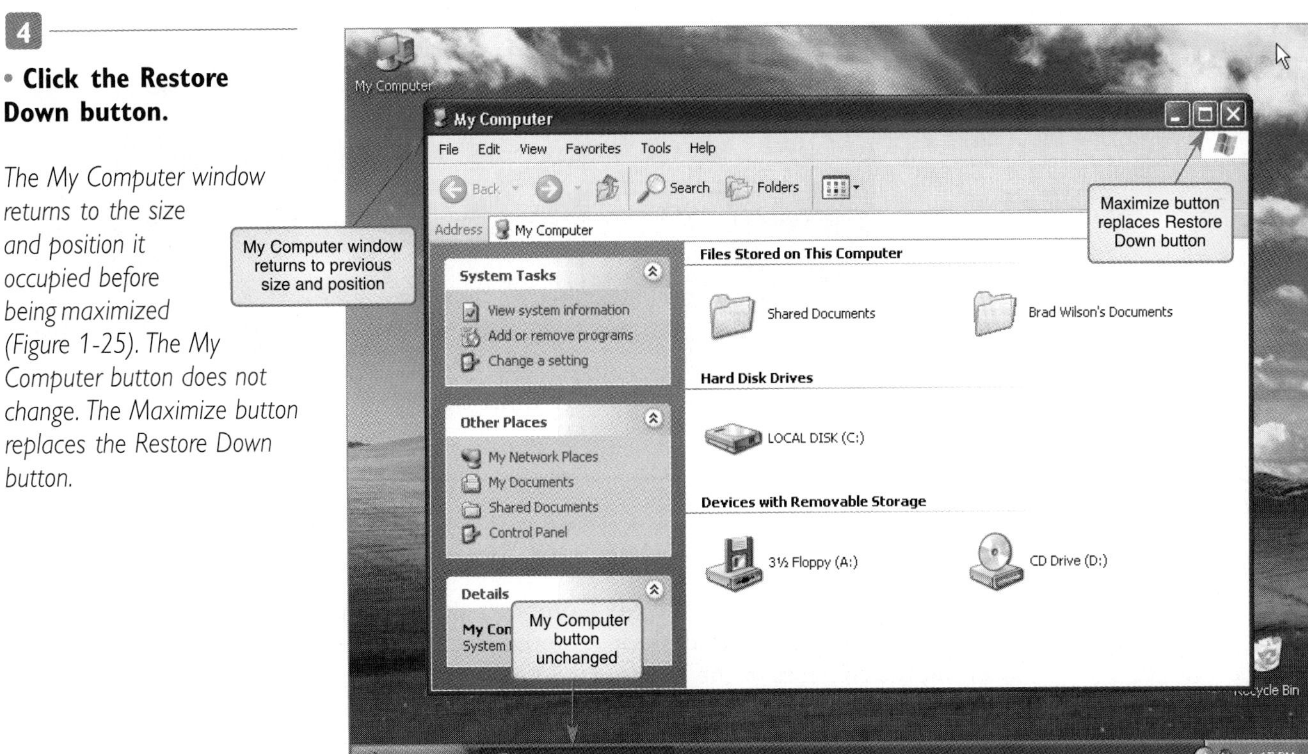

FIGURE 1-25

When a window is maximized, such as in Figure 1-23, you also can minimize the window by clicking the Minimize button. If, after minimizing the window, you click its button in the taskbar button area, the window will return to its maximized size.

More About

Opening and Closing a Window

Windows XP remembers the size of a window when you close the window. When you reopen the window, it will display in the same size you closed it.

Closing a Window

The **Close button** on the title bar of a window closes the window and removes the taskbar button from the taskbar. The following steps show how to close the My Computer window.

To Close a Window

1

• **Point to the Close button on the title bar of the My Computer window.**

The mouse pointer points to the Close button on the My Computer window title bar and the color of the Close button changes to light red (Figure 1-26). A ToolTip is displayed below the Close button.

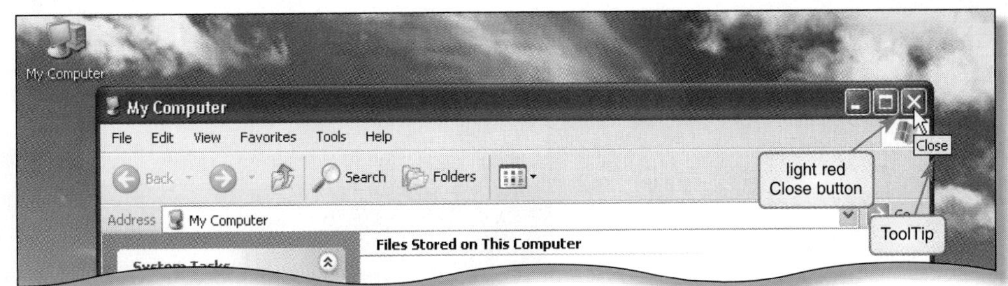

FIGURE 1-26

2

• **Click the Close button.**

The My Computer window closes and the My Computer button no longer is displayed in the taskbar button area (Figure 1-27).

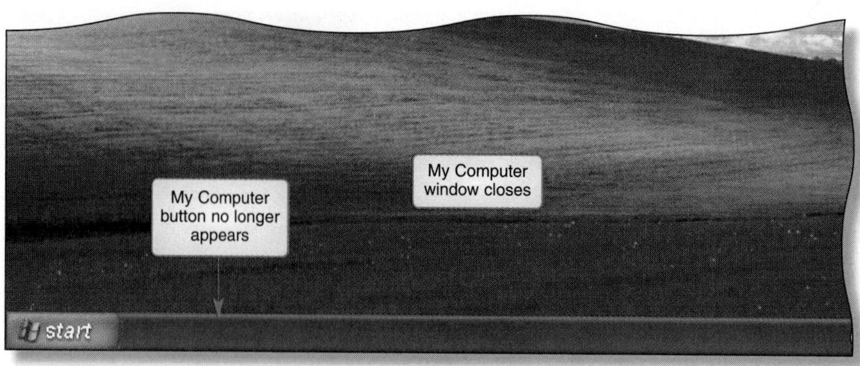

FIGURE 1-27

Other Ways

1. Click icon on left side of title bar, click Close
2. Right-click title bar, click Close on shortcut menu
3. Press ALT+F4

Opening a Window Using the Start Menu

Previously, you opened the My Computer window by double-clicking the My Computer icon on the desktop. Another method of opening a window and viewing the contents of the window is to click a command on the Start menu. The steps below show how to open the My Documents window using the My Documents command on the Start menu.

To Open a Window Using the Start Menu

1

• **Click the Start button on the taskbar and then point to the My Documents command on the Start menu.**

The Start menu is displayed, the Start button is recessed on the taskbar, the color of the button changes to dark green, and the mouse pointer points to the highlighted My Documents command on the Start menu (Figure 1-28).

More About

Opening a Window

Although the preferred method of opening a window in previous Windows versions was double-clicking a desktop icon, using the redesigned Start menu now makes it easier to open those windows.

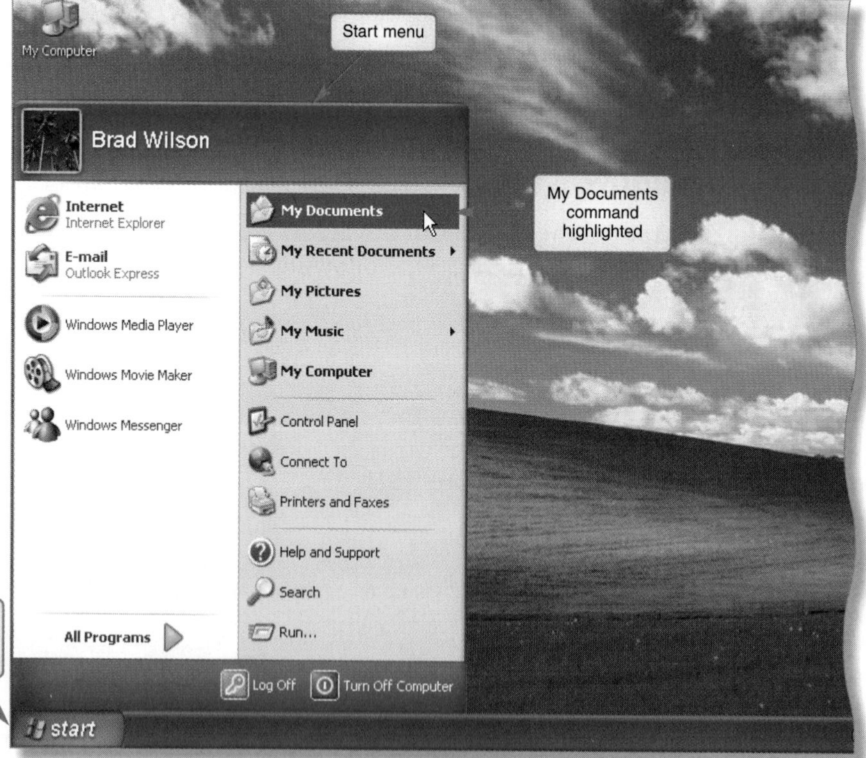

FIGURE 1-28

2

• **Click My Documents on the Start menu.**

The My Documents window opens, the recessed dark blue My Documents button is displayed in the taskbar button area, and the My Documents window is the active window (Figure 1-29). You may find more, fewer, or different folder icons in the right pane on your computer.

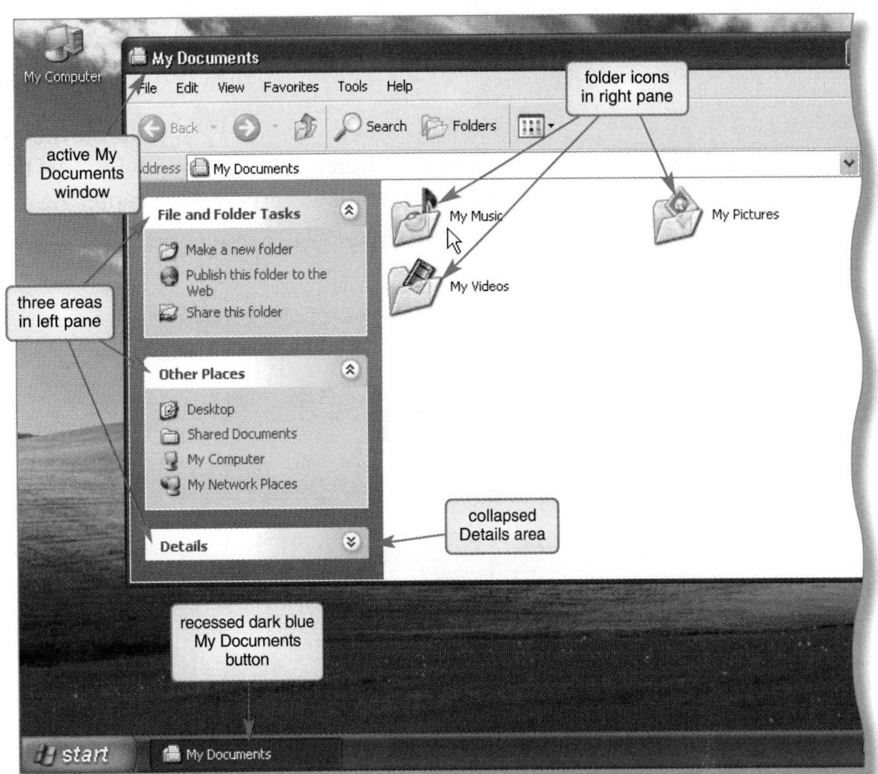

FIGURE 1-29

Other Ways

1. Click Start button, right-click window icon, click Open on shortcut menu

The My Documents Window

The **My Documents window** shown in Figure 1-29 is a central location for the storage and management of documents. The title bar at the top of the My Documents window identifies the window and the color of the title bar (dark blue) and the recessed dark blue My Documents button in the taskbar button area indicate the My Documents window is the active window.

The File and Folders Tasks, Other Places, and Details areas display in the left pane. The **File and Folders Tasks area** contains three tasks (Make a new folder, Publish this folder to the Web, and Share this folder). The **Other Places area** contains links to four folders (Desktop, Shared Documents, My Computer, and My Network Places). The **Details area** is collapsed and only the title and a double down arrow button appear in the area.

The right pane of the My Documents window contains the My Music, My Pictures, and My Videos folders. Clicking a folder icon in the right pane highlights the icon in the right pane and changes the files and folder tasks in the File and Folder Tasks area in the left pane. Double-clicking a folder icon displays the contents of the corresponding folder in the right pane, adds another area to the folder (My Music Tasks area, My Pictures Tasks area, or My Videos Tasks area) in the left pane, and changes the file and folder information in the left pane.

More About

Dragging

Dragging is the second-most difficult mouse skill to learn. You may want to practice dragging a few times so you will be comfortable with it. Do not let dragging become a drag — PRACTICE!!

Moving a Window by Dragging

Drag means you point to an item, hold down the left mouse button, move the item to the desired location, and then release the left mouse button. You can move any open window to another location on the desktop by pointing to the title bar of the window and then dragging the window. The following steps illustrate dragging the My Documents window to the center of the desktop.

To Move a Window by Dragging

1

- **Point to the My Documents window title bar (Figure 1-30).**

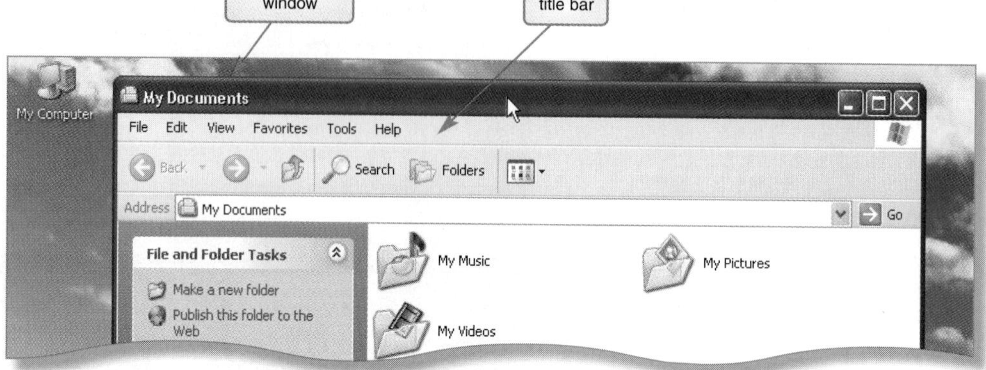

FIGURE 1-30

2

- **Hold down the left mouse button, move the mouse down so the window moves to the center of the desktop, and then release the left mouse button.**

As you drag the My Documents window, the window moves across the desktop. When you release the left mouse button, the window is displayed in its new location on the desktop (Figure 1-31).

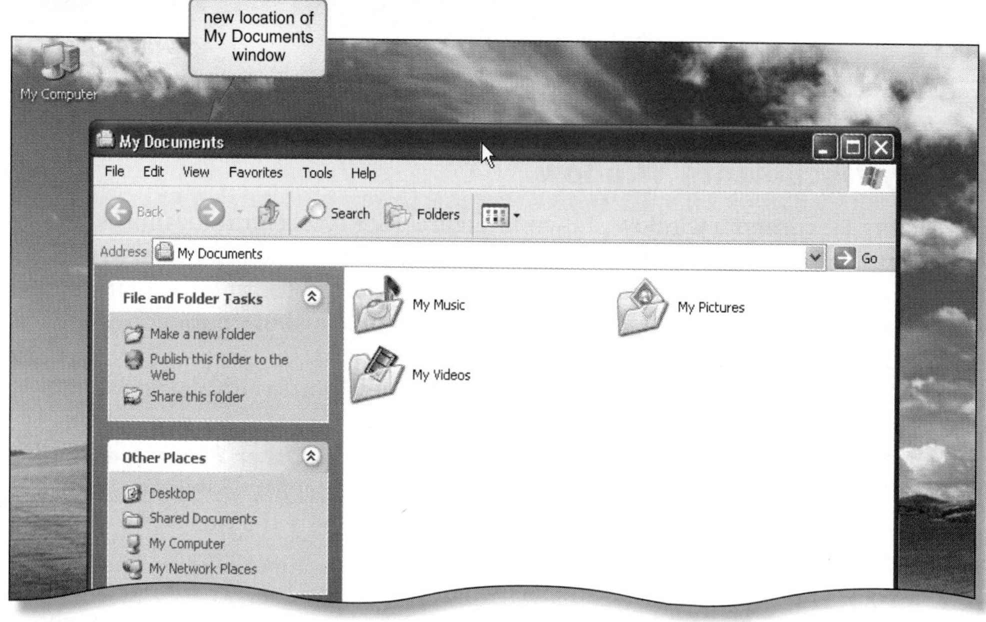

FIGURE 1-31

Other Ways

1. Click icon on left side of title bar, click Move, drag window

Expanding an Area

The Details area in the My Documents window is collapsed and a double down arrow button appears to the right of the Details title (see Figure 1-32). Clicking the button or the area title expands the Details area and reveals the window title (My Documents) and folder type (System Folder) in the Details area. Similarly, clicking the double up arrow button or the area title collapses the area so only the area title and double down arrow button appear in the area. The steps on the next page illustrate how to expand the Details area in the left pane of the My Documents window.

To Expand an Area

1

• **Point to the double down arrow button in the Details area.**

The mouse pointer changes to a hand icon and points to the double down arrow button in the Details area and the color of the Details title and button changes to light blue (Figure 1-32).

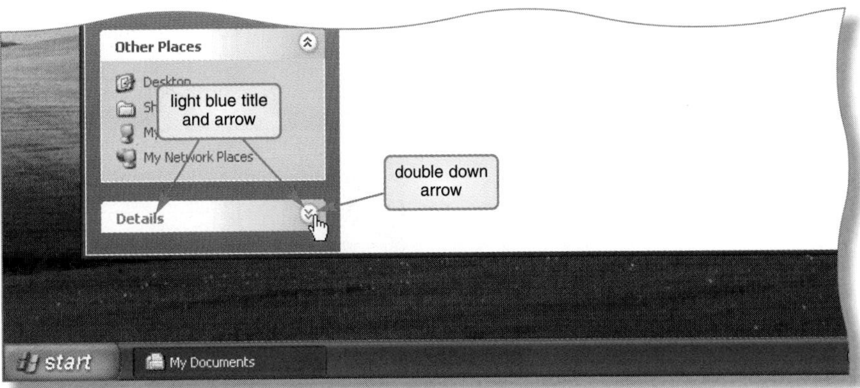

FIGURE 1-32

2

• **Click the double down arrow button.**

The Details area expands, the window title (My Documents) and folder type (System Folder) is displayed in the area, the double down arrow on the button changes to a double up arrow, a portion of the left pane is not visible, and a scroll bar is displayed in the area (Figure 1-33).

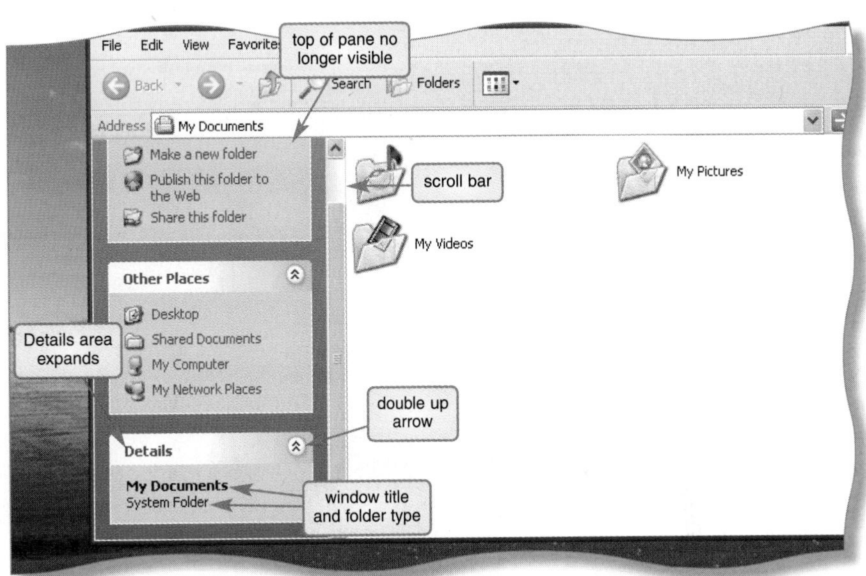

FIGURE 1-33

A **scroll bar** is a bar that appears when the contents of a pane or window are not completely visible. A vertical scroll bar contains an **up scroll arrow**, a **down scroll arrow**, and a **scroll box** that enable you to view areas that currently are not visible. A vertical scroll bar is displayed along the right side of the left pane in the My Documents window shown in Figure 1-33. In some cases, the vertical scroll bar also may appear along the right side of the right pane in a window.

Q: Is scrolling a window the most efficient way to view objects in a window?

A: No. There are other more efficient methods. You can either maximize a window or size it so that all the objects in the window are visible. It is better to avoid scrolling because scrolling takes time.

Scrolling in a Window

Previously, the My Documents window was maximized to display information that was not completely visible in the My Documents window. Another method of viewing information that is not visible in a window is to use the scroll bar.

Scrolling can be accomplished in three ways: (1) click the scroll arrows; (2) click the scroll bar; and (3) drag the scroll box. On the following pages, you will use the scroll bar to scroll the contents of the left pane of the My Documents window. The steps on the next page show how to scroll the left pane using the scroll arrows.

To Scroll Using Scroll Arrows

1

• **Point to the up scroll arrow on the vertical scroll bar.**

The color of the up scroll arrow changes to light blue (Figure 1-34).

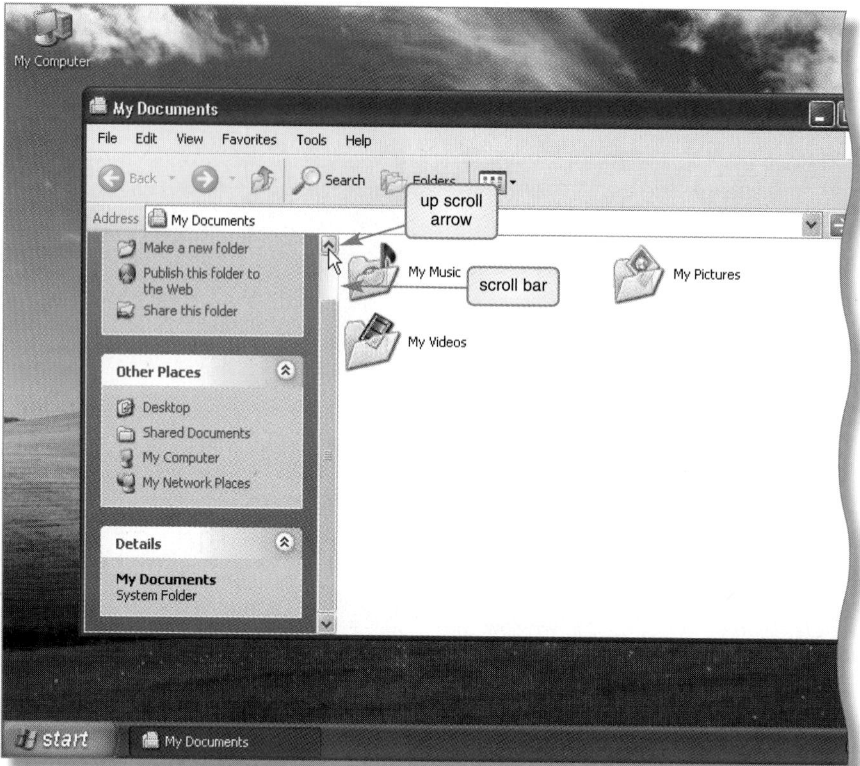

FIGURE 1-34

2

• **Click the up scroll arrow two times.**

The left pane scrolls down (the contents in the left pane move up) and displays a portion of the text in the File and Folder Tasks area at the top of the pane that previously was not visible (Figure 1-35). Because the size of the left pane does not change when you scroll, the contents in the left pane will change, as seen in the difference between Figures 1-35 and 1-34.

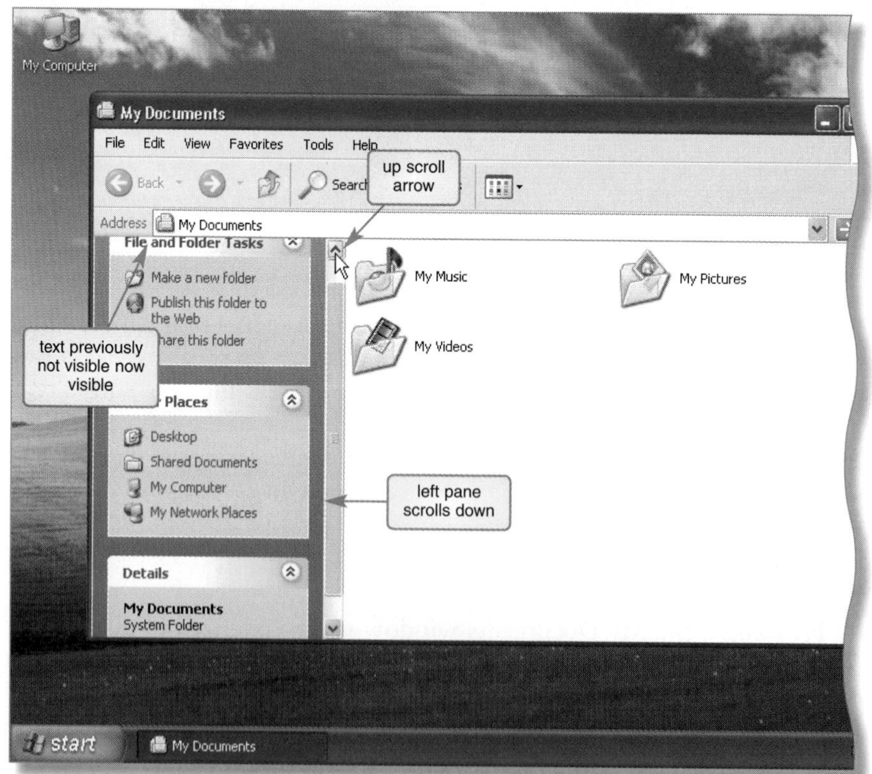

FIGURE 1-35

3

• **Click the up scroll arrow three more times.**

The scroll box moves to the top of the scroll bar and the remaining text in the File and Folder Tasks area is displayed (Figure 1-36).

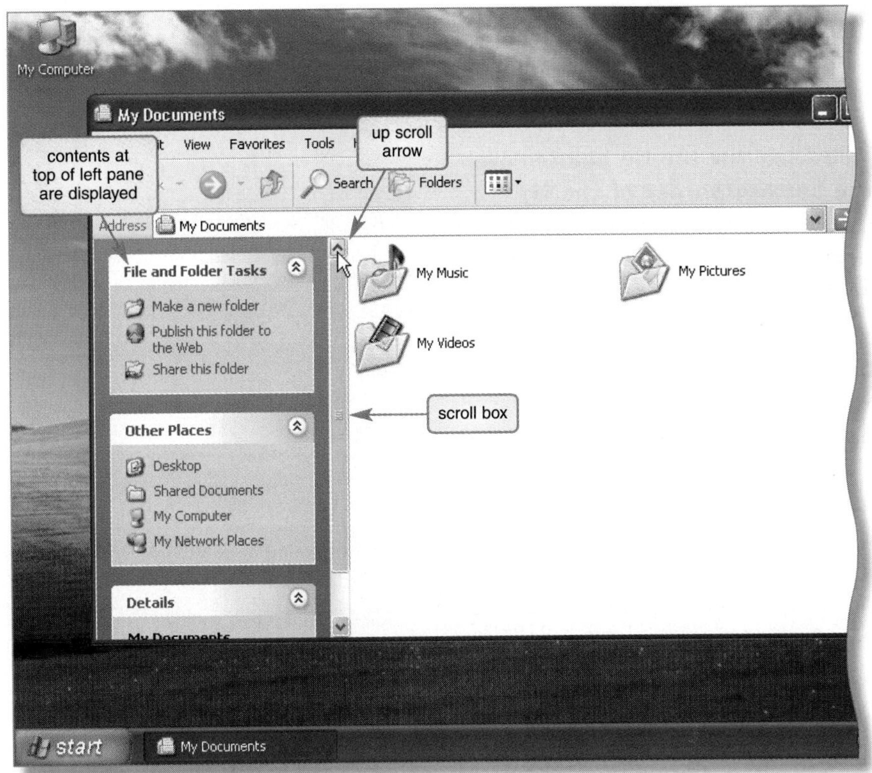

FIGURE 1-36

You can scroll continuously using scroll arrows by pointing to the up or down scroll arrow and holding down the left mouse button. The area being scrolled continues to scroll until you release the left mouse button or you reach the top or bottom of the area. You also can scroll by clicking the scroll bar itself. When you click the scroll bar, the area being scrolled moves up or down a greater distance than when you click the scroll arrows.

The third way in which you can scroll is by dragging the scroll box. When you drag the scroll box, the area being scrolled moves up or down as you drag.

Being able to view the contents of a window by scrolling is an important Windows XP skill because in many cases, the entire contents of a window are not visible.

More About

The Scroll Box

Dragging the scroll box is the most efficient technique to scroll long distances. In many application programs, such as Microsoft Word, as you scroll using the scroll box, the page number of the document appears next to the scroll box.

Sizing a Window by Dragging

As previously mentioned, sometimes when information is displayed in a window, the information is not completely visible. A third method of displaying information that is not visible is to change the size of the window by dragging the border of a window. The step on the next page illustrates changing the size of the My Documents window.

More About

Scrolling Guidelines

General scrolling guidelines: (1) To scroll short distances (line by line), click the scroll arrows; (2) To scroll one screen at a time, click the scroll bar; and (3) To scroll long distances, drag the scroll box.

To Size a Window by Dragging

1

- **Position the mouse pointer over the bottom border of the My Documents window until the mouse pointer changes to a two-headed arrow.**
- **Drag the bottom border downward until the Details area on your desktop resembles the Details area shown in Figure 1-37.**

As you drag the bottom border, the My Documents window, vertical scroll bar, and scroll box change size. After dragging, the Details area is visible and the vertical scroll bar no longer is visible (Figure 1-37).

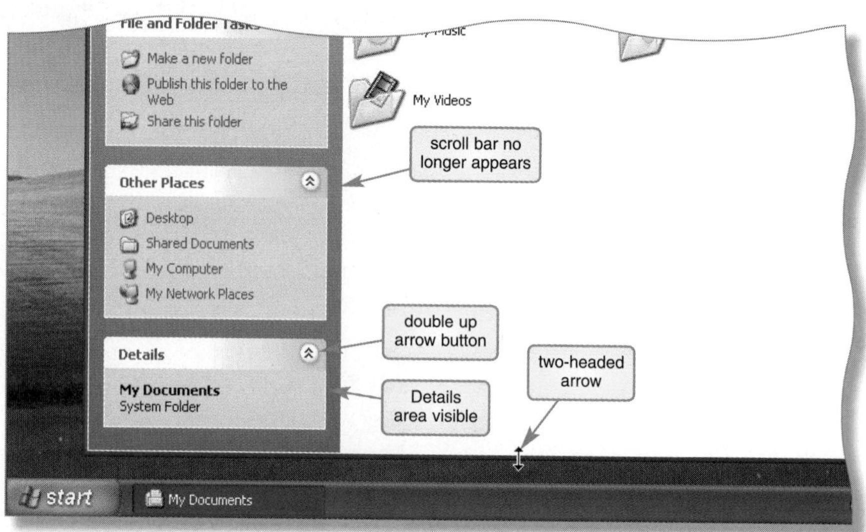

FIGURE 1-37

In addition to dragging the bottom border of a window, you also can drag the other borders (left, right, and top) and any window corner. If you drag a vertical border (left or right), you can move the border left or right. If you drag a horizontal border (top or bottom), you can move the border of the window up or down. If you drag a corner, you can move the corner up, down, left, or right.

Collapsing an Area

The Details area in the My Documents window is expanded and a double up arrow button displays to the right of the Details title (Figure 1-37). Clicking the button or the area title collapses the Details area and removes the window title (My Documents) and folder type (System Folder) from the Details area. The following steps show how to collapse the Details area in the My Documents window.

To Collapse an Area

1

- **Point to the double up arrow button in the Details area.**

The mouse pointer changes to a hand icon, points to the double up arrow button in the Details area, and the color of the Details title and button changes to light blue (Figure 1-38).

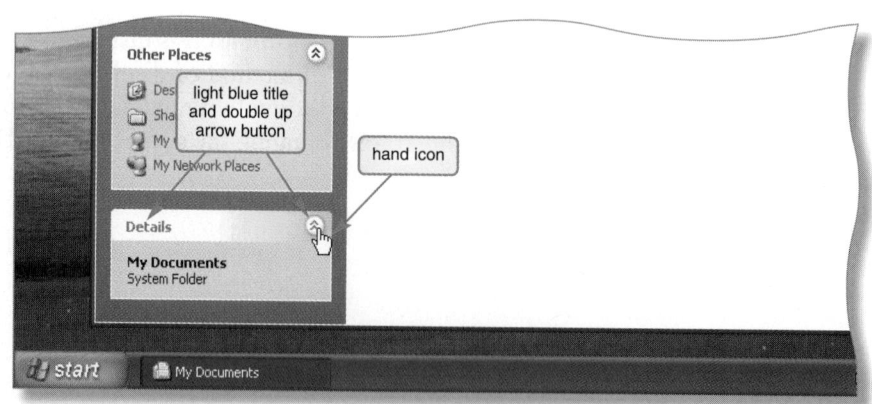

FIGURE 1-38

2

• **Click the double up arrow button.**

The Details area collapses and only the Details title and the double down arrow button are displayed (Figure 1-39).

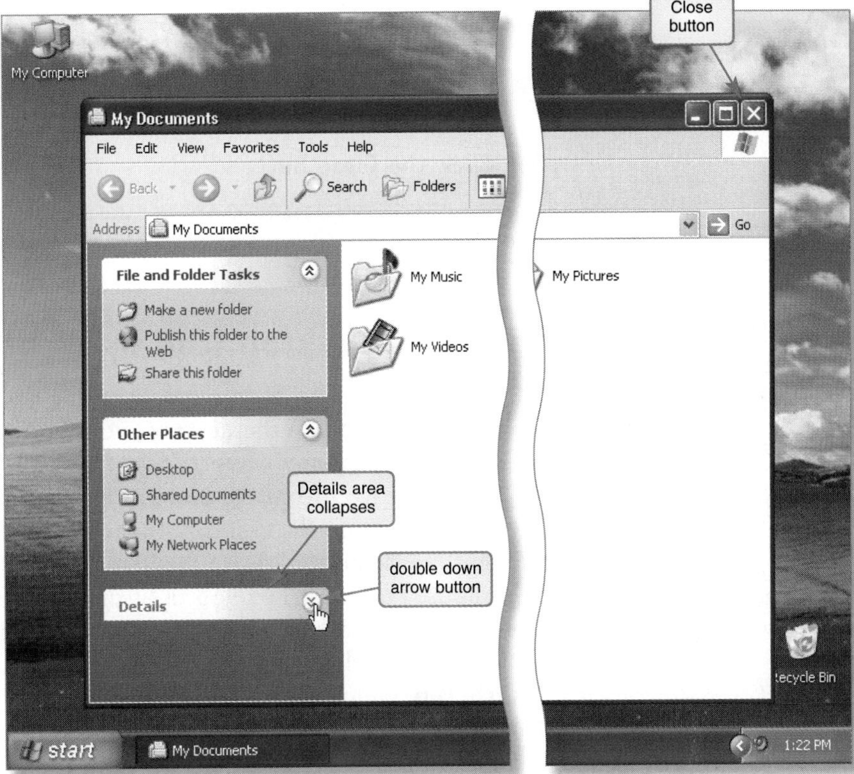

FIGURE 1-39

Resizing a Window

After moving and resizing a window, you may wish to return the window to approximately its original size. To return the My Documents window to about its original size, complete the following steps.

To Resize a Window

1. **Position the mouse pointer over the bottom border of the My Documents window border until the mouse pointer changes to a two-headed arrow.**
2. **Drag the bottom border of the My Documents window up until the window is the same size as shown in Figure 1-29 on page WIN 25 and then release the mouse button.**

The My Documents window is approximately the same size as it was before you made it smaller.

Closing a Window

After you have completed work in a window, normally you will close the window. The steps on the next page show how to close the My Documents window.

To Close a Window

1. **Point to the Close button on the right of the title bar in the My Documents window.**
2. **Click the Close button.**

The My Documents window closes and the desktop contains no open windows.

> *More About*
>
> **Right-Dragging**
>
> Right-dragging was not available on some earlier versions of Windows, so you might find people who are familiar with Windows not even considering right-dragging. Because it always produces a shortcut menu, right-dragging is the safest way to drag.

Deleting a Desktop Icon by Right-Dragging

The My Computer icon remains on the desktop. In many cases after you have placed an icon on the desktop, you will want to delete the icon. Although Windows XP has many ways to delete desktop icons, one method of removing the My Computer icon from the desktop is to right-drag the My Computer icon to the Recycle Bin icon on the desktop. **Right-drag** means you point to an item, hold down the right mouse button, move the item to the desired location, and then release the right mouse button. When you right-drag an object, a shortcut menu is displayed. The shortcut menu contains commands specifically for use with the object being dragged.

When you delete an icon from the desktop, Windows XP places the item in the **Recycle Bin**, which is an area on the hard disk that contains all the items you have deleted not only from the desktop but also from the hard disk. When the Recycle Bin becomes full, you can empty it. Up until the time you empty the Recycle Bin, you can recover deleted items from the Recycle Bin. The following steps illustrate how to delete the My Computer icon by right-dragging the icon to the Recycle Bin icon.

To Delete a Desktop Icon by Right-Dragging

1

- **Point to the My Computer icon on the desktop, hold down the right mouse button, drag the My Computer icon over the Recycle Bin icon.**
- **Release the right mouse button and then point to Move Here on the shortcut menu.**

The My Computer icon is displayed on the desktop as you drag the icon. When you release the right mouse button, a shortcut menu is displayed on the desktop (Figure 1-40). Pointing to the Move Here command on the shortcut menu highlights the Move Here command.

FIGURE 1-40

2

• **Click Move Here and then point to the Yes button in the Confirm Delete dialog box.**

The shortcut menu closes, and the Confirm Delete dialog box is displayed on the desktop (Figure 1-41). A dialog box is displayed whenever Windows XP needs to supply information to you or wants you to enter information or select among several options. The Confirm Delete dialog box contains a question, a message, and the Yes and No buttons.

3

• **Click the Yes button.**

The Confirm Delete dialog box closes, the My Computer icon no longer is displayed on the desktop, and the My Computer icon now is contained in the Recycle Bin.

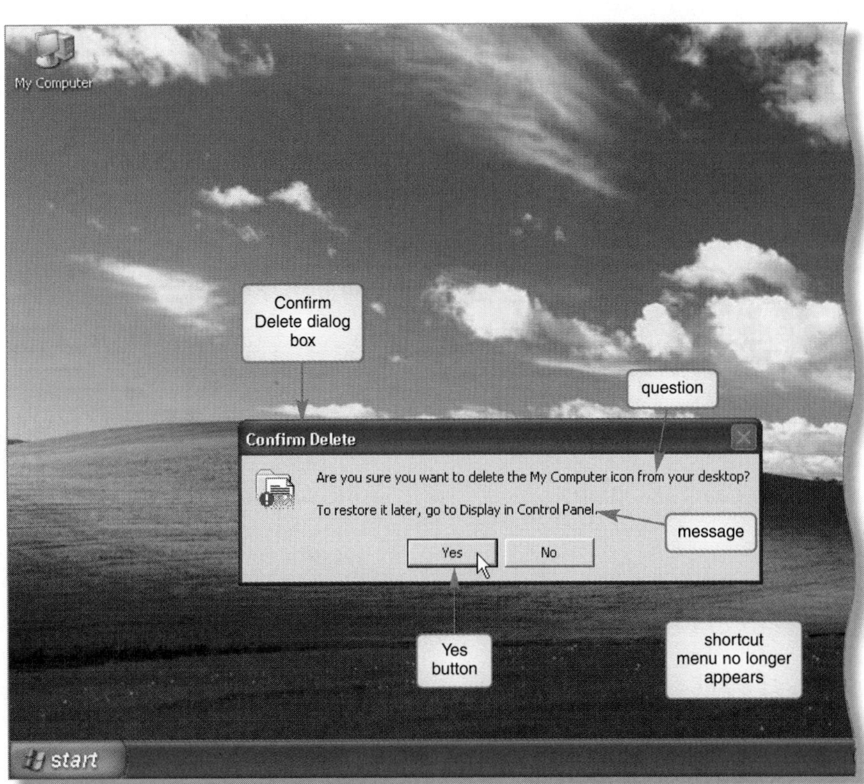

FIGURE 1-41

Other Ways

1. Drag icon to Recycle Bin, click Yes button
2. Right-click icon, click Delete, click Yes button

If you click **Move Here** on the shortcut menu shown in Figure 1-40, Windows XP will move the icon from its current location to the new location. If you click Cancel, the operation will be terminated, and the **Cancel command** will reset anything you have done during the operation.

In Figure 1-41, the Confirm Delete dialog box contains the Yes button and the No button. Clicking the Yes button completes the operation and clicking the No button terminates the operation.

Although you can move icons by dragging with the primary (left) mouse button and by right-dragging with the secondary (right) mouse button, it is strongly suggested you right-drag because a shortcut menu appears and, in most cases, you can specify the exact operation you want to occur. When you drag using the left mouse button, a default operation takes place and that operation may not be the operation you intended to perform.

Summary of Mouse and Windows Operations

You have seen how to use the mouse to point, click, right-click, double-click, drag, and right-drag in order to accomplish certain tasks on the desktop. The use of a mouse is an important skill when using Windows XP. In addition, you have learned how to move around and use windows on the Windows XP desktop.

More About

The Microsoft Office Keyboard

When using the Single Touch pad, Microsoft Office users place their left hand on the pad and their right hand on the mouse. These hand positions allow them to get more work done in less time. They also report that when using Hot Keys, they can increase productivity because they do not have to take their hand off the keyboard as frequently to use a mouse.

The Keyboard and Keyboard Shortcuts

The **keyboard** is an input device on which you manually key in, or type, data. Figure 1-42 shows the Microsoft Office keyboard designed specifically for use with Microsoft Office and the Internet. The Single Touch pad along the left side of the keyboard contains keys to browse the Internet, copy and paste text, and switch between applications. A scroll wheel allows you to move quickly within a document window. The Hot Keys along the top of the keyboard allow you to start a Web browser or e-mail program, play multimedia, and adjust the system volume.

FIGURE 1-42

More About

Microsoft Keyboards

For additional information about Microsoft Keyboards, visit the Microsoft Windows XP More About Web Page (scsite.com/winoff20032e/more) and then click Microsoft Keyboards.

Many tasks you accomplish with a mouse also can be accomplished using a keyboard. To perform tasks using the keyboard, you must understand the notation used to identify which keys to press. This notation is used throughout Windows XP to identify a **keyboard shortcut**.

Keyboard shortcuts consist of (1) pressing a single key (such as press the ENTER key); or (2) pressing and holding down one key and pressing a second key, as shown by two key names separated by a plus sign (such as press CTRL+ESC). For example, to obtain help about Windows XP, you can press the F1 key and to display the Start menu, hold down the CTRL key and then press the ESC key (press CTRL+ESC).

Often, computer users will use keyboard shortcuts for operations they perform frequently. For example, many users find pressing the F1 key to start Help and Support easier than using the Start menu as shown later in this project. As a user, you probably will find the combination of keyboard and mouse operations that particularly suits you, but it is strongly recommended that generally you use the mouse.

Starting an Application Program

One of the basic tasks you can perform using Windows XP is starting an application program. A **program** is a set of computer instructions that carries out a task on the computer. An **application program** is a set of specific computer instructions that is designed to allow you to accomplish a particular task. For example, a **word processing program** is an application program that allows you to create written documents; a **presentation graphics program** is an application program that allows you to create graphic presentations for display on a computer; and a **Web browser program** is an application program that allows you to search for and display Web pages.

The **default Web browser program** (Internet Explorer) appears in the pinned items list on the Start menu shown in Figure 1-43. Because the default **Web browser** is selected during the installation of the Windows XP operating system, the default Web browser on your computer may be different. In addition, you can easily select another Web browser as the default Web browser. Another frequently used Web browser program is **MSN Explorer**.

More About

Application Programs

Several application programs (Internet Explorer, Movie Maker, Media Player, and Windows Messenger) are part of Windows XP. Most application programs, such as the Microsoft Office applications, must be purchased separately from Windows XP, however.

Starting an Application Using the Start Menu

The most common activity performed on a computer is starting an application program to accomplish specific tasks. You can start an application program by using the Start menu. To illustrate the use of the Start menu to start an application program, the default Web browser program (Internet Explorer) will be started. The following steps illustrate starting Internet Explorer using the Internet command on the Start menu.

To Start an Application Using the Start Menu

1

- **Click the Start button on the taskbar and then point to Internet on the pinned items list on the Start menu.**

The Start menu is displayed (Figure 1-43). The pinned items list on the Start menu contains the Internet command to start the default Web browser program and the name of the default Web browser program (Internet Explorer). The default Web browser program on your computer may be different.

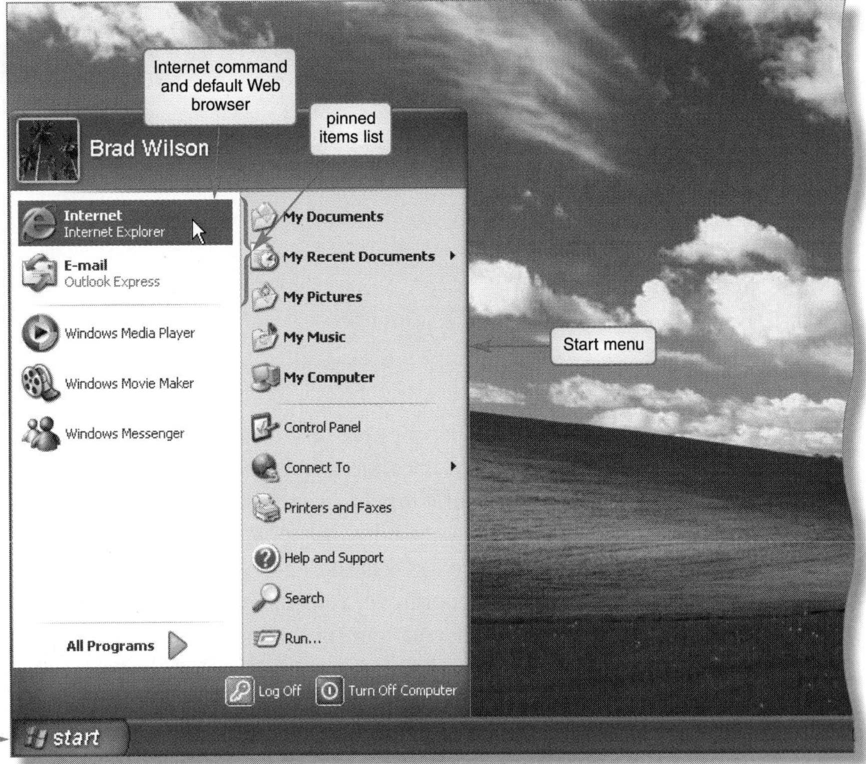

FIGURE 1-43

2

• **Click Internet.**

Windows XP starts the Internet Explorer program by displaying the Welcome to MSN.com – Microsoft Internet Explorer window, displaying the MSN home page in the window, and adding a recessed button on the taskbar (Figure 1-44). The URL for the Web page is displayed in the Address bar. Because you can select the default Web browser and the Web page to display when you start the Web browser, the Web page that is displayed on your desktop may be different.

FIGURE 1-44

3

• **Click the Close button in the Microsoft Internet Explorer window.**

The Microsoft Internet Explorer window closes.

Other Ways

1. Click Start button, in frequently used program list click Internet Explorer
2. Click Start button, point to All Programs, click Internet Explorer
3. Press CTRL+ESC, press I

Any computer connected to the Internet that contains Web pages you can reference is called a **Web site**. The **MSN.com Web site**, one of millions of Web sites around the world, is stored on a computer operated by Microsoft Corporation and can be accessed using a Web browser. The Welcome to MSN.com **Web page** shown in Figure 1-44 is the first Web page you see when you access the MSN.com Web site and is, therefore, referred to as a **home page**, or **start page.** The Web page that displays on your computer may be different.

After you have started a Web browser, you can use the program to search for and display additional Web pages located on different Web sites around the world.

In the preceding section, you started Internet Explorer and then quit the Internet Explorer program by closing the Microsoft Internet Explorer window. In the next section, you will learn about hierarchical format, USB flash drives, and the Windows Explorer application program.

Windows Explorer

Windows Explorer is an application program included with Windows XP. It allows you to view the contents of the computer, the hierarchy of drives and folders on the computer, and the files and folders in each folder. In this project, you will use Windows Explorer to (1) expand and collapse drives and folders; (2) display drive and folder contents; (3) create a new folder; (4) copy a file between folders; and (5) rename and then delete a file. These are common operations that you should understand how to perform.

Starting Windows Explorer

As with many other operations, Windows XP offers a variety of ways to start Windows Explorer. The following steps show how to start Windows Explorer using the Folders button in the My Computer window.

To Start Windows Explorer and Maximize Its Window

1

- **Click the Start button on the taskbar and then click My Computer on the Start menu.**
- **Maximize the My Computer window.**
- **If the status bar does not appear at the bottom of the My Computer window, click View on the menu bar and then click Status Bar.**
- **Point to the Folders button on the Standard Buttons toolbar.**

The maximized My Computer window is displayed (Figure 1-45). The status bar is located at the bottom of the window. Pointing to the Folders button on the Standard Buttons toolbar displays a three-dimensional button.

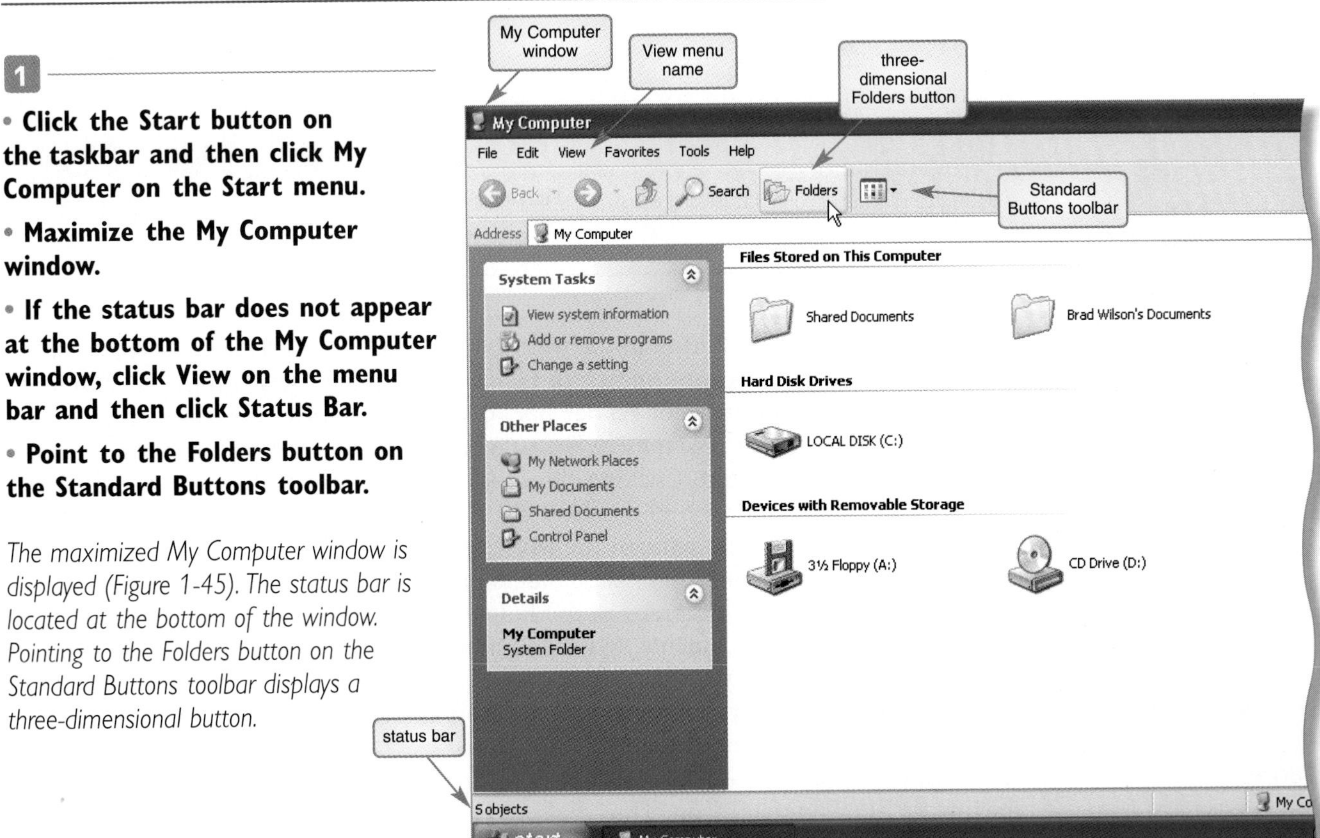

FIGURE 1-45

2

• **Click the Folders button.**

The Folders pane is displayed in place of the left pane in the My Computer window (Figure 1-46).

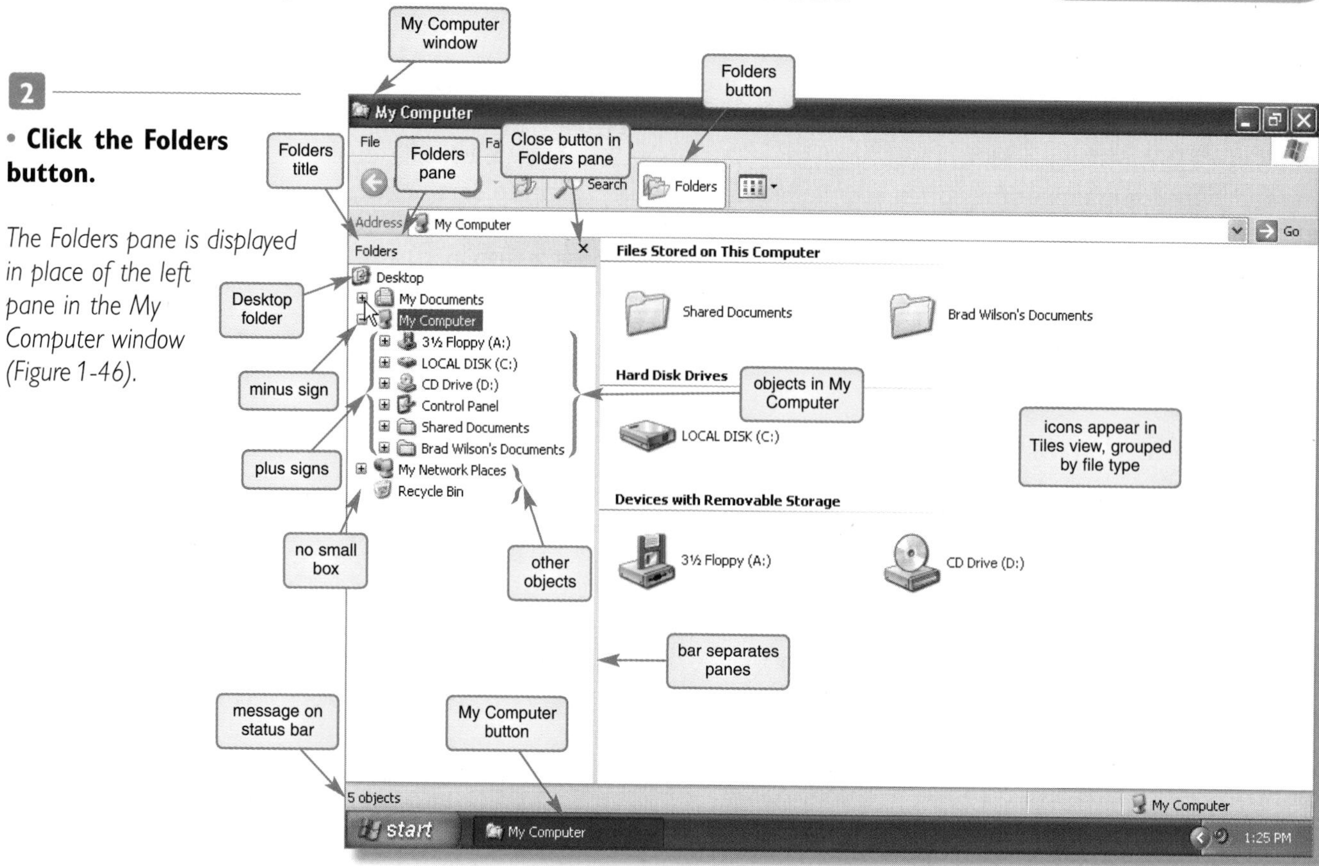

FIGURE 1-46

Other Ways

1. Click Start button, right-click My Computer, click Explore on shortcut menu
2. Right-click Start button or any desktop icon, click Explore on shortcut menu
3. Click Start button, point to All Programs, point to Accessories, click Windows Explorer, click My Computer
4. Press WINDOWS+E

More About

Icons

In many cases, you may not recognize a particular icon because hundreds of icons are developed by software vendors to represent their products. Each icon is supposed to be unique and eye-catching. You can purchase thousands of icons on floppy disk or CD-ROM to use to represent the documents you create.

Clicking the Folders button in the My Computer window selects the Folders button, displays the Folders pane shown in Figure 1-46, and allows you to use Windows Explorer. The **Folders pane** (or **Folder bar**) displays the **hierarchical structure** of folders and drives on the computer. The title bar in the Folders pane contains a title (Folders) and Close button. Clicking the Close button removes the Folders pane from the My Computer window and deselects the Folders button. A bar separates the Folders pane and the right pane of the My Computer window. You can drag the bar left or right to change the size of the Folders pane.

The top level of the hierarchy in the Folders pane is the Desktop. Below the Desktop are the My Documents, My Computer, My Network Places, and Recycle Bin icons. The icons on your computer may be different.

To the left of the My Computer icon is a minus sign in a small box. The **minus sign** indicates that the drive or folder represented by the icon next to it, in this case My Computer, contains additional folders or drives and these folders or drives appear below the My Computer icon. Thus, below the My Computer icon are the 3½ Floppy (A:), LOCAL DISK (C:), CD Drive (D:), Control Panel, Shared Documents, and Brad Wilson's Documents icons. Each of these icons has a small box with a plus sign next to it. The **plus sign** indicates that the drive or folder represented by the icon has more folders within it but the folders do not appear in the Folders pane. As you will see shortly, clicking the box with the plus sign will display the folders within the drive or folder represented by the icon. If an item contains no folders, such as the Recycle Bin, no hierarchy exists and no small box is displayed next to the icon.

The right pane in the My Computer window illustrated in Figure 1-46 contains three groups of icons. The Files Stored on This Computer group contains the Shared Documents icon and Brad Wilson's Documents icon. The Hard Disk Drives group contains the LOCAL DISK (C:) icon. The Devices with Removable Storage group contains the 3½ Floppy (A:) and CD Drive (D:) icons.

The **status bar** appears at the bottom of the window and contains information about the documents, folders, and programs in a window. A message on the left of the status bar located at the bottom of the window indicates the right pane contains five objects.

Windows Explorer displays the drives and folders on the computer in hierarchical structure in the Folders pane. This arrangement allows you to move and copy files and folders using only the Folders pane and the contents of the right pane.

As mentioned earlier, being able to create and organize folders on the computer is an important skill that every student should understand. On the following pages, you will learn about removable media and DOS paths, plug a USB flash drive into a USB port on the computer, create and name a folder on a removable drive, and download the remaining folders in the hierarchical structure (see Figure 1-47) into the Freshman folder.

Using a Hierarchical Format to Organize Files and Folders

One of the more important tasks for a beginning student is to be able to create and organize the files and folders on the computer. A file may contain a spreadsheet assignment given by the computer teacher, a research paper assigned by the English teacher, an electronic quiz given by the Business teacher, or a study sheet designed by the Math teacher. These files should be organized and stored in folders to reduce the possibility of misplacing or losing a file and to quickly find a file.

Assume you are a freshman and are taking four classes (Business, Computer, English, and Math). You want to design a series of folders for the four classes you are taking in the first semester of the freshman year. To accomplish this, you arrange the folders in a **hierarchical format**. The hierarchical structure of folders for the Freshman year is shown in Figure 1-47.

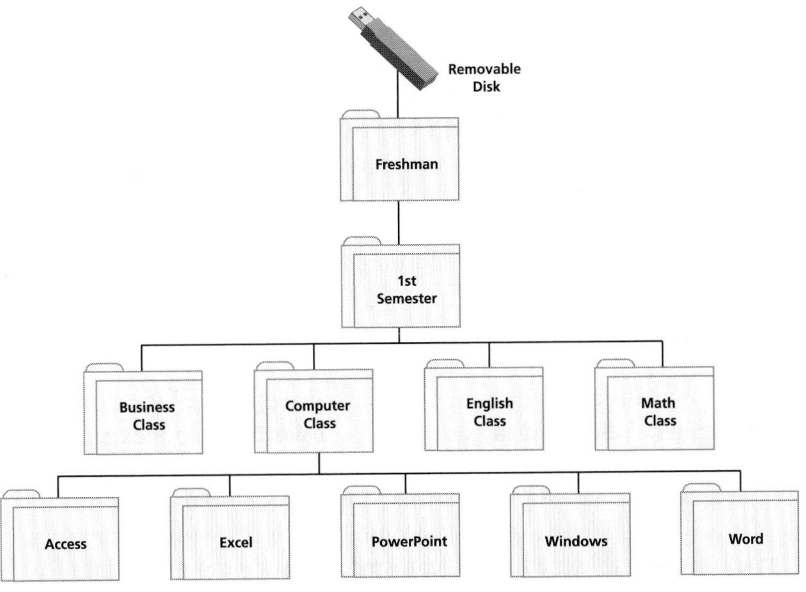

FIGURE 1-47

The hierarchy contains five levels. Each rectangular box is represented by a folder icon and vertical and horizontal lines connect the folders. The first level contains the

Removable Disk drive, the second level contains the Freshman folder, the third level contains the 1st Semester folder, the fourth level contains four folders (Business Class, Computer Class, English Class, and Math Class), the fifth level contains five folders (Access, Excel, PowerPoint, Windows, and Word).

The vertical and horizontal lines in the hierarchy chart form a pathway that allows you to navigate to a drive or folder. Each pathway, or **DOS path**, is a means of navigation to a specific location on a computer or network. The acronym, DOS, comes from the name of Microsoft's first operating system (**D**isk **O**perating **S**ystem). A path consists of a drive letter and colon (C:), a backslash (\), and one or more folders. Each drive or folder in the hierarchy chart has a corresponding path. When you click a drive or folder icon in the Folders pane, the corresponding path appears in the Address box on the Address bar. Table 1-1 contains examples of path names and their corresponding drives and folders.

Table 1-1 Path Names and Corresponding Drives and Folders

PATH	DRIVE AND FOLDER
E:\	Drive E (Removable Disk)
E:\Freshman	Freshman folder on drive E
E:\Freshman\1st Semester	1st Semester folder in Freshman folder on drive E
E:\Freshman\1st Semester\Computer Class\Word	Word folder in Computer Class folder in 1st Semester folder in Freshman folder on Drive E

In Table 1-1, the E:\ path represents the Removable Disk (E:) drive, the E:\Freshman folder represents the Freshman folder on the Removable Disk (E:) drive, the E:\Freshman\1st Semester folder represents the 1st Semester folder in the Freshman folder on the Removable Disk (E:) drive, and so on.

When this hierarchy is created on the computer, the Removable Disk drive is said "to contain" the Freshman folder, the Freshman folder is said "to contain" the 1st Semester folder, and so on. In addition, this hierarchy can easily be expanded to include folders for the Sophomore, Junior, and Senior years and additional semesters.

When clicking a drive or folder icon in the Folders pane while performing the steps in this project, look at the path in the Address box to better understand the relationship between the folders and drives on the computer.

Removable Media and Network Drives

A removable media (floppy disk, Zip disk, or USB flash drive) is ideal for storing files and folders on a computer. A **floppy disk**, also called a **diskette**, is an inexpensive, portable storage medium that consists of a thin, circular, flexible plastic disk with a magnetic coating enclosed in a square-shaped plastic shell. Although still in use, floppy disks are not as widely used as they were ten years ago because of their low storage capacity.

A **Zip disk** is a type of removable media that can store a large amount of data. A Zip disk stores 500 times more than a floppy disk. A **USB flash drive**, sometimes called a **keychain drive**, is a flash memory storage device that plugs into a USB port on a computer. A **USB port**, short for universal serial bus port, can be found on either the front or back of most computers. USB flash drives are convenient for mobile users because they are small and lightweight enough to be transported on a keychain or in a pocket.

A **network** is a collection of computers and devices connected together for the purpose of sharing information between computer users. In some cases, students might be required to store their files on a network drive found on the school's computer network. A **network drive** is a storage device that is connected to the server on the computer network. A **server** controls access to the hardware, software, and other resources on the network and provides a centralized storage area for programs, data, and information. If student files reside on the network drive on the school's network, files may be accessed from a school computer, or from a personal computer with permission from the school. Ask your teacher if the school requires students to use a network drive.

Plugging a USB Flash Drive into a USB Port

Although other removable media may be used for storage, the USB flash drive is one of the more popular drives (Figure 1-48). To store files and folders on the USB flash drive, you must plug the USB flash drive into a USB port on the computer. Plugging a USB flash drive into a USB port causes the Removable Disk (E:) window to display on the desktop. The removable media drive name on your computer may be different.

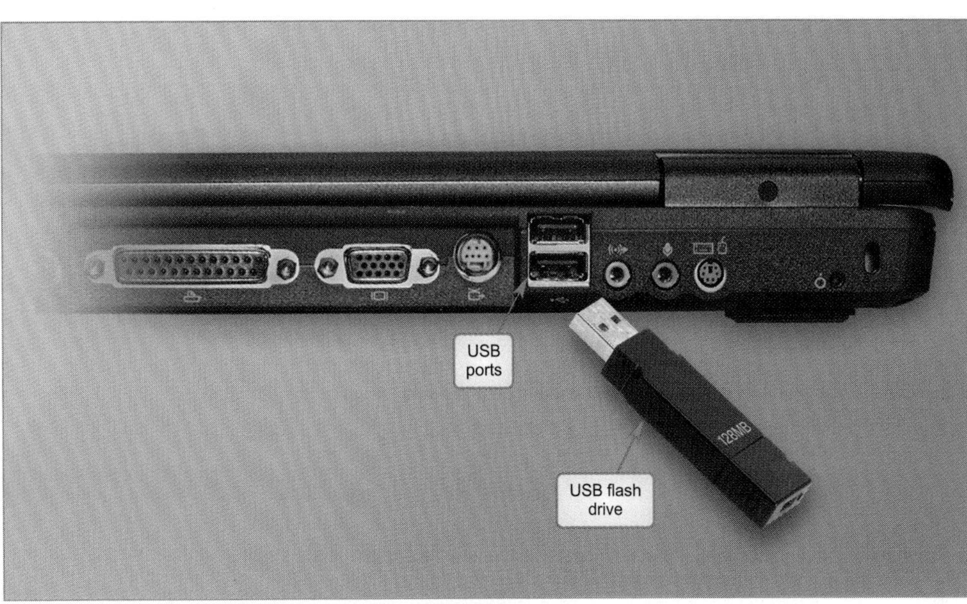

FIGURE 1-48

To Plug a USB Flash Drive into a USB Port

1

• **Plug the USB flash drive into a USB port on the computer.**

When you plug the USB flash drive into the USB port, the Auto Play dialog box displays momentarily, the Removable Disk (E:) icon is displayed in the Folders pane, the Removable Disk (E:) dialog box displays, and the Play command is selected in the dialog box (Figure 1-49). The My Computer button and Removable Disk (E:) button appear on the taskbar.

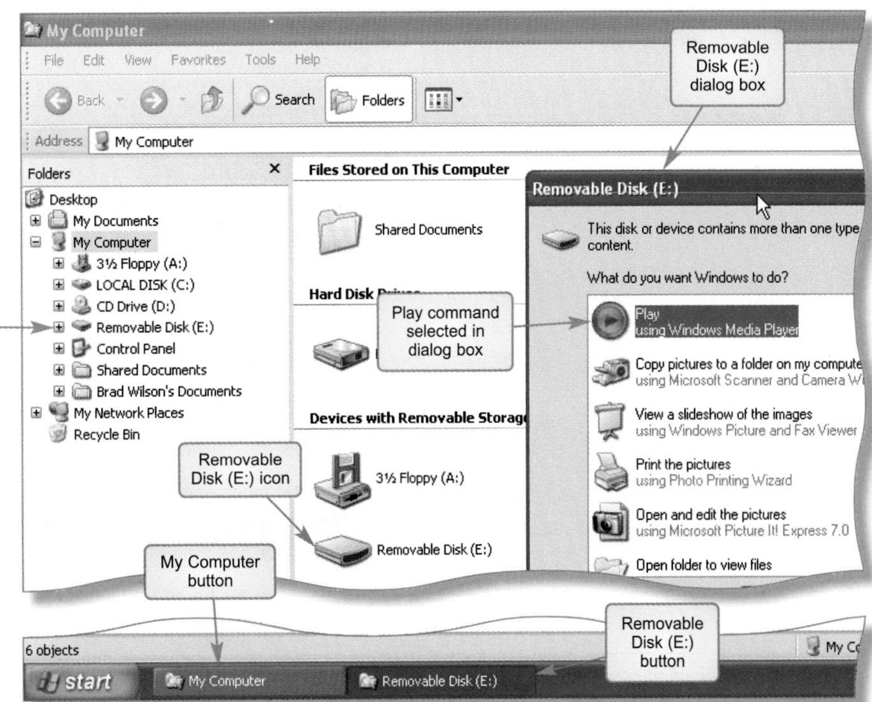

FIGURE 1-49

2

• **Scroll to the bottom of the What do you want Windows to do? list box and click the Take no action command.**

The Take no action command is selected in the What do you want Windows to do? list box (Figure 1-50).

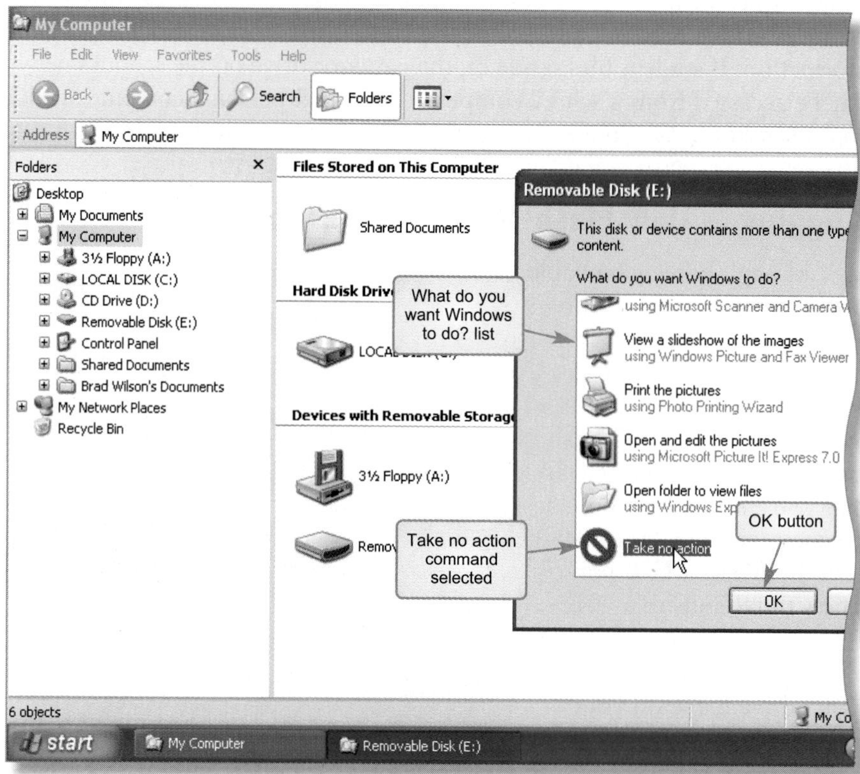

FIGURE 1-50

3

• **Click the OK button in the What do you want Windows to do? list box.**

The Removable Disk (E:) dialog box closes and the Removable Disk (E:) icon is displayed in the right pane (Figure 1-51).

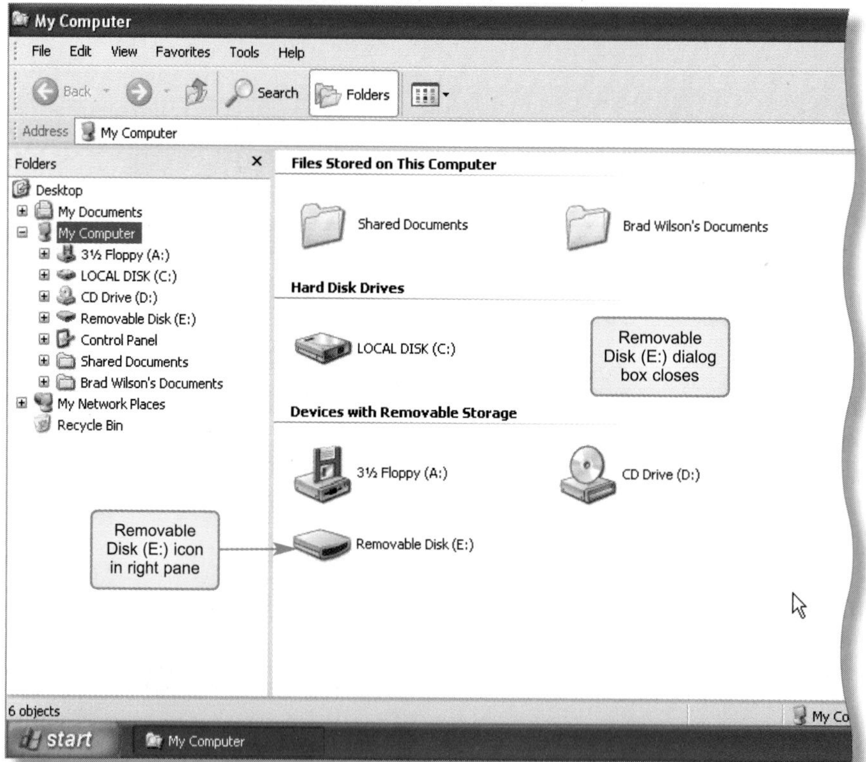

FIGURE 1-51

The USB flash drive is inserted into the USB port, the Removable Disk (E:) drive entry displays in the Folders pane and the Removable Disk (E:) drive icon displays in the right pane.

After inserting the USB flash drive into the USB port, the next step is to create the Freshman folder on the Removable Disk (E:) drive (see Figure 1-47 on page WIN 39). The next two sections explain the rules for naming a folder and illustrate how to create the Freshman folder on the Removable Disk (E:) drive.

Naming a Folder

When you create a folder, you must assign a name to the folder. A folder name should be descriptive of the folder. Examples of folder names are Word 2003 Student Data Files, Windows XP Features, and Office Supplies. A folder name can contain up to 255 characters, including spaces. Any uppercase or lowercase character is valid when creating a folder name, except a backslash (\), slash (/), colon (:), asterisk (*), question mark (?), quotation marks ("), less than symbol (<), greater than symbol (>), or vertical bar (|). Folder names cannot be CON, AUX, COM1, COM2, COM3, COM4, LPT1, LPT2, LPT3, PRN, or NUL. The same rules for naming folders also apply to naming files.

Creating a Folder on a Removable Drive

To create a folder on a removable drive, you must select the Removable Disk (E:) drive icon in the Folders pane and then create the folder in the right pane. The following steps show how to create the Freshman folder on the Removable Disk (E:) drive.

To Create a Folder on a Removable Drive

1

• **Click the Removable Drive (E:) icon in the Folders pane, right-click an open area of the right pane to display a shortcut menu, point to New on the shortcut menu, and then point to Folder on the New submenu.**

A shortcut menu containing the highlighted New command and the New submenu containing the highlighted Folder command are displayed (Figure 1-52). The path to the Removable Disk (E:) drive is displayed in the Address box.

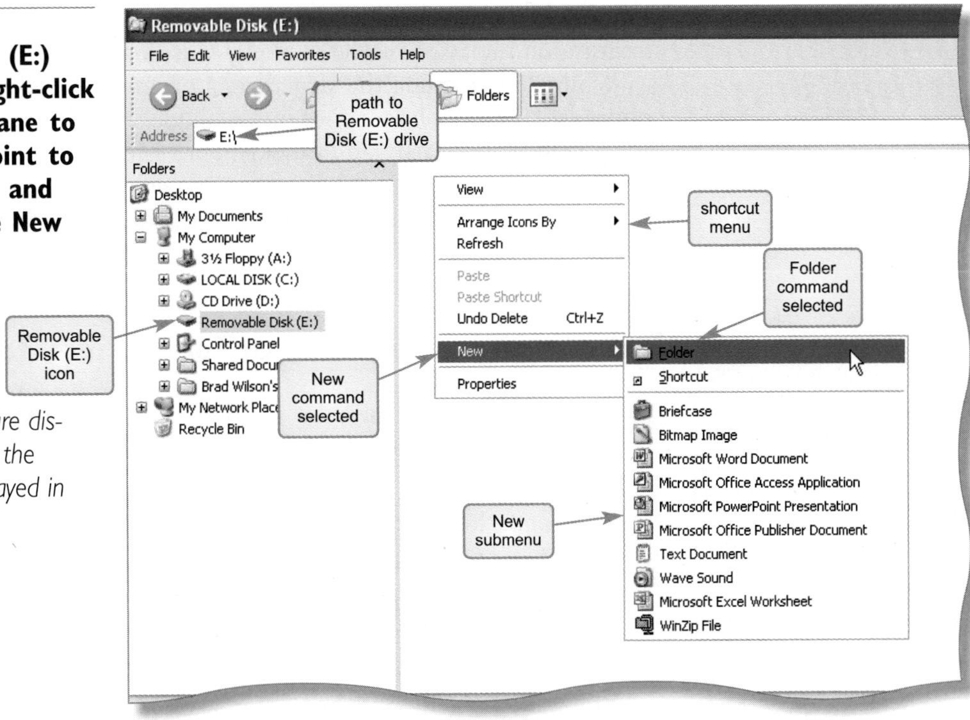

FIGURE 1-52

2

- **Click Folder on the New submenu, type** `Freshman` **in the icon title text box, and then press the ENTER key.**

The shortcut menu and Folder submenu close, the Freshman folder is selected in the right pane, and the Freshman folder is created on the Removable Disk (E:) drive (Figure 1-53).

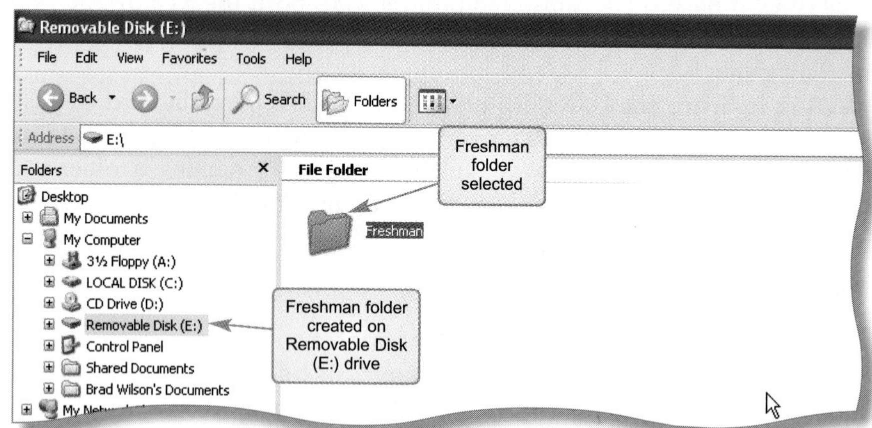

FIGURE 1-53

Other Ways

1. On File menu point to New, click Folder, type file name, press ENTER
2. Press ALT+F, press W, press F, type file name, press ENTER
3. Click Folders button, click Make a new folder in File and Folder Tasks area, type file name, press ENTER

Downloading a Hierarchy of Folders into the Freshman Folder

After creating the Freshman folder on the Removable Disk (E:) drive, the remaining folders in the hierarchical structure (see Figure 1-47 on page WIN 39), starting with the 1st Semester folder, should be downloaded to the Freshman folder. **Downloading** is the process of a computer receiving information, such as a set of files or folders from a Web site, from a server on the Internet.

The remaining folders could be created by double-clicking the Freshman folder and then creating the 1st Semester folder in the Freshman folder, double-clicking the 1st Semester folder and then creating the next four folders (Business, Computer, English, and Math) in the 1st Semester folder, and so on. To make the task of creating the folders easier, the folders have been created and stored in a hierarchical structure on the SCSITE.COM Shelly Cashman Series Student Resources Web site.

While downloading the structure, a program called WinZip is used. **WinZip** compresses, or **zips**, larger files into a single smaller file, allowing the folders to be downloaded more easily and quickly. Performing the download causes the hierarchy of folders to be stored in the Freshman folder.

The following steps show how to download the folders in the hierarchical structure into the Freshman folder.

More About

Downloading from a Web Site

A variety of media are available to store the downloaded folders and files from scsite.com. You may use a USB flash drive, floppy disk, or Zip disk. In addition, a network drive located on the school's computer may be available. If necessary, check with your instructor to determine which devices are available at your school.

To Download a Hierarchy of Folders into the Freshman Folder

1. **Start Internet Explorer by clicking the Start button on the taskbar and then clicking Internet on the Start menu.**
2. **Click the Address box on the Address bar, type** `scsite.com` **in the Address box, and then click the Go button.**
3. **When the SCSITE.COM Shelly Cashman Series Student Resources Web page is displayed, scroll down to view the Browse by Subject area, and then click the Office Suites link.**
4. **When the expanded Office Suites link is displayed, click the link containing the name of your textbook (for example, Microsoft Office 2003: Introductory Concepts and Techniques).**
5. **Scroll down to display the Data Files for Students (Windows) area and then click the Windows XP Project 1 Folders and Files link.**

6 **When the File Download – Security Warning dialog box is displayed, click the Run button.**

7 **When the Internet Explorer – Security Warning dialog box is displayed, click the Run button.**

8 **When the WinZip Self-Extractor dialog box is displayed, type the removable media drive letter of your removable media drive followed by a colon, backslash, and folder name (Freshman) (for example, E:\Freshman).**

9 **Click the Unzip button in the WinZip Self-Extractor dialog box.**

10 **When a smaller WinZip Self-Extractor dialog box is displayed, click the OK button.**

11 **Click the Close button in the WinZip Self-Extractor dialog box.**

12 **Click the Close button in the SCSITE.COM Shelly Cashman Series Student Resources window.**

The Windows XP Project 1 Folders and Files are downloaded from the SCSITE.COM Shelly Cashman Series Student Resources Web site to the Freshman folder in the right pane (Figure 1-54). Even though you cannot see the folders and files in the Freshman folder, the folders and files are contained in the Freshman folder. Some folders contain files to be used later in this project.

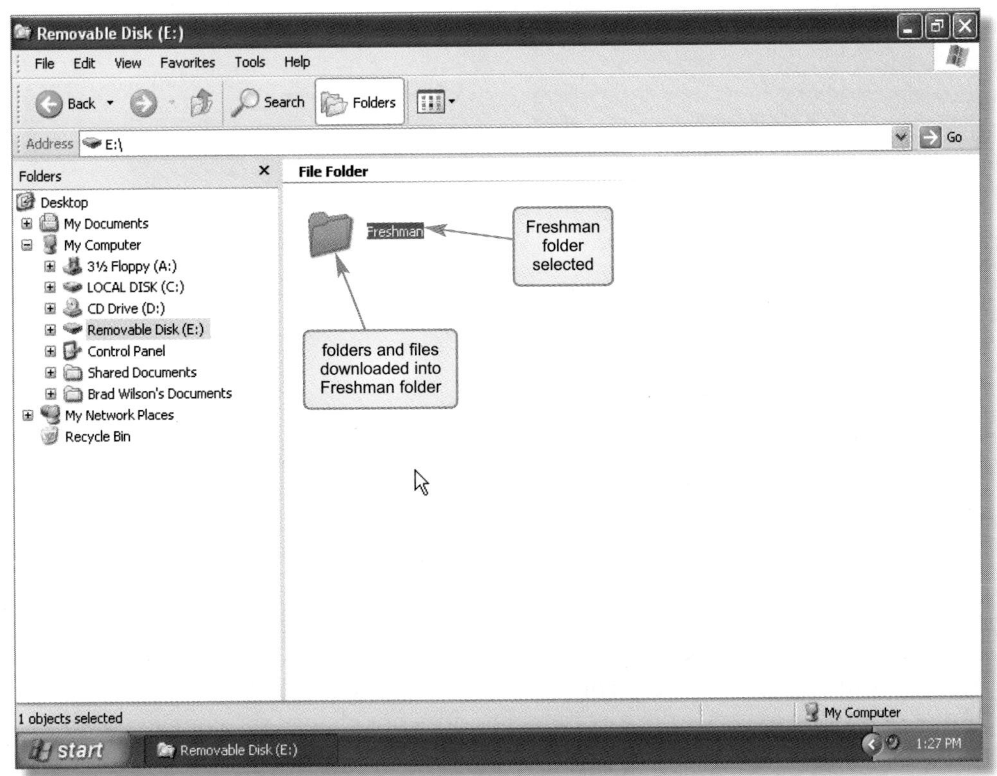

FIGURE 1-54

Expanding a Drive

Explorer displays the hierarchy of items in the Folders pane and the contents of drives and folders in the right pane. To expand a drive or folder in the Folders pane, click the plus sign in the small box to the left of the drive or folder icon. Clicking the plus sign expands the hierarchy in the Folders pane. The contents of the right pane remain the same. The steps on the next page show how to expand a drive.

To Expand a Drive

1

• **Point to the plus sign in the small box to the left of the Removable Disk (E:) icon in the Folders pane (Figure 1-55).**

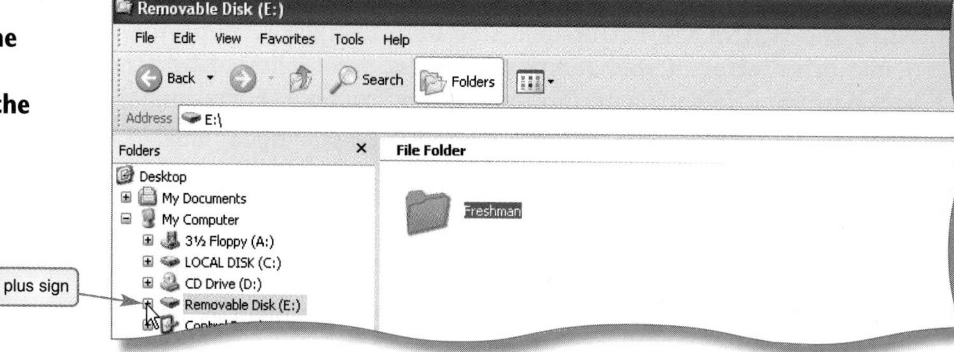

FIGURE 1-55

2

• **Click the plus sign.**

The hierarchy below the Removable Disk (E:) icon expands to display the Freshman folder (Figure 1-56). The minus sign to the left of the Removable Disk (E:) drive indicates the drive is expanded. The plus sign to the left of the Freshman folder indicates the folder contains additional folders.

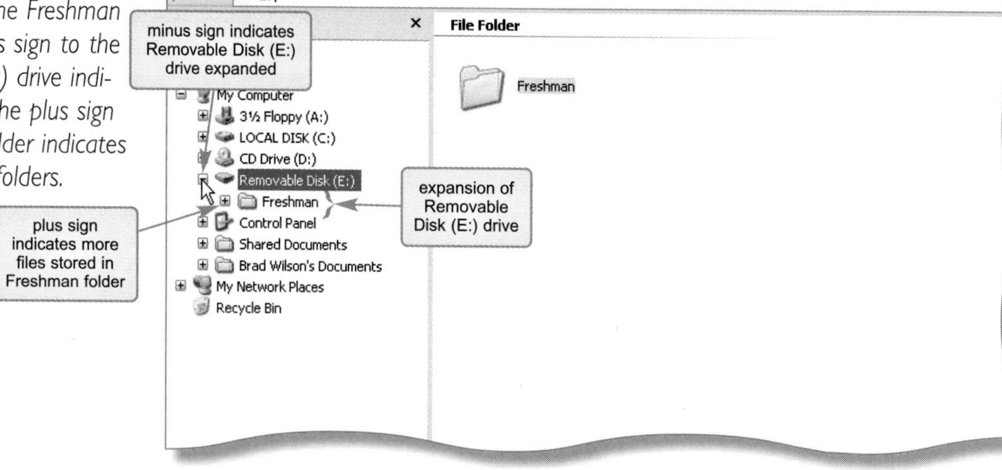

FIGURE 1-56

Other Ways

1. Click drive icon in Folders pane
2. Select drive to expand using ARROW keys, press PLUS on numeric keyboard
3. Select drive to expand, press RIGHT ARROW

In Figure 1-56, the Removable Disk (E:) drive is expanded and the right pane still contains the contents of the Removable Disk (E:) drive. Clicking the plus sign next to a drive icon expands the hierarchy but does not change the contents of the right pane.

Expanding a Folder

When a plus sign in a small box displays to the left of a folder icon in the Folders pane, you can expand the folder to show all the folders it contains. The steps on the next page illustrate expanding the Freshman folder to view the contents of the Freshman folder.

To Expand a Folder

1

• **Point to the plus sign in the small box to the left of the Freshman icon (Figure 1-57).**

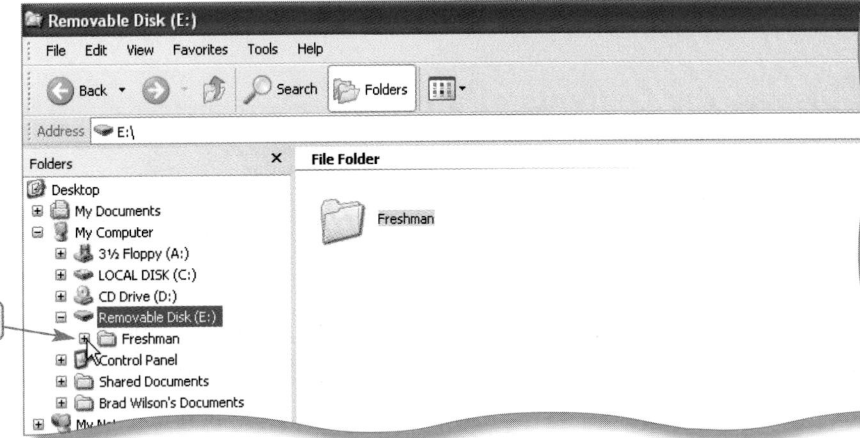

FIGURE 1-57

2

• **Click the plus sign.**

The hierarchy below the Freshman icon expands to display the 1st Semester folder contained in the Freshman folder (Figure 1-58). The folder is indented below the Freshman icon and the minus sign to the left of the Freshman icon indicates the folder has been expanded. A folder with a plus sign contains more folders.

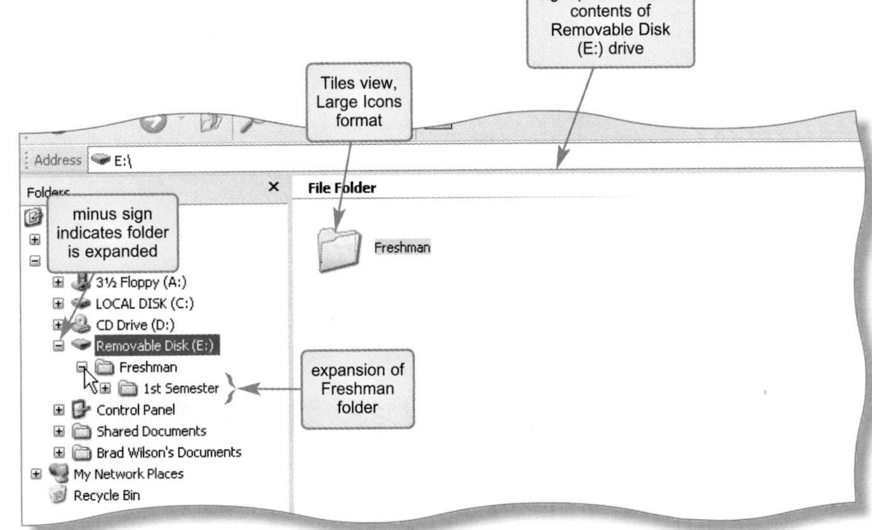

FIGURE 1-58

In Figure 1-58, the Freshman folder is expanded and the right pane still contains the contents of the Removable Disk (E:) folder. Clicking the plus sign next to a folder icon expands the hierarchy but does not change the contents of the right pane.

When a folder is expanded, the folders contained within the expanded folder display in the Folders pane. You can continue this expansion to view further levels of the hierarchy.

You can display files and folders in the right pane in several different views. Currently, the Freshman folder displays in Tiles view using Large Icons format.

Displaying Drive and Folder Contents

Explorer displays the hierarchy of items in the left, or Folders, pane and the contents of drives and folders in the right pane. To display the contents of a drive or folder in the right pane, click the drive or folder icon in the Folders pane. Clicking the icon displays the contents of the drive or folder in the right pane, expands the hierarchy in the Folders pane, and displays the path in the Address box. The following step shows how to display the contents of the 1st Semester folder.

To Display the Contents of a Folder

1

- **Click the 1st Semester icon in the Folders pane.**

The highlighted 1st Semester name is displayed in the Folders pane, the hierarchy below the 1st Semester icon expands, and the right pane contains the contents of the 1st Semester folder (Figure 1-59). The window title changes to 1st Semester, the 1st Semester button replaces the My Computer button on the taskbar, the status bar indicates four objects are displayed in the right pane, and the path to the 1st Semester folder displays in the Address box.

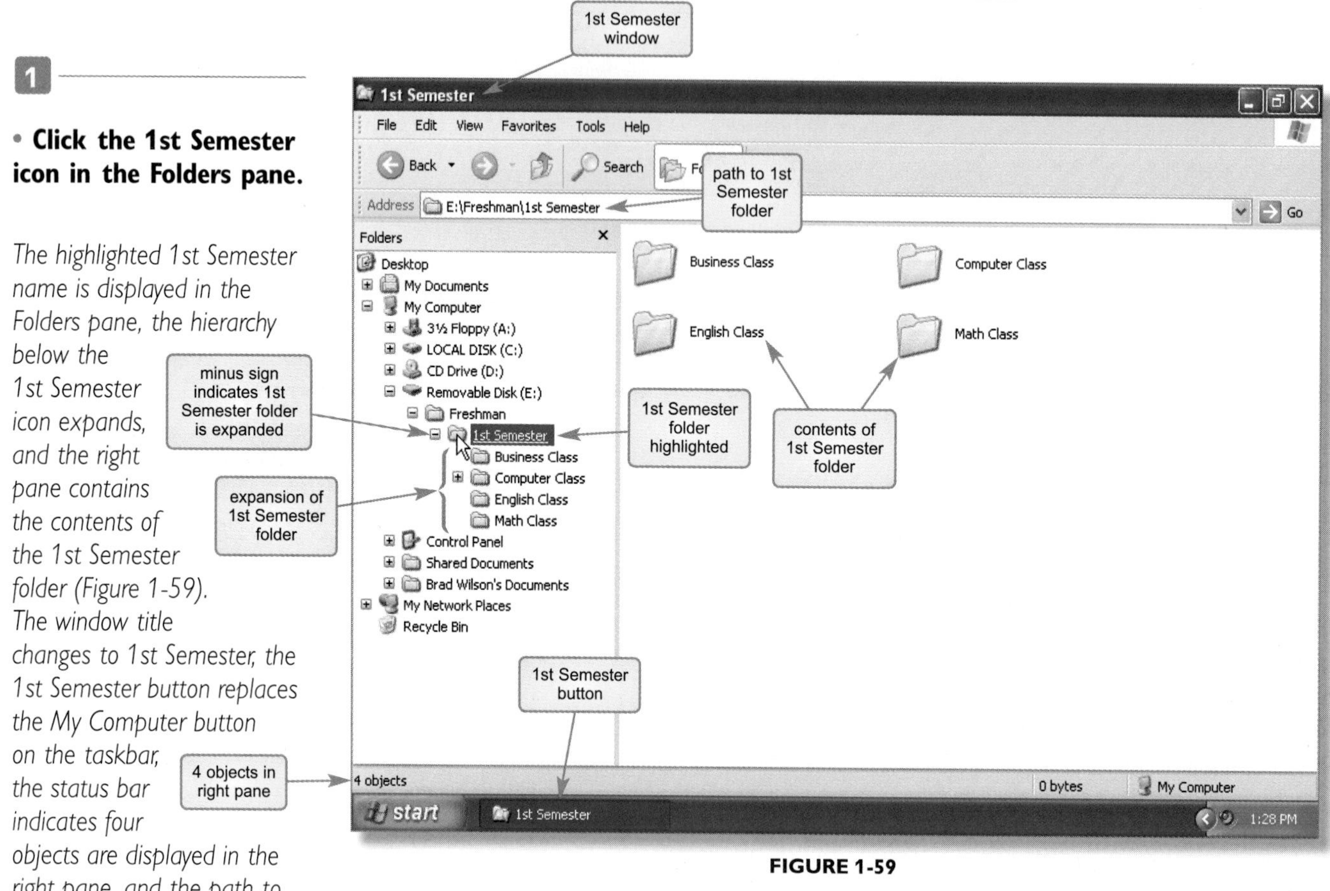

FIGURE 1-59

Other Ways

1. Right-click 1st Semester icon, click Explore on shortcut menu

Whenever files or folders display in the right pane of a window, you can display the contents of the file or folder by double-clicking the icon of the file or folder.

Creating a Document and Folder in Microsoft Word

Previously, the Freshman folder was created in the Removable Disk (E:) drive using Windows Explorer. You also can create a folder anytime you save a file in a Windows application. For example, you can use Microsoft Office Word 2003 to create a document and then save the document in a folder. Microsoft Office Word 2003 is one of the five basic applications included in Microsoft Office 2003. Word is a full-featured word processing program that allows you to create a variety of personal and business documents.

The following section illustrates how to start Word, type text into a Word document, save the document in a new folder, and verify the document was saved in the folder. For example, you may want to type the Monday, April 10 assignment for your computer class in a Word document and then save the document in a newly created Homework folder.

More About

Word 2003

For more information about the features of Microsoft Office Word 2003, visit the Word 2003 More About Web page (scsite.com/wd2003/more) and then click Microsoft Word 2003 Features.

More About

Task Panes

When you first start Word, a small window called a task pane may be displayed docked on the right side of the screen. You can drag a task pane title bar to float the pane in your work area or dock it on either the left or right side of a screen, depending on your personal preference.

Starting Word

To create the Monday, April 10 document, you must start Word. You may need to ask your instructor how to start Word on your system.

To Start Word

1

- **Click the Start button on the Windows taskbar, point to All Programs on the Start menu, point to Microsoft Office on the All Programs submenu, and then point to Microsoft Office Word 2003 on the Microsoft Office submenu.**

The Start menu, All Programs submenu, and Microsoft Office submenu are displayed (Figure 1-60). The Microsoft Office submenu contains the Microsoft Office Word 2003 command to start the Microsoft Word program.

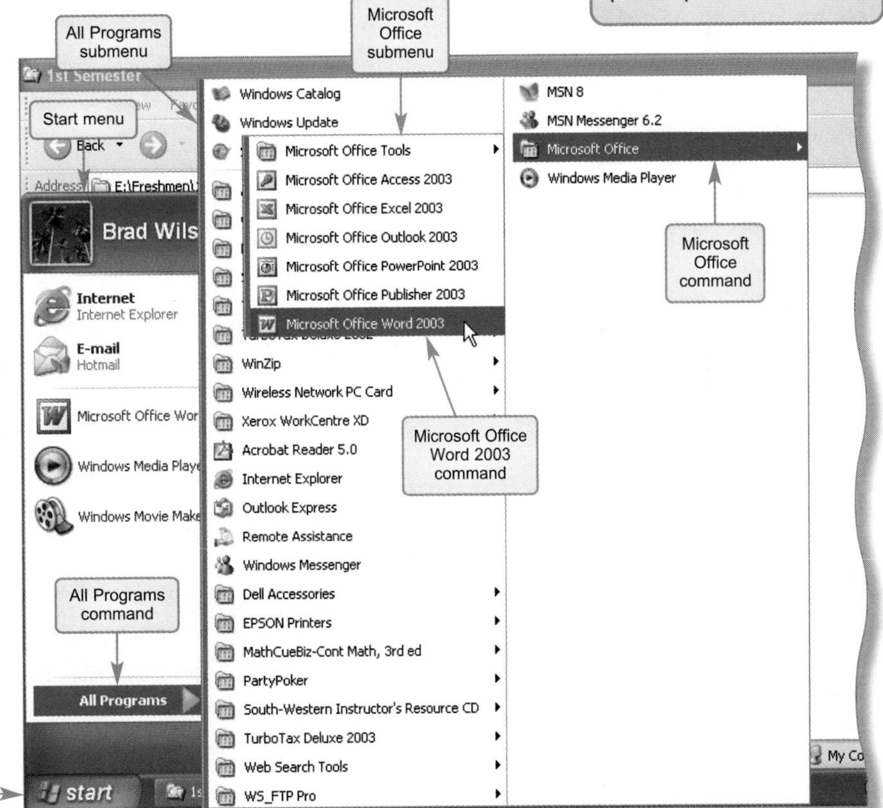

FIGURE 1-60

• **Click Microsoft Office Word 2003.**

Word starts. After a few moments, Word displays a blank document titled Document1 in the Microsoft Word window (Figure 1-61). The Windows taskbar displays the Microsoft Word program button, indicating Word is running.

3

• **If the Microsoft Word window is not maximized, double-click its title bar to maximize it.**

• **If the Office Assistant appears, right-click it and then click Hide on the shortcut menu.**

• **If the Getting Started task pane appears, click the Close button in the upper-right corner of the Getting Started pane.**

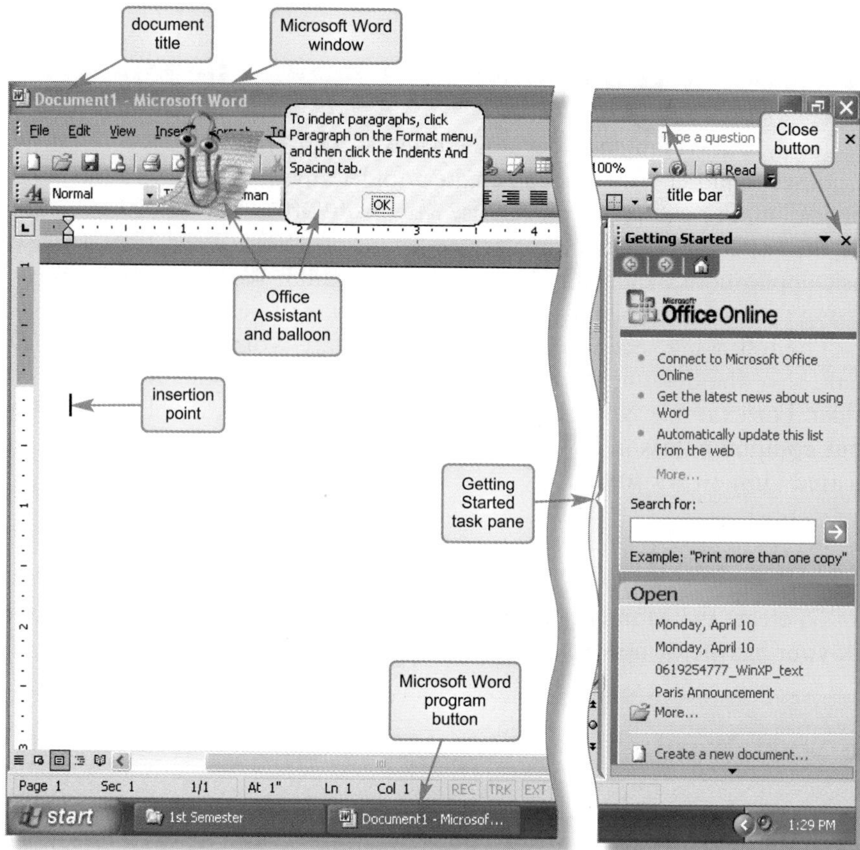

FIGURE 1-61

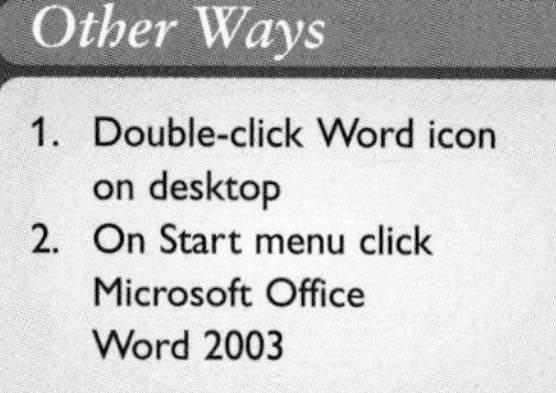

Other Ways

1. Double-click Word icon on desktop
2. On Start menu click Microsoft Office Word 2003

Typing Text

After starting Word, you can enter the text for the Monday, April 10 assignment in a Word document. To enter text in the document, you type on the keyboard. The following steps illustrate how to type the text of the Monday, April 10 assignment in a Word document.

To Type Text in a Word Document

1

• **Type** `Monday, April 10` **and then press the ENTER key twice. Type** `Finish - More Birds Data Base` **and then press the ENTER key. Type** `Read - Next Project` **and then press the ENTER key.**

The Word document is complete (Figure 1-62).

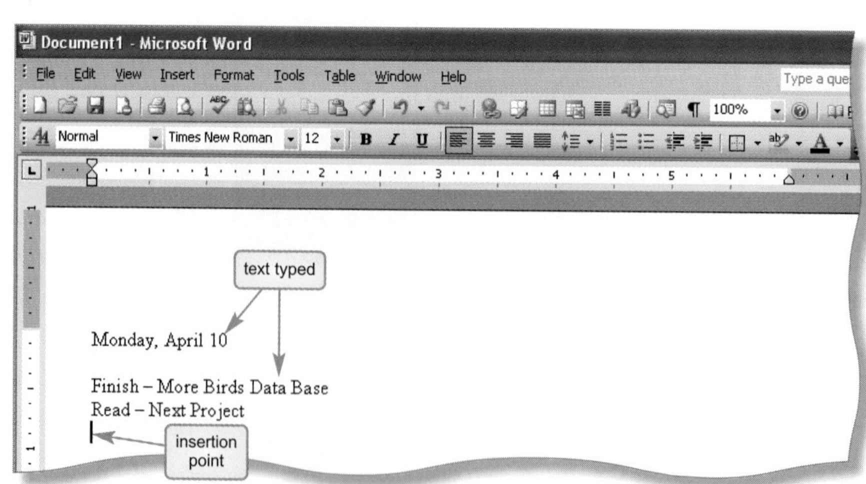

FIGURE 1-62

Saving a Document in a New Folder

After typing text in the Word document, you should name the document using the Monday, April 10 name, create the Homework folder in the Computer Class folder, (see the hierarchy in Figure 1-47 on page WIN 39), and save the Monday, April 10 document in the Homework folder. The following steps show how to create the Homework folder and save the Monday, April 10 document in the Homework folder.

To Save a Word Document in a New Folder

1

- **Click the Save button on the Standard toolbar.**

Word displays the Save As dialog box (Figure 1-63). The first word from the document (Monday) is selected in the File name text box as the default file name. You can change this selected file name by immediately typing the new name.

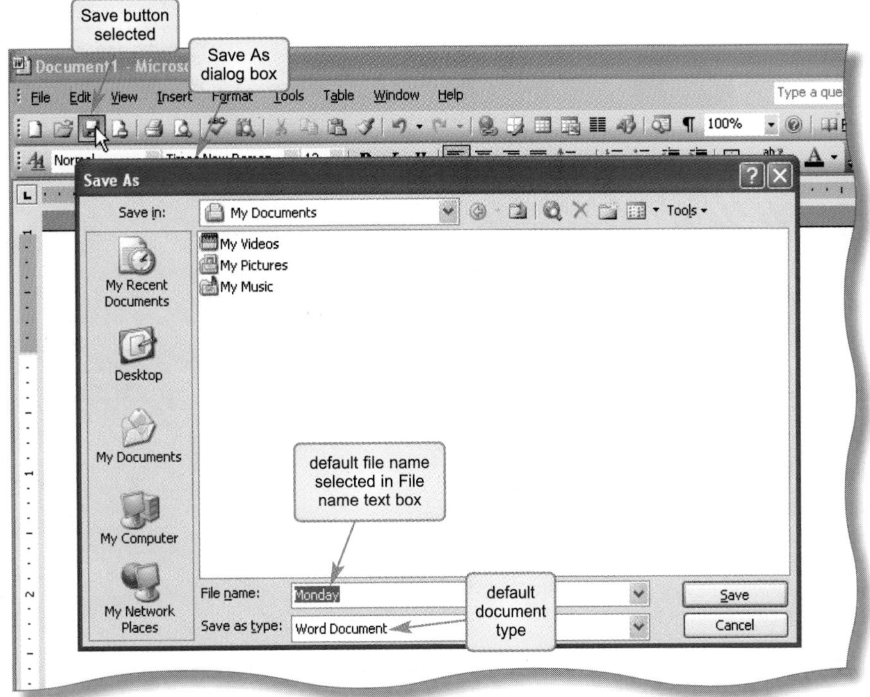

FIGURE 1-63

2

- **Type** `Monday, April 10` **in the File name text box. Do not press the ENTER key after typing the file name.**

The file name, Monday, April 10, replaces the text, Monday, in the file name text box (Figure 1-64).

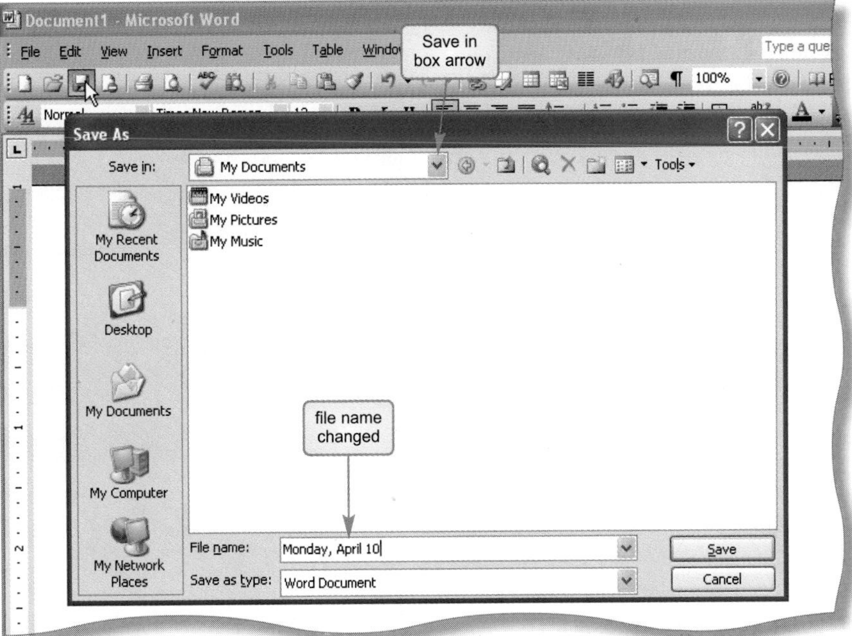

FIGURE 1-64

3

• **Click the Save in box arrow.**

Word displays a list of the available drives and folders in the Save in list (Figure 1-65). The Brad Wilson's Documents folder is selected in the Save in list. The Brad Wilson's Documents folder displays in the Save in list because a computer administrator previously created a user account for Brad Wilson. Your list may differ depending on your computer's configuration.

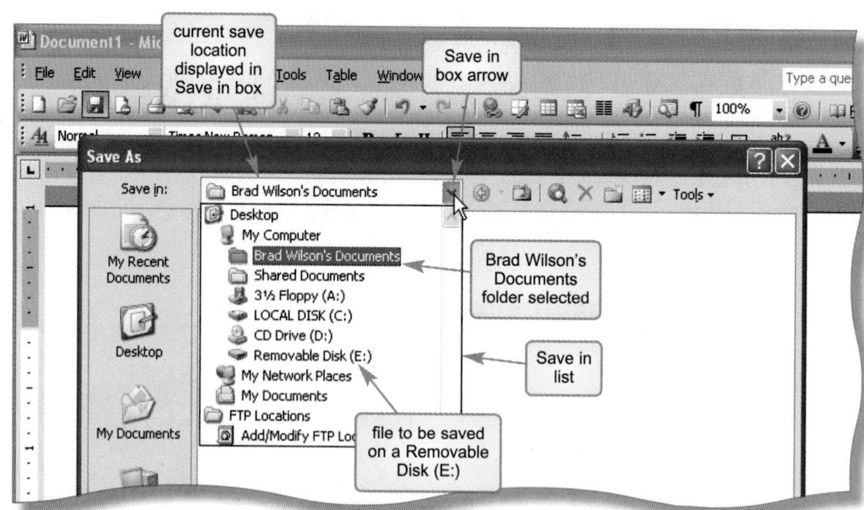

FIGURE 1-65

4

• **Click Removable Disk (E:) in the Save in list.**

Drive E becomes the new save location (Figure 1-66). The Save As dialog box now shows names of existing folders stored on drive E. In Figure 1-66, the Freshman folder is stored on drive E.

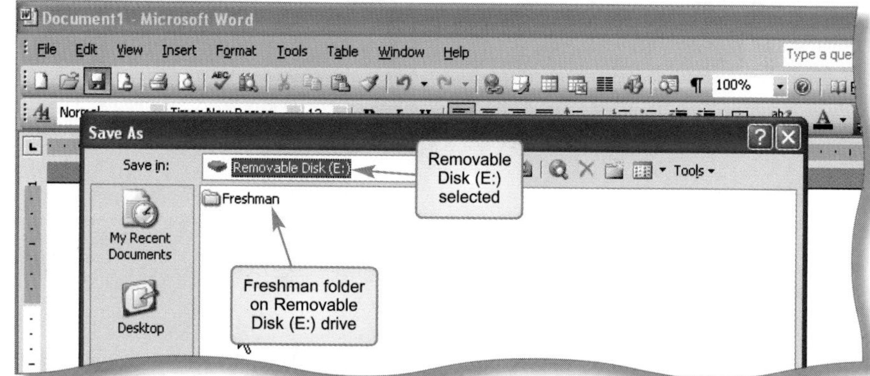

FIGURE 1-66

5

• **Double-click Freshman in the Save As dialog box.**

The Freshman folder is displayed in the Save in box, and the 1st Semester folder is displayed in the Save As dialog box (Figure 1-67). The 1st Semester folder is contained in the Freshman folder.

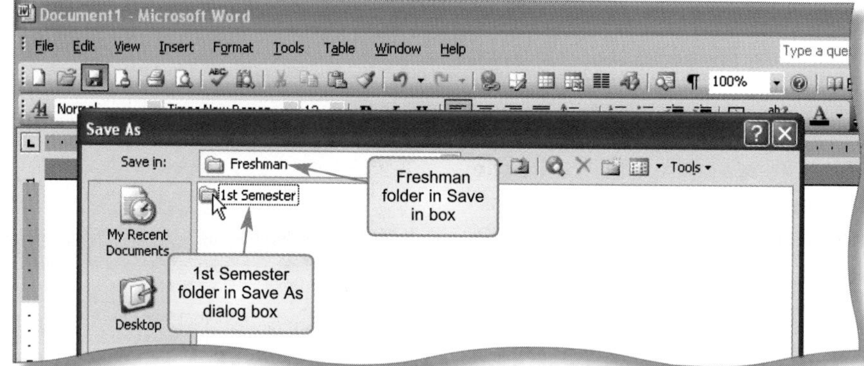

FIGURE 1-67

6

• **Double-click 1st Semester in the Save As dialog box.**

The 1st Semester folder is displayed in the Save in box and the Math Class, English Class, Computer Class, and Business Class folders are displayed in the Save As dialog box (Figure 1-68). The four folders are contained in the 1st Semester folder.

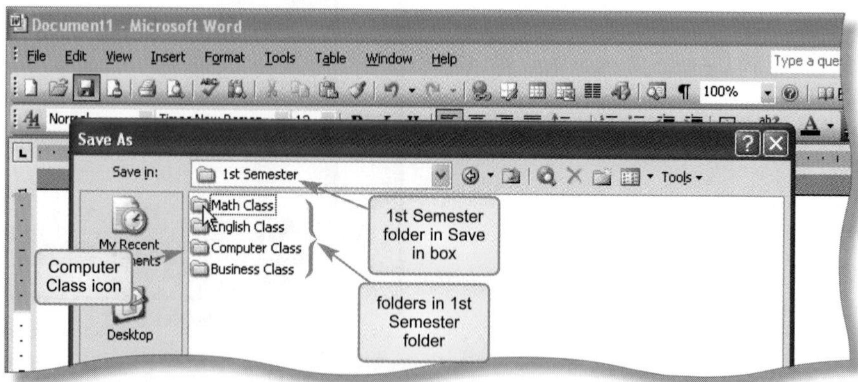

FIGURE 1-68

7

• **Double-click Computer Class in the Save As dialog box.**

The Computer Class folder is displayed in the Save in box and the Word, Windows, PowerPoint, Excel, and Access folders are displayed in the Save As dialog box (Figure 1-69). The five folders are contained in the Computer Class folder.

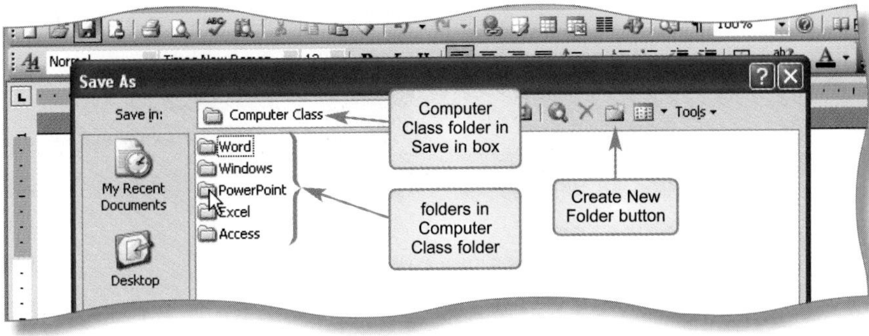

FIGURE 1-69

8

• **Click the Create New Folder button on the Save As dialog box toolbar. Type** `Homework` **in the Name text box in the New Folder dialog box.**

The New Folder dialog box is displayed and the Homework folder name appears in the Name text box (Figure 1-70).

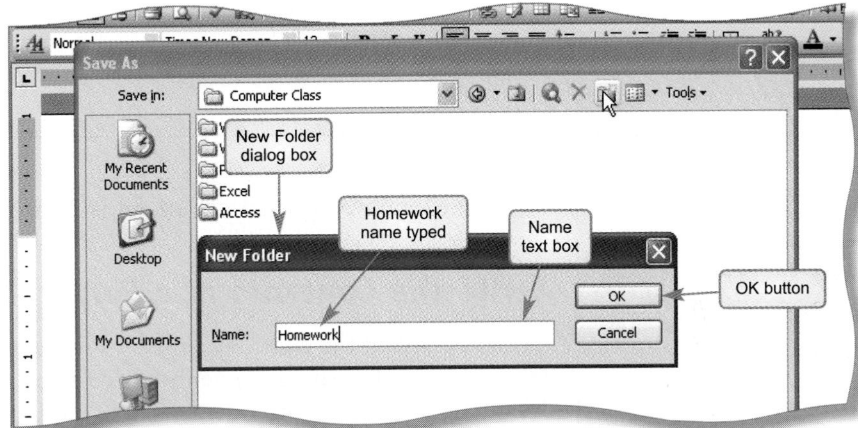

FIGURE 1-70

9

• **Click the OK button in the New Folder dialog box.**

The New Folder dialog box closes and the Homework folder is displayed in the Save in box (Figure 1-71).

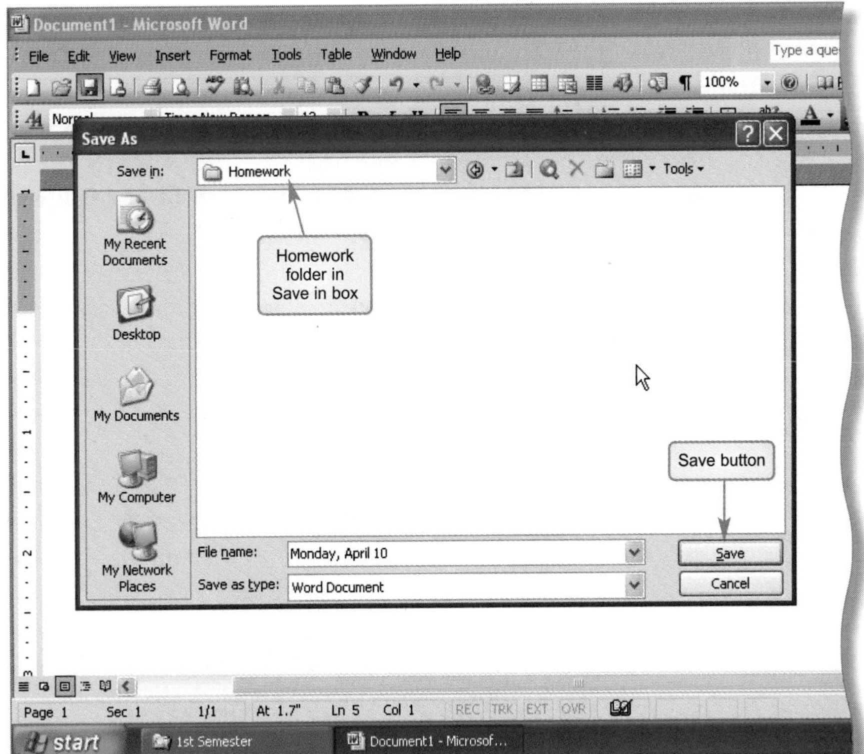

FIGURE 1-71

10

• **Click the Save button in the Save As dialog box.**

The Save As dialog box closes and the Monday, April 10 - Microsoft Word window is displayed (Figure 1-72).

11

• **Click the Close button in the Monday, April 10 - Microsoft Word window.**

The Microsoft Word window closes.

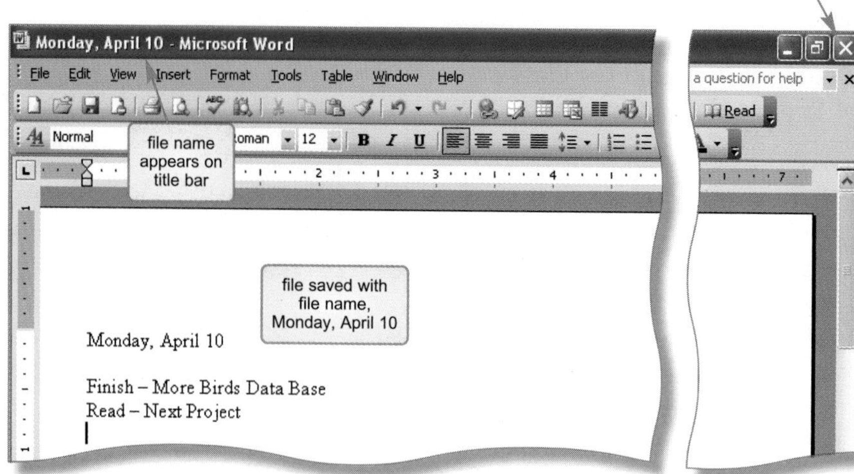

FIGURE 1-72

Other Ways

1. On File menu click Save As, type file name, click Save In box arrow, select drive or folder, click Create New Folder button on toolbar, type folder name, click Save button in Save As dialog box
2. Press CTRL+S, type file name, click Save In box arrow, select drive or folder, click Create New Folder button on toolbar, type folder name, click Save button in Save As dialog box

The Monday, April 10 document is created and stored in the Homework folder.

Verify the Contents of a Folder

After saving the Monday, April 10 document in the Homework folder, you should verify that the document was correctly saved in the Homework folder. The following steps illustrate how to verify the Homework folder contains the Monday, April 10 document.

To Verify the Contents of a Folder

1 **Click the plus sign in the small box next to the Computer Class icon in the Folders pane.**

2 **Click the Homework icon in the Folders pane.**

The Homework folder is selected in the Folders pane, the Monday, April 10 document is displayed in the right pane, Monday, April 10 is correctly saved in the Homework folder, and the path to the Homework folder displays in the Address box (Figure 1-73).

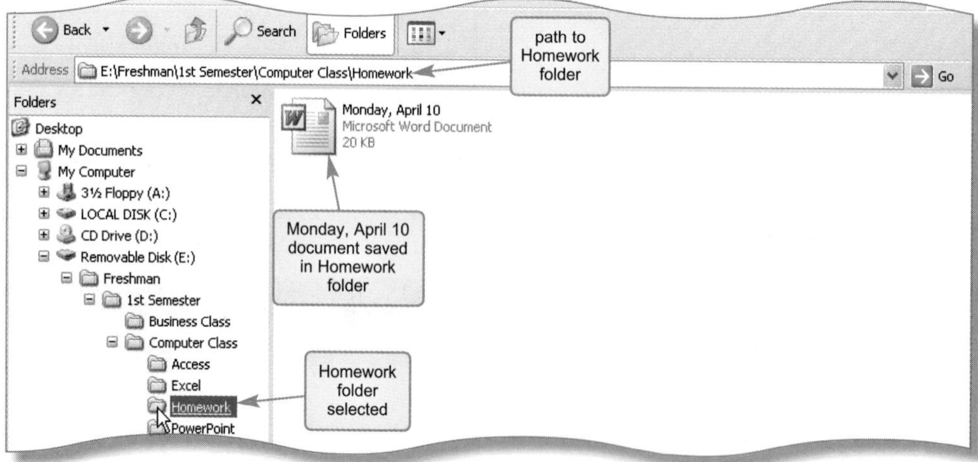

FIGURE 1-73

File Management in Windows Explorer

Being able to manage the files on the computer is one of the more important computer skills a student can have. **File management** includes copying, moving, renaming, and deleting files and folders on the computer. These are common operations that you should understand how to perform. The following pages show how to copy a file between folders, display the contents of a folder, rename a file, and then delete a file.

Copying Files in Windows Explorer

When copying files, the drive and folder containing the files to be copied are called the **source drive** and **source folder**, respectively. The drive and folder to which the files are copied are called the **destination drive** and **destination folder**, respectively. In the following steps, the Access folder is the source folder, the Homework folder is the destination folder, and the Removable Disk (E:) drive is both the source drive and the destination drive. The Access folder contains two of the nine Access database files (Begon Pest Control and More Birds) required to perform the lab assignments in the Access section of this book.

One method of copying files in Windows Explorer is to right-drag a file icon from the right pane to a folder or drive icon in the Folders pane. The following steps show how to copy the More Birds file in the Access folder (source folder) to the Homework folder (destination folder).

To Copy a File in Windows Explorer by Right-Dragging

1

• **Click the Access icon in the Folders pane.**

The Access folder is selected, the contents of the Access folder, including the Begon Pest Control and More Birds files, are displayed in the right pane, and the path to the Access folder appears in the Address box (Figure 1-74).

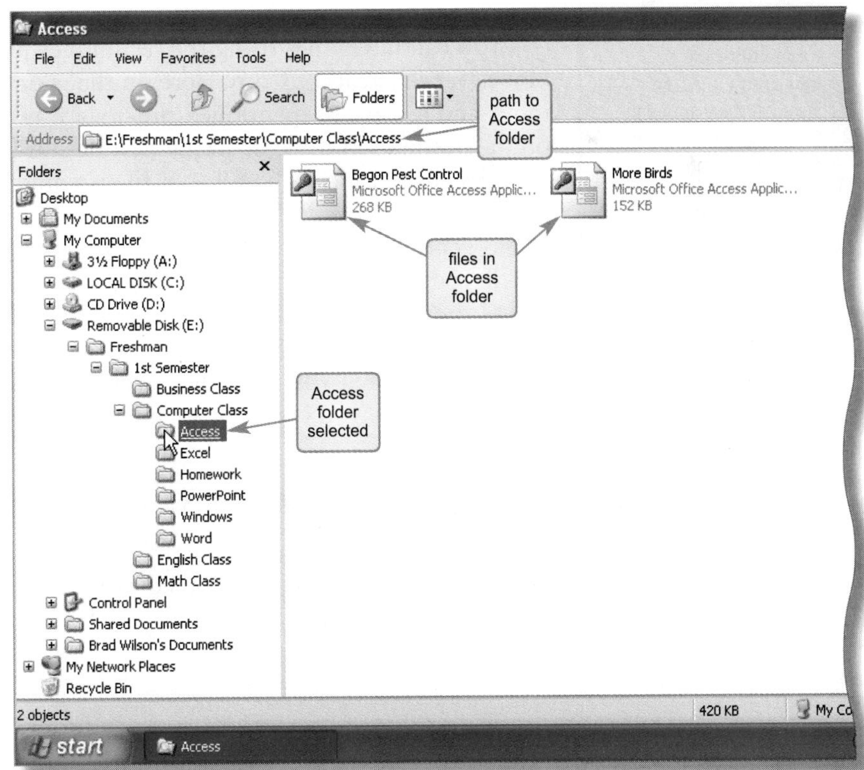

FIGURE 1-74

2

• **Right-drag the More Birds icon onto the top of the Homework folder.**

The dimmed image of the More Birds icon is displayed as you right-drag the icon onto the top of the Homework folder, the shortcut menu appears, and the dimmed image no longer is displayed (Figure 1-75).

3

• **Click Copy Here on the shortcut menu.**

The More Birds file is copied to the Homework folder.

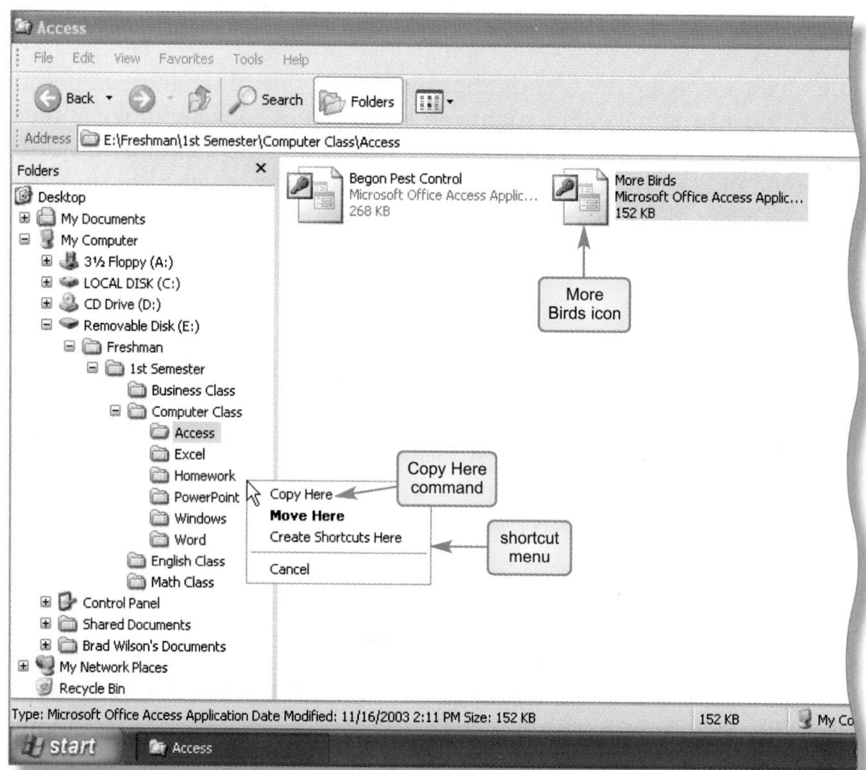

FIGURE 1-75

Other Ways

1. Right-click file to copy, click Copy on shortcut menu, right-click Homework icon, click Paste on shortcut menu
2. Click file to copy, on Edit menu click Copy, click Homework icon, on Edit menu click Paste
3. Select file to copy, press CTRL+C, select Homework icon, press CTRL+V

You can move files using the techniques just discussed except that you click **Move Here** instead of Copy Here on the shortcut menu. The difference between a move and a copy, as mentioned previously, is that when you move a file, it is placed on the destination drive or in the destination folder and is permanently removed from its current location. When a file is copied, it is placed on the destination drive or in the destination folder as well as remaining stored in its current location.

In general, you should right-drag to copy or move a file instead of dragging a file. If you drag a file from one folder to another on the same drive, Windows XP moves the file. If you drag a file from one folder to another folder on a different drive, Windows XP copies the file. Because of the different ways this is handled, it is strongly suggested you right-drag when moving or copying files.

In addition, you can copy or move a folder using the techniques just discussed.

Displaying the Contents of the Homework Folder

After copying a file, you might want to examine the folder or drive where the file was copied to ensure it was copied properly. The following step illustrates how to display the contents of the Homework folder.

To Display the Contents of a Folder

1

• **Click the Homework icon in the Folders pane.**

The Homework folder name is selected in the Folders pane, the More Birds file is displayed in the right pane, and the Homework name replaces the Access name in the window title and on the taskbar button (Figure 1-76). The path to the Homework folder displays in the Address box.

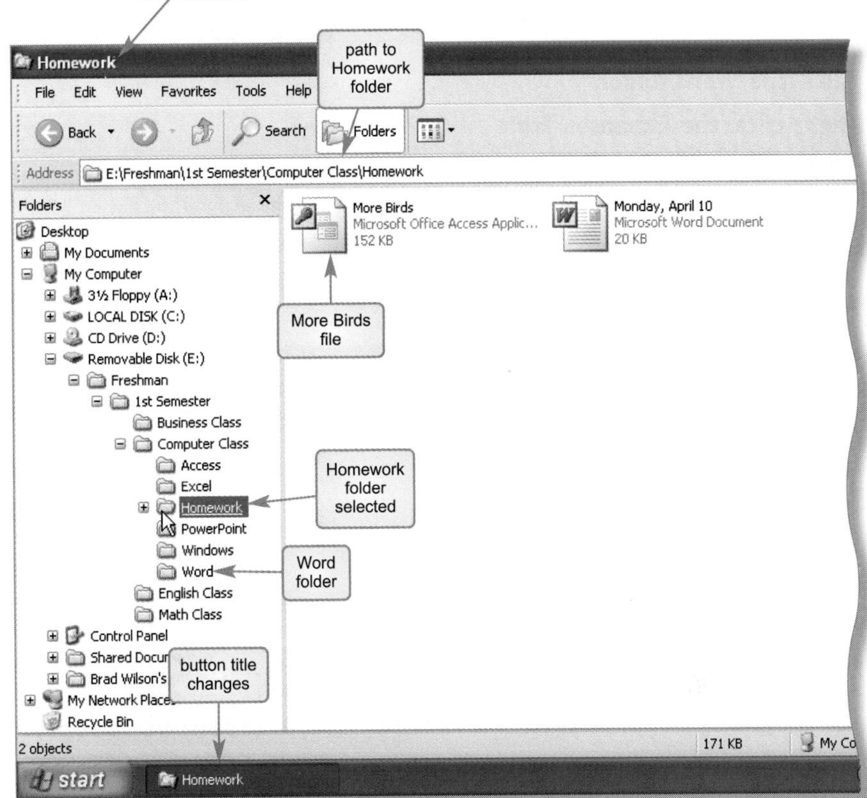

FIGURE 1-76

Renaming Files and Folders

In some circumstances, you may want to **rename** a file or a folder. This could occur when you want to distinguish a file in one folder or drive from a copy, or if you decide you need a better name to identify a file.

The Word folder in Figure 1-77 on the next page contains the three Word document files (Authentication Paragraph, Expenses Table, and Paris Announcement) required to perform the lab assignments in the Word section of this book. In this case, you decide to personalize the Expenses Table name by adding the word, Personal, to the beginning of the name. The following steps illustrate how to change the name of the Expenses Table file in the Word folder to Personal Expenses Table file.

To Rename a File

1

- **Click the Word folder.**
- **Right-click the Expenses Table icon in the right pane.**

The Expenses Table file name is selected, a shortcut menu appears, and the Word name replaces the Access name in the window title and taskbar button (Figure 1-77). The path to the Word folder displays in the Address box.

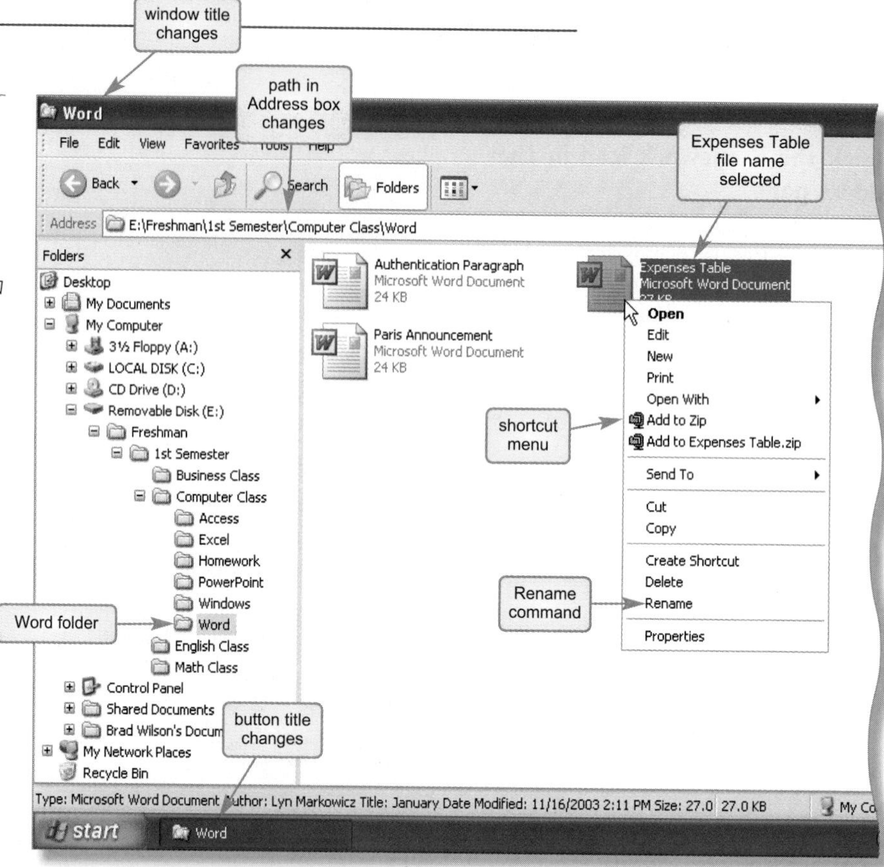

FIGURE 1-77

2

- **Click Rename on the shortcut menu.**
- **Type** `Personal Expenses Table` **and then press the ENTER key.**

The file is renamed Personal Expenses Table (Figure 1-78).

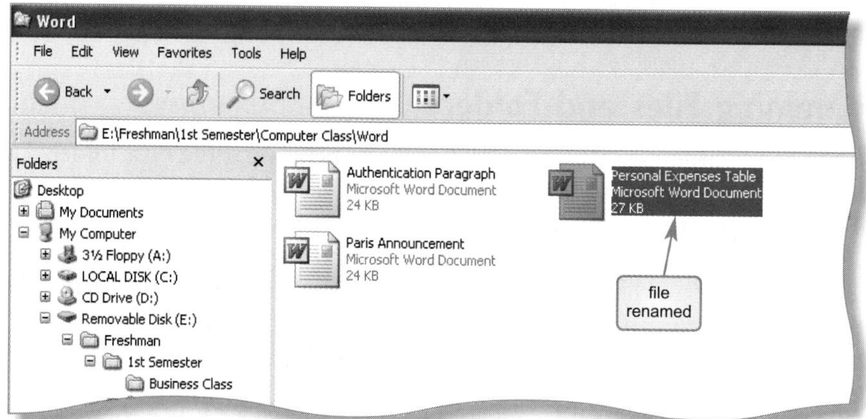

FIGURE 1-78

Other Ways

1. Right-click icon, press M, type name, press ENTER
2. Click icon, press F2, type name, press ENTER
3. Click icon, on File menu click Rename, type name, press ENTER
4. Select icon, press ALT+F, press M, type name, press ENTER

You can rename a folder using the techniques just discussed. To rename a folder, right-click the folder icon, click Rename on the shortcut menu, type the new folder name, and then press the ENTER key.

Deleting Files in Windows Explorer

A final operation that you may want to perform in Windows Explorer is to delete a file. Exercise extreme caution when deleting a file or files. When you delete a file from a hard drive, the deleted file is stored in the Recycle Bin where you can recover it until you empty the Recycle Bin. If you delete a file from a removable media, the file is gone permanently once you delete it.

Assume you have decided you no longer want the Paris Announcement file and would like to delete the file from the Word folder. The following steps show how to delete the Paris Announcement file by right-clicking the Paris Announcement icon.

More About

Deleting Files

Someone proposed that the Delete command be removed from operating systems after an employee, who thought he knew what he was doing, deleted an entire database, which cost the company millions of dollars to replace. You should regard the Delete command as something to be used with extreme caution.

To Delete a File by Right-Clicking

1

- **Right-click the Paris Announcement icon in the right pane.**

The Paris Announcement icon in the right pane is selected and a shortcut menu is displayed (Figure 1-79).

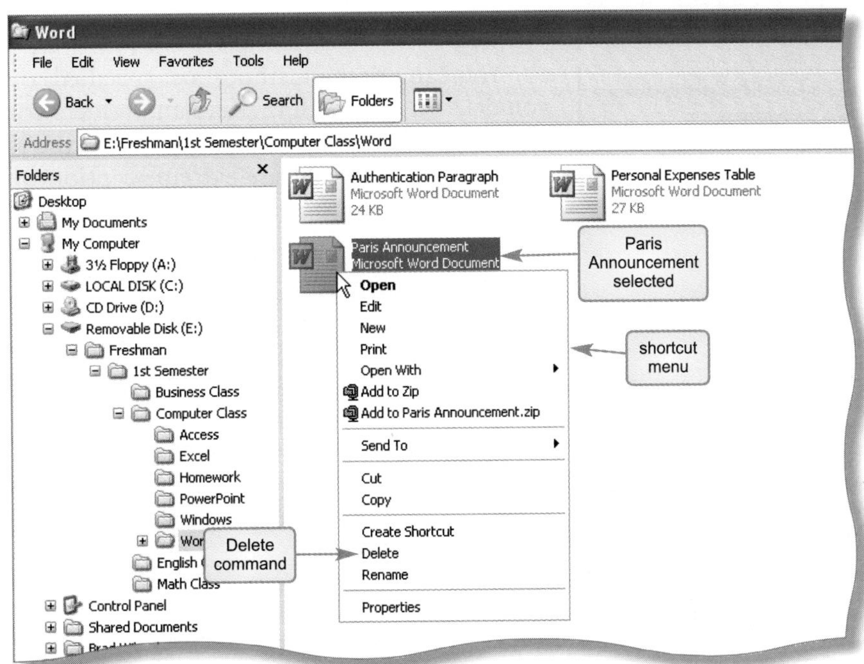

FIGURE 1-79

2

- **Click Delete on the shortcut menu.**

Windows displays the Confirm File Delete dialog box (Figure 1-80). The dialog box contains the question, Are you sure you want to delete 'Paris Announcement'?, and the Yes and No buttons.

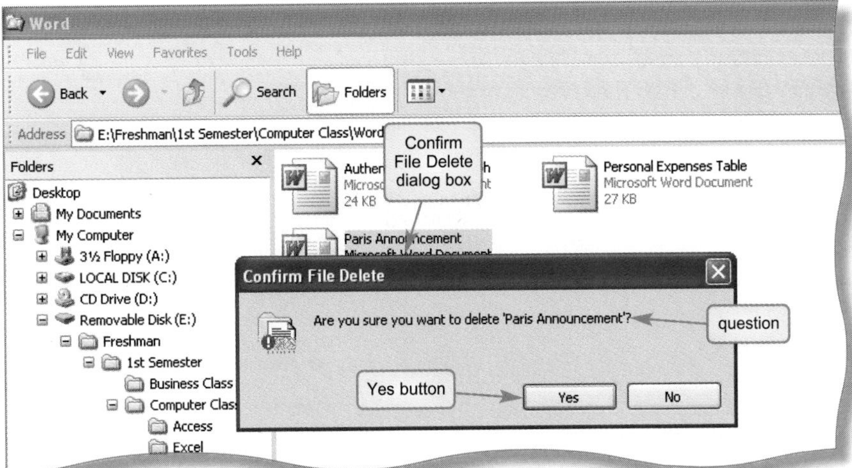

FIGURE 1-80

3

• **Click the Yes button in the Confirm File Delete dialog box.**

The Paris Announcement icon is removed from the right pane (Figure 1-81). Remember – if you delete a file on a removable media (flash drive), the file is gone permanently once you delete it.

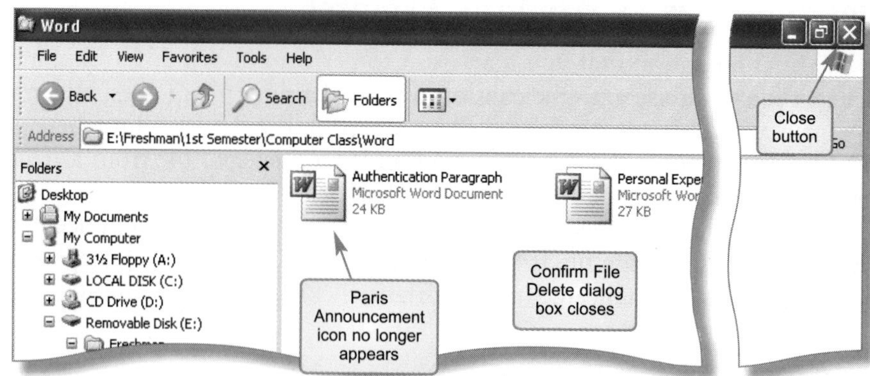

FIGURE 1-81

Other Ways

1. Drag icon to Recycle Bin
2. Click icon, on File menu click Delete, click Yes button
3. Select icon, press ALT+F, press D, press Y

You can use the methods just specified to delete folders on a disk drive. When you delete a folder, all the files and folders contained in the folder you are deleting, together with all the files and folders on the lower hierarchical levels, are deleted.

Again, you should use extreme caution when deleting files and folders to ensure you do not delete something you may not be able to recover.

Closing Folder Expansions

Sometimes, after you have completed work with expanded folders, you will want to close the expansions while still leaving the Explorer window open. The following steps illustrate how to close the Computer Class folder, 1st Semester folder, Freshman folder, and Removable Disk (E:) drive.

To Close Expanded Folders

1

• **Click the minus sign to the left of the Computer Class icon.**

The expansion of the Computer Class folder collapses and the minus sign changes to a plus sign (Figure 1-82). The contents of the right pane do not change.

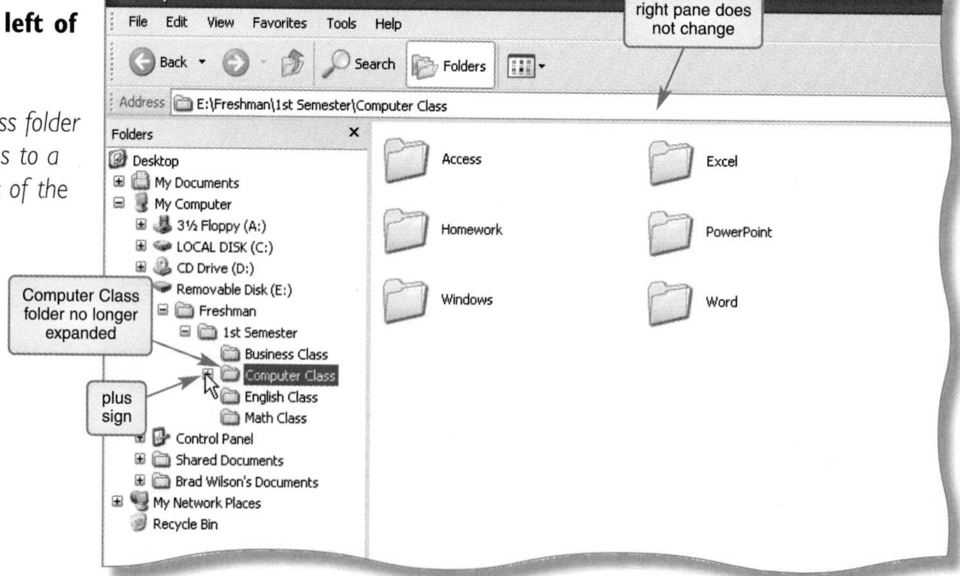

FIGURE 1-82

To Close All Expanded Folders

1. **Click the minus sign to the left of the 1st Semester icon.**
2. **Click the minus sign to the left of the Freshman icon.**
3. **Click the minus sign to the left of the Removable Disk (E:) icon.**

The expansion of the 1st Semester folder, Freshman folder, and Removable Disk (E:) drive collapses and the minus signs change to a plus signs.

Other Ways

1. Click expanded folder icon, press MINUS SIGN on numeric keypad
2. Click expanded folder icon, press LEFT ARROW

Moving through the Folders pane and right pane is an important skill because you will find that you use Windows Explorer to perform a significant amount of file maintenance on the computer.

More About

Deleting Files

This is your last warning! Be EXTREMELY careful when deleting files. Hours of work can be lost with one click of a mouse button. If you are going to delete files or folders from your hard disk, make a backup of those files to ensure that if you inadvertently delete something you need, you will be able to recover the file.

Quitting Windows Explorer

When you have finished working with Windows Explorer, you can quit Windows Explorer by closing the Folders pane or by closing the Windows Explorer (Removable Disk (E:)) window. The following step illustrates how to quit Windows Explorer by closing the Removable Disk (E:) window.

To Quit Windows Explorer

1. **Click the Close button on the Removable Disk (E:) window title bar.**

Windows XP closes the Removable Disk (E:) window and quits Windows Explorer.

Finding Files or Folders

You know the location of files you use often and can locate the folder that contains them. In some cases, however, you may know you have a certain file on the computer but you have no idea in what folder it is located. To search every folder manually on the computer to find the file would be time consuming and almost impossible. Fortunately, Windows XP provides Search Companion.

Search Companion allows you to search for files and folders by name, type, or size. You can search for a file based on when you last worked on the file or search for files containing specific text. You also can choose to search with the help of an animated character.

Searching for a File by Name

If you know the name or partial name of a file, you can use Search Companion to locate the file. For example, a file named Personal Expenses Table exists on the Removable Disk (E:) drive. The following steps show how to search for a file on the Removable Disk (E:) drive knowing only a part of the file name.

To Search for a File by Name

1

- **Click the Start button on the taskbar.**

The Start menu and Search command are displayed (Figure 1-83).

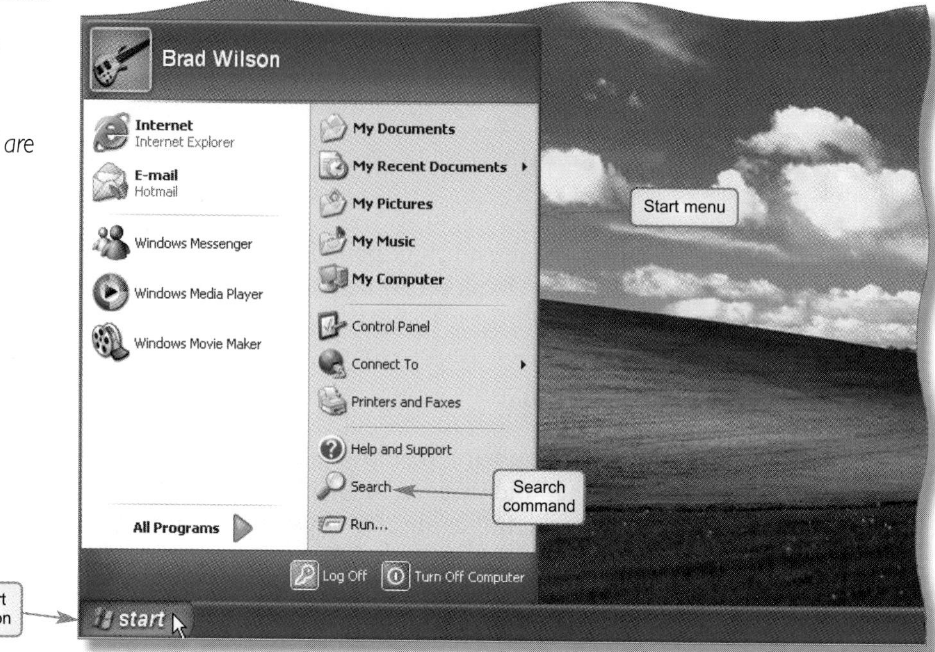

FIGURE 1-83

2

- **Click Search on the Start menu. If necessary, maximize the Search Results window.**

The Search Companion pane is displayed in the Search Results window (Figure 1-84). The pane contains the Search Companion balloon and an animated dog named Rover. The right pane contains a message about starting a search.

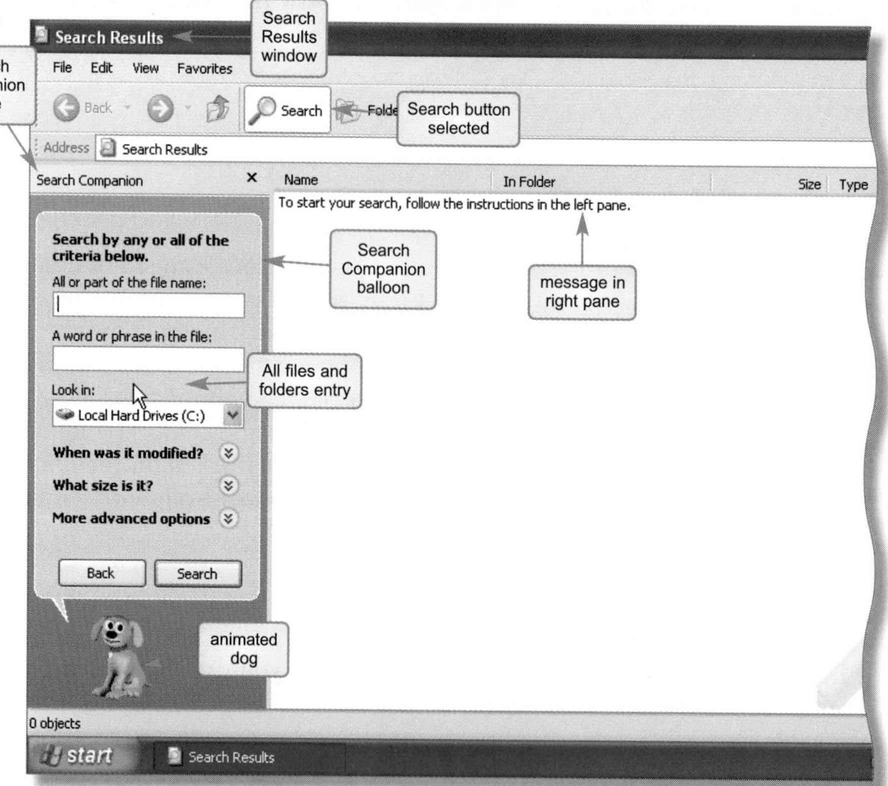

FIGURE 1-84

3

• **Click All files and folders in the Search Companion balloon. Type** `Expenses Table` **in the All or part of the file name text box.**

The contents of the Search Companion balloon change (Figure 1-85). The keywords, Expenses Table, appears in the All or part of the file name text box. The Local Hard Drives (C:) entry in the Look in box indicates all of Local Hard Drives (C:) will be searched.

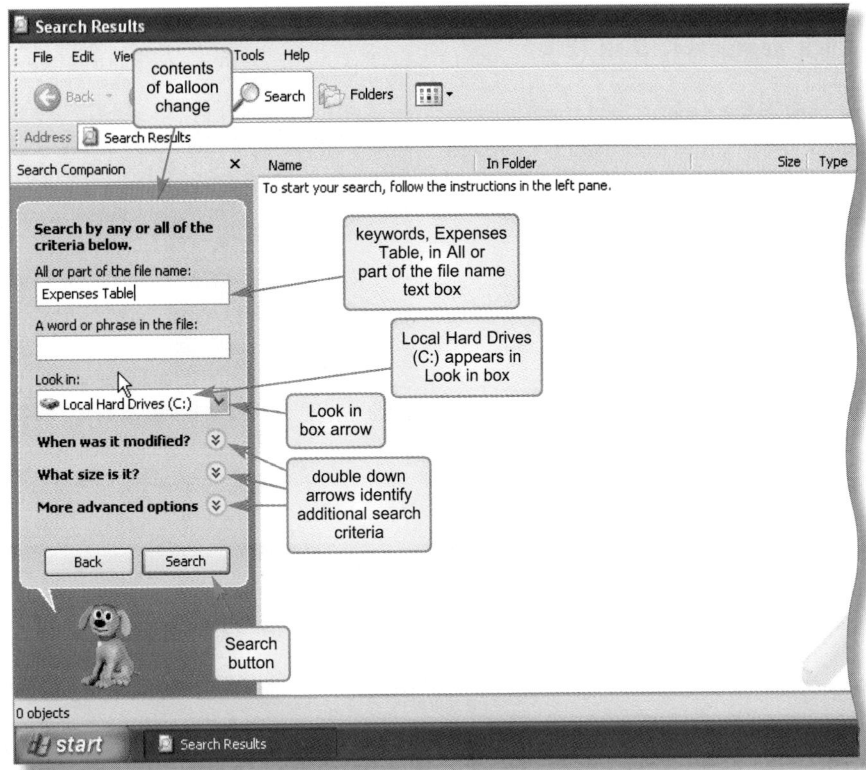

FIGURE 1-85

4

• **Click the Look in box arrow in the Search Companion pane.**

The Look in list is displayed, the Local Hard Drives (C:) entry is selected, and the Removable Disk (E:) drive name appears (Figure 1-86).

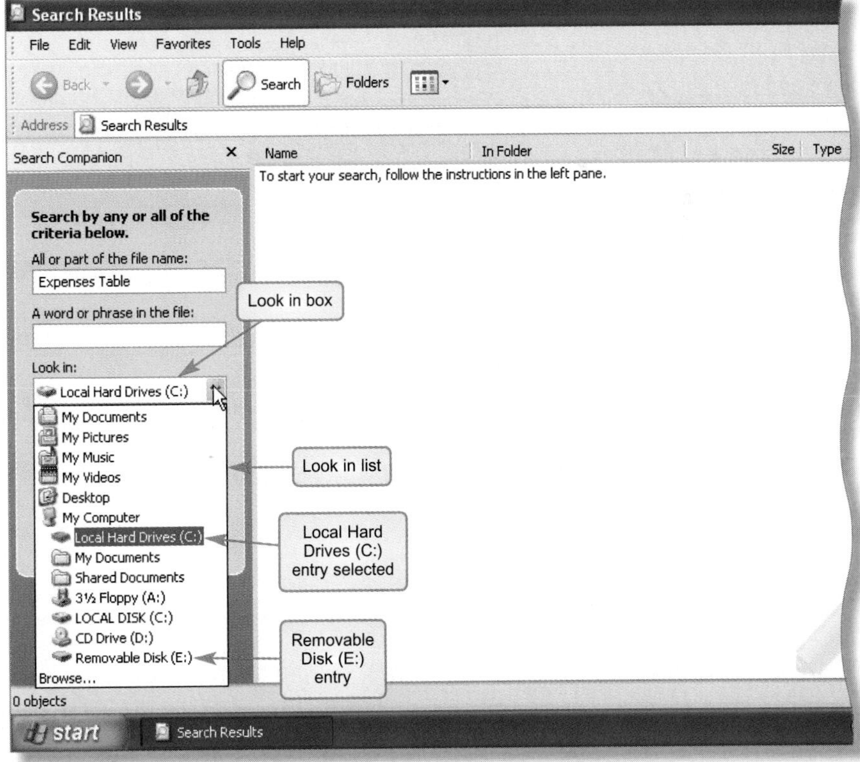

FIGURE 1-86

5

• **Click Removable Disk (E:).**

The Look in list is closed and the highlighted Removable Disk (E:) drive name is selected in the Look in box (Figure 1-87).

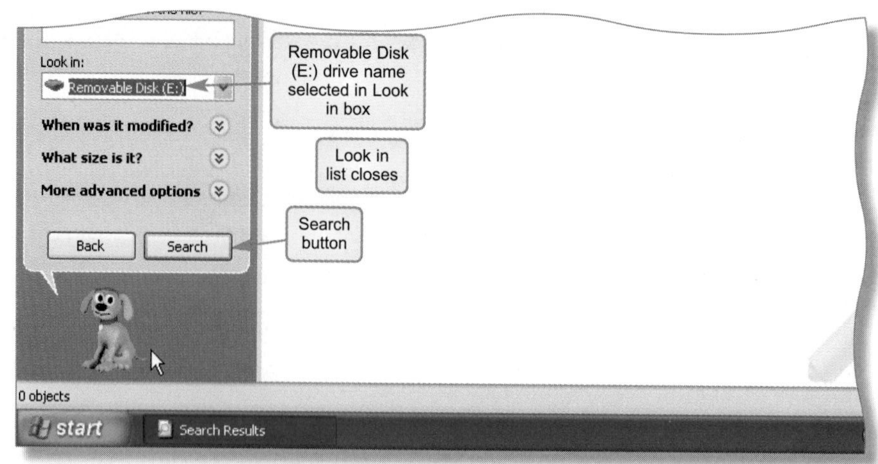

FIGURE 1-87

6

• **Click the Search button.**

While the search continues, Windows momentarily displays a message, locations being searched, a progress bar, and a Stop button in the balloon. Windows XP searches drive E: for the Expenses Table file (Figure 1-88). One file is found, and the right pane displays the file name (Personal Expenses Table), folder path (E:\Freshman\1st Semester\Computer Class\Word), file size (27KB), file type (Microsoft Word Document), and modification date (10/25/2006). The modification date is not visible in the right pane.

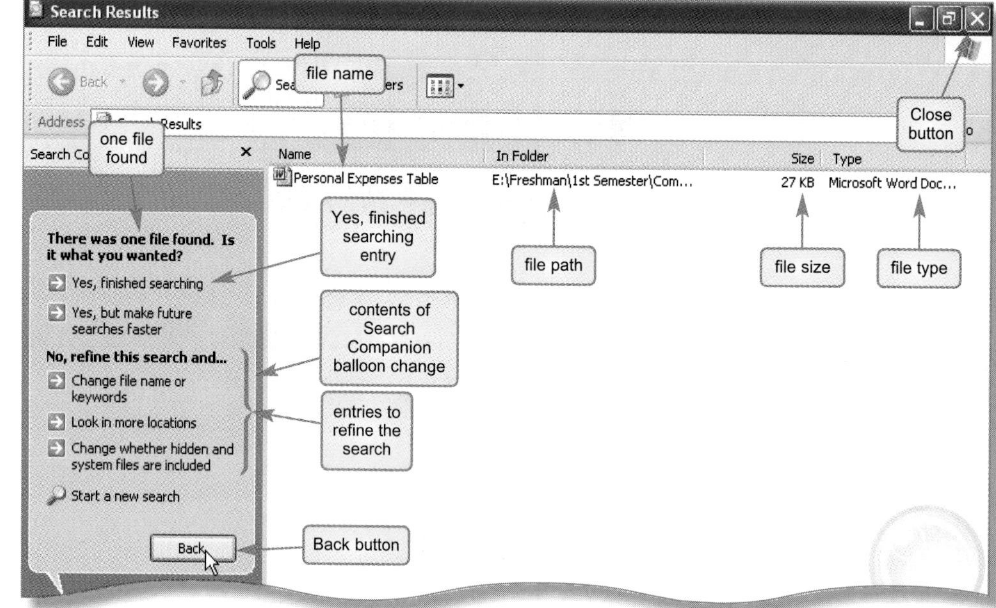

FIGURE 1-88

7

• **Click the Close button on the Search Results window title bar.**

The Search Results window is closed.

Other Ways

1. Click Search button on Standard Buttons toolbar, click All files and folders, select search criteria, click Search button
2. Press F3 or WINDOWS+F, select search criteria, press ENTER

If the search results were not satisfactory, you can refine the search by changing the file name, looking in more locations, or changing whether hidden and system files are included in the search.

In the right pane of the Search Results window shown in Figure 1-88, after the search is complete, you can work with the files found in any manner desired. For example, you can open the file by double-clicking the file icon, or by right-clicking the file icon and then clicking Open on the shortcut menu. You can print the file by right-clicking the file icon and then clicking Print on the shortcut menu. You can copy or move the file with the same method as shown for files in My Computer or Windows Explorer. In summary, any operation you can accomplish from My Computer or from Windows Explorer can be performed on the files displayed in the right pane of the Search Results window.

If the file you are searching for is an executable program file, such as Microsoft Word, you can start the program by double-clicking the file icon in the right pane of the Search Results window.

If you know only a portion of a file's name, you can use an asterisk in the name to represent the remaining characters. For example, if you know a file starts with the letters WIN, you can type **win*** in the All or part of the file name text box. All files that begin with the letters win, regardless of what letters follow, will be displayed.

You may use three additional criteria when searching for all files and folders: modification date, file size, and advanced options. These criteria are identified by double down arrow buttons at the bottom of the balloon shown in Figure 1-85 on page WIN 63. Searching by modification date allows you to display all files that were created or modified within the last week, past month, past year, or on a specific date. Searching by file size allows you to search for files based on file size in kilobytes. Advanced options allow you to search system folders, hidden files or folders, subfolders, and tape backup, and perform case-sensitive searches. If no files are found in the search, a message (Search is complete. There are no results to display.) appears in the right pane of the Search Results window. In this case, you may want to check the file name you entered or examine a different drive to continue the search.

Searching for a File by Using a Word or Phrase in the File

If you want to search for a file knowing only a word or phrase in the file, you can search by typing the word or phrase in the A word or phrase in the file text box in the Search Companion balloon. Assume you want to find all files containing the word, apply, on the Removable Disk (E:) drive. The following steps illustrate how to search for all files containing the word, apply.

To Search for a File Using a Word or Phrase in the File

1

- **Click the Start button on the taskbar. Click Search on the Start menu. If necessary, maximize the Search Results window. Click All files and folders in the Search Companion balloon.**

The Search Companion balloon is displayed in the maximized Search Results window (Figure 1-89). The insertion point is blinking in the All or part of the file name box.

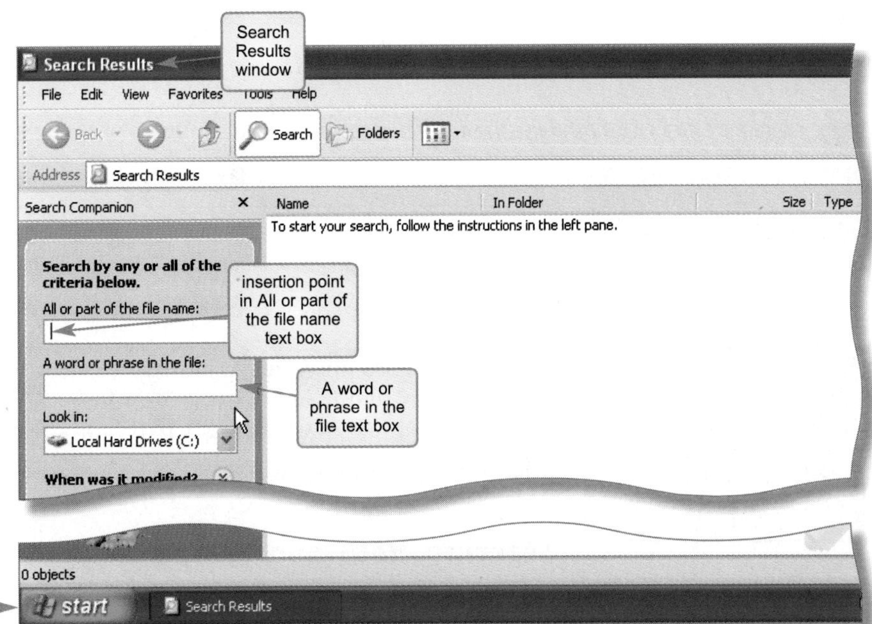

FIGURE 1-89

2

• **Click the A word or phrase in the file text box.**

• **Type** `apply` **in the A word or phrase in the file text box, click the Look in box arrow, and then click Removable Disk (E:) in the Look in list.**

The word, apply, is displayed in the A word or phrase in the file text box and Removable Disk (E:) is displayed in the Look in box (Figure 1-90).

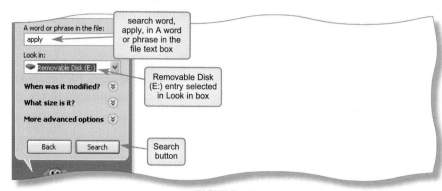

FIGURE 1-90

3

• **Click the Search button in the Search Companion balloon.**

While the search progresses, Windows displays the search criteria and locations being searched in the balloon along with the path of the folder currently being searched. When the search is complete, four Word document files containing the word, apply, on the Removable Disk (E:) drive are displayed in the Search Results window (Figure 1-91). Different files may appear on your computer.

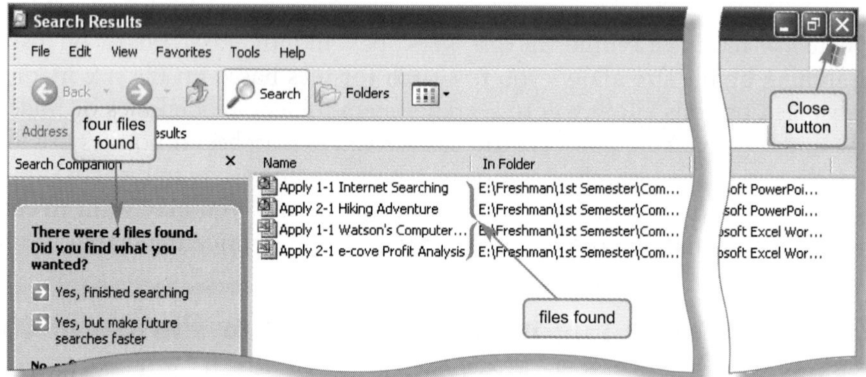

FIGURE 1-91

• **Click the Close button on the Search Results window title bar.**

The Search Results window closes.

• **Remove the USB flash drive from the USB port.**

When you remove the USB flash drive, a sound indicating the flash drive has been removed may sound.

Other Ways

1. Click Search button on Standard Buttons toolbar, click All files and folders, select search criteria, click Search button
2. Press F3 or WINDOWS+F, select search criteria, press ENTER
3. Press WINDOWS+F, press L, select search criteria, press ENTER

Using Help and Support

One of the more powerful Windows XP features is Help and Support. **Help and Support** is available when using Windows XP, or when using any application program running under Windows XP. It contains answers to many questions you may ask with respect to Windows XP.

Starting Help and Support

Before you can access the Help and Support Center services, you must start Help and Support. One method of starting Help and Support uses the Start menu. The following steps show how to start Help and Support.

To Start Help and Support

1

- **Click the Start button on the taskbar and then point to Help and Support on the Start menu.**

Windows XP displays the Start menu and highlights the Help and Support command (Figure 1-92).

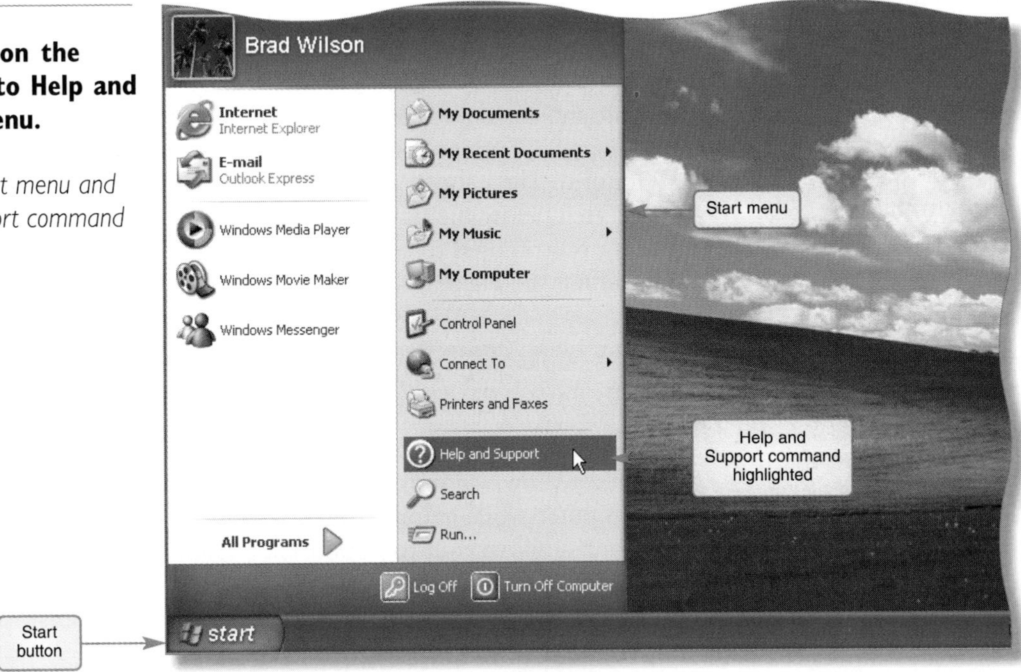

FIGURE 1-92

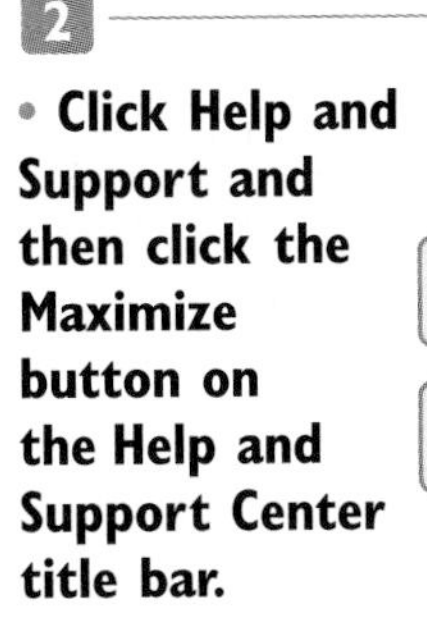

2

- **Click Help and Support and then click the Maximize button on the Help and Support Center title bar.**

The Help and Support Center window opens and maximizes (Figure 1-93). The window contains the Help viewer. The Help viewer includes the navigation toolbar, Search text box and Set search options link, and table of contents. The table of contents contains four areas (Pick a Help topic, Ask for assistance, Pick a task, and Did you know?).

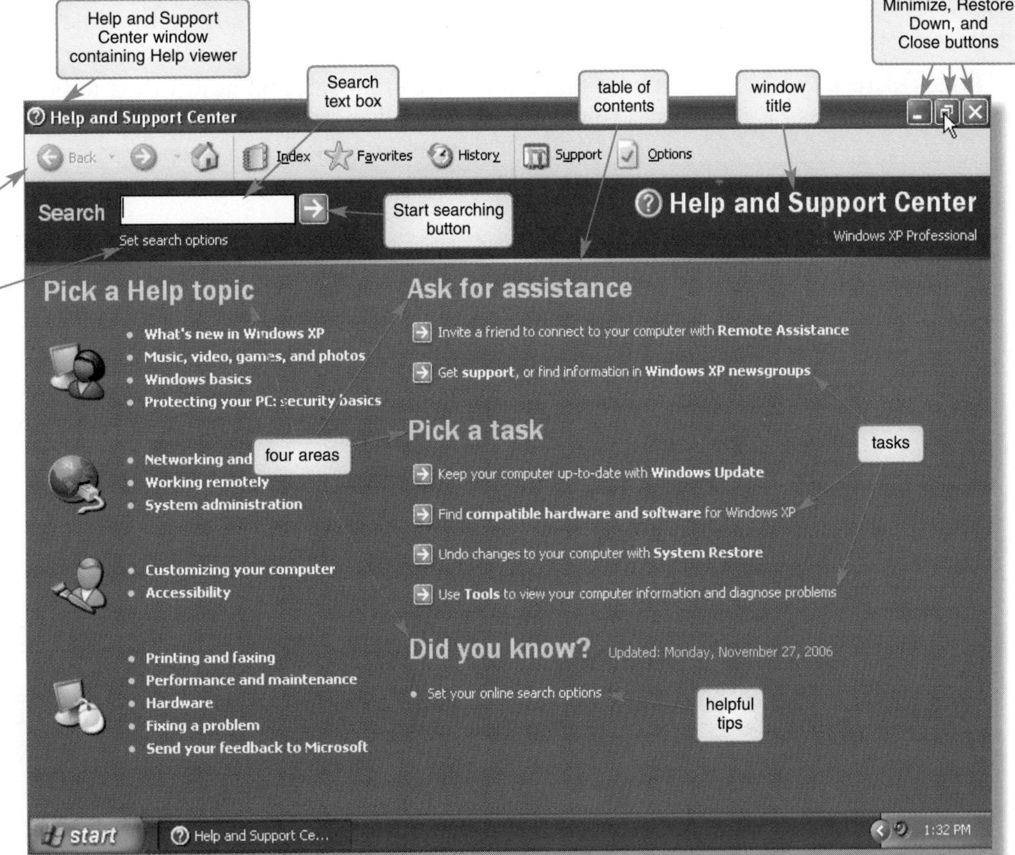

FIGURE 1-93

Other Ways

1. Press F1
2. Press CTRL+ESC, press H
3. Press WINDOWS+F1

More About

Windows XP Help and Support

If you purchased an operating system or application program nine years ago, you received at least one, and more often several, heavy thick technical manuals that explained the software. With Windows XP, you receive a booklet with only 34 pages. The Help and Support feature of Windows XP replaces the reams and reams of printed pages in hard-to-understand technical manuals.

More About

The Table of Contents

The table of contents in Windows XP resembles the Contents sheet in previous versions of Windows. To display the Contents sheet, you had to click the Contents tab in the Help window. Now, the table of contents appears in a prominent position and contains links to online Help and Support topics.

The Help and Support Center title bar shown in Figure 1-93 on the previous page contains a Minimize button, Restore Down button, and Close button. You can minimize or restore the Help and Support Center window as needed and also close the Help and Support Center window.

The navigation toolbar is displayed below the title bar. The **navigation toolbar** allows you to navigate through Help topics and pages, browse and save Help topics and pages, view previously saved Help topics and pages, get online support for questions and problems, and customize the Help viewer. An icon identifies each button on the navigation toolbar. Six buttons contain a text label (Back, Index, Favorites, History, Support, and Options). The buttons on the navigation toolbar on your computer may be different.

The area below the navigation toolbar contains the Search text box and Start searching button used to search for help, the Set search options link to set the criteria for searching the Help and Support Center, and the window's title (Help and Support Center).

The **table of contents** contains four areas. The **Pick a Help topic area** contains four category groups. A unique icon identifies each group. Clicking a category in a group displays a list of subcategories and Help topics related to the category.

The **Ask for assistance area** contains two tasks. The first task (**Remote Assistance**) allows an individual at another computer to connect and control your computer while helping to solve a problem. The second task (**Windows XP newsgroups**) allows you to obtain Help from product support experts or discuss your questions with other Windows XP users in newsgroups.

The **Pick a task area** contains four tasks. The first task (**Windows Update**) allows you to access a catalog of items such as device drivers, security fixes, critical updates, the latest Help files, and Internet products that you can download to keep your computer up-to-date. The second task (**compatible hardware and software**) allows you to search for hardware and software that are compatible with Windows XP. The third task (**System Restore**) allows you to store the current state of your computer and restore your computer to that state without losing important information. The fourth task (**Tools**) contains a collection of eight helpful tools to keep your computer running smoothly. The **Did you know? area** is updated daily with helpful tips for using Windows XP.

Browsing for Help Topics in the Table of Contents

After starting Help and Support, the next step is to find the Help topic in which you are interested. Assume you want to know more about finding information using the Help and Support Center. The following steps illustrate how to use the table of contents to find a Help topic that describes how to find what you need in the Help and Support Center.

To Browse for Help Topics in the Table of Contents

1

• **Point to Windows basics in the Pick a Help topic area.**

The mouse pointer changes to a hand icon when positioned on the Windows basics category, and the category is underlined (Figure 1-94).

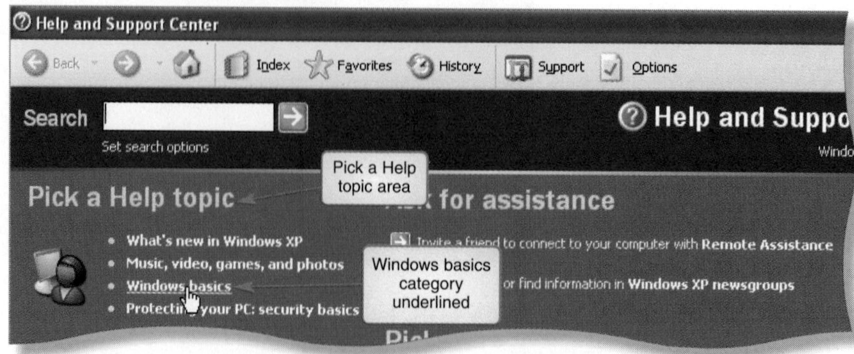

FIGURE 1-94

2

- **Click Windows basics and then point to Tips for using Help.**

The navigation pane and topic pane are displayed in the Help and Support Center window (Figure 1-95). The Windows basics area in the navigation pane contains five categories and the underlined Tips for using Help category. The See Also area contains four Help topics. The topic pane contains the Help and Support toolbar and the Windows basics page.

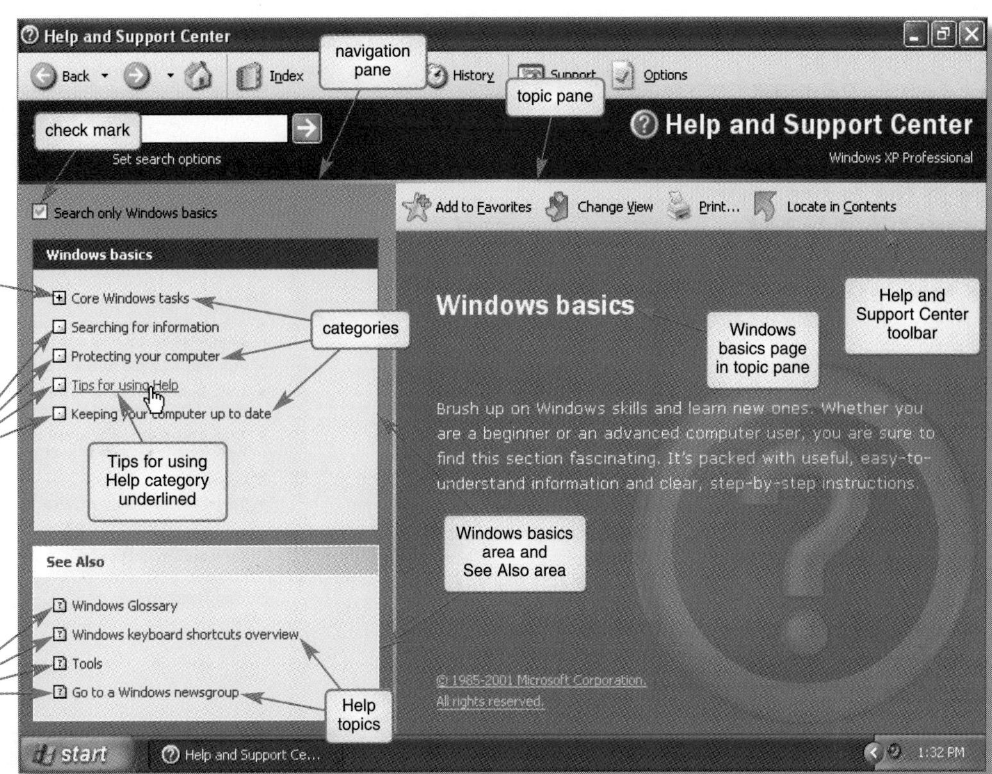

FIGURE 1-95

3

- **Click Tips for using Help and then point to Find what you need in Help and Support Center in the topic pane.**

Windows XP highlights the Tips for using Help category in the Windows basics area, displays the Tips for using Help page in the topic pane, and underlines the Find what you need in Help and Support Center task (Figure 1-96). The Add to Favorites button and Print button on the Help and Support Center toolbar are dimmed to indicate the page cannot be added to the favorites list or printed.

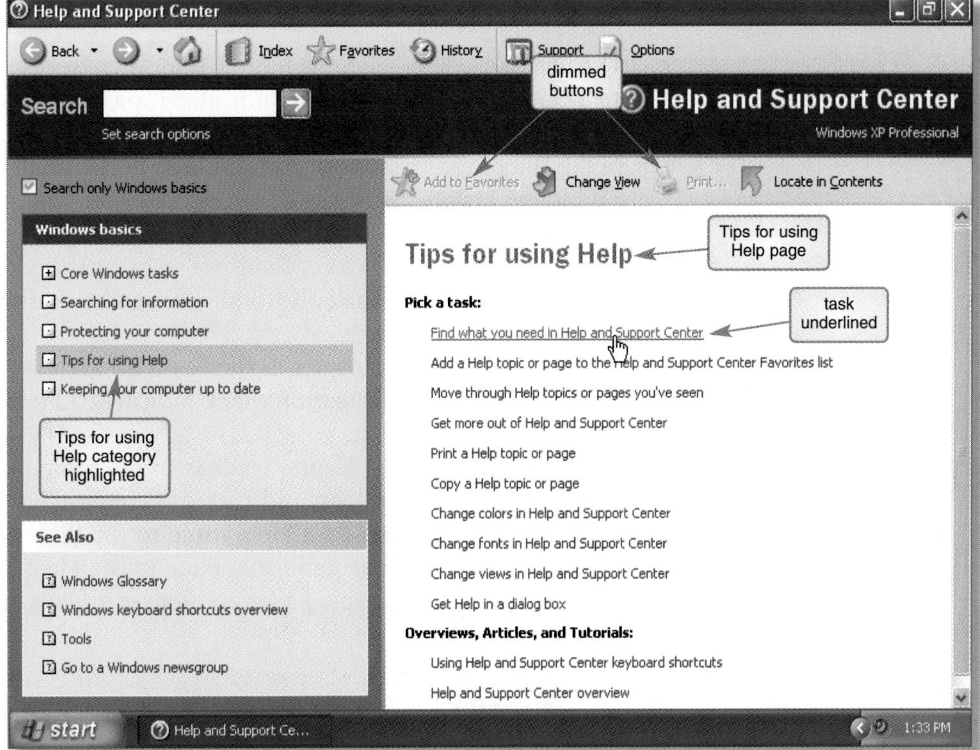

FIGURE 1-96

4

• **Click Find what you need in Help and Support Center and then read the information in the To find what you need in Help and Support Center topic in the topic pane.**

Windows XP removes the dotted rectangle surrounding the Tips for using Help category in the Windows basics area and displays the To find what you need in Help and Support Center topic in the topic pane (Figure 1-97). Clicking the Related Topics link displays a list of related Help topics.

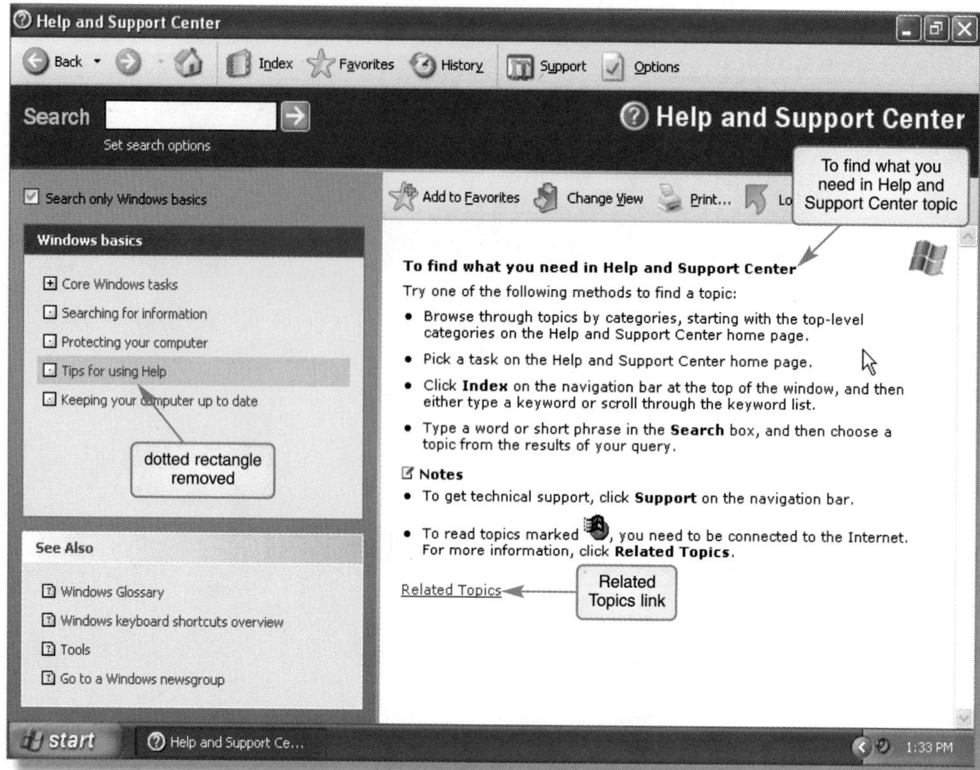

FIGURE 1-97

Other Ways

1. Press TAB until category or topic is highlighted, press ENTER, repeat for each category or topic

The check mark in the Search only Windows basics check box shown in Figure 1-95 on the previous page indicates topics in the Windows basics category will be searched.

In the Windows basics area, the **plus sign** in the small box to the left of the Core Windows tasks category indicates the category contains subcategories but the subcategories do not appear in the area. Clicking the box with the plus sign displays a list of subcategories below the Core Windows tasks category. A **bullet** in a small box indicates a category. Clicking the bullet within a small box displays a list of tasks in the topic pane.

Each of the four Help topics in the See Also area is identified by a question mark in a document icon. The **question mark** indicates a Help topic without further subdivision.

The Help and Support Center toolbar in the topic pane shown in Figure 1-95 contains four buttons. An icon and text label identify each button on the toolbar. The buttons allow you to add a Help topic to the favorites list, display only the Help and Support Center toolbar and topic pane in the Help and Support Center window, print a Help topic in the topic pane, and locate a Help topic in the topic pane in the table of contents.

More About

The Index

The Index is probably the best source of information in Windows Help and Support, because you can enter the name of the subject in which you are interested. Sometimes, however, you will have to be creative to discover the index entry that answers your question, because the most obvious entry will not always lead to your answer.

Using the Help and Support Center Index

A second method of finding answers to your questions about Windows XP is to use the Help and Support Center Index. The **Help and Support Center Index** contains a list of index entries, each of which references one or more Help topics. Assume you want more information about home networking. The following steps illustrate how to learn more about home networking.

To Search for Help Topics Using the Index

1

- **Click the Index button on the navigation toolbar, type** home networking **in the Type in the keyword to find text box, and then point to overview in the list box.**

The Index area, containing a text box, list box, and Display button, is displayed in the navigation pane and the Index page is displayed in the topic pane (Figure 1-98). When you type an entry in the text box, the list of index entries in the list box automatically scrolls and the entry you type is highlighted in the list. Several entries appear indented below the home networking entry.

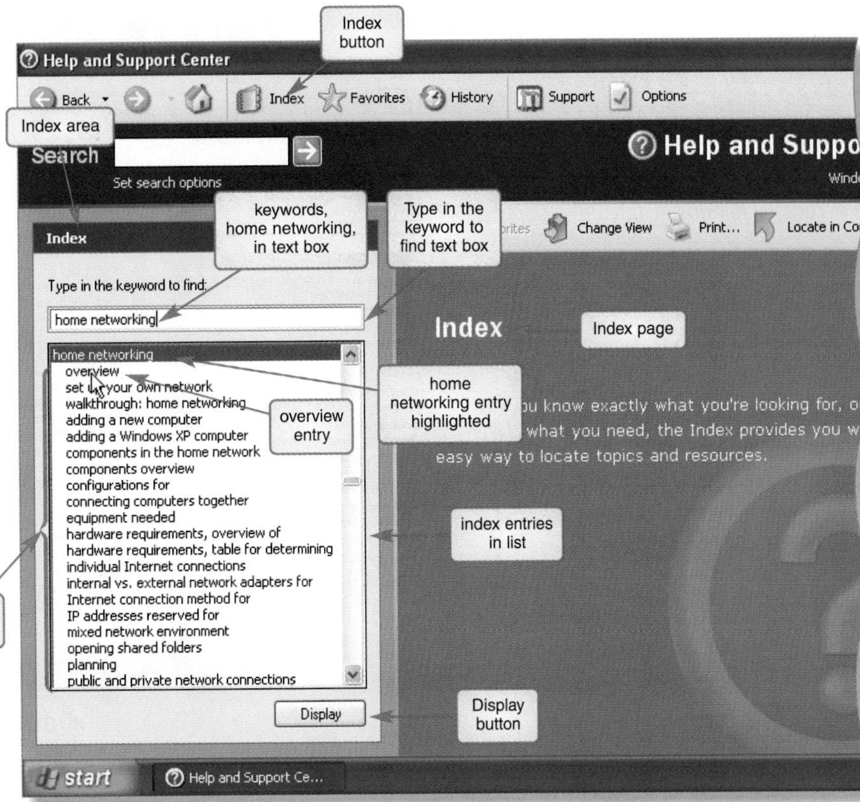

FIGURE 1-98

2

- **Click overview in the list and then point to the Display button.**

Windows XP displays the overview entry in the text box and highlights the overview entry in the list (Figure 1-99). The yellow outline surrounding the Display button indicates the button is selected.

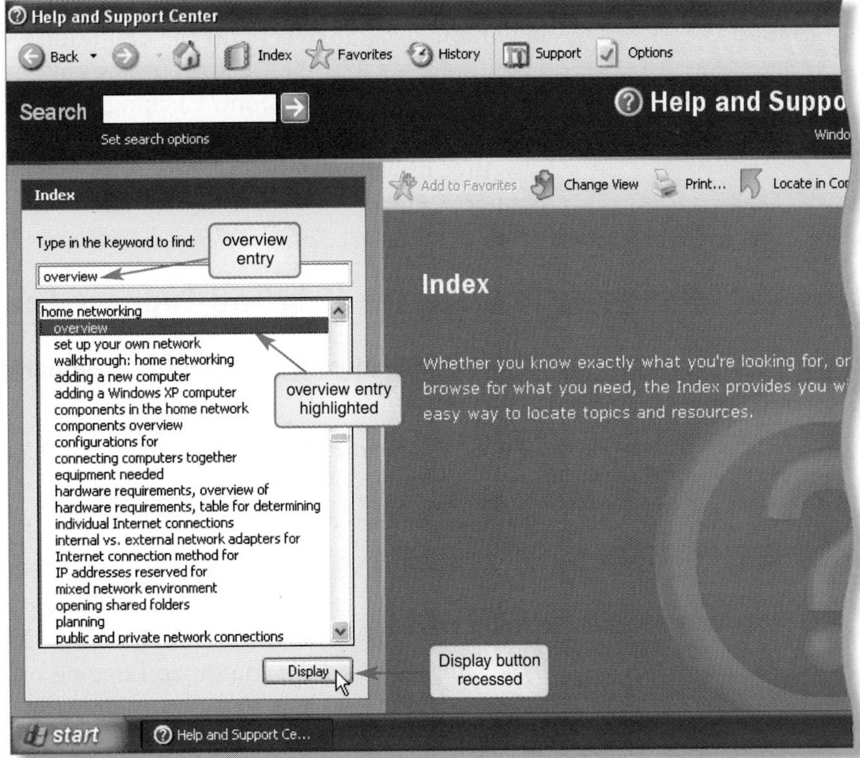

FIGURE 1-99

• **Click the Display button.**

The Home or small office network overview topic is displayed in the topic pane (Figure 1-100). The topic contains an overview of home and small office networks. Additional information is available by using the vertical scroll bar in the topic pane.

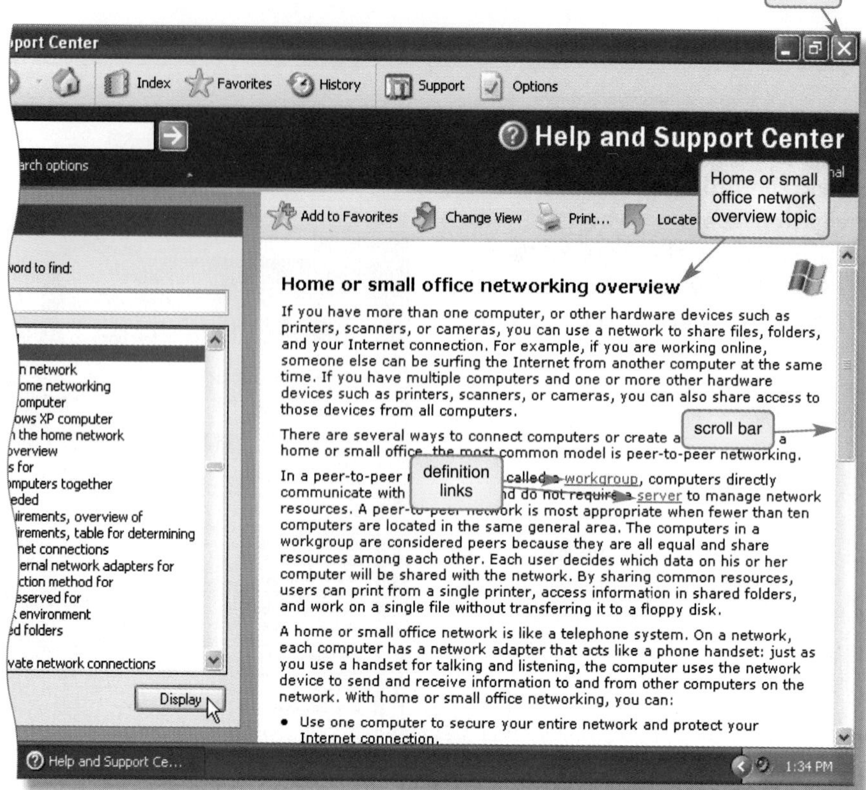

FIGURE 1-100

Other Ways

1. Press ALT+N, type keyword, press DOWN ARROW until topic is highlighted, press ALT+D (or ENTER)

In Figure 1-100, the workgroup and server links are underlined and displayed in green font to indicate that clicking the link will display its definition. To remove the definition, click anywhere off the definition. Although not visible in Figure 1-100, other links, such as the Related Topics link, appear at the bottom of the page, underlined, and in blue font. Clicking the Related Topics link displays a pop-up window that contains topics related to the home or small office network overview.

After using the Help and Support Center, normally you will close the Help and Support Center. The following step shows how to close the Help and Support Center.

To Close the Help and Support Center

1 **Click the Close button on the title bar of the Help and Support Center window.**

Windows XP closes the Help and Support Center window.

Logging Off and Turning Off the Computer

After completing your work with Windows XP, you should close your user account by logging off from the computer. Logging off from the computer closes any open applications, allows you to save any unsaved documents, ends the Windows XP session, and makes the computer available for other users. Perform the following steps to log off from the computer.

To Log Off from the Computer

1

• **Click the Start button on the taskbar and then point to Log Off on the Start menu.**

Windows XP displays the Start menu and highlights the Log Off command (Figure 1-101).

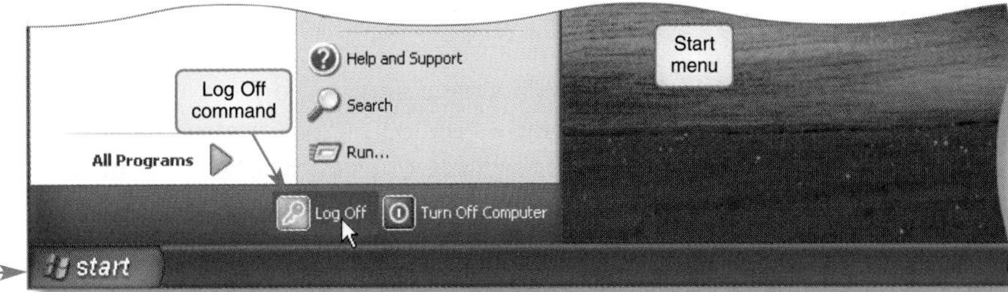

FIGURE 1-101

2

• **Click Log Off.**

• **Point to the Log Off button in the Log Off Windows dialog box.**

Windows XP displays the Log Off Windows dialog box (Figure 1-102). The dialog box contains three buttons (Switch User, Log Off, and Cancel). Pointing to the Log Off button changes the color of the button to light orange and displays the Log Off balloon. The balloon contains the balloon name, Log Off, and the text, Closes your programs and ends your Windows session. The Cancel button is hidden behind the balloon.

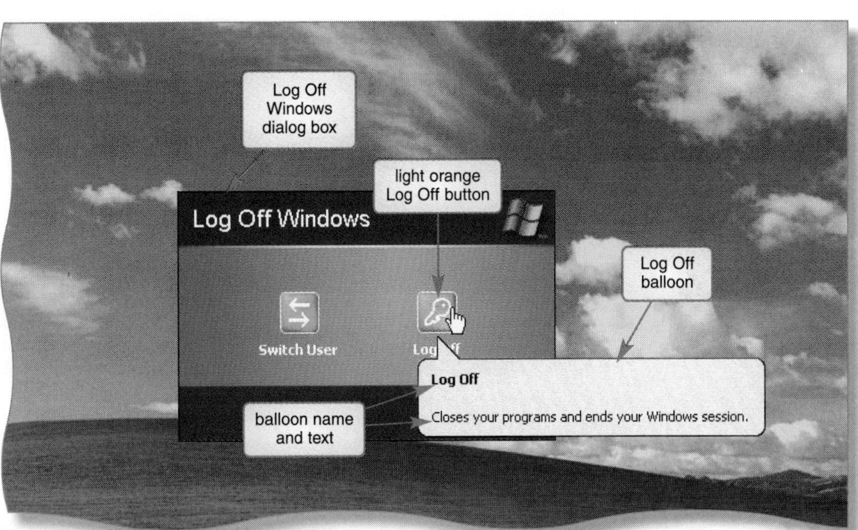

FIGURE 1-102

3

• **Click the Log Off button.**

Windows XP logs off from the computer and displays the Welcome screen (Figure 1-103). A message is displayed below the Brad Wilson name on the Welcome screen to indicate the user has unread e-mail messages. Your user name will be displayed instead of the Brad Wilson name on the Welcome screen.

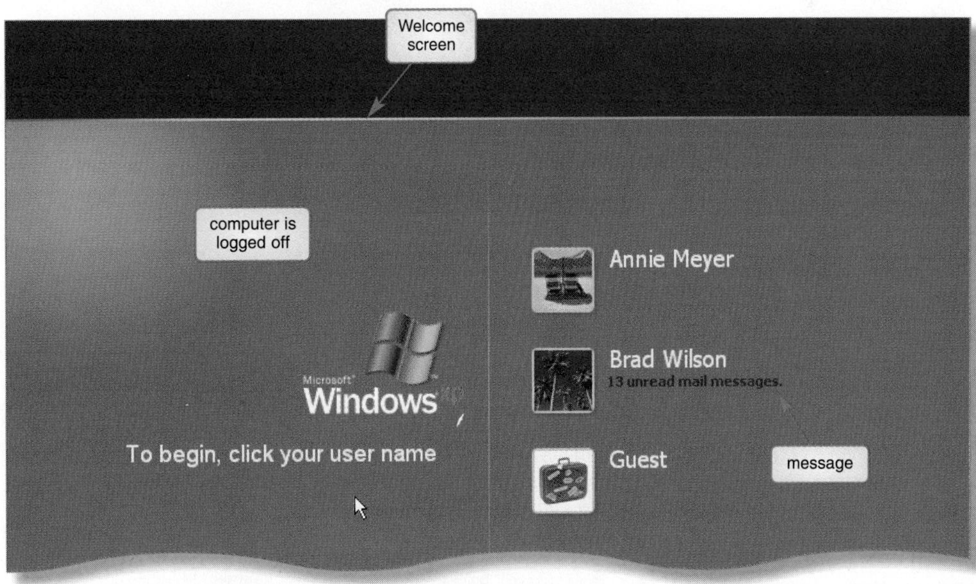

FIGURE 1-103

Other Ways

1. Press CTRL+ESC, press L, press L

Q: Why is it important to log off the computer?

A: It is important to log off the computer so you do not lose your work. Some users of Windows XP have turned off their computers without following the log off procedure only to find data they thought they had stored on disk was lost.

While Windows XP is logging off, a blue screen containing the word, Welcome, appears on the desktop and the messages, Logging off..., and Saving your settings..., appear on the screen momentarily. The blue screen closes and the Welcome screen (Figure 1-103 on the previous page) appears on the desktop. At this point, another user can log on.

If you accidentally click Log Off on the Start menu as shown in Figure 1-101 on the previous page and you do not want to log off, click the Cancel button in the Log Off Windows dialog box to return to normal Windows XP operation.

After logging off, you also may want to turn off the computer using the **Turn off computer link** on the Welcome screen. Turning off the computer shuts down Windows XP so you can turn off the power to the computer. Many computers turn the power off automatically. The following steps illustrate how to turn off the computer. If you are not sure about turning off the computer, simply read the steps.

To Turn Off the Computer

• **Point to the Turn off computer link on the Welcome screen.**

Pointing to the Turn off computer link underlines the Turn off computer link (Figure 1-104).

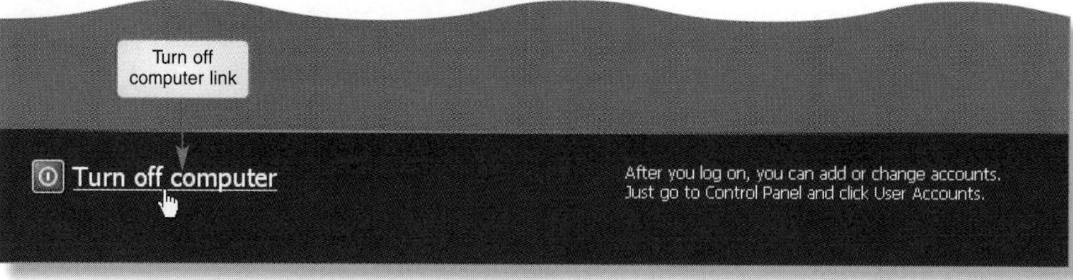

FIGURE 1-104

2

• **Click Turn off computer.**

The Welcome screen darkens and the Turn off computer dialog box is displayed (Figure 1-105). The dialog box contains four buttons (Stand By, Turn Off, Restart, and Cancel). The buttons allow you to perform different operations, such as placing the computer in stand by mode (Stand By), shutting down Windows XP (Turn Off), restarting the computer (Restart), and canceling the process of shutting down Windows XP (Cancel).

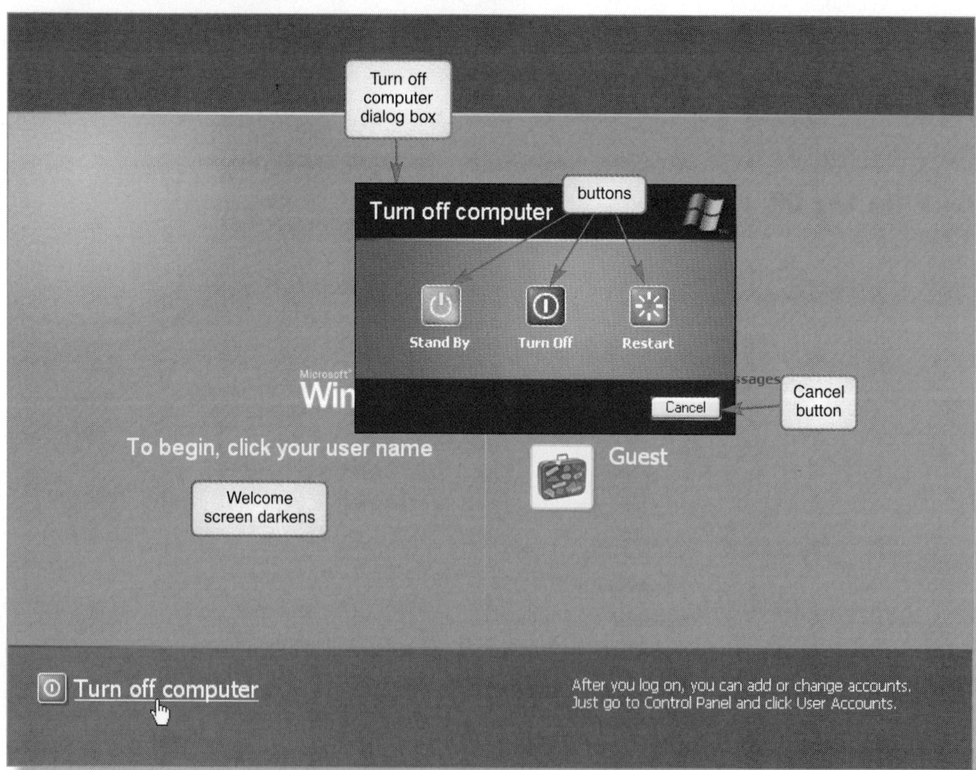

FIGURE 1-105

3

- **Point to the Turn Off button in the Turn off computer dialog box.**

The color of the Turn Off button changes to light red and the Turn Off balloon is displayed (Figure 1-106). The balloon contains the balloon name, Turn Off, and the text, Shuts down Windows so that you can safely turn off the computer.

4

- **Click the Turn Off button.**

Windows XP is shut down.

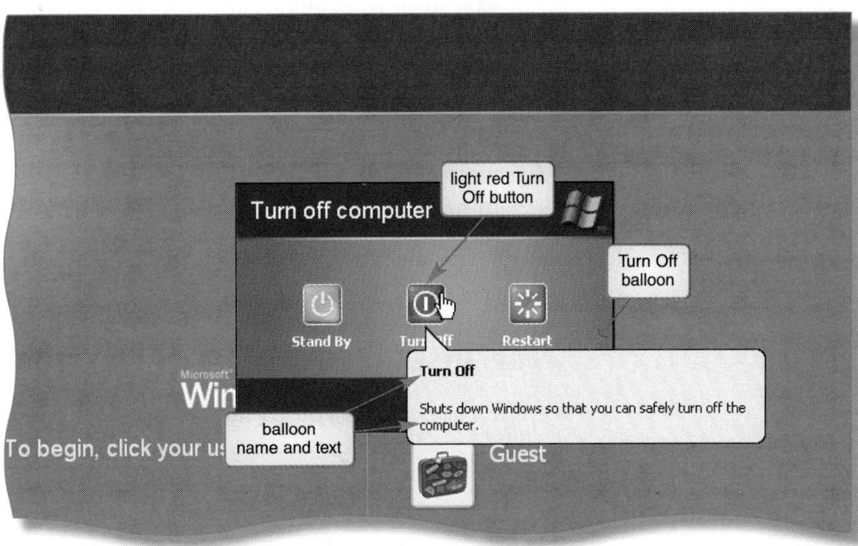

FIGURE 1-106

Other Ways

1. Press CTRL+ESC, press U, use ARROW keys to select Turn Off, press ENTER
2. Press ALT+F4, use ARROW keys to select Turn Off, press ENTER

While Windows XP is shutting down, a blue screen containing the word, Welcome, is displayed on the desktop and the message, Windows is shutting down..., appears momentarily. At this point, you can turn off the computer. When shutting down Windows XP, you should never turn off the computer before these messages appear.

If you accidentally click Turn off computer on the Welcome screen as shown in Figure 1-104 and you do not want to shut down Windows XP, click the Cancel button in the Turn off computer dialog box shown in Figure 1-105 to return to normal Windows XP operation.

What Is Microsoft Office 2003?

Microsoft Office 2003 is a collection of the more popular Microsoft application software products and is available in Standard, Small Business, Professional, Student and Teacher, and Developer editions. The **Microsoft Office Professional Edition 2003** includes the five basic applications, which are Microsoft Office Word 2003, Microsoft Office Excel 2003, Microsoft Office Access 2003, Microsoft Office PowerPoint 2003, and Microsoft Office Outlook 2003. Office allows you to work more efficiently, communicate more effectively, and improve the appearance of each document you create.

Office contains a collection of media files (art, sound, animation, and movies) that you can use to enhance documents. **Microsoft Clip Organizer** allows you to organize the media files on your computer and search for specific files, as well as search for and organize media files located on the Internet. Clip art and media files are accessible from the Microsoft Office Online Web site, which contains thousands of additional media files.

With the **Office Speech Recognition** software installed and a microphone, you can speak the names of toolbar buttons, menus, and menu commands, and list items, screen alerts, and dialog box controls, such as OK and Cancel. You also can dictate text and numbers to insert them as well as delete them. If you have speakers, you can instruct the computer to speak a document or worksheet to you. In addition, you can translate a word, phrase, or an entire document from English into Japanese, Chinese, French, Spanish, or German.

Menus and toolbars adjust to the way in which you work. As Office detects which commands you use more frequently, these commands are displayed at the top of the menu, and the infrequently used commands are placed in reserve. A button at the bottom of the menu allows you to expand the menu in order to view all its commands. More frequently used buttons on a toolbar appear on the toolbar, while less frequently used buttons are not displayed.

In addition, Office integrates its applications with the power of the Internet so you can share information, communicate and collaborate on projects over long distances, and conduct online meetings.

The Internet, World Wide Web, and Intranets

Office allows you to take advantage of the Internet, the World Wide Web, and intranets. The **Internet** is a worldwide network of thousands of computer networks and millions of commercial, educational, government, and personal computers. The **World Wide Web** is an easy-to-use graphical interface for exploring the Internet. The World Wide Web consists of many individual Web sites. A **Web site** consists of a single **Web page** or multiple Web pages linked together. The first Web page in the Web site is called the **home page** and a unique address, called a **Uniform Resource Locator** (**URL**), identifies each Web page. Web sites are located on computers called Web servers.

A software tool, called a **browser**, allows you to locate and view a Web page. One method of viewing a Web page is to use the browser to enter the URL for the Web page. A widely used browser, called **Internet Explorer**, is included with Office. Another method of viewing a Web page is clicking a hyperlink. A **hyperlink** is colored or underlined text or a graphic that, when clicked, connects to another Web page.

An **intranet** is a special type of Web site that is available only to the users of a particular type of computer network, such as a network used within a company or organization for internal communication. Like the Internet, hyperlinks are used within an intranet to access documents, pages, and other destinations on the intranet.

Office and the Internet

Office was designed in response to customer requests to streamline the process of information sharing and collaboration within their organizations. Organizations that, in the past, made important information available only to a select few, now want their information accessible to a wider range of individuals who are using tools such as Office and Internet Explorer. Office allows users to utilize the Internet or an intranet as a central location to view documents, manage files, and work together.

Each of the Office applications makes publishing documents on a Web server as simple as saving a file on a hard disk. Once the file is placed on the Web server, users can view and edit the documents, and conduct Web discussions and live online meetings.

An explanation of each Office application along with how it is used to access an intranet or the Internet is given on the following pages.

Microsoft Office Word 2003

Microsoft Office Word 2003 is a full-featured word processing program that allows you to create many types of personal and business communications, including announcements, letters, resumes, business documents, and academic reports, as well as other forms of written documents. Figure 1-107 illustrates the top portion of the announcement that students create in Project 1 of the Word section of this book. The steps to create the announcement also are shown in Project 1 of the Word section of this book.

FIGURE 1-107

The Word AutoCorrect, Spelling, and Grammar features allow you to proofread documents for errors in spelling and grammar by identifying the errors and offering corrections as you type. As you create a specific document, such as a business letter or resume, Word provides wizards, which ask questions and then use your answers to format the document before you type the text of the document.

Word automates many often-used tasks and provides you with powerful desktop publishing tools to use as you create professional looking brochures, advertisements, and newsletters. The drawing tools allow you to design impressive 3-D effects by including shadows, textures, and curves.

Word makes it easier for you to share documents in order to collaborate on a document. The Send for Review and Markup features allow you to send a document for review and easily track the changes made to the document.

Word and the Internet

Word makes it possible to design and publish Web pages on an intranet or the Internet, insert a hyperlink to a Web page in a word processing document, as well as access other Web pages to search for and retrieve information and pictures from them. Figure 1-108 on the next page illustrates the top portion of a cover letter that contains a hyperlink (e-mail address) that allows you to send an e-mail message to the sender.

Clicking the hyperlink starts the Outlook mail program, through which you can send an e-mail message to the author of the cover letter. In Figure 1-109, the Resume and Cover Letter - Message window that allows you to compose a new e-mail message contains the recipient's e-mail address (okamoto@earth.net), subject of the e-mail message (Resume and Cover Letter), and a brief message.

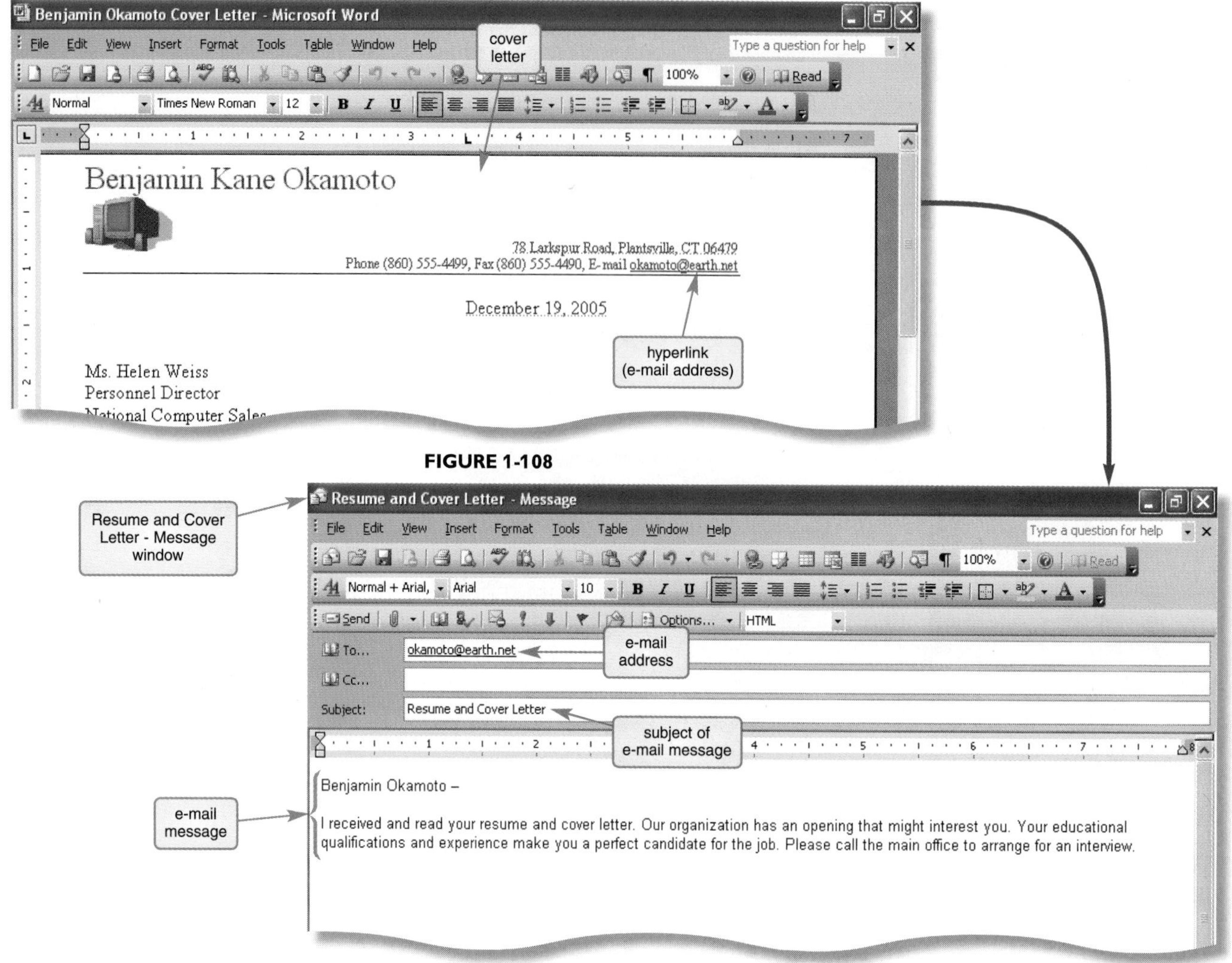

FIGURE 1-108

FIGURE 1-109

Microsoft Office Excel 2003

Microsoft Office Excel 2003 is a spreadsheet program that allows you to organize data, complete calculations, graph data, develop professional looking reports, publish organized data to the Web, access real-time data from Web sites, and make decisions. Figure 1-110 illustrates the Excel window that contains the worksheet and 3-D Column chart created in one of the exercises in Project 1 of the Excel section of this book.

Excel and the Internet

Using Excel, you can create hyperlinks within a worksheet to access other Office documents on the network, an organization's intranet, or the Internet. You also can save worksheets as static or dynamic Web pages that can be viewed using a browser.

Static Web pages cannot be changed by the person viewing them. Dynamic Web pages give the person viewing them in their browser many capabilities to modify them using Excel. In addition, you can create and run queries to retrieve information from a Web page directly into a worksheet.

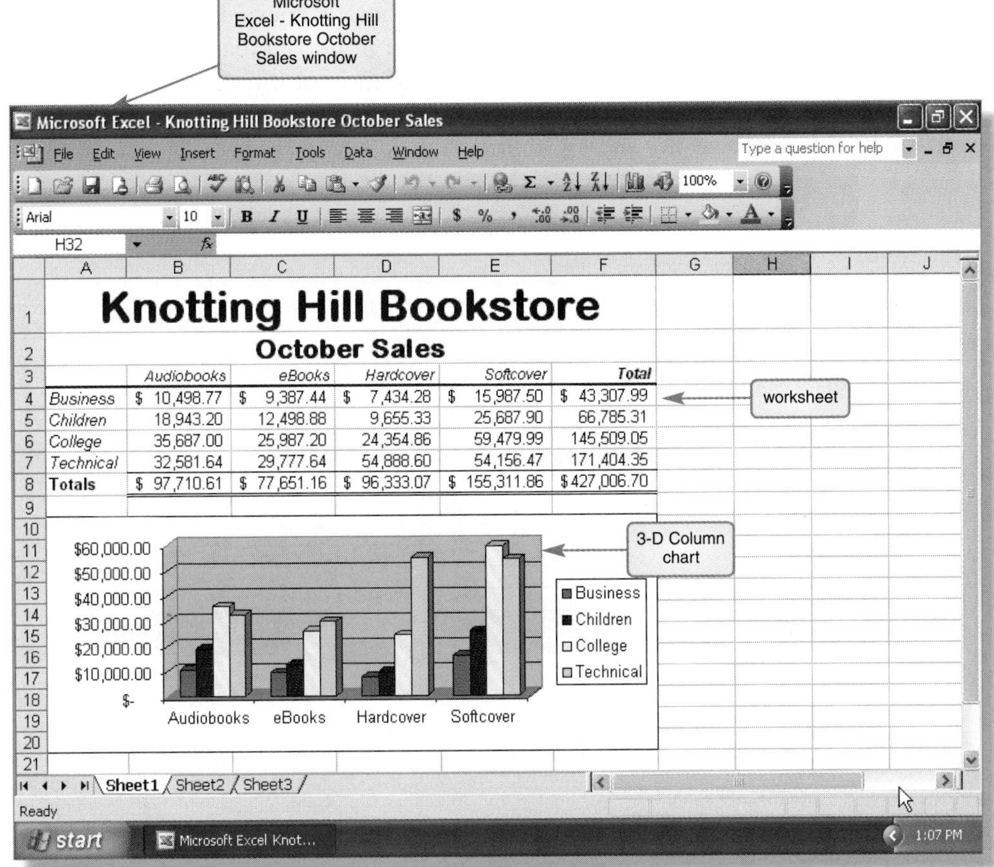

FIGURE 1-110

Figure 1-111 on the next page illustrates a worksheet created by running a Web query to retrieve stock market information for two stocks (XM Satellite Radio Holdings Inc. and Sirius Satellite Radio Inc.). The two hyperlinks were created using the Insert Hyperlink button on the Standard toolbar, and the information in the worksheet was obtained from the MSN Money Web site.

The Refresh All button on the External Data toolbar allows you to update the last price of the stocks (Last). Clicking the Refresh All button locates the MSN Money Web site, retrieves current information for the stocks listed in the worksheet, and displays the updated information in the worksheet (Figure 1-112 on the next page). Notice that the stock prices and information in this worksheet differ from what was displayed in the worksheet shown in Figure 1-111.

Microsoft Office Access 2003

Microsoft Office Access 2003 is a comprehensive database management system (DBMS). A **database** is a collection of data organized in a manner that allows access, retrieval, and use of that data. Access allows you to create a database; add, change, and delete data in the database; sort data in the database; retrieve data from the database; and create forms and reports using the data in the database.

The database created in Project 1 of the Access section of this book is displayed in the Microsoft Access - [Client : Table] window illustrated in Figure 1-113. The steps to create this database are shown in Project 1 of Access.

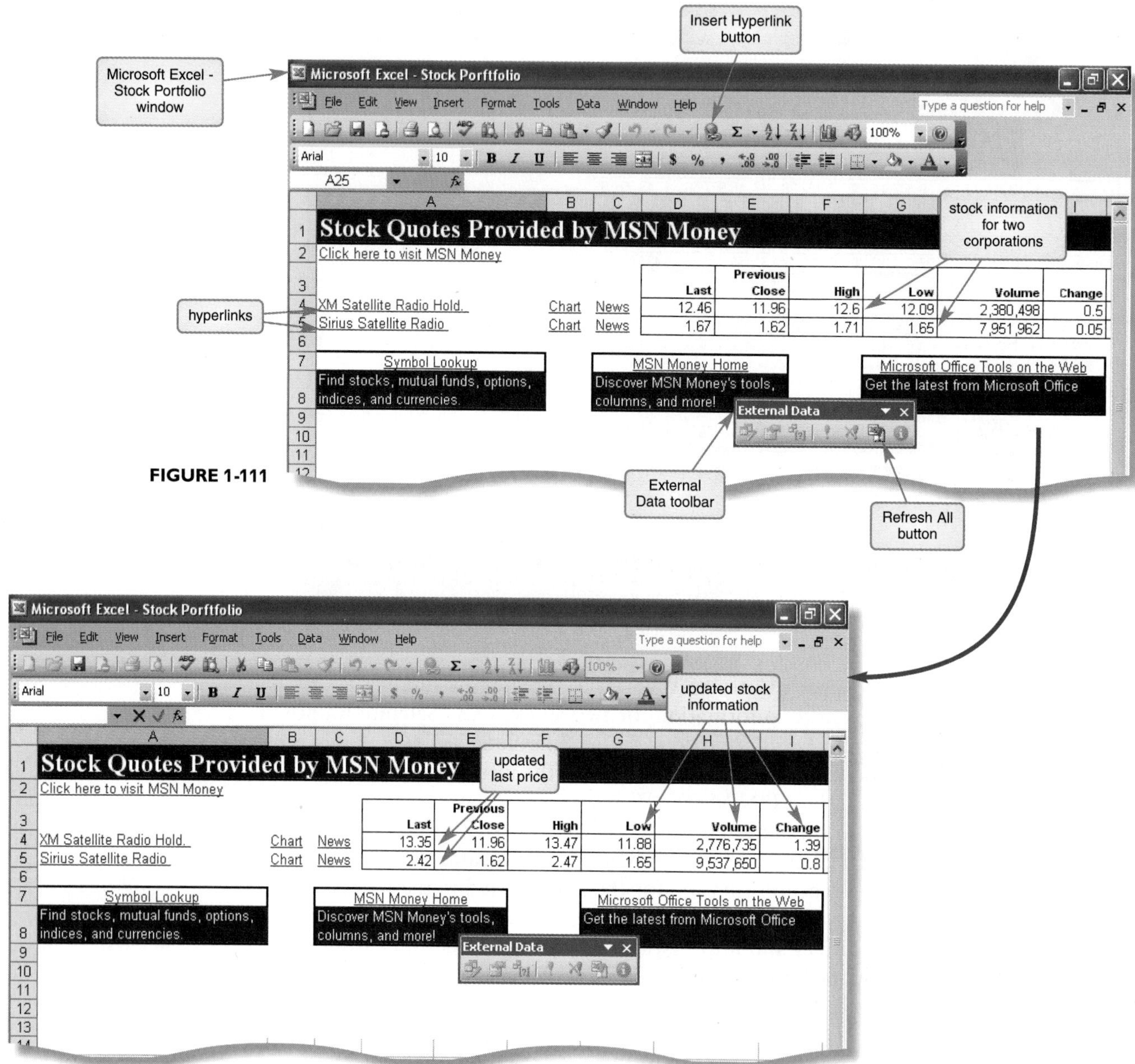

FIGURE 1-111

FIGURE 1-112

Access and the Internet

Databases provide a central location to store related pieces of information. Access simplifies the creation of a database with a wizard that quickly can build one of more than a dozen types of databases. You also can transform lists or worksheets into databases using Access wizards. Data access pages permit you to share a database with other computer users on a network, intranet, or over the Internet, as well as allowing the users to view and edit the database. The database shown in Figure 1-114 contains information (order number, customer number, order date, product number, and quantity) about three orders entered over the Internet using the Internet Explorer browser.

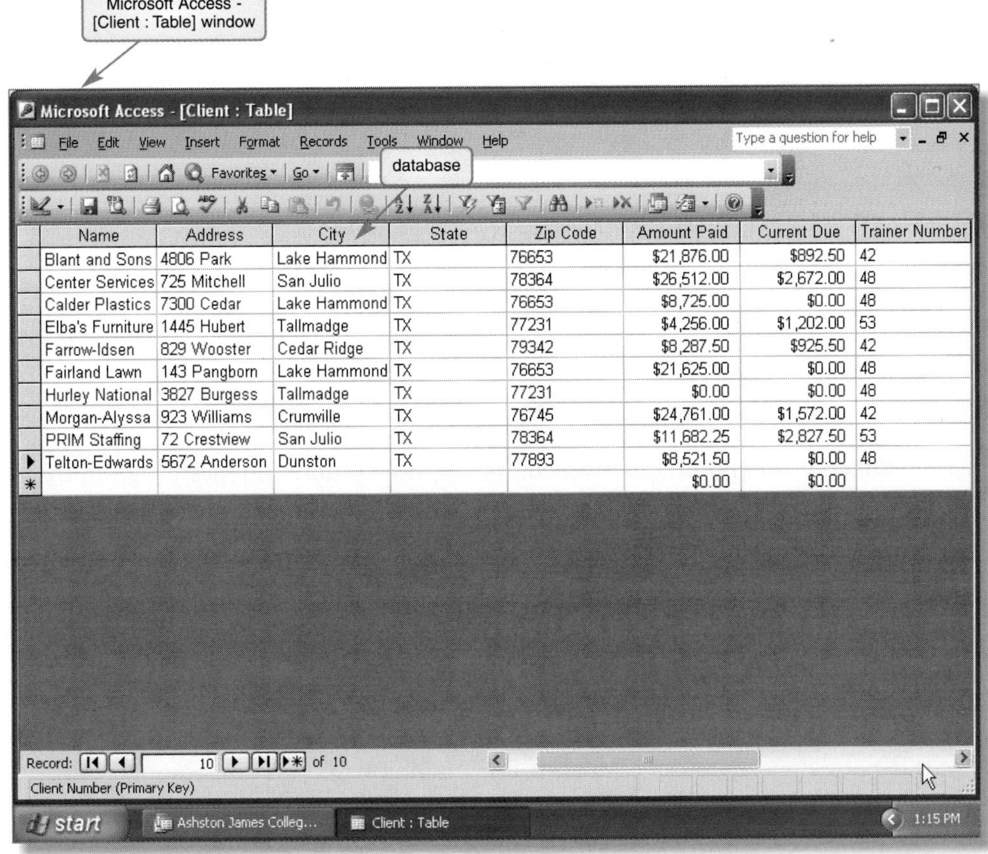

FIGURE 1-113

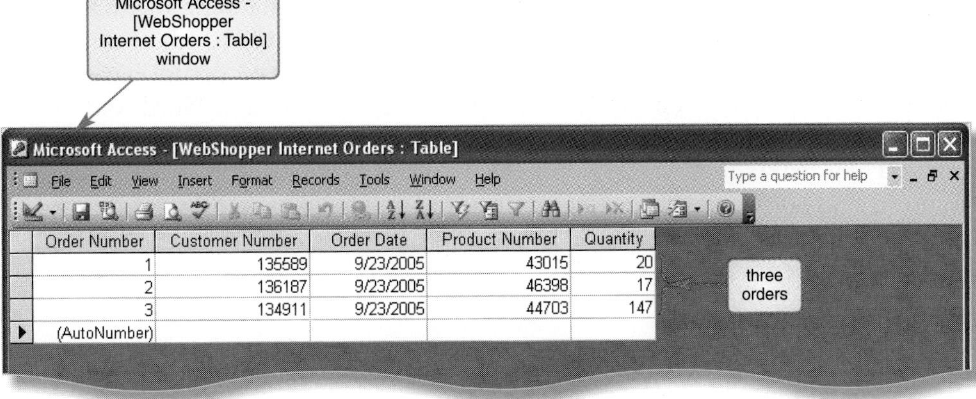

FIGURE 1-114

Figure 1-115 illustrates a simple online order form created to enter order information into the database shown in Figure 1-114 on the previous page. The order form, containing information about order number 4, is displayed in the WebShopper Internet Orders - Microsoft Internet Explorer window.

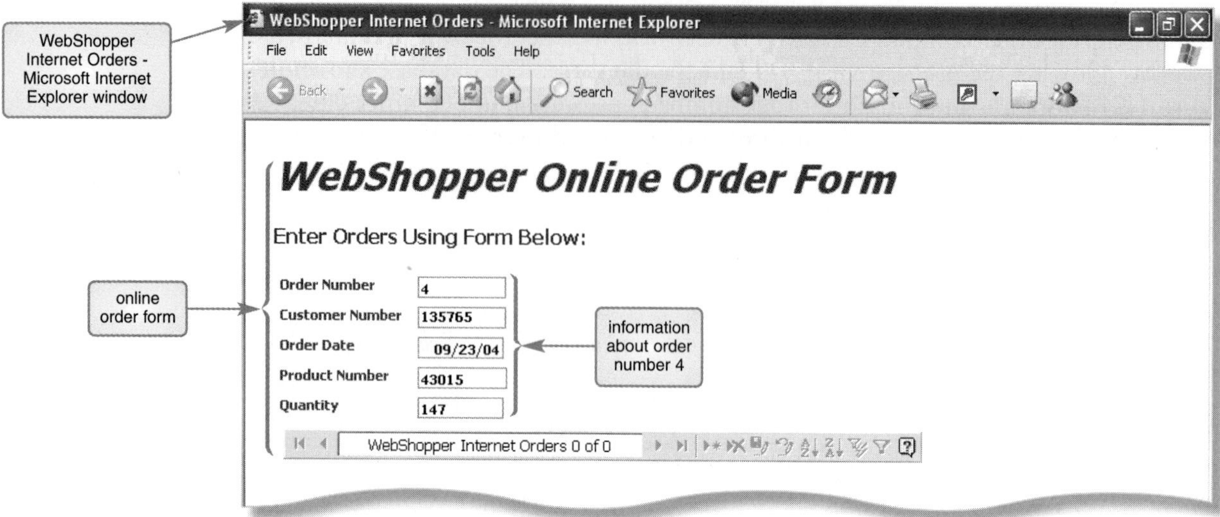

FIGURE 1-115

Microsoft Office PowerPoint 2003

Microsoft Office PowerPoint 2003 is a complete presentation graphics program that allows you to produce professional looking presentations. PowerPoint provides the flexibility that lets you make informal presentations using overhead transparencies, make electronic presentations using a projection device attached to a personal computer, make formal presentations using 35mm slides or a CD, or run virtual presentations on the Internet.

In PowerPoint, you create a presentation in Normal view. **Normal view** allows you to view the tabs pane, slide pane, and notes pane at the same time. The first slide in the presentation created in one of the exercises in Project 1 of the PowerPoint section of this book appears in the Microsoft PowerPoint - [Rivercrest Community Center] window illustrated in Figure 1-116. The full window contains the Outline tab with the presentation outline, the slide pane displaying the first slide in the presentation, and the notes pane showing a note about the presentation.

PowerPoint allows you to create dynamic presentations easily that include multimedia features such as sounds, movies, and pictures. PowerPoint comes with templates that assist you in designing a presentation that you can use to create a slide show. PowerPoint also contains formatting for tables, so that you do not have to create the tables using Excel or Word. The Table Draw tool used in Word to draw tables also is available in PowerPoint.

PowerPoint makes it easier for you to share presentations and collaborate on those presentations. The Send for Review feature and Compare and Merge feature allow you to send a presentation for review and easily merge comments and revisions from multiple reviewers.

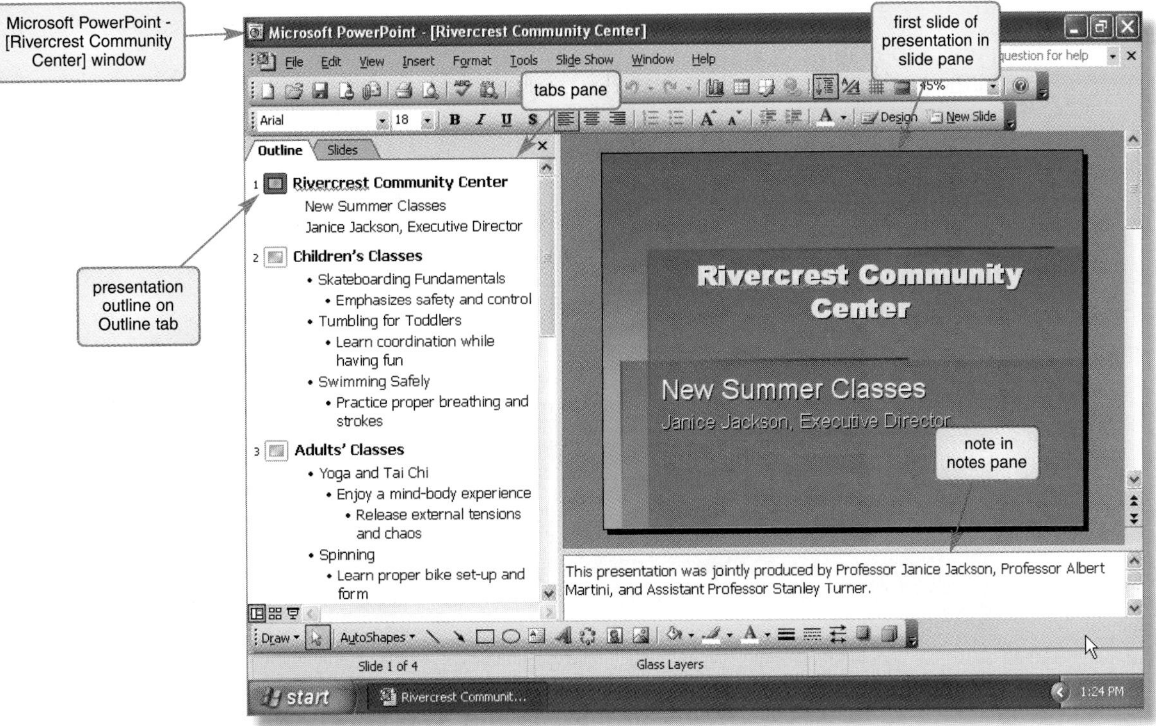

FIGURE 1-116

PowerPoint and the Internet

PowerPoint allows you to publish presentations on the Internet or an intranet. Figure 1-117 illustrates the first slide in a presentation to be published on the Internet. The slide appears in slide view and contains a title (Computers 4 U), a subtitle (Complete Repairs and Service), and a presenter message (Elliott Dane and Lynn Verone). The additional slides in this presentation do not appear in Figure 1-117.

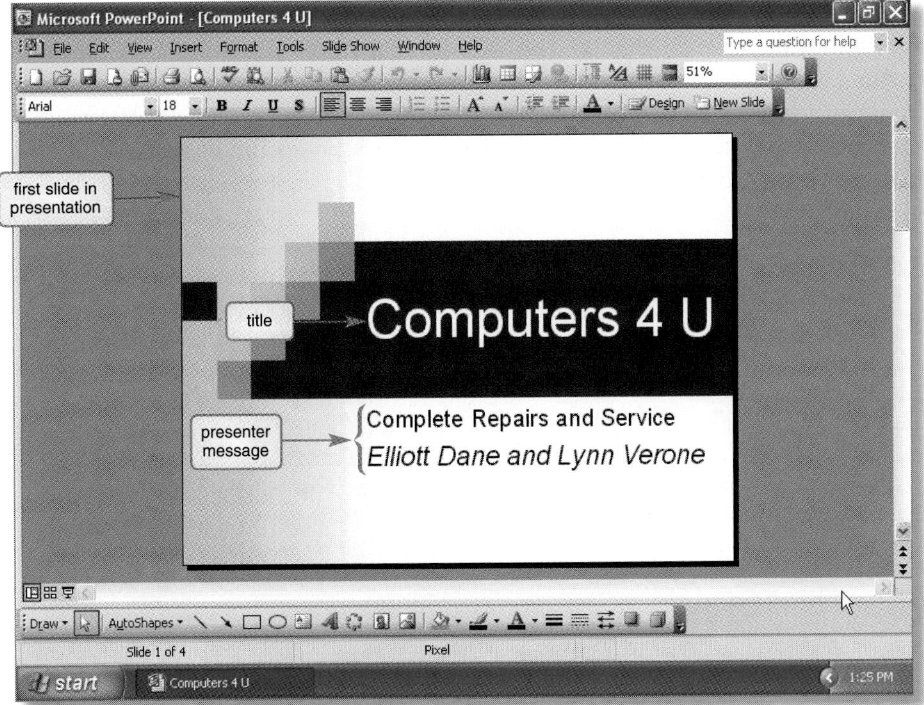

FIGURE 1-117

Figure 1-118 shows the first Web page in a series of Web pages created from the presentation illustrated in Figure 1-117 on the previous page. The Web page appears in the Computers 4 U window in the Internet Explorer browser window. Navigation buttons below the Web page allow you to view additional Web pages in the presentation.

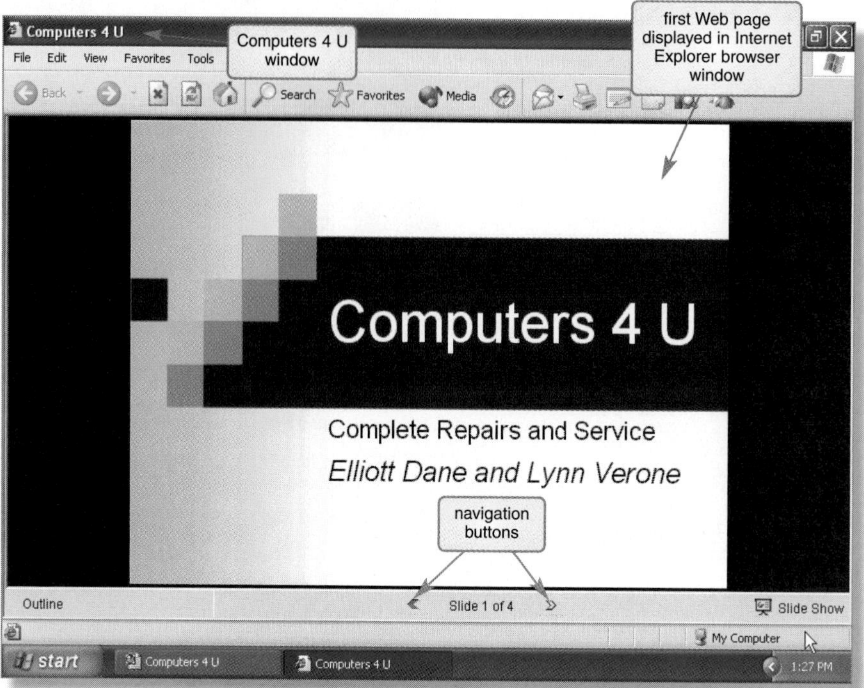

FIGURE 1-118

The Web Toolbar

The easiest method of navigating an intranet or the Internet is to use the Web toolbar. The Web toolbar allows you to search for and open Office documents that you have placed on an intranet or the Internet. The Web toolbar in the Benjamin Okamoto Cover Letter - Microsoft Word window shown in Figure 1-119 is available in all Office applications except FrontPage. Currently, a Word document (cover letter) is displayed in the window, and the path and file name of the document appear in the text box on the Web toolbar.

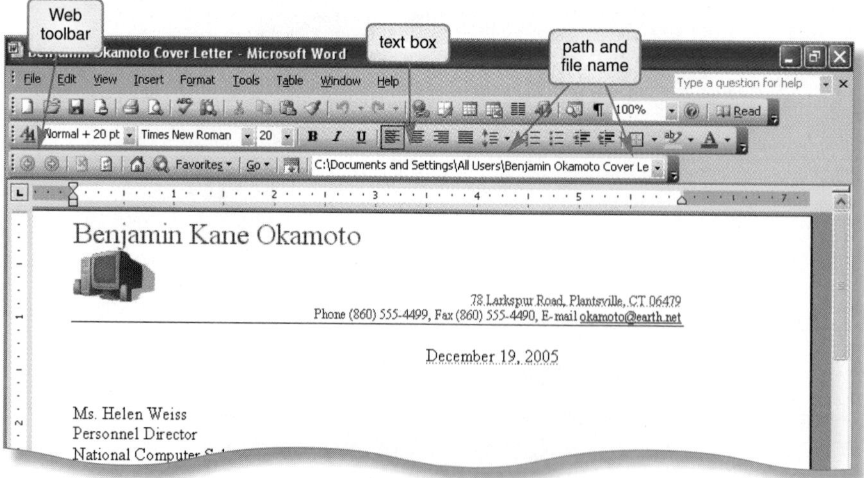

FIGURE 1-119

The buttons and text box on the Web toolbar allow you to jump to Web pages you have viewed previously, cancel a jump to a Web page, update the contents of the current Web page, or replace all other toolbars with the Web toolbar. In addition, you can view the first Web page displayed, search the Web for new Web sites, and add any Web pages you select to the Favorites folder, so you can return to them quickly in the future.

Microsoft Office Publisher 2003

Microsoft Office Publisher 2003 is a desktop publishing program (DTP) that allows you to design and produce professional quality documents (newsletters, flyers, brochures, business cards, Web sites, and so on) that combine text, graphics, and photographs. Desktop publishing software provides a variety of tools, including design templates, graphic manipulation tools, color schemes or libraries, and various page wizards and templates. For large jobs, businesses use desktop publishing software to design publications that are **camera ready**, which means the files are suitable for production by outside commercial printers. Publisher also allows you to locate commercial printers, service bureaus, and copy shops willing to accept customer files created in Publisher.

Publisher allows you to design a unique image, or logo, using one of more than 45 master design sets. This, in turn, permits you to use the same design for all your printed documents (letters, business cards, brochures, and advertisements) and Web pages. Publisher includes 60 coordinated color schemes, more than 10,000 high-quality clip art images, 1,500 photographs, 1,000 Web-art graphics, 175 fonts, 340 animated graphics, and hundreds of unique Design Gallery elements (quotations, sidebars, and so on). If you wish, you also can download additional images from the Microsoft Office Online Web page on the Microsoft Web site.

In the Business Card - Hank Landers - Microsoft Publisher window illustrated in Figure 1-120, a business card that was created using the Business Card wizard and the Arcs design set is displayed.

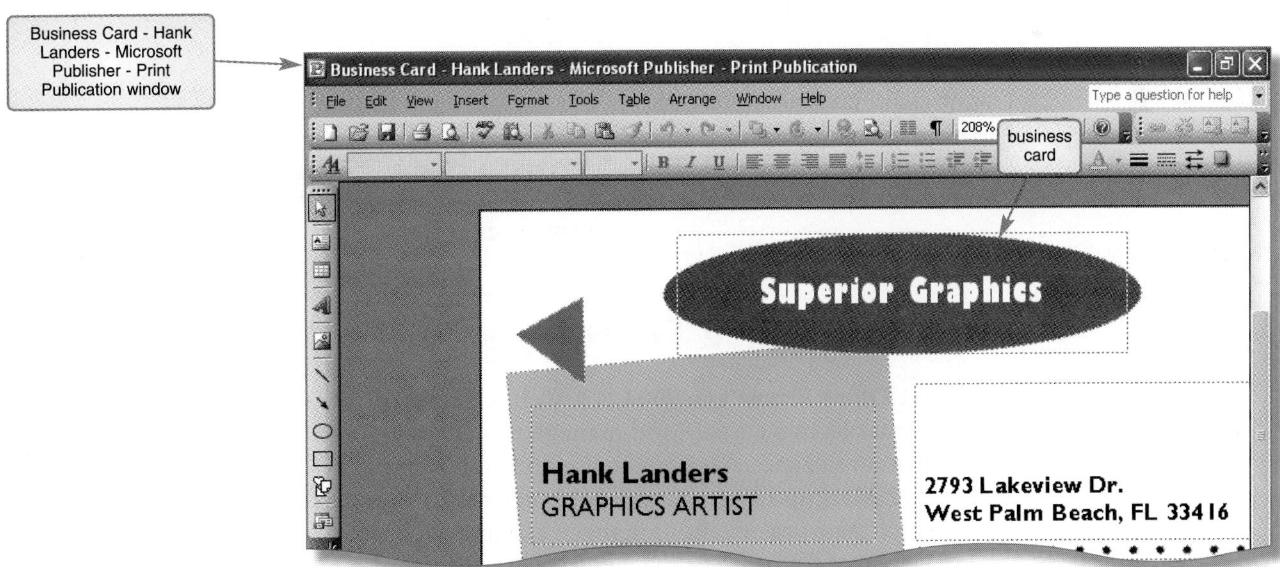

FIGURE 1-120

Publisher and the Internet

Publisher allows you easily to create a multipage Web site with custom color schemes, photo images, animated images, and sounds. Figure 1-121 illustrates the Superior Graphics - Microsoft Internet Explorer window displaying the top portion of the home page in a Web site created using the Web page wizard and Arcs design set.

The home page in the Superior Graphics Web site contains text, graphic images, animated graphic images, and displays using the same design set (Arcs) as the business card illustrated in Figure 1-120 on the previous page.

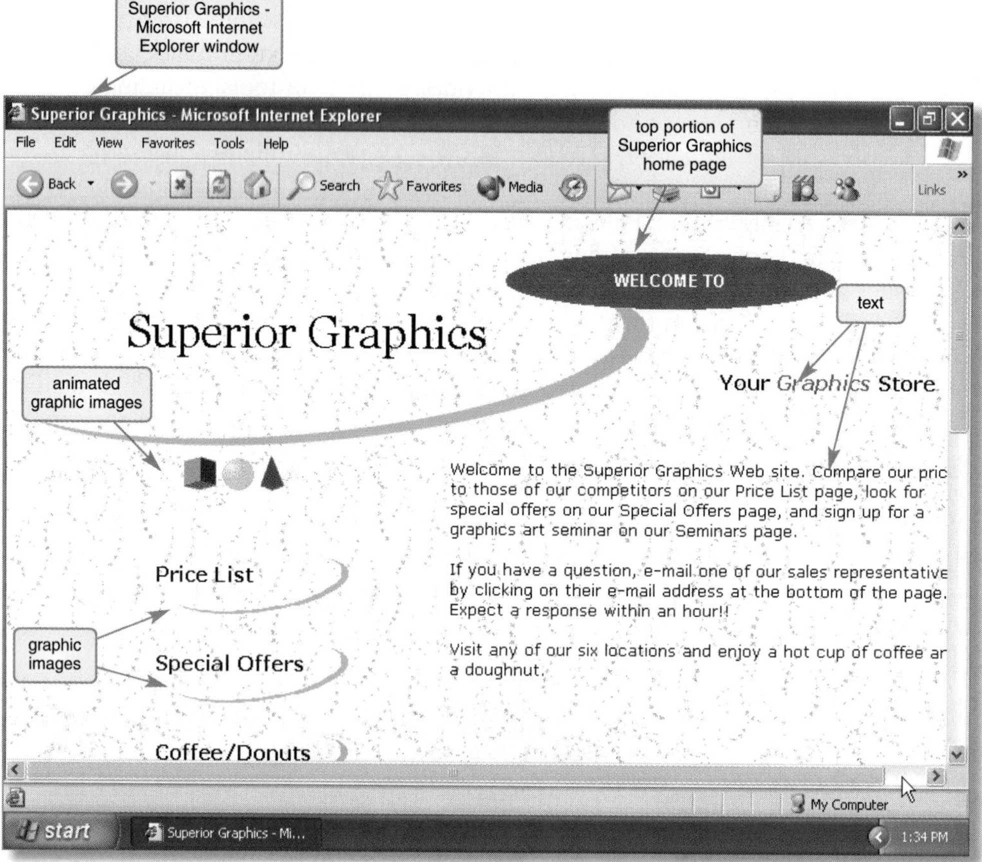

FIGURE 1-121

Microsoft Office FrontPage 2003

Microsoft Office FrontPage 2003 is a Web page authoring and site management program that lets you create and manage professional looking Web sites on the Internet or an intranet. You can create and edit Web pages without knowing HyperText Markup Language (HTML), view the pages and files in the Web site and control their organization, manage existing Web sites, import and export files, and diagnose and correct problems. A variety of templates, including the Workgroup Web template that allows you to set up and maintain the basic structure of a workgroup Web, are available to facilitate managing the Web site.

Figure 1-122 illustrates the top portion of a Web page created using FrontPage that contains information about the Shelly Cashman Series developed by Course Technology. It appears in the SCSITE.COM Shelly Cashman Series Student Resources - Microsoft Internet Explorer window.

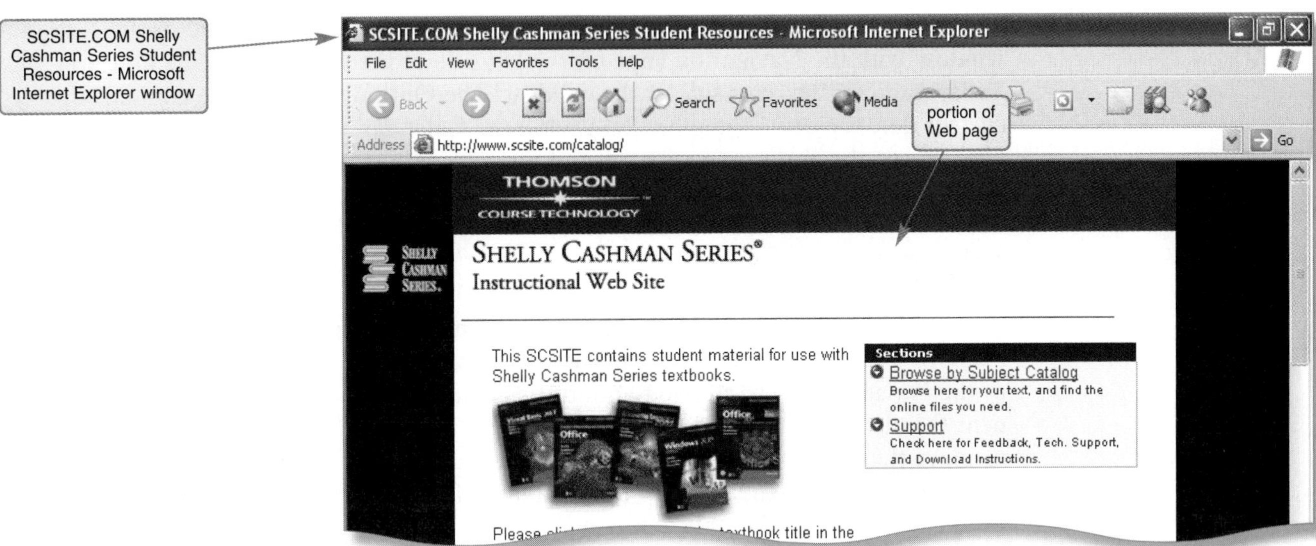

FIGURE 1-122

Microsoft Office Outlook 2003

Microsoft Office Outlook 2003 is a powerful communications and scheduling program that helps you communicate with others, keep track of your contacts, and organize your busy schedule. Outlook allows you to send and receive electronic mail and permits you to engage in real-time messaging with family, friends, or coworkers using instant messaging. Outlook also provides you with the means to organize your contacts. Users easily can track e-mail messages, meetings, and notes with a particular contact. Outlook's Calendar, Contacts, Tasks, and Notes components aid in this organization. Contact information readily is available from the Outlook Calendar, Mail, Contacts, and Task components by accessing the Find a Contact feature. **Personal information management** (**PIM**) programs such as Outlook provide a way for individuals and workgroups to organize, find, view, and share information easily.

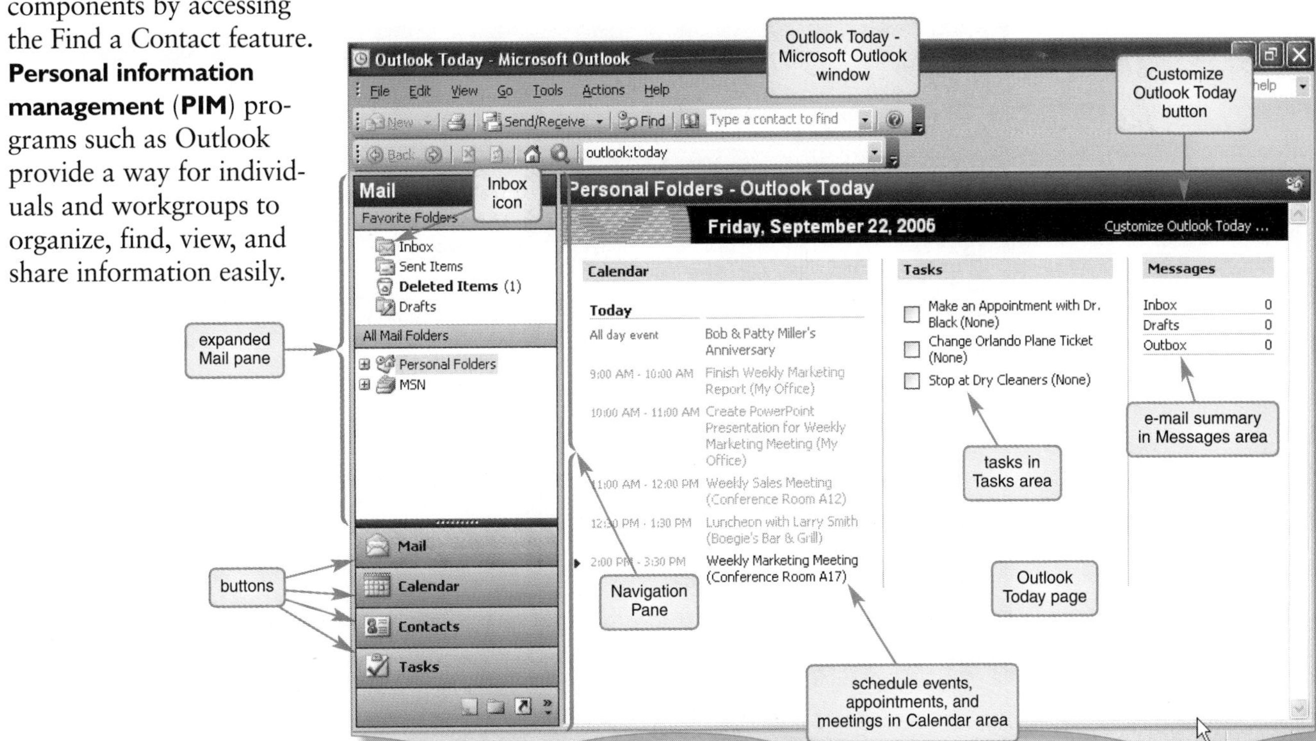

FIGURE 1-123

Figure 1-123 on the previous page shows the Outlook Today - Microsoft Outlook window with the Navigation Pane on the left side of the window and the **Outlook Today page** on the right side of the window. The Outlook Today page contains the current date (Friday, September 22, 2006); the Calendar area with the currently scheduled events; the Tasks area with a list of tasks to perform; and the Messages area that summarizes the users e-mail messages by folder. You can customize this page by clicking the Customize Outlook Today button in the upper-right corner of the Outlook Today page.

The **Navigation Pane** is a new feature in Outlook. It is set up to help you navigate Outlook while using any of the components. It comprises one or more panes and two sets of buttons. Although the two sets of buttons remain constant, the area of the Navigation Pane above the buttons changes depending on the active component (Mail, Calendar, Contacts, or Tasks). In Figure 1-123, the expanded Mail pane displays the Favorite Folders pane and the All Mail Folders pane. Clicking a button in the Navigation Pane displays the contents of the component's folder with its associated panes in the Outlook window.

Outlook allows you to click the Mail button in the Navigation Pane to view e-mail messages, click the Calendar button to schedule activities (events, appointments, and meetings), click the Contacts button to maintain a list of contacts and e-mail addresses, and click the Tasks button to view a detailed list of tasks.

When you click the Inbox icon in the Mail pane, the Inbox - Microsoft Outlook window is displayed and the contents of the Inbox folder (your e-mail messages) and the Reading Pane are displayed in the window (Figure 1-124).

The Inbox message pane contains two e-mail messages. The second e-mail message is highlighted. The contents of the highlighted e-mail message are displayed in the Reading Pane.

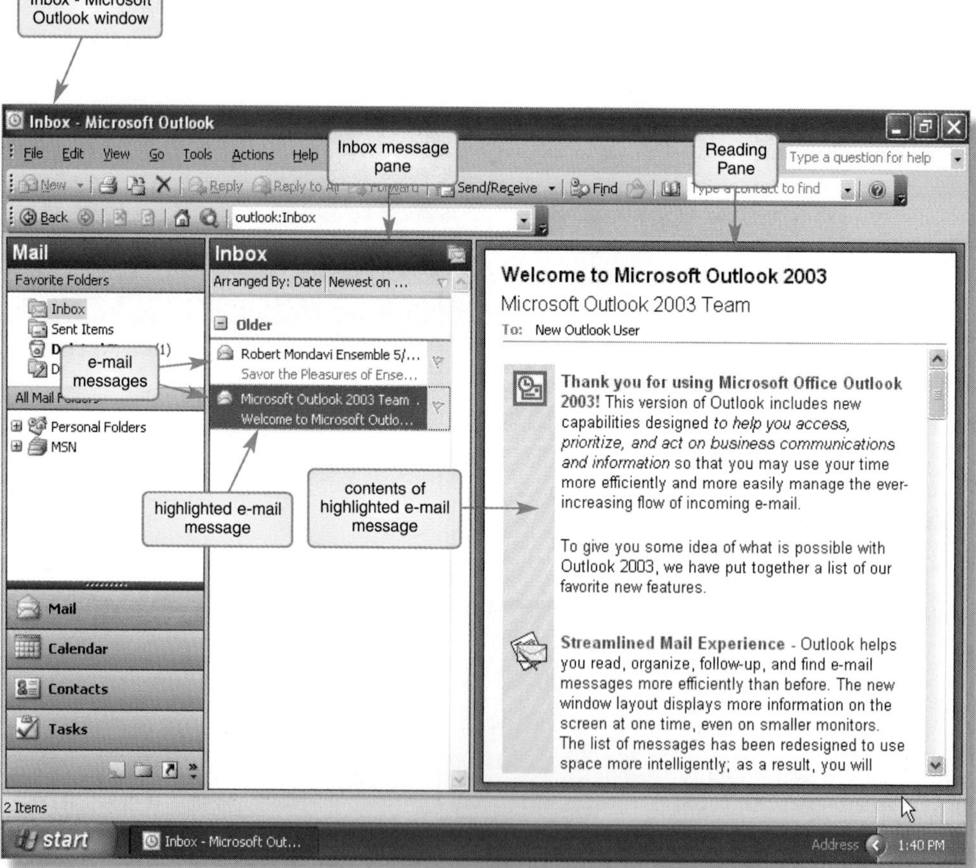

FIGURE 1-124

The Microsoft Office 2003 Help System

At any time while you are using one of the Office applications, you can interact with the **Microsoft Office 2003 Help system** for that application and display information on any topic associated with the application. Several categories of help are available to you. One of the easiest methods to obtain help is to use the Type a question for help box. The **Type a question for help box** on the right side of the menu bar lets you type free-form questions, such as how do I save or how do I create a Web page, or you can type terms, such as template, smart tags, or speech. The Help system responds by displaying a list of topics relating to the question or term in the Search Results task pane. The Type a question for help box that appears in the Grand Prix Announcement – Microsoft Word window is illustrated in Figure 1-125.

When you type the question, How do I check Spelling, in the Type a question for help box shown in Figure 1-125, the Help system displays a list of topics relating to the question. Clicking a topic in the list opens a Help window that provides Help information about spell checking. Detailed instructions for using the Type a question for help box and the other categories of Help are explained in Appendix A of this book.

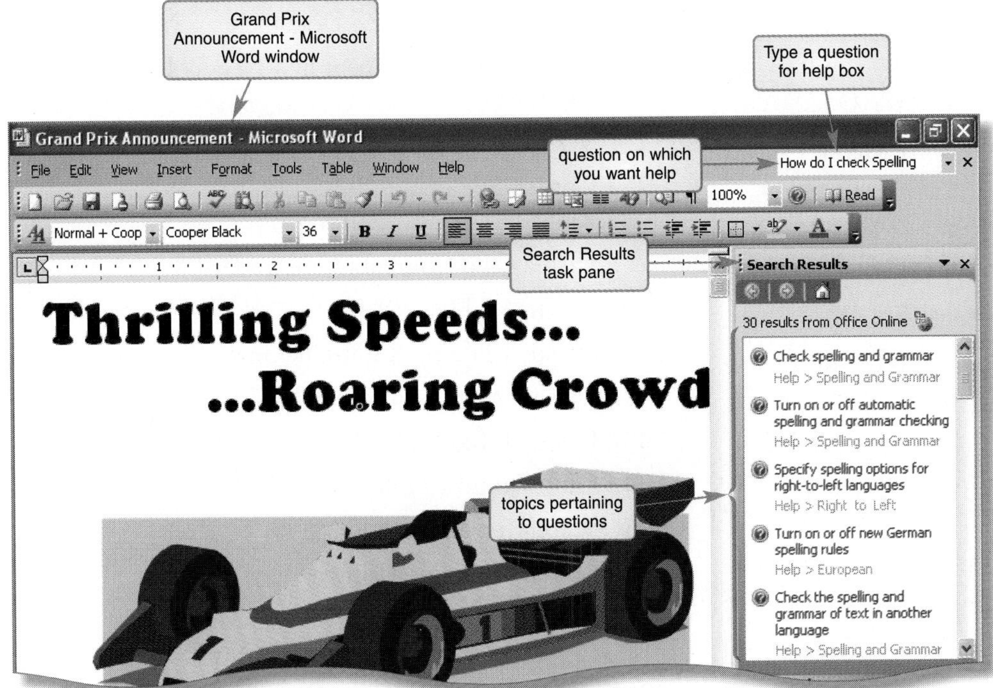

FIGURE 1-125

Project Summary

Project 1 illustrated the Microsoft Windows XP graphical user interface and the Microsoft Office 2003 applications. You launched Windows XP, learned the components of the desktop and the six mouse operations. You opened, closed, moved, resized, minimized, maximized, and scrolled a window. You used Windows Explorer to expand and collapse drives and folders, display drive and folder contents, create a folder, copy a file between folders, and rename and then delete a file. You learned about hierarchical format, removable media, flash drives, and used Microsoft Word to type and save a document in a newly created folder. You searched for files using a word or phrase in the file or by name, you obtained help about using Microsoft Windows XP, and shut down Windows XP.

Brief explanations of the Word, Excel, Access, PowerPoint, Publisher, FrontPage, and Outlook applications and examples of how these applications interact with the Internet were given. With this introduction, you now are ready to begin a more in-depth study of each Office application explained in this book.

If you have a SAM user profile, you may have access to hands-on instruction, practice, and assessment of the skills covered in this project. Log in to your SAM account and go to your assignments page to see what your instructor has assigned.

What You Should Know

Having completed this project, you should be able to perform the tasks below. The tasks are listed in the same order they were presented in this project. For a list of the buttons, menus, toolbars, and commands introduced in this project, see the Quick Reference Summary at the back of this book and refer to the Page Number column.

1. Log On to the Computer (WIN 9)
2. Display the Start Menu (WIN 12)
3. Add an Icon to the Desktop (WIN 15)
4. Open a Window Using a Desktop Icon (WIN 17)
5. Minimize and Redisplay a Window (WIN 20)
6. Maximize and Restore a Window (WIN 22)
7. Close a Window (WIN 23, WIN 32)
8. Open a Window Using the Start Menu (WIN 24)
9. Move a Window by Dragging (WIN 26)
10. Expand an Area (WIN 27)
11. Scroll Using Scroll Arrows (WIN 28)
12. Size a Window by Dragging (WIN 30)
13. Collapse an Area (WIN 30)
14. Resize a Window (WIN 31)
15. Delete a Desktop Icon by Right-Dragging (WIN 32)
16. Start an Application Using the Start Menu (WIN 35)
17. Start Windows Explorer and Maximize Its Window (WIN 37)
18. Plug a USB Flash Drive into a USB Port (WIN 41)
19. Create a Folder on a Removable Drive (WIN 43)
20. Download a Hierarchy of Folders into the Freshman folder (WIN 44)
21. Expand a Drive (WIN 46)
22. Expand a Folder (WIN 47)
23. Display the Contents of a Folder (WIN 48, WIN 57)
24. Start Word (WIN 49)
25. Type Text in a Word Document (WIN 50)
26. Save a Word Document in a New Folder (WIN 51)
27. Verify the Contents of a Folder (WIN 54)
28. Copy a File in Windows Explorer by Right-Dragging (WIN 55)
29. Display the Contents of a Folder (WIN 57)
30. Rename a File (WIN 58)
31. Delete a File by Right-Clicking (WIN 59)
32. Close Expanded Folders (WIN 60)
33. Close all Expanded Folders (WIN 61)
34. Quit Windows Explorer (WIN 61)
35. Search for a File by Name (WIN 62)
36. Search for a File Using a Word or Phrase in the File (WIN 65)
37. Start Help and Support (WIN 67)
38. Browse for Help Topics in the Table of Contents (WIN 68)
39. Search for Help Topics Using the Index (WIN 71)
40. Close the Help and Support Center (WIN 72)
41. Log Off from the Computer (WIN 73)
42. Turn Off the Computer (WIN 74)

Learn It Online

Instructions: To complete the Learn It Online exercises, start your browser, click the Address bar, and then enter the Web address scsite.com/winoff20032e/learn. When the Windows/Office Learn It Online page is displayed, follow the instructions in the exercises below. Each exercise has instructions for printing your results, either for your own records or for submission to your instructor.

1 Project Reinforcement TF, MC, and SA

Below Project 1, click the Project Reinforcement link. Print the quiz by clicking Print on the File menu for each page. Answer each question.

2 Flash Cards

Below Project 1, click the Flash Cards link and read the instructions. Type 20 (or a number specified by your instructor) in the Number of playing cards text box, type your name in the Enter your Name text box, and then click the Flip Card button. When the flash card is displayed, read the question and then click the ANSWER box arrow to select an answer. Flip through Flash Cards. If your score is 15 (75%) correct or greater, click Print on the File menu to print your results. If your score is less than 15 (75%) correct, then redo this exercise by clicking the Replay button.

3 Practice Test

Below Project 1, click the Practice Test link. Answer each question, enter your first and last name at the bottom of the page, and then click the Grade Test button. When the graded practice test is displayed on your screen, click Print on the File menu to print a hard copy. Continue to take practice tests until you score 80% or better.

4 Who Wants To Be a Computer Genius?

Below Project 1, click the Computer Genius link. Read the instructions, enter your first and last name at the bottom of the page, and then click the PLAY button. When your score is displayed, click the PRINT RESULTS link to print a hard copy.

5 Wheel of Terms

Below Project 1, click the Wheel of Terms link. Read the instructions, and then enter your first and last name and your school name. Click the PLAY button. When your score is displayed, right-click the score and then click Print on the shortcut menu to print a hard copy.

6 Crossword Puzzle Challenge

Below Project 1, click the Crossword Puzzle Challenge link. Read the instructions, and then enter your first and last name. Click the SUBMIT button. Work the crossword puzzle. When you are finished, click the Submit button. When the crossword puzzle is redisplayed, click the Print Puzzle button to print a hard copy.

7 Tips and Tricks

Below Project 1, click the Tips and Tricks link. Click a topic that pertains to Project 1. Right-click the information and then click Print on the shortcut menu. Construct a brief example of what the information relates to in Windows XP to confirm you understand how to use the tip or trick.

8 Newsgroups

Below Project 1, click the Newsgroups link. Click a topic that pertains to Project 1. Print three comments.

9 Expanding Your Horizons

Below Project 1, click the Expanding Your Horizons link. Click a topic that pertains to Project 1. Print the information. Construct a brief example of what the information relates to in Windows XP to confirm you understand the contents of the article.

10 Search Sleuth

Below Project 1, click the Search Sleuth link. To search for a term that pertains to this project, select a term below the Project 1 title and then use the Google search engine at google.com (or any major search engine) to display and print two Web pages that present information on the term.

11 Windows XP Online Training

Below Project 1, click the Windows/Office Online Training link. When your browser displays the Microsoft Office Online Web page, click the Windows XP link. Click one of the Windows XP courses that covers one or more of the objectives listed at the beginning of the project on page WIN 4. Print the first page of the course before stepping through it.

12 Office Marketplace

Below Project 1, click the Office Marketplace link. When your browser displays the Microsoft Office Online Web page, click the Office Marketplace link. Click a topic that relates to one of the Office 2003 applications. Print the first page.

1 Taking the Windows XP Tour

Instructions: Use a computer to perform the following tasks.

Part 1: ***Starting the Windows XP Tour***

1. If necessary, launch Microsoft Windows XP and log on to the computer.
2. Click the Start button and then click Help and Support on the Start menu.
3. Click the Maximize button on the Help and Support Center title bar.
4. Click What's new in Windows XP in the navigation pane.
5. Click Taking a tour or tutorial in the navigation pane. The Taking a tour or tutorial page appears in the topic pane.
6. Click Take the Windows XP tour in the topic pane. The Windows XP Tour dialog box appears.
7. If your computer does not have speakers or earphones, proceed to step 8 below. If your computer has speakers or earphones, follow the steps in Part 2.
8. If your computer does not have speakers or earphones, follow the steps in Part 3.

Part 2: ***Taking the Windows XP Tour with Sound and Animation***

1. Verify the Play the animated tour that features text, animation, music, and voice narration button is selected in the Windows XP Tour dialog box and then click the Next button.
2. Listen to the voice narration of the introduction to the Windows XP tour.
3. Click the gray Windows XP Basics button and answer the following questions.
   a. What is the narrow band at the bottom of the desktop called? ____________________
   b. What identifies a shortcut icon? ____________________
   c. What icons appear on the desktop the first time you launch Windows? ____________________
   d. What is contained in the notification area? ____________________
   e. How does Windows keep the taskbar tidy? ____________________
   f. What does a right-facing arrow on a Start menu command signify? ____________________
   ____
   g. In which folders are text, image, and music files placed? ____________________
   ____
   h. What does the Restore Down button do? ____________________
   i. What appears when a program needs some information from you before it can complete a command?
   ____
   j. What do you use to set up user accounts? ____________________
   k. Where do you go when you want to interrupt your Windows session and let someone else use the computer? ____________________
4. Click the Skip Intro button in the lower corner of the desktop to skip the introduction to the Windows XP tour.
5. Click the yellow Best for Business button and listen to the narration.
6. Click the red Safe and Easy Personal Computing button and listen to the narration.
7. Click the green Unlock the World of Digital Media button and listen to the narration.
8. Click the blue The Connected Home and Office button and listen to the narration.
9. Click the red Exit Tour button on the desktop to exit the Windows XP tour.
10. Click the Close button in the Help and Support center window.
11. You have completed this lab assignment.

Part 3: ***Taking the Windows XP Tour without Sound or Animation***

1. Click the Play the non-animated tour that features text and images only button in the Windows XP Tour dialog box and then click the Next button.

2. Click the Start Here button to read about the basics of the Windows XP operating system.
3. Scroll the Windows XP Basics window and read the paragraph below the Windows Desktop heading. Click the Next button to display the next topic.
4. Scroll the Windows XP Basics window and read the paragraph below the Icons heading. Answer the following questions.
   a. What icon displays on the desktop the first time you launch Windows? ____________
   b. Does deleting a shortcut icon affect the actual program or file? ____________
5. Click the Next button to display the next topic. Scroll the Windows XP Basics window and read the paragraphs below the Taskbar heading. Answer the following question.
   a. Where is the notification area located? ____________
6. Click the Next button to display the next topic. Scroll the Windows XP Basics window and read the paragraph below the Start Menu heading. Answer the following question.
   a. What does a right-facing arrow mean? ____________
7. Click the Next button to display the next topic. Scroll the Windows XP Basics window and read the paragraph below the Files and Folder heading. Answer the following question.
   a. In which folders are text, image, and music files placed?

   ____
8. Click the Next button to display the next topic. Scroll the Windows XP Basics window and read the paragraphs below the Windows heading. Answer the following question.
   a. What appears if a program needs some information from you before it can complete a command?

   ____
9. Click the Next button to display the next topic. Scroll the Windows XP Basics window and read the paragraphs below the Control Panel heading. Answer the following questions.
   a. What Windows feature do you use to customize computer settings? ____________
   b. Where is this feature located? ____________
10. Click the Next button to display the next topic. Scroll the Windows XP Basics window and read the paragraphs below the Ending Your Session heading. Answer the following question.
    a. What do you do when you want to interrupt your Windows session and let someone else use the computer? ____________
11. Click the Next button repeatedly to display the topics in the remaining four sections of the Windows XP tour.
12. Click the Close button in the window to end the tour.
13. Click the Close button in the Help and Support Center window.
14. You have completed this lab assignment.

2 Windows Explorer

Instructions: Use a computer to perform the following tasks.

1. Launch Microsoft Windows XP and connect to the Internet.
2. Right-click the Start button on the Windows taskbar, click Explore on the shortcut menu, and then maximize the Start Menu window.
3. If necessary, scroll to the left in the Folders pane so the Start Menu and Programs icons are visible.
4. Click the Programs icon in the Start Menu folder.
5. Double-click the Internet Explorer Shortcut icon in the Contents pane to start the Internet Explorer application. What is the URL of the Web page that appears in the Address bar in the Microsoft Internet Explorer window? ____________

(continued)

Windows Explorer *(continued)*

6. Click the URL in the Address bar in the Internet Explorer window to select it. Type `scsite.com` and then press the ENTER key.
7. Scroll the Web page to display the Browse by Subject area containing the subject categories. Clicking a subject category displays the book titles in that category.
8. Click Operating Systems in the Browse by Subject area.
9. Click the Microsoft Windows XP Comprehensive Concepts and Techniques link.
10. Right-click the Microsoft Windows XP textbook cover image on the Web page, click Save Picture As on the shortcut menu, type `Windows XP Cover` in the File name box, and then click the Save button in the Save Picture dialog box to save the image in the My Pictures folder.
11. Click the Close button in the Microsoft Internet Explorer window.
12. If necessary, scroll to the top of the Folders pane to make the drive C icon visible.
13. Click the minus sign in the box to the left of the drive C icon. The 3½ Floppy (A:) and My Documents icons should be visible in the Folders pane.
14. Click the plus sign in the box to the left of the My Documents icon.
15. Click the My Pictures folder name in the Folders pane.
16. Right-click the Windows XP Cover icon and then click Properties on the shortcut menu.
    a. What type of file is the Windows XP Cover file? ____________________
    b. When was the file last modified? ____________________
    c. With what application does this file open? ____________________
17. Click the Cancel button in the Windows XP Cover Properties dialog box.
18. Insert a formatted floppy disk in drive A of your computer.
19. Right-drag the Windows XP Cover icon to the 3½ Floppy (A:) icon in the Folders pane. Click Move Here on the shortcut menu. Click the 3½ Floppy (A:) icon in the Folders pane.
    a. Is the Windows XP Cover file stored on drive A? ____________________
20. Click the Close button in the 3½ Floppy (A:) window.

3 Using the Help and Support Center

Instructions: Use Windows Help and Support to perform the following tasks.

Part 1: Using the Question Mark Button

1. If necessary, launch Microsoft Windows XP and then log on to the computer.
2. Right-click an open area of the desktop to display a shortcut menu.
3. Click Properties on the shortcut menu to display the Display Properties dialog box.
4. Click the Desktop tab in the Display Properties dialog box.
5. Click the Help button on the title bar. The mouse pointer changes to a block arrow with a question mark.
6. Click the list box in the Desktop sheet. A pop-up window appears explaining the list box. Read the information in the pop-up window and then summarize the function of the list box.

    ____

7. Click an open area of the Desktop sheet to remove the pop-up window.
8. Click the Help button on the title bar and then click the Customize Desktop button. A pop-up window appears explaining what happens when you click this button. Read the information in the pop-up window and then summarize the function of the button.

    ____

9. Click an open area in the Desktop sheet to remove the pop-up window.

10. Click the Help button on the title bar and then click the monitor icon in the Desktop sheet. A pop-up window appears explaining the function of the monitor. Read the information in the pop-up window and then summarize the function of the monitor.

    ____

11. Click an open area in the Desktop sheet to remove the pop-up window.
12. Click the Help button on the title bar and then click the Cancel button. A pop-up window appears explaining what happens when you click the button. Read the information in the pop-up window and then summarize the function of the Cancel button.

    ____

13. Click an open area in the Desktop sheet to remove the pop-up window.
14. Click the Cancel button in the Display Properties dialog box.

Part 2: ***Finding What's New in Windows XP***

1. Click the Start button and then click Help and Support on the Start menu.
2. If necessary, click the Maximize button on the Help and Support Center title bar.
3. Click What's new in Windows XP in the navigation pane.
4. Click What's new topics in the navigation pane. Ten topics appear in the topic pane.
5. Click What's new on your desktop in the topic pane.
6. Click Start menu (or the plus sign in the small box preceding Start menu) to expand the entry. Read the information about the Start menu.
7. Click the Using the Start menu link.
8. Click the Print button on the Help and Support toolbar to print the topic. Click the Print button in the Print dialog box.
9. If necessary, scroll the topic pane to display the Related Topics link. Click the Related Topics link to display a pop-up window containing three related topics. List the three topics.

    ____

    ____

10. Click Display a program at the top of the Start menu in the pop-up window.
11. Click the Print button on the Help and Support toolbar to print the topic. Click the Print button in the Print dialog box.

Part 3: ***Viewing Windows XP Articles***

1. Click Windows XP articles: Walk through ways to use your PC in the What's new in Windows XP area in the navigation pane. A list of overviews, articles, and tutorials appears in the topic pane.
2. Click Walkthrough: Making music in the topic pane. Read the Making music article in the topic pane. List four ways in which you can use Windows XP musically.

    ____

    ____

3. Click Play music in the Making Music area. Scroll to display the Display details about a CD area. List the three steps to display details about a CD.

    ____

    ____

4. Scroll to the top of the window to display the Making Music area.

(continued)

Using the Help and Support Center *(continued)*

5. Click Create CDs in the Making Music area. Scroll to display the steps to burn your own CD. List the six steps to burn a CD.

____
____
____
____
____
____

6. Read other articles of interest to you in the Making music area.
7. Click the Close button in the Help and Support Center window.

4 Downloading the Word 2003 Project 1-3 Data Files

Instructions: Use the SCSITE.COM Shelly Cashman Series Student Resources Web site to download the Word 2003 Project 1-3 Data Files into the Word folder.

Part 1:* *Plug the USB Flash Drive into the USB Port

1. If necessary, launch Microsoft Windows XP and log on to the computer.
2. Plug the USB flash drive into the USB port on the computer. The removable disk window should display on the desktop and should contain the Freshman folder.
3. If the Freshman folder does not display in the removable disk window, follow the steps in Project One to create the hierarchy of folders shown in Figure 1-47 on page WIN 39.

Part 2:* *Download the Word 2003 Project 1-3 Data Files into the Word Folder

1. Start Internet Explorer by clicking the Start button on the taskbar and then clicking Internet on the Start menu.
2. Click the Address box on the Address bar, type `scsite.com` in the Address box, and then click the Go button.
3. When the SCSITE.COM Shelly Cashman Series Student Web page is displayed, scroll down to view the Browse by Subject area, and then click the Office Suites link.
4. When the expanded Office Suites link appears, click the link containing the name of your textbook (for example, Microsoft Office 2003: Introductory Concepts and Techniques.
5. Scroll down to display the Data Files for Students (Windows) area and then click the Word 2003 Project 1-3 Data Files link.
6. When the File Download – Security Warning dialog box is displayed, click the Run button.
7. When the Internet Explorer – Security Warning dialog box is displayed, click the Run button.
8. When the WinZip Self-Extractor dialog box displays, click the Browse button.
9. Click the plus sign to the left of the removable drive, click the plus sign to the left of the Freshman folder, click the plus sign to the left of the 1st Semester folder, click the plus sign to the left of the Computer Class folder, and then click the Word folder.
10. Click the OK button in the Browse for Folder dialog box.
11. Click the Unzip button in the WinZip Self-Extractor dialog box.
12. When a smaller WinZip Self-Extractor dialog box appears, click the OK button.
13. Click the Close button in the WinZip Self-Extractor dialog box.
14. Click the Close button in the SCSITE.COM Shelly Cashman Series Student Resources window.
15. Verify the Word 2003 Student Data Files folder is contained in the Word folder.
16. Close the Word window.
17. Unplug the USB flash drive from the USB port.

MICROSOFT OFFICE

Word 2003

MICROSOFT OFFICE WORD

MICROSOFT OFFICE

Word 2003

Creating and Editing a Word Document

PROJECT

1

CASE PERSPECTIVE

Racing fans everywhere proclaim the Formula One Grand Prix as the most exhilarating racing competition in the world. Formula One Grand Prix events typically run for three days in a variety of countries including Brazil, Canada, England, Germany, Italy, Spain, and the United States. On the first day of each event, drivers practice on the tracks. Qualifying sessions begin on the second day. The fastest 26 drivers participate in a drivers' parade and then compete in the Formula One Grand Prix race on Sunday. During the race of nearly 200 miles, Formula One cars reach speeds that exceed 220 miles per hour.

When the Formula One Grand Prix season approaches, travel agents begin taking reservations for race packages. Jill Hall is a senior travel agent at Beacon Travel, where you are employed as a summer intern. Jill knows you have learned the guidelines for designing announcements in your marketing classes and has asked you to prepare a one-page flier announcing Beacon's Grand Prix race packages. You decide to use thick, bold characters to emphasize the headline and title. To attract attention to the announcement, you plan to include a large graphic of a Formula One race car. When you show the finished document to Jill, she is quite impressed. After Jill approves the completed flier, she wants you to distribute it to businesses for display on bulletin boards and in window fronts.

As you read through this project, you will learn how to use Word to create, save, and print a document that includes a graphical image.

Creating and Editing a Word Document

PROJECT

Objectives

You will have mastered the material in this project when you can:

- Start and quit Word
- Describe the Word window
- Enter text in a document
- Check spelling as you type
- Save a document
- Format text and paragraphs
- Undo and redo commands or actions
- Insert clip art in a document
- Print a document
- Open a document
- Correct errors in a document
- Use Word's Help to answer questions

What Is Microsoft Office Word 2003?

Microsoft Office Word 2003 is a full-featured word processing program that allows you to create professional looking documents and revise them easily. With Word, you can develop announcements, letters, memos, resumes, reports, fax cover sheets, mailing labels, newsletters, and many other types of documents. Word also provides tools that enable you to create Web pages with ease. From within Word, you can place these Web pages directly on a Web server.

Word has many features designed to simplify the production of documents and make documents look visually appealing. Using Word, you easily can change the shape, size, and color of text. You also can include borders, shading, tables, images, pictures, and Web addresses in documents. With proper hardware, you can dictate or handwrite text instead of typing it in Word. You also can speak instructions to Word.

While you are typing, Word performs many tasks automatically. For example, Word detects and corrects spelling and grammar errors in several languages. Word's thesaurus allows you to add variety and precision to your writing. Word also can format text such as headings, lists, fractions, borders, and Web addresses as you type them. Within Word, you can e-mail a copy of a Word document to an e-mail address.

This latest version of Word has many new features to make you more productive. It supports XML documents, improves readability of documents, supports ink input from devices such as the Tablet PC, provides more control for protecting documents, allows two documents to be compared side by side, and includes the capability to search a variety of reference information.

Project One — Grand Prix Announcement

To illustrate the features of Word, this book presents a series of projects that use Word to create documents similar to those you will encounter in academic and business environments. Project 1 uses Word to produce the announcement shown in Figure 1-1.

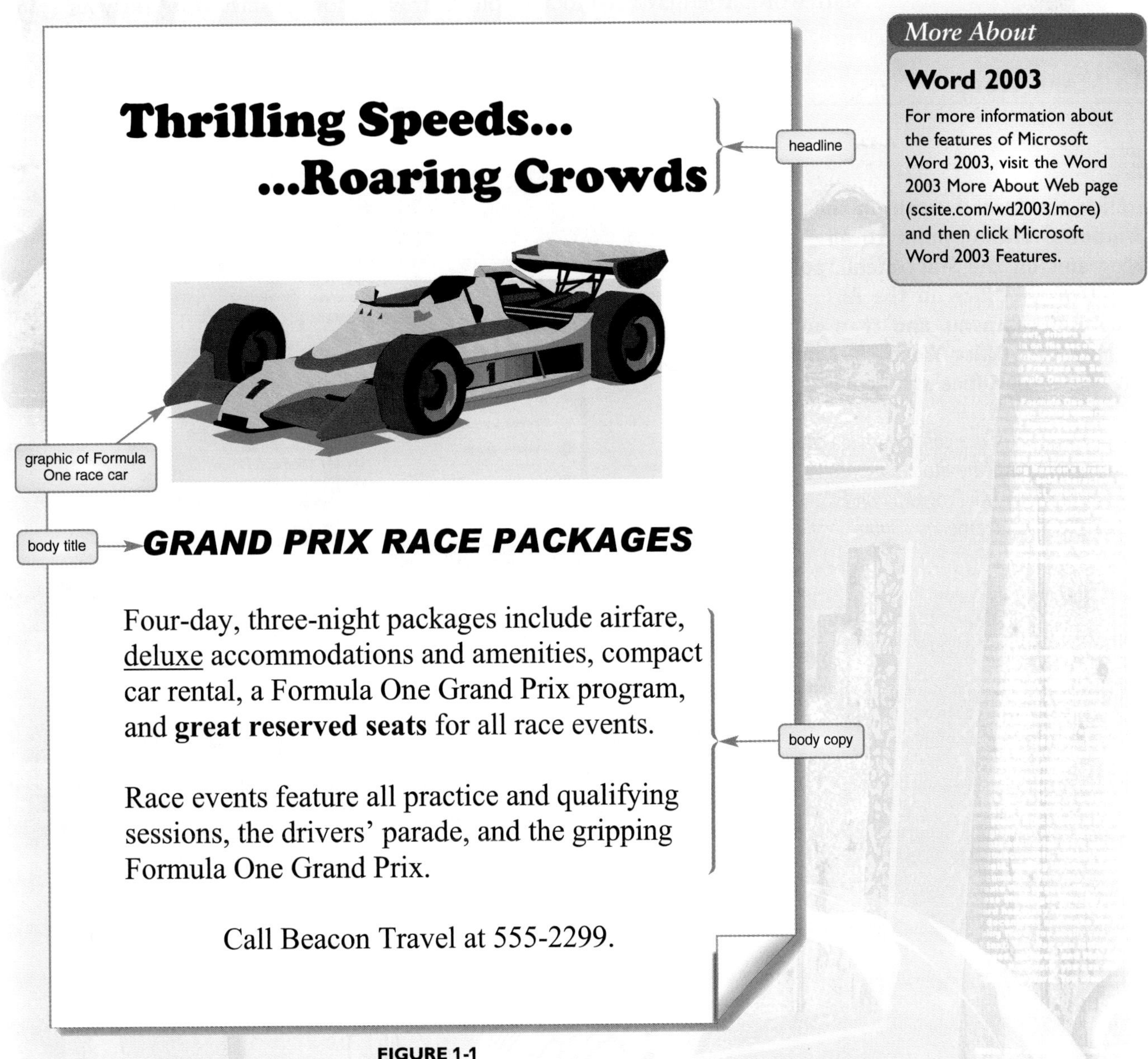

Thrilling Speeds...
...Roaring Crowds
headline
graphic of Formula One race car
body title
GRAND PRIX RACE PACKAGES
Four-day, three-night packages include airfare, deluxe accommodations and amenities, compact car rental, a Formula One Grand Prix program, and great reserved seats for all race events.
body copy
Race events feature all practice and qualifying sessions, the drivers' parade, and the gripping Formula One Grand Prix.
Call Beacon Travel at 555-2299.

FIGURE 1-1

More About

Word 2003

For more information about the features of Microsoft Word 2003, visit the Word 2003 More About Web page (scsite.com/wd2003/more) and then click Microsoft Word 2003 Features.

The announcement informs potential customers about Grand Prix race packages available through Beacon Travel. The announcement begins with a headline in large, thick characters. Below the headline is a graphic of a Formula One race car, followed by the body title, GRAND PRIX RACE PACKAGES. The paragraphs of body copy below the body title briefly discuss the items included in the race packages. Finally, the last line of the announcement lists the telephone number of Beacon Travel.

Starting and Customizing Word

If you are stepping through this project on a computer and you want your screen to match the figures in this book, then you should change your computer's resolution to 800 × 600. For more information about how to change the resolution on your computer, read Appendix D.

To start Word, Windows must be running. The following steps show how to start Word. You may need to ask your instructor how to start Word for your system.

To Start Word

1

- **Click the Start button on the Windows taskbar, point to All Programs on the Start menu, point to Microsoft Office on the All Programs submenu, and then point to Microsoft Office Word 2003 on the Microsoft Office submenu.**

Windows displays the commands on the Start menu above the Start button and then displays the All Programs and Microsoft Office submenus (Figure 1-2).

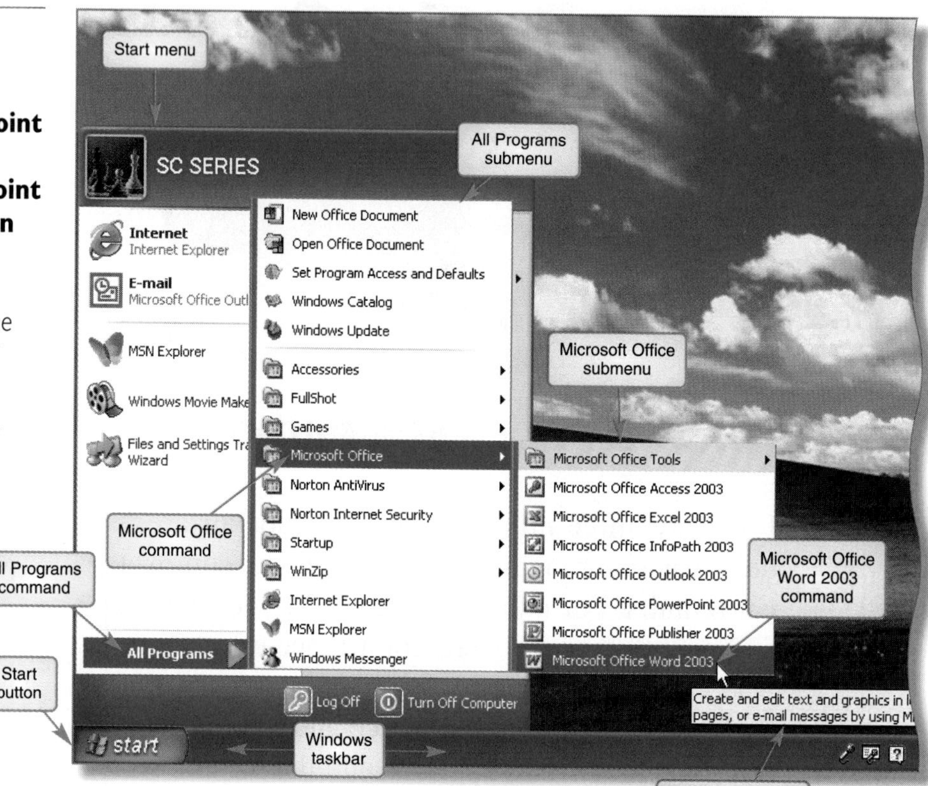

FIGURE 1-2

2

• **Click Microsoft Office Word 2003.**

Word starts. After a few moments, Word displays a new blank document titled Document1 in the Word window (Figure 1-3). The Windows taskbar displays the Word program button, indicating Word is running.

3

• **If the Word window is not maximized, double-click its title bar to maximize it.**

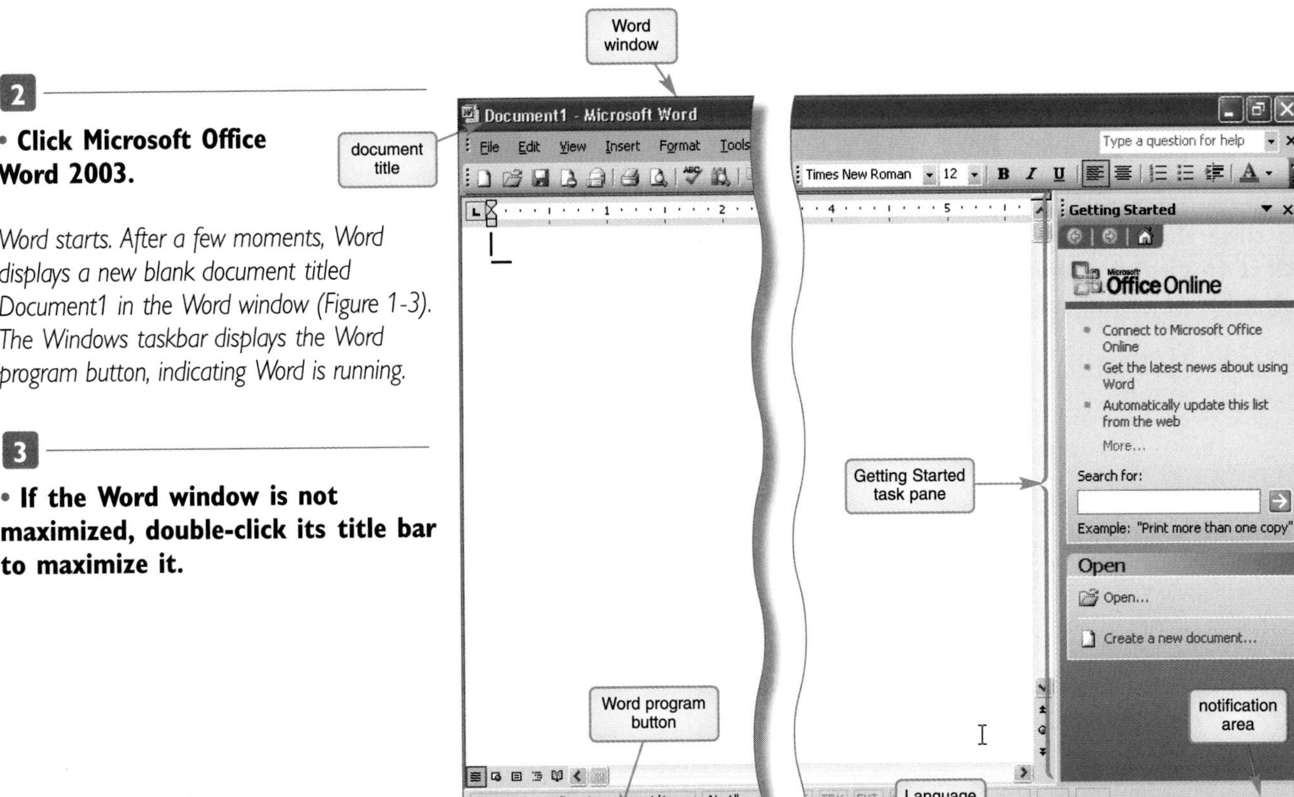

FIGURE 1-3

Other Ways

1. Double-click Word icon on desktop
2. Click Microsoft Office Word 2003 on Start menu
3. Click Start button, point to All Programs on Start menu, click New Office Document, click General tab, double-click Blank Document icon

The screen in Figure 1-3 shows how the Word window looks the first time you start Word after installation on most computers. If the Office Speech Recognition software is installed and active on your computer, then when you start Word the Language bar is displayed on the screen. The **Language bar** contains buttons that allow you to speak commands and dictate text. It usually is located on the right side of the Windows taskbar next to the notification area, and it changes to include the speech recognition functions available in Word. In this book, the Language bar is closed because it takes up computer resources and with the Language bar active, the microphone can be turned on accidentally by clicking the Microphone button, causing your computer to act in an unstable manner. For additional information about the Language bar, see page WD 16 and Appendix B.

As shown in Figure 1-3, Word may display a task pane on the right side of the screen. A **task pane** is a separate window that enables users to carry out some Word tasks more efficiently. When you start Word, it automatically may display the Getting Started task pane, which is a task pane that allows you to search for Office-related topics on the Microsoft Web site, open files, or create new documents. In this book, the Getting Started task pane is closed to allow the maximum typing area in Word.

After installation, Word displays the toolbar buttons on a single row. A **toolbar** contains buttons and boxes that allow you to perform frequent tasks quickly. For more efficient use of the buttons, the toolbars should be displayed on two separate rows instead of sharing a single row.

The steps on the next page show how to customize the Word window by closing the Language bar, closing the Getting Started task pane, and displaying the toolbar buttons on two separate rows.

More About

Task Panes

When you first start Word, a small window called a task pane may be displayed docked on the right side of the screen. You can drag a task pane title bar to float the pane in your work area or dock it on either the left or right side of a screen, depending on your personal preference.

To Customize the Word Window

1

- **To close the Language bar, right-click it to display a shortcut menu with a list of commands.**

The Language bar shortcut menu appears (Figure 1-4).

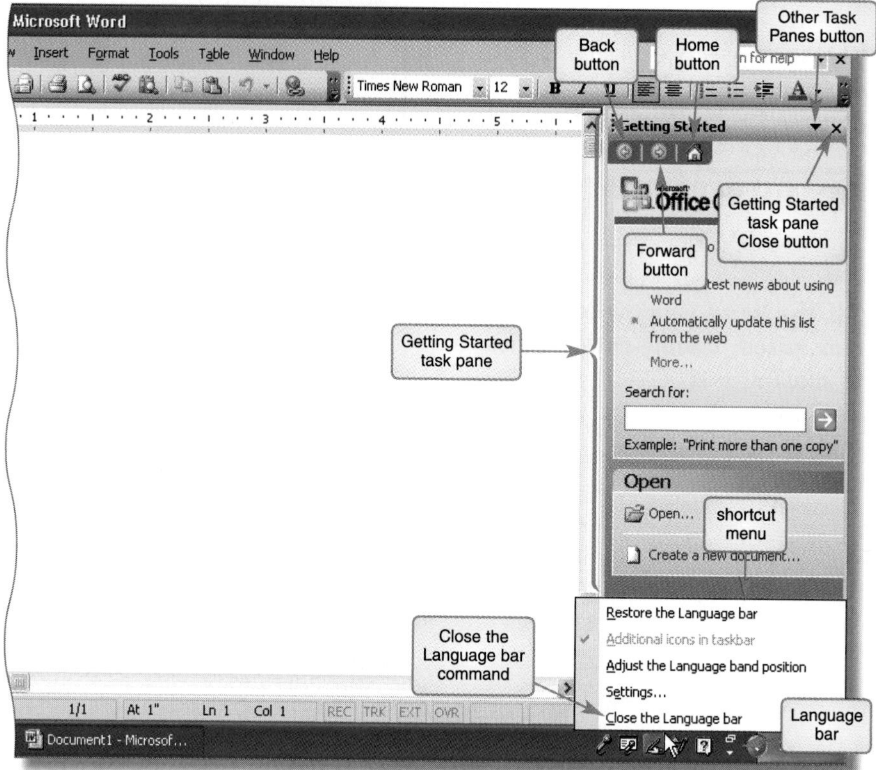

FIGURE 1-4

2

- **Click Close the Language bar on the shortcut menu.**
- **If the Getting Started task pane is displayed, click the Close button in the upper-right corner of the task pane.**

The Language bar disappears. Word removes the Getting Started task pane from the screen (Figure 1-5).

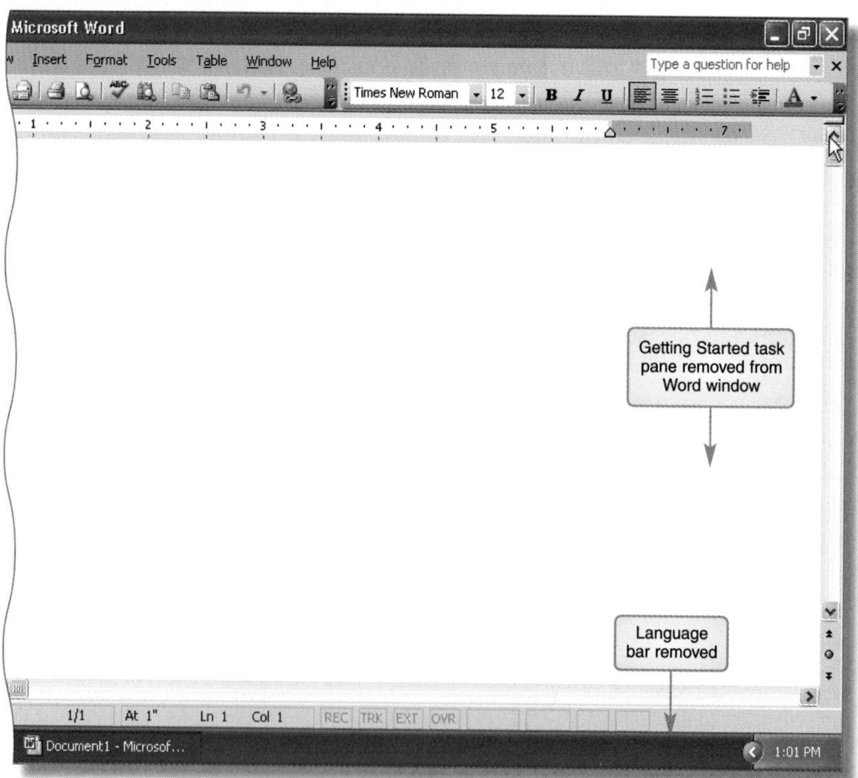

FIGURE 1-5

3

• If the toolbar buttons are displayed on one row, click the Toolbar Options button.

Word displays the Toolbar Options list, which shows the buttons that do not fit on the toolbars when they are displayed on one row (Figure 1-6).

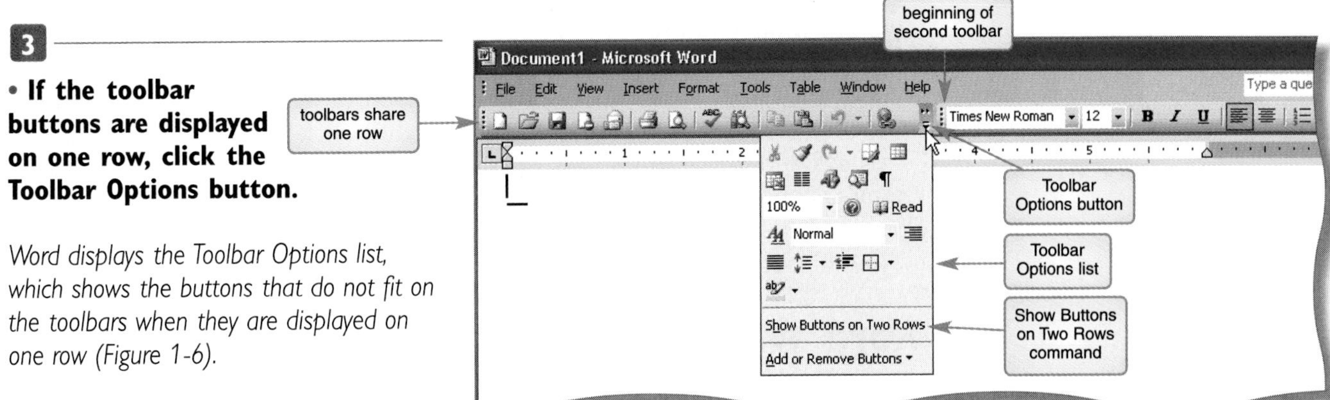

FIGURE 1-6

4

• Click Show Buttons on Two Rows in the Toolbar Options list.

• If your screen differs from Figure 1-7, click the Normal View button on the horizontal scroll bar.

Word displays the toolbars on two separate rows (Figure 1-7). The Toolbar Options list now is empty because all of the buttons fit on the toolbars when they display on two rows.

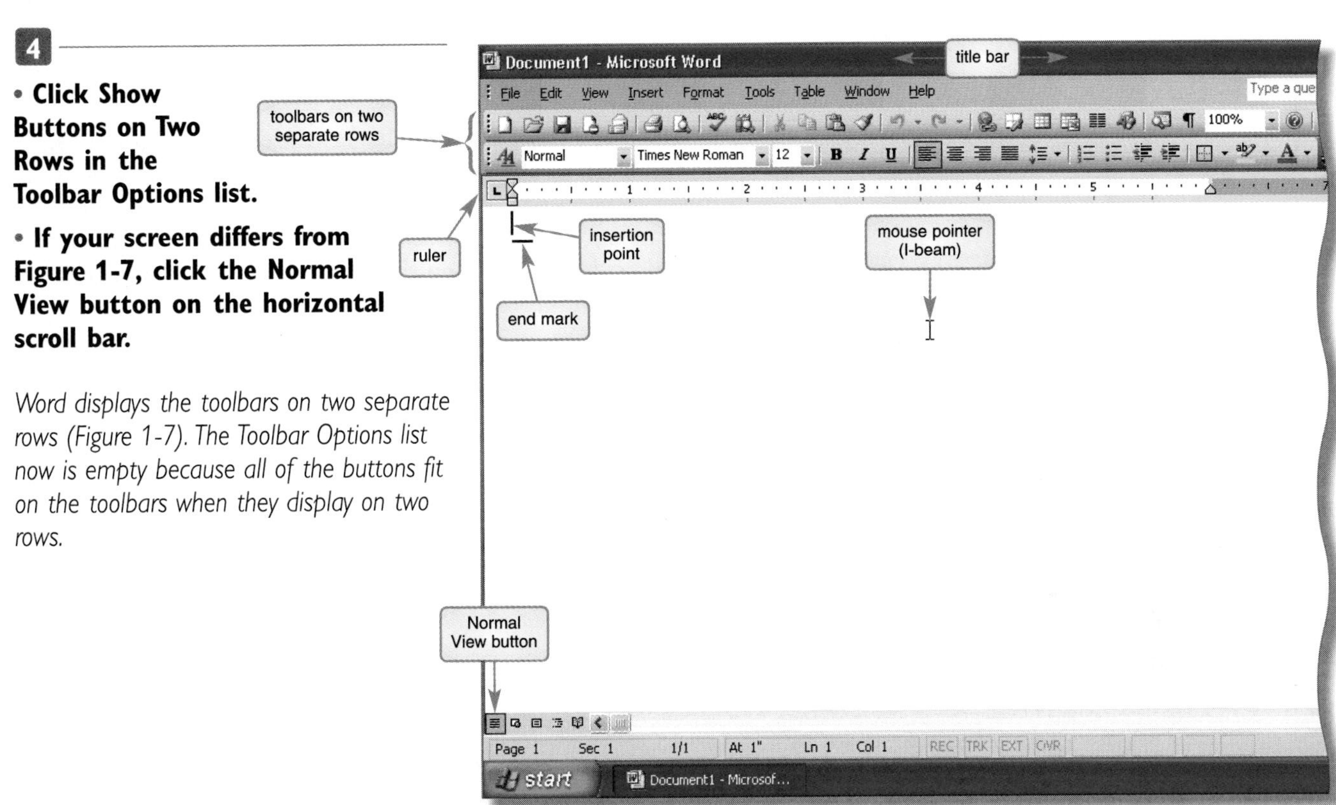

FIGURE 1-7

As an alternative to Steps 3 and 4 above, you can point to the beginning of the second toolbar (Figure 1-6), and when the mouse pointer changes to a four-headed arrow, drag the toolbar down to create two rows of toolbars.

Each time you start Word, the Word window appears the same way it did the last time you used Word. If the toolbar buttons are displayed on one row, then they will be displayed on one row the next time you start Word.

As you work through creating a document, you will find that certain Word operations automatically display a task pane. In addition to the Getting Started task pane shown in Figure 1-4, Word provides 13 other task panes. Some of the more important ones are the Help, Clip Art, Clipboard, and Research task panes. These task panes are discussed as they are used throughout the book.

More About

The Office Assistant

The Office Assistant is an animated object that can answer questions for you. On some installations, the Office Assistant may appear when Word starts. If the Office Assistant appears on your screen and you do not want to use it, right-click it and then click Hide on the shortcut menu.

At any point while working with Word, you can open or close a task pane by clicking View on the menu bar and then clicking Task Pane. To display a different task pane, click the Other Task Panes button to the left of the Close button on the task pane title bar (Figure 1-4 on page WD 8) and then click the desired task pane in the list. The Back and Forward buttons below the task pane title bar allow you to switch among task panes you have opened during a Word session. The Home button causes Word to display the Getting Started task pane.

The Word Window

The Word window consists of a variety of components to make your work more efficient and documents more professional. The following sections discuss these components, which are identified in either Figure 1-7 on the previous page or Figure 1-8.

Document Window

The **document window** displays text, tables, graphics, and other items as you type or insert them in a document. Only a portion of a document, however, appears on the screen at one time. You view the portion of the document displayed on the screen through a document window (Figure 1-8).

Thrilling Speeds...
...Roaring Crowds
GRAND PRIX RACE PACKAGES
Four-day, three-night packages include airfare, deluxe accommodations and amenities, compact car rental, a Formula One Grand Prix program, and great reserved seats for all race events.
Race events feature all practice and q
sessions, the drivers' parade, and the
Formula One Grand Prix.
Call Beacon Travel at 555-22
stored document
Grand Prix Announcement - Microsoft Word 2003
ruler
scroll box
document window
scroll bars
scroll arrows
status bar
buttons to change view of document
OVR status indicator

FIGURE 1-8

A document window contains several elements commonly found in other application software, as well as some elements unique to Word. The main elements of the Word document window are the insertion point, end mark, mouse pointer, rulers, scroll bars, and status bar.

INSERTION POINT The **insertion point** (Figure 1-7 on page WD 9) is a blinking vertical bar that indicates where text will be inserted as you type. As you type, the insertion point moves to the right and, when you reach the end of a line, it moves downward to the beginning of the next line. You also insert graphics, tables, and other items at the location of the insertion point.

END MARK The **end mark** (Figure 1-7) is a short horizontal line that indicates the end of the document. Each time you begin a new line, the end mark moves downward.

MOUSE POINTER The **mouse pointer** becomes different shapes depending on the task you are performing in Word and the pointer's location on the screen (Figure 1-7). The mouse pointer in Figure 1-7 has the shape of an I-beam. Other mouse pointer shapes are described as they appear on the screen during this and subsequent projects.

RULERS At the top edge of the document window is the horizontal ruler (Figure 1-8). You use the **horizontal ruler**, usually simply called the **ruler**, to set tab stops, indent paragraphs, adjust column widths, and change page margins.

An additional ruler, called the **vertical ruler**, sometimes is displayed at the left edge of the Word window when you perform certain tasks. The purpose of the vertical ruler is discussed in a later project. If your screen displays a vertical ruler, click View on the menu bar and then click Normal.

SCROLL BARS By using the **scroll bars**, you display different portions of your document in the document window (Figure 1-8). At the right edge of the document window is a vertical scroll bar. At the bottom of the document window is a horizontal scroll bar. On both the vertical and horizontal scroll bars, the position of the **scroll box** reflects the location of the portion of the document that is displayed in the document window.

On the left edge of the horizontal scroll bar are five buttons that change the view of a document. On the bottom of the vertical scroll bar are three buttons you can use to scroll through a document. These buttons are discussed as they are used in later projects.

STATUS BAR The **status bar** displays at the bottom of the document window, above the Windows taskbar (Figure 1-8). The status bar presents information about the location of the insertion point and the progress of current tasks, as well as the status of certain commands, keys, and buttons.

From left to right, Word displays the following information on the status bar in Figure 1-8: the page number, the section number, the page containing the insertion point followed by the total number of pages in the document, the position of the insertion point in inches from the top of the page, the line number and column number of the insertion point, and then several status indicators.

More About

The Horizontal Ruler

If the horizontal ruler is not displayed on your screen, click View on the menu bar and then click Ruler. To hide the ruler, also click View on the menu bar and then click Ruler.

More About

Scroll Bars

You can use the vertical scroll bar to scroll through multi-page documents. As you drag the scroll box up or down the scroll bar, Word displays a page indicator to the left of the scroll box. When you release the mouse button, the document window displays the page shown in the page indicator.

More About

Languages

If multiple languages have been installed on your computer, the status bar also displays the language format, which shows the name of the language you are using to create the document. You add languages through the Control Panel in Windows.

You use the **status indicators** to turn certain keys or modes on or off. Word displays the first four status indicators (REC, TRK, EXT, and OVR) darkened when they are on and dimmed when they are off. For example, the dimmed OVR indicates overtype mode is off. To turn these four status indicators on or off, double-click the status indicator on the status bar. Each of these status indicators is discussed as it is used in the projects.

The remaining status indicators display icons as you perform certain tasks. For example, when you begin typing in the document window, Word displays a Spelling and Grammar Status icon. When Word is saving your document, it displays a Background Save icon. When you print a document, Word displays a Background Print icon. If you perform a task that requires several seconds (such as saving a document), the status bar usually displays a message informing you of the progress of the task.

Menu Bar and Toolbars

The menu bar and toolbars display at the top of the screen just below the title bar (Figure 1-9).

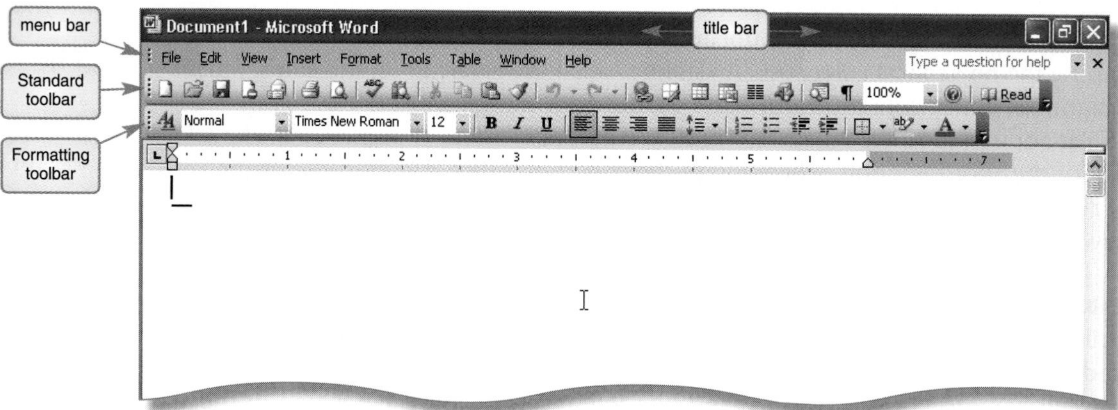

FIGURE 1-9

MENU BAR The **menu bar** is a special toolbar that displays the Word menu names. Each menu name represents a menu. A **menu** contains a list of commands you use to perform tasks such as retrieving, storing, printing, and formatting data in a document.

When you point to a menu name on the menu bar, the area of the menu bar containing the name is displayed as a selected button. Word shades selected buttons in light orange and surrounds them with a blue outline.

To display a menu, click the menu name on the menu bar. For example, to display the Edit menu, click the Edit menu name on the menu bar. When you click a menu name on the menu bar, Word initially displays a **short menu** listing your most recently used commands (Figure 1-10a). If you wait a few seconds or click the arrows at the bottom of the short menu, it expands into a full menu. A **full menu** lists all the commands associated with a menu (Figure 1-10b). You also can display a full menu immediately by double-clicking the menu name on the menu bar.

More About

Menus

Right-clicking an object displays a shortcut menu (also called a context-sensitive or object menu). Depending on the object, the commands in the shortcut menu vary.

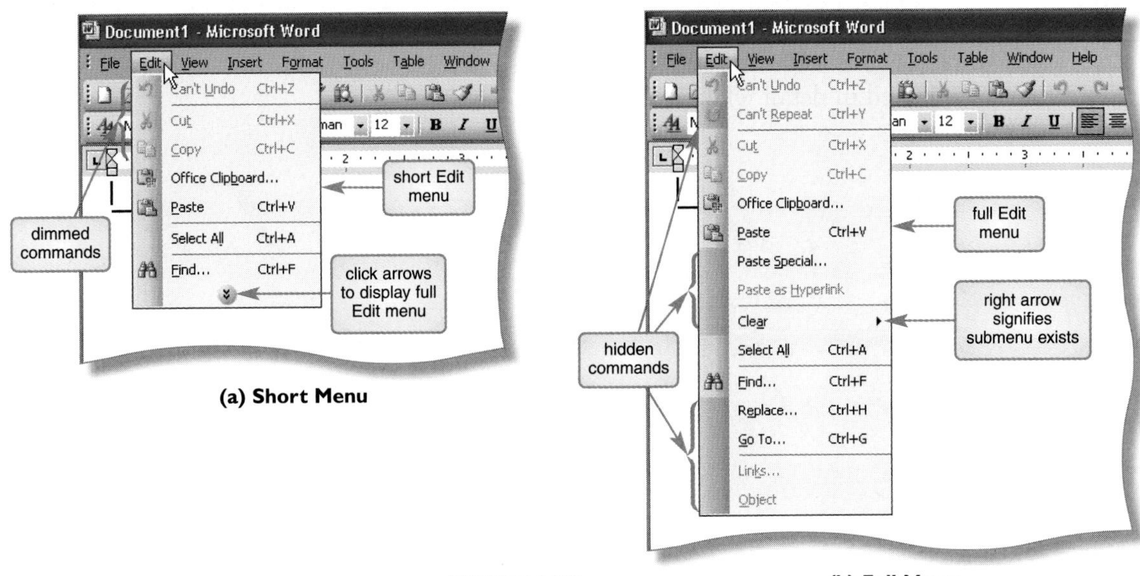

(a) Short Menu

FIGURE 1-10

(b) Full Menu

In this book, when you display a menu, use one of the following techniques to ensure that Word always displays a full menu:

1. Click the menu name on the menu bar and then wait a few seconds.
2. Click the menu name on the menu bar and then click the arrows at the bottom of the short menu.
3. Click the menu name on the menu bar and then point to the arrows at the bottom of the short menu.
4. Double-click the menu name on the menu bar.

Both short and full menus may display some dimmed commands. A **dimmed command** appears gray, or dimmed, instead of black, which indicates it is not available for the current selection. A command with medium blue shading in the rectangle to its left on a full menu is called a **hidden command** because it does not appear on a short menu. As you use Word, it automatically personalizes the short menus for you based on how often you use commands. That is, as you use hidden commands on the full menu, Word *unhides* them and places them on the short menu.

Some commands have an arrow at the right edge of the menu. If you point to this arrow, Word displays a **submenu**, which is a list of additional commands associated with the selected command.

TOOLBARS Word has many predefined, or built-in, toolbars. A toolbar contains buttons, boxes, and menus that allow you to perform tasks more quickly than using the menu bar. For example, to print a document, you can click the Print button on a toolbar instead of navigating through the File menu to reach the Print command.

Each button on a toolbar displays an image to help you remember its function. Also, when you position the mouse pointer on, or point to, a button or box, Word displays the name of the button or box in a ScreenTip. A **ScreenTip** is a short on-screen note associated with the object to which you are pointing.

Two built-in toolbars are the Standard toolbar and the Formatting toolbar. Figure 1-11a shows the **Standard toolbar** and identifies its buttons and boxes. Figure 1-11b shows the **Formatting toolbar**. Each of these buttons and boxes will be explained in detail when it is used in this book.

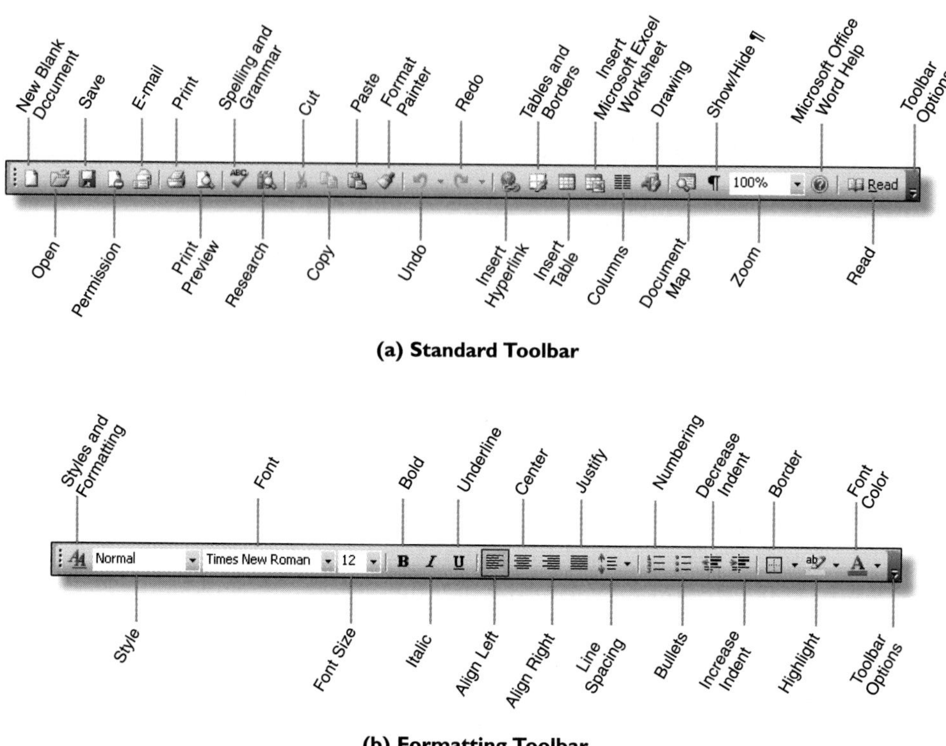

(a) Standard Toolbar

(b) Formatting Toolbar

FIGURE 1-11

When you first install Word, the buttons on both the Standard and Formatting toolbars are preset to display on the same row immediately below the menu bar (Figure 1-12a). Unless the resolution of your display device is greater than 800 × 600, many of the buttons that belong to these toolbars are hidden when the two toolbars share one row. The buttons that display on the toolbar are the more frequently used buttons. Hidden buttons display in the Toolbar Options list (Figure 1-12b). You can display all the buttons on either toolbar by double-clicking the **move handle**, which is the vertical dotted line on the left edge of the toolbar.

As an alternative, you can instruct Word to display the buttons on the Standard and Formatting toolbars on separate rows, one below the other, by clicking the Show Buttons on Two Rows command in the Toolbar Options list (Figure 1-12b). In this book, the Standard and Formatting toolbars are shown on separate rows so that all buttons are displayed on a screen with the resolution set to 800 × 600 (Figure 1-12c).

In the previous figures, the Standard and Formatting toolbars are docked. A **docked toolbar** is a toolbar that is attached to an edge of the Word window. Depending on the task you are performing, Word may display additional toolbars on the screen. These additional toolbars either are docked or floating in the Word window. A **floating toolbar** is not attached to an edge of the Word window; that is, it appears in the middle of the Word window. You can rearrange the order of docked toolbars and can move floating toolbars anywhere in the Word window. Later in this book, steps are presented that show you how to float a docked toolbar or dock a floating toolbar.

More About

The Word Help System

Need Help? It is no further away than the Type a question for help box on the menu bar in the upper-right corner of the window. Click the box that contains the text, Type a question for help (Figure 1-12c), type `help`, and then press the ENTER key. Word responds with a list of topics you can click to learn about obtaining help on any Word-related topic. To find out what is new in Word 2003, type `what is new in Word` in the Type a question for help box.

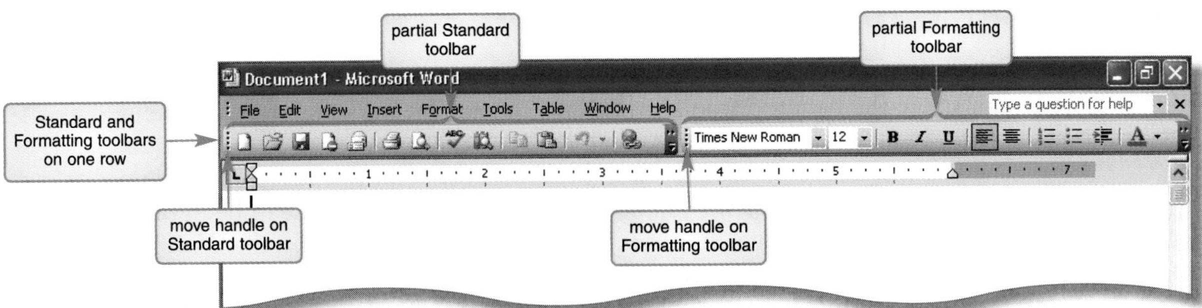

(a) Standard and Formatting Toolbars on One Row

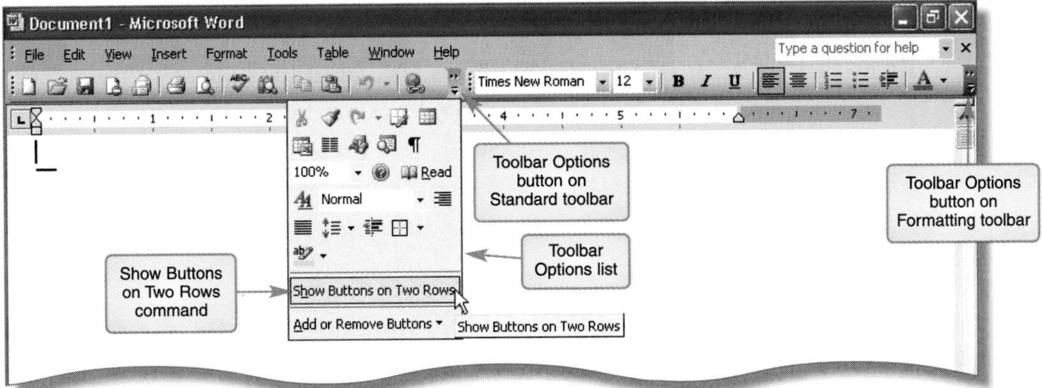

(b) Toolbar Options List

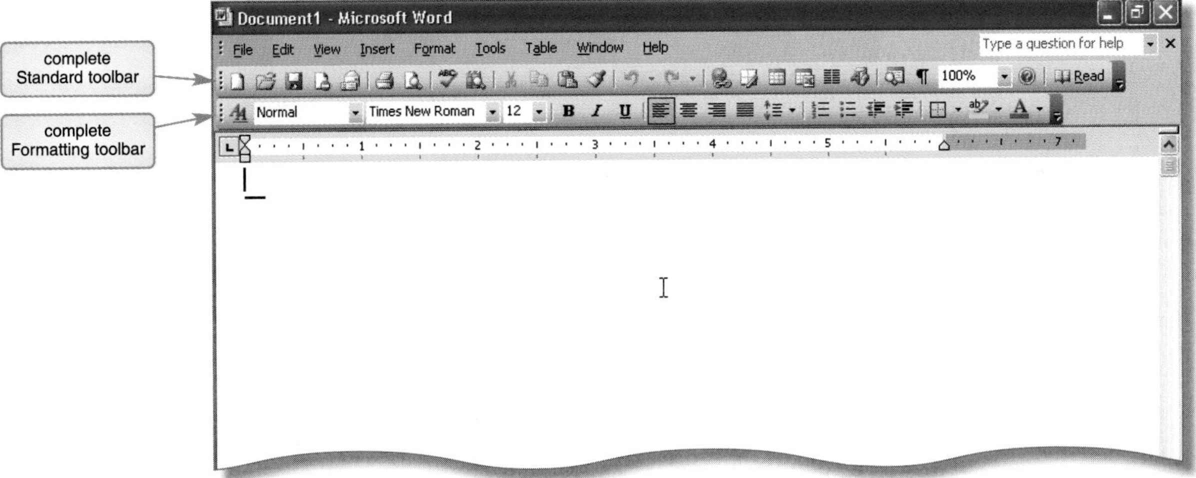

(c) Standard and Formatting Toolbars on Two Rows

FIGURE 1-12

Resetting Menus and Toolbars

Each project in this book begins with the menus and toolbars appearing as they did at the initial installation of the software. If you are stepping through this project on a computer and you want your menus and toolbars to match the figures in this book, then you should reset your menus and toolbars. For more information about how to reset menus and toolbars, read Appendix D.

More About

Toolbar Buttons

If you have difficulty seeing the small buttons on the toolbars, you can increase their size. Click View on the menu bar, point to Toolbars, click Customize on the Toolbars submenu, click the Options tab, place a check mark in the Large icons check box, and then click the Close button.

More About

Speech Recognition

If Office Speech Recognition software is installed on your computer, you can speak instructions to Word including toolbar button names, menu names and commands, and items in dialog boxes and task panes. You also can dictate so Word writes exactly what you say. The microphone picks up others' voices and background sounds, so speech recognition is most effective when used in a quiet environment.

Speech Recognition

With the **Office Speech Recognition software** installed and a microphone, you can speak the names of toolbar buttons, menus, menu commands, list items, alerts, and dialog box controls, such as OK and Cancel. You also can dictate text, such as words and sentences. To indicate whether you want to speak commands or dictate text, you use the Language bar. The Language bar can be in one of four states: (1) **restored**, which means it is displayed somewhere in the Word window (Figure 1-13a); (2) **minimized**, which means it is displayed on the Windows taskbar (Figure 1-13b); (3) **hidden**, which means you do not see it on the screen but it will be displayed the next time you start your computer; or (4) **closed**, which means it is hidden permanently until you enable it. If the Language bar is hidden and you want it to be displayed, then do the following:

1. Right-click an open area on the Windows taskbar at the bottom of the screen.
2. Point to Toolbars and then click Language bar on the Toolbars submenu.

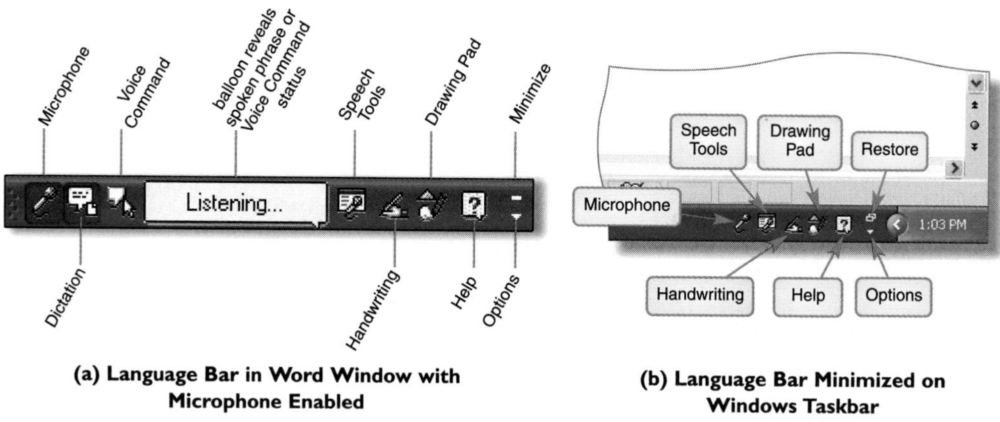

(a) Language Bar in Word Window with Microphone Enabled

(b) Language Bar Minimized on Windows Taskbar

FIGURE 1-13

If the Language bar command is dimmed on the Toolbars submenu or if the Speech command is dimmed on the Tools menu, the Office Speech Recognition software is not installed.

In this book, the Language bar does not appear in the figures. If you want to close the Language bar so that your screen is identical to what you see in the book, right-click the Language bar and then click Close the Language bar on the shortcut menu. Additional information about the speech recognition capabilities of Word is available in Appendix B.

Q&A

Q: What font size should I use in an announcement?

A: An announcement usually is posted on a bulletin board. Thus, its font size should be as large as possible so that all potential readers easily can see the announcement.

Entering Text

Characters that display on the screen are a specific shape, size, and style. The **font**, or typeface, defines the appearance and shape of the letters, numbers, and special characters. The preset, or **default**, font is Times New Roman (Figure 1-14). **Font size** specifies the size of the characters and is determined by a measurement system called points. A single **point** is about 1/72 of one inch in height. Thus, a character with a font size of 12 is about 12/72 or 1/6 of one inch in height. On most computers, the default font size in Word is 12.

If more of the characters in your document require a larger font size than the default, you easily can change the font size before you type. In Project 1, many of the characters in the body copy of the announcement are a font size of 22. The following steps show how to increase the font size before you begin typing text.

To Increase the Font Size before Typing

1

- **Click the Font Size box arrow on the Formatting toolbar.**

Word displays a list of available font sizes in the Font Size list (Figure 1-14). The available font sizes depend on the current font, which is Times New Roman.

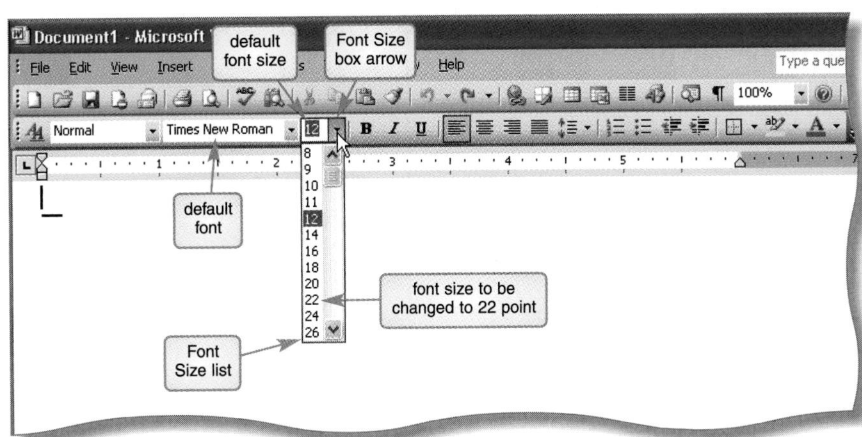

FIGURE 1-14

2

- **Click 22 in the Font Size list.**

The font size for characters to be entered in this document changes to 22 (Figure 1-15). The size of the insertion point increases to reflect the new font size.

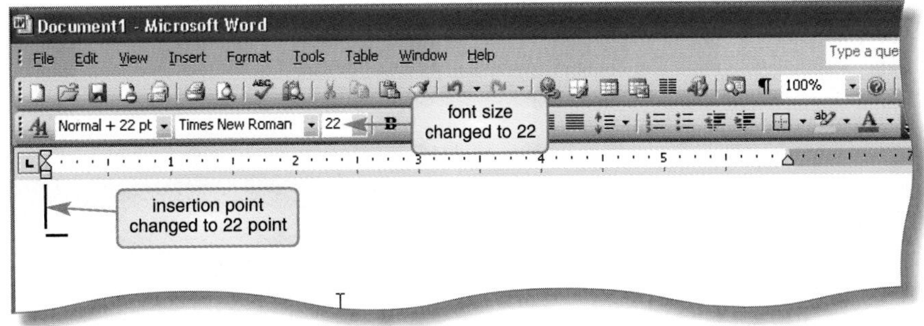

FIGURE 1-15

Other Ways

1. On Format menu click Font, click Font tab, select desired font size in Size list, click OK button
2. Right-click paragraph mark above end mark, click Font on shortcut menu, click Font tab, select desired font size in Size list, click OK button
3. Press CTRL+SHIFT+P, type desired font size, press ENTER
4. Press CTRL+SHIFT+> repeatedly
5. In Voice Command mode, say "Font Size, [select font size]"

The new font size takes effect immediately in the document. Word uses this font size for characters you enter in this announcement.

Typing Text

To enter text in a document, you type on the keyboard or speak into the microphone. The example on the next page illustrates the steps required to type both lines of the headline in the announcement. By default, Word positions these lines at the left margin. In a later section, this project will show how to make all of the characters in the headline larger and thicker, and how to position the second line of the headline at the right margin.

The steps on the next page show how to begin typing text in the announcement.

To Type Text

1

• **Type** `Thrilling Speeds` **and then press the PERIOD (.) key three times. If you make an error while typing, press the BACKSPACE key until you have deleted the text in error and then retype the text correctly.**

As you type, the insertion point moves to the right (Figure 1-16).

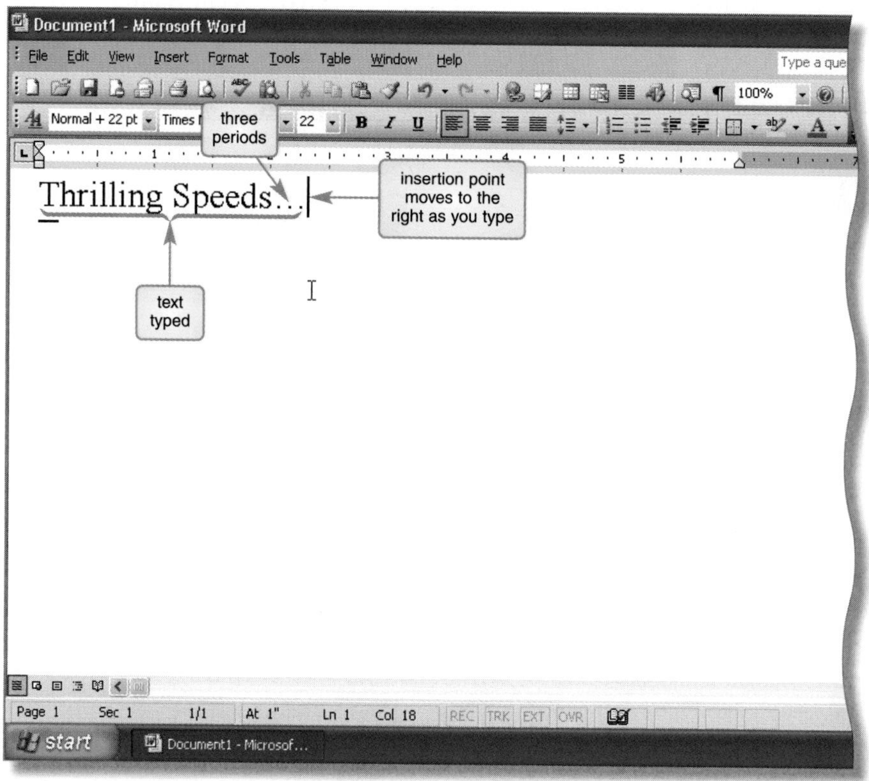

FIGURE 1-16

2

• **Press the ENTER key.**

Word moves the insertion point to the beginning of the next line (Figure 1-17). Notice the status bar indicates the current position of the insertion point. That is, the insertion point currently is on line 2 column 1.

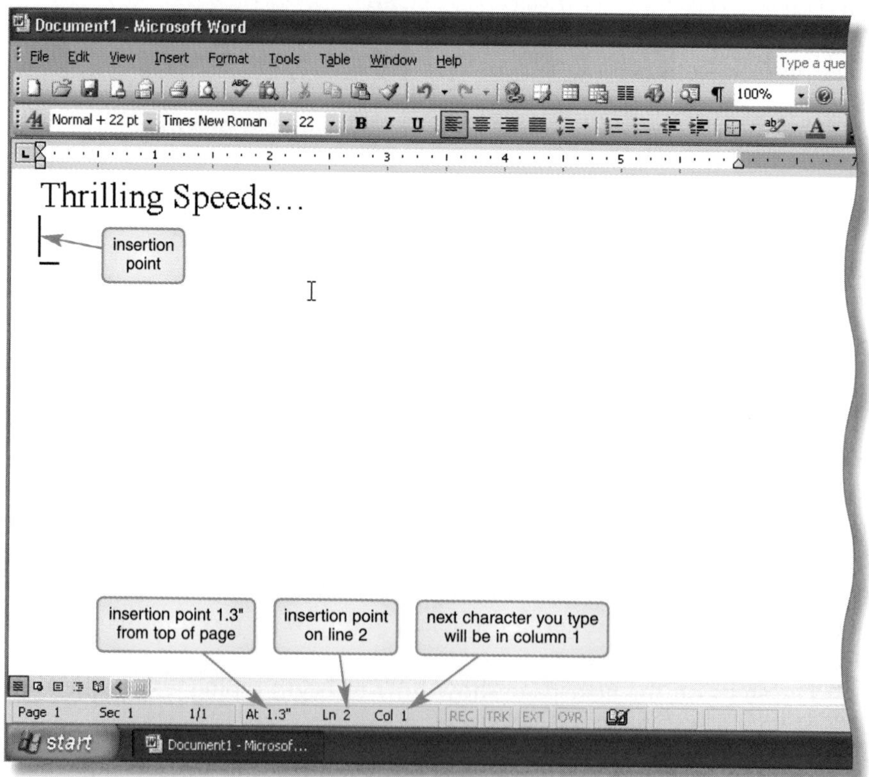

FIGURE 1-17

3

- **Press the PERIOD key three times.**
- **Type** `Roaring Crowds` **and then press the ENTER key.**

The headline is complete (Figure 1-18). The insertion point is on line 3.

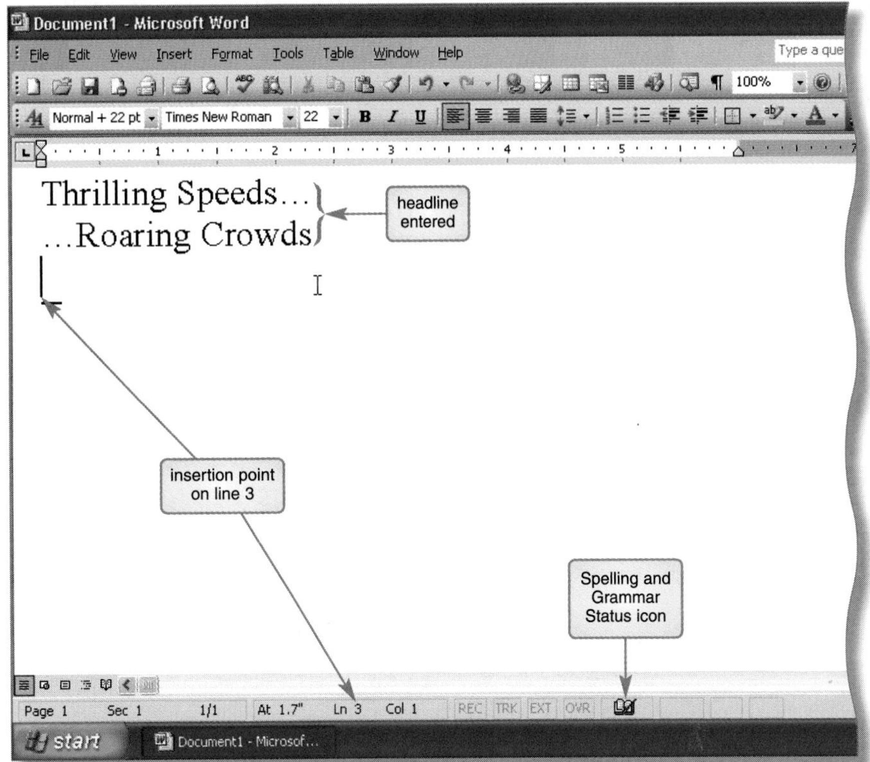

FIGURE 1-18

> *Other Ways*
>
> 1. In Dictation mode, say "Thrilling Speeds, Period, Period, Period, New Line, Period, Period, Period, Roaring Crowds, New Line"

When you begin entering text in a document, the **Spelling and Grammar Status icon** appears at the right of the status bar (Figure 1-18). As you type, the Spelling and Grammar Status icon shows an animated pencil writing on paper, which indicates Word is checking for possible errors. When you stop typing, the pencil changes to either a red check mark or a red X. In Figure 1-18, the Spelling and Grammar Status icon contains a red check mark.

In general, if all of the words you have typed are in Word's dictionary and your grammar is correct, the Spelling and Grammar Status icon contains a red check mark. If you type a word not in the dictionary (because it is a proper name or misspelled), a red wavy underline appears below the word. If you type text that may be incorrect grammatically, a green wavy underline appears below the text. When Word flags a possible spelling or grammar error, it also changes the red check mark on the Spelling and Grammar Status icon to a red X. As you enter text in a document, your Spelling and Grammar Status icon may show a red X instead of a red check mark. Later, this project will show how to check the spelling of these flagged words. At that time, the red X returns to a red check mark.

> *More About*
>
> **Entering Text**
>
> In the days of typewriters, the letter l was used for both the letter l and the numeral one. Keyboards, however, have both a numeral one and the letter l. Keyboards also have both a numeral zero and the letter o. Be careful to press the correct keyboard character when creating a word processing document.

Entering Blank Lines in a Document

To enter a blank line in a document, press the ENTER key without typing any text on the line. The following example shows how to enter three blank lines below the headline.

To Enter Blank Lines in a Document

1

• **Press the ENTER key three times.**

Word inserts three blank lines in the document below the headline (Figure 1-19).

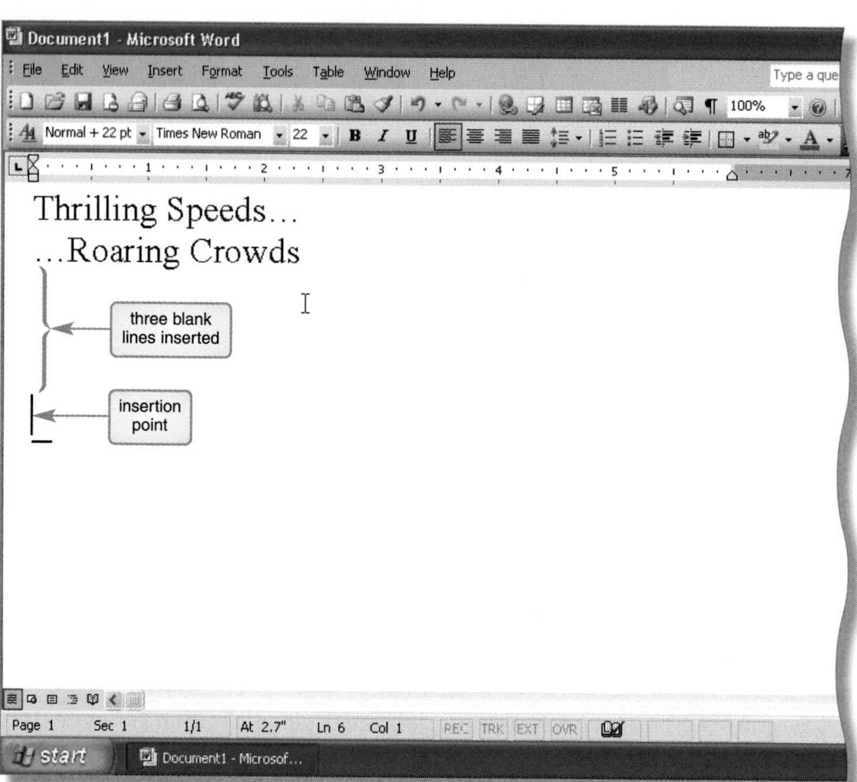

FIGURE 1-19

Other Ways

1. In Dictation mode, say "New Line, New Line, New Line"

More About

Hidden Text

When you display formatting marks, Word also displays hidden text. Text formatted as hidden shows on the screen but does not print. Hidden text is useful if you want to write a note to yourself in a document. To format text as hidden, select the text, click Format on the menu bar, click Font, click the Font tab, place a check mark in the Hidden check box, and then click the OK button.

Displaying Formatting Marks

To indicate where in a document you press the ENTER key or SPACEBAR, you may find it helpful to display formatting marks. A **formatting mark**, sometimes called a **nonprinting character**, is a character that Word displays on the screen but is not visible on a printed document. For example, the paragraph mark (¶) is a formatting mark that indicates where you pressed the ENTER key. A raised dot (•) shows where you pressed the SPACEBAR. Other formatting marks are discussed as they appear on the screen.

Depending on settings made during previous Word sessions, the Word screen already may display formatting marks (Figure 1-20). The following step shows how to display formatting marks, if they are not displayed already on the screen.

To Display Formatting Marks

1

- **If it is not selected already, click the Show/Hide ¶ button on the Standard toolbar.**

Word displays formatting marks on the screen (Figure 1-20). The Show/Hide ¶ button is selected. That is, the button is light orange and surrounded with a blue outline.

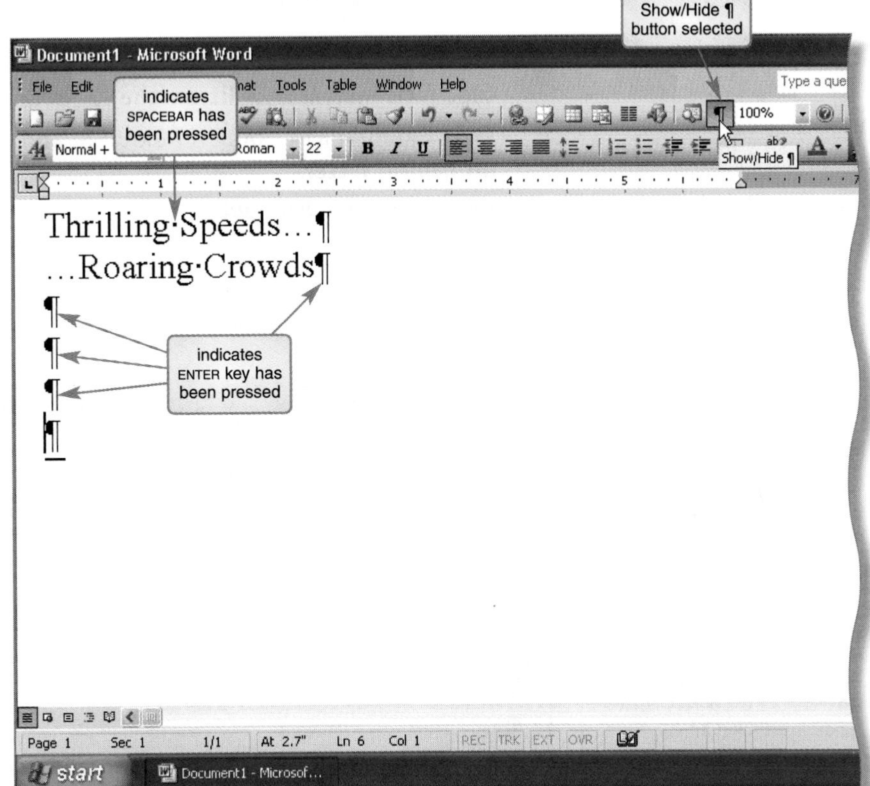

FIGURE 1-20

Notice several changes to the Word document window (Figure 1-20). A paragraph mark appears at the end of each line to indicate you pressed the ENTER key. Each time you press the ENTER key, Word creates a new paragraph. The size of paragraph marks is 22 point because the font size was changed earlier in the project. Between each word, a raised dot appears, indicating you pressed the SPACEBAR. Finally, the Show/Hide ¶ button changes from blue to light orange and has a blue outline, which indicates it is selected.

If you feel the formatting marks clutter the screen, you can hide them by clicking the Show/Hide ¶ button again. It is recommended that you display formatting marks; therefore, the document windows presented in this book show the formatting marks.

Other Ways

1. On Tools menu click Options, click View tab, click All check box, click OK button
2. Press CTRL+SHIFT+ASTERISK (*)
3. In Voice Command mode, say "Show Hide Paragraph"

More About

Zooming

If text is too small to read on the screen, you can zoom the document by clicking View on the menu bar, clicking Zoom, selecting the desired percentage, and then clicking the OK button. Changing the zoom percent has no effect on the printed document.

More About

Caps Lock

If you leave the CAPS LOCK key on and begin typing a new sentence, Word automatically corrects the problem for you. That is, it disengages the CAPS LOCK key and capitalizes only the first letter of the first word in the next sentence.

Entering More Text

Every character in the body title (GRAND PRIX RACE PACKAGES) of the announcement is in capital letters. The next step is to enter this body title in all capital letters in the document window, as explained below.

To Type More Text

1. **Press the CAPS LOCK key on the keyboard to turn on capital letters. Verify the caps lock indicator is lit on the keyboard.**
2. **Type** GRAND PRIX RACE PACKAGES **and then press the CAPS LOCK key to turn off capital letters.**
3. **Press the ENTER key twice.**

Word displays the body title on line 6 (Figure 1-21). Depending on your Word settings, your screen may not display the smart tag indicator below the word, RACE.

More About

Smart Tags

A smart tag is a button that automatically appears on the screen when Word performs a certain action. You then can use the smart tag to perform tasks more efficiently. Word notifies you of a smart tag by displaying a smart tag indicator, such as the purple dotted underline shown in Figure 1-21.

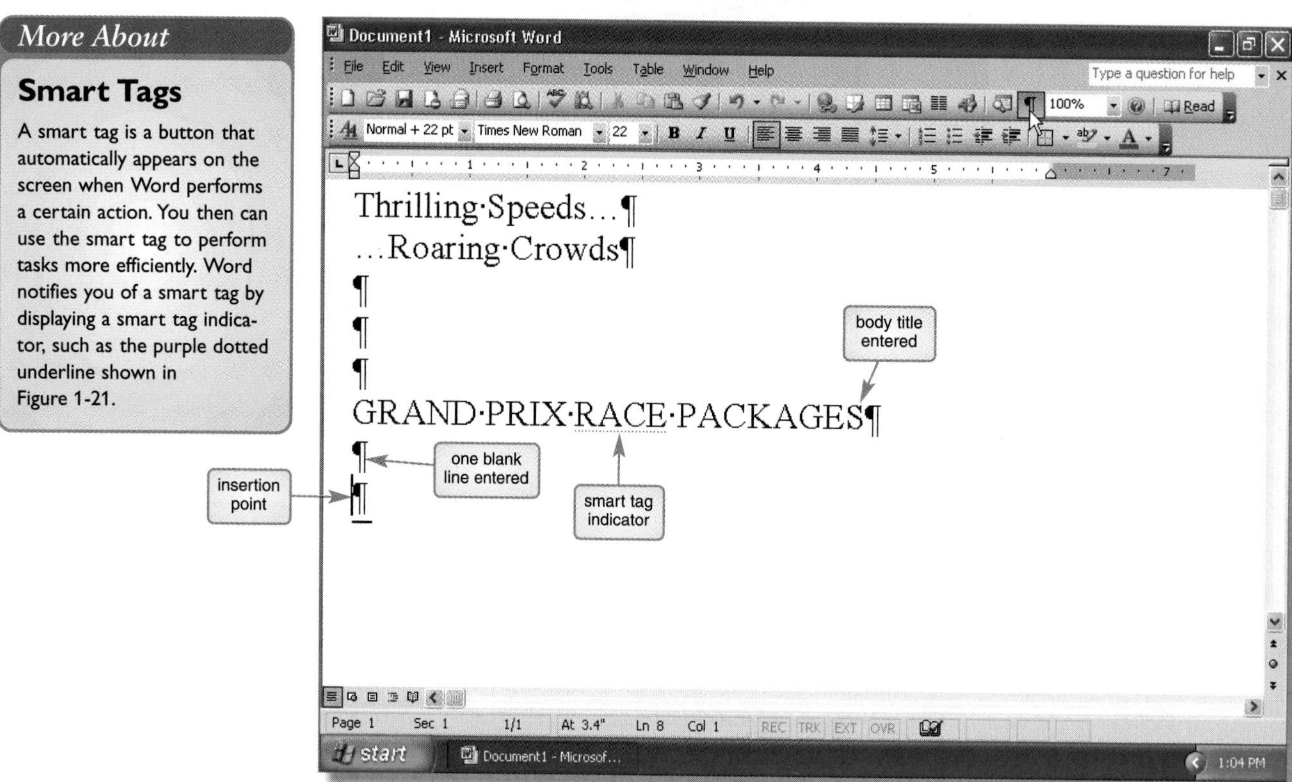

FIGURE 1-21

Using Wordwrap

Wordwrap allows you to type words in a paragraph continually without pressing the ENTER key at the end of each line. When the insertion point reaches the right margin, Word automatically positions the insertion point at the beginning of the next line. As you type, if a word extends beyond the right margin, Word also automatically positions that word on the next line with the insertion point.

As you type text in the document window, do not press the ENTER key when the insertion point reaches the right margin. Word creates a new paragraph each time you press the ENTER key. Thus, press the ENTER key only in these circumstances:

1. To insert blank lines in a document
2. To begin a new paragraph
3. To terminate a short line of text and advance to the next line
4. In response to certain Word commands

The following step illustrates wordwrap.

More About

Wordwrap

Your printer controls where wordwrap occurs for each line in your document. For this reason, it is possible that the same document could wordwrap differently if printed on different printers.

To Wordwrap Text as You Type

1

- **Type** `Four-day, three-night packages include airfare, deluxe` **and then press the SPACEBAR.**

The word, deluxe, wraps to the beginning of line 9 because it is too long to fit on line 8 (Figure 1-22). Your document may wordwrap differently depending on the type of printer you are using.

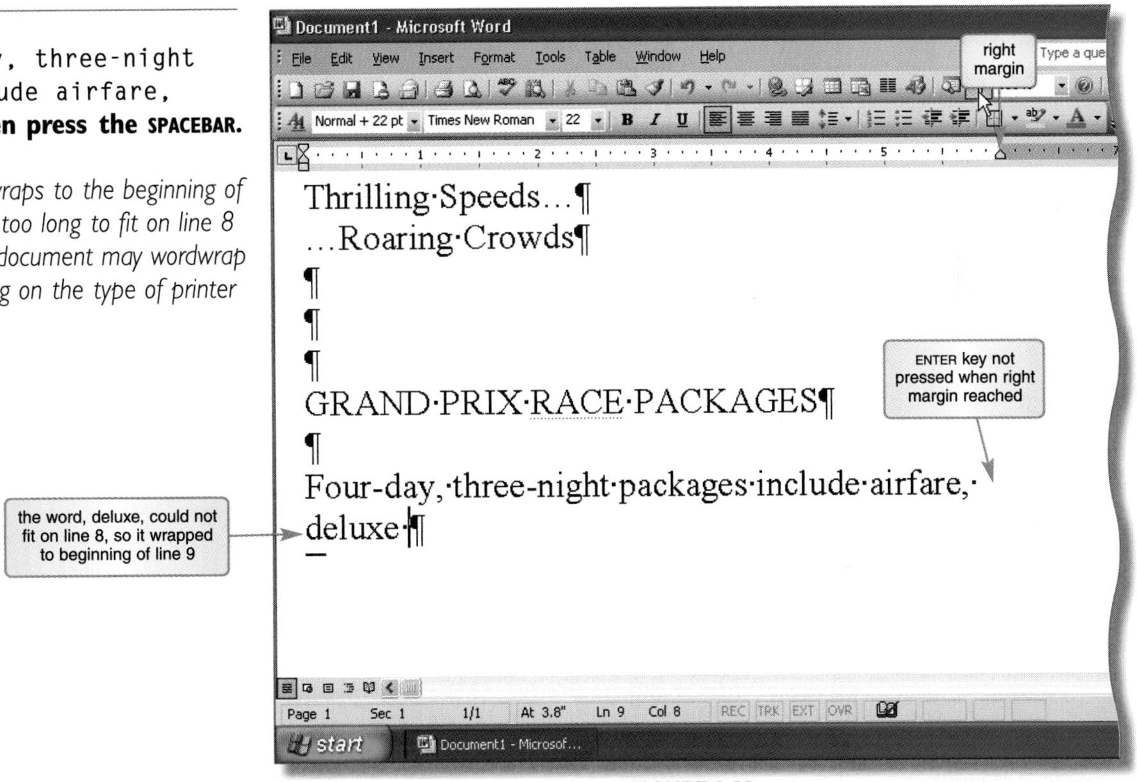

FIGURE 1-22

Other Ways

1. In Dictation mode, say "Four Hyphen day Comma three Hyphen night packages include airfare Comma deluxe Spacebar"

Entering Text that Scrolls the Document Window

As you type more lines of text than Word can display in the document window, Word **scrolls** the top portion of the document upward off the screen. Although you cannot see the text once it scrolls off the screen, it remains in the document. As previously discussed, the document window allows you to view only a portion of your document at one time (Figure 1-8 on page WD 10).

The following step shows how Word scrolls text through the document window.

To Enter Text that Scrolls the Document Window

1

- **Type** `accommodations and amenities, compact car rental, a Formula One Grand Prix program, and great reserved seats for all race events.`
- **Press the ENTER key twice.**

Word scrolls the headline off the top of the screen (Figure 1-23). Your screen may scroll differently depending on the type of monitor you are using.

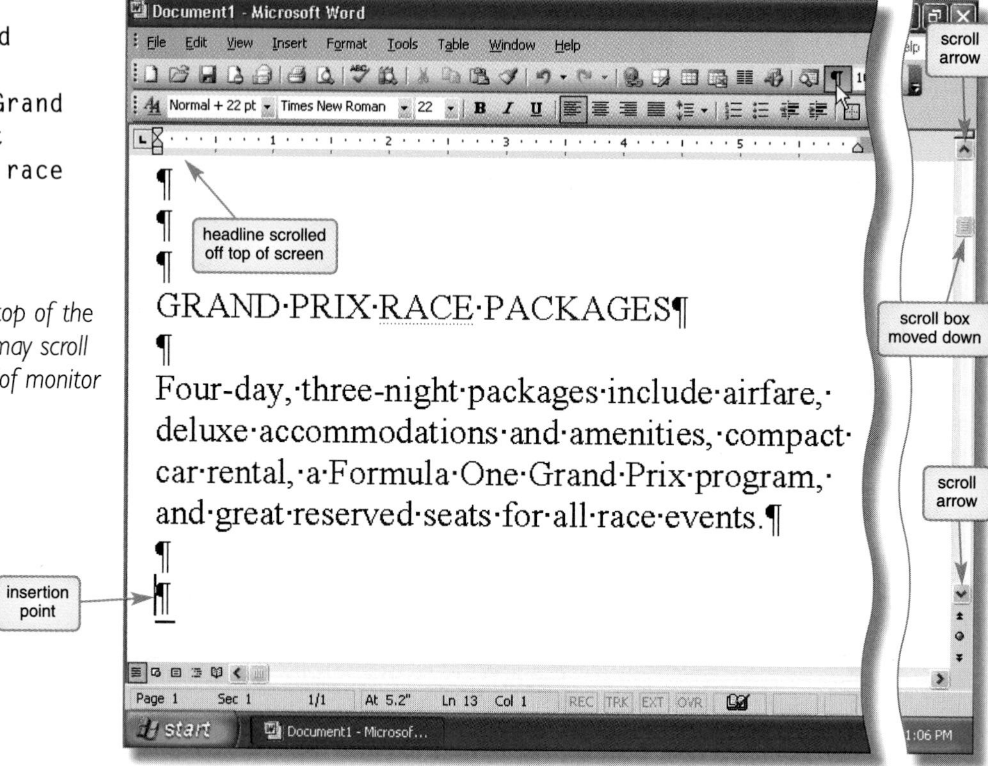

FIGURE 1-23

Other Ways

1. In Dictation mode, say "accommodations and amenities Comma compact car rental Comma a Formula One Grand Prix program Comma and great reserved seats for all race events Period, New Line, New Line"

When Word scrolls text off the top of the screen, the scroll box on the vertical scroll bar at the right edge of the document window moves downward (Figure 1-23). The scroll box indicates the current relative location of the portion of the document that is displayed in the document window. You may use either the mouse or the keyboard to scroll to a different location in a document.

With the mouse, you can use the scroll arrows or the scroll box on the scroll bar to display a different portion of the document in the document window, and then click the mouse to move the insertion point to that location. Table 1-1 explains various techniques for using the scroll bar to scroll vertically with the mouse.

More About

Healthy Computing

For more information about healthy computing, visit the Word 2003 More About Web page (scsite.com/wd2003/more) and then click Healthy Computing.

Table 1-1 Using the Scroll Bar to Scroll with the Mouse

SCROLL DIRECTION	MOUSE ACTION
Up	Drag the scroll box upward.
Down	Drag the scroll box downward.
Up one screen	Click anywhere above the scroll box on the vertical scroll bar.
Down one screen	Click anywhere below the scroll box on the vertical scroll bar.
Up one line	Click the scroll arrow at the top of the vertical scroll bar.
Down one line	Click the scroll arrow at the bottom of the vertical scroll bar.

When you use the keyboard to scroll, the insertion point automatically moves when you press the appropriate keys. Table 1-2 outlines various techniques to scroll through a document using the keyboard.

Table 1-2 Scrolling with the Keyboard

SCROLL DIRECTION	KEY(S) TO PRESS
Left one character	LEFT ARROW
Right one character	RIGHT ARROW
Left one word	CTRL+LEFT ARROW
Right one word	CTRL+RIGHT ARROW
Up one line	UP ARROW
Down one line	DOWN ARROW
To end of a line	END
To beginning of a line	HOME
Up one paragraph	CTRL+UP ARROW
Down one paragraph	CTRL+DOWN ARROW
Up one screen	PAGE UP
Down one screen	PAGE DOWN
To top of document window	ALT+CTRL+PAGE UP
To bottom of document window	ALT+CTRL+PAGE DOWN
To beginning of a document	CTRL+HOME
To end of a document	CTRL+END

Q&A

Q: How can I help prevent wrist injury while working on a computer?

A: Typical computer users frequently switch between the keyboard and the mouse during a word processing session, an action that strains the wrist. To help prevent wrist injury, minimize switching. If your fingers already are on the keyboard, use keyboard keys to scroll. If your hand already is on the mouse, use the mouse to scroll.

Checking Spelling and Grammar as You Type

As you type text in the document window, Word checks your typing for possible spelling and grammar errors. If a word you type is not in the dictionary, a red wavy underline appears below the word. Similarly, if text you type contains a possible grammar error, a green wavy underline appears below the text. In both cases, the Spelling and Grammar Status icon on the status bar shows a red X, instead of a check mark. Although you can check the entire document for spelling and grammar errors at once, you also can check these flagged errors immediately.

To verify that the check spelling as you type feature is enabled, right-click the Spelling and Grammar Status icon on the status bar and then click Options on the shortcut menu. When Word displays the Spelling & Grammar dialog box, be sure Check spelling as you type has a check mark and Hide spelling errors in this document does not have a check mark.

When a word is flagged with a red wavy underline, it is not in Word's dictionary. To display a list of suggested corrections for a flagged word, you right-click the word. A flagged word, however, is not necessarily misspelled. For example, many names, abbreviations, and specialized terms are not in Word's main dictionary. In these cases, you tell Word to ignore the flagged word. As you type, Word also detects duplicate words. For example, if your document contains the phrase, to the the store, Word places a red wavy underline below the second occurrence of the word, the.

In the example on the next page, the word, feature, has been misspelled intentionally as feture to illustrate Word's check spelling as you type. If you are doing this project on a personal computer, your announcement may contain different misspelled words, depending on the accuracy of your typing.

To Check Spelling and Grammar as You Type

1

• **Type** Race events feture **and then press the SPACEBAR.**

• **Position the mouse pointer in the flagged word (feture, in this case).**

Word flags the misspelled word, feture, by placing a red wavy underline below it (Figure 1-24). The Spelling and Grammar Status icon on the status bar now contains a red X, indicating Word has detected a possible spelling or grammar error.

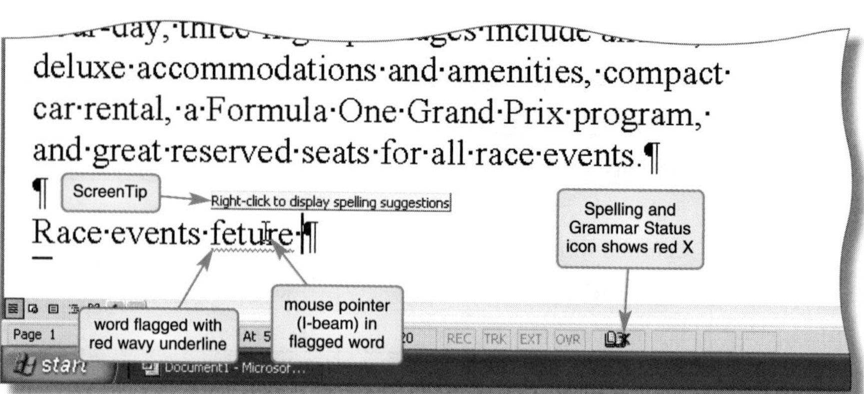

FIGURE 1-24

2

• **Right-click the flagged word, feture.**

Word displays a shortcut menu that lists suggested spelling corrections for the flagged word (Figure 1-25).

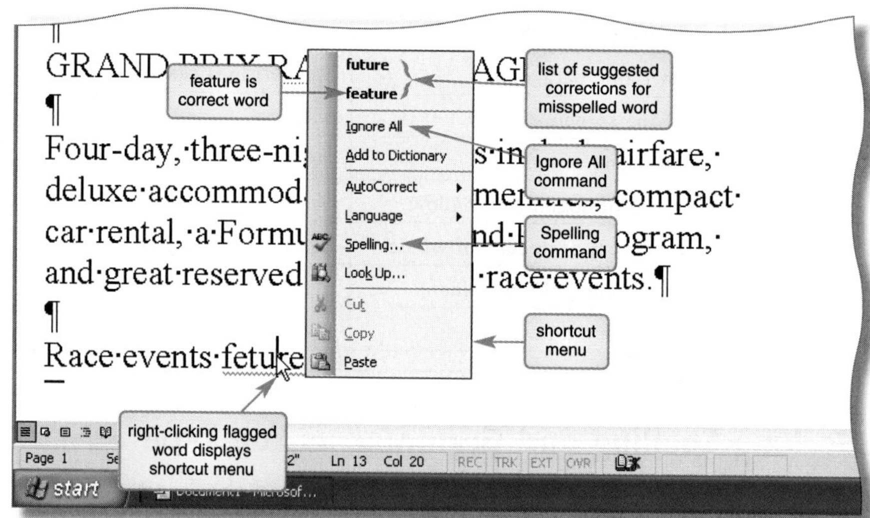

FIGURE 1-25

3

• **Click feature on the shortcut menu.**

Word replaces the misspelled word with the word selected on the shortcut menu (Figure 1-26). The Spelling and Grammar Status icon once again contains a red check mark.

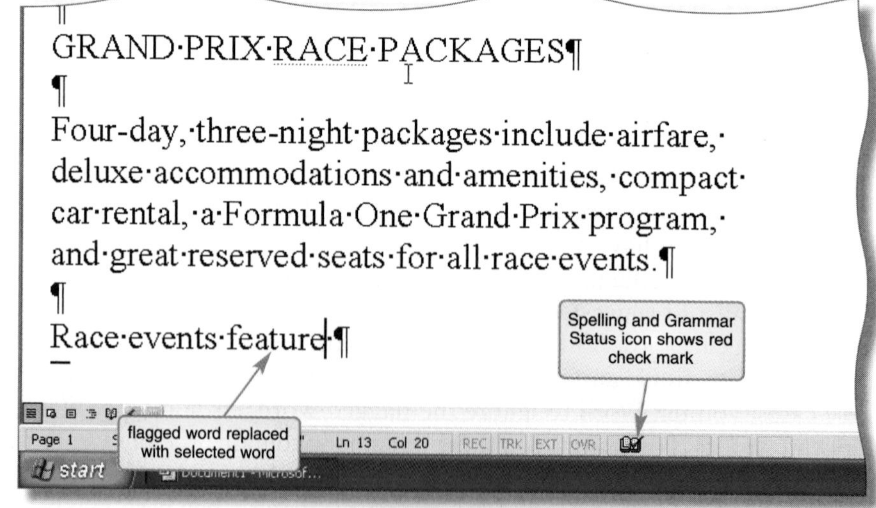

FIGURE 1-26

Other Ways

1. Double-click Spelling and Grammar Status icon on status bar, click correct word on shortcut menu
2. In Voice Command mode, say "Spelling and Grammar"

If a flagged word actually is spelled correctly and, for example, is a proper name, you can right-click it and then click Ignore All on the shortcut menu (Figure 1-25). If, when you right-click the misspelled word, your desired correction is not in the list on the shortcut menu, you can click outside the shortcut menu to close the menu and then retype the correct word, or you can click Spelling on the shortcut menu to display the Spelling dialog box. Project 2 discusses the Spelling dialog box.

If you feel the wavy underlines clutter the document window, you can hide them temporarily until you are ready to check for spelling and grammar errors. To hide spelling errors, right-click the Spelling and Grammar Status icon on the status bar and then click Hide Spelling Errors on the shortcut menu. To hide grammar errors, right-click the Spelling and Grammar Status icon on the status bar and then click Hide Grammatical Errors on the shortcut menu.

The next step is to type the remainder of text in the announcement, as described in the following steps.

More About

Correcting Spelling

As you type, Word automatically corrects some misspelled words. For example, if you type recieve, Word automatically fixes the misspelling and displays the word, receive, when you press the SPACEBAR or type a punctuation mark. To see a complete list of automatically corrected words, click Tools on the menu bar, click AutoCorrect Options on the Tools menu, click the AutoCorrect tab, and then scroll through the list of words near the bottom of the dialog box.

To Enter More Text

1. **Press the END key to move the insertion point to the end of the line.**
2. **Type** `all practice and qualifying sessions, the drivers' parade, and the gripping Formula One Grand Prix.`
3. **Press the ENTER key twice.**
4. **Type** `Call Beacon Travel at 555-2299.`

The text of the announcement is complete (Figure 1-27).

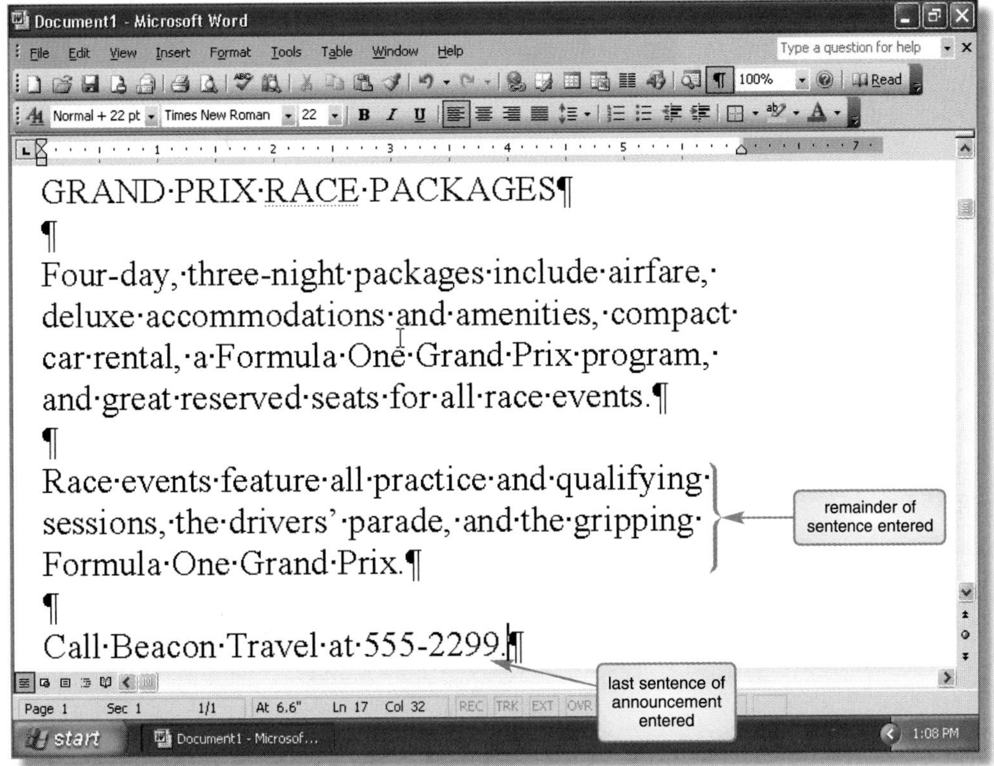
Document1 - Microsoft Word
GRAND·PRIX·RACE·PACKAGES¶
Four-day,·three-night·packages·include·airfare,· deluxe·accommodations·and·amenities,·compact· car·rental,·a·Formula·One·Grand·Prix·program,· and·great·reserved·seats·for·all·race·events.¶
Race·events·feature·all·practice·and·qualifying· sessions,·the·drivers'·parade,·and·the·gripping· Formula·One·Grand·Prix.¶
Call·Beacon·Travel·at·555-2299.¶
remainder of sentence entered
last sentence of announcement entered
Page 1 Sec 1 1/1 At 6.6" Ln 17 Col 32
start
1:08 PM

FIGURE 1-27

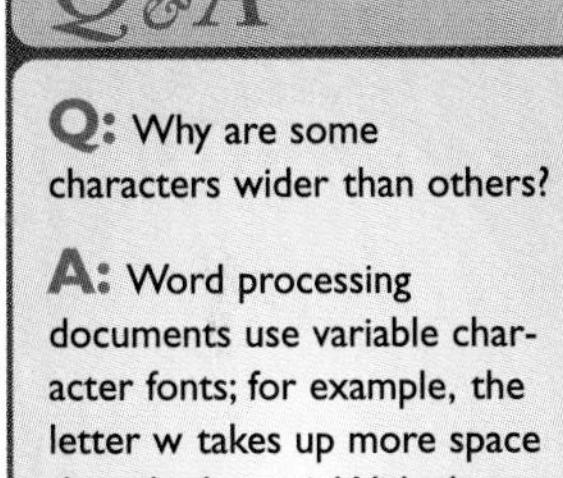
Q&A

Q: Why are some characters wider than others?

A: Word processing documents use variable character fonts; for example, the letter w takes up more space than the letter i. With these fonts, it often is difficult to determine how many times someone has pressed the SPACEBAR between sentences. Thus, the rule is to press the SPACEBAR only once after periods, colons, and other punctuation marks.

Saving a Document

As you create a document in Word, the computer stores it in memory. If the computer is turned off or if you lose electrical power, the document in memory is lost. Hence, if you plan to use the document later, you must save it on disk.

A saved document is called a **file**. A **file name** is the name assigned to a file when it is saved. This project saves the announcement with the file name, Grand Prix Announcement. Depending on your Windows settings, the file type .doc may display immediately after the file name. The file type **.doc** indicates the file is a Word document.

The following steps illustrate how to save a document on a floppy disk in drive A using the Save button on the Standard toolbar.

To Save a New Document

1

• **With a formatted floppy disk in drive A, click the Save button on the Standard toolbar.**

Word displays the Save As dialog box (Figure 1-28). The first line from the document (Thrilling Speeds) is selected in the File name text box as the default file name. You can change this selected file name by immediately typing the new name.

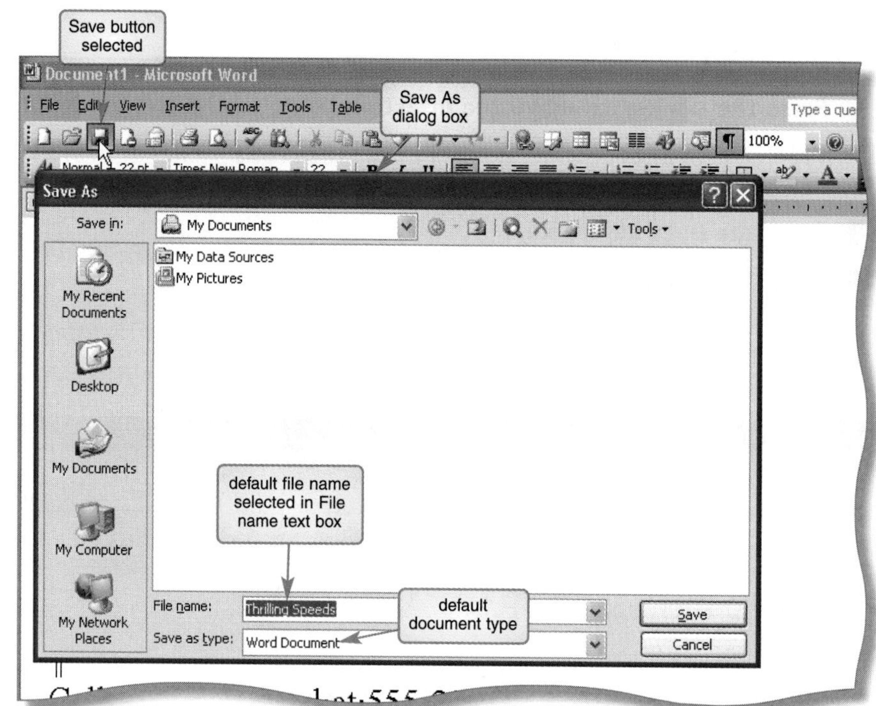

FIGURE 1-28

2

• **Type** `Grand Prix Announcement` **in the File name text box. Do not press the ENTER key after typing the file name.**

The file name, Grand Prix Announcement, replaces the text, Thrilling Speeds, in the File name text box (Figure 1-29).

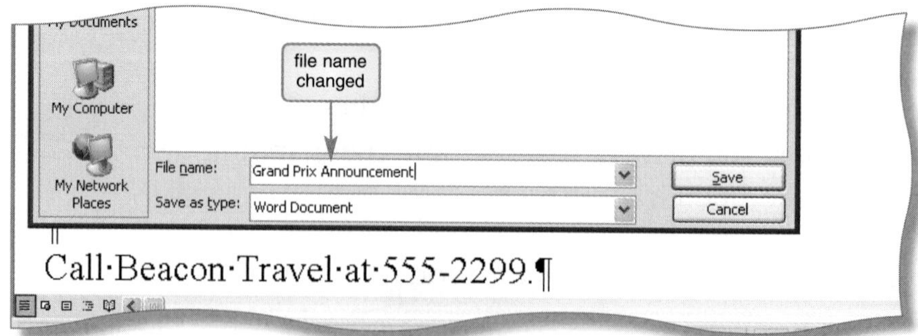

FIGURE 1-29

3

• **Click the Save in box arrow.**

Word displays a list of the available drives and folders in which you can save the document (Figure 1-30). A ***folder*** *is a specific location on a disk. Your list may differ depending on your computer's configuration.*

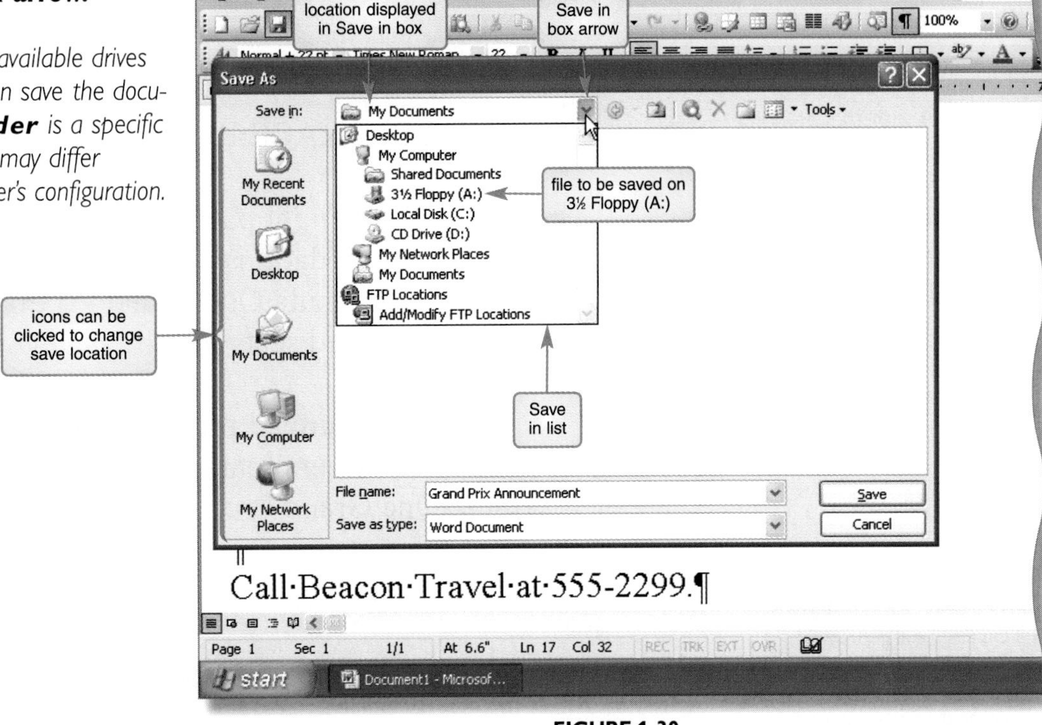

FIGURE 1-30

4

• **Click 3½ Floppy (A:) in the Save in list.**

Drive A becomes the new save location (Figure 1-31). The Save As dialog box now shows names of existing files stored on the floppy disk in drive A. In Figure 1-31, the list is empty because no Word files currently are stored on the floppy disk in drive A.

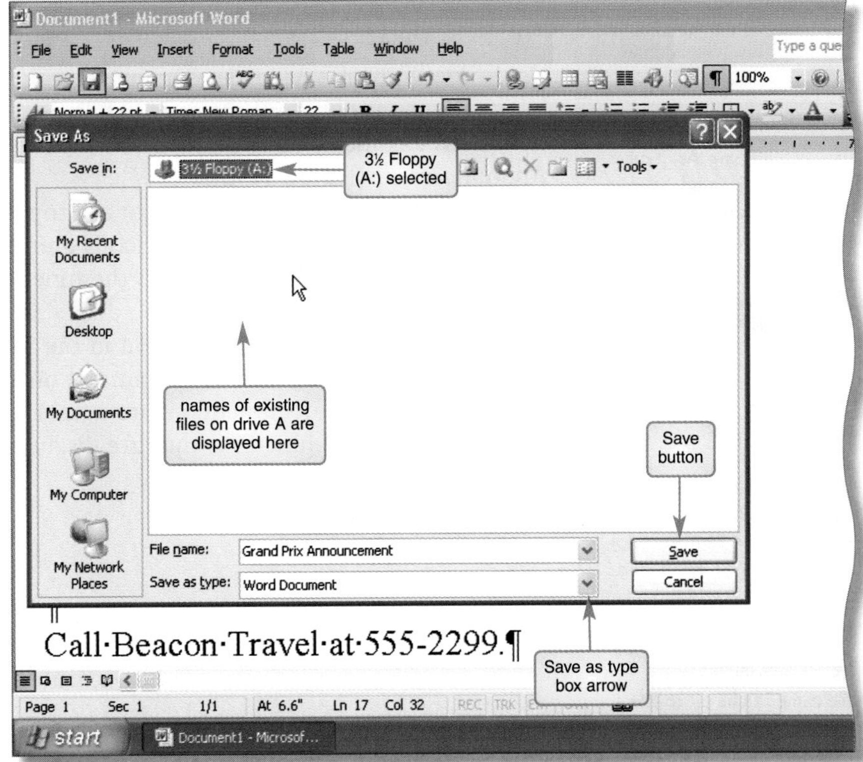

FIGURE 1-31

5

- **Click the Save button in the Save As dialog box.**

Word saves the document on the floppy disk in drive A with the file name, Grand Prix Announcement (Figure 1-32). Although the announcement is saved on a floppy disk, it also remains in main memory and on the screen.

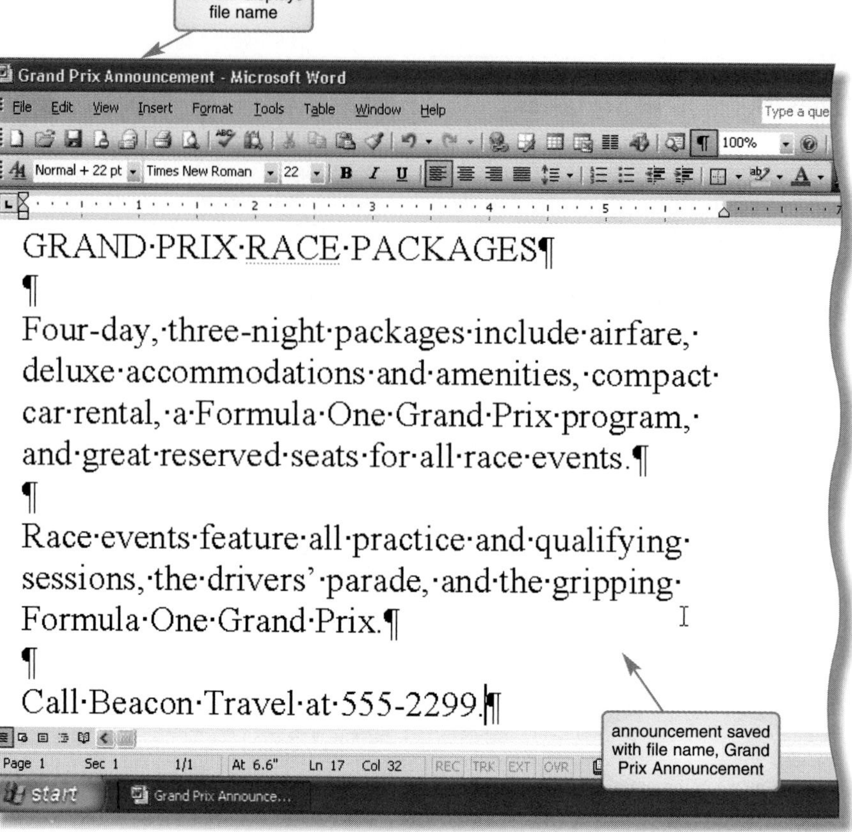
title bar displays file name
Grand Prix Announcement - Microsoft Word
GRAND·PRIX·RACE·PACKAGES¶
¶
Four-day,·three-night·packages·include·airfare,·deluxe·accommodations·and·amenities,·compact·car·rental,·a·Formula·One·Grand·Prix·program,·and·great·reserved·seats·for·all·race·events.¶
¶
Race·events·feature·all·practice·and·qualifying·sessions,·the·drivers'·parade,·and·the·gripping·Formula·One·Grand·Prix.¶
¶
Call·Beacon·Travel·at·555-2299.¶
announcement saved with file name, Grand Prix Announcement

FIGURE 1-32

Other Ways

1. On File menu click Save As, type file name, select drive or folder using either the Save in list or the My Computer icon, click Save button in dialog box
2. Press CTRL+S, type file name, select location in Save in list, click Save button in dialog box
3. In Voice Command mode, say "File, Save As, [type file name], Save In, [select folder], Save"

While Word is saving the document, it displays a message on the status bar indicating the progress of the save. After the save operation is complete, Word changes the name of the document on the title bar from Document1 to Grand Prix Announcement (Figure 1-32).

You can use the seven buttons at the top of the Save As dialog box (Figure 1-30 on the previous page) and the five icons along the left edge to change the save location and other tasks. Table 1-3 lists the function of the buttons and icons in the Save As dialog box.

When you click the Tools button in the Save As dialog box, Word displays the Tools menu. The Save Options command on the Tools menu allows you to save a backup copy of the document, create a password to limit access to the document, and carry out other functions that are discussed later.

More About

Saving

Word allows you to save a document in more than 10 different file formats. Choose the file format by clicking the Save as type box arrow at the bottom of the Save As dialog box (Figure 1-31 on the previous page). Word Document is the default file format. When you save a document, use meaningful file names. A file name can be up to 255 characters, including spaces. The only invalid characters are the backslash (\), slash (/), colon (:), asterisk (*), question mark (?), quotation mark ("), less than symbol (<), greater than symbol (>), and vertical bar (|).

Table 1-3 Save As Dialog Box Buttons and Icons

BUTTON OR ICON	BUTTON OR ICON NAME	FUNCTION
	Default File Location	Displays contents of default file location
	Up One Level	Displays contents of folder one level up from current folder
	Search the Web	Starts Web browser and displays search engine
	Delete	Deletes selected file or folder
	Create New Folder	Creates new folder
	Views	Changes view of files and folders
Tools	Tools	Lists commands to print or modify file names and folders
My Recent Documents	My Recent Documents	Displays contents of My Recent Documents in Save in list (you cannot save to this location)
Desktop	Desktop	Displays contents of Windows desktop folder in Save in list to save quickly to the Windows desktop
My Documents	My Documents	Displays contents of My Documents in Save in list to save quickly to the My Documents folder
My Computer	My Computer	Displays contents of My Computer in Save in list to save quickly to another drive on the computer
My Network Places	My Network Places	Displays contents of My Network Places in Save in list to save quickly to My Network Places

Formatting Paragraphs and Characters in a Document

The text for Project 1 now is complete. The next step is to format the paragraphs and characters in the announcement.

Paragraphs encompass the text up to and including a paragraph mark (¶). **Paragraph formatting** is the process of changing the appearance of a paragraph. For example, you can center or indent a paragraph.

Characters include letters, numbers, punctuation marks, and symbols. **Character formatting** is the process of changing the way characters appear on the screen and in print. You use character formatting to emphasize certain words and improve readability of a document. For example, you can italicize or underline characters.

In many cases, you apply both paragraph and character formatting to the same text. For example, you may center a paragraph (paragraph formatting) and bold the characters in a paragraph (character formatting).

With Word, you can format paragraphs and characters before you type, or you can apply new formats after you type. Earlier, this project showed how to change the font size (character formatting) before you typed any text. This section shows how to format existing text.

Q: What is the difference between character formatting and paragraph formatting?

A: Character formatting includes changing the font, font style, font size; adding an underline, color, strikethrough, shadow, or outline; embossing; engraving; making a superscript or subscript; and changing the case of the letters. Paragraph formatting includes alignment; indentation; and spacing above, below, and in between lines.

Figure 1-33a shows the announcement before formatting its paragraphs and characters. Figure 1-33b shows the announcement after formatting. As you can see from the two figures, a document that is formatted is easier to read and looks more professional.

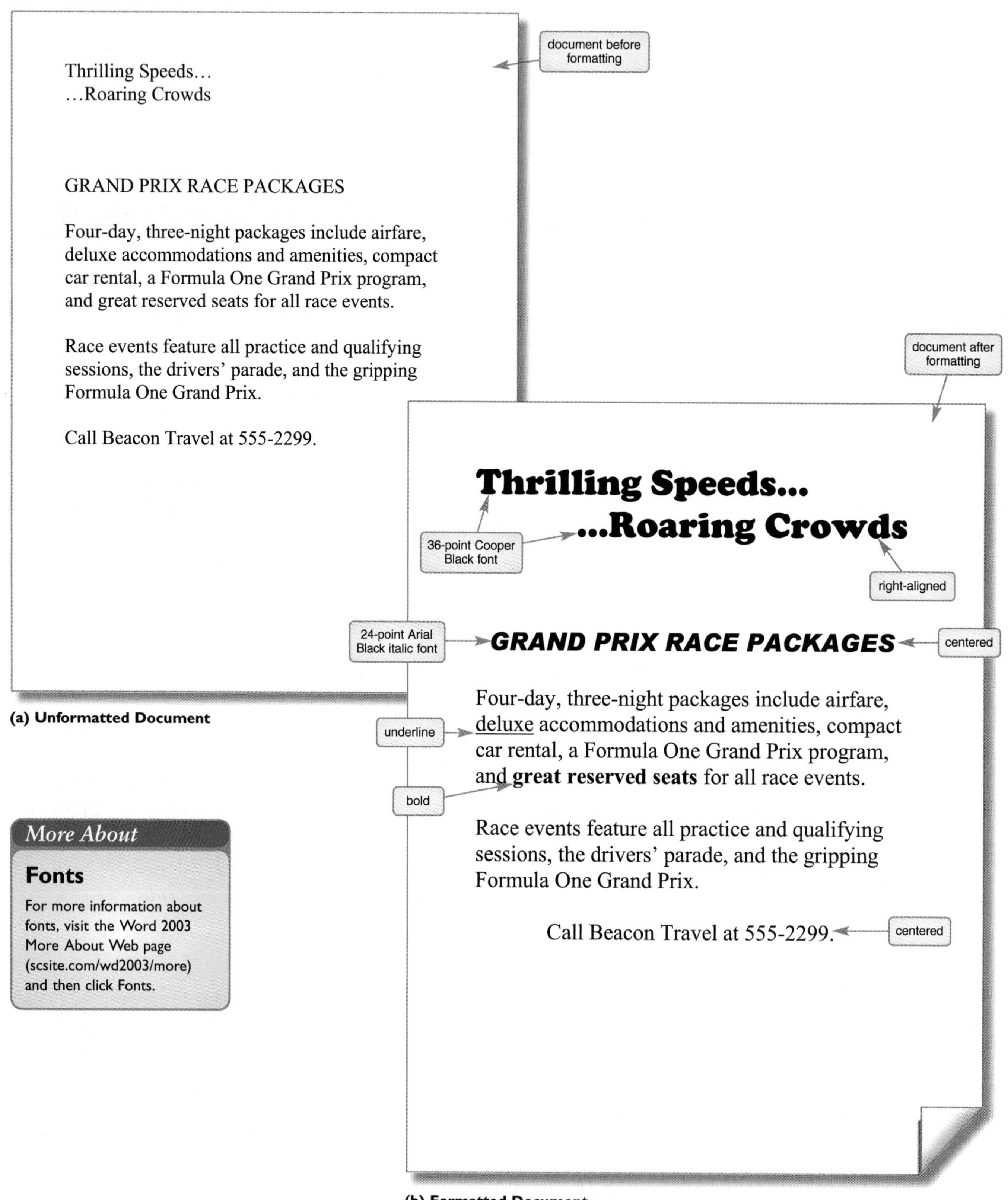

document before formatting
Thrilling Speeds...
...Roaring Crowds
GRAND PRIX RACE PACKAGES
Four-day, three-night packages include airfare, deluxe accommodations and amenities, compact car rental, a Formula One Grand Prix program, and great reserved seats for all race events.
Race events feature all practice and qualifying sessions, the drivers' parade, and the gripping Formula One Grand Prix.
Call Beacon Travel at 555-2299.
document after formatting
Thrilling Speeds...
...Roaring Crowds
36-point Cooper Black font
right-aligned
24-point Arial Black italic font
GRAND PRIX RACE PACKAGES
centered
Four-day, three-night packages include airfare, deluxe accommodations and amenities, compact car rental, a Formula One Grand Prix program, and great reserved seats for all race events.
underline
bold
Race events feature all practice and qualifying sessions, the drivers' parade, and the gripping Formula One Grand Prix.
Call Beacon Travel at 555-2299.
centered

(a) Unformatted Document

(b) Formatted Document

FIGURE 1-33

More About

Fonts

For more information about fonts, visit the Word 2003 More About Web page (scsite.com/wd2003/more) and then click Fonts.

Selecting and Formatting Paragraphs and Characters

To format a single paragraph, move the insertion point in the paragraph and then format the paragraph. That is, you do not need to select a single paragraph to format it. To format *multiple* paragraphs, however, you first must select the paragraphs you want to format and then format them. In the same manner, to format a single word, position the insertion point in the word and then format the word. To format multiple characters or words, however, you first must select the characters or words to be formatted and then format the selection.

Selected text is highlighted text. If your screen normally displays dark letters on a light background, then selected text displays light letters on a dark background.

Selecting Multiple Paragraphs

The first formatting step in this project is to change the font size of the characters in the headline. The headline consists of two separate lines, each ending with a paragraph mark. As previously discussed, Word creates a new paragraph each time you press the ENTER key. Thus, the headline actually is two separate paragraphs.

To change the font size of the characters in the headline, you first must **select** (highlight) both paragraphs in the headline, as shown in the following steps.

To Select Multiple Paragraphs

1

- **Press CTRL+HOME; that is, press and hold down the CTRL key, press the HOME key, and then release both keys.**
- **Move the mouse pointer to the left of the first paragraph to be selected until the mouse pointer changes to a right-pointing block arrow.**

CTRL+HOME *is a keyboard shortcut that positions the insertion point at the top of the document. The mouse pointer changes to a right-pointing block arrow when positioned to the left of a paragraph (Figure 1-34).*

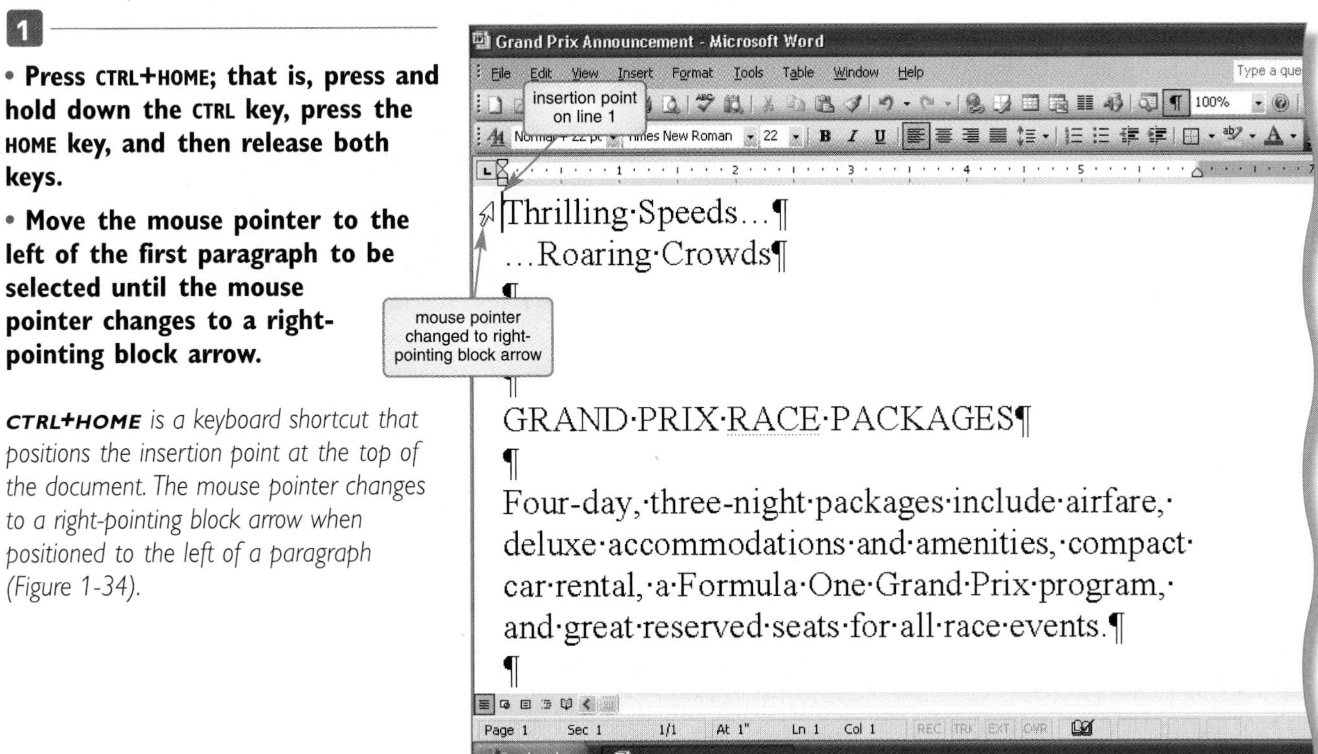
Grand Prix Announcement - Microsoft Word
insertion point on line 1
mouse pointer changed to right-pointing block arrow
Thrilling·Speeds…¶
…Roaring·Crowds¶
GRAND·PRIX·RACE·PACKAGES¶
Four-day,·three-night·packages·include·airfare,·deluxe·accommodations·and·amenities,·compact·car·rental,·a·Formula·One·Grand·Prix·program,·and·great·reserved·seats·for·all·race·events.¶

FIGURE 1-34

2

• **Drag downward until both paragraphs are selected.**

Word selects (highlights) both of the paragraphs (Figure 1-35). Dragging is the process of holding down the mouse button while moving the mouse and then releasing the mouse button.

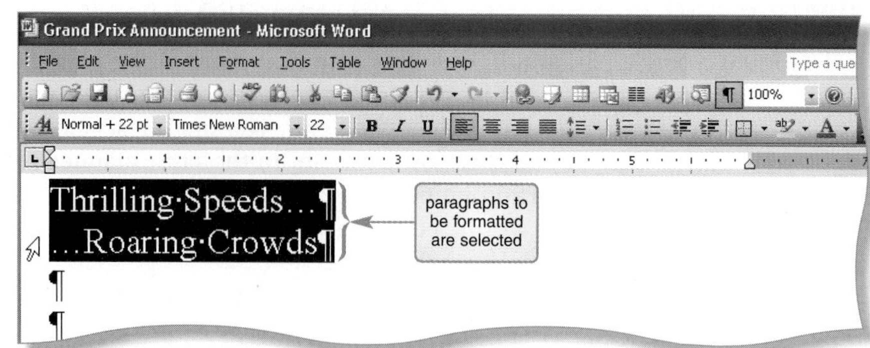
Grand Prix Announcement - Microsoft Word
Thrilling·Speeds...¶
...Roaring·Crowds¶
paragraphs to be formatted are selected

FIGURE 1-35

Other Ways

1. With insertion point at beginning of first paragraph, press CTRL+SHIFT+DOWN ARROW
2. In Voice Command mode, say "Select Paragraph"

Changing the Font Size of Text

The next step is to increase the font size of the characters in the selected headline. Recall that the font size specifies the size of the characters. Earlier, this project showed how to change the font size to 22 for characters typed in the entire announcement. To give the headline more impact, it has a font size larger than the body copy. The following steps show how to increase the font size of the headline from 22 to 36 point.

To Change the Font Size of Text

1

• **With the text selected, click the Font Size box arrow on the Formatting toolbar.**

Word displays a list of available font sizes (Figure 1-36). Available font sizes vary depending on the current font and the printer driver.

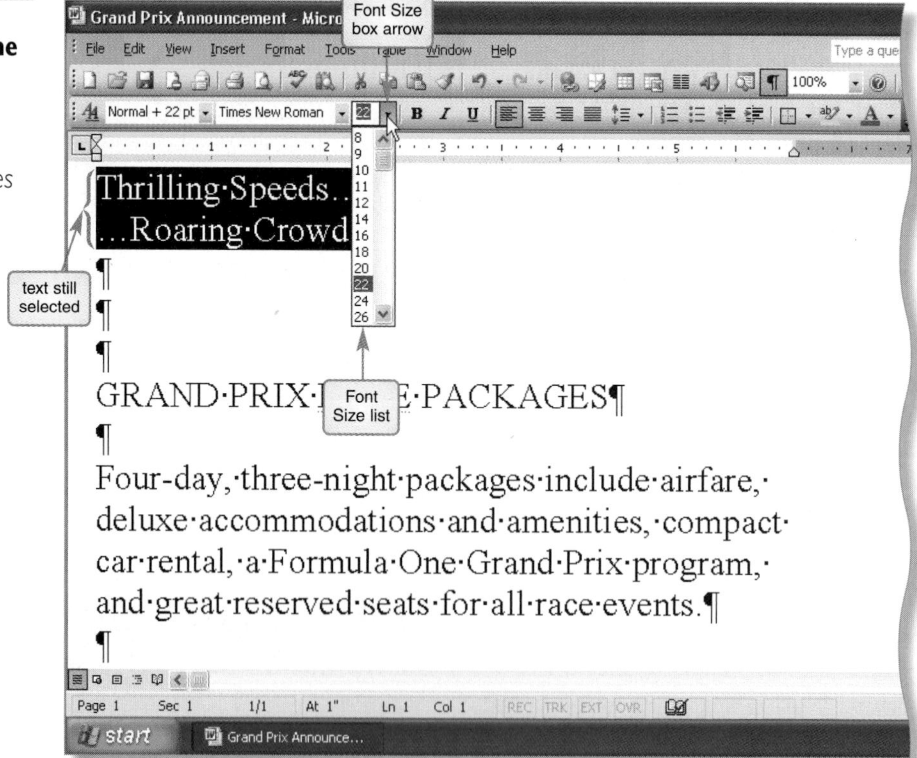
Font Size box arrow
Thrilling·Speeds..
...Roaring·Crowd
text still selected
Font Size list
GRAND·PRIX·
E·PACKAGES¶
Four-day,·three-night·packages·include·airfare,·
deluxe·accommodations·and·amenities,·compact·
car·rental,·a·Formula·One·Grand·Prix·program,·
and·great·reserved·seats·for·all·race·events.¶

FIGURE 1-36

2

- **Click the down scroll arrow on the Font Size scroll bar until 36 appears in the list (Figure 1-37).**

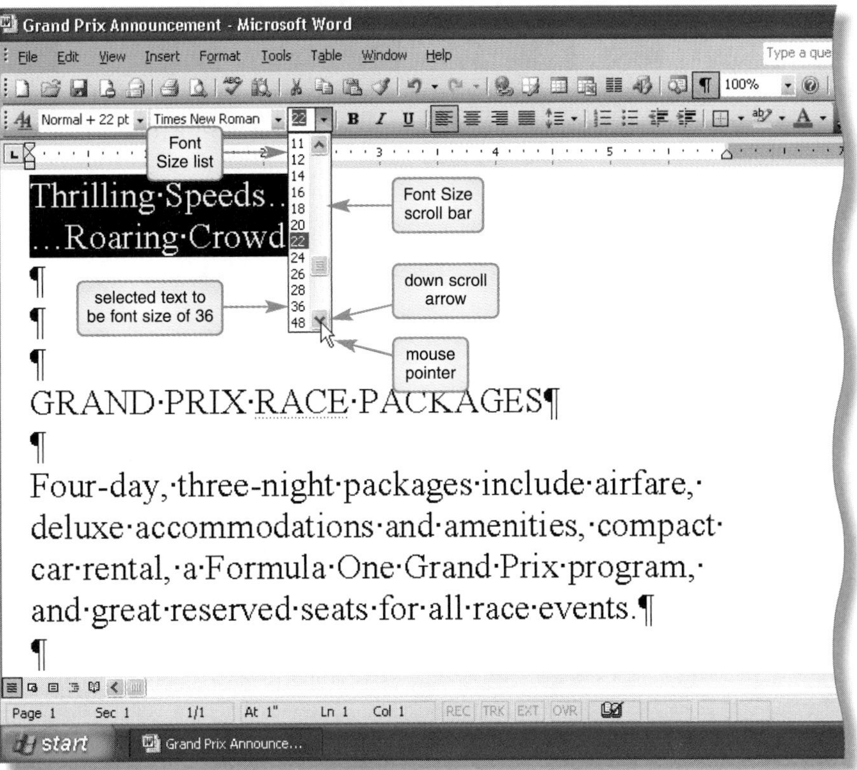
Grand Prix Announcement - Microsoft Word
Font Size list
Font Size scroll bar
selected text to be font size of 36
down scroll arrow
mouse pointer
Thrilling·Speeds...
...Roaring·Crowd
GRAND·PRIX·RACE·PACKAGES¶
Four-day,·three-night·packages·include·airfare,·deluxe·accommodations·and·amenities,·compact·car·rental,·a·Formula·One·Grand·Prix·program,·and·great·reserved·seats·for·all·race·events.¶

FIGURE 1-37

3

- **Click 36 in the Font Size list.**

Word increases the font size of the headline to 36 (Figure 1-38). The Font Size box on the Formatting toolbar displays 36, indicating the selected text has a font size of 36. Notice that when the mouse pointer is positioned in selected text, its shape is a left-pointing block arrow.

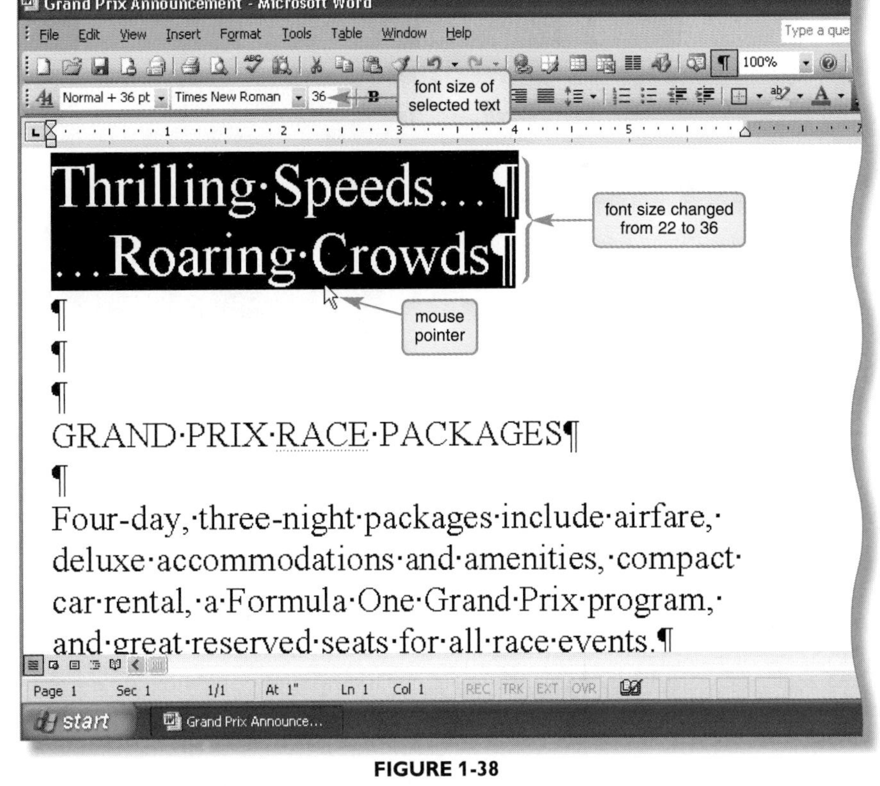
Grand Prix Announcement - Microsoft Word
font size of selected text
font size changed from 22 to 36
mouse pointer
Thrilling·Speeds...¶
...Roaring·Crowds¶
GRAND·PRIX·RACE·PACKAGES¶
Four-day,·three-night·packages·include·airfare,·deluxe·accommodations·and·amenities,·compact·car·rental,·a·Formula·One·Grand·Prix·program,·and·great·reserved·seats·for·all·race·events.¶

FIGURE 1-38

Other Ways

1. On Format menu click Font, click Font tab, select desired font size in Size list, click OK button
2. Right-click selected text, click Font on shortcut menu, click Font tab, select desired font size in Size list, click OK button
3. Press CTRL+SHIFT+P, type desired font size, press ENTER
4. In Voice Command mode, say "Font Size, [select font size]"

Changing the Font of Text

As mentioned earlier in this project, the default font in Word is Times New Roman. Word, however, provides many other fonts to add variety to your documents. The following steps show how to change the font of the headline in the announcement from Times New Roman to Cooper Black.

To Change the Font of Text

1

- **With the text selected, click the Font box arrow on the Formatting toolbar and then scroll through the Font list until Cooper Black (or a similar font) is displayed.**

Word displays a list of available fonts (Figure 1-39). Your list of available fonts may differ, depending on the type of printer you are using.

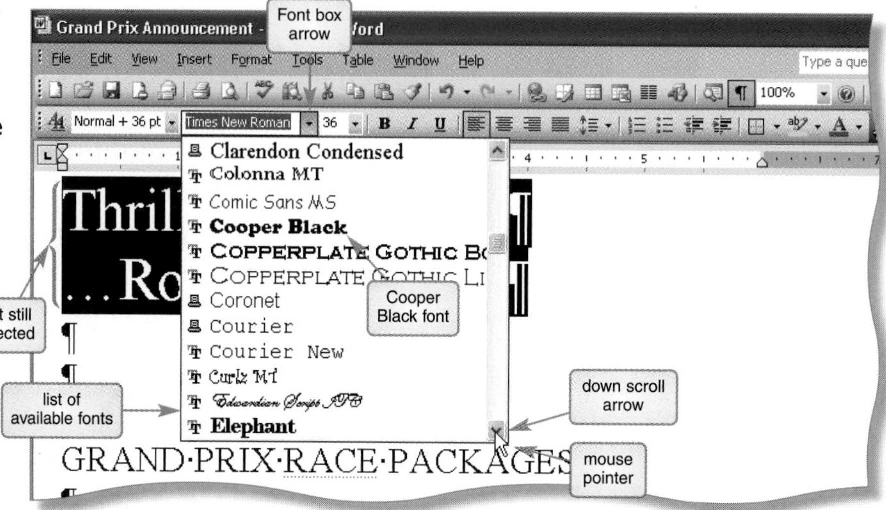

FIGURE 1-39

2

- **Click Cooper Black (or a similar font).**

Word changes the font of the selected text to Cooper Black (Figure 1-40).

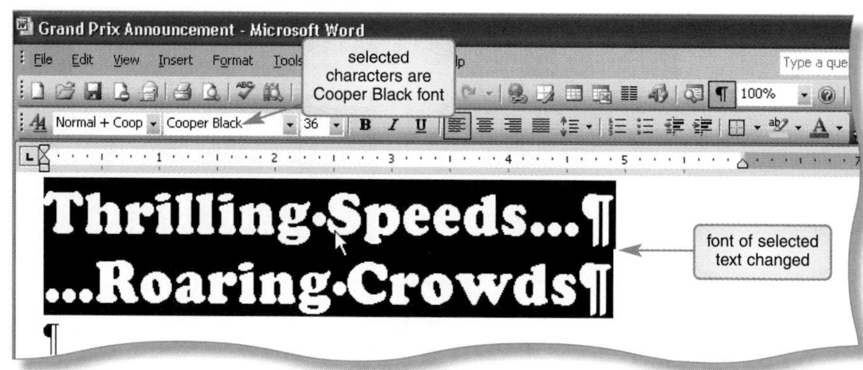

FIGURE 1-40

Other Ways

1. On Format menu click Font, click Font tab, click font name in Font list, click OK button
2. Right-click selected text, click Font on shortcut menu, click Font tab, click font name in Font list, click OK button
3. Press CTRL+SHIFT+F, press DOWN ARROW to font name, press ENTER
4. In Voice Command mode, say "Font, [select font name]"

Right-Align a Paragraph

The default alignment for paragraphs is **left-aligned**, that is, flush at the left margin of the document with uneven right edges. In Figure 1-41, the Align Left button is selected to indicate the paragraph containing the insertion point is left-aligned.

The second line of the headline, however, is to be **right-aligned**, that is, flush at the right margin of the document with uneven left edges. Recall that the second line of the headline is a paragraph, and paragraph formatting does not require you to select the paragraph prior to formatting. Just position the insertion point in the paragraph to be formatted and then format it accordingly.

The following steps show how to right-align the second line of the headline.

To Right-Align a Paragraph

1

- **Click somewhere in the paragraph to be right-aligned.**

Word positions the insertion point at the location you clicked (Figure 1-41).

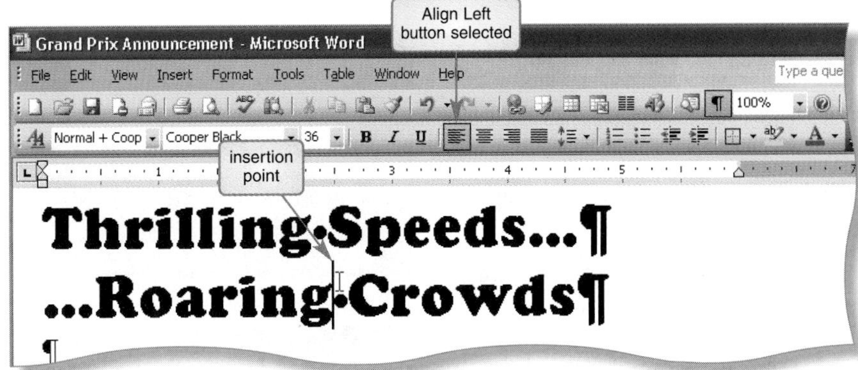

FIGURE 1-41

2

- **Click the Align Right button on the Formatting toolbar.**

The second line of the headline now is right-aligned (Figure 1-42). Notice that you did not have to select the paragraph before right-aligning it. Formatting a single paragraph requires only that the insertion point be positioned somewhere in the paragraph.

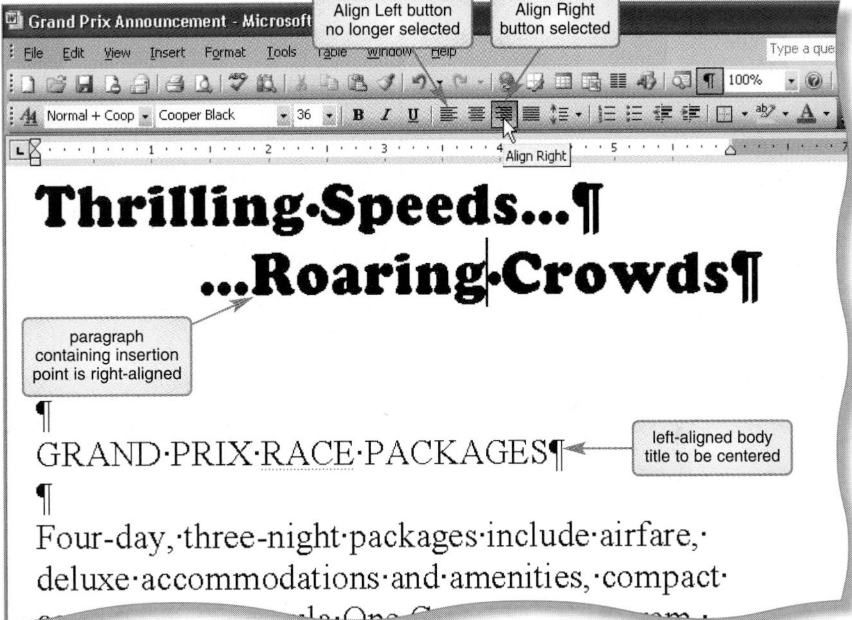

FIGURE 1-42

When a paragraph is right-aligned, the Align Right button on the Formatting toolbar is selected. If, for some reason, you wanted to return the paragraph to left-aligned, you would click the Align Left button on the Formatting toolbar.

Other Ways

1. On Format menu click Paragraph, click Indents and Spacing tab, click Alignment box arrow, click Right, click OK button
2. Right-click paragraph, click Paragraph on shortcut menu, click Indents and Spacing tab, click Alignment box arrow, click Right, click OK button
3. Press CTRL+R
4. In Voice Command mode, say "Align Right"

Center a Paragraph

The body title currently is left-aligned (Figure 1-42 on the previous page). The following step shows how to **center** the paragraph, that is, position its text horizontally between the left and right margins on the page.

To Center a Paragraph

1

- **Click somewhere in the paragraph to be centered.**
- **Click the Center button on the Formatting toolbar.**

Word centers the body title between the left and right margins (Figure 1-43). The Center button on the Formatting toolbar is selected, which indicates the paragraph containing the insertion point is centered.

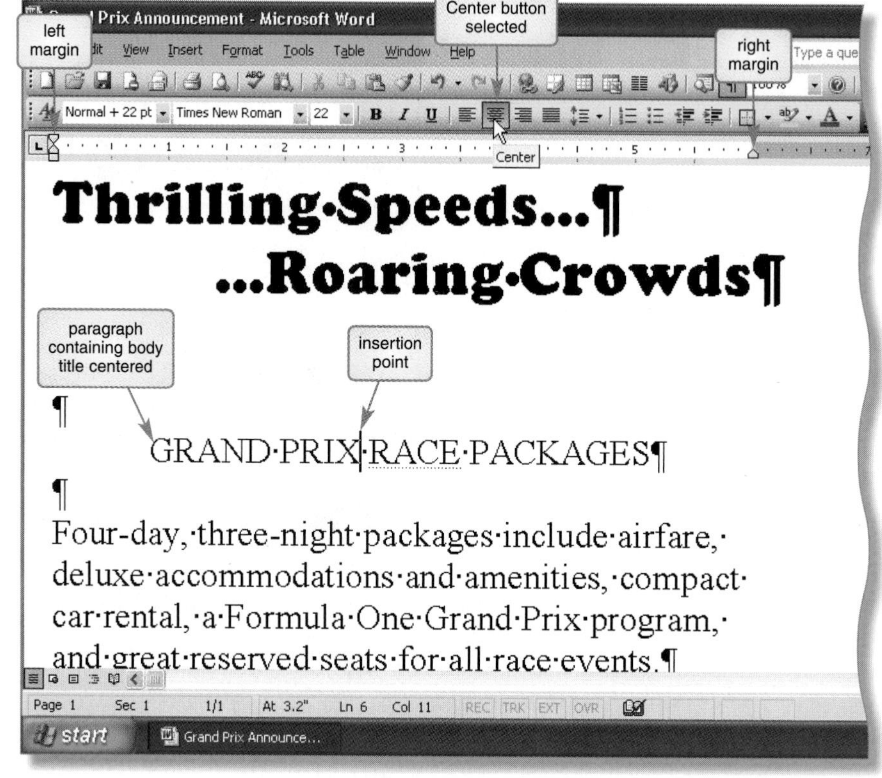
Center button selected
left margin
right margin
Center
Thrilling·Speeds...¶
...Roaring·Crowds¶
paragraph containing body title centered
insertion point
GRAND·PRIX·RACE·PACKAGES¶
Four-day,·three-night·packages·include·airfare,·
deluxe·accommodations·and·amenities,·compact·
car·rental,·a·Formula·One·Grand·Prix·program,·
and·great·reserved·seats·for·all·race·events.¶

FIGURE 1-43

Other Ways

1. On Format menu click Paragraph, click Indents and Spacing tab, click Alignment box arrow, click Centered, click OK button
2. Right-click paragraph, click Paragraph on shortcut menu, click Indents and Spacing tab, click Alignment box arrow, click Centered, click OK button
3. Press CTRL+E
4. In Voice Command mode, say "Center"

When a paragraph is centered, the Center button on the Formatting toolbar is selected. If, for some reason, you wanted to return the paragraph to left-aligned, you would click the Align Left button on the Formatting toolbar.

More About

Centering

The Center button on the Formatting toolbar centers text horizontally between the left and right margins. You also can center text vertically between the top and bottom margins. To do this, click File on the menu bar, click Page Setup, click the Layout tab, click the Vertical alignment box arrow, click Center in the list, and then click the OK button.

Undoing, Redoing, and Repeating Commands or Actions

Word provides an Undo button on the Standard toolbar that you can use to cancel your recent command(s) or action(s). For example, if you format text incorrectly, you can undo the format and try it again. If, after you undo an action, you decide you did not want to perform the undo, you can use the Redo button to redo the undo. Word prevents you from undoing or redoing some actions, such as saving or printing a document.

The following steps show how to undo the center format to the body title using the Undo button and then re-center it using the Redo button.

To Undo and Redo an Action

• **Click the Undo button on the Standard toolbar.**

Word returns the body title to its formatting before you issued the center command (Figure 1-44). That is, Word left-aligns the body title.

2

• **Click the Redo button on the Standard toolbar.**

Word reapplies the center format to the body title (shown in Figure 1-43).

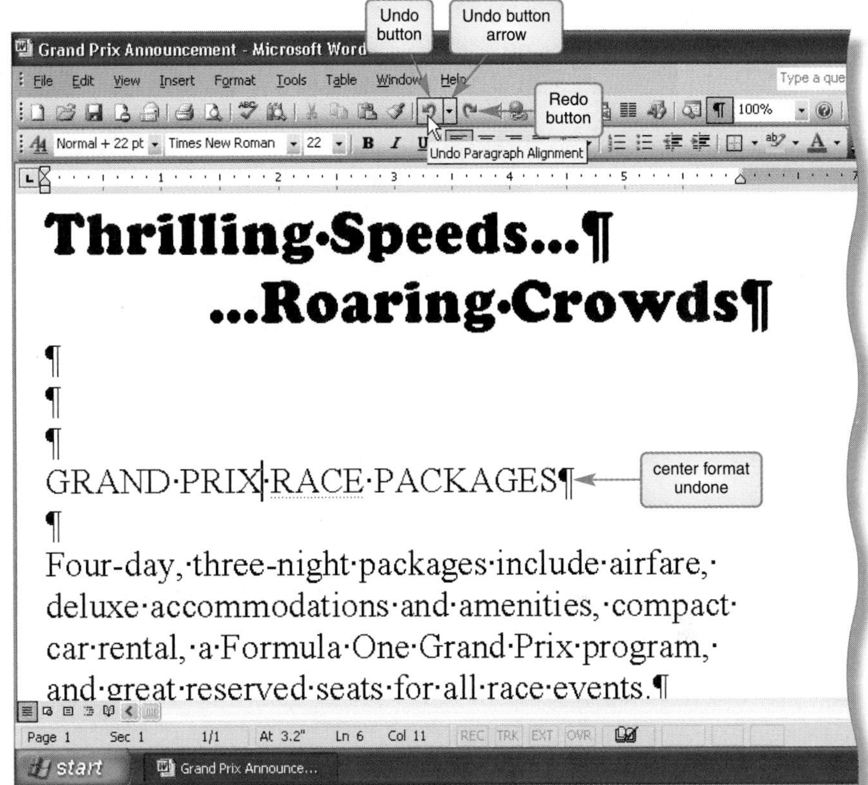
Undo button
Undo button arrow
Redo button
Undo Paragraph Alignment
center format undone
Thrilling·Speeds...¶
...Roaring·Crowds¶
GRAND·PRIX·RACE·PACKAGES¶
Four-day,·three-night·packages·include·airfare,·deluxe·accommodations·and·amenities,·compact·car·rental,·a·Formula·One·Grand·Prix·program,·and·great·reserved·seats·for·all·race·events.¶

FIGURE 1-44

Other Ways

1. On Edit menu click Undo
2. Press CTRL+Z
3. In Voice Command mode, say "Undo"

You also can cancel a series of prior actions by clicking the Undo button arrow on the Standard toolbar (Figure 1-44) to display the list of undo actions and then dragging through the actions you wish to undo.

Whereas the Undo command cancels an action you did not want to perform, Word also provides a **Repeat command** on the Edit menu, which duplicates your last command so you can perform it again. For example, if you centered a paragraph and wish to format another paragraph the exact same way, you could click in the second paragraph to format, click Edit on the menu bar, and then click Repeat Paragraph Alignment. The text listed after Repeat varies, depending on your most recent action. If the action cannot be repeated, Word displays the text, Can't Repeat, on the Edit menu.

Selecting a Line and Formatting It

The characters in the body title, GRAND PRIX RACE PACKAGES, are to be a different font, larger font size, and italicized. To make these changes, you must select the line of text containing the body title, as shown in the following step.

To Select a Line

1

- **Move the mouse pointer to the left of the line to be selected (in this case, GRAND PRIX RACE PACKAGES) until it changes to a right-pointing block arrow and then click.**

Word selects the entire line to the right of the mouse pointer (Figure 1-45).

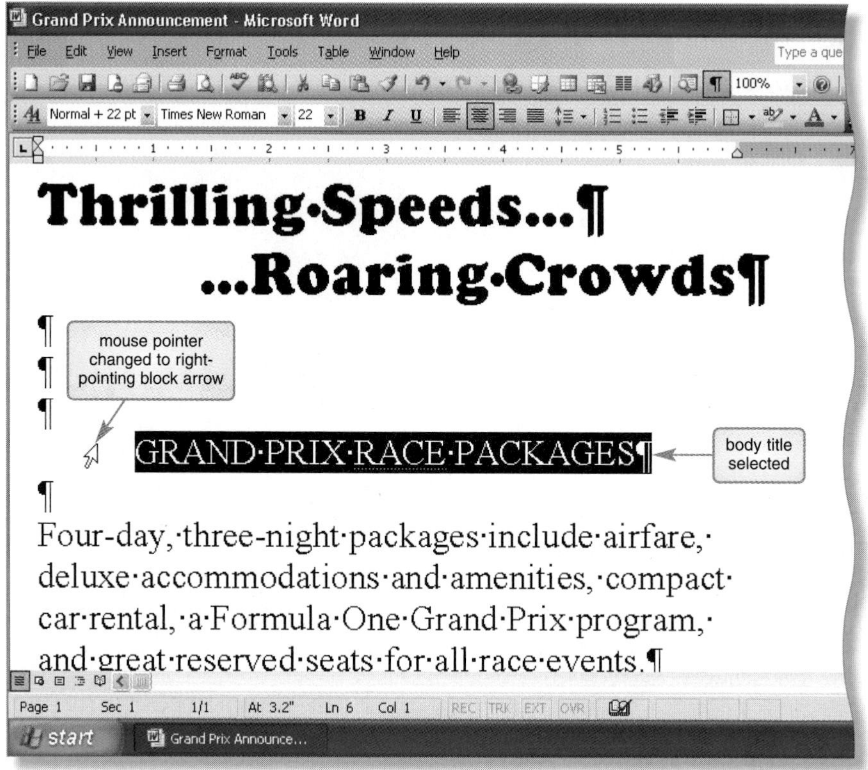
Grand Prix Announcement - Microsoft Word
Thrilling·Speeds...¶
...Roaring·Crowds¶
mouse pointer changed to right-pointing block arrow
GRAND·PRIX·RACE·PACKAGES¶
body title selected
Four-day,·three-night·packages·include·airfare,· deluxe·accommodations·and·amenities,·compact· car·rental,·a·Formula·One·Grand·Prix·program,· and·great·reserved·seats·for·all·race·events.¶

FIGURE 1-45

Other Ways

1. Drag through the line
2. With insertion point at beginning of desired line, press SHIFT+DOWN ARROW
3. In Voice Command mode, say "Select Line"

The next step is to change the font of the selected characters from Times New Roman to Arial Black and increase the font size of the selected characters from 22 to 24, as explained below.

To Format a Line of Text

1 **With the text selected, click the Font box arrow on the Formatting toolbar and then scroll to Arial Black (or a similar font) in the list. Click Arial Black (or a similar font).**

2 **With the text selected, click the Font Size box arrow on the Formatting toolbar and then click 24 in the list.**

Word changes the characters in the body title to 24-point Arial Black (Figure 1-46).

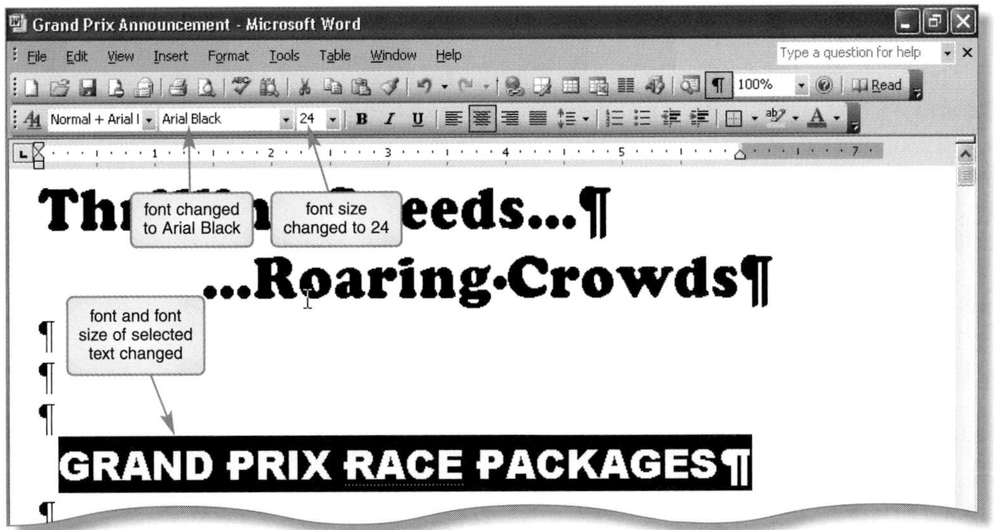

FIGURE 1-46

More About

Fonts

With some fonts, the formatting marks are not displayed on the screen properly. For example, the raised dot in each space may be displayed behind a character instead of in the space between two characters, causing the characters to look incorrect. Notice in Figure 1-46 that the formatting marks in the body title run into the characters. Recall that formatting marks do not print. Thus, the line will print fine.

Italicizing Text

Italicized text has a slanted appearance. The following step shows how to italicize the selected characters in the body title.

To Italicize Text

1

- **With the text still selected, click the Italic button on the Formatting toolbar.**

Word italicizes the text (Figure 1-47). The Italic button on the Formatting toolbar is selected.

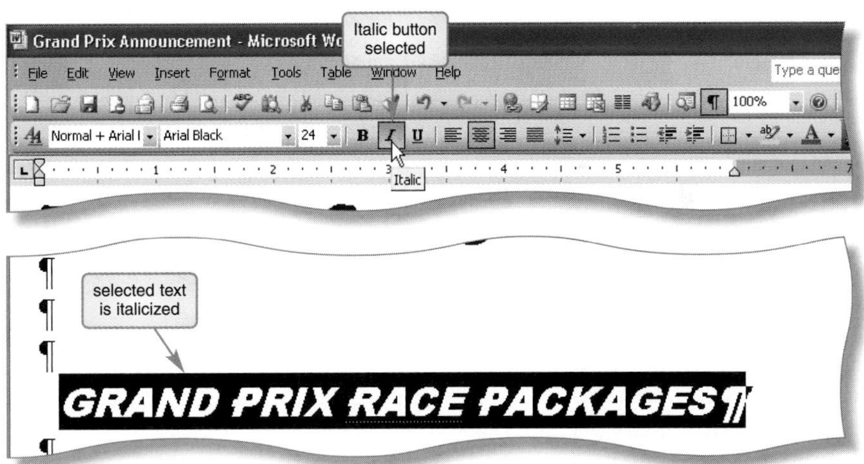

FIGURE 1-47

Other Ways

1. On Format menu click Font, click Font tab, click Italic in Font style list, click OK button
2. Right-click selected text, click Font on shortcut menu, click Font tab, click Italic in Font style list, click OK button
3. Press CTRL+I
4. In Voice Command mode, say "Italic"

When the selected text is italicized, the Italic button on the Formatting toolbar is selected. If, for some reason, you wanted to remove the italic format from the selected text, you would click the Italic button a second time, or you immediately could click the Undo button on the Standard toolbar.

Underlining Text

The next step is to underline a word in the first paragraph below the body title. **Underlined** text prints with an underscore (_) below each character. Underlining is used to emphasize or draw attention to specific text.

As with a single paragraph, if you want to format a single word, you do not need to select the word. Simply position the insertion point somewhere in the word and apply the desired format. The following step shows how to underline a word.

To Underline a Word

1

- **Click somewhere in the word to be underlined (deluxe, in this case).**
- **Click the Underline button on the Formatting toolbar.**

Word underlines the word containing the insertion point (Figure 1-48). The Underline button on the Formatting toolbar is selected.

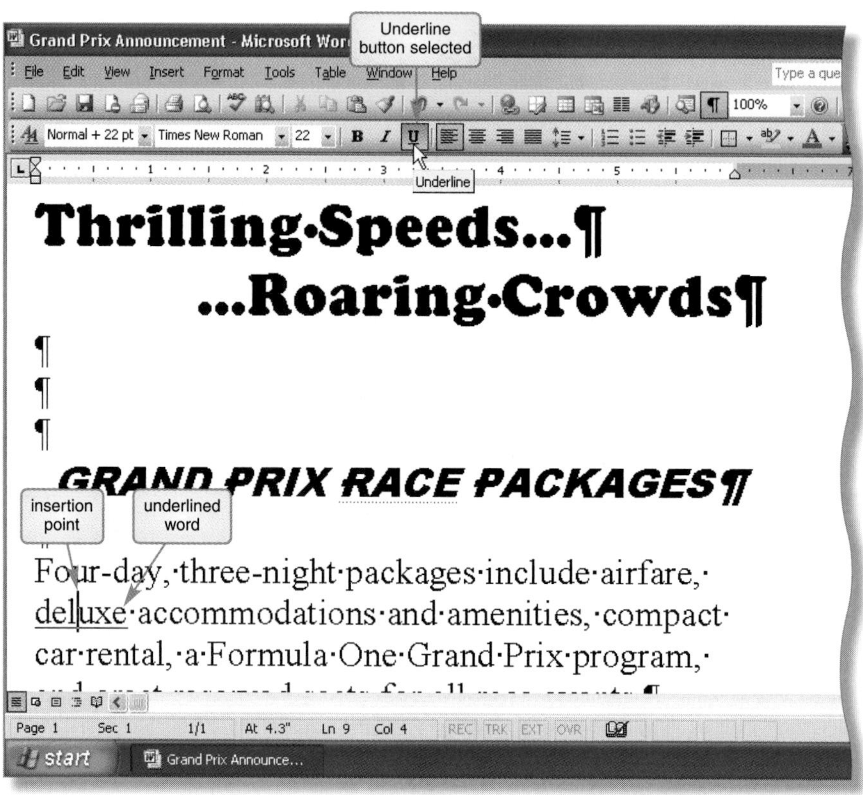

FIGURE 1-48

Other Ways

1. On Format menu click Font, click Font tab, click Underline style box arrow, click desired underline style, click OK button
2. Right-click selected text, click Font on shortcut menu, click Font tab, click Underline style box arrow, click desired underline style, click OK button
3. Press CTRL+U
4. In Voice Command mode, say "Underline"

When the text containing the insertion point is underlined, the Underline button on the Formatting toolbar is selected. If, for some reason, you wanted to remove the underline from the text, you would click the Underline button a second time, or you immediately could click the Undo button on the Standard toolbar.

In addition to the basic underline shown in Figure 1-48, Word has many decorative underlines that are available through the Font dialog box. For example, you can use double underlines, dotted underlines, and wavy underlines. In the Font dialog box, you also can change the color of an underline and instruct Word to underline only the words and not the spaces between the words. To display the Font dialog box, click Format on the menu bar and then click Font.

Scrolling

The next text to format is in the lower portion of the announcement, which currently is not showing in the document window. To continue formatting the document, scroll down so the lower portion of the announcement is displayed in the document window, as shown in the following step.

To Scroll through a Document

1

- **Click the down scroll arrow on the vertical scroll bar nine times.**

Word scrolls through the document (Figure 1-49). Depending on your monitor type, your screen may scroll differently.

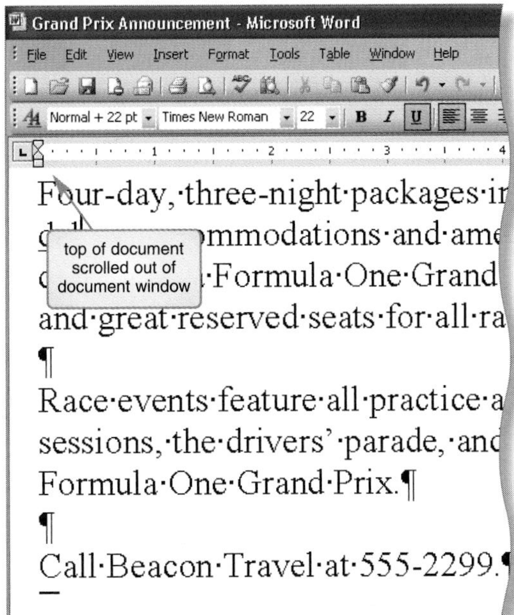
Grand Prix Announcement - Microsoft Word
top of document scrolled out of document window
Four-day, three-night packages in
and great reserved seats for all ra
Race events feature all practice a
sessions, the drivers' parade, and
Formula One Grand Prix.
Call Beacon Travel at 555-2299.

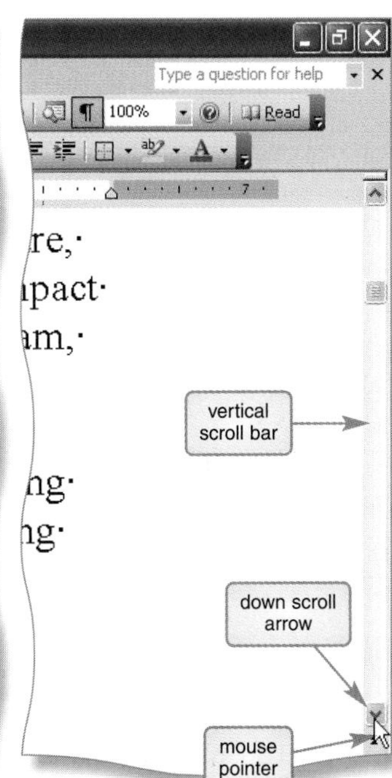
Type a question for help
vertical scroll bar
down scroll arrow
mouse pointer

FIGURE 1-49

Other Ways

1. See Tables 1-1 and 1-2 on pages WD 24 and WD 25
2. In Dictation mode, say key name(s) in Table 1-2

Selecting a Group of Words

The next step is to bold the words, great reserved seats, in the announcement. To do this, you first must select this group of words. The following steps show how to select a group of words.

To Select a Group of Words

1

- **Position the mouse pointer immediately to the left of the first character of the text to be selected (in this case, the g in great).**

The mouse pointer's shape is an I-beam when positioned in unselected text in the document window (Figure 1-50).

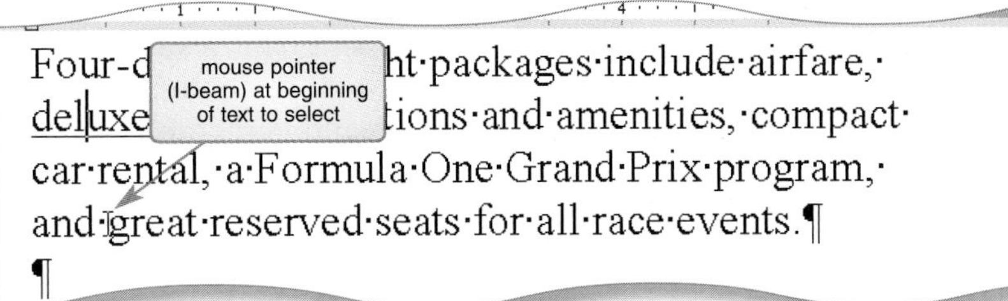
mouse pointer (I-beam) at beginning of text to select
Four-d ht packages include airfare,
delux tions and amenities, compact
car rental, a Formula One Grand Prix program,
and great reserved seats for all race events.

FIGURE 1-50

2

• **Drag the mouse pointer through the last character of the text to be selected (in this case, the second s in seats).**

Word selects the phrase, great reserved seats (Figure 1-51).

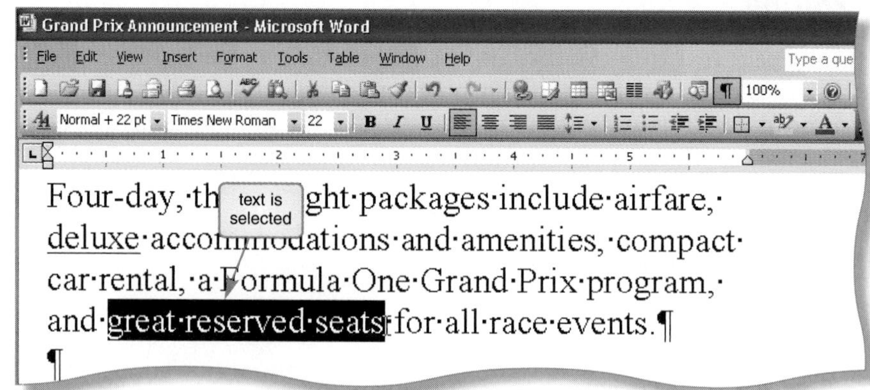
Grand Prix Announcement - Microsoft Word
text is selected
Four-day, three-night packages include airfare, deluxe accommodations and amenities, compact car rental, a Formula One Grand Prix program, and great reserved seats for all race events.

FIGURE 1-51

Other Ways

1. With insertion point at beginning of first word in the group, press CTRL+SHIFT+RIGHT ARROW until words are selected
2. In Voice Command mode, repeatedly say "Select Word"

Bolding Text

Bold characters display somewhat thicker and darker than those that are not bold. The following step shows how to bold the selected phrase, great reserved seats.

To Bold Text

1

• **With the text selected, click the Bold button on the Formatting toolbar.**

• **Click inside the selected text to remove the selection (highlight).**

Word formats the selected text in bold and positions the insertion point inside the bold text (Figure 1-52). The Bold button on the Formatting toolbar is selected.

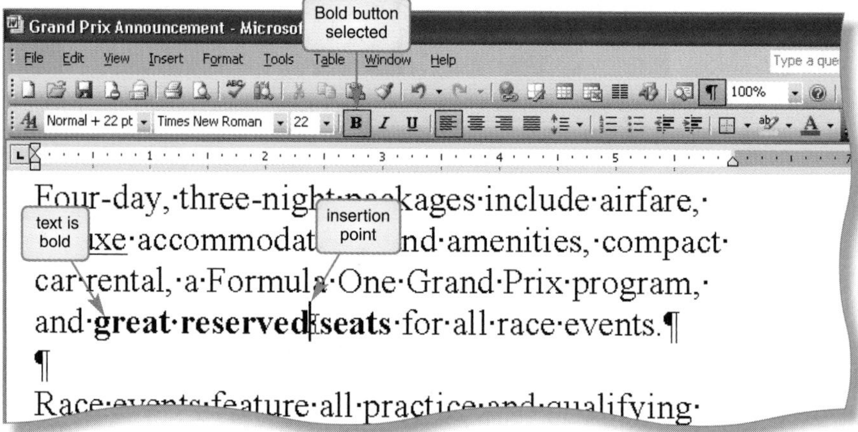
Grand Prix Announcement - Microsof
Bold button selected
text is bold
insertion point
and great reserved seats for all race events.

FIGURE 1-52

Other Ways

1. On Format menu click Font, click Font tab, click Bold in Font style list, click OK button
2. Right-click selected text, click Font on shortcut menu, click Font tab, click Bold in Font style list, click OK button
3. Press CTRL+B
4. In Voice Command mode, say "Bold"

When you click in the document, Word positions the insertion point at the location you clicked and removes the selection (highlight) from the screen. If you click inside the selection, the Formatting toolbar displays the formatting characteristics of the characters and paragraphs containing the insertion point. For example, at the location of the insertion point, the characters are a 22-point Times New Roman bold font, and the paragraph is left-aligned.

When the selected text is bold, the Bold button on the Formatting toolbar is selected. If, for some reason, you wanted to remove the bold format from the selected text, you would click the Bold button a second time, or you immediately could click the Undo button on the Standard toolbar.

The next step is to center the last line of the announcement, as described in the following steps.

> *More About*
>
> **Toolbar Buttons**
>
> Many of the buttons on the Formatting toolbar are toggles; that is, click them once to format the selected text, and click them again to remove the format from the selected text. For example, clicking the Bold button bolds selected text; clicking the Bold button again removes the bold format.

To Center a Paragraph

1. **Click somewhere in the paragraph to be centered (in this case, the last line of the announcement).**
2. **Click the Center button on the Formatting toolbar.**

Word centers the last line of the announcement (Figure 1-53).

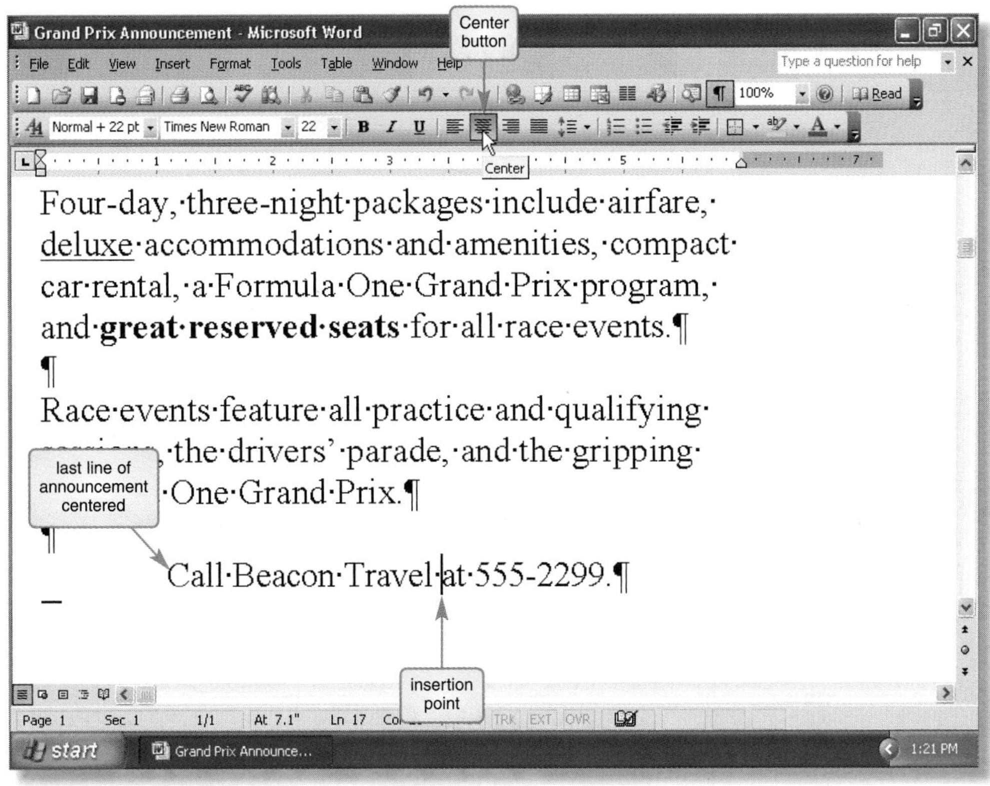
Grand Prix Announcement - Microsoft Word
Center button
Center
Four-day,·three-night·packages·include·airfare,·
deluxe·accommodations·and·amenities,·compact·
car·rental,·a·Formula·One·Grand·Prix·program,·
and·great·reserved·seats·for·all·race·events.¶
Race·events·feature·all·practice·and·qualifying·
·the·drivers'·parade,·and·the·gripping·
·One·Grand·Prix.¶
last line of announcement centered
Call·Beacon·Travel·at·555-2299.¶
insertion point
Page 1 Sec 1 1/1 At 7.1" Ln 17
Grand Prix Announce...
1:21 PM

FIGURE 1-53

The formatting for the announcement now is complete.

> *More About*
>
> **Graphics**
>
> If you have a scanner or digital camera attached to your computer, Word can insert a graphic directly from these devices. You also can scan a graphic into a file and then insert the scanned file into the Word document.

Inserting Clip Art in a Word Document

Files containing graphical images, also called **graphics**, are available from a variety of sources. Word includes many predefined graphics, called **clip art**, that you can insert in a document. Clip art is located in the **Clip Organizer**, which contains a collection of clips, including clip art, as well as photographs, sounds, and video clips.

Inserting Clip Art

The next step in the project is to insert clip art of a race car in the announcement between the headline and the body title. Recall that Word has 14 task panes, some of which automatically appear as you perform certain operations. When you use the Clip Art command, Word automatically displays the Clip Art task pane. The following steps show how to use the Clip Art task pane to insert clip art in a document.

To Insert Clip Art in a Document

1

- **To position the insertion point where you want the clip art to be located, press CTRL+HOME and then press the DOWN ARROW key three times.**
- **Click Insert on the menu bar.**

Word positions the insertion point on the second paragraph mark below the headline, and displays the Insert menu (Figure 1-54). Remember that a short menu initially displays, which expands into a full menu after a few seconds.

FIGURE 1-54

2

- **Point to Picture on the Insert menu.**

Word displays the Picture submenu (Figure 1-55). As discussed earlier, when you point to a command that has a small arrow to its right, Word displays a submenu associated with that command.

FIGURE 1-55

3

- **Click Clip Art on the Picture submenu.**
- **If the Search for text box contains text, drag through the text to select it.**
- **Type** `race car` **in the Search for text box.**

Word displays the Clip Art task pane at the right edge of the Word window (Figure 1-56). Recall that a task pane is a separate window that enables you to carry out some Word tasks more efficiently. When you click the Go button, Word searches the Clip Organizer for clips that match the description you type in the Search for text box.

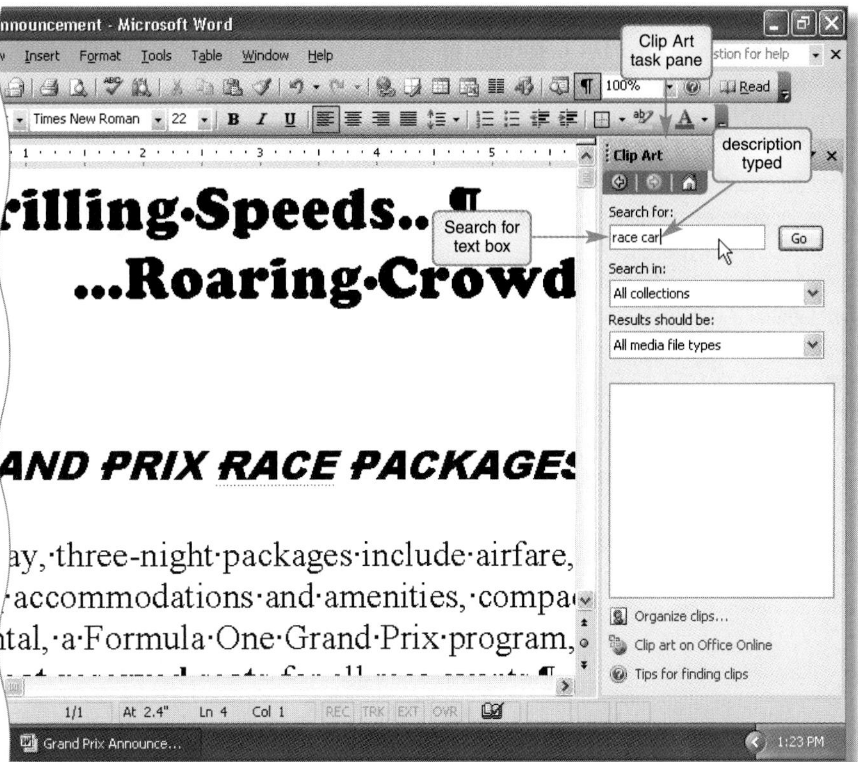

FIGURE 1-56

4

- **Click the Go button.**

Word displays a list of clips that match the description, race car (Figure 1-57). If you are connected to the Web, the Clip Art task pane displays clips from the Web, as well as those installed on your hard disk.

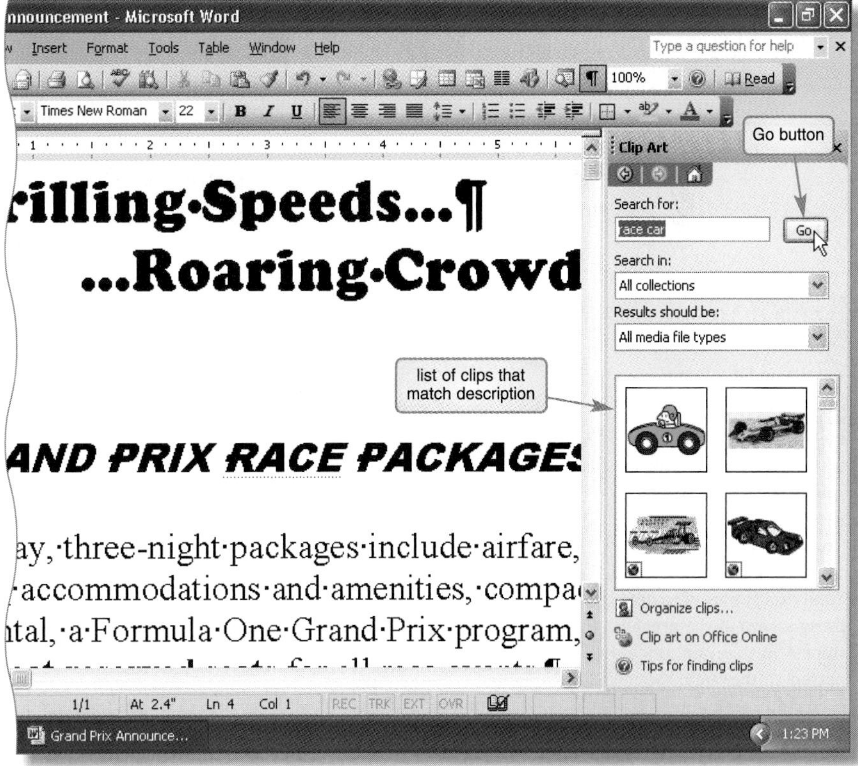

FIGURE 1-57

• **Click the image to be inserted in the document (in this case, the Formula One race car).**

Word inserts the clip art in the document at the location of the insertion point (Figure 1-58). In the Clip Art task pane, the selected clip art has a box arrow at its right edge.

6

• **Click the Close button on the Clip Art task pane title bar.**

Word removes the Clip Art task pane from the screen.

FIGURE 1-58

Other Ways

1. In Voice Command mode, say "Insert, Picture, Clip Art"

The clip art in the announcement is part of a paragraph. Because that paragraph is left-aligned, the clip art also is left-aligned. Notice the Align Left button on the Formatting toolbar is selected (Figure 1-58). You can use any of the paragraph alignment buttons on the Formatting toolbar to reposition the clip art. The following step shows how to center a graphic that is part of a paragraph.

More About

Clip Art

If you are not connected to the Web, Word displays clip art from your hard disk. If you are connected to the Web, Word displays clip art from your hard disk and also from Microsoft's Web site. Your results may differ from those shown in the preceding steps if you are not connected to the Web. When clip art images display in the Clip Art task pane, Web clips are identified by a small globe displayed in their lower-left corner (Figure 1-58).

To Center a Paragraph Containing a Graphic

1 **With the insertion point on the paragraph mark containing the clip art, click the Center button on the Formatting toolbar.**

Word centers the paragraph, which also centers the graphic in the paragraph (Figure 1-59).

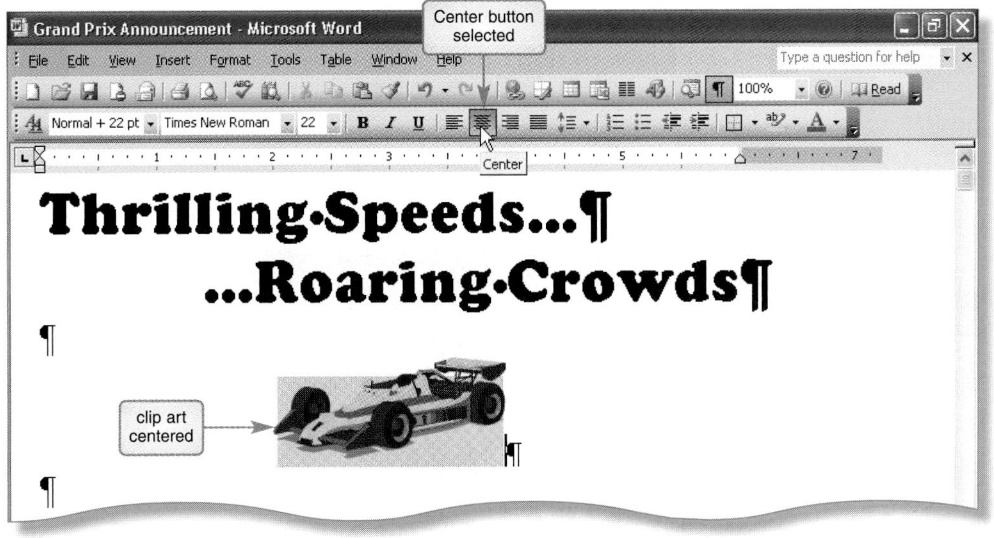

FIGURE 1-59

More About

Clip Art Packages

For more information about the clip art available for purchase, visit the Word 2003 More About Web page (scsite.com/wd2003/more) and then click Clip Art.

Q&A

Q: Where should a graphic be positioned in an announcement?

A: Emphasize a graphic by placing it at the optical center of the page. To determine optical center, divide the page in half horizontally and vertically. The optical center is located one third of the way up the vertical line from the point of intersection of the two lines.

Resizing a Graphic

The clip art in this announcement is to be a larger size. Once you have inserted a graphic in a document, you easily can change its size. **Resizing** includes both enlarging and reducing the size of a graphic. To resize a graphic, you first must select it. Thus, the following step shows how to select a graphic.

To Select a Graphic

1

- **Click anywhere in the graphic.**
- **If your screen does not display the Picture toolbar, click View on the menu bar, point to Toolbars, and then click Picture.**

Word selects the graphic (Figure 1-60). A selected graphic is displayed surrounded by a ***selection rectangle****, which has small squares, called* ***sizing handles****, at each corner and middle location. You use the sizing handles to change the size of the graphic. When a graphic is selected, the Picture toolbar automatically should appear on the screen.*

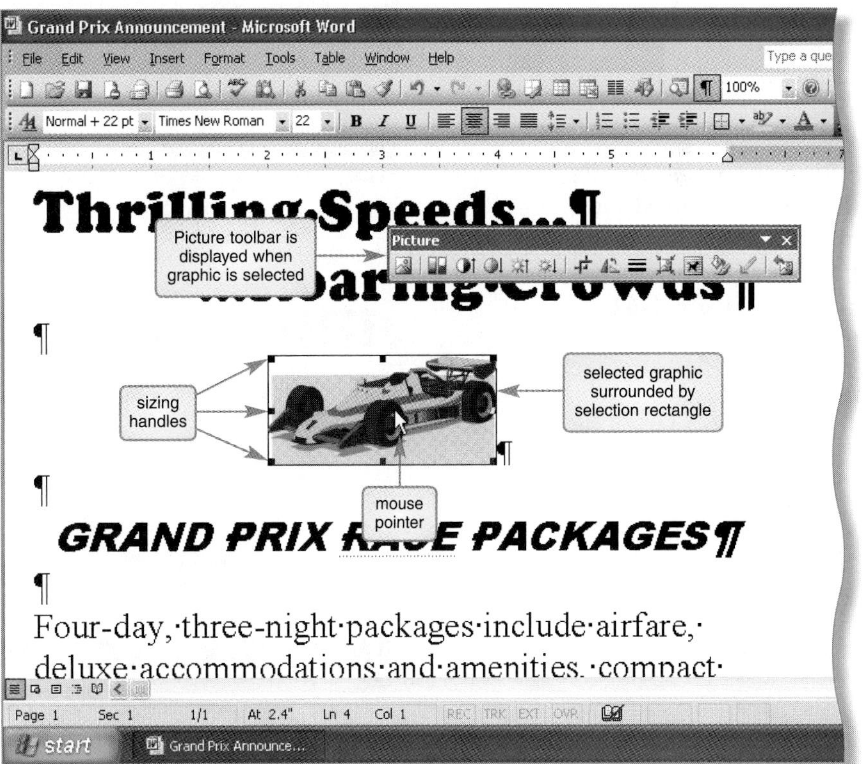

FIGURE 1-60

The following steps show how to resize the graphic just inserted and selected.

To Resize a Graphic

1

- **With the graphic still selected, point to the upper-right corner sizing handle.**

The mouse pointer shape changes to a two-headed arrow when it is on a sizing handle (Figure 1-61). To resize a graphic, you drag the sizing handle(s) until the graphic is the desired size.

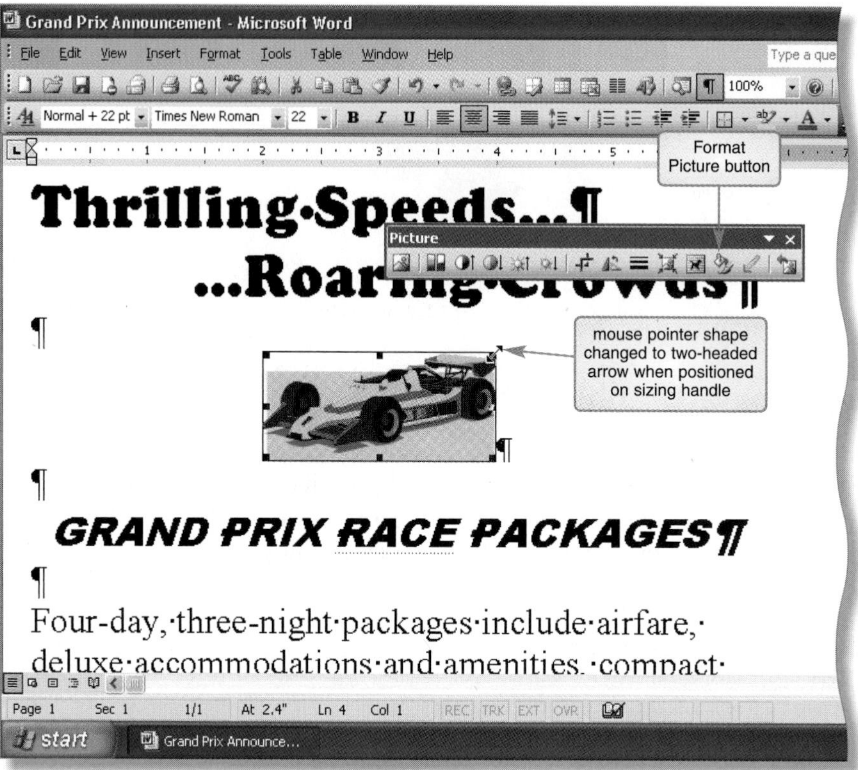

FIGURE 1-61

2

- **Drag the sizing handle diagonally outward until the dotted selection rectangle is positioned approximately as shown in Figure 1-62.**

When you drag a corner sizing handle, the proportions of the graphic remain intact.

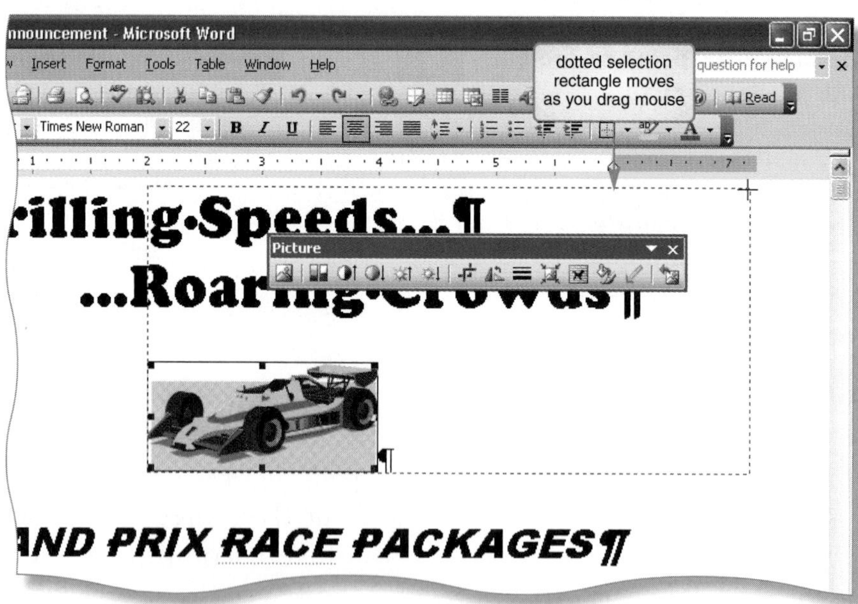

FIGURE 1-62

3

• **Release the mouse button. Press CTRL+HOME.**

Word resizes the graphic (Figure 1-63). When you click outside of a graphic or press a key to scroll through a document, Word deselects the graphic. The Picture toolbar disappears from the screen when you deselect a graphic.

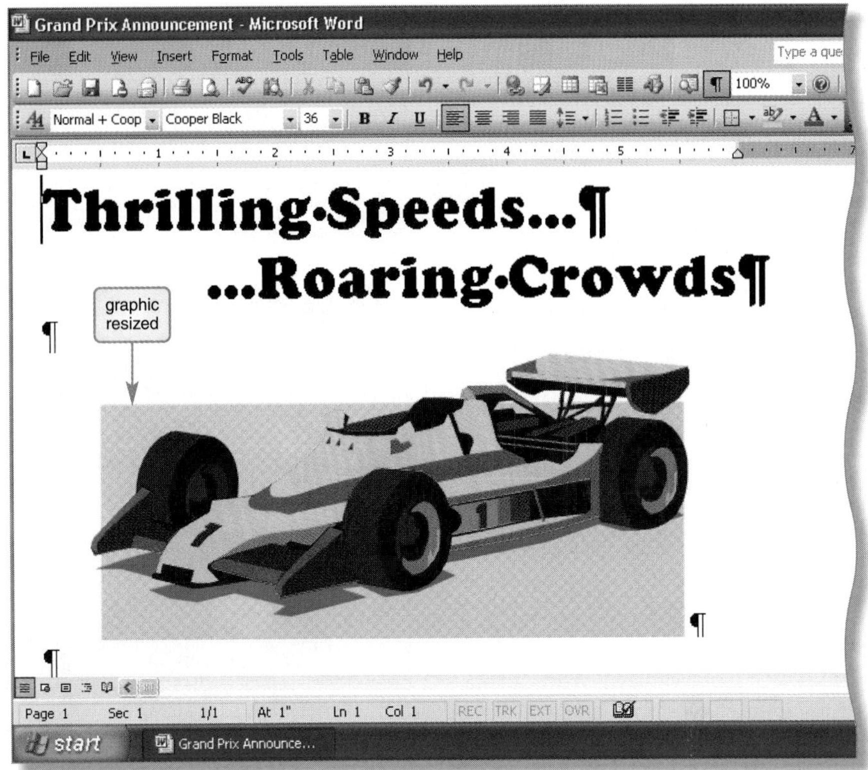

FIGURE 1-63

Other Ways

1. Click Format Picture button on Picture toolbar, click Size tab, enter desired height and width, click OK button
2. On Format menu click Picture, click Size tab, enter desired height and width, click OK button
3. In Voice Command mode, say "Format, Picture"

Instead of resizing a selected graphic by dragging a sizing handle with the mouse, you also can use the Format Picture dialog box to resize a graphic by clicking the Format Picture button on the Picture toolbar (Figure 1-61) and then clicking the Size tab. In the Size sheet, you can enter exact height and width measurements. If you have a precise measurement for a graphic, use the Format Picture dialog box; otherwise, drag the sizing handles to resize a graphic.

Sometimes, you might resize a graphic and realize it is the wrong size. In this case, you may want to return the graphic to its original size and start again. To restore a resized graphic to its exact original size, click the graphic to select it and then click the Format Picture button on the Picture toolbar to display the Format Picture dialog box. Click the Size tab, click the Reset button, and then click the OK button.

More About

The Picture Toolbar

The Picture toolbar is a floating toolbar. Thus, you can drag its title bar to move the toolbar to a different location on the screen.

Saving an Existing Document with the Same File Name

The announcement for Project 1 now is complete. To transfer the modified document with the formatting changes and graphic to the floppy disk in drive A, you must save the document again. When you saved the document the first time, you assigned a file name to it (Grand Prix Announcement). When you use the procedure on the next page, Word automatically assigns the same file name to the document each time you subsequently save it.

To Save an Existing Document with the Same File Name

1

• **Click the Save button on the Standard toolbar.**

Word saves the document on a floppy disk inserted in drive A using the currently assigned file name, Grand Prix Announcement (Figure 1-64).

FIGURE 1-64

Other Ways

1. On File menu click Save
2. Press CTRL+S
3. In Voice Command mode, say "Save"

While Word is saving the document, the Background Save icon appears near the right edge of the status bar. When the save is complete, the document remains in memory and on the screen.

If, for some reason, you want to save an existing document with a different file name, click Save As on the File menu to display the Save As dialog box. Then, fill in the Save As dialog box as discussed in Steps 2 through 5 on pages WD 28 through WD 30.

More About

Print Preview

To view a document before you print it, click the Print Preview button on the Standard toolbar. To return to the document window, click the Close Preview button on the Print Preview toolbar.

Printing a Document

The next step is to print the document you created. A printed version of the document is called a **hard copy** or **printout**. The following steps show how to print the announcement created in this project.

To Print a Document

1

- **Ready the printer according to the printer instructions.**
- **Click the Print button on the Standard toolbar.**

The mouse pointer briefly changes to an hourglass shape as Word prepares to print the document. While the document is printing, a printer icon appears in the notification area on the Windows taskbar (Figure 1-65).

2

- **When the printer stops printing the document, retrieve the printout, which should look like Figure 1-1 on page WD 5.**

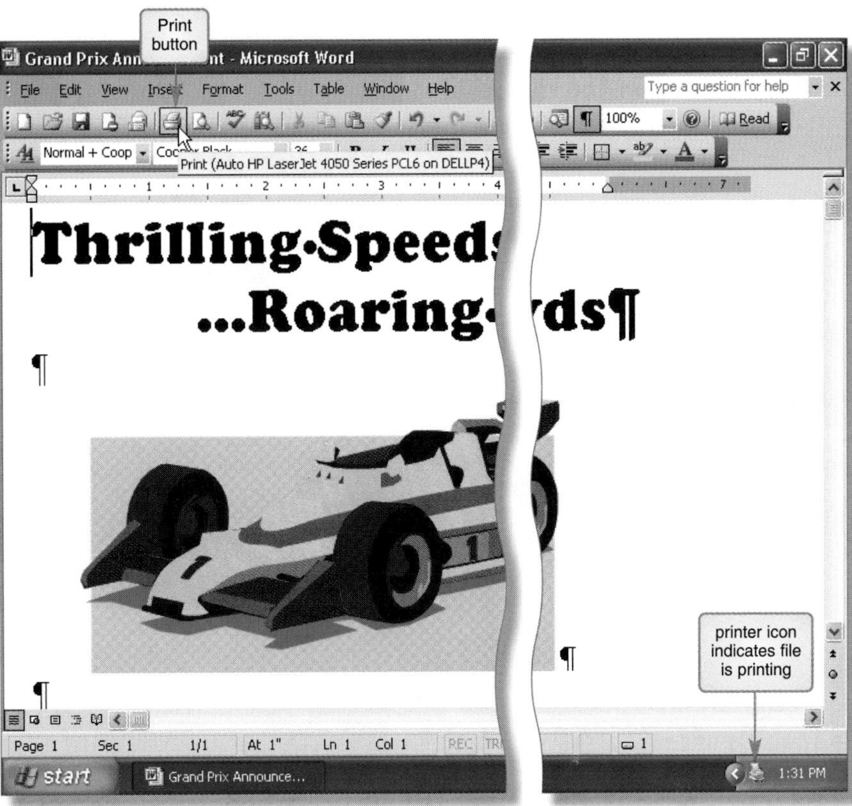

FIGURE 1-65

Other Ways

1. On File menu click Print, click OK button
2. Press CTRL+P, press ENTER
3. In Voice Command mode, say "Print"

When you use the Print button to print a document, Word prints the entire document automatically. You then may distribute the printout or keep it as a permanent record of the document.

If you wanted to print multiple copies of the document, display the Print dialog box by clicking File on the menu bar and then clicking Print. In addition to the number of copies, the Print dialog box has several printing options.

If you wanted to cancel your job that is printing or one you have waiting to be printed, double-click the printer icon on the taskbar (Figure 1-65). In the printer window, click the job to be canceled and then click Cancel on the Document menu.

Q: How can I save ink, print faster, or decrease printer overrun errors?

A: Print a draft. Click File on the menu bar, click Print, click the Options button, place a check mark in the Draft output check box, and then click the OK button in each dialog box.

Quitting Word

After you create, save, and print the announcement, Project 1 is complete. The following steps show how to quit Word and return control to Windows.

To Quit Word

1

- **Position the mouse pointer on the Close button on the right side of the title bar (Figure 1-66).**

2

- **Click the Close button.**

The Word window closes.

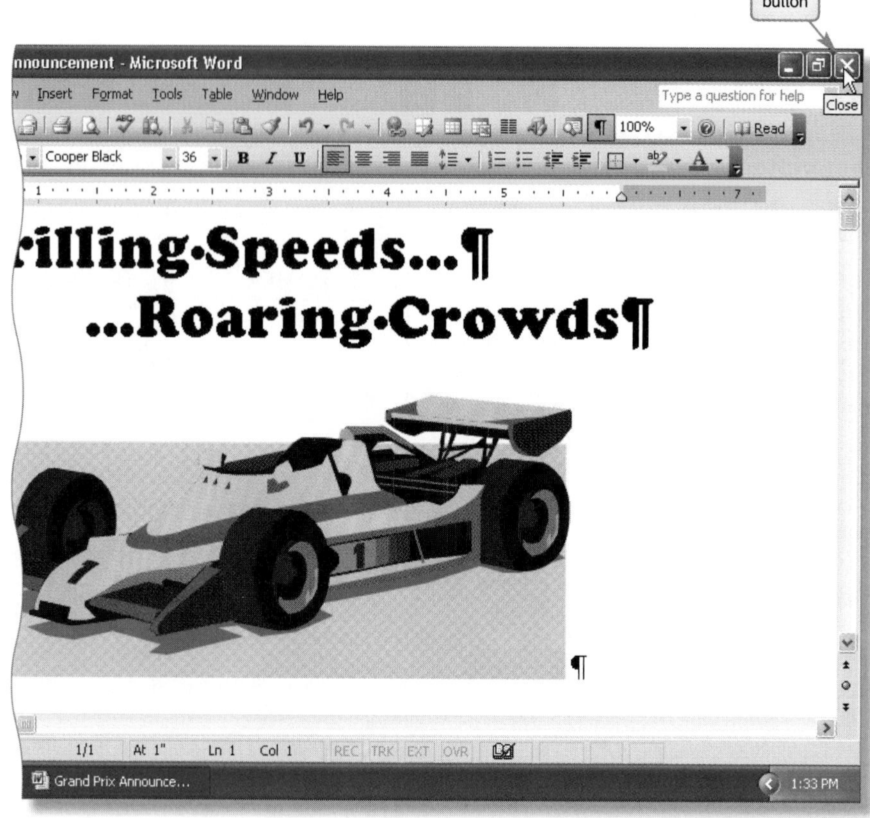

FIGURE 1-66

Other Ways

1. On File menu click Exit
2. Right-click Microsoft Word button on Windows taskbar, click Close on shortcut menu
3. Press ALT+F4
4. In Voice Command mode, say "File, Exit"

When you quit Word, a dialog box may display asking if you want to save the changes. This occurs if you made changes to the document since the last save. Clicking the Yes button in the dialog box saves the changes; clicking the No button ignores the changes; and clicking the Cancel button returns to the document. If you did not make any changes since you saved the document, this dialog box usually is not displayed.

Starting Word and Opening a Document

Once you have created and saved a document, you often will have reason to retrieve it from disk. For example, you might want to revise the document or print it again. Earlier, you saved the Word document created in Project 1 on a floppy disk using the file name, Grand Prix Announcement.

The following steps, which assume Word is not running, show how to open the Grand Prix Announcement file from a floppy disk in drive A.

To Open a Document

1

- **With your floppy disk in drive A, click the Start button on the Windows taskbar, point to All Programs on the Start menu, point to Microsoft Office on the All Programs submenu, and then click Microsoft Office Word 2003 on the Microsoft Office submenu.**

Word starts. The Open area of the Getting Started task pane lists up to four of the most recently used files (Figure 1-67).

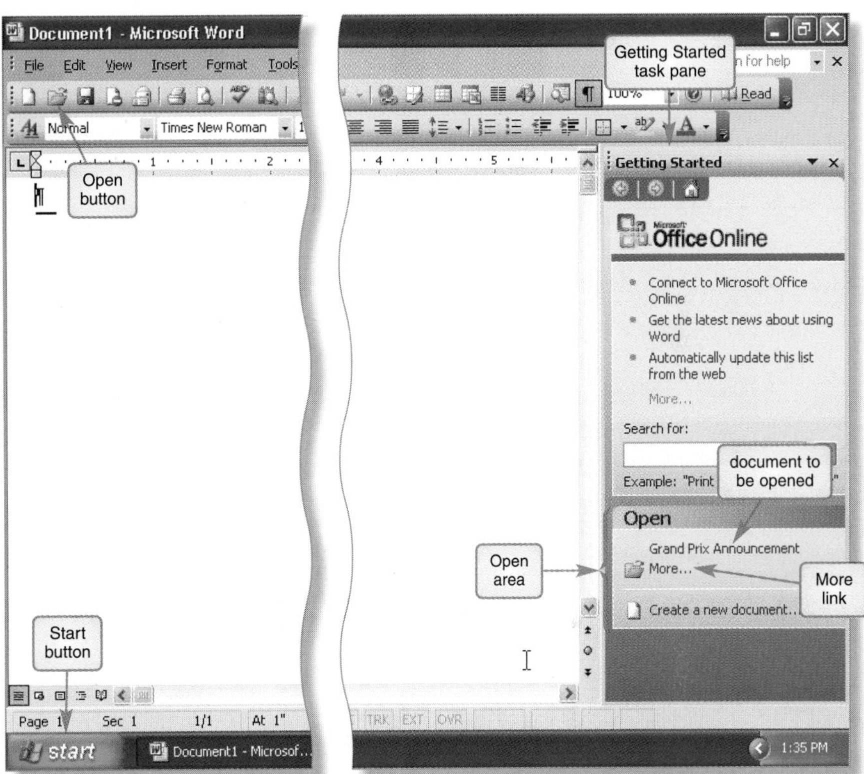

FIGURE 1-67

More About

Opening Files

In Word, you can open a recently used file by clicking File on the menu bar and then clicking the file name on the File menu. To instruct Word to show the recently used documents on the File menu, click Tools on the menu bar, click Options, click the General tab, click Recently used file list to place a check mark in the check box, and then click the OK button.

2

- **Click Grand Prix Announcement in the Getting Started task pane.**

Word opens the document, Grand Prix Announcement, from the floppy disk in drive A and displays it in the Word window (Figure 1-68). The Getting Started task pane closes.

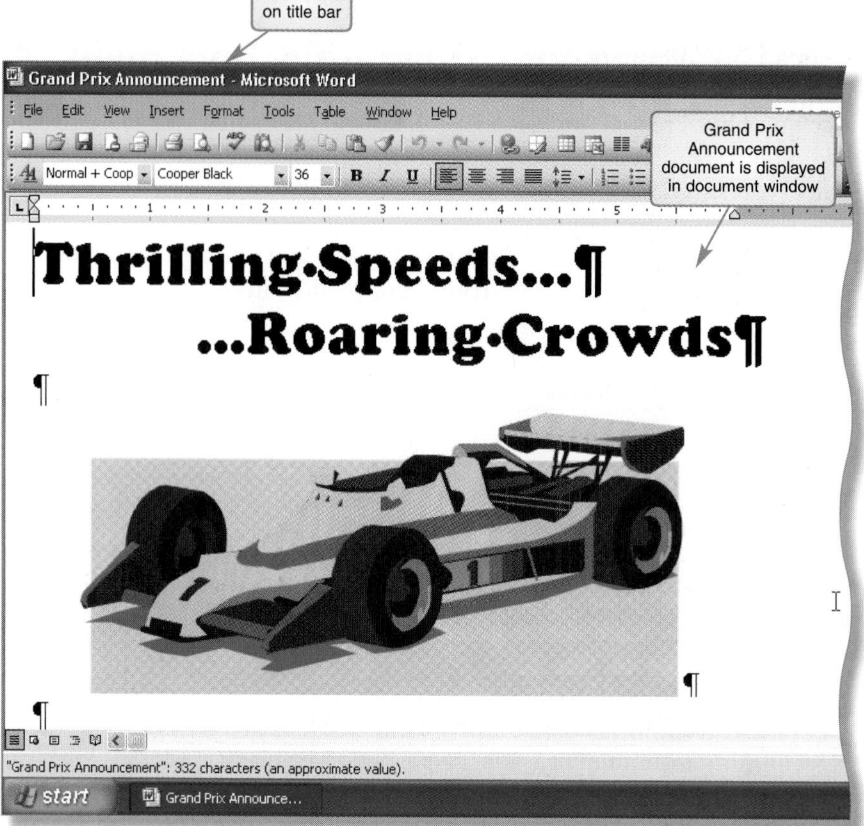

FIGURE 1-68

Other Ways

1. Click Start Button, point to All Programs on Start menu, click Open Office Document, select desired drive, double-click file name
2. Right-click Start button, click Explore, display contents of desired drive and folder, double-click file name
3. In Word, click Open button on Standard toolbar, select file name, click Open button in dialog box
4. In Word, on File menu click Open, select file name, click Open button in dialog box
5. In Word, press CTRL+O, select file name, press ENTER
6. In Word, in Voice Command mode, say "Open, [select file name], Open"

If you want to open a document other than one of the four most recently opened ones, click the Open button on the Standard toolbar or the More link in the Getting Started task pane. Clicking the Open button or the More link displays the Open dialog box, which allows you to navigate to a document stored on disk.

Correcting Errors

After creating a document, you often will find you must make changes to it. For example, the document may contain an error or new circumstances may require you add text to the document.

Types of Changes Made to Documents

The types of changes made to documents normally fall into one of the three following categories: additions, deletions, or modifications.

ADDITIONS Additional words, sentences, or paragraphs may be required in a document. Additions occur when you omit text from a document and want to insert it later. For example, the travel agency may decide to add breakfast as part of its Grand Prix race packages.

DELETIONS Sometimes, text in a document is incorrect or is no longer needed. For example, the travel agency may stop including car rental in their Grand Prix race packages. In this case, you would delete the words, compact car rental, from the announcement.

MODIFICATIONS If an error is made in a document or changes take place that affect the document, you might have to revise a word(s) in the text. For example, the travel agency might change the Grand Prix race packages from four-day, three-night to five-day, four-night.

Inserting Text in an Existing Document

Word inserts text to the left of the insertion point. The text to the right of the insertion point moves to the right and downward to fit the new text. The following steps show how to insert the word, fun, to the left of the word, drivers', in the announcement.

To Insert Text in an Existing Document

1

- **Scroll through the document and then click to the left of the location of text to be inserted (in this case, the d in drivers').**

Word positions the insertion point at the clicked location (Figure 1-69).

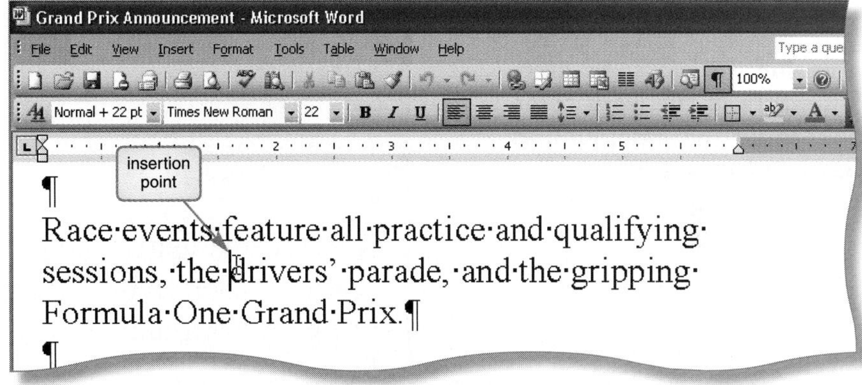
Grand Prix Announcement - Microsoft Word
insertion point
Race·events·feature·all·practice·and·qualifying·
sessions,·the·drivers'·parade,·and·the·gripping·
Formula·One·Grand·Prix.¶

FIGURE 1-69

2

- **Type** `fun` **and then press the SPACEBAR.**

Word inserts the word, fun, to the left of the insertion point (Figure 1-70).

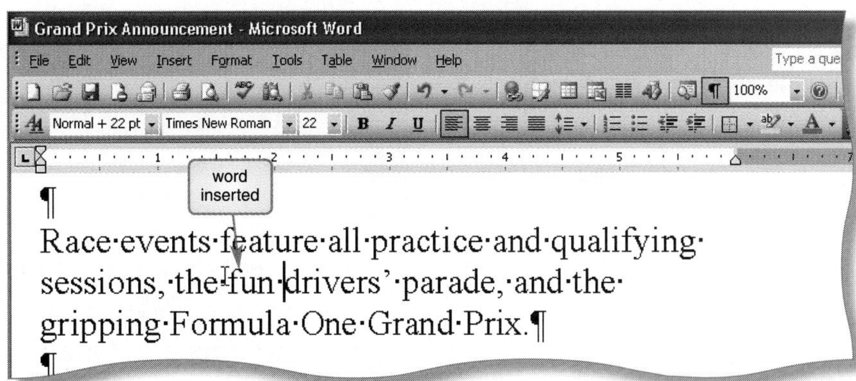
Grand Prix Announcement - Microsoft Word
word inserted
Race·events·feature·all·practice·and·qualifying·
sessions,·the·fun·drivers'·parade,·and·the·
gripping·Formula·One·Grand·Prix.¶

FIGURE 1-70

In Word, the default typing mode is insert mode. In **insert mode**, as you type a character, Word inserts the character and moves all the characters to the right of the typed character one position to the right. You can change to overtype mode by double-clicking the OVR status indicator on the status bar (Figure 1-8 on page WD 10). In **overtype mode,** Word replaces characters to the right of the insertion point. Double-clicking the OVR status indicator again returns Word to insert mode.

More About

Overtype

As you type, if existing text is overwritten with new text, you probably are in overtype mode. Double-click the OVR status indicator to turn overtype mode off. You also can press the INSERT key on the keyboard to turn off overtype mode.

More About

The Clipboard Task Pane

If you click the Cut button (or Copy button) twice in a row, Word displays the Clipboard task pane. You use the Clipboard task pane to copy and paste items within a document or from one Office document to another. To close the Clipboard task pane, click the Close button on the task pane title bar.

Deleting Text from an Existing Document

It is not unusual to type incorrect characters or words in a document. As discussed earlier in this project, you can click the Undo button on the Standard toolbar to immediately undo a command or action — this includes typing. Word also provides other methods of correcting typing errors.

To delete an incorrect character in a document, simply click next to the incorrect character and then press the BACKSPACE key to erase to the left of the insertion point, or press the DELETE key to erase to the right of the insertion point.

To delete a word or phrase you first must select the word or phrase. The following steps show how to select the word, fun, that was just added in the previous steps and then delete the selection.

To Select a Word

1

- **Position the mouse pointer somewhere in the word to be selected (in this case, fun), as shown in Figure 1-71.**

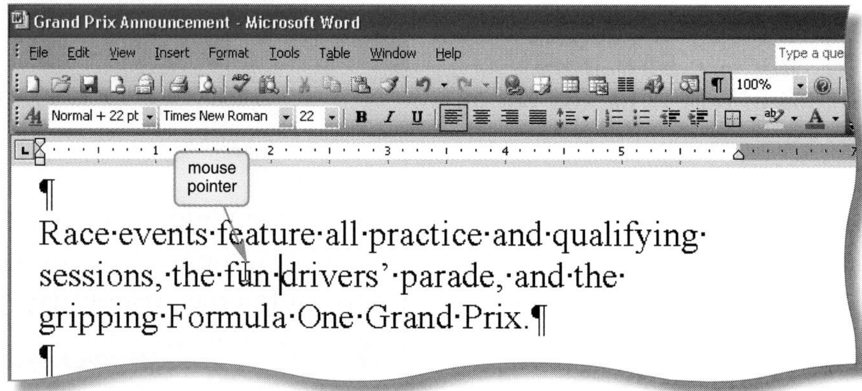
Grand Prix Announcement - Microsoft Word
mouse pointer
Race·events·feature·all·practice·and·qualifying·
sessions,·the·fun·drivers'·parade,·and·the·
gripping·Formula·One·Grand·Prix.¶

FIGURE 1-71

2

- **Double-click the word to be selected.**

The word, fun, is selected (Figure 1-72).

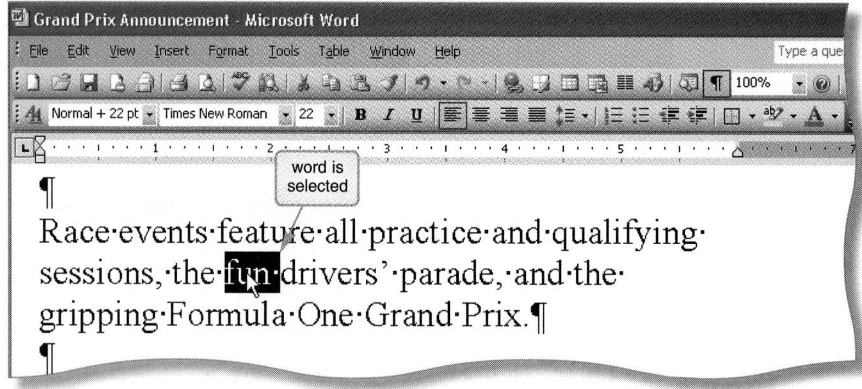
Grand Prix Announcement - Microsoft Word
word is selected
Race·events·feature·all·practice·and·qualifying·
sessions,·the·fun·drivers'·parade,·and·the·
gripping·Formula·One·Grand·Prix.¶

FIGURE 1-72

Other Ways

1. Drag through the word
2. With insertion point at beginning of desired word, press CTRL+SHIFT+RIGHT ARROW
3. With insertion point at beginning of desired word, in Voice Command mode, say "Select Word"

The next step is to delete the selected text.

To Delete Text

1

• **With the text selected, press the DELETE key.**

Word deletes the selected word from the document (Figure 1-73).

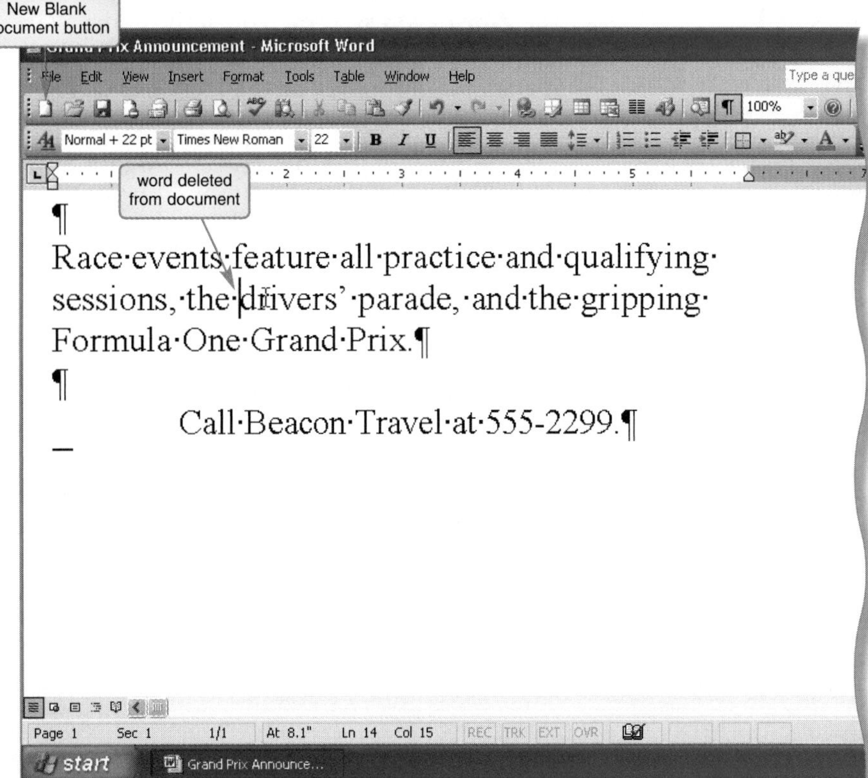

FIGURE 1-73

Other Ways

1. On Edit menu click Cut
2. Right-click selected text, click Cut on shortcut menu
3. Press CTRL+X or BACKSPACE
4. In Voice Command mode, say "DELETE"

Closing the Entire Document

Sometimes, everything goes wrong. If this happens, you may want to close the document entirely and start over. You also may want to close a document when you are finished with it so you can begin your next document.

To Close the Entire Document and Start Over

1. Click File on the menu bar and then click Close.
2. If Word displays a dialog box, click the No button to ignore the changes since the last time you saved the document.
3. Click the New Blank Document button (Figure 1-73) on the Standard toolbar.

You also can close the document by clicking the Close button at the right edge of the menu bar.

More About

The Word Help System

The best way to become familiar with the Word Help system is to use it. Appendix A includes detailed information on the Word Help system and exercises that will help you gain confidence in using it.

Word Help System

At anytime while you are using Word, you can get answers to questions through the **Word Help system**. You activate the Word Help system by using the Type a question for help box on the menu bar, the Microsoft Office Word Help button on the Standard toolbar, or the Help menu (Figure 1-74). Used properly, this form of online assistance can increase your productivity and reduce your frustrations by minimizing the time you spend learning how to use Word.

The following section shows how to obtain answers to your questions using the Type a question for help box. Additional information about using the Word Help system is available in Appendix A.

Using the Type a Question for Help Box

Through the Type a question for help box on the right side of the menu bar (Figure 1-66 on page WD 54), you type free-form questions, such as *how do I save* or *how do I create a Web page*, or you type terms, such as *copy*, *save*, or *format*. Word responds by displaying a list of topics related to the word or phrase you typed. The following steps show how to use the Type a question for help box to obtain information about shortcut keys.

To Use the Type a Question for Help Box

1

• **Click the Type a question for help box on the right side of the menu bar and then type** shortcut keys **(Figure 1-74).**

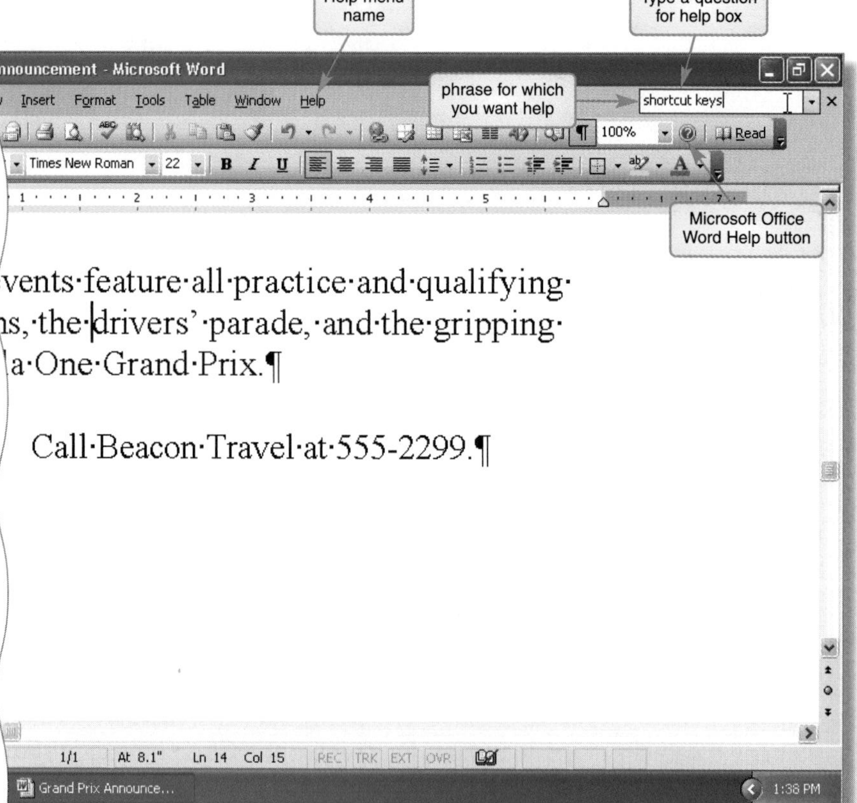

FIGURE 1-74

2

- **Press the ENTER key.**
- **When Word displays the Search Results task pane, if necessary, scroll to display the topic, About shortcut keys.**
- **Click About shortcut keys.**
- **If the Microsoft Office Help window has an Auto Tile button, click it so the Word window and Help window display side-by-side.**

Word displays the Search Results task pane with a list of topics relating to the phrase, shortcut keys. When the About shortcut keys link is clicked, Word opens the Microsoft Office Word Help window on the right side of the screen (Figure 1-75).

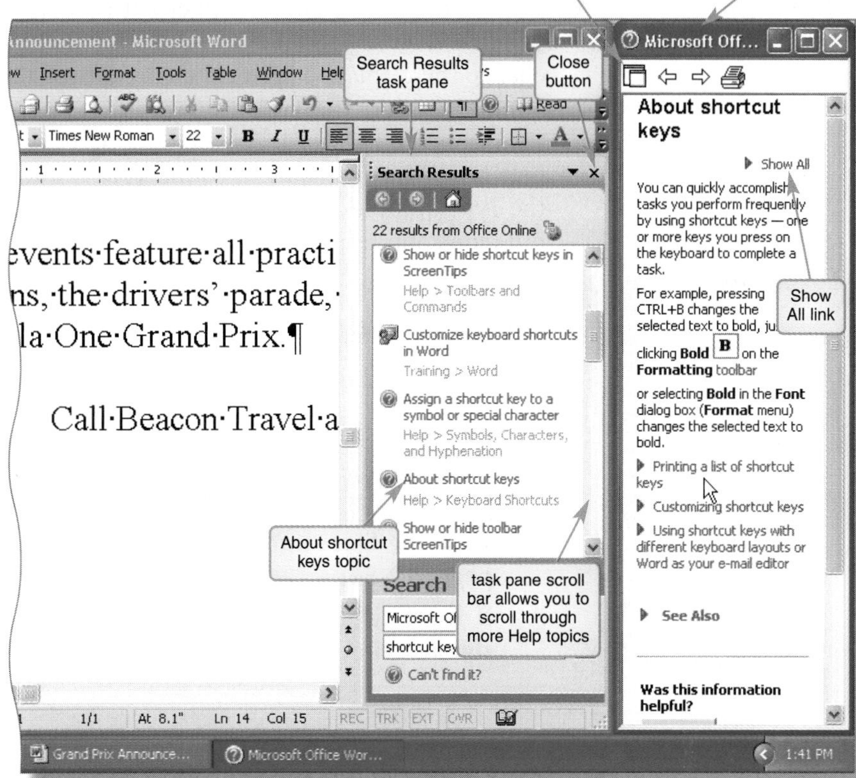

FIGURE 1-75

3

- **Click the Show All link on the right side of the Microsoft Office Word Help window to expand the links in the window.**
- **Double-click the Microsoft Office Word Help window title bar to maximize the window.**

The links in the Microsoft Office Word Help window are expanded and the window is maximized (Figure 1-76).

4

- **Click the Close button on the Microsoft Office Word Help window title bar.**
- **Click the Close button on the Search Results task pane.**

Word closes the Microsoft Office Word Help window. The Word document window again is active.

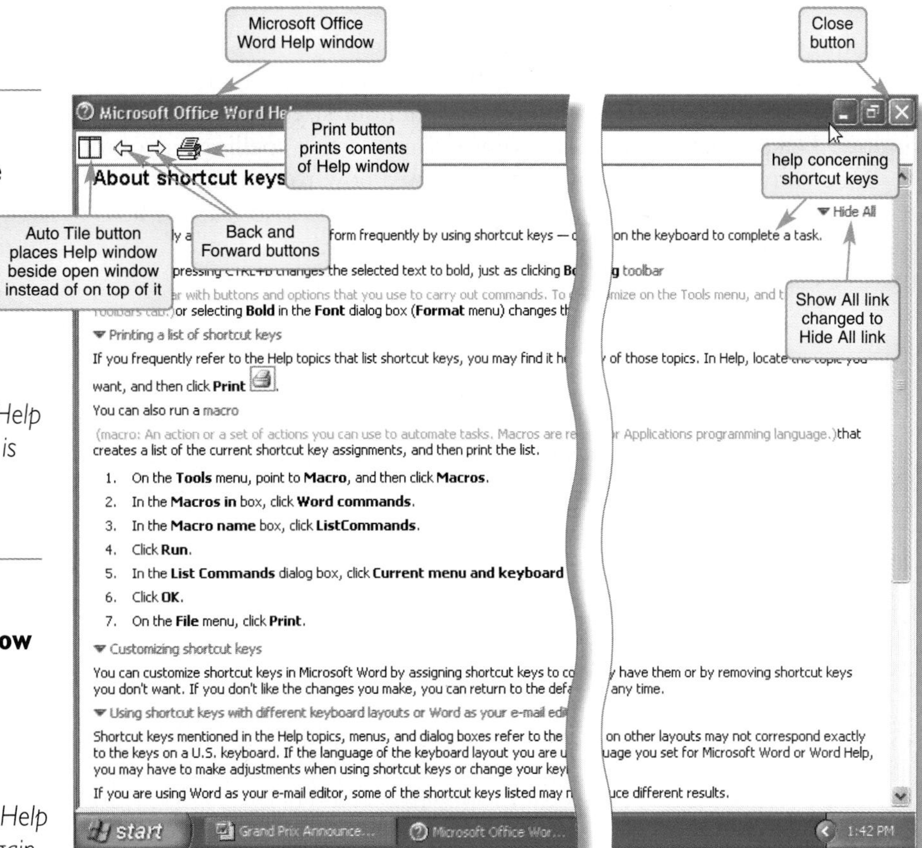

FIGURE 1-76

Use the buttons in the upper-left corner of the Microsoft Office Word Help window (Figure 1-76 on the previous page) to navigate through the Help system, change the display, or print the contents of the window.

You can use the Type a question for help box to search for Help about any topic concerning Word. As you enter questions and terms in the Type a question for help box, Word adds them to the Type a question for help list. Thus, if you click the Type a question for help box arrow, Word displays a list of previously typed questions and terms.

More About

Certification

The Microsoft Office Specialist Certification program provides an opportunity for you to obtain a valuable industry credential — proof that you have the Word 2003 skills required by employers. For more information, see Appendix E or visit the Word 2003 Certification Web page (scsite.com/wd2003/cert).

Quitting Word

The final step in this project is to quit Word.

To Quit Word

1. **Click the Close button on the right side of the Word title bar (Figure 1-66 on page WD 54).**
2. **If Word displays a dialog box, click the No button to ignore the changes since the last time you saved the document.**

The Word window closes.

Project Summary

In creating the Grand Prix Announcement document in this project, you gained a broad knowledge of Word. First, you were introduced to starting Word. You learned about the Word window. Before entering any text in the document, you learned how to change the font size. You then learned how to type in the Word document window. The project showed how to use Word's check spelling as you type feature.

Once you saved the document, you learned how to format its paragraphs and characters. Then, the project showed how to insert and resize a clip art image. You also learned how to save the document again, print it, and then quit Word. You learned how to open a document, and insert, delete, and modify text. Finally, you learned how to use the Word Help system to answer questions.

If you have a SAM user profile, you may have access to hands-on instruction, practice, and assessment of the skills covered in this project. Log in to your SAM account and go to your assignments page to see what your instructor has assigned.

What You Should Know

Having completed this project, you should be able to perform the tasks below. The tasks are listed in the same order they were presented in this project. For a list of the buttons, menus, toolbars, and commands introduced in this project, see the Quick Reference Summary at the back of this book and refer to the Page Number column.

1. Start Word (WD 6)
2. Customize the Word Window (WD 8)
3. Increase the Font Size before Typing (WD 17)
4. Type Text (WD 18)
5. Enter Blank Lines in a Document (WD 20)
6. Display Formatting Marks (WD 21)
7. Type More Text (WD 22)
8. Wordwrap Text as You Type (WD 23)
9. Enter Text that Scrolls the Document Window (WD 24)
10. Check Spelling and Grammar as You Type (WD 26)
11. Enter More Text (WD 27)
12. Save a New Document (WD 28)
13. Select Multiple Paragraphs (WD 33)
14. Change the Font Size of Text (WD 34)
15. Change the Font of Text (WD 36)
16. Right-Align a Paragraph (WD 37)
17. Center a Paragraph (WD 38)
18. Undo and Redo an Action (WD 39)
19. Select a Line (WD 40)
20. Format a Line of Text (WD 40)
21. Italicize Text (WD 41)
22. Underline a Word (WD 42)
23. Scroll through a Document (WD 43)
24. Select a Group of Words (WD 43)
25. Bold Text (WD 44)
26. Center a Paragraph (WD 45)
27. Insert Clip Art in a Document (WD 46)
28. Center a Paragraph Containing a Graphic (WD 48)
29. Select a Graphic (WD 49)
30. Resize a Graphic (WD 50)
31. Save an Existing Document with the Same File Name (WD 52)
32. Print a Document (WD 53)
33. Quit Word (WD 54, WD 62)
34. Open a Document (WD 55)
35. Insert Text in an Existing Document (WD 57)
36. Select a Word (WD 58)
37. Delete Text (WD 59)
38. Close the Entire Document and Start Over (WD 59)
39. Use the Type a Question for Help Box (WD 60)

More About

Quick Reference

For a table that lists how to complete the tasks covered in this book using the mouse, menu, shortcut menu, and keyboard, see the Quick Reference Summary at the back of this book, or visit the Word 2003 Quick Reference Web page (scsite.com/wd2003/qr).

Learn It Online

Instructions: To complete the Learn It Online exercises, start your browser, click the Address bar, and then enter the Web address `scsite.com/wd2003/learn`. When the Word 2003 Learn It Online page is displayed, follow the instructions in the exercises below. Each exercise has instructions for printing your results, either for your own records or for submission to your instructor.

1 Project Reinforcement TF, MC, and SA

Below Word Project 1, click the Project Reinforcement link. Print the quiz by clicking Print on the File menu for each page. Answer each question.

2 Flash Cards

Below Word Project 1, click the Flash Cards link and read the instructions. Type 20 (or a number specified by your instructor) in the Number of playing cards text box, type your name in the Enter your Name text box, and then click the Flip Card button. When the flash card is displayed, read the question and then click the ANSWER box arrow to select an answer. Flip through Flash Cards. If your score is 15 (75%) correct or greater, click Print on the File menu to print your results. If your score is less than 15 (75%) correct, then redo this exercise by clicking the Replay button.

3 Practice Test

Below Word Project 1, click the Practice Test link. Answer each question, enter your first and last name at the bottom of the page, and then click the Grade Test button. When the graded practice test is displayed on your screen, click Print on the File menu to print a hard copy. Continue to take practice tests until you score 80% or better.

4 Who Wants To Be a Computer Genius?

Below Word Project 1, click the Computer Genius link. Read the instructions, enter your first and last name at the bottom of the page, and then click the PLAY button. When your score is displayed, click the PRINT RESULTS link to print a hard copy.

5 Wheel of Terms

Below Word Project 1, click the Wheel of Terms link. Read the instructions, and then enter your first and last name and your school name. Click the PLAY button. When your score is displayed, right-click the score and then click Print on the shortcut menu to print a hard copy.

6 Crossword Puzzle Challenge

Below Word Project 1, click the Crossword Puzzle Challenge link. Read the instructions, and then enter your first and last name. Click the SUBMIT button. Work the crossword puzzle. When you are finished, click the Submit button. When the crossword puzzle is redisplayed, click the Print Puzzle button to print a hard copy.

7 Tips and Tricks

Below Word Project 1, click the Tips and Tricks link. Click a topic that pertains to Project 1. Right-click the information and then click Print on the shortcut menu. Construct a brief example of what the information relates to in Word to confirm you understand how to use the tip or trick.

8 Newsgroups

Below Word Project 1, click the Newsgroups link. Click a topic that pertains to Project 1. Print three comments.

9 Expanding Your Horizons

Below Word Project 1, click the Expanding Your Horizons link. Click a topic that pertains to Project 1. Print the information. Construct a brief example of what the information relates to in Word to confirm you understand the contents of the article.

10 Search Sleuth

Below Word Project 1, click the Search Sleuth link. To search for a term that pertains to this project, select a term below the Project 1 title and then use the Google search engine at google.com (or any major search engine) to display and print two Web pages that present information on the term.

11 Word Online Training

Below Word Project 1, click the Word Online Training link. When your browser displays the Microsoft Office Online Web page, click the Word link. Click one of the Word courses that covers one or more of the objectives listed at the beginning of the project on page WD 4. Print the first page of the course before stepping through it.

12 Office Marketplace

Below Word Project 1, click the Office Marketplace link. When your browser displays the Microsoft Office Online Web page, click the Office Marketplace link. Click a topic that relates to Word. Print the first page.

Apply Your Knowledge

1 Checking Spelling and Grammar, Modifying Text, and Formatting a Document

Instructions: Start Word. Open the document, Apply 1-1 Paris Announcement Unformatted, on the Data Disk. See page xxiv at the front of this book for instructions for downloading the Data Disk or see your instructor for information about accessing files required in this book.

The document on the Data Disk is an unformatted announcement that contains some spelling errors. You are to fix the spelling mistakes, modify text, format paragraphs and characters, and insert clip art in the announcement, so it looks like Figure 1-77 on the next page.

1. Correct each spelling and grammar error by right-clicking the flagged word and then clicking the appropriate correction on the shortcut menu, so the announcement text matches Figure 1-77 on the next page. The unformatted announcement on the Data Disk contains several spelling errors (red wavy underline) and grammar errors (green wavy underline). Word may flag some proper names that are spelled correctly. In these cases, click Ignore Once or Ignore All on the shortcut menu. If your screen does not display the wavy underlines, right-click the Spelling and Grammar Status icon on the status bar and be sure Hide Spelling Errors and Hide Grammatical Errors do not have check marks beside them. If they do, remove the check mark(s) by the appropriate command. If your screen still does not display the wavy underlines, right-click the Spelling and Grammar Status icon on the status bar, click Options on the shortcut menu, click the Recheck Document button, and then click the OK button.
2. At the end of the first sentence of body copy, change the period to an exclamation point. The sentence should read: See Paris this spring – on a shoestring!
3. Delete the word, morning, in the first sentence of the second paragraph of body copy.
4. Insert the word, event, between the text, Discount tickets, in the second sentence of the second paragraph of body copy. The text should read: Discount event tickets…
5. Change the font and font size of the first line of the headline to 72-point Lucida Calligraphy, or a similar font.
6. Change the font and font size of the second line of the headline to 48-point Lucida Calligraphy, or a similar font.
7. Right-align the second line of the headline.
8. Change the font size of the two paragraphs of body copy to 20 point.
9. Change the font and font size of the last line of the announcement to 24-point Arial.
10. Italicize the word, shoestring, in the first paragraph of body copy.
11. Bold the phrase, unbelievably low price, in the same paragraph.
12. Underline the telephone number in the last line of the announcement.
13. Italicize the text in the last line of the announcement.
14. Center the last line of the announcement.
15. Insert the clip art between the first and second lines of the headline. Use the search text, Paris, to locate this, or a similar, clip art image. Center the clip art.
16. Click File on the menu bar and then click Save As. Save the document using Apply 1-1 Paris Announcement Formatted as the file name.
17. Print the revised document, shown in Figure 1-77.

(continued)

Apply Your Knowledge

Checking Spelling and Grammar, Modifying Text, and Formatting a Document *(continued)*

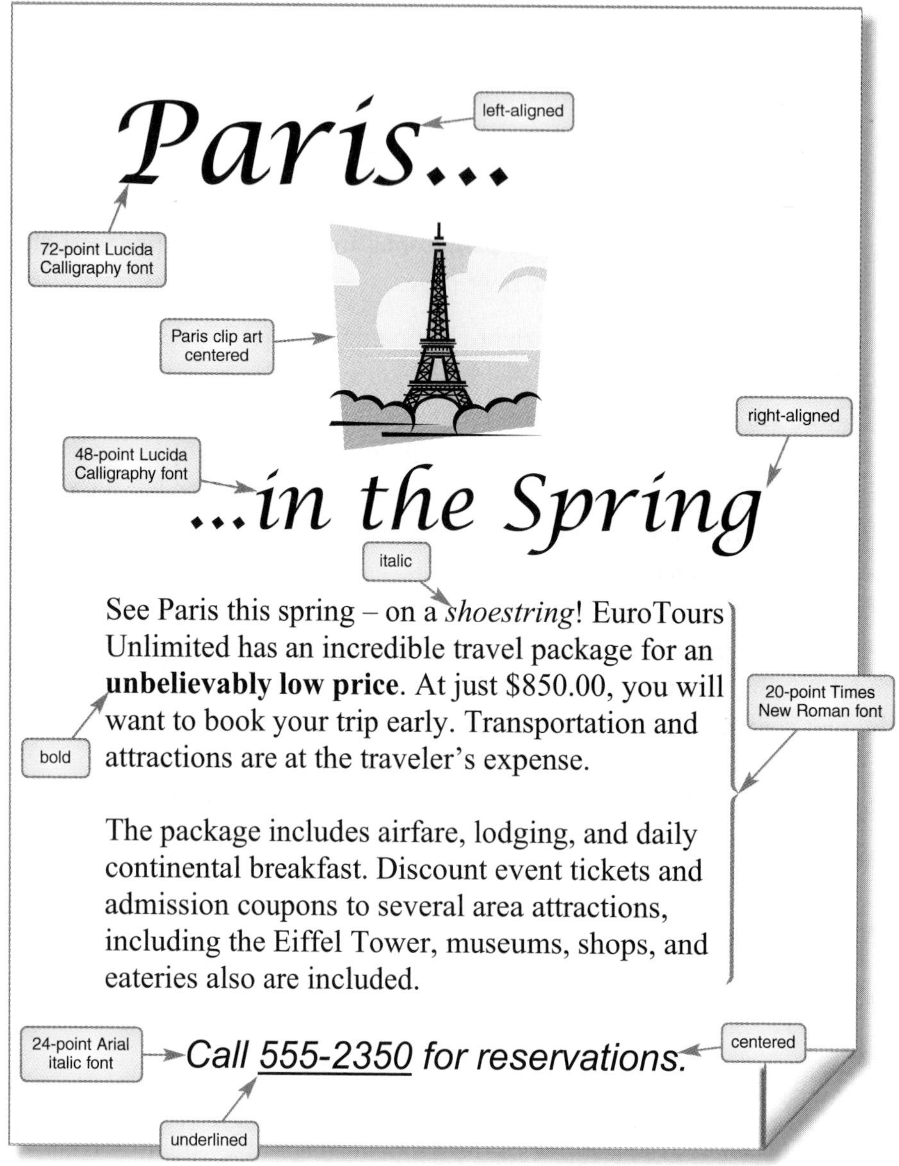

Paris...
left-aligned
72-point Lucida Calligraphy font
Paris clip art centered
right-aligned
48-point Lucida Calligraphy font
...in the Spring
italic
See Paris this spring – on a shoestring! EuroTours Unlimited has an incredible travel package for an unbelievably low price. At just $850.00, you will want to book your trip early. Transportation and attractions are at the traveler's expense.
bold
20-point Times New Roman font
The package includes airfare, lodging, and daily continental breakfast. Discount event tickets and admission coupons to several area attractions, including the Eiffel Tower, museums, shops, and eateries also are included.
24-point Arial italic font
Call 555-2350 for reservations.
centered
underlined

FIGURE 1-77

In the Lab

1 Creating an Announcement with Clip Art

Problem: You work as an assistant to the vice president at Reid Construction Company. She has asked you to prepare an announcement for part-time construction work. First, you prepare the unformatted announcement shown in Figure 1-78a, and then you format it so it looks like Figure 1-78b on the next page. ***Hint:*** Remember, if you make a mistake while formatting the announcement, you can click the Undo button on the Standard toolbar to undo your last action.

1. Before entering any text, change the font size from 12 to 20.
2. Display formatting marks on the screen.
3. Type the unformatted announcement shown in Figure 1-78a. If Word flags any misspelled words as you type, check the spelling of these words and correct them.
4. Save the document on a floppy disk with Lab 1-1 Reid Construction Announcement as the file name.

Want to work…
…outdoors?

Reid Construction

Reid Construction Company is looking for a few good part-time laborers. Join us for an information session on Saturday, March 11, at 1:00 p.m. at our corporate offices in Hamilton.

Interested parties should be available on weekends. Employment is needed for new home construction and remodeling work. Some experience preferred.

Call us at 555-0928 for directions.

FIGURE 1-78a Unformatted Document

5. Change the font of both lines of the headline to Britannic Bold, or a similar font. Change the font size from 20 to 48.
6. Right-align the second line of the headline.
7. Center the body title line.

(continued)

In the Lab

Creating an Announcement with Clip Art *(continued)*

8. Change the font of the body title line to Arial Black, or a similar font. Change the font size to 36. Bold the body title line.
9. In the first paragraph of the body copy, bold the text, part-time.
10. In the second paragraph, italicize the sentence, Some experience preferred.
11. In the same paragraph, underline the word, weekends.
12. Center the last line of the announcement.
13. Insert the clip art of a construction worker between the headline and the body title line. Search for the text, construction, in the Clip Art task pane to locate this, or a similar, graphic.
14. Center the clip art.
15. Save the announcement again with the same file name.
16. Print the formatted announcement, as shown in Figure 1-78b.

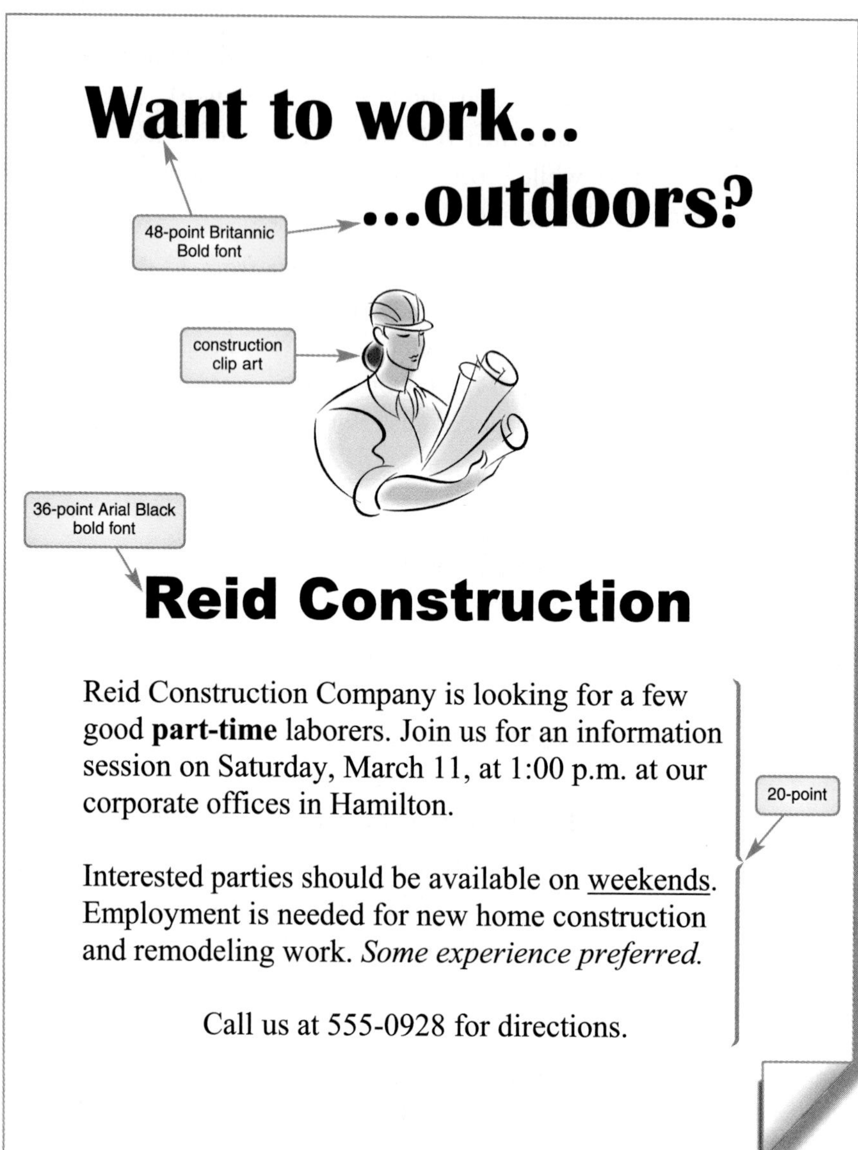

FIGURE 1-78b Formatted Document

2 Creating an Announcement with Resized Clip Art

Problem: Your professor at University Animal Clinic has requested that you prepare an announcement for an upcoming free veterinarian exam day. You prepare the announcement shown in Figure 1-79. ***Hint:*** Remember, if you make a mistake while formatting the announcement, you can click the Undo button on the Standard toolbar to undo your last action.

1. Before entering any text, change the font size from 12 to 20.
2. Display formatting marks on the screen.

In the Lab

3. Create the announcement shown in Figure 1-79. Enter the text of the document first without the clip art and unformatted; that is, without any bold, underlined, italicized, right-aligned, or centered text. If Word flags any misspelled words as you type, check the spelling of these words and correct them.
4. Save the document on a floppy disk with Lab 1-2 University Animal Clinic Announcement as the file name.
5. Change the font of both lines of the headline to Matura MT Script Capitals, or a similar font. Change the font size from 20 to 36.
6. Right-align the second line of the headline.
7. Center the body title line.
8. Change the font and font size of the body title line to 36-point Arial Rounded MT Bold. Bold the body title line.
9. Underline the word, only, in the first paragraph of the body copy.
10. In the next paragraph, italicize the sentence: Walk-ins accepted.

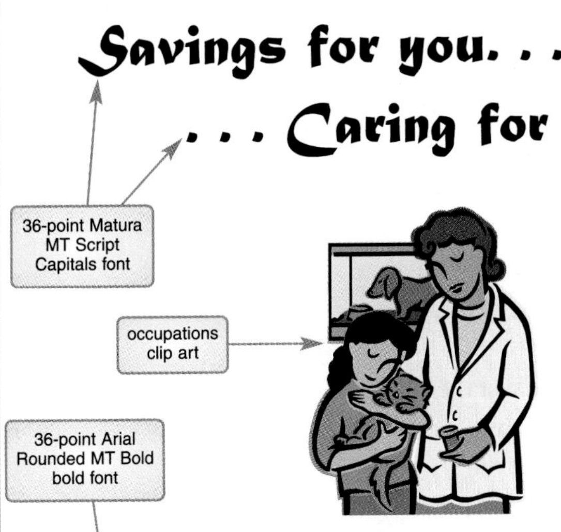

FIGURE 1-79

11. Center the last line of the announcement.
12. Insert the clip art between the headline and the body title line. Search for the text, occupations, in the Clip Art task pane to locate this, or a similar, graphic. Center the graphic.
13. Enlarge the graphic. If you make the graphic too large, the announcement may flow onto two pages. If this occurs, reduce the size of the graphic so the announcement fits on a single page. ***Hint:*** Use Help to learn about print preview, which is a way to see the page before you print it. To exit print preview and return to the document window, click the Close button on the Print Preview toolbar.
14. Save the announcement again with the same file name.
15. Print the announcement.

In the Lab

3 Creating an Announcement with Resized Clip Art, a Bulleted List, and Color

Problem: The Grishman College of Business has requested that each student in your class prepare an announcement advertising their pre-game party. The student that creates the winning announcement will receive a complimentary ticket to the buffet. You prepare the announcement shown in Figure 1-80. ***Hint:*** Remember, if you make a mistake while formatting the announcement, you can click the Undo button on the Standard toolbar to undo your last action.

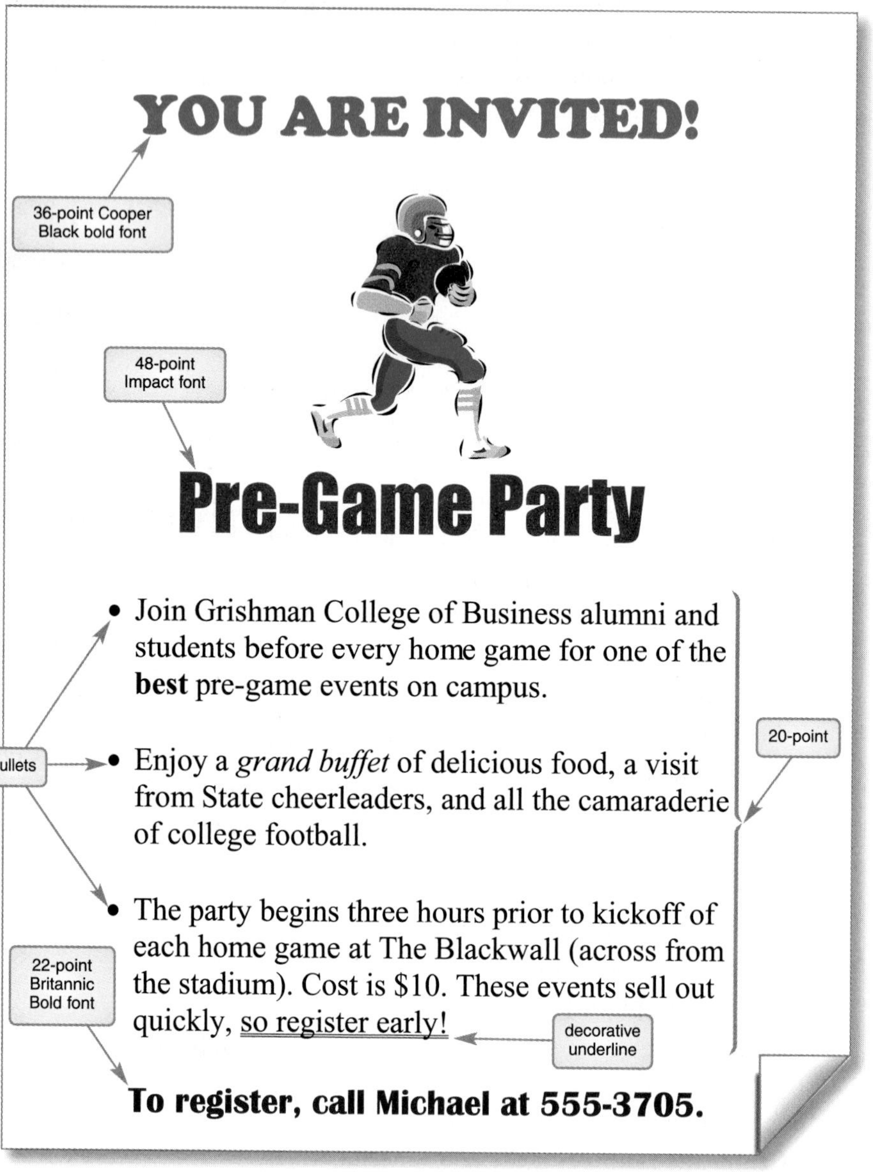

FIGURE 1-80

1. Type the announcement shown in Figure 1-80, using the fonts and font sizes indicated in the figure. Check spelling as you type.
2. Save the document on a floppy disk with Lab 1-3 Pre-Game Party Announcement as the file name.
3. Change the font color of the headline to green, the body title to red, and the last line of the announcement to blue. ***Hint:*** Use Help to learn how to change the font color of text.
4. Add a blue double underline below the text, so register early. ***Hint:*** Use Help to learn how to add a decorative underline to text.
5. Add bullets to the three paragraphs of body copy. ***Hint:*** Use Help to learn how to add bullets to a list of paragraphs.
6. Insert clip art related to football between the headline and the body title line. If you have access to the Web, select the clip art from the Web. Otherwise, select the clip art from the hard disk. In the Clip Art task pane, images from the Web display an icon of a small globe in their lower-left corner.
7. Enlarge the football graphic. If you make the graphic too large, the announcement may flow onto two pages. If this occurs, reduce the size of the graphic so the announcement fits on a single page. ***Hint:*** Use Help to learn about print preview, which is a way to see the page before you print it. To exit print preview and return to the document window, click the Close button on the Print Preview toolbar.
8. Save the announcement again with the same file name.
9. Print the announcement.

Cases and Places

The difficulty of these case studies varies:
■ are the least difficult and ■■ are more difficult. The last exercise is a group exercise.

1 ■ You have been assigned the task of preparing an announcement for The Gridiron Club. The announcement is to contain clip art related to football. Use the following text: first line of headline – Gridiron Club…; second line of headline – …Tailgate Party; body title – GO TROJANS!; first paragraph of body copy – Join us on Friday, October 28, for a pre-game tailgate party. Help us celebrate our beloved Trojans' undefeated season! The Gridiron Club will provide grills, brats, hamburgers, hot dogs, and buns. Please bring a side dish to share and your own nonalcoholic beverages.; second paragraph of body copy – The party starts at 5:30 p.m. in the parking lot by the Administration Center. Kick-off for the first playoff game is at 7:00 p.m.; and last line – Call 555-1995 for more information. Use the concepts and techniques presented in this project to create and format this announcement. Be sure to check spelling and grammar in the announcement.

2 ■ You have been assigned the task of preparing an announcement for an upcoming camp at the Sherman Planetarium. The announcement is to contain clip art of a telescope. Use the following text: first line of headline – Reach for…; second line of headline – …the Stars; body title – Space, Stars, and Skies Camp; first paragraph of body copy – Have you always been fascinated by the planets, stars, and space travel? Enroll in our Space, Stars, and Skies Camp to learn more about the cosmos. The camp will meet June 6 through June 9 from 8:30 a.m. until 12:30 p.m. at the Sherman Planetarium.; second paragraph of body copy – Our facilities include simulators, lecture halls, virtual rooms, and a planetarium. Learn about space travel from our staff, two of whom are former astronauts.; third paragraph of body copy – Register early to reserve your seat. Space is limited to 25 participants.; and last line – Call 555-9141 to register. Use the concepts and techniques presented in this project to create and format this announcement. Be sure to check spelling and grammar in the announcement.

3 ■■ Your boss at Cornucopia Health Foods has asked you to prepare an announcement for a grand opening. You are to include appropriate clip art. He gives you the following information for the announcement. The doors of its newest store will open in Centerbrook Mall at 9:00 a.m. on Monday, September 26. You will find great deals throughout the store. Discount coupons and free samples will be distributed all day. The first 50 customers at the register will receive a free bottle of vitamin C tablets. Cornucopia Health Foods offers a huge selection of health food and organics. Tofu, carob, soy products, herbal teas, vitamin supplements, and organically grown produce are just a few items in our extensive product line. The store's slogan is as follows: Cornucopia ~ good food for good health! Use the concepts and techniques presented in this project to create the announcement. Change the color of text in the headline, body title, and last line of the announcement. Use a decorative underline in the announcement. Add bullets to the paragraphs of the body copy. Be sure to check spelling and grammar in the announcement.

Cases and Places

4 You have been assigned the task of preparing an announcement for Stone Bay Apartments advertising an apartment for rent. You are to include appropriate clip art. These details have been provided. Stone Bay Apartments has a two-bedroom apartment available for rent now. This upper-level unit has an eat-in kitchen, central air, and a large living room with southern exposure. Rent is $925.00 a month. Utilities are included in rent. Pets are welcome. Interested parties should call 555-8265 to arrange a showing. Stone Bay Apartments provide amenities galore, including laundry facilities, garage parking, clubhouse, pool, and tennis courts. We are located close to Lake Park Mall, grocery stores, restaurants, and Victor Community College. Use the concepts and techniques presented in this project to create the announcement. Change the color of text in the headline, body title, and last line of the announcement. Use a decorative underline in the announcement. Add bullets to some of the paragraphs of the body copy. Be sure to check spelling and grammar in the announcement.

5 **Working Together** Schools, churches, libraries, grocery stores, and other public places have bulletin boards for announcements and other postings. Often, these bulletin boards have so many announcements that some go unnoticed. Look at a bulletin board at one of the locations mentioned above and find a posted announcement that you think might be overlooked. Copy the text from the announcement and distribute it to each team member. Each member then independently should use this text, together with the techniques presented in this project, to create an announcement that would be more likely to catch a reader's eye. Be sure to check spelling and grammar. As a group, critique each announcement and have each member redesign their announcement based on the group's recommendations. Hand in printouts of each team member's original and final announcements.

MICROSOFT OFFICE

Excel 2003

MICROSOFT OFFICE EXCEL

MICROSOFT OFFICE
Excel 2003

Creating a Worksheet and an Embedded Chart

PROJECT 1

CASE PERSPECTIVE

In the late 1970s, Extreme Blading pioneered the sport of inline skating as an off-season training tool for hockey players. The sport quickly caught on with fitness enthusiasts, aggressive skaters, and the population in general. Today, nearly 50 million inline skaters participate in the activity worldwide and the sport continues to grow.

The Extreme Blading product line includes a variety of skates, including inline, quad, and custom models for all age levels, as well as a complete line of protective gear and other accessories.

For years, the company sold their goods via direct mail, telesales, and company-owned outlets in major cities across the country. Thanks to the popularity of personal computers and the World Wide Web, the company added an e-commerce Web site last year. This new sales channel has given the company access to more than 600 million people worldwide and has resulted in a significant increase in sales.

Sales continued to grow during the first half of this year, thus driving senior management to ask their financial analyst, Maria Lopez, to develop a better sales tracking system. As a first step, Maria has asked you to prepare an easy-to-read worksheet that shows product sales for the second quarter by sales channel (Figure 1-1 on page EX 5). In addition, Maria has asked you to create a chart showing second quarter sales, because the president of the company likes to have a graphical representation of sales that allows her quickly to identify stronger and weaker product groups by sales channel.

As you read through this project, you will learn how to use Excel to create, save, and print a financial report that includes a 3-D Column chart.

Creating a Worksheet and an Embedded Chart

PROJECT

Objectives

You will have mastered the material in this project when you can:

- Start and Quit Excel
- Describe the Excel worksheet
- Enter text and numbers
- Use the AutoSum button to sum a range of cells
- Copy a cell to a range of cells using the fill handle
- Format a worksheet
- Create a 3-D Clustered column chart
- Save a workbook and print a worksheet
- Open a workbook
- Use the AutoCalculate area to determine statistics
- Correct errors on a worksheet
- Use the Excel Help system to answer questions

What Is Microsoft Office Excel 2003?

Microsoft Office Excel 2003 is a powerful spreadsheet program that allows users to organize data, complete calculations, make decisions, graph data, develop professional looking reports (Figure 1-1), publish organized data to the Web, and access real-time data from Web sites. The four major parts of Excel are:

- **Worksheets** Worksheets allow users to enter, calculate, manipulate, and analyze data such as numbers and text. The term worksheet means the same as spreadsheet.
- **Charts** Excel can draw a variety of charts.
- **Lists** Lists organize and store data. For example, once a user enters data into a worksheet, Excel can sort the data, search for specific data, and select data that satisfies defined criteria.
- **Web Support** Web support allows users to save Excel worksheets or parts of a worksheet in HTML format, so a user can view and manipulate the worksheet using a browser. Excel Web support also provides access to real-time data, such as stock quotes, using Web queries.

This latest version of Excel makes it much easier to create and manipulate lists of data. It also offers industry-standard XML support that simplifies the sharing of data within and outside an organization; improved statistical functions; smart documents that automatically fill with data; information rights management; allows two workbooks to be compared side by side; and includes the capability of searching a variety of reference information.

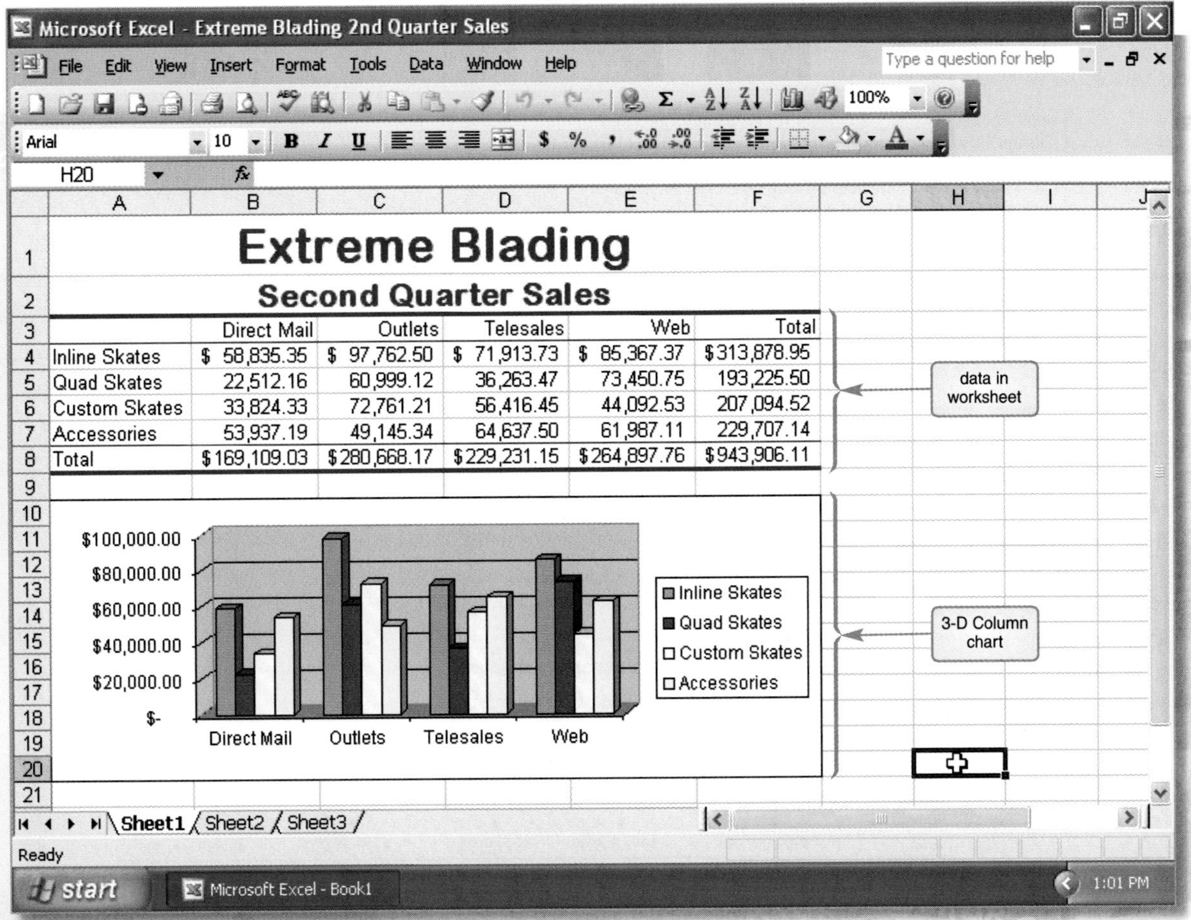

FIGURE 1-1

Project One — Extreme Blading Second Quarter Sales

The first step in creating an effective worksheet is to make sure you understand what is required. The person or persons requesting the worksheet should supply their requirements in a requirements document. A **requirements document** includes a needs statement, source of data, summary of calculations, and any other special requirements for the worksheet, such as charting and Web support. Figure 1-2 on the next page shows the requirements document for the new worksheet to be created in this project.

After carefully reviewing the requirements document, the next step is to design a solution or draw a sketch of the worksheet based on the requirements, including titles, column and row headings, location of data values, and the 3-D Column chart, as shown in Figure 1-3 on the next page. The dollar signs, 9s, and commas that you see in the sketch of the worksheet indicate formatted numeric values.

More About

Worksheet Development Cycle

Spreadsheet specialists do not sit down and start entering text, formulas, and data into a blank Excel worksheet as soon as they have a spreadsheet assignment. Instead, they follow an organized plan, or methodology, that breaks the development cycle into a series of tasks. The recommended methodology for creating worksheets includes (1) analyze requirements (supplied in a requirements document); (2) design solution; (3) validate design; (4) implement design; (5) test solution; and (6) document solution.

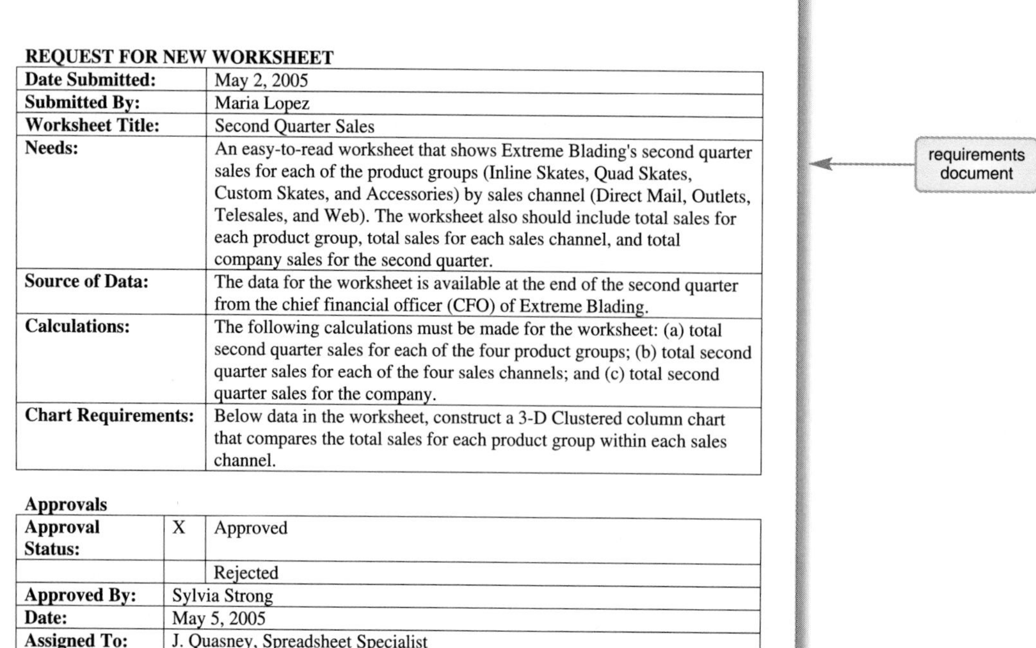

REQUEST FOR NEW WORKSHEET

Date Submitted:	May 2, 2005
Submitted By:	Maria Lopez
Worksheet Title:	Second Quarter Sales
Needs:	An easy-to-read worksheet that shows Extreme Blading's second quarter sales for each of the product groups (Inline Skates, Quad Skates, Custom Skates, and Accessories) by sales channel (Direct Mail, Outlets, Telesales, and Web). The worksheet also should include total sales for each product group, total sales for each sales channel, and total company sales for the second quarter.
Source of Data:	The data for the worksheet is available at the end of the second quarter from the chief financial officer (CFO) of Extreme Blading.
Calculations:	The following calculations must be made for the worksheet: (a) total second quarter sales for each of the four product groups; (b) total second quarter sales for each of the four sales channels; and (c) total second quarter sales for the company.
Chart Requirements:	Below data in the worksheet, construct a 3-D Clustered column chart that compares the total sales for each product group within each sales channel.

Approvals

Approval Status:	X	Approved
		Rejected
Approved By:	Sylvia Strong	
Date:	May 5, 2005	
Assigned To:	J. Quasney, Spreadsheet Specialist	

requirements document

FIGURE 1-2

sketch of worksheet

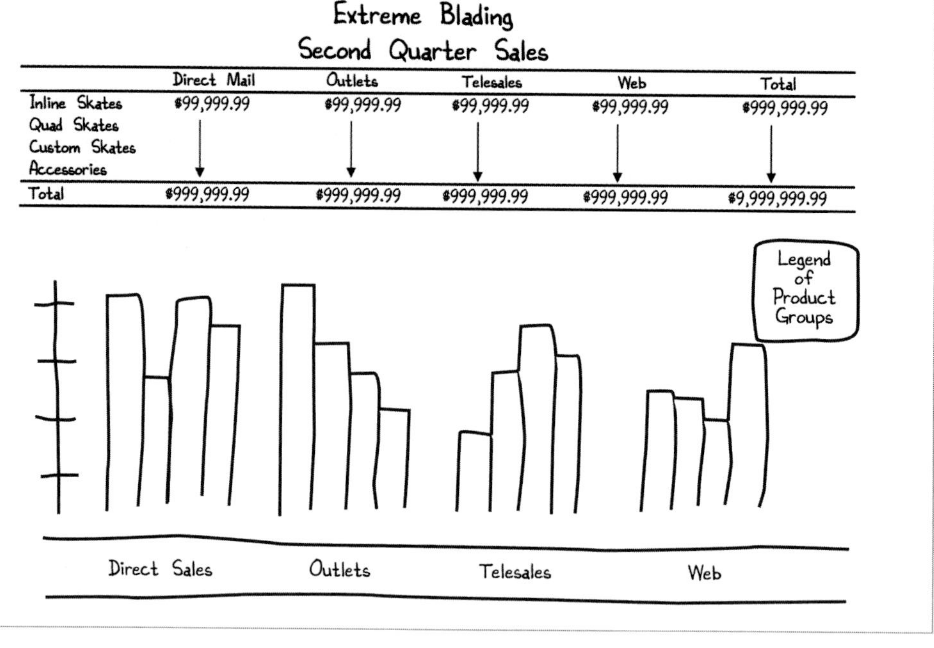

FIGURE 1-3

> ***More About***
>
> **Excel 2003 Features**
>
> With its what-if analysis tools, research capabilities, collaboration tools, XML support, smart tags, speech recognition, charting features, toolbars, Web capabilities, hundreds of functions, and speech playback, Excel 2003 is one of the easier and more powerful spreadsheet packages available. Its dynamic analytical features make it possible to answer complicated what-if questions. Its Web capabilities allow you to create, publish, view, and analyze data on an intranet or the World Wide Web.

With a good understanding of the requirements document and a sketch of the worksheet, the next step is to use Excel to create the worksheet and chart.

Starting and Customizing Excel

If you are stepping through this project on a computer and you want your screen to match the figures in this book, then you should change your computer's resolution to 800 × 600. For more information on how to change the resolution on your computer, see Appendix D. The following steps show how to start Excel.

To Start Excel

1

- **Click the Start button on the Windows taskbar, point to All Programs on the Start menu, point to Microsoft Office on the All Programs submenu, and then point to Microsoft Office Excel 2003 on the Microsoft Office submenu.**

Windows displays the Start menu, the All Programs submenu, and the Microsoft Office submenu (Figure 1-4).

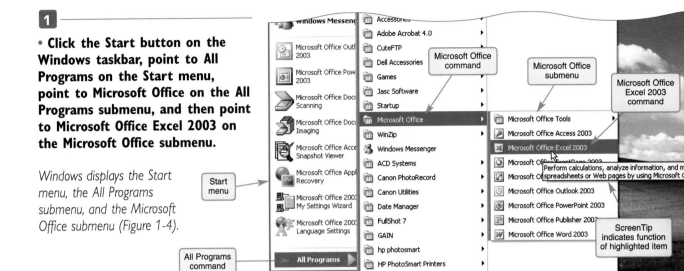

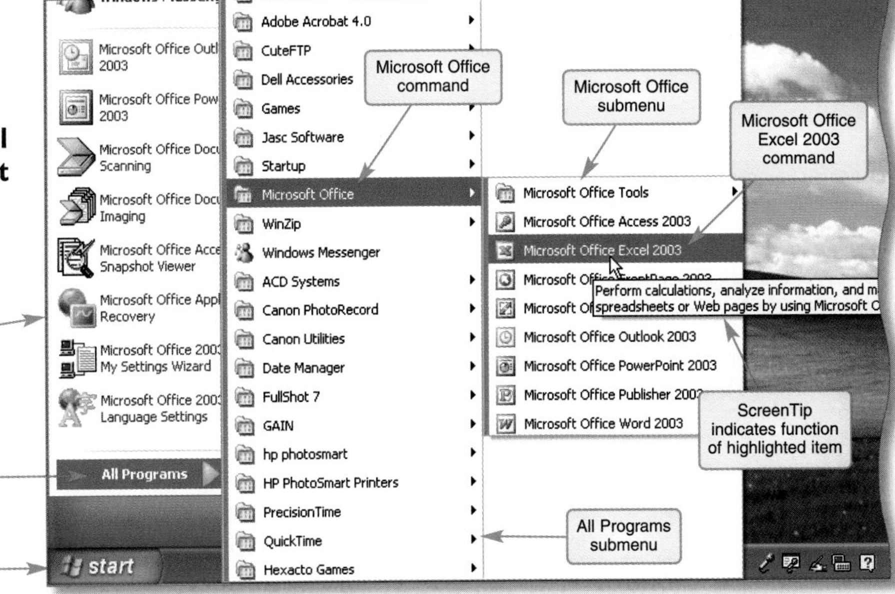

FIGURE 1-4

2

- **Click Microsoft Office Excel 2003.**

Excel starts. After several seconds, Excel displays a blank workbook titled Book1 in the Excel window (Figure 1-5).

3

- **If the Excel window is not maximized, double-click its title bar to maximize it.**

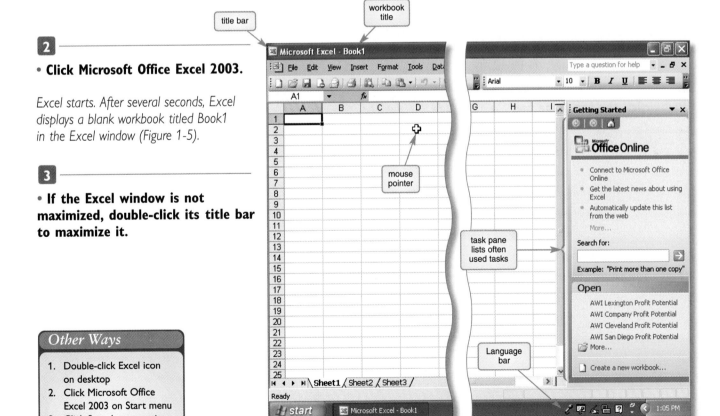

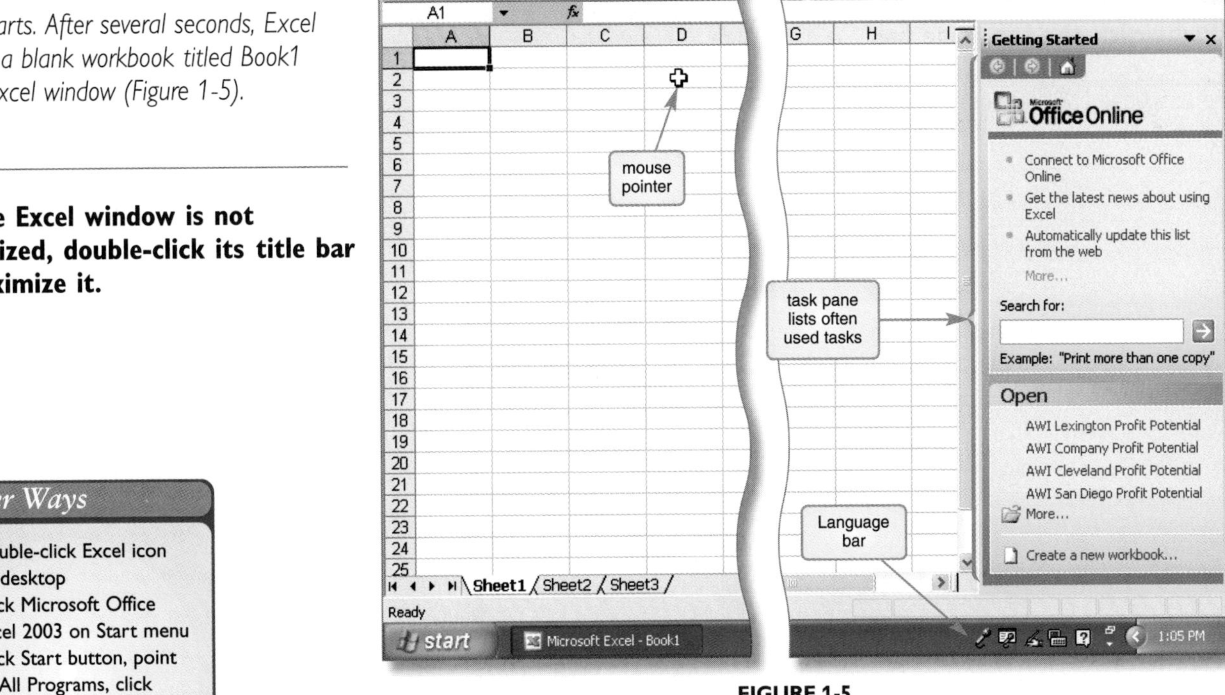

FIGURE 1-5

Other Ways

1. Double-click Excel icon on desktop
2. Click Microsoft Office Excel 2003 on Start menu
3. Click Start button, point to All Programs, click New Office Document, click General tab, double-click Blank Workbook icon

The screen shown in Figure 1-5 on the previous page illustrates how the Excel window looks the first time you start Excel after installation on most computers. If the Office Speech Recognition software is installed and active on your computer, then when you start Excel, the Language bar is displayed on the screen. The **Language bar** contains buttons that allow you to speak commands and dictate text. It usually is located on the right side of the Windows taskbar next to the notification area, and it changes to include the speech recognition functions available in Excel. In this book, the Language bar is closed because it takes up computer resources and with the Language bar active, the microphone can be turned on accidentally by clicking the Microphone button causing your computer to act in an unstable manner. For additional information about the Language bar, see page EX 15 and Appendix B.

More About

Task Panes

You can drag a task pane title bar to float the pane in your work area or dock it on either the left or right side of a screen, depending on your personal preference.

As shown in Figure 1-5, Excel displays a task pane on the right side of the screen. A **task pane** is a separate window that enables users to carry out some Excel tasks more efficiently. When you start Excel, it displays the Getting Started task pane, which is a small window that provides commonly used links and commands that allow you to open files, create new files, or search Office-related topics on the Microsoft Web site. In this book, the Getting Started task pane is hidden to allow the maximum number of columns to appear in Excel.

At startup, Excel also displays two toolbars on a single row. A **toolbar** contains buttons, boxes, and menus that allow you to perform tasks quickly. To allow for more efficient use of the buttons, the toolbars should appear on two separate rows, instead of sharing a single row. The following steps show how to close the Language bar, close the Getting Started task pane, and instruct Excel to display the toolbars on two separate rows.

To Customize the Excel Window

1

- **Right-click the Language bar.**

The Language bar shortcut menu appears (Figure 1-6).

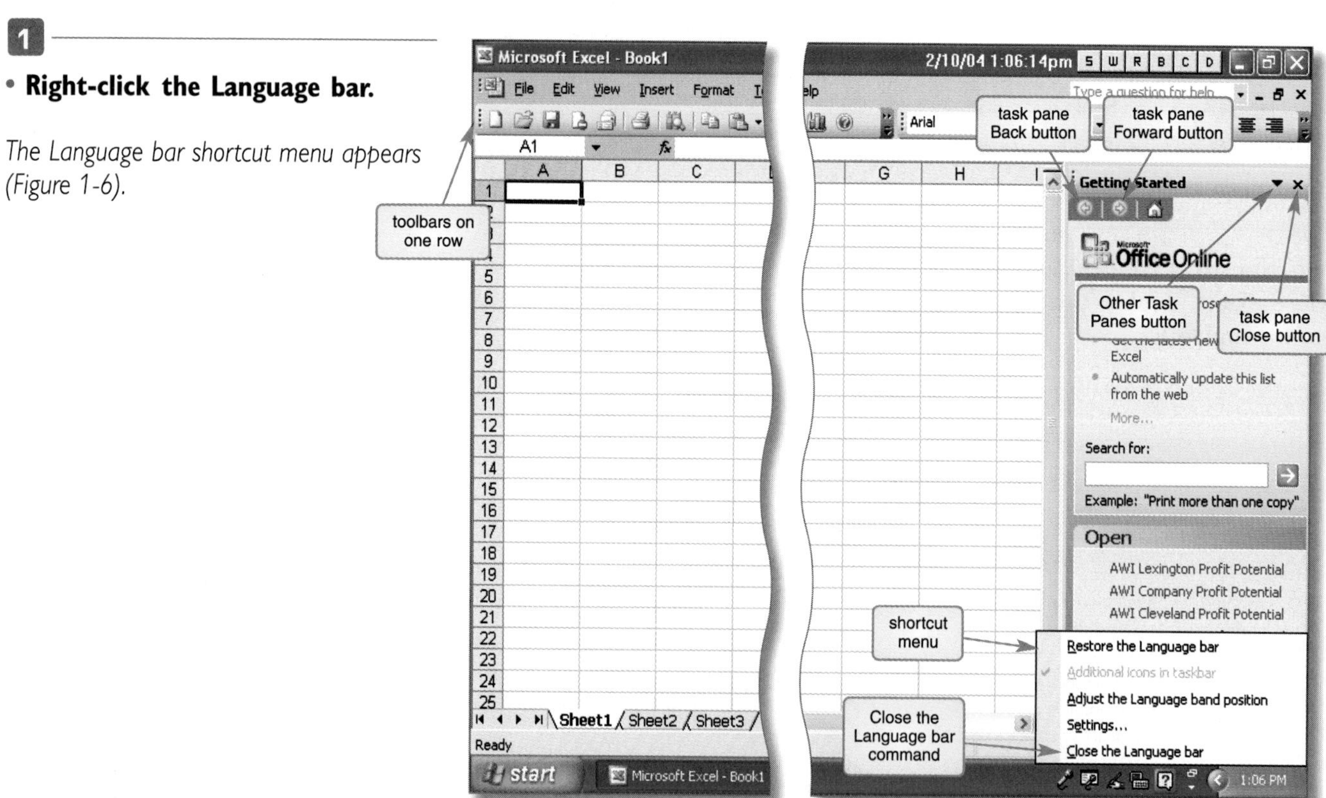

FIGURE 1-6

2

- **Click Close the Language bar.**
- **Click the Getting Started task pane Close button in the upper-right corner of the task pane.**
- **If the toolbars are positioned on the same row, click the Toolbar Options button.**

The Language bar disappears. Excel closes the Getting Started task pane and displays additional columns. Excel also displays the Toolbar Options list showing the buttons that do not fit on the toolbars when toolbars appear on one row (Figure 1-7).

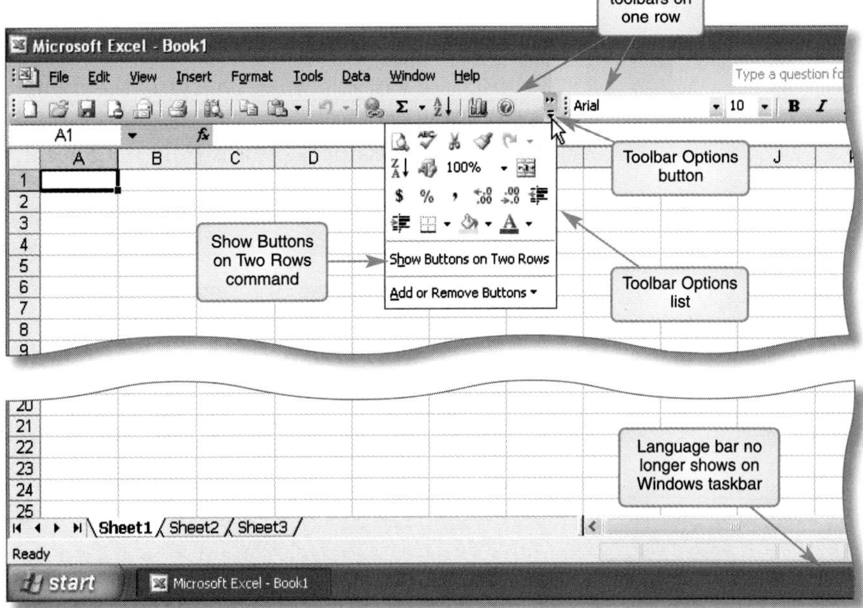

FIGURE 1-7

3

- **Click Show Buttons on Two Rows.**

Excel displays the toolbars on two separate rows (Figure 1-8). With the toolbars on two separate rows, all of the buttons fit on the two toolbars.

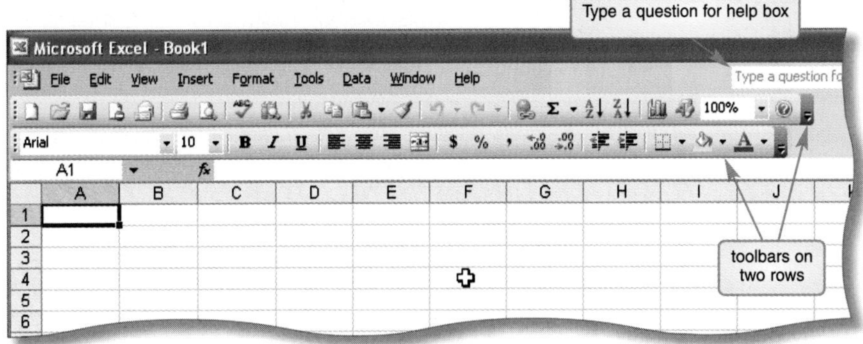

FIGURE 1-8

As you work through creating a worksheet, you will find that certain Excel operations cause Excel to display a task pane. Excel provides eleven task panes, in addition to the Getting Started task pane shown in Figure 1-6. Some of the more important ones are the Clipboard task pane, the Excel Help task pane, and the Clip Art task pane. Throughout the book, these task panes are discussed when they are used.

At any point while working with an Excel worksheet, you can open or close a task pane by clicking the Task Pane command on the View menu. You can activate additional task panes by clicking the Other Task Panes button to the left of the Close button on the task pane title bar (Figure 1-6) and then selecting a task pane in the Other Task Panes list. The Back and Forward buttons below the task pane title bar allow you to switch between task panes that you opened during a session.

More About

The Excel Help System

Need Help? It is no further away than the Type a question for help box on the menu bar in the upper-right corner of the window. Click the box that contains the text, Type a question for help (Figure 1-8), type `help`, and then press the ENTER key. Excel responds with a list of topics you can click to learn about obtaining help on any Excel-related topic. To find out what is new in Excel 2003, type `what is new in Excel` in the Type a question for help box.

The Excel Worksheet

When Excel starts, it creates a new blank workbook, called Book1. The **workbook** (Figure 1-9 on the next page) is like a notebook. Inside the workbook are sheets, each of which is called a **worksheet**. Excel opens a new workbook with three worksheets.

If necessary, you can add additional worksheets to a maximum of 255. Each worksheet has a sheet name that appears on a **sheet tab** at the bottom of the workbook. For example, Sheet1 is the name of the active worksheet displayed in the Book1 workbook. If you click the sheet tab labeled Sheet2, Excel displays the Sheet2 worksheet. This project uses only the Sheet1 worksheet.

The Worksheet

The worksheet is organized into a rectangular grid containing vertical columns and horizontal rows. A column letter above the grid, also called the **column heading**, identifies each column. A row number on the left side of the grid, also called the **row heading**, identifies each row. With the screen resolution set to 800 × 600 and the Excel window maximized, Excel displays 12 columns (A through L) and 23 rows (1 through 23) of the worksheet on the screen, as shown in Figure 1-9.

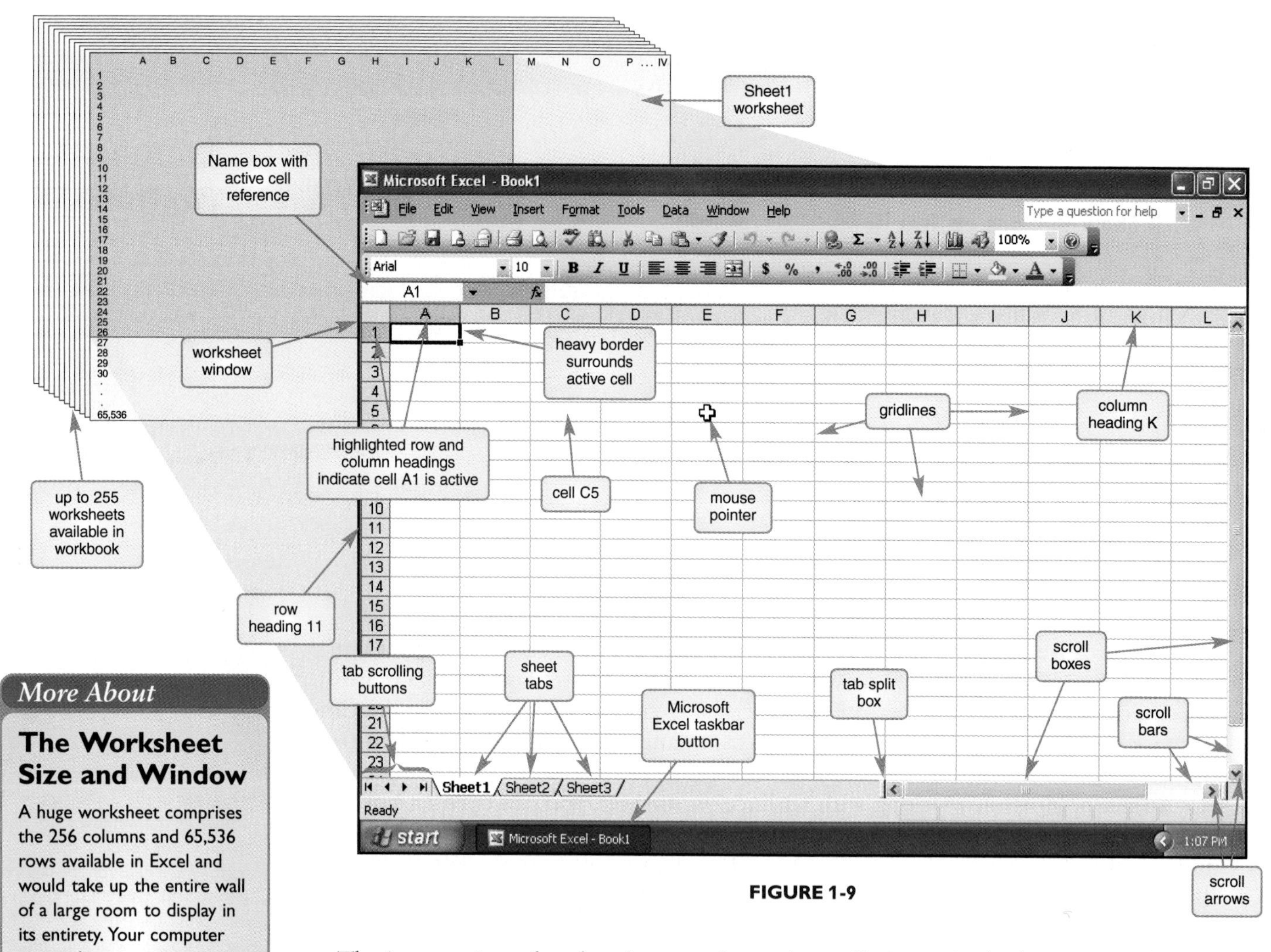

FIGURE 1-9

More About

The Worksheet Size and Window

A huge worksheet comprises the 256 columns and 65,536 rows available in Excel and would take up the entire wall of a large room to display in its entirety. Your computer screen, by comparison, is a small window that allows you to view only a minute area of the worksheet at one time. While you cannot see the entire worksheet, you can move the window over the worksheet to view any part of it.

The intersection of each column and row is a cell. A **cell** is the basic unit of a worksheet into which you enter data. Each worksheet in a workbook has 256 columns and 65,536 rows for a total of 16,777,216 cells. The column headings begin with A and end with IV. The row headings begin with 1 and end with 65,536. Only a small fraction of the active worksheet appears on the screen at one time.

A cell is referred to by its unique address, or **cell reference**, which is the coordinates of the intersection of a column and a row. To identify a cell, specify the column letter first, followed by the row number. For example, cell reference C5 refers to the cell located at the intersection of column C and row 5 (Figure 1-9).

One cell on the worksheet, designated the **active cell**, is the one into which you can enter data. The active cell in Figure 1-9 is A1. The active cell is identified in three ways. First, a heavy border surrounds the cell; second, the active cell reference shows immediately above column A in the Name box; and third, the column heading A and row heading 1 are highlighted so it is easy to see which cell is active (Figure 1-9).

The horizontal and vertical lines on the worksheet itself are called **gridlines**. Gridlines make it easier to see and identify each cell in the worksheet. If desired, you can turn the gridlines off so they do not show on the worksheet, but it is recommended that you leave them on for now.

The mouse pointer in Figure 1-9 has the shape of a block plus sign. The mouse pointer appears as a block plus sign whenever it is located in a cell on the worksheet. Another common shape of the mouse pointer is the block arrow. The mouse pointer turns into the block arrow whenever you move it outside the worksheet or when you drag cell contents between rows or columns. The other mouse pointer shapes are described when they appear on the screen.

More About

The Mouse Pointer

The mouse pointer can change to one of more than 15 different shapes, such as a block arrow, cross hair, or chart symbol, depending on the task you are performing in Excel and the mouse pointer's location on the screen.

Worksheet Window

You view the portion of the worksheet displayed on the screen through a **worksheet window** (Figure 1-9). Below and to the right of the worksheet window are **scroll bars**, **scroll arrows**, and **scroll boxes** that you can use to move the worksheet window around to view different parts of the active worksheet. To the right of the sheet tabs at the bottom of the screen is the tab split box. You can drag the **tab split box** to increase or decrease the view of the sheet tabs (Figure 1-9). When you decrease the view of the sheet tabs, you increase the length of the horizontal scroll bar, and vice versa.

The menu bar, Standard toolbar, Formatting toolbar, and formula bar appear at the top of the screen, above the worksheet window and below the title bar.

Q&A

Q: Can the Excel window or viewing area be increased to show more of the worksheet?

A: Yes. Two ways exist to increase what you can see in the viewing area: (1) on the View menu, click Full Screen; and (2) change to a higher resolution. See Appendix D for information about how to change to a higher resolution.

Menu Bar

The **menu bar** is a special toolbar that includes the menu names as shown in Figure 1-10a on the next page. Each **menu name** represents a menu. A **menu** is a list of commands that you can use to retrieve, store, print, and manipulate data on the worksheet. When you point to a menu name on the menu bar, the area of the menu bar containing the name changes to a button. To display a menu, such as the Edit menu, click the Edit menu name on the menu bar (Figures 1-10b and 1-10c on the next page). If you point to a menu command with an arrow to its right, Excel displays a **submenu** from which you can choose a command.

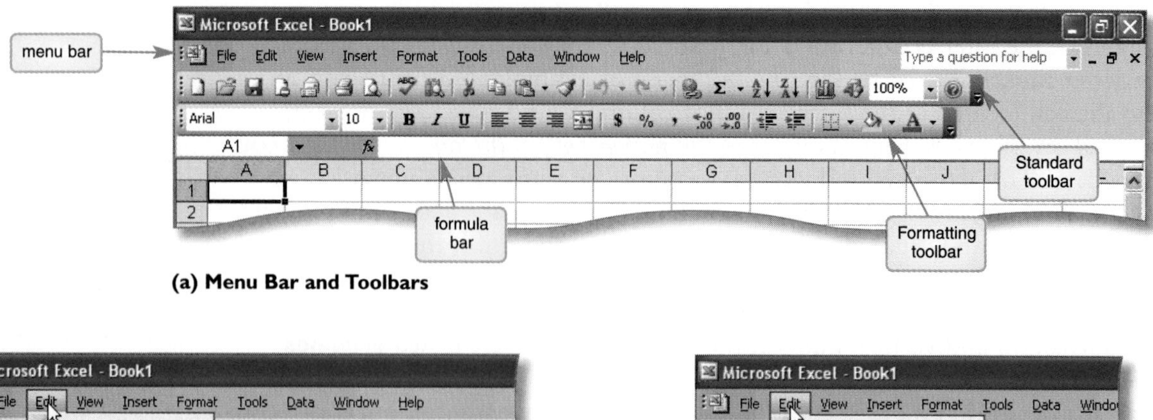

(a) Menu Bar and Toolbars

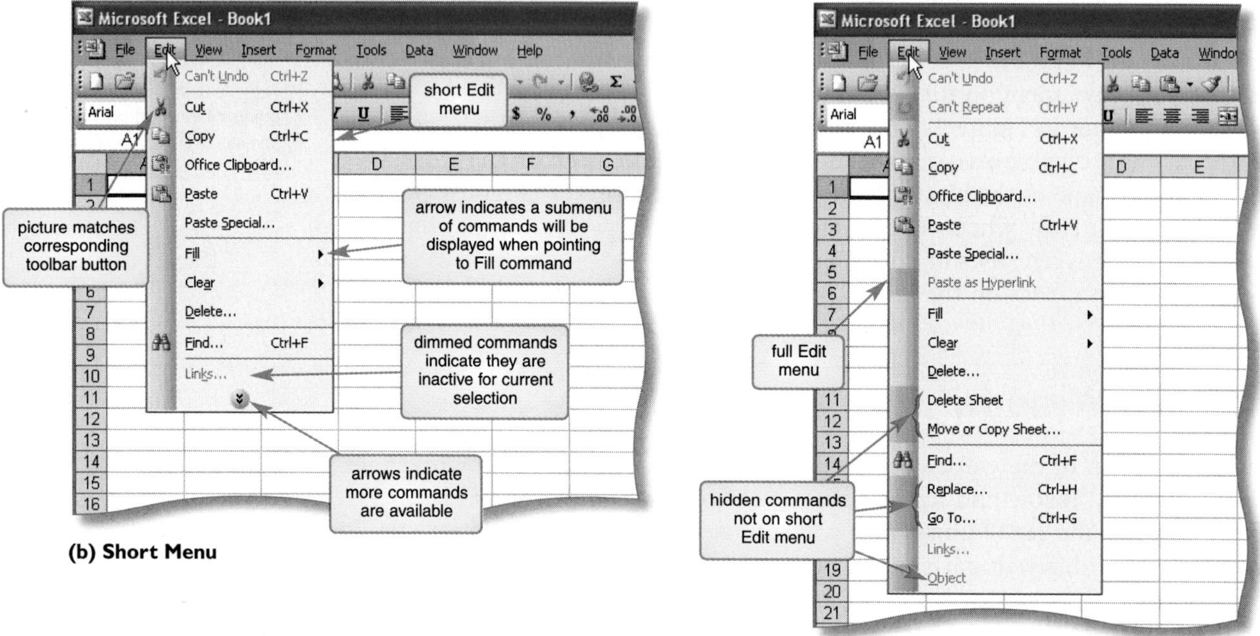

(b) Short Menu

(c) Full Menu

FIGURE 1-10

When you click a menu name on the menu bar, Excel displays a **short menu** listing the most recently used commands (Figure 1-10b). If you wait a few seconds or click the arrows at the bottom of the short menu, Excel displays the full menu. The **full menu** lists all of the commands associated with a menu (Figure 1-10c). You also can display a full menu immediately by double-clicking the menu name on the menu bar. In this book, use one of the following techniques to ensure that Excel always displays the full menu.

1. Click the menu name on the menu bar and then wait a few seconds.
2. Click the menu name on the menu bar and then click the arrows at the bottom of the short menu.
3. Click the menu name on the menu bar and then point to the arrows at the bottom of the short menu.
4. Double-click the menu name on the menu bar.

Both short and full menus display some dimmed commands. A **dimmed command** appears gray, or dimmed, instead of black, which indicates it is not available for the current selection. A command with medium blue shading to the left of it on a full menu is called a **hidden command** because it does not appear on a short menu. As you use Excel, it automatically personalizes the short menus for you based on how often you use commands. That is, as you use hidden commands, Excel *unhides* them and places them on the short menu.

The menu bar can change to include other menu names depending on the type of work you are doing in Excel. For example, if you are working with a chart sheet rather than a worksheet, Excel displays the Chart menu bar with menu names that reflect charting commands.

More About

Toolbars

You can move a toolbar to any location on the screen. Drag the move handle (Figure 1-12a on the next page) to the desired location. Once the toolbar is in the window area, drag the title bar to move it. Each side of the screen is called a dock. You can drag a toolbar to a dock so it does not clutter the window.

Standard Toolbar and Formatting Toolbar

The Standard toolbar and the Formatting toolbar (Figure 1-11) contain buttons and boxes that allow you to perform frequent tasks more quickly than when using the menu bar. For example, to print a worksheet, you click the Print button on the Standard toolbar. Each button has a picture on the button face to help you remember the button's function. Also, when you move the mouse pointer over a button or box, Excel displays the name of the button or box below it in a **ScreenTip**.

Figures 1-11a and 1-11b illustrate the Standard and Formatting toolbars and describe the functions of the buttons. Each of the buttons and boxes will be explained in detail when they are used.

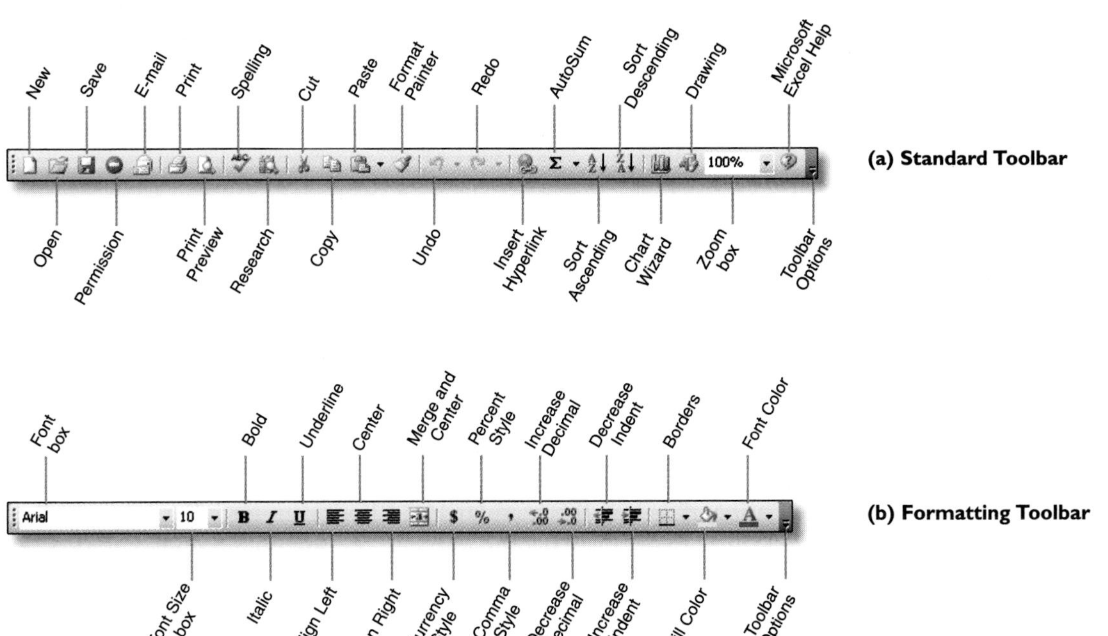

FIGURE 1-11

When you first install Excel, both the Standard and Formatting toolbars are preset to display on the same row (Figure 1-12a on the next page), immediately below the menu bar. Unless the resolution of your display device is greater than 800 × 600, many of the buttons that belong on these toolbars are hidden. Hidden buttons appear in the Toolbar Options list (Figure 1-12b on the next page). In this mode, you also can display all the buttons on either toolbar by double-clicking the **move handle** on the left of each toolbar (Figure 1-12a).

More About

Resetting Toolbars

If your toolbars have a different set of buttons than shown in Figure 1-11, it probably means that a previous user added or deleted buttons. To reset the toolbars to their default, see Appendix D.

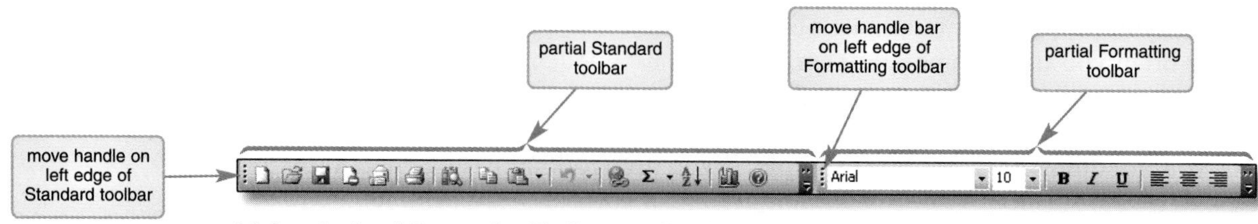

(a) Standard and Formatting Toolbars on One Row

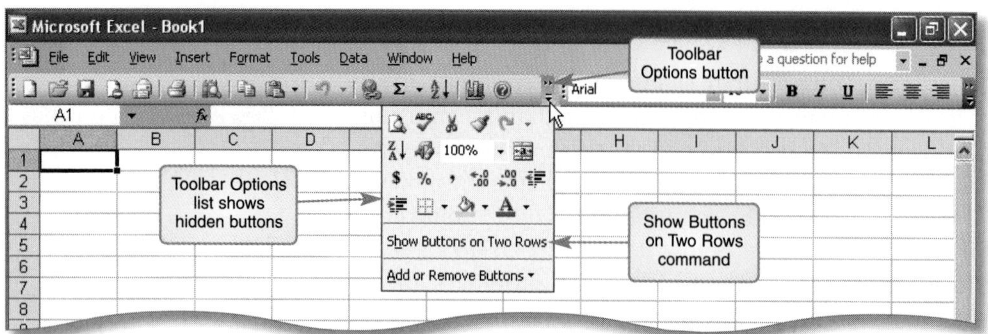

(b) Toolbar Options List

(c) Standard and Formatting Toolbars on Two Rows

FIGURE 1-12

More About

Sizing Toolbar Buttons

If you have difficulty seeing the small buttons on the toolbars, you can increase their size by clicking View on the menu bar, pointing to Toolbars, clicking Customize on the Toolbars submenu, clicking the Options tab, clicking the Large icons check box, and then clicking the Close button.

In this book, the Standard and Formatting toolbars are shown on two rows, one below the other, so that all buttons appear on a screen with the resolution set to 800 × 600 (Figure 1-12c). You can show the two toolbars on two rows by clicking the Show Buttons on Two Rows command in the Toolbar Options list (Figure 1-12b).

Formula Bar

The formula bar appears below the Standard and Formatting toolbars (Figure 1-13). As you type, Excel displays the entry in the **formula bar**. Excel also displays the active cell reference in the Name box on the left side of the formula bar.

Status Bar

The status bar is located immediately above the Windows taskbar at the bottom of the screen (Figure 1-13). The **status bar** displays a brief description of the command selected (highlighted) on a menu, the function of the button the mouse pointer is pointing to, or the mode of Excel. **Mode indicators**, such as Enter and Ready, appear on the status bar and specify the current mode of Excel. When the mode is **Ready**, Excel is ready to accept the next command or data entry. When the mode indicator reads **Enter**, Excel is in the process of accepting data through the keyboard into the active cell.

In the middle of the status bar is the AutoCalculate area. The **AutoCalculate area** can be used in place of a calculator or formula to view the sum, average, or other types of totals of a group of numbers on the worksheet. The AutoCalculate area is discussed in detail later in this project.

Keyboard indicators, such as CAPS (Caps Lock), NUM (Num Lock), and SCRL (Scroll), show which keys are engaged. Keyboard indicators appear in the small rectangular boxes on the right side of the status bar (Figure 1-13).

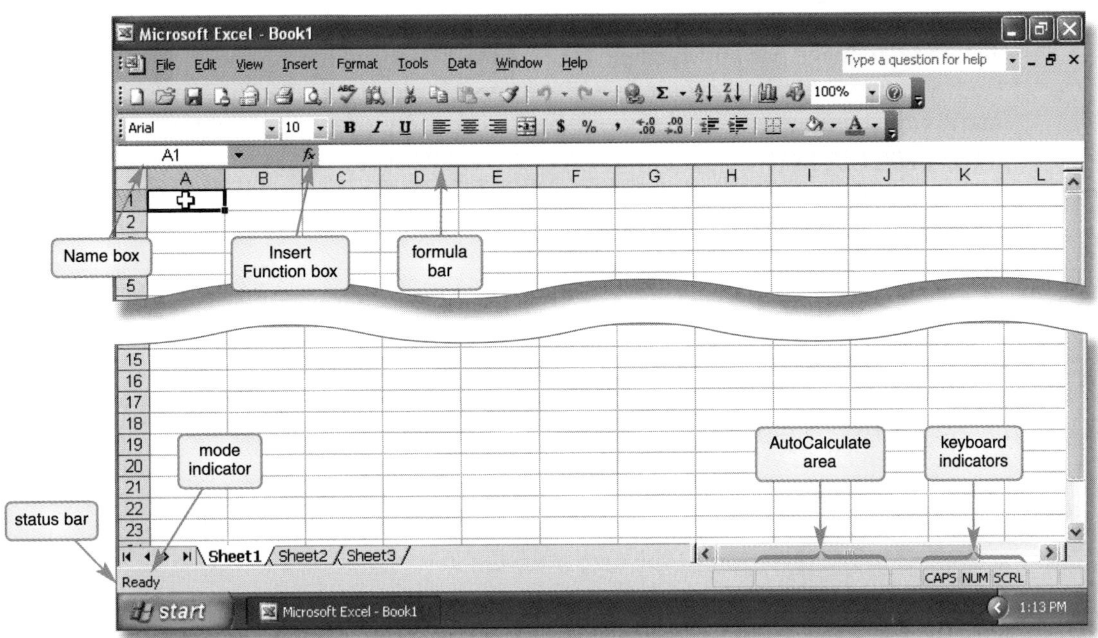

FIGURE 1-13

Speech Recognition and Speech Playback

With the **Office Speech Recognition software** installed and a microphone, you can speak the names of toolbar buttons, menus, menu commands, list items, alerts, and dialog box controls, such as OK and Cancel. You also can dictate cell entries, such as text and numbers. To indicate whether you want to speak commands or dictate cell entries, you use the Language bar. The Language bar can be in one of four states: (1) **restored**, which means it is displayed somewhere in the Excel window (Figure 1-14a); (2) **minimized**, which means it is displayed on the Windows taskbar (Figure 1-14b); (3) **hidden**, which means you do not see it on the screen but it will be displayed the next time you start your computer; (4) **closed**, which means it is hidden permanently until you enable it. If the Language bar is hidden or closed and you want it to display, then do the following:

1. Right-click an open area on the Windows taskbar at the bottom of the screen.
2. Point to Toolbars on the shortcut menu and then click Language bar on the Toolbars submenu.

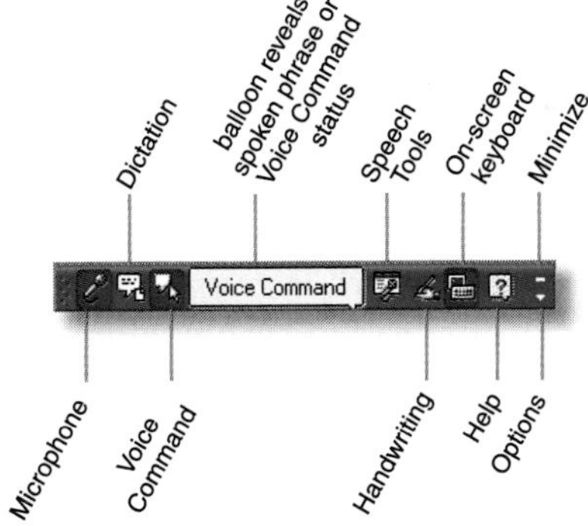

(a) Language Bar in Excel Window with Microphone Enabled

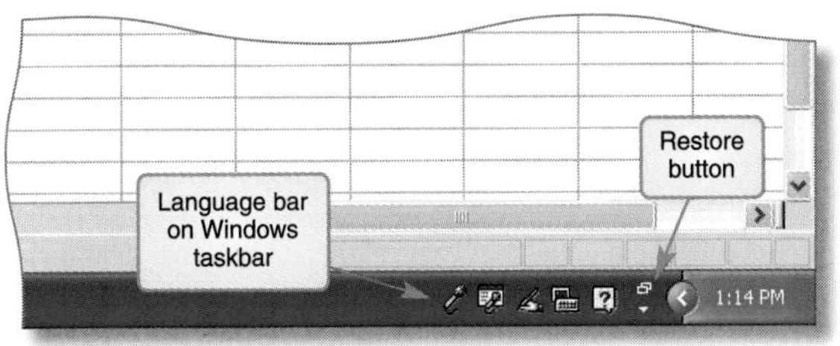

(b) Language Bar Minimized on Windows Taskbar

FIGURE 1-14

If the Language bar command is dimmed on the Toolbars submenu or if the Speech command is dimmed on the Tools menu, the Office Speech Recognition software is not installed.

In this book, the Language bar does not appear in the figures. If you want to close the Language bar so that your screen is identical to what you see in the book, right-click the Language bar and then click Close the Language bar on the shortcut menu.

If you have speakers, you can use the **speech playback** functions of Excel to instruct the computer to read a worksheet to you. By selecting the appropriate option, you can have the worksheet read in a male or female voice. Additional information about the speech recognition and speech playback capabilities of Excel is available in Appendix B.

More About

Selecting a Cell

You can select any cell by entering its cell reference, such as b4, in the Name box on the left side of the formula bar.

Selecting a Cell

To enter data into a cell, you first must select it. The easiest way **to select a cell** (make it active) is to use the mouse to move the block plus sign mouse pointer to the cell and then click.

An alternative method is to use the arrow keys that are located just to the right of the typewriter keys on the keyboard. An arrow key selects the cell adjacent to the active cell in the direction of the arrow on the key.

You know a cell is selected, or active, when a heavy border surrounds the cell and the active cell reference appears in the Name box on the left side of the formula bar. Excel also changes the active cell's column heading and row heading to a gold color.

Q&A

Q: What is the maximum allowable length of a text entry?

A: A text entry in a cell can contain from 1 to 32,767 characters. Although text entries primarily are used to identify parts of a worksheet, some worksheet applications use text entries as data that you dissect, string together, and manipulate using text functions.

Entering Text

In Excel, any set of characters containing a letter, hyphen (as in a telephone number), or space is considered text. **Text** is used to place titles, such as worksheet titles, column titles, and row titles, on the worksheet. For example, as shown in Figure 1-15, the worksheet title, Extreme Blading, identifies the worksheet created in Project 1. The worksheet subtitle, Second Quarter Sales, identifies the type of report. The column titles in row 3 (Direct Mail, Outlets, Telesales, Web, and Total) identify the numbers in each column. The row titles in column A (Inline Skates, Quad Skates, Custom Skates, Accessories, and Total) identify the numbers in each row.

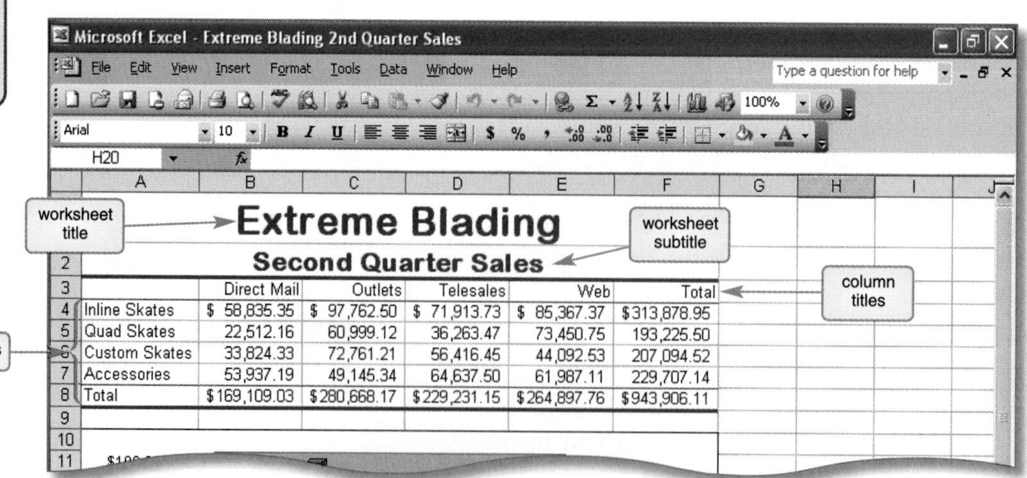

	A	B	C	D	E	F
3		Direct Mail	Outlets	Telesales	Web	Total
4	Inline Skates	$ 58,835.35	$ 97,762.50	$ 71,913.73	$ 85,367.37	$313,878.95
5	Quad Skates	22,512.16	60,999.12	36,263.47	73,450.75	193,225.50
6	Custom Skates	33,824.33	72,761.21	56,416.45	44,092.53	207,094.52
7	Accessories	53,937.19	49,145.34	64,637.50	61,987.11	229,707.14
8	Total	$169,109.03	$280,668.17	$229,231.15	$264,897.76	$943,906.11

FIGURE 1-15

Entering the Worksheet Titles

The following steps show how to enter the worksheet titles in cells A1 and A2. Later in this project, the worksheet titles will be formatted so they appear as shown in Figure 1-15.

To Enter the Worksheet Titles

• **Click cell A1.**

Cell A1 becomes the active cell and a heavy border surrounds it (Figure 1-16).

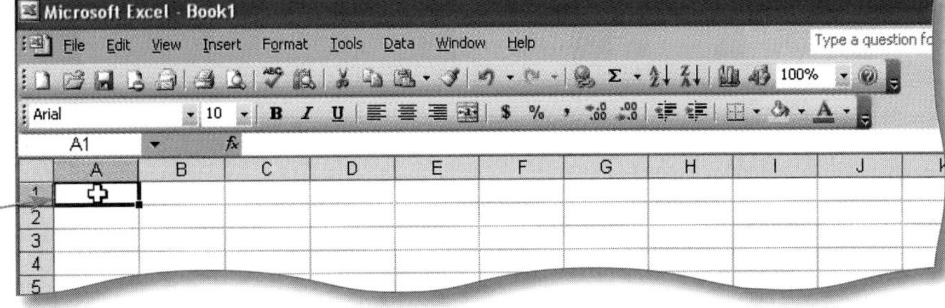

FIGURE 1-16

2

• **Type** `Extreme Blading` **in cell A1 and then point to the Enter box in the formula bar.**

Excel displays the title in the formula bar and in cell A1 (Figure 1-17). When you begin typing a cell entry, Excel displays two additional boxes in the formula bar: the Cancel box and the Enter box.

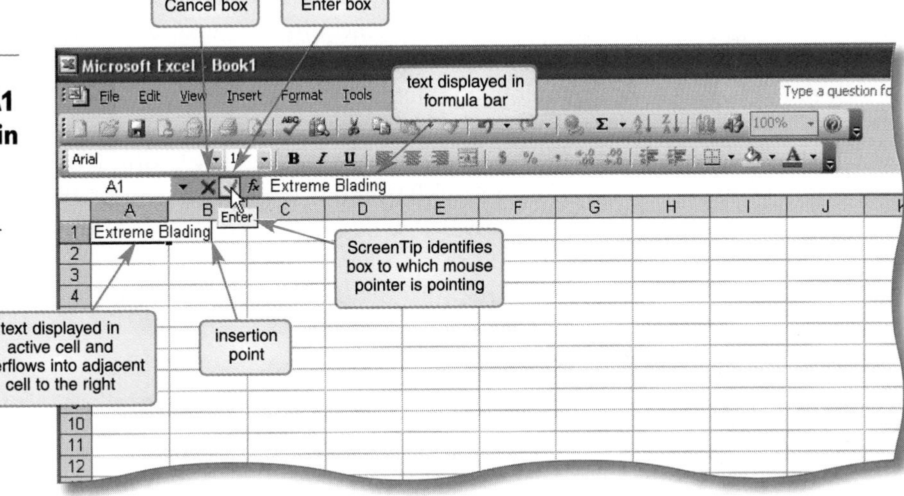

FIGURE 1-17

3

• **Click the Enter box to complete the entry.**

Excel enters the worksheet title in cell A1 (Figure 1-18).

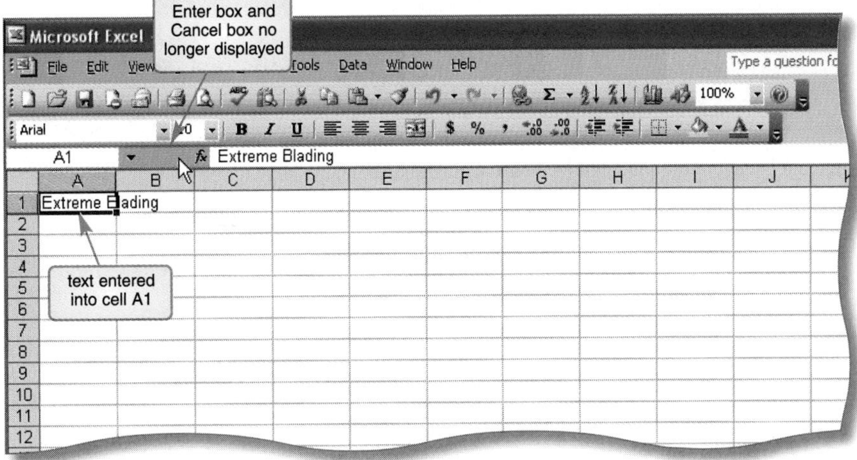

FIGURE 1-18

4

• **Click cell A2 to select it. Type** `Second Quarter Sales` **as the cell entry. Click the Enter box to complete the entry.**

Excel enters the worksheet subtitle in cell A2 (Figure 1-19).

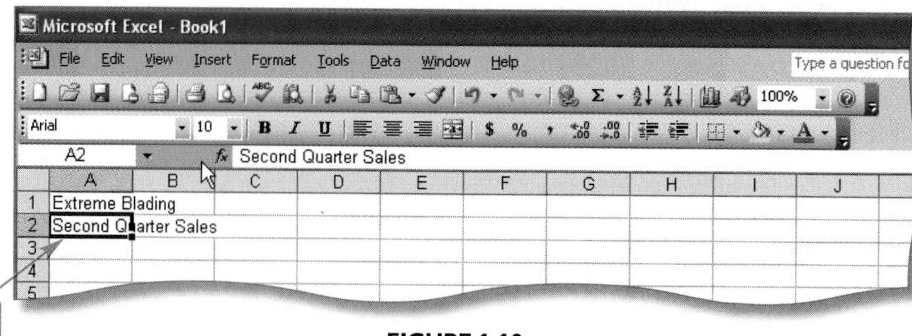

FIGURE 1-19

Other Ways

1. To complete entry, click any cell other than active cell
2. To complete entry, press ENTER key
3. To complete entry, press HOME, PAGE UP, PAGE DOWN, or END key
4. To complete entry, in Voice Command mode, say "Enter"

In Figure 1-17 on the previous page, the text in cell A1 is followed by the insertion point. The **insertion point** is a blinking vertical line that indicates where the next typed character will appear. In Steps 3 and 4, clicking the **Enter box** completes the entry. Clicking the **Cancel box** cancels the entry.

When you complete a text entry into a cell, a series of events occurs. First, Excel positions the text left-aligned in the cell. **Left-aligned** means the cell entry is positioned at the far left in the cell. Therefore, the E in the worksheet title, Extreme Blading, begins in the leftmost position of cell A1.

Second, when the text is longer than the width of a column, Excel displays the overflow characters in adjacent cells to the right as long as these adjacent cells contain no data. In Figure 1-19, the width of cell A1 is approximately 9 characters. The text consists of 15 characters. Therefore, Excel displays the overflow characters from cell A1 in cell B1, because cell B1 is empty. If cell B1 contained data, Excel would hide the overflow characters, so that only the first 9 characters in cell A1 would appear on the worksheet. Excel stores the overflow characters in cell A1 and displays them in the formula bar whenever cell A1 is the active cell.

Third, when you complete an entry by clicking the Enter box, the cell in which the text is entered remains the active cell.

More About

The ENTER Key

When you first install Excel, the ENTER key not only completes the entry, but it also moves the selection to an adjacent cell. You can instruct Excel not to move the selection after pressing the ENTER key by clicking Options on the Tools menu, clicking the Edit tab, removing the check mark from the Move Selection after Enter check box, and then clicking the OK button.

Correcting a Mistake while Typing

If you type the wrong letter and notice the error before clicking the Enter box or pressing the ENTER key, use the BACKSPACE key to delete all the characters back to and including the incorrect letter. To cancel the entire entry before entering it into the cell, click the Cancel box in the formula bar or press the ESC key. If you see an error in a cell after entering the text, select the cell and retype the entry. Later in this project, additional error-correction techniques are discussed.

AutoCorrect

The **AutoCorrect feature** of Excel works behind the scenes, correcting common mistakes when you complete a text entry in a cell. AutoCorrect makes three types of corrections for you:

1. Corrects two initial capital letters by changing the second letter to lowercase.
2. Capitalizes the first letter in the names of days.
3. Replaces commonly misspelled words with their correct spelling. For example, it will change the misspelled word *recieve* to *receive* when you complete the entry. AutoCorrect will correct the spelling of hundreds of commonly misspelled words automatically.

Entering Column Titles

To enter the column titles in row 3, select the appropriate cell and then enter the text, as described in the following steps.

To Enter Column Titles

1

- **Click cell B3.**

Cell B3 becomes the active cell. The active cell reference in the Name box changes from A2 to B3 (Figure 1-20).

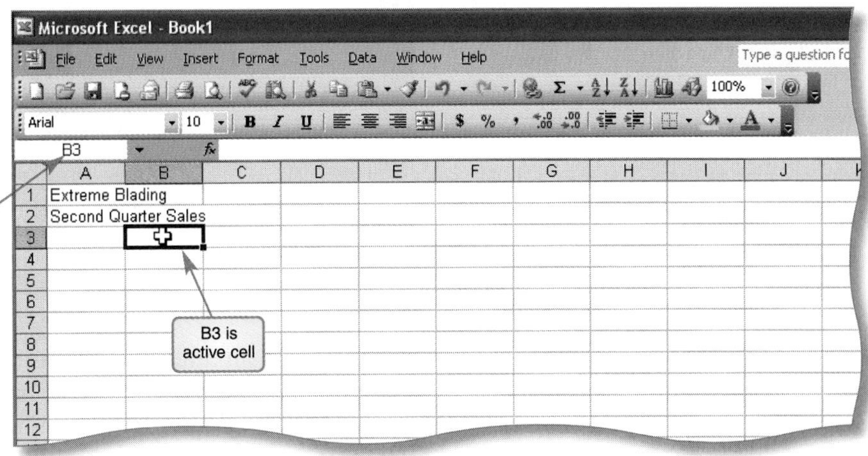

FIGURE 1-20

2

- **Type** `Direct Mail` **in cell B3.**

Excel displays Direct Mail in the formula bar and in cell B3 (Figure 1-21).

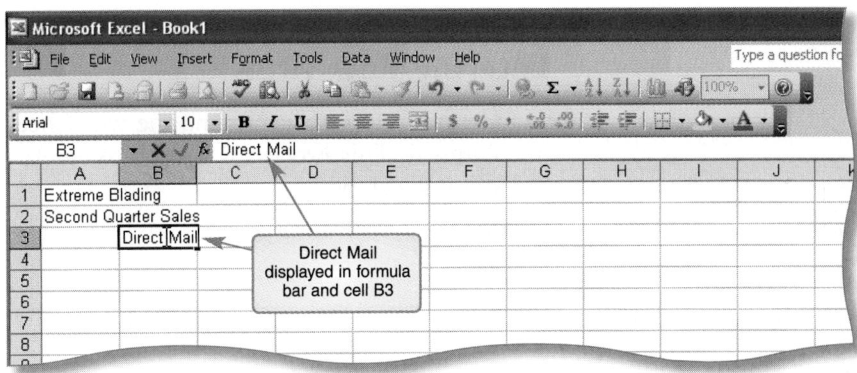

FIGURE 1-21

3

- **Press the RIGHT ARROW key.**

Excel enters the column title, Direct Mail, in cell B3 and makes cell C3 the active cell (Figure 1-22).

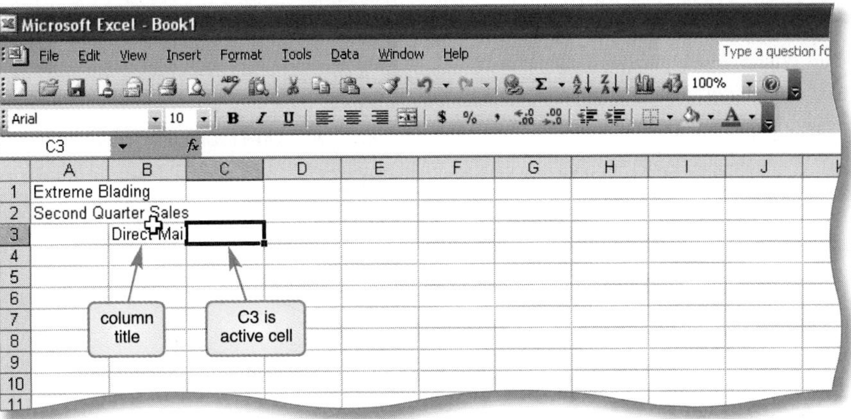

FIGURE 1-22

4

• **Repeat Steps 2 and 3 for the remaining column titles in row 3; that is, enter** `Outlets` **in cell C3,** `Telesales` **in cell D3,** `Web` **in cell E3, and** `Total` **in cell F3 (complete the last entry in cell F3 by clicking the Enter box in the formula bar).**

Excel displays the column titles left-aligned as shown in Figure 1-23.

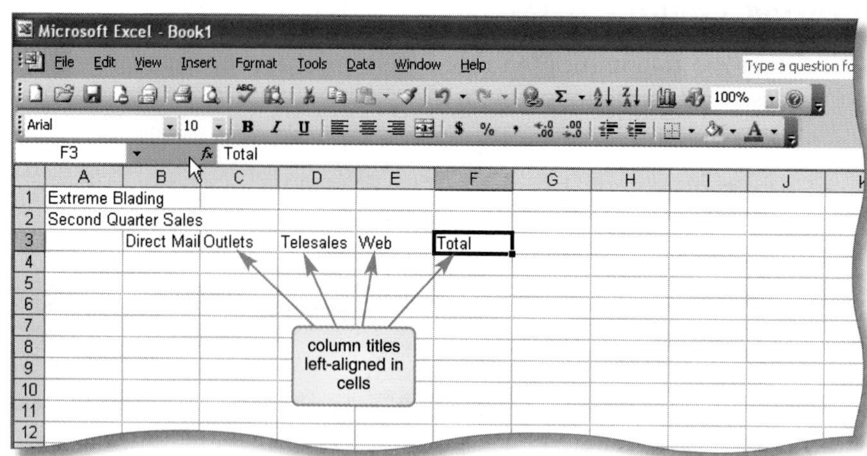

FIGURE 1-23

If the next entry is in an adjacent cell, use the arrow keys to complete the entry in a cell. When you press an arrow key to complete an entry, the adjacent cell in the direction of the arrow (up, down, left, or right) becomes the active cell. If the next entry is in a nonadjacent cell, complete an entry by clicking the next cell in which you plan to enter data. You also can click the Enter box or press the ENTER key and then click the appropriate cell for the next entry.

Entering Row Titles

The next step in developing the worksheet in Project 1 is to enter the row titles in column A. This process is similar to entering the column titles and is described in the following steps.

To Enter Row Titles

1

• **Click cell A4. Type** `Inline Skates` **and then press the DOWN ARROW key.**

Excel enters the row title, Inline Skates, in cell A4, and cell A5 becomes the active cell (Figure 1-24).

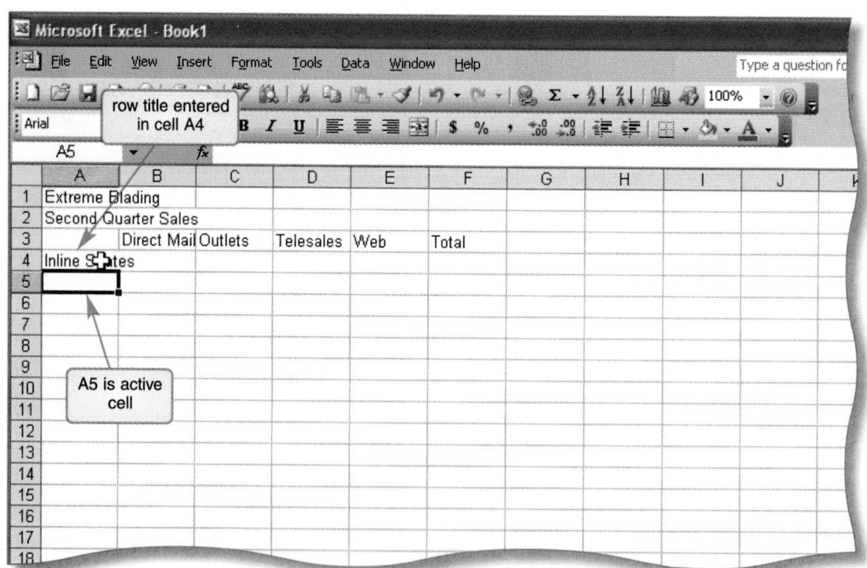

FIGURE 1-24

2

• **Repeat Step 1 for the remaining row titles in column A; that is, enter** `Quad Skates` **in cell A5,** `Custom Skates` **in cell A6,** `Accessories` **in cell A7, and** `Total` **in cell A8.**

Excel displays the row titles as shown in Figure 1-25.

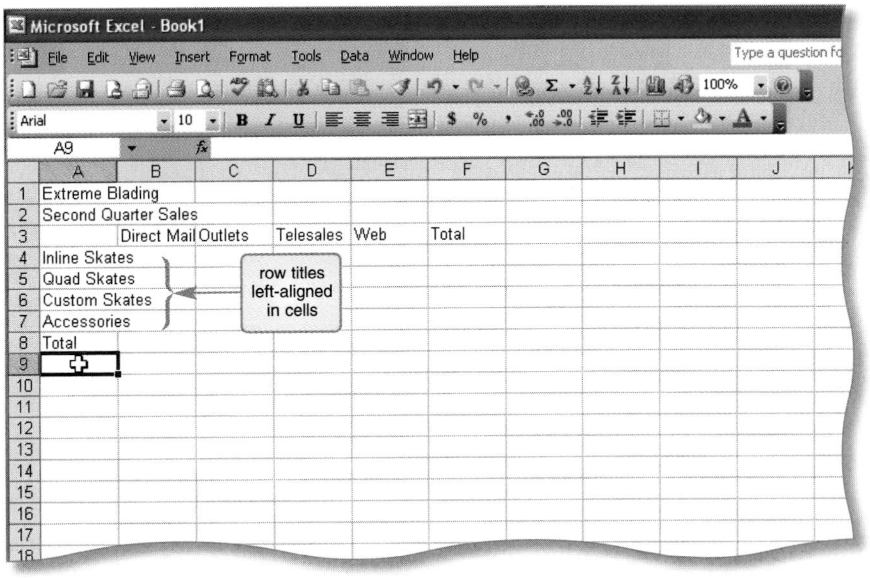

FIGURE 1-25

When you enter text, Excel automatically left-aligns the text in the cell. Excel treats any combination of numbers, spaces, and nonnumeric characters as text. For example, the following entries are text:

401AX21, 921-231, 619 321, 883XTY

You can change the text alignment in a cell by realigning it. Several alignment techniques are discussed later in the project.

More About

Entering Numbers as Text

Sometimes, you will want Excel to treat numbers, such as Zip codes and telephone numbers, as text. To enter a number as text, start the entry with an apostrophe (').

Entering Numbers

In Excel, you can enter numbers into cells to represent amounts. A **number** can contain only the following characters:

0 1 2 3 4 5 6 7 8 9 + - ( ) , / . $ % E e

If a cell entry contains any other keyboard character (including spaces), Excel interprets the entry as text and treats it accordingly. The use of the special characters is explained when they are used in the project.

The Extreme Blading Second Quarter numbers used in Project 1 are summarized in Table 1-1. These numbers, which represent second quarter sales for each of the sales channels and product groups, must be entered in rows 4, 5, 6, and 7. The steps on the next page enter the numbers in Table 1-1 one row at a time.

Table 1-1 Extreme Blading Second Quarter Data

	Direct Mail	Outlets	Telesales	Web
Inline Skates	58835.35	97762.50	71913.73	85367.37
Quad Skates	22512.16	60999.12	36263.47	73450.75
Custom Skates	33824.33	72761.21	56416.45	44092.53
Accessories	53937.19	49145.34	64637.50	61987.11

To Enter Numbers

1

- **Click cell B4.**
- **Type** `58835.35` **and then press the RIGHT ARROW key.**

Excel enters the number 58835.35 in cell B4 and changes the active cell to cell C4 (Figure 1-26).

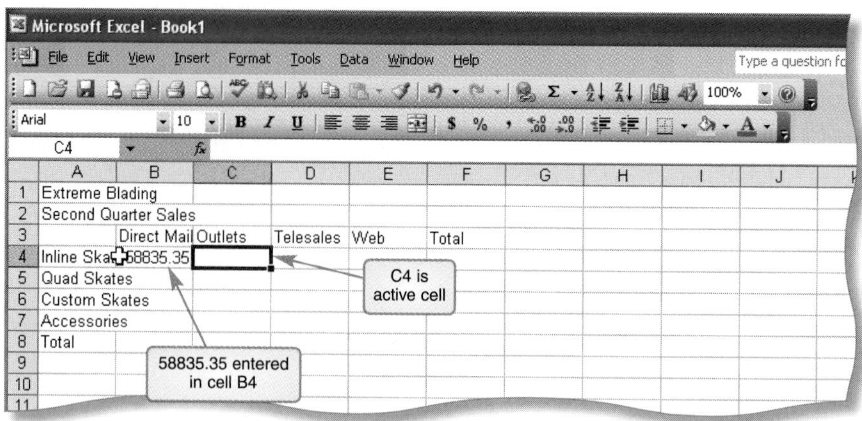

FIGURE 1-26

2

- **Enter** `97762.50` **in cell C4,** `71913.73` **in cell D4, and** `85367.37` **in cell E4.**

Row 4 now contains the second quarter sales by sales channel for the Inline Skates product group (Figure 1-27). The numbers in row 4 are right-aligned, which means Excel displays the cell entry to the far right in the cell.

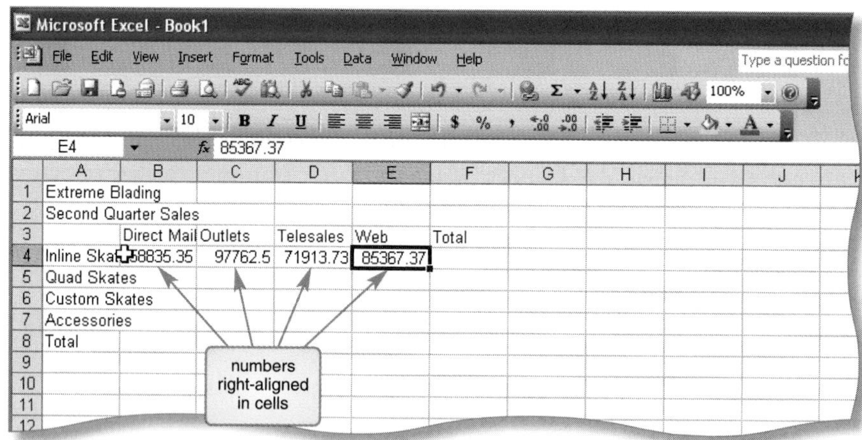

FIGURE 1-27

3

- **Click cell B5.**
- **Enter the remaining second quarter sales provided in Table 1-1 on the previous page for each of the three remaining product groups in rows 5, 6, and 7.**

Excel displays the second quarter sales as shown in Figure 1-28.

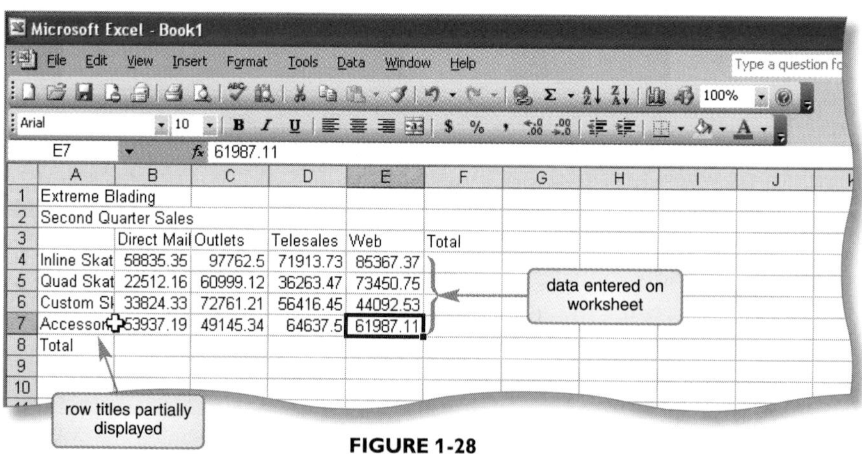

FIGURE 1-28

When the numbers are entered into the cells in column B, Excel only partially displays the row titles in column A. When the worksheet is formatted later in the project, the row titles will appear in their entirety.

Steps 1 through 3 complete the numeric entries. As shown in Figure 1-28, Excel does not display trailing zeros in cells C4 and D7. You are not required to type dollar signs, commas, or trailing zeros. When you enter a dollar value that has cents, however, you must add the decimal point and the numbers representing the cents. Later in this project, the numbers will be formatted to use dollar signs, commas, and trailing zeros to improve the appearance and readability of the numbers.

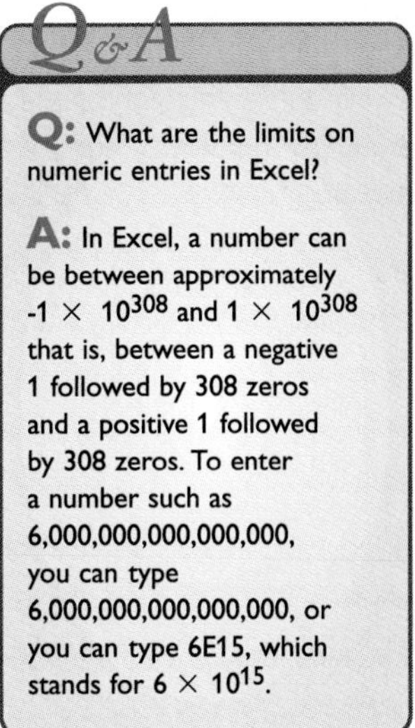

Q&A

Q: What are the limits on numeric entries in Excel?

A: In Excel, a number can be between approximately -1×10^{308} and 1×10^{308} that is, between a negative 1 followed by 308 zeros and a positive 1 followed by 308 zeros. To enter a number such as 6,000,000,000,000,000, you can type 6,000,000,000,000,000, or you can type 6E15, which stands for 6×10^{15}.

Calculating a Sum

The next step in creating the worksheet is to determine the total second quarter sales for the Direct Mail sales channel in column B. To calculate this value in cell B8, Excel must add, or sum, the numbers in cells B4, B5, B6, and B7. Excel's **SUM function**, which adds all of the numbers in a range of cells, provides a convenient means to accomplish this task.

A **range** is a series of two or more adjacent cells in a column or row or a rectangular group of cells. For example, the group of adjacent cells B4, B5, B6, and B7 is called a range. Many Excel operations, such as summing numbers, take place on a range of cells.

The following steps show how to sum the numbers in column B.

To Sum a Column of Numbers

1

- **Click cell B8.**

Cell B8 becomes the active cell (Figure 1-29).

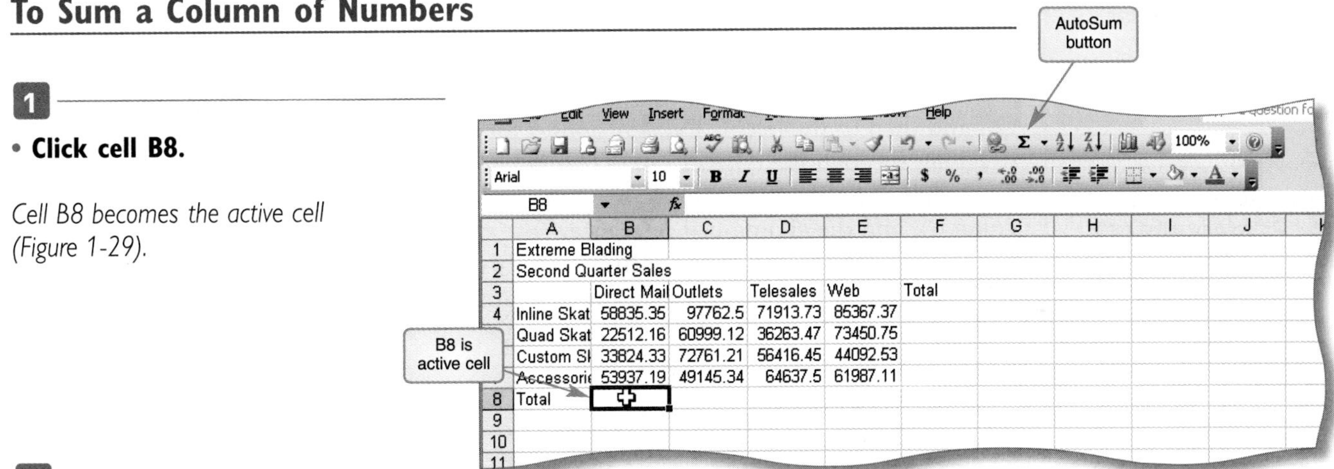

FIGURE 1-29

2

- **Click the AutoSum button on the Standard toolbar.**

Excel responds by displaying =SUM(B4:B7) in the formula bar and in the active cell B8 (Figure 1-30). Excel displays a ScreenTip below the active cell. The B4:B7 within parentheses following the function name SUM is Excel's way of identifying that the SUM function will add the numbers in the range B4 through B7. Excel also surrounds the proposed cells to sum with a moving border, called a ***marquee****.*

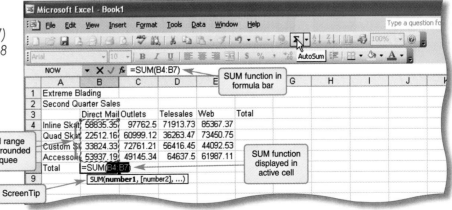

SUM function in formula bar
proposed range to sum surrounded by marquee
SUM function displayed in active cell
ScreenTip

FIGURE 1-30

3

• **Click the AutoSum button a second time.**

Excel enters the sum of the second quarter sales for the Direct Mail sales channel in cell B8 (Figure 1-31). The SUM function assigned to cell B8 appears in the formula bar when cell B8 is the active cell.

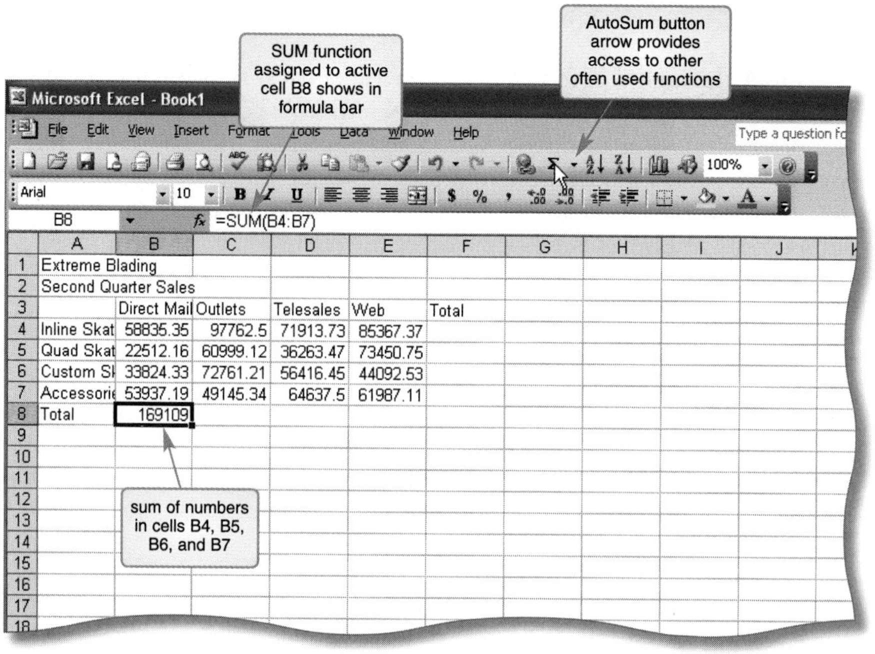

SUM function assigned to active cell B8 shows in formula bar

AutoSum button arrow provides access to other often used functions

sum of numbers in cells B4, B5, B6, and B7

FIGURE 1-31

Other Ways

1. Click Insert Function button in formula bar, select SUM in Select a function list, click OK button, select range, click OK button
2. On Insert menu click Function, select SUM in Select a function list, click OK button, select range, click OK button
3. Press ALT+EQUAL SIGN (=) twice
4. In Voice Command mode, say "AutoSum, Sum, Enter"

When you enter the SUM function using the AutoSum button, Excel automatically selects what it considers to be your choice of the range to sum. When proposing the range to sum, Excel first looks for a range of cells with numbers above the active cell and then to the left. If Excel proposes the wrong range, you can correct it by dragging through the correct range before clicking the AutoSum button a second time. You also can enter the correct range by typing the beginning cell reference, a colon (:), and the ending cell reference.

If you click the AutoSum button arrow on the right side of the AutoSum button, Excel displays a list of often used functions from which you can choose. The list includes functions that allow you to determine the average, the minimum value, or the maximum value of a range of numbers.

Using the Fill Handle to Copy a Cell to Adjacent Cells

Excel also must calculate the totals for Outlets in cell C8, Telesales in cell D8, and for Web in cell E8. Table 1-2 illustrates the similarities between the entry in cell B8 and the entries required to sum the totals in cells C8, D8, and E8.

Table 1-2 Sum Function Entries in Row 8

CELL	SUM FUNCTION ENTRIES	REMARK
B8	=SUM(B4:B7)	Sums cells B4, B5, B6, and B7
C8	=SUM(C4:C7)	Sums cells C4, C5, C6, and C7
D8	=SUM(D4:D7)	Sums cells D4, D5, D6, and D7
E8	=SUM(E4:E7)	Sums cells E4, E5, E6, and E7

To place the SUM functions in cells C8, D8, and E8, follow the same steps shown previously in Figures 1-29 through 1-31. A second, more efficient method is to copy the SUM function from cell B8 to the range C8:E8. The cell being copied is called the **source area** or **copy area**. The range of cells receiving the copy is called the **destination area** or **paste area.**

Although the SUM function entries in Table 1-2 are similar, they are not exact copies. The range in each SUM function entry uses cell references that are one column to the right of the previous column. When you copy cell references, Excel automatically adjusts them for each new position, resulting in the SUM function entries illustrated in Table 1-2. Each adjusted cell reference is called a **relative reference.**

The easiest way to copy the SUM formula from cell B8 to cells C8, D8, and E8 is to use the fill handle. The **fill handle** is the small black square located in the lower-right corner of the heavy border around the active cell. The following steps show how to use the fill handle to copy cell B8 to the adjacent cells C8:E8.

To Copy a Cell to Adjacent Cells in a Row

1

- **With cell B8 active, point to the fill handle.**

The mouse pointer changes to a cross hair (Figure 1-32).

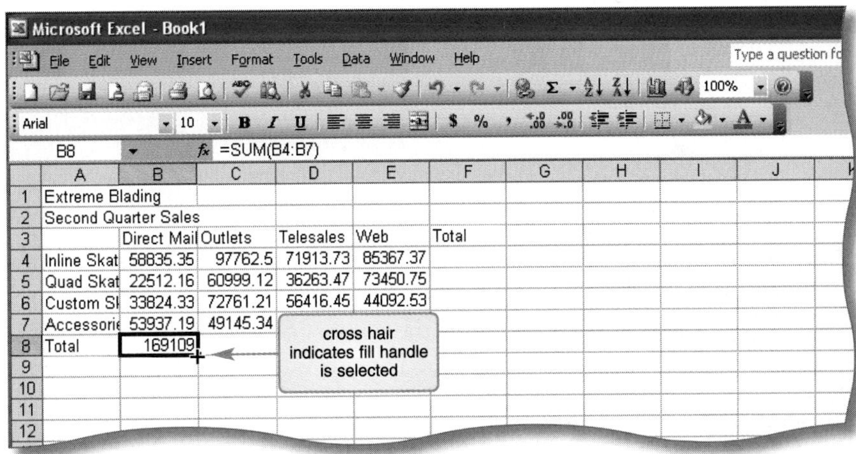

FIGURE 1-32

2

- **Drag the fill handle to select the destination area, range C8:E8. Do not release the mouse button.**

Excel displays a shaded border around the destination area, range C8:E8, and the source area, cell B8 (Figure 1-33).

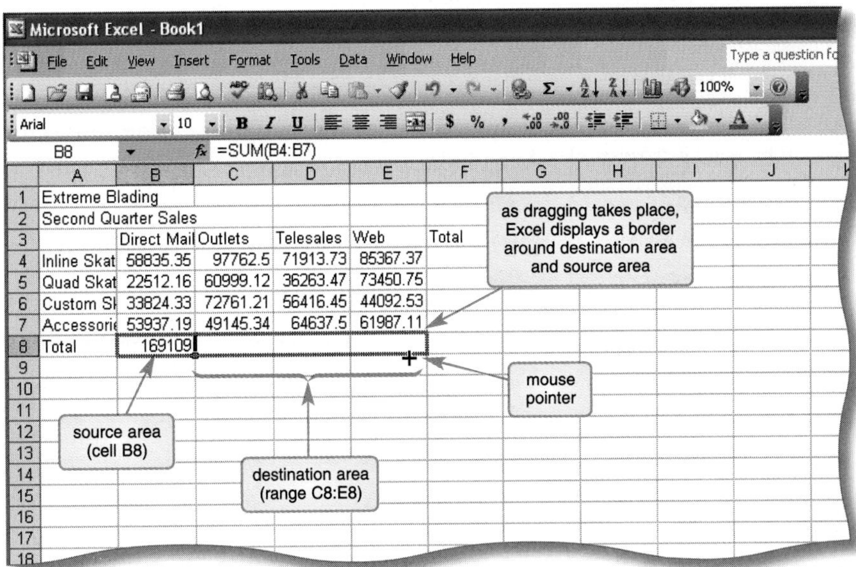

FIGURE 1-33

3

• **Release the mouse button.**

Excel copies the SUM function in cell B8 to the range C8:E8 (Figure 1-34). In addition, Excel calculates the sums and enters the results in cells C8, D8, and E8. The Auto Fill Options button appears to the right and below the destination area.

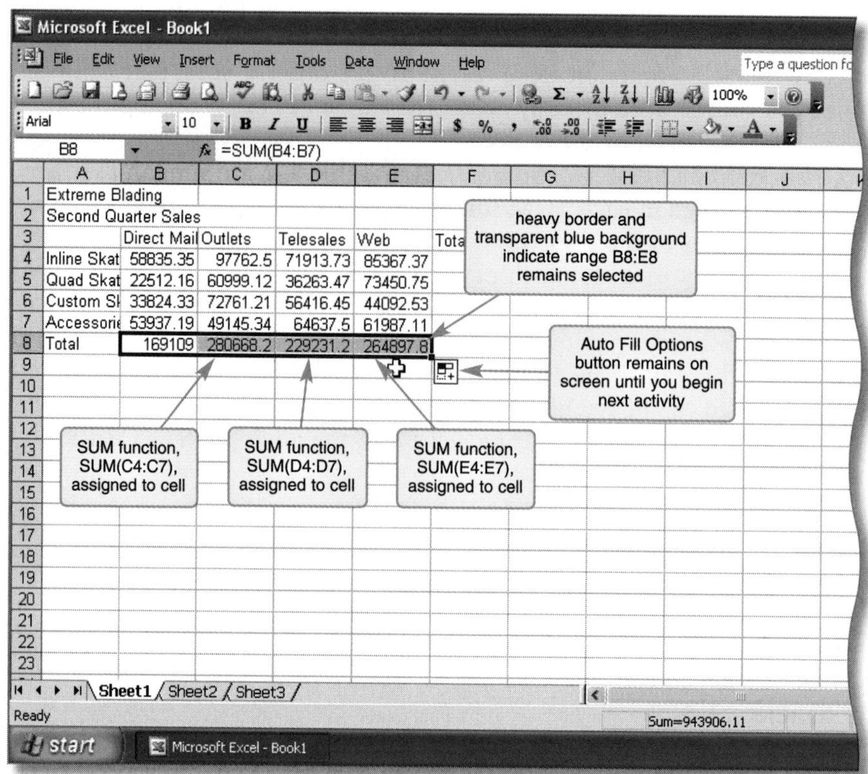

FIGURE 1-34

Other Ways

1. Select source area, on Edit menu click Copy, select destination area, on Edit menu click Paste
2. Right-click source area, click Copy on shortcut menu, right-click destination area, click Paste on shortcut menu
3. Select source area and then point to border of range; while holding down CTRL key, drag source area to destination area
4. Select source area, press CTRL+C, select destination area, press CTRL+V
5. In Voice Command mode, [select source area], say "Copy", [select destination area], say "Paste"

Once the copy is complete, Excel continues to display a heavy border and transparent blue background around cells B8:E8. The heavy border and transparent blue background are called **see-through view** and indicates a selected range. Excel does not display the transparent blue background around cell B8, the first cell in the range, because it is the active cell. If you click any cell, Excel will remove the heavy border and transparent blue background of the see-through view.

When you copy one range to another, Excel displays an Auto Fill Options button to the right and below the destination area (Figure 1-34). The Auto Fill Options button allows you to choose whether you want to copy the values from the source area to the destination area with formatting, without formatting, or only copy the format. To view the available fill options, click the Auto Fill Options button. The Auto Fill Options button disappears when you begin another activity.

Determining Multiple Totals at the Same Time

The next step in building the worksheet is to determine total second quarter sales for each product group and total second quarter sales for the company in column F. To calculate these totals, you can use the SUM function much as you used it to total the sales by sales channel in row 8. In this example, however, Excel will determine totals for all of the rows at the same time. The following steps illustrate this process.

To Determine Multiple Totals at the Same Time

1

• **Click cell F4.**

Cell F4 becomes the active cell (Figure 1-35).

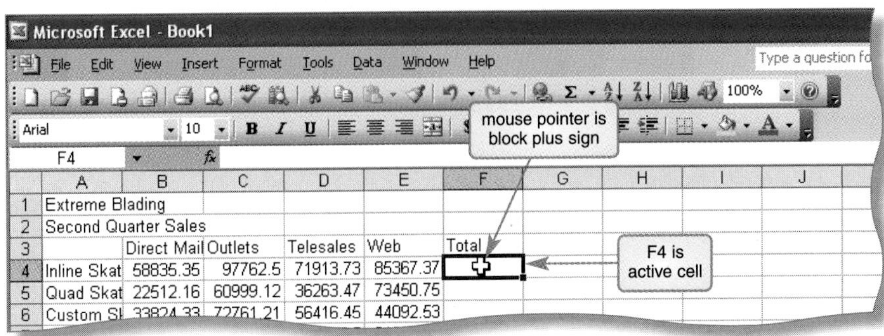

FIGURE 1-35

2

• **With the mouse pointer in cell F4 and in the shape of a block plus sign, drag the mouse pointer down to cell F8.**

Excel highlights the range F4:F8 with a see-through view (Figure 1-36).

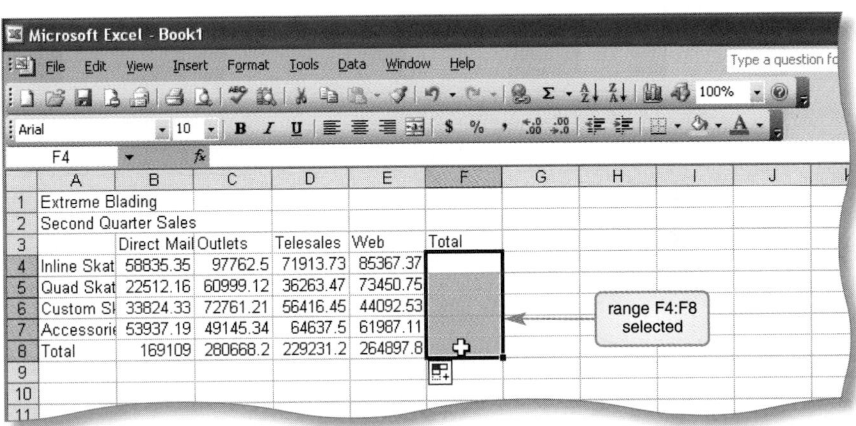

FIGURE 1-36

3

• **Click the AutoSum button on the Standard toolbar.**

Excel assigns the appropriate SUM functions to cells F4, F5, F6, F7, and F8, and then calculates and displays the sums in the respective cells (Figure 1-37).

4

• **Select cell A9 to deselect the range F4:F8.**

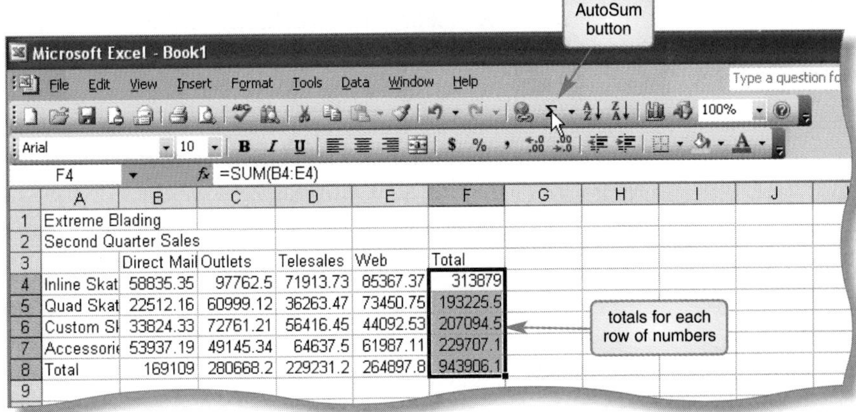

FIGURE 1-37

If each cell in a selected range is next to a row of numbers, Excel assigns the SUM function to each cell when you click the AutoSum button. Thus, as shown in the previous steps, each of the five cells in the selected range is assigned a SUM function with a different range, based on its row. This same procedure could have been used earlier to sum the columns. That is, instead of clicking cell B8, clicking the AutoSum button twice, and then copying the SUM function to the range C8:E8, the range B8:E8 could have been selected and then the AutoSum button clicked once, which would have assigned the SUM function to the entire range.

More About

Summing Columns and Rows

A more efficient way to determine the totals in row 8 and column F in Figure 1-37 is to select the range (B4:F8) and then click the AutoSum button on the Standard toolbar.

Formatting the Worksheet

The text, numeric entries, and functions for the worksheet now are complete. The next step is to format the worksheet. You **format** a worksheet to emphasize certain entries and make the worksheet easier to read and understand.

Figure 1-38a shows the worksheet before formatting. Figure 1-38b shows the worksheet after formatting. As you can see from the two figures, a worksheet that is formatted not only is easier to read, but also looks more professional.

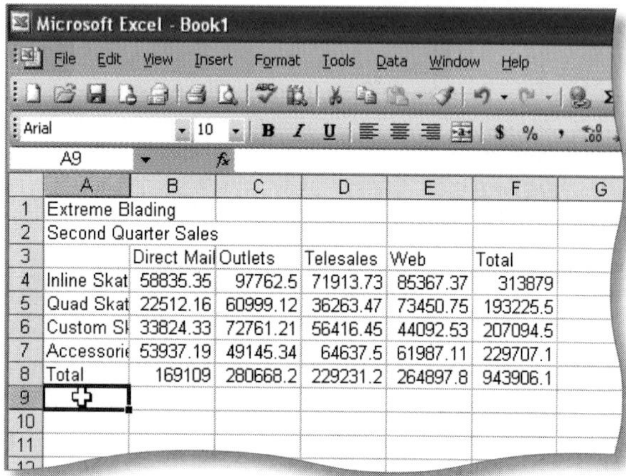

(a) Before Formatting

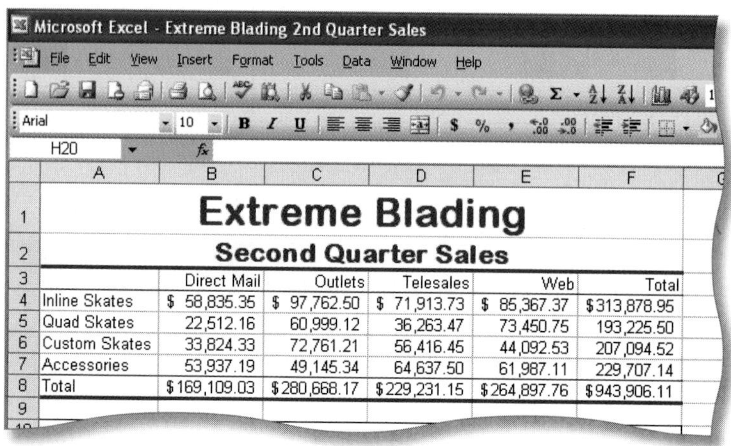

(b) After Formatting

FIGURE 1-38

To change the unformatted worksheet in Figure 1-38a to the formatted worksheet in Figure 1-38b, the following tasks must be completed:

1. Change the font type, change the font style to bold, increase the font size, and change the font color of the worksheet titles in cells A1 and A2.
2. Center the worksheet titles in cells A1 and A2 across columns A through F.
3. Format the body of the worksheet. The body of the worksheet, range A3:F8, includes the column titles, row titles, and numbers. Formatting the body of the worksheet changes the numbers to use a dollars-and-cents format, with dollar signs in the first row (row 4) and the total row (row 8); adds underlining that emphasizes portions of the worksheet; and modifies the column widths to make the text and numbers readable.

The remainder of this section explains the process required to format the worksheet. Although the format procedures are explained in the order described above, you should be aware that you can make these format changes in any order.

Font Type, Style, Size, and Color

More About

Fonts

In general, use no more than two font types in a worksheet.

The characters that Excel displays on the screen are a specific font type, style, size, and color. The **font type**, or font face, defines the appearance and shape of the letters, numbers, and special characters. Examples of font types include Times New Roman, Arial, and Courier. **Font style** indicates how the characters are formatted. Common font styles include regular, bold, underline, or italic. The **font size** specifies the size of the characters on the screen. Font size is gauged by a measurement system called points. A single point is about 1/72 of one inch in height. Thus, a character with a **point size** of 10 is about 10/72 of one inch in height. The **font color** defines the color of the characters. Excel can display characters in a wide variety of colors, including black, red, orange, and blue.

When Excel begins, the preset font type for the entire workbook is Arial, with a font size and font style of 10-point regular black. Excel allows you to change the font characteristics in a single cell, a range of cells, the entire worksheet, or the entire workbook.

Other Ways

1. On Format menu click Cells, click Font tab, click desired font type in Font box, click OK button
2. Right-click cell, click Format Cells on shortcut menu, click Font tab, click desired font type in Font box, click OK button
3. In Voice Command mode, say "Font, [select font type]"

Changing the Font Type

Different font types often are used in a worksheet to make it more appealing to the reader. The following steps show how to change the worksheet title font type from Arial to Arial Rounded MT Bold.

To Change the Font Type

1

- **Click cell A1 and then point to the Font box arrow on the Formatting toolbar.**

Cell A1 is the active cell (Figure 1-39).

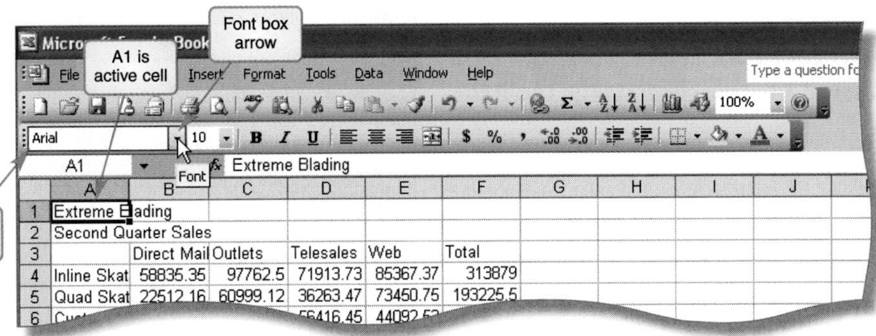

FIGURE 1-39

2

- **Click the Font box arrow and then point to Arial Rounded MT Bold.**

Excel displays the Font list with Arial Rounded MT Bold highlighted (Figure 1-40).

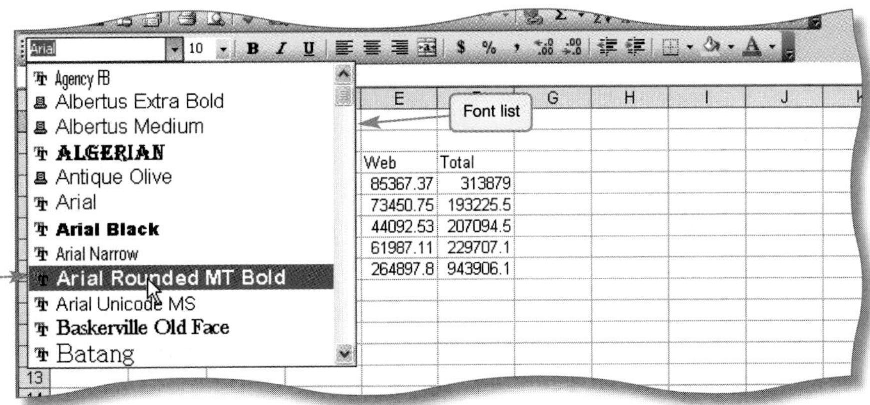

FIGURE 1-40

3

- **Click Arial Rounded MT Bold.**

Excel changes the font type of cell A1 from Arial to Arial Rounded MT Bold (Figure 1-41).

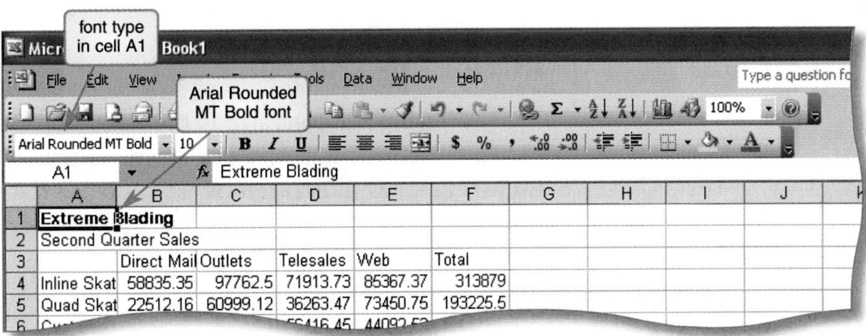

FIGURE 1-41

Because many applications supply additional font types beyond what comes with the Windows operating system, the number of font types available on your computer will depend on the applications installed. This book only uses font types that come with the Windows operating system.

Bolding a Cell

You **bold** an entry in a cell to emphasize it or make it stand out from the rest of the worksheet. The following step shows how to bold the worksheet title in cell A1.

To Bold a Cell

1

• **With cell A1 active, click the Bold button on the Formatting toolbar.**

Excel changes the font style of the worksheet title, Extreme Blading, to bold. With the mouse pointer pointing to the Bold button, Excel displays a ScreenTip immediately below the Bold button to identify the function of the button (Figure 1-42).

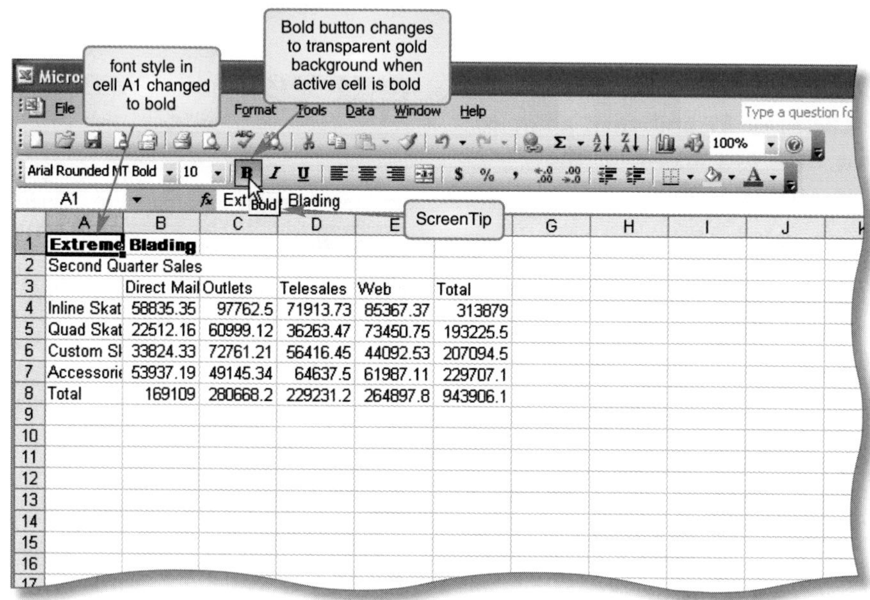

FIGURE 1-42

Other Ways

1. On Format menu click Cells, click Font tab, click Bold in Font style box, click OK button
2. Right-click cell, click Format Cells on shortcut menu, click Font tab, click Bold in Font style box, click OK button
3. Press CTRL+B
4. In Voice Command mode, say "Bold"

When the active cell is bold, Excel displays the Bold button on the Formatting toolbar with a transparent gold background (Figure 1-42). If you point to the Bold button and the active cell is already bold, then Excel displays the button with a transparent red background. Clicking the Bold button a second time removes the bold font style.

Increasing the Font Size

Increasing the font size is the next step in formatting the worksheet title. You increase the font size of a cell so the entry stands out and is easier to read. The following steps illustrate how to increase the font size of the worksheet title in cell A1.

To Increase the Font Size of a Cell Entry

1

• **With cell A1 selected, click the Font Size box arrow on the Formatting toolbar.**

Excel displays the Font Size list as shown in Figure 1-43.

FIGURE 1-43

2

• **Click 24 in the Font Size list.**

The font size of the characters in cell A1 increase from 10 point to 24 point (Figure 1-44). The increased font size makes the worksheet title easier to read.

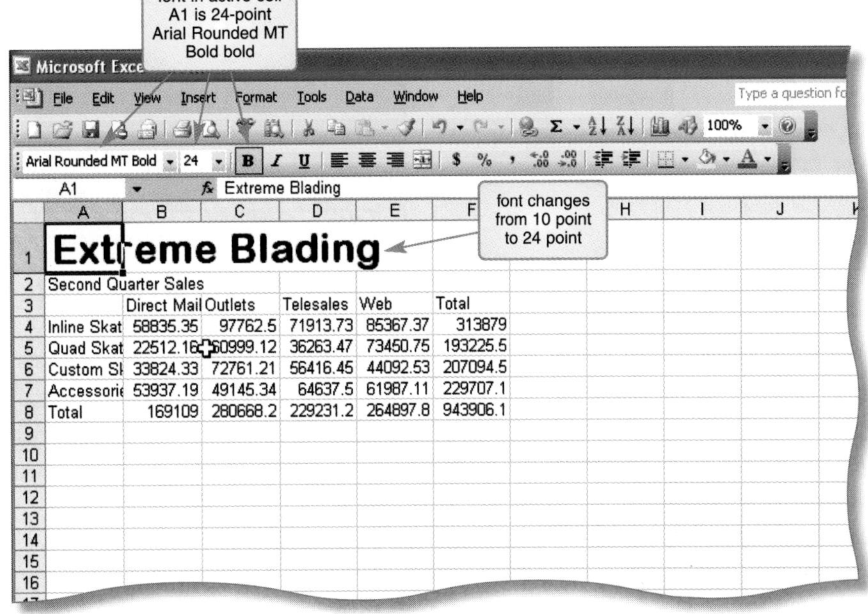

FIGURE 1-44

Other Ways

1. On Format menu click Cells, click Font tab, select font size in Size box, click OK button
2. Right-click cell, click Format Cells on shortcut menu, click Font tab, select font size in Size box, click OK button
3. In Voice Command mode, say "Font Size, [desired font size]"

An alternative to clicking a font size in the Font Size list is to click the Font Size box, type the font size, and then press the ENTER key. This procedure allows you to assign a font size not available in the Font Size list to a selected cell entry. With cell A1 selected (Figure 1-44), the Font Size box shows that the new font size is 24 and the transparent gold Bold button shows that the font style is bold.

Changing the Font Color of a Cell Entry

The next step is to change the color of the font in cell A1 from black to violet. The steps on the next page show how to change the font color of a cell entry.

To Change the Font Color of a Cell Entry

1

• **With cell A1 selected, click the Font Color button arrow on the Formatting toolbar.**

Excel displays the Font Color palette (Figure 1-45).

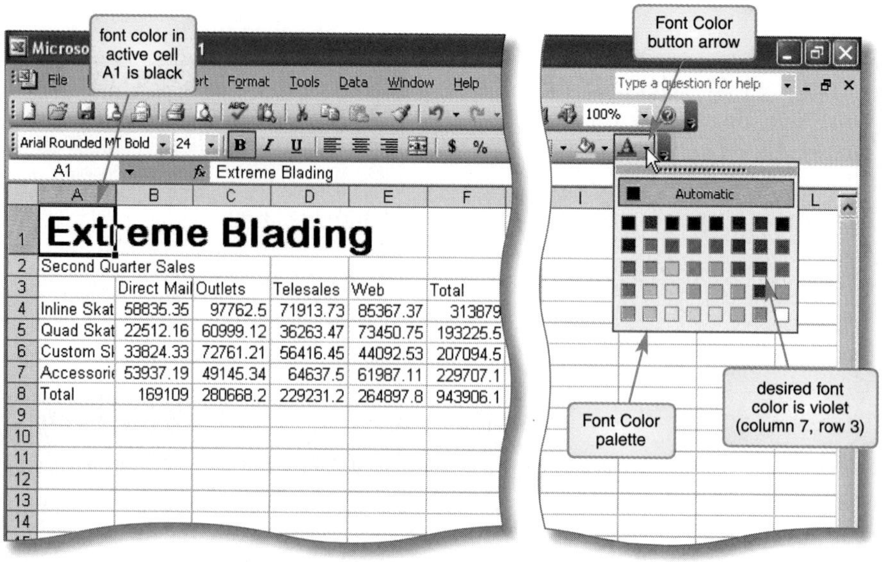

FIGURE 1-45

2

• **Click Violet (column 7, row 3) on the Font Color palette.**

The font in the worksheet title in cell A1 changes from black to violet (Figure 1-46).

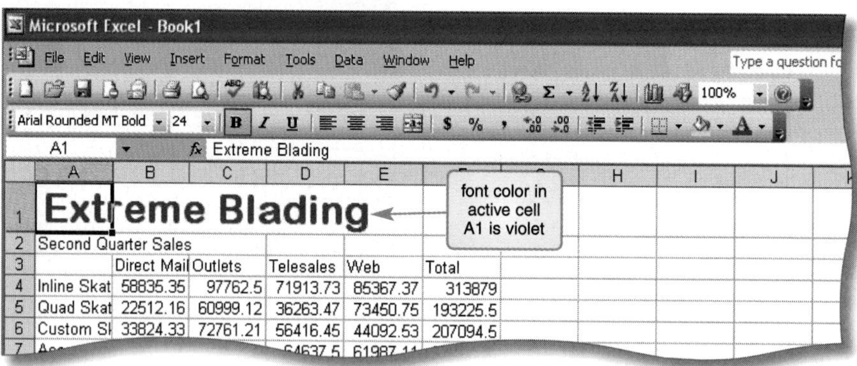

FIGURE 1-46

Other Ways

1. On Format menu click Cells, click Font tab, click Color box arrow, select color on Color palette, click OK button
2. Right-click cell, click Format Cells on shortcut menu, click Font tab, click Color box arrow, select color on Color palette, click OK button
3. In Voice Command mode, say "Font Color, [desired color]"

As shown in Figure 1-45, you can choose from 40 different font colors on the Font Color palette. Your Font Color palette may have more or fewer colors, depending on color settings of your operating system. When you choose a color on the Font Color palette, Excel changes the Font Color button on the Formatting toolbar to the chosen color. Thus, to change the font color of the cell entry in another cell to the same color, you only need to select the cell and then click the Font Color button.

Centering a Cell Entry across Columns by Merging Cells

The final step in formatting the worksheet title is to center it across columns A through F. Centering a worksheet title across the columns used in the body of the worksheet improves the worksheet's appearance. To do this, the six cells in the range A1:F1 are combined, or merged, into a single cell that is the width of the columns in the body of the worksheet. **Merging cells** involves creating a single cell by combining two or more selected cells. The following steps illustrate how to center the worksheet title across columns by merging cells.

To Center a Cell Entry across Columns by Merging Cells

1

- **With cell A1 selected, drag to cell F1.**

Excel highlights the selected cells (Figure 1-47).

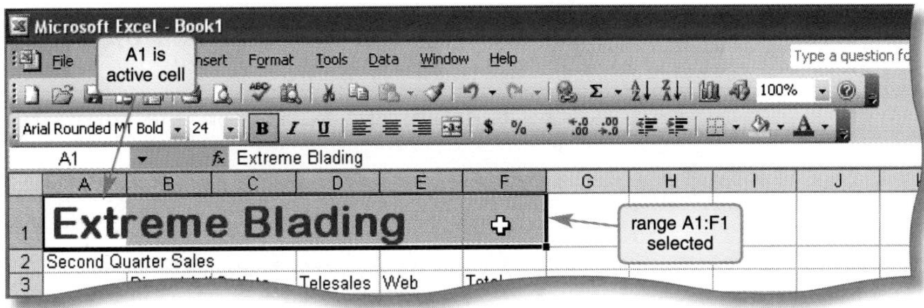

FIGURE 1-47

2

- **Click the Merge and Center button on the Formatting toolbar.**

Excel merges the cells A1 through F1 to create a new cell A1 and centers the contents of cell A1 across columns A through F (Figure 1-48). After the merge, cells B1 through F1 no longer exist on the worksheet.

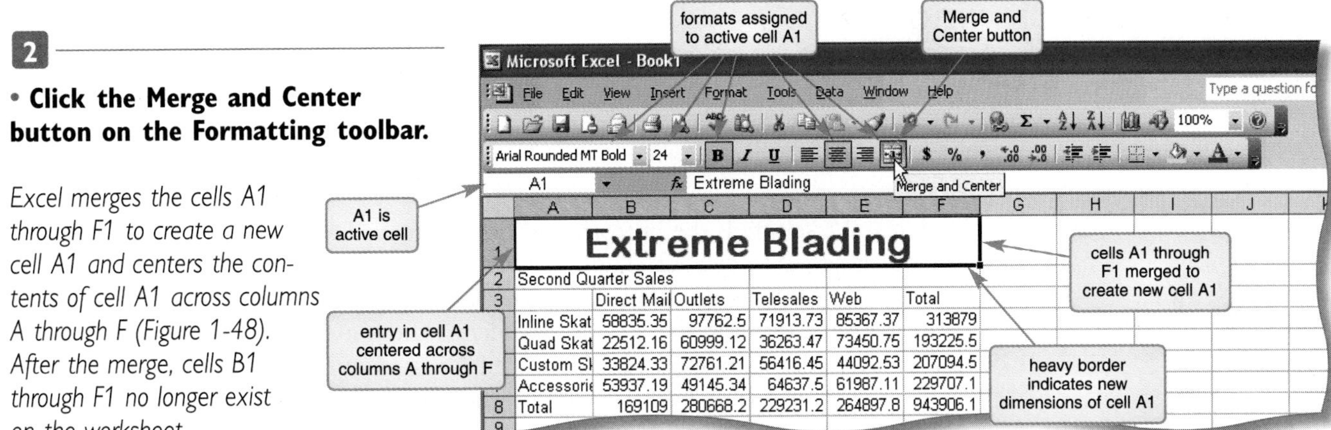

FIGURE 1-48

Other Ways

1. On Format menu click Cells, click Alignment tab, select Center in Horizontal list, click Merge cells check box, click OK button
2. Right-click cell, click Format Cells on shortcut menu, click Alignment tab, select Center in Horizontal list, click Merge cells check box, click OK button
3. In Voice Command mode, say "Merge and Center"

Excel not only centers the worksheet title across the range A1:F1, but it also merges cells A1 through F1 into one merged cell, cell A1. For the Merge and Center button to work properly, all the cells except the leftmost cell in the selected range must be empty.

The opposite of merging cells is **splitting a merged cell**. After you have merged multiple cells to create one merged cell, you can unmerge, or split, the merged cell to display the original cells on the worksheet. You split a merged cell by selecting it and clicking the Merge and Center button. For example, if you click the Merge and Center button a second time in Step 2, it will split the merged cell A1 to cells A1, B1, C1, D1, E1, and F1.

Most formats assigned to a cell will appear on the Formatting toolbar when the cell is selected. For example, with cell A1 selected in Figure 1-48, Excel displays the font type and font size of the active cell in their appropriate boxes. Transparent gold buttons on the Formatting toolbar indicate other assigned formatting. To determine if less frequently used formats are assigned to a cell, right-click the cell, click Format Cells on the shortcut menu, and then click each of the tabs in the Format Cells dialog box.

Formatting the Worksheet Subtitle

The worksheet subtitle in cell A2 is to be formatted the same as the worksheet title in cell A1, except that the font size should be 16 rather than 24. The steps on the next page show how to format the worksheet subtitle in cell A2.

To Format the Worksheet Subtitle

1. **Select cell A2.**
2. **Click the Font box arrow on the Formatting toolbar and then click Arial Rounded MT Bold.**
3. **Click the Bold button on the Formatting toolbar.**
4. **Click the Font Size box arrow on the Formatting toolbar and then click 16.**
5. **Click the Font Color button on the Formatting toolbar.**
6. **Select the range A2:F2 and then click the Merge and Center button on the Formatting toolbar.**

Excel displays the worksheet subtitle in cell A2 as shown in Figure 1-49.

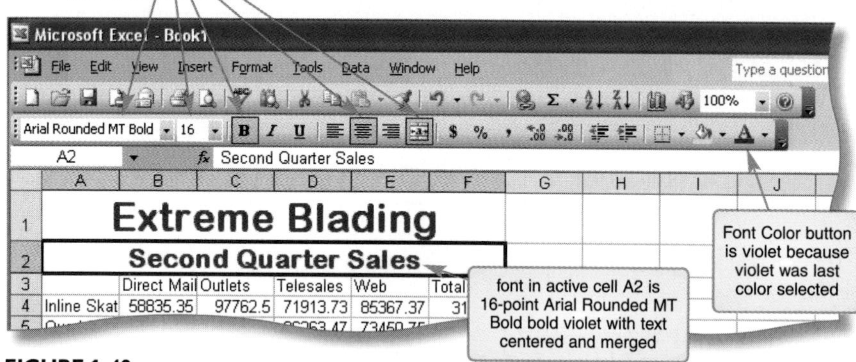

FIGURE 1-49

With cell A2 selected, the buttons and boxes on the Formatting toolbar describe the formats assigned to cell A2. The steps used to format the worksheet subtitle in cell A2 were the same as the steps used to assign the formats to the worksheet title in cell A1, except for the step that assigned violet as the font color. The step to change the font color of the worksheet subtitle in cell A2 used only the Font Color button, rather than the Font Color button arrow. Recall that, when you choose a color on the Font Color palette, Excel assigns the last font color used (in this case, violet) to the Font Color button.

Using AutoFormat to Format the Body of a Worksheet

Excel has customized autoformats that allow you to format the body of the worksheet to give it a professional look. An **autoformat** is a built-in collection of formats such as font style, font color, borders, and alignment, which you can apply to a range of cells. The following steps format the range A3:F8 using the AutoFormat command on the Format menu.

To Use AutoFormat to Format the Body of a Worksheet

1.
- **Select cell A3, the upper-left corner cell of the rectangular range to format.**
- **Drag the mouse pointer to cell F8, the lower-right corner cell of the range to format.**

Excel highlights the range to format with a heavy border and transparent blue background (Figure 1-50).

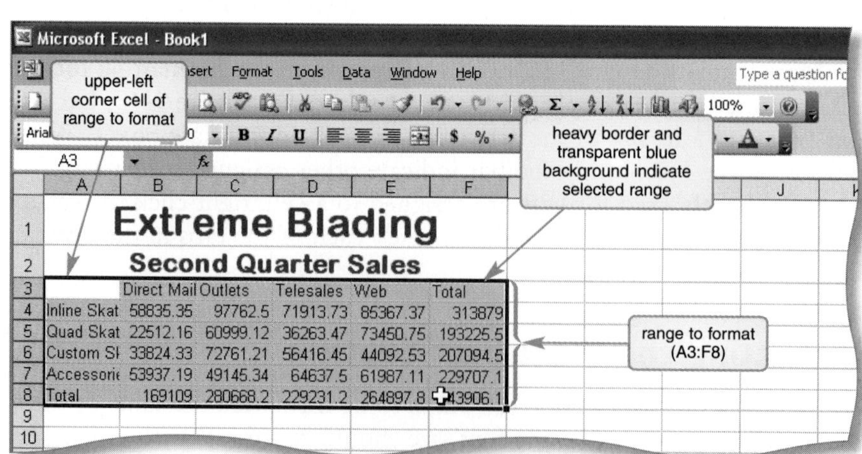

FIGURE 1-50

2

- **Click Format on the menu bar.**

Excel displays the Format menu (Figure 1-51).

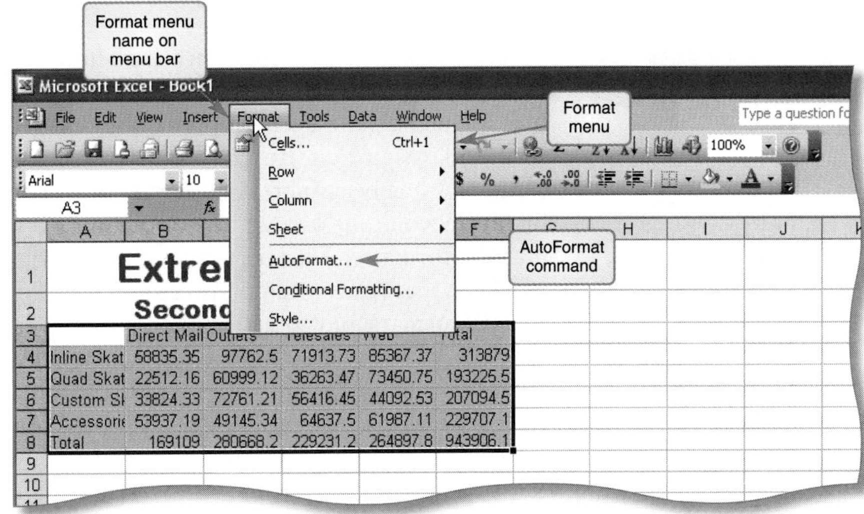

FIGURE 1-51

3

- **Click AutoFormat on the Format menu.**
- **When Excel displays the AutoFormat dialog box, click the Accounting 2 format.**

Excel displays the AutoFormat dialog box with a list of available autoformats (Figure 1-52). For each autoformat, Excel provides a sample to illustrate how the body of the worksheet will appear if that autoformat is chosen.

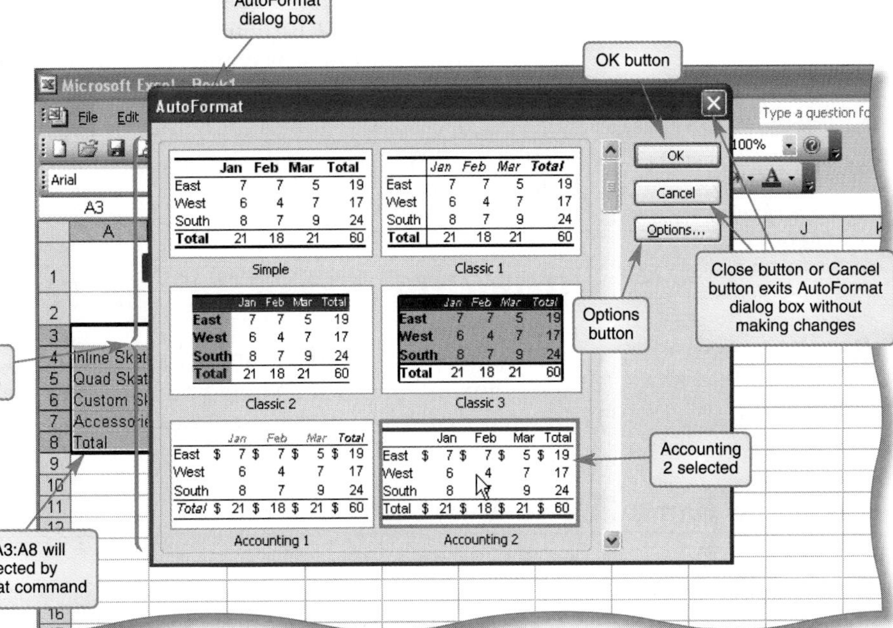

FIGURE 1-52

4

- **Click the OK button.**
- **Select cell A10 to deselect the range A3:F8.**

Excel displays the worksheet with the range A3:F8 formatted using the autoformat, Accounting 2 (Figure 1-53).

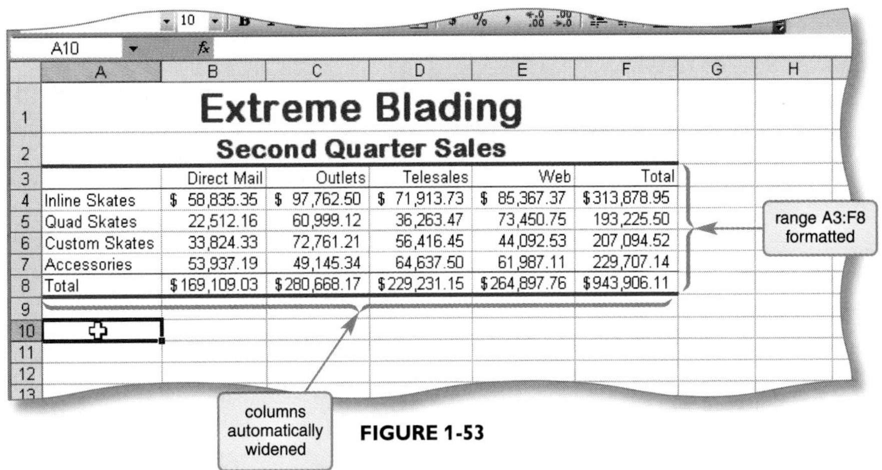

FIGURE 1-53

More About

Merging Table Formats

It is not uncommon to apply two or more of the table formats (Figure 1-52 on the previous page) to the same range. If you assign two table formats to a range, Excel does not remove the original format from the range; it simply adds the second table format to the first. Thus, if you decide to change a table format to another, select the table format None from the bottom of the list to clear the first table format.

The formats associated with the autoformat Accounting 2 include right-aligned column titles; numbers displayed as dollars and cents with comma separators; numbers aligned on the decimal point; the first row and total row of numbers displayed with dollar signs; and top and bottom rows displayed with borders. The width of column A has been increased so the longest row title in cell A6, Custom Skates, just fits in the column. The widths of columns B through F also have been increased so that the formatted numbers will fit in the cells.

The AutoFormat dialog box shown in Figure 1-52 on the previous page includes 17 autoformats and four buttons. Use the vertical scroll bar in the dialog box to view the autoformats that are not displayed when the dialog box first opens. Each one of these autoformats offers a different look. The one you choose depends on the worksheet you are creating. The last autoformat in the list, called None, removes all formats.

The four buttons in the AutoFormat dialog box allow you to complete the entries, modify an autoformat, or cancel changes and close the dialog box. The Close button on the title bar and the Cancel button both terminate the current activity and close the AutoFormat dialog box without making changes. The Options button allows you to deselect formats, such as fonts or borders, within an autoformat.

The worksheet now is complete. The next step is to chart the second quarter sales for the four product groups by sales channel. To create the chart, you must select the cell in the upper-left corner of the range to chart (cell A3). Rather than clicking cell A3 to select it, the next section describes how to use the Name box to select the cell.

More About

Navigation

For more information about selecting cells that contain certain entries, such as constants or formulas, visit the Excel 2003 More About Web page (scsite.com/ex2003/more) and click Using Go To Special.

Using the Name Box to Select a Cell

As previously noted, the Name box is located on the left side of the formula bar. To select any cell, click the Name box and enter the cell reference of the cell you want to select. The following steps show how to select cell A3.

To Use the Name Box to Select a Cell

1

• **Click the Name box in the formula bar and then type** a3 **as the cell to select.**

Even though cell A10 is the active cell, Excel displays the typed cell reference a3 in the Name box (Figure 1-54).

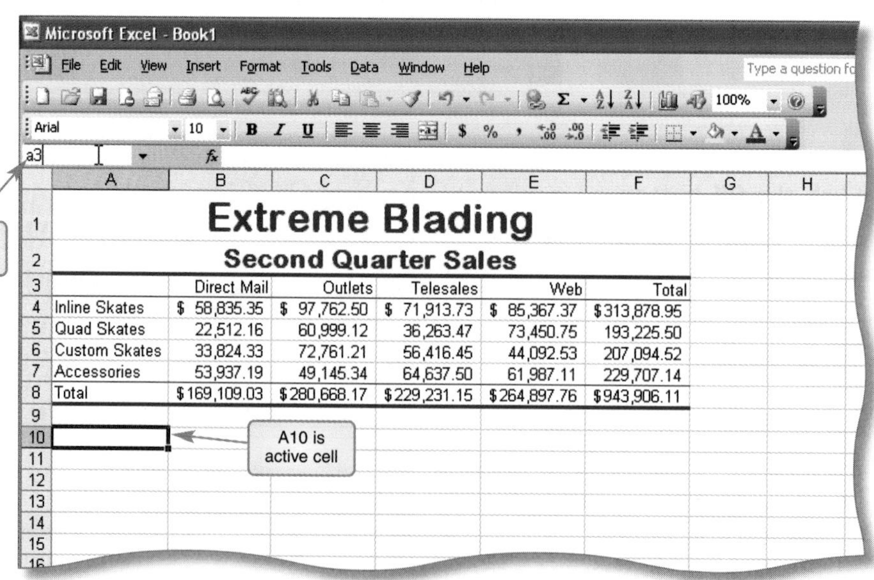

FIGURE 1-54

2

- **Press the ENTER key.**

Excel changes the active cell from cell A10 to cell A3 (Figure 1-55).

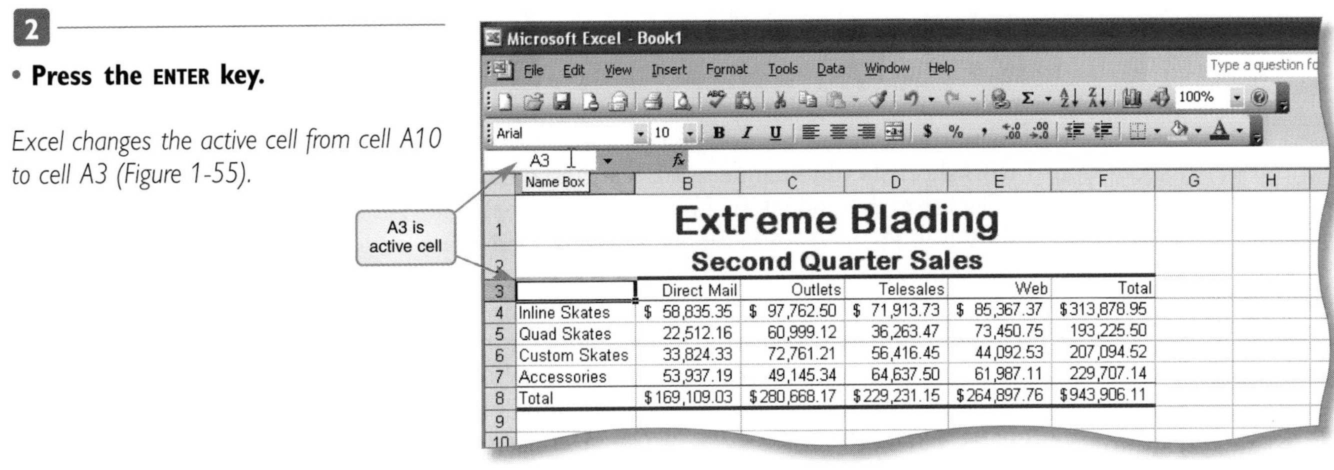

FIGURE 1-55

As you will see in later projects, in addition to using the Name box to select any cell in a worksheet, you also can use it to assign names to a cell or range of cells. Excel supports several additional ways to select a cell, as summarized in Table 1-3.

Table 1-3 Selecting Cells in Excel

KEY, BOX, OR COMMAND	FUNCTION
ALT+PAGE DOWN	Selects the cell one worksheet window to the right and moves the worksheet window accordingly.
ALT+PAGE UP	Selects the cell one worksheet window to the left and moves the worksheet window accordingly.
ARROW	Selects the adjacent cell in the direction of the arrow on the key.
CTRL+ARROW	Selects the border cell of the worksheet in combination with the arrow keys and moves the worksheet window accordingly. For example, to select the rightmost cell in the row that contains the active cell, press CTRL+RIGHT ARROW. You also can press the END key, release it, and then press the appropriate arrow key to accomplish the same task.
CTRL+HOME	Selects cell A1 or the cell one column and one row below and to the right of frozen titles and moves the worksheet window accordingly.
Find command on Edit menu or SHIFT+F5	Finds and selects a cell that contains specific contents that you enter in the Find dialog box. If necessary, Excel moves the worksheet window to display the cell. You also can press CTRL+F to display the Find dialog box.
Go To command on Edit menu or F5	Selects the cell that corresponds to the cell reference you enter in the Go To dialog box and moves the worksheet window accordingly. You also can press CTRL+G to display the Go To dialog box.
HOME	Selects the cell at the beginning of the row that contains the active cell and moves the worksheet window accordingly.
Name box	Selects the cell in the workbook that corresponds to the cell reference you enter in the Name box.
PAGE DOWN	Selects the cell down one worksheet window from the active cell and moves the worksheet window accordingly.
PAGE UP	Selects the cell up one worksheet window from the active cell and moves the worksheet window accordingly.

Adding a 3-D Clustered Column Chart to the Worksheet

As outlined in the requirements document in Figure 1-2 on page EX 6, the worksheet should include a 3-D Clustered column chart to graphically represent sales for each product group by sales channel. The 3-D Clustered column chart shown in Figure 1-56 is called an **embedded chart** because it is drawn on the same worksheet as the data.

The chart uses different colored columns to represent sales for different product groups. For the Direct Mail sales channel, for example, the light blue column represents the second quarter sales for the Inline Skates product group ($58,835.35); for the Outlets sales channel, the purple column represents the second quarter sales for Quad Skates ($60,999.12); for the Telesales sales channel, the light yellow column represents the second quarter sales for Custom Skates ($56,416.45); and for the Web sales channel, the turquoise column represents the second quarter sales for Accessories ($61,987.11). For the Outlets, Telesales, and Web sales channels, the columns follow the same color scheme to represent the comparable second quarter sales. The totals from the worksheet are not represented because the totals are not in the range specified for charting.

Excel derives the chart scale based the values in the worksheet and then displays the scale along the vertical axis (also called the **y-axis** or **value axis**) of the chart. For example, no value in the range B4:E7 is less than 0 or greater than $100,000.00, so the scale ranges from 0 to $100,000.00. Excel also determines the $20,000.00 increments of the scale automatically. For the numbers along the y-axis, Excel uses a format that includes representing the 0 value with a dash (Figure 1-56).

Q&A

Q: If I change a cell value on which the chart is dependent, will Excel redraw the chart?

A: Yes. Excel redraws the chart instantaneously, unless automatic recalculation is disabled. If automatic recalculation is disabled, then you must press function key F9 to redraw the chart. To enable or disable automatic recalculation, invoke the Options command on the Tools menu and click the Calculation tab.

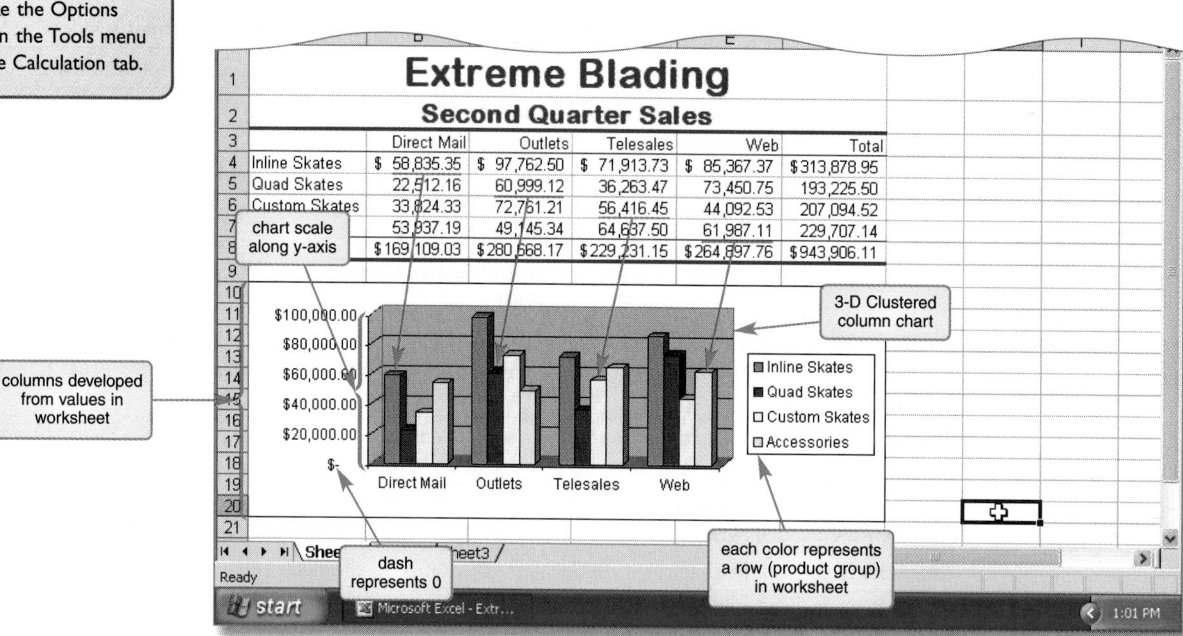

FIGURE 1-56

With the range to chart selected, you click the Chart Wizard button on the Standard toolbar to initiate drawing the chart. The area on the worksheet where the chart appears is called the **chart location**. As shown in Figure 1-56, the chart location in this worksheet is the range A10:F20, immediately below the worksheet data.

The following steps show how to draw a 3-D Clustered column chart that compares the second quarter sales by product group for the four sales channels.

To Add a 3-D Clustered Column Chart to the Worksheet

1

- **With cell A3 selected, position the block plus sign mouse pointer within the cell's border and drag the mouse pointer to the lower-right corner cell (cell E7) of the range to chart (A3:E7).**

Excel highlights the range to chart (Figure 1-57).

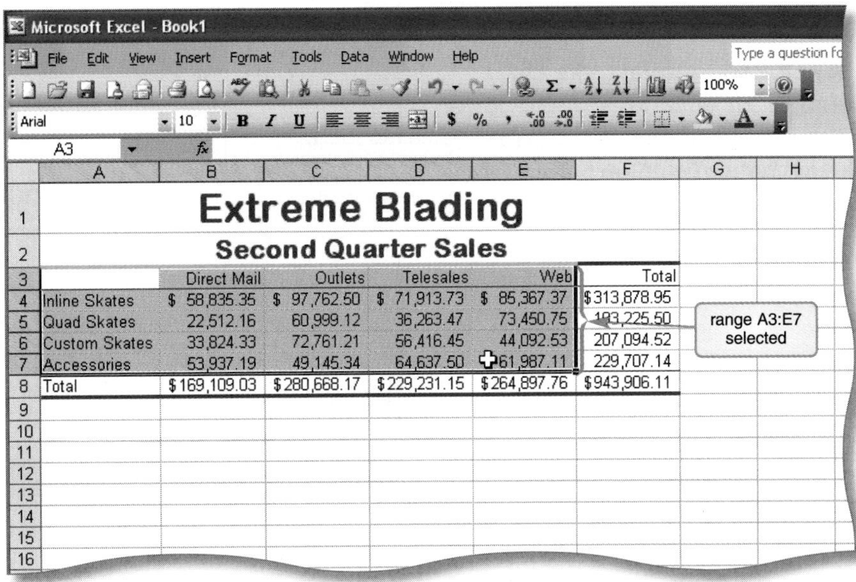

FIGURE 1-57

2

- **Click the Chart Wizard button on the Standard toolbar.**
- **When Excel displays the Chart Wizard - Step 1 of 4 - Chart Type dialog box, and with Column selected in the Chart type list, click Clustered column with a 3-D visual effect (column 1, row 2) in the Chart sub-type area.**

Excel displays the Chart Wizard - Step 1 of 4 - Chart Type dialog box as shown in Figure 1-58.

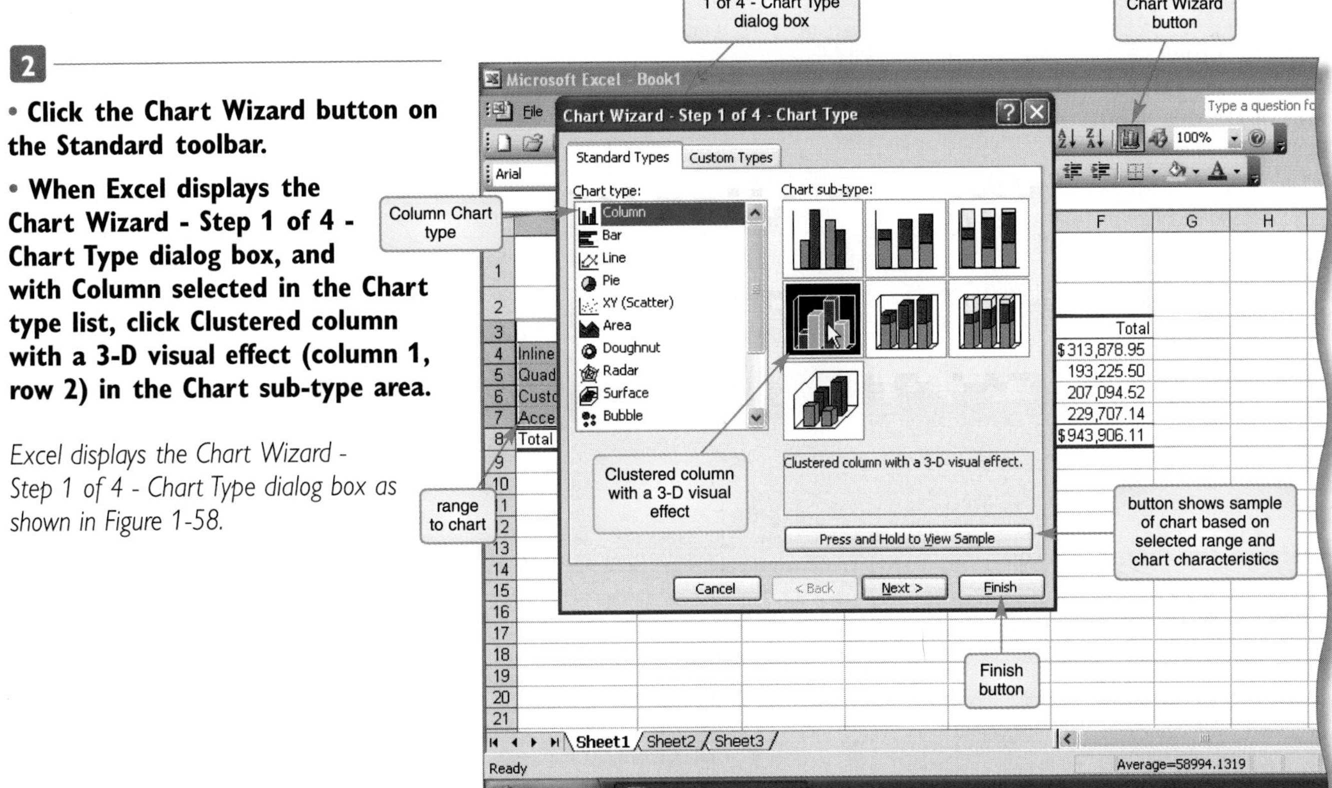

FIGURE 1-58

3

- **Click the Finish button.**
- **If the Chart toolbar appears, click its Close button.**
- **When Excel displays the chart, point to an open area in the lower-right section of the chart area so the ScreenTip, Chart Area, appears next to the mouse pointer.**

Excel draws the 3-D Clustered column chart (Figure 1-59). The chart appears in the middle of the worksheet window in a selection rectangle. The small sizing handles at the corners and along the sides of the selection rectangle indicate the chart is selected.

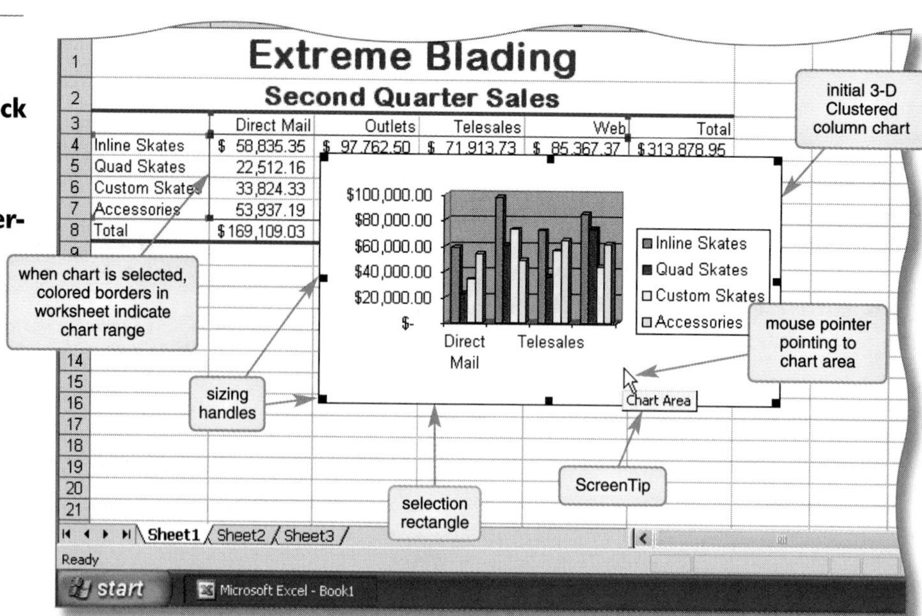

FIGURE 1-59

4

- **Drag the chart down and to the left to position the upper-left corner of the dotted line rectangle over the upper-left corner of cell A10. Do not release the mouse button (Figure 1-60).**

As you drag the selected chart, Excel displays a dotted line rectangle showing the new chart location and the mouse pointer changes to a cross hair with four arrowheads.

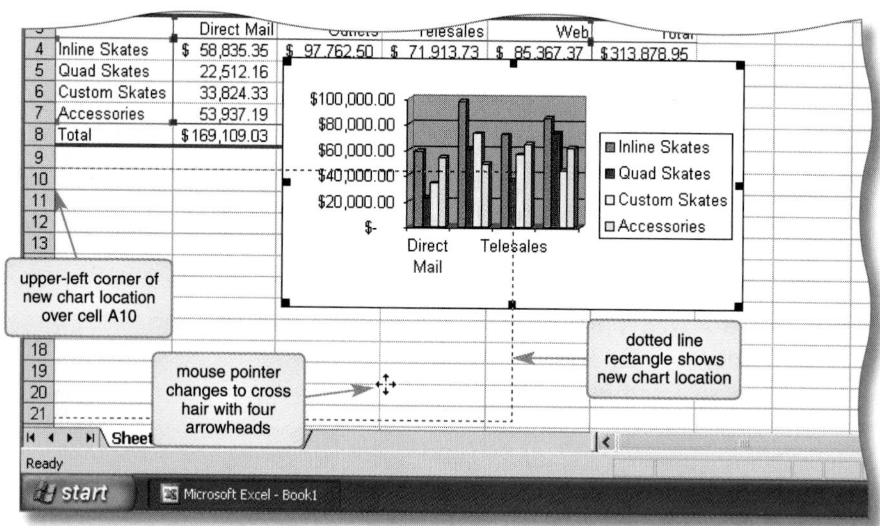

FIGURE 1-60

5

- **Release the mouse button.**
- **Point to the middle sizing handle on the right edge of the selection rectangle.**

The chart appears in a new location (Figure 1-61). The mouse pointer changes to a horizontal line with two arrowheads when it points to a sizing handle.

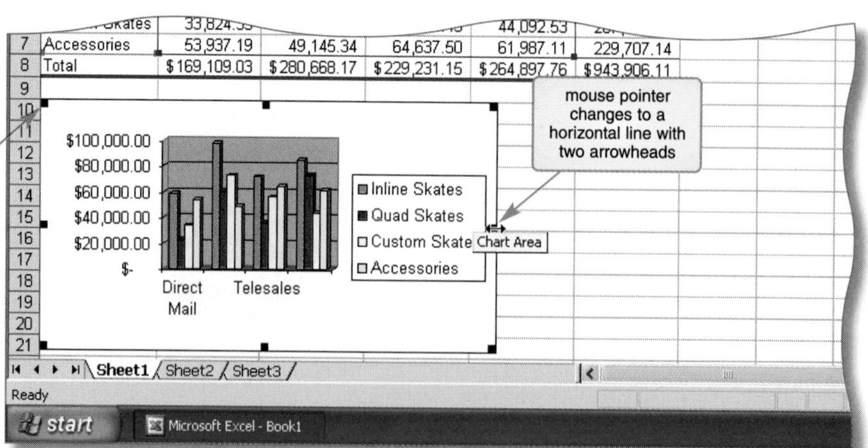

FIGURE 1-61

6

• **While holding down the ALT key, drag the sizing handle to the right edge of column F.**

While you drag, the dotted line rectangle shows the new chart location (Figure 1-62). Holding down the ALT key while you drag a chart ***snaps*** *(aligns) the edge of the chart area to the worksheet gridlines.*

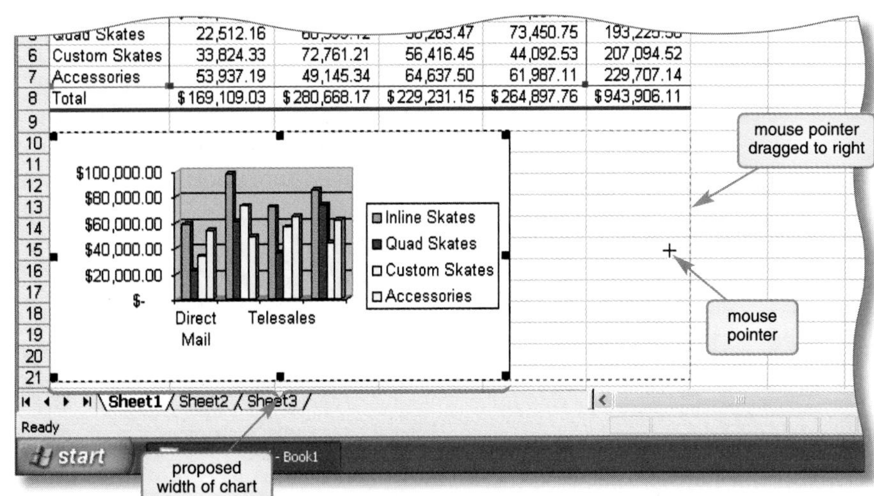

FIGURE 1-62

7

• **If necessary, hold down the ALT key and drag the lower-middle sizing handle up to the bottom border of row 20.**

• **Click cell H20 to deselect the chart.**

The new chart location extends from the top of cell A10 to the bottom of cell F20 (Figure 1-63).

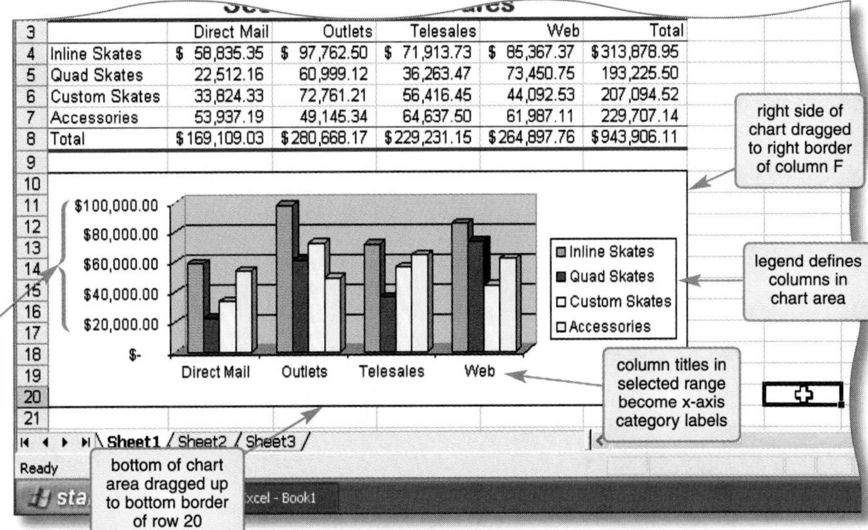

FIGURE 1-63

The embedded 3-D Clustered column chart in Figure 1-63 compares the second quarter sales for the four product groups by each sales channel. It also allows you to compare second quarter sales for the four product groups among the sales channels.

Excel automatically selects the entries in the topmost row of the chart range (row 3) as the titles for the horizontal axis (also called the **x-axis** or **category axis**) and draws a column for each of the 16 cells in the range containing numbers. The small box to the right of the column chart in Figure 1-63 contains the **legend**, which identifies the colors assigned to each bar in the chart. Excel automatically selects the entries in the leftmost column of the chart range (column A) as titles within the legend. As indicated earlier, Excel also automatically derives the chart scale on the y-axis based on the highest and lowest numbers in the chart range.

Excel offers 14 different chart types (Figure 1-58 on page EX 39). The **default chart type** is the chart Excel draws if you click the Finish button in the first Chart Wizard dialog box. When you install Excel on a computer, the default chart type is the 2-D (two-dimensional) Column chart.

Other Ways

1. On Insert menu click Chart
2. Press F11
3. In Voice Command mode, say "Chart Wizard"

More About

Printing Only the Chart

To print the embedded chart without printing the worksheet, select the chart, click File on the menu bar, click Page Setup, click the Chart tab, click the Scale to fit page in the Printed chart size area, click the Print button, and then click the OK button.

Saving a Workbook

While you are building a workbook, the computer stores it in memory. If the computer is turned off or if you lose electrical power, the workbook is lost. Hence, if you plan to use the workbook later, you must save the workbook on a floppy disk or hard disk. A saved workbook is referred to as a **file.** The following steps illustrate how to save a workbook on a floppy disk in drive A using the Save button on the Standard toolbar.

To Save a Workbook

1

- **With a floppy disk in drive A, click the Save button on the Standard toolbar.**

Excel displays the Save As dialog box (Figure 1-64). The default Save in folder is Documents (your Save in folder may be different), the default file name is Book1, and the default file type is Microsoft Office Excel Workbook.

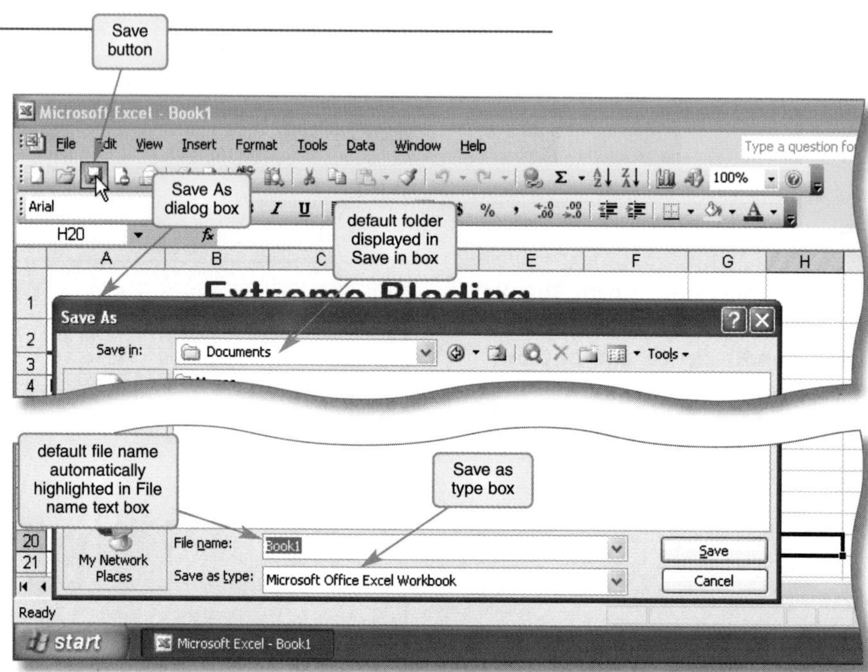

FIGURE 1-64

2

- **Type** `Extreme Blading 2nd Quarter Sales` **in the File name text box.**
- **Click the Save in box arrow.**

The new file name replaces Book1 in the File name text box (Figure 1-65). A file name can be up to 255 characters and can include spaces. Excel displays a list of available drives and folders.

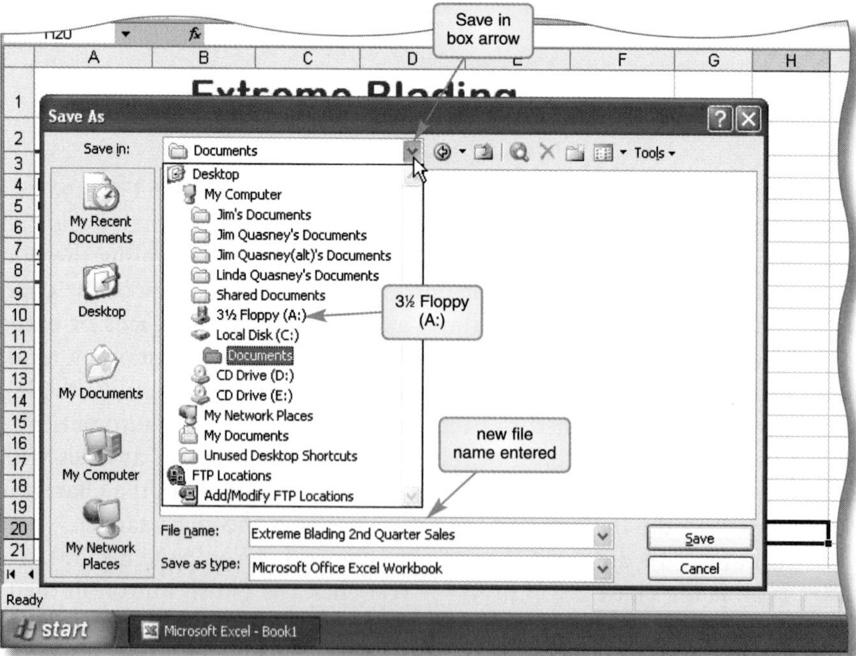

FIGURE 1-65

3

• **Click 3½ Floppy (A:) in the Save in list.**

Drive A becomes the selected drive (Figure 1-66). The buttons on the top and on the side of the dialog box are used to select folders, change the appearance of file names, and complete other tasks.

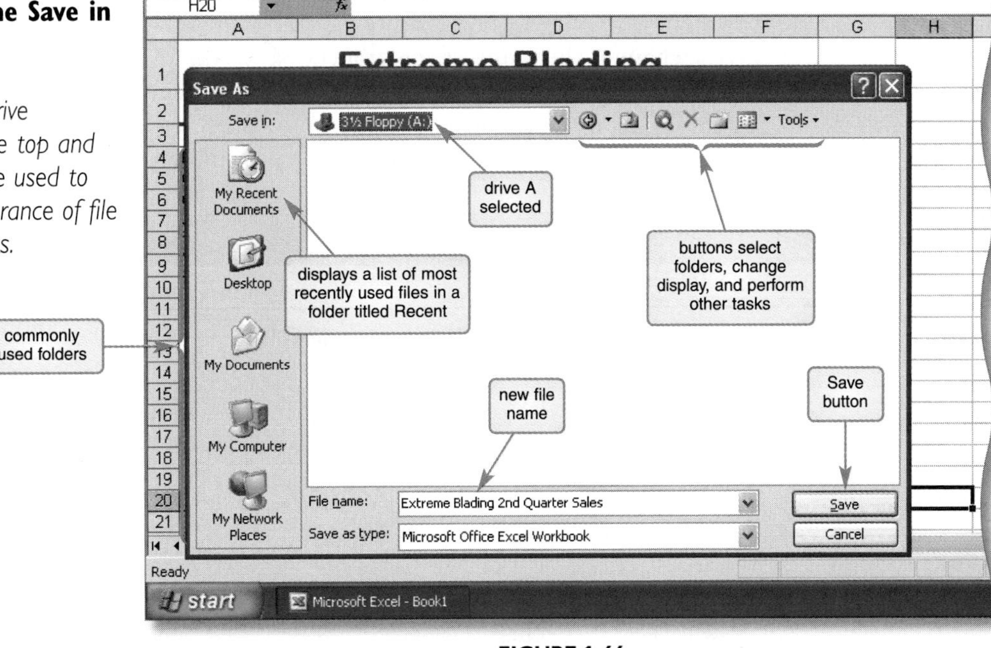

FIGURE 1-66

4

• **Click the Save button in the Save As dialog box.**

*Excel saves the workbook on the floppy disk in drive A using the file name, Extreme Blading 2nd Quarter Sales. Excel automatically appends the extension **.xls** to the file name you entered in Step 2, which stands for Excel workbook. Although the workbook is saved on a floppy disk, it also remains in memory and is displayed on the screen (Figure 1-67). Excel displays the new file name on the title bar.*

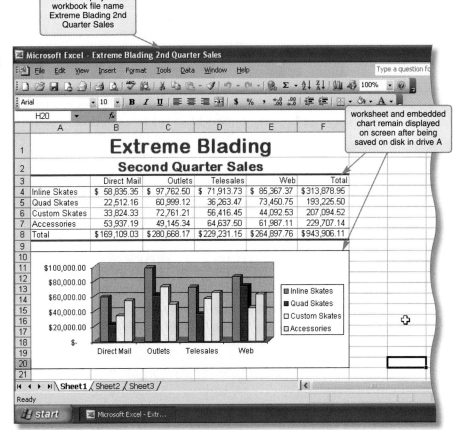

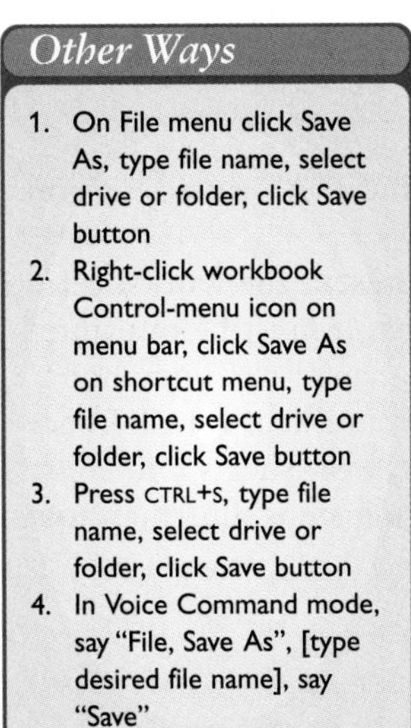

Other Ways

1. On File menu click Save As, type file name, select drive or folder, click Save button
2. Right-click workbook Control-menu icon on menu bar, click Save As on shortcut menu, type file name, select drive or folder, click Save button
3. Press CTRL+S, type file name, select drive or folder, click Save button
4. In Voice Command mode, say "File, Save As", [type desired file name], say "Save"

title bar displays new workbook file name Extreme Blading 2nd Quarter Sales

Microsoft Excel - Extreme Blading 2nd Quarter Sales

worksheet and embedded chart remain displayed on screen after being saved on disk in drive A

Extreme Blading

Second Quarter Sales

	Direct Mail	Outlets	Telesales	Web	Total
Inline Skates	$ 58,835.35	$ 97,762.50	$ 71,913.73	$ 85,367.37	$313,878.95
Quad Skates	22,512.16	60,999.12	36,263.47	73,450.75	193,225.50
Custom Skates	33,824.33	72,761.21	56,416.45	44,092.53	207,094.52
Accessories	53,937.19	49,145.34	64,637.50	61,987.11	229,707.14
Total	$169,109.03	$280,668.17	$229,231.15	$264,897.76	$943,906.11

FIGURE 1-67

While Excel is saving the workbook, it momentarily changes the word Ready on the status bar to Saving. It also displays a horizontal bar on the status bar indicating the amount of the workbook saved. After the save operation is complete, Excel changes the name of the workbook on the title bar from Book1 to Extreme Blading 2nd Quarter Sales (Figure 1-67 on the previous page).

The seven buttons at the top of the Save As dialog box in Figure 1-66 on the previous page and their functions are summarized in Table 1-4.

Table 1-4 Save As Dialog Box Toolbar Buttons

BUTTON	BUTTON NAME	FUNCTION
	Default File Location	Displays contents of default file location
	Up One Level	Displays contents of folder one level up from current folder
	Search the Web	Starts browser and displays search engine
	Delete	Deletes selected file or folder
	Create New Folder	Creates new folder
	Views	Changes view of files and folders
Tools ▾	Tools	Lists commands to print or modify file names and folders

When you click the Tools button in the Save As dialog box, Excel displays the Tools menu. The General Options command on the menu allows you to save a backup copy of the workbook, create a password to limit access to the workbook, and carry out other functions that are discussed later. Saving a **backup copy** of the workbook means that each time you save a workbook, Excel copies the current version of the workbook on disk to a file with the same name, but with the words, Backup of, appended to the front of the file name. In the case of a power failure or some other problem, you can use the backup copy to restore your work.

You also can use the General Options command on the Tools menu to assign a password to a workbook so others cannot open it. A password is case-sensitive and can be up to 15 characters long. **Case-sensitive** means Excel can differentiate between uppercase and lowercase letters. If you assign a password and forget the password, you cannot access the workbook.

The five buttons on the left of the Save As dialog box in Figure 1-66 allow you to select frequently used folders. The My Recent Documents button displays a list of shortcuts (pointers) to the most recently used files in a folder titled Recent.

More About

Saving

Excel allows you to save a workbook in more than 30 different file formats. Choose the file format by clicking the Save as type box arrow at the bottom of the Save As dialog box (Figure 1-66). Microsoft Office Excel Workbook is the default file format.

Printing a Worksheet

Once you have created the worksheet, you might want to print it. A printed version of the worksheet is called a **hard copy** or **printout**.

You might want a printout for several reasons. First, to present the worksheet and chart to someone who does not have access to a computer, it must be in printed form. A printout, for example, can be handed out in a management meeting about second quarter sales. In addition, worksheets and charts often are kept for reference by people other than those who prepare them. In many cases, worksheets and charts are printed and kept in binders for use by others. The following steps illustrate how to print the worksheet.

To Print a Worksheet

1

- **Ready the printer according to the printer instructions and then click the Print button on the Standard toolbar (Figure 1-68).**

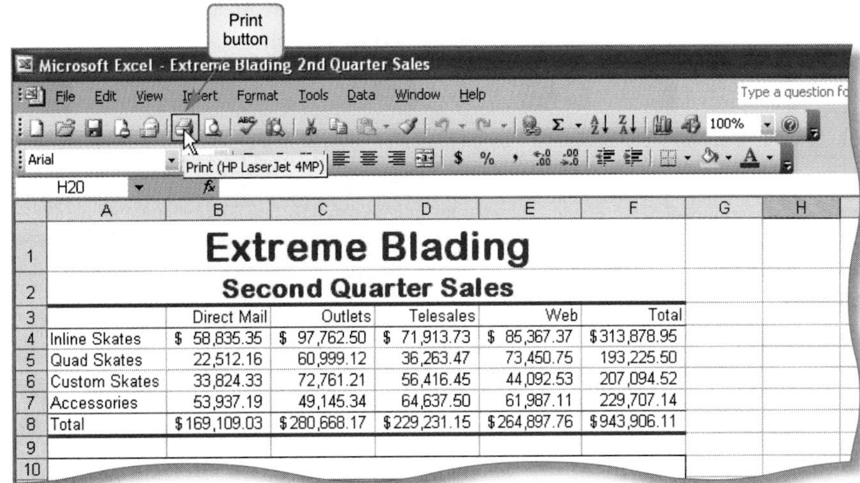

FIGURE 1-68

2

- **When the printer stops printing the worksheet and the chart, retrieve the printout.**

Excel sends the worksheet to the printer, which prints it (Figure 1-69).

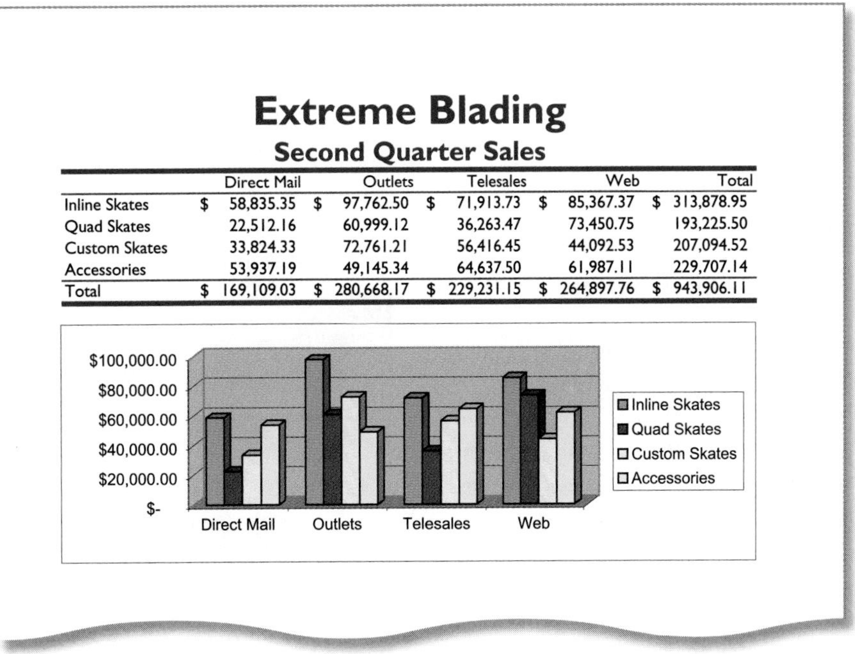

	Direct Mail	Outlets	Telesales	Web	Total
Inline Skates	$ 58,835.35	$ 97,762.50	$ 71,913.73	$ 85,367.37	$ 313,878.95
Quad Skates	22,512.16	60,999.12	36,263.47	73,450.75	193,225.50
Custom Skates	33,824.33	72,761.21	56,416.45	44,092.53	207,094.52
Accessories	53,937.19	49,145.34	64,637.50	61,987.11	229,707.14
Total	$ 169,109.03	$ 280,668.17	$ 229,231.15	$ 264,897.76	$ 943,906.11

FIGURE 1-69

Prior to clicking the Print button, you can select which columns and rows in the worksheet to print. The range of cells you choose to print is called the **print area**. If you do not select a print area, as was the case in the previous set of steps, Excel automatically selects a print area on the basis of used cells. As you will see in future projects, Excel has many different print options, such as allowing you to preview the printout on the screen to see if the printout is satisfactory before sending it to the printer.

Other Ways

1. On File menu click Print, click OK button
2. Right-click workbook Control-menu icon on menu bar, click Print on shortcut menu, click OK button
3. Press CTRL+P, click OK button
4. In Voice Command mode, say "Print"

Quitting Excel

The Project 1 worksheet and embedded chart are complete. The following steps show how to quit Excel.

To Quit Excel

1

• **Point to the Close button on the right side of the title bar (Figure 1-70).**

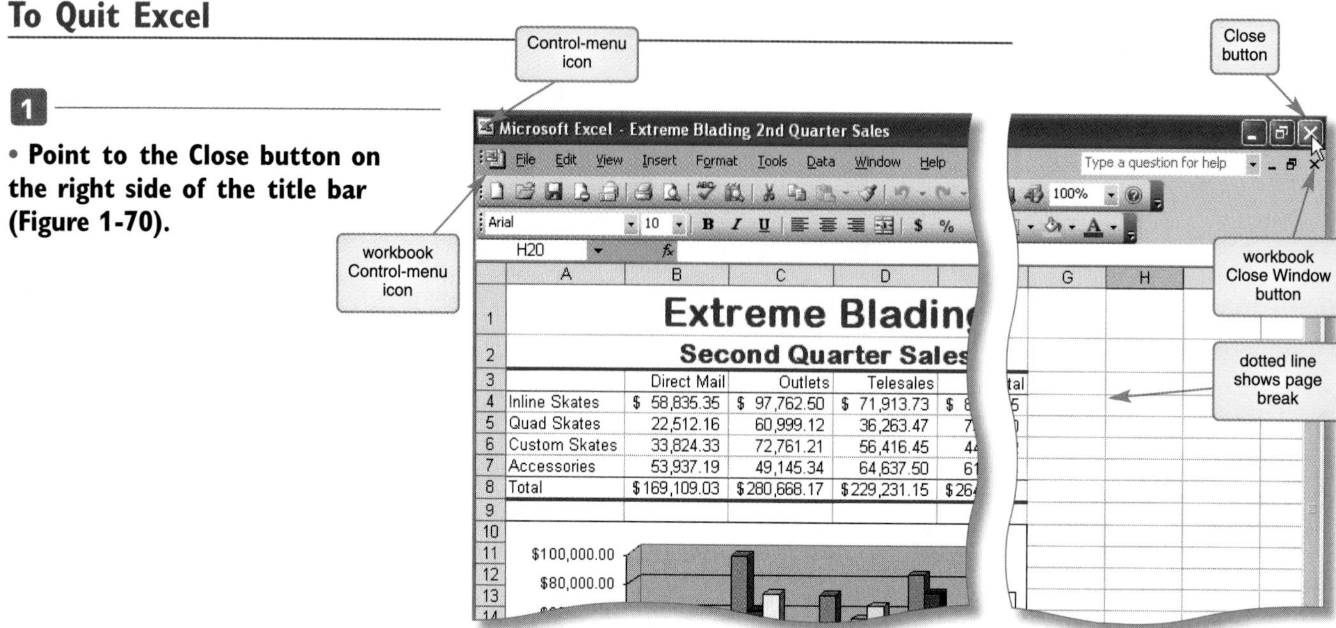

FIGURE 1-70

2

• **Click the Close button.**

If the worksheet was changed or printed, the Microsoft Excel dialog box displays the question, Do you want to save the changes you made to 'Extreme Blading 2nd Quarter Sales.xls'? (Figure 1-71). Clicking the Yes button saves the changes before quitting Excel. Clicking the No button quits Excel without saving the changes. Clicking the Cancel button closes the dialog box and returns control to the worksheet without saving the changes.

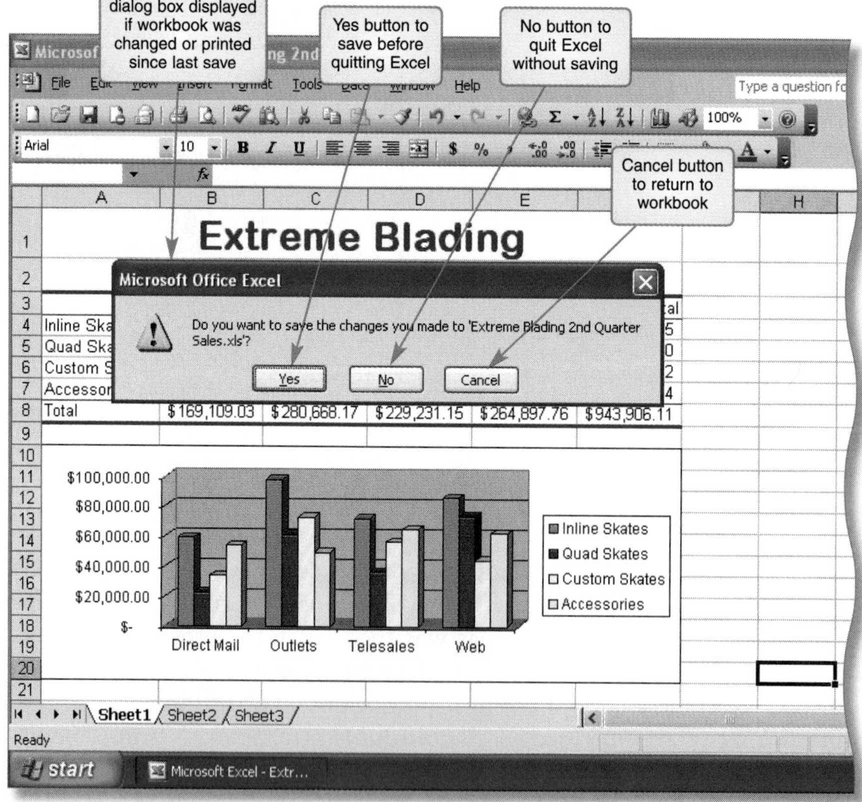

FIGURE 1-71

3

• **Click the No button.**

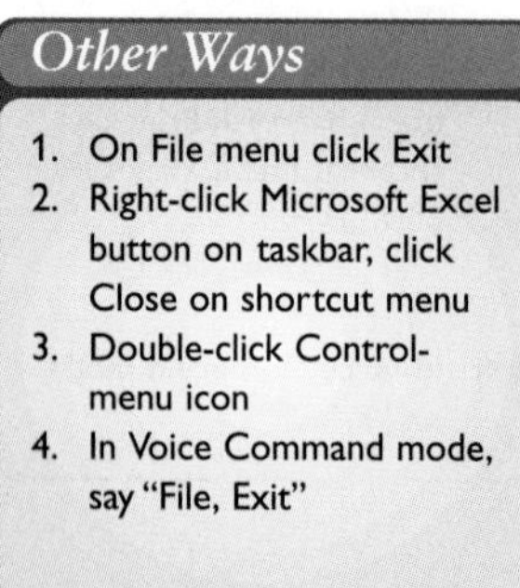

Other Ways

1. On File menu click Exit
2. Right-click Microsoft Excel button on taskbar, click Close on shortcut menu
3. Double-click Control-menu icon
4. In Voice Command mode, say "File, Exit"

In Figure 1-70, you can see that the Excel window includes two Close buttons and two Control-menu icons. The Close button and Control-menu icon on the title bar can be used to quit Excel. The Close Window button and Control-menu icon on the menu bar can be used to close the workbook, but not to quit Excel.

> **Q&A**
>
> **Q:** Does a way exist to circumvent the heavy use of paper and ink with computers?
>
> **A:** Yes. You can preview the printout on your screen using the Print Preview button on the Standard toolbar, make adjustments to the worksheet, and then print it only when it appears exactly as you want. Each time you preview rather than print, you save both ink and paper.

Starting Excel and Opening a Workbook

After creating and saving a workbook, you often will have reason to retrieve it from a floppy disk. For example, you might want to review the calculations on the worksheet and enter additional or revised data. The following steps assume Excel is not running.

To Start Excel and Open a Workbook

1

• **With your floppy disk in drive A, click the Start button on the Windows taskbar, point to All Programs on the Start menu, point to Microsoft Office on the All Programs submenu, and then click Microsoft Office Excel 2003 on the Microsoft Office submenu.**

Excel starts. The Getting Started task pane lists the four most recently used files in the Open area (Figure 1-72).

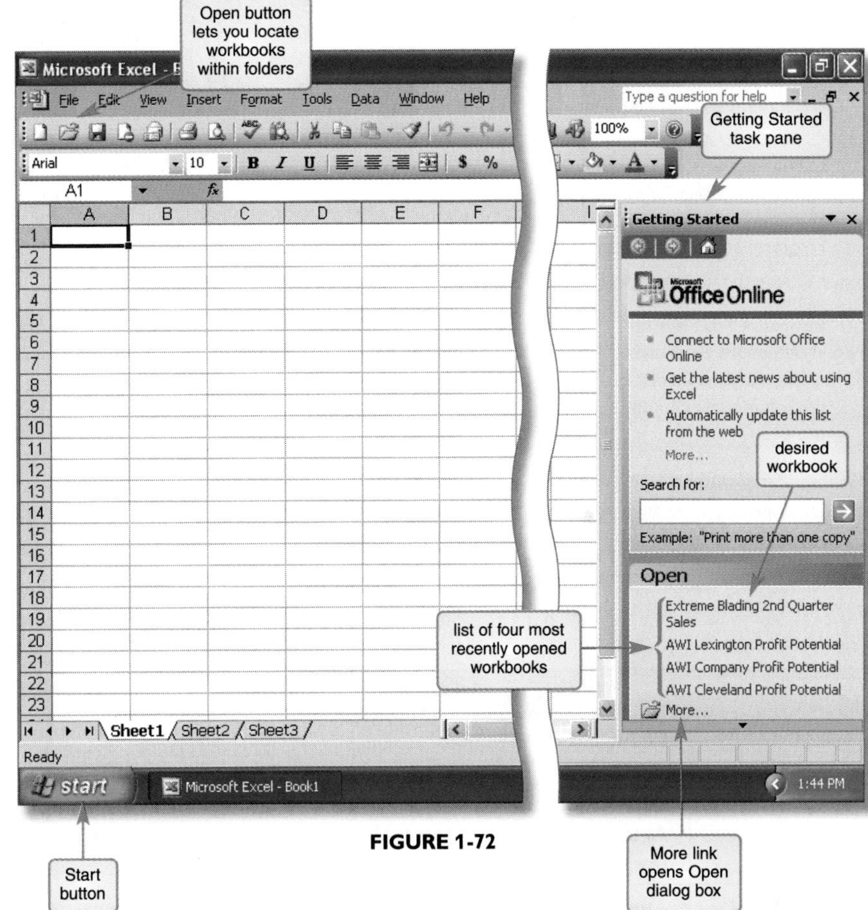

FIGURE 1-72

2

• **Click Extreme Blading 2nd Quarter Sales in the Open area in the Getting Started task pane.**

Excel opens the workbook Extreme Blading 2nd Quarter Sales (Figure 1-73). The Getting Started task pane closes.

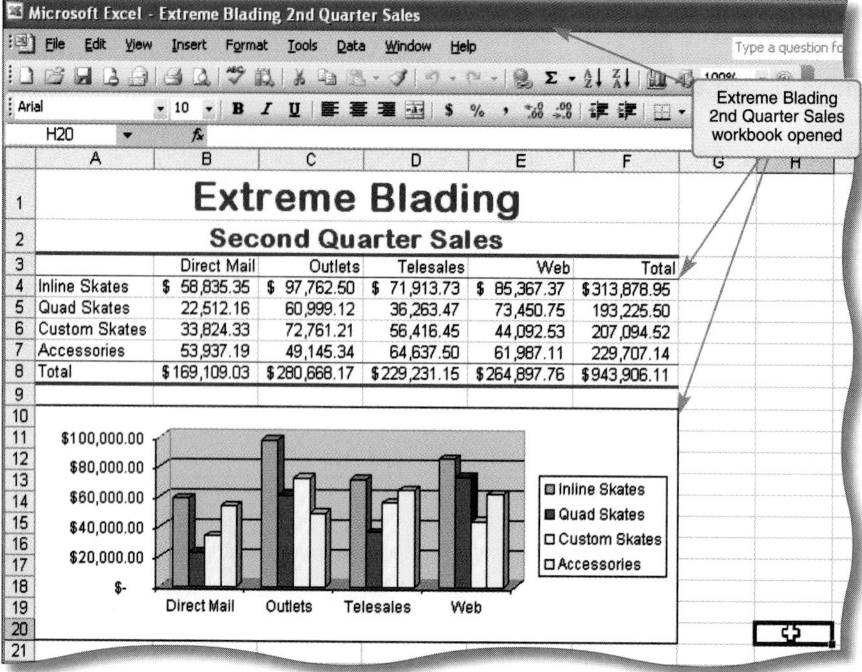

FIGURE 1-73

Other Ways

1. Click Start button, point to All Programs on Start menu, click Open Office Document on All Programs submenu, select drive A, double-click file name
2. Right-click Start button, click Explore on shortcut menu, display contents of drive A, double-click file name
3. With Excel active, in Voice Command mode, say "Open", [select file name], say "Open"

If you want to open a workbook other than one of the four most recently opened ones, click the Open button on the Standard toolbar or the More link in the Getting Started task pane. Clicking the Open button or the More link displays the Open dialog box, which allows you to navigate to a workbook stored on disk.

AutoCalculate

You easily can obtain a total, an average, or other information about the numbers in a range by using the **AutoCalculate area** on the status bar. First, select the range of cells containing the numbers you want to check. Next, right-click the AutoCalculate area to display the shortcut menu (Figure 1-74). The check mark to the left of the active function (Sum) indicates that the sum of the selected range is displayed in the AutoCalculate area on the status bar. The function of the commands on the AutoCalculate shortcut menu are described in Table 1-5.

The following steps show how to display the average second quarter sales for the Custom Skates product group.

Table 1-5 AutoCalculate Shortcut Menu Commands

COMMAND	FUNCTION
None	No value is displayed in the AutoCalculate area
Average	AutoCalculate area displays the average of the numbers in the selected range
Count	AutoCalculate area displays the number of nonblank cells in the selected range
Count Nums	AutoCalculate area displays the number of cells containing numbers in the selected range
Max	AutoCalculate area displays the highest value in the selected range
Min	AutoCalculate area displays the lowest value in the selected range
Sum	AutoCalculate area displays the sum of the numbers in the selected range

To Use the AutoCalculate Area to Determine an Average

1

• **Select the range B6:E6 and then right-click the AutoCalculate area on the status bar.**

The sum of the numbers in the range B6:E6 is displayed (207,094.52) in the AutoCalculate area, because Sum is the active function (Figure 1-74). Excel displays a shortcut menu listing the other available functions above the AutoCalculate area. If another function is active on your shortcut menu, you may see a different value in the AutoCalculate area.

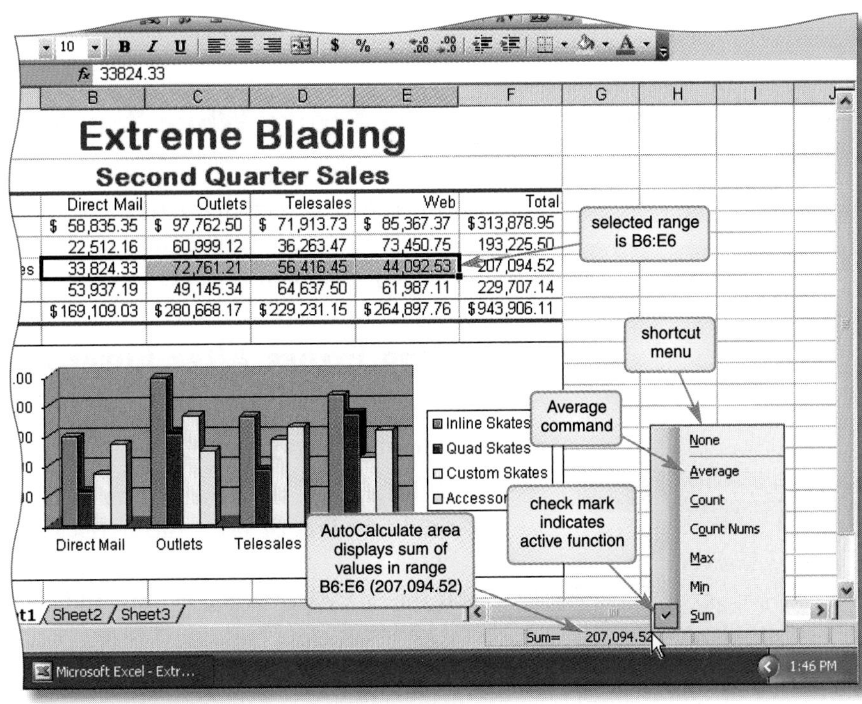

FIGURE 1-74

2

• **Click Average on the shortcut menu.**

Excel displays the average of the numbers in the range B6:E6 (51,773.63) in the AutoCalculate area (Figure 1-75).

3

• **Right-click the AutoCalculate area and then click Sum on the shortcut menu.**

The AutoCalculate area displays the sum as shown earlier in Figure 1-74.

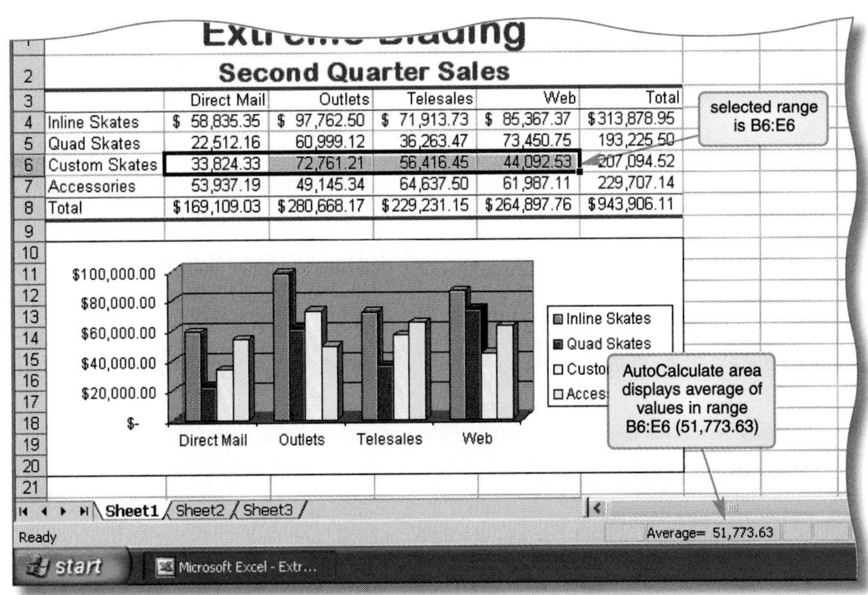

FIGURE 1-75

To change to any one of the other five functions for the range B6:E6, right-click the AutoCalculate area and then click the desired function. Clicking None at the top of the AutoCalculate shortcut menu in Figure 1-74 turns off the AutoCalculate area. Thus, if you select None, then no value will be displayed in the AutoCalculate area when you select a range.

More About

Shortcut Menus

Shortcut menus contain the most frequently used commands that relate to the object to which the mouse pointer is pointing.

Correcting Errors

You can correct errors on a worksheet using one of several methods. The method you choose will depend on the extent of the error and whether you notice it while typing the data or after you have entered the incorrect data into the cell.

Correcting Errors While You Are Typing Data into a Cell

If you notice an error while you are typing data into a cell, press the BACKSPACE key to erase the incorrect characters and then type the correct characters. If the error is a major one, click the Cancel box in the formula bar or press the ESC key to erase the entire entry and then reenter the data from the beginning.

Correcting Errors After Entering Data into a Cell

If you find an error in the worksheet after entering the data, you can correct the error in one of two ways:

> *More About*
>
> **In-Cell Editing**
>
> An alternative to double-clicking the cell to edit is to select the cell and then press F2.

1. If the entry is short, select the cell, retype the entry correctly, and then click the Enter box or press the ENTER key. The new entry will replace the old entry.
2. If the entry in the cell is long and the errors are minor, using Edit mode may be a better choice than retyping the cell entry. Use the Edit mode as described below.
   a. Double-click the cell containing the error to switch Excel to Edit mode. In **Edit mode**, Excel displays the active cell entry in the formula bar and a flashing insertion point in the active cell (Figure 1-76). With Excel in Edit mode, you can edit the contents directly in the cell — a procedure called **in-cell editing**.
   b. Make changes using in-cell editing, as indicated below.
      (1) To insert new characters between two characters, place the insertion point between the two characters and begin typing. Excel inserts the new characters at the location of the insertion point.
      (2) To delete a character in the cell, move the insertion point to the left of the character you want to delete and then press the DELETE key or place the insertion point to the right of the character you want to delete and then press the BACKSPACE key. You also can use the mouse to drag through the character or adjacent characters you want to delete and then press the DELETE key or click the Cut button on the Standard toolbar.
      (3) When you are finished editing an entry, click the Enter box or press the ENTER key.

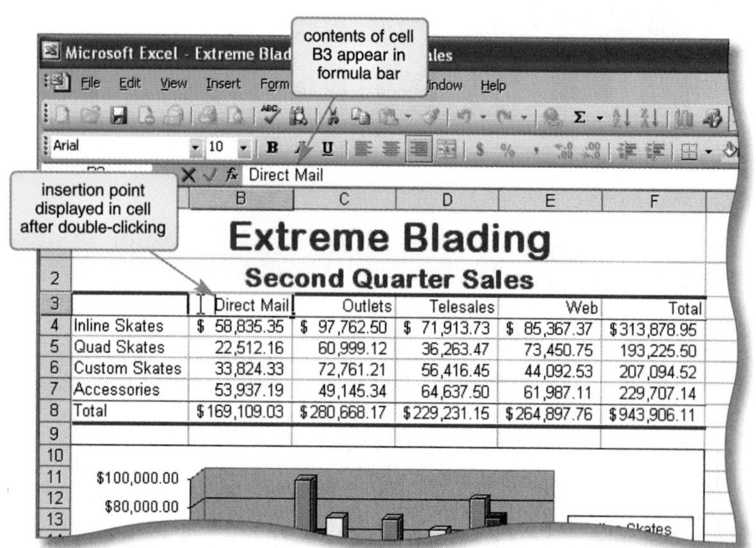

FIGURE 1-76

When Excel enters the Edit mode, the keyboard usually is in Insert mode. In **Insert mode**, as you type a character, Excel inserts the character and moves all characters to the right of the typed character one position to the right. You can change to Overtype mode by pressing the INSERT key. In **Overtype mode**, Excel overtypes, or replaces, the character to the right of the insertion point. The INSERT key toggles the keyboard between Insert mode and Overtype mode.

While in Edit mode, you may have reason to move the insertion point to various points in the cell, select portions of the data in the cell, or switch from inserting characters to overtyping characters. Table 1-6 summarizes the more common tasks used during in-cell editing.

More About

Editing the Contents of a Cell

Rather than using in-cell editing, you can select the cell and then click the formula bar to edit the contents.

Table 1-6 Summary of In-Cell Editing Tasks

	TASK	MOUSE	KEYBOARD
1	Move the insertion point to the beginning of data in a cell.	Point to the left of the first character and click.	Press HOME
2	Move the insertion point to the end of data in a cell.	Point to the right of the last character and click.	Press END
3	Move the insertion point anywhere in a cell.	Point to the appropriate position and click the character.	Press RIGHT ARROW or LEFT ARROW
4	Highlight one or more adjacent characters.	Drag the mouse pointer through adjacent characters.	Press SHIFT+RIGHT ARROW or SHIFT+LEFT ARROW
5	Select all data in a cell.	Double-click the cell with the insertion point in the cell.	
6	Delete selected characters.	Click the Cut button on the Standard toolbar.	Press DELETE
7	Delete characters to the left of the insertion point.		Press BACKSPACE
8	Toggle between Insert and Overtype modes.		Press INSERT

Undoing the Last Cell Entry

Excel provides the Undo command on the Edit menu and the Undo button on the Standard toolbar (Figure 1-77), both of which allow you to erase recent cell entries. Thus, if you enter incorrect data in a cell and notice it immediately, click the Undo command or Undo button and Excel changes the cell entry to what it was prior to the incorrect data entry.

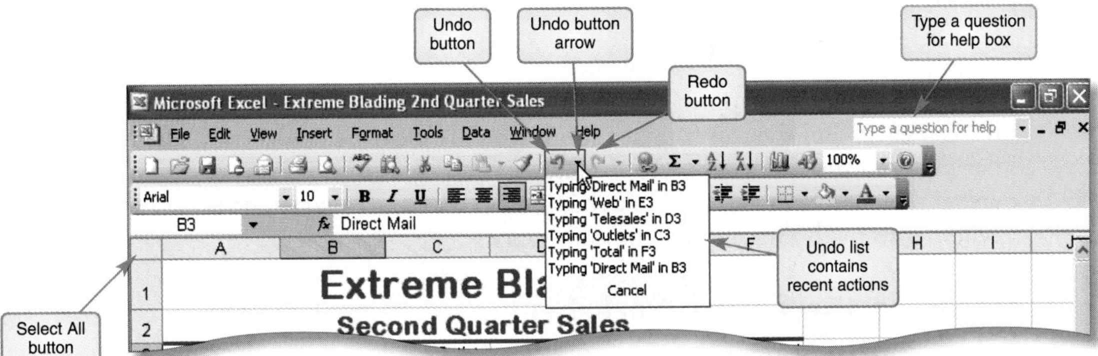

FIGURE 1-77

More About

The Undo Button

The Undo button can undo far more complicated worksheet activities than just removing the latest entry from a cell. In fact, most commands can be undone if you click the Undo button before you make another entry or issue another command. You cannot undo a save or print, but, as a rule, the Undo button can restore the worksheet data and settings to what they were the last time Excel was in Ready mode. With Excel, you have multiple-level undo and redo capabilities.

Excel remembers the last 16 actions you have completed. Thus, you can undo up to 16 previous actions by clicking the Undo button arrow to display the Undo list and then clicking the action to be undone (Figure 1-77 on the previous page). You can drag through several actions in the Undo list to undo all of them at once. If no actions are available for Excel to undo, then the Undo button is dimmed and inoperative.

The Redo button, next to the Undo button on the Standard toolbar, allows you to repeat previous actions. You also can click Redo on the Edit menu, instead of using the Redo button.

Clearing a Cell or Range of Cells

If you enter data into the wrong cell or range of cells, you can erase, or **clear**, the data using one of the first four methods listed below. The fifth method clears the formatting from the selected cells.

To Clear Cell Entries Using the Fill Handle

1. Select the cell or range of cells and then point to the fill handle so the mouse pointer changes to a cross hair.
2. Drag the fill handle back into the selected cell or range until a shadow covers the cell or cells you want to erase. Release the mouse button.

More About

Getting Back to Normal

If you accidentally assign unwanted formats to a range of cells, you can use the Clear command on the Edit menu to delete the formats of a selected range. Doing so changes the format to Normal style. To view the characteristics of the Normal style, click Style on the Format menu or press ALT+APOSTROPHE (').

To Clear Cell Entries Using the Shortcut Menu

1. Select the cell or range of cells to be cleared.
2. Right-click the selection.
3. Click Clear Contents on the shortcut menu.

To Clear Cell Entries Using the DELETE Key

1. Select the cell or range of cells to be cleared.
2. Press the DELETE key.

To Clear Cell Entries Using the Clear Command

1. Select the cell or range of cells to be cleared.
2. Click Edit on the menu bar and then point to Clear.
3. Click All on the Clear submenu.

More About

The Quick Reference

For a table that lists how to complete the tasks covered in this book using the mouse, menu, shortcut menu, and keyboard, see the Quick Reference Summary at the back of this book, or visit the Excel 2003 Quick Reference Web page (scsite.com/ex2003/qr).

To Clear Formatting Using the Clear Command

1. Select the cell or range of cells that you want to remove the formatting from.
2. Click Edit on the menu bar and then point to Clear.
3. Click Formats on the Clear submenu.

The All command on the Clear submenu is the only command that clears both the cell entry and the cell formatting. As you are clearing cell entries, always remember that you should ***never press the*** SPACEBAR ***to clear a cell.*** Pressing the SPACEBAR enters a blank character. A blank character is text and is different from an empty cell, even though the cell may appear empty.

Clearing the Entire Worksheet

If required worksheet edits are extremely extensive, you may want to clear the entire worksheet and start over. To clear the worksheet or delete an embedded chart, use the following steps.

To Clear the Entire Worksheet

1. Click the Select All button on the worksheet (Figure 1-77 on page EX 51).
2. Press the DELETE key to delete all the entries. Click Edit on the menu bar, point to Clear, and then click All on the Clear submenu to delete both the entries and formats.

The Select All button selects the entire worksheet. Instead of clicking the Select All button, you also can press CTRL+A. To clear an unsaved workbook, click the workbook's Close Window button or click the Close command on the File menu. Click the No button if the Microsoft Excel dialog box asks if you want to save changes. To start a new, blank workbook, click the New button on the Standard toolbar or click the New command on the File menu and begin working on a new workbook.

To delete an embedded chart, complete the following steps.

To Delete an Embedded Chart

1. Click the chart to select it.
2. Press the DELETE key.

> *More About*
> **Microsoft Certification**
> The Microsoft Office Specialist Certification program provides an opportunity for you to obtain a valuable industry credential — proof that you have the Excel 2003 skills required by employers. For more information, see Appendix E, or visit the Excel 2003 Certification Web page (scsite.com/ex2003/cert).

Excel Help System

At any time while you are using Excel, you can get answers to questions using the **Excel Help** system. You can activate the Excel Help system by using the Type a question for help box on the menu bar, the Microsoft Excel Help button on the Standard toolbar, or by clicking Help on the menu bar (Figure 1-78). Used properly, this form of online assistance can increase your productivity and reduce your frustrations by minimizing the time you spend learning how to use Excel.

The following section shows how to get answers to your questions using the Type a question for help box. Additional information on using the Excel Help system is available in Appendix A.

> *More About*
> **The Excel Help System**
> The best way to become familiar with the Excel Help system is to use it. Appendix A includes detailed information on the Excel Help system and exercises that will help you gain confidence in using it.

Obtaining Help Using the Type a Question for Help Box on the Menu Bar

The Type a question for help box on the right side of the menu bar (see Figure 1-77 on page EX 51) lets you type free-form questions such as, how do I save or how do I create a Web page, phrases such as save a workbook or print a worksheet, or key terms such as, copy, save, or formatting. Excel responds by displaying a list of topics related to the question or terms you entered in the Search Results task pane. The following steps show how to use the Type a question for help box to obtain information on saving a workbook.

> *More About*
> **Tips and Tricks**
> To receive a free newsletter titled ExcelTips regularly via e-mail, visit the Excel 2003 More About Web page (scsite.com/ex2003/more) and click ExcelTips.

To Obtain Help Using the Type a Question for Help Box

1

- **Type** `save a workbook` **in the Type a question for help box on the right side of the menu bar (Figure 1-78).**

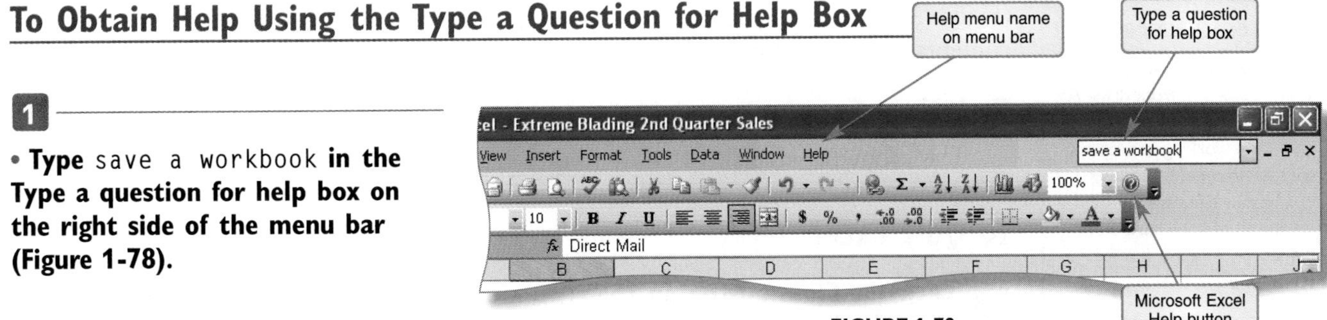

FIGURE 1-78

2

- **Press the ENTER key.**
- **When Excel displays the Search Results task pane, scroll down and then click the link Save a file.**
- **If necessary, click the AutoTile button (see Figure 1-80) to tile the windows.**

Excel displays the Search Results task pane with a list of topics related to the term, save. Excel found 30 search results (Figure 1-79). When the Save a file link is clicked, Excel opens the Microsoft Excel Help window on the left side of the screen.

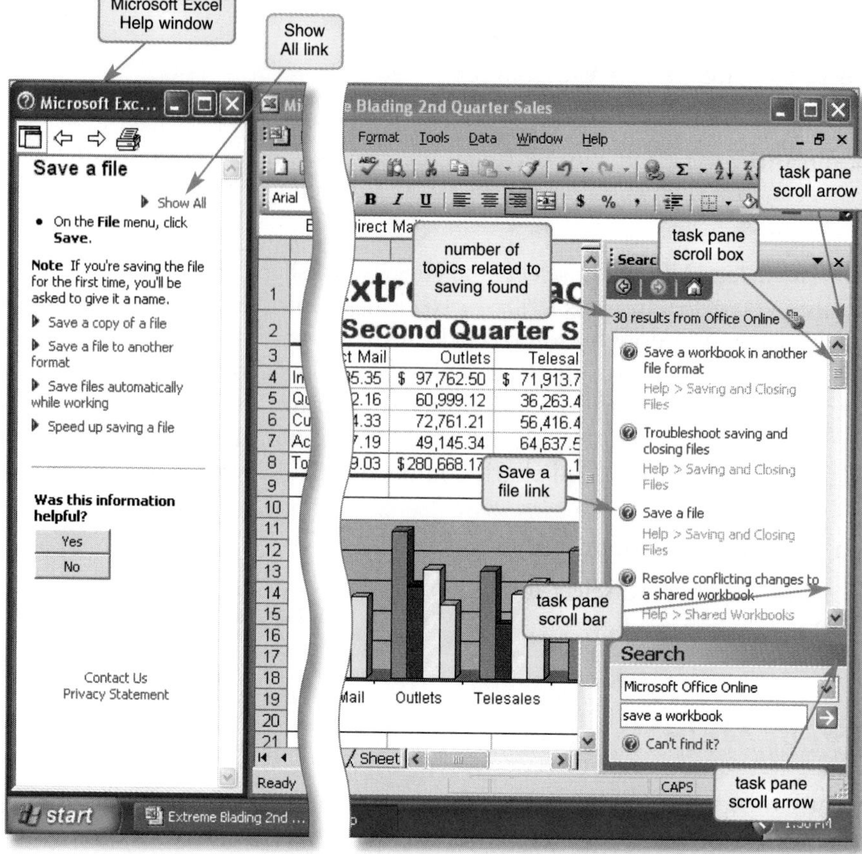

FIGURE 1-79

3

- **Click the Show All link on the right side of the Microsoft Excel Help window to expand the links in the window.**
- **Double-click the Microsoft Excel Help title bar to maximize it.**

The links in the Microsoft Excel Help window are expanded. Excel maximizes the window that provides Help information about saving a file (Figure 1-80).

4

- **Click the Close button on the Microsoft Excel Help window title bar.**

The Microsoft Excel Help window closes and the worksheet is active.

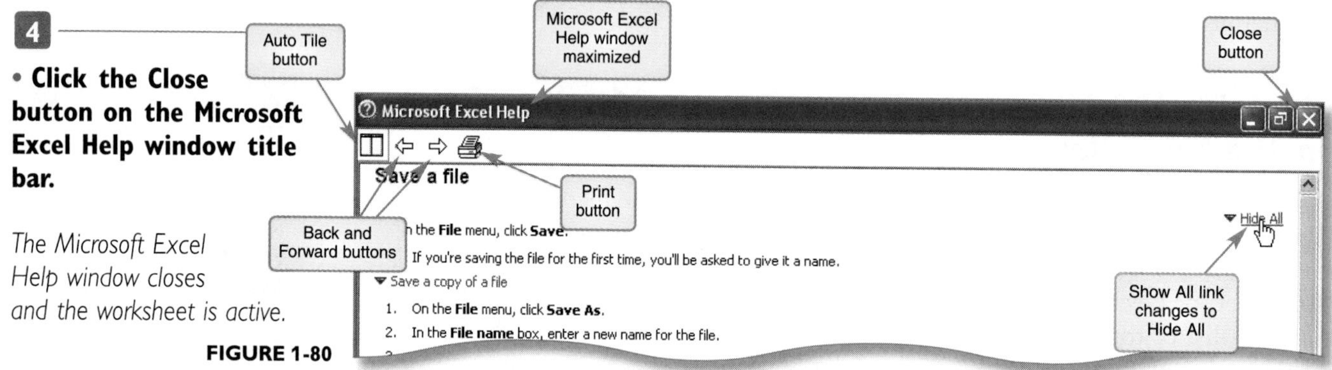

FIGURE 1-80

> **More About**
>
> **Quitting Excel**
>
> Do not forget to remove your floppy disk from drive A after quitting Excel, especially if you are working in a laboratory environment. Nothing can be more frustrating than leaving all of your hard work behind on a floppy disk for the next user.

Use the buttons in the upper-left corner of the Microsoft Excel Help window (Figure 1-80) to navigate through the Help system, change the display, and print the contents of the window.

Quitting Excel

The following step shows how to quit Excel.

To Quit Excel

1 **Click the Close button on the right side of the title bar, and if necessary, click the No button in the Microsoft Excel dialog box.**

Project Summary

This project presented Excel basics. First, you were introduced to starting Excel. You learned about the Excel window and how to enter text and numbers to create a worksheet. You learned how to select a range and how to use the AutoSum button to sum numbers in a column or row. Using the fill handle, you learned how to copy a cell to adjacent cells. Once the worksheet was built, you learned how to format cells one at a time using buttons on the Formatting toolbar and how to format a range using the AutoFormat command. You then learned how to use the Chart Wizard to add a 3-D Clustered column chart to the worksheet. After completing the worksheet, you learned how to save the workbook on a floppy disk, print the worksheet and chart, and then quit Excel. You also learned how to start Excel by opening an Excel document, use the AutoCalculate area, and edit data in cells. Finally, you learned how to use the Excel Help system to answer your questions.

If you have a SAM user profile, you may have access to hands-on instruction, practice, and assessment of the skills covered in this project. Log in to your SAM account and go to your assignments page to see what your instructor has assigned.

What You Should Know

Having completed this project, you should be able to perform the tasks below. The tasks are listed in the same order they were presented in this project. For a list of the buttons, menus, toolbars, and commands introduced in this project, see the Quick Reference Summary at the back of this book and refer to the Page Number column.

1. Start Excel (EX 7)
2. Customize the Excel Window (EX 8)
3. Enter the Worksheet Titles (EX 17)
4. Enter Column Titles (EX 19)
5. Enter Row Titles (EX 20)
6. Enter Numbers (EX 22)
7. Sum a Column of Numbers (EX 23)
8. Copy a Cell to Adjacent Cells in a Row (EX 25)
9. Determine Multiple Totals at the Same Time (EX 27)
10. Change the Font Type (EX 29)
11. Bold a Cell (EX 30)
12. Increase the Font Size of a Cell Entry (EX 31)
13. Change the Font Color of a Cell Entry (EX 32)
14. Center a Cell Entry across Columns by Merging Cells (EX 33)
15. Format the Worksheet Subtitle (EX 34)
16. Use AutoFormat to Format the Body of a Worksheet (EX 34)
17. Use the Name Box to Select a Cell (EX 36)
18. Add a 3-D Clustered Column Chart to the Worksheet (EX 39)
19. Save a Workbook (EX 42)
20. Print a Worksheet (EX 45)
21. Quit Excel (EX 46)
22. Start Excel and Open a Workbook (EX 47)
23. Use the AutoCalculate Area to Determine an Average (EX 49)
24. Clear Cell Entries Using the Fill Handle (EX 52)
25. Clear Cell Entries Using the Shortcut Menu (EX 52)
26. Clear Cell Entries Using the DELETE Key (EX 52)
27. Clear Cell Entries Using the Clear Command (EX 52)
28. Clear the Entire Worksheet (EX 53)
29. Delete an Embedded Chart (EX 53)
30. Obtain Help Using the Type a Question for Help Box (EX 53)
31. Quit Excel (EX 54)

Learn It Online

Instructions: To complete the Learn It Online exercises, start your browser, click the Address bar, and then enter the Web address scsite.com/ex2003/learn. When the Excel 2003 Learn It Online page is displayed, follow the instructions in the exercises below. Each exercise has instructions for printing your results, either for your own records or for submission to your instructor.

1 Project Reinforcement TF, MC, and SA

Below Excel Project 1, click the Project Reinforcement link. Print the quiz by clicking Print on the File menu for each page. Answer each question.

2 Flash Cards

Below Excel Project 1, click the Flash Cards link and read the instructions. Type 20 (or a number specified by your instructor) in the Number of playing cards text box, type your name in the Enter your Name text box, and then click the Flip Card button. When the flash card is displayed, read the question and then click the ANSWER box arrow to select an answer. Flip through Flash Cards. If your score is 15 (75%) correct or greater, click Print on the File menu to print your results. If your score is less than 15 (75%) correct, then redo this exercise by clicking the Replay button.

3 Practice Test

Below Excel Project 1, click the Practice Test link. Answer each question, enter your first and last name at the bottom of the page, and then click the Grade Test button. When the graded practice test is displayed on your screen, click Print on the File menu to print a hard copy. Continue to take practice tests until you score 80% or better.

4 Who Wants To Be a Computer Genius?

Below Excel Project 1, click the Computer Genius link. Read the instructions, enter your first and last name at the bottom of the page, and then click the PLAY button. When your score is displayed, click the PRINT RESULTS link to print a hard copy.

5 Wheel of Terms

Below Excel Project 1, click the Wheel of Terms link. Read the instructions, and then enter your first and last name and your school name. Click the PLAY button. When your score is displayed, right-click the score and then click Print on the shortcut menu to print a hard copy.

6 Crossword Puzzle Challenge

Below Excel Project 1, click the Crossword Puzzle Challenge link. Read the instructions, and then enter your first and last name. Click the SUBMIT button. Work the crossword puzzle. When you are finished, click the Submit button. When the crossword puzzle is redisplayed, click the Print Puzzle button to print a hard copy.

7 Tips and Tricks

Below Excel Project 1, click the Tips and Tricks link. Click a topic that pertains to Project 1. Right-click the information and then click Print on the shortcut menu. Construct a brief example of what the information relates to in Excel to confirm you understand how to use the tip or trick.

8 Newsgroups

Below Excel Project 1, click the Newsgroups link. Click a topic that pertains to Project 1. Print three comments.

9 Expanding Your Horizons

Below Excel Project 1, click the Expanding Your Horizons link. Click a topic that pertains to Project 1. Print the information. Construct a brief example of what the information relates to in Excel to confirm you understand the contents of the article.

10 Search Sleuth

Below Excel Project 1, click the Search Sleuth link. To search for a term that pertains to this project, select a term below the Project 1 title and then use the Google search engine at google.com (or any major search engine) to display and print two Web pages that present information on the term.

11 Excel Online Training

Below Excel Project 1, click the Excel Online Training link. When your browser displays the Microsoft Office Online Web page, click the Excel link. Click one of the Excel courses that covers one or more of the objectives listed at the beginning of the project on page EX 4. Print the first page of the course before stepping through it.

12 Office Marketplace

Below Excel Project 1, click the Office Marketplace link. When your browser displays the Microsoft Office Online Web page, click the Office Marketplace link. Click a topic that relates to Excel. Print the first page.

Apply Your Knowledge

1 Changing the Values in a Worksheet

Instructions: Start Excel. Open the workbook Apply 1-1 Watson's Computer Discount Annual Sales from the Data Disk. See page xxiv at the front of this book for instructions for downloading the Data Disk or see your instructor for information on accessing the files required in this book.

Make the changes to the worksheet described in Table 1-7 so that the worksheet appears as shown in Figure 1-81. As you edit the values in the cells containing numeric data, watch the totals in row 7, the totals in column F, and the chart change.

Change the worksheet title in cell A1 to 20-point Arial Black brown, bold font and then center it across columns A through F. Change the worksheet subtitle in cell A2 to 14-point Arial Black brown, bold font and then center it across columns A through F.

Enter your name, course, laboratory assignment number, date, and instructor name in cells A21 through A25. Save the workbook using the file name, Apply 1-1 Babbage's Computer Discount Annual Sales. Print the revised worksheet and hand in the printout to your instructor.

Table 1-7 New Worksheet Data

CELL	CHANGE CELL CONTENTS TO
A1	Babbage's Computer Discount
B4	43200.75
C4	17563.52
D5	38152.43
E5	28968.78
E6	38751.49

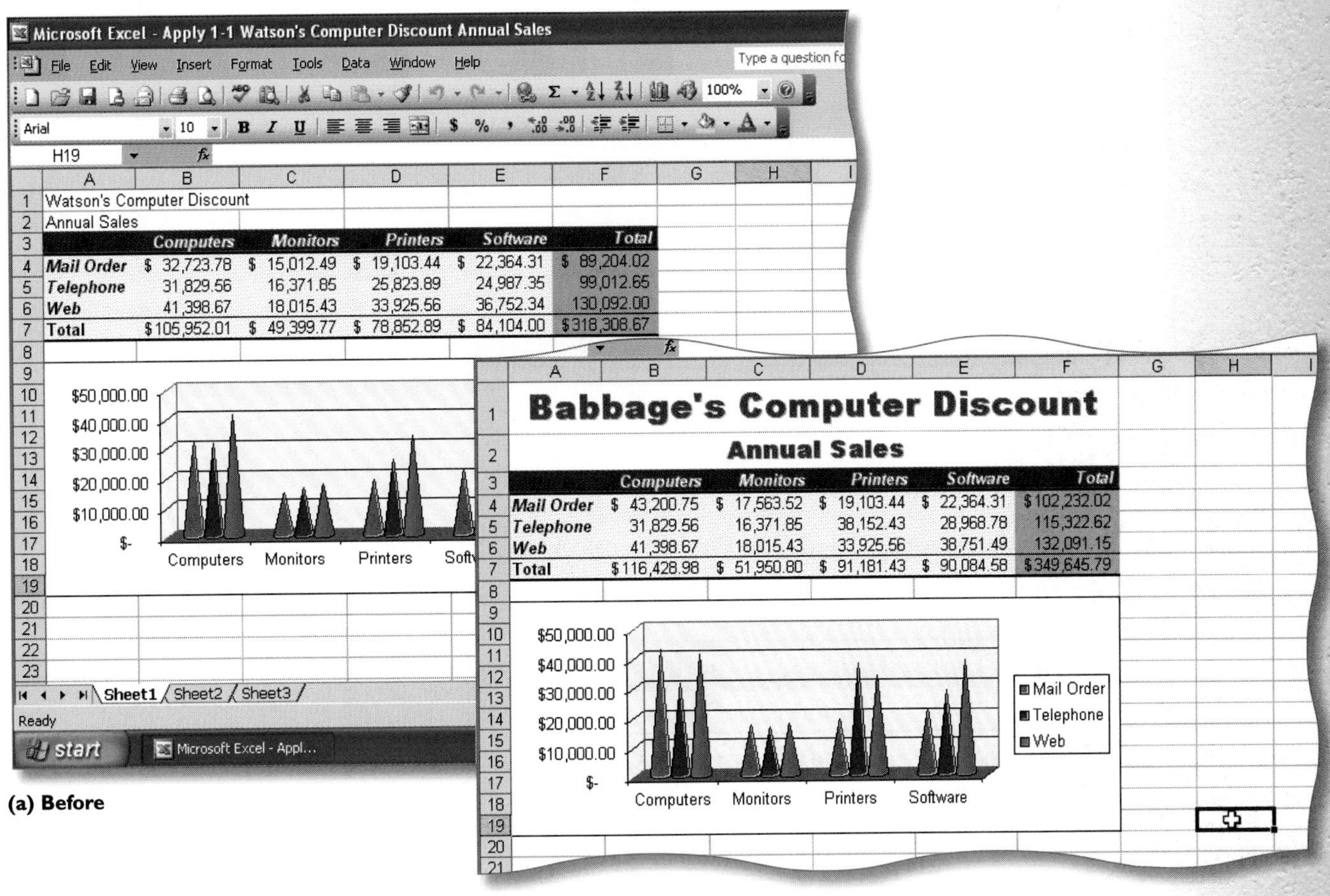

(a) Before

(b) After

FIGURE 1-81

1 Quarterly Sales Analysis Worksheet

Problem: You work part-time as a spreadsheet specialist for Trevor's Global Golf Outlet, one of the larger golf retail stores in the world. Your manager has asked you to develop a quarterly sales analysis worksheet similar to the one shown in Figure 1-82.

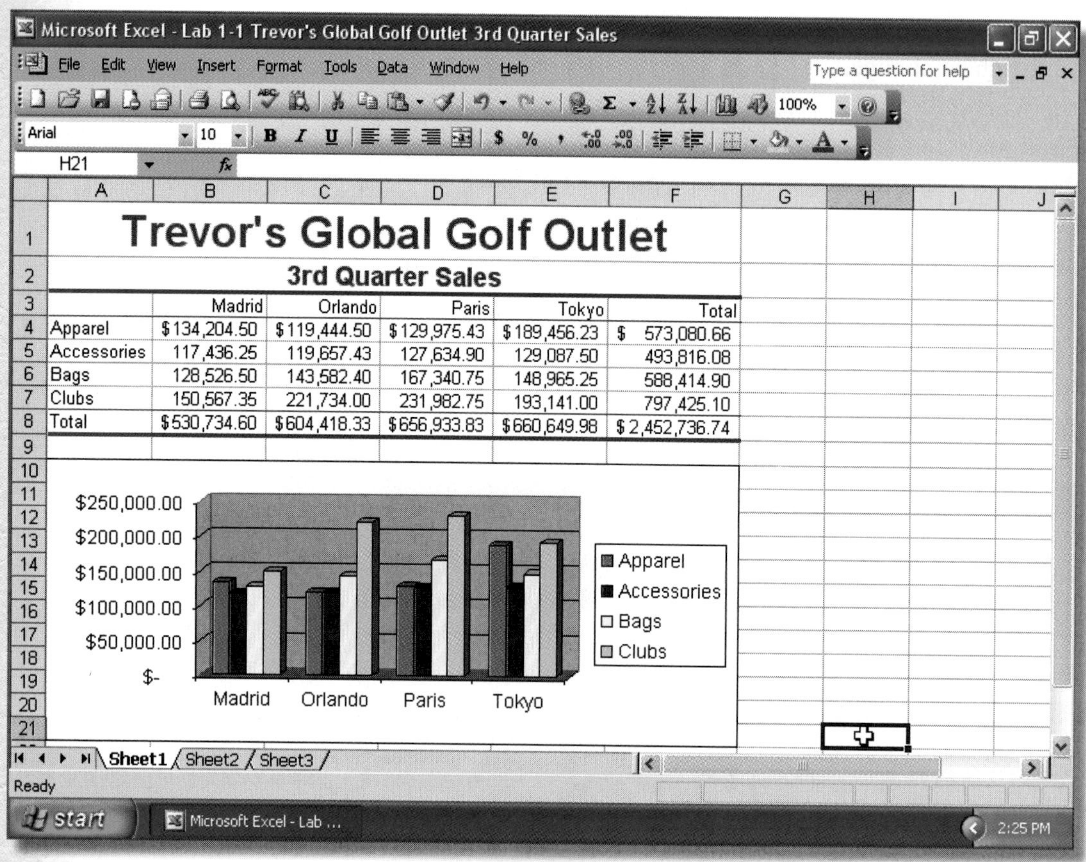

FIGURE 1-82

Instructions: Perform the following tasks.

1. Enter the worksheet title Trevor's Global Golf Outlet in cell A1 and the worksheet subtitle 3rd Quarter Sales in cell A2. Beginning in row 3, enter the sales amounts and categories shown in Table 1-8.

Table 1-8 Trevor's Global Golf Outlet 3rd Quarter Sales

	Madrid	Orlando	Paris	Tokyo
Apparel	134204.50	119444.50	129975.43	189456.23
Accessories	117436.25	119657.43	127634.90	129087.50
Bags	128526.50	143582.40	167340.75	148965.25
Clubs	150567.35	221734.00	231982.75	193141.00

2. Use the SUM function to determine the totals for the cities, golf gear, and company totals.
3. Format the worksheet title to 24-point Arial plum color, bold font and center it across columns A through F. Do not be concerned if the edges of the worksheet title are not displayed.
4. Format the worksheet subtitle to 14-point Arial plum color, bold font and center it across columns A through F.
5. Format the range A3:F8 using the AutoFormat command. Select the Accounting 2 autoformat.
6. Select the range A3:E7 and then use the Chart Wizard button on the Standard toolbar to draw a Clustered column with a 3-D visual effect chart (column 1, row 2 in the Chart sub-type list). Move and resize the chart so that it appears in the range A10:F21. If the labels along the horizontal axis (x-axis) do not appear as shown in Figure 1-82, then drag the right side of the chart so that it is displayed in the range A10:H20.
7. Enter your name, course, laboratory assignment number, date, and instructor name in cells A23 through A27.
8. Save the workbook using the file name Lab 1-1 Trevor's Global Golf Outlet 3rd Quarter.
9. Print the worksheet.
10. Make the following two corrections to the sales amounts: $152,600.25 for Orlando Bag Sales (cell C6), $201,375.55 for Tokyo Apparel Sales (cell E4). After you enter the corrections, the company totals in cell F8 should equal $2,473,673.91.
11. Print the revised worksheet. Close the workbook without saving the changes.

2 Annual Business Expense Analysis Worksheet

Problem: As the chief accountant for Hitchcox Electronics, you have been asked by the vice president to create a worksheet to analyze the annual business expenses for the company by office and expense category (Figure 1-83 on the next page). The office locations and corresponding annual business expenses are shown in Table 1-9.

Table 1-9 Hitchcox Electronics Annual Business Expenses

	Chicago	Dallas	New York	San Diego
Marketing	38895.34	34182.56	56781.60	38367.30
Rent	63925.65	77345.28	88950.45	61819.25
Supplies	21782.60	15375.00	21919.25	18374.50
Travel	7192.75	9341.57	11435.00	6819.25
Wages	72011.65	62198.10	58410.45	85357.15

Instructions: Perform the following tasks.

1. Enter the worksheet title Hitchcox Electronics in cell A1 and the worksheet subtitle Annual Business Expenses in cell A2. Beginning in row 3, enter the annual business expenses and categories shown in Table 1-9.
2. Use the SUM function to determine totals expenses for the four offices, the totals for each expense category, and the company total. Add column and row headings for the totals, as appropriate.

(continued)

Annual Business Expense Analysis Worksheet *(continued)*

3. Change the worksheet title to 28-point Arial Rounded MT Bold red, bold font, and center it across columns A through F. Format the worksheet subtitle to 18-point Arial Rounded MT Bold red, bold font, and center it across columns A through F.

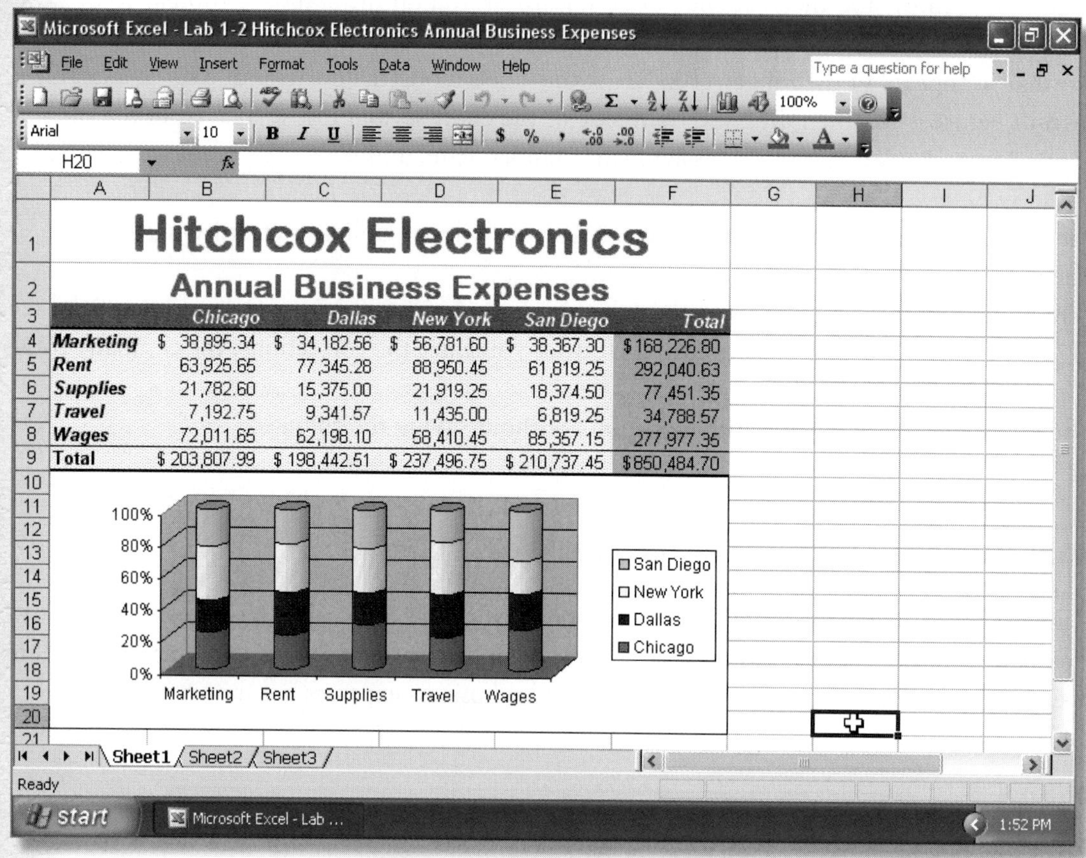

FIGURE 1-83

4. Format the range A3:F9 using the AutoFormat command on the Format menu as follows: (a) apply the autoformat Accounting 3; and (b) with the range A3:F9 still selected, apply the autoformat Colorful 2. If you make a mistake, apply the autoformat None and then apply the autoformats again. Change the background color of the range A3:F3 to red.
5. Chart the range A3:E8. Draw the 100% Stacked column with a cylindrical shape chart, as shown in Figure 1-83, by clicking the Chart Wizard button on the Standard toolbar. When Excel displays the Chart Wizard dialog box, select Cylinder in the Chart type list, and then select column 3, row 1 in the Chart sub-type list. Use the chart location A10:F20.
6. Enter your name, course, laboratory assignment number, date, and instructor name in cells A23 through A27.
7. Save the workbook using the file name, Lab 1-2 Hitchcox Electronics Annual Business Expenses. Print the worksheet.
8. Two corrections to the expenses were sent in from the accounting department. The correct expenses are $67,856.34 for the Dallas rent (cell C5) and $8,561.60 for San Diego travel expenses (cell E7). After you enter the two corrections, the company total in cell F9 should equal $842,738.11. Print the revised worksheet.

In the Lab

9. Use the Undo button to change the worksheet back to the original numbers in Table 1-9. Use the Redo button to change the worksheet back to the revised state.
10. Close Excel without saving the latest changes. Start Excel and open the workbook saved in step 7. Double-click cell D6 and use in-cell editing to change the New York supplies expense to $25,673.17. Write the company total in cell F9 at the top of the first printout. Click the Undo button.
11. Click cell A1 and then click the Merge and Center button to split cell A1 into cells A1, B1, C1, D1, E1, and F1. To re-merge the cells into one, select the range A1:F1 and then click the Merge and Center button.
12. Hand in the two printouts to your instructor. Close the workbook without saving the changes.

3 College Cash Flow Analysis Worksheet

Problem: Attending college is an expensive proposition and your resources are limited. To plan for your four-year college career, you have decided to organize your anticipated resources and expenses in a worksheet. The data required to prepare your worksheet is shown in Table 1-10.

Table 1-10 College Resources and Expenses

Resources	Freshman	Sophomore	Junior	Senior
Financial Aid	6050.00	6655.00	7320.50	8052.55
Job	1650.00	1815.00	1996.50	2196.15
Parents	2800.00	3080.00	3388.00	3726.80
Savings	1300.00	1430.00	1573.00	1730.30
Other	500.00	550.00	605.00	665.50
Expenses				
Clothes	540.00	594.00	653.40	718.74
Entertainment	830.00	913.00	1004.30	1104.73
Miscellaneous	400.00	440.00	484.00	532.40
Room & Board	3880.00	4,268.00	4694.80	5164.28
Tuition & Books	6650.00	7315.00	8046.50	8851.15

Instructions Part 1: Using the numbers in Table 1-10, create the worksheet shown in columns A through F in Figure 1-84 on the next page. Format the worksheet title in cell A1 to 24-point Algerian (or a font style of your choice) green bold font. Format the worksheet subtitles in cells A2 and A10 to 18-point Algerian (or a font style of your choice) red bold font. Format the range A3:F9 using the AutoFormat command on the Format menu as follows: (a) select the range A3:F9 and then apply the autoformat Accounting 3; and (b) with the range A3:F9 still selected, apply the autoformat List 2. Use the same autoformats for the range A11:F17.

Enter your identification on the worksheet and save the workbook using the file name Lab 1-3 Part 1 College Cash Flow Analysis. Print the worksheet in landscape orientation. You print in landscape orientation by invoking the Page Setup command on the File menu and then clicking Landscape on the Page sheet in the Page Setup dialog box. Click the Save button on the Standard toolbar to save the workbook with the new print settings.

(continued)

College Cash Flow Analysis Worksheet *(continued)*

After reviewing the numbers, you realize you need to increase manually each of the Junior-year expenses in column D by $600. Manually change the Junior-year expenses to reflect this change. Manually change the financial aid for the Junior year by the amount required to cover the increase in expenses. The totals in cells F9 and F17 should equal $60,084.30. Print the worksheet. Close the workbook without saving changes. Hand in the two printouts to your instructor.

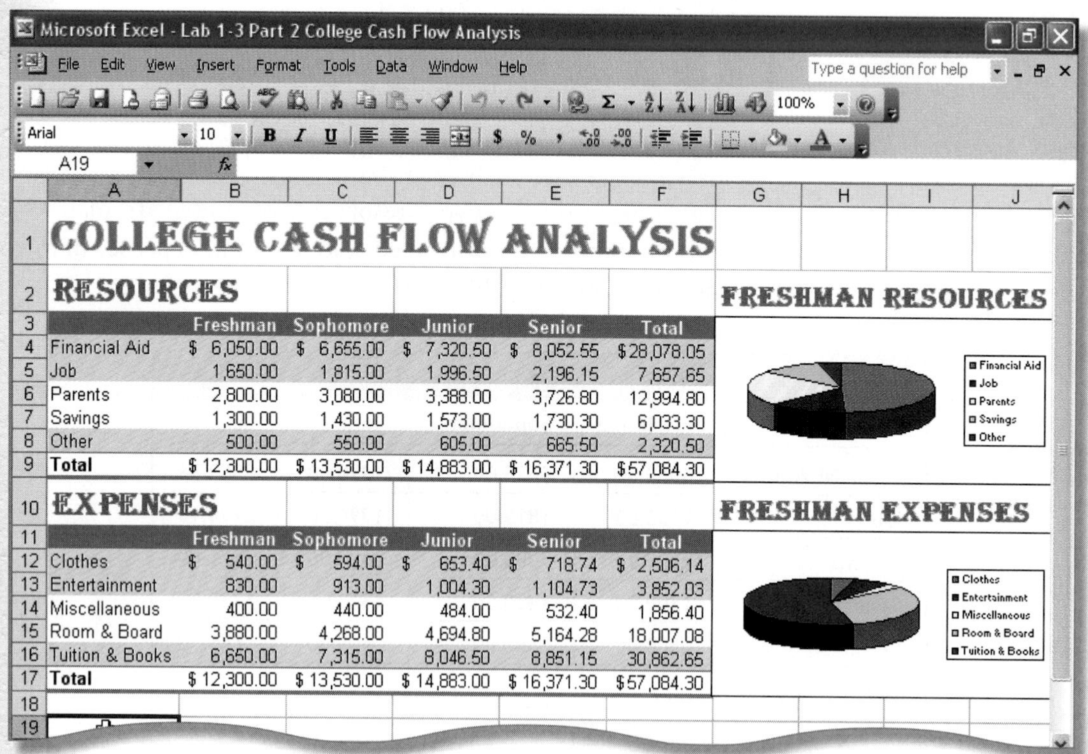

	A	B	C	D	E	F	G
1	COLLEGE CASH FLOW ANALYSIS						
2	RESOURCES						FRESHMAN RESOURCES
3		Freshman	Sophomore	Junior	Senior	Total	
4	Financial Aid	$ 6,050.00	$ 6,655.00	$ 7,320.50	$ 8,052.55	$28,078.05	
5	Job	1,650.00	1,815.00	1,996.50	2,196.15	7,657.65	
6	Parents	2,800.00	3,080.00	3,388.00	3,726.80	12,994.80	
7	Savings	1,300.00	1,430.00	1,573.00	1,730.30	6,033.30	
8	Other	500.00	550.00	605.00	665.50	2,320.50	
9	Total	$ 12,300.00	$ 13,530.00	$ 14,883.00	$ 16,371.30	$57,084.30	
10	EXPENSES						FRESHMAN EXPENSES
11		Freshman	Sophomore	Junior	Senior	Total	
12	Clothes	$ 540.00	$ 594.00	$ 653.40	$ 718.74	$ 2,506.14	
13	Entertainment	830.00	913.00	1,004.30	1,104.73	3,852.03	
14	Miscellaneous	400.00	440.00	484.00	532.40	1,856.40	
15	Room & Board	3,880.00	4,268.00	4,694.80	5,164.28	18,007.08	
16	Tuition & Books	6,650.00	7,315.00	8,046.50	8,851.15	30,862.65	
17	Total	$ 12,300.00	$ 13,530.00	$ 14,883.00	$ 16,371.30	$57,084.30	

FIGURE 1-84

Instructions Part 2: Open the workbook Lab 1-3 Part 1 College Cash Flow Analysis. Draw a 3-D Pie chart in the range G3:J9 to show the contribution of each category of resources for the Freshman year. Chart the range A4:B8. Add the Pie chart title as shown in cell G2 in Figure 1-84. Draw a 3-D Pie chart in the range G11:J17 to show the contribution of each category of expenses for the Freshman year. Chart the range A12:B16. Add the Pie chart title shown in cell G10 in Figure 1-84. Save the workbook using the file name, Lab 1-3 Part 2 College Cash Flow Analysis. Print the worksheet. Hand in the printout to your instructor.

Instructions Part 3: Open the workbook Lab 1-3 Part 2 College Cash Flow Analysis. A close inspection of Table 1-10 on the previous page shows that both expenses and resources increase 10% each year. Use the Type a question for help box on the menu bar to learn how to enter the data for the last three years using a formula and the Copy command. For example, the formula to enter in cell C4 is =B4 * 1.1. Enter formulas to replace all the numbers in the range C4:E8 and C12:E16. If necessary, reformat the tables using the autoformats, as described in Part 1. The worksheet should appear as shown in Figure 1-84. Save the worksheet using the file name, Lab 1-3 Part 3 College Cash Flow Analysis. Print the worksheet. Press CTRL+ACCENT MARK(`) to display the formulas. Print the formulas version. Close the workbook without saving changes. Hand in both printouts to your instructor.

Cases and Places

The difficulty of these case studies varies:
■ are the least difficult and ■■ are more difficult. The last exercise is a group exercise.

1 ■ You are employed by the Reggae Music Company. Your manager has asked you to prepare a worksheet to help her analyze monthly sales by store and by type of reggae music (Table 1-11). Use the concepts and techniques presented in this project to create the worksheet and an embedded Clustered bar chart with a 3-D visual effect.

Table 1-11 Reggae Music Company Monthly Sales

	Boston	Kansas City	Portland	San Diego
Dancehall	6734	7821	4123	7989
Dub	5423	2134	6574	3401
Dub Poetry	3495	6291	7345	7098
Lovers Rock	6789	4523	9102	7812
Ragga	8920	9812	5637	3456
Rocksteady	2134	2190	3401	2347
Ska	5462	2923	8034	5135

2 ■ To estimate the funds you need to make it through the upcoming year, you decide to create a personal budget itemizing your expected quarterly expenses. The anticipated expenses are listed in Table 1-12. Use the concepts and techniques presented in this project to create the worksheet and an embedded 100% Stacked column chart with a conical shape that compares the quarterly cost of each expense. If necessary, reduce the size of the font in the chart so that each expense category name appears on the horizontal axis (x-axis). Use the AutoCalculate area to determine the average amount spent per quarter on each expense. Manually insert the averages with appropriate titles in an empty area on the worksheet.

Table 1-12 Quarterly Personal Budget

	Jan – Mar	April – June	July – Sept	Oct – Dec
Mortgage	1500	1500	1500	1500
Food	900	950	950	1000
Car & Ins.	600	600	600	600
Clothes	567	433	200	459
Utilities	600	400	400	550
Miscellaneous	149	121	159	349

Cases and Places

3 The Magic Theater is a movie house that shows movies at weekday evening, weekend matinee, and weekend evening screenings. Three types of tickets are sold at each presentation: general admission, senior citizen, and children. The theater management has asked you to prepare a worksheet, based on the revenue from a typical week, that can be used to reevaluate its ticket structure. During an average week, weekday evening shows generate $7,250 from general admission ticket sales, $6,715 from senior citizen ticket sales, and $1,575 from children ticket sales. Weekend matinee shows make $6,723 from general admission ticket sales, $2,050 from senior citizen ticket sales, and $2,875 from children ticket sales. Weekend evening shows earn $9,415 from general admission ticket sales, $9,815 from senior citizen ticket sales, and $1,235 from children ticket sales. Use the concepts and techniques presented in this project to prepare a worksheet that includes total revenues for each type of ticket and for each presentation time, and a Clustered Bar chart illustrating ticket revenues.

4 Jasmine's Floral Shop on Michigan Avenue in Chicago sells floral arrangments to an exclusive clientele. The company is trying to decide whether it is feasible to open another boutique in the Chicago area. You have been asked to develop a worksheet totaling all the revenue received last year from customers living in the Chicago area. The revenue from customers living in the Chicago area by quarter is: Quarter 1, $221,565.56; Quarter 2, $182,704.34; Quarter 3, $334,116.31; and Quarter 4, $421,333.50. Create a Pie chart with a 3-D visual effect to illustrate Chicago-area revenue contribution by quarter. Use the AutoCalculate area to find the average, maximum, and minimum quarterly revenue and manually enter them and their corresponding identifiers in an empty area on the worksheet.

5 **Working Together** Visit the Registrar's office at your school and obtain data, such as age, gender, and resident status, for the students majoring in at least five different academic departments this semester. Have each member of your team divide the data into different categories. For example, separate the data by:

1. Age, divided into four different age groups
2. Gender, divided into male and female
3. Resident status, divided into resident and nonresident

After coordinating the data as a group, have each member independently use the concepts and techniques presented in this project to create a worksheet and appropriate chart to show the total students by characteristics by academic department. As a group, critique each worksheet and have each member re-do his or her worksheet based on the group recommendations. Hand in printouts of your original worksheet and final worksheet.

MICROSOFT OFFICE

Access 2003

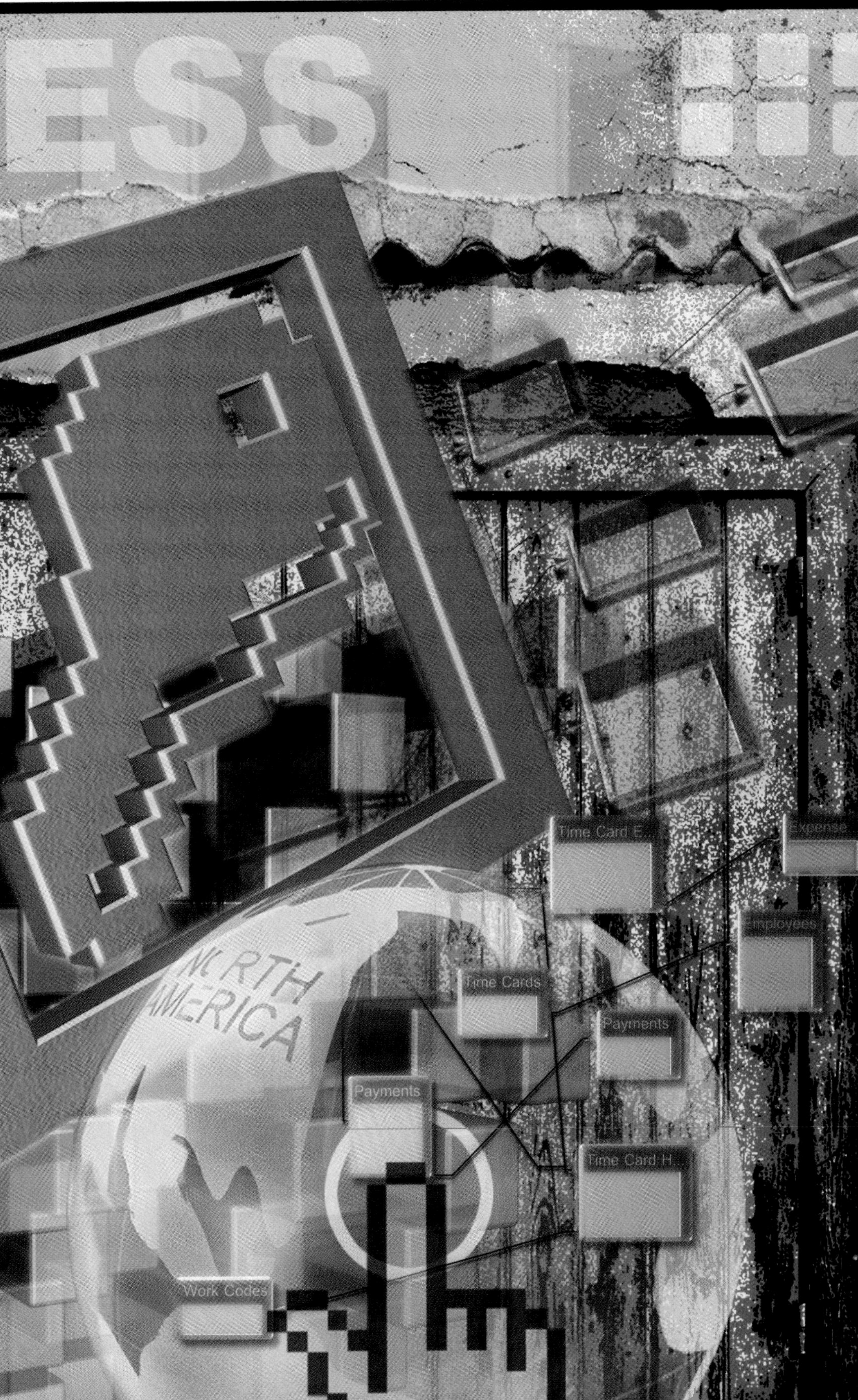

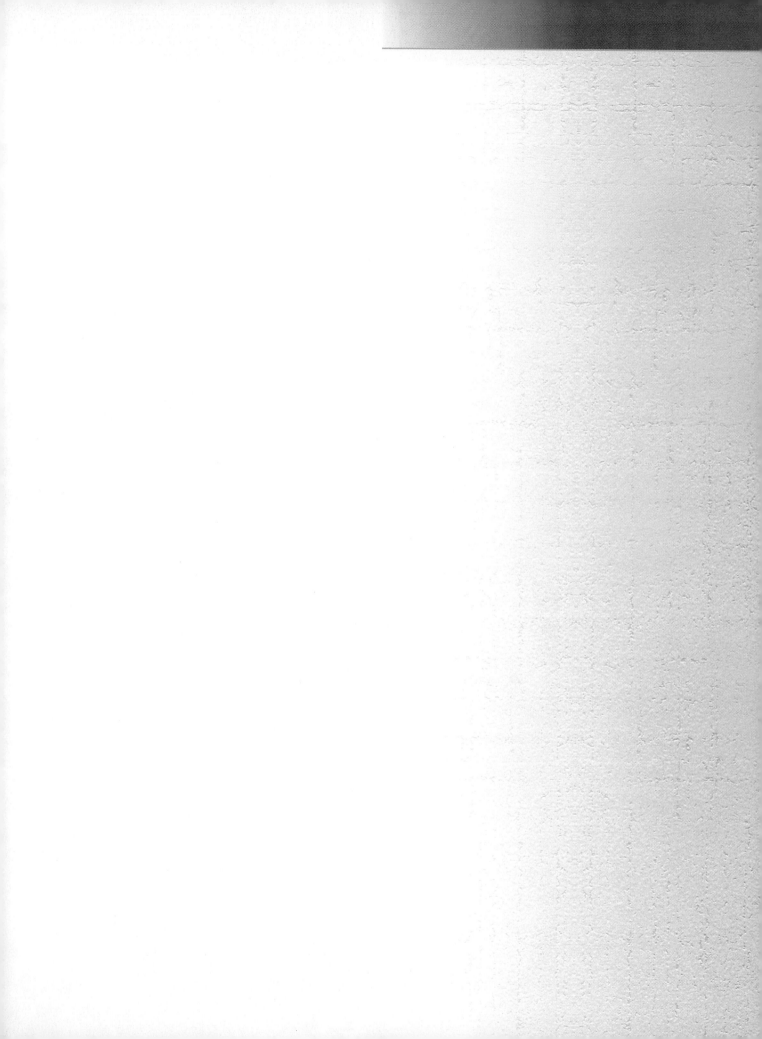

MICROSOFT OFFICE

Access 2003

Creating and Using a Database

PROJECT

1

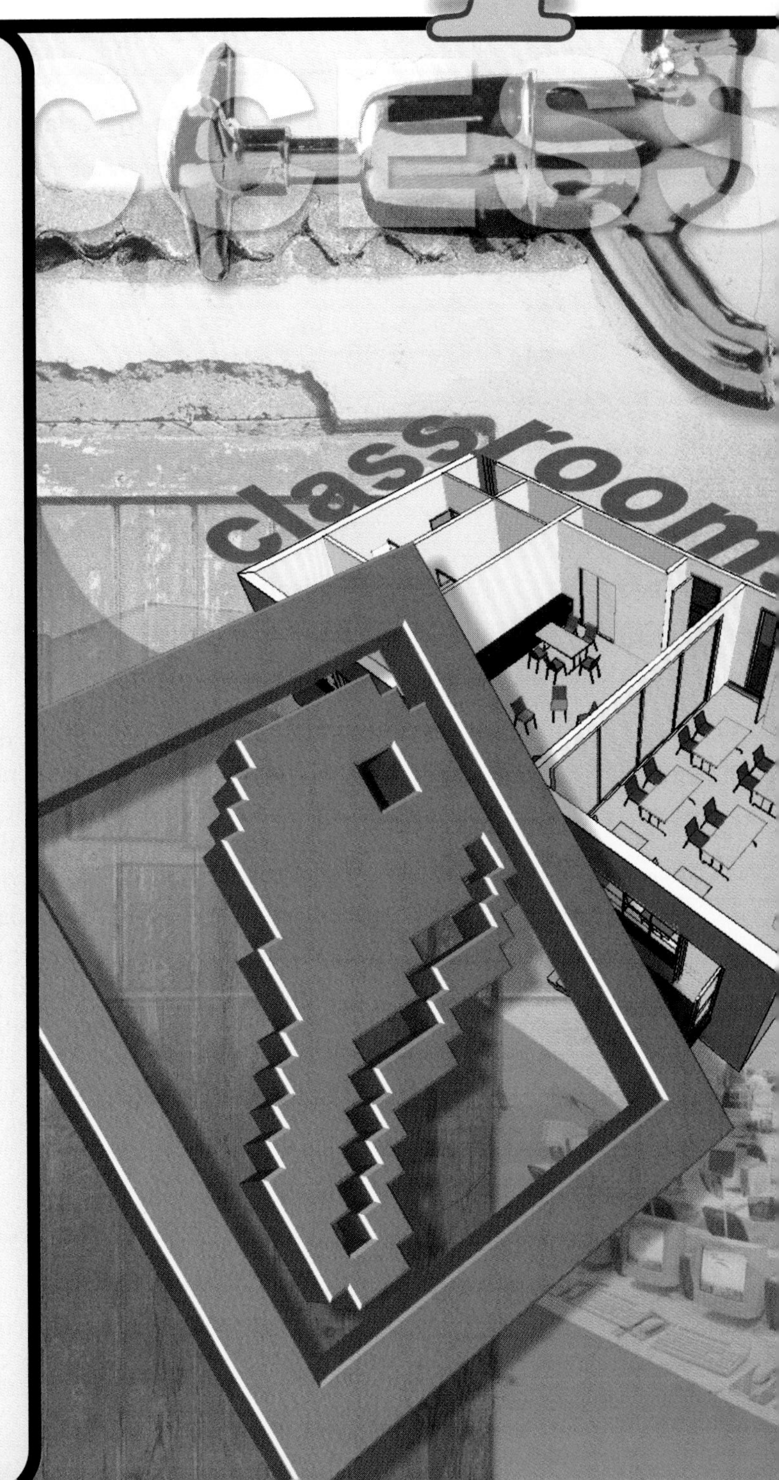

CASE PERSPECTIVE

Ashton James College (AJC) has a solid reputation in the community, delivers quality computer courses, and has a faculty of highly professional, dedicated instructors. Its graduates are among the top achievers in the state. Recently, at the urging of area businesses that depend on the college-educated workforce, AJC has begun to offer corporate computer training through its Continuing Education department. The programs have proved to be very popular, and the client list is growing rapidly.

AJC employs several trainers to teach these corporate courses. It assigns each client to a specific trainer. The trainer contacts the client to determine the particular course the client requires. The trainer then customizes a program for that particular client. The trainer will schedule all the necessary training sessions.

To ensure that operations run smoothly, Ashton James College needs to maintain data on its trainers and their clients. The AJC administration wants to organize the data in a database, managed by a database management system such as Access. In this way, AJC can keep its data current and accurate while program administrators analyze the data for trends and produce a variety of useful reports. Your task is to help the director of continuing education at Ashton James College, Dr. Robert Gernaey, create and use the database.

As you read through this project, you will learn how to use Access to create a database.

Creating and Using a Database

PROJECT

Objectives

You will have mastered the material in this project when you can:

- Describe databases and database management systems
- Start Access
- Describe the features of the Access desktop
- Create a database
- Create a table and add records
- Close a table
- Close a database and quit Access
- Open a database
- Print the contents of a table
- Create and use a simple query
- Create and use a simple form
- Create and print a custom report
- Design a database to eliminate redundancy

What Is Microsoft Office Access 2003?

Microsoft Office Access 2003 is a powerful database management system (DBMS) that functions in the Windows environment and allows you to create and process data in a database. Some of the key features are:

- **Data entry and update** Access provides easy mechanisms for adding, changing, and deleting data, including the capability of making mass changes in a single operation.
- **Queries (questions)** Access makes it possible to ask complex questions concerning the data in the database and then receive instant answers.
- **Forms** Access allows the user to produce attractive and useful forms for viewing and updating data.
- **Reports** Access report creation tools make it easy to produce sophisticated reports for presenting data.
- **Web support** Access allows you to save objects, reports, and tables in HTML format so they can be viewed using a browser. You also can import and export documents in XML format. Access's capability of creating data access pages allows real-time access to data in the database via the Internet.

What Is New in Access?

This latest version of Access has many new features to make you more productive. You can view information on dependencies between various database objects. You can enable error checking for many common errors in forms and reports. You can add smart tags to fields in tables, queries, forms, or data access pages. Access now has a command to backup a database. Many wizards provide more options for sorting data. You can export to, import from, or link to a Windows SharePoint Services list. Access now offers enhanced XML support.

Project One — Ashton James College Database

Creating, storing, sorting, and retrieving data are important tasks. In their personal lives, many people keep a variety of records such as names, addresses, and telephone numbers of friends and business associates, records of investments, records of expenses for tax purposes, and so on. For effective use of this data, users must have quick access to it. Businesses also must be able to store and access information quickly and easily.

The term **database** describes a collection of data organized in a manner that allows access, retrieval, and use of that data. A **database management system**, such as Access, is a software tool that allows you to use a computer to create a database; add, change, and delete data in the database; sort the data in the database; retrieve data in the database; and create forms and reports using the data in the database.

In Access, a database consists of a collection of tables. Figure 1-1 shows a sample database for Ashton James College, which consists of two tables. The Client table contains information about the clients to which Ashton James College provides services. The college assigns each client to a specific trainer. The Trainer table contains information about the trainers to whom these clients are assigned.

CLIENT NUMBER	NAME	ADDRESS	CITY	STATE	ZIP CODE	AMOUNT PAID	CURRENT DUE	TRAINER NUMBER
BS27	Blant and Sons	4806 Park	Lake Hammond	TX	76653	$21,876.00	$892.50	42
CE16	Center Services	725 Mitchell	San Julio	TX	78364	$26,512.00	$2,672.00	48
CP27	Calder Plastics	7300 Cedar	Lake Hammond	TX	76653	$8,725.00	$0.00	48
EU28	Elba's Furniture	1445 Hubert	Tallmadge	TX	77231	$4,256.00	$1,202.00	53
FI28	Farrow-Idsen	829 Wooster	Cedar Ridge	TX	79342	$8,287.50	$925.50	42
FL93	Fairland Lawn	143 Pangborn	Lake Hammond	TX	76653	$21,625.00	$0.00	48
HN83	Hurley National	3827 Burgess	Tallmadge	TX	77231	$0.00	$0.00	48
MC28	Morgan-Alyssa	923 Williams	Crumville	TX	76745	$24,761.00	$1,572.00	42
PS82	PRIM Staffing	72 Crestview	San Julio	TX	78364	$11,682.25	$2,827.50	53
TE26	Telton-Edwards	5672 Anderson	Dunston	TX	77893	$8,521.50	$0.00	48

TRAINER NUMBER	LAST NAME	FIRST NAME	ADDRESS	CITY	STATE	ZIP CODE	HOURLY RATE	YTD EARNINGS
42	Perry	Belinda	261 Porter	Burdett	TX	76734	$23.00	$27,620.00
48	Stevens	Michael	3135 Gill	Rockwood	TX	78884	$21.00	$23,567.50
53	Gonzalez	Manuel	265 Maxwell	Camino	TX	76574	$24.00	$29,885.00
67	Danville	Marty	1827 Maple	Dunston	TX	77893	$20.00	$0.00

FIGURE 1-1

More About

Databases in Access 2003

In some DBMSs, every table, query, form, or report is stored in a separate file. This is not the case in Access 2003, in which a database is stored in a single file on disk. The file contains all the tables, queries, forms, reports, and programs created for this database.

The rows in the tables are called **records**. A record contains information about a given person, product, or event. A row in the Client table, for example, contains information about a specific client.

The columns in the tables are called fields. A **field** contains a specific piece of information within a record. In the Client table, for example, the fourth field, City, contains the city where the client is located.

The first field in the Client table is the Client Number. Ashton James College assigns a number to each client. As is common to the way in which many organizations format client numbers, Ashton James College calls it a *number*, although it actually contains letters. The AJC client numbers consist of two uppercase letters followed by a two-digit number.

These numbers are unique; that is, no two clients are assigned the same number. Such a field can be used as a **unique identifier**. This simply means that a given client number will appear only in a single record in the table. Only one record exists, for example, in which the client number is CP27. A unique identifier also is called a **primary key**. Thus, the Client Number field is the primary key for the Client table.

The next seven fields in the Client table are Name, Address, City, State, Zip Code, Amount Paid, and Current Due. The Amount Paid field contains the amount that the client has paid Ashton James College year-to-date (YTD), but before the current period. The Current Due field contains the amount due to AJC for the current period.

For example, client BS27 is Blant and Sons. The address is 4806 Park in Lake Hammond, Texas. The Zip code is 76653. The client has paid $21,876.00 for training services so far this year. The amount due for the current period is $892.50.

AJC assigns each client a single trainer. The last field in the Client table, Trainer Number, gives the number of the client's trainer.

The first field in the Trainer table, Trainer Number, is the number Ashton James College assigns to the trainer. These numbers are unique, so Trainer Number is the primary key of the Trainer table.

The other fields in the Trainer table are Last Name, First Name, Address, City, State, Zip Code, Hourly Rate, and YTD Earnings. The Hourly Rate field gives the trainer's hourly billing rate, and the YTD Earnings field contains the total amount that AJC has paid the trainer for services so far this year.

For example, Trainer 42 is Belinda Perry. Her address is 261 Porter in Burdett, Texas. The Zip code is 76734. Her hourly billing rate is $23.00, and her YTD earnings are $27,620.00.

The trainer number appears in both the Client table and the Trainer table. It relates clients and trainers. For example, in the Client table, you see that the trainer number for client BS27 is 42. To find the name of this trainer, look for the row in the Trainer table that contains 42 in the Trainer Number field. After you have found it, you know the client is assigned to Belinda Perry. To find all the clients assigned to Belinda Perry, however, you must look through the Client table for all the clients that contain 42 in the Trainer Number field. Her clients are BS27 (Blant and Sons), FI28 (Farrow-Idsen), and MC28 (Morgan-Alyssa).

The last trainer in the Trainer table, Marty Danville, has not been assigned any clients yet; therefore, his trainer number, 67, does not appear on any row in the Client table.

Figure 1-1 on page AC 5 shows the data that must be maintained in the database. The first step is to create the database and the tables it contains. In the process, you must define the fields included in the two tables, as well as the type of data each field will contain. Then, you must add the appropriate records to the tables. Finally, you will print the contents of the tables. After you have completed these tasks, you will create a query, a form, and a report.

More About

The Access Help System

Need Help? It is no further than the Type a question for help box on the menu bar in the upper-right corner of the window. Click the box that contains the text, Type a question for help (Figure 1-3 on the next page), type `help`, and then press the ENTER key. Access responds with a list of topics you can click to learn about obtaining help on any Access-related topic. To find out what is new in Access 2003, type `what is new in Access` in the Type a question for help box.

Starting Access

If you are stepping through this project on a computer, and you want your screen to agree with the figures in this book, then you should change your computer's resolution to 800 × 600. For more information on how to change the resolution on your computer, see Appendix D. To start Access, Windows must be running. The following steps show how to start Access.

To Start Access

1

- **Click the Start button on the Windows taskbar, point to All Programs on the Start menu and then point to Microsoft Office on the All Programs submenu.**

Windows displays the Start menu, the All Programs submenu, and the Microsoft Office submenu (Figure 1-2).

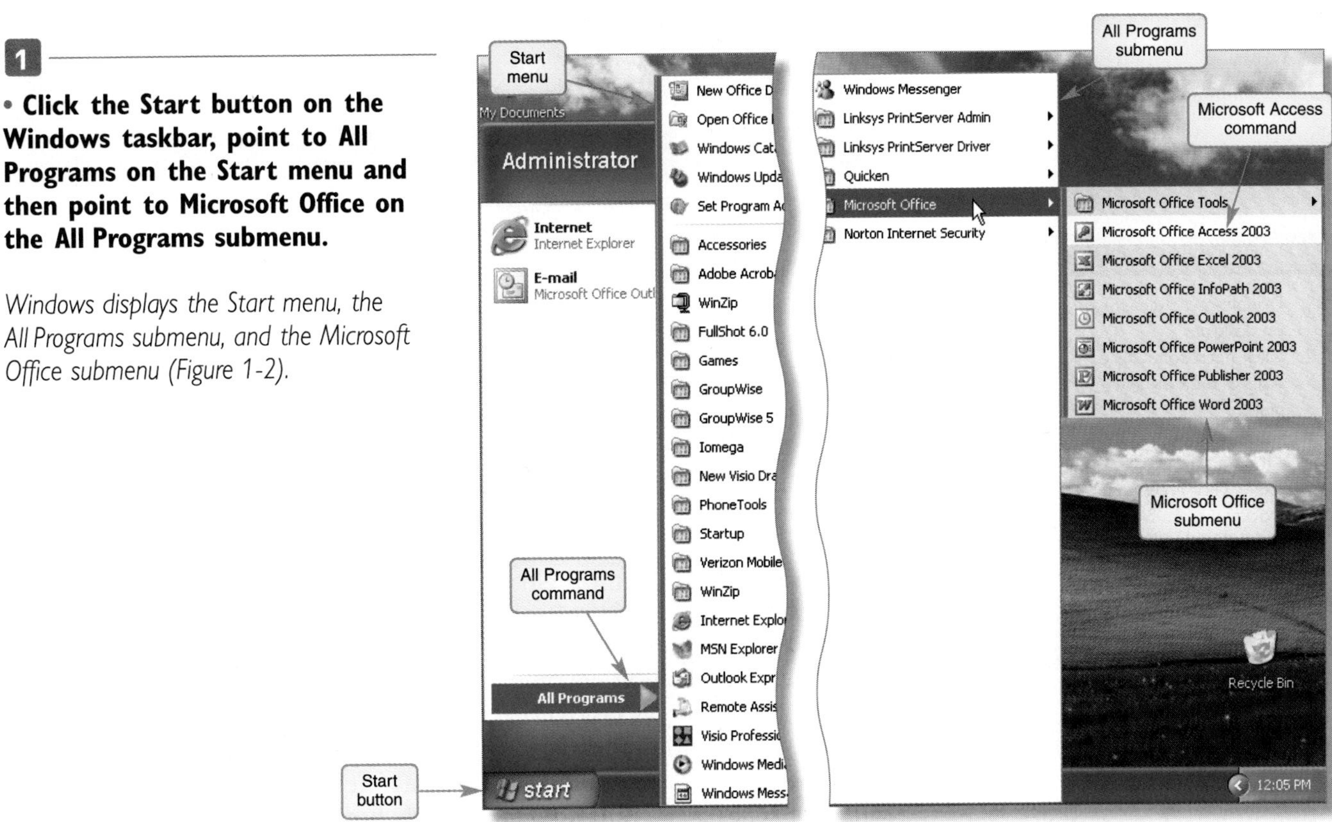

FIGURE 1-2

2

• **Click Microsoft Office Access 2003.**

Access starts. After several seconds, the Access window appears (Figure 1-3).

3

• **If the Access window is not maximized, double-click its title bar to maximize it.**

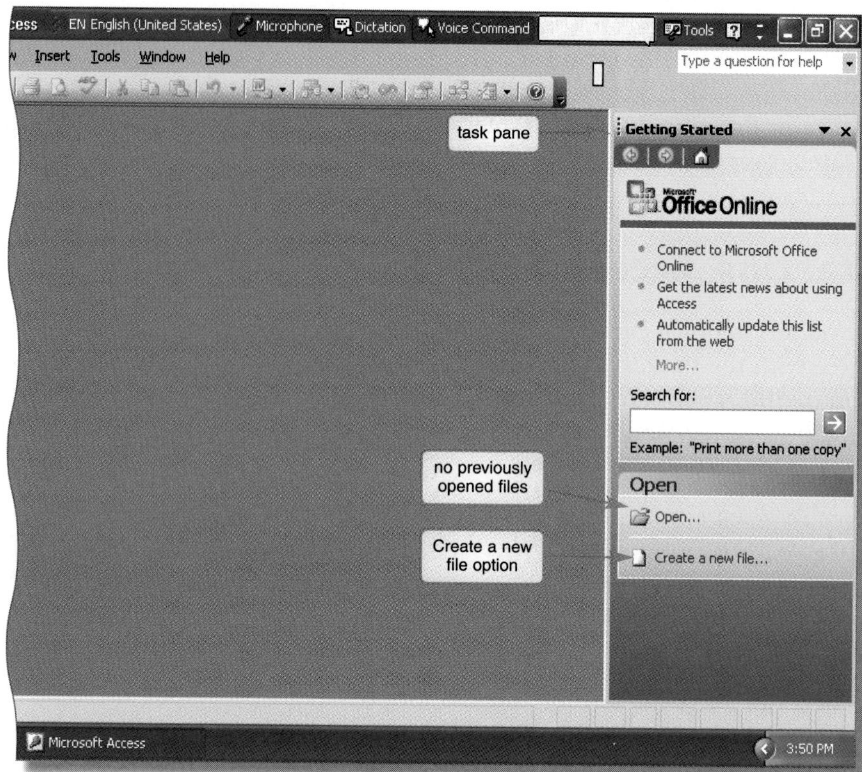

FIGURE 1-3

Other Ways

1. Double-click Access icon on desktop
2. Click Microsoft Office Access 2003 on Start menu
3. Click Start button, click All Programs on Start menu, click New Office Document, double-click Blank Database icon

More About

Task Panes

You can drag a task pane title bar to float the pane in your work area or dock it on either the left or right side of a screen, depending on your personal preference.

The screen in Figure 1-3 illustrates how the Access window looks the first time you start Access after installation on most computers. Access displays a task pane on the right side of the screen at startup. A **task pane** is a separate window that enables users to carry out some Access tasks more efficiently. When you start Access, it displays the Getting Started task pane, which is a small window that provides commonly used links and commands that allow you to open files, create new files, or search Office-related topics on the Microsoft Web site. The task pane is used only to create a new database and then it is closed.

If the Office Speech Recognition software is installed and active on your computer, then when you start Access the Language bar is displayed on the screen. The **Language bar** allows you to speak commands and dictate text. It usually is located on the right side of the Windows taskbar next to the notification area and changes to include the speech recognition functions available in Access. In this book, the Language bar is closed. For additional information about the Language bar, see the next page and Appendix B. The following steps show how to close the Language bar if it appears on the screen.

To Close the Language Bar

1

- **Right-click the Language bar to display a list of commands.**

The Language bar shortcut menu appears (Figure 1-4).

2

- **Click Close the Language bar.**
- **Click the OK button.**

The Language bar disappears.

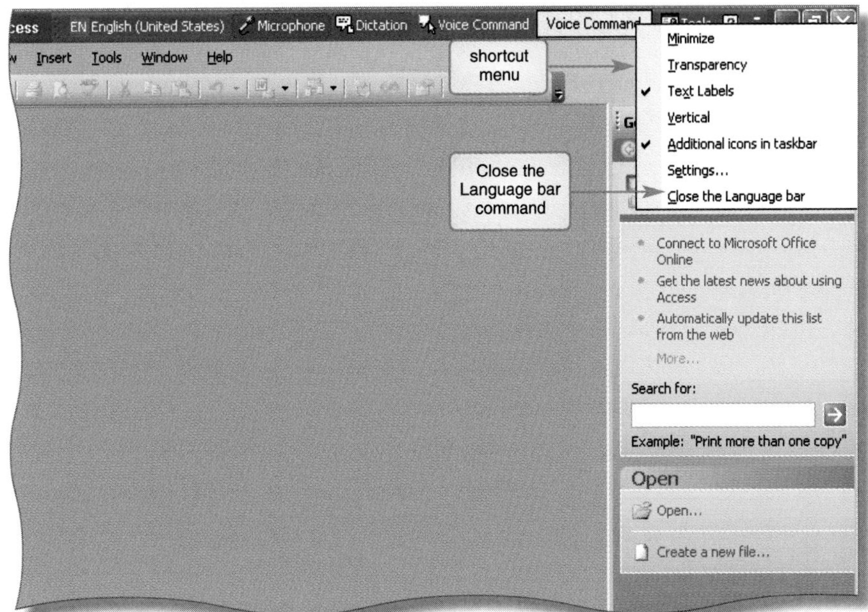

FIGURE 1-4

Speech Recognition

With the **Office Speech Recognition software** installed and a microphone, you can speak the names of toolbar buttons, menus, menu commands, list items, alerts, and dialog box controls, such as OK and Cancel. You also can dictate field entries, such as text and numbers. To indicate whether you want to speak commands or dictate cell entries, you use the Language bar. The Language bar can be in one of three states: (1) **restored**, which means it is displayed somewhere in the Access window (Figure 1-5a); (2) **minimized**, which means it is displayed on the Windows taskbar (Figure 1-5b); or (3) **hidden**, which means you do not see it on the screen. If the Language bar is hidden and you want it to display, then do the following:

1. Right-click an open area on the Windows taskbar at the bottom of the screen.
2. Point to Toolbars and then click Language bar on the Toolbars submenu.

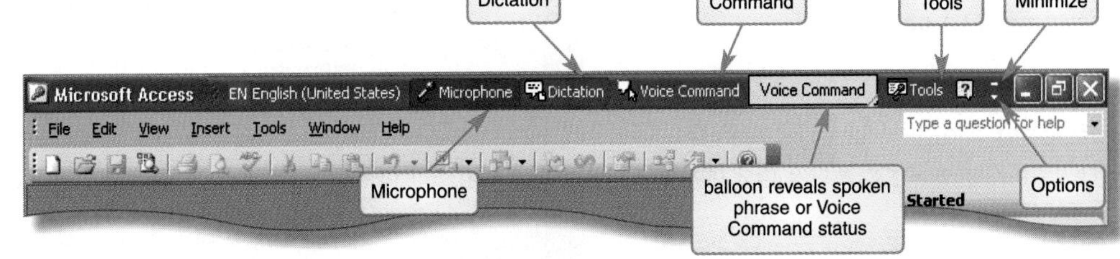

(a) Language Bar in Access Window with Microphone Enabled

(b) Language Bar Minimized on Windows Taskbar

FIGURE 1-5

If the Language bar command is dimmed on the Toolbars submenu or if the Speech command is dimmed on the Tools menu, the Office Speech Recognition software is not installed.

Creating a New Database

In Access, all the tables, reports, form, and queries that you create are stored in a single file called a database. Thus, before creating any of these objects, you first must create the database that will hold them. You can use either the Database Wizard or the Blank database option in the task pane to create a new database. The Database Wizard can guide you by suggesting some commonly used databases. If you choose to create a database using the Database Wizard, you would use the following steps.

To Create a Database Using the Database Wizard

1. Click the New button on the Database toolbar and then click the On my computer link in the New File task pane.
2. When Access displays the Template dialog box, click the Databases tab, and then click the database that is most appropriate for your needs.
3. Follow the instructions in the Database Wizard dialog box to create the database.

Because you already know the tables and fields you want in the Ashton James College database, you would use the Blank database option in the task pane rather than the Database Wizard. The following steps illustrate how to use the Blank database option to create a database on a floppy disk in drive A.

To Create a New Database

1

- **Insert a formatted floppy disk in drive A.**
- **Click the New button on the Database toolbar to display the task pane.**
- **Click the Blank database option in the task pane, and then click the Save in box arrow.**

Access displays the File New Database dialog box and the Save in list appears (Figure 1-6a). Your File name text box may display db1.mdb, rather than db1.

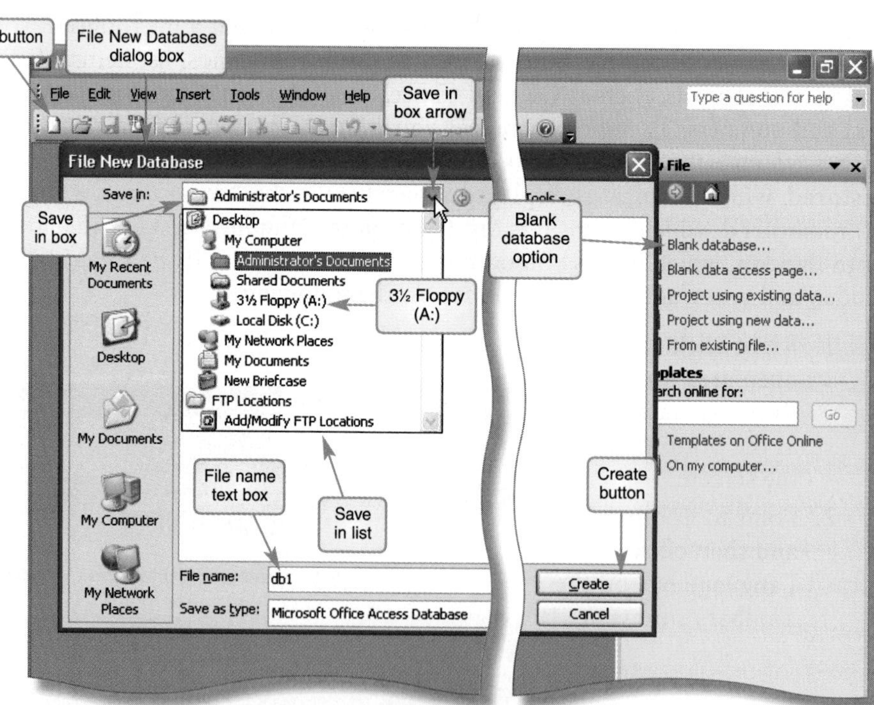

FIGURE 1-6a

2

- **Click 3½ Floppy (A:).**
- **Click the File name text box.**
- **Use the BACKSPACE key or the DELETE key to delete db1 and then type** `Ashton James College` **as the file name.**

The file name is changed to Ashton James College (Figure 1-6b).

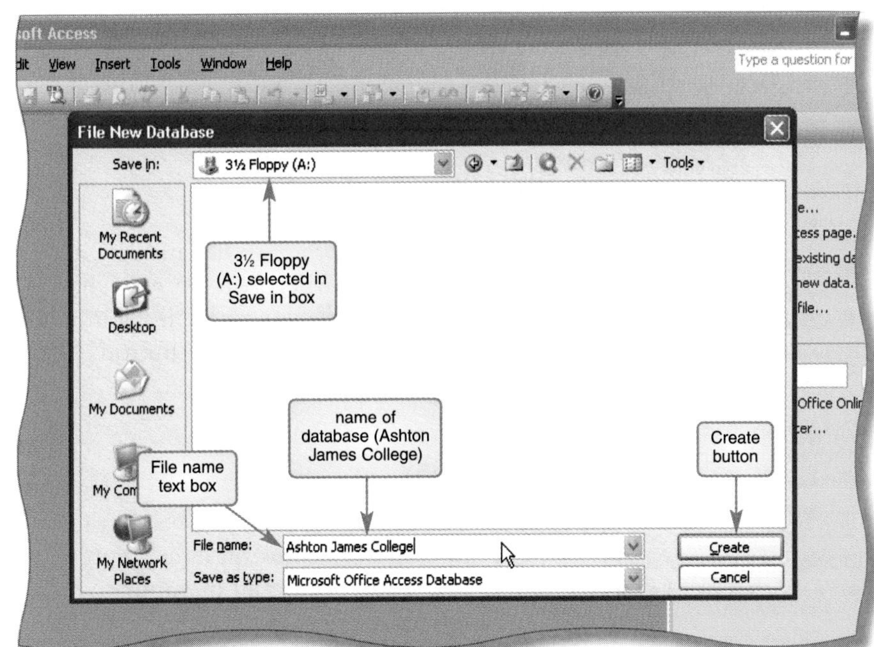

FIGURE 1-6b

3

- **Click the Create button to create the database.**

The Ashton James College database is created. The Ashton James College : Database window appears in the Microsoft Access window (Figure 1-7). The task pane does not appear.

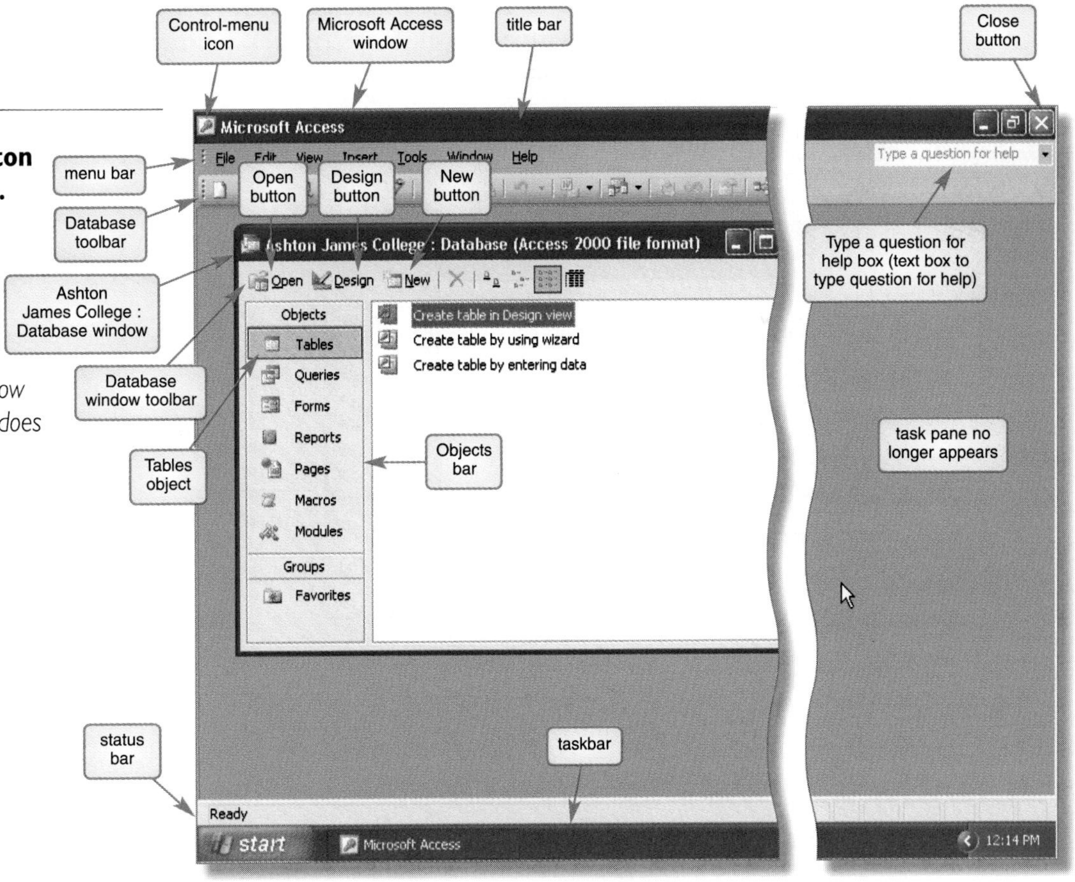

Control-menu icon
Microsoft Access window
title bar
Close button
menu bar
Database toolbar
Open button
Design button
New button
Ashton James College : Database window
Database window toolbar
Tables object
Type a question for help box (text box to type question for help)
Objects bar
task pane no longer appears
status bar
taskbar
Microsoft Access
Ashton James College : Database (Access 2000 file format)
Objects
Tables
Queries
Forms
Reports
Pages
Macros
Modules
Groups
Favorites
Create table in Design view
Create table by using wizard
Create table by entering data
Ready
start
12:14 PM

FIGURE 1-7

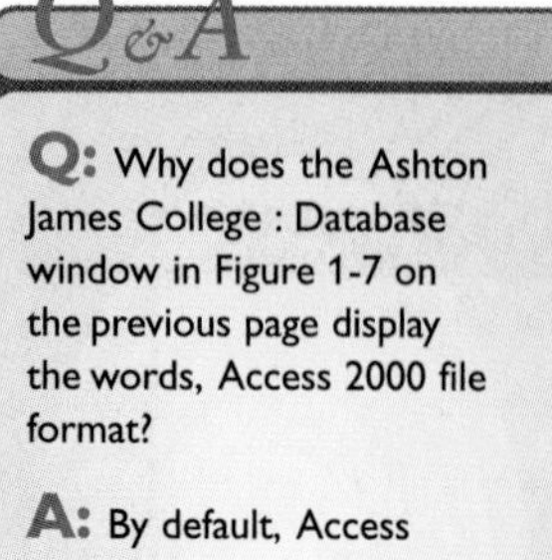

Q: Why does the Ashton James College : Database window in Figure 1-7 on the previous page display the words, Access 2000 file format?

A: By default, Access creates a new database in Access 2000 format. A file in Access 2000 format can be opened in Access 2000, Access 2002, or Access 2003. This allows you to share your database with users who do not have Access 2003. You can open a file in Access 2002-2003 only in Access 2002 or later. Certain features of Access 2003 are not available if the database is in Access 2000 file format.

The Access Window

The Access window (Figure 1-7 on the previous page) contains a variety of features that play important roles when you are working with a database.

Title Bar

The **title bar** is the top bar in the Microsoft Access window. It includes the title of the application, Microsoft Access. The icon on the left is the Control-menu icon. Clicking this icon displays a menu from which you can close the Access window. The button on the right is the Close button. Clicking the Close button closes the Access window.

Menu Bar

The **menu bar** is displayed below the title bar. It is a special toolbar that displays the menu names. Each menu name represents a menu of commands that you can use to retrieve, store, print, and manipulate data. When you point to a menu name on the menu bar, the area of the menu bar is displayed as a selected button. Access shades selected buttons in light orange and surrounds them with a blue outline. To display a menu, such as the Edit menu, click the Edit menu name on the menu bar (Figures 1-8a and 1-8b). A **menu** is a list of commands. If you point to a command on the menu with an arrow to its right, a **submenu** is displayed from which you can choose a command.

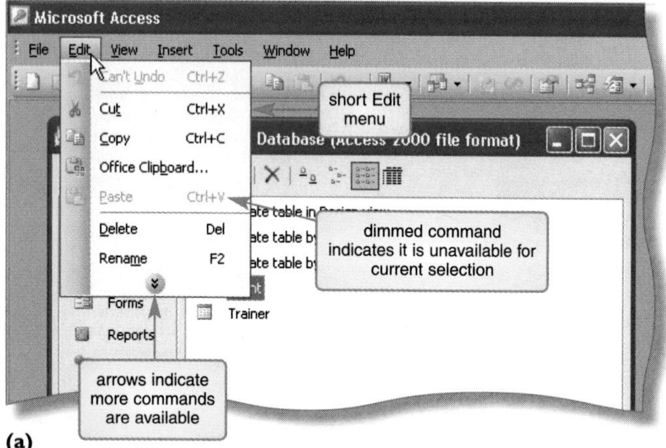

(a)

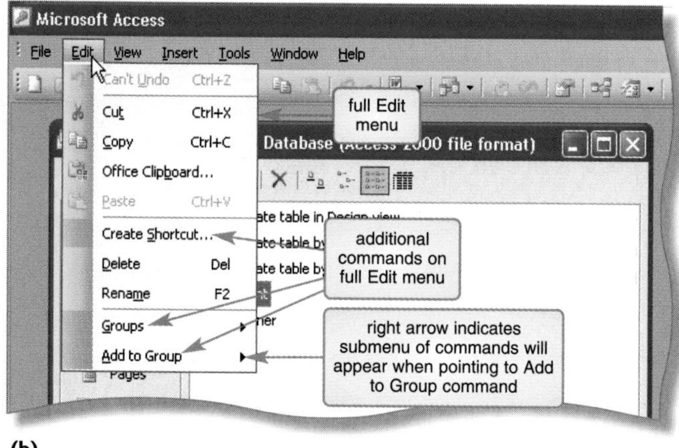

(b)

FIGURE 1-8

When you click a menu name on the menu bar, Access displays a **short menu** listing the most recently used commands (Figure 1-8a). If you wait a few seconds or click the arrows at the bottom of the short menu, the full menu appears. The **full menu** lists all the commands associated with a menu (Figure 1-8b). You also can display a full menu immediately by double-clicking the menu name on the menu bar. In this book, always have Access display the full menu using one of the following techniques.

1. Click the menu name on the menu bar and then wait a few seconds.
2. Click the menu name and then click the arrows at the bottom of the short menu.

3. Click the menu name and then point to the arrows at the bottom of the short menu.
4. Double-click the menu name.

Both short and full menus display some **dimmed commands** that appear gray, or dimmed, instead of black, which indicates they are not available for the current selection. A command with a medium blue shading to the left of it on a full menu is called a **hidden command** because it does not display on a short menu. As you use Access, it automatically personalizes the short menus for you based on how often you use commands. That is, as you use hidden commands, Access *unhides* them and places them on the short menu.

More About

Toolbars

Normally, the correct Access 2003 toolbar will display automatically. If it does not, click View on the menu bar, and then click Toolbars. On the Toolbars submenu, select the toolbar for the activity in which you are engaged. See Appendix D for additional details.

Toolbars

Below the menu bar is a toolbar. A **toolbar** contains buttons that allow you to perform certain tasks more quickly than using the menu bar. Each button contains a picture, or **icon**, depicting its function. When you move the mouse pointer over a button, the name of the button appears below it in a **ScreenTip**. The toolbar shown in Figure 1-7 on page AC 11 is the Database toolbar. The specific toolbar or toolbars that appear will vary, depending on the task on which you are working. Access routinely displays the toolbar or toolbars you will need for the task. If you want to change these or simply to determine what toolbars are available for the given task, consult Appendix D.

Taskbar

The Windows **taskbar** at the bottom of the screen displays the Start button, any active windows, and the current time.

Status Bar

Immediately above the Windows taskbar is the **status bar**. It contains special information that is appropriate for the task on which you are working. Currently, it contains the word, Ready, which means Access is ready to accept commands.

Database Window

The **Database window**, referred to in Figure 1-7 as the Ashton James College : Database window, is a special window that allows you to access easily and rapidly a variety of objects such as tables, queries, forms, and reports. To do so, you will use the various components of the window.

Shortcut Menus

Rather than use toolbars to accomplish a given task, you also can use **shortcut menus**, which are menus that display the actions available for a particular item. To display the shortcut menu for an item, right-click the item; that is, point to the item and then click the right mouse button. Figures 1-9a and 1-9b on the next page illustrate the use of toolbars and shortcut menus to perform the same task, namely to print the contents of the Client table. In the figure, the tables you will create in this project already have been created.

More About

Shortcut Menus

Shortcut menus contain the most frequently used commands that relate to the object to which the mouse pointer is pointing.

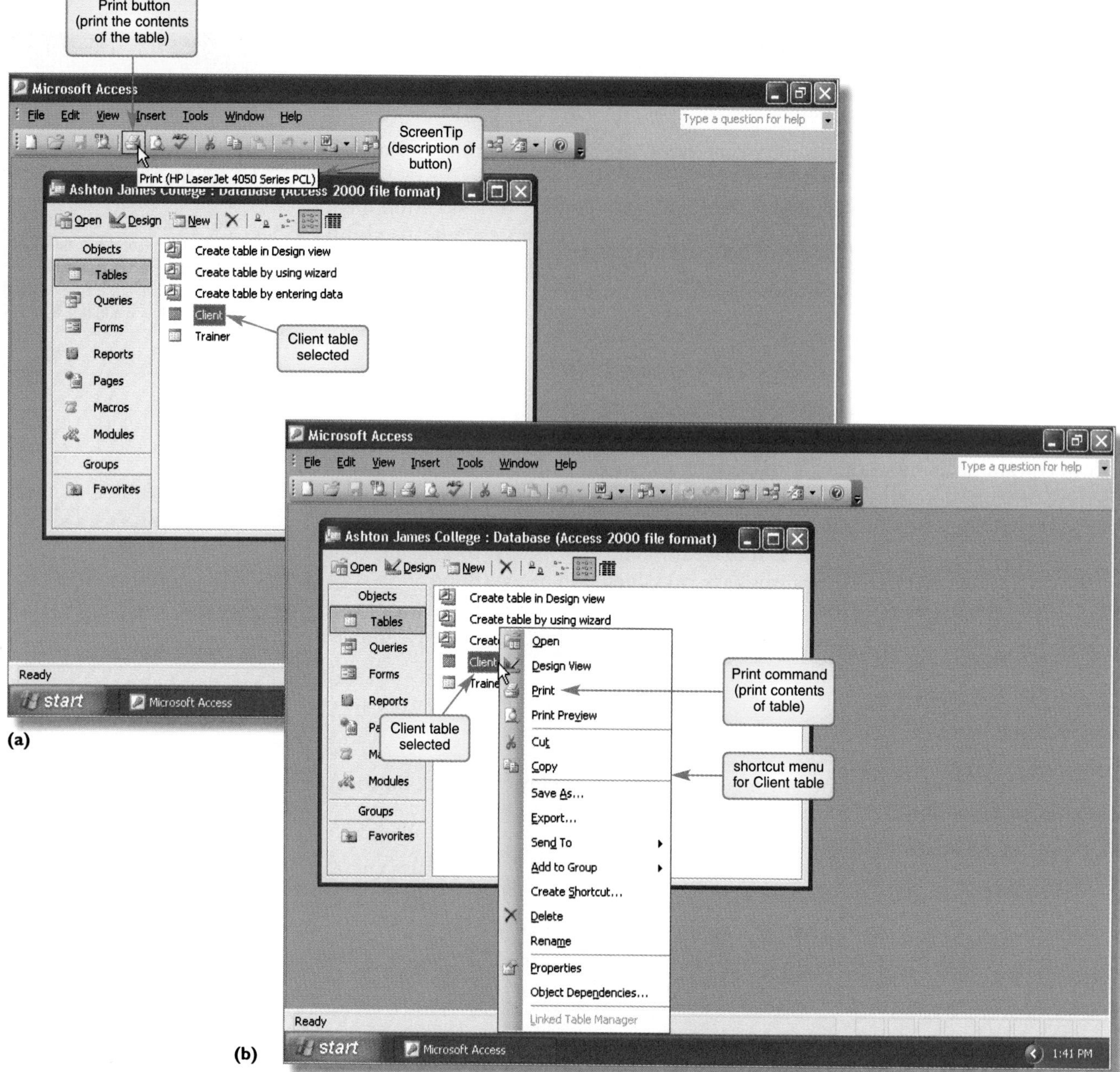

FIGURE 1-9

Before the action illustrated in Figure 1-9a, you would have to select the Client table by clicking it. Then, you would point to the Print button on the toolbar as shown in the figure. When you point to a button on a toolbar, the ScreenTip appears, indicating the purpose of the button, in this case Print. When you click the button, the corresponding action takes place. In this case, Access will print the contents of the Client table.

To use a shortcut menu to perform the same task, you would right-click the Client table, which produces the shortcut menu shown in Figure 1-9b. You then would click the desired command, in this case the Print command, on the shortcut menu. The corresponding action then takes place.

You can use whichever option you prefer. Many professionals who use Access will use a combination. If it is simplest to use the shortcut menu, which often is the case, they will use the shortcut menu. If it is simpler just to click a toolbar button, they will do that. The steps in this text follow this approach; that is, using a combination of both options. The text indicates how to accomplish the task using the other approach, as well. Thus, if the steps use a shortcut menu, the Other Ways box at the end of the steps will indicate how you could accomplish the task using a toolbar button. If the steps use a button, the Other Ways box will indicate how you could accomplish the task with a shortcut menu.

AutoCorrect

Not visible in the Access window, the **AutoCorrect** feature of Access works behind the scenes, correcting common mistakes when you complete a text entry in a cell. AutoCorrect makes three types of corrections for you:

1. Corrects two initial capital letters by changing the second letter to lowercase.
2. Capitalizes the first letter in the names of days.
3. Replaces commonly misspelled words with their correct spelling. For example, it will change the misspelled word *recieve* to *receive* when you complete the entry. AutoCorrect will correct the spelling automatically of more than 400 commonly misspelled words.

More About

AutoCorrect

Using the Office AutoCorrect feature, you can create entries that will replace abbreviations with spelled-out names and phrases automatically. For example, you can create the abbreviated entry *dbms* for *database management system.* Whenever you type dbms followed by a space or punctuation mark, Access automatically replaces dbms with database management system. AutoCorrect works with text in a datasheet or in a form. To specify AutoCorrect rules and exceptions to the rules, click Tools on the menu bar and then click AutoCorrect Options.

Creating a Table

An Access database consists of a collection of tables. After you have created the database, you must create each of the tables within it. In this project, for example, you must create both the Client and Trainer tables shown in Figure 1-1 on page AC 5.

To create a table, you describe the structure of the table to Access by describing the fields within the table. For each field, you indicate the following:

1. **Field name** — Each field in the table must have a unique name. In the Client table (Figure 1-10a and 1-10b on the next page), for example, the field names are Client Number, Name, Address, City, State, Zip Code, Amount Paid, Current Due, and Trainer Number.

More About

Creating a Table: The Table Wizard

Access includes a Table Wizard that guides you by suggesting some commonly used tables and fields. To use the Table Wizard, click Tables on the Objects bar and then click Create table by using wizard. Follow the directions in the Table Wizard dialog boxes. After you create the table, you can modify it at any time by opening the table in Design view.

Structure of Client table

FIELD NAME	DATA TYPE	FIELD SIZE	PRIMARY KEY?	DESCRIPTION
Client Number	Text	4	Yes	Client Number (Primary Key)
Name	Text	20		Client Name
Address	Text	15		Street Address
City	Text	15		City
State	Text	2		State (Two-Character Abbreviation)
Zip Code	Text	5		Zip Code (Five-Character Version)
Amount Paid	Currency			Amount Paid by Client This Year
Current Due	Currency			Current Due from Client This Period
Trainer Number	Text	2		Number of Client's Trainer

FIGURE 1-10a

Client table

CLIENT NUMBER	NAME	ADDRESS	CITY	STATE	ZIP CODE	AMOUNT PAID	CURRENT DUE	TRAINER NUMBER
BS27	Blant and Sons	4806 Park	Lake Hammond	TX	76653	$21,876.00	$892.50	42
CE16	Center Services	725 Mitchell	San Julio	TX	78364	$26,512.00	$2,672.00	48
CP27	Calder Plastics	7300 Cedar	Lake Hammond	TX	76653	$8,725.00	$0.00	48
EU28	Elba's Furniture	1445 Hubert	Tallmadge	TX	77231	$4,256.00	$1,202.00	53
FI28	Farrow-Idsen	829 Wooster	Cedar Ridge	TX	79342	$8,287.50	$925.50	42
FL93	Fairland Lawn	143 Pangborn	Lake Hammond	TX	76653	$21,625.00	$0.00	48
HN83	Hurley National	3827 Burgess	Tallmadge	TX	77231	$0.00	$0.00	48
MC28	Morgan-Alyssa	923 Williams	Crumville	TX	76745	$24,761.00	$1,572.00	42
PS82	PRIM Staffing	72 Crestview	San Julio	TX	78364	$11,682.25	$2,827.50	53
TE26	Telton-Edwards	5672 Anderson	Dunston	TX	77893	$8,521.50	$0.00	48

FIGURE 1-10b

2. **Data type** — Data type indicates to Access the type of data the field will contain. Some fields can contain only numbers. Others, such as Amount Paid and Current Due, can contain numbers and dollar signs. Still others, such as Name and Address, can contain letters.
3. **Description** — Access allows you to enter a detailed description of the field.

Q: Do all database management systems use the same data types?

A: No. Different database management systems have different available data types. Even data types that are essentially the same can have different names. The Access 2003 Text data type, for example, is referred to as Character in some systems and Alpha in others.

You also can assign field widths to text fields (fields whose data type is Text). This indicates the maximum number of characters that can be stored in the field. If you do not assign a width to such a field, Access assumes the width is 50.

You also must indicate which field or fields make up the primary key; that is, the unique identifier, for the table. In the Ashton James College database, the Client Number field is the primary key of the Client table and the Trainer Number field is the primary key of the Trainer table.

The rules for field names are:

1. Names can be up to 64 characters in length.
2. Names can contain letters, digits, and spaces, as well as most of the punctuation symbols.
3. Names cannot contain periods, exclamation points (!), accent graves (`), or square brackets ([ ]).
4. The same name cannot be used for two different fields in the same table.

More About

Primary Keys

In some cases, the primary key consists of a combination of fields rather than a single field. For more information about determining primary keys in such situations, visit the Access 2003 More About Web page (scsite.com/ac2003/more) and click Primary Keys.

Each field has a **data type**. This indicates the type of data that can be stored in the field. The data types you will use in this project are:

1. **Text** — The field can contain any characters. A maximum number of 255 characters is allowed in a field whose data type is Text.
2. **Number** — The field can contain only numbers. The numbers either can be positive or negative. Fields are assigned this type so they can be used in arithmetic operations. Fields that contain numbers but will not be used for arithmetic operations usually are assigned a data type of Text. The Trainer Number field, for example, is a text field because the trainer numbers will not be involved in any arithmetic.

3. **Currency** — The field can contain only monetary data. The values will appear with currency symbols, such as dollar signs, commas, decimal points, and with two digits following the decimal point. Like numeric fields, you can use currency fields in arithmetic operations. Access assigns a size to currency fields automatically.

Table 1-1 shows the other data types that are available.

Table 1-1 Additional Data Types

DATA TYPE	DESCRIPTION
Memo	Field can store a variable amount of text or combinations of text and numbers where the total number of characters may exceed 255.
Date/Time	Field can store dates and times.
AutoNumber	Field can store a unique sequential number that Access assigns to a record. Access will increment the number by 1 as each new record is added.
Yes/No	Field can store only one of two values. The choices are Yes/No, True/False, or On/Off.
OLE Object	Field can store an OLE object, which is an object linked to or embedded in the table.
Hyperlink	Field can store text that can be used as a hyperlink address.
Lookup Wizard	Field can store a value from another table or from a list of values by using a list box or combo box. Choosing this data type starts the Lookup Wizard, which assists in the creation of the field. The field then is a Lookup field. The data type is set based on the values you selected in the wizard. If the values are text for example, the field is assigned the Text data type.

The field names, data types, field widths, primary key information, and descriptions for the Client table are shown in Figure 1-10a on page AC 15.

With the information in Figures 1-10a and 1-10b, you are ready to begin creating the table. The following steps illustrate how to create a table.

To Create a Table

1

- **Click the New button on the Database window toolbar.**

The New Table dialog box appears (Figure 1-11).

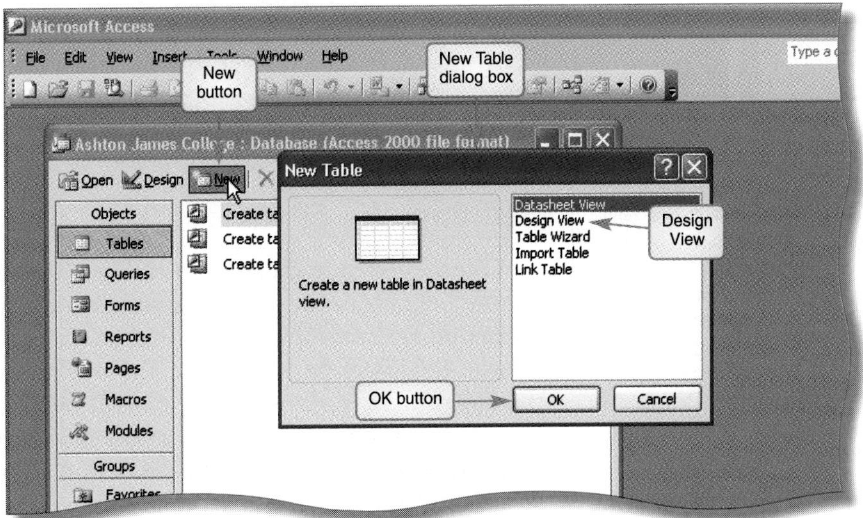

FIGURE 1-11

2

• **Click Design View and then click the OK button.**

The Table1 : Table window appears (Figure 1-12).

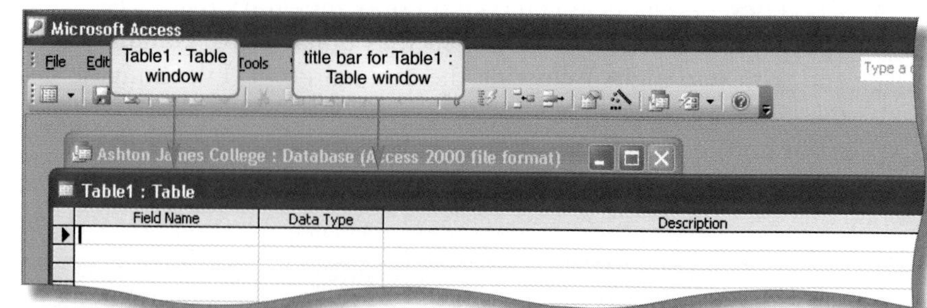

FIGURE 1-12

3

• **Double-click the title bar of the Table1 : Table window to maximize the window.**

Access displays the maximized Table1 : Table window (Figure 1-13).

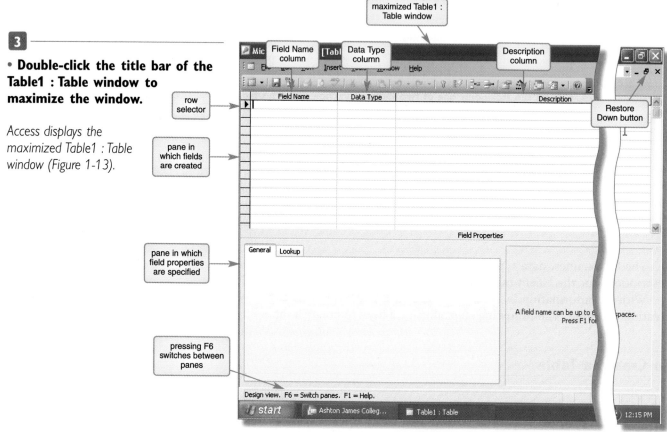

FIGURE 1-13

Other Ways

1. On Insert menu click Table
2. Double-click Create table in Design view
3. Press ALT+N
4. In Voice Command mode, say "Insert, Table"

Defining the Fields

The next step in creating the table is to define the fields by specifying the required details in the Table window, which include entries in the Field Name, Data Type, and Description columns and additional information in the Field Properties pane in the lower portion of the Table window. You press the F6 key to move from the upper **pane** (portion of the screen), the one where you define the fields, to the lower pane, the one where you define field properties. As you define the fields, the **row selector** (Figure 1-13), the small box or bar that, when you click it, selects the entire row, indicates the field you currently are describing. It is positioned on the first field, indicating Access is ready for you to enter the name of the first field in the Field Name column.

The following steps show how to define the fields in the table.

To Define the Fields in a Table

1

• **Type** `Client Number` **(the name of the first field) in the Field Name column, and then press the TAB key.**

The words, Client Number, appear in the Field Name column and the insertion point advances to the Data Type column, indicating you can enter the data type (Figure 1-14). The word, Text, one of the possible data types, currently appears. The arrow indicates a list of data types is available by clicking the arrow.

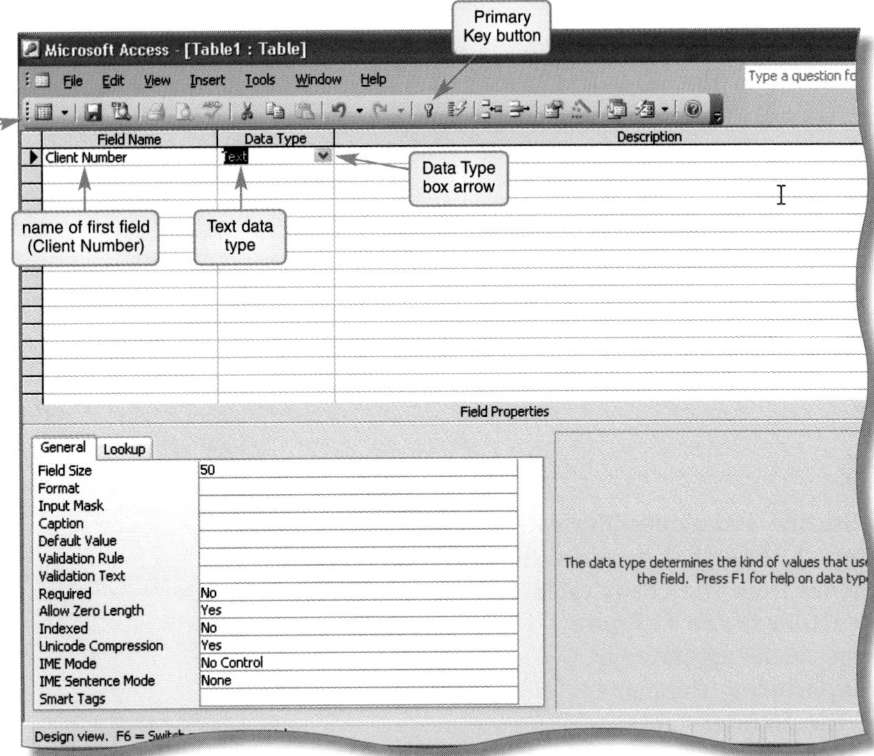

FIGURE 1-14

2

• **Because Text is the correct data type, press the TAB key to move the insertion point to the Description column, type** `Client Number (Primary Key)` **as the description, and then click the Primary Key button on the Table Design toolbar.**

The Client Number field is the primary key as indicated by the key symbol that appears in the row selector (Figure 1-15). A ScreenTip, which is a description of the button, appears.

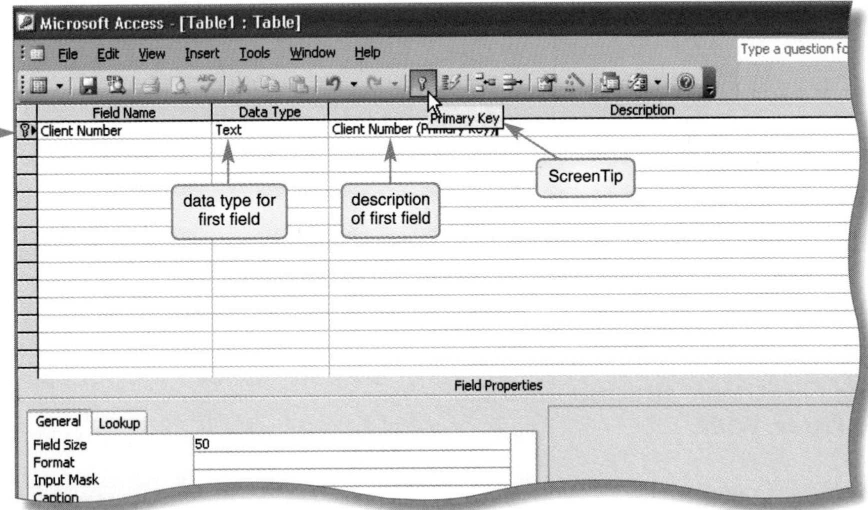

FIGURE 1-15

3

• **Press the F6 key.**

The current entry in the Field Size property box (50) is selected (Figure 1-16).

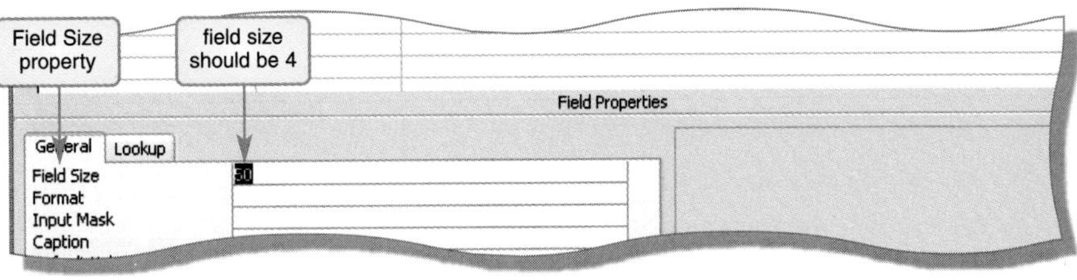

FIGURE 1-16

4

- **Type** 4 **as the size of the Client Number field.**
- **Press the F6 key to return to the Description column for the Client Number field, and then press the TAB key to move to the Field Name column in the second row.**

The insertion point moves to the second row just below the field name Client Number (Figure 1-17).

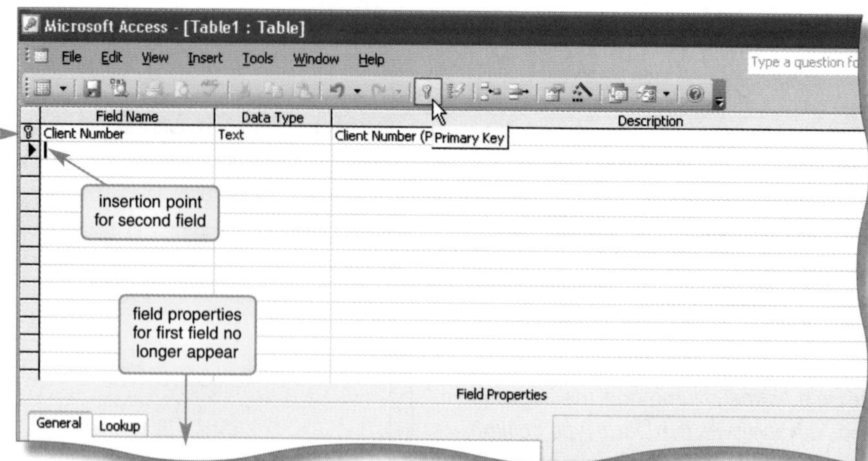

FIGURE 1-17

5

- **Use the techniques illustrated in Steps 1 through 4 to make the entries from the Client table structure shown in Figure 1-10a on page AC 15 up through and including the name of the Amount Paid field.**
- **Click the Data Type box arrow.**

The additional fields are entered (Figure 1-18). A list of available data types appears in the Data Type column for the Amount Paid field.

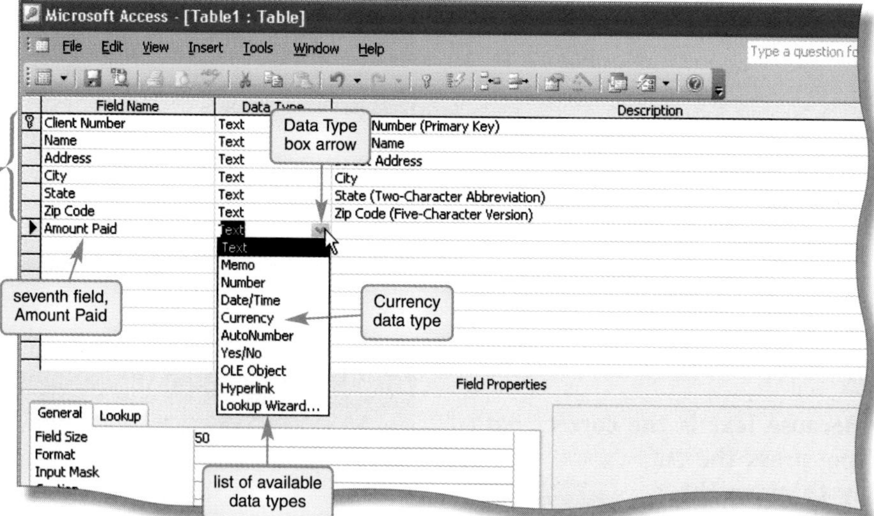

FIGURE 1-18

6

- **Click Currency and then press the TAB key.**
- **Make the remaining entries from the Client table structure shown in Figure 1-10a.**

All the fields are entered (Figure 1-19).

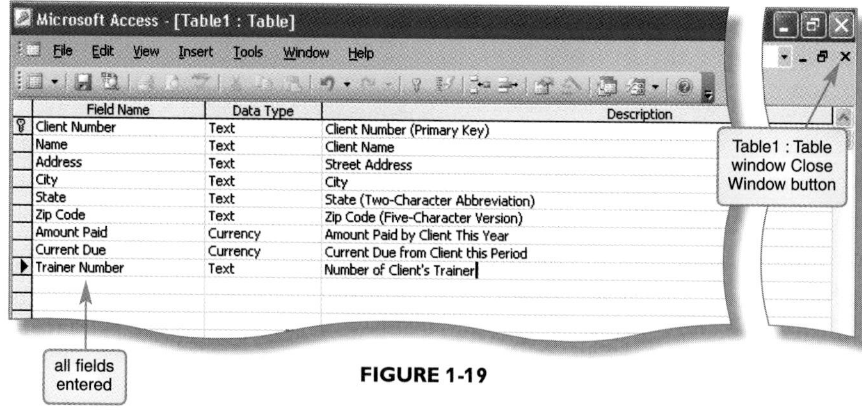

FIGURE 1-19

The description of the table is now complete.

Correcting Errors in the Structure

When creating a table, check the entries carefully to ensure they are correct. If you make a mistake and discover it before you press the TAB key, you can correct the error by repeatedly pressing the BACKSPACE key until the incorrect characters are removed. Then, type the correct characters. If you do not discover a mistake until later, you can click the entry, type the correct value, and then press the ENTER key.

If you accidentally add an extra field to the structure, select the field by clicking the row selector (the leftmost column on the row that contains the field to be deleted). After you have selected the field, press the DELETE key. This will remove the field from the structure.

If you forget a field, select the field that will follow the field you want to add by clicking the row selector, and then press the INSERT key. The remaining fields move down one row, making room for the missing field. Make the entries for the new field in the usual manner.

If you made the wrong field a primary key field, click the correct primary key entry for the field and then click the Primary Key button on the Table Design toolbar.

As an alternative to these steps, you may want to start over. To do so, click the Close Window button for the Table1 : Table window and then click the No button in the Microsoft Office Access dialog box. The initial Microsoft Access window is displayed and you can repeat the process you used earlier.

More About

Correcting Errors in the Structure

You also can correct errors by using the Undo button on the Table Design toolbar. Access displays a list of the 20 most recent actions you can undo. When you undo an action, you also undo all actions above it in the list. If you later decide you did not want to undo an action, click Redo.

Q: Why is the data type for Zip Code Text instead of Number?

A: Zip codes are not used in arithmetic operations. You do not add Zip codes or find an average Zip code, for example.

Closing and Saving a Table

The Client table structure now is complete. The final step is to close and save the table within the database. At this time, you should give the table a name.

Table names are from 1 to 64 characters in length and can contain letters, numbers, and spaces. The two table names in this project are Client and Trainer.

The following steps close and save the table.

To Close and Save a Table

1

- **Click the Close Window button for the Table1 : Table window (see Figure 1-19). (Be sure not to click the Close button on the Microsoft Access title bar, because this would close Microsoft Access.)**

The Microsoft Office Access dialog box appears (Figure 1-20).

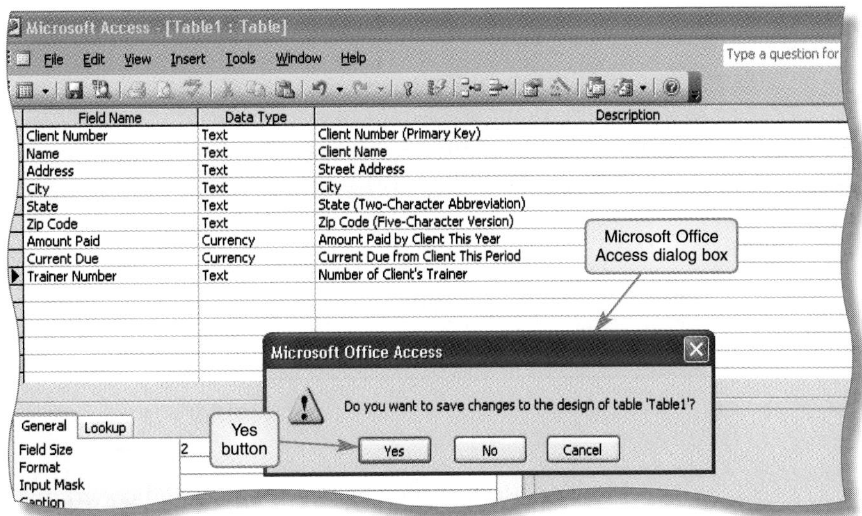

FIGURE 1-20

2

• **Click the Yes button in the Microsoft Office Access dialog box, and then type `Client` as the name of the table.**

The Save As dialog box appears (Figure 1-21). The table name is entered.

3

• **Click the OK button in the Save As dialog box.**

The table is saved. The window containing the table design no longer is displayed.

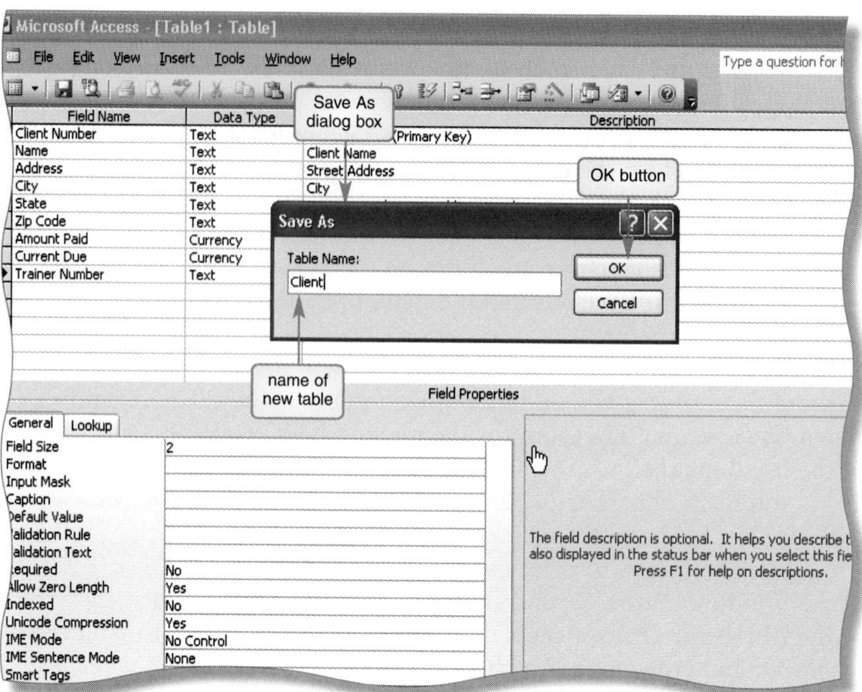

FIGURE 1-21

Other Ways

1. On File menu click Save
2. Press CTRL+S
3. In Voice Command mode, say "Save"

Adding Records to a Table

Creating a table by building the structure and saving the table is the first step in a two-step process. The second step is to add records to the table. To add records to a table, the table must be open. When making changes to tables, you work in Datasheet view. In **Datasheet view**, the table is represented as a collection of rows and columns called a **datasheet**. It looks very much like the tables shown in Figure 1-1 on page AC 5.

You often add records in phases. You may, for example, not have enough time to add all the records in one session. To illustrate this process, this project begins by adding the first two records in the Client table (Figure 1-22). The remaining records are added later.

Client table (first 2 records)

CLIENT NUMBER	NAME	ADDRESS	CITY	STATE	ZIP CODE	AMOUNT PAID	CURRENT DUE	TRAINER NUMBER
BS27	Blant and Sons	4806 Park	Lake Hammond	TX	76653	$21,876.00	$892.50	42
CE16	Center Services	725 Mitchell	San Julio	TX	78364	$26,512.00	$2,672.00	48

FIGURE 1-22

The following steps illustrate how to open the Client table and then add records.

To Add Records to a Table

1

- **Right-click the Client table in the Ashton James College : Database window.**

The shortcut menu for the Client table appears (Figure 1-23). The Ashton James College : Database window is maximized because the previous window, the Client : Table window, was maximized. (If you wanted to restore the Database window to its original size, you would click the Restore Window button.)

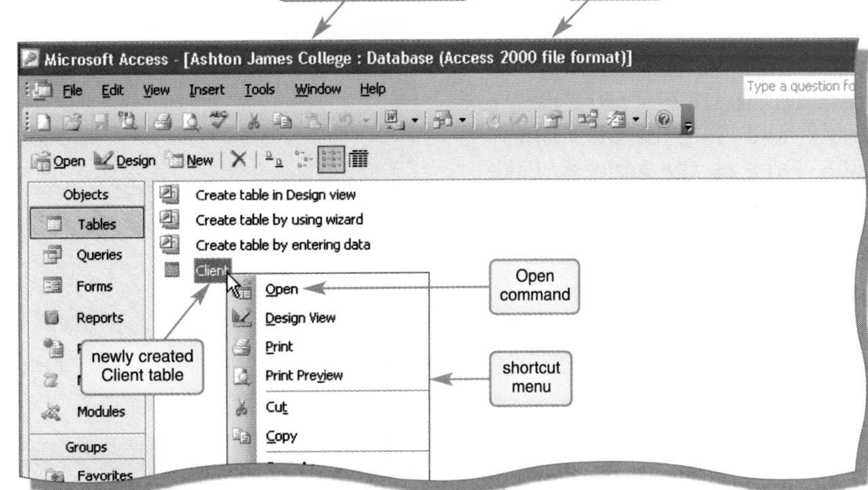

FIGURE 1-23

2

- **Click Open on the shortcut menu.**

Access displays the Client : Table window (Figure 1-24). The window contains the Datasheet view for the Client table. The ***record selector****, the small box or bar that, when clicked, selects the entire record, is positioned on the first record. The status bar at the bottom of the window also indicates that the record selector is positioned on record 1.*

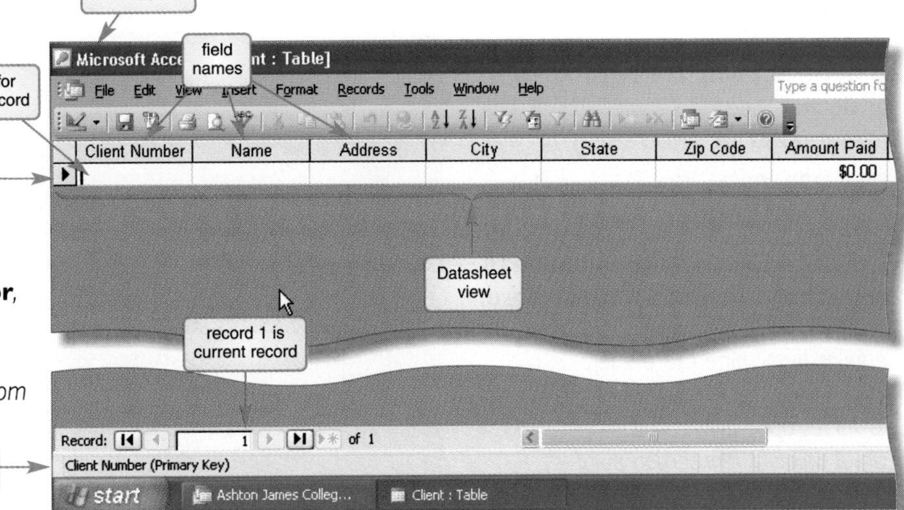

FIGURE 1-24

3

- **Type** BS27 **as the first client number (see Figure 1-22). Be sure you type the letters in uppercase as shown in the table in Figure 1-22 so they are entered in the database correctly.**

The client number is entered, but the insertion point is still in the Client Number field (Figure 1-25). The pencil icon in the record selector column indicates that the record is being edited but changes to the record are not saved yet. Microsoft Access also creates a row for a new record.

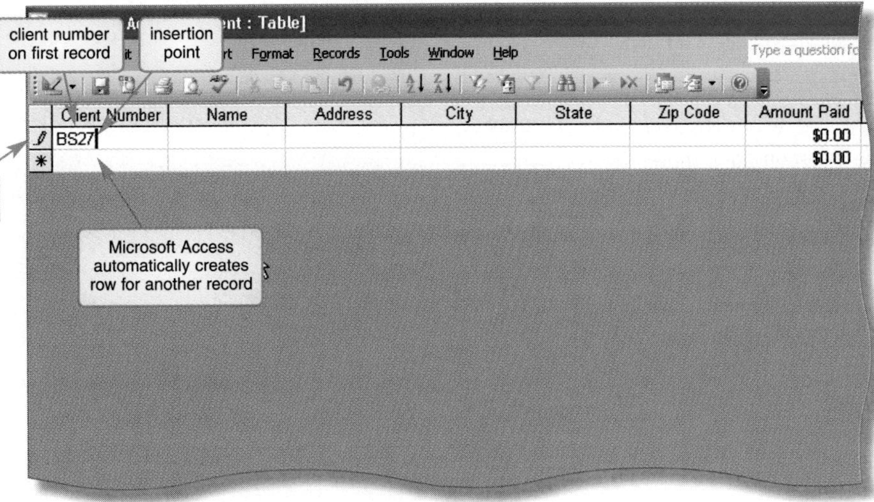

FIGURE 1-25

• **Press the TAB key to complete the entry for the Client Number field.**

• **Type the following entries, pressing the TAB key after each one:** `Blant and Sons` **as the name,** `4806 Park` **as the address,** `Lake Hammond` **as the city,** `TX` **as the state, and** `76653` **as the Zip code.**

The Name, Address, City, State, and Zip Code fields are entered (Figure 1-26).

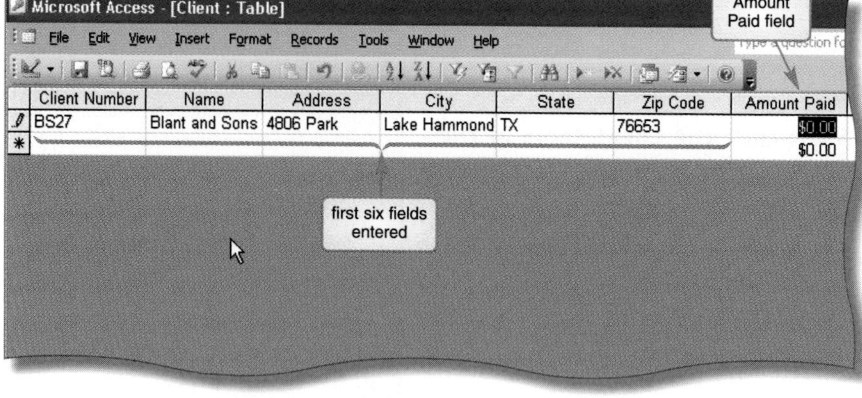

FIGURE 1-26

• **Type** `21876` **as the Amount Paid amount and then press the TAB key. (You do not need to type dollar signs or commas. In addition, because the digits to the right of the decimal point are both zeros, you do not need to type either the decimal point or the zeros.)**

• **Type** `892.50` **as the current due amount and then press the TAB key.**

• **Type** `42` **as the trainer number to complete data entry for the record.**

The fields have shifted to the left (Figure 1-27). The Amount Paid and Current Due values appear with dollar signs and decimal points. The insertion point is positioned in the Trainer Number field.

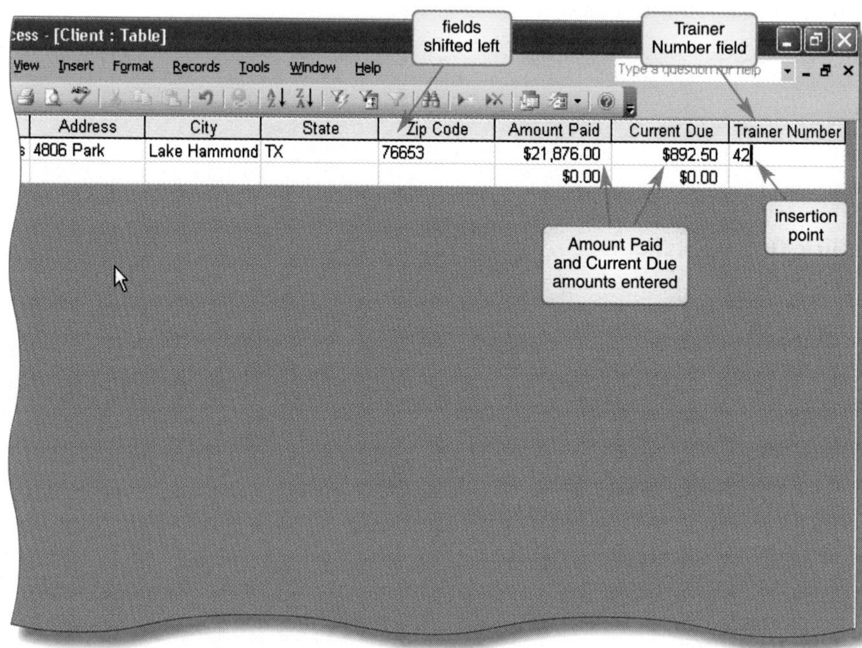

FIGURE 1-27

• **Press the TAB key.**

The fields shift back to the right, the record is saved, and the insertion point moves to the client number field on the second row (Figure 1-28).

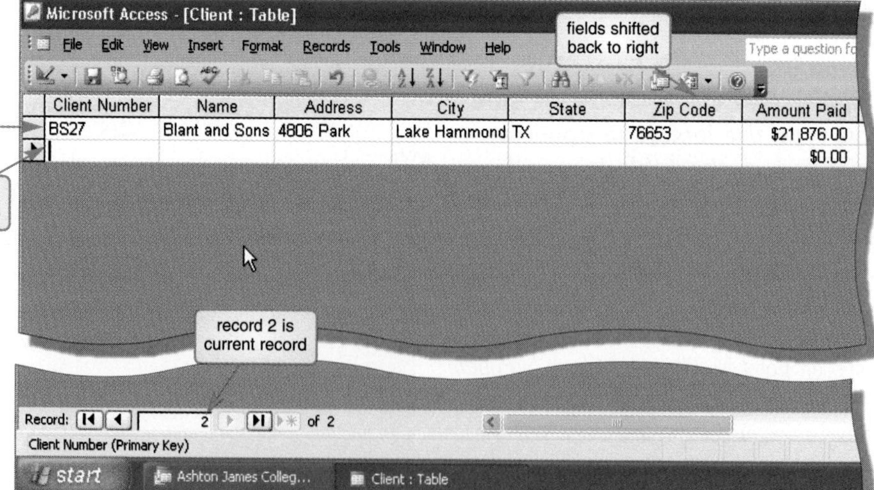

FIGURE 1-28

7

• Use the techniques shown in Steps 3 through 6 to add the data for the second record shown in Figure 1-22 on page AC 22.

The second record is added and the insertion point moves to the Client Number field on the third row (Figure 1-29).

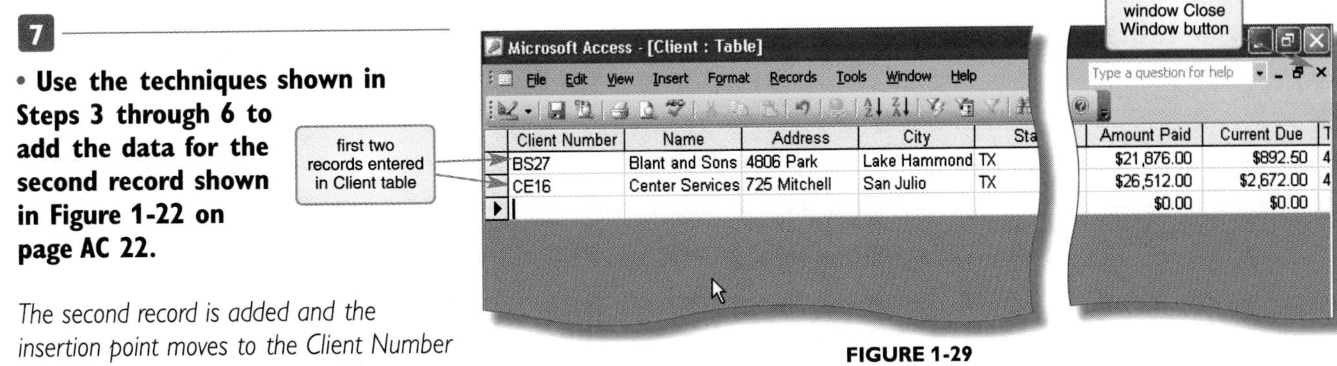

FIGURE 1-29

As soon as you have entered or modified a record and moved to another record, the original record is saved. This is different from other applications. The rows entered in a spreadsheet, for example, are not saved until the entire spreadsheet is saved.

Correcting Errors in the Data

Check your entries carefully to ensure they are correct. If you make a mistake and discover it before you press the TAB key, correct it by pressing the BACKSPACE key until the incorrect characters are removed and then typing the correct characters.

If you discover an incorrect entry later, correct the error by clicking the incorrect entry and then making the appropriate correction. If the record you must correct is not on the screen, use any technique, such as the UP ARROW and DOWN ARROW keys to move to it. If the field you want to correct is not visible on the screen, use the horizontal scroll bar along the bottom of the screen to shift all the fields until the one you want appears. Then make the correction.

If you add an extra record accidentally, select the record by clicking the record selector that immediately precedes the record. Then, press the DELETE key. This will remove the record from the table. If you forget a record, add it using the same procedure as for all the other records. Access will place it in the correct location in the table automatically.

If you cannot determine how to correct the data, you are, in effect, stuck on the record. Access neither allows you to move to any other record until you have made the correction, nor allows you to close the table. If you encounter this situation, simply press the ESC key. Pressing the ESC key will remove from the screen the record you are trying to add. You then can move to any other record, close the table, or take any other action you desire.

More About

Correcting Errors in the Data

You also can undo changes to a field by clicking the Undo typing button on the Table Datasheet toolbar. If you already have moved to another record and want to delete the record you just added, click Edit on the menu bar and then click Undo Saved Record.

Closing a Table and Database and Quitting Access

It is a good idea to close a table as soon as you have finished working with it. It keeps the screen from getting cluttered and prevents you from making accidental changes to the data in the table. If you no longer will work with the database, you should close the database as well. With the creation of the Client table complete, you also can quit Access at this point.

The steps on the next page close the table and the database and then quit Access.

To Close a Table and Database and Quit Access

1

- **Click the Close Window button for the Client : Table window.**

The datasheet for the Client table no longer appears (Figure 1-30).

2

- **Click the Close Window button for the Ashton James College : Database window.**

The Ashton James College : Database window no longer appears.

3

- **Click the Close button for the Microsoft Access window.**

The Microsoft Access window closes and the Windows desktop appears.

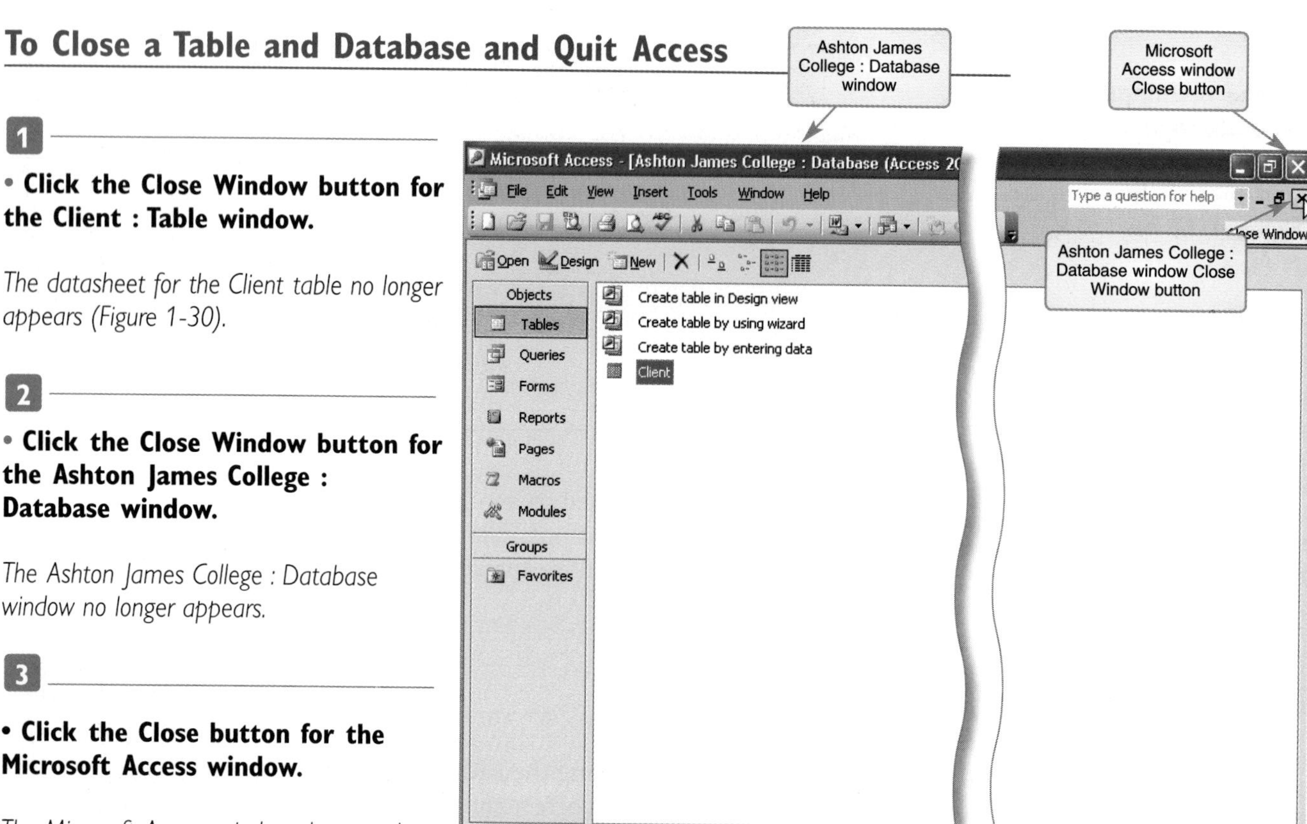

FIGURE 1-30

Opening a Database

To work with any of the tables, reports, or forms in a database, the database must be open. The following steps open the database from within Access.

To Open a Database

1

- **Start Access following the steps on pages AC 7 and AC 8.**
- **If the task pane appears, click its Close button.**
- **Click the Open button on the Database toolbar.**

The Open dialog box appears (Figure 1-31).

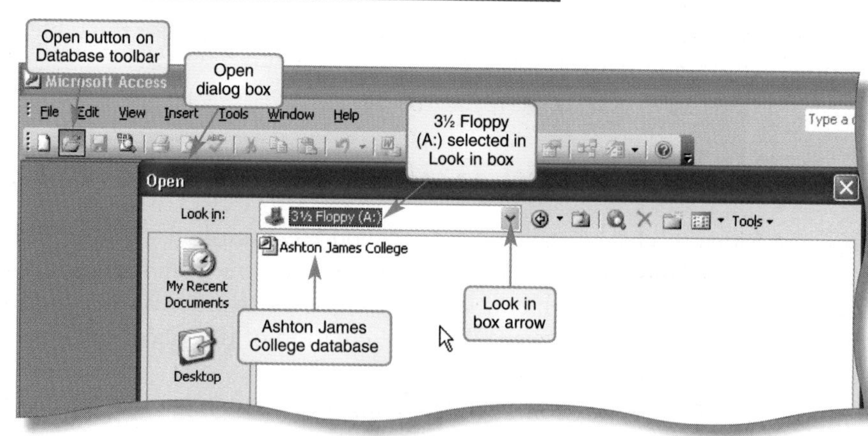

FIGURE 1-31

2

- **Be sure 3½ Floppy (A:) folder appears in the Look in box. If not, click the Look in box arrow and click 3½ Floppy (A:).**
- **Click Ashton James College.**

Access displays the Open dialog box (Figure 1-32). The 3½ Floppy (A:) folder appears in the Look in box and the files on the floppy disk in drive A are displayed. (Your list may be different.)

3

- **Click the Open button in the Open dialog box.**
- **If a Security Warning dialog box appears, click the Open button.**

The database opens and the Ashton James College : Database window appears.

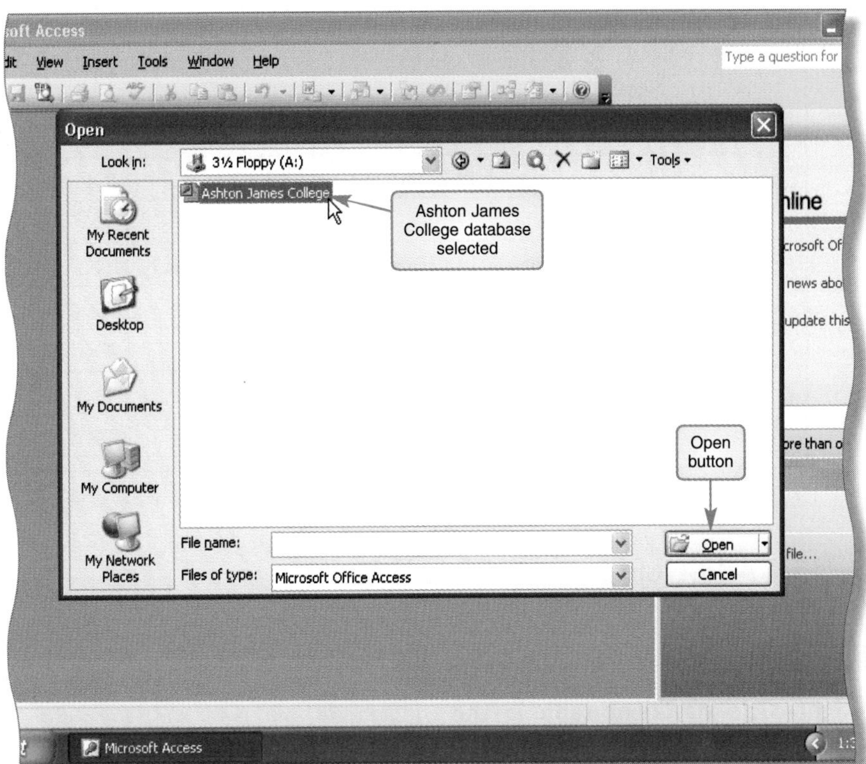

FIGURE 1-32

Other Ways

1. On File menu click Open
2. In Getting Started task pane, click name of database
3. Press CTRL + O
4. In Voice Command mode, say "Open"

Adding Additional Records

You can add records to a table that already contains data using a process almost identical to that used to add records to an empty table. The only difference is that you place the insertion point after the last data record before you enter the additional data. To do so, use the **Navigation buttons**, which are buttons used to move within a table, found near the lower-left corner of the screen shown in Figure 1-34 on the next page. The purpose of each of the Navigation buttons is described in Table 1-2.

Table 1-2 Navigation Buttons in Datasheet View

BUTTON	PURPOSE
First Record	Moves to the first record in the table
Previous Record	Moves to the previous record
Next Record	Moves to the next record
Last Record	Moves to the last record in the table
New Record	Moves to the end of the table to a position for entering a new record

The steps on the next page add the remaining records (Figure 1-33 on the next page) to the Client table.

Q: Why click the New Record button? Could you just click the Client Number on the first open record and then add the record?

A: You could click the Client Number on the first open record, provided that record appears on the screen. With only two records in the table, this is not a problem. Once a table contains more records than will fit on the screen, it is easier to click the New Record button.

Client table (last 8 records)

CLIENT NUMBER	NAME	ADDRESS	CITY	STATE	ZIP CODE	AMOUNT PAID	CURRENT DUE	TRAINER NUMBER
CP27	Calder Plastics	7300 Cedar	Lake Hammond	TX	76653	$8,725.00	$0.00	48
EU28	Elba's Furniture	1445 Hubert	Tallmadge	TX	77231	$4,256.00	$1,202.00	53
FI28	Farrow-Idsen	829 Wooster	Cedar Ridge	TX	79342	$8,287.50	$925.50	42
FL93	Fairland Lawn	143 Pangborn	Lake Hammond	TX	76653	$21,625.00	$0.00	48
HN83	Hurley National	3827 Burgess	Tallmadge	TX	77231	$0.00	$0.00	48
MC28	Morgan-Alyssa	923 Williams	Crumville	TX	76745	$24,761.00	$1,572.00	42
PS82	PRIM Staffing	72 Crestview	San Julio	TX	78364	$11,682.25	$2,827.50	53
TE26	Telton-Edwards	5672 Anderson	Dunston	TX	77893	$8,521.50	$0.00	48

FIGURE 1-33

To Add Additional Records to a Table

1

- **Right-click the Client table in the Ashton James College : Database window, and then click Open on the shortcut menu.**
- **When the Client table appears, maximize the window by double-clicking its title bar.**

The datasheet appears (Figure 1-34).

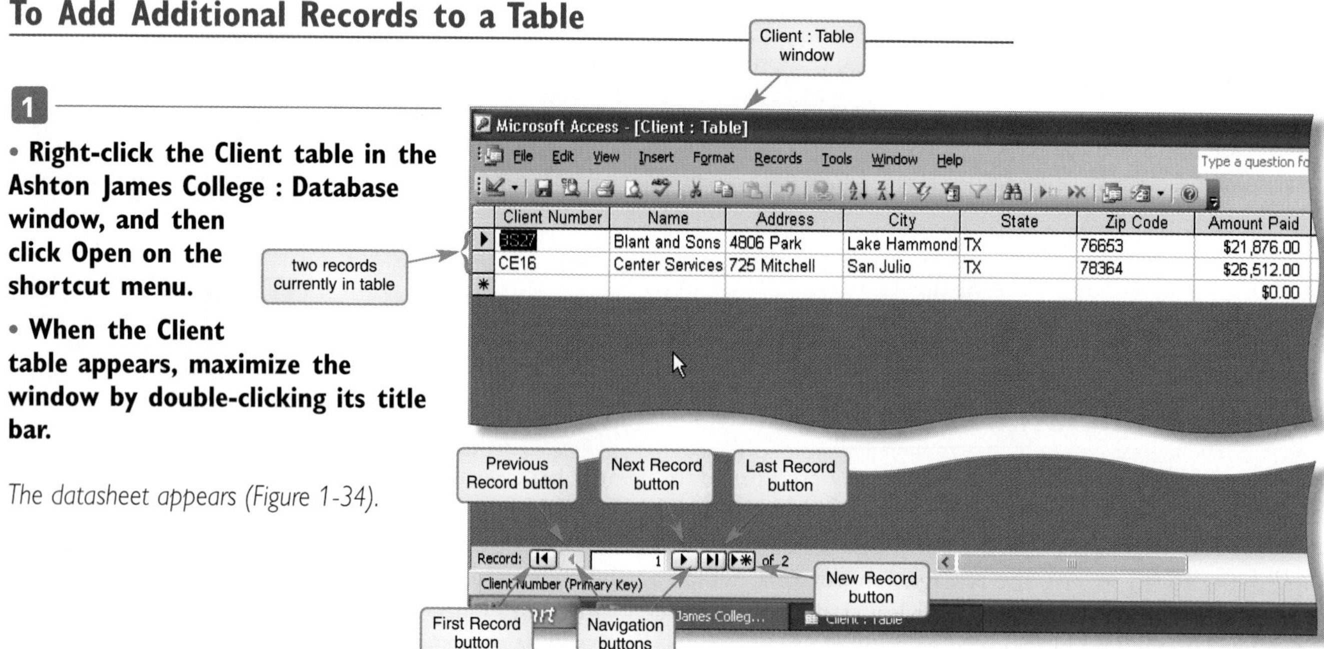

FIGURE 1-34

2

- **Click the New Record button.**

Access places the insertion point in position to enter a new record (Figure 1-35).

FIGURE 1-35

3

• **Add the records from Figure 1-33 using the same techniques you used to add the first two records.**

The additional records are added (Figure 1-36).

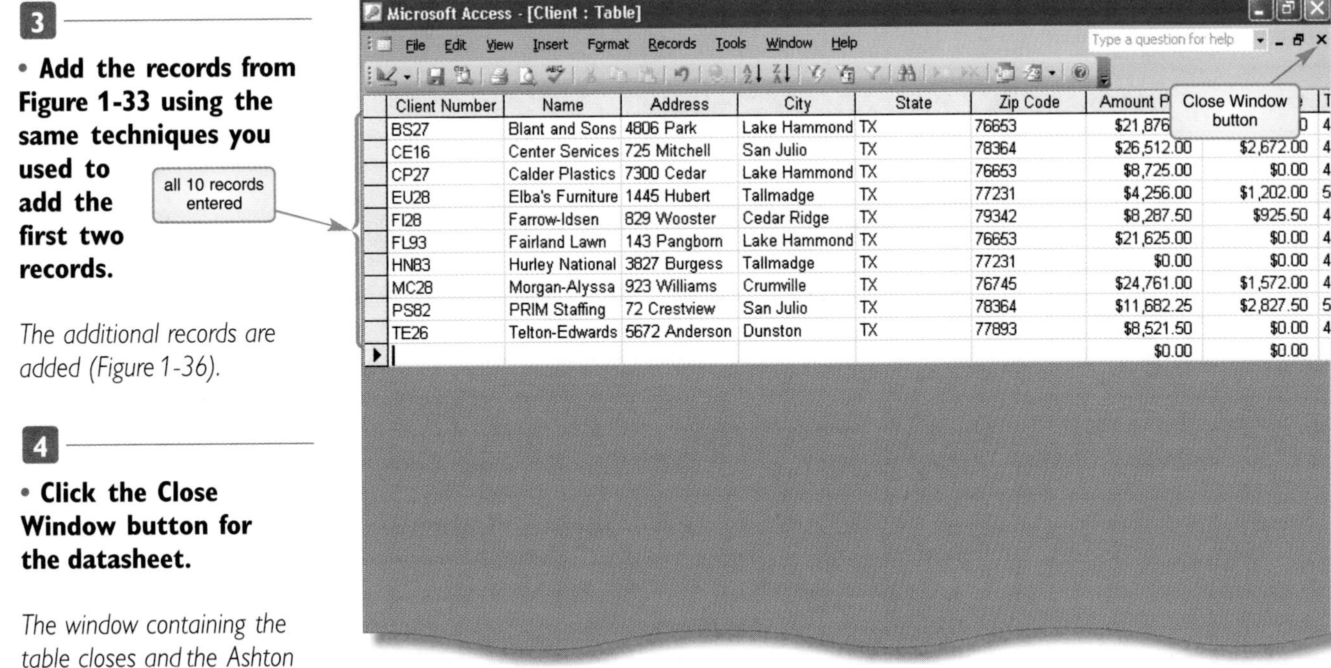

4

• **Click the Close Window button for the datasheet.**

The window containing the table closes and the Ashton James College : Database window appears.

FIGURE 1-36

> ***Other Ways***
>
> 1. Click New Record button on Table Datasheet toolbar
> 2. On Insert menu click New Record
> 3. Press CTRL+PLUS SIGN (+)
> 4. In Voice Command mode, say "Insert, New Record"

Previewing and Printing the Contents of a Table

When working with a database, you often will need to print a copy of the table contents. Figure 1-37 shows a printed copy of the contents of the Client table. (Yours may look slightly different, depending on your printer.) Because the Client table is wider substantially than the screen, it also will be wider than the normal printed page in portrait orientation. **Portrait orientation** means the printout is across the width of the page. **Landscape orientation** means the printout is across the length of the page. Thus, to print the wide database table, use landscape orientation. If you are printing the contents of a table that fit on the screen, you will not need landscape orientation. A convenient way to change to landscape orientation is to preview what the printed copy will look like by using Print Preview. This allows you to determine whether landscape orientation is necessary and, if it is, to change the orientation easily to landscape. In addition, you also can use Print Preview to determine whether any adjustments are necessary to the page margins.

Client　　　9/15/05

Client Number	Name	Address	City	State	Zip Code	Amount Paid	Current Due	Trainer Number
BS27	Blant and Sons	4806 Park	Lake Hammon	TX	76653	$21,876.00	$892.50	42
CE16	Center Service	725 Mitchell	San Julio	TX	78364	$26,512.00	$2,672.00	48
CP27	Calder Plastics	7300 Cedar	Lake Hammon	TX	76653	$8,725.00	$0.00	48
EU28	Elba's Furniture	1445 Hubert	Tallmadge	TX	77231	$4,256.00	$1,202.00	53
FI28	Farrow-Idsen	829 Wooster	Cedar Ridge	TX	79342	$8,287.50	$925.50	42
FL93	Fairland Lawn	143 Pangborn	Lake Hammon	TX	76653	$21,625.00	$0.00	48
HN83	Hurley National	3827 Burgess	Tallmadge	TX	77231	$0.00	$0.00	48
MC28	Morgan-Alyssa	923 Williams	Crumville	TX	76745	$24,761.00	$1,572.00	42
PS82	PRIM Staffing	72 Crestview	San Julio	TX	78364	$11,682.25	$2,827.50	53
TE26	Telton-Edwards	5672 Anderson	Dunston	TX	77893	$8,521.50	$0.00	48

FIGURE 1-37

The following steps illustrate using Print Preview to preview and then print the Client table.

To Preview and Print the Contents of a Table

1

- **Right-click the Client table.**

The shortcut menu for the Client table appears (Figure 1-38).

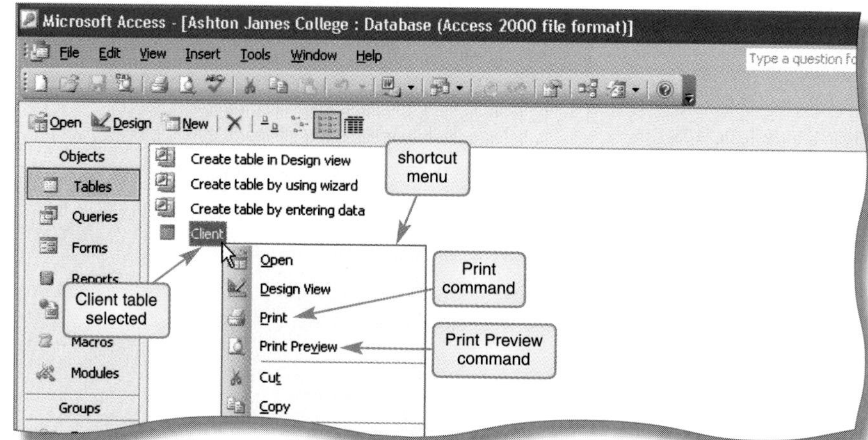

FIGURE 1-38

2

- **Click Print Preview on the shortcut menu.**
- **Point to the approximate position shown in Figure 1-39.**

The preview of the report appears. The mouse pointer shape changes to a magnifying glass, indicating you can magnify a portion of the report.

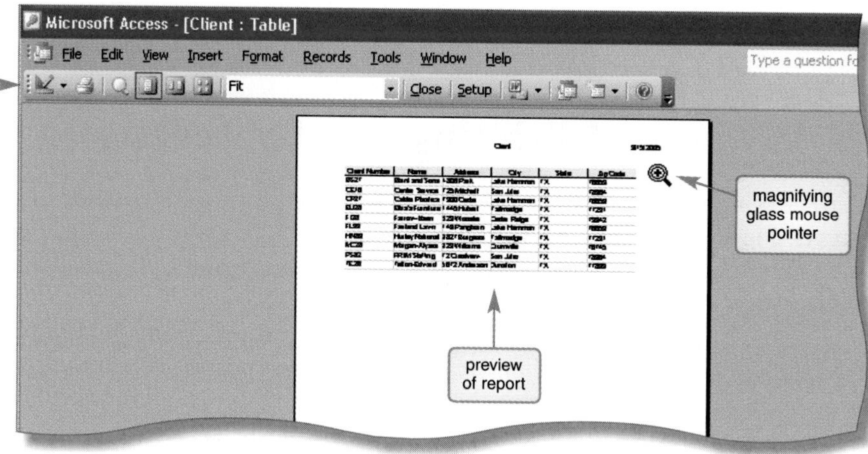

FIGURE 1-39

3

- **Click the magnifying glass mouse pointer in the approximate position shown in Figure 1-39.**

The portion surrounding the mouse pointer is magnified (Figure 1-40). The last field that appears is the Zip Code field. The Amount Paid, Current Due, and Trainer Number fields do not appear. To display the additional fields, you will need to switch to landscape orientation.

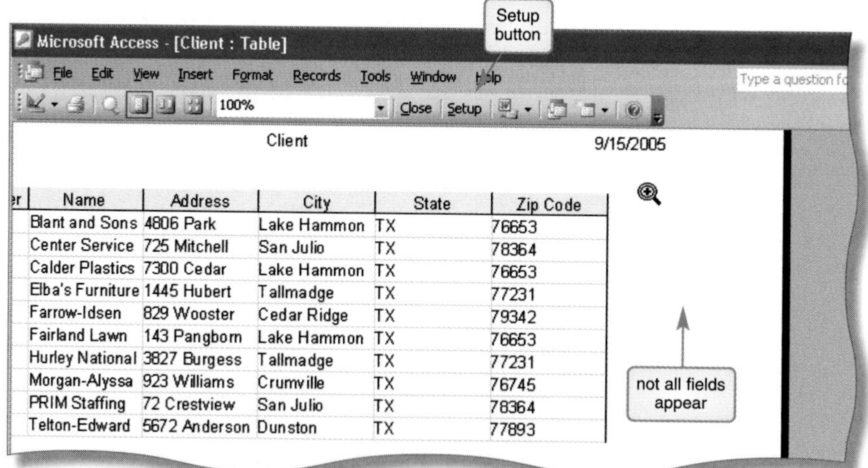

Name	Address	City	State	Zip Code
Blant and Sons	4806 Park	Lake Hammon	TX	76653
Center Service	725 Mitchell	San Julio	TX	78364
Calder Plastics	7300 Cedar	Lake Hammon	TX	76653
Elba's Furniture	1445 Hubert	Tallmadge	TX	77231
Farrow-Idsen	829 Wooster	Cedar Ridge	TX	79342
Fairland Lawn	143 Pangborn	Lake Hammon	TX	76653
Hurley National	3827 Burgess	Tallmadge	TX	77231
Morgan-Alyssa	923 Williams	Crumville	TX	76745
PRIM Staffing	72 Crestview	San Julio	TX	78364
Telton-Edward	5672 Anderson	Dunston	TX	77893

FIGURE 1-40

- **Click the Setup button on the Print Preview toolbar.**

Access displays the Page Setup dialog box (Figure 1-41).

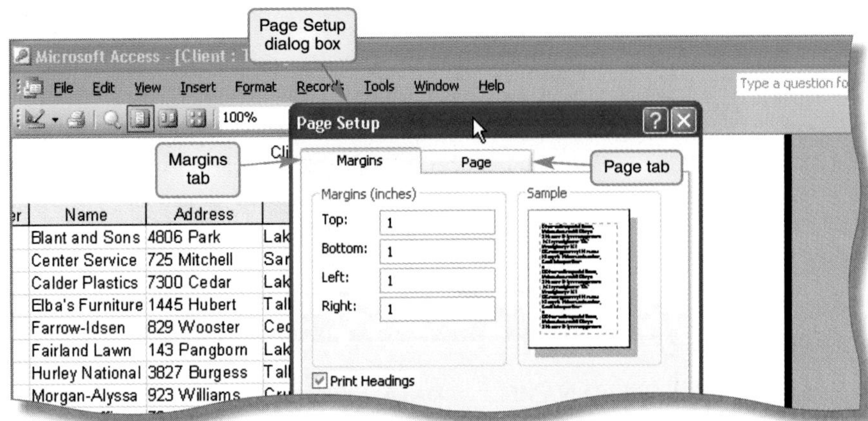

FIGURE 1-41

- **Click the Page tab.**

*The Page sheet appears (Figure 1-42). The Portrait option button currently is selected. (**Option button** refers to the round button that indicates choices in a dialog box. When the corresponding option is selected, the button contains within it a solid circle. Clicking an option button selects it, and deselects all others.)*

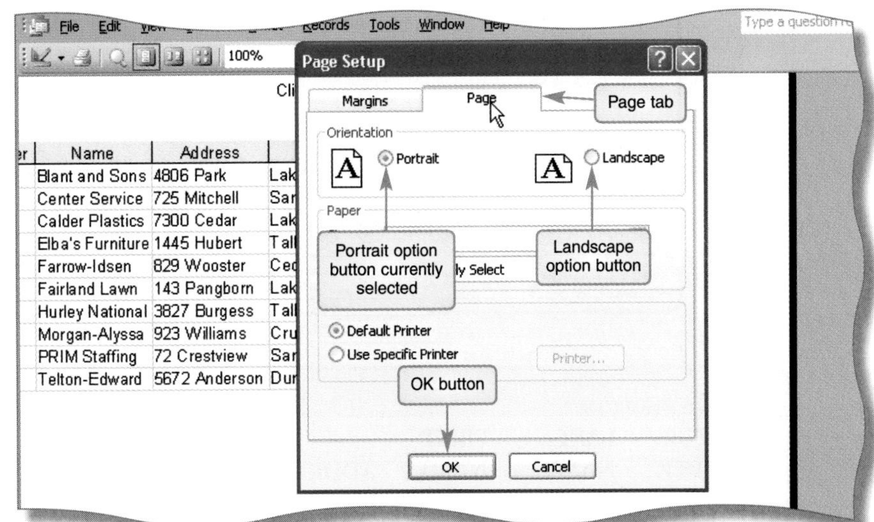

FIGURE 1-42

- **Click Landscape, and then click the OK button.**

The orientation is changed to landscape as shown by the report that appears on the screen (Figure 1-43). The last field that is displayed is the Trainer Number field; so all fields currently appear. If they did not, you could decrease the left and right margins; that is, the amount of space left by Access on the left and right edges of the report.

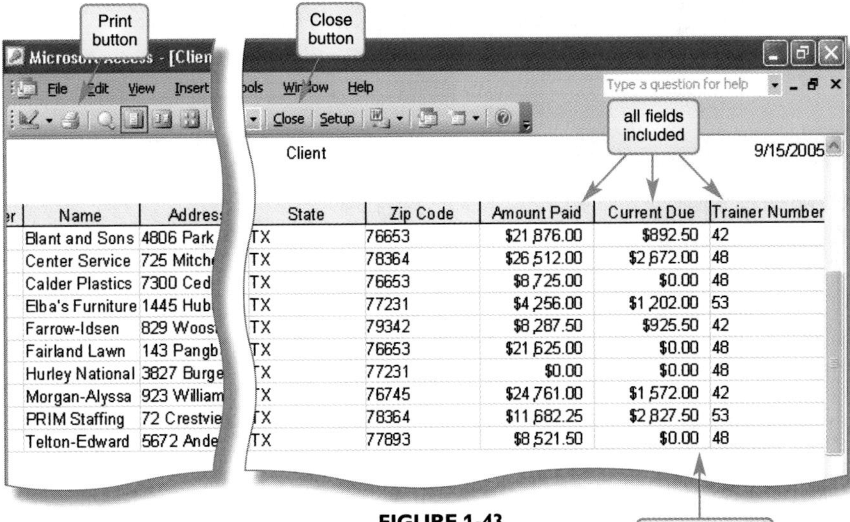

FIGURE 1-43

7

- **Click the Print button to print the report, and then click the Close button on the Print Preview toolbar.**

The report prints. It looks like the report shown in Figure 1-37 on page AC 29. The Print Preview window closes and the Ashton James College : Database window appears.

Creating Additional Tables

A database typically consists of more than one table. The Ashton James College database contains two, the Client table and the Trainer table. You need to repeat the process of creating a table and adding records for each table in the database. In the Ashton James College database, you need to create and add records to the Trainer table. The structure and data for the table are given in Figure 1-44.

Structure of Trainer table

FIELD NAME	DATA TYPE	FIELD SIZE	PRIMARY KEY?	DESCRIPTION
Trainer Number	Text	2	Yes	Trainer Number (Primary Key)
Last Name	Text	10		Last Name of Trainer
First Name	Text	8		First Name of Trainer
Address	Text	15		Street Address
City	Text	15		City
State	Text	2		State (Two-Character Abbreviation)
Zip Code	Text	5		Zip Code (Five-Character Version)
Hourly Rate	Currency			Hourly Rate of Trainer
YTD Earnings	Currency			YTD Earnings of Trainer

Trainer table

TRAINER NUMBER	LAST NAME	FIRST NAME	ADDRESS	CITY	STATE	ZIP CODE	HOURLY RATE	YTD EARNINGS
42	Perry	Belinda	261 Porter	Burdett	TX	76734	$23.00	$27,620.00
48	Stevens	Michael	3135 Gill	Rockwood	TX	78884	$21.00	$23,567.50
53	Gonzalez	Manuel	265 Maxwell	Camino	TX	76574	$24.00	$29,885.00
67	Danville	Marty	1827 Maple	Dunston	TX	77893	$20.00	$0.00

FIGURE 1-44

The following steps show how to create the table.

More About

Printing the Contents of a Table

You can change the margins, paper size, paper source, or the printer that will be used to print the report. To change the margins, select the Margins sheet in the Page Setup dialog box and then enter the appropriate margin size. To change the paper size, paper source, or the printer, select the Page sheet in the Page Setup dialog box, click the appropriate down arrow, and then select the desired option.

To Create an Additional Table

1

• **Make sure the Ashton James College database is open.**

• **Click the New button on the Database window toolbar, click Design View, and then click the OK button.**

• **Enter the data for the fields for the Trainer table from Figure 1-44. Be sure to click the Primary Key button when you enter the Trainer Number field.**

The entries appear (Figure 1-45).

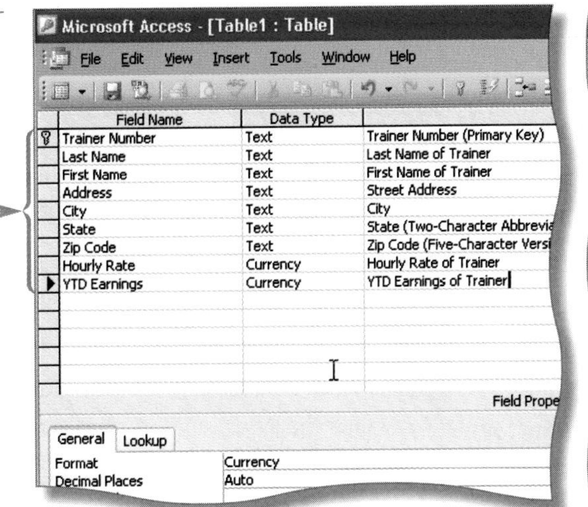

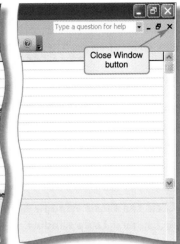

FIGURE 1-45

• **Click the Close Window button, click the Yes button in the Microsoft Office Access dialog box when asked if you want to save the changes, and then type** `Trainer` **as the name of the table.**

The Save As dialog box appears (Figure 1-46). The table name is entered.

• **Click the OK button.**

The table is saved in the Ashton James College database. The window containing the table structure no longer appears.

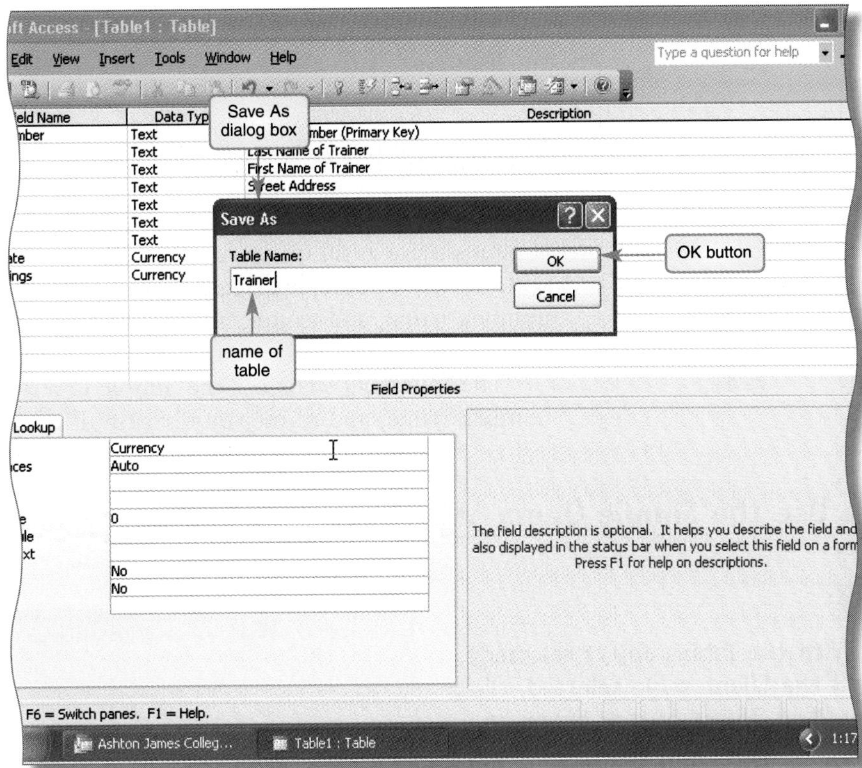

FIGURE 1-46

Adding Records to the Additional Table

Now that you have created the Trainer table, use the steps on the next page to add records to it.

To Add Records to an Additional Table

1

• **Right-click the Trainer table, and then click Open on the shortcut menu. Enter the Trainer data from Figure 1-44 on page AC 32 into the Trainer table.**

The datasheet displays the entered records (Figure 1-47).

2

• **Click the Close Window button for the Trainer : Table window.**

Access closes the table and removes the datasheet from the screen.

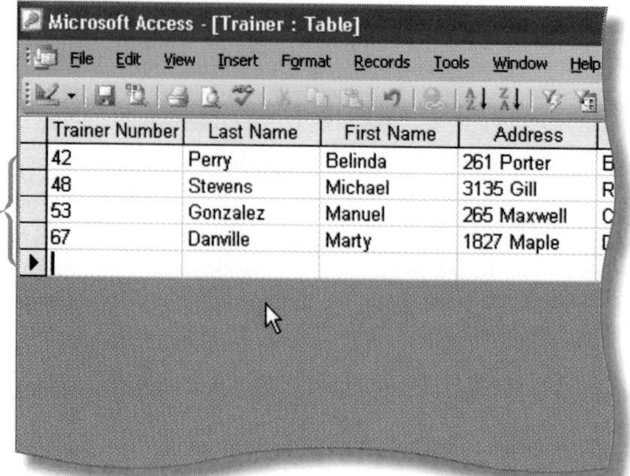

Microsoft Access - [Trainer : Table]
all records entered
Trainer Number
Last Name
First Name
Address
42
Perry
Belinda
261 Porter
48
Stevens
Michael
3135 Gill
53
Gonzalez
Manuel
265 Maxwell
67
Danville
Marty
1827 Maple

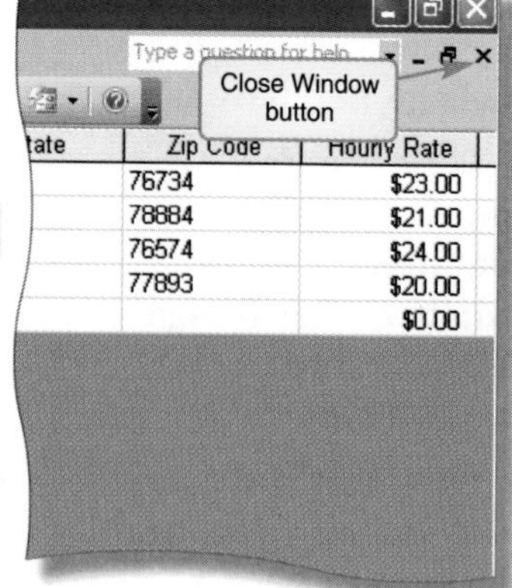

FIGURE 1-47

The records are now in the table.

Using Queries

Queries are simply questions, the answers to which are in the database. Access contains a powerful query feature. Through the use of this feature, you can ask a wide variety of complex questions. For simple requests, however, such as listing the number, name, and trainer number of all clients, you do not need to use the query feature, but instead can use the Simple Query wizard.

The following steps use the Simple Query wizard to create a query to display the number, name, and trainer number of all clients.

To Use the Simple Query Wizard to Create a Query

1

• **With the Tables object selected and the Client table selected, click the New Object button arrow on the Database toolbar.**

A list of objects that can be created is displayed (Figure 1-48).

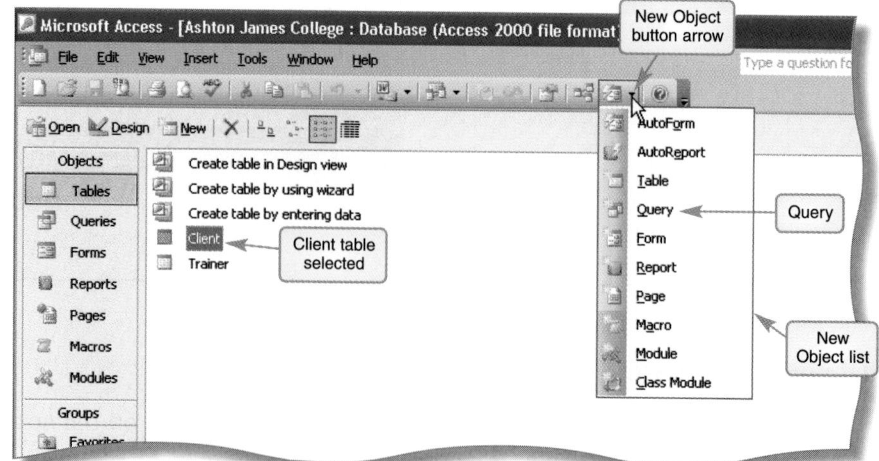

FIGURE 1-48

2

- **Click Query on the New Object list.**

The New Query dialog box appears (Figure 1-49).

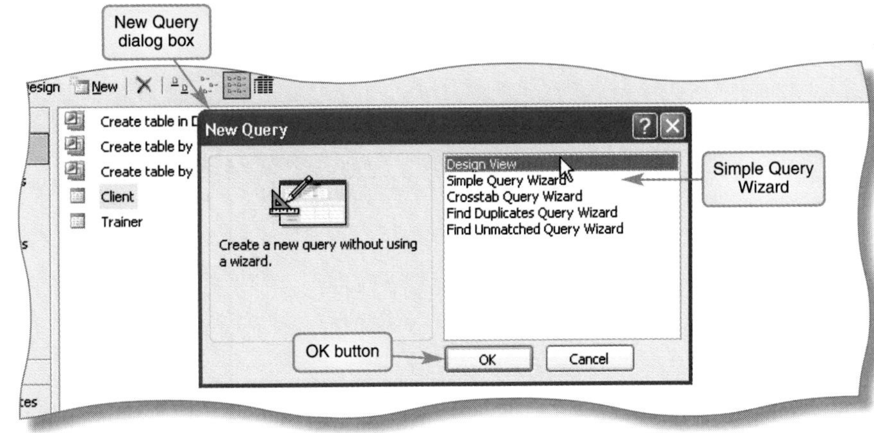

FIGURE 1-49

3

- **Click Simple Query Wizard, and then click the OK button.**

Access displays the Simple Query Wizard dialog box (Figure 1-50). It contains a list of available fields and a list of selected fields. Currently no fields are selected for the query.

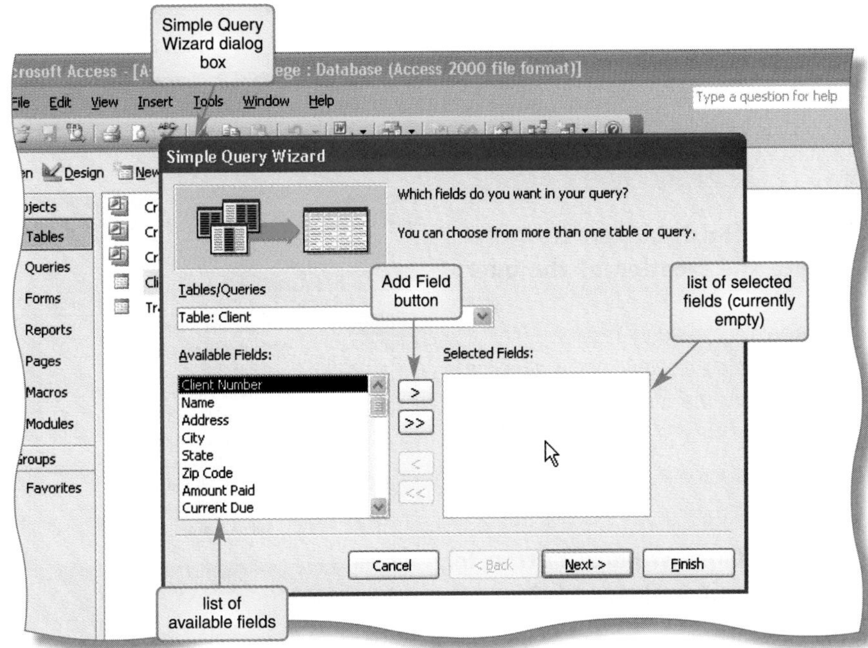

FIGURE 1-50

4

- **Click the Add Field button to add the Client Number field.**
- **Click the Add Field button a second time to add the Name field.**
- **Click the Trainer Number field, and then click the Add Field button to add the Trainer Number field.**

The fields are selected (Figure 1-51).

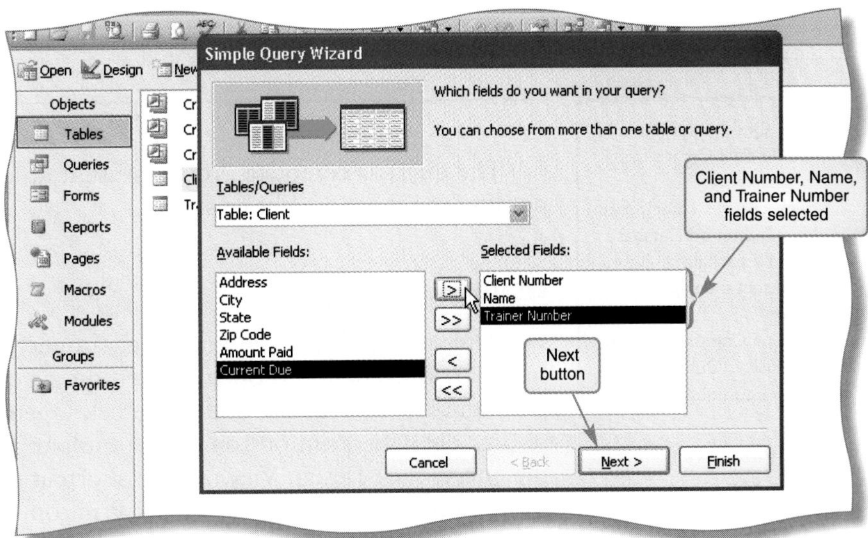

FIGURE 1-51

5

• **Click the Next button, and then type** `Client-Trainer Query` **as the name for the query.**

The Simple Query Wizard dialog box displays the new query name (Figure 1-52).

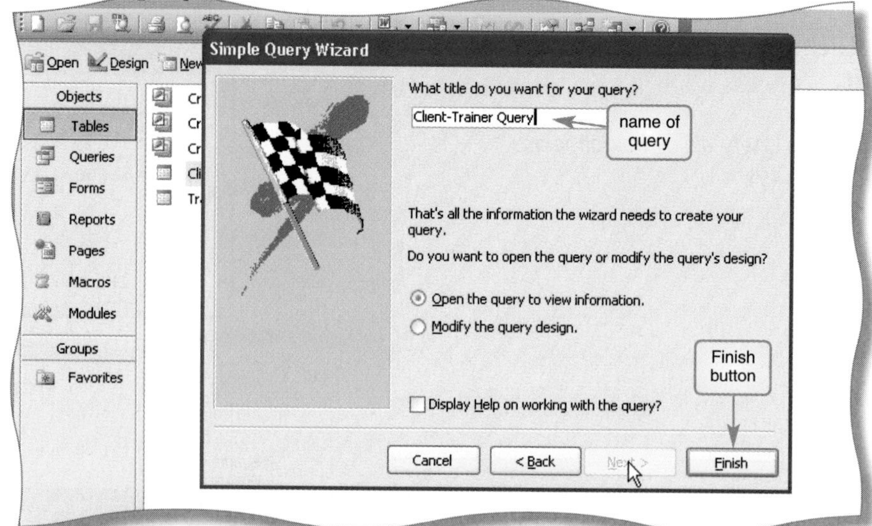

FIGURE 1-52

6

• **Click the Finish button to complete the creation of the query.**

Access displays the query results (Figure 1-53). The results contain all records, but only contain the Client Number, Name, and Trainer Number fields.

7

• **Click the Close Window button for the Client-Trainer Query : Select Query window.**

Access closes the query and the Ashton James College : Database window appears.

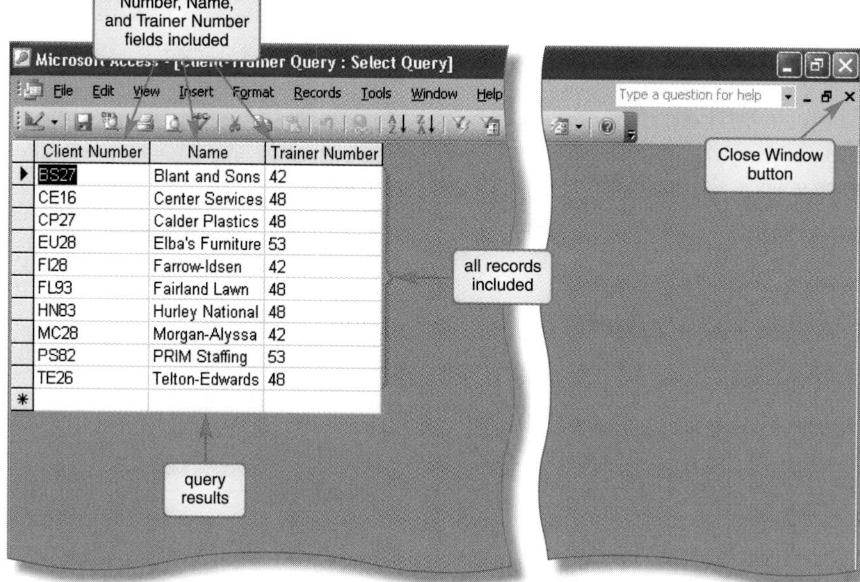

FIGURE 1-53

Other Ways

1. Click Queries object, double-click Create query by using wizard
2. Click Queries object, click New button on Database window toolbar
3. On Insert menu click Query
4. In Voice Command mode, say "Insert, Query"

The query is complete. You can use it at any time you like in the future without needing to repeat the above steps.

Using a Query

After you have created and saved a query, you can use it at any time in the future by opening it. To open a saved query, click the Queries object on the Objects bar, right-click the query, and then click Open on the shortcut menu. To print the results, click the Print button on the toolbar. If you want to change the design of the query, click Design View on the shortcut menu rather than Open. To print the query without first opening it, click Print on the shortcut menu.

You often want to restrict the records that are included. For example, you might only want to include those clients whose trainer number is 42. In such a case, you need to enter the 42 as a **criterion**, which is a condition that the records to be included must satisfy. To do so, you will open the query in Design view, enter the criterion below the appropriate field, and then run the query. The following steps show how to enter a criterion to include only clients of trainer 42 and then run the query.

To Use a Query

1

- **If necessary, click the Queries object. Right-click the Client-Trainer Query.**

The shortcut menu for the Client-Trainer Query is displayed (Figure 1-54).

Queries object selected

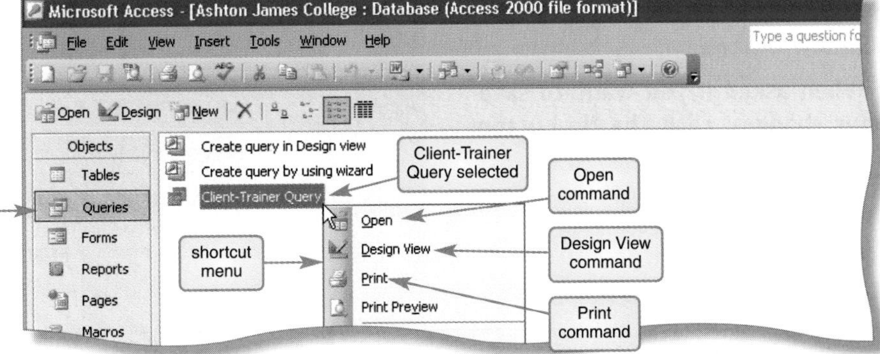

FIGURE 1-54

2

- **Click Design View on the shortcut menu.**

The query appears in Design view (Figure 1-55).

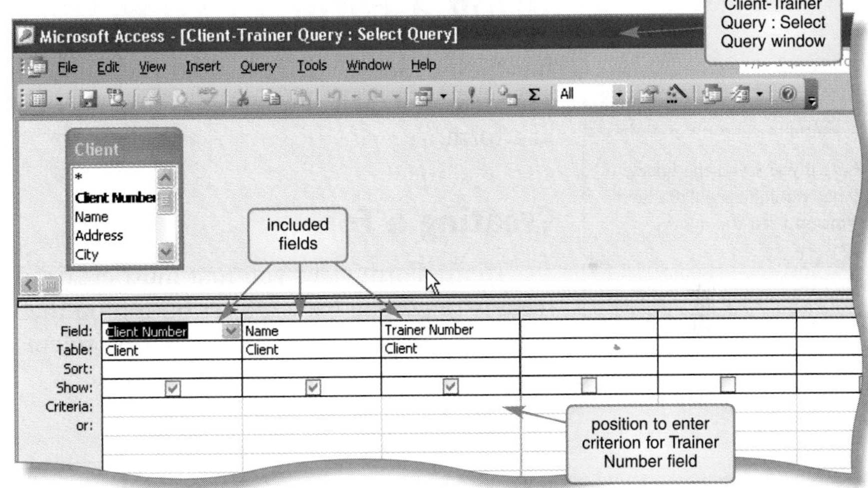

FIGURE 1-55

3

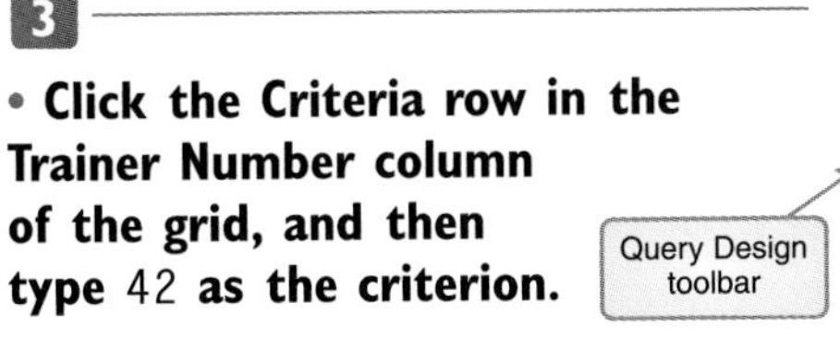

- **Click the Criteria row in the Trainer Number column of the grid, and then type** 42 **as the criterion.**

The criterion is typed (Figure 1-56).

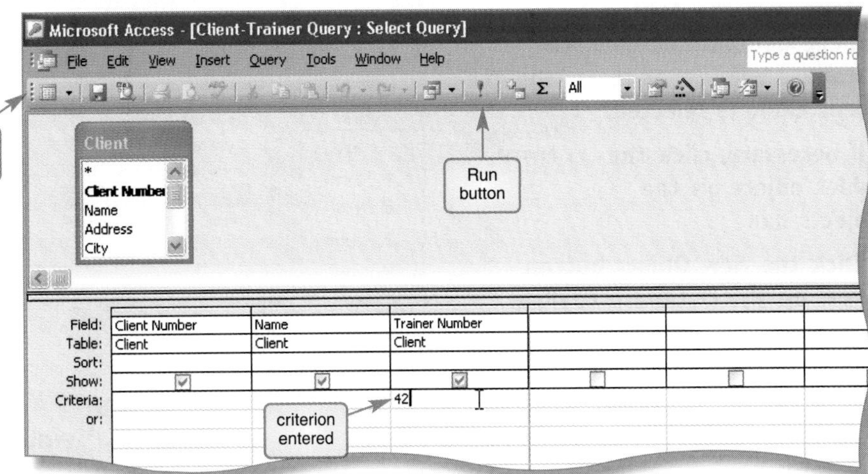

FIGURE 1-56

4

• **Click the Run button on the Query Design toolbar.**

Access displays the results (Figure 1-57). Only the clients of trainer 42 are included.

5

• **Close the window containing the query results by clicking its Close Window button.**

• **When asked if you want to save your changes, click the No button.**

The results no longer appear. The changes to the query are not saved.

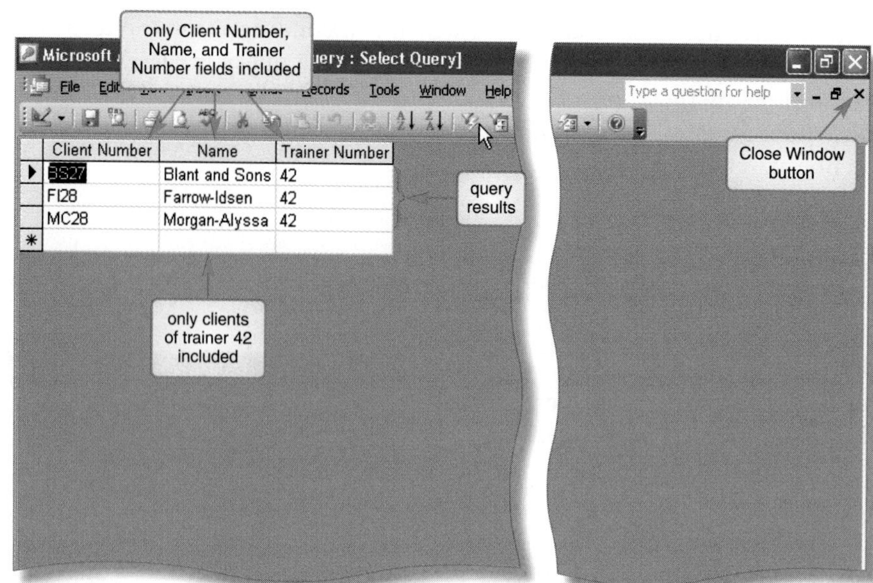

FIGURE 1-57

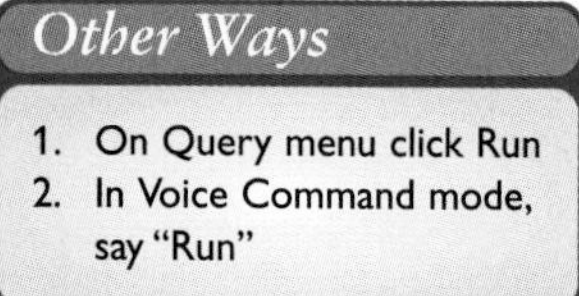

Other Ways

1. On Query menu click Run
2. In Voice Command mode, say "Run"

Using a Form to View Data

In creating tables, you have used Datasheet view; that is, the data on the screen appeared as a table. You also can use **Form view**, in which you see data contained in a form.

Q&A

Q: If you saved the query, what would happen the next time you ran the query?

A: You would see only clients of trainer 42.

Creating a Form

To use Form view, you first must create a form. The simplest way to create a form is to use the New Object button on the Database toolbar. The following steps illustrate using the New Object button to create a form for the Client table.

To Use the New Object Button to Create a Form

1

• **Make sure the Ashton James College database is open, the Database window appears, and the Client table is selected.**

• **If necessary, click the Tables object on the Objects bar.**

• **Click the New Object button arrow on the Database toolbar.**

A list of objects that can be created appears (Figure 1-58).

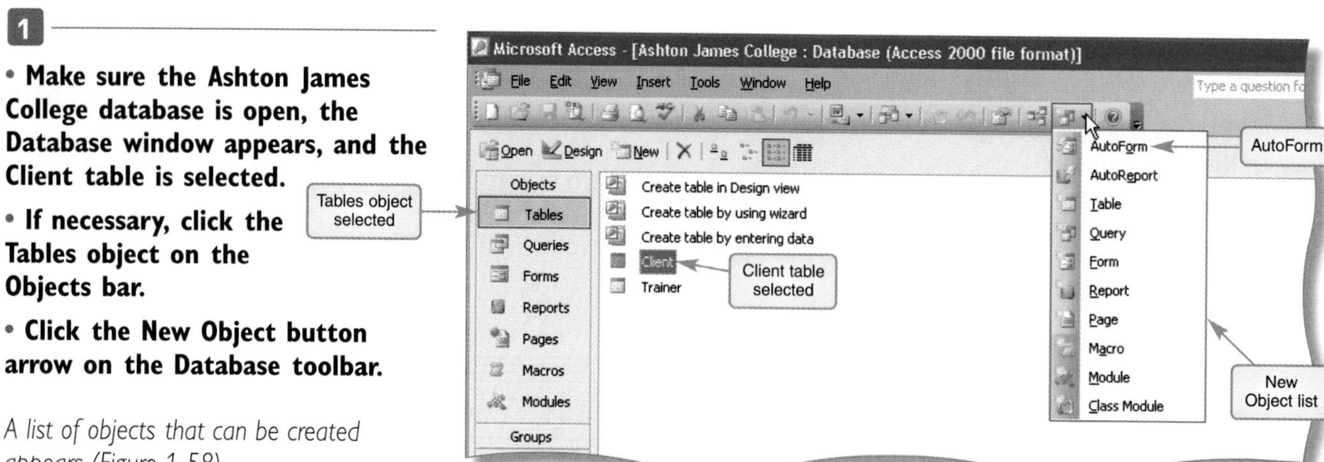

FIGURE 1-58

2

• **Click AutoForm on the New Object list.**

After a brief delay, the form appears (Figure 1-59). If you do not move the mouse pointer after clicking the New Object button, the ScreenTip for the Properties button may appear when the form opens. Access displays the Formatting toolbar when a form is created. (When you close the form, this toolbar no longer appears.)

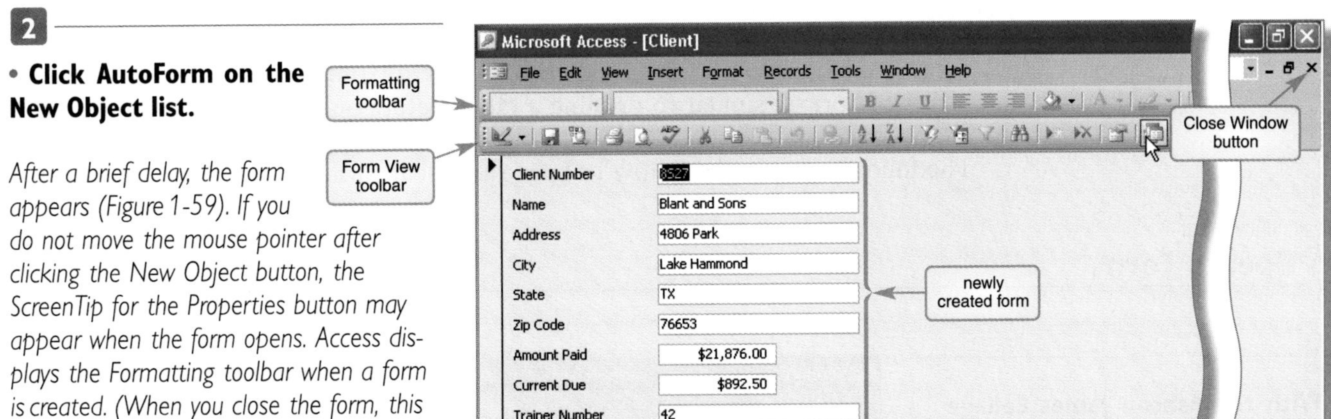

FIGURE 1-59

Other Ways

1. On Insert menu click AutoForm
2. In Voice Command mode, say "New Object, AutoForm"
3. In Voice Command mode, say "Insert, AutoForm"

Closing and Saving the Form

Closing a form is similar to closing a table. The only difference is that you will be asked if you want to save the form unless you previously have saved it. The following steps close the form and save it as Client.

To Close and Save a Form

1

• **Click the Close Window button for the Client window (see Figure 1-59).**

Access displays the Microsoft Office Access dialog box (Figure 1-60).

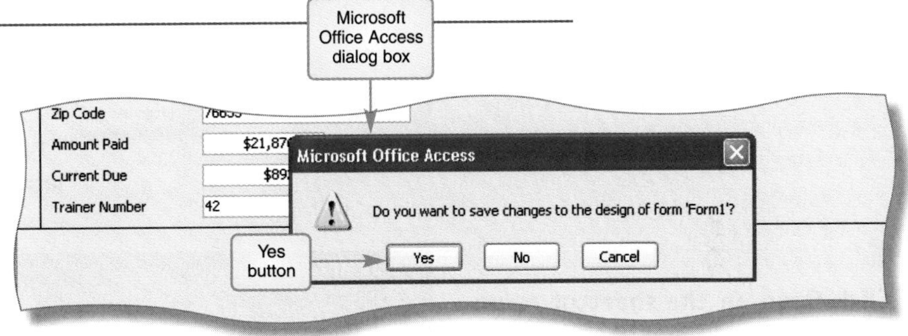

FIGURE 1-60

2

• **Click the Yes button.**

The Save As dialog box appears (Figure 1-61). The name of the table (Client) becomes the name of the form automatically. This name could be changed, if desired.

3

• **Click the OK button.**

The form is saved as part of the database and the form closes. The Ashton James College : Database window is redisplayed.

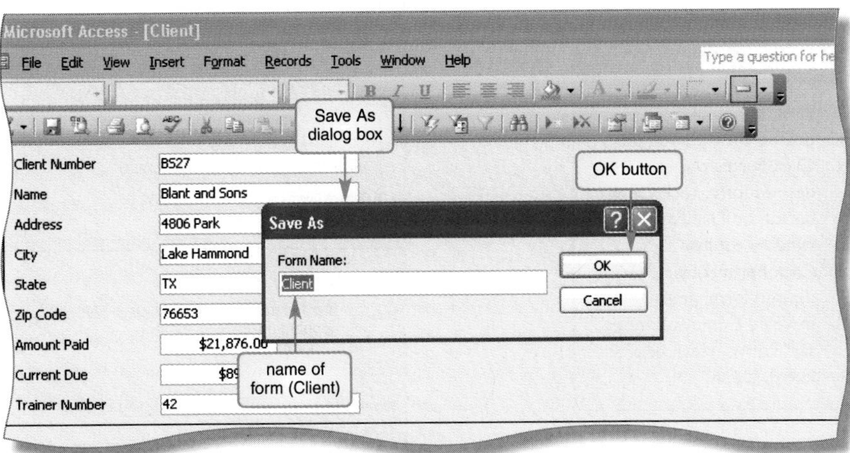

FIGURE 1-61

Opening the Saved Form

After you have saved a form, you can use it at any time in the future by opening it. Opening a form is similar to opening a table. Before opening the form, however, the Forms object, rather than the Tables object, must be selected.

The following steps show how to open the Client form.

To Open a Form

1

- **With the Ashton James College database open and the Database window on the screen, click Forms on the Objects bar, and then right-click the Client form.**

The list of forms appears (Figure 1-62). The shortcut menu for the Client form appears.

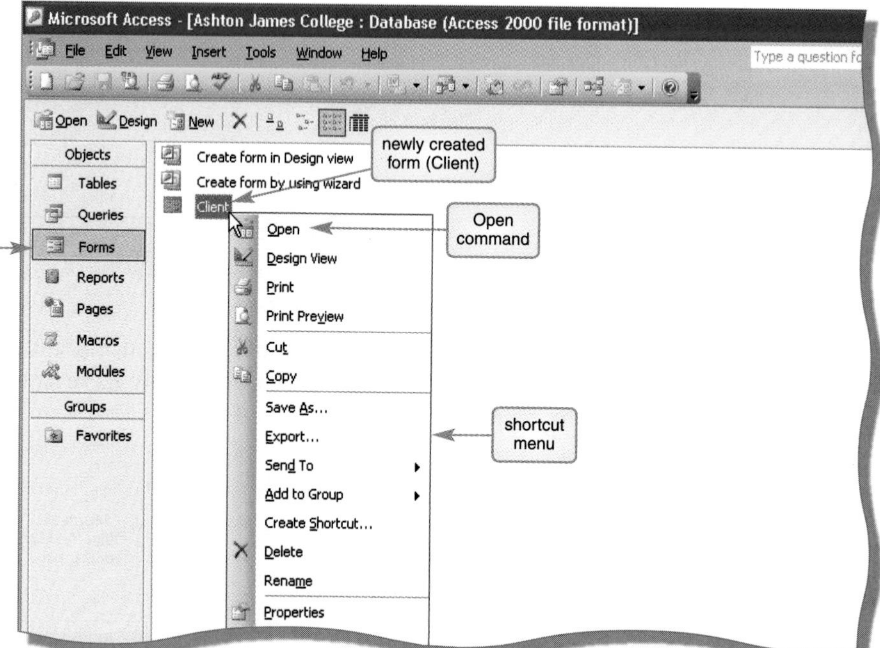

FIGURE 1-62

2

- **Click Open on the shortcut menu.**

The Client form appears (Figure 1-63).

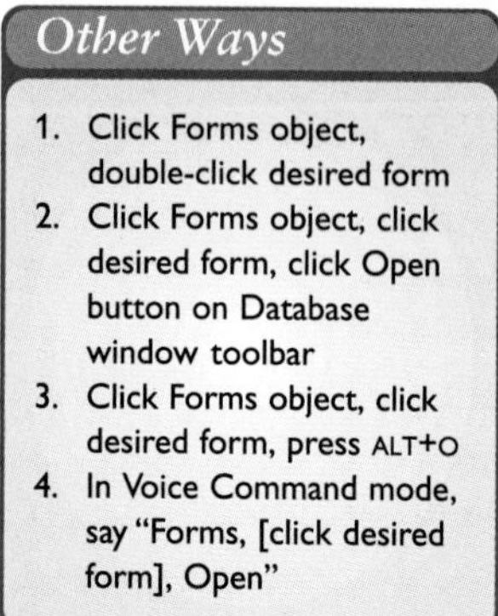

Other Ways
1. Click Forms object, double-click desired form
2. Click Forms object, click desired form, click Open button on Database window toolbar
3. Click Forms object, click desired form, press ALT+O
4. In Voice Command mode, say "Forms, [click desired form], Open"

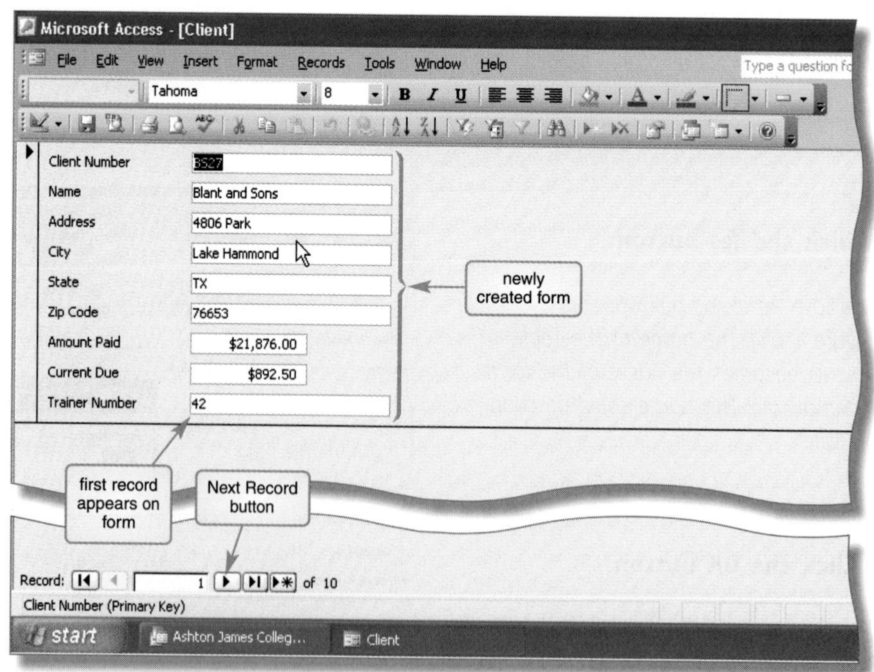

FIGURE 1-63

Using the Form

You can use the form just as you used Datasheet view. You use the Navigation buttons to move between records. You can add new records or change existing ones. To delete the record appearing on the screen, after selecting the record by clicking its record selector, press the DELETE key. Thus, you can perform database operations using either Form view or Datasheet view.

Because you can see only one record at a time in Form view, to see a different record, such as the fifth record, you must use the Navigation buttons to move to it. The following step illustrates moving from record to record in Form view.

To Use a Form

- **Click the Next Record button four times.**

Access displays the fifth record on the form (Figure 1-64).

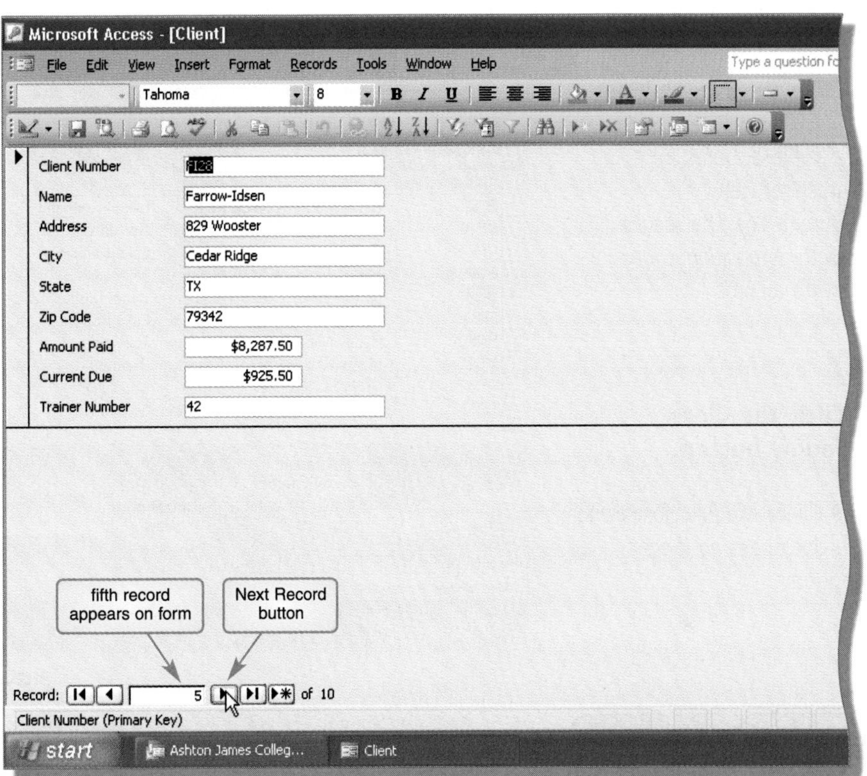

FIGURE 1-64

Switching Between Form View and Datasheet View

In some cases, after you have seen a record in Form view, you will want to switch to Datasheet view to see the collection of records. The steps on the next page show how to switch from Form view to Datasheet view.

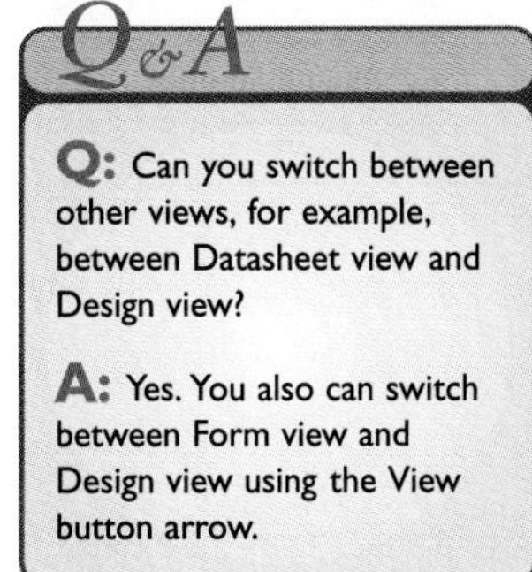

Q&A

Q: Can you switch between other views, for example, between Datasheet view and Design view?

A: Yes. You also can switch between Form view and Design view using the View button arrow.

To Switch from Form View to Datasheet View

1

• **Click the View button arrow on the Form View toolbar.**

The list of available views appears (Figure 1-65).

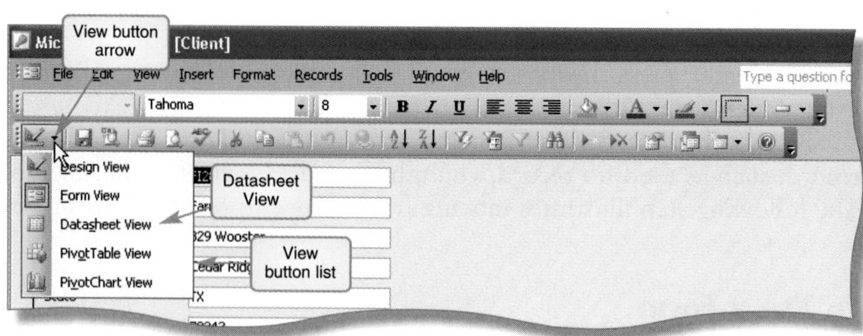

FIGURE 1-65

2

• **Click Datasheet View.**

The table appears in Datasheet view (Figure 1-66). The record selector is positioned on the fifth record.

3

• **Click the Close Window button.**

The Client window closes and the datasheet no longer appears.

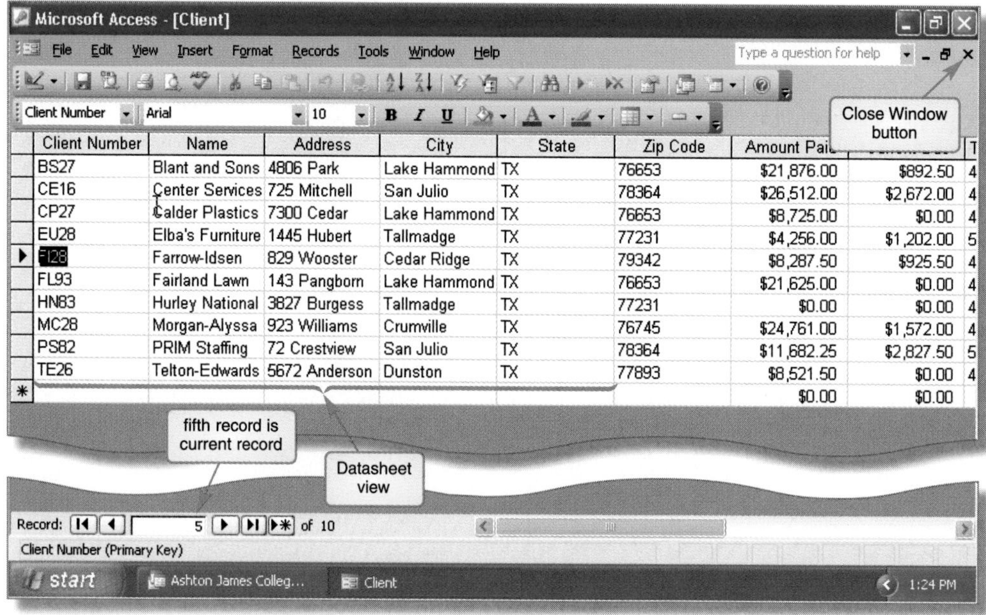

FIGURE 1-66

Other Ways

1. On View menu click Datasheet View
2. In Voice Command mode, say "View, Datasheet View"

Creating a Report

Earlier in this project, you printed a table using the Print button. The report you produced was shown in Figure 1-37 on page AC 29. While this type of report presented the data in an organized manner, the format is very rigid. You cannot select the fields to appear, for example; the report automatically includes all the fields and they appear in precisely the same order as in the table. A way to change the title of the table is not available. Therefore, it will be the same as the name of the table.

In this section, you will create the report shown in Figure 1-67. This report features significant differences from the one in Figure 1-37. The portion at the top of the report in Figure 1-67, called a **page header**, contains a custom title. The contents of this page header appear at the top of each page. The **detail lines**, which are the lines that are printed for each record, contain only those fields you specify and in the order you specify.

Client Amount Report

Client Number	Name	Amount Paid	Current Due
BS27	Blant and Sons	$21,876.00	$892.50
CE16	Center Services	$26,512.00	$2,672.00
CP27	Calder Plastics	$8,725.00	$0.00
EU28	Elba's Furniture	$4,256.00	$1,202.00
FI28	Farrow-Idsen	$8,287.50	$925.50
FL93	Fairland Lawn	$21,625.00	$0.00
HN83	Hurley National	$0.00	$0.00
MC28	Morgan-Alyssa	$24,761.00	$1,572.00
PS82	PRIM Staffing	$11,682.25	$2,827.50
TE26	Telton-Edwards	$8,521.50	$0.00

FIGURE 1-67

The following steps show how to create the report in Figure 1-67.

To Create a Report

1

- **Click Tables on the Objects bar, and then make sure the Client table is selected.**
- **Click the New Object button arrow on the Database toolbar.**

The list of available objects appears (Figure 1-68).

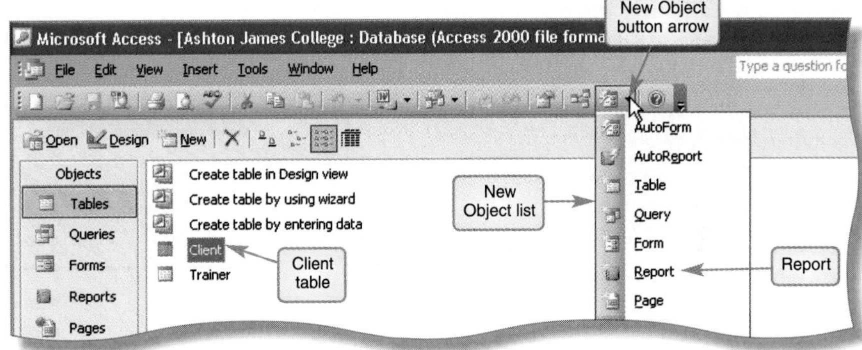

FIGURE 1-68

2

- **Click Report.**

Access displays the New Report dialog box (Figure 1-69).

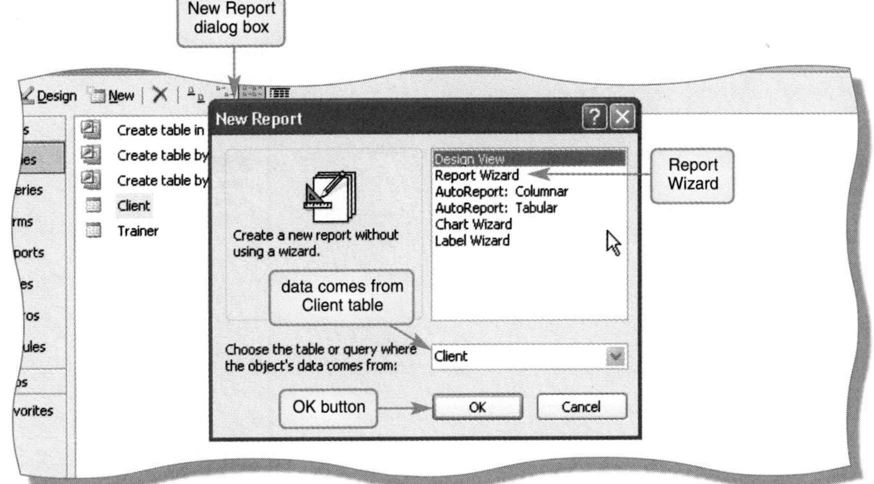

FIGURE 1-69

3

- **Click Report Wizard, and then click the OK button.**

Access displays the Report Wizard dialog box (Figure 1-70). As you click the Next button in this dialog box, a series of options helps you create the report.

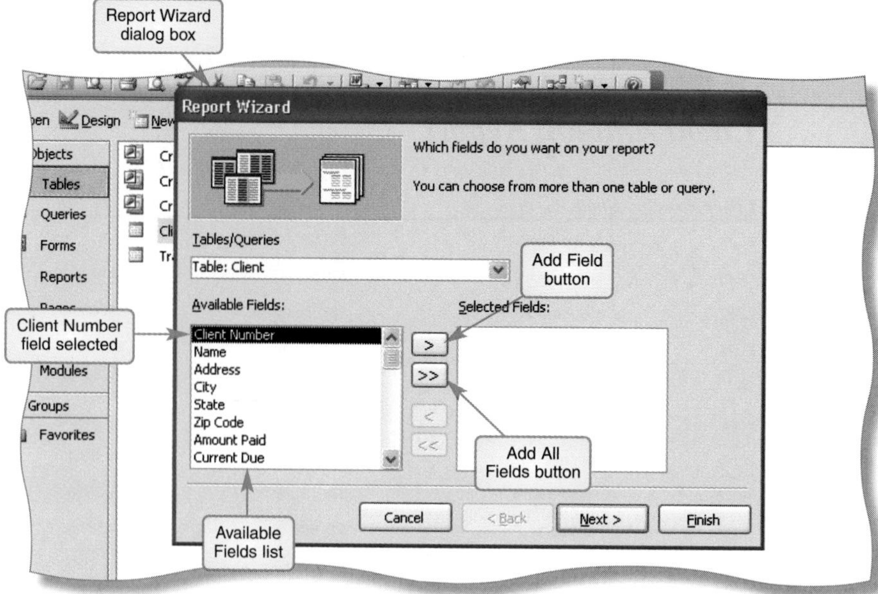

FIGURE 1-70

4

- **Click the Add Field button to add the Client Number field.**
- **Click the Add Field button to add the Name field.**
- **Add the Amount Paid and Current Due fields by clicking each field and then clicking the Add Field button.**

The fields for the report appear in the Selected Fields box (Figure 1-71).

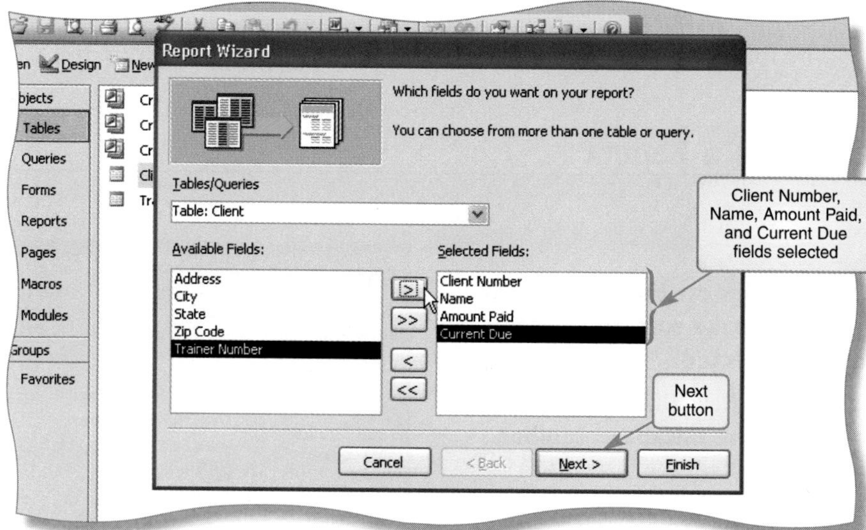

FIGURE 1-71

5

- **Click the Next button.**

The Report Wizard dialog box displays options to specify any grouping that is to take place (Figure 1-72).

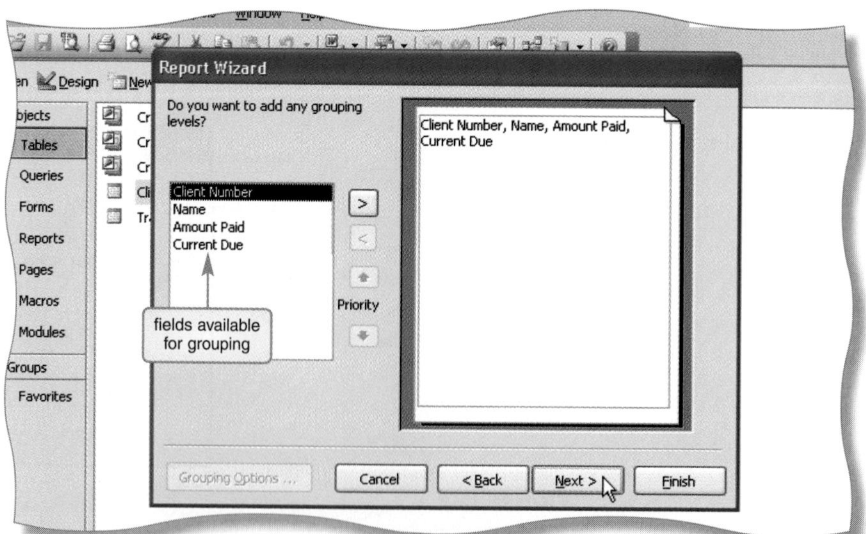

FIGURE 1-72

6

- **Because you will not specify any grouping, click the Next button in the Report Wizard dialog box.**
- **Click the Next button a second time because you will not need to change the sort order for the records.**

The Report Wizard dialog box displays options for changing the layout and orientation of the report (Figure 1-73).

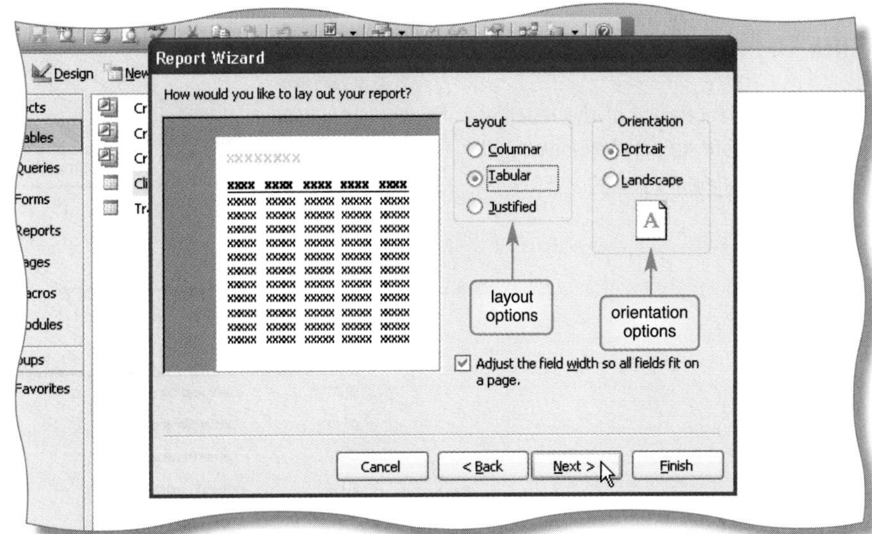

FIGURE 1-73

7

- **Make sure that Tabular is selected as the Layout and Portrait is selected as the Orientation, and then click the Next button.**

The Report Wizard dialog box displays options you can select for the style of the report (Figure 1-74).

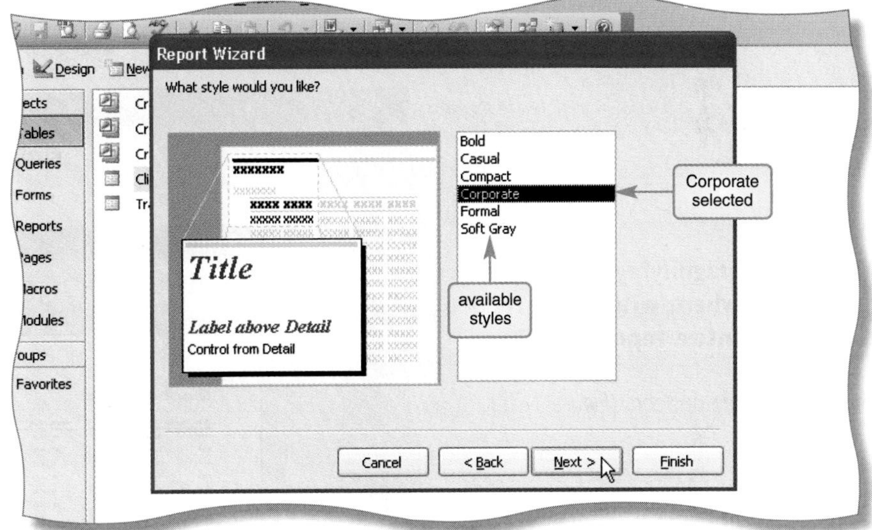

FIGURE 1-74

8

- **Be sure the Corporate style is selected, click the Next button, and then type** `Client Amount Report` **as the new title.**

The Report Wizard dialog box displays the new title of the report (Figure 1-75).

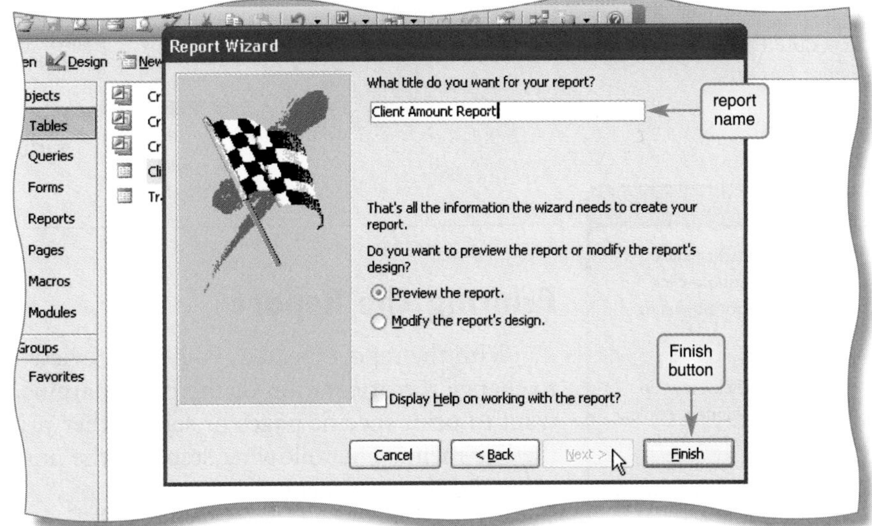

FIGURE 1-75

9

• **Click the Finish button.**

Access displays a preview of the report (Figure 1-76). Your report may look slightly different, depending on your printer.

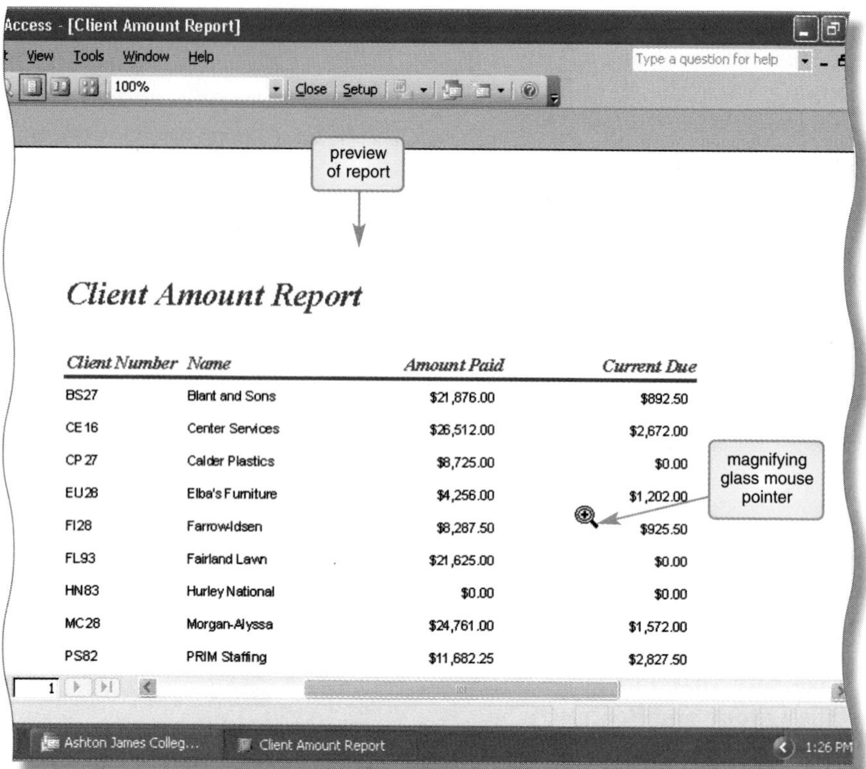

FIGURE 1-76

• **Click the magnifying glass mouse pointer anywhere within the report to see the entire report.**

The entire report appears (Figure 1-77).

• **Click the Close Window button in the Client Amount Report window.**

The report no longer appears. It has been saved automatically using the name Client Amount Report.

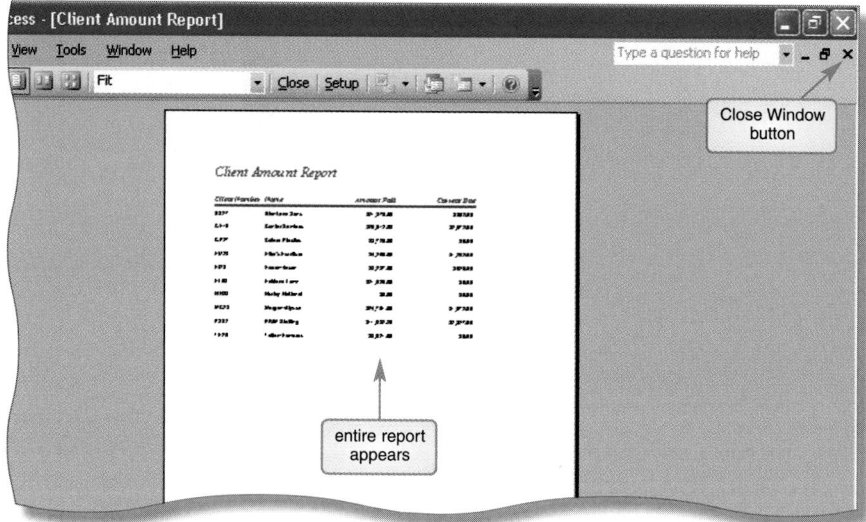

FIGURE 1-77

Other Ways

1. On Objects bar click Reports, double-click Create report by using wizard
2. On Objects bar click Reports, click New on Database window toolbar
3. On Insert menu click Report
4. In Voice Command mode, say "Insert, Report"

Printing the Report

With the report created, you can preview the report to determine if you need to change the orientation or the page margins. You also can print the report. If you want to print specific pages or select other print options, use the Print command on the File menu. The following steps on the next page show how to print a report using the shortcut menu.

To Print a Report

1

- **If necessary, click Reports on the Objects bar in the Database window.**
- **Right-click the Client Amount Report.**

The Client Amount Report is selected and the shortcut menu appears (Figure 1-78).

2

- **Click Print on the shortcut menu.**

The report prints. It should look similar to the one shown in Figure 1-67 on page AC 43.

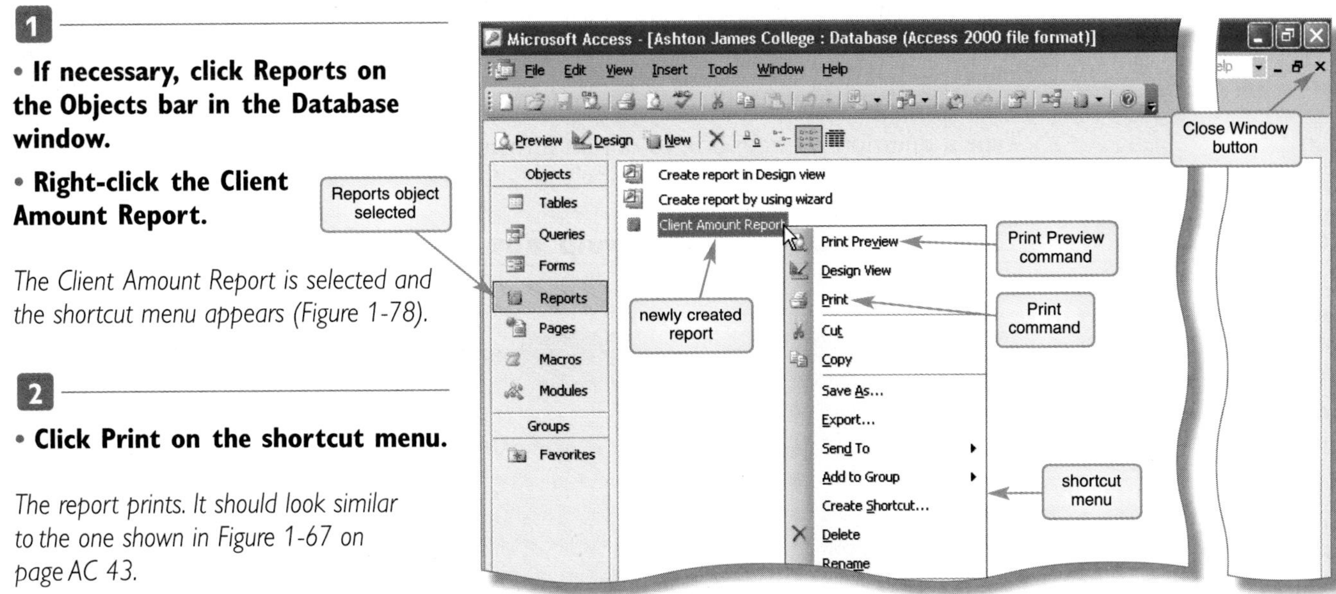

FIGURE 1-78

Closing the Database

After you have finished working with a database, you should close it. The following step closes the database by closing its Database window.

To Close a Database

1 **Click the Close Window button for the Ashton James College : Database window.**

Access Help System

At any time while you are using Access, you can get answers to questions by using the Access Help system. You can activate the Access Help system by using the Type a question for help box on the menu bar, by clicking the Microsoft Access Help button on the toolbar, or by clicking Help on the menu bar (Figure 1-79 on the next page). Used properly, this form of online assistance can increase your productivity and reduce your frustrations by minimizing the time you spend learning how to use Access.

The section on the next page shows how to get answers to your questions using the Type a question for help box. Additional information about using the Access Help system is available in Appendix A.

More About

The Access Help System

The best way to become familiar with the Access Help system is to use it. Appendix A includes detailed information on the Access Help system and exercises that will help you gain confidence in using it.

Obtaining Help Using the Type a Question for Help Box on the Menu Bar

The Type a question for help box on the right side of the menu bar lets you type in free-form questions, such as *how do I save* or *how do I create a Web page* or, you can type in terms, such as *copy*, *save*, or *formatting*. Access responds by displaying a list of topics related to what you entered. The following steps show how to use the Type a question for help box to obtain information on removing a primary key.

To Obtain Help Using the Type a Question for Help Box

1

- **Click the Type a question for help box on the right side of the menu bar.**
- **Type** how do I remove a primary key **in the box (Figure 1-79).**

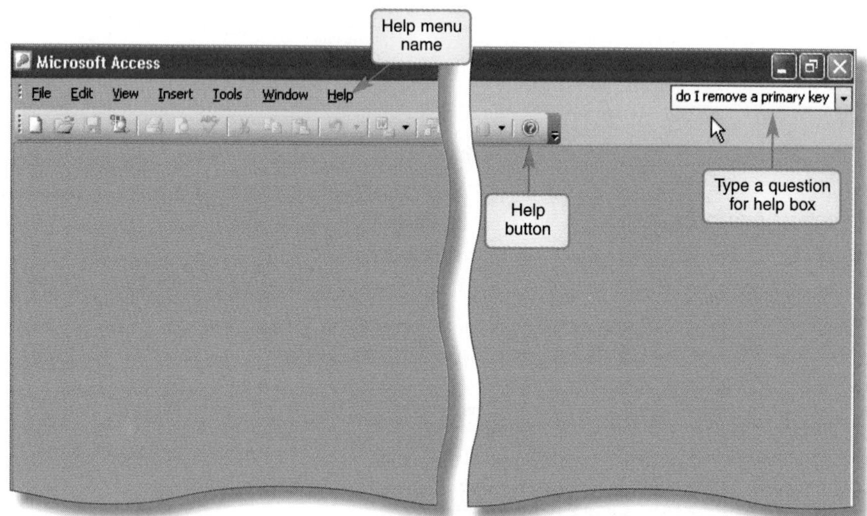

FIGURE 1-79

2

- **Press the ENTER key.**

Access displays the Search Results task pane, which includes a list of topics relating to the question, how do I remove a primary key (Figure 1-80). Your list may be different.

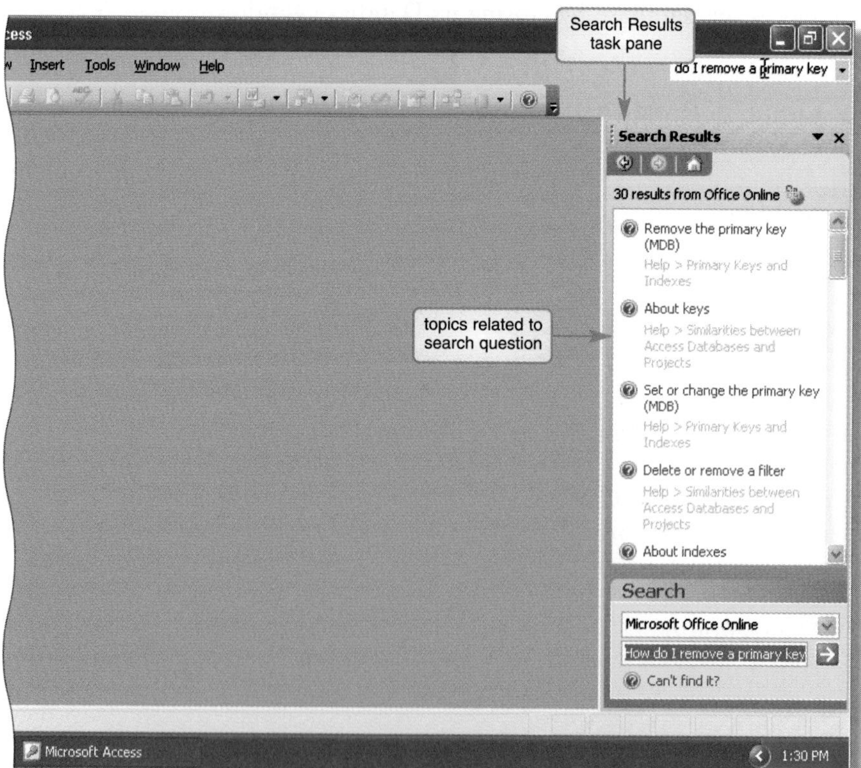

FIGURE 1-80

3

• **Point to the Remove the primary key (MDB) topic.**

The mouse pointer changes to a hand indicating it is pointing to a link (Figure 1-81).

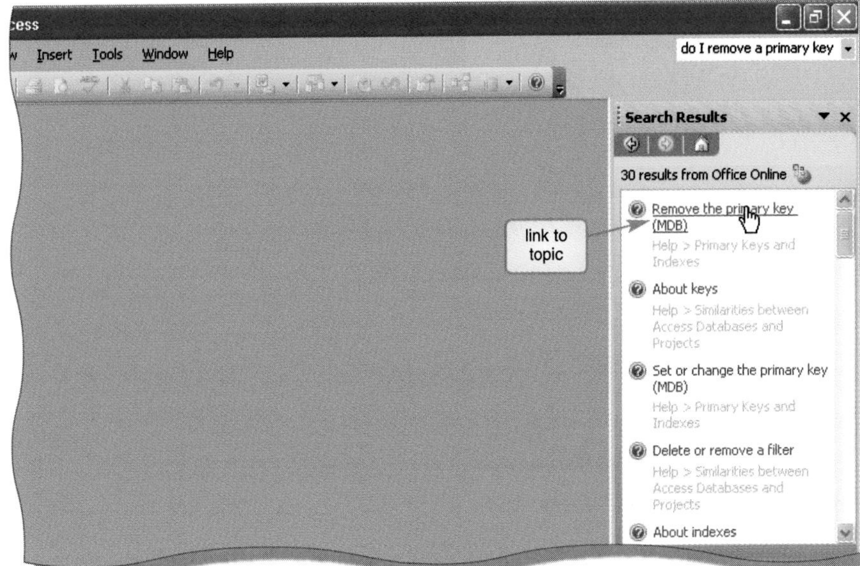

FIGURE 1-81

4

• **Click Remove the primary key (MDB).**

Access displays a Microsoft Office Access Help window that provides Help information about removing the primary key (Figure 1-82). Your window may be in a different position.

• **Click the Close button on the Microsoft Office Access Help window title bar.**

The Microsoft Access Help window closes.

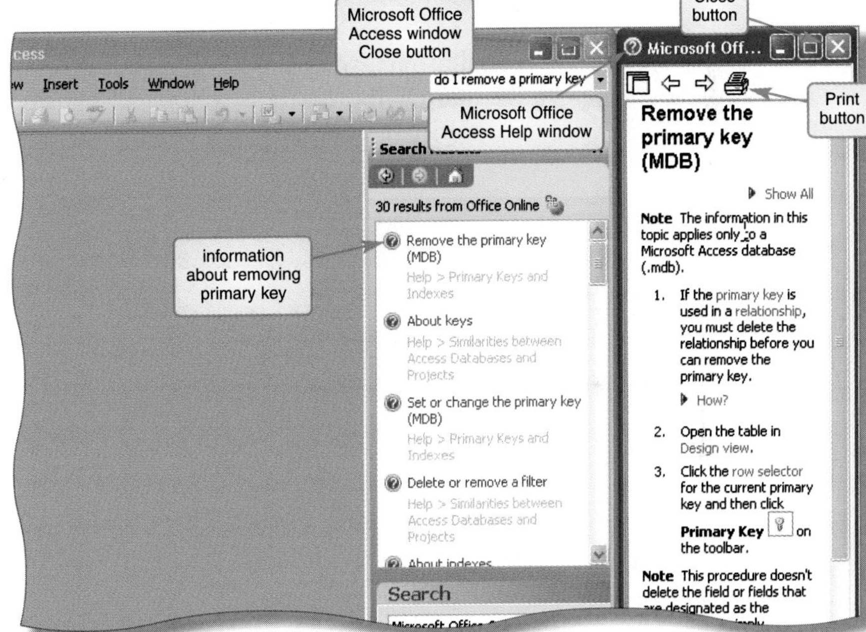

FIGURE 1-82

Use the buttons in the upper-left corner of the Microsoft Office Access Help window (Figure 1-82) to navigate through the Help system, and change the appearance and print the contents of the window.

As you enter questions and terms in the Type a question for help box, Access adds them to its list. Thus, if you click the Type a question for help box arrow, a list of previously asked questions and terms will appear.

Quitting Access

After you close a database, you can open another database, create a new database, or simply quit Access and return to the Windows desktop. The following step quits Access.

To Quit Access

1. **Click the Close button in the Microsoft Access window (see Figure 1-82 on the previous page).**

More About

Database Design: Design Method

A variety of methods have been developed for designing complex databases given a set of input and output requirements. For more information about database design methods, visit the Access 2003 More About Web page (scsite.com/ac2003/more) and click Database Design.

Designing a Database

Database design refers to the arrangement of data into tables and fields. In the example in this project, the design is specified, but in many cases, you will have to determine the design based on what you want the system to accomplish.

With large, complex databases, the database design process can be extensive. Major sections of advanced database textbooks are devoted to this topic. Often, however, you should be able to design a database effectively by keeping one simple principle in mind: design to remove redundancy. **Redundancy** means storing the same fact in more than one place.

To illustrate, you need to maintain the following information shown in Figure 1-83. In the figure, all the data is contained in a single table. Notice that the data for a given trainer (number, name, address, and so on) occurs on more than one record.

Client table

duplicate trainer names

CLIENT NUMBER	NAME	ADDRESS	...	CURRENT DUE	TRAINER NUMBER	LAST NAME	FIRST NAME	...
BS27	Blant and Sons	4806 Park	...	$892.50	42	Perry	Belinda	...
CE16	Center Services	725 Mitchell	...	$2,672.00	48	Stevens	Michael	...
CP27	Calder Plastics	7300 Cedar	...	$0.00	48	Stevens	Michael	...
EU28	Elba's Furniture	1445 Hubert	...	$1,202.00	53	Gonzalez	Manuel	...
FI28	Farrow-Idsen	829 Wooster	...	$925.50	42	Perry	Belinda	...
FL93	Fairland Lawn	143 Pangborn	...	$0.00	48	Stevens	Michael	
HN83	Hurley National	3827 Burgess	...	$0.00	48	Stevens	Michael	
MC28	Morgan-Alyssa	923 Williams	...	$1,572.00	42	Perry	Belinda	...
PS82	PRIM Staffing	72 Crestview	...	$2,827.50	53	Gonzalez	Manuel	
TE26	Telton-Edwards	5672 Anderson	...	$0.00	48	Stevens	Michael	

FIGURE 1-83

More About

The Quick Reference

For a table that lists how to complete tasks covered in this book using the mouse, menu, shortcut menu, and keyboard, see the Quick Reference Summary at the back of this book, or visit the Access 2003 Quick Reference Web page (scsite.com/ac2003/qr).

Storing this data on multiple records is an example of redundancy, which causes several problems, including:

1. Redundancy wastes space on the disk. The name of trainer 42 (Belinda Perry), for example, should be stored only once. Storing this fact several times is wasteful.
2. Redundancy makes updating the database more difficult. If, for example, Belinda Perry's name changes, her name would need to be changed in several different places.

3. A possibility of inconsistent data exists. If, for example, you change the name of Belinda Perry on client FI28's record to Belinda Martin, but do not change it on client BS27's record, the data is inconsistent. In both cases, the trainer number is 42, but the names are different.

The solution to the problem is to place the redundant data in a separate table, one in which the data no longer will be redundant. If, for example, you place the data for trainers in a separate table (Figure 1-84), the data for each trainer will appear only once.

More About

Database Design: Normalization

A special technique, called normalization, identifies and eliminates redundancy. For more information about normalization, visit the Access 2003 More About Web page (scsite.com/ac2003/more) and click Normalization.

trainer data is in separate table

Trainer table

TRAINER NUMBER	LAST NAME	FIRST NAME	ADDRESS	CITY	STATE	ZIP CODE	HOURLY RATE	YTD EARNINGS
42	Perry	Belinda	261 Porter	Burdett	TX	76734	$23.00	$27,620.00
48	Stevens	Michael	3135 Gill	Rockwood	TX	78884	$21.00	$23,567.50
53	Gonzalez	Manuel	265 Maxwell	Camino	TX	76574	$24.00	$29,885.00

Client table

CLIENT NUMBER	NAME	ADDRESS	CITY	STATE	ZIP CODE	AMOUNT PAID	CURRENT DUE	TRAINER NUMBER
BS27	Blant and Sons	4806 Park	Lake Hammond	TX	76653	$21,876.00	$892.50	42
CE16	Center Services	725 Mitchell	San Julio	TX	78364	$26,512.00	$2,672.00	48
CP27	Calder Plastics	7300 Cedar	Lake Hammond	TX	76653	$8,725.00	$0.00	48
EU28	Elba's Furniture	1445 Hubert	Tallmadge	TX	77231	$4,256.00	$1,202.00	53
FI28	Farrow-Idsen	829 Wooster	Cedar Ridge	TX	79342	$8,287.50	$925.50	42
FL93	Fairland Lawn	143 Pangborn	Lake Hammond	TX	76653	$21,625.00	$0.00	48
HN83	Hurley National	3827 Burgess	Tallmadge	TX	77231	$0.00	$0.00	48
MC28	Morgan-Alyssa	923 Williams	Crumville	TX	76745	$24,761.00	$1,572.00	42
PS82	PRIM Staffing	72 Crestview	San Julio	TX	78364	$11,682.25	$2,827.50	53
TE26	Telton-Edwards	5672 Anderson	Dunston	TX	77893	$8,521.50	$0.00	48

FIGURE 1-84

Notice that you need to have the trainer number in both tables. Without it, no way exists to tell which trainer is associated with which client. The remaining trainer data, however, was removed from the Client table and placed in the Trainer table. This new arrangement corrects the problems of redundancy in the following ways:

1. Because the data for each trainer is stored only once, space is not wasted.
2. Changing the name of a trainer is easy. You have only to change one row in the Trainer table.
3. Because the data for a trainer is stored only once, inconsistent data cannot occur.

Designing to omit redundancy will help you to produce good and valid database designs.

More About

Microsoft Certification

The Microsoft Office Specialist Certification program provides an opportunity for you to obtain a valuable industry credential — proof that you have the Access 2003 skills required by employers. For more information, see Appendix E, or visit the Access 2003 Certification Web page (scsite.com/ac2003/cert).

Project Summary

In Project 1, you learned about databases and database management systems. You learned how to create a database and how to create the tables within a database. You saw how to define the fields in a table by specifying the characteristics of the fields. You learned how to open a table, how to add records to it, and how to close it. You also printed the contents of a table. You learned how to use the Simple Query wizard to create a query that included columns from a table as well as how to enter a criterion to restrict the rows that were included. You created a form to view data on the screen and also created a custom report. You learned how to use Microsoft Access Help. Finally, you learned how to design a database to eliminate redundancy.

If you have a SAM user profile, you may have access to hands-on instruction, practice, and assessment of the skills covered in this project. Log in to your SAM account and go to your assignments page to see what your instructor has assigned.

What You Should Know

Having completed this project, you should be able to perform the tasks below. The tasks are listed in the same order they were presented in this project. For a list of the buttons, menus, toolbars, and commands introduced in this project, see the Quick Reference Summary at the back of this book and refer to the Page Number column.

1. Start Access (AC 7)
2. Close the Language Bar (AC 9)
3. Create a New Database (AC 10)
4. Create a Table (AC 17)
5. Define the Fields in a Table (AC 19)
6. Close and Save a Table (AC 21)
7. Add Records to a Table (AC 23)
8. Close a Table and Database and Quit Access (AC 26)
9. Open a Database (AC 26)
10. Add Additional Records to a Table (AC 28)
11. Preview and Print the Contents of a Table (AC 30)
12. Create an Additional Table (AC 33)
13. Add Records to an Additional Table (AC 34)
14. Use the Simple Query Wizard to Create a Query (AC 34)
15. Use a Query (AC 37)
16. Use the New Object Button to Create a Form (AC 38)
17. Close and Save a Form (AC 39)
18. Open a Form (AC 40)
19. Use a Form (AC 41)
20. Switch from Form View to Datasheet View (AC 42)
21. Create a Report (AC 43)
22. Print a Report (AC 47)
23. Close a Database (AC 47)
24. Obtain Help Using the Type a Question for Help Box (AC 48)
25. Quit Access (AC 50)

Learn It Online

Instructions: To complete the Learn It Online exercises, start your browser, click the Address bar, and then enter the Web address scsite.com/ac2003/learn. When the Access 2003 Learn It Online page is displayed, follow the instructions in the exercises below. Each exercise has instructions for printing your results, either for your own records or for submission to your instructor.

1 Project Reinforcement TF, MC, and SA

Below Access Project 1, click the Project Reinforcement link. Print the quiz by clicking Print on the File menu for each page. Answer each question.

2 Flash Cards

Below Access Project 1, click the Flash Cards link and read the instructions. Type 20 (or a number specified by your instructor) in the Number of playing cards text box, type your name in the Enter your Name text box, and then click the Flip Card button. When the flash card is displayed, read the question and then click the ANSWER box arrow to select an answer. Flip through Flash Cards. If your score is 15 (75%) correct or greater, click Print on the File menu to print your results. If your score is less than 15 (75%) correct, then redo this exercise by clicking the Replay button.

3 Practice Test

Below Access Project 1, click the Practice Test link. Answer each question, enter your first and last name at the bottom of the page, and then click the Grade Test button. When the graded practice test is displayed on your screen, click Print on the File menu to print a hard copy. Continue to take practice tests until you score 80% or better.

4 Who Wants To Be a Computer Genius?

Below Access Project 1, click the Computer Genius link. Read the instructions, enter your first and last name at the bottom of the page, and then click the PLAY button. When your score is displayed, click the PRINT RESULTS link to print a hard copy.

5 Wheel of Terms

Below Access Project 1, click the Wheel of Terms link. Read the instructions, and then enter your first and last name and your school name. Click the PLAY button. When your score is displayed, right-click the score and then click Print on the shortcut menu to print a hard copy.

6 Crossword Puzzle Challenge

Below Access Project 1, click the Crossword Puzzle Challenge link. Read the instructions, and then enter your first and last name. Click the SUBMIT button. Work the crossword puzzle. When you are finished, click the Submit button. When the crossword puzzle is redisplayed, click the Print Puzzle button to print a hard copy.

7 Tips and Tricks

Below Access Project 1, click the Tips and Tricks link. Click a topic that pertains to Project 1. Right-click the information and then click Print on the shortcut menu. Construct a brief example of what the information relates to in Access to confirm you understand how to use the tip or trick.

8 Newsgroups

Below Access Project 1, click the Newsgroups link. Click a topic that pertains to Project 1. Print three comments.

9 Expanding Your Horizons

Below Access Project 1, click the Expanding Your Horizons link. Click a topic that pertains to Project 1. Print the information. Construct a brief example of what the information relates to in Access to confirm you understand the contents of the article.

10 Search Sleuth

Below Access Project 1, click the Search Sleuth link. To search for a term that pertains to this project, select a term below the Project 1 title and then use the Google search engine at google.com (or any major search engine) to display and print two Web pages that present information on the term.

11 Access Online Training

Below Access Project 1, click the Access Online Training link. When your browser displays the Microsoft Office Online Web page, click the Access link. Click one of the Access courses that covers one or more of the objectives listed at the beginning of the project on page AC 4. Print the first page of the course before stepping through it.

12 Office Marketplace

Below Access Project 1, click the Office Marketplace link. When your browser displays the Microsoft Office Online Web page, click the Office Marketplace link. Click a topic that relates to Access. Print the first page.

Apply Your Knowledge

1 Changing Data, Creating Queries, and Creating Reports

Instructions: Start Access. Open the database Begon Pest Control from the Data Disk. See page xxiv at the front of this book for instructions for downloading the Data Disk or see your instructor for information about accessing the files required in this book.

Begon Pest Control is a company that performs pest control services for commercial businesses. Begon has a database that keeps track of its technicians and customers. The database has two tables. The Customer table contains data on the customers who use the services of Begon. The Technician table contains data on the individuals employed by Begon. The structure and data are shown for the Customer table in Figure 1-85 and for the Technician table in Figure 1-86.

Structure of Customer table

FIELD NAME	DATA TYPE	FIELD SIZE	PRIMARY KEY?	DESCRIPTION
Customer Number	Text	4	Yes	Customer Number (Primary Key)
Name	Text	20		Customer Name
Address	Text	15		Street Address
City	Text	15		City
State	Text	2		State (Two-Character Abbreviation)
Zip Code	Text	5		Zip Code (Five-Character Version)
Balance	Currency			Amount Owed by Customer
Technician Number	Text	3		Number of Customer's Technician

Customer table

CUSTOMER NUMBER	NAME	ADDRESS	CITY	STATE	ZIP CODE	BALANCE	TECHNICIAN NUMBER
AT23	Atlas Repair	220 Beard	Kady	TN	42514	$335.00	203
AZ01	AZ Auto	412 Beechwood	Conradt	TN	42547	$300.00	210
BL35	Blanton Shoes	443 Chedder	Kady	TN	42514	$290.00	210
CJ45	C Joe Diner	87 Fletcher	Carlton	TN	52764	$0.00	214
CM90	Cramden Co.	234 Fairlawn	Conradt	TN	42546	$355.00	203
HI25	Hill Crafts	245 Beard	Kady	TN	42514	$334.00	210
KL50	Klean n Dri	378 Stout	Carlton	TN	52764	$365.00	210
MC10	Moss Carpet	109 Fletcher	Carlton	TN	52764	$398.00	203
PV83	Prime Video	734 Lanton	Conradt	TN	42547	$0.00	214
SE05	Servete Mfg Co.	879 Redfern	Kady	TN	42515	$343.00	210

FIGURE 1-85

Apply Your Knowledge

Structure of Technician table

FIELD NAME	DATA TYPE	FIELD SIZE	PRIMARY KEY?	DESCRIPTION
Technician Number	Text	3	Yes	Technician Number (Primary Key)
Last Name	Text	10		Last Name of Technician
First Name	Text	8		First Name of Technician
Address	Text	15		Street Address
City	Text	15		City
State	Text	2		State (Two-Character Abbreviation)
Zip Code	Text	5		Zip Code (Five-Character Version)
Hourly Rate	Currency			Hourly Pay Rate

Technician table

TECHNICIAN NUMBER	LAST NAME	FIRST NAME	ADDRESS	CITY	STATE	ZIP CODE	HOURLY RATE
203	Estevez	Miguel	467 Clay	Kady	TN	42517	$11.50
210	Hillsdale	Rachel	78 Parkton	Conradt	TN	42547	$11.75
214	Liu	Chou	897 North	Carlton	TN	52764	$11.65
220	Short	Chris	111 Maple	Conradt	TN	42547	$11.50

FIGURE 1-86

Instructions: Perform the following tasks:

1. Open the Customer table and change the Technician Number for customer KL50 to 214.
2. Print the Customer table.
3. Use the Simple Query Wizard to create a new query to display and print the customer number, name, and technician number for records in the Customer table as shown in Figure 1-87 on the next page.
4. Save the query as Customer-Technician Query and then close the query.
5. Open the Customer-Technician Query in Design View and restrict the query results to only those customers whose technician number is 210.
6. Print the query but do not save the changes.
7. Create the report shown in Figure 1-88 on the next page for the Customer table.
8. Print the report.

(continued)

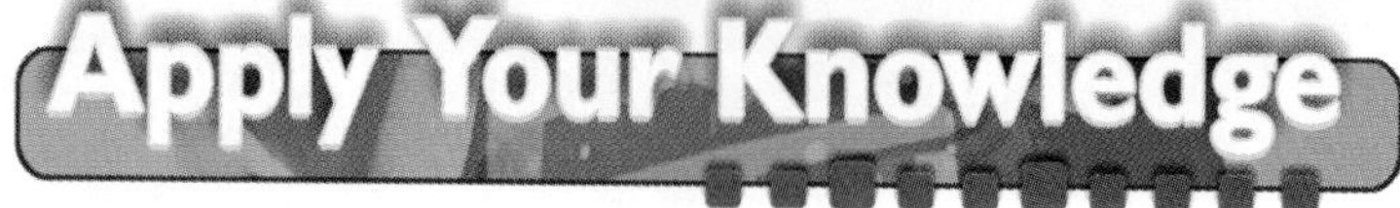

Changing Data, Creating Queries, and Creating Reports *(continued)*

Microsoft Access - [Customer-Technician Query :

Customer Numb	Name	Technician Num
AT23	Atlas Repair	203
AZ01	AZ Auto	210
BL35	Blanton Shoes	210
CJ45	C Joe Diner	214
CM90	Cramden Co.	203
HI25	Hill Crafts	210
KL50	Klean n Dri	214
MC10	Moss Carpet	203
PV83	Prime Video	214
SE05	Servete Mfg Co.	210

FIGURE 1-87

Customer Amount Report

Customer Number	*Name*	*Balance*
AT23	Atlas Repair	$335.00
AZ01	AZ Auto	$300.00
BL35	Blanton Shoes	$290.00
CJ45	C Joe Diner	$0.00
CM90	Cramden Co.	$355.00
HI25	Hill Crafts	$334.00
KL50	Klean n Dri	$365.00
MC10	Moss Carpet	$398.00
PV83	Prime Video	$0.00
SE05	Servete Mfg Co.	$343.00

FIGURE 1-88

1 Creating the Birds2U Database

Problem: Birds2U is a new online retailer. The company specializes in products for bird and nature enthusiasts. The database consists of two tables. The Item table contains information on items available for sale. The Supplier table contains information on the companies that supply the items.

Instructions: Perform the following tasks:

1. Create a new database in which to store all the objects related to the items for sale. Call the database Birds2U.
2. Create the Item table using the structure shown in Figure 1-89. Use the name Item for the table.
3. Add the data shown in Figure 1-89 to the Item table.
4. Print the Item table.

Structure of Item table

FIELD NAME	DATA TYPE	FIELD SIZE	PRIMARY KEY?	DESCRIPTION
Item Code	Text	4	Yes	Item Code (Primary Key)
Description	Text	20		Description of Item
On Hand	Number			Number of Units On Hand
Cost	Currency			Cost of Item
Selling Price	Currency			Selling Price of Item
Supplier Code	Text	2		Code of Item's Supplier

Item table

ITEM CODE	DESCRIPTION	ON HAND	COST	SELLING PRICE	SUPPLIER CODE
BA35	Bat House	14	$43.50	$45.50	21
BB01	Bird Bath	2	$82.10	$86.25	13
BE19	Bee Box	7	$39.80	$42.50	21
BL06	Bluebird House	9	$14.35	$15.99	13
BU24	Butterfly Box	6	$36.10	$37.75	21
GF12	Globe Feeder	12	$14.80	$16.25	05
HF01	Hummingbird Feeder	5	$11.35	$14.25	05
PM05	Purple Martin House	3	$67.10	$69.95	13
SF03	Suet Feeder	7	$8.05	$9.95	05
WF10	Window Feeder	10	$14.25	$15.95	05

FIGURE 1-89

5. Create the Supplier table using the structure shown in Figure 1-90 on the next page. Use the name Supplier for the table.
6. Add the data shown in Figure 1-90 to the Supplier table.
7. Print the Supplier table.
8. Create a form for the Supplier table. Use the name Supplier for the form.
9. Open the form you created and change the address for Supplier Code 17 to 56 Beechtree. Print the Supplier table.
10. Create and print the report shown in Figure 1-91 on the next page for the Item table.

(continued)

Creating the Birds2U Database *(continued)*

Structure of Supplier table

FIELD NAME	DATA TYPE	FIELD SIZE	PRIMARY KEY?	DESCRIPTION
Supplier Code	Text	2	Yes	Supplier Code (Primary Key)
Name	Text	20		Supplier Name
Address	Text	15		Street Address
City	Text	15		City
State	Text	2		State (Two-Character Abbreviation)
Zip Code	Text	5		Zip Code (Five-Character Version)
Telephone Number	Text	12		Telephone Number (999-999-9999 Version)

Supplier table

SUPPLIER CODE	NAME	ADDRESS	CITY	STATE	ZIP CODE	TELEPHONE NUMBER
05	All Birds Supply	234 Southward	Elgin	AZ	85165	602-555-6756
13	Bird Casa Ltd	38 Junction	Grandber	TX	78628	512-555-3402
17	Lawn Fixtures	56 Beecham	Holligan	CA	95418	707-555-4545
21	Natural Woods	67 Main	Ghostman	MI	49301	610-555-3333

FIGURE 1-90

Inventory Report

Item Code	*Description*	*On Hand*	*Cost*
BA35	Bat House	14	$43.50
BB01	Bird Bath	2	$82.10
BE19	Bee Box	7	$39.80
BL06	Bluebird House	9	$14.35
BU24	Butterfly Box	6	$36.10
GF12	Globe Feeder	12	$14.80
HF01	Hummingbird Feeder	5	$11.35
PM05	Purple Martin House	3	$67.10
SF03	Suet Feeder	7	$8.05
WF10	Window Feeder	10	$14.25

FIGURE 1-91

2 Creating the Babbage Bookkeeping Database

Problem: Babbage Bookkeeping is a local company that provides bookkeeping services to several small businesses in the area. The database consists of two tables. The Client table contains information on the businesses that use Babbage's services. The Bookkeeper table contains information on the bookkeeper assigned to the business.

Instructions: Perform the following tasks:

1. Create a new database in which to store all the objects related to the bookkeeping data. Call the database Babbage Bookkeeping.
2. Create and print the Client table using the structure and data shown in Figure 1-92. Then, create and print the Bookkeeper table using the structure and data shown in Figure 1-93 on the next page.

Structure of Client table

FIELD NAME	DATA TYPE	FIELD SIZE	PRIMARY KEY?	DESCRIPTION
Client Number	Text	3	Yes	Client Number (Primary Key)
Name	Text	20		Name of Client
Address	Text	15		Street Address
City	Text	15		City
Zip Code	Text	5		Zip Code (Five-Character Version)
Balance	Currency			Amount Currently Owed for Services
Bookkeeper Number	Text	2		Number of Client's Bookkeeper

Client table

CLIENT NUMBER	NAME	ADDRESS	CITY	ZIP CODE	BALANCE	BOOKKEEPER NUMBER
A54	Afton Mills	612 Revere	Grant City	58120	$315.50	22
A62	Atlas Suppliers	227 Dandelion	Empeer	58216	$525.00	24
B26	Blake-Scripps	557 Maum	Grant City	58120	$229.50	24
D76	Dege Grocery	446 Linton	Portage	59130	$485.75	34
G56	Grand Cleaners	337 Abelard	Empeer	58216	$265.00	22
H21	Hill Shoes	247 Fulton	Grant City	58121	$228.50	24
J77	Jones Plumbing	75 Getty	Portage	59130	$0.00	24
M26	Mohr Crafts	665 Maum	Empeer	58216	$312.50	22
S56	SeeSaw Ind.	31 Liatris	Portage	59130	$362.50	34
T45	Tate Repair	824 Revere	Grant City	58120	$254.00	24

FIGURE 1-92

(continued)

Creating the Babbage Bookkeeping Database *(continued)*

Structure of Bookkeeper table

FIELD NAME	DATA TYPE	FIELD SIZE	PRIMARY KEY?	DESCRIPTION
Bookkeeper Number	Text	2	Yes	Bookkeeper Number (Primary Key)
Last Name	Text	10		Last Name of Bookkeeper
First Name	Text	8		First Name of Bookkeeper
Address	Text	15		Street Address
City	Text	15		City
Zip Code	Text	5		Zip Code (Five-Character Version)
Hourly Rate	Currency			Hourly Rate
YTD Earnings	Currency			Year-to-Date Earnings

Bookkeeper table

BOOKKEEPER NUMBER	LAST NAME	FIRST NAME	ADDRESS	CITY	ZIP CODE	HOURLY RATE	YTD EARNINGS
22	Lewes	Johanna	26 Cotton	Portage	59130	$14.50	$18,245.00
24	Rodriguez	Mario	79 Marsden	Grant City	58120	$13.50	$17,745.50
34	Wong	Choi	263 Topper	Empeer	58216	$14.00	$16,750.25

FIGURE 1-93

3. Change the Bookkeeper Number for client J77 to 34.
4. Use the Simple Query Wizard to create a new query to display and print the Client Number, Name, and Bookkeeper Number for all clients where the bookkeeper number is 34.
5. Create and print the report shown in Figure 1-94 for the Client table.

Balance Due Report

Client Number	*Name*	*Balance*
A54	Afton Mills	$315.50
A62	Atlas Suppliers	$525.00
B26	Blake-Scripps	$229.50
D76	Dege Grocery	$485.75
G56	Grand Cleaners	$265.00
H21	Hill Shoes	$228.50
J77	Jones Plumbing	$0.00
M26	Mohr Crafts	$312.50
S56	SeeSaw Ind.	$362.50
T45	Tate Repair	$254.00

FIGURE 1-94

In the Lab

3 Creating the City Guide Database

Problem: The local chamber of commerce publishes a guide for newcomers. To help finance the guide, the chamber includes advertisements from local businesses. Advertising representatives receive a commission based on the advertising revenues they generate. The database consists of two tables. The Advertiser table contains information on the businesses that advertise in the guide. The Ad Rep table contains information on the advertising representative assigned to the account.

Instructions Part 1: Using the data shown in Figures 1-95 and 1-96 on the next page create the City Guide database, the Advertiser table, and the Ad Rep table. Note that the Ad Rep table uses the number data type. Print the tables. Then, create a form for the Advertiser table.

Structure of Advertiser table

FIELD NAME	DATA TYPE	FIELD SIZE	PRIMARY KEY?	DESCRIPTION
Advertiser Number	Text	4	Yes	Advertiser Number (Primary Key)
Name	Text	20		Name of Advertiser
Address	Text	15		Street Address
Zip Code	Text	5		Zip Code (Five-Character Version)
Telephone Number	Text	8		Telephone Number (999-9999 Version)
Balance	Currency			Amount Currently Owed
Amount Paid	Currency			Amount Paid Year-to-Date
Ad Rep Number	Text	2		Number of Advertising Representative

Data for Advertiser table

ADVERTISER NUMBER	NAME	ADDRESS	ZIP CODE	TELEPHONE NUMBER	BALANCE	AMOUNT PAID	AD REP NUMBER
A228	Adam's Music	47 Berton	19363	555-0909	$90.00	$565.00	26
B103	Barbecue Joint	483 Cantor	19363	555-8990	$185.00	$825.00	29
C048	Chloe's Salon	10 Main	19362	555-2334	$0.00	$375.00	29
C135	Creative Toys	26 Jefferson	19362	555-1357	$130.00	$865.00	32
D217	Dog Groomers	33 Maple	19362	555-2468	$290.00	$515.00	26
G346	Gold's Clothes	196 Lincoln	19364	555-3579	$0.00	$805.00	29
M321	Meat Shoppe	234 Magnolia	19363	555-6802	$215.00	$845.00	29
P124	Palace Theatre	22 Main	19364	555-8024	$65.00	$180.00	26
S111	Suds n Spuds	10 Jefferson	19365	555-5791	$465.00	$530.00	32
W456	Western Wear	345 Oaktree	19363	555-7913	$105.00	$265.00	26

FIGURE 1-95

(continued)

Creating the City Guide Database *(continued)*

Structure for Ad Rep table

FIELD NAME	DATA TYPE	FIELD SIZE	PRIMARY KEY?	DESCRIPTION
Ad Rep Number	Text	2	Yes	Advertising Rep Number (Primary Key)
Last Name	Text	10		Last Name of Advertising Rep
First Name	Text	8		First Name of Advertising Rep
Address	Text	15		Street Address
City	Text	15		City
Zip Code	Text	5		Zip Code (Five-Character Version)
Comm Rate	Number	Double		Commission Rate on Advertising Sales
Commission	Currency			Year-to-Date Total Commissions

Data for Ad Rep table

AD REP NUMBER	LAST NAME	FIRST NAME	ADDRESS	CITY	ZIP CODE	COMM RATE	COMMISSION
26	Febo	Jen	57 Barton	Crescent	19111	0.09	$6,500.00
29	Martinson	Kyle	87 Pearl	Newton	19124	0.08	$6,250.00
32	Rogers	Elena	45 Magret	San Luis	19362	0.09	$7,000.00

FIGURE 1-96

Instructions Part 2: Correct the following error. The ad rep assigned to the Meat Shoppe account should be Elena Rogers. Use the form you created to make the correction, and then print the form showing the corrected record. To print the form, open the form, click File on the menu bar, and then click Print. Click Selected Records(s) as the Print Range. Click the OK button.

Instructions Part 3: Create a query to find which accounts Jen Febo represents. Print the results. Prepare an advertiser status report that lists the advertiser's number, name, balance currently owed, and amount paid to date.

Cases and Places

The difficulty of these case studies varies:
■ are the least difficult and ■■ are more difficult. The last exercise is a group exercise.

1 ■ To help finance your college education, you formed a small business. You provide dog-walking services to local residents. Dog walkers are paid by the walk for each dog they walk. The business has grown rapidly and you now have several other students working for you. You realize that you need to computerize your business.

Design and create a database to store the data that College Dog Walkers needs to manage its business. Then create the necessary tables and enter the data from the Case 1-1 College Dog Walkers Word document on the Data Disk. Print the tables. See page xxiv at the front of this book for instructions for downloading the Data Disk or see your instructor for information on accessing the files required in this book.

2 ■ The Health and Physical Education department at your college recognized early that personal training would be a growth field. One of your friends graduated from the program and has started a company, InPerson Fitness Company. The company specializes in personal training in the comfort of the customer's home. It designs exercise programs for clients based on each person's health history, abilities, and fitness objectives. The company is expanding rapidly and you have been hired to computerize the business.

Design and create a database to store the data that InPerson Fitness needs to manage its business. Then create the necessary tables and enter the data from the Case 1-2 InPerson Fitness Word document on the Data Disk. Print the tables. See page xxiv at the front of this book for instructions for downloading the Data Disk or see your instructor for information on accessing the files required in this book.

3 ■■ Regional Books is a local bookstore that specializes in books that are of local interest. These are books that are set in the region or are written by authors who live in the area. The owner has asked you to create and update a database that she can use to keep track of the books she has in stock.

Design and create a database to store the book data. To create the Books table, use the Table Wizard and select the Books table. You do not need to select all the fields the Table Wizard provides and you can rename the fields in the table. (***Hint***: See More About Creating a Table: The Table Wizard on page AC 15.) Enter the data from the Case 1-3 Regional Books Word document on the Data Disk. Print the tables. Prepare a sample query and a sample report to illustrate to the owner the types of tasks that can be done with a database management system. See page xxiv at the front of this book for instructions for downloading the Data Disk or see your instructor for information on accessing the files required in this book.

Cases and Places

4 ■■ The Campus Housing office at the local university provides a listing of available off-campus rentals by private owners. The office would like to make this listing available on the campus Web site. The administrator has asked you to create and update a database that can store information about available off-campus housing. The housing list is in the Case 1-4 Campus Housing Word document on the Data Disk. A listing that has 0 bedrooms is either an efficiency apartment or a room for rent in a home. Distance indicates the rental unit's distance in miles from the university. Parking signifies whether reserved parking is available with the unit.

Design and create a database to meet the needs of the Campus Housing office. Then create the necessary tables, enter the data from the Case 1-4 Campus Housing Word document on the Data Disk. Print the tables. Prepare a sample form, sample query, and sample report to illustrate to the office the types of tasks that can be done with a database management system. See page xxiv at the front of this book for instructions for downloading the Data Disk or see your instructor for information on accessing the files required in this book.

5 ■■ **Working Together** Conducting a job search requires careful preparation. In addition to preparing a resume and cover letter, you will need to research the companies for which you are interested in working and contact these companies to let them know of your interest and qualifications. Microsoft Access can help you manage the job search process. The Database Wizard includes a Contact Management template that can create a database that will help you keep track of your job contacts.

Have each member of your team explore the features of the Database Wizard and determine individually which fields should be included in a Contact Management database. As a group, review your choices and decide on one common design. Prepare a short paper for your instructor that explains why your team chose those particular fields to include in the database.

After agreeing on the database design, assign one member to create the database using the Database Wizard. Every other team member should research a company and add the data to the database. Print the alphabetical contact listing that the Database Wizard creates. Turn in the short paper and the report to your instructor.

MICROSOFT OFFICE

PowerPoint 2003

MICROSOFT OFFICE POWERPOINT

MICROSOFT OFFICE
PowerPoint 2003

Using a Design Template and Text Slide Layout to Create a Presentation

PROJECT 1

CASE PERSPECTIVE

Do you use the 168 hours in each week effectively? From attending class, doing homework, attending school events, exercising, eating, watching television, and sleeping, juggling the demands of school and personal lives can be daunting. Odds are that one of every three students will fail a course at one point in their college career due to poor study habits.

The ability to learn effectively is the key to college success. What matters is not how long people study but how well they use their time in the classroom and while preparing for class assignments and tests. Students with good academic skills maximize their time and, consequently, achieve the highest grades on exams and homework assignments. They ultimately earn higher incomes than their less organized peers because good academic practices carry over to the working environment.

Advisers in the Academic Skills Center at your college are aware of this fact and are developing seminars to help students succeed. Their first presentation focuses on getting organized, enhancing listening skills, and taking tests effectively. Dr. Traci Johnson, the dean of the Academic Skills Center, has asked you to help her create a PowerPoint slide show to use at next month's lunchtime study skills session (Figure 1-1 on page PPT 5). In addition, she would like handouts of the slides to distribute to these students.

As you read through this project, you will learn how to use PowerPoint to create, save, and print a slide show that is composed of single- and multi-level bulleted lists.

MICROSOFT OFFICE

PowerPoint 2003

Using a Design Template and Text Slide Layout to Create a Presentation

PROJECT

1

Objectives

You will have mastered the material in this project when you can:

- Start and customize PowerPoint
- Describe the PowerPoint window
- Select a design template
- Create a title slide and text slides with single- and multi-level bulleted lists
- Change the font size and font style
- Save a presentation
- End a slide show with a black slide
- View a presentation in slide show view
- Quit PowerPoint and then open a presentation
- Display and print a presentation in black and white
- Use the PowerPoint Help system

What Is Microsoft Office PowerPoint 2003?

Microsoft Office PowerPoint 2003 is a complete presentation graphics program that allows you to produce professional-looking presentations (Figure 1-1). A PowerPoint **presentation** also is called a **slide show**.

PowerPoint contains several features to simplify creating a slide show. For example, you can instruct PowerPoint to create a predesigned presentation, and then you can modify the presentation to fulfill your requirements. You quickly can format a slide show using one of the professionally designed presentation design templates. To make your presentation more impressive, you can add tables, charts, pictures, video, sound, and animation effects. Additional PowerPoint features include the following:

- **Word processing** create bulleted lists, combine words and images, find and replace text, and use multiple fonts and type sizes.
- **Outlining** develop your presentation using an outline format. You also can import outlines from Microsoft Word or other word processing programs.
- **Charting** create and insert charts into your presentations. The two chart types are: standard, which includes bar, line, pie, and xy (scatter) charts; and custom, which shows such objects as floating bars and colored lines.
- **Drawing** form and modify diagrams using shapes such as arcs, arrows, cubes, rectangles, stars, and triangles.
- **Inserting multimedia** insert artwork and multimedia effects into your slide show. The Microsoft Clip Organizer contains hundreds of media files, including pictures, photos, sounds, and movies.

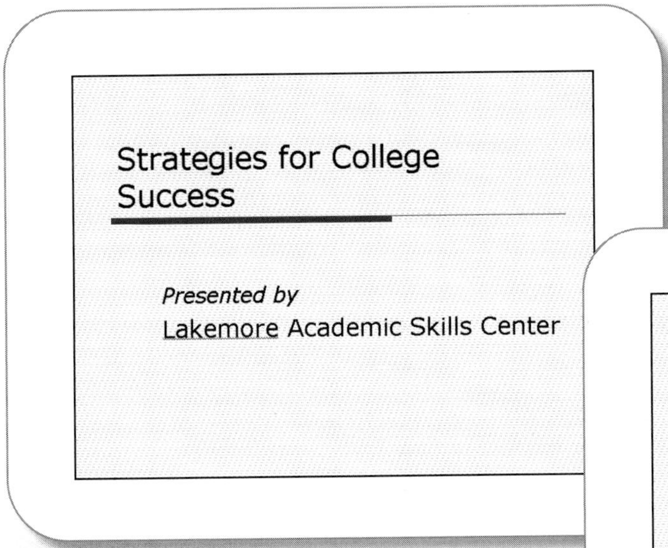

Strategies for College Success

Presented by
Lakemore Academic Skills Center

(a) Slide 1 (Title Slide)

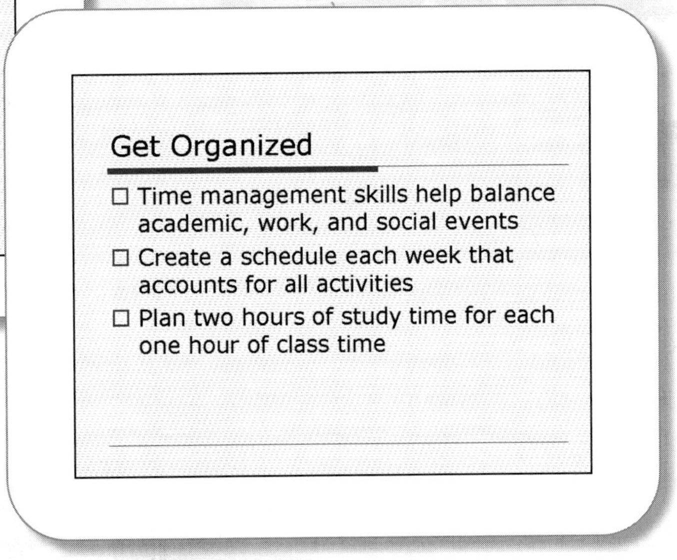

Get Organized

- Time management skills help balance academic, work, and social events
- Create a schedule each week that accounts for all activities
- Plan two hours of study time for each one hour of class time

(b) Slide 2 (Single-Level Bulleted List)

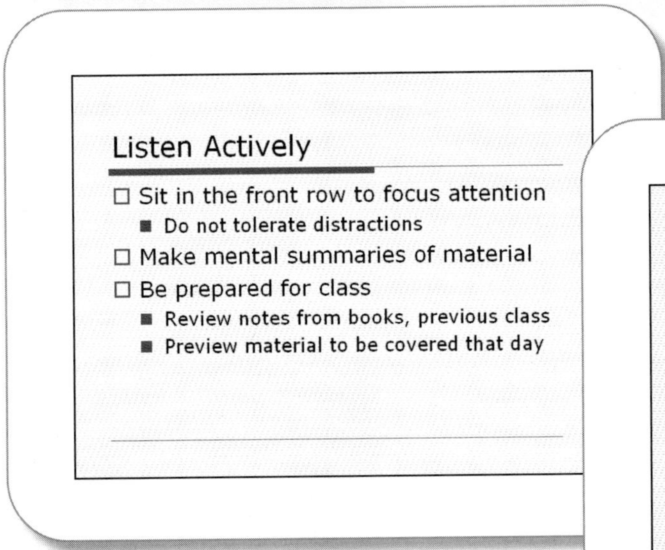

Listen Actively

- Sit in the front row to focus attention
  - Do not tolerate distractions
- Make mental summaries of material
- Be prepared for class
  - Review notes from books, previous class
  - Preview material to be covered that day

(c) Slide 3 (Multi-Level Bulleted List)

Excel on Exams

- Review test material throughout week
  - Cramming before exam is ineffective
    - Facts remain only in short-term memory
- Review entire test before answering
  - Start with the material you know
    - Think positively and stay focused

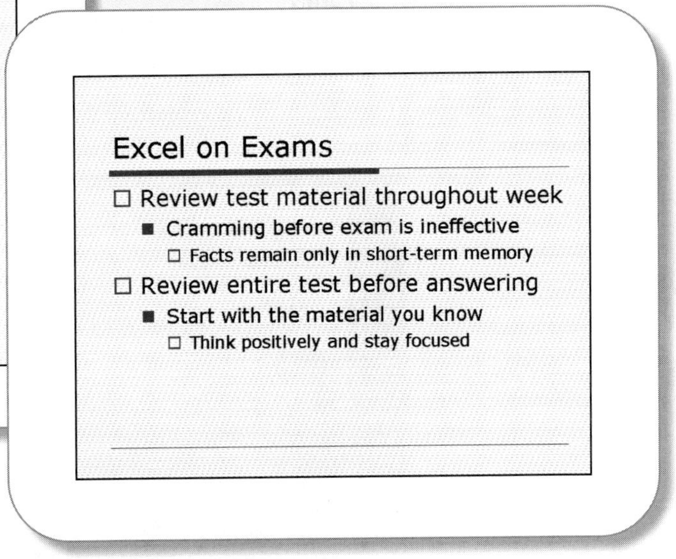

(d) Slide 4 (Multi-Level Bulleted List)

FIGURE 1-1

More About

Portable Projection Devices

New multimedia projectors weigh less than three pounds and can be held in one hand. Some projectors allow users to control the projector wirelessly from 300 feet away using a PDA. For more information about projectors, visit the PowerPoint 2003 More About Web page (scsite.com/ppt2003/more) and then click Projectors.

- **Web support** save presentations or parts of a presentation in HTML format so they can be viewed and manipulated using a browser. You can publish your slide show to the Internet or to an intranet.
- **E-mailing** send your entire slide show as an attachment to an e-mail message.
- **Using Wizards** create a presentation quickly and efficiently by answering prompts for specific content criteria. For example, the **AutoContent Wizard** gives prompts for the type of slide show you are planning, such as communicating serious news or motivating a team, and the type of output, such as an on-screen presentation or black and white overheads.

PowerPoint gives you the flexibility to make presentations using a projection device attached to a personal computer (Figure 1-2a) and using overhead transparencies (Figure 1-2b). In addition, you can take advantage of the World Wide Web and run virtual presentations on the Internet (Figure 1-2c). PowerPoint also can create paper printouts of the individual slides, outlines, and speaker notes.

This latest version of PowerPoint has many new features to make you more productive. It saves the presentation to a CD; uses pens, highlighters, arrows, and pointers for emphasis; and includes a thesaurus and other research tools.

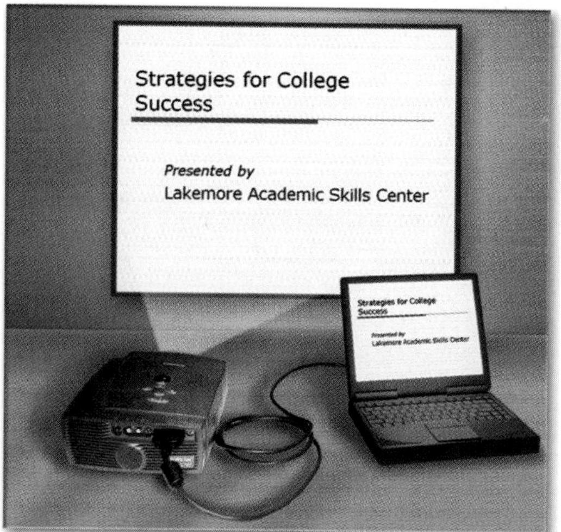

(a) Projection Device Connected to a Personal Computer

(b) Overhead Transparencies

(c) PowerPoint Presentation on the World Wide Web

FIGURE 1-2

Project One — Strategies for College Success

PowerPoint allows you to produce slides to use in an academic, business, or other environment. In Project 1, you create the presentation shown in Figures 1-1a through 1-1d. The objective is to produce a presentation, called Strategies for College Success, to be displayed using a projection device. As an introduction to PowerPoint, this project steps you through the most common type of presentation, which is a **text slide** consisting of a bulleted list. A **bulleted list** is a list of paragraphs, each preceded by a bullet. A **bullet** is a symbol such as a heavy dot (•) or other character that precedes text when the text warrants special emphasis.

> **Q&A**
>
> **Q:** Can I change the bullet characters?
>
> **A:** Yes. While default bullets are part of the design templates, they can be modified or deleted. You can use symbols, numbers, and picture files as revised bullets. You also can change their size and color.

Starting and Customizing PowerPoint

If you are stepping through this project on a computer and you want your screen to agree with the figures in this book, then you should change your computer's resolution to 800 × 600. To change the resolution on your computer, see Appendix D.

To start PowerPoint, Windows must be running. The quickest way to begin a new presentation is to use the Start button on the **Windows taskbar** at the bottom of the screen. The following steps show how to start PowerPoint and a new presentation.

To Start PowerPoint

1

- **Click the Start button on the Windows taskbar, point to All Programs on the Start menu, point to Microsoft Office on the All Programs submenu, and then point to Microsoft Office PowerPoint 2003 on the Microsoft Office submenu.**

Windows displays the commands on the Start menu above the Start button, the All Programs submenu, and the Microsoft Office submenu (Figure 1-3).

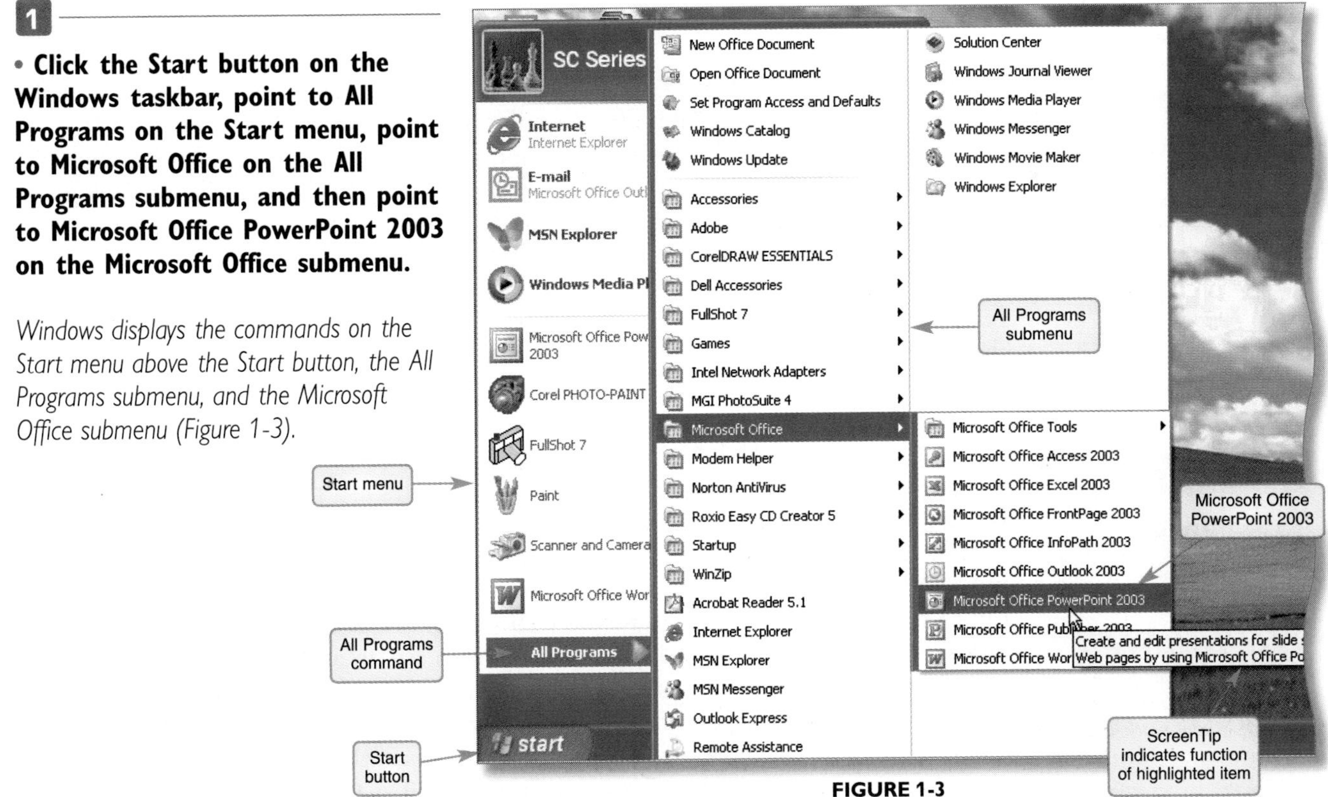

FIGURE 1-3

2

• **Click Microsoft Office PowerPoint 2003.**

PowerPoint starts. While PowerPoint is starting, the mouse pointer changes to the shape of an hourglass. After several seconds, PowerPoint displays a blank presentation titled Presentation1 in the PowerPoint window (Figure 1-4).

3

• **If the PowerPoint window is not maximized, double-click its title bar to maximize it.**

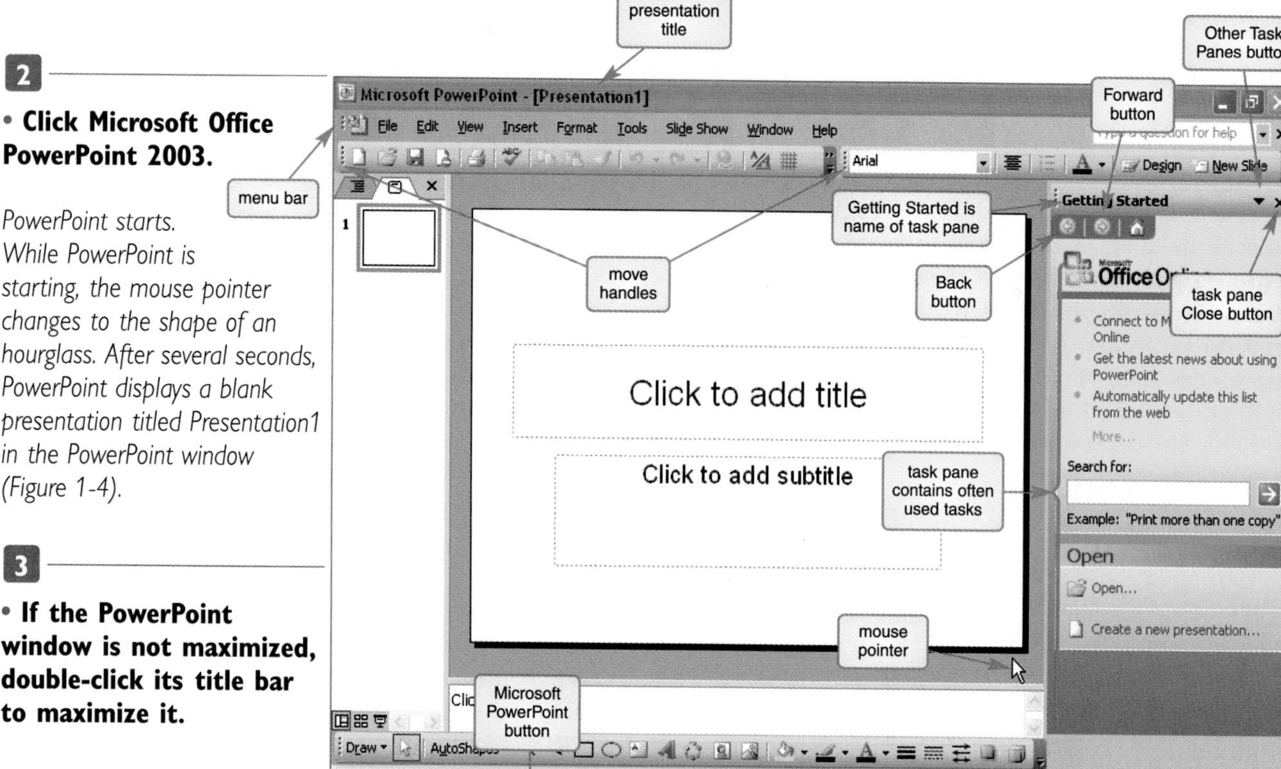

FIGURE 1-4

Other Ways

1. Double-click PowerPoint icon on desktop
2. On Start menu click Microsoft Office PowerPoint 2003
3. On Windows taskbar menu click Start button, point to All Programs, click New Office Document, double-click Blank Presentation icon

The screen shown in Figure 1-4 illustrates how the PowerPoint window looks the first time you start PowerPoint after installation on most computers. If the Office Speech Recognition software is installed and active on your computer, then, when you start PowerPoint, the Language bar is displayed on the screen. The **Language bar** contains buttons that allow you to speak commands and dictate text. It usually is located on the right side of the Windows taskbar next to the notification area, and it changes to include the speech recognition functions available in PowerPoint. In this book, the Language bar is closed because it takes up computer resources, and with the Language bar active, the microphone can be turned on accidentally by clicking the Microphone button, causing your computer to act in an unstable manner. For additional information about the Language bar, see page PPT 16 and Appendix B.

As shown in Figure 1-4, PowerPoint displays a task pane on the right side of the screen. A **task pane** is a separate window that enables users to carry out some PowerPoint tasks more efficiently. When you start PowerPoint, it displays the Getting Started task pane, which is a small window that provides commonly used links and commands that allow you to open files, create new files, or search Office-related topics on the Microsoft Web site. In this book, the Getting Started task pane is hidden to allow the maximum screen size to appear in PowerPoint.

At startup, PowerPoint also displays two toolbars on a single row. A **toolbar** contains buttons, boxes, and menus that allow you to perform frequent tasks quickly. To allow for more efficient use of the buttons, the toolbars should appear on two separate rows, instead of sharing a single row. The following steps show how to close the Language bar, close the Getting Started task pane, and instruct PowerPoint to display the toolbars on two separate rows.

More About

Task Panes

When you first start PowerPoint, a small window called a task pane may be docked on the right side of the screen. You can drag a task pane title bar to float the pane in your work area or dock it on either the left or right side or the top or bottom of a screen, depending on your personal preference.

To Customize the PowerPoint Window

1

- **If the Language bar appears, right-click it to display a list of commands.**

The Language bar shortcut menu appears (Figure 1-5).

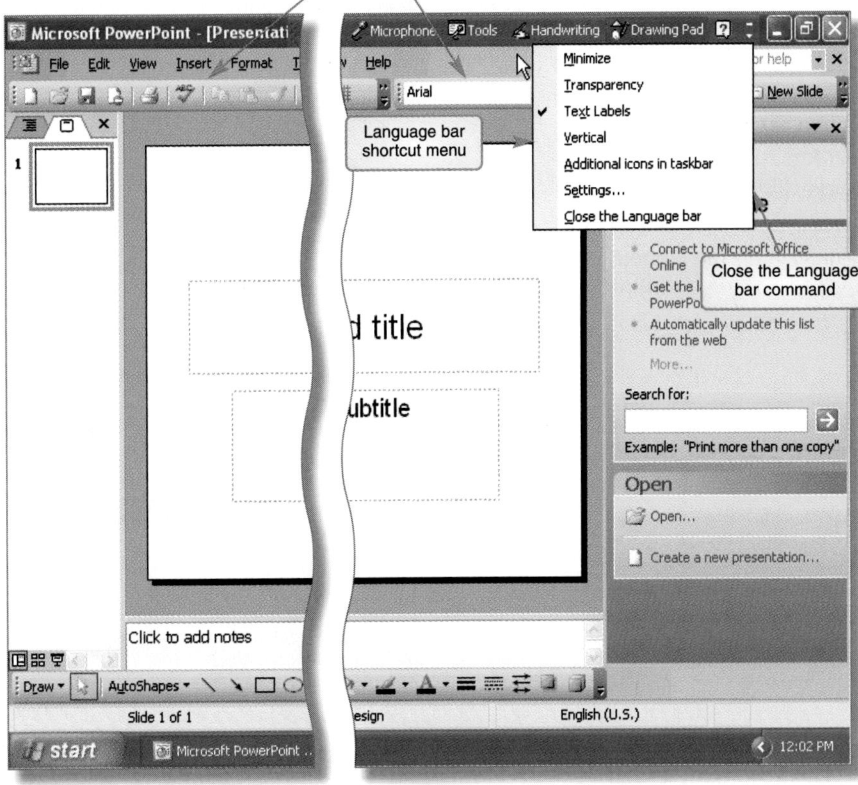

FIGURE 1-5

2

- **Click the Close the Language bar command.**
- **If necessary, click the OK button in the Language Bar dialog box.**
- **Click the Getting Started task pane Close button in the upper-right corner of the task pane.**
- **If the Standard and Formatting toolbars are positioned on the same row, click the Toolbar Options button on the Standard toolbar.**

The Language bar disappears. PowerPoint closes the Getting Started task pane and increases the size of the PowerPoint window. PowerPoint also displays the Toolbar Options list showing the buttons that do not fit on the toolbars when the toolbars are displayed on one row (Figure 1-6).

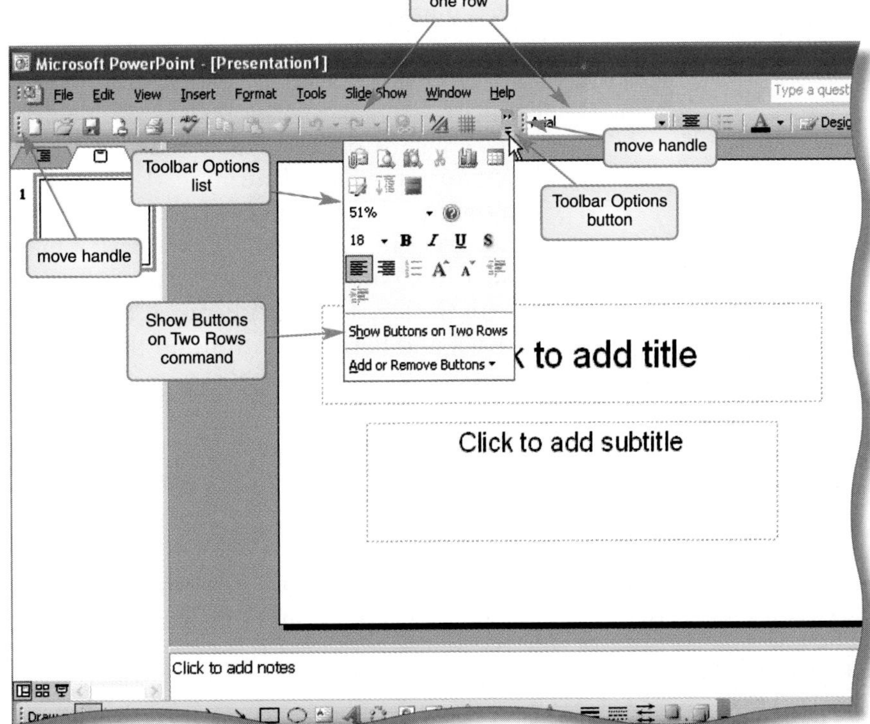

FIGURE 1-6

3

• **Click Show Buttons on Two Rows.**

PowerPoint displays the buttons on two separate rows (Figure 1-7). The Toolbar Options list shown in Figure 1-6 on the previous page is empty because all the buttons are displayed on two rows.

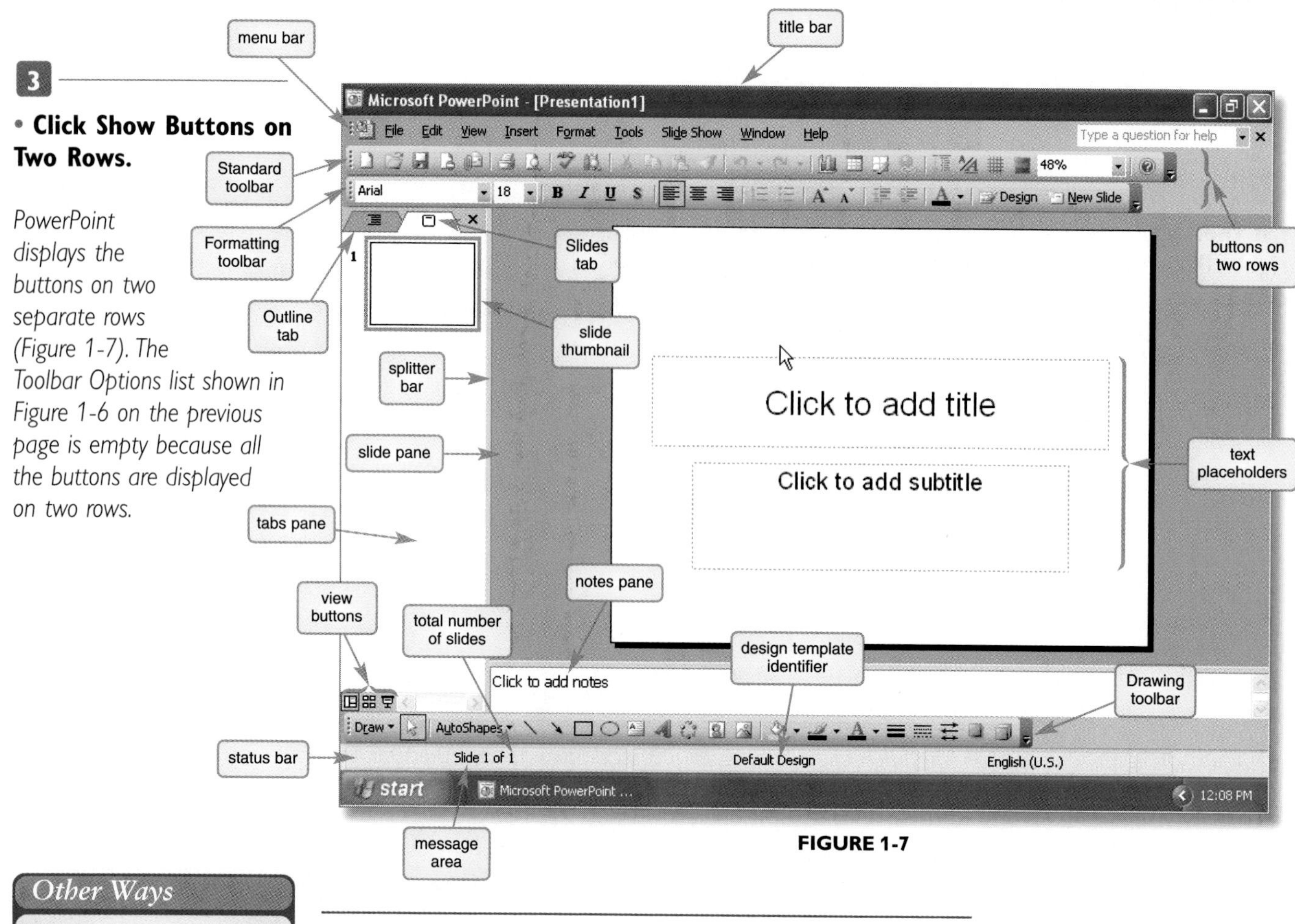

FIGURE 1-7

Other Ways

1. Double-click move handle on toolbar

As you work through creating a presentation, you will find that certain PowerPoint operations result in displaying a task pane. Besides the Getting Started task pane shown in Figure 1-4 on page PPT 8, PowerPoint provides 15 additional task panes: Help, Search Results, Clip Art, Research, Clipboard, New Presentation, Template Help, Shared Workspace, Document Updates, Slide Layout, Slide Design, Slide Design - Color Schemes, Slide Design - Animation Schemes, Custom Animation, and Slide Transition. These task panes are discussed when they are used. You can show or hide a task pane by clicking the Task Pane command on the View menu. You can activate additional task panes by clicking the down arrow to the left of the Close button on the task pane title bar (Figure 1-4) and then selecting a task pane in the list. To switch between task panes that you opened during a session, use the Back and Forward buttons on the left side of the task pane title bar.

More About

Resolution

Resolution refers to the number of pixels, or dots, that can fit into one square inch of a monitor. It is measured, consequently, in dots per inch, which is abbreviated, dpi. PowerPoint's default screen resolution is 72 dpi, and it can be set as high as 1,200 dpi. Use a resolution of 150 dpi if you are going to print handouts of your slides.

The PowerPoint Window

The basic unit of a PowerPoint presentation is a **slide**. A slide contains one or many **objects**, such as a title, text, graphics, tables, charts, and drawings. An object is the building block for a PowerPoint slide. PowerPoint assumes the first slide in a new presentation is the **title slide**. The title slide's purpose is to introduce the presentation to the audience.

In PowerPoint, you have the option of using the PowerPoint default settings or establishing your own. A **default setting** is a particular value for a variable that PowerPoint assigns initially. It controls the placement of objects, the color scheme, the transition between slides, and other slide attributes, and it remains in effect unless you cancel or override it. **Attributes** are the properties or characteristics of an object. For example, if you underline the title of a slide, the title is the object, and the underline is the attribute. When you start PowerPoint, the default **slide layout** is **landscape orientation**, where the slide width is greater than its height. In landscape orientation, the slide size is preset to 10 inches wide and 7.5 inches high. You can change the slide layout to **portrait orientation**, so the slide height is greater than its width, by clicking Page Setup on the File menu. In portrait orientation, the slide width is 7.5 inches, and the height is 10 inches.

When a PowerPoint window is open, its name appears in an icon on the Windows taskbar. The **active application** is the one displaying in the foreground of the desktop. That application's corresponding icon on the Windows taskbar is displayed recessed.

PowerPoint Views

PowerPoint has three main views: normal view, slide sorter view, and slide show view. A **view** is the mode in which the presentation appears on the screen. You may use any or all views when creating a presentation, but you can use only one at a time. You also can select one of these views to be the default view. Change views by clicking one of the view buttons located at the lower-left of the PowerPoint window above the Drawing toolbar (Figure 1-7). The PowerPoint window display varies depending on the view. Some views are graphical while others are textual.

You generally will use normal view and slide sorter view when you are creating a presentation. **Normal view** is composed of three working areas that allow you to work on various aspects of a presentation simultaneously (Figure 1-7). The left side of the screen has a tabs pane that consists of an **Outline tab** and a **Slides tab** that alternate between views of the presentation in an outline of the slide text and a thumbnail, or miniature, view of the slides. You can type the text of the presentation on the Outline tab and easily rearrange bulleted lists, paragraphs, and individual slides. As you type, you can view this text in the **slide pane**, which shows a large view of the current slide on the right side of the window. You also can enter text, graphics, animations, and hyperlinks directly in the slide pane. The **notes pane** at the bottom of the window is an area where you can type notes and additional information. This text can consist of notes to yourself or remarks to share with your audience.

More About

Sizing Panes

The three panes in normal view allow you to work on all aspects of your presentation simultaneously. You can drag the splitter bar and the pane borders to make each area larger or smaller.

In normal view, you can adjust the width of the slide pane by dragging the **splitter bar** and the height of the notes pane by dragging the pane borders. After you have created at least two slides, **scroll bars**, **scroll arrows**, and **scroll boxes** will be displayed below and to the right of the windows, and you can use them to view different parts of the panes.

Slide sorter view is helpful when you want to see all the slides in the presentation simultaneously. A thumbnail version of each slide is displayed, and you can rearrange their order, add transitions and timings to switch from one slide to the next in a presentation, add and delete slides, and preview animations.

Slide show view fills the entire screen and allows you to see the slide show just as your audience will view it. Transition effects, animation, graphics, movies, and timings are shown as they will appear during an actual presentation.

Table 1-1 identifies the view buttons and provides an explanation of each view.

Table 1-1 View Buttons and Functions

BUTTON	BUTTON NAME	FUNCTION
	Normal View	Shows three panes: the tabs pane with either the Outline tab or the Slides tab, the slide pane, and the notes pane.
	Slide Sorter View	Shows thumbnail versions of all slides in a presentation. You then can copy, cut, paste, or otherwise change the slide position to modify the presentation. Slide sorter view also is used to add timings, to select animated transitions, and to preview animations.
	Slide Show View	Shows the slides as an electronic presentation on the full screen of your computer's monitor. Looking much like a slide projector display, this view can show you the effect of transitions, build effects, slide timings, and animations.

More About

The 7 × 7 Rule

All slide shows in the projects and exercises in this textbook follow the 7 x 7 rule. This guideline states that each slide should have a maximum of seven lines, and each of these lines should have a maximum of seven words. This rule requires PowerPoint designers to choose their words carefully and, in turn, helps viewers read the slides easily.

Placeholders, Text Areas, Mouse Pointer, and Scroll Bars

The PowerPoint window contains elements similar to the document windows in other Microsoft Office applications. Other features are unique to PowerPoint. The main elements are the placeholders, text areas, mouse pointer, and scroll bars.

PLACEHOLDERS **Placeholders** are boxes that are displayed when you create a new slide. All layouts except the Blank slide layout contain placeholders. Depending on the particular slide layout selected, placeholders are displayed for the slide title, body text, charts, tables, organization charts, media clips, and clip art. You type titles, body text, and bulleted lists in **text placeholders**; you place graphic elements in chart placeholders, table placeholders, organizational chart placeholders, and clip art placeholders. A placeholder is considered an **object**, which is a single element of a slide.

TEXT AREAS **Text areas** are surrounded by a dotted outline. The title slide in Figure 1-7 on page PPT 10 has two text areas that contain the text placeholders where you will type the main heading, or title, of a new slide and the subtitle, or other object. Other slides in a presentation may use a layout that contains text areas for a title and bulleted lists.

MOUSE POINTER The **mouse pointer** can become one of several different shapes depending on the task you are performing in PowerPoint and the pointer's location on the screen. The different shapes are discussed when they appear.

SCROLL BARS When you add a second slide to a presentation, a **vertical scroll bar** appears on the right side of the slide pane. PowerPoint allows you to use the scroll bar to move forward or backward through the presentation.

The **horizontal scroll bar** also may be displayed. It is located on the bottom of the slide pane and allows you to display a portion of the slide when the entire slide does not fit on the screen.

Status Bar, Menu Bar, Standard Toolbar, Formatting Toolbar, and Drawing Toolbar

The status bar is displayed at the bottom of the screen above the Windows taskbar (Figure 1-7). The menu bar, Standard toolbar, and Formatting toolbar are displayed at the top of the screen just below the title bar. The Drawing toolbar is displayed above the status bar.

STATUS BAR Immediately above the Windows taskbar at the bottom of the screen is the status bar. The **status bar** consists of a message area and a presentation design template identifier (Figure 1-7). Generally, the message area shows the current slide number and the total number of slides in the slide show. For example, in Figure 1-7 the message area shows Slide 1 of 1. Slide 1 is the current slide, and of 1 indicates the slide show contains only one slide. The template identifier shows Default Design, which is the template PowerPoint uses initially.

More About

Selecting Fonts

Designers recommend using a maximum of two fonts and two font styles or effects in a slide show. This design philosophy maintains balance and simplicity.

MENU BAR The **menu bar** is a special toolbar that includes the PowerPoint menu names (Figure 1-8a). Each **menu name** represents a menu of commands that you can use to perform tasks such as retrieving, storing, printing, and manipulating objects in a presentation. When you point to a menu name on the menu bar, the area of the menu bar containing the name changes to a button. To display a menu, such as the Edit menu, click the Edit menu name on the menu bar. A **menu** is a list of commands. If you point to a command on a menu that has an arrow to its right edge, a **submenu** shows another list of commands.

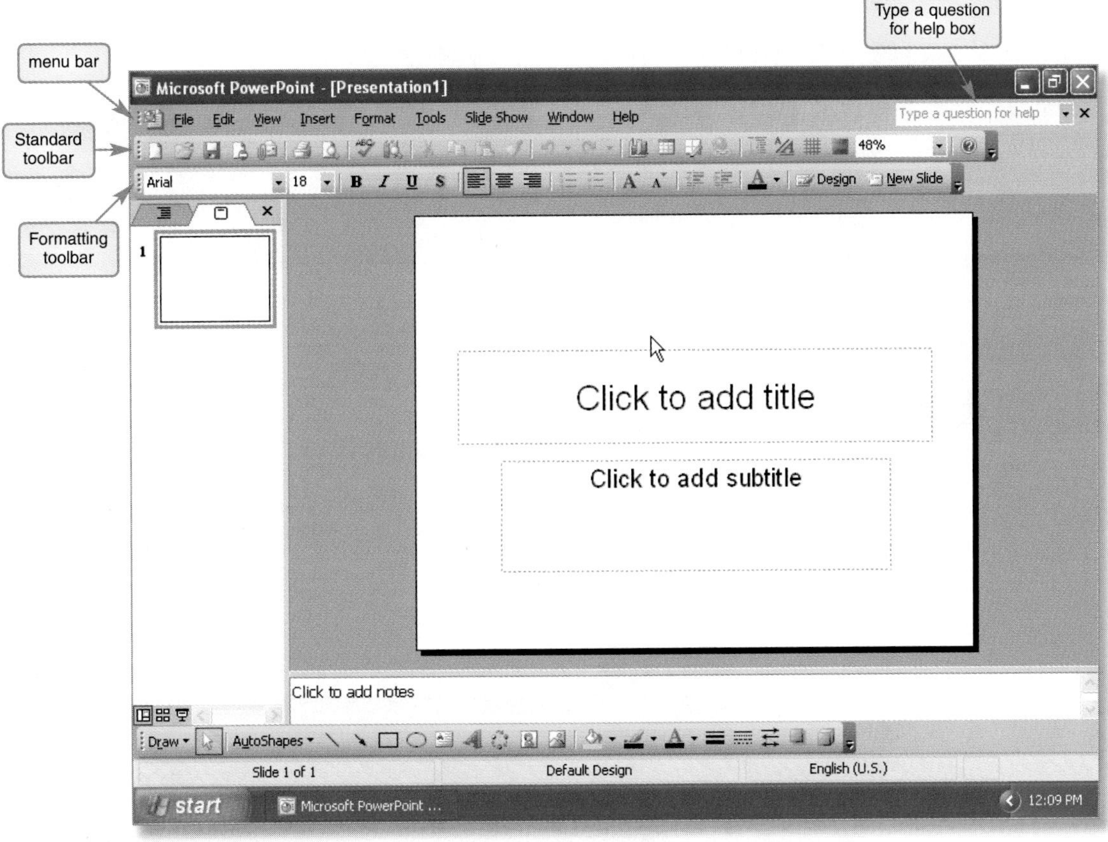

(a) Menu Bar and Toolbars

FIGURE 1-8

When you click a menu name on the menu bar, PowerPoint displays a **short menu** listing the most recently used commands (Figure 1-8b). If you wait a few seconds or click the arrows at the bottom of the short menu, it expands into a full menu. A **full menu** lists all the commands associated with a menu (Figure 1-8c). You also can display a full menu immediately by double-clicking the menu name on the menu bar. In this book, always have PowerPoint show the full menu by using one of the following techniques:

1. Click the menu name on the menu bar and then wait a few seconds.
2. Click the menu name on the menu bar and then click the arrows at the bottom of the short menu.
3. Click the menu name on the menu bar and then point to the arrows at the bottom of the short menu.
4. Double-click the menu name on the menu bar.

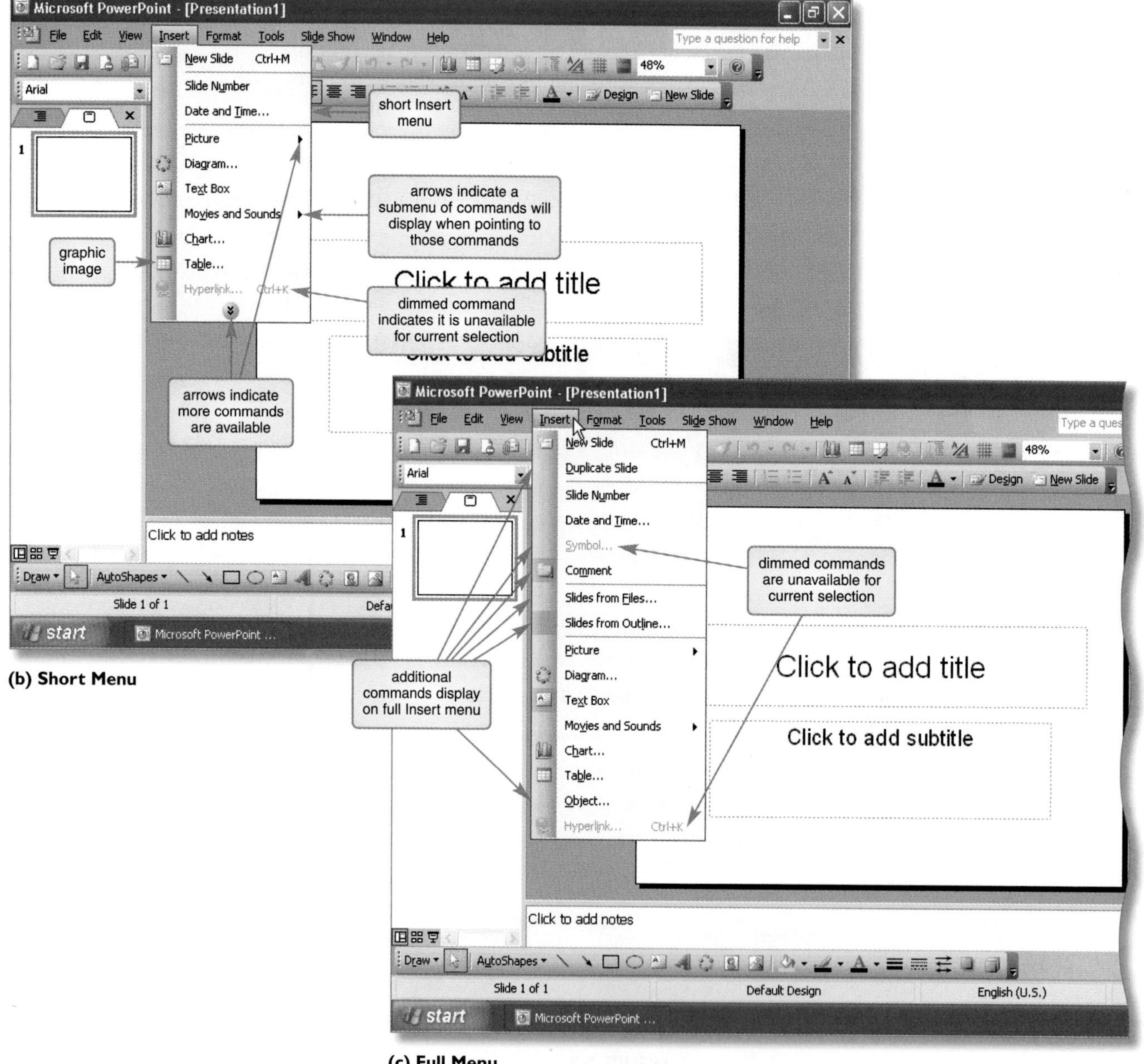

(b) Short Menu

(c) Full Menu

FIGURE 1-8 ***(continued)***

Both short and full menus display some **dimmed commands** that appear gray, or dimmed, instead of black, which indicates they are not available for the current selection. A command with a dark gray shading to the left of it on a full menu is a **hidden command** because it does not appear on a short menu. As you use PowerPoint, it automatically personalizes the short menus for you based on how often you use commands. That is, as you use hidden commands, PowerPoint *unhides* them and places them on the short menu.

The menu bar can change to include other menu names depending on the type of work you are doing in PowerPoint. For example, if you are adding a chart to a slide, Data and Chart menu names are added to the menu bar with commands that reflect charting options.

STANDARD, FORMATTING, AND DRAWING TOOLBARS The **Standard toolbar** (Figure 1-9a), **Formatting toolbar** (Figure 1-9b), and **Drawing toolbar** (Figure 1-9c on the next page) contain buttons and boxes that allow you to perform frequent tasks more quickly than when using the menu bar. For example, to print a slide show, you click the Print button on the Standard toolbar. Each button has an image on the button face that helps you remember the button's function. Also, when you move the mouse pointer over a button or box, the name of the button or box appears below it in a ScreenTip. A **ScreenTip** is a short on-screen note associated with the object to which you are pointing. For examples of ScreenTips, see Figures 1-3 and 1-13 on pages PPT 7 and PPT 19.

Figure 1-9 illustrates the Standard, Formatting, and Drawing toolbars and describes the functions of the buttons. Each of the buttons and boxes will be explained in detail when they are used.

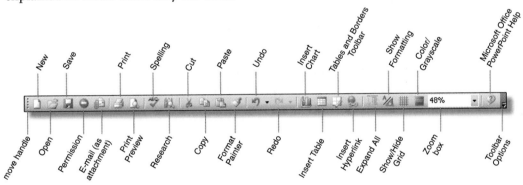

More About

Hiding Toolbars

To display more of the PowerPoint window, you can hide a toolbar you no longer need. To hide a toolbar, right-click any toolbar and then click the check mark next to the toolbar you want to hide on the shortcut menu.

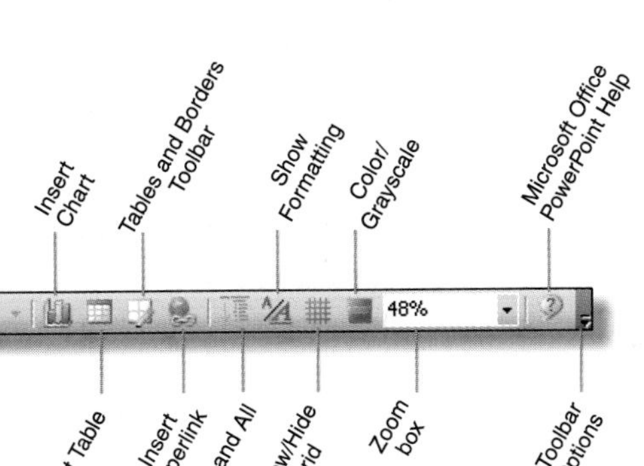

(a) Standard Toolbar

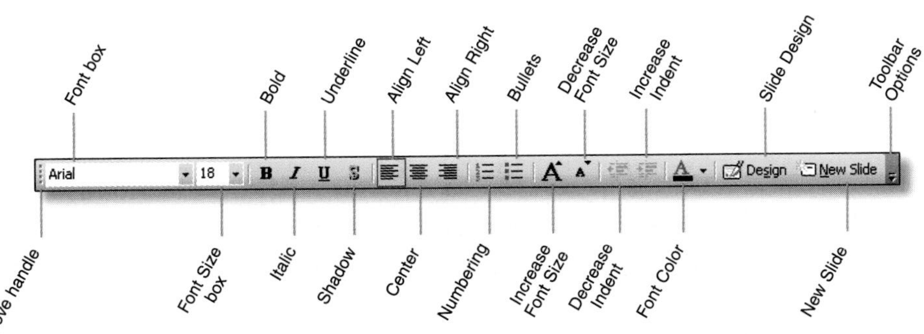

(b) Formatting Toolbar

FIGURE 1-9

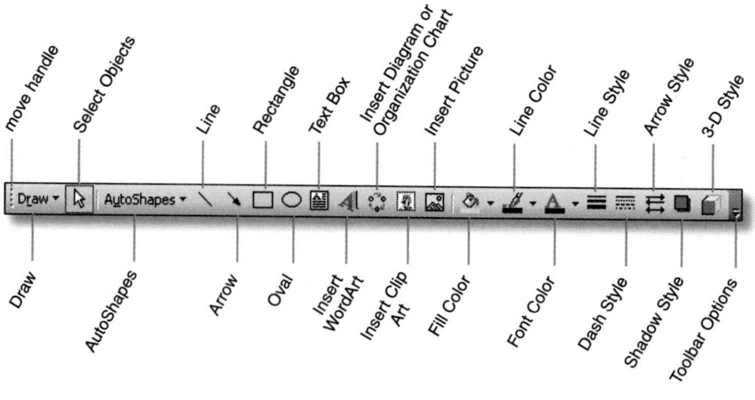

(c) Drawing Toolbar

FIGURE 1-9 ***(continued)***

More About

Shortcut Menus

When you point to or select an item and right-click, a shortcut menu usually displays. This special menu contains frequently used commands related to that object. In some cases, you also can display the shortcut menu by selecting an object, such as a paragraph, and then pressing SHIFT+F10. To hide a shortcut menu, click outside the shortcut menu or press the ESC key.

PowerPoint has several additional toolbars you can display by pointing to Toolbars on the View menu and then clicking the respective name on the Toolbars submenu. You also may display a toolbar by pointing to a toolbar and right-clicking to display a shortcut menu, which lists the available toolbars. A **shortcut menu** contains a list of commands or items that relate to the item to which you are pointing when you right-click.

Speech Recognition

With the **Office Speech Recognition software** installed and a microphone, you can speak the names of toolbar buttons, menus, menu commands, list items, alerts, and dialog box controls, such as OK and Cancel. You also can dictate words to fill the placeholders. To indicate whether you want to speak commands or dictate placeholder entries, you use the Language bar. The Language bar can be in one of four states: (1) **restored**, which means it is displayed somewhere in the PowerPoint window (Figure 1-10a); (2) **minimized**, which means it is displayed on the Windows taskbar (Figure 1-10b); (3) **hidden**, which means you do not see it on the screen but it will be displayed the next time you start your computer; (4) **closed**, which means it is hidden permanently until you enable it. If the Language bar is hidden or closed and you want it to display, then do the following:

1. Right-click an open area on the Windows taskbar at the bottom of the screen.
2. Point to Toolbars and then click Language bar on the Toolbars submenu.

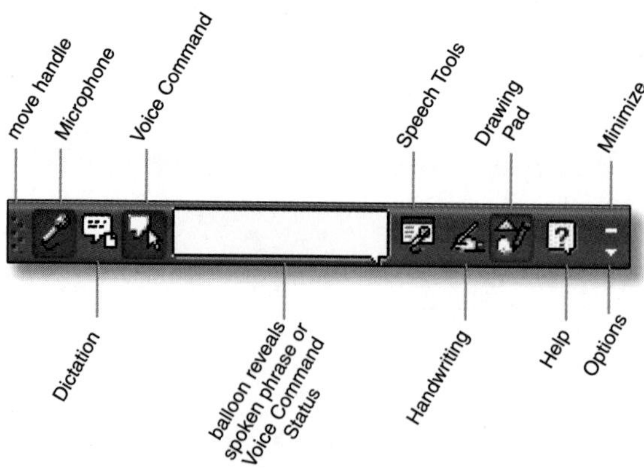

(a) Language Bar Restored

FIGURE 1-10

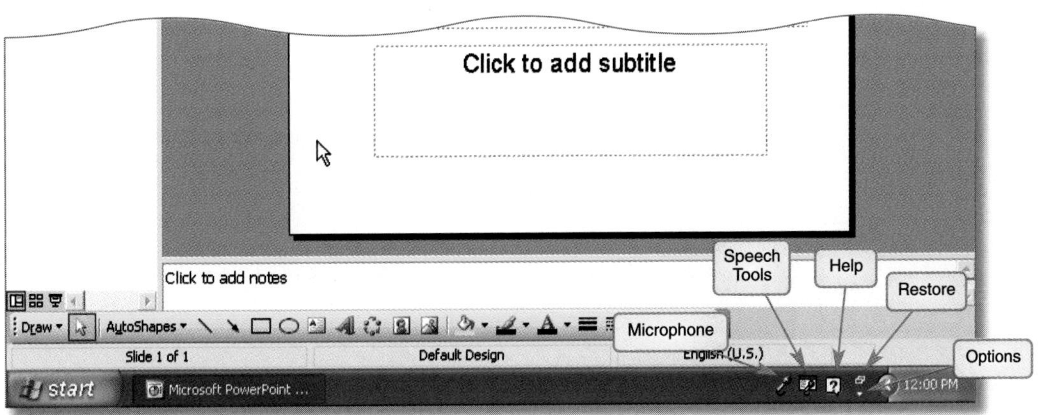

(b) Language Bar Minimized on Windows Taskbar

FIGURE 1-10 *(continued)*

If the Language bar command is dimmed on the Toolbars submenu or if the Speech command is dimmed on the Tools menu, the Office Speech Recognition software is not installed.

In this book, the Language bar does not appear in the figures. If you want to close the Language bar so that your screen is identical to what you see in the book, right-click the Language bar and then click Close the Language bar on the shortcut menu.

Additional information about the speech recognition capabilities of PowerPoint is available in Appendix B.

Choosing a Design Template

A **design template** provides consistency in design and color throughout the entire presentation. It determines the color scheme, font and font size, and layout of a presentation. PowerPoint has three Slide Design task panes that allow you to choose and change the appearance of slides in your presentation. The **Slide Design task pane** shows a variety of styles. You can alter the colors used in the design templates by using the **Slide Design – Color Schemes task pane.** In addition, you can animate elements of your presentation by using the **Slide Design – Animation Schemes task pane.**

In this project, you will select a particular design template by using the Slide Design task pane. The top section of the task pane, labeled Used in This Presentation, shows the template currently used in the slide show. PowerPoint uses the **Default Design** template until you select a different style. When you place your mouse over a template, the name of the template appears. Once a PowerPoint slide show has been created on the computer, the next section of the task pane displayed is the Recently Used templates. This area shows the four templates you have used in your newest slide shows. The Available For Use area shows additional templates. The templates are displayed in alphabetical order in the two columns.

You want to change the template for this presentation from the Default Design to Profile. The steps on the next page apply the Profile design template.

More About

The Default Design Template

Some PowerPoint slide show designers create presentations using the Default Design template. This blank design allows them to concentrate on the words being used to convey the message and does not distract them with colors and various text attributes. Once the text is entered, the designers then select an appropriate design template.

To Choose a Design Template

1

• **Point to the Slide Design button on the Formatting toolbar (Figure 1-11).**

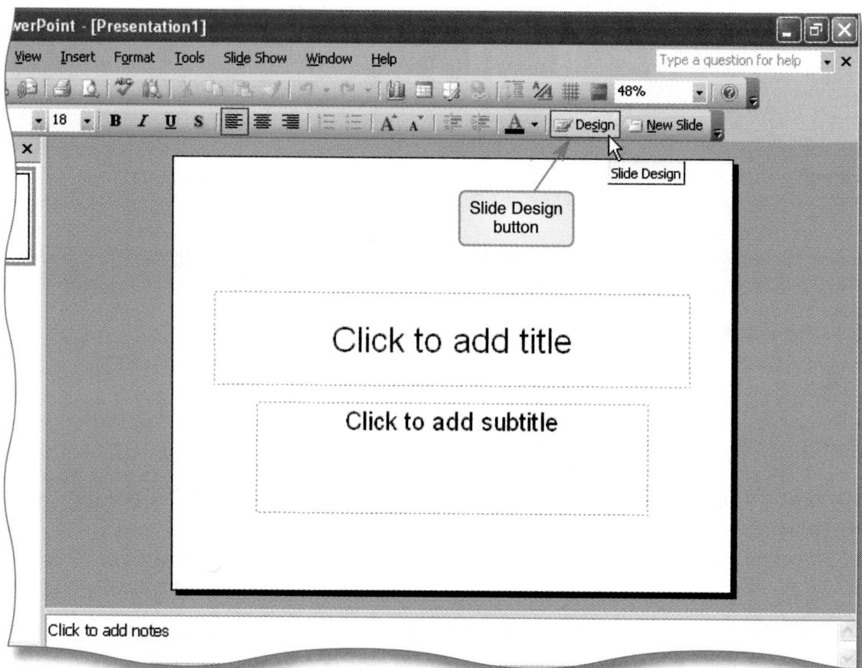

FIGURE 1-11

2

• **Click the Slide Design button and then point to the down scroll arrow in the Apply a design template list.**

The Slide Design task pane appears (Figure 1-12). The Apply a design template list shows thumbnail views of numerous design templates. Your list may look different depending on your computer. The Default Design template is highlighted in the Used in This Presentation area. Other templates display in the Available For Use area and possibly in the Recently Used area. The Close button in the Slide Design task pane can be used to close the task pane if you do not want to apply a new template.

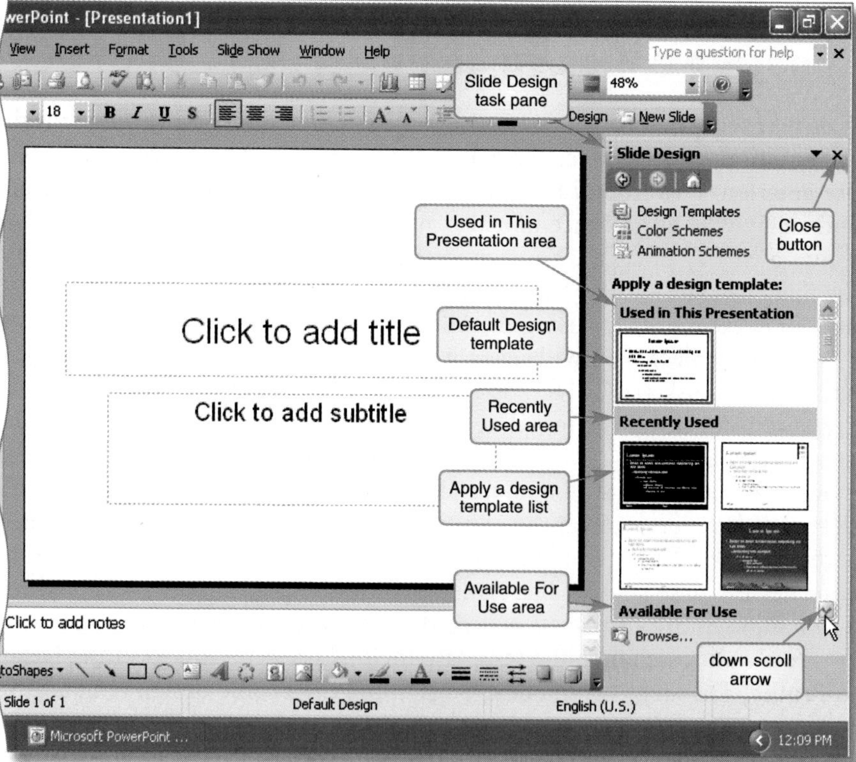

FIGURE 1-12

3

- **Click the down scroll arrow to scroll through the list of design templates until Profile appears in the Available For Use area. Point to the Profile template.**

The Profile template is selected, as indicated by the blue box around the template and the arrow button on the right side (Figure 1-13). PowerPoint provides 45 templates in the Available For Use area. Additional templates are available on the Microsoft Office Online Web site. A ScreenTip shows the template's name. Your system may display the ScreenTip, Profile.pot, which indicates the design template's file extension (.pot).

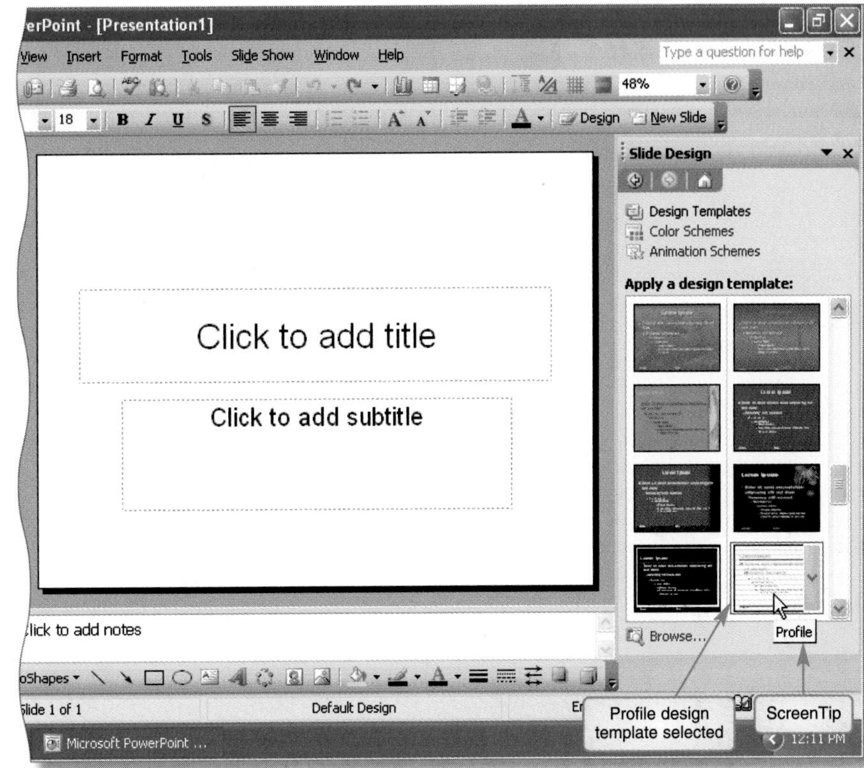

FIGURE 1-13

4

- **Click Profile.**
- **Point to the Close button in the Slide Design task pane.**

The template is applied to Slide 1, as shown in the slide pane and Slides tab (Figure 1-14).

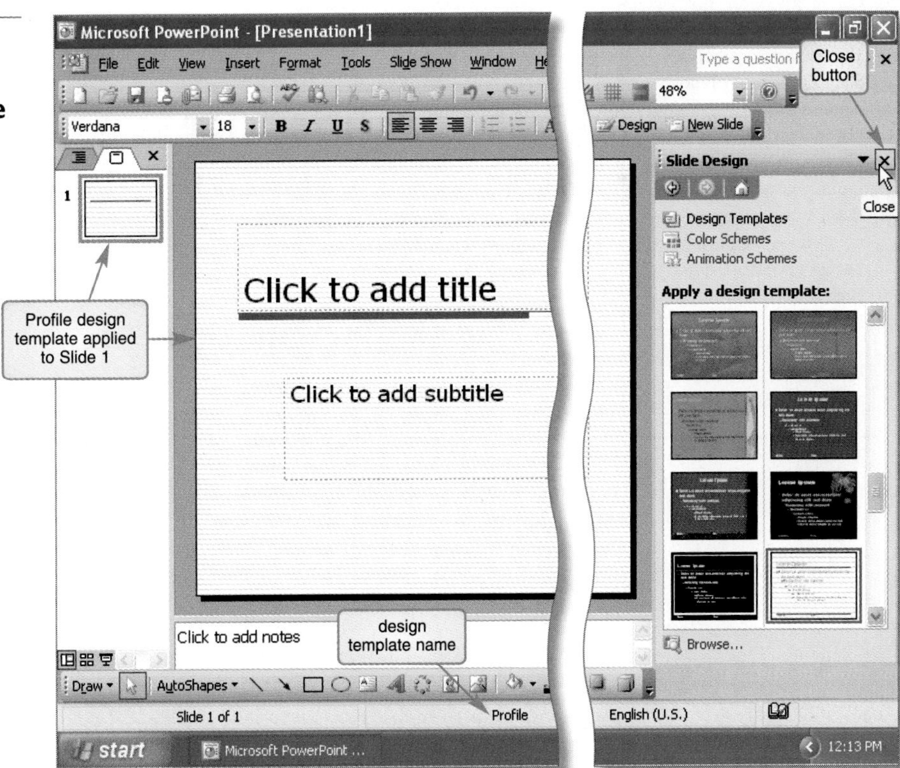

FIGURE 1-14

5

• **Click the Close button.**

Slide 1 is displayed in normal view with the Profile design template (Figure 1-15).

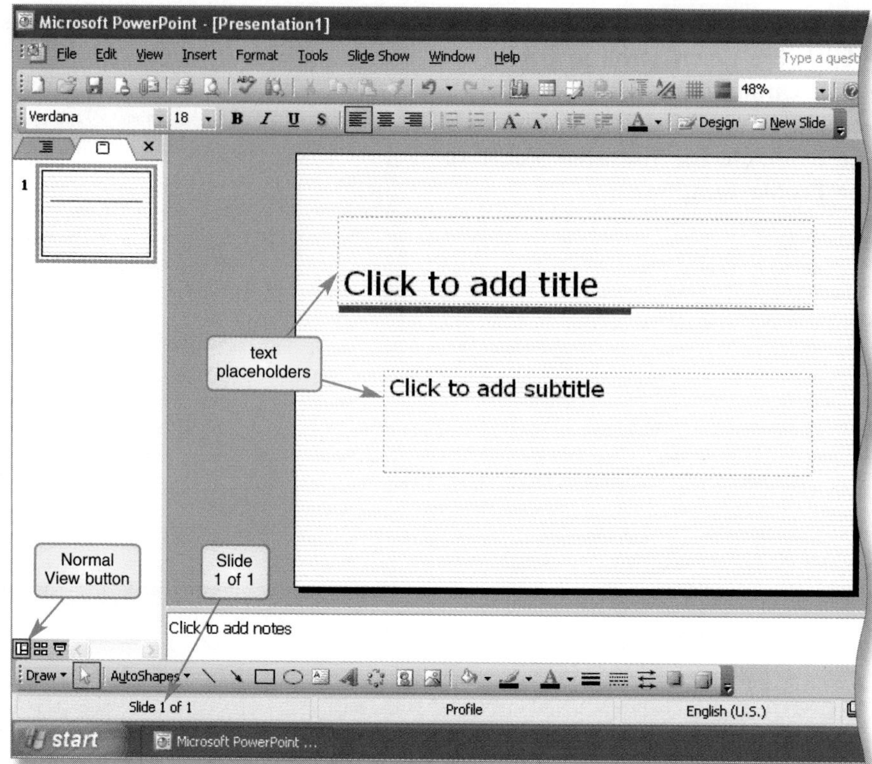

FIGURE 1-15

Other Ways

1. On Format menu click Slide Design, scroll down Apply a design template list and click Profile, click Close button
2. Double-click Default Design on status bar, scroll down Apply a design template list and click Profile, click Close button
3. In Voice Command mode, say "Design, [desired design template name]"

Creating a Title Slide

With the exception of a blank slide, PowerPoint assumes every new slide has a title. To make creating a presentation easier, any text you type after a new slide appears becomes title text in the title text placeholder.

Entering the Presentation Title

The presentation title for Project 1 is Strategies for College Success. To enter text in your slide, you type on the keyboard or speak into the microphone. As you begin entering text in the title text placeholder, the title text is displayed immediately in the Slide 1 thumbnail in the Slides tab. The following steps create the title slide for this presentation.

To Enter the Presentation Title

1

- **Click the label, Click to add title, located inside the title text placeholder.**

The insertion point is in the title text placeholder (Figure 1-16). The ***insertion point*** *is a blinking vertical line (|), which indicates where the next character will display. The mouse pointer changes to an I-beam. A* ***selection rectangle*** *appears around the title text placeholder. The placeholder is selected as indicated by the border and sizing handles displaying on the edges.*

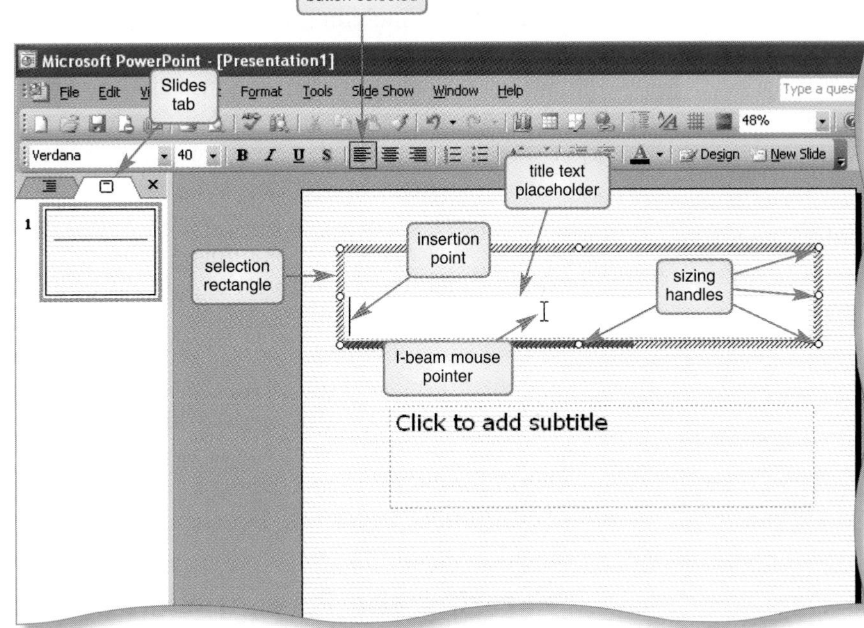

FIGURE 1-16

2

- **Type** `Strategies for College Success` **in the title text placeholder. Do not press the ENTER key.**

The title text, Strategies for College Success, appears on two lines in the title text placeholder and in the Slides tab (Figure 1-17). The insertion point appears after the final letter s in Success. The title text is displayed aligned left in the placeholder with the default text attributes of the Verdana font and font size 40.

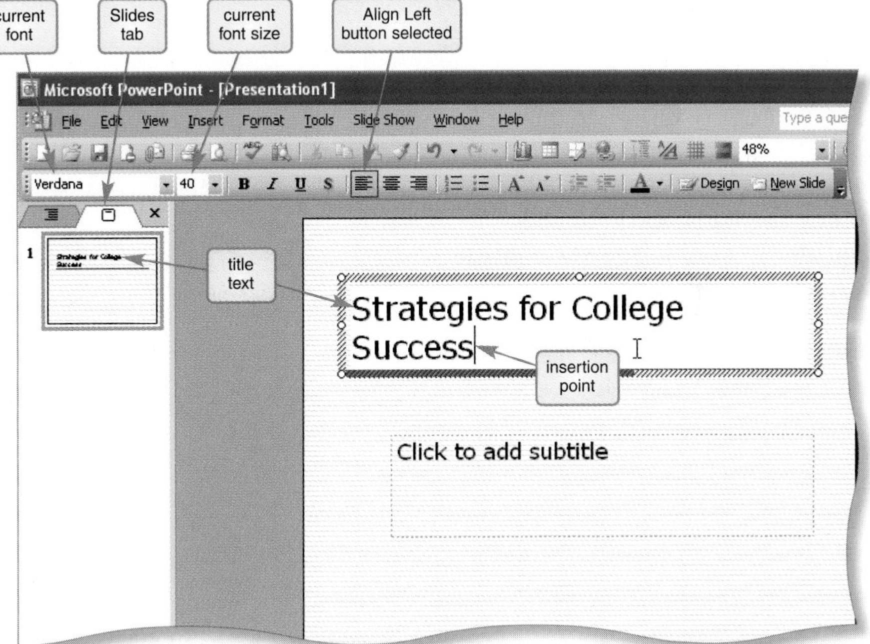

FIGURE 1-17

Other Ways

1. In Dictation mode, say "Strategies for College Success"

PowerPoint **line wraps** text that exceeds the width of the placeholder. One of PowerPoint's features is **text AutoFit**. If you are creating a slide and need to squeeze an extra line in the text placeholder, PowerPoint will prompt you to resize the existing text in the placeholder so the spillover text will fit on the slide.

Correcting a Mistake When Typing

If you type the wrong letter, press the BACKSPACE key to erase all the characters back to and including the one that is incorrect. If you mistakenly press the ENTER key after typing the title and the insertion point is on the new line, simply press the BACKSPACE key to return the insertion point to the right of the letter s in the word Success.

When you install PowerPoint, the default setting allows you to reverse up to the last 20 changes by clicking the Undo button on the Standard toolbar. The ScreenTip that appears when you point to the Undo button changes to indicate the type of change just made. For example, if you type text in the title text placeholder and then point to the Undo button, the ScreenTip that appears is Undo Typing. For clarity, when referencing the Undo button in this project, the name displaying in the ScreenTip is referenced. Another way to reverse changes is to click the Undo command on the Edit menu. As with the Undo button, the Undo command reflects the last type of change made to the presentation.

You can reapply a change that you reversed with the Undo button by clicking the Redo button on the Standard toolbar. Clicking the Redo button reverses the last undo action. The ScreenTip name reflects the type of reversal last performed.

Q&A

Q: Can I change the capitalization of letters and words?

A: Yes. Simply select the text you want to change, click Change Case on the Format menu, and then click the desired option. For example, you can change all uppercase letters to lowercase letters or capitalize the first letter in each word.

Entering the Presentation Subtitle

The next step in creating the title slide is to enter the subtitle text into the subtitle text placeholder. Complete the following steps to enter the presentation subtitle.

To Enter the Presentation Subtitle

1

- **Click the label, Click to add subtitle, located inside the subtitle text placeholder.**

The insertion point appears in the subtitle text placeholder (Figure 1-18). The mouse pointer changes to an I-beam, indicating the mouse is in a text placeholder. The selection rectangle indicates the placeholder is selected.

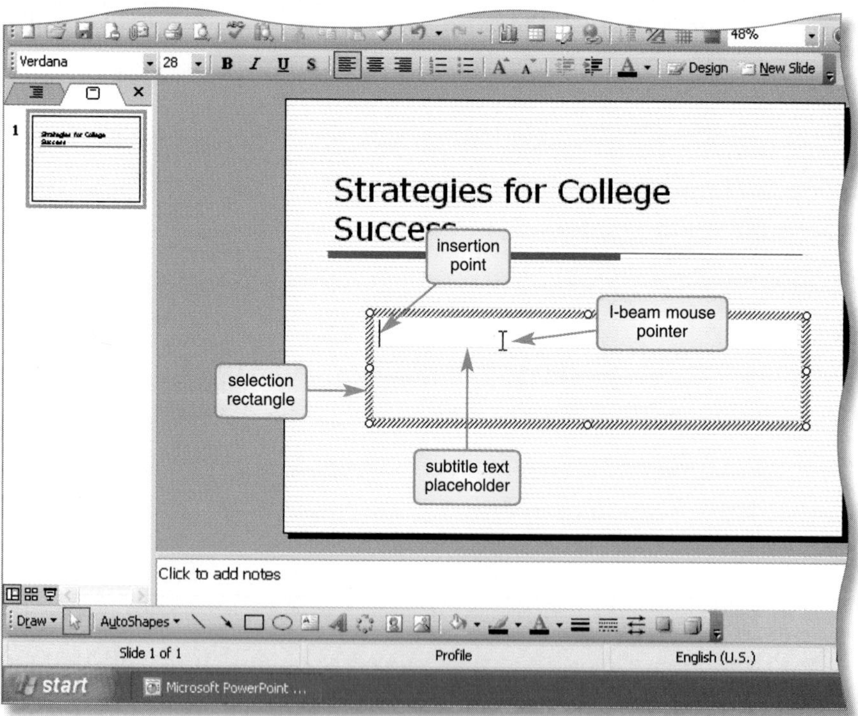

FIGURE 1-18

2

- **Type** `Presented by` **and then press the ENTER key.**
- **Type** `Lakemore Academic Skills Center` **but do not press the ENTER key.**

The subtitle text appears in the subtitle text placeholder and the Slides tab (Figure 1-19). The insertion point appears after the letter r in Center. A red wavy line appears below the word, Lakemore, to indicate a possible spelling error.

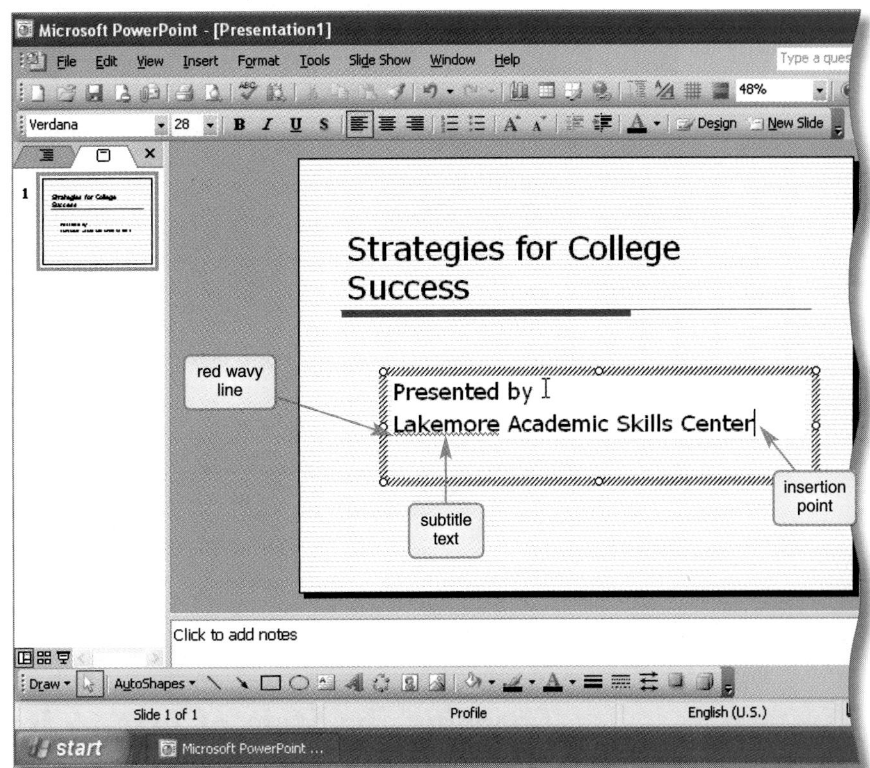

FIGURE 1-19

Other Ways

1. In Dictation mode, say "Presented by, New Line, Lakemore Academic Skills Center"

After pressing the ENTER key in Step 2, PowerPoint created a new line, which is the second paragraph in the placeholder. A **paragraph** is a segment of text with the same format that begins when you press the ENTER key and ends when you press the ENTER key again.

Text Attributes

This presentation uses the Profile design template. Each design template has its own text attributes. A **text attribute** is a characteristic of the text, such as font, font size, font style, or text color. You can adjust text attributes any time before, during, or after you type the text. Recall that a design template determines the color scheme, font and font size, and layout of a presentation. Most of the time, you use the design template's text attributes and color scheme. Occasionally, you may want to change the way a presentation looks, however, and still keep a particular design template. PowerPoint gives you that flexibility. You can use the design template and change the font and the font's color, effects, size, and style. Text may have one or more font styles and effects simultaneously. Table 1-2 on the next page explains the different text attributes available in PowerPoint.

More About

Text Attributes

The Microsoft Web site contains a comprehensive glossary of typography terms. The information includes a diagram illustrating text attributes. For more information, visit the PowerPoint 2003 More About Web page (`scsite.com/ppt2003/more`) and then click Attributes.

Table 1-2 Design Template Text Attributes

ATTRIBUTE	DESCRIPTION
Color	Defines the color of text. Printing text in color requires a color printer or plotter.
Effects	Effects include underline, shadow, emboss, superscript, and subscript. Effects can be applied to most fonts.
Font	Defines the appearance and shape of letters, numbers, and special characters.
Size	Specifies the height of characters on the screen. Character size is gauged by a measurement system called points. A single point is about 1/72 of an inch in height. Thus, a character with a point size of 18 is about 18/72 (or 1/4) of an inch in height.
Style	Font styles include regular, bold, italic, and bold italic.

The next two sections explain how to change the font size and font style attributes.

Changing the Style of Text to Italic

Text font styles include plain, italic, bold, shadowed, and underlined. PowerPoint allows you to use one or more text font styles in a presentation. The following steps add emphasis to the first line of the subtitle text by changing regular text to italic text.

To Change the Text Font Style to Italic

1

- **Triple-click the paragraph, Presented by, in the subtitle text placeholder, and then point to the Italic button on the Formatting toolbar.**

The paragraph, Presented by, is highlighted (Figure 1-20). The Italic button is surrounded by a blue box. You select an entire paragraph quickly by triple-clicking any text within the paragraph.

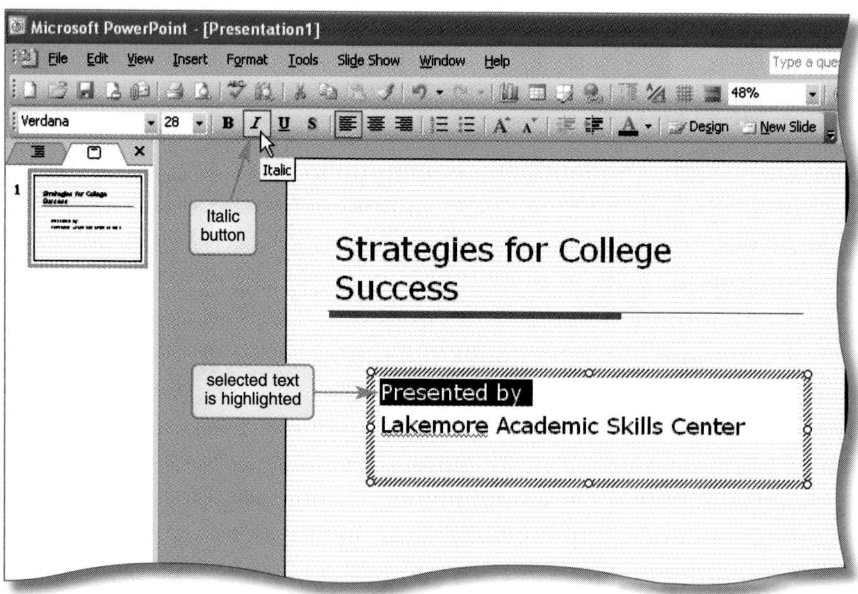

FIGURE 1-20

2

• **Click the Italic button.**

The text is italicized on the slide and the slide thumbnail (Figure 1-21).

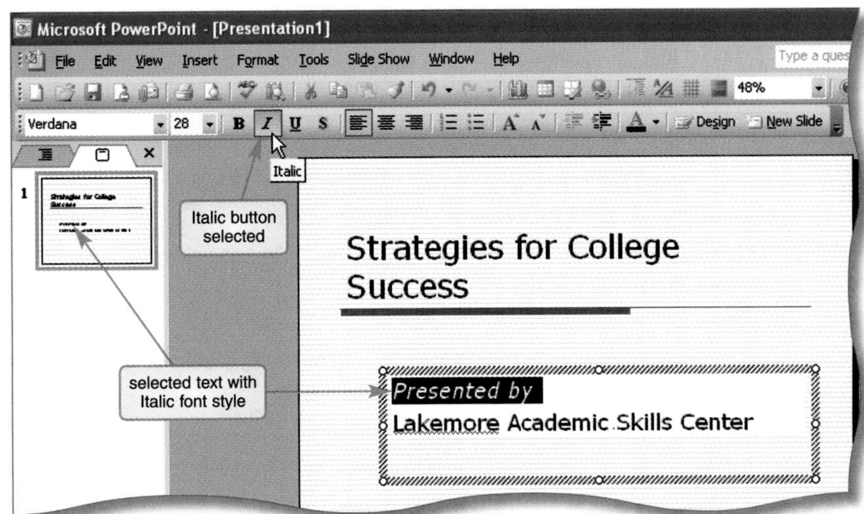

FIGURE 1-21

Other Ways

1. Right-click selected text, click Font on shortcut menu, click Italic in Font style list
2. On Format menu click Font, click Italic in Font style list
3. Press CTRL+I
4. In Voice Command mode, say "Italic"

To remove the italic style from text, select the italicized text and then click the Italic button. As a result, the Italic button is not selected, and the text does not have the italic font style.

Changing the Font Size

The Profile design template default font size is 40 point for title text and 28 point for body text. A point is 1/72 of an inch in height. Thus, a character with a point size of 40 is 40/72 (or 5/9) of an inch in height. Slide 1 requires you to increase the font size for the paragraph, Lakemore Academic Skills Center. The following steps illustrate how to increase the font size.

To Increase Font Size

1

• **Position the mouse pointer in the paragraph, Lakemore Academic Skills Center, and then triple-click.**

PowerPoint selects the entire paragraph (Figure 1-22).

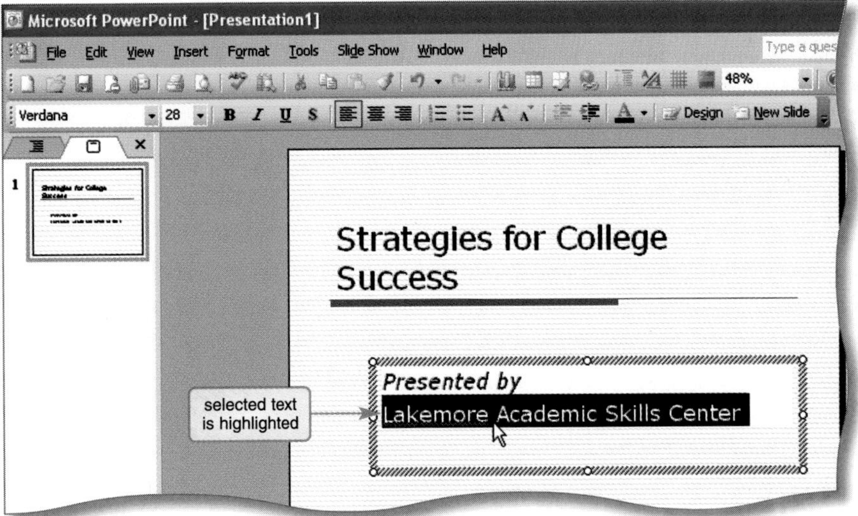

FIGURE 1-22

2

• **Point to the Font Size box arrow on the Formatting toolbar.**

*The ScreenTip shows the words, Font Size (Figure 1-23). The **Font Size box** is surrounded by a box and indicates that the subtitle text is 28 point.*

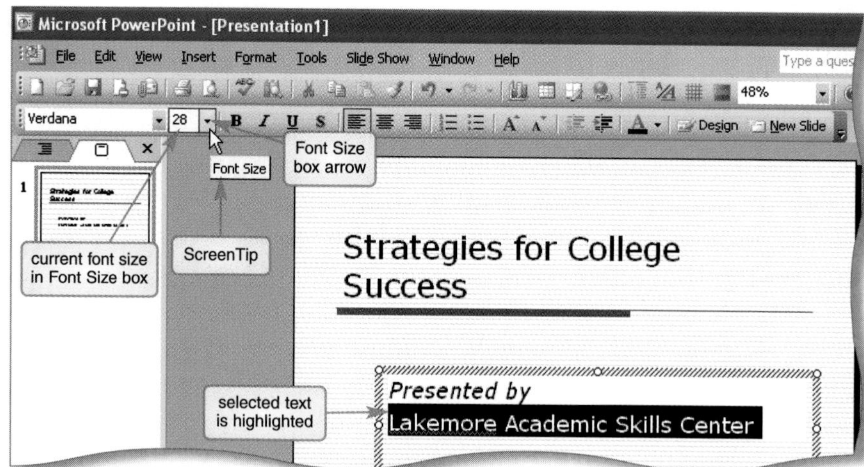

FIGURE 1-23

3

• **Click the Font Size box arrow, click the Font Size box scroll bar, and then point to 32 in the Font Size list.**

When you click the Font Size box, a list of available font sizes is displayed in the Font Size list (Figure 1-24). The font sizes displayed depend on the current font, which is Verdana. Font size 32 is highlighted.

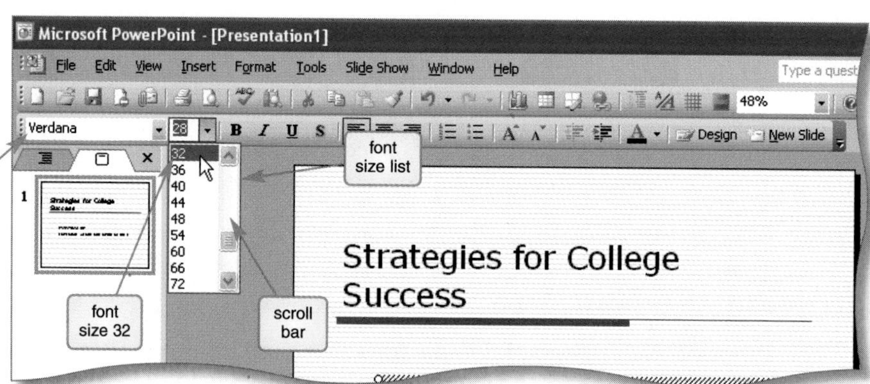

FIGURE 1-24

4

• **Click 32.**

The font size of the subtitle text, Lakemore Academic Skills Center, increases to 32 point (Figure 1-25). The Font Size box on the Formatting toolbar shows 32, indicating the selected text has a font size of 32.

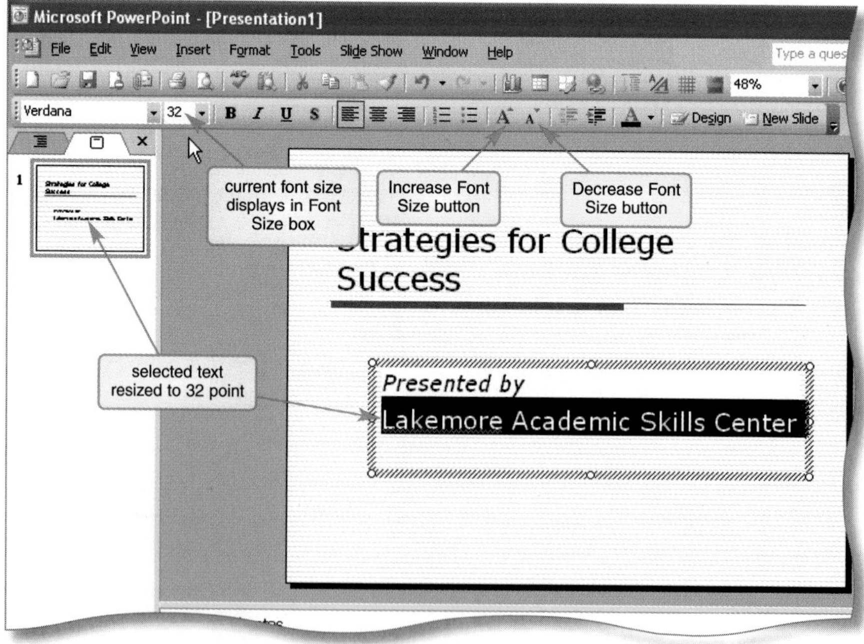

FIGURE 1-25

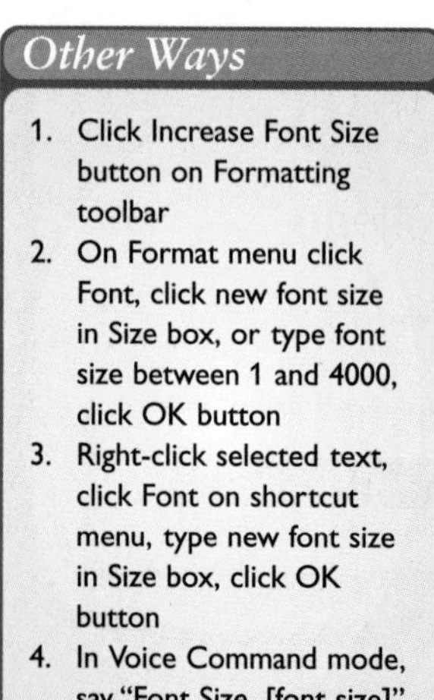

Other Ways

1. Click Increase Font Size button on Formatting toolbar
2. On Format menu click Font, click new font size in Size box, or type font size between 1 and 4000, click OK button
3. Right-click selected text, click Font on shortcut menu, type new font size in Size box, click OK button
4. In Voice Command mode, say "Font Size, [font size]"

The Increase Font Size button on the Formatting toolbar (Figure 1-25) increases the font size in preset increments each time you click the button. If you need to decrease the font size, click the Font Size box arrow and then select a size smaller than 32. The Decrease Font Size button on the Formatting toolbar (Figure 1-25) also decreases the font size in preset increments each time you click the button.

Saving the Presentation on a Floppy Disk

While you are building a presentation, the computer stores it in memory. It is important to save the presentation frequently because the presentation will be lost if the computer is turned off or you lose electrical power. Another reason to save your work is that if you run out of lab time before completing your project, you may finish the project later without starting over. Therefore, always save any presentation you will use later on a floppy disk or hard disk. A saved presentation is referred to as a **file.** Before you continue with Project 1, save the work completed thus far. The following steps illustrate how to save a presentation on a floppy disk in drive A using the Save button on the Standard toolbar.

Q&A

Q: Does PowerPoint save files automatically?

A: Yes. Every 10 minutes PowerPoint saves a copy of your presentation. To check or change the save interval, click Options on the Tools menu and then click the Save tab. Click the Save AutoRe cover info every check box and then type the specific time in the minutes box.

To Save a Presentation on a Floppy Disk

1

- **With a formatted floppy disk in drive A, click the Save button on the Standard toolbar.**

The Save As dialog box is displayed (Figure 1-26). The default folder, My Documents, appears in the Save in box. Strategies for College Success appears highlighted in the File name text box because PowerPoint uses the words in the title text placeholder as the default file name. Presentation appears in the Save as type box. The buttons on the top and on the side are used to select folders and change the appearance of file names and other information.

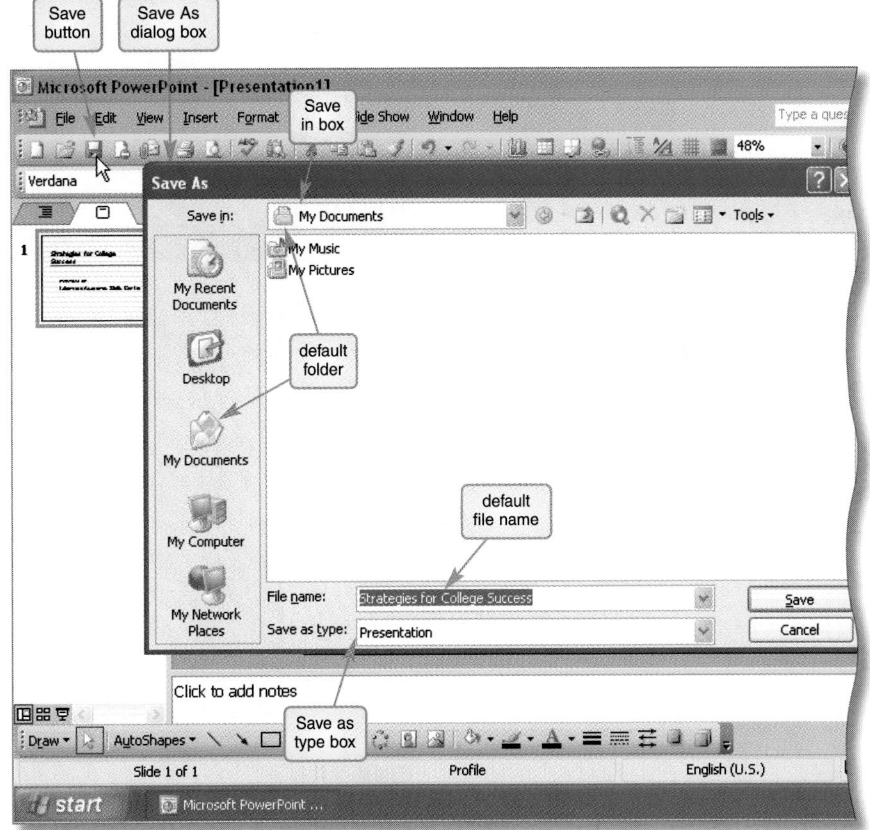

FIGURE 1-26

2

- **Type** `College Success` **in the File name text box. Do not press the ENTER key after typing the file name.**
- **Click the Save in box arrow.**

The name, College Success, appears in the File name text box (Figure 1-27). A file name can be up to 255 characters and can include spaces. The Save in list shows a list of locations in which to save a presentation. Your list may look different depending on the configuration of your system. Clicking the Cancel button closes the Save As dialog box.

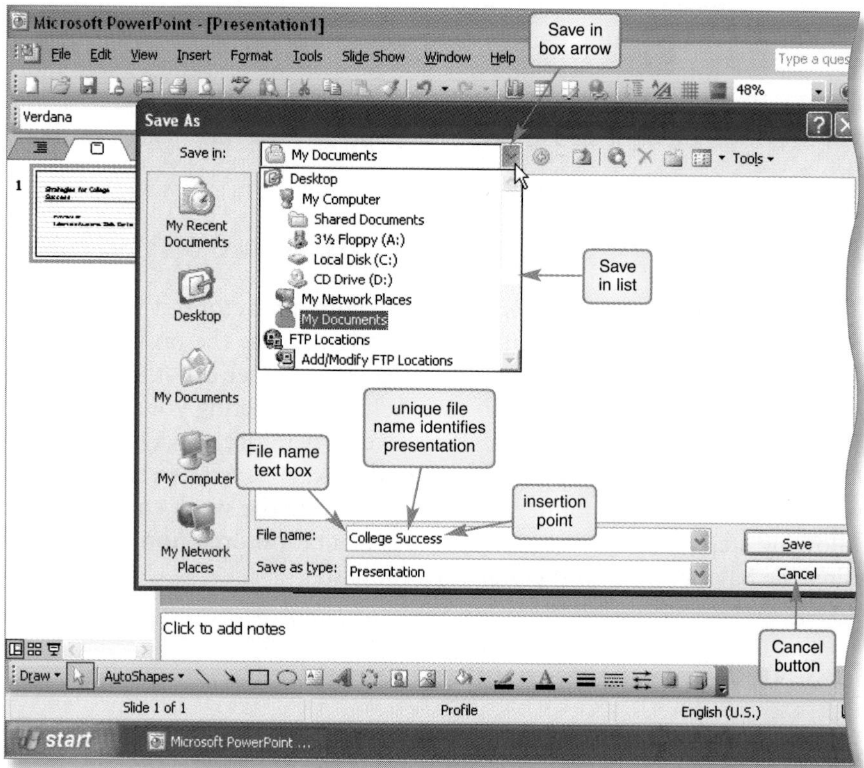

FIGURE 1-27

3

- **Click 3½ Floppy (A:) in the Save in list.**

Drive A becomes the selected drive (Figure 1-28).

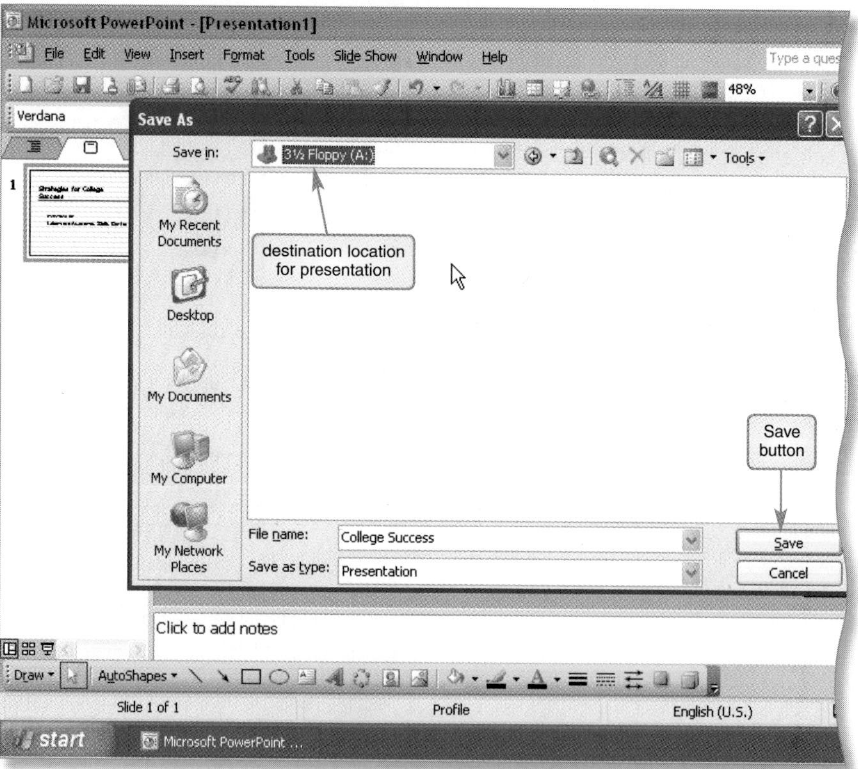

FIGURE 1-28

4

• **Click the Save button in the Save As dialog box.**

PowerPoint saves the presentation on the floppy disk in drive A. The title bar shows the file name used to save the presentation, College Success (Figure 1-29).

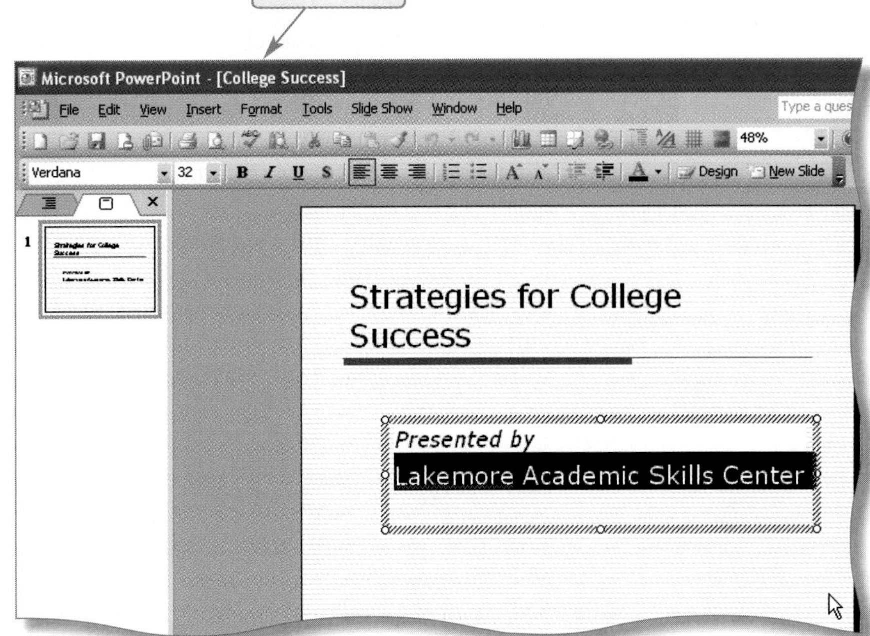

FIGURE 1-29

Other Ways

1. On File menu click Save As, type file name, select drive or folder, click Save button
2. On File menu click Save As, click My Computer button, select drive or folder, click Save button
3. Press CTRL+S or press SHIFT+F12, type file name, select drive or folder, click OK button
4. In Voice Command mode, say "File, Save As, [type desired file name], Save"

PowerPoint automatically appends the extension .ppt to the file name, College Success. The **.ppt** extension stands for **P**ower**P**oin**t**. Although the slide show, College Success, is saved on a floppy disk, it also remains in memory and is displayed on the screen.

It is a good practice to save periodically while you are working on a project. By doing so, you protect yourself from losing all the work you have done since the last time you saved.

The seven buttons at the top and to the right in the Save As dialog box in Figure 1-28 and their functions are summarized in Table 1-3.

Table 1-3 Save As Dialog Box Toolbar Buttons

BUTTON	BUTTON NAME	FUNCTION
	Default File Location	Displays contents of default file location
	Up One Level	Displays contents of folder one level up from current folder
	Search the Web	Starts browser and displays search engine
	Delete	Deletes selected file or folder
	Create New Folder	Creates new folder
	Views	Changes view of files and folders
Tools	Tools	Lists commands to print or modify file names and folders

More About

Passwords

The most common word used for a password is the word, password. When choosing a password for your files, experts recommend using a combination of letters and numbers and making the word at least eight characters. Avoid using your name and the names of family members or pets.

When you click the Tools button in the Save As dialog box, PowerPoint displays a list. The Save Options command in the list allows you to save the presentation automatically at a specified time interval and to reduce the file size. The Security Options command allows you to modify the security level for opening files that may contain harmful computer viruses and to assign a password to limit access to the file. A password is case-sensitive and can be up to 15 characters long. **Case-sensitive** means PowerPoint can differentiate between uppercase and lowercase letters. If you assign a password and then forget the password, you cannot access the file.

The file buttons on the left of the Save As dialog box in Figure 1-28 on page PPT 28 allow you to select frequently used folders. The My Recent Documents button displays a list of shortcuts (pointers) to the most recently used files in a folder titled Recent. You cannot save presentations to the Recent folder.

Adding a New Slide to a Presentation

With the title slide for the presentation created, the next step is to add the first text slide immediately after the title slide. Usually, when you create a presentation, you add slides with text, graphics, or charts. When you add a new slide, PowerPoint uses the Title and Text slide layout. Some placeholders allow you to double-click the placeholder and then access other objects, such as media clips, charts, diagrams, and organization charts.

The following steps add a new Text slide layout with a bulleted list. The default PowerPoint setting will display the Slide Layout task pane each time a new slide is added. Your system may not display this task pane if the setting has been changed.

To Add a New Text Slide with a Bulleted List

1

• **Click the New Slide button on the Formatting toolbar.**

The Slide Layout task pane opens. The Title and Text slide layout is selected. Slide 2 of 2 appears on the status bar (Figure 1-30).

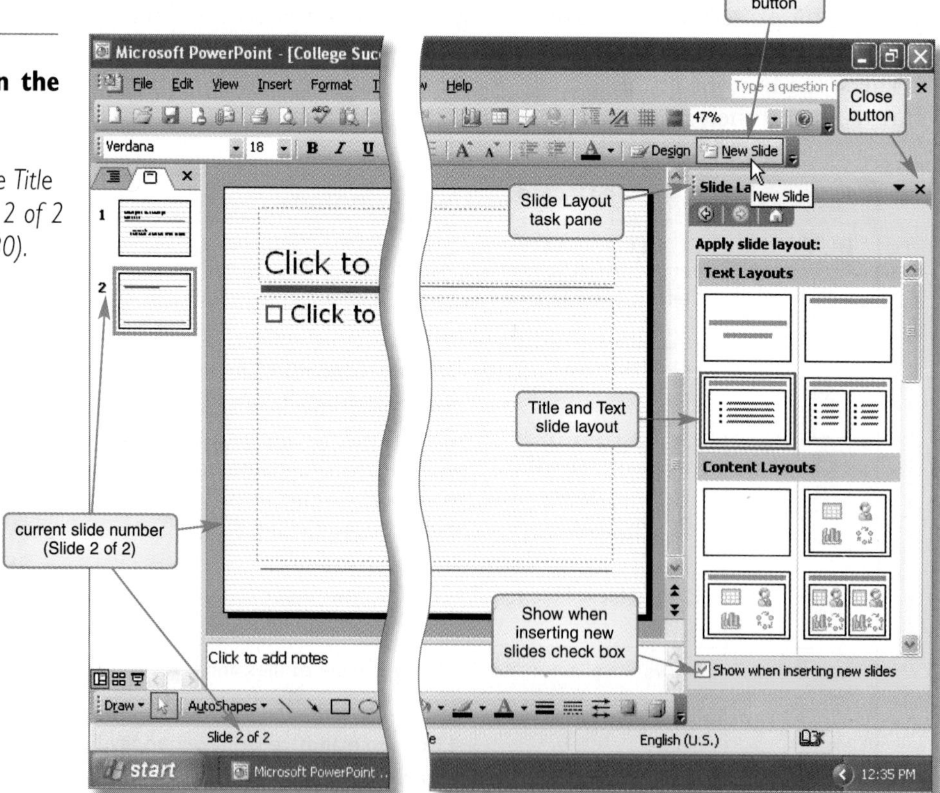

FIGURE 1-30

2

• **If necessary, click the Show when inserting new slides check box to remove the check mark, and then click the Close button on the Slide Layout task pane.**

Slide 2 appears in both the slide pane and Slides tab retaining the attributes of the Profile design template (Figure 1-31). The vertical scroll bar appears in the slide pane. The bullet appears as an outline square.

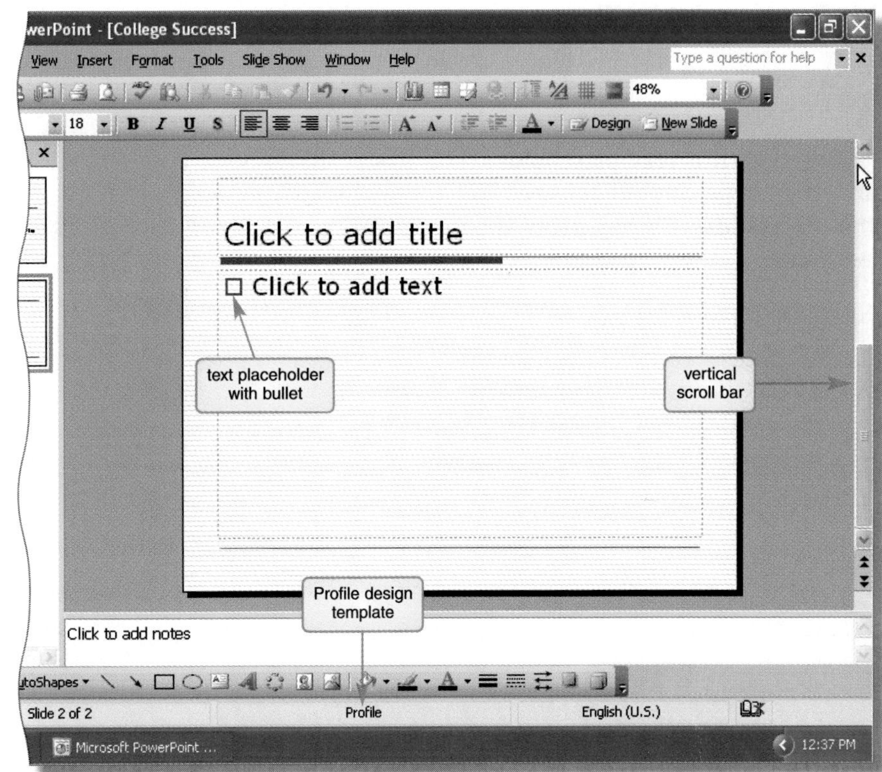

FIGURE 1-31

Other Ways

1. On Insert menu click New Slide
2. Press CTRL+M
3. In Voice Command mode, say "New Slide"

Slide 2 appears with a title text placeholder and a text placeholder with a bullet. You can change the layout for a slide at any time during the creation of a presentation by clicking Format on the menu bar and then clicking Slide Layout. You also can click View on the menu bar and then click Task Pane. You then can double-click the slide layout of your choice from the Slide Layout task pane.

Creating a Text Slide with a Single-Level Bulleted List

The information in the Slide 2 text placeholder is presented in a bulleted list. All the bullets appear on one level. A **level** is a position within a structure, such as an outline, that indicates the magnitude of importance. PowerPoint allows for five paragraph levels. Each paragraph level has an associated bullet. The bullet font is dependent on the design template.

More About

Deleting Bullets

If you do not want bullets to display on a particular paragraph, select the paragraph and then click the Bullets button on the Formatting toolbar.

Entering a Slide Title

PowerPoint assumes every new slide has a title. The title for Slide 2 is Get Organized. The step on the next page shows how to enter this title.

To Enter a Slide Title

1

- **Click the title text placeholder and then type** `Get Organized` **in the placeholder. Do not press the ENTER key.**

The title, Get Organized, appears in the title text placeholder and in the Slides tab (Figure 1-32). The insertion point appears after the d in Organized. The selection rectangle indicates the title text placeholder is selected.

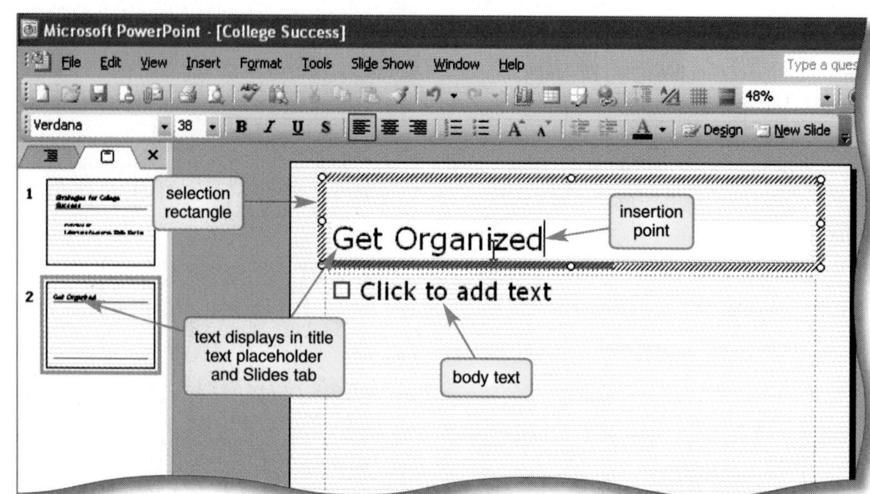

FIGURE 1-32

Other Ways

1. In Dictation mode, say "Get Organized"

Selecting a Text Placeholder

Before you can type text into the text placeholder, you first must select it. The following step selects the text placeholder on Slide 2.

To Select a Text Placeholder

1

- **Click the bulleted paragraph labeled, Click to add text.**

The insertion point appears immediately to the right of the bullet on Slide 2 (Figure 1-33). The mouse pointer may change shape if you move it away from the bullet. The selection rectangle indicates the text placeholder is selected.

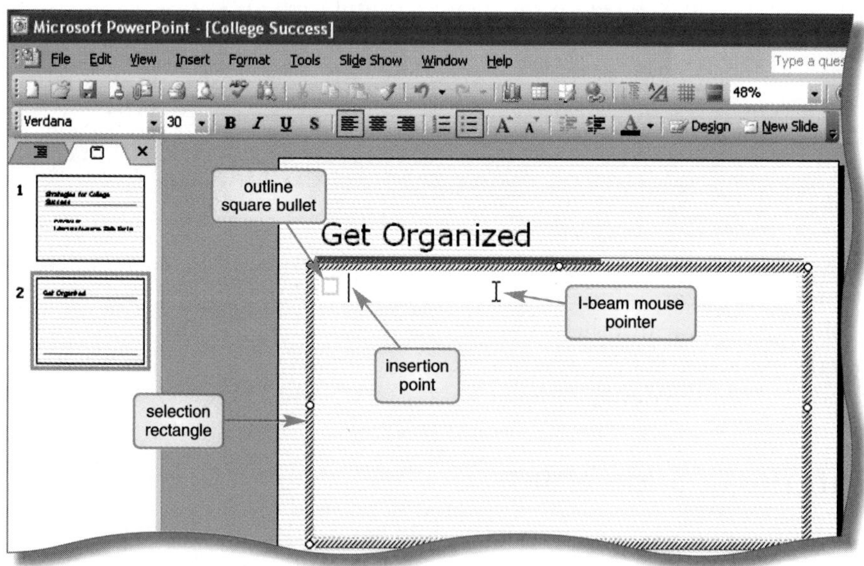

FIGURE 1-33

Other Ways

1. Press CTRL+ENTER

Typing a Single-Level Bulleted List

As discussed previously, a bulleted list is a list of paragraphs, each of which is preceded by a bullet. A paragraph is a segment of text ended by pressing the ENTER key. The next step is to type the single-level bulleted list, which consists of three entries (Figure 1-1b on page PPT 5). The following steps illustrate how to type a single-level bulleted list.

To Type a Single-Level Bulleted List

1

- **Type** `Time management skills help balance academic, work, and social events` **and then press the ENTER key.**

The paragraph, Time management skills help balance academic, work, and social events, appears (Figure 1-34). The font size is 30. The insertion point appears after the second bullet. When you press the ENTER key, PowerPoint ends one paragraph and begins a new paragraph. With the Title and Text slide layout, PowerPoint places an outline square bullet in front of the new paragraph.

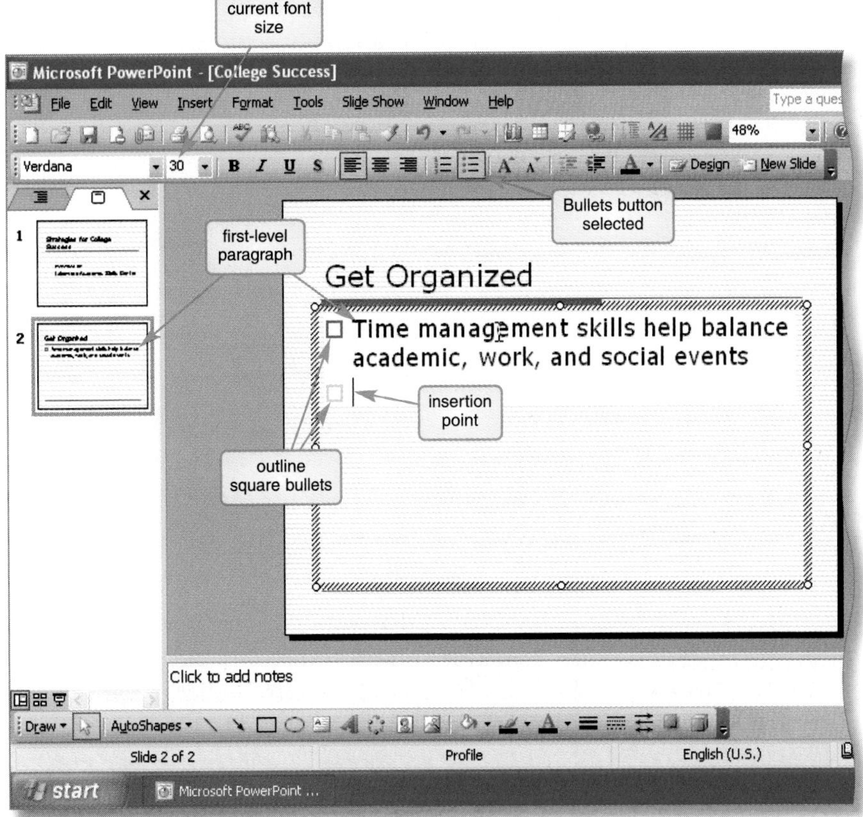

FIGURE 1-34

2

• **Type** `Create a schedule each week that accounts for all activities` **and then press the ENTER key.**

• **Type** `Plan two hours of study time for each one hour of class time` **but do not press the ENTER key.**

• **Point to the New Slide button on the Formatting toolbar.**

The insertion point is displayed after the e in time (Figure 1-35). Three new first-level paragraphs are displayed with outline square bullets in both the text placeholder and the Slides tab. When you press the ENTER key, PowerPoint adds a new paragraph at the same level as the previous paragraph.

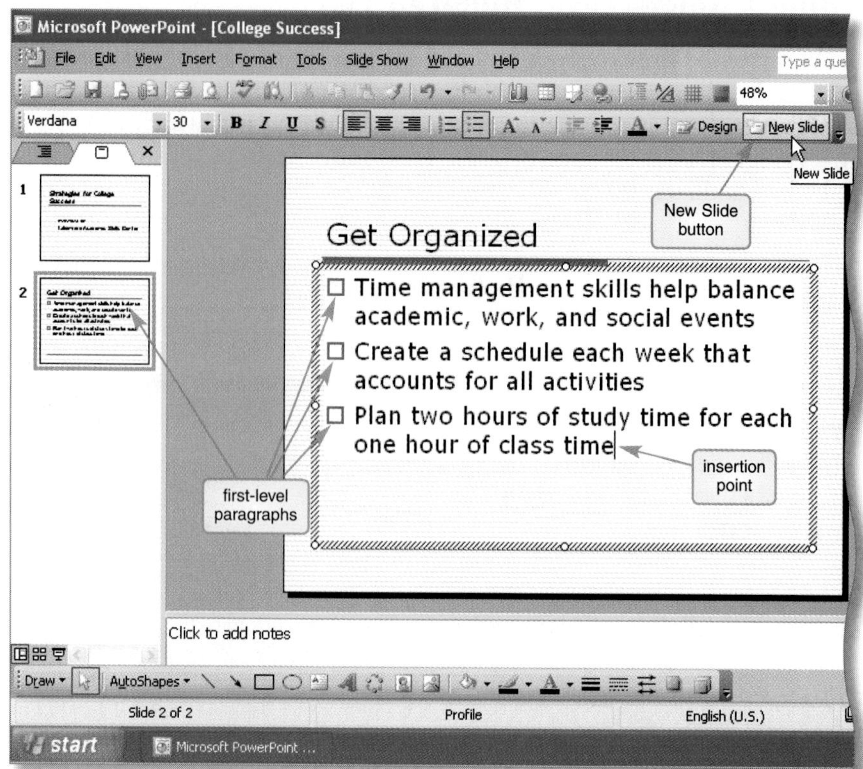

FIGURE 1-35

Other Ways

1. In Dictation mode, say "Time management skills help balance academic, work, and social events, New Line, Create a schedule each week that accounts for all activities, New Line, Plan two hours of study time for each one hour of class time"

Notice that you did not press the ENTER key after typing the last paragraph in Step 2. If you press the ENTER key, a new bullet appears after the last entry on this slide. To remove an extra bullet, press the BACKSPACE key.

Creating a Text Slide with a Multi-Level Bulleted List

Slides 3 and 4 in Figure 1-1 on page PPT 5 contain more than one level of bulleted text. A slide that consists of more than one level of bulleted text is called a **multi-level bulleted list slide**. Beginning with the second level, each paragraph indents to the right of the preceding level and is pushed down to a lower level. For example, if you increase the indent of a first-level paragraph, it becomes a second-level paragraph. This lower-level paragraph is a subset of the higher-level paragraph. It usually contains information that supports the topic in the paragraph immediately above it. You increase the indent of a paragraph by clicking the Increase Indent button on the Formatting toolbar.

When you want to raise a paragraph from a lower level to a higher level, you click the Decrease Indent button on the Formatting toolbar.

Creating a text slide with a multi-level bulleted list requires several steps. Initially, you enter a slide title in the title text placeholder. Next, you select the body text placeholder. Then, you type the text for the multi-level bulleted list, increasing and decreasing the indents as needed. The next several sections explain how to add a slide with a multi-level bulleted list.

Adding New Slides and Entering Slide Titles

When you add a new slide to a presentation, PowerPoint keeps the same layout used on the previous slide. PowerPoint assumes every new slide has a title. The title for Slide 3 is Listen Actively. The following steps show how to add a new slide (Slide 3) and enter a title.

To Add a New Slide and Enter a Slide Title

1

- **Click the New Slide button.**

Slide 3 of 3 appears in the slide pane and Slides tab (Figure 1-36).

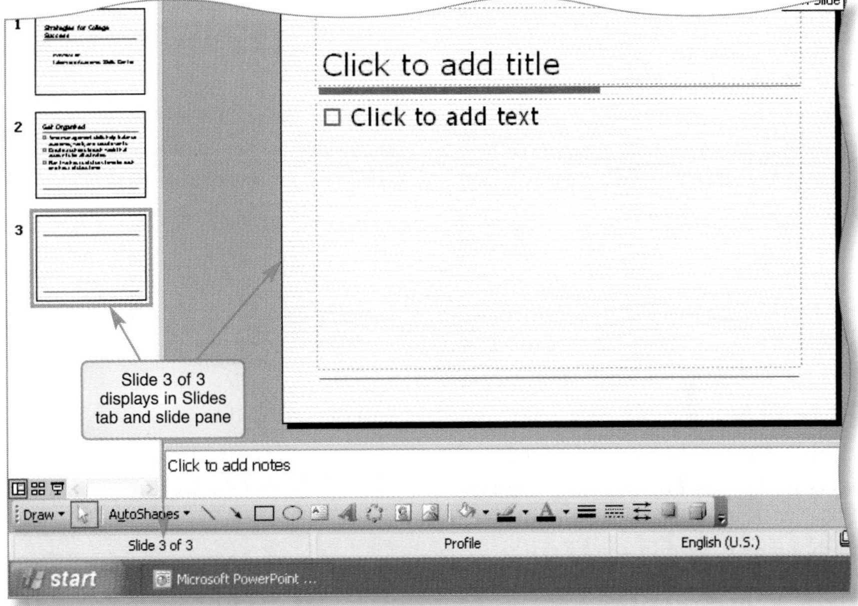

FIGURE 1-36

2

- **Type** `Listen Actively` **in the title text placeholder. Do not press the ENTER key.**

Slide 3 shows the Title and Text slide layout with the title, Listen Actively, in the title text placeholder and in the Slides tab (Figure 1-37). The insertion point appears after the y in Actively.

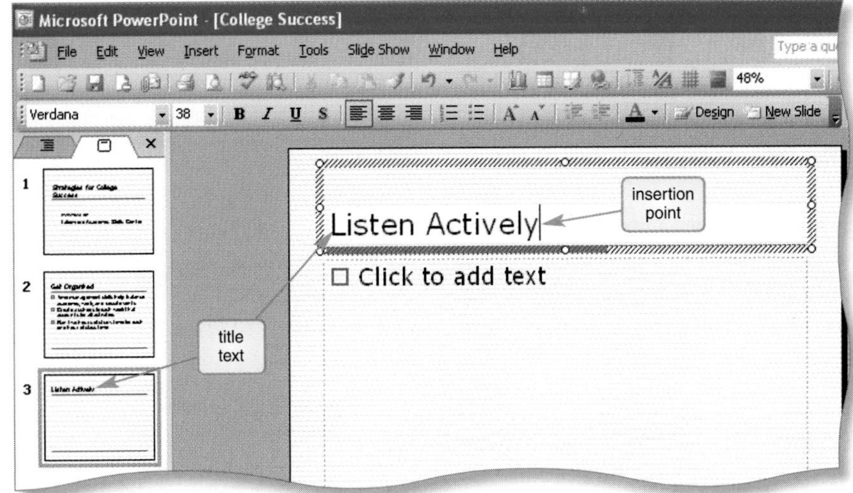

FIGURE 1-37

Slide 3 is added to the presentation with the desired title.

Other Ways

1. Press SHIFT+CTRL+M
2. In Dictation mode, say "New Slide, Listen Actively"

Typing a Multi-Level Bulleted List

The next step is to select the body text placeholder and then type the multi-level bulleted list, which consists of six entries (Figure 1-1c on page PPT 5). The following steps show how to create a list consisting of three levels.

To Type a Multi-Level Bulleted List

1

- **Click the bulleted paragraph labeled, Click to add text.**

The insertion point appears immediately to the right of the bullet on Slide 3. The mouse pointer may change shape if you move it away from the bullet.

2

- **Type** `Sit in the front row to focus attention` **and then press the ENTER key.**
- **Point to the Increase Indent button on the Formatting toolbar.**

The paragraph, Sit in the front row to focus attention, appears (Figure 1-38). The font size is 30. The insertion point appears to the right of the second bullet.

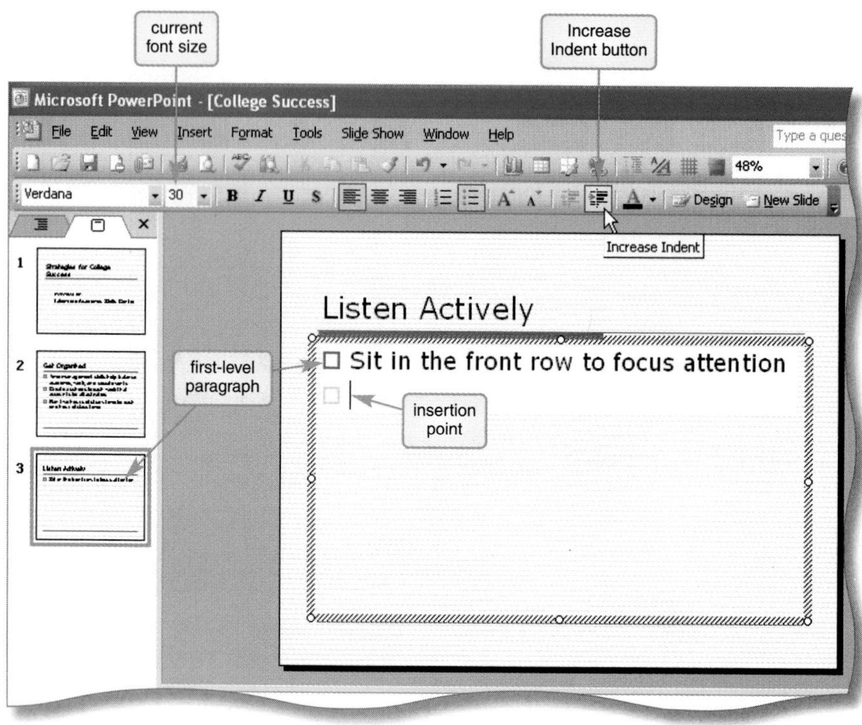

FIGURE 1-38

3

- **Click the Increase Indent button.**

The second paragraph indents below the first and becomes a second-level paragraph (Figure 1-39). The bullet to the left of the second paragraph changes from an outline square to a solid square, and the font size for the paragraph now is 26. The insertion point appears to the right of the solid square.

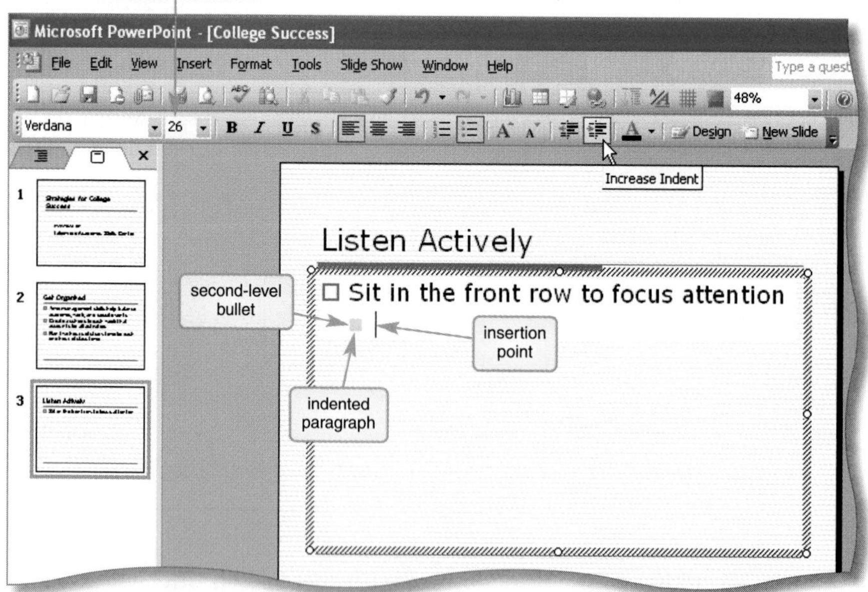

FIGURE 1-39

4

- **Type** `Do not tolerate distractions` **and then press the ENTER key.**
- **Point to the Decrease Indent button on the Formatting toolbar.**

The first second-level paragraph appears with a solid orange square bullet in both the slide pane and the Slides tab (Figure 1-40). When you press the ENTER key, PowerPoint adds a new paragraph at the same level as the previous paragraph.

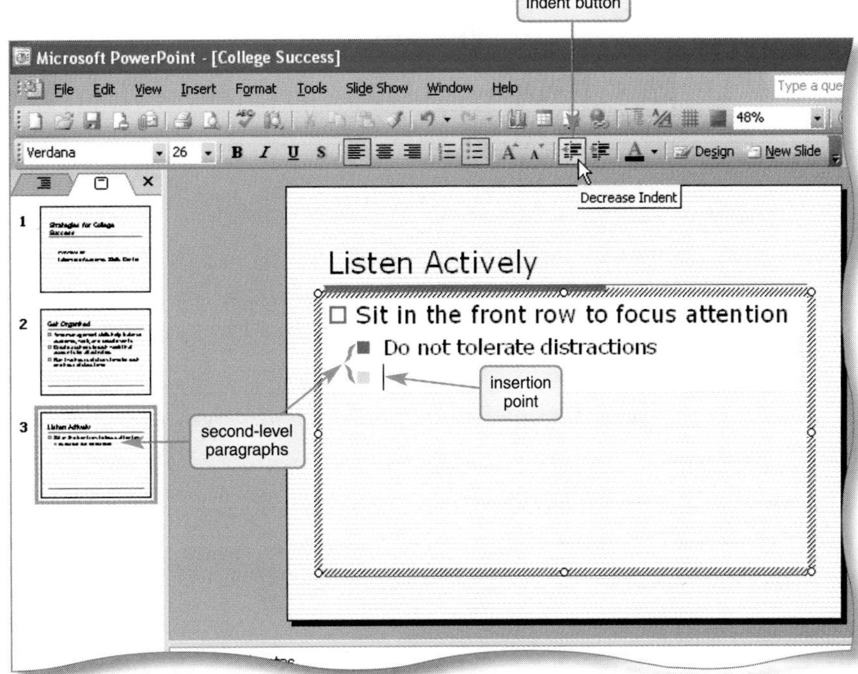

FIGURE 1-40

5

- **Click the Decrease Indent button.**

The second-level paragraph becomes a first-level paragraph (Figure 1-41). The bullet of the new paragraph changes from a solid orange square to an outline square, and the font size for the paragraph is 30. The insertion point appears to the right of the outline square bullet.

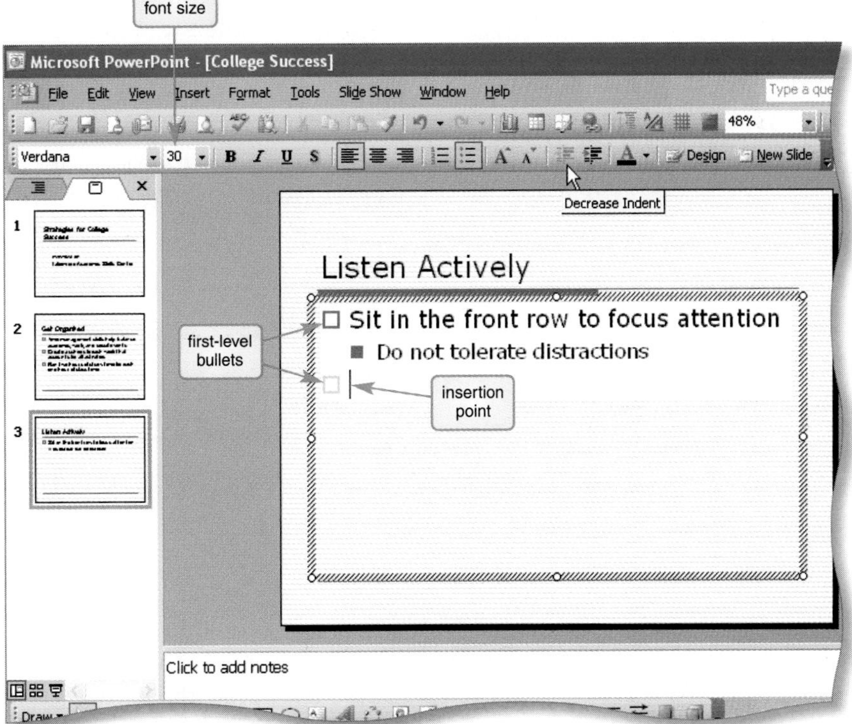

FIGURE 1-41

The steps on the next page complete the text for Slide 3.

Other Ways

1. In Dictation mode, say, "Sit in the front row to focus attention, New Line, Increase Indent, Do not tolerate distractions, New Line, Decrease Indent"

To Type the Remaining Text for Slide 3

1. **Type** `Make mental summaries of material` **and then press the ENTER key.**
2. **Type** `Be prepared for class` **and then press the ENTER key.**
3. **Click the Increase Indent button on the Formatting toolbar.**
4. **Type** `Review notes from books, previous class` **and then press the ENTER key.**
5. **Type** `Preview material to be covered that day` **but do not press the ENTER key.**

Slide 3 is displayed as shown in Figure 1-42. The insertion point appears after the y in day.

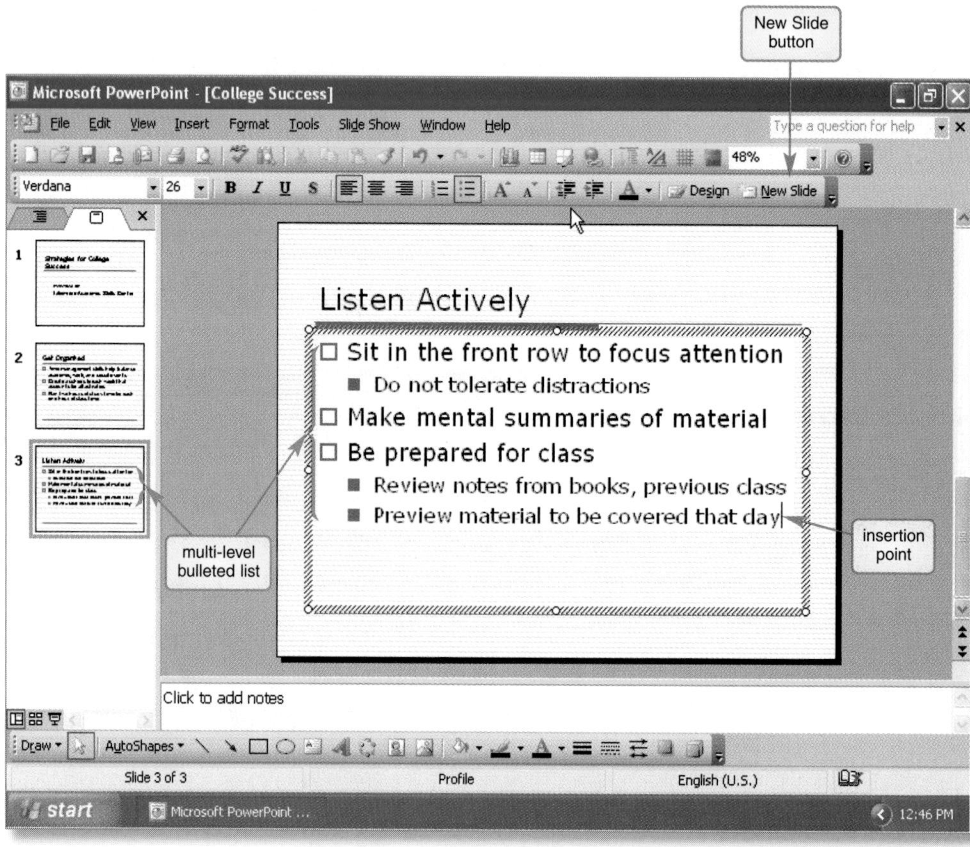

FIGURE 1-42

Other Ways

1. In Dictation mode, say "Make mental summaries of material, New Line, Be prepared for class, Increase Indent, Review notes from books comma previous class, New Line, Preview material to be covered that day"

In Step 4 above, you did not press the ENTER key after typing the last paragraph. If you press the ENTER key, a new bullet appears after the last entry on this slide. To remove an extra bullet, press the BACKSPACE key.

Slide 4 is the last slide in this presentation. It also is a multi-level bulleted list and has three levels. The following steps create Slide 4.

To Create Slide 4

1. **Click the New Slide button on the Formatting toolbar.**
2. **Type** `Excel on Exams` **in the title text placeholder.**
3. **Press CTRL+ENTER to move the insertion point to the body text placeholder.**
4. **Type** `Review test material throughout week` **and then press the ENTER key.**
5. **Click the Increase Indent button on the Formatting toolbar. Type** `Cramming before exams is ineffective` **and then press the ENTER key.**

The title and first two levels of bullets are added to Slide 4 (Figure 1-43).

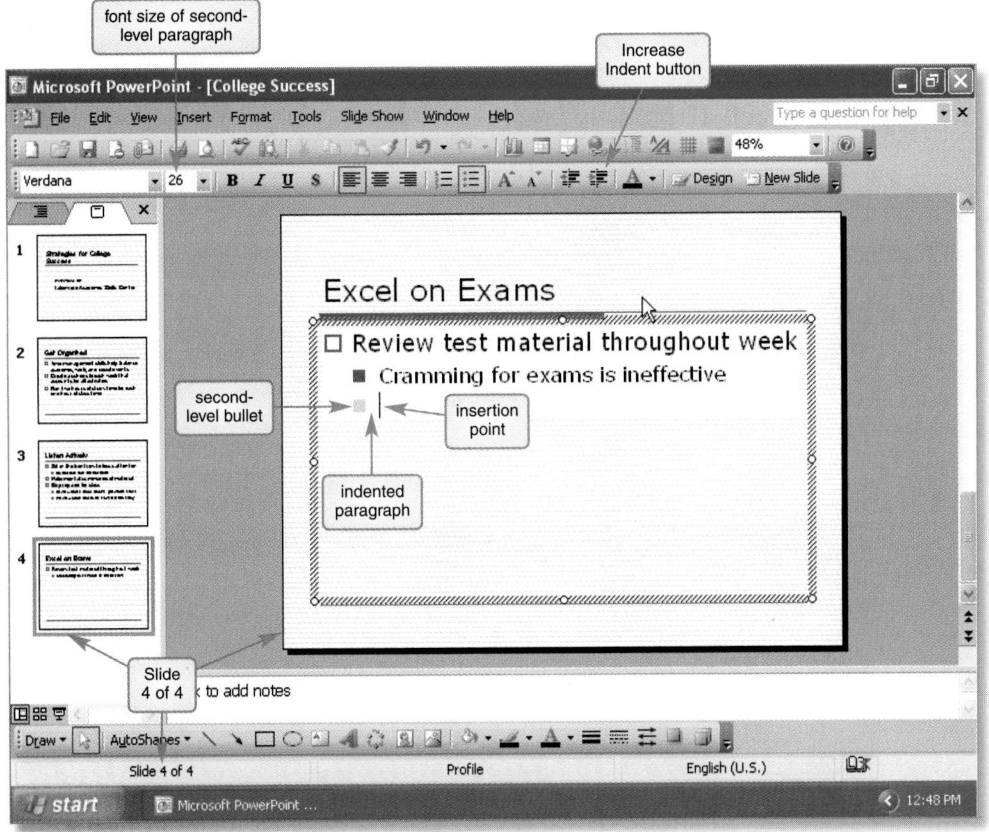

FIGURE 1-43

Other Ways

1. In Dictation mode, say "New Slide, Excel on Exams, [type CTRL+ENTER], Review test material throughout week, New Line, Increase Indent, Cramming before exams is ineffective"

Creating a Third-Level Paragraph

The next line in Slide 4 is indented an additional level, to the third level. The steps on the next page create an additional level.

To Create a Third-Level Paragraph

1

• **Click the Increase Indent button on the Formatting toolbar.**

The second-level paragraph becomes a third-level paragraph (Figure 1-44). The bullet to the left of the new paragraph changes from a solid square to an outline square, and the font size for the paragraph is 23. The insertion point appears after the outline square bullet.

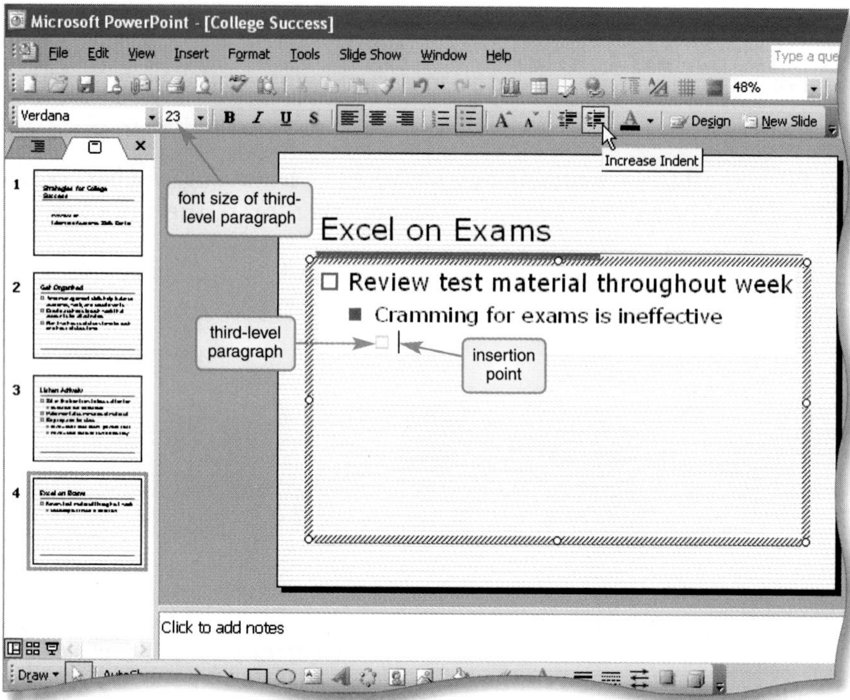

FIGURE 1-44

2

• **Type** `Facts remain only in short-term memory` **and then press the ENTER key.**

• **Point to the Decrease Indent button on the Formatting toolbar.**

The first third-level paragraph, Facts remain only in short-term memory, is displayed with the bullet for a second third-level paragraph (Figure 1-45).

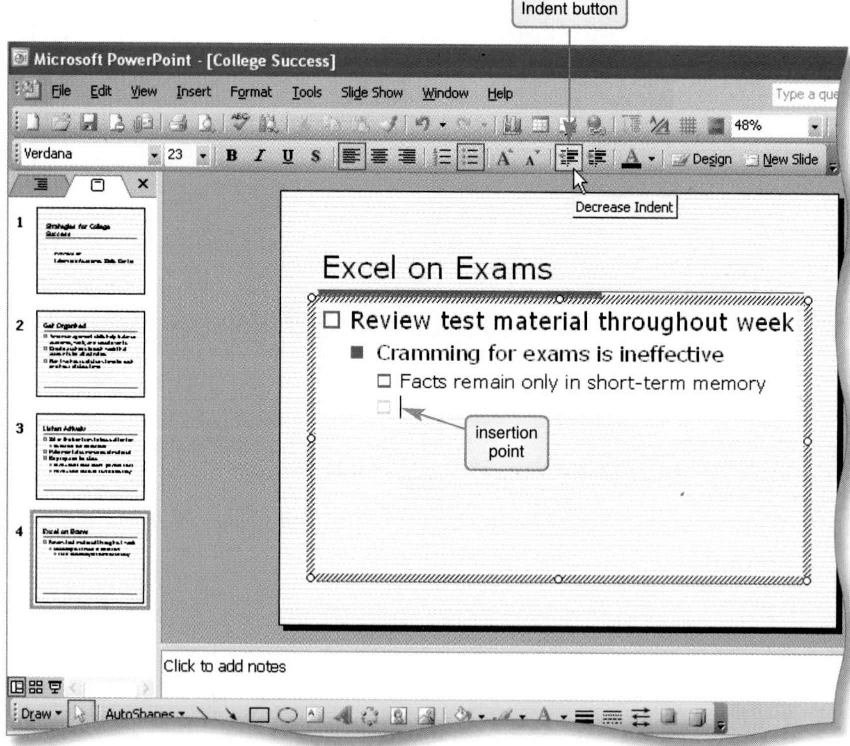

FIGURE 1-45

3

- **Click the Decrease Indent button two times.**

The insertion point appears at the first level (Figure 1-46).

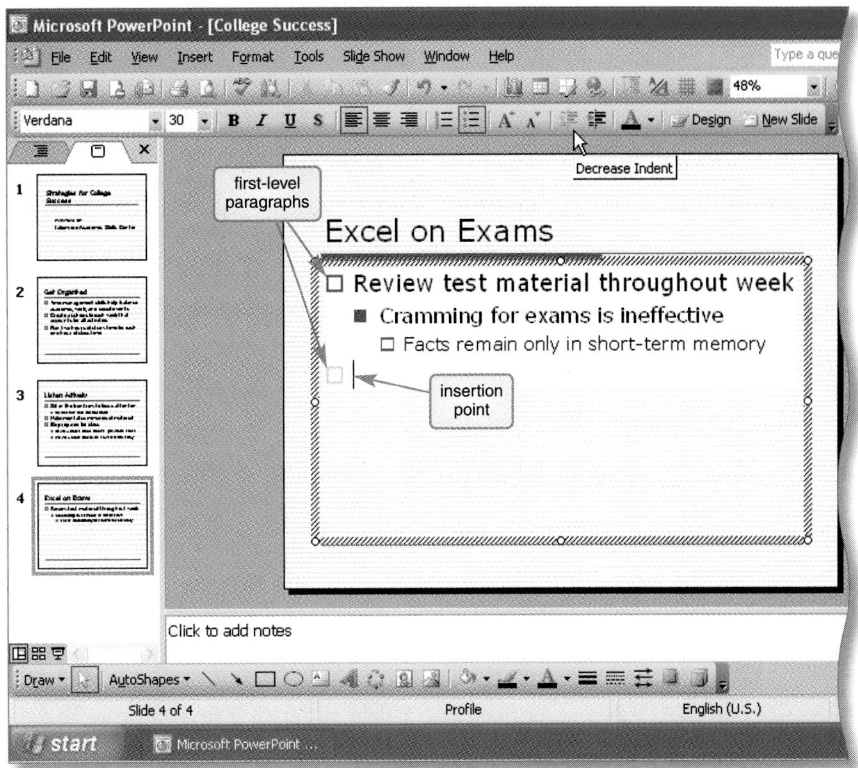

FIGURE 1-46

Other Ways

1. In Dictation mode, say "Tab, Facts remain only in short-term memory, New Line, [type backspace]"

The title text and three levels of paragraphs discussing preparing for exams are complete. The next three paragraphs concern strategies for taking tests. As an alternative to clicking the Increase Indent button, you can press the TAB key. Likewise, instead of clicking the Decrease Indent button, you can press the SHIFT+TAB keys. The following steps illustrate how to type the remaining text for Slide 4.

To Type the Remaining Text for Slide 4

1. **Type** `Review entire test before answering` **and then press the ENTER key.**
2. **Press the TAB key to increase the indent to the second level.**
3. **Type** `Start with the material you know` **and then press the ENTER key.**
4. **Press the TAB key to increase the indent to the third level.**
5. **Type** `Think positively and stay focused` **but do not press the ENTER key.**

The Slide 4 title text and body text are displayed in the slide pane and Slides tabs (Figure 1-47 on the next page). The insertion point appears after the d in focused.

Other Ways

1. In Dictation mode, say "Review entire test before answering, New Line, Tab, Start with the material you know, New Line, Tab, Think positively and stay focused"

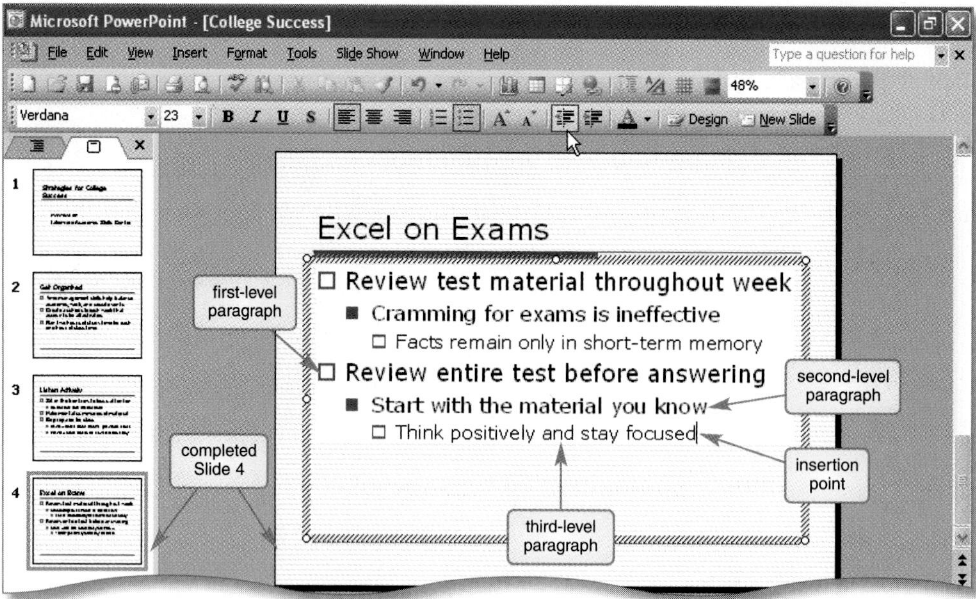

FIGURE 1-47

All the slides are created for the College Success slide show. This presentation consists of a title slide, one text slide with a single-level bulleted list, and two text slides with a multi-level bulleted list.

Ending a Slide Show with a Black Slide

After the last slide in the slide show appears, the default PowerPoint setting is to end the presentation with a black slide. This black slide appears only when the slide show is running and concludes the slide show gracefully so your audience never sees the PowerPoint window. A **black slide** ends all slide shows unless the option setting is deselected. The following steps verify that the End with black slide option is activated.

To End a Slide Show with a Black Slide

1

- **Click Tools on the menu bar and then point to Options (Figure 1-48).**

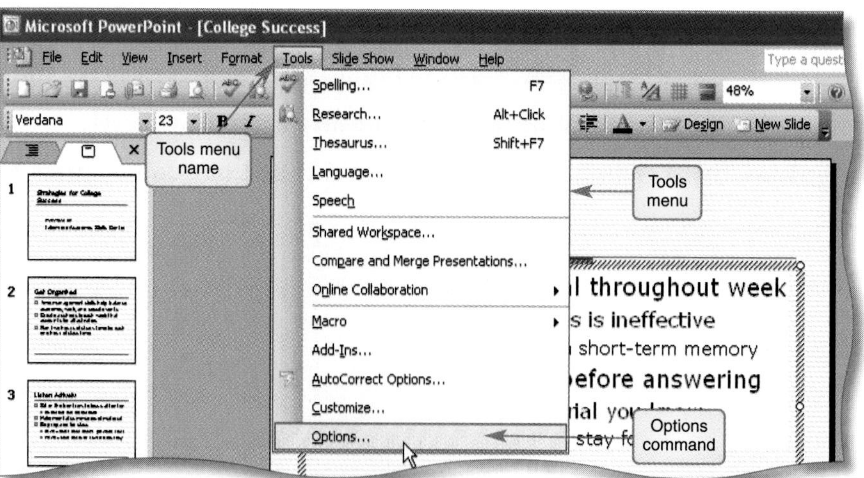

FIGURE 1-48

- **Click Options.**
- **If necessary, click the View tab when the Options dialog box appears.**
- **Verify that the End with black slide check box is selected.**
- **If a check mark does not show, click End with black slide.**
- **Point to the OK button.**

The Options dialog box appears (Figure 1-49). The View sheet contains settings for the overall PowerPoint display and for a particular slide show.

3

- **Click the OK button.**

The End with black slide option will cause the slide show to end with a black slide until it is deselected.

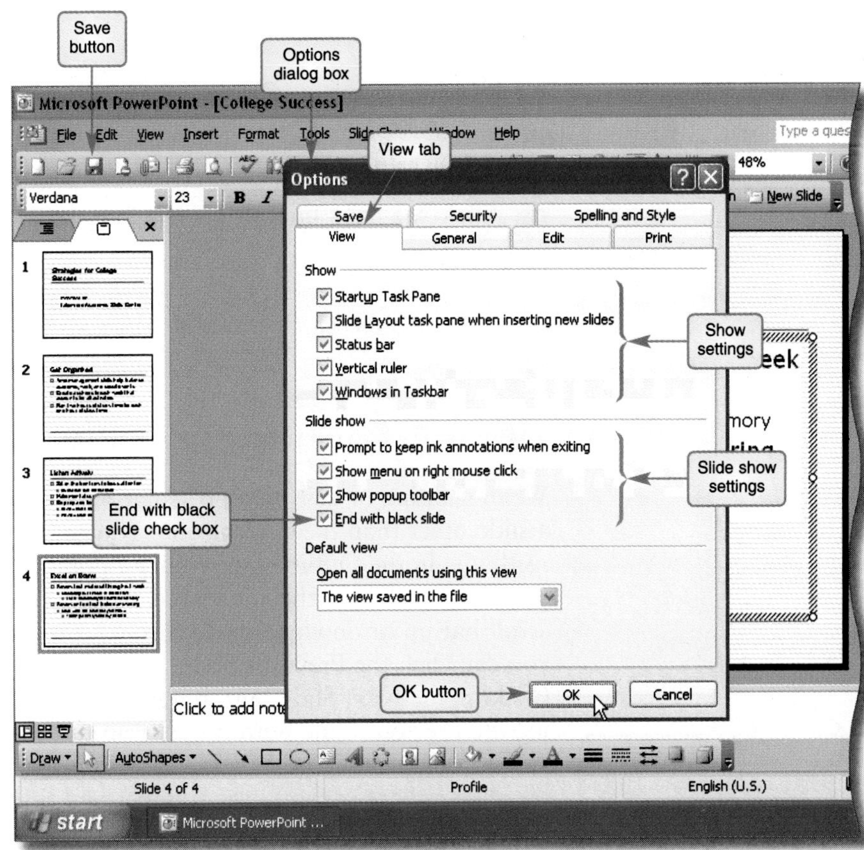

FIGURE 1-49

With all aspects of the presentation complete, it is important to save the additions and changes you have made to the College Success presentation.

Saving a Presentation with the Same File Name

Saving frequently cannot be overemphasized. When you first saved the presentation, you clicked the Save button on the Standard toolbar, and the Save dialog box appeared. When you want to save the changes made to the presentation after your last save, you again click the Save button. This time, however, the Save dialog box does not appear because PowerPoint updates the document called College Success.ppt on the floppy disk. The steps on the next page illustrate how to save the presentation again.

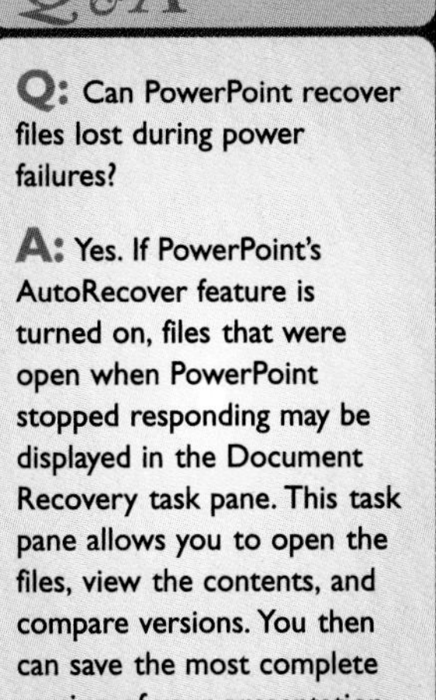

Q&A

Q: Can PowerPoint recover files lost during power failures?

A: Yes. If PowerPoint's AutoRecover feature is turned on, files that were open when PowerPoint stopped responding may be displayed in the Document Recovery task pane. This task pane allows you to open the files, view the contents, and compare versions. You then can save the most complete version of your presentation.

To Save a Presentation with the Same File Name

1. **Be certain your floppy disk is in drive A.**
2. **Click the Save button on the Standard toolbar.**

PowerPoint overwrites the old College Success.ppt document on the floppy disk in drive A with the revised presentation document. Slide 4 is displayed in the PowerPoint window.

Other Ways

1. In Voice Command mode, say "Save"

Moving to Another Slide in Normal View

When creating or editing a presentation in normal view, you often want to display a slide other than the current one. You can move to another slide using several methods. In the Outline tab, you can point to any of the text in a particular slide to display that slide in the slide pane, or you can drag the scroll box on the vertical scroll bar up or down to move through the text in the presentation. In the slide pane, you can click the Previous Slide or Next Slide button on the vertical scroll bar. Clicking the Next Slide button advances to the next slide in the presentation. Clicking the Previous Slide button backs up to the slide preceding the current slide. You also can drag the scroll box on the vertical scroll bar. When you drag the scroll box, the **slide indicator** shows the number and title of the slide you are about to display. Releasing the mouse button shows the slide.

A slide's **Zoom setting** affects the portion of the slide displaying in the slide pane. PowerPoint defaults to a setting of approximately 50 percent so the entire slide is displayed. This percentage depends on the size and type of your monitor. If you want to display a small portion of the current slide, you would zoom in by clicking the **Zoom box arrow** and then clicking the desired magnification. You can display the entire slide in the slide pane by clicking **Fit** in the Zoom list. The Zoom setting affects the action of the vertical and horizontal scroll bars. If Zoom is set so the entire slide is not visible in the slide pane, clicking the up scroll arrow on the vertical scroll bar shows the next portion of the slide, not the previous slide.

Q&A

Q: Can I enlarge the slide size on my monitor?

A: Yes. You can increase your Zoom setting as large as 400% when you want to see details on small objects. Likewise, you can decrease your Zoom setting as small as 10%. When you want to redisplay the entire slide, click Fit in the Zoom list.

Using the Scroll Box on the Slide Pane to Move to Another Slide

Before continuing with Project 1, you want to display the title slide. The following steps show how to move from Slide 4 to Slide 1 using the scroll box on the slide pane vertical scroll bar.

To Use the Scroll Box on the Slide Pane to Move to Another Slide

1

- **Position the mouse pointer on the scroll box.**
- **Press and hold down the mouse button.**

Slide: 4 of 4 Excel on Exams appears in the slide indicator (Figure 1-50). When you click the scroll box, the Slide 4 thumbnail has no gray border in the Slides tab.

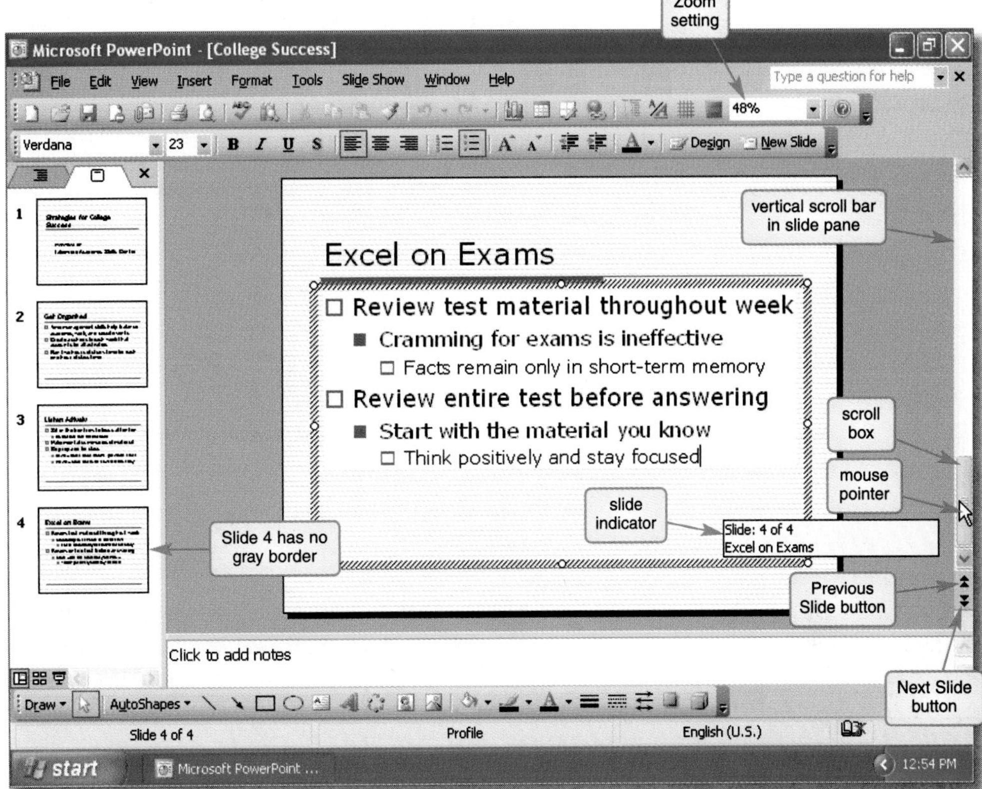

FIGURE 1-50

2

- **Drag the scroll box up the vertical scroll bar until Slide: 1 of 4 Strategies for College Success appears in the slide indicator.**

Slide: 1 of 4 Strategies for College Success appears in the slide indicator (Figure 1-51). Slide 4 still is displayed in the PowerPoint window.

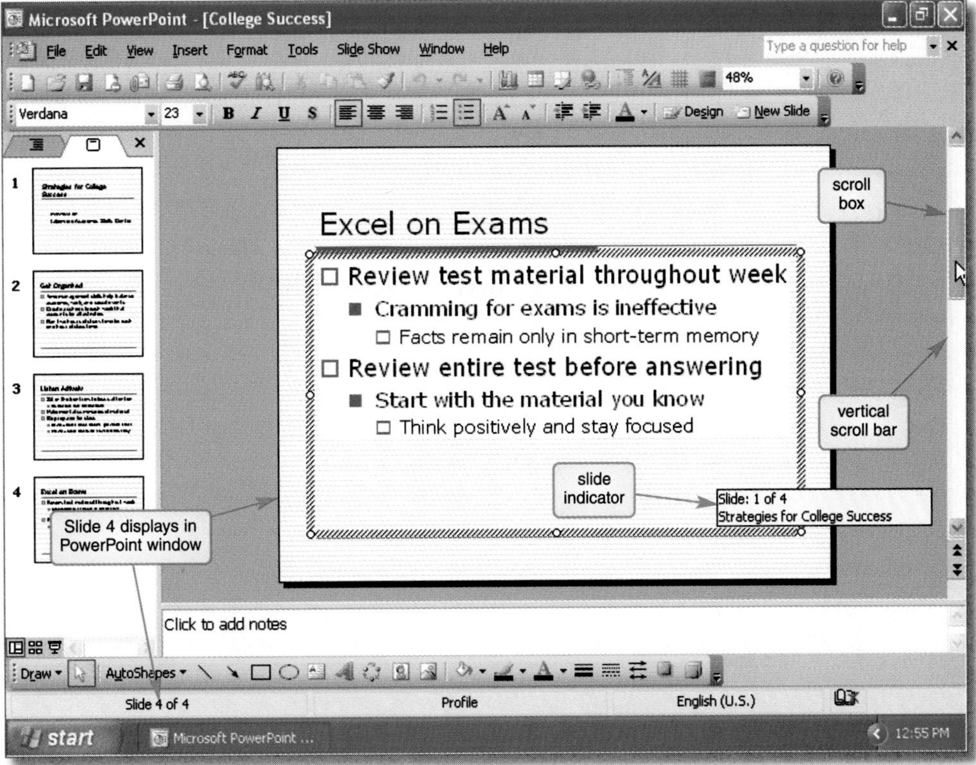

FIGURE 1-51

3

• **Release the mouse button.**

Slide 1, titled Strategies for College Success, appears in the PowerPoint window (Figure 1-52). The Slide 1 thumbnail has a gray border in the Slides tab, indicating it is selected.

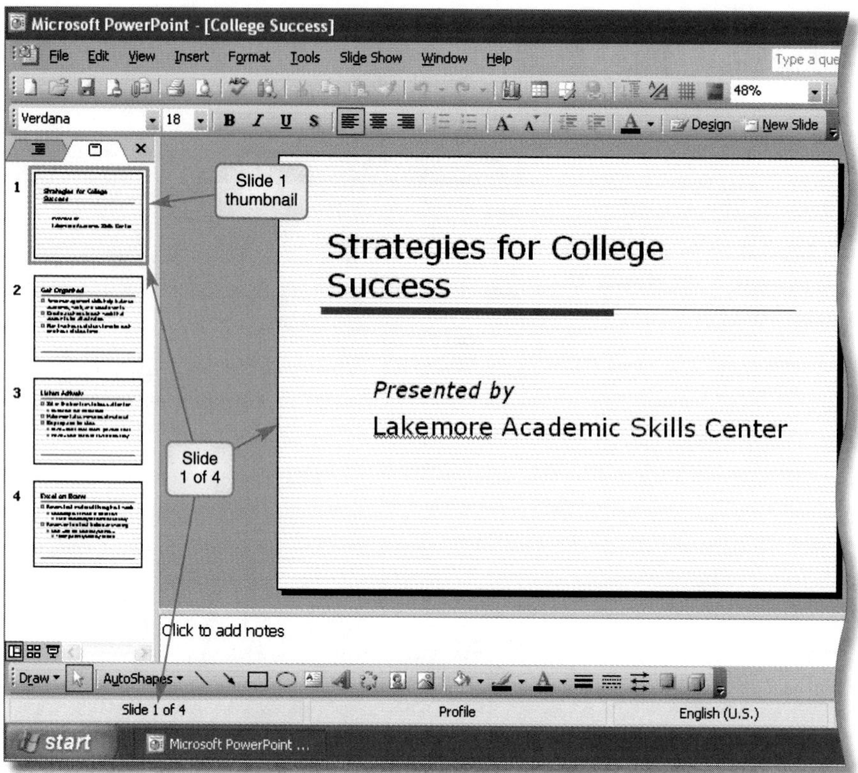

FIGURE 1-52

Other Ways

1. Click Next Slide button or Previous Slide button to move forward or back one slide
2. Press PAGE DOWN or PAGE UP to move forward or back one slide
3. In Voice Command mode, say "Next page" or "Previous page"

Viewing the Presentation in Slide Show View

The Slide Show button, located in the lower-left of the PowerPoint window above the status bar, allows you to show a presentation using a computer. The computer acts like a slide projector, displaying each slide on a full screen. The full-screen slide hides the toolbars, menus, and other PowerPoint window elements. When making a presentation, you use **slide show view**. You can start slide show view from normal view or slide sorter view.

Starting Slide Show View

Slide show view begins when you click the Slide Show button in the lower-left of the PowerPoint window above the status bar. PowerPoint then shows the current slide on the full screen without any of the PowerPoint window objects, such as the menu bar or toolbars. The following steps show how to start slide show view.

To Start Slide Show View

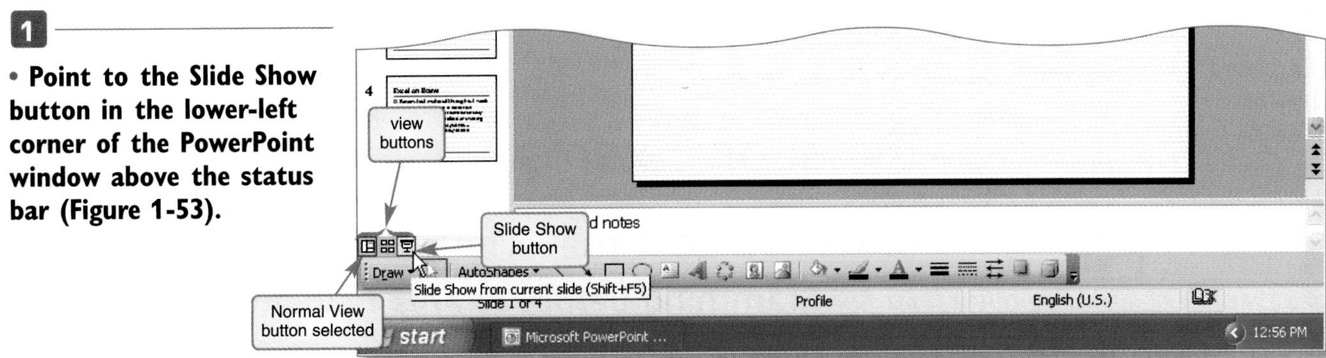

1

- **Point to the Slide Show button in the lower-left corner of the PowerPoint window above the status bar (Figure 1-53).**

FIGURE 1-53

2

- **Click the Slide Show button.**

A starting slide show message may display momentarily, and then the title slide fills the screen (Figure 1-54). The PowerPoint window is hidden.

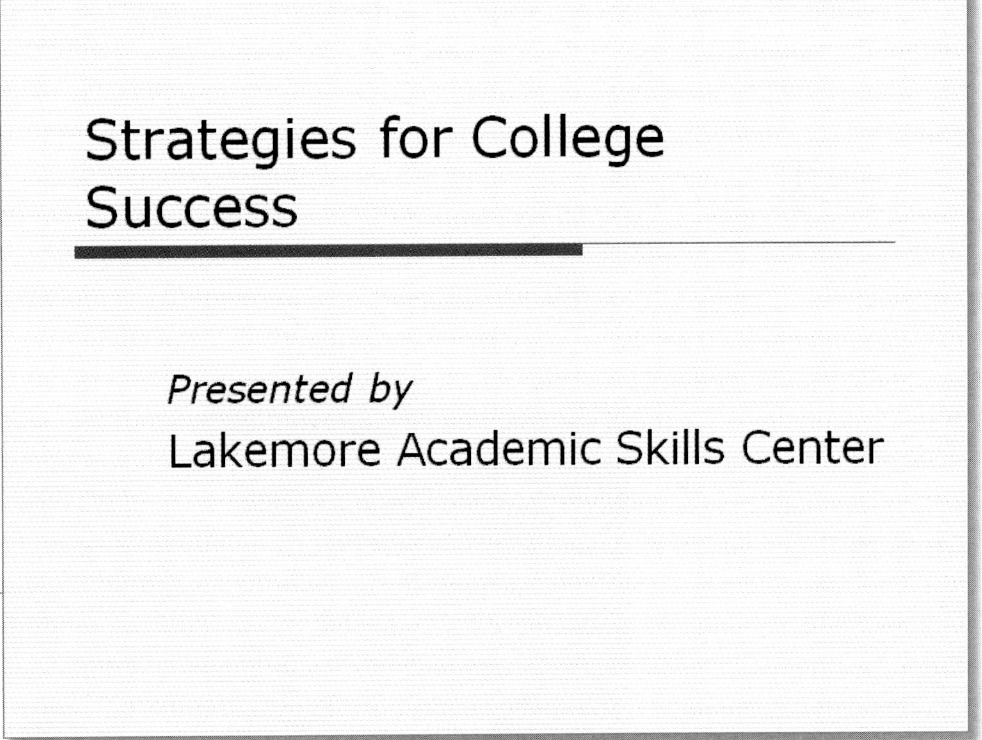

FIGURE 1-54

Other Ways

1. On View menu click Slide Show
2. Press F5
3. In Voice Command mode, say "View show"

Advancing Through a Slide Show Manually

After you begin slide show view, you can move forward or backward through the slides. PowerPoint allows you to advance through the slides manually or automatically. The steps on the next page illustrate how to move manually through the slides.

To Move Manually Through Slides in a Slide Show

1

- **Click each slide until the Excel on Exams slide (Slide 4) is displayed.**

Slide 4 is displayed (Figure 1-55). Each slide in the presentation shows on the screen, one slide at a time. Each time you click the mouse button, the next slide appears.

Excel on Exams

- Review test material throughout week
  - Cramming before exams is ineffective
    - Facts remain only in short-term memory
- Review entire test before answering
  - Start with the material you know
    - Think positively and stay focused

Slide 4 displays in slide show view

FIGURE 1-55

2

- **Click Slide 4.**

The black slide appears (Figure 1-56). The message at the top of the slide announces the end of the slide show. If you wanted to end the presentation at this point and return to normal view, you would click the black slide.

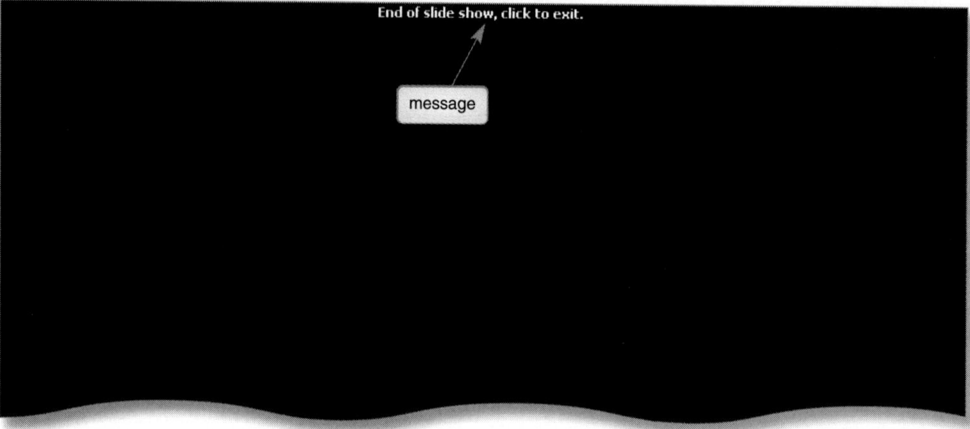

FIGURE 1-56

Other Ways

1. Press PAGE DOWN to advance one slide at a time, or press PAGE UP to go backward one slide at a time
2. Press RIGHT ARROW or DOWN ARROW key to advance one slide at a time, or press LEFT ARROW or UP ARROW key to go back one slide at a time

Using the Popup Menu to Go to a Specific Slide

Slide show view has a shortcut menu, called the Popup menu, that appears when you right-click a slide in slide show view. This menu contains commands to assist you during a slide show. For example, clicking the Next command moves to the next slide. Clicking the Previous command moves to the previous slide. Pointing to the Go to Slide command and then clicking the desired slide allows you to move to any slide in the presentation. The Go to Slide submenu contains a list of the slides in the presentation. You can go to the requested slide by clicking the name of that slide. The following steps illustrate how to go to the title slide (Slide 1) in the College Success presentation.

To Display the Popup Menu and Go to a Specific Slide

1

- **With the black slide displaying in slide show view, right-click the slide.**
- **Point to Go to Slide on the Popup menu, and then point to 1 Strategies for College Success in the Go to Slide submenu.**

The Popup menu appears on the black slide, and the Go to Slide submenu shows a list of slides in the presentation (Figure 1-57). Your screen may look different because the Popup menu appears near the location of the mouse pointer at the time you right-click.

2

- **Click 1 Strategies for College Success.**

The title slide, Strategies for College Success (shown in Figure 1-54 on page PPT 47), is displayed.

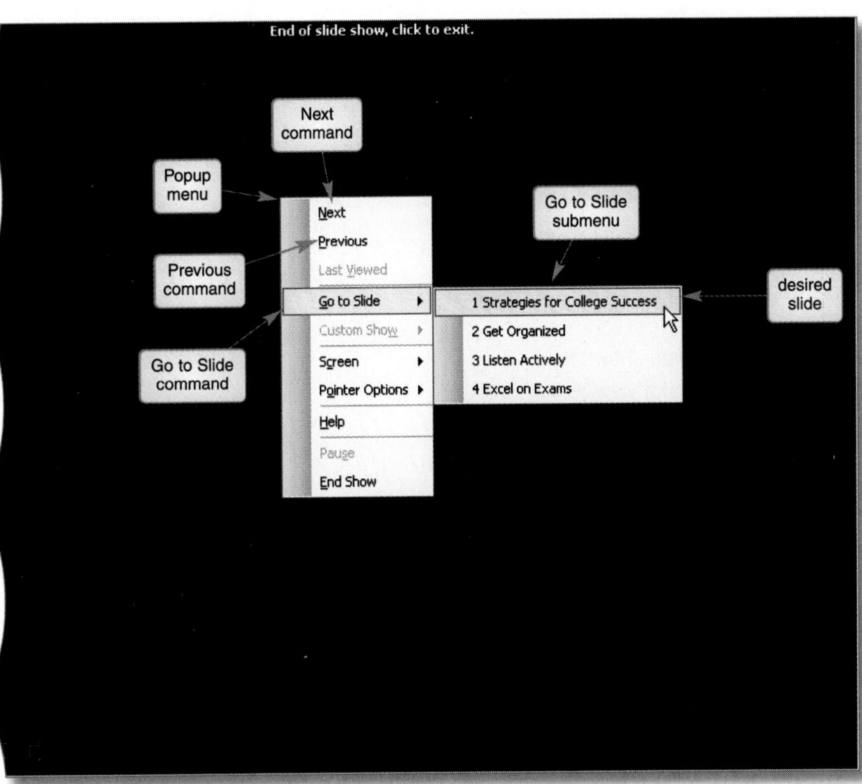

FIGURE 1-57

Additional Popup menu commands allow you to change the mouse pointer to a ballpoint or felt tip pen or highlighter that draws in various colors, make the screen black or white, create speaker notes, and end the slide show. Popup menu commands are discussed as they are used.

Using the Popup Menu to End a Slide Show

The End Show command on the Popup menu ends slide show view and returns to the same view as when you clicked the Slide Show button. The steps on the next page show how to end slide show view and return to normal view.

To Use the Popup Menu to End a Slide Show

1

- **Right-click the title slide and then point to End Show on the Popup menu.**

The Popup menu appears on Slide 1 (Figure 1-58).

2

- **Click End Show.**
- **If the Microsoft Office PowerPoint dialog box appears, click the Yes button.**

PowerPoint ends slide show view and returns to normal view (shown in Figure 1-59 below). Slide 1 is displayed because it is the last slide displayed in slide show view.

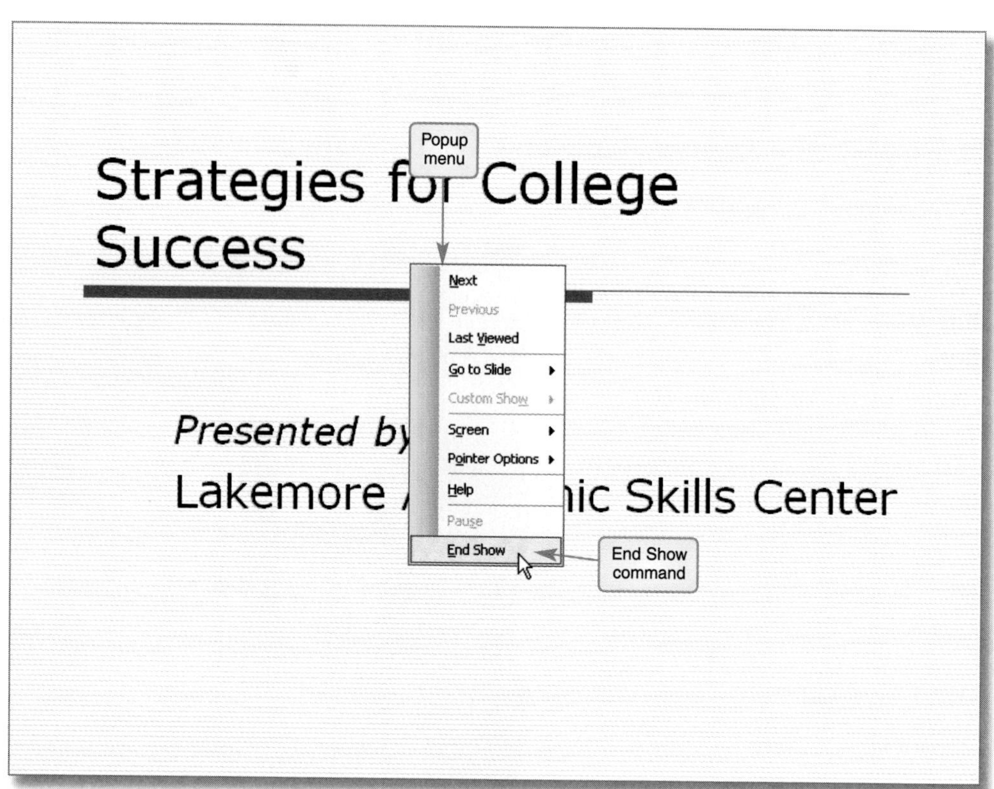

FIGURE 1-58

Other Ways

1. Press ESC (shows slide last viewed in slide show view)
2. In Voice Command mode say "Escape"

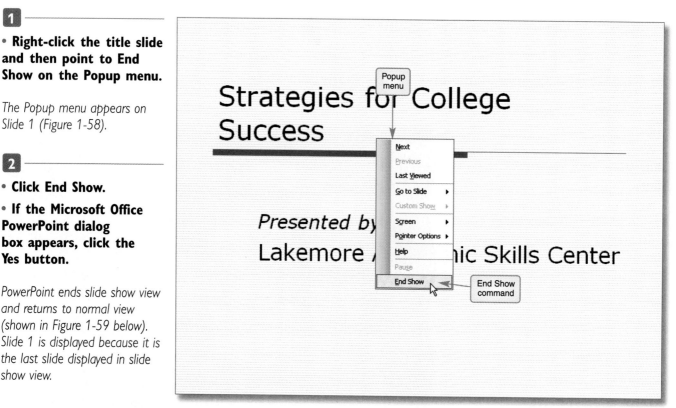

Quitting PowerPoint

The College Success presentation now is complete. When you quit PowerPoint, you are prompted to save any changes made to the presentation since the last save. The program then closes all PowerPoint windows, quits, and returns control to the desktop. The following steps quit PowerPoint.

To Quit PowerPoint

1

- **Point to the Close button on the PowerPoint title bar (Figure 1-59).**

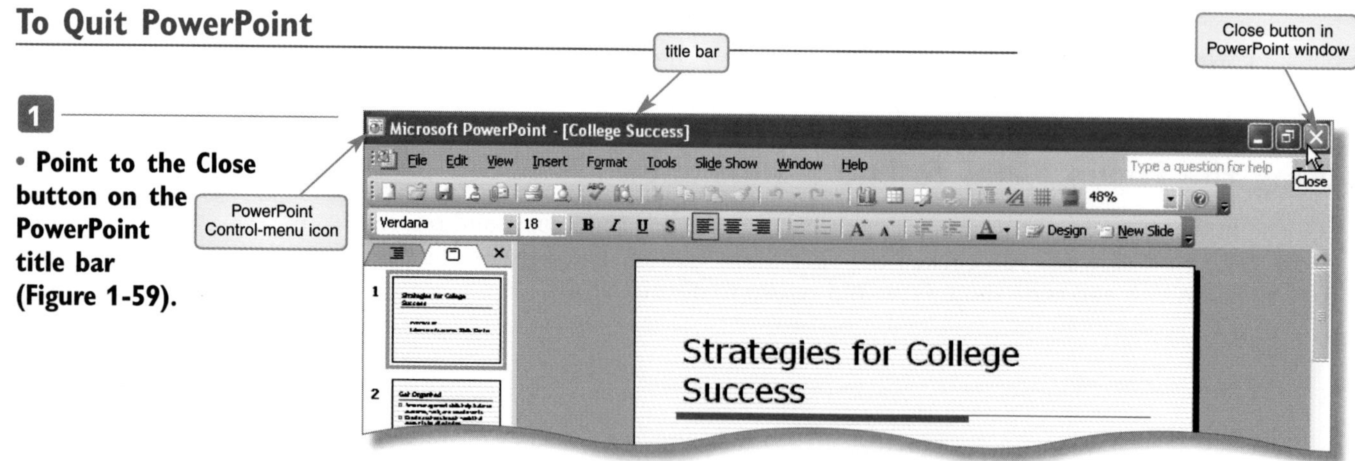

FIGURE 1-59

2

• **Click the Close button.**

PowerPoint closes and the Windows desktop is displayed (Figure 1-60). If you made changes to the presentation since your last save, a Microsoft Office PowerPoint dialog box appears asking if you want to save changes. Clicking the Yes button saves the changes to the presentation before quitting PowerPoint. Clicking the No button quits PowerPoint without saving the changes. Clicking the Cancel button cancels the exit and returns control to the presentation.

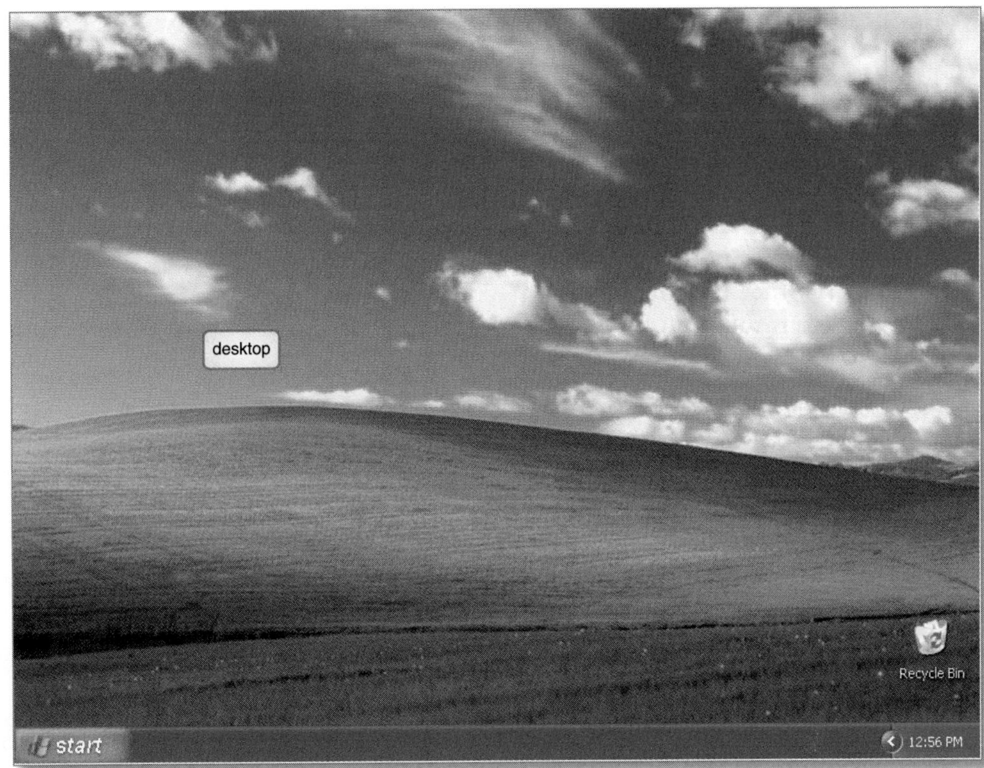

FIGURE 1-60

Other Ways

1. On File menu click Exit
2. Right-click Microsoft PowerPoint button on taskbar, click Close on shortcut menu
3. Double-click PowerPoint Control-menu icon; or click PowerPoint Control-menu icon, on Control menu click Close
4. In Voice Command mode, say "File, Exit"

Starting PowerPoint and Opening a Presentation

Once you have created and saved a presentation, you may need to retrieve it from the floppy disk to make changes. For example, you may want to replace the design template or modify some text. The steps on the next page assume PowerPoint is not running.

To Start PowerPoint and Open an Existing Presentation

1

- **With your floppy disk in drive A, click the Start button on the taskbar, point to All Programs, point to Microsoft Office, and then click Microsoft Office PowerPoint 2003 on the Microsoft Office submenu.**
- **When the Getting Started task pane opens, point to the Open link in the Open area.**

PowerPoint starts. The Getting Started task pane opens (Figure 1-61).

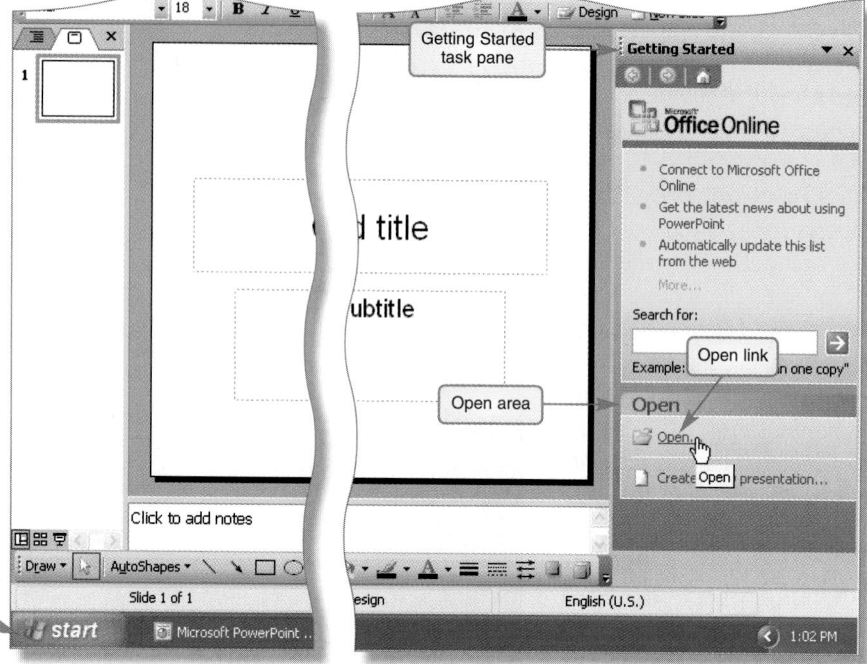

FIGURE 1-61

2

- **Click the Open link. Click the Look in box arrow, click 3½ Floppy (A:), and then double-click College Success.**

PowerPoint opens the presentation College Success and shows the first slide in the PowerPoint window (Figure 1-62). The presentation is displayed in normal view because PowerPoint opens a presentation in the same view in which it was saved. The Getting Started task pane disappears.

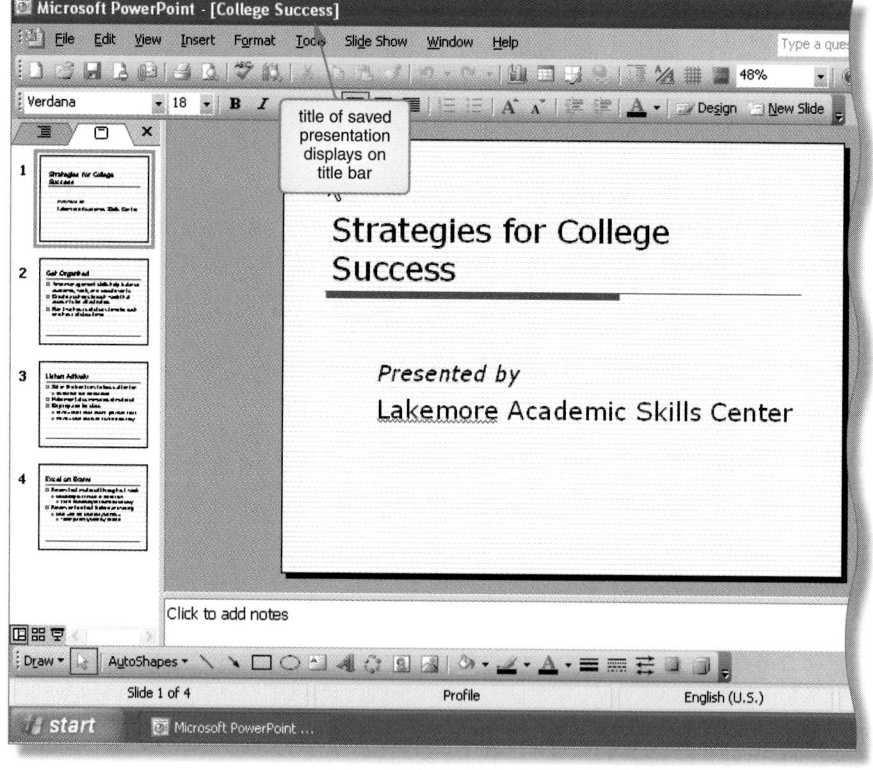

FIGURE 1-62

Other Ways

1. Right-click Start button, click Explore, display contents of drive A, double-click file name
2. Click Open button on Standard toolbar, select file name, click Open button in Open Office Document dialog box
3. On File menu click Open, select file name, click Open button in Open dialog box
4. In Voice Command mode, say "Open, [file name], Open"

When you start PowerPoint and open the College Success file, the application name and file name are displayed on a recessed button on the Windows taskbar. When more than one application is open, you can switch between applications by clicking the appropriate application button. If you want to open a presentation other than a recent one, click the Open button on the Standard toolbar or in the Getting Started task pane. Either button lets you navigate to a slide show stored on a disk.

Checking a Presentation for Spelling and Consistency

After you create a presentation, you should check it visually for spelling errors and style consistency. In addition, you can use PowerPoint's Spelling and Style tools to identify possible misspellings and inconsistencies.

Q: Can I rely on the spelling checker?

A: While PowerPoint's Spelling checker is a valuable tool, it is not infallible. You should proofread your presentation carefully by pointing to each word and saying it aloud as you point to it. Be mindful of commonly misused words such as its and it's, through and though, and to and too.

Checking a Presentation for Spelling Errors

PowerPoint checks the entire presentation for spelling mistakes using a standard dictionary contained in the Microsoft Office group. This dictionary is shared with the other Microsoft Office applications such as Word and Excel. A **custom dictionary** is available if you want to add special words such as proper names, cities, and acronyms. When checking a presentation for spelling errors, PowerPoint opens the standard dictionary and the custom dictionary file, if one exists. When a word appears in the Spelling dialog box, you perform one of the actions listed in Table 1-4.

Table 1-4 Summary of Spelling Checker Actions

ACTION	DESCRIPTION
Ignore the word	Click the Ignore button when the word is spelled correctly but not found in the dictionaries. PowerPoint continues checking the rest of the presentation.
Ignore all occurrences of the word	Click the Ignore All button when the word is spelled correctly but not found in the dictionaries. PowerPoint ignores all occurrences of the word and continues checking the rest of the presentation.
Select a different spelling	Click the proper spelling of the word from the list in the Suggestions box. Click the Change button. PowerPoint corrects the word and continues checking the rest of the presentation.
Change all occurrences of the misspelling to a different spelling	Click the proper spelling of the word from the list in the Suggestions box. Click the Change All button. PowerPoint changes all occurrences of the misspelled word and continues checking the rest of the presentation.
Add a word to the custom dictionary	Click the Add button. PowerPoint opens the custom dictionary, adds the word, and continues checking the rest of the presentation.
View alternative spellings	Click the Suggest button. PowerPoint lists suggested spellings. Click the correct word from the Suggestions box or type the proper spelling. Then click the Change button. PowerPoint continues checking the rest of the presentation.
Add spelling error to AutoCorrect list	Click the AutoCorrect button. PowerPoint adds the spelling error and its correction to the AutoCorrect list. Any future misspelling of the word is corrected automatically as you type.
Close	Click the Close button to close the Spelling checker and return to the PowerPoint window.

The standard dictionary contains commonly used English words. It does not, however, contain proper names, abbreviations, technical terms, poetic contractions, or antiquated terms. PowerPoint treats words not found in the dictionaries as misspellings.

Starting the Spelling Checker

The following steps illustrate how to start the Spelling checker and check the entire presentation.

To Start the Spelling Checker

1

- **Point to the Spelling button on the Standard toolbar (Figure 1-63).**

FIGURE 1-63

2

- **Click the Spelling button.**
- **When the Spelling dialog box appears, point to the Ignore button.**

PowerPoint starts the Spelling checker and displays the Spelling dialog box (Figure 1-64). The word, Lakemore, appears in the Not in Dictionary box. Depending on the custom dictionary, Lakemore may not be recognized as a misspelled word.

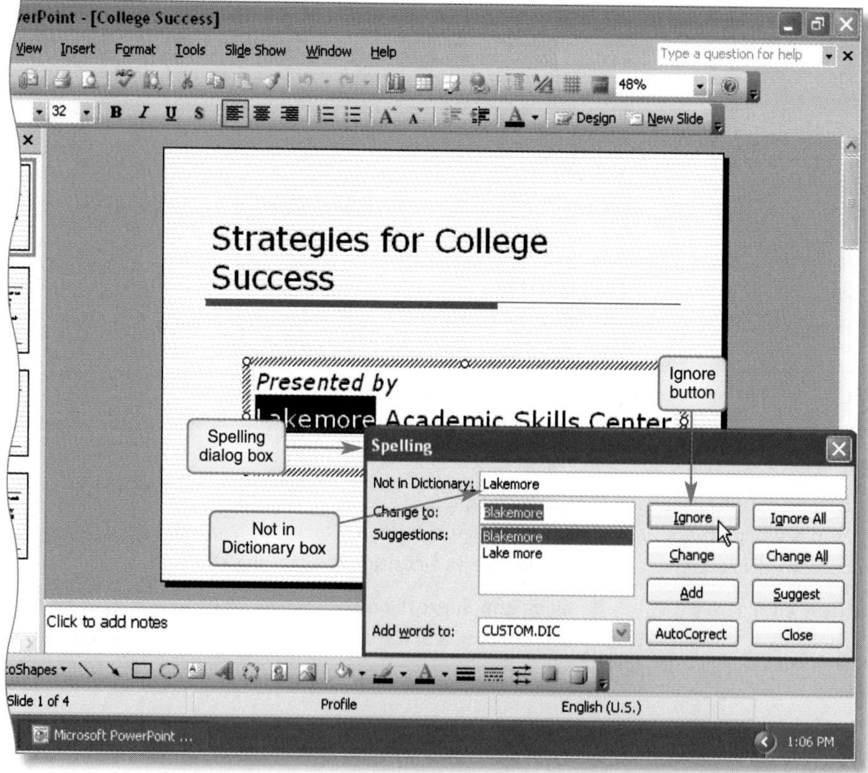

FIGURE 1-64

3

- **Click the Ignore button.**
- **When the Microsoft Office PowerPoint dialog box appears, point to the OK button.**

PowerPoint ignores the word, Lakemore, and continues searching for additional misspelled words. PowerPoint may stop on additional words depending on your typing accuracy. When PowerPoint has checked all slides for misspellings, the Microsoft Office PowerPoint dialog box informs you that the spelling check is complete (Figure 1-65).

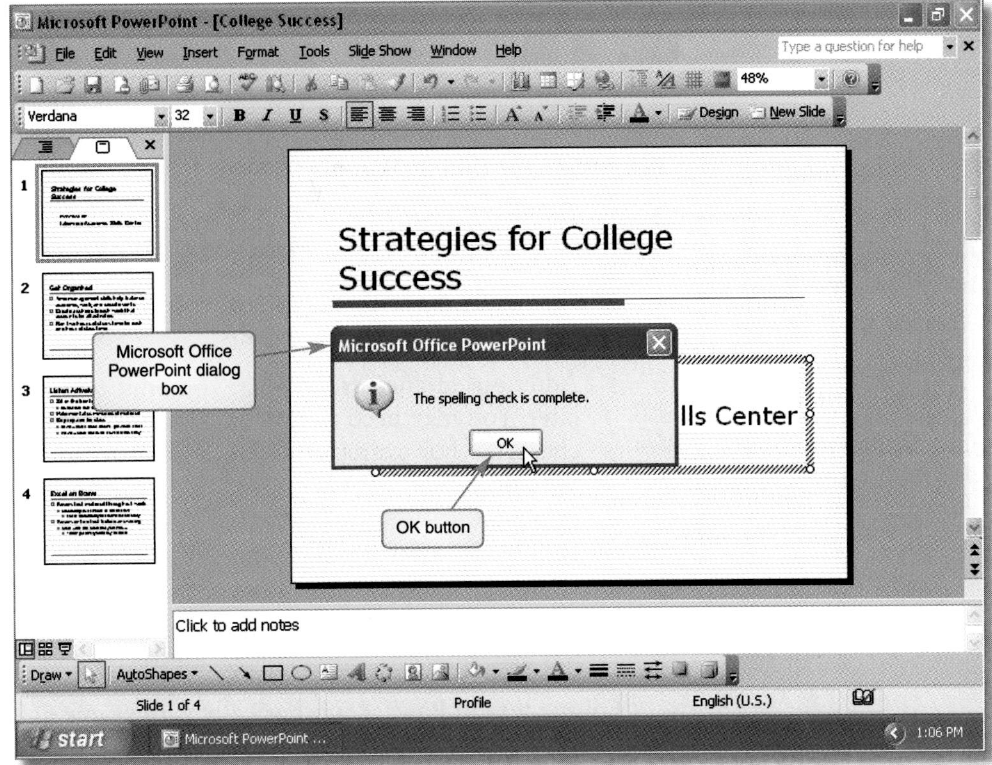

FIGURE 1-65

4

- **Click the OK button.**
- **Click the slide to remove the highlight from the word, Lakemore.**

PowerPoint closes the Spelling checker and returns to the current slide, Slide 1 (Figure 1-66), or to the slide where a possible misspelled word displayed.

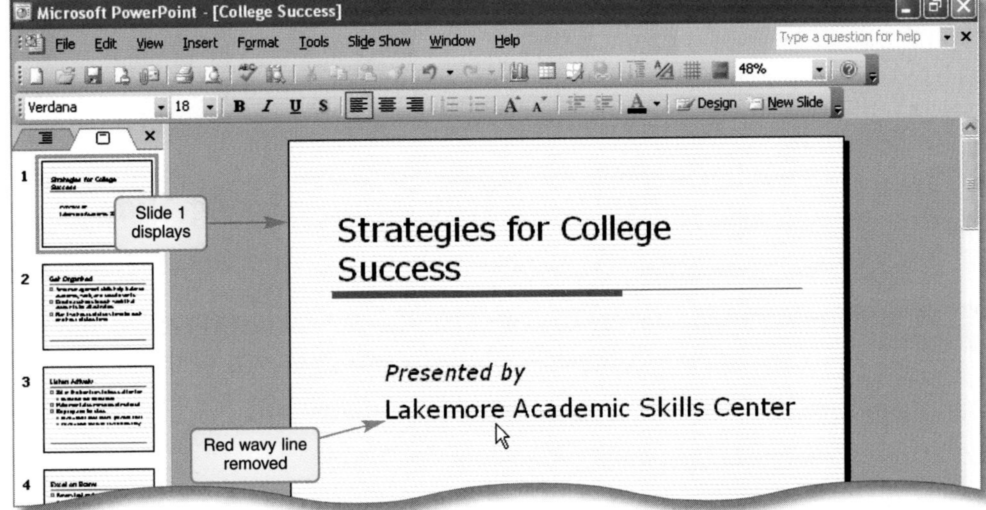

FIGURE 1-66

The red wavy line below the word, Lakemore, is gone because you instructed PowerPoint to ignore that word, which does not appear in the standard dictionary. You also could have added that word to the dictionary so it would not be flagged as a possible misspelled word in subsequent presentations you create using that word.

Other Ways

1. On Tools menu click Spelling
2. Press ALT+T, press S; when finished, press ENTER
3. Press F7
4. In Voice Command mode, say "Spelling"

Correcting Errors

After creating a presentation and running the Spelling checker, you may find that you must make changes. Changes may be required because a slide contains an error, the scope of the presentation shifts, or the style is inconsistent. This section explains the types of errors that commonly occur when creating a presentation.

More About

Quick Reference

For more information, see the Quick Reference Summary at the back of this book, or visit the PowerPoint 2003 Quick Reference Web page (scsite.com/ppt2003/qr).

Types of Corrections Made to Presentations

You generally make three types of corrections to text in a presentation: additions, deletions, and replacements.

- Additions are necessary when you omit text from a slide and need to add it later. You may need to insert text in the form of a sentence, word, or single character. For example, you may want to add the presenter's middle name on the title slide.
- Deletions are required when text on a slide is incorrect or no longer is relevant to the presentation. For example, a slide may look cluttered. Therefore, you may want to remove one of the bulleted paragraphs to add more space.
- Replacements are needed when you want to revise the text in a presentation. For example, you may want to substitute the word, their, for the word, there.

Editing text in PowerPoint basically is the same as editing text in a word processing package. The following sections illustrate the most common changes made to text in a presentation.

Deleting Text

You can delete text using one of three methods. One is to use the BACKSPACE key to remove text just typed. The second is to position the insertion point to the left of the text you wish to delete and then press the DELETE key. The third method is to drag through the text you wish to delete and then press the DELETE key. (Use the third method when deleting large sections of text.)

Replacing Text in an Existing Slide

When you need to correct a word or phrase, you can replace the text by selecting the text to be replaced and then typing the new text. As soon as you press any key on the keyboard, the highlighted text is deleted and the new text is displayed.

PowerPoint inserts text to the left of the insertion point. The text to the right of the insertion point moves to the right (and shifts downward if necessary) to accommodate the added text.

More About

Microsoft Certification

The Microsoft Office Specialist Certification program provides an opportunity for you to obtain a valuable industry credential – proof that you have the PowerPoint skills required by employers. For more information, see Appendix E, or visit the PowerPoint 2003 Certification Web page (scsite.com/ppt2003/cert).

Displaying a Presentation in Black and White

Printing handouts of a presentation allows you to use them to make overhead transparencies. The Color/Grayscale button on the Standard toolbar shows the presentation in black and white before you print. Table 1-5 identifies how PowerPoint objects display in black and white.

Table 1-5 Appearance in Black and White View

OBJECT	APPEARANCE IN BLACK AND WHITE VIEW
Bitmaps	Grayscale
Embossing	Hidden
Fills	Grayscale
Frame	Black
Lines	Black
Object shadows	Grayscale
Pattern fills	Grayscale
Slide backgrounds	White
Text	Black
Text shadows	Hidden

The following steps show how to display the presentation in black and white.

To Display a Presentation in Black and White

1

- **Click the Color/Grayscale button on the Standard toolbar and then point to Pure Black and White in the list.**

The Color/Grayscale list is displayed (Figure 1-67). Pure Black and White alters the slides' appearance so that only black lines display on a white background. Grayscale shows varying degrees of gray.

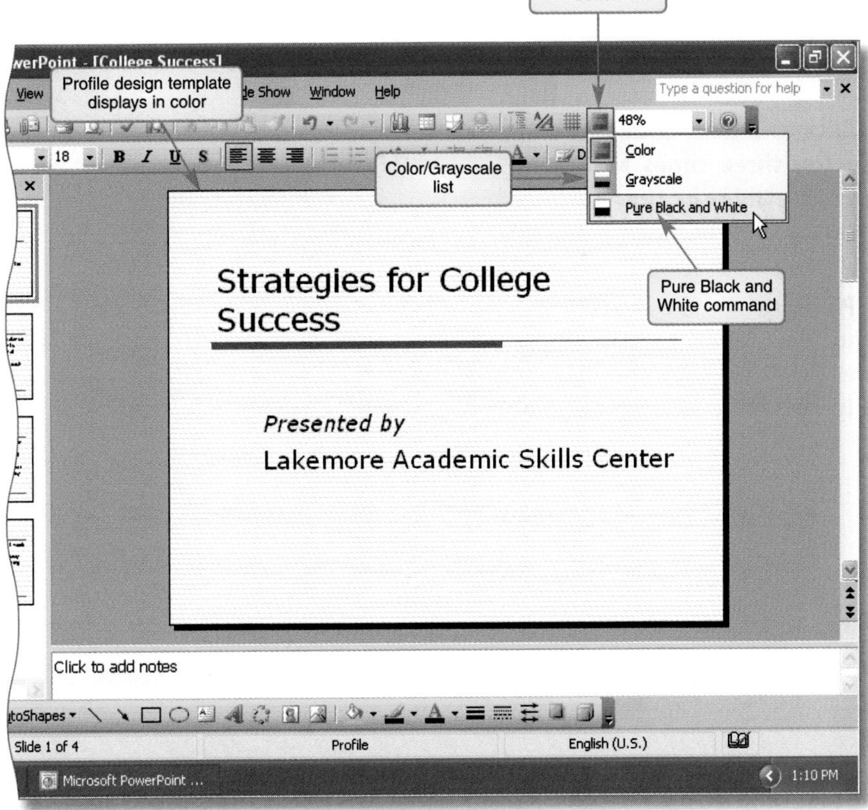

FIGURE 1-67

2

• **Click Pure Black and White.**

Slide 1 is displayed in black and white in the slide pane (Figure 1-68). The four thumbnail slides are displayed in color in the Slides tab. The Grayscale View toolbar appears. The Color/Grayscale button on the Standard toolbar changes from color bars to black and white.

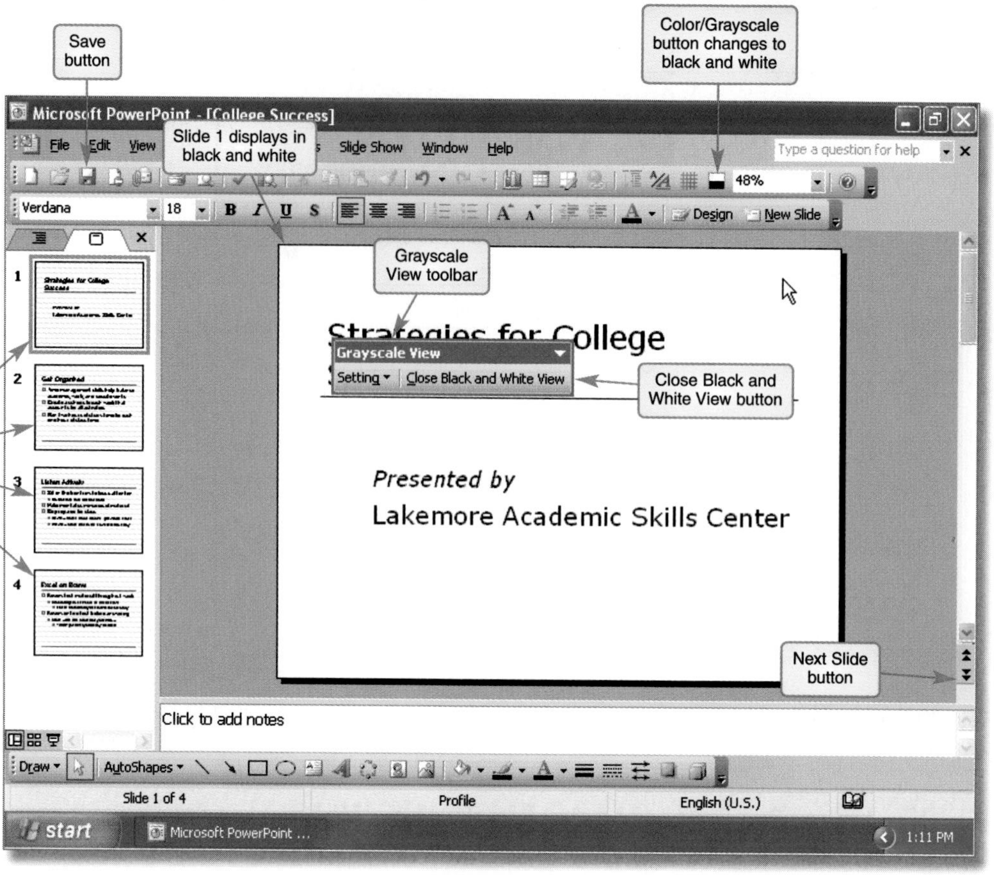

Save button

Color/Grayscale button changes to black and white

Slide 1 displays in black and white

Grayscale View toolbar

Close Black and White View button

thumbnail slides display in color

Next Slide button

Microsoft PowerPoint - [College Success]

Grayscale View

Setting ▾ | Close Black and White View

Strategies for College Success

Presented by

Lakemore Academic Skills Center

Click to add notes

Slide 1 of 4 | Profile | English (U.S.)

FIGURE 1-68

3

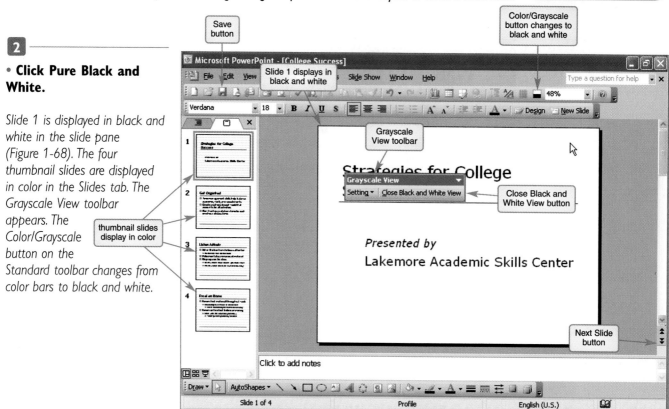

• **Click the Next Slide button three times to view all slides in the presentation in black and white.**

• **Point to the Close Black and White View button on the Grayscale View toolbar (Figure 1-69).**

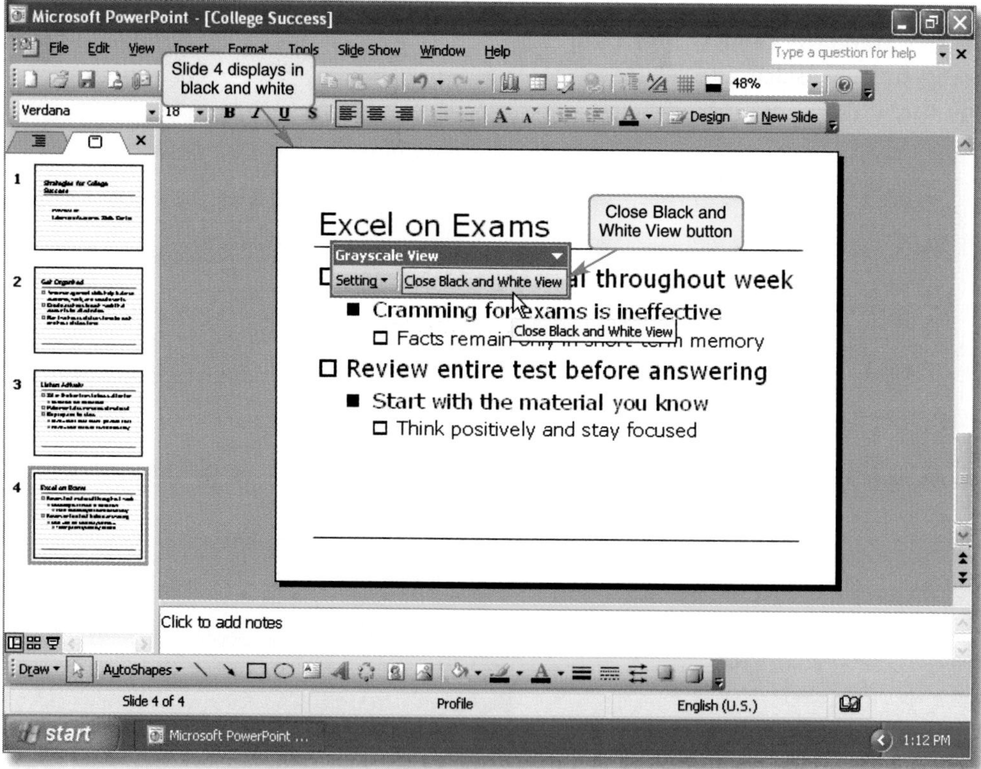

FIGURE 1-69

4

• **Click the Close Black and White View button.**

Slide 4 is displayed with the default Profile color scheme (Figure 1-70).

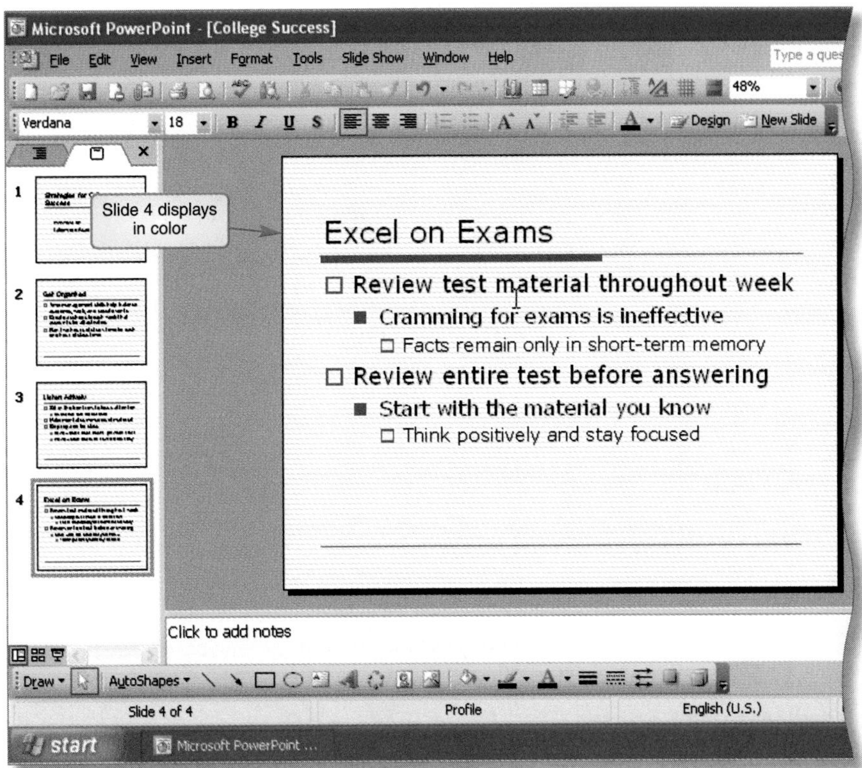

FIGURE 1-70

Other Ways

1. On View menu point to Color/Grayscale and then click Pure Black and White
2. In Voice Command mode, say "View, Color Grayscale, Pure Black and White"

After you view the text objects in the presentation in black and white, you can make any changes that will enhance printouts produced from a black and white printer or photocopier.

Printing a Presentation

After you create a presentation, you often want to print it. A printed version of the presentation is called a **hard copy**, or **printout**. The first printing of the presentation is called a **rough draft**. The rough draft allows you to proofread the presentation to check for errors and readability. After correcting errors, you print the final copy of the presentation.

Saving Before Printing

Before printing a presentation, you should save your work in the event you experience difficulties with the printer. You occasionally may encounter system problems that can be resolved only by restarting the computer. In such an instance, you will need to reopen the presentation. As a precaution, always save the presentation before you print. The steps on the next page save the presentation before printing.

More About

Printing in Black and White

If you have a color printer, you can avoid wasting ink by printing a presentation in black and white. You print in black and white by clicking Color/Grayscale on the View menu and then clicking either Grayscale or Pure Black and White.

To Save a Presentation Before Printing

1 **Verify that the floppy disk is in drive A.**

2 **Click the Save button on the Standard toolbar.**

All changes made after your last save now are saved on the floppy disk.

Printing the Presentation

After saving the presentation, you are ready to print. Clicking the Print button on the Standard toolbar causes PowerPoint to print all slides in the presentation. The following steps illustrate how to print the presentation slides.

To Print a Presentation

1

- **Ready the printer according to the printer instructions.**
- **Click the Print button on the Standard toolbar.**

The printer icon in the tray status area on the Windows taskbar indicates a print job is processing (Figure 1-71). This icon may not display on your system, or it may display on your status bar. After several moments, the slide show begins printing on the printer. When the presentation is finished printing, the printer icon in the tray status area on the Windows taskbar no longer is displayed.

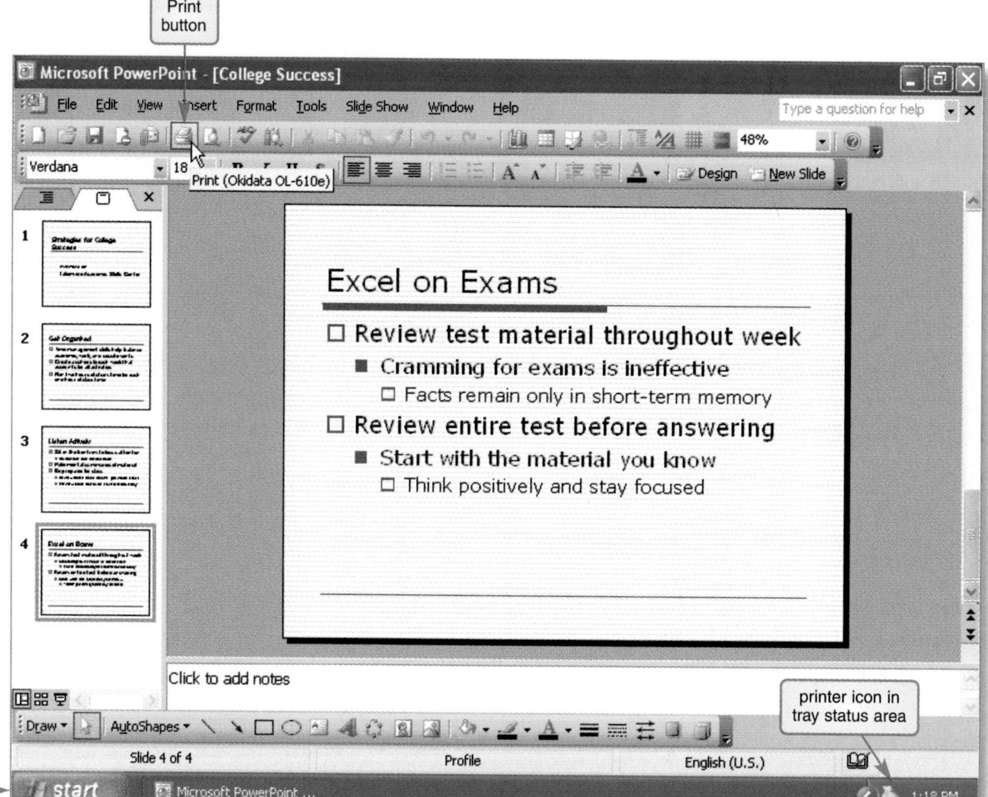

FIGURE 1-71

2

• **When the printer stops, retrieve the printouts of the slides.**

The presentation, College Success, prints on four pages (Figures 1-72a through 1-72d).

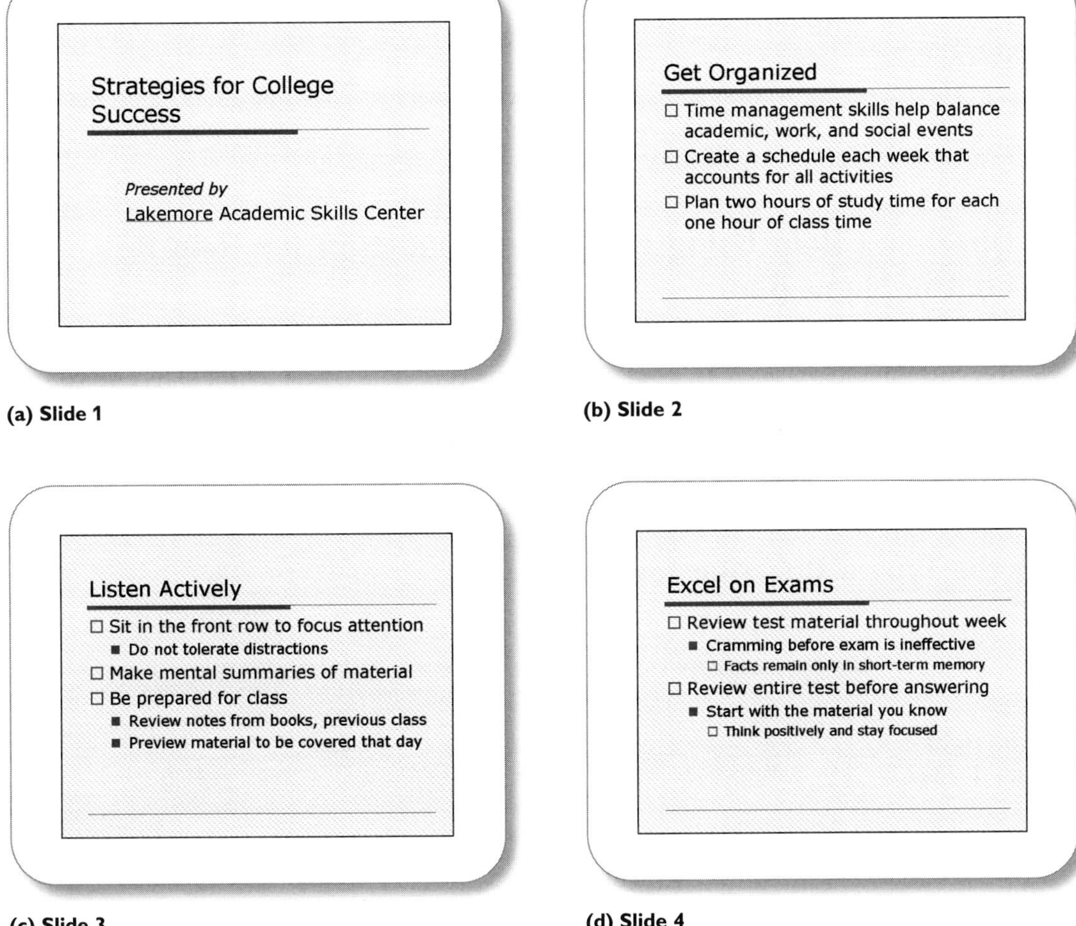

(a) Slide 1 (b) Slide 2 (c) Slide 3 (d) Slide 4

FIGURE 1-72

Other Ways

1. On File menu click Print
2. Press CTRL+P or press CTRL+SHIFT+F12
3. In Voice Command mode, say "Print"

You can click the printer icon next to the clock in the tray status area on the Windows taskbar to obtain information about the presentations printing on your printer and to delete files in the print queue that are waiting to be printed.

Making a Transparency

With the handouts printed, you now can make overhead transparencies using one of several devices. One device is a printer attached to your computer, such as an inkjet printer or a laser printer. Transparencies produced on a printer may be in black and white or color, depending on the printer. Another device is a photocopier. Because each of these devices requires a special transparency film, check the user's manual for the film requirement of your specific device, or ask your instructor.

More About

The PowerPoint Help System

Need Help? It is no further away than the Type a question for help box on the menu bar in the upper-right corner of the window. Click the box that contains the text, Type a question for help (Figure 1-73), type `help`, and then press the ENTER key. PowerPoint responds with a list of topics you can click to learn about obtaining help on any PowerPoint-related topic. To find out what is new in PowerPoint 2003, type `what is new in PowerPoint` in the Type a question for help box.

PowerPoint Help System

You can get answers to PowerPoint questions at any time by using the PowerPoint Help system. You can activate the PowerPoint Help system by using the Type a question for help box on the menu bar, by using the Microsoft PowerPoint Help button on the Standard toolbar, or by clicking Help on the menu bar (Figure 1-73). Used properly, this form of online assistance can increase your productivity and reduce your frustrations by minimizing the time you spend learning how to use PowerPoint.

The following section shows how to get answers to your questions using the Type a question for help box. Additional information on using the PowerPoint Help system is available in Appendix A and Table 1-6 on page PPT 65.

Obtaining Help Using the Type a Question for Help Box on the Menu Bar

The Type a question for help box on the right side of the menu bar lets you type free-form questions such as, *how do I save* or *how do I create a Web page*, or you can type terms such as, *copy*, *save*, or *format*. PowerPoint responds by displaying a list of topics related to what you typed. The following steps show how to use the Type a question for help box to obtain information on formatting bullets.

To Obtain Help Using the Type a Question for Help Box

1

• **Type** `bullet` **in the Type a question for help box on the right side of the menu bar (Figure 1-73).**

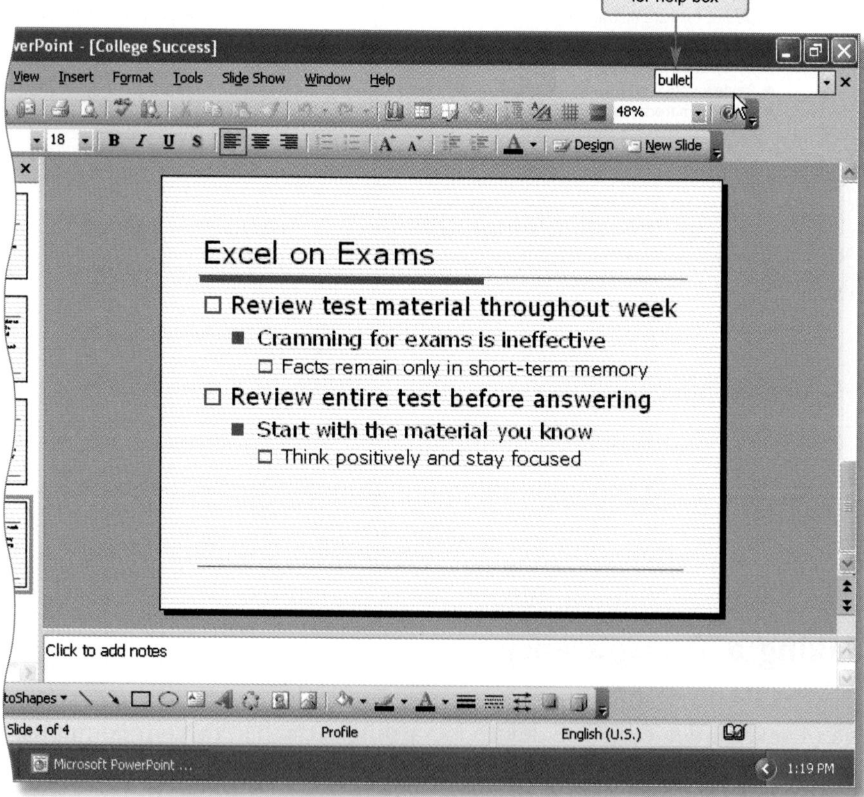

FIGURE 1-73

2

- **Press the ENTER key.**
- **When PowerPoint displays the Search Results task pane, scroll down and then point to the topic, Change the bullet style in a list.**

PowerPoint displays the Search Results task pane with a list of topics relating to the term, bullet. PowerPoint found 30 results from Microsoft Office Online. The mouse pointer changes to a hand, which indicates it is pointing to a link (Figure 1-74).

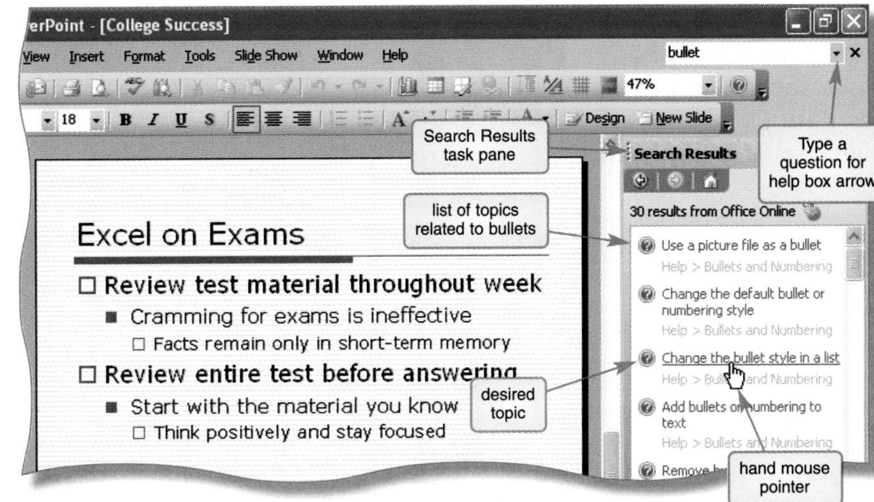

FIGURE 1-74

3

- **Click Change the bullet style in a list.**
- **When the Microsoft Office PowerPoint Help window is displayed, double-click its title bar to maximize it.**

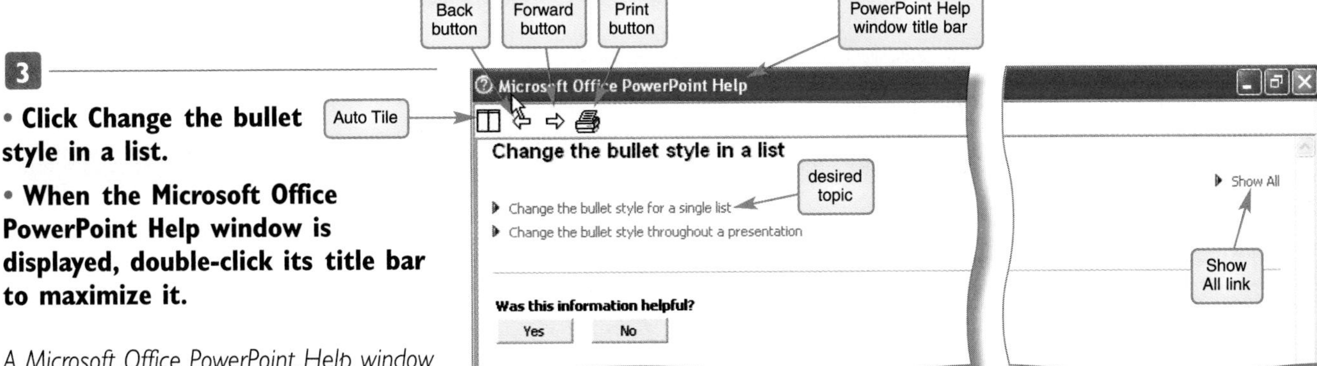

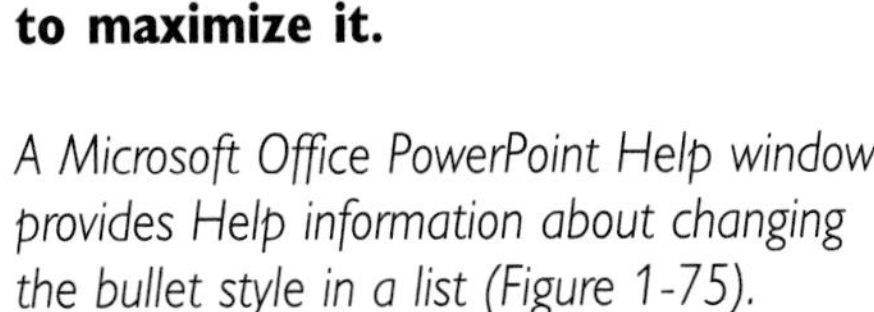

A Microsoft Office PowerPoint Help window provides Help information about changing the bullet style in a list (Figure 1-75).

FIGURE 1-75

4

- **Click the Show All link.**

Directions for changing a bullet style for a single list are displayed. Options include change the bullet character, change the bullet size, and change the bullet color (Figure 1-76).

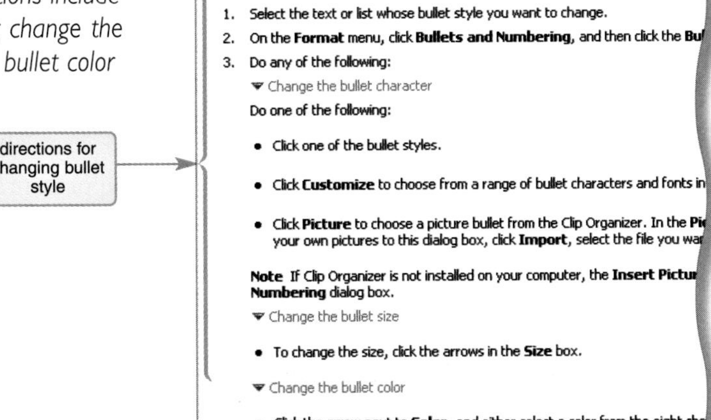

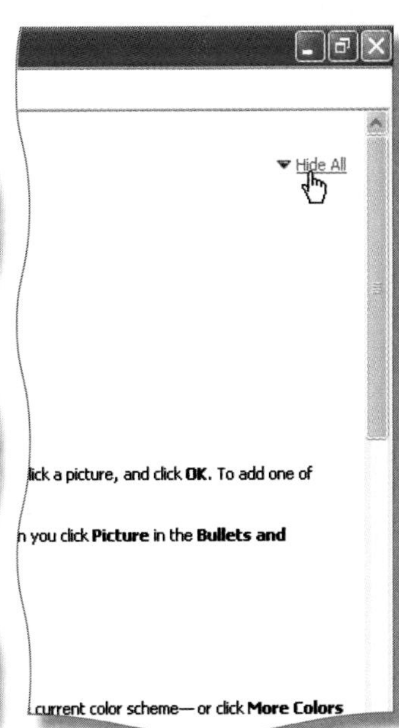

FIGURE 1-76

• **Drag the scroll box down the vertical scroll bar until Change the bullet color is displayed.**

PowerPoint displays specific details of changing the color of the bullets on a slide (Figure 1-77).

• **Click the Close button on the Microsoft Office PowerPoint Help window title bar.**

• **Click the Close button on the Search Results task pane.**

The PowerPoint Help window closes, and the PowerPoint presentation is displayed.

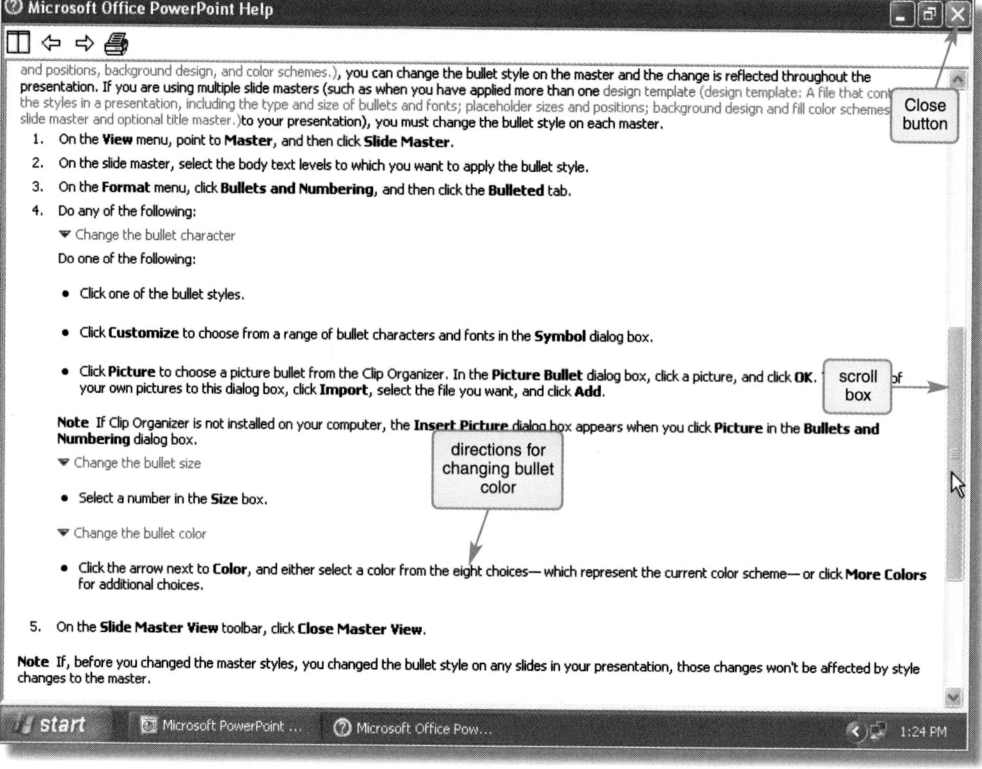

FIGURE 1-77

Other Ways

1. Click Microsoft Office PowerPoint Help button on Standard toolbar; or on Help menu click Microsoft Office PowerPoint Help
2. Press F1

Use the buttons in the upper-left corner of the Microsoft Office PowerPoint Help window (Figure 1-75 on the previous page) to navigate through the Help system, change the display, and print the contents of the window.

As you enter questions and terms in the Type a question for help box, PowerPoint adds them to its list. Thus, if you click the Type a question for help box arrow (Figure 1-74 on the previous page), PowerPoint will display a list of previously asked questions and terms.

Table 1-6 summarizes the major categories of Help available to you. Because of the way the PowerPoint Help system works, be certain to review the rightmost column of Table 1-6 if you have difficulties activating the desired category of Help. Additional information on using the PowerPoint Help system is available in Appendix A.

Quitting PowerPoint

Project 1 is complete. The final task is to close the presentation and quit PowerPoint. The following steps quit PowerPoint.

To Quit PowerPoint

1. **Click the Close button on the title bar.**
2. **If prompted to save the presentation before quitting PowerPoint, click the Yes button in the Microsoft Office PowerPoint dialog box.**

Table 1-6 PowerPoint Help System

TYPE	DESCRIPTION	HOW TO ACTIVATE
Microsoft Office PowerPoint Help	Displays PowerPoint Help task pane. Answers questions or searches for terms that you type in your own words.	Click the Microsoft Office PowerPoint Help button on the Standard toolbar or click Microsoft Office PowerPoint Help on the Help menu.
Office Assistant	Similar to the Type a question for help box. The Office Assistant answers questions that you type in your own words, offers tips, and provides help for a variety of PowerPoint features.	Click the Office Assistant icon. If the Office Assistant does not display, click Show the Office Assistant on the Help menu.
Type a question for help box	Answers questions or searches for terms that you type in your own words.	Type a question or term in the Type a question for help box on the menu bar and then press the ENTER key.
Table of Contents	Groups Help topics by general categories. Use when you know only the general category of the topic in question.	Click the Microsoft Office PowerPoint Help button on the Standard toolbar or click Microsoft Office PowerPoint Help on the Help menu, and then click the Table of Contents link on the PowerPoint Help task pane.
Microsoft Office Online	Used to access technical resources and download free product enhancements on the Web.	Click Microsoft Office Online on the Help menu.
Detect and Repair	Automatically finds and fixes errors in the application.	Click Detect and Repair on the Help menu.

Project Summary

In creating the Strategies for College Success slide show in this project, you gained a broad knowledge of PowerPoint. First, you were introduced to starting PowerPoint and creating a presentation consisting of a title slide and single- and multi-level bulleted lists. You learned about PowerPoint design templates, objects, and attributes.

This project illustrated how to create an interesting introduction to a presentation by changing the text font style to italic and increasing font size on the title slide. Completing these tasks, you saved the presentation. Then, you created three text slides with bulleted lists, two with multi-level bullets, to explain effective academic skills. Next, you learned how to view the presentation in slide show view. Then, you learned how to quit PowerPoint and how to open an existing presentation. You used the Spelling checker to search for spelling errors. You learned how to display the presentation in black and white. You also learned how to print hard copies of the slides in order to make handouts and overhead transparencies. Finally, you learned how to use the PowerPoint Help system to answer your questions.

If you have a SAM user profile, you may have access to hands-on instruction, practice, and assessment of the skills covered in this project. Log in to your SAM account and go to your assignments page to see what your instructor has assigned.

What You Should Know

Having completed this project, you should be able to perform the tasks below. The tasks are listed in the same order they were presented in this project. For a list of the buttons, menus, toolbars, and commands introduced in this project, see the Quick Reference Summary at the back of this book and refer to the Page Number column.

1. Start PowerPoint (PPT 7)
2. Customize the PowerPoint Window (PPT 9)
3. Choose a Design Template (PPT 18)
4. Enter the Presentation Title (PPT 21)
5. Enter the Presentation Subtitle (PPT 22)
6. Change the Text Font Style to Italic (PPT 24)
7. Increase Font Size (PPT 25)
8. Save a Presentation on a Floppy Disk (PPT 27)
9. Add a New Text Slide with a Bulleted List (PPT 30)
10. Enter a Slide Title (PPT 32)
11. Select a Text Placeholder (PPT 32)
12. Type a Single-Level Bulleted List (PPT 33)
13. Add a New Slide and Enter a Slide Title (PPT 35)
14. Type a Multi-Level Bulleted List (PPT 36)
15. Type the Remaining Text for Slide 3 (PPT 38)
16. Create Slide 4 (PPT 39)
17. Create a Third-Level Paragraph (PPT 40)
18. Type the Remaining Text for Slide 4 (PPT 41)
19. End a Slide Show with a Black Slide (PPT 42)
20. Save a Presentation with the Same File Name (PPT 44)
21. Use the Scroll Box on the Slide Pane to Move to Another Slide (PPT 45)
22. Start Slide Show View (PPT 47)
23. Move Manually Through Slides in a Slide Show (PPT 48)
24. Display the Popup Menu and Go to a Specific Slide (PPT 49)
25. Use the Popup Menu to End a Slide Show (PPT 50)
26. Quit PowerPoint (PPT 50)
27. Start PowerPoint and Open an Existing Presentation (PPT 52)
28. Start the Spelling Checker (PPT 54)
29. Display a Presentation in Black and White (PPT 57)
30. Save a Presentation Before Printing (PPT 60)
31. Print a Presentation (PPT 60)
32. Obtain Help Using the Type a Question for Help Box (PPT 62)
33. Quit PowerPoint (PPT 64)

Learn It Online

Instructions: To complete the Learn It Online exercises, start your browser, click the Address bar, and then enter the Web address `scsite.com/ppt2003/learn`. When the PowerPoint 2003 Learn It Online page is displayed, follow the instructions in the exercises below. Each exercise has instructions for printing your results, either for your own records or for submission to your instructor.

1 Project Reinforcement TF, MC, and SA

Below PowerPoint Project 1, click the Project Reinforcement link. Print the quiz by clicking Print on the File menu for each page. Answer each question.

2 Flash Cards

Below PowerPoint Project 1, click the Flash Cards link and read the instructions. Type 20 (or a number specified by your instructor) in the Number of playing cards text box, type your name in the Enter your Name text box, and then click the Flip Card button. When the flash card is displayed, read the question and then click the ANSWER box arrow to select an answer. Flip through Flash Cards. If your score is 15 (75%) correct or greater, click Print on the File menu to print your results. If your score is less than 15 (75%) correct, then redo this exercise by clicking the Replay button.

3 Practice Test

Below PowerPoint Project 1, click the Practice Test link. Answer each question, enter your first and last name at the bottom of the page, and then click the Grade Test button. When the graded practice test is displayed on your screen, click Print on the File menu to print a hard copy. Continue to take practice tests until you score 80% or better.

4 Who Wants To Be a Computer Genius?

Below PowerPoint Project 1, click the Computer Genius link. Read the instructions, enter your first and last name at the bottom of the page, and then click the PLAY button. When your score is displayed, click the PRINT RESULTS link to print a hard copy.

5 Wheel of Terms

Below PowerPoint Project 1, click the Wheel of Terms link. Read the instructions, and then enter your first and last name and your school name. Click the PLAY button. When your score is displayed, right-click the score and then click Print on the shortcut menu to print a hard copy.

6 Crossword Puzzle Challenge

Below PowerPoint Project 1, click the Crossword Puzzle Challenge link. Read the instructions, and then enter your first and last name. Click the SUBMIT button. Work the crossword puzzle. When you are finished, click the Submit button. When the crossword puzzle is redisplayed, click the Print Puzzle button to print a hard copy.

7 Tips and Tricks

Below PowerPoint Project 1, click the Tips and Tricks link. Click a topic that pertains to Project 1. Right-click the information and then click Print on the shortcut menu. Construct a brief example of what the information relates to in PowerPoint to confirm you understand how to use the tip or trick.

8 Newsgroups

Below PowerPoint Project 1, click the Newsgroups link. Click a topic that pertains to Project 1. Print three comments.

9 Expanding Your Horizons

Below PowerPoint Project 1, click the Expanding Your Horizons link. Click a topic that pertains to Project 1. Print the information. Construct a brief example of what the information relates to in PowerPoint to confirm you understand the contents of the article.

10 Search Sleuth

Below PowerPoint Project 1, click the Search Sleuth link. To search for a term that pertains to this project, select a term below the Project 1 title and then use the Google search engine at google.com (or any major search engine) to display and print two Web pages that present information on the term.

11 PowerPoint Online Training

Below PowerPoint Project 1, click the PowerPoint Online Training link. When your browser displays the Microsoft Office Online Web page, click the PowerPoint link. Click one of the PowerPoint courses that covers one or more of the objectives listed at the beginning of the project on page PPT 4. Print the first page of the course before stepping through it.

12 Office Marketplace

Below PowerPoint Project 1, click the Office Marketplace link. When your browser displays the Microsoft Office Online Web page, click the Office Marketplace link. Click a topic that relates to PowerPoint. Print the first page.

Apply Your Knowledge

1 Searching on the World Wide Web

Instructions: Start PowerPoint. Open the presentation Apply 1-1 Internet Searching from the Data Disk. See page xxiv at the front of this book for instructions for downloading the Data Disk or see your instructor for information on accessing the files required for this book. The two slides in the presentation give information on tools to search the Web. Make the following changes to the slides so they appear as shown in Figure 1-78.

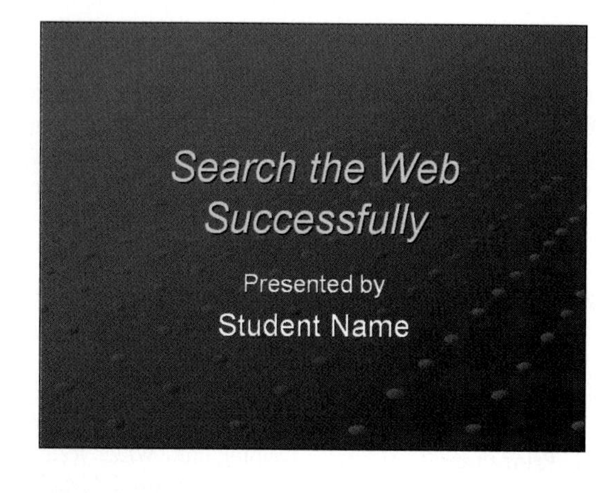

(a) Slide 1 (Title Slide)

Two Search Tools

- Subject Directory
  - Categorized lists of links arranged by subject and displayed in series of menus
- Search Engine
  - Requires search text: a word, words, phrase
    - Carefully craft keywords to limit search

(b) Slide 2 (Multi-Level Bulleted List)

FIGURE 1-78

Change the design template to Digital Dots. On the title slide, use your name in place of Student Name and change the font size to 40. Italicize the title text.

On Slide 2, increase the indent of the second and fourth paragraphs, Categorized lists of links arranged by subject and displayed in series of menus, and Requires search text: a word, words, phrase, to second-level paragraphs. Then change the last paragraph, Carefully craft keywords to limit search, to a third-level paragraph.

Display the revised presentation in black and white, and then print the two slides.

Save the presentation using the file name, Apply 1-1 Search Tools. Hand in the hard copy to your instructor.

In the Lab

Note: These labs require you to create presentations based on notes. When you design these slide shows, use the 7 × 7 rule, which states that each line should have a maximum of seven words, and each slide should have a maximum of seven lines.

1 Proper Tire Care Presentation

Problem: Your tires are one of the most important safety features on your car. Regarding tire maintenance, the Rubber Manufacturers Association recommends you "play your PART": Pressure, Alignment, Rotation, Tread. Terry Quinn, the owner of the local tire dealer in your community, is concerned that approximately 10 percent of cars have at least one worn out or bald tire, according to the National Highway Traffic Safety Administration. He has asked you to prepare a short PowerPoint presentation and handouts to educate drivers about how to care for their tires. He hands you the outline shown in Figure 1-79 and asks you to create the presentation shown in Figures 1-80a through 1-80f on the following pages.

I.) Tire Maintenance
Presented by
Terry Quinn

II.) Play Your PART in Tire Maintenance
- Pressure
- Alignment
- Rotation
- Tread

III.) Proper Pressure
- Check monthly when tires are cold
- Information placard has correct pressure
  - o Mounted in drivers' door frame or glove box
  - o Front and rear pressures may differ
- Use reliable tire pressure gauge
  - o Do not rely on air pump gauge

IV.) Alignment Action
- Vehicles can become misaligned over time
  - o Bumps, potholes create suspension problems
  - o Apply brakes as you approach hole
  - o Release just before striking it
- Misalignment causes tires to ride at angle
  - o May experience handling problems

V.) Rotation Rules
- Each tire wears out at different rate
  - o Rotating keeps wear even
- Should be done every 6,000 – 8,000 miles
- Pattern depends on type of vehicle, tires
  - o Consult owner's manual
  - o Adjust air pressure after rotation

VI.) Tread Tactics
- Uneven tread wear indicates problems
  - o Incorrect balance, underinflation, misalignment
- Shallow tread
  - o Should be at least 1/16-inch deep
- Check tread wear indicators
  - o When tread is even with bars, replace tire

FIGURE 1-79

(continued)

Proper Tire Care Presentation *(continued)*

Tire Maintenance

Presented by
Terry Quinn

(a) Slide 1

Play Your PART in Tire Maintenance

- Pressure
- Alignment
- Rotation
- Tread

(b) Slide 2

Proper Pressure

- Check monthly when tires are cold
- Information placard has correct pressure
  - Mounted in drivers' door frame or glove box
  - Front and rear pressures may differ
- Use reliable tire pressure gauge
  - Do not rely on air pump gauge

(c) Slide 3

Alignment Action

- Vehicles can become misaligned over time
  - Bumps, potholes create suspension problems
  - Apply brakes as you approach hole
  - Release just before striking it
- Misalignment causes tires to ride at angle
  - May experience handling problems

(d) Slide 4

FIGURE 1-80

In the Lab

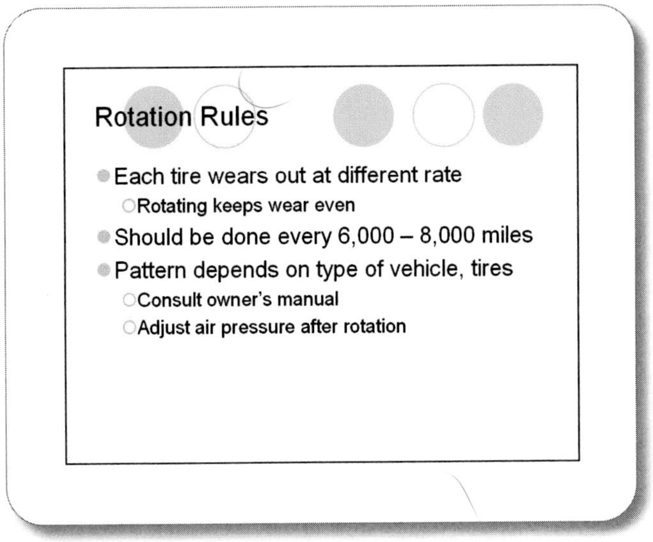

Rotation Rules
- Each tire wears out at different rate
  - Rotating keeps wear even
- Should be done every 6,000 – 8,000 miles
- Pattern depends on type of vehicle, tires
  - Consult owner's manual
  - Adjust air pressure after rotation

(e) Slide 5

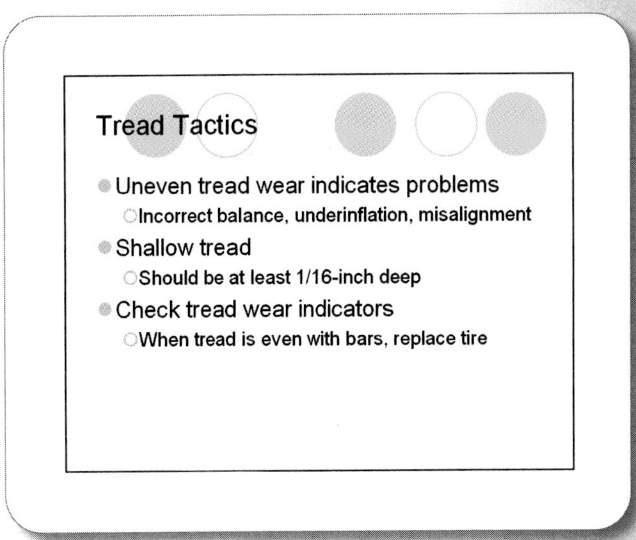

Tread Tactics
- Uneven tread wear indicates problems
  - Incorrect balance, underinflation, misalignment
- Shallow tread
  - Should be at least 1/16-inch deep
- Check tread wear indicators
  - When tread is even with bars, replace tire

(f) Slide 6

FIGURE 1-80 ***(continued)***

Instructions: Perform the following tasks.

1. Create a new presentation using the Watermark design template.
2. Using the typed notes illustrated in Figure 1-79 on page PPT 69, create the title slide shown in Figure 1-80a using your name in place of Terry Quinn. Italicize the title paragraph, Tire Maintenance, and increase the font size to 60. Increase the font size of the first paragraph of the subtitle text, Presented by, to 36. Italicize your name, and increase the font size to 40.
3. Using the typed notes in Figure 1-79, create the five text slides with bulleted lists shown in Figures 1-80b through 1-80f.
4. Click the Spelling button on the Standard toolbar. Correct any errors.
5. Drag the scroll box to display Slide 1. Click the Slide Show button to start slide show view. Then click to display each slide.
6. Save the presentation using the file name, Lab 1-1 Tire Maintenance.
7. Display and print the presentation in black and white. Close the presentation. Hand in the hard copy to your instructor.

2 Credit Card Safety Measures Presentation

Problem: The credit union on your campus issues many credit cards to students. Brian Brown, the branch manager, desires to inform these students about using their credit cards safely, especially because the Federal Trade Commission found recently that nearly 30 percent of identity theft was reported by people 18 to 29 years old. He has asked you to help him design a PowerPoint presentation that he can show during student orientation. He has typed information about wise credit habits (Figure 1-81) and has asked you to create the presentation shown in Figures 1-82a through 1-82d.

1) Credit Card Safety
Guard Your Card
Brian Brown
Credit Union Manager

2) Check Your Monthly Statements

- Compare receipts with billing statements
  - Evaluate whether all purchases are yours
- Check personal information
- Thieves often make small purchases
  - If not detected, they then charge large amounts
- Shred all documents and receipts

3) Secure Your Cards

- Do not
  - Put credit cards in glove compartment
  - Lend your card to anyone
  - Write your password on your card
  - Write your account number on an envelope
  - Leave receipts lying around

4) Take Security Measures

- Forward mail if you move
- Hold mail if leaving town for extended time
- Record account numbers, expiration dates, and customer service numbers
  - Store in safe location
  - Call immediately when problems arise

FIGURE 1-81

In the Lab

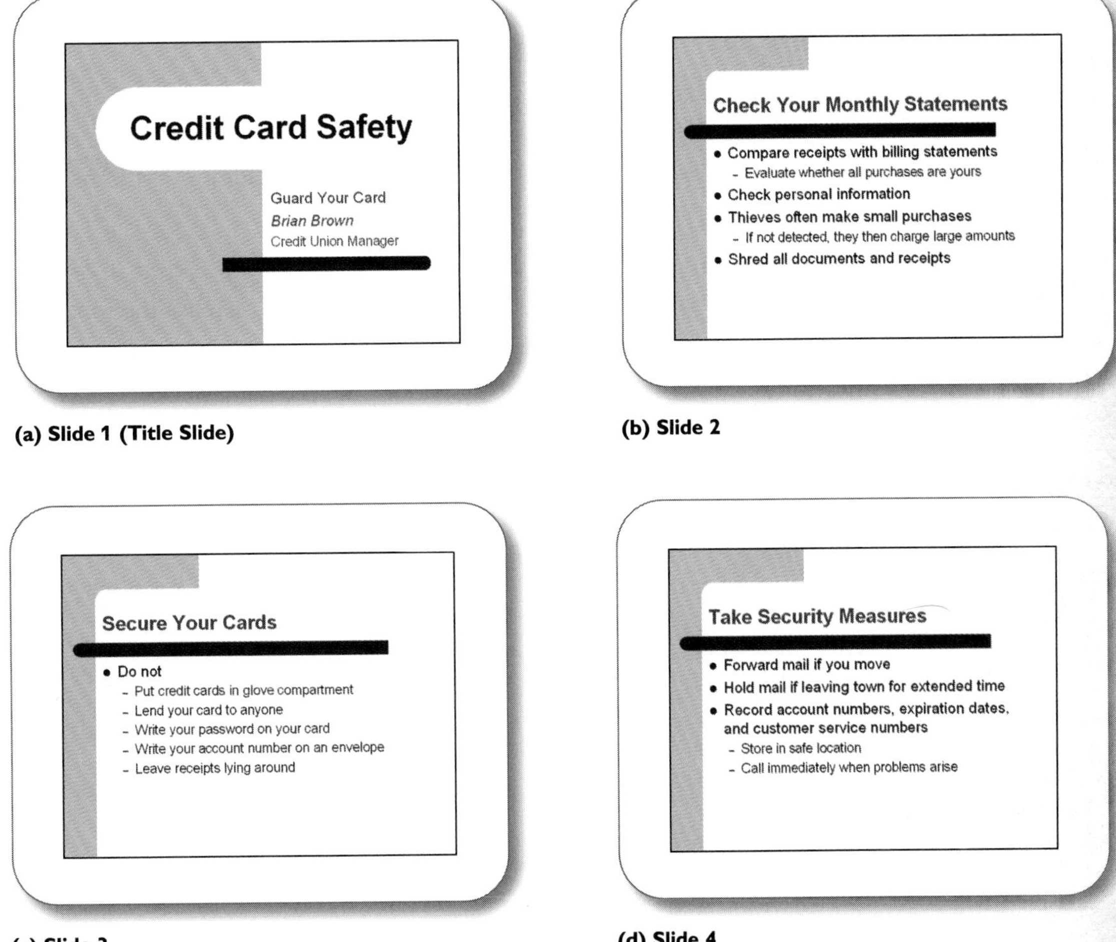

(a) Slide 1 (Title Slide) **(b) Slide 2**

(c) Slide 3 **(d) Slide 4**

FIGURE 1-82

Instructions: Perform the following tasks.

1. Create a new presentation using the Capsules design template.
2. Using the typed notes illustrated in Figure 1-81, create the title slide shown in Figure 1-82a using your name in place of Brian Brown. Italicize your name. Increase the font size of the title paragraph, Credit Card Safety, to 60. Decrease the font size of the third paragraph of the subtitle text, Credit Union Manager, to 24.
3. Using the typed notes in Figure 1-81, create the three text slides with bulleted lists shown in Figures 1-82b through 1-82d.
4. Click the Spelling button on the Standard toolbar. Correct any errors.
5. Save the presentation using the file name, Lab 1-2 Credit Card.
6. Display the presentation in black and white.
7. Print the black and white presentation. Close the presentation. Hand in the hard copy to your instructor.

3 Bodacious Bikers City Tour Presentation

Problem: The members of the Bodacious Bikers sponsor several activities throughout the year to raise money for community organizations in their city. One of their most popular events is a three-day bicycle tour that winds through major metropolitan cities. Bikers stay at a college campus the first night and at a campground the second night.

Instructions Part 1: Using the outline in Figure 1-83, create the presentation shown in Figure 1-84. Use the Studio design template. On the title slide, type your name in place of Louisa Garcia. Increase the font size of the title paragraph, Bodacious Bikers, to 54, and underline and italicize that text. Increase the font size of the subtitle paragraph, Spring City Tour, to 36. Create the three text slides with multi-level bulleted lists shown in Figures 1-84b through 1-84d.

Correct any spelling mistakes, and then view the slide show. Save the presentation using the file name, Lab 1-3 Part One Spring Bikers. Display and print the presentation in black and white.

1. Bodacious Bikers
Spring City Tour
April 10 – 12
Louisa Garcia, President

2. Day 1
- Meet at Midtown Mall parking lot
  - 8 a.m. check-in; 9 a.m. start
    - Light snack provided before ride starts
- End at Stevens College
- Approximately 62 miles
- Accommodations at Conference Center

3. Day 2
- Leave Stevens College at 9 a.m.
- End at Joseph Bay on Lake Echo
- Approximately 60 miles
- Accommodations at Dunes Campground
  - Tents and sleeping bags provided
  - Barbecue dinner served

4. Day 3
- Leave Joseph Bay at 8:30 a.m.
- Arrive at Midland Mall
- Approximately 55 miles
- Enjoy a celebration dinner
  - Awards ceremony for fundraisers
    - First prize: Cannondale Sport Road Bicycle

FIGURE 1-83

In the Lab

Bodacious Bikers
Spring City Tour
April 10 – 12
Louisa Garcia, President

(a) Slide 1 (Title Slide)

Day 1
Meet at Midtown Mall parking lot
8 a.m. check-in; 9 a.m. start
Light snack provided before ride starts
End at Stevens College
Approximately 62 miles
Accommodations at Conference Center

(b) Slide 2

Day 2
Leave Stevens College at 9 a.m.
End at Joseph Bay on Lake Echo
Approximately 60 miles
Accommodations at Dunes Campground
Tents and sleeping bags provided
Barbecue dinner served

(c) Slide 3

Day 3
Leave Joseph Bay at 8:30 a.m.
Arrive at Midland Mall
Approximately 55 miles
Enjoy a celebration dinner
Awards ceremony for fundraisers
First prize: Cannondale Sport Road Bicycle

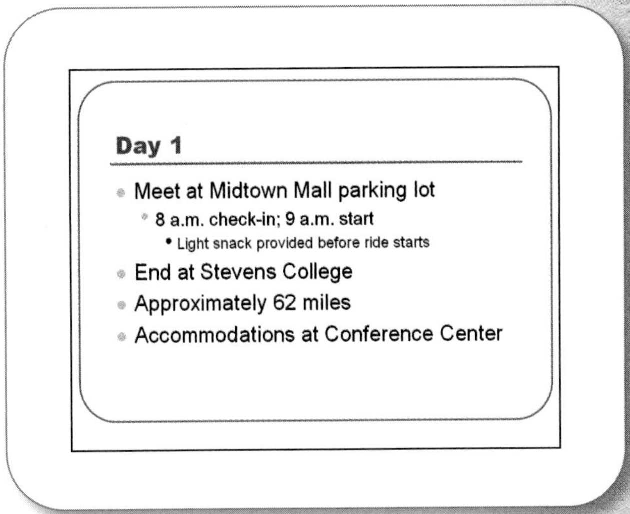

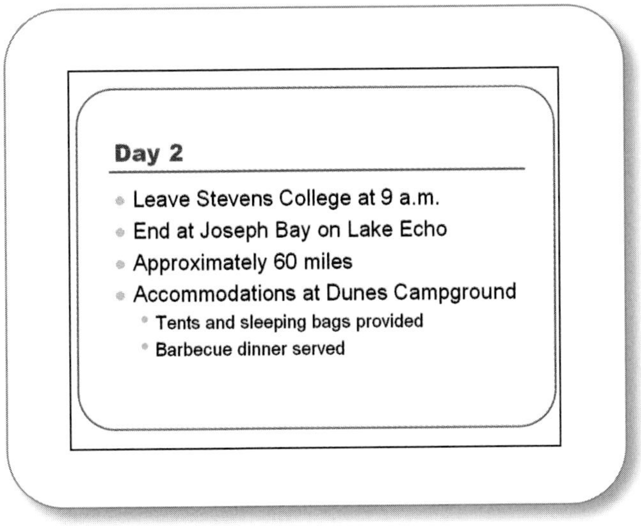

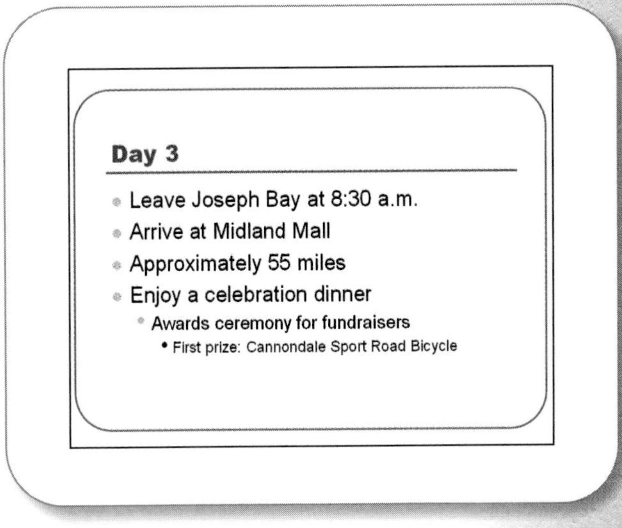

(d) Slide 4

FIGURE 1-84

(continued)

Bodacious Bikers City Tour Presentation *(continued)*

Instructions Part 2: The Bodacious Bikers want to update their presentation to promote the Fall bicycle tour. Modify the presentation created in Part 1 to create the presentation shown in Figure 1-85. Change the design template to Maple.

On the title slide, remove the underline from the title paragraph, Bodacious Bikers, decrease the font size to 60, and align the text on the left side of the placeholder. Change the first subtitle paragraph to, Fall City Tour. Change the dates in the second subtitle paragraph to, October 9 – 11. Then change your title in the third subtitle paragraph to, Treasurer, and decrease the font size of that paragraph to 28.

On Slide 2, delete the first first-level paragraph regarding the Midtown Mall and replace it with the paragraph, Arrive at Community Recreational Center. Delete the last paragraph on the slide and replace it with the paragraph, Lodging at Stevens Memorial Union.

On Slide 3, change the second first-level paragraph to, End at Twilight Shores on Lake Baker. Then change the last paragraph to, Enjoy a fresh fish dinner.

On Slide 4, change the first paragraph to, Leave Twilight Shores at 9 a.m., and then change the last paragraph to, Grand Prize: Rocky Mountain Ski Trip.

Correct any spelling mistakes, and then view the slide show. Save the presentation using the file name, Lab 1-3 Part Two Fall Bikers. Display and print the presentation in black and white. Close the presentation. Hand in both presentation printouts to your instructor.

In the Lab

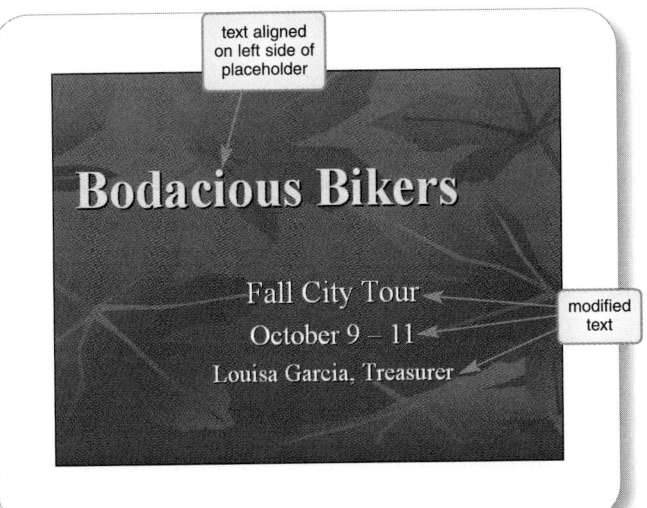

(a) Slide 1

Day 1

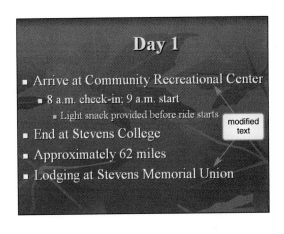

- Arrive at Community Recreational Center
  - 8 a.m. check-in; 9 a.m. start
    - Light snack provided before ride starts
- End at Stevens College
- Approximately 62 miles
- Lodging at Stevens Memorial Union

modified text

(b) Slide 2

Day 2

- Leave Stevens College at 9 a.m.
- End at Twilight Shores on Lake Baker
- Approximately 60 miles
- Accommodations at Dunes Campground
  - Tents and sleeping bags provided
  - Enjoy a fresh fish dinner

modified text

(c) Slide 3

Day 3

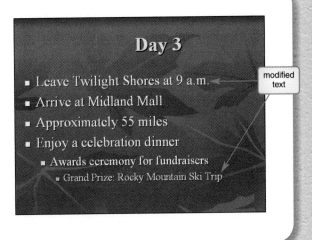

- Leave Twilight Shores at 9 a.m.
- Arrive at Midland Mall
- Approximately 55 miles
- Enjoy a celebration dinner
  - Awards ceremony for fundraisers
    - Grand Prize: Rocky Mountain Ski Trip

modified text

(d) Slide 4

FIGURE 1-85

The difficulty of these case studies varies:
■ are the least difficult and ■■ are more difficult. The last exercise is a group exercise.

Note: Remember to use the 7 × 7 rule as you design the presentations: a maximum of seven words on a line and a maximum of seven lines on one slide.

1 ■ The dispatcher at the Imperial Grove Police Station is noticing an increase in the number of calls made to the emergency 911 telephone number. These calls, unfortunately, are not always emergencies. Community residents have been calling the number to obtain information on everything from the times of movies at the local theatre to the names of the local city trustees. Police Chief Gina Colatta wants to inform homeowners of the importance of using the 911 service correctly. She created the outline shown in Figure 1-86 and asks you to help her prepare an accompanying PowerPoint presentation to show at the local mall and food stores. Using the concepts and techniques introduced in this project, together with Chief Colatta's outline, develop a slide show with a title slide and three text slides with bulleted lists. Print the slides so they can be distributed to residents at the conclusion of the presentation.

1) 911 – A Call for Help
- Presented by
- Chief Gina Colatta
- Imperial Grove Police Department

2) What It Is For
- When you need an emergency response
  - Fire
  - Police
  - Emergency Medical Personnel
- When disaster occurs
  - Tornadoes, earthquakes, floods

3) How to Help
- Do not call for general information
  - Consult local telephone directories
- If you call by mistake:
  - Tell the dispatcher you have misdialed
- Wait if you hear a recording

4) Other Information
- Tell the telephone company if you change your name or address
  - This info displays on the dispatcher's screen
  - The dispatcher relies on this information
- Be certain your house number can be seen from the street

FIGURE 1-86

Cases and Places

2 ■ Your school is planning a job fair to occur during the week of midterm exams. The Placement Office has invited 100 companies and local businesses to promote its current and anticipated job openings. The Placement Office director, Latasha Prince, hands you the outline shown in Figure 1-87 and asks you to prepare a presentation and handouts to promote the event. Use this list to design and create a presentation with a title slide and three text slides with bulleted lists.

1. Brookville College Career Fair
Presented by
Brookville College Placement Office
Latasha Prince, Director

2. Who Is Coming?
National corporations
    Progressive companies looking for high-quality candidates
Local companies
    Full-time and part-time
      - Hundreds of jobs

3. When Is It?
Midterm week
    Monday through Friday
Brookville College Cafeteria
Convenient hours
    9:00 a.m. to 8:00 p.m.

4. How Should I Prepare?
Bring plenty of resumes
    More than 100 companies expected
Dress neatly
View the Placement Office Web site
    Up-to-date information
    Company profiles

FIGURE 1-87

Cases and Places

3 In-line skating is a popular recreational sport throughout the world. In 1989, three million skaters spent $20 million on these skates and protective gear. In 1994, sales soared when nearly 14 million skaters spent $250 million. Today, the more than 27 million in-line skaters are purchasing more than $300 million in equipment yearly. Females account for 52 percent of skaters, and youths ranging in age from 7 to 17 are 58 percent of the total skaters. In-line skaters can participate more safely if they follow these steps: Wear full protective gear, including a helmet, wrist guards, and knee and elbow pads; practice basic skills, including braking, turning, and balancing, in a parking lot or other flat surface; always skate under control; and avoid hills until mastering speed control. The public relations director of your local park district has asked you to prepare a slide show emphasizing these safety tips and illustrating the in-line skating popularity surge. You decide to develop a slide show to run at the sporting goods store. Prepare a short presentation aimed at encouraging skaters to practice safe skating.

4 About 25 percent of the population suffers from the flu each year from October through May. Flu-related symptoms generally last for two weeks and include sudden headaches, chills, dry coughs, high fevers, and body aches. Serious complications are common, and an estimated 20,000 Americans die each year from the disease. Annual flu shots can help prevent the illness, and they are recommended for high-risk individuals such as the elderly and healthcare workers. Some drugs will help shorten the duration of the illness and decrease its severity if given within 48 hours after symptoms appear. General health tips include eating a balanced diet, getting enough rest, staying home when ill, exercising frequently, and washing hands frequently with warm, soapy water. Your campus' health services department wants to develop a presentation for students informing them about the flu and giving advice to stay healthy. Using the techniques introduced in the project, create a presentation about the flu.

5 **Working Together** Volunteers can make a contribution to society while they gain much fulfillment in return. Community organizations and non-for-profit businesses frequently seek volunteers for various projects. Have each member of your team visit or telephone several local civic groups to determine volunteer opportunities. Gather data about:

1) Required duties
2) Number of required hours
3) Contact person
4) Address
5) Telephone number

After coordinating the data, create a presentation with at least one slide showcasing the charitable organization. As a group, critique each slide. Hand in a hard copy of the final presentation.

Appendix A

Microsoft Office Help System

Using the Microsoft Office Help System

This appendix shows you how to use the Microsoft Office Help system. At anytime while you are using one of the Microsoft Office 2003 applications, you can interact with its Help system and display information on any topic associated with the application. To illustrate the use of the Office Help system, you will use the Microsoft Word application in this appendix. The Help systems in other Office applications respond in a similar fashion.

As shown in Figure A-1, five methods for accessing Word's Help system are available:

1. Microsoft Office Word Help button on the Standard toolbar
2. Microsoft Office Word Help command on the Help menu
3. Function key F1 on the keyboard
4. Type a question for help box on the menu bar
5. Office Assistant

1 MICROSOFT OFFICE WORD HELP BUTTON ON STANDARD TOOLBAR

2 MICROSOFT OFFICE WORD HELP COMMAND ON HELP MENU

3 FUNCTION KEY F1 ON KEYBOARD

4 TYPE A QUESTION FOR HELP BOX ON MENU BAR

5 OFFICE ASSISTANT

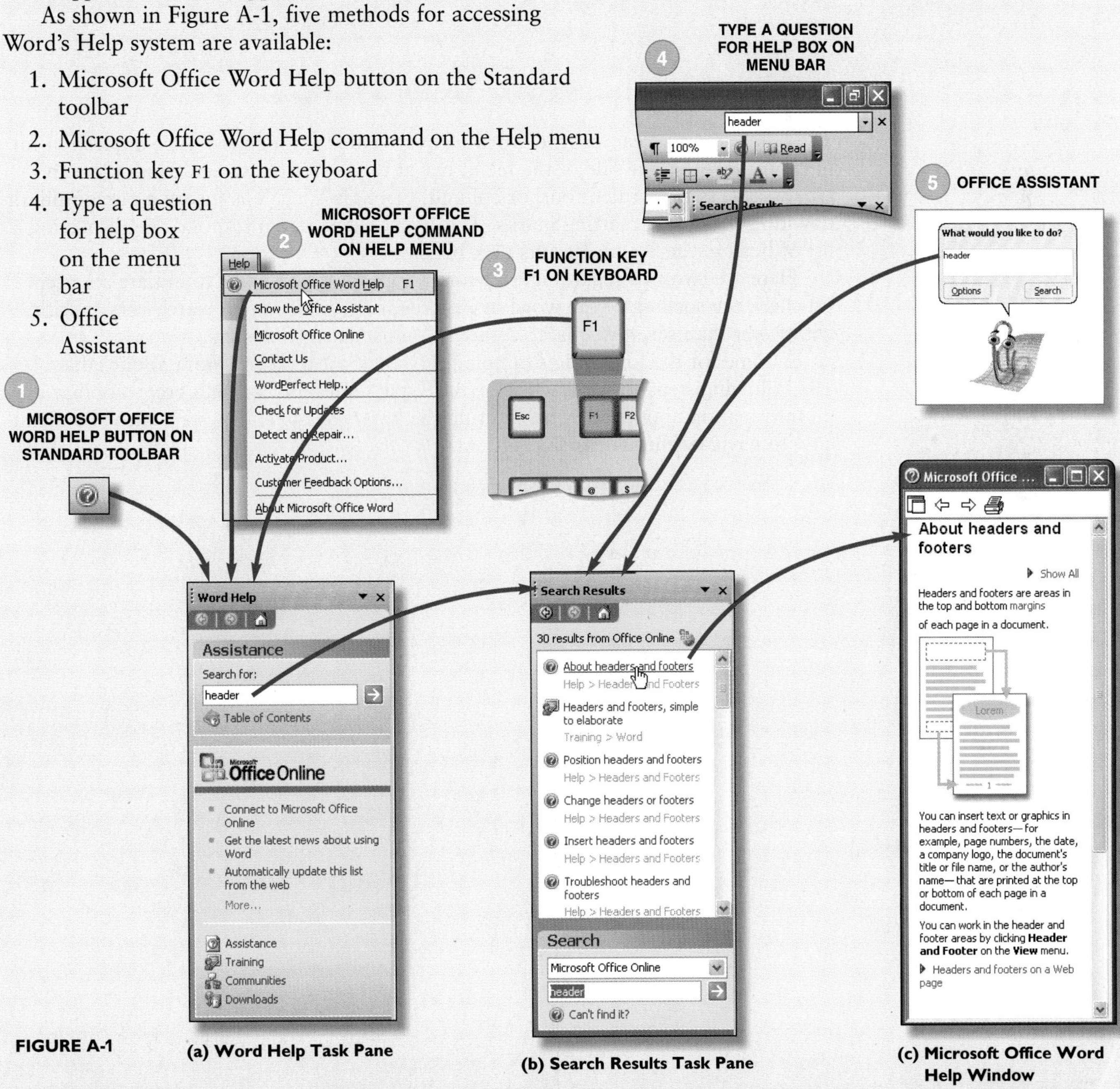

FIGURE A-1

(a) Word Help Task Pane

(b) Search Results Task Pane

(c) Microsoft Office Word Help Window

All five methods result in the Word Help system displaying a task pane on the right side of the Word window. The first three methods cause the **Word Help task pane** to display (Figure A-1a on the previous page). This task pane includes a Search text box in which you can enter a word or phrase on which you want help. Once you enter the word or phrase, the Word Help system displays the Search Results task pane (Figure A-1b on the previous page). With the Search Results task pane displayed, you can select specific Help topics.

As shown in Figure A-1, methods 4 and 5 bypass the Word Help task pane and display the **Search Results task pane** (Figure A-1b) with a list of links that pertain to the selected topic. Thus, any of the five methods for accessing the Word Help system results in displaying the Search Results task pane. Once the Word Help system displays this task pane, you can choose links that relate to the word or phrase on which you searched. In Figure A-1, for example, header was the searched topic (About headers and footers), which resulted in the Word Help system displaying the Microsoft Office Word Help window with information about headers and footers (Figure A-1c on the previous page).

Navigating the Word Help System

The quickest way to access the Word Help system is through the Type a question for help box on the right side of the menu bar at the top of the screen. Here you can type words, such as ruler, font, or column, or phrases, such as justify a paragraph, or how do I display formatting marks. The Word Help system responds by displaying a list of links in the Search Results task pane.

Here are two tips regarding the words or phrases you enter to initiate a search: (1) check the spelling of the word or phrase; and (2) keep your search very specific, with fewer than seven words, to return the most accurate results.

Assume for the following example that you want to know more about tables. The following steps show how to use the Type a question for help box to obtain useful information about tables by entering the keyword table. The steps also show you how to navigate the Word Help system.

To Obtain Help Using the Type a Question for Help Box

1

- **Click the Type a question for help box on the right side of the menu bar, type** `table`**, and then press the ENTER key (Figure A-2).**

The Word Help system displays the Search Results task pane on the right side of the window. The Search Results task pane contains a list of 30 links (Figure A-2). If you do not find what you are looking for, you can modify or refine the search in the Search area at the bottom of the task pane. The topics displayed in your Search Results task pane may be different.

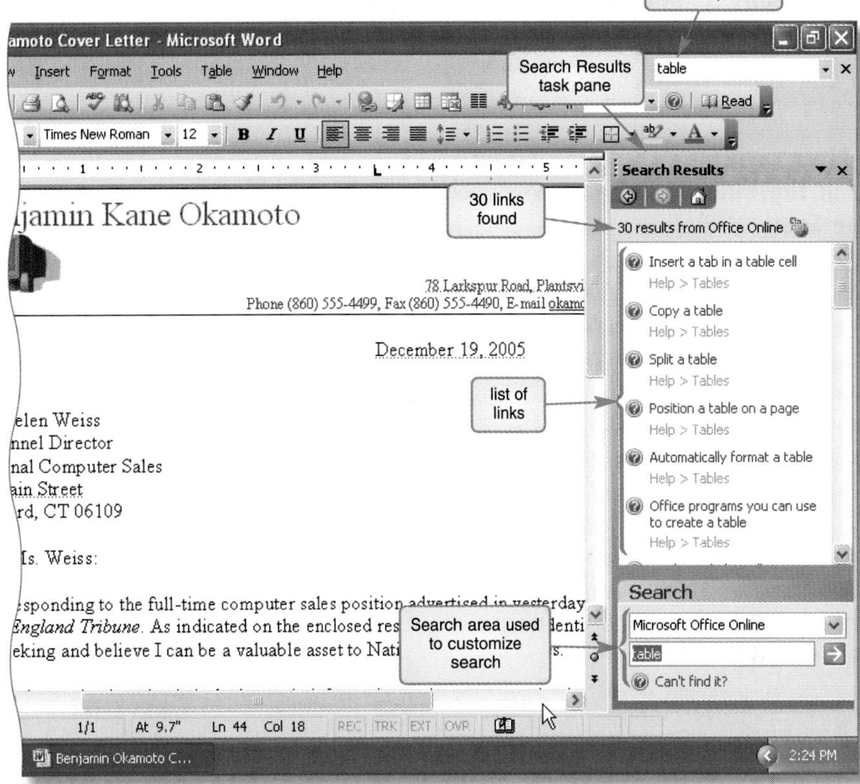

FIGURE A-2

2

Scroll down the list of links in the Search Results task pane and then click the About tables link.

- **When Word displays the Microsoft Office Help Word window, click its Auto Tile button in the upper-left corner of the window (Figure A-4 on the next page), if necessary, to tile the windows.**

Word displays the Microsoft Office Word Help window with the desired information about tables (Figure A-3). With the Microsoft Office Word Help window and Microsoft Word window tiled, you can read the information in one window and complete the task in the other window.

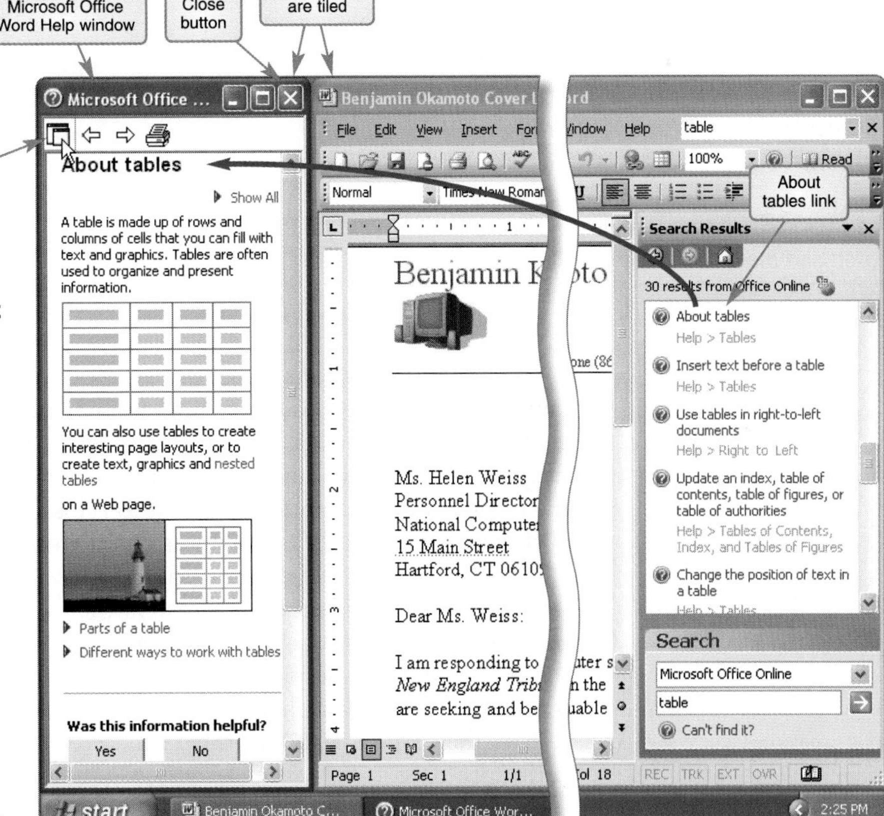

FIGURE A-3

3

- **Double-click the Microsoft Office Word Help window title bar.**
- **Click the Show All link in the upper-right corner of the window.**
- **After reviewing the information, click the Hide All link that replaced the Show All link.**

The Microsoft Office Word Help window is maximized so it fills the entire screen (Figure A-4). If you are connected to the Internet, you can give Microsoft your opinion as to whether the information was helpful by clicking the Yes or No button at the bottom of the page. The Show All link expands the coverage of information and the Hide all link condenses the information displayed on the topic in the Microsoft Office Word Help window.

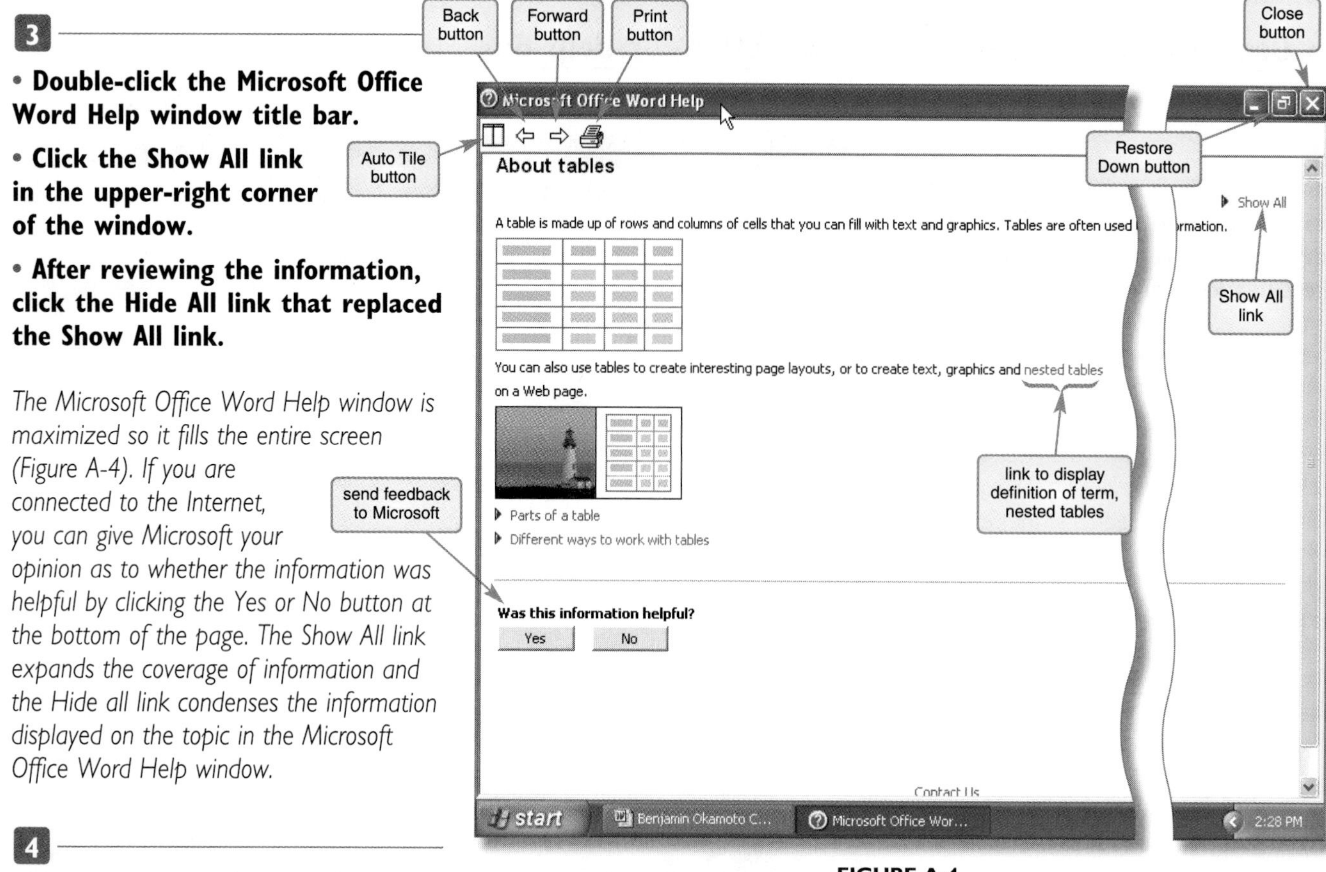

FIGURE A-4

4

- **Click the Restore Down button on the right side of the Microsoft Office Word Help window title bar to return to the tiled state shown in Figure A-3 on the previous page.**
- **Click the Close button on the Microsoft Office Word Help window title bar.**

The Microsoft Office Word Help window is closed and the Word document is active.

Use the four buttons in the upper-left corner of the Microsoft Office Word Help window (Figure A-4) to tile or untile, navigate through the Help system, or print the contents of the window. As you click links in the Search Results task pane, the Word Help system displays new pages of information. The Word Help System remembers the links you visited and allows you to redisplay the pages visited during a session by clicking the Back and Forward buttons (Figure A-4).

If none of the links presents the information you want, you can refine the search by entering another word or phrase in the Search text box in the Search Results task pane (Figure A-2 on the previous page). If you have access to the Web, then the scope is global for the initial search. **Global** means all of the categories listed in the Search box of the Search area in Figure A-2 are searched. For example, you can, restrict the scope to **Offline Help**, which results in a search of related links only on your hard disk.

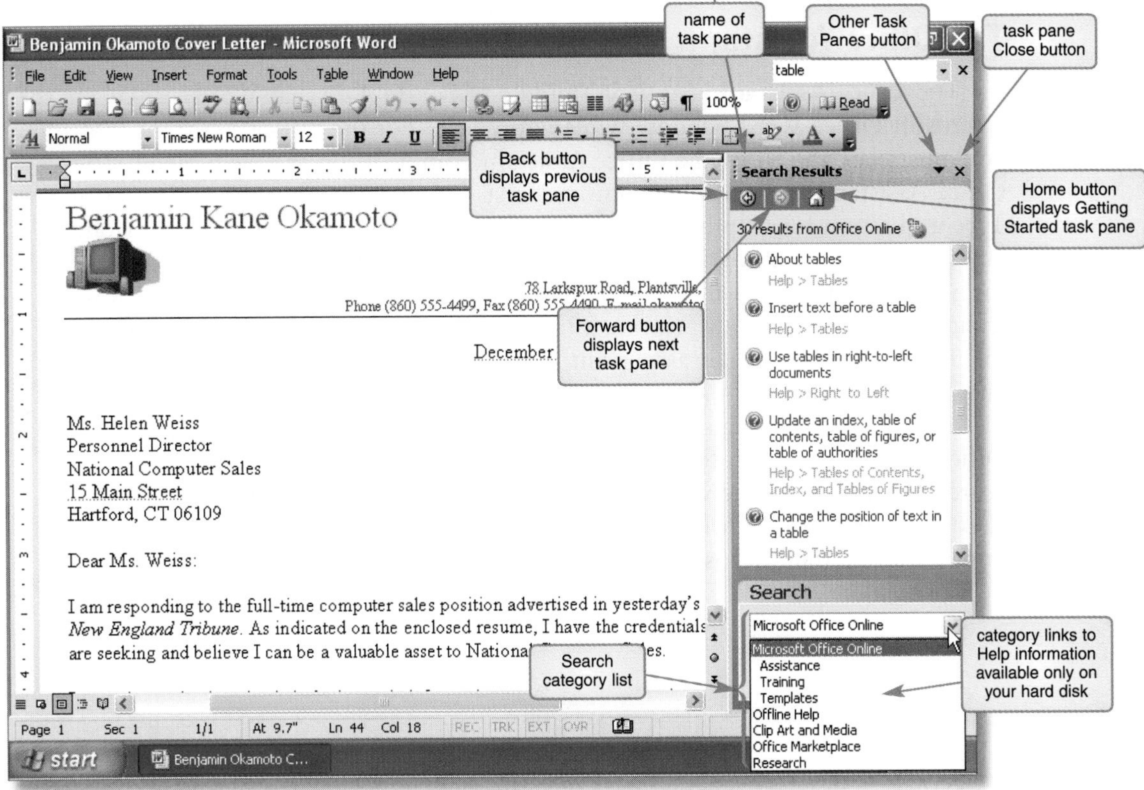

FIGURE A-5

Figure A-5 shows several additional features of the Search Results task pane. The Other Task Panes button and Close button on the Search Results task pane title bar allow you to display other task panes and close the Search Results task pane. The three buttons below the Search Results task pane title bar allow you to navigate between task panes (Back button and Forward button) and display the Getting Started task pane (Home button).

As you enter words and phrases in the Type a question for help box, the Word Help system adds them to the Type a question for help list. To display the list of previously typed words and phrases, click the Type a question for help box arrow (Figure A-6).

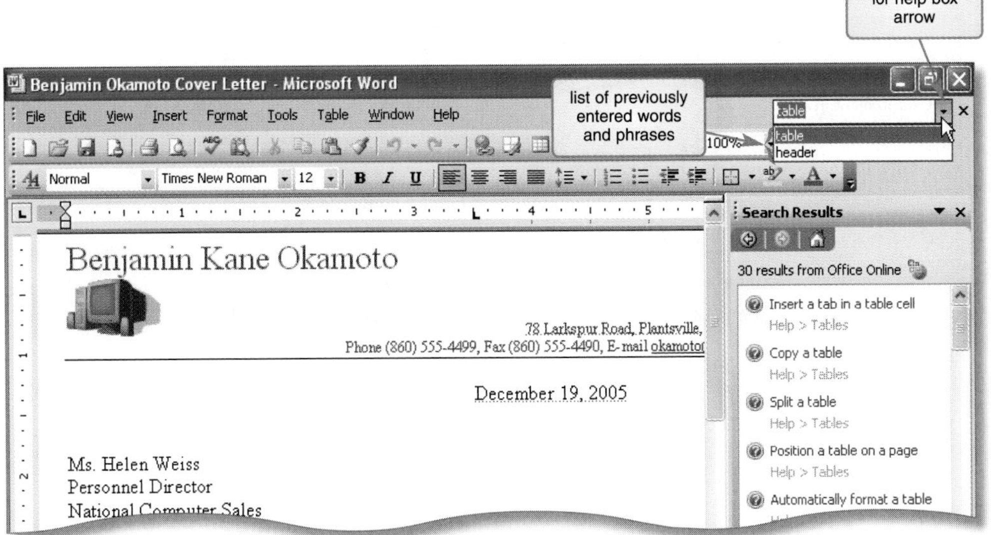

FIGURE A-6

The Office Assistant

The **Office Assistant** is an icon (middle of Figure A-7) that Word displays in the Microsoft Office Word window while you work. For the Office Assistant to display, you must click the Show the Office Assistant command on the Help menu. The Office Assistant has multiple functions. First, it will respond in the same way as the Type a question for help box with a list of topics that relate to the word or phrase you enter in the text box in the Office Assistant balloon. The entry can be in the form of a word or phrase as if you were talking to a person. For example, if you want to learn more about printing a file, in the balloon text box, you can type any of the following words or phrases: print, print a document, how do I print a file, or anything similar.

In the example in Figure A-7, the phrase, print a document, is entered into the Office Assistant balloon text box. The Office Assistant responds by displaying the Search Results task pane with a list of links from which you can choose. Once you click a link in the Search Results task pane, the Word Help system displays the information in the Microsoft Office Word Help window (Figure A-7).

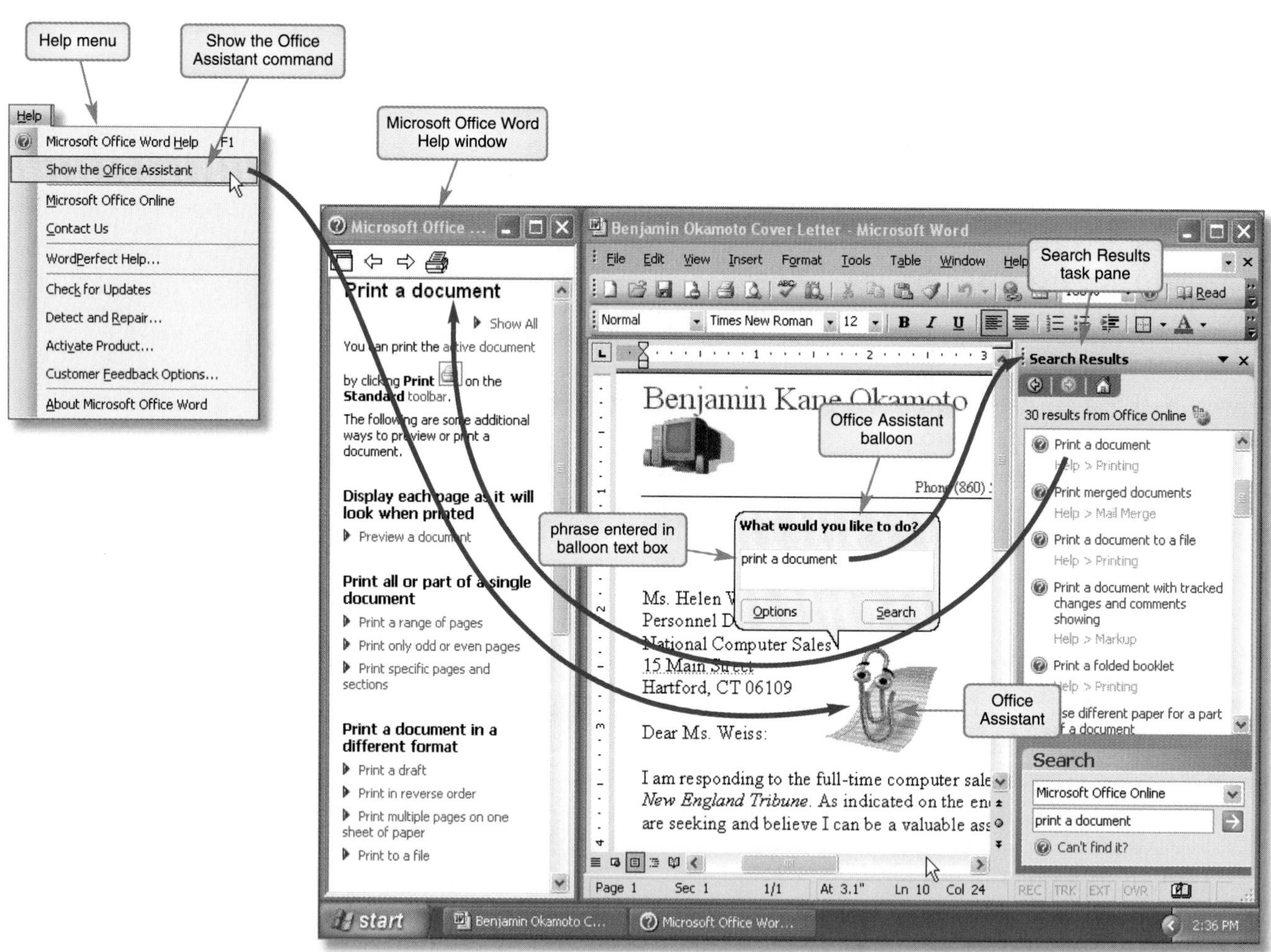

FIGURE A-7

In addition, the Office Assistant monitors your work and accumulates tips during a session on how you might increase your productivity and efficiency. The accumulation of tips must be enabled. You enable the accumulation of tips by right-clicking the Office Assistant, clicking Options on the shortcut menu, and then selecting the types of tips you want accumulated. You can view the tips at anytime. The accumulated tips appear when you activate the Office Assistant balloon. Also, if at anytime you see a light bulb above the Office Assistant, click it to display the most recent tip. If the Office Assistant is hidden, then the light bulb shows on the Microsoft Office Word Help button on the Standard toolbar.

You hide the Office Assistant by invoking the Hide the Office Assistant command on the Help menu or by right-clicking the Office Assistant and then clicking Hide on the shortcut menu. The Hide the Office Assistant command shows on the Help menu only when the Office Assistant is active in the Word window. If the Office Assistant begins showing up on your screen without you instructing it to show, then right-click the Office Assistant, click Options on the shortcut menu, click the Use the Office Assistant check box to remove the check mark, and then click the OK button.

If the Office Assistant is active in the Word window, then Word displays all program and system messages in the Office Assistant balloon.

You may or may not want the Office Assistant to display on the screen at all times. As indicated earlier, you can hide it and then show it later through the Help menu. For more information about the Office Assistant, type `office assistant` in the Type a question for help box and then click the links in the Search Results task pane.

Question Mark Button in Dialog Boxes and Help Icon in Task Panes

You use the Question Mark button with dialog boxes. It is located in the upper-right corner on the title bar of the dialog boxes, next to the Close button. For example, in Figure A-8 on the next page, the Print dialog box appears on the screen. If you click the Question Mark button in the upper-right corner of the dialog box, the Microsoft Office Word Help window is displayed and provides information about the options in the Print dialog box.

Some task panes include a Help icon. It can be located in various places within the task pane. For example, in the Clip Art task pane shown in Figure A-8, the Help icon appears at the bottom of the task pane and the Tips for finding clips link appears to the right of the Help icon. When you click the link, the Microsoft Office Word Help window is displayed and provides tips for finding clip art.

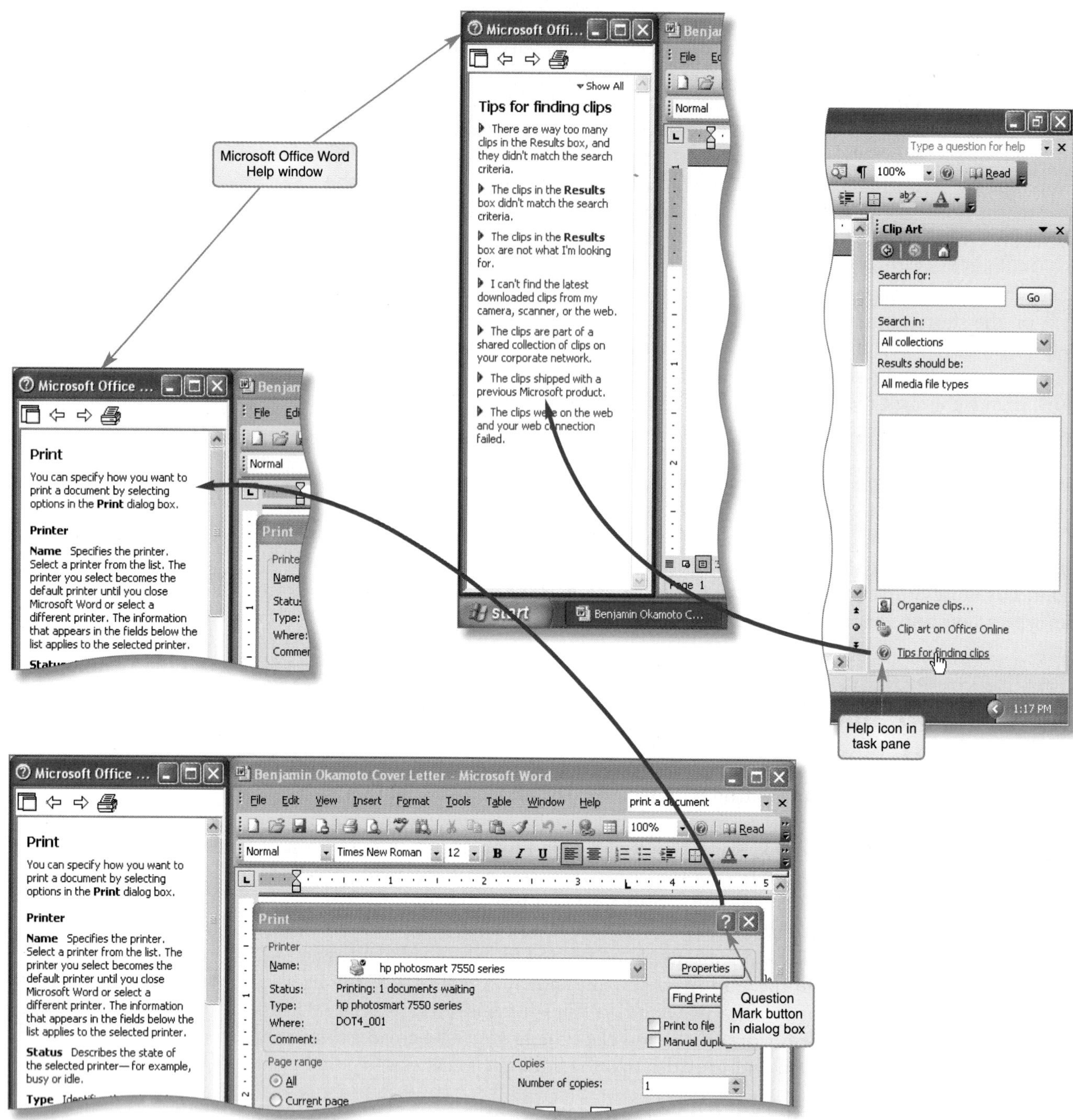

FIGURE A-8

Other Help Commands on the Help Menu

Thus far, this appendix has discussed the first two commands on the Help menu: (1) the Microsoft Office Word Help command (Figure A-1 on page APP 1) and (2) the Show the Office Assistant command (Figure A-7 on page APP 6). Several additional commands are available on the Help menu as shown in Figure A-9. Table A-1 summarizes these commands.

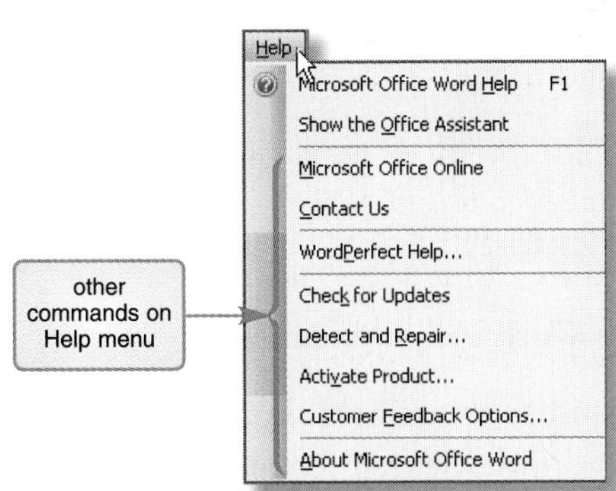

FIGURE A-9

Table A-1 Summary of Other Help Commands on the Help Menu

COMMAND ON HELP MENU	FUNCTION
Microsoft Office Online	Activates the browser, which displays the Microsoft Office Online Home page. The Microsoft Office Online Home page contains links that can improve Office productivity.
Contact Us	Activates the browser, which displays Microsoft contact information and a list of useful links.
WordPerfect Help	Displays the Help for WordPerfect Users dialog box, which includes information about carrying out commands in Word.
Check for Updates	Activates the browser, which displays a list of updates to Office 2003. These updates can be downloaded and installed to improve the efficiency of Office or to fix an error in one or more of the Office applications.
Detect and Repair	Detects and repairs errors in the Word program.
Activate Product	Activates Word if it has not already been activated.
Customer Feedback Options	Gives or denies Microsoft permission to collect anonymous information about the hardware.
About Microsoft Office Word	Displays the About Microsoft Word dialog box. The dialog box lists the owner of the software and the product identification. You need to know the product identification if you call Microsoft for assistance. The three buttons below the OK button are the System Info button, Tech Support button, and Disabled Items button. The System Info button displays system information, including hardware resources, components, software environment, and applications. The Tech Support button displays technical assistance information. The Disabled Items button displays a list of disabled items that prevents Word from functioning properly.

1 Using the Type a Question for Help Box

Instructions: Perform the following tasks using the Word Help system.

1. Use the Type a question for help box on the menu bar to get help on adding a bullet.
2. Click Add bullets or numbering in the list of links in the Search Results task pane. If necessary, tile the windows. Double-click the Microsoft Office Word Help window title bar to maximize it. Click the Show All link. Read and print the information. At the top of the printout, write down the number of links the Word Help system found.
3. Click the Restore Down button on the Microsoft Office Word Help title bar to restore the Microsoft Office Word Help window.
4. One at a time, click two additional links in the Search Results task pane and print the information. Hand in the printouts to your instructor. Use the Back and Forward buttons to return to the original page.
5. Use the Type a question for help box to search for information on adjusting line spacing. Click the Adjust line or paragraph spacing link in the Search Results task pane. Maximize the Microsoft Office Word Help window. Read and print the contents of the window. One at a time, click the links on the page and print the contents of the window. Close the Microsoft Office Word Help window.
6. For each of the following words and phrases, click one link in the Search Results task pane, click the Show All link, and then print the page: page zoom; date; print preview; office clipboard; word count; and themes.

2 Expanding on the Word Help System Basics

Instructions: Use the Word Help system to understand the topics better and answer the questions listed below. Answer the questions on your own paper, or hand in the printed Help information to your instructor.

1. Show the Office Assistant. Right-click the Office Assistant and then click Animate! on the shortcut menu. Repeat invoking the Animate! command to see various animations.
2. Right-click the Office Assistant, click Options on the shortcut menu, click the Reset my tips button, and then click the OK button. If necessary, repeatedly click the Office Assistant and then click off the Office Assistant until a light bulb appears above the Office Assistant. When you see the light bulb, it indicates that the Office Assistant has a tip to share with you.
3. Use the Office Assistant to find help on undoing. Click the Undo mistakes link and then print the contents of the Microsoft Office Word Help window. Close the window. Hand in the printouts to your instructor. Hide the Office Assistant.
4. Press the F1 key. Search for information on Help. Click the first two links in the Search Results task pane. Read and print the information for both links.
5. Display the Help menu. One at a time, click the Microsoft Office Online, Contact Us, and Check for Updates commands. Print the contents of each Internet Explorer window that displays and then close the window. Hand in the printouts to your instructor.
6. Click About Microsoft Office Word on the Help menu. Click the Tech Support button, print the contents of the Microsoft Office Word Help window, and then close the window. Click the System Info button. If necessary, click the plus sign to the left of Components in the System Summary list to display the Components category. Click CD-ROM and then print the information. Click Display and then print the information. Hand in the printouts to your instructor.

Appendix B

Speech and Handwriting Recognition and Speech Playback

Introduction

This appendix discusses the Office capability that allows users to create and modify worksheets using its alternative input technologies available through **text services.** Office provides a variety of text services, which enable you to speak commands and enter text in an application. The most common text service is the keyboard. Other text services include speech recognition and handwriting recognition.

The Language Bar

The **Language bar** allows you to use text services in the Office applications. You can utilize the Language bar in one of three states: (1) in a restored state as a floating toolbar in the Word window (Figure B-1a or Figure B-1b if Text Labels are enabled); (2) in a minimized state docked next to the notification area on the Windows taskbar (Figure B-1c); or (3) hidden (temporarily closed and out of the way). If the Language bar is hidden, you can activate it by right-clicking the Windows taskbar, pointing to Toolbars on the shortcut menu (Figure B-1d), and then clicking Language bar on the Toolbars submenu. If you want to close the Language bar, right-click the Language bar and then click Close the Language bar on the shortcut menu (Figure B-1e).

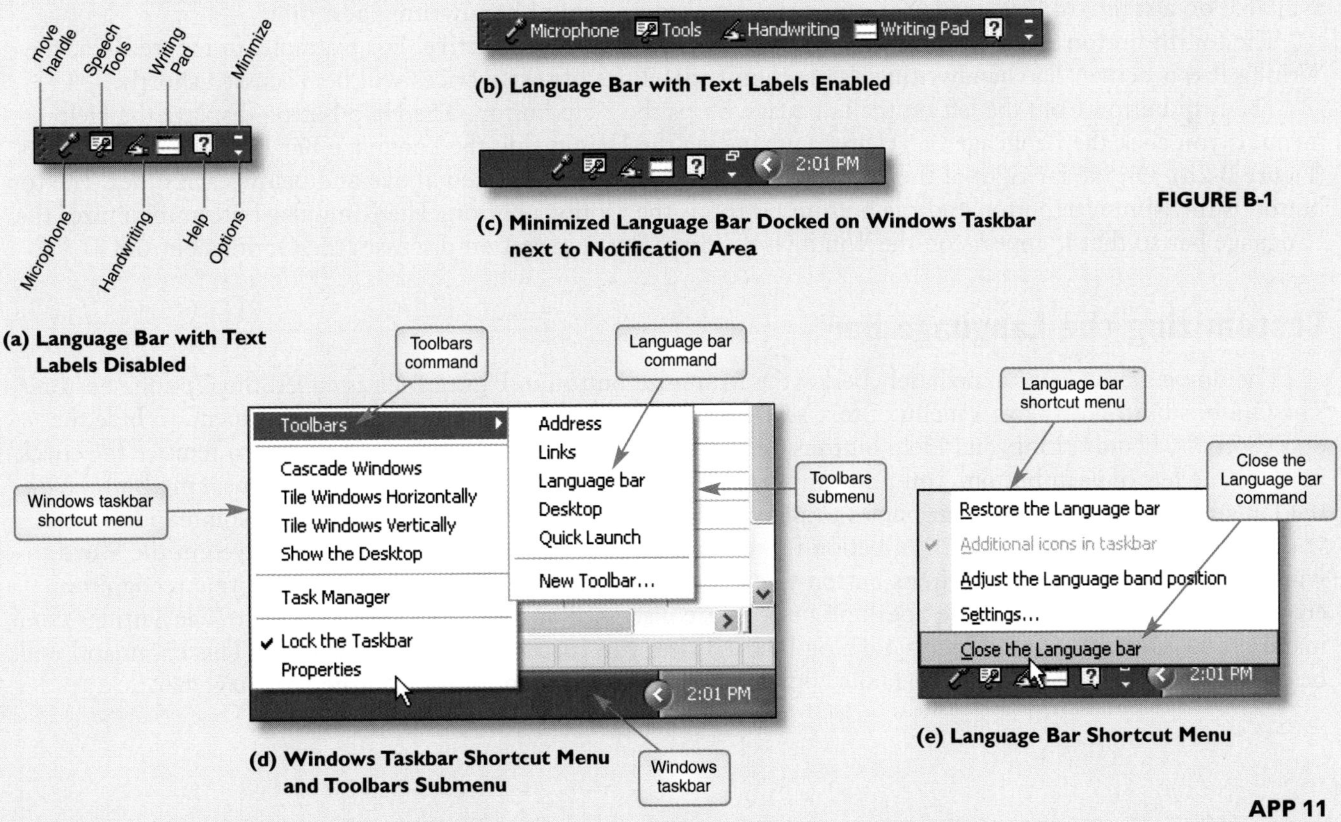

move handle
Speech Tools
Writing Pad
Minimize
Microphone
Handwriting
Help
Options

(a) Language Bar with Text Labels Disabled

Microphone Tools Handwriting Writing Pad

(b) Language Bar with Text Labels Enabled

2:01 PM

(c) Minimized Language Bar Docked on Windows Taskbar next to Notification Area

FIGURE B-1

Toolbars command
Language bar command
Windows taskbar shortcut menu
Toolbars submenu
Toolbars
Cascade Windows
Tile Windows Horizontally
Tile Windows Vertically
Show the Desktop
Task Manager
Lock the Taskbar
Properties
Address
Links
Language bar
Desktop
Quick Launch
New Toolbar...
2:01 PM
Windows taskbar

(d) Windows Taskbar Shortcut Menu and Toolbars Submenu

Language bar shortcut menu
Close the Language bar command
Restore the Language bar
Additional icons in taskbar
Adjust the Language band position
Settings...
Close the Language bar
2:01 PM

(e) Language Bar Shortcut Menu

When Windows was installed on your computer, the installer specified a default language. For example, most users in the United States select English (United States) as the default language. You can add more than 90 additional languages and varying dialects such as Basque, English (Zimbabwe), French (France), French (Canada), German (Germany), German (Austria), and Swahili. With multiple languages available, you can switch from one language to another while working in Word. If you change the language or dialect, then text services may change the functions of the keys on the keyboard, adjust speech recognition, and alter handwriting recognition. If a second language is activated, then a Language icon appears immediately to the right of the move handle on the Language bar and the language name is displayed on the Word status bar. This appendix assumes that English (United States) is the only language installed. Thus, the Language icon does not appear in the examples in Figure B-1 on the previous page.

Buttons on the Language Bar

The Language bar shown in Figure B-2a contains seven buttons. The number of buttons on your Language bar may be different. These buttons are used to select the language, customize the Language bar, control the microphone, control handwriting, and obtain help.

The first button on the left is the Microphone button, which enables and disables the microphone. When the microphone is enabled, text services adds two buttons and a balloon to the Language bar (Figure B-2b). These additional buttons and the balloon will be discussed shortly.

The second button from the left is the Speech Tools button. The Speech Tools button displays a menu of commands (Figure B-2c) that allow you to scan the current document looking for words to add to the speech recognition dictionary; hide or show the balloon on the Language bar; train the Speech Recognition service so that it can interpret your voice better; add and delete specific words to and from its dictionary, such as names and other words not understood easily; and change the user profile so more than one person can use the microphone on the same computer.

The third button from the left on the Language bar is the Handwriting button. The Handwriting button displays the Handwriting menu (Figure B-2d), which lets you choose the Writing Pad (Figure B-2e), Write Anywhere (Figure B-2f), or the on-screen keyboard (Figure B-2g). The On-Screen Symbol Keyboard command on the Handwriting menu displays an on-screen keyboard that allows you to enter special symbols that are not available on a standard keyboard. You can choose only one form of handwriting at a time.

The fourth button indicates which one of the handwriting forms is active. For example, in Figure B-2a, the Writing Pad is active. The handwriting recognition capabilities of text services will be discussed shortly.

The fifth button from the left on the Language bar is the Help button. The Help button displays the Help menu. If you click the Language Bar Help command on the Help menu, the Language Bar Help window appears (Figure B-2h). On the far right of the Language bar are two buttons stacked above and below each other. The top button is the Minimize button and the bottom button is the Options button. The Minimize button minimizes the Language bar so that it appears on the Windows taskbar. The next section discusses the Options button.

Customizing the Language Bar

The down arrow icon immediately below the Minimize button in Figure B-2a is called the Options button. The Options button displays a menu of text services options (Figure B-2i). You can use this menu to hide the Speech Tools, Handwriting, and Help buttons on the Language bar by clicking their names to remove the check mark to the left of each button. You also can show the Correction, Speak Text, and Pause Speaking buttons on the Language bar by clicking their names to place a check mark to the left of the respective command. When you select text and then click the Correction button, a list of correction alternatives is displayed in the Word window. You can use the Corrections button to correct both speech recognition and handwriting recognition errors. The Speak Text and Pause Speaking buttons are discussed at the end of this Appendix. The Settings command on the Options menu displays a dialog box that lets you customize the Language bar. This command will be discussed shortly. The Restore Defaults command redisplays hidden buttons on the Language bar.

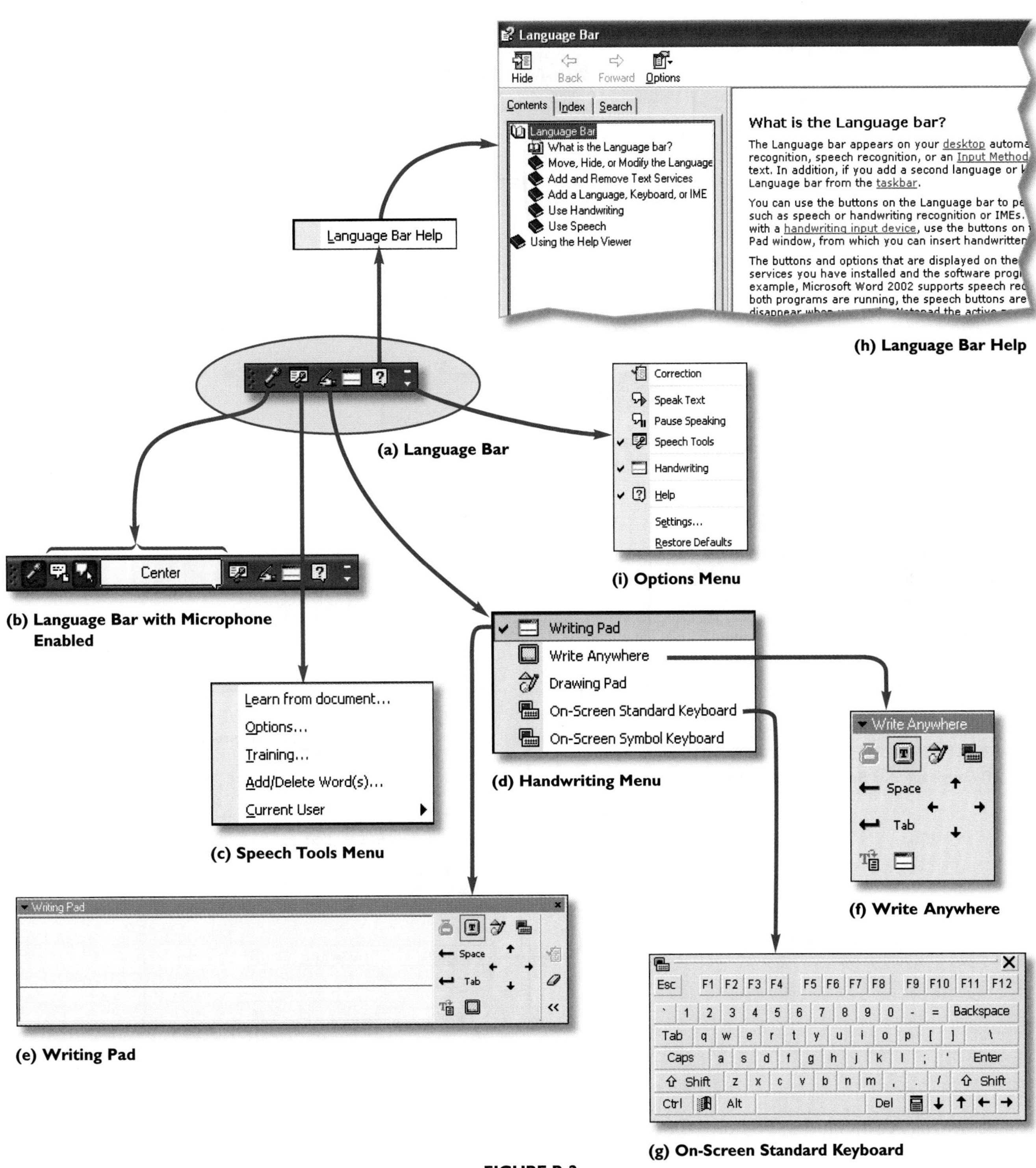

(h) Language Bar Help

(a) Language Bar

(i) Options Menu

(b) Language Bar with Microphone Enabled

(d) Handwriting Menu

(c) Speech Tools Menu

(f) Write Anywhere

(e) Writing Pad

(g) On-Screen Standard Keyboard

FIGURE B-2

If you right-click the Language bar, a shortcut menu appears (Figure B-3a on the next page). This shortcut menu lets you further customize the Language bar. The Minimize command on the shortcut menu docks the Language bar on the Windows taskbar. The Transparency command in Figure B-3a toggles the Language bar between being solid and transparent. You can see through a transparent Language bar (Figure B-3b). The Text Labels command toggles on text labels on the Language bar (Figure B-3c) and off (Figure B-3b). The Vertical command displays the Language bar vertically on the screen (Figure B-3d).

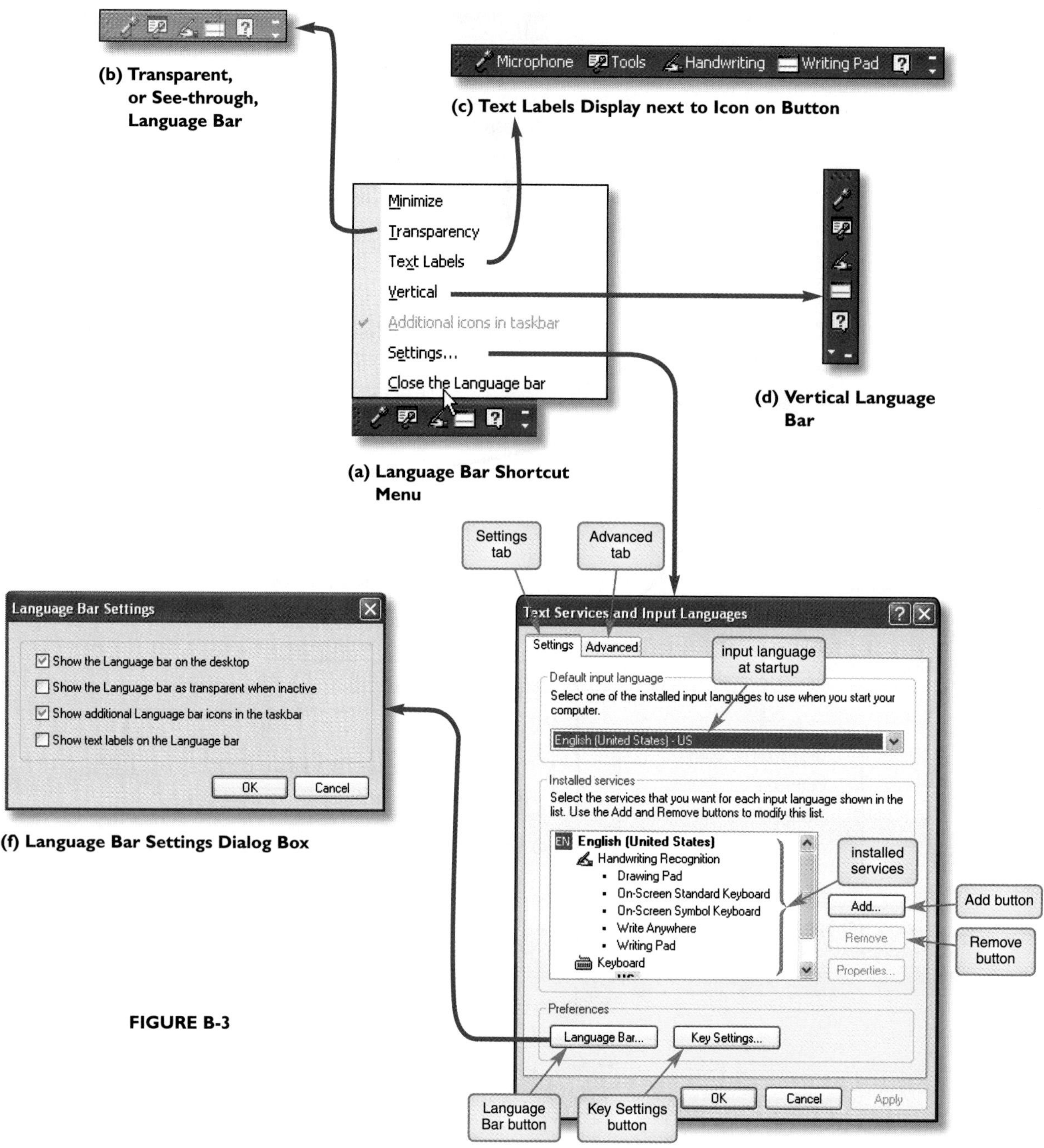

FIGURE B-3

The Settings command in Figure B-3a displays the Text Services and Input Languages dialog box (Figure B-3e). The Text Services and Input Languages dialog box allows you to add additonal languages, add and remove text services, modify keys on the keyboard, modify the Language bar, and extend support of advanced text services to all programs, including Notepad and other programs that normally do not support text services (through the Advanced tab). If you want to remove any one of the services in the Installed services list, select the service, and then click the Remove button. If you want to add a service, click the Add button. The Key Settings button allows you to modify the keyboard. If you click the Language Bar button in the Text Services and Input Languages dialog box, the Language Bar Settings dialog box appears (Figure B-3f). This dialog box contains Language bar options, some of which are the same as the commands on the Language bar shortcut menu shown in Figure B-3a.

The Close the Language bar command on the shortcut menu shown in Figure B-3a closes or hides the Language bar. If you close the Language bar and want to redisplay it, see Figure B-1d on page APP 11.

Speech Recognition

The **Speech Recognition service** available with Office enables your computer to recognize human speech through a microphone. The microphone has two modes: dictation and voice command (Figure B-4). You switch between the two modes by clicking the Dictation button and the Voice Command button on the Language bar. These buttons appear only when you turn on Speech Recognition by clicking the Microphone button on the Language bar (Figure B-5a on the next page). If you are using the Microphone button for the very first time in Word, it will require that you check your microphone settings and step through voice training before activating the Speech Recognition service.

The Dictation button places the microphone in Dictation mode. In **Dictation mode**, whatever you speak is entered as text at the location of the insertion point. The Voice Command button places the microphone in Voice Command mode. In **Voice Command mode**, whatever you speak is interpreted as a command. If you want to turn off the microphone, click the Microphone button on the Language bar or in Voice Command mode say, "Mic off" (pronounced mike off). It is important to remember that minimizing the Language bar does not turn off the microphone.

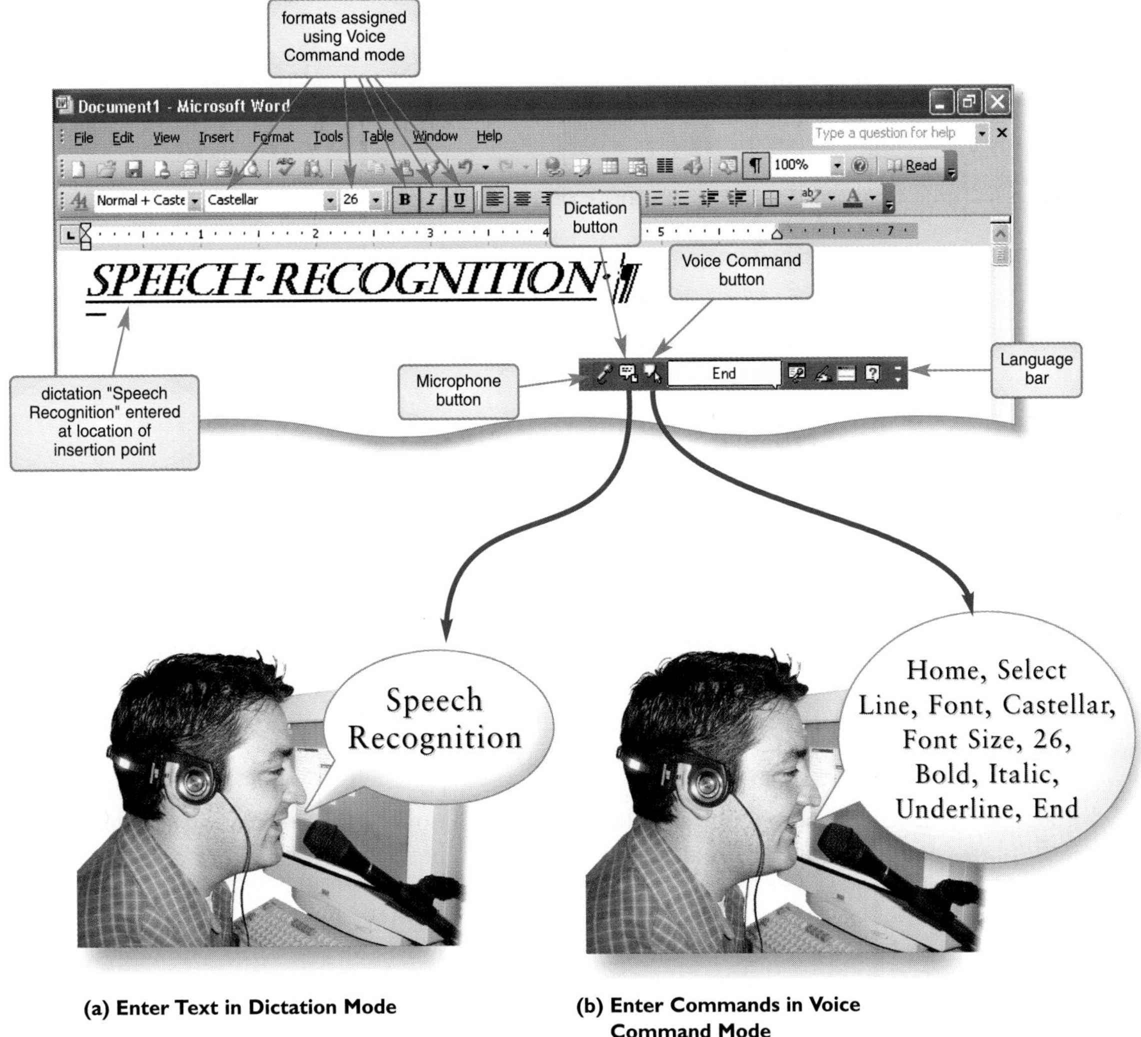

(a) Enter Text in Dictation Mode

(b) Enter Commands in Voice Command Mode

FIGURE B-4

The Language bar speech message balloon shown in Figure B-5b displays messages that may offer help or hints. In Voice Command mode, the name of the last recognized command you said appears. If you use the mouse or keyboard instead of the microphone, a message will appear in the Language bar speech message balloon indicating the word you could say. In Dictation mode, the message, Dictating, usually appears. The Speech Recognition service, however, will display messages to inform you that you are talking too soft, too loud, too fast, or to ask you to repeat what you said by displaying, What was that?

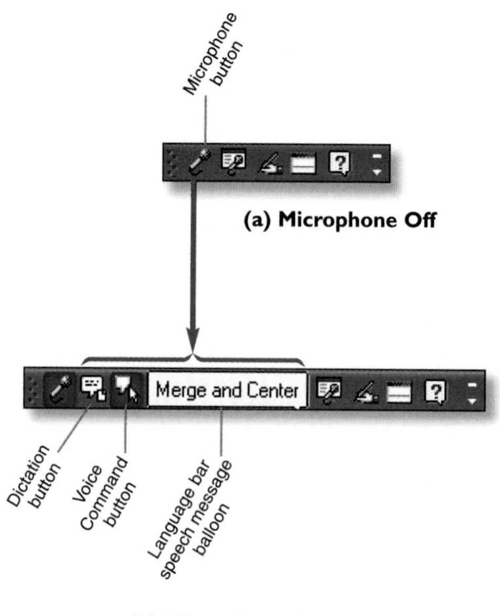

FIGURE B-5

Getting Started with Speech Recognition

For the microphone to function properly, you should follow these steps:

1. Make sure your computer meets the minimum requirements.
2. Start Word. Activate Speech Recognition by clicking Tools on the menu bar and then clicking Speech.
3. Set up and position your microphone, preferably a close-talk headset with gain adjustment support.
4. Train Speech Recognition.

The following sections describe these steps in more detail.

SPEECH RECOGNITION SYSTEM REQUIREMENTS For Speech Recognition to work on your computer, it needs the following:

1. Microsoft Windows 98 or later or Microsoft Windows NT 4.0 or later
2. At least 128 MB RAM
3. 400 MHz or faster processor
4. Microphone and sound card

SETUP AND POSITION YOUR MICROPHONE Set up your microphone as follows:

1. Connect your microphone to the sound card in the back of the computer.
2. Position the microphone approximately one inch out from and to the side of your mouth. Position it so you are not breathing into it.
3. On the Language bar, click the Speech Tools button and then click Options on the Speech Tools menu (Figure B-6a).
4. When text services displays the Speech input settings dialog box (Figure B-6b), click the Advanced Speech button. When text services displays the Speech Properties dialog box (Figure B-6c), click the Speech Recognition tab.
5. Click the Configure Microphone button. Follow the Microphone Wizard directions as shown in Figures B-6d, B-6e, and B-6f. The Next button will remain dimmed in Figure B-6e until the volume meter consistently stays in the green area.
6. If someone else installed Speech Recognition, click the New button in the Speech Properties dialog box and enter your name. Click the Train Profile button and step through the Voice Training dialog boxes. The Voice Training dialog boxes will require that you enter your gender and age group. It then will step you through voice training.

You can adjust the microphone further by clicking the Settings button in the Speech Properties dialog box (Figure B-6c). The Settings button displays the Recognition Profile Settings dialog box that allows you to adjust the pronunciation sensitivity and accuracy versus recognition response time.

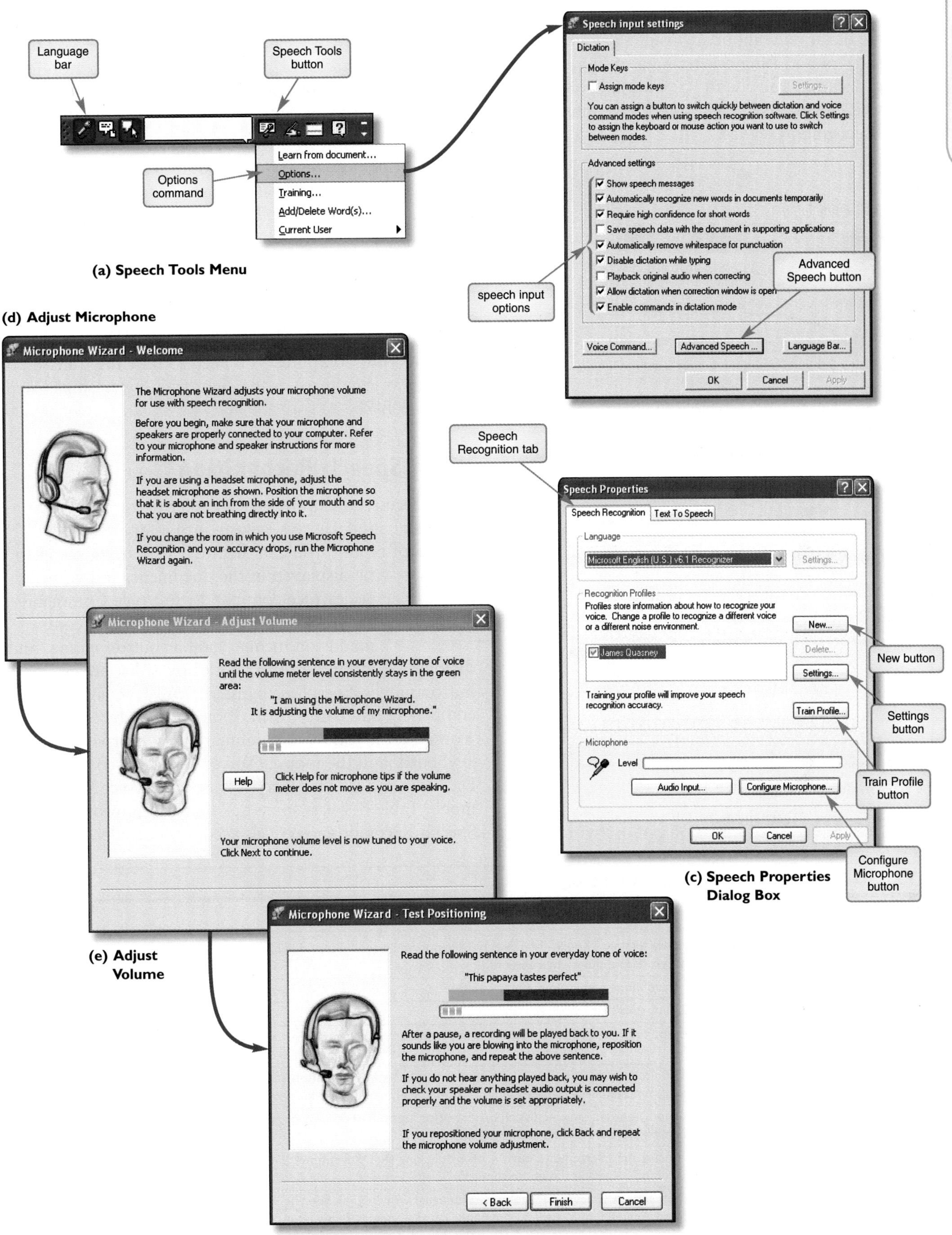
Language bar
Speech Tools button
Learn from document...
Options...
Training...
Add/Delete Word(s)...
Current User
Options command
(a) Speech Tools Menu
Speech input settings
Dictation
Mode Keys
Assign mode keys
Settings...
You can assign a button to switch quickly between dictation and voice command modes when using speech recognition software. Click Settings to assign the keyboard or mouse action you want to use to switch between modes.
Advanced settings
Show speech messages
Automatically recognize new words in documents temporarily
Require high confidence for short words
Save speech data with the document in supporting applications
Automatically remove whitespace for punctuation
Disable dictation while typing
Playback original audio when correcting
Allow dictation when correction window is open
Enable commands in dictation mode
speech input options
Advanced Speech button
Voice Command...
Advanced Speech...
Language Bar...
OK
Cancel
Apply
(d) Adjust Microphone
Microphone Wizard - Welcome
The Microphone Wizard adjusts your microphone volume for use with speech recognition.
Before you begin, make sure that your microphone and speakers are properly connected to your computer. Refer to your microphone and speaker instructions for more information.
If you are using a headset microphone, adjust the headset microphone as shown. Position the microphone so that it is about an inch from the side of your mouth and so that you are not breathing directly into it.
If you change the room in which you use Microsoft Speech Recognition and your accuracy drops, run the Microphone Wizard again.
Speech Recognition tab
Speech Properties
Speech Recognition
Text To Speech
Language
Microsoft English (U.S.) v6.1 Recognizer
Settings...
Recognition Profiles
Profiles store information about how to recognize your voice. Change a profile to recognize a different voice or a different noise environment.
New...
James Quasney
Delete...
Settings...
Training your profile will improve your speech recognition accuracy.
Train Profile...
Microphone
Level
Audio Input...
Configure Microphone...
OK
Cancel
Apply
New button
Settings button
Train Profile button
Configure Microphone button
(c) Speech Properties Dialog Box
Microphone Wizard - Adjust Volume
Read the following sentence in your everyday tone of voice until the volume meter level consistently stays in the green area:
"I am using the Microphone Wizard. It is adjusting the volume of my microphone."
Help
Click Help for microphone tips if the volume meter does not move as you are speaking.
Your microphone volume level is now tuned to your voice. Click Next to continue.
(e) Adjust Volume
Microphone Wizard - Test Positioning
Read the following sentence in your everyday tone of voice:
"This papaya tastes perfect"
After a pause, a recording will be played back to you. If it sounds like you are blowing into the microphone, reposition the microphone, and repeat the above sentence.
If you do not hear anything played back, you may wish to check your speaker or headset audio output is connected properly and the volume is set appropriately.
If you repositioned your microphone, click Back and repeat the microphone volume adjustment.
< Back
Finish
Cancel
(f) Test Microphone

FIGURE B-6

TRAIN THE SPEECH RECOGNITION SERVICE The Speech Recognition service will understand most commands and some dictation without any training at all. It will recognize much more of what you speak, however, if you take the time to train it. After one training session, it will recognize 85 to 90 percent of your words. As you do more training, accuracy will rise to 95 percent. If you feel that too many mistakes are being made, then continue to train the service. The more training you do, the more accurately it will work for you. Follow these steps to train the Speech Recognition service:

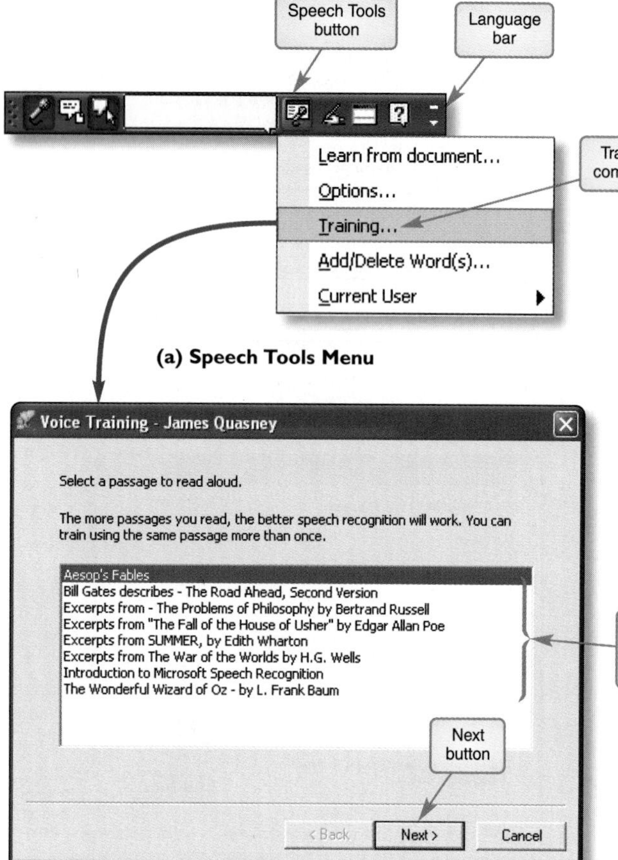

(a) Speech Tools Menu

(b) Voice Training Dialog Box

FIGURE B-7

1. Click the Speech Tools button on the Language bar and then click Training (Figure B-7a).
2. When the Voice Training dialog box appears (Figure B-7b), click one of the sessions and then click the Next button.
3. Complete the training session, which should take less than 15 minutes.

If you are serious about using a microphone to speak to your computer, you need to take the time to go through at least three of the eight training sessions listed in Figure B-7b.

Using Speech Recognition

Speech recognition lets you enter text into a document similarly to speaking into a tape recorder. Instead of typing, you can dictate text that you want to be displayed in the document, and you can issue voice commands. In Voice Command mode, you can speak menu names, commands on menus, toolbar button names, and dialog box option buttons, check boxes, list boxes, and button names. Speech recognition, however, is not a completely hands-free form of input. Speech recognition works best if you use a combination of your voice, the keyboard, and the mouse. You soon will discover that Dictation mode is far less accurate than Voice Command mode. Table B-1 lists some tips that will improve the Speech Recognition service's accuracy considerably.

Table B-1 Tips to Improve Speech Recognition

NUMBER	TIP
1	The microphone hears everything. Though the Speech Recognition service filters out background noise, it is recommended that you work in a quiet environment.
2	Try not to move the microphone around once it is adjusted.
3	Speak in a steady tone and speak clearly.
4	In Dictation mode, do not pause between words. A phrase is easier to interpret than a word. Sounding out syllables in a word will make it more difficult for the Speech Recognition service to interpret what you are saying.
5	If you speak too loudly or too softly, it makes it difficult for the Speech Recognition service to interpret what you said. Check the Language bar speech message balloon for an indication that you may be speaking too loudly or too softly.
6	If you experience problems after training, adjust the recognition options that control accuracy and rejection by clicking the Settings button shown in Figure B-6c on the previous page.
7	When you are finished using the microphone, turn it off by clicking the Microphone button on the Language bar or in Voice Command mode, say "Mic off." Leaving the microphone on is the same as leaning on the keyboard.
8	If the Speech Recognition service is having difficulty with unusual words, then add the words to its dictionary by using the Learn from document and Add/Delete Word(s) commands on the Speech Tools menu (Figure B-8a). The last names of individuals and the names of companies are good examples of the types of words you should add to the dictionary.
9	Training will improve accuracy; practice will improve confidence.

The last command on the Speech Tools menu is the Current User command (Figure B-8a). The Current User command is useful for multiple users who share a computer. It allows them to configure their own individual profiles, and then switch between users as they use the computer.

For additional information about the Speech Recognition service, enter `speech recognition` in the Type a question for help box on the menu bar.

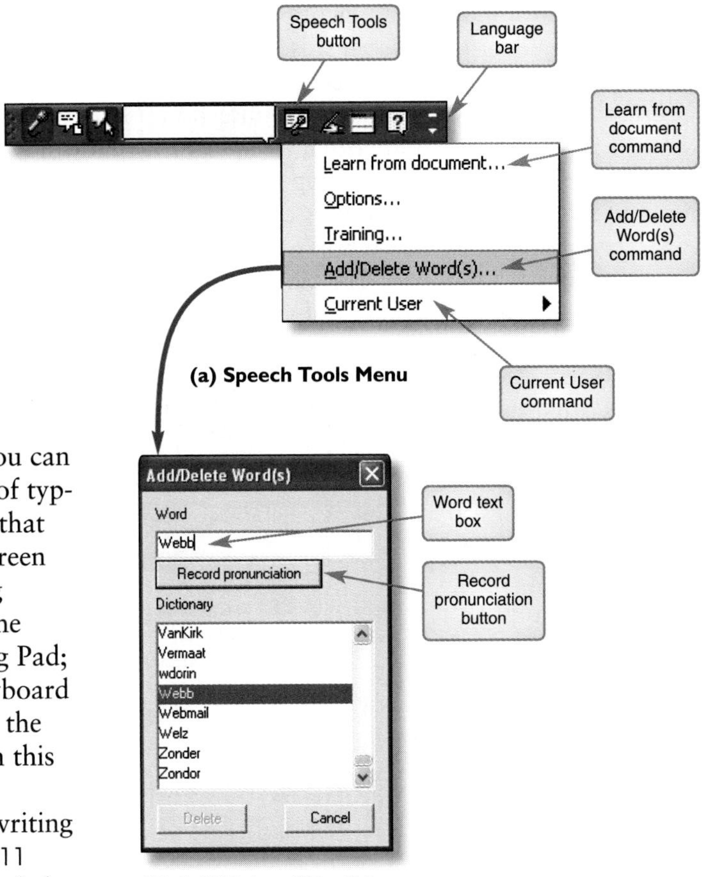

(a) Speech Tools Menu

(b) Add/Delete Word(s) Dialog Box

FIGURE B-8

Handwriting Recognition

Using the Office **Handwriting Recognition service**, you can enter text and numbers into Word by writing instead of typing. You can write using a special handwriting device that connects to your computer or you can write on the screen using your mouse. Four basic methods of handwriting are available by clicking the Handwriting button on the Language bar: Writing Pad; Write Anywhere; Drawing Pad; and On-Screen Keyboard. Although the on-screen keyboard does not involve handwriting recognition, it is part of the Handwriting menu and, therefore, will be discussed in this section.

If your Language bar does not include the Handwriting button, then for installation instructions, enter `install handwriting recognition` in the Type a question for help box on the menu bar.

Writing Pad

To display the Writing Pad, click the Handwriting button on the Language bar and then click Writing Pad (Figure B-9). The **Writing Pad** resembles a notepad with one or more lines on which you can use freehand to print or write in cursive. With the Text button enabled, you can form letters on the line by moving the mouse while holding down the mouse button. To the right of the notepad is a rectangular toolbar. Use the buttons on this toolbar to adjust the Writing Pad, select cells, and activate other handwriting applications.

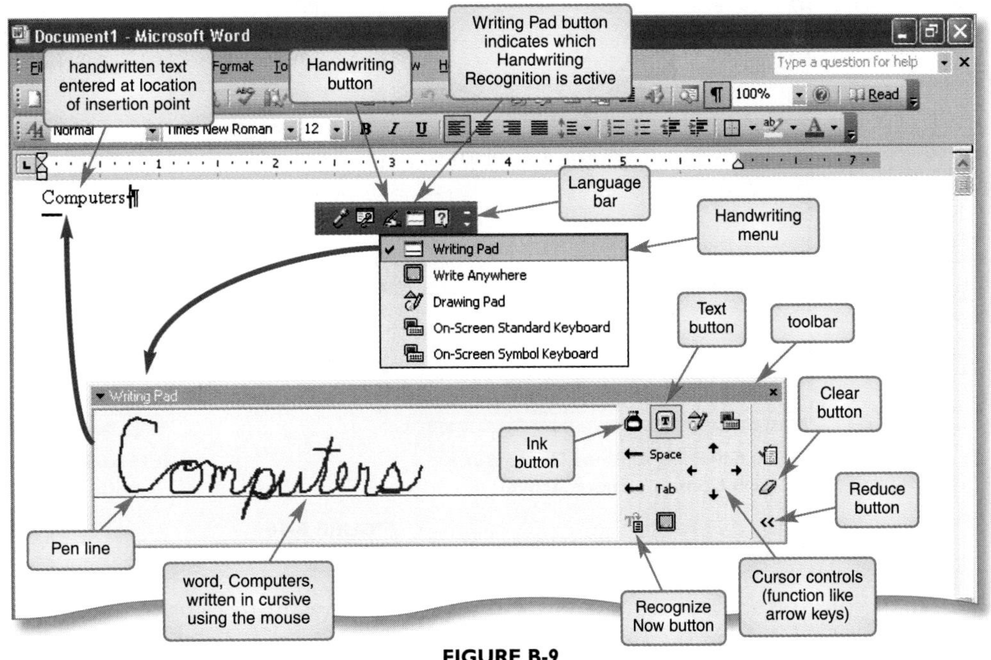

FIGURE B-9

Consider the example in Figure B-9 on the previous page. With the insertion point at the top of the document, the word, Computers, is written in cursive on the **Pen line** in the Writing Pad. As soon as the word is complete, the Handwriting Recognition service automatically converts the handwriting to typed characters and inserts the text at the location of the insertion point. With the Ink button enabled, instead of the Text button, the text is inserted in handwritten form in the document.

You can customize the Writing Pad by clicking the Options button on the left side of the Writing Pad title bar and then clicking the Options command (Figure B-10a). Invoking the Options command causes the Handwriting Options dialog box to be displayed. The Handwriting Options dialog box contains two sheets: Common and Writing Pad. The Common sheet lets you change the pen color and pen width, adjust recognition, and customize the toolbar area of the Writing Pad. The Writing Pad sheet allows you to change the background color and the number of lines that are displayed in the Writing Pad. Both sheets contain a Restore Default button to restore the settings to what they were when the software was installed initially.

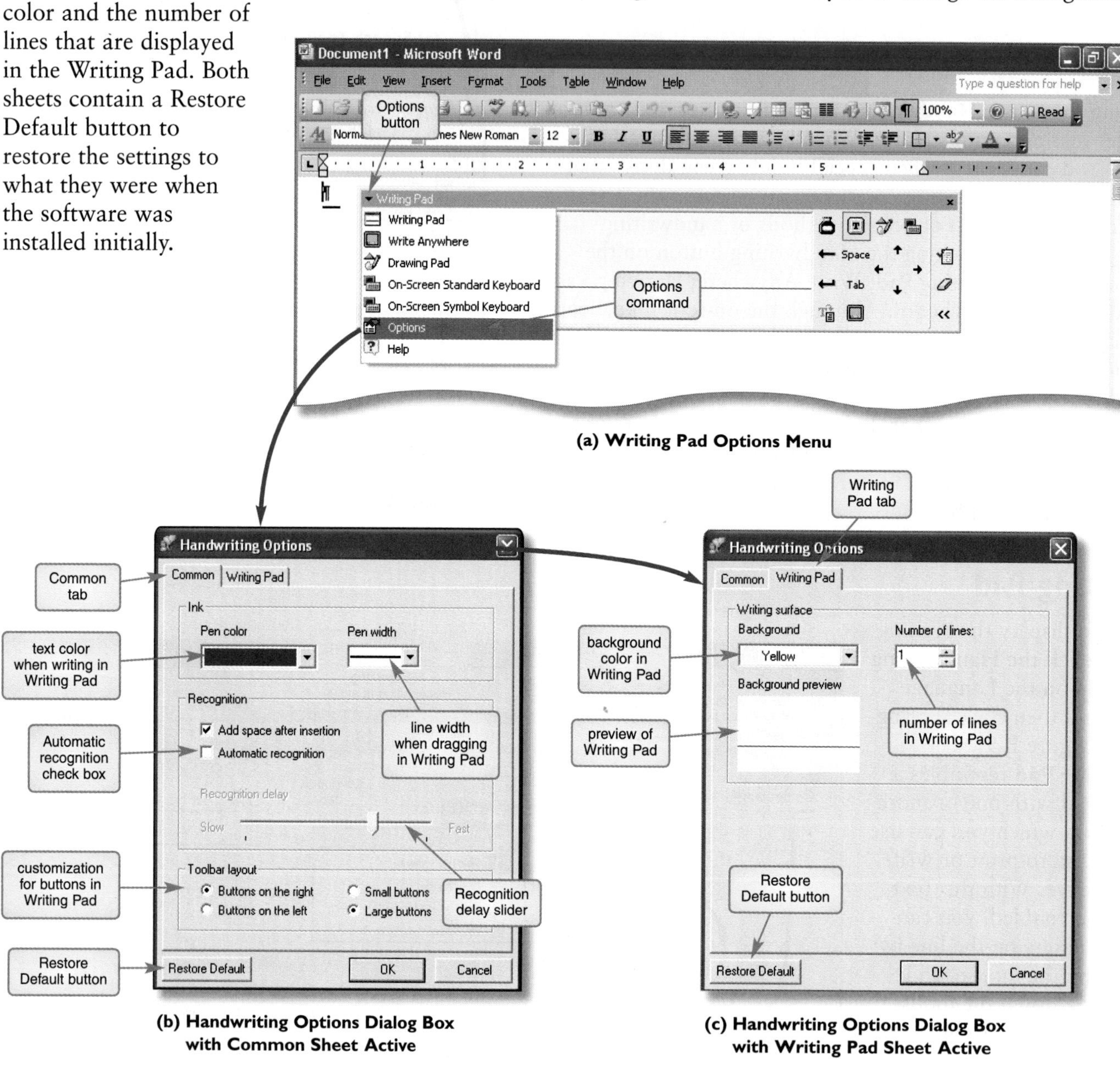

(a) Writing Pad Options Menu

(b) Handwriting Options Dialog Box with Common Sheet Active

(c) Handwriting Options Dialog Box with Writing Pad Sheet Active

FIGURE B-10

When you first start using the Writing Pad, you may want to remove the check mark from the Automatic recognition check box in the Common sheet in the Handwriting Options dialog box (Figure B-10b). With the check mark removed, the Handwriting Recognition service will not interpret what you write in the Writing Pad until you click the Recognize Now button on the toolbar (Figure B-9 on the previous page). This allows you to pause and adjust your writing.

The best way to learn how to use the Writing Pad is to practice with it. Also, for more information, enter `handwriting recognition` in the Type a question for help box on the menu bar.

Write Anywhere

Rather than use Writing Pad, you can write anywhere on the screen by invoking the Write Anywhere command on the Handwriting menu (Figure B-11) that appears when you click the Handwriting button on the Language bar. In this case, the entire window is your writing pad.

In Figure B-11, the word, Report, is written in cursive using the mouse button. Shortly after the word is written, the Handwriting Recognition service interprets it, assigns it to the location of the insertion point, and erases what was written.

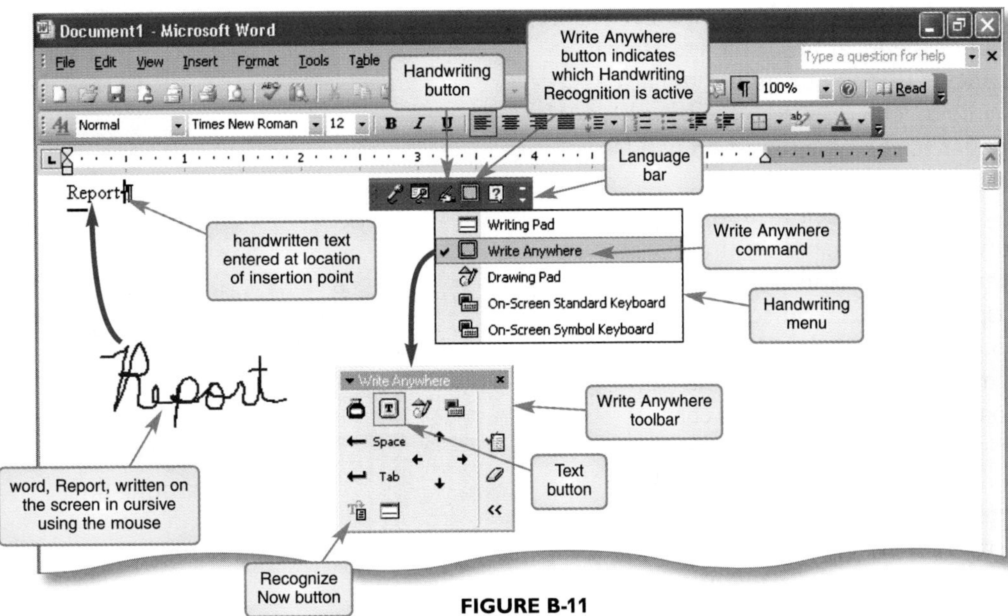

FIGURE B-11

It is recommended that when you first start using the Write Anywhere service that you remove the check mark from the Automatic recognition check box in the Common sheet in the Handwriting Options dialog box (Figure B-10b). With the check mark removed, the Handwriting Recognition service will not interpret what you write on the screen until you click the Recognize Now button on the toolbar (Figure B-11).

Write Anywhere is more difficult to use than the Writing Pad, because when you click the mouse button, Word may interpret the action as moving the insertion point rather than starting to write. For this reason, it is recommended that you use the Writing Pad.

Drawing Pad

With the Drawing Pad, you can insert a freehand drawing or sketch in a Word document. To display the Drawing Pad, click the Handwriting button on the Language bar and then click Drawing Pad (Figure B-12). Create a drawing by dragging the mouse in the Drawing Pad. In Figure B-12, the mouse was used to draw a tic-tac-toe game. When you click the Insert Drawing button on the Drawing Pad toolbar, Word inserts the drawing in the document at the location of the insertion point. Other buttons on the toolbar allow you to erase a drawing, erase your last drawing stroke, copy the drawing to the Office Clipboard, or activate the Writing Pad.

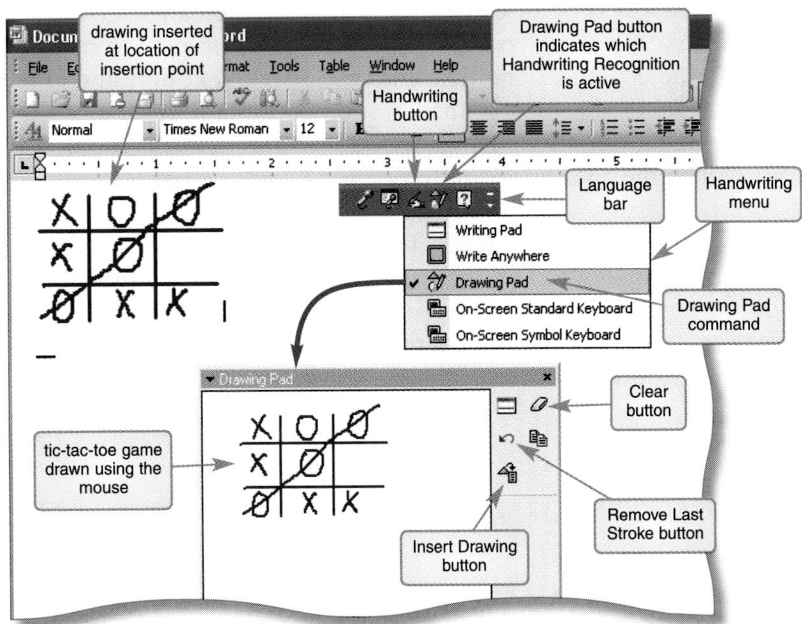

FIGURE B-12

The best way to learn how to use the Drawing Pad is to practice with it. Also, for more information, enter `drawing pad` in the Type a question for help box on the menu bar.

On-Screen Keyboard

The On-Screen Standard Keyboard command on the Handwriting menu (Figure B-13) displays an on-screen keyboard. The **on-screen keyboard** lets you enter data at the location of the insertion point by using your mouse to click the keys. The on-screen keyboard is similar to the type found on handheld computers or PDAs.

The On-Screen Symbol Keyboard command on the Handwriting menu (Figure B-13) displays a special on-screen keyboard that allows you to enter symbols that are not on your keyboard, as well as Unicode characters. **Unicode characters** use a coding scheme capable of representing all the world's current languages.

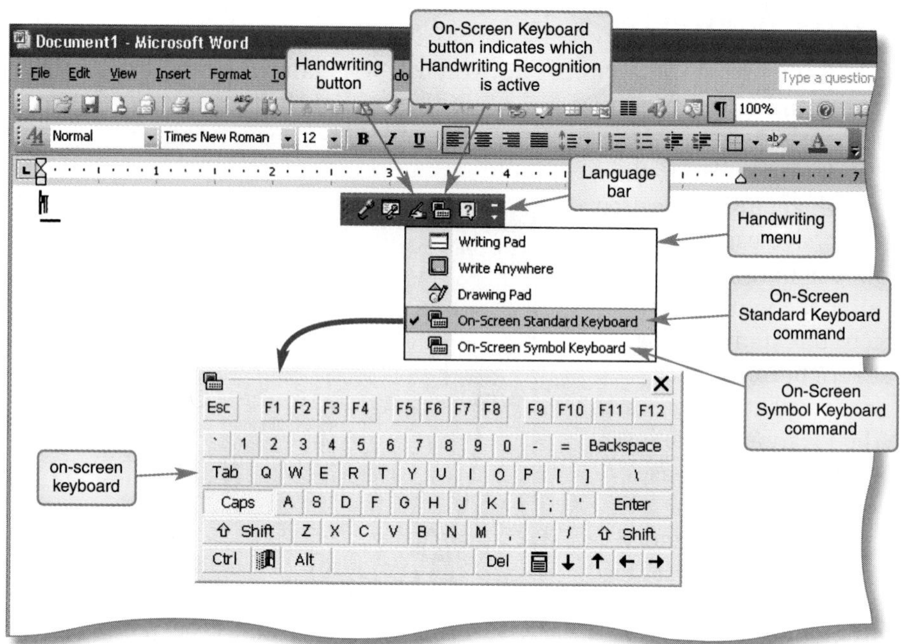

FIGURE B-13

Speech Playback

Using **speech playback**, you can have your computer read back the text in a document. Word provides two buttons for speech playback: Speak Text and Pause Speaking. To show the Speak Text button on the Language bar, click the Options button on the Language bar (Figure B-14) and then click Speak Text on the Options menu. Similarly, click the Options button on the Language bar and then click Pause Speaking on the Options menu to show the Pause Speaking button on the Language bar.

To use speech playback, position the insertion point where you want the computer to start reading back the text in the document and then click the Speak Text button on the Language bar (Figure B-14). The computer reads from the location of the insertion point until the end of the document or until you click the Pause Speaking button on the Language bar. An alternative is to select the text you want the computer to read and then click the Speak Text button on the Language bar. After the computer reads back the selected text, it stops speech playback.

When you click the Speak Text button on the Language bar, it changes to a Stop Speaking button. Click the Stop Speaking button on the Language bar to stop the speech playback. If you click the Pause Speaking button on the Language bar to stop speech playback, the Pause Speaking button changes to a Resume Speaking button that you click when you want the computer to continue reading the document from the location at which it stopped reading.

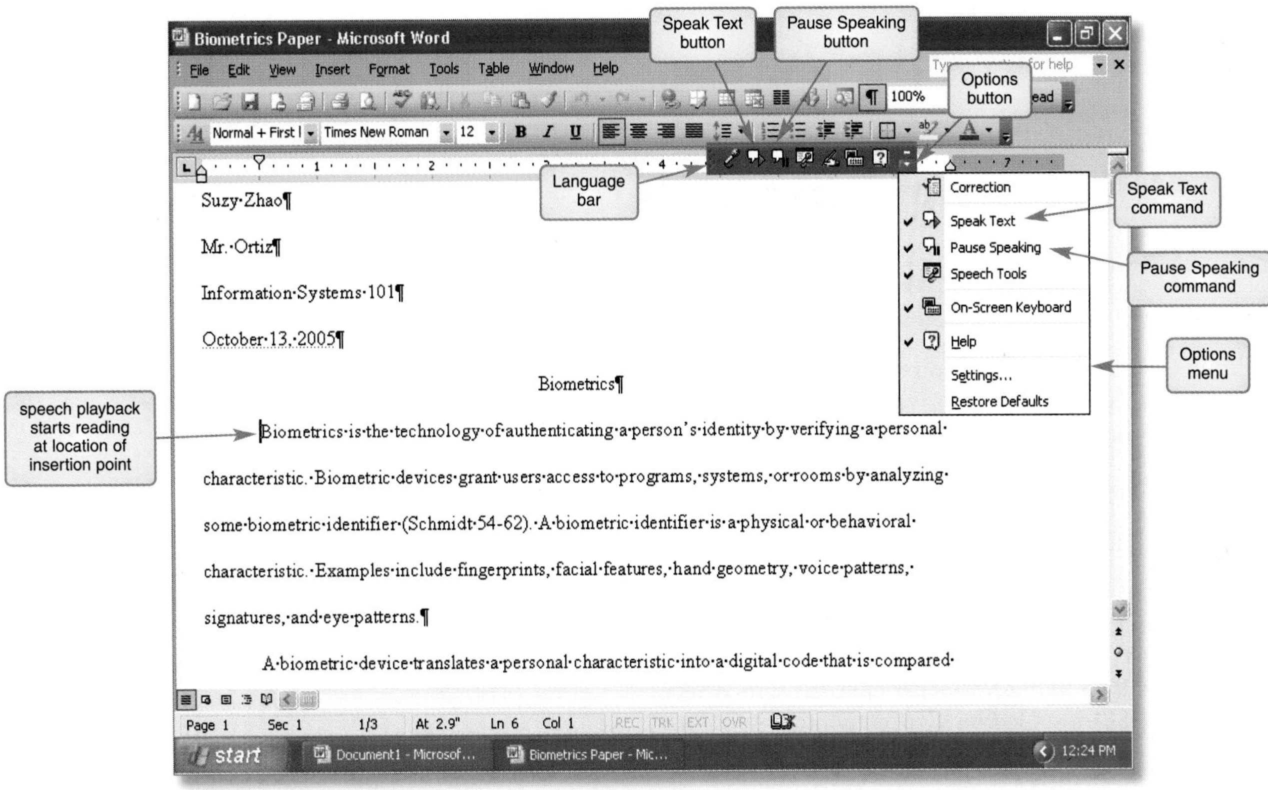

FIGURE B-14

Customizing Speech Playback

You can customize speech playback through the Speech Properties dialog box. Click the Speech Tools button on the Language bar and then click Options on the Speech Tools menu (Figure B-6a on page APP 17). When text services displays the Speech input settings dialog box (Figure B-6b), click the Advanced Speech button. When text services displays the Speech Properties dialog box, click the Text To Speech tab (Figure B-15). The Text To Speech sheet has two areas: Voice selection and Voice speed. The Voice selection area lets you choose between two male voices and one female voice. You can click the Preview Voice button to hear a sample of the voice. The Voice speed area contains a slider. Drag the slider to slow down or speed up the pace of the speaking voice.

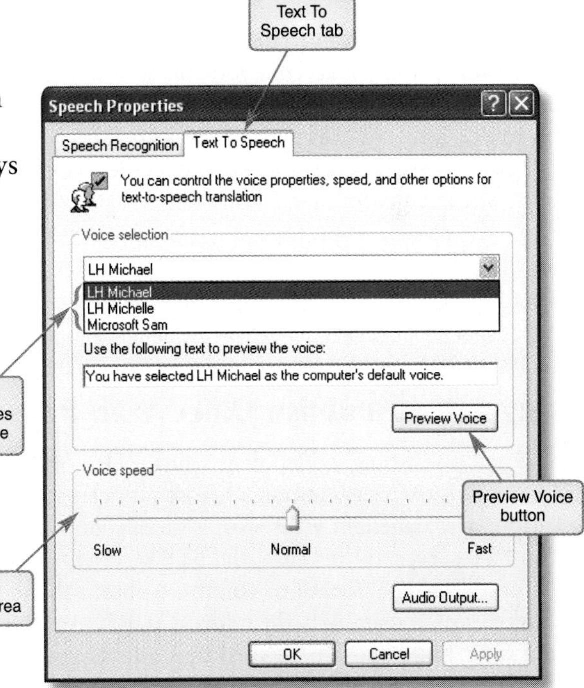

FIGURE B-15

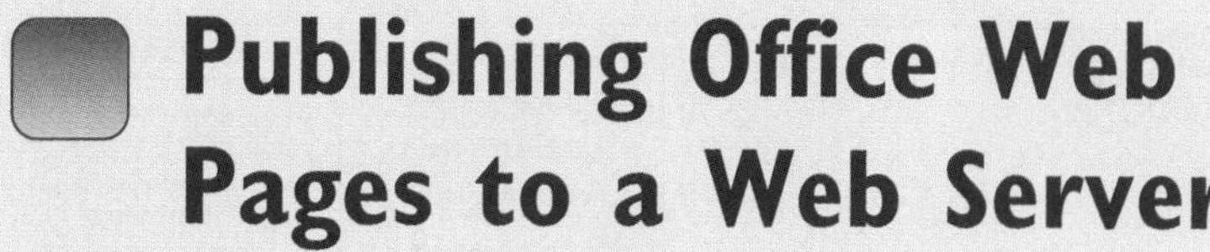

Publishing Office Web Pages to a Web Server

With the Office applications, you use the Save as Web Page command on the File menu to save the Web page to a Web server using one of two techniques: Web folders or File Transfer Protocol. A **Web folder** is an Office shortcut to a Web server. **File Transfer Protocol** (**FTP**) is an Internet standard that allows computers to exchange files with other computers on the Internet.

You should contact your network system administrator or technical support staff at your ISP to determine if their Web server supports Web folders, FTP, or both, and to obtain necessary permissions to access the Web server. If you decide to publish Web pages using a Web folder, you must have the Office Server Extensions (OSE) installed on your computer.

Using Web Folders to Publish Office Web Pages

When publishing to a Web folder, someone first must create the Web folder before you can save to it. If you are granted permission to create a Web folder, you must obtain the URL of the Web server, a user name, and possibly a password that allows you to access the Web server. You also must decide on a name for the Web folder. Table C-1 explains how to create a Web folder.

Office adds the name of the Web folder to the list of current Web folders. You can save to this folder, open files in the folder, rename the folder, or perform any operations you would to a folder on your hard disk. You can use your Office program or Windows Explorer to access this folder. Table C-2 explains how to save to a Web folder.

Using FTP to Publish Office Web Pages

When publishing a Web page using FTP, you first must add the FTP location to your computer before you can save to it. An FTP location, also called an **FTP site**, is a collection of files that reside on an FTP server. In this case, the FTP server is the Web server.

To add an FTP location, you must obtain the name of the FTP site, which usually is the address (URL) of the FTP server, and a user name and a password that allows you to access the FTP server. You save and open the Web pages on the FTP server using the name of the FTP site. Table C-3 explains how to add an FTP site.

Office adds the name of the FTP site to the FTP locations list in the Save As and Open dialog boxes. You can open and save files using this list. Table C-4 explains how to save to an FTP location.

Table C-1 Creating a Web Folder

1. Click File on the menu bar and then click Save As (or Open).
2. When the Save As dialog box (or Open dialog box) appears, click My Network Places on the My Places bar, and then click the Create New Folder button on the toolbar.
3. When the Add Network Place Wizard dialog box appears, click the Next button. If necessary, click Choose another network location. Click the Next button. Click the View some examples link, type the Internet or network address, and then click the Next button. Click Log on anonymously to deselect the check box, type your user name in the User name text box, and then click the Next button. Enter the name you want to call this network place and then click the Next button. Click the Finish button.

Table C-2 Saving to a Web Folder

1. Click File on the menu bar and then click Save As.
2. When the Save As dialog box appears, type the Web page file name in the File name text box. Do not press the ENTER key.
3. Click My Network Places on the My Places bar.
4. Double-click the Web folder name in the Save in list.
5. If the Enter Network Password dialog box appears, type the user name and password in the respective text boxes and then click the OK button.
6. Click the Save button in the Save As dialog box.

Table C-3 Adding an FTP Location

1. Click File on the menu bar and then click Save As (or Open).
2. In the Save As dialog box, click the Save in box arrow and then click Add/Modify FTP Locations in the Save in list; or in the Open dialog box, click the Look in box arrow and then click Add/Modify FTP Locations in the Look in list.
3. When the Add/Modify FTP Locations dialog box appears, type the name of the FTP site in the Name of FTP site text box. If the site allows anonymous logon, click Anonymous in the Log on as area; if you have a user name for the site, click User in the Log on as area and then enter the user name. Enter the password in the Password text box. Click the OK button.
4. Close the Save As or the Open dialog box.

Table C-4 Saving to an FTP Location

1. Click File on the menu bar and then click Save As.
2. When the Save As dialog box appears, type the Web page file name in the File name text box. Do not press the ENTER key.
3. Click the Save in box arrow and then click FTP Locations.
4. Double-click the name of the FTP site to which you wish to save.
5. When the FTP Log On dialog box appears, enter your user name and password and then click the OK button.
6. Click the Save button in the Save As dialog box.

Appendix D

Changing Screen Resolution and Resetting the Word Toolbars and Menus

This appendix explains how to change your screen resolution in Windows to the resolution used in this book. It also describes how to reset the Word toolbars and menus to their installation settings.

Changing Screen Resolution

The **screen resolution** indicates the number of pixels (dots) that your computer uses to display the letters, numbers, graphics, and background you see on your screen. The screen resolution usually is stated as the product of two numbers, such as 800 × 600 (pronounced 800 by 600). An 800 × 600 screen resolution results in a display of 800 distinct pixels on each of 600 lines, or about 480,000 pixels. The figures in this book were created using a screen resolution of 800 × 600.

The screen resolutions most commonly used today are 800 × 600 and 1024 × 768, although some Office specialists operate their computers at a much higher screen resolution, such as 2048 × 1536. The following steps show how to change the screen resolution from 1024 × 768 to 800 × 600.

To Change the Screen Resolution

1

- **If necessary, minimize all applications so that the Windows desktop appears.**
- **Right-click the Windows desktop.**

Windows displays the Windows desktop shortcut menu (Figure D-1).

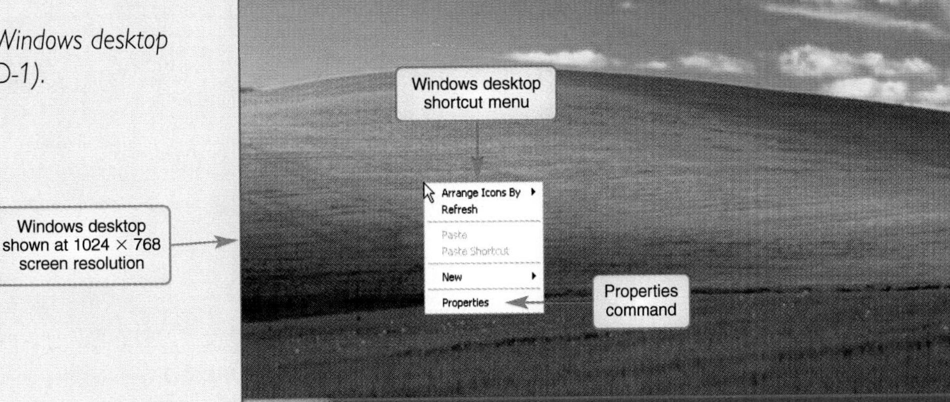

FIGURE D-1

2

• **Click Properties on the shortcut menu.**

• **When Windows displays the Display Properties dialog box, click the Settings tab.**

Windows displays the Settings sheet in the Display Properties dialog box (Figure D-2). The Settings sheet shows a preview of the Windows desktop using the current screen resolution (1024 x 768). The Settings sheet also shows the screen resolution and the color quality settings.

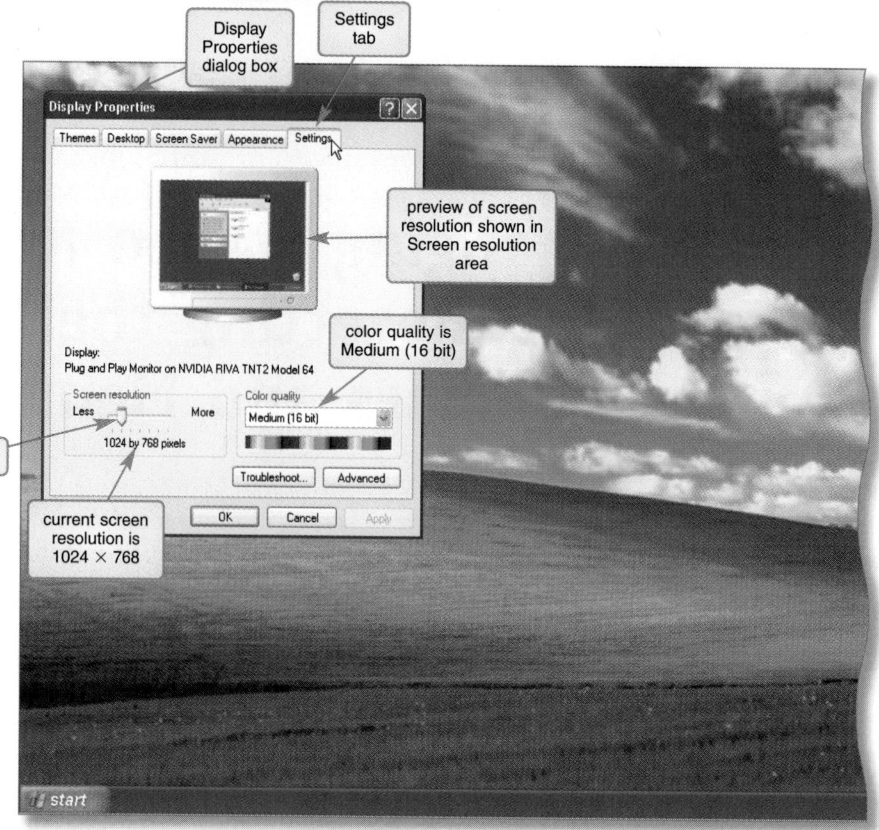

FIGURE D-2

3

• **Drag the slider in the Screen resolution area to the left so that the screen resolution changes to 800 x 600.**

The screen resolution in the Screen resolution area changes to 800 × 600 (Figure D-3). The Settings sheet shows a preview of the Windows desktop using the new screen resolution (800 × 600).

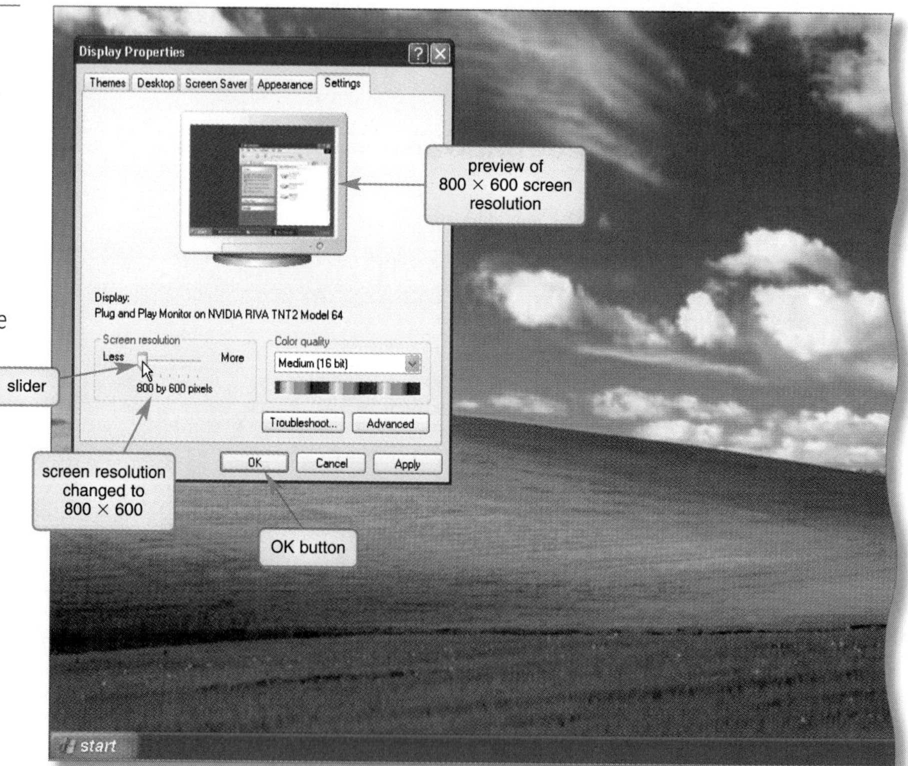

FIGURE D-3

4

- **Click the OK button.**
- **If Windows displays the Monitor Settings dialog box, click the Yes button.**

Windows changes the screen resolution from 1024 × 768 to 800 × 600 (Figure D-4).

FIGURE D-4

As shown in the previous steps, as you decrease the screen resolution, Windows displays less information on your screen, but the information increases in size. The reverse also is true: as you increase the screen resolution, Windows displays more information on your screen, but the information decreases in size.

Resetting the Word Toolbars and Menus

Word customization capabilities allow you to create custom toolbars by adding and deleting buttons and personalize menus based on their usage. Each time you start Word, the toolbars and menus are displayed using the same settings as the last time you used it. The figures in this book were created with the Word toolbars and menus set to the original, or installation, settings.

Resetting the Standard and Formatting Toolbars

The steps on the next page show how to reset the Standard and Formatting toolbars.

To Reset the Standard and Formatting Toolbars

1

- **Start Word.**
- **Click the Toolbar Options button on the Standard toolbar and then point to Add or Remove Buttons on the Toolbar Options menu.**

Word displays the Toolbar Options menu and the Add or Remove Buttons submenu (Figure D-5).

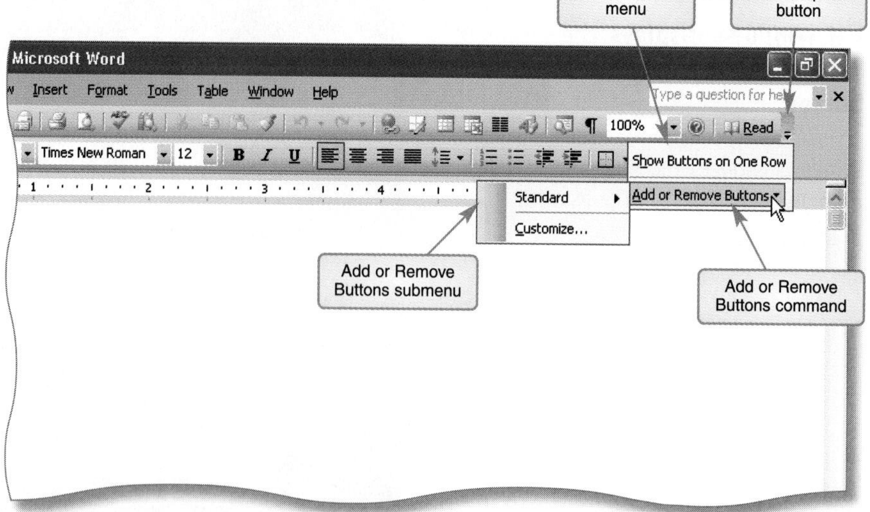

FIGURE D-5

- **Point to Standard on the Add or Remove Buttons submenu.**
- **When Word displays the Standard submenu, scroll down and then point to Reset Toolbar.**

The Standard submenu indicates the buttons and boxes that are displayed on the Standard toolbar (Figure D-6). To remove a button from the Standard toolbar, click a button name with a check mark to the left of the name to remove the check mark.

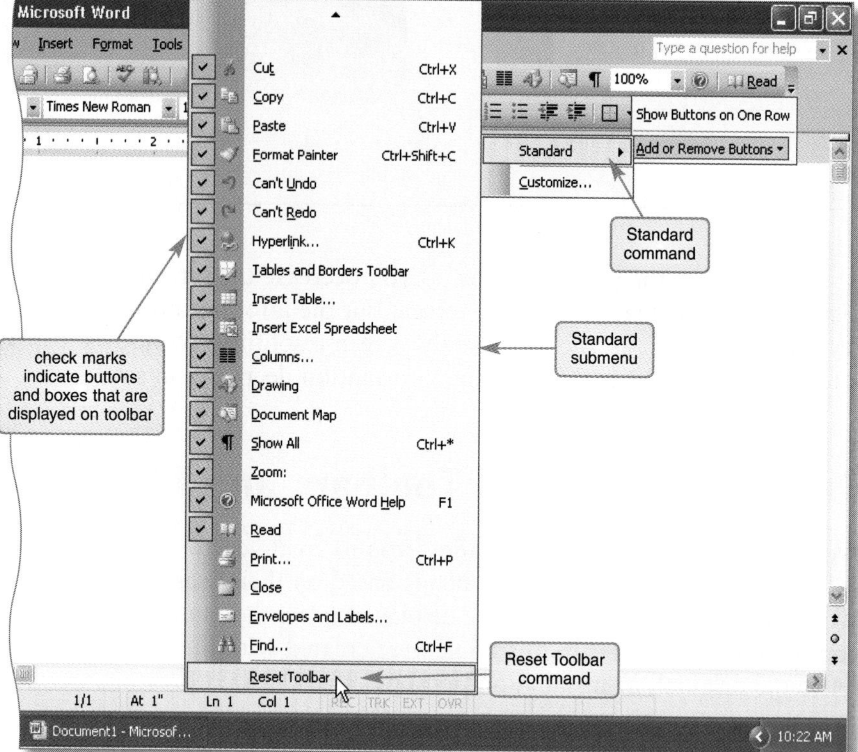

FIGURE D-6

3

- **Click Reset Toolbar.**
- **If a Microsoft Word dialog box is displayed, click the Yes button.**

Word resets the Standard toolbar to its original settings.

- **Reset the Formatting toolbar by following Steps 1 through 3 and replacing any reference to the Standard toolbar with the Formatting toolbar.**

Not only can you use the Standard submenu shown in Figure D-6 to reset the Standard toolbar to its original settings, but you also can use it to customize the Standard toolbar by adding and deleting buttons. To add or delete buttons, click the button name on the Standard submenu to add or remove the check mark. Buttons with a check mark to the left currently are displayed on the Standard toolbar; buttons without a check mark are not displayed on the Standard toolbar. You can complete the same tasks for the Formatting toolbar, using the Formatting submenu to add and delete buttons from the Formatting toolbar.

Other Ways

1. On View menu point to Toolbars, click Customize on Toolbars submenu, click Toolbars tab, click toolbar name, click Reset button, click OK button, click Close button
2. Right-click toolbar, click Customize on shortcut menu, click Toolbars tab, click toolbar name, click Reset button, click OK button, click Close button
3. In Voice Command mode, say "View, Toolbars, Customize, Toolbars, [desired toolbar name], Reset, OK, Close"

Resetting the Word Menus

The following steps show how to reset the Word menus to their original settings.

To Reset the Word Menus

1

- **Click the Toolbar Options button on the Standard toolbar and then point to Add or Remove Buttons on the Toolbar Options menu.**

Word displays the Toolbar Options menu and the Add or Remove Buttons submenu (Figure D-7).

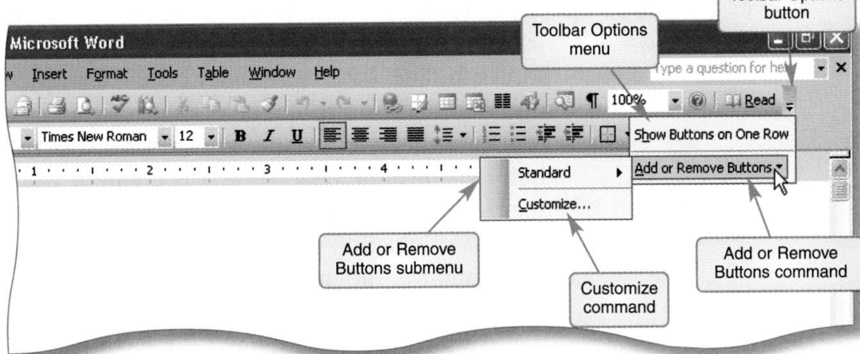

FIGURE D-7

2

- **Click Customize on the Add or Remove Buttons submenu.**
- **When Word displays the Customize dialog box, click the Options tab.**

The Customize dialog box contains three sheets used for customizing the Word toolbars and menus (Figure D-8).

3

- **Click the Reset menu and toolbar usage data button.**
- **When Word displays the Microsoft Word dialog box, click the Yes button.**
- **Click the Close button in the Customize dialog box.**

Word resets the menus to the original settings.

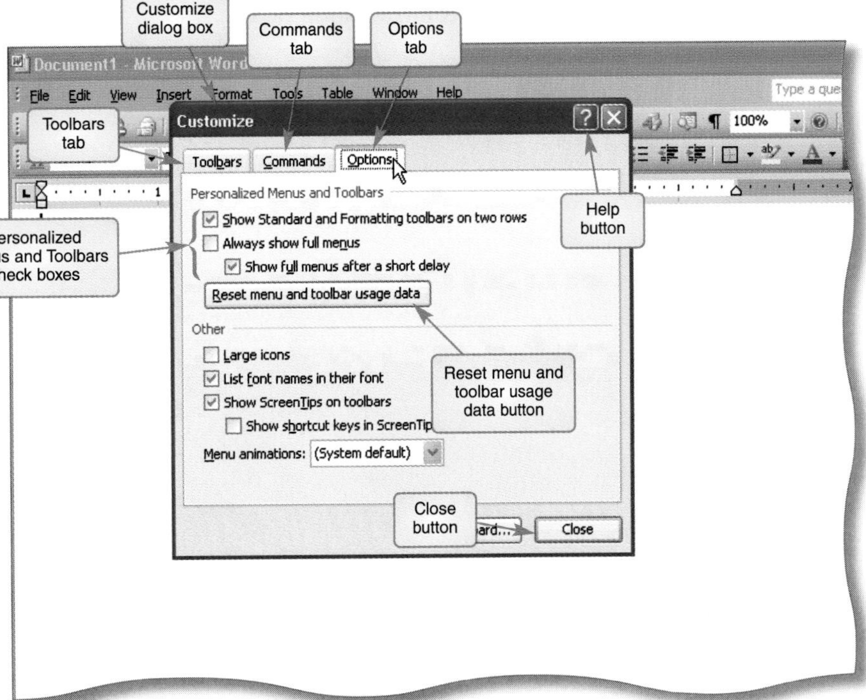

FIGURE D-8

Other Ways

1. On View menu point to Toolbars, click Customize on Toolbars submenu, click Options tab, click Reset menu and toolbar usage data button, click Yes button, click Close button
2. Right-click toolbar, click Customize on shortcut menu, click Options tab, click Reset menu and toolbar usage data button, click Yes button, click Close button
3. In Voice Command mode, say "View, Toolbars, Customize, Options, Reset menu and toolbar usage data, Yes, Close"

Using the Options sheet in the Customize dialog box, as shown in Figure D-8 on the previous page, you can select options to personalize menus and toolbars. For example, you can select or deselect a check mark that instructs Word to display the Standard and Formatting toolbars on two rows. You also can select whether Word always displays full menus or displays short menus followed by full menus, after a short delay. Other options available on the Options sheet including settings to instruct Word to display toolbars with large icons; to use the appropriate font to display font names in the Font list; and to display a ScreenTip when a user points to a toolbar button. Clicking the Help button in the upper-right corner of the Customize dialog box displays Help topics that will assist you in customizing toolbars and menus.

Using the Commands sheet in the Customize dialog box, you can add buttons to toolbars and commands to menus. Recall that the menu bar at the top of the Word window is a special toolbar. To add buttons to a toolbar, click a category name in the Categories list and then drag the command name in the Commands list to a toolbar. To add commands to a menu, click a category name in the Categories list, drag the command name in the Commands list to a menu name on the menu bar, and then, when the menu is displayed, drag the command to the desired location in the list of menu commands.

Using the Toolbars sheet in the Customize dialog box, you can add new toolbars and reset existing toolbars and the menu. To add a new toolbar, click the New button, enter a toolbar name in the New Toolbar dialog box, and then click the OK button. Once the new toolbar is created, you can use the Commands sheet to add or remove buttons, as you would with any other toolbar. If you add one or more buttons to an existing toolbar and want to reset the toolbar to its original settings, click the toolbar name in the Toolbars list so a check mark is displayed to the left of the name and then click the Reset button. If you add commands to one or more menus and want to reset the menus to their default settings, click Menu Bar in the Toolbars list on the Toolbars sheet so a check mark is displayed to the left of the name and then click the Reset button. When you have finished, click the Close button to close the Customize dialog box.

Appendix E

Microsoft Office Specialist Certification

What Is Microsoft Office Specialist Certification?

Microsoft Office Specialist certification provides a framework for measuring your proficiency with the Microsoft Office 2003 applications, such as Microsoft Office Word 2003, Microsoft Office Excel 2003, Microsoft Office Access 2003, Microsoft Office PowerPoint 2003, and Microsoft Office Outlook 2003. The levels of certification are described in Table E-1.

Table E-1 Levels of Microsoft Office Specialist Certification

LEVEL	DESCRIPTION	REQUIREMENTS	CREDENTIAL AWARDED
Microsoft Office Specialist	Indicates that you have an understanding of the basic features in a specific Microsoft Office 2003 application	Pass any ONE of the following: Microsoft Office Word 2003 Microsoft Office Excel 2003 Microsoft Office Access 2003 Microsoft Office PowerPoint 2003 Microsoft Office Outlook 2003	Candidates will be awarded one certificate for each of the Specialist-level exams they have passed: Microsoft Office Word 2003 Microsoft Office Excel 2003 Microsoft Office Access 2003 Microsoft Office PowerPoint 2003 Microsoft Office Outlook 2003
Microsoft Office Expert	Indicates that you have an understanding of the advanced features in a specific Microsoft Office 2003 application	Pass any ONE of the following: Microsoft Office Word 2003 Expert Microsoft Office Excel 2003 Expert	Candidates will be awarded one certificate for each of the Expert-level exams they have passed: Microsoft Office Word 2003 Expert Microsoft Office Excel 2003 Expert
Microsoft Office Master	Indicates that you have a comprehensive understanding of the features of four of the five primary Microsoft Office 2003 applications	Pass the following: Microsoft Office Word 2003 Expert Microsoft Office Excel 2003 Expert Microsoft Office PowerPoint 2003 And pass ONE of the following: Microsoft Office Access 2003 or Microsoft Office Outlook 2003	Candidates will be awarded the Microsoft Office Master certificate for fulfilling the requirements.

Why Should You Be Certified?

Being Microsoft Office certified provides a valuable industry credential — proof that you have the Office 2003 applications skills required by employers. By passing one or more Microsoft Office Specialist certification exams, you demonstrate your proficiency in a given Office 2003 application to employers. With more than 400 million people in 175 nations and 70 languages using Office applications, Microsoft is targeting Office 2003 certification to a wide variety of companies. These companies include temporary employment agencies that want to prove the expertise of their workers, large corporations looking for a way to measure the skill set of employees, and training companies and educational institutions seeking Microsoft Office 2003 teachers with appropriate credentials.

The Microsoft Office Specialist Certification Exams

You pay $50 to $100 each time you take an exam, whether you pass or fail. The fee varies among testing centers. The **Microsoft Office Expert** exams, which you can take up to 60 minutes to complete, consist of between 40 and 60 tasks that you perform on a personal computer in a simulated environment. The tasks require you to use the application just as you would in doing your job. The **Microsoft Office Specialist** exams contain fewer tasks, and you will have slightly less time to complete them. The tasks you will perform differ on the two types of exams. After passing designated Expert and Specialist exams, candidates are awarded the **Microsoft Office Master** certificate (see the requirements in Table E-1 on the previous page).

How to Prepare for the Microsoft Office Specialist Certification Exams

The Shelly Cashman Series offers several Microsoft-approved textbooks that cover the required objectives of the Microsoft Office Specialist certification exams. For a listing of the textbooks, visit the Shelly Cashman Series Microsoft Office Specialist Center at scsite.com/winoff2003/cert. Click the link Shelly Cashman Series Microsoft Office 2003-Approved Microsoft Office Textbooks (Figure E-1). After using any of the books listed in an instructor-led course, you should be prepared to take the indicated Microsoft Office Specialist certification exam.

How to Find an Authorized Testing Center

To locate a testing center, call 1-800-933-4493 in North America, or visit the Shelly Cashman Series Microsoft Office Specialist Center at scsite.com/winoff2003/cert. Click the link Locate an Authorized Testing Center Near You (Figure E-1). At this Web site, you can look for testing centers around the world.

Shelly Cashman Series Microsoft Office Specialist Center

The Shelly Cashman Series Microsoft Office Specialist Center (Figure E-1) lists more than 15 Web sites you can visit to obtain additional information about certification. The Web page (scsite.com/winoff2003/cert) includes links to general information about certification, choosing an application for certification, preparing for the certification exam, and taking and passing the certification exam.

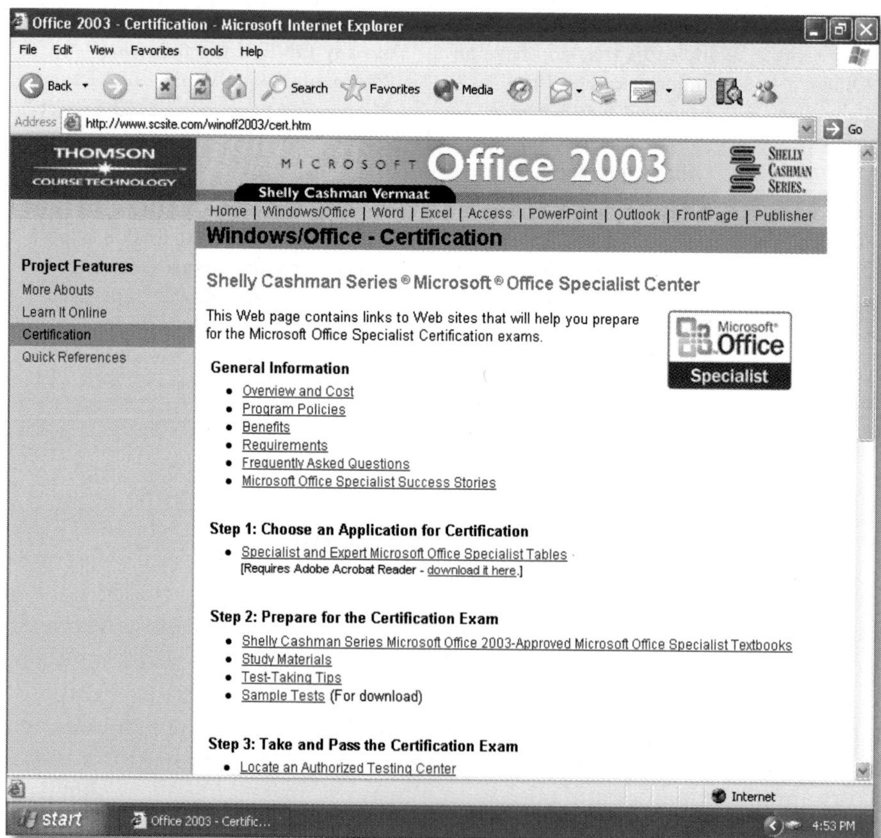

FIGURE E-1

Microsoft Office Specialist Certification Maps

The tables on the following pages list the skill sets and activities you should be familiar with if you plan to take one of the Microsoft Office Specialist certification examinations. Each activity is accompanied by page numbers on which the activity is illustrated and page numbers on which the activity is part of an exercise.

Microsoft Office Word 2003

Table E-2 lists the skill sets and activities you should be familiar with if you plan to take the Microsoft Office Specialist examination for Microsoft Office Word 2003. Table E-3 on the next page lists the skill sets and activities you should be familiar with if you plan to take the Microsoft Office Expert examination for Microsoft Office Word 2003. **ADV** means that the activity is demonstrated in the companion textbook *Microsoft Office 2003: Advanced Concepts and Techniques* (ISBN 0-619-20025-1 or ISBN 0-619-20026-X). **POST-ADV** means that the activity is demonstrated in the companion textbook *Microsoft Office 2003: Post-Advanced Concepts and Techniques* (ISBN 0-619-20027-8).

Table E-2 Microsoft Office Specialist Skill Sets, Activities, and Locations in Book for Microsoft Office Word 2003

SKILL SET	SKILL BEING MEASURED	SKILL DEMONSTRATED IN BOOK	SKILL EXERCISE IN BOOK
I. Creating Content	A. Insert and edit text, symbols and special characters	WD 18-20, WD 22-27, WD 57, WD 58-59, WD 83, WD 107, WD 112-114, WD 118-120, WD 125, WD 152, WD 156-157, WD 154-155, WD 166-172, WD 180, **ADV**	WD 65 (Apply Your Knowledge Steps 1-4), WD 67 (In the Lab 1 Step 3), WD 69 (In the Lab 2 Step 3), WD 70 (In the Lab 3 Step 1), WD 78 (Cases and Places 1-3, last sentence), WD 129 (Apply Your Knowledge Steps 1, 7-8, and 10 - 3rd sentence), WD 131 (In the Lab 1 Steps 8-9), WD 133 (In the Lab 2, Part 1 Steps 3b and 4, Part 2 Step 1), WD 134 (In the Lab 3 Steps 2-3), WD 136 (Cases and Places 5 - 4th sentence from end), WD 199 (In the Lab 1 Steps 1-2), WD 202 (Cases and Places 5 - 3rd sentence from end), **ADV**
	B. Insert frequently used and pre-defined text	WD 84 (2nd paragraph), WD 89-90, WD 91-93, WD 177-179, WD 181-182	WD 129 (Apply Your Knowledge Step 10 - 4th sentence), WD 134 (In the Lab 3 Step 1 - 4th sentence), WD 135 (Cases and Places 1 - 2nd to last sentence), WD 200 (In the Lab 2 Step 2 - 3rd and 4th sentences)
	C. Navigate to specific content	WD 110-112, WD 116-117, **ADV**	WD 129 (Apply Your Knowledge Step 6), WD 131 (In the Lab 1 Step 11), WD 133 (In the Lab 2 Part 2 Steps 2 and 4), **ADV**
	D. Insert, position and size graphics	WD 46-50, **ADV**	WD 65 (Apply Your Knowledge Step 15), WD 68 (In the Lab 1 Steps 13-14), WD 60 (In the Lab 2 Steps 12-13), WD 70 (In the Lab 3 Steps 6-7), **ADV**
	E. Create and modify diagrams and charts	**ADV**	**ADV**
	F. Locate, select and insert supporting information	WD 118, WD 124, WD 125	WD 129 (Apply Your Knowledge Step 13), WD 134 (In the Lab 3 Step 3), WD 135 (Cases and Places 2-4)
II. Organizing Content	A. Insert and modify tables	WD 150-151, WD 182-187, **ADV**	WD 198 (Apply Your Knowledge Steps 4-13), WD 200 (In the Lab 2 Step 2), WD 200 (In the Lab 3 Step 2), **ADV**
	B. Create bulleted lists, numbered lists and outlines	WD 153-154, WD 156, WD 187-189, **ADV**	WD 70 (In the Lab 1 Step 5), WD 72 (Cases and Places 4 - next to last sentence), WD 199 (In the Lab 1), WD 200 (In the Lab 2), WD 200 (In the Lab 3 Step 2), WD 202 (Cases and Places 5 - 4th sentence), **ADV**
	C. Insert and modify hyperlinks	WD 108, WD 122, WD 174, WD 207, WD 212-213	WD 131 (In the Lab 1 Step 8), WD 133 (In the Lab 2 Step 3b), WD 200 (In the Lab 2 Step 2 - 2nd to last sentence), WD 216 (In the Lab 2 Steps 2 and 4)

Table E-2 Microsoft Office Specialist Skill Sets, Activities, and Locations in Book for Microsoft Office Word 2003 *(continued)*

SKILL SET	SKILL BEING MEASURED	SKILL DEMONSTRATED IN BOOK	SKILL EXERCISE IN BOOK
III. Formatting Content	A. Format text	WD 17, WD 34-36, WD 40-42, WD 44, WD 87, WD 117, WD 161, WD 173, WD 213, **ADV**	WD 65 (Apply Your Knowledge Steps 5-6, and 8-13), WD 67-68 (In the Lab 1 Steps 1, 5, and 8-11), WD 68-69 (In the Lab 2 Steps 1, 5, and 8-10), WD 70 (In the Lab 3 Steps 1, 3-4), WD 71 (Cases and Places 3 - 3rd & 4th sentences from end), WD 72 (Cases and Places 4 - 4th and 5th sentences from end), WD 129 (Apply Your Knowledge Steps 2 and 9), WD 198 (Apply Your Knowledge Steps 3 and 9), WD 200 (In the Lab 2 Step 2), **ADV**
	B. Format paragraphs	WD 37-38, WD 79-80, WD 82-83, WD 86-89, WD 104-105, WD 163-165, WD 172-173, WD 176-177, **ADV**	WD 65 (Apply Your Knowledge Steps 7 and 14), WD 67 (In the Lab 1 Steps 6-7, 12), WD 69 (In the Lab 2 Steps 6-7, 11), WD 129 (Apply Your Knowledge Steps 3-4), WD 131 (In the Lab 1 Steps 3, 5-8), WD 133 (In the Lab 2 Part 1 Steps 1-3, Part 2 Step 2), WD 134 (In the Lab 3), WD 135-136 (Cases and Places 1-5), WD 198 (Apply Your Knowledge Steps 1-2), WD 199-200 (In the Lab 2 Step 2), **ADV**
	C. Apply and format columns	**ADV**	**ADV**
	D. Insert and modify content in headers and footers	WD 81-84, **ADV**	WD 129 (Apply Your Knowledge Step 10), WD 131 (In the Lab 1 Step 4), WD 133 (In the Lab 2 Part 1 Step 1 - Part 3 Step 2), WD 134 (In the Lab 3 Step 1), WD 135-136 (Cases and Places 1-5), **ADV**
	E. Modify document layout and page setup	WD 77-79, WD 103, **ADV**	WD 131 (In the Lab 1 Steps 2 and 7), WD 133 (In the Lab 2 Part 1 Steps 1 and 2, Part 3 Step 2), WD 134 (In the Lab 3), WD 135-136 (Cases and Places 1-5), **ADV**
IV. Collaborating	A. Circulate documents for review	WD 123, **ADV**	WD 134 (In the Lab 3 Step 5), **ADV**
	B. Compare and merge documents	**ADV**	**ADV**
	C. Insert, view and edit comments	**ADV**	**ADV**
	D. Track, accept and reject proposed changes	**ADV**	**ADV**
V. Formatting and Managing Documents	A. Create new documents using templates	WD 142-148, WD 175 (More About Saving), **ADV**	WD 199 (In the Lab 1 Steps 1 and 2), WD 201-202 (Cases and Places 1-5), **ADV**
	B. Review and modify document properties	WD 100-101, WD 102, WD 193-194	WD 131 (In the Lab 1 Step 12), WD 133 (In the Lab 2 Part 1 Step 7, Part 2 Step 6, Part 3 Step 5), WD 134 (In the Lab 3 Step 4), WD 200 (In the Lab 2 Steps 3 and 6)
	C. Organize documents using file folders	**ADV**	**ADV**
	D. Save documents in appropriate formats for different uses	WD 30, WD 205, WD 206, **ADV**	WD 216 (In the Lab 1 Steps 2, 5-6), WD 216 (In the Lab 2 Step 2)
	E. Print documents, envelopes and labels	WD 53, WD 190-191, **ADV**	WD 65 (Apply Your Knowledge Step 17), WD 68 (In the Lab 1 Step 16), WD 69 (In the Lab 2 Step 15), WD 70 (In the Lab 3 Step 9), WD 131 (In the Lab 1 Step 12), WD 200 (In the Lab 2 Step 7), WD 200 (In the Lab 3 Step 3), **ADV**
	F. Preview documents and Web pages	WD 52, WD 158-159, WD 208-209	WD 70 (In the Lab 3 Step 7), WD 199 (In the Lab 1 Step 5), WD 200 (In the Lab 2 Step 5), WD 216 (In the Lab 1 Step 3), WD 216 (In the Lab 2 Step 5), **ADV**
	G. Change and organize document views and windows	WD 9 Step 4, WD 20-21, WD 77, WD 148-149, WD 169-170, WD 172, **ADV**	WD 67 (In the Lab 1 Step 2), WD 68 (In the Lab 2 Step 2), WD 71-72 (Cases and Places 1-5), WD 133 (In the Lab 2 Part 3 Step 1), WD 135-136 (Cases and Places 1-5), WD 199 (In the Lab 1 Step 2), **ADV**

Table E-3 Microsoft Office Expert Skill Sets, Activities, and Locations in Book for Microsoft Office Word 2003

SKILL SET	SKILL BEING MEASURED	SKILL DEMONSTRATED IN BOOK	SKILL EXERCISE IN BOOK
I. Formatting Content	A. Create custom styles for text, tables and lists	WD 96-98, **ADV**, **POST-ADV**	WD 133 (In the Lab 2 Part 1 Step 2, Part 2 Step 2), WD 135-136 (Cases and Places 2-5), **ADV**, **POST-ADV**
	B. Control pagination	WD 103, WD 154-155, **ADV**, **POST-ADV**	WD 131 (In the Lab 1 Step 7), WD 133 (In the Lab 2 Part 1 Step 2, Part 3 Step 2), WD 134 (In the Lab 3 Step 1), WD 135-136 (Cases and Places 1-5), WD 199 (In the Lab 1 Step 2), **ADV**, **POST-ADV**
	C. Format, position and resize graphics using advanced layout features	WD 49-51, **ADV**, **POST-ADV**	WD 69 (In the Lab 2 Step 13), WD 70 (In the Lab 3 Step 7), WD 199-200 (In the Lab 2 Step 1), WD 201 (Cases and Places 1), **ADV**, **POST-ADV**
	D. Insert and modify objects	**ADV**, **POST-ADV**	**ADV**, **POST-ADV**
	E. Create and modify diagrams and charts using data from other sources	**POST-ADV**	**POST-ADV**
II. Organizing Content	A. Sort content in lists and tables	WD 109-110, **ADV**, **POST-ADV**	WD 133 (In the Lab 2 Part 1, Step 3), WD 134 (In the Lab 3 Step 1 last sentence), WD 135-136 (Cases and Places 1-5), **ADV**, **POST-ADV**
	B. Perform calculations in tables	**ADV**	WD 198 (Apply Your Knowledge Step 7), **ADV**
	C. Modify table formats	**ADV**, **POST-ADV**	**ADV**, **POST-ADV**
	D. Summarize document content using automated tools	**POST-ADV**	**POST-ADV**
	E. Use automated tools for document navigation	**POST-ADV**	**POST-ADV**
	F. Merge letters with other data sources	**ADV**	**ADV**
	G. Merge labels with other data sources	**ADV**	**ADV**
	H. Structure documents using XML	**POST-ADV**	**POST-ADV**
III. Formatting Documents	A. Create and modify forms	**POST-ADV**	**POST-ADV**
	B. Create and modify document background	WD 207-208, **ADV**, **POST-ADV**	WD 216 (In the Lab 2 Steps 2-3), **ADV**, **POST-ADV**
	C. Create and modify document indexes and tables	**POST-ADV**	**POST-ADV**
	D. Insert and modify endnotes, footnotes, captions, and cross-references	WD 93-99, **POST-ADV**	WD 131 (In the Lab 1 Step 7), WD 133 (In the Lab 2 Part 1 Step 2, Part 2 Steps 3 and 4, Part 3 Steps 1-3), WD 134 (In the Lab 3 Step 1), WD 135-136 (Cases and Places 1-5), **POST-ADV**
	E. Create and manage master documents and subdocuments	**POST-ADV**	**POST-ADV**
IV. Collaborating	A. Modify track changes options	**ADV**	**ADV**
	B. Publish and edit Web documents	WD 205-215, WD 209-212, Appendix C	WD 216 (In the Lab 1 Steps 2-5), WD 216 (In the Lab 2 Steps 2, 7)
	C. Manage document versions	**POST-ADV**	**POST-ADV**
	D. Protect and restrict forms and documents	**POST-ADV**	**POST-ADV**
	E. Attach digital signatures to documents	**POST-ADV**	**POST-ADV**
	F. Customize document properties	**POST-ADV**	**POST-ADV**
V. Customizing Word	A. Create, edit, and run macros	**POST-ADV**	**POST-ADV**
	B. Customize menus and toolbars	**POST-ADV**	**POST-ADV**
	C. Modify Word default settings	WD 121, **ADV**, **POST-ADV**	WD 136 (Cases and Places 5), **ADV**, **POST-ADV**

Microsoft Office Excel 2003

Table E-4 lists the skill sets and activities you should be familiar with if you plan to take the Microsoft Office Specialist examination for Microsoft Office Excel 2003. Table E-5 on the next page lists the skill sets and activities you should be familiar with if you plan to take the Microsoft Office Expert examination for Microsoft Office Excel 2003. **ADV** means that the activity is demonstrated in the companion textbook *Microsoft Office 2003: Advanced Concepts and Techniques* (ISBN 0-619-20025-1 or ISBN 0-619-20026-X). **POST-ADV** means that the activity is demonstrated in the companion textbook *Microsoft Office 2003: Post-Advanced Concepts and Techniques* (ISBN 0-619-20027-8).

Table E-4 Microsoft Office Specialist Skill Sets, Activities, and Locations in Book for Microsoft Office Excel 2003

SKILL SET	SKILL BEING MEASURED	SKILL DEMONSTRATED IN BOOK	SKILL EXERCISE IN BOOK
I. Creating Data and Content	A. Enter and edit cell content	EX 16-23, EX 50-53, EX 72-88, EX 151-154, **ADV**	EX 57 (Apply Your Knowledge 1), EX 58-64 (In the Labs 1-3 and Cases and Places 1-5), EX 212 (In the Lab 1 Step 2), **ADV**
	B. Navigate to specific cell content	EX 36-37, **ADV**	EX 57(Apply Your Knowledge 1), EX 58-64 (In the Labs 1-3 and Cases and Places 1-5), **ADV**
	C. Locate, select and insert supporting information	**ADV**	**ADV**
	D. Insert, position, and size graphics	**ADV**	**ADV**
II. Analyzing Data	A. Filter lists using AutoFilter	**ADV**	**ADV**
	B. Sort lists	**ADV**	**ADV**
	C. Insert and modify formulas	EX 72-77, EX 79-80, EX 80-87, EX 168-172, EX 173, EX 174-175, **ADV**	EX 62 (In the Lab Part 3), EX 130 (In the Lab 1 Part 1), EX 130 (In the Lab 1 Part 1), EX 133 (In the Lab 1 Part 1 Steps 2 and 4), EX 135 (In the Lab 2 Part 1 Steps 3 and 5), EX 140-143 (Cases and Places 1-5), EX 211 (Apply Your Knowledge 1 Steps 5-8), EX 212 (In the Lab 1 Part 1), EX 217 (In the Lab 2 Part 1), EX 220 (In the Lab 3 Part 1 Step 11), **ADV**
	D. Use statistical, date and time, financial, and logical functions	EX 23-24, EX 26-27, EX 80-87, EX 165-167, EX 170-172, **ADV**	EX 59 (In the Lab 1 Step 2), EX 59 (In the Lab 2 Step 2), EX 130 (Apply Your Knowledge 1 Part 1), EX 133 (In the Lab 1 Part 1 Step 4), EX 135 (In the Lab 2 Part 1 Step 5), EX 212 (In the Lab 1 Part 1 Step 1), EX 216 (In the Lab 2 Part 1 Step 1), **ADV**
	E. Create, modify, and position diagrams and charts based on worksheet data	EX 38-41, EX 187-199, **ADV**	EX 59 (In the Lab 1 Step 6), EX 60 (In the Lab 2 Step 5), EX 62 (In the Lab 3 Part 2), EX 214 (In the Lab 1 Part 2), EX 217 (In the Lab 2 Part 2), **ADV**
III. Formatting Data and Content	A. Apply and modify cell formats	EX 28-36, EX 90-110, EX 177-186, **ADV**	EX 59 (In the Lab 1 Step 5), EX 60 (In the Lab 2 Step 5), EX 61 (In the Lab 3 Part 1), EX 63-64 (Cases and Places 1-5), EX 131 (Apply Your Knowledge 1), EX 133 (In the Lab 1 Steps 6-8), EX 135 (In the Lab 2 Part 1 Steps 6-9), EX 140-143 (Cases and Places 1-5), EX 214 (In the Lab 1 Step 8), EX 217 (In the Lab 2 Steps 8-10), **ADV**
	B. Apply and modify cell styles	**ADV**	**ADV**
	C. Modify row and column formats	EX 32-33, EX 91-94, EX 96-97, EX 107-111, EX 155-156, EX 159-162, **ADV**	EX 59 (In the Lab 1 Step 4), EX 60 (In the Lab 2 Step 3), EX 133 (In the Lab 1 Steps 6 and 7), EX 135 (In the Lab 3 Step 1), EX 135 (In the Lab 2 Step 6), EX 212 (In the Lab 1 Step 4), EX 216 (In the Lab 2 Steps 3 and 4), EX 219 (In the Lab 3 Steps 1-3), **ADV**
	D. Format worksheets	EX 124, EX 197-199, **ADV**	EX 135 (In the Lab 2 Step 10), EX 137-139 (In the Lab 3 Parts 1-4), EX 214 (In the Lab 1 Part 2), EX 217 (In the Lab 2 Step 11), **ADV**

Table E-4 Microsoft Office Specialist Skill Sets, Activities, and Locations in Book for Microsoft Office Excel 2003

SKILL SET	SKILL BEING MEASURED	SKILL DEMONSTRATED IN BOOK	SKILL EXERCISE IN BOOK
IV. Collaborating	A. Insert, view and edit comments	**ADV**	**ADV**
V. Managing Workbooks	A. Create new workbooks from templates	**ADV**	**ADV**
	B. Insert, delete and move cells	EX 24-27, EX 157-159, EX 161-162, EX 174-175, **ADV**	EX 62 (In the Lab 3 Part 3), EX 212 (In the Lab 1 Step 7), EX 216 (In the Lab 2 Step 6), EX 221 (In the Lab 3 Steps 1-3), **ADV**
	C. Create and modify hyperlinks	**ADV**	**ADV**
	D. Organize worksheets	EX 197-199, **ADV**	EX 214 (In the Lab 1 Part 2), EX 217 (In the Lab 2 Step 11), **ADV**
	E. Preview data in other views	EX 113-116, EX 228-230, **ADV**	EX 133 (In the Lab 1 Step 10), EX 137 (In the Lab 3 Part 2), EX 138 (In the Lab 2 Part 3), EX 239 (In the Lab 1 Part 1 Step 1), EX 240 (In the Lab 2 Part 1 Step 1), **ADV**
	F. Customize Window layout	EX 163-164, EX 175-176, EX 202-207, **ADV**	EX 215 (In the Lab 1 Part 3), EX 216-217 (In the Lab 2 Steps 2, 11, and 14), EX 219-220 (In the Lab 3 Steps 6 and 17), **ADV**
	G. Setup pages for printing	EX 113-116, **ADV**	EX 131 (Apply Your Knowledge 1), EX 133 (In the Lab 1 Step 11), EX 137 (In the Lab 3 Part 1), **ADV**
	H. Print data	EX 113-120, **ADV**	**ADV**
	I. Organize workbooks using file folders	EX 230-232	EX 240 (In the Lab 3)
	J. Save data in appropriate formats for different uses	EX 228-238, **ADV**	EX 239 (In the Lab 1 Parts 1 and 2), EX 240 (In the Lab 2 Parts 1 and 2), **ADV**

Table E-5 Microsoft Office Expert Skill Sets, Activities, and Locations in Book for Microsoft Office Excel 2003

SKILL SET	SKILL BEING MEASURED	SKILL DEMONSTRATED IN BOOK	SKILL EXERCISE IN BOOK
I. Organizing and Analyzing Data	A. Use subtotals	**ADV**	**ADV**
	B. Define and apply advanced filters	**ADV**	**ADV**
	C. Group and outline data	**ADV**	**ADV**
	D. Use data validation	**ADV, POST-ADV**	**ADV, POST-ADV**
	E. Create and modify list ranges	**ADV**	**ADV**
	F. Add, show, close, edit, merge and summarize scenarios	**POST-ADV**	**POST-ADV**
	G. Perform data analysis using automated tools	EX 204-208, **ADV, POST-ADV**	EX 215 (In the Lab 1 Part 3), EX 218 (In the Lab 2 Part 3), EX 221 (In the Lab 3 Part 2), EX 223-224 (Cases and Places 3-5), **ADV, POST-ADV**
	H. Create PivotTable and PivotChart reports	**POST-ADV**	**POST-ADV**
	I. Use Lookup and Reference functions	**ADV**	**ADV**
	J. Use Database functions	**ADV**	**ADV**
	K. Trace formula precedents, dependents and errors	**POST-ADV**	**POST-ADV**
	L. Locate invalid data and formulas	EX 89-90, EX 292-294, **POST-ADV**	EX 131 (Apply Your Knowledge 1 Part 1), **ADV, POST-ADV**

Table E-5 Microsoft Office Expert Skill Sets, Activities, and Locations in Book for Microsoft Office Excel 2003 *(continued)*

SKILL SET	SKILL BEING MEASURED	SKILL DEMONSTRATED IN BOOK	SKILL EXERCISE IN BOOK
	M. Watch and evaluate formulas	**POST-ADV**	**POST-ADV**
	N. Define, modify and use named ranges	**ADV**	**ADV**
	O. Structure workbooks using XML	**POST-ADV**	**POST-ADV**
II. Formatting z Data and Content	A. Create and modify custom data formats	**ADV**	**ADV**
	B. Use conditional formatting	EX 103-106, **ADV**	EX 133 (In the Lab 1 Step 8), EX 135 (In the Lab 2 Step 8), **ADV**
	C. Format and resize graphics	ADV	ADV
	D. Format charts and diagrams	EX 192-198, **ADV**	EX 214 (In the Lab 1, Part 2), EX 217-218, (In the Lab 2 Part 2), **ADV**
III. Collaborating	A. Protect cells, worksheets, and workbooks	**ADV, POST-ADV**	**ADV, POST-ADV**
	B. Apply workbook security settings	**POST-ADV**	**POST-ADV**
	C. Share workbooks	**POST-ADV**	**POST-ADV**
	D. Merge workbooks	**POST-ADV**	**POST-ADV**
	E. Track, accept, and reject changes to workbooks	**POST-ADV**	**POST-ADV**
IV. Managing Data and Workbooks	A. Import data to Excel	EX 120-123, **POST-ADV**	EX 136-139 (In the Lab 3), EX 143 (Cases and Places 5), **ADV, POST-ADV**
	B. Export data from Excel	**POST-ADV**	**POST-ADV**
	C. Publish and edit Web worksheets and workbooks	EX 225-239, **POST-ADV**	EX 239 (In the Lab 1), EX 240 (In the Lab 2), **POST-ADV**
	D. Create and edit templates	**ADV**	**ADV**
	E. Consolidate data	**ADV**	**ADV**
	F. Define and modify workbook properties	**POST-ADV**	**POST-ADV**
V. Customizing Excel	A. Customize toolbars and menus	**POST-ADV**	**POST-ADV**
	B. Create, edit, and run macros	**POST-ADV**	**POST-ADV**
	C. Modify Excel default settings	**ADV**	**ADV**

Microsoft Office Access 2003

Table E-6 lists the skill sets and activities you should be familiar with if you plan to take the Microsoft Office Specialist examination for Microsoft Office Access 2003. **ADV** means that the activity is demonstrated in the companion textbook *Microsoft Office 2003: Advanced Concepts and Techniques* (ISBN 0-619-20025-1 or ISBN 0-619-20026-X). Expert certification is not available for Microsoft Office Access 2003.

Table E-6 Microsoft Office Specialist Skill Sets, Activities, and Locations in Book for Microsoft Office Access 2003

SKILL SET	SKILL BEING MEASURED	SKILL DEMONSTRATED IN BOOK	SKILL EXERCISE IN BOOK
I. Structuring Databases	A. Create Access databases	AC 10	AC 56-64 (In The Lab 1, 2, 3; Cases and Places 1-5)
	B. Create and modify tables	AC 15, AC 159, AC 127-130	AC 63 (Cases and Places 3), AC 171 (Cases and Places 3), AC 167-172 (All Exercises)

Table E-6 Microsoft Office Specialist Skill Sets, Activities, and Locations in Book for Microsoft Office Access 2003

SKILL SET	SKILL BEING MEASURED	SKILL DEMONSTRATED IN BOOK	SKILL EXERCISE IN BOOK
	C. Define and modify field types	AC 130, AC 147	AC 169 (In The Lab 2 Step 5f, In The Lab 3 part 1), AC 172 (Cases and Places 5)
	D. Modify field properties	AC 127-128, AC 140, AC 141, 143, AC 142, AC 144, AC 160, **ADV**	AC 167-172 (All Exercises), **ADV**
	E. Create and modify one-to-many relationships	AC 151, AC 342	AC 171-172 (Cases and Places 1-4), **ADV**
	F. Enforce referential integrity	AC 152, **ADV**	AC 167 (Apply Your Knowledge Step 17), AC 169 (In The Lab 1 Step 13), AC 170 (In The Lab 2 Step 11), AC 170 (In The Lab 3 part 3), AC 171-172 (Cases and Places 1-4), **ADV**
	G. Create and modify queries	AC 34, AC 37, AC 104, AC 154,	AC 55 (Apply Your Knowledge Steps 3-6), AC 60 (In The Lab 2 Step 2), AC 62 (In The Lab Part 3), AC 63-64 (Cases and Places 3, 4), AC 109 (Apply Your Knowledge Step 8), AC 111 (In The Lab 2 Step 12), AC 112 (Cases and Places 5), AC 172 (Cases and Places 4), AC 171 (Cases and Places 3), AC 172 (Cases and Places 5), **ADV**
	H. Create forms	AC 38, **ADV**	AC 57 (In The Lab 1 Step 8), AC 61 (In the Lab 3 Part 1), AC 64 (Cases and Places 4), **ADV**
	I. Add and modify form controls and properties	**ADV**	**ADV**
	J. Create reports	AC 43, **ADV**	AC 55-64 (All Exercises), **ADV**
	K. Add and modify report control properties	**ADV**	**ADV**
	L. Create a data access page	**ADV**	**ADV**
II. Entering Data	A. Enter, edit and delete records	AC 23, AC 28, AC 116, AC 119, AC 125	AC 54-64 (All Exercises), AC 167-172 (All Exercises)
	B. Find and move among records	AC 27	AC 55 (Apply Your Knowledge Step 1), AC 57 (In The Lab 1 Step 9), AC 60 (In The Lab 2 Step 3), AC 62 (In The Lab 3 part 2)
	C. Import data to Access	AC 176-180	AC 191 (In The Lab 1)
III. Organizing Data	A. Create and modify calculated fields and aggregate functions	AC 96-97, AC 99-103	AC 110 (In The Lab 1 Step 11), AC 111 (In The Lab 3 part 3), AC 112 (Cases and Places 3), AC 110 (In The Lab 1 Steps 12, 13), AC 111 (In The Lab 2 Step 11, In The Lab 3 part 3), AC 112 (Cases and Places 1-4)
	B. Modify form layout	**ADV**	**ADV**
	C. Modify report layout and page setup	AC 30-31, **ADV**	AC 170 (In The Lab 3 Parts 2-3), **ADV**
	D. Format datasheets	AC 131-135	AC 171 (Cases and Places 2)
	E. Sort records	AC 86-89, AC 155, **ADV**	AC 167 (Apply Your Knowledge Step 15), AC 171-172 (Cases and Places 2, 4), **ADV**
	F. Filter records	AC 121, AC 123	AC 167 (Apply Your Knowledge Step 13), AC 169 (In The Lab 2 Step 9)
IV. Managing Databases	A. Identify object dependencies	**ADV**	**ADV**
	B. View objects and object data in other views	AC 23, AC 29-31, AC 42, **ADV**	AC 54-64 (All Exercises), AC 170 (In The Lab 3), **ADV**
	C. Print database objects and data	AC 29-31, AC 47, AC 72, **ADV**	AC 54-64 (All Exercises, AC 109-112 (All Exercises), **ADV**
	D. Export data from Access	AC 181, AC 183, AC 184, AC 185-187	AC 192 (In The Lab 2)
	E. Back up a database	AC 162-163	AC 167 (Apply Your Knowledge Step 18), AC 170 (In The Lab 2 Step 12), AC 171 (Cases and Places 1-2)
	F. Compact and repair databases	AC 163-164	AC 169 (In The Lab 1 Step 14), AC 170 (In The Lab 2 Step 12), AC 171 (Cases and Places 1-2)

Microsoft Office PowerPoint 2003

Table E-7 lists the skill sets and activities you should be familiar with if you plan to take the Microsoft Office Specialist examination for Microsoft Office PowerPoint 2003. **ADV** means that the activity is demonstrated in the companion textbook *Microsoft Office 2003: Advanced Concepts and Techniques* (ISBN 0-619-20025-1 or ISBN 0-619-20026-X). Expert certification is not available for Microsoft Office PowerPoint 2003.

Table E-7 Microsoft Office Specialist Skill Sets, Activities, and Locations in Book for Microsoft Office PowerPoint 2003

SKILL SET	SKILL BEING MEASURED	SKILL DEMONSTRATED IN BOOK	SKILL EXERCISE IN BOOK
I. Creating Content	A. Create new presentations from templates	PPT 18-43, PPT 85-11, PPT 111, **ADV**	PPT 69-71 (In the Lab 1 Steps 1-3), PPT 132-133 (In the Lab 1 Steps 1-4), **ADV**
	B. Insert and edit text-based content	PPT 20-24, PPT 31-42, PPT 53-55, PPT 56, PPT 88-94, **ADV**	PPT 69-71 (In the Lab 1 Steps 2-4), PPT 72-73 (In the Lab 2 Step 4), PPT 74-77 (In the Lab 3, Part 1 and Part 2), PPT 132-134 (In the Lab 1 Steps 2-4), **ADV**
	C. Insert tables, charts and diagrams	**ADV**	**ADV**
	D. Insert pictures, shapes and graphics	PPT 99-106, **ADV**	PPT 132-134 (In the Lab 1 Steps 2-3, 5-6), PPT 134-135 (In the Lab 2 Steps 2-5), **ADV**
	E. Insert objects	**ADV**	**ADV**
II. Formatting Content	A. Format text-based content	PPT 23-27, PPT 153-155, **ADV**	PPT 69-71 (In the Lab 1 Step 2), PPT 72-73 (In the Lab 2 Step 2), **ADV**
	B. Format pictures, shapes and graphics	PPT 108-111, PPT 116-119, **ADV**	PPT 132-134 (In the Lab 1 Steps 2-3, 5-6), PPT 134-135 (In the Lab 2 Steps 2-5, and 8), PPT 136-137 (In the Lab 3 Steps 2-5), **ADV**
	C. Format slides	PPT 17-20, PPT 85, PPT 97-99, PPT 144, **ADV**	PPT 69-71 (In the Lab 1 Step 1), PPT 131-132 (Apply Your Knowledge 1 Steps 3, 5), PPT 132-134 (In the Lab 1 Steps 3, 5, 6), PPT 134-135 (In the Lab 2 Step 1), **ADV**
	D. Apply animation schemes	PPT 114-116, **ADV**	PPT 131-132 (Apply Your Knowledge 1 Step 6), PT 136-137 (In the Lab 3 Step 7), **ADV**
	E. Apply slide transitions	**ADV**	**ADV**
	F. Customize slide templates	**ADV**	**ADV**
	G. Work with masters	PPT 112-113, **ADV**	PPT 132-134 (In the Lab 1 Step 7), PPT 134-135 (In the Lab 2 Step 6), PPT 136-137 (In the Lab 3 Step 6), **ADV**
III. Collaborating	A. Track, accept and reject changes in a presentation	**ADV**	**ADV**
	B. Add, edit and delete comments in a presentation	**ADV**	**ADV**
	C. Compare and merge presentations	**ADV**	**ADV**
IV. Managing and Delivering Presentations	A. Organize a presentation	PPT 30-31, PPT 89-97, **ADV**	PPT 69-71 (In the Lab 1 Step 3), PPT 132-134 (In the Lab 1 Steps 3-4), **ADV**
	B. Set up slide shows for delivery	**ADV**	**ADV**
	C. Rehearse timing	**ADV**	**ADV**
	D. Deliver presentations	PPT 46-50, **ADV**	PPT 74-77 (In the Lab 3 Part 1 Step 2, Part 2 Step 6), **ADV**
	E. Prepare presentations for remote delivery	**ADV**	**ADV**

Table E-7 Microsoft Office Specialist Skill Sets, Activities, and Locations in Book for Microsoft Office PowerPoint 2003

SKILL SET	SKILL BEING MEASURED	SKILL DEMONSTRATED IN BOOK	SKILL EXERCISE IN BOOK
	F. Save and publish presentations	PPT 146-149, PPT 154-157, Appendix C, **ADV**	PPT 158 (In the Lab 1 Steps 2-3, and 6), PPT 158 (In the Lab 2 Steps 2-3, and 8), PPT 159 (In the Lab 3 Steps 2-3), **ADV**
	G. Print slides, outlines, handouts, and speaker notes	PPT 56-61, PPT 122-126, **ADV**	PPT 69-71 (In the Lab 1 Step 7), PPT 72-73 (In the Lab 2 Steps 6-8), PPT 158 (In the Lab 1 Step 7), **ADV**
	H. Export a presentation to another Microsoft Office program	**ADV**	**ADV**

Microsoft Office Outlook 2003

Table E-8 lists the skill sets and activities you should be familiar with if you plan to take the Microsoft Office Specialist examination for Microsoft Office Outlook 2003. **ADV** means that the activity is demonstrated in the companion textbook *Microsoft Office 2003: Advanced Concepts and Techniques* (ISBN 0-619-20025-1 or ISBN 0-619-20026-X). Expert certification is not available for Microsoft Office Outlook 2003.

Table E-8 Microsoft Office Specialist Skill Sets, Activities, and Locations in Book for Microsoft Office Outlook 2003

SKILL SET	SKILL BEING MEASURED	SKILL DEMONSTRATED IN BOOK	SKILL EXERCISE IN BOOK
I. Messaging	A. Originate and respond to e-mail and instant messages	OUT 13-16, OUT 23-25, OUT 51-53, **ADV**	OUT 62 (In the Lab 1 Part 2 Step 1), OUT 63 (In the Lab 3 Part 2), OUT 64 (Cases and Places 3), **ADV**
	B. Attach files to items	OUT 27-29, **ADV**	OUT 62 (In the Lab 1 Part 2 Step 3), **ADV**
	C. Create and modify a personal signature for messages	OUT 19-23	OUT 63 (In the Lab 3 Part 1 and Part 3 Step 4
	D. Modify e-mail message settings and delivery options	OUT 15, OUT 29-31, OUT 34-38	OUT 62 (In the Lab 1 Part 2 Steps 2, 4-5), OUT 62 (In the Lab 2), OUT 63 (In the Lab 3 Part 2)
	E. Create and edit contacts	OUT 41-44, **ADV**	OUT 61 (Apply Your Knowledge 1), OUT 64 (Cases and Places 1-5), **ADV**
	F. Accept, decline, and delegate tasks	**ADV**	**ADV**
II. Scheduling	A. Create and modify appointments, meetings, and events	**ADV**	**ADV**
	B. Update, cancel, and respond to meeting requests	**ADV**	**ADV**
	C. Customize Calendar settings	**ADV**	**ADV**
	D. Create, modify, and assign tasks	**ADV**	**ADV**
III. Organizing	A. Create and modify distribution lists	OUT 53-56	OUT 61 (Apply Your Knowledge 1 and In the Lab 1 Part 1)
	B. Link contacts to other items	OUT 58	OUT 64 (Cases and Places 3)
	C. Create and modify notes	**ADV**	**ADV**
	D. Organize items	OUT 31-34, OUT 44-48, **ADV**	OUT 61 (Apply Your Knowledge 1), OUT 62 (In the Lab 2), OUT 64 (Cases and Places 3 and 5), **ADV**
	E. Organize items using folders	OUT 39-41, **ADV**	OUT 61 (Apply Your Knowledge 1), OUT 64 (Cases and Places 4), **ADV**
	F. Search for items	OUT 38, OUT 46-47	OUT 63 (In the Lab 3 Part 3 Step 2), OUT 64 (Cases and Places 2)

Table E-8 Microsoft Office Specialist Skill Sets, Activities, and Locations in Book for Microsoft Office Outlook 2003 *(continued)*

SKILL SET	SKILL BEING MEASURED	SKILL DEMONSTRATED IN BOOK	SKILL EXERCISE IN BOOK
	G. Save items in different file formats	OUT 56-58	OUT 62 (In the Lab 1 Part 3)
	H. Assign items to categories	OUT 47-49	OUT 64 (Cases and Places 4)
	I. Preview and print items	OUT 12, OUT 49-50, **ADV**	OUT 61-62 (Apply Your Knowledge 1, In the Lab 1 Part 1, and Part 2 Step 6), OUT 63 (In the Lab 3 Part 1, Part 2, and Part 3 Step 5), OUT 64 (Cases and Places 1-5), **ADV**

Index

Abbreviations, AutoCorrect entries for, WD 92
Absolute addressing, relative addressing versus, EX 168-170
Absolute cell reference, **EX 168**
copying formula with, EX 174-175
Access 2003, **AC 4**, WIN 80-82
Help system, AC 47-49, AC 68, AC 116
new features, AC 4-5
quitting, AC 25-26, AC 49-50
starting, AC 7-8
Access window
elements of, AC 12-15
maximizing, AC 8
new database in, AC 11
Accessories command, WIN 13
Action buttons, **INT 29**
Action query, AC 135
Active application, **PPT 11**
Active cell, **EX 11**, EX 16, EX 20
bold, EX 30
worksheet title in, EX 17
Active cell reference, in Name box, EX 16
Active document, WD 160
Active window, AC 13, **WIN 17**
Activities, tracking for contacts, OUT 58
Address Cards view, **OUT 39**, OUT 44
Address bar, WIN 18
Advanced Filter/Sort, **AC 123-125**
Aggregate function, **AC 99**
Align Left button (Excel Formatting toolbar), EX 96
Align Left button (Word Formatting toolbar), WD 37
Align Right button (Excel Formatting toolbar), EX 96
Align Right button (Word Formatting toolbar), WD 37
Alignment
cell contents, EX 96
centering, *see* Centering
date, EX 167
decimal point, WD 165
horizontal, EX 92, 96
left, WD 36, WD 37
paragraph using shortcut keys, WD 86
right, WD 36-37
rotating text, EX 151
shrink to fit, EX 157
tab stops and, WD 163
table, WD 186-187
text in table cells, WD 183
text in worksheet cell, EX 18
vertical, EX 92, EX 96
worksheet title using Format Cells dialog box, EX 92-93
See also Indentation
All Mail Folders pane, **OUT 8**, OUT 9
All Programs submenu (Start menu)
Microsoft Office, Microsoft Office Access 2003 command, AC 7-8
Microsoft Office, Microsoft Office Excel 2003 command, EX 7
Microsoft Office, Microsoft Office PowerPoint 2003 command, PPT 7
Microsoft Office, Microsoft Office Word 2003 command, WD 6, WIN 49
New Office Document command, starting Access, AC 8
New Office Document command, starting PowerPoint, PPT 8
Alternate, scrolling text behavior, **INT 20**
American Psychological Association (APA), **WD 74**, WD 75, WD 76
AND criterion, **AC 83-84**
Animate, **PPT 116**
Animated slide show
creating, PPT 114-119
running, PPT 120-121
Animation, **PPT 114**
clip art, PPT 116-119
custom, PPT 114, PPT 116-119
preset, PPT 114
See also Slide Design – Animation Schemes task pane
Animation schemes, PPT 114-116
Animation Schemes command (Slide Show menu), PPT 114
Antonym, **WD 119**
APA, *see* American Psychological Association
Append query, AC 135, **AC 139**
Application, active, PPT 11
Application programs, **WIN 6**, WIN 34-36
Applying style, WD 98
Aquatics Wear worksheet, EX 145-208
Arguments, **EX 81**
IF function, EX 171
Arithmetic operations
database, AC 16, AC 17
worksheet, EX 74
Arrange By command (Outlook shortcut menu), OUT 10
Arrange By command (Outlook View menu), OUT 31, OUT 32
Arrangement, **OUT 10**, OUT 31
Arrow keys
advancing through slide show using, PPT 48
completing entry using, EX 20
selecting cell using, EX 16
Ascending sort order
database, AC 86, AC 89
document, **WD 110**
Ashton James College database
creating and using, AC 3-52
maintaining, AC 115-164
querying using Select Query window, AC 66-107
Ask a Question box, AC 48
Aspect ratio, INT 19, PPT 108
Assumptions, **EX 146**
Asterisk (*)
multiplication and, **EX 74**
wildcard, **AC 76**
Attachment
Biometrics research paper as, WD 123
creating, OUT 27-29
paper clip icon and, OUT 10
slide show as, PPT 126-128
viewing, OUT 18-19
workbook, 125-126
Attributes, **PPT 11**
text, PPT 23-27
Audience handout, outline as, PPT 112
Auditing command (Excel Tools menu), EX 148
Auto Fill Options button, EX 26
month name series, EX 153
Auto Fill Options menu (Excel) options available on, EX 153
AutoCalculate area (status bar), **EX 14**, **EX 48**, EX 49
AutoCalculate shortcut menu, EX 48
AutoComplete tip, **WD 85**, **WD 182**
AutoContent Wizard, **PPT 6**, **PPT 142**
AutoCorrect, AC 15, EX 18, WD 89-93
creating entries, WD 90, WD 91-93
spell checking using, EX 113, WD 27
symbols, WD 106
turning off, WD 92
AutoCorrect entries, **WD 106**
AutoCorrect Options button, **WD 90-91**
AutoCorrect Options command (Excel Tools menu), smart tags, EX 78
AutoCorrect Options command (Word Tools menu), WD 92
AutoFormat As You Type, WD 156
smart tags, WD 115
spell checking, WD 27
AutoFit command (Word shortcut menu), columns, WD 185
AutoFit command (Word Table menu), columns, WD 185
AutoFit to contents, **INT 10**
Autoformat, **EX 34-36**
AutoFormat, WD 155
bulleted list, WD 187
superscript, WD 156-157
table, WD 187
worksheet, EX 34-35
AutoFormat As You Type, WD 155
AutoFormat command (Excel Format menu), EX 34-35
Automatic Layout Options button, undoing layout change using, PPT 107
Automatic page breaks, **WD 101**-102
AutoRecover feature, PPT 43
AutoSum button (Excel Standard toolbar), EX 165
determining totals using, EX 23-24, EX 27, EX 79-80
functions and, EX 84, EX 85
AutoText command (Word Insert menu), WD 179, WD 181
AutoText entry, **WD 178**-179
Average, determining using AutoCalculate area, EX 49
Average command (Excel shortcut menu), EX 49
AVERAGE function, **EX 81-82**

Back Up Database command (Access File menu), AC 162-163
Background
Blue Chip Stock Club worksheet, EX 94-95
scrolling text, **INT 22**
Background repagination, **WD 101**
Backing up (database), **AC 162**-163
backspace key
deleting bullet using, PPT 34, PPT 38
deleting characters using, EX 18, EX 50
erasing field contents using, AC 146
erasing text using, WD 58
Backup copy
database, AC 5, **AC 162**-163
document, WD 30
worksheet, **EX 44**
Bar chart, EX 187
embedding into Word document, INT 14-19
Base style, **WD 95**
Behavior, scrolling text, INT 20

Best fit (worksheet column), **EX 107**
Best fit (table column), **AC 131**
Bibliographical references, WD 104
Biometrics research paper, WD 73-126
Black and white, printing in, EX 116, EX 200, PPT 59
Black and white view, displaying presentation in, PPT 56-59
Black slide, **PPT 42-43**
Blank cell, **EX 80**
statistical functions and, EX 81
Blank characters, EX 52
Blank database option (task pane), AC 10
Blank lines, entering using enter key, WD 20, WD 23
Blue Chip Stock Club Investment Analysis worksheet, EX 65-128
Body, of research paper, WD 84
Bold, EX 29, **EX 30, WD 44**
alternatives to, EX 150
Blue Chip Stock Club worksheet, EX 92, EX 93, EX 96
column titles using Formatting toolbar, EX 96
entire worksheet, EX 150
row titles, EX 100
Bold button (Excel Formatting toolbar), EX 30
Bold button (Word Formatting toolbar), WD 44
Border, **WD 172**
bottom, *see* Bottom border
deleting, WD 173
table, INT 10-11
worksheet title, EX 95
Border button arrow (Word Formatting toolbar), letterhead, WD 172
Borders palette, EX 95
Bottom border, WD 172
column titles, EX 96
row, EX 100
Break command (Word Insert menu), WD 103
Browser, *see* Web browser
Browsing document, WD 110-112
B-tree indexes, AC 157
Build command (Access shortcut menu), AC 97
Bullet, **PPT 7, WD 154,** WD 187-189
changing, PPT 7
deleting, PPT 31, PPT 34, PPT 38
Bulleted list, **PPT 7, WD 154**
cover letter, WD 187-189
multi-level, PPT 34-42
single-level, PPT 31-34
Strategies for College Success presentation, PPT 30-42
Bullets button (PowerPoint Formatting toolbar), PPT 31
Business cards, creating with Publisher 2003, WIN 85
Business letter, components of, WD 175
Buttons
Double down arrow button, WIN 27
Minimize, Maximize, WIN 19-21
mouse, WIN 8-9

Calculated field, **AC 96-97**
Calculations, used in queries, AC 96-103
Cancel box (formula bar), EX 17, **EX 18,** EX 50
Canceling actions, WD 39. *See also* Undo
Capitalization, PPT 22
changing, AC 135
entering using caps lock key, WD 22
errors, WD 92
caps lock key, WD 22, WD 92
Caption, query results, AC 98
Cascade the delete, **AC 150**
Cascade the update, **AC 151**
Case-sensitive, **EX 44, PPT 30**
Category axis, *see* X-axis
Category names, **EX 187**
Cell (Excel worksheet), **EX 10**
active, *see* Active cell
aligning contents of, EX 96
blank, EX 80
clearing, EX 52
color, EX 105
copying format using Format Painter button, EX 154-156
copying to adjacent cells, using fill handle, EX 24-26
deleting versus clearing, EX 161
editing using formula bar, EX 51
editing using in-cell editing, EX 50
formatting, EX 28-34
formatting nonadjacent, EX 184-185
hiding, EX 109
inserting, EX 159-161
merge, *see* Merge cells
merging, centering cell entry across columns by, EX 32-33
rotating entries, EX 98
rotating text in, EX 151-152
selecting, EX 16
selecting for formula, EX 75
shrinking entries, EX 98
undoing last entry, EX 51-52
wrapping text in, EX 71
Cell (Word table), **WD 151,** WD 183
changing contents of, WD 184
Cell reference, **EX 11,** EX 16
absolute, EX 168
copying formulas and, EX 78
deleted cells and, EX 162
errors, EX 162
formulas, EX 74
inserting rows and, EX 161
mixed, EX 168
Range Finder verifying, EX 89
relative, EX 25, EX 78, EX 168
selecting cell by typing in Name box, EX 36
Cells command (Excel Format menu)
alignment, EX 33
font color, EX 32
font size, EX 31
font style, EX 30
font type, EX 29
formatting, EX 93
numbers, EX 163
shrink to fit, EX 157
Cells command (Excel Insert menu), EX 161
Center (paragraph), **WD 38,** WD 45
Center button (Excel Formatting toolbar), EX 96
Center button (Word Formatting toolbar), **WD 38,** WD 45
Centering
cell entry across columns by merging cells, EX 32-33
column titles using Formatting toolbar, EX 96
horizontal, EX 92, EX 96
paragraph containing graphic, WD 48
paragraph containing text, WD 38, WD 45
paragraph using shortcut keys, WD 86
table, WD 187
title of works cited page, WD 104
vertical, EX 92, EX 96
worksheet title using Format Cells dialog box, EX 92-93
Change Case command (PowerPoint Format menu), PPT 22
Character, **EX 107**
blank, EX 52
deleting, EX 18, EX 50
formatting, WD 31-45
inserting, EX 50
nonprinting, WD 20
shrink to fit, EX 157
special, searching for, WD 117
wildcards, AC 76-77
See also Text
Character formatting, **WD 31**
Grand Prix announcement document, WD 31-45
shortcut keys for, WD 87
Character styles, **WD 152**
Chart location, **EX 38**
Chart menu (Excel), 3-D View command, EX 195
Chart sheet, **EX 187**
Chart Wizard button (Excel Standard toolbar)
3-D clustered column chart, EX 39
3-D Pie chart, EX 188-192
Charting, PPT 4
Charts, **EX 4**
bar, EX 187
default type, EX 41
deleting, EX 52-53
embedded, EX 38-41
embedding into Word document, INT 14-19
formatting, EX 41
legend, *see* Legend
location, EX 191
moving, EX 40-41
rotating, EX 194-196
saving as dynamic Web page, EX 234-236
selected, EX 40
3-D clustered column, EX 39
3-D Pie, EX 187-197
tilting, EX 194-196
title, EX 189, EX 192
Citations
footnote, WD 93
MLA style, WD 76
Clear command (Excel Edit menu), EX 52
Clear Grid command (Access Edit menu), AC 70, AC 75, AC 86, AC 103, AC 138
Clearing
design grid, AC 70, AC 75, AC 86, AC 103, AC 138
entire worksheet, EX 52-53
formatting, WD 173
Clearing cells or ranges, EX 52
deleting versus, EX 161
Click and Type, **WD 82-83**
Clip art, PPT 99, WD 45
adding using content placeholder, 100-103
adding using Drawing toolbar, PPT 100, PPT 104-105
animation, PPT 116-119
inserting in Grand Prix announcement document, WD 45-51
moving, PPT 108
Nutrition and Fitness presentation, PPT 99-105
searching, PPT 100, PPT 101, PPT 105, WD 47
size of, PPT 108-110
on Web, WD 48

Clip Art task pane, WD 47-48
Clip Organizer, **WD 45**
Clipboard, **WD 112**
Office, *see* Office Clipboard
Windows, *see* Windows Clipboard
Clipboard task pane, WD 168-169
Clips, **PPT 84**
Close button (Excel title bar), EX 46
Close button (PowerPoint title bar), PPT 50-51, PPT 64
Close button (Word title bar), WD 54, WD 59, WD 62
Close command (Word File menu), WD 59
Close the Language bar command (shortcut menu), WD 8
Closed (Language bar), **EX 15, PPT 16, WD 16**
Closed envelope icon, **OUT 10**
Closing
database, AC 25-26, AC 47
document and not saving, WD 59
e-mail, OUT 12-13
expanded folders, 60-61
form, AC 39
Getting Started task pane, WD 8
Help and Support Center, WIN 72
Language bar, AC 9, EX 9, PPT 8, PPT 9, PPT 16, PPT 17, WD 8, WD 16
note pane, WD 99
query, AC 73
table, AC 21-22, AC 25-26
task pane, EX 9
windows, WIN 23-24, WIN 31-32
Closing slide, **PPT 93**
clip art on, PPT 110-111
creating on Outline tab, PPT 93-94
Collapsing areas, WIN 30-31
Collect, **WD 165**
Color
cells, EX 105
choosing for worksheet, EX 91
font, *see* Font color
gridline, AC 134
sheet tab, EX 198
slices in pie chart, EX 193
See also Slide Design – Color Schemes task pane
Color printer, black and white printing on, PPT 59
Color/Grayscale button (PowerPoint Standard toolbar), PPT 56, PPT 57, PPT 58
Color/Grayscale command (PowerPoint View menu), black and white printing, PPT 59
Column boundary, **WD 186**
Column command (Excel Format menu), width, EX 109
Column heading, **EX 10**
active cell, EX 16
Column number, displayed on status bar, WD 11
Column titles
Blue Chip Stock Club worksheet, EX 70-71
Blue Chip Stock Club worksheet, EX 96
bottom border, EX 96
centering using Formatting toolbar, EX 96
entering, EX 19-20
freezing, EX 163-164
Column width
Aquatics Wear worksheet, EX 155-156
best fit, EX 107
Blue Chip Stock Club worksheet, EX 107-109
increasing after entering values, EX 107-109
increasing before entering values, EX 155-156
text and, EX 18
Column Width command (Access Format menu), AC 133
Column Width command (Excel shortcut menu), EX 109
Columns (Access table)
best fit, AC 131
fields imported and, AC 174, AC 177
resizing, AC 131
Columns (Excel worksheet)
deleting, EX 161
hidden, EX 109, EX 110
inserting, EX 161
number of, EX 10
summing, EX 23-24, EX 27
titles, EX 16
Columns (Word table), INT 10, WD 150, WD 182
AutoFit, INT 10
adding, WD 185
resizing, WD 185-186
Columns, database, *see* Field
Columns command (Excel Insert menu), EX 161
Comb Horizontal slide transition effect, PPT 120
Comma Style button (Excel Formatting toolbar), EX 99
Comma style format, **EX 98**
Command-line switch, starting Excel using, EX 70
dimmed, AC 13, EX 12, PPT 15, WD 13
hidden, AC 13, EX 12-13, PPT 15, WD 13
redoing, WD 39
smart tag, WD 116
speaking, *see* Office Speech Recognition software
toggle, EX 175
undoing, WD 39, WD 58
Commands
Delete, WIN 59
on Start menu, WIN 14
Compact (database), **AC 163-164**
Comparing workbooks, EX 4
Comparison operator
database, **AC 82-83**
worksheet, EX 171
Complimentary close, **WD 175**, 189
Compound criterion, **AC 83-85**
Computer
logging off, turning off, WIN 72-75
logging on, WIN 9-10
software, hardware, WIN 6
Condition, **EX 104**
Conditional formatting, **EX 103**-106
Conditional Formatting command (Excel Format menu), EX 104
Confirm Delete dialog box, WIN 33, WIN 60
Constant, replacing formula with, EX 173
Contact Index, **OUT 44**
Contact list, **OUT 38**
addressing e-mail message using, OUT 51-53
creating, OUT 41-44
previewing, OUT 49-50
printing, OUT 49-50
saving as text file, OUT 56-57
sorting, OUT 44-45
Contacts, **OUT 38-58**
displaying. OUT 49
finding, OUT 46-47
organizing, OUT 47-48
tracking activities for, OUT 58
Contacts button (Navigation pane), OUT 40
Contacts component, **OUT 38**
Content Layouts (Slide Layout task pane), PPT 97
Content placeholder, adding clip art using, PPT 100-103
Context-sensitive menu, WD 12
Control-menu icon, AC 12
Control Panel, WIN 8
Copy area, *see* Source area
Copy button (Excel Standard toolbar)
formats, EX 155
Office Clipboard, EX 157-158
Copy command (Excel Edit menu)
cell, EX 26
functions, EX 88
Office Clipboard and, EX 157, EX 158
Copying
cell format using Format Painter button, EX 154-156
cell to adjacent cells using fill handle, EX 24-26
cells between workbooks, EX 157
chart to Word document, INT 15
copy and paste used in, EX 157-158
cut and paste used in, EX 159
database to other applications, AC 181-187
drag and drop used in, EX 159
files in Windows Explorer, WIN 55-56
formulas using fill handle, EX 77-78
formulas with absolute cell references, EX 174-175
functions using fill handle, EX 87-88
moving versus, EX 159
Office Clipboard and, WD 165-171
range, EX 26
range to nonadjacent destination area, EX 157-158
text as hyperlink, INT 11
text from Research task pane, WD 125
Copyright, clip art and, PPT 108
Corporate style report, AC 45
Correcting errors
AutoCorrect and, AC 15, WD 89-93
debugging, EX 119
document, WD 18, WD 56-59
e-mail messages, OUT 25
formulas, EX 77, EX 90, EX 113, EX 148
presentation, PPT 22, PPT 56
queries, AC 75
records, AC 25
spelling, *see* Spell checking
table structure, AC 21
Trace Error, EX 79
worksheet, EX 18, EX 50-53
Cover letter, **WD 138**, WD 139
creating, WD 175-190
elements of, WD 140, WD 175
envelopes for, WD 190-191
letterhead for, WD 160-175
Create button (File New Database dialog box), AC 11
Criteria, AC 37, AC 75-80
calculating statistics and, AC 101-102
compound, AC 83-85
filtering and, AC 123-125
Criterion, **AC 37**
Crosstab query, **AC 104-106**
CTRL key, selecting nonadjacent ranges using, EX 177
CTRL+clicking, hyperlink and, **WD 107**
CTRL+enter, manual page break using, **WD 103**

CTRL+home, **WD 33**
Currency field, AC 17, AC 20
Currency style
with floating dollar sign, EX 177
using Format Cells command, EX 100-101
using Formatting toolbar, **EX 98**
Current date, WD 177
Custom animation, **PPT 114,** PPT 116-117
Custom Animation command (PowerPoint shortcut menu), PPT 117
Custom Animation command (Slide Show menu), PPT 119
Custom Animation dialog box, animating clip art using, PPT 116
Custom dictionary, **PPT 53**
Custom show, **PPT 157**
Custom tab stop, **WD 164,** WD 176-177
Cut button (Excel Standard toolbar), EX 50, EX 52, EX 159
Cut button (Word Standard toolbar), WD 114
Cut command (Word Edit menu), WD 59, WD 114
Cutting, **WD 112**

Data
importing using Web query, EX 120-123
refreshing external, EX 123
validation rules, AC 139-146
Data access page, **INT 30-38**
Data entry, AC 4
Data labels
formatting, EX 192, EX 197
leader lines with, EX 197
3-D Pie chart, EX 190, EX 197
Data menu (Excel), Import External Data command, EX 121
Data redundancy, AC 50-51
Data series, **EX 187**
Data type, **AC 16**
changing, AC 130
Database, AC 5, **WIN 80**
Ashton James College, AC 3-52, AC 115-164
backing up, AC 162-163
closing, AC 25-26, AC 47
compacting, AC 163-164
copying to other applications, AC 181-187
creating using New button, AC 10, AC 32-33
data access page from, INT 30-38
designing, AC 50-51
exporting query to Word document, AC 175, AC 182-183
file, AC 10
form, *see* Form
importing worksheet into, AC 176-180
live, AC 162
maintaining, AC 114-164
opening, AC 26-27, AC 68
queries, *see* Queries
recovery, AC 162-163
repairing, AC 163-164
restructuring, AC 114
sorting, AC 5
updates, *see* Updating
worksheet conversion, AC 173-182
Database design, **AC 50-51**
Database management system (DBMS), AC 4, **AC 5**
file system versus, AC 91
Database Utilities command (Access Tools menu), Compact and Repair Database, AC 164
Database window, **AC 13**
Datasheet, **AC 22**
changing appearance of, AC 131-135
Print Preview, AC 135
sub-, AC 153-154
Datasheet view, **AC 22**
switching between Form view and, AC 41-42, AC 119-120
Datasheet View command (Access View menu), AC 120
Date
current, WD 177
formatting, EX 96-97
in outline, PPT 112
system, EX 165-167
Date and Time command (Word Insert menu), WD 177
Date line, **WD 175,** WD 176-177
Date stamp, **EX 165**
DBMS, *see* Database management system
Debugging, **EX 118**
Decimal places
date, EX 167
decreasing, EX 100
increasing, EX 99-100, 102-103
Decimal point, alignment on, WD 165
Decision making, EX 170
Decrease Decimal button (Excel Formatting toolbar), EX 100
Decrease Font Size button (PowerPoint Formatting toolbar), PPT 27
Decrease Indent button (Excel Formatting toolbar), EX 156
Decrease Indent button (PowerPoint Formatting toolbar), PPT 34, PPT 37, PPT 40-41
Default (font), **WD 16**
Default chart type, **EX 41**
Default Design (template), **PPT 17**
Default setting, **PPT 11**
Default value, **AC 139,** AC 149-142
Delete, cascade the, AC 150
Delete button (Outlook Standard toolbar), OUT 17
Delete command (Excel Edit menu), EX 161-162
DELETE key
clearing cell entries using, EX 52
deleting characters using, EX 50, WD 58, WD 59
deleting record using, AC 25, AC 41
Delete query, AC 135, **AC 137-138,** AC 139
Delete Query command (Query menu), AC 139
Delete the records, **AC 125-126**
Deleted Items folder, **OUT 8,** OUT 17
Deleting
border, WD 173
bullets, PPT 31, PPT 34, PPT 38
characters, EX 18, EX 50
chart, EX 52-53
columns, EX 161
desktop icons, WIN 32-33
files in Windows Explorer, WIN 59-61
drop shadow, EX 186
e-mail, OUT 16-18
field, AC 21, AC 130
fields in query, AC 70
filter, AC 122
formatting, EX 52
note, WD 99
range, EX 162
records, AC 25, AC 41, AC 125-126
referential integrity and, AC 150-153
rows, EX 161-162
toolbar button, EX 91
Deleting cells
clearing cells versus, EX 161
formulas and, EX 162
Deleting text
from PowerPoint presentation, PPT 56
from Word document, WD 56, WD 58-59
Demote button (Outlining toolbar), PPT 88-89, PPT 90, PPT 91
Descending sort order
database, AC 89
document, **WD 110**
Description, field, AC 16
Design grid, **AC 69,** AC 70
clearing, AC 70, AC 75, AC 86, AC 103
Design mode, **INT 22**
Design Mode button (Web Tools toolbar), INT 22
Design template, **PPT 17**
choosing, PPT 17-20
Design view
creating table in, AC 18, AC 33
database structure and, AC 126-130
query in, AC 36, AC 37, AC 69
Design View command (Access View menu), query, AC 73
Desktop, **WIN 10,** WIN 15-17
Destination area, **EX 25,** EX 88
copying range to nonadjacent, EX 157-158
Destination document, **INT 14,** INT 17
Destination files, folders, **WIN 55**
Detail lines, **AC 42**
Details area, My Documents window, WIN 25, WIN 30-31
Dialog boxes
option buttons in, AC 31
use described, WIN 33
Diamond animation effect, PPT 116-119
Dictating, AC 8, AC 9, PPT 8, PPT 16, WD 7, WD 16
Dictionary
custom, EX 111, PPT 53, WD 121
main, WD 19, WD 25, WD 121
Digital camera, WD 45
Dimension, of table, **WD 182**
Dimmed command, AC 13, EX 12, PPT 15, WD 13
Direction, scrolling text, **INT 22**
Directories in Windows Explorer, WIN 38
Disks, removable, *see* Removable media
Displaying
Clipboard task pane, WD 168-169
contacts, OUT 49
drive, folder contents, WIN 47, WIN 56-57
Drawing toolbar, EX 181-182
formatting marks, WD 20-21
Getting Started task pane, WD 10
header area, WD 81-82
help topics, WIN 69-70
hidden columns, EX 109
hidden rows, EX 111
Language bar, EX 15
menu, WD 12-13
Outlining toolbar, PPT 86-87
presentation in black and white, PPT 56-59
slide, PPT 44
smart tags, WD 115
Start menu, WIN 11-13
system date, EX 165-167

toolbar buttons on two rows, PPT 8, PPT 9, WD 9, WD 14
toolbars, PPT 16
Distribution list, **OUT 53-56**
.doc extension, **WD 28**
Dock, **WD 82**
Docked toolbar, EX 182, **WD 14,** WD 82
Docking task pane title bar, WD 7
Document (Word)
active, WD 160
Biometrics research paper, WD 73-126
browsing, WD 110-112
changes made to, WD 56-59
clip art in, *see* Clip art
closing but not saving, WD 59
destination, INT 14
embedding Excel chart into, INT 14-19
entering text, WD 16-27, WIN 50
formatting, *see* Formatting
going to specific location in, WD 110-112
Grand Prix announcement, WD 3-62
hyperlinks in integrated, INT 8-14
importing query from database using drag-and-drop, AC 175, AC 182-183
inserting table, INT 9-10
multiple open, WD 160
opening existing, WD 55-56
saving as Web page, WD 203
saving existing, WD 51-52
saving new, WD 28-31, WIN 51-54
scrolling, WD 23-25, WD 43
scrolling text added to, INT 19-23
source, INT 17
statistics about, WD 101
zooming, WD 21
Document name, on title bar, WD 30
Document summary, **WD 193-194**
Document window, **WD 10-12**
scrolling, WD 23-25
Dollar sign
fixed, EX 98, EX 102
floating, EX 98, EX 100-102, EX 177
DOS path, WIN 40
Double-click, WIN 17-18
Double down arrow button, WIN 27
Double-space, **WD 79-80**
footnote, WD 96, WD 97
Downloading files, folders, 44-45
Drafts folder, **OUT 8**
averaging range of numbers using, EX 81
column width changed using, EX 107-109
moving clip art using, PPT 108
ranges, EX 161
row height changed using, EX 110
Drag and drop, **EX 159, PPT 88**
exporting query to Word document using, AC 175, AC 182-183
moving windows, WIN 26
right-dragging, WIN 32
sizing windows, WIN 29-30
Drag-and-drop editing, **WD 112**-114
Draw Table feature, WD 183
Drawing, PPT 4
Drawing button (Excel Standard toolbar), EX 181-182
Drawing toolbar (Excel), **EX 181**
displaying, EX 181-182
docking, EX 182-183
hiding, EX 187
Drawing toolbar (PowerPoint), **PPT 15**
adding clip art using, PPT 100, PPT 104-105
Drives
copying between, WIN 55
creating folders on removable, WIN 43
drive icons, WIN 19
expanding, WIN 45-46
network, WIN 40-41
pathways to, WIN 40
Drop shadow, EX 183-184
deleting, EX 186
DTP, *see* Desktop publishing program
Duplicate records, AC 154
indexes and, AC 160
Dynamic Web page, **EX 226,** EX 234-238, WIN 79
modifying worksheet on, EX 237-238
saving chart as, EX 234-236
viewing and manipulating, EX 236-237

Edit menu (Access)
Clear Grid command, AC 70, AC 75, AC 86, AC 103, AC 138
Find command, AC 118
Edit menu (Excel)
Clear command, EX 52
Copy command, cells, EX 26
Copy command, functions, EX 88
Copy command, Office Clipboard, EX 157, EX 158
Delete command, EX 161-162
Paste command, cells, EX 26
Paste command, functions, EX 88
Paste command, Office Clipboard, EX 157, EX 158
Paste Special command, formats, EX 155
Redo command, EX 52
Undo command, EX 51
Undo Paste command, EX 158
Edit menu (Word)
Cut command, WD 59, WD 114
Go To command, WD 111
Office Clipboard command, WD 166-167
Paste command, WD 114
Paste command, Clipboard task pane, WD 171
Paste Special command, Excel chart, INT 15-16
Repeat command, WD 39
Replace command, WD 117
Undo command, WD 39
Edit mode, **EX 50-51**
Editing
cell contents, WD 184
drag-and-drop, PPT 88, WD 112-114
hyperlink, 213
in-cell, EX 50-51
note, WD 99
presentation, PPT 56
using formula bar, EX 51
Web page through browser, PPT 151-153
Electronic mail, *see* E-mail
E-mail (electronic mail), **EX 125, OUT 6**-38, PPT 6
attachment, *see* Attachment
Biometrics research paper, WD 123
closing, OUT 12-13
composing, OUT 23-25
contact list used to address, OUT 51-53
deleting, OUT 16-18
distribution list, OUT 53-56
flagging, OUT 29-31
formatting, OUT 15, OUT 19, OUT 23, OUT 26-27
forwarding, OUT 15-16
message importance, OUT 34-38
message sensitivity, OUT 34-38
opening, OUT 11
printing, OUT 12
reading, OUT 11
replying to, OUT 13-14
report, AC 175, AC 184
rules, OUT 34
sending, OUT 29
slide show, PPT 126-128
sorting, OUT 31-32
spam filters, OUT 15, OUT 29
view filter, OUT 32-34
workbook attachment, EX 125-126
E-mail (as Attachment) button (PowerPoint Standard toolbar), PPT 127
E-mail address
formatting as hyperlink, WD 206-207
links to, INT 12, INT 13, INT 14
removing hyperlink, WD 174
E-mail button (Excel Standard toolbar), EX 126
E-mail button (Word Standard toolbar), WD 123
E-mail signature, **OUT 19**-23
E-Mail toolbar, **OUT 15**
Embedded chart, **EX 38**-41, INT 14-19
En dash, WD 158
End mark, **WD 11**
line spacing and, WD 80
End Show command (Popup menu), PPT 49-50
Endnote, **WD 93,** WD 94
End-of-cell mark, **WD 151,** WD 183
Enter box, EX 17, **EX 18,** EX 20
ENTER key
AutoComplete tip and, WD 85, WD 182
blank lines, WD 20, WD 23
bulleted list and, WD 154, WD 188
completing entry by pressing, EX 18, EX 20
creating new bullet using, PPT 38
creating new line using, PPT 23
creating new paragraph using, PPT 33, PPT 34, WD 18, WD 21
displaying formatting marks and, WD 20
hyperlink and, WD 108
paragraph formatting and, WD 89
paragraph in cell using, WD 183
paste operation and, EX 159
Enter mode, **EX 14**
Entry-level resume, WD 144
Envelopes, WD 190-191
Equal sign (=), **EX 74**
Error Checking command (Excel Tools menu), EX 90, EX 113, EX 148
Error messages, formulas and, EX 175
Errors, *see* Correcting errors
ESC key, removing record using, AC 25, AC 146
Excel 2003, **EX 4**-55, WIN 78-79
Help system, EX 9, EX 53-54
new features, EX 4, EX 6
quitting, EX 46, EX 54
starting, EX 6-8, EX 47
starting using command-line switch, EX 70
tips and tricks, EX 53
Excel window
customizing, EX 8-9
splitting into panes, EX 202-204
Exit command (Excel File menu), EX 46
Exit command (PowerPoint File menu), PPT 51
Exit command (Word File menu), WD 54
Expand and Collapse indicators, **INT 38**

Expand/Collapse Outline button, PPT 150
Expanding
areas in My Documents window, WIN 26-27
drives in My Documents window, WIN 45-46
Explorer, *see* Windows Explorer
Exploded Pie chart, **EX 187,** EX 194
Export command (Access File menu), query to Word document, AC 175
Export command (Access shortcut menu)
database to worksheet, AC 181
snapshot of report, AC 184
XML data, AC 186
Exporting
database to other applications, AC 181-187
query to Word document using drag-and-drop, AC 175, AC 182-183
records, AC 181
to Windows SharePoint Services list, AC 5
XML data, AC 185-186
Expression Builder, AC 96
Extensible Markup Language, *see* XML
External Data toolbar, EX 123
Extreme Blading Second Quarter Sales worksheet, EX 3-55

F3 key (AutoText entry), WD 181
F4 key (absolute cell reference), EX 169
F6 key (moving between panes), AC 18, AC 19
Fast saves, **PPT 111**
Favorite Folders pane, **OUT 8**
Field, **AC 6**
adding to database, AC 128-129
adding to query, AC 35
calculated, AC 96-97
correcting, AC 25
data access page, INT 32
defining, AC 18-20
deleting, AC 21, AC 130
description, AC 16
format, AC 143-144
including all, in query, AC 74
index key, AC 157-158
inserting, AC 21
lookup, AC 146-150
moving, AC 130
in multiple tables, AC 6
ordering records on multiple, AC 156
queries, AC 69-71
report, AC 42, AC 44
selecting, AC 18, AC 21
size of, AC 20, AC 127-128
updating contents of, AC 119, AC 130
validation rules, AC 139-140
worksheet columns, AC 174, AC 177
Field name, **AC 15,** AC 16, AC 18, AC 19
Field selector, **AC 131**
ordering records and, AC 156
File, EX 42, WD 28
database, AC 10
deleting in Windows Explorer, WIN 59-61
finding, WIN 61-66
moving, copying, WIN 55-56
naming, WIN 43
opening database, AC 27
RTF (Rich Text Format), PPT 87
File attachment, *see* Attachment
File formats, EX 44, EX 89, OUT 56-58, PPT 105-106, PPT 149, WD 30
File management tools, EX 232, PPT 149
File menu (Access)
Back Up Database command, AC 162-163
Export command, query to Word document, AC 175
Get External Data command, AC 179
Open command. database, AC 26
Save command, database, AC 22
Save command, query, AC 80
File menu (Excel)
Exit command, EX 46
Page Setup command, black and white printing, EX 116
Page Setup command, print scaling, EX 120
Print Area command, EX 117
Print command, worksheet, EX 45
Print Preview command, EX 115
Save As command, EX 43
Save as Web Page command, EX 231, EX 234-235
Send To command, e-mail, EX 125-126
Web Page Preview command, EX 228-229
File menu (PowerPoint)
Exit command, PPT 51
Open command, PPT 52
Print command, outlines, PPT 122
Print command, slides, PPT 61
Print Preview command, outline, PPT 124
Save As command, PPT 29
Save as Web Page command, PPT 147
Web Page Preview command, INT 28, PPT 143, PPT 144
File menu (Word)
Close command, WD 59
Exit command, WD 54
file names on, WD 55
New command, Resume Wizard, WD 142
Page Setup command, margins, WD 78
Print command, WD 13, WD 53
Print Preview command, WD 159
Properties command, document summary, WD 193
Properties command, statistics, WD 101
Save As command, WD 30
Save as Web Page command, WD 205
Send To command, WD 123
Web Page Preview command, INT 24, WD 209
File name (Access), AC 10-11
File name (Excel)
saving workbook with new, EX 42, EX 43
saving workbook with same, EX 88-90
File name (PowerPoint)
saving presentation with new, PPT 27-30
saving presentation with same, PPT 43-44
File name (Word), **WD 28**
on File menu, WD 55
saving existing document with new, WD 52
saving existing document with same, WD 51-52
File New Database dialog box, AC 10-11
File properties, **WD 193-194**
File systems, database management systems versus, AC 91
File Transfer Protocol, *see* FTP
Fill color
font, EX 94-95
slices in pie chart, EX 193
Fill Color button, EX 180
Fill handle, **EX 25**
clearing cell entries using, EX 52
copying cell to adjacent cells using, EX 24-26
copying formulas using, EX 77-78
copying formulas with absolute cell references using, EX 174
copying functions using, EX 87-88
creating series of month names, EX 152-153
Filter, **AC 120-125**
removing, AC 122
Filter By Form, **AC 122-123**
Filter By Selection, **AC 121-122**
Filter command (Records menu), AC 123, AC 124
Filtered Web Page format, **WD 206**
Find and Replace dialog box, WD 116
Find button (Form View toolbar), AC 117, AC 118
Find command (Access Edit menu), AC 118
Find Duplicates Query Wizard, **AC 154**
Find option, contacts and, **OUT 38**
Find Unmatched Query Wizard, **AC 154**
Finding files, folders, WIN 61-66
First-line indent, **WD 87,** WD 88
footnote, WD 96, WD 98
First Line Indent marker, **WD 87,** WD 88
centering and, WD 104
Fixed dollar sign, **EX 98,** EX 102
Flag icon, **OUT 10**
Flag Status column, **OUT 29**
Flagged word, WD 26, WD 27, WD 119
Flagging e-mail, OUT 29-31
Float animation effect, PPT 115
Floating dollar sign, **EX 98,** EX 100-102, EX 177
Floating task pane title bar, WD 7
Floating toolbar, **EX 182, WD 14,** WD 82
Folder, **WD 29, WIN 14**
closed, expanded, 60-61
e-mail, OUT 8
expanding, WIN 46-47
finding, WIN 61-66
moving, copying, WIN 55
naming, WIN 43
pathways to, WIN 40
saving documents in, WIN 51-54
verifying contents of, WIN 54
Web, EX 228
in Windows Explorer, WIN 38
Folder bar, *see* Folders pane
Font, **WD 16**
Blue Chip Stock Club worksheet, EX 91-94
choosing, PPT 13
datasheet, AC 133
formatting marks, WD 41
variable character, WD 27
Font box arrow (Excel Formatting toolbar), EX 29
Font box arrow (Word Formatting toolbar), WD 36
Font color, **EX 28**
worksheet, EX 31-32, EX 94-95
letterhead, WD 161
Font command (PowerPoint Format menu), font size, PPT 26
Font command (Word Format menu)
bold, WD 44
font size, WD 17, WD 35
font style, WD 35
hidden text, WD 20
italics, WD 41
underline, WD 42
Font size, **EX 28, WD 16-17**
Blue Chip Stock Club worksheet, EX 92, EX 93
e-mail, **OUT 26**
Extreme Blading Second Quarter Sales worksheet, EX 30-31
footnote, WD 96, WD 97

Grand Prix announcement, WD 34-35
letterhead, WD 161, WD 162
Strategies for College Success presentation, PPT 25-27
Font Size box, **PPT 26**
Font Size box arrow (Excel Formatting toolbar), EX 31
Font Size box arrow (PowerPoint Formatting toolbar), PPT 26
Font Size box arrow (Word Formatting toolbar), WD 17, WD 34
Font style, **EX 28**
Grand Prix announcement, WD 36
Strategies for College Success presentation, PPT 24
Font type, **EX 28**
Footer, PPT 112, WD 81, WD 84
Footnote, **WD 93**-95
deleting, WD 99
editing, WD 99
formatting, WD 95-99
For Follow Up, **OUT 38**
Foreign key, **AC 150**
key index and, AC 159
Forms, AC 4
adding records using, AC 116-117
based on query, AC 81
closing, AC 39
creating, AC 38-39
name, AC 39
opening saved, AC 40
saving, AC 39
using, AC 41
viewing data using, AC 38-41
Form view, AC 38, AC 116
creating form, AC 38-39
deleting record in, AC 126
switching between Datasheet view and, AC 41-42
switching to Datasheet view from, AC 119-120
updating records using, AC 116
Format (database), **AC 143**-144
Format (e-mail), **OUT 23**
Format (worksheet), **EX 28**
Format Cells command (Excel shortcut menu)
date, EX 97, EX 167
formatting numbers using, EX 100-102
Format Cells dialog box
centering worksheet title using, EX 92-93
rotating text, EX 151-152
Format menu (Access), Column Width command, AC 133
Format menu (Excel)
AutoFormat command, EX 34-35
Cells command, alignment, EX 33
Cells command, font color, EX 32
Cells command, font size, EX 31
Cells command, font style, EX 30
Cells command, font type, EX 29
Cells command, formatting, EX 93
Cells command, numbers, EX 163
Cells command, shrink to fit, EX 157
Column command, width, EX 109
Conditional Formatting command, EX 104
Format menu (PowerPoint)
Change Case command, PPT 22
Font command, font size, PPT 26
Font command, font style, PPT 25
Picture command, size, PPT 110
Slide Design command, PPT 20
Slide Layout command, PPT 31, PPT 98
Format menu (Word)
Font command, bold, WD 44
Font command, font size, WD 17
Font command, font size, WD 35
Font command, font style, WD 35
Font command, hidden text, WD 20
Font command, italics, WD 41
Font command, underline, WD 42
Frames command, WD 210
Object command, size, INT 17
Paragraph command, alignment, WD 37
Paragraph command, centering, WD 38
Paragraph command, hanging indent, WD 105
Paragraph command, indents, WD 89
Paragraph command, line spacing, WD 80
Tabs command, WD 164, WD 176
Theme command, WD 208, WD 211
Format Object dialog box, Excel chart, INT 16-19
Format Painter button (Excel Standard toolbar), EX 107, EX 154-156
Format Picture button (Word Picture toolbar), WD 51
Format Picture command (PowerPoint shortcut menu) clip art, PPT 109
Format Picture dialog box, resizing graphic using, PPT 108-110, WD 162-163
Format symbol, **AC 143, EX 162**-163
Formatting
Aquatics Wear worksheet, EX 177-187
AutoFormat As You Type, WD 155-157
Biometrics research paper, WD 77-89
Blue Chip Stock Club worksheet, EX 90-11
characters, WD 31-45
chart, EX 41
chart title, EX 192
clearing, WD 173
column titles, EX 96
conditional, EX 103-106
data labels, EX 192, EX 197
datasheet, AC 133-134
date, EX 96-97, EX 165, EX 167
deleting, EX 52
e-mail, OUT 15, OUT 19, OUT 23, OUT 26-27
e-mail address as hyperlink, WD 206-207
footnote, WD 95-99
Grand Prix announcement document, WD 31-45
inserted row and, EX 161
letterhead, WD 161
line, WD 40
multiple paragraphs, WD 33-35
negative numbers, EX 180
numbers, EX 177
numbers as they are entered, EX 100
numbers using Format Cells command, EX 100-102
numbers using Formatting toolbar, EX 98-100
object, INT 16-19
painting, EX 107, EX 154-156
paragraph, WD 31-45
query, AC 98
scrolling text, INT 20
searching for, WD 117
shortcut keys for, WD 85-87
style, *see* Style
styles and, WD 151-152
table, WD 186-187
themes and, WD 207-208
using autoformat, EX 34-36
using Formatting toolbar, EX 28-34
using shortcut keys, WD 85-87
Web page, WD 206-207
worksheet, EX 72
worksheet subtitle, EX 33-34
Formatting mark, **WD 20**
displaying, WD 20-21
fonts, WD 41
Formatting toolbar
Excel, EX 13-14, EX 28-34, EX 98-100
PowerPoint, **PPT 15,** PPT 24-27
Word, **WD 14,** WD 34-45
Formula, **EX 73**
absolute cell reference, EX 168-170
Blue Chip Stock Club worksheet, EX 72-80
changing to number, EX 77
checking, EX 90, EX 148
copying, with absolute cell references, EX 174-175
copying using fill handle, EX 77-78
correcting errors, EX 77, EX 113
deleted cells and, EX 162
entering using keyboard, EX 73-74
entering using Point mode, EX 75-77
equal sign (=) and, EX 74
error messages, EX 175
inserting rows and, EX 161
order of operations, EX 74-75
replacing with constant, EX 173
values versus, EX 118
verifying using Range Finder, EX 89-90
Formula Auditing toolbar, EX 118
Formula bar, **EX 14**
editing cell using, EX 51
Formula Palette, EX 82
Formulas version, **EX 118**
displaying, EX 118
printing, EX 119
Forward button (Outlook Standard toolbar), OUT 16
Forwarding e-mail, OUT 15-16
Frame, **WD 203**-204
properties, WD 214
Frames command (Word Format menu), WD 210
Frames page, **WD 203**
creating, WD 209-210
resizing, WD 211
Freeze Panes command (Excel Window menu), EX 163-164
Freeze the titles, **EX 163**
FrontPage 2003, WIN 86-87
FTP (File Transfer Protocol), **PPT 141,** PPT 149
FTP locations, EX 228, EX 232, WD 204
Full menu, **AC 12, EX 12, PPT 14, WD 12**-13
Full Screen command (Excel View menu), viewing area, EX 11
Function, **EX 81**
aggregate, AC 99
arguments, EX 81
AVERAGE, EX 81-82
copying using fill handle, EX 87-88
IF, EX 170-172
MAX, EX 82-84
MIN, EX 84-87
NOW, EX 165-167
ROUND, EX 100
Function command (Excel Insert menu), EX 24, EX 84, EX 86, EX 167

General format, date, EX 167
Get External Data command (Access File menu), AC 179
Getting Started task pane, EX 8, AC 8, PPT 8
closing, WD 8
displaying, WD 10
hiding, WD 141
Go To command (Word Edit menu), WD 111
Go to Slide command (Popup menu), PPT 49
Goal Seek command (Excel Tools menu), EX 206-207
Goal seeking, **EX 206**-208
Grammar checking, WD 19, WD 25, WD 119-120
Grand Prix announcement document, WD 3-62
Graphical user interface (GUI), **WIN 7**
Graphics, **WD 45**
centering paragraph containing, WD 48
inserting in letterhead, WD 162
line spacing and, WD 80
position of, WD 49
resizing, WD 49-51
restoring size, WD 51
selecting, WD 49
Grayscale View toolbar, PPT 58
Gridlines
database, AC 134
document, **WD 151**
worksheet, **EX 11**
Group of words, selecting, WD 43-44
Grouping, **AC 102**-103
report, AC 44-45
Grouping levels, data access page, **INT 32**, INT 33
GUI, *see* Graphical user interface

Handout
outline as, PPT 112
printing, PPT 125, PPT 156
Handwritten input, WD 4
Hanging indent, **WD 104**-105
Hanging Indent marker, **WD 104**-105
Hard copy, EX 44, PPT 59, WD 53
Hard page break, *see* Manual page break
Header
message, OUT 10, OUT 11
presentation, **PPT 112**-113
Header (Word document), **WD 81**
page number in, WD 81-82, WD 83-84
viewing, WD 102
Header and Footer command (Word View menu), WD 81-82, WD 102
Header and Footer dialog box, Notes and Handouts sheet, PPT 112
Header and Footer toolbar, WD 82, WD 83-84
Header area, displaying, WD 81-82
Headings, resume, WD 147
Height, clip art, PPT 110
Help and Support Center, WIN 66-72, WIN 94-95
Help system
Access, AC 47-49, AC 68, AC 116
Excel, EX 9, EX 53-54
Microsoft Office 2003, WIN 89
PowerPoint, PPT 62-64
Windows XP, WIN 68-69
Word, WD 14, **WD 60**-62
Hidden (Language bar), AC 9, EX 15, PPT 16, WD 16
Hidden columns, EX 109, EX 110
Hidden command, AC 13, EX 12-13, PPT 15, WD 13
Hidden rows, EX 111
Hidden text, WD 20
Hidden toolbar buttons, WD 14
Hide White Space button, WD 149
Hiding
cells, **EX 109**
Drawing toolbar, EX 187
Getting Started task pane, WD 141
Office Assistant, WD 9
spelling error underlines, WD 27
toolbars, PPT 15
white space, WD 149
Hierarchy, **PPT 85**
file and folder organization, WIN 39
Highlighting text, WD 213
Home page, INT 8, WIN 36
hyperlink, INT 27
Horizontal alignment, EX 92, 96
Horizontal ruler, **WD 11**
amount displayed, WD 169
hanging indent and, WD 104-105
indent markers on, WD 87, WD 88
tab stops on, WD 163-164, WD 176-177
Horizontal scroll bar, **PPT 12**
Horizontal split bar, **EX 204**
.htm format, PPT 157
HTML (Hypertext Markup Language), **INT 25**, **OUT 26**, **PPT 146**, **WD 206**, **WIN 86**
HTML format
message in, OUT 15, OUT 19, OUT 26
presentation in, AC 4
workbook in, EX 232
Hyperlink, AC 180, INT 8, WD 107-108, WIN 19, **WIN 76**
automatic format, WD 109
converting to regular text, WD 174
creating while typing, WD 108
data access page, INT 36-37
editing, WD 213
formatting e-mail address as, WD 206-207
fresh, INT 27
navigating to, WD 122-123
PowerPoint Web pages, INT 12-14
presentation, INT 26-28
resume, WD 204, WD 206-207, WD 212
text, INT 11-12
verifying, INT 39
Word document, INT 8-14
workbook, EX 237
Hyperlink button (Word Standard toolbar), WD 108
Hyperlink command (Word Insert menu), INT 13
Hypertext Markup Language, *see* HTML
Hyphen, WD 158
nonbreaking, WD 180

Icon, **AC 13**
adding to, deleting from desktop, WIN 15-17, WIN 32-33
drive, WIN 19
opening windows using, WIN 17
in Windows Explorer, WIN 38
IF function, EX 170, **EX 171**-172
nested, EX 176
Import command (Access shortcut menu)
worksheet, AC 177
XML data, AC 187-188
Import External Data command (Excel Data menu), EX 121
Import Spreadsheet Wizard, **AC 176**
Importing, **AC 176**
data using Web query, EX 120-123
linking versus, AC 180
to Windows SharePoint Services list, AC 5
worksheet into database, AC 176-180
XML data, AC 187-188
Inbox folder, **OUT 8**
Inbox message pane opening e-mail, OUT 11
Inbox – Microsoft Office Outlook 2003 window, OUT 8-10
In-cell editing, **EX 50**-51
Increase Decimal button (Excel Formatting toolbar), EX 99-100, 102-103
Increase Font Size button (PowerPoint Formatting toolbar), PPT 26, PPT 27
Increase Indent button (Excel Formatting toolbar), row titles, EX 156
Increase Indent button (PowerPoint Formatting toolbar), PPT 36, PPT 40, PPT 41
Indentation
decreasing, PPT 34, PPT 37, PPT 40-41
first-line, *see* First-line indent
hanging, WD 104-105
increasing, PPT 34, PPT 36, PPT 40, PPT 41
left, WD 87
paragraphs in MLA style, WD 87-89
row titles, EX 156
tab stops and, WD 163
Index (contacts), OUT 44
Index (presentation), AC 114, **AC 157**-162
B-tree, AC 157
multiple-field, AC 160-161
single-field, AC 159-160
Index key, **AC 157**-158
Index, Windows XP Help and Support, WIN 70
Indexed property box (Field Properties pane), AC 160
Indexes button (Table Design toolbar), AC 161
Indexes command (Access View menu), AC 161
Information rights management, EX 4
Ink input, WD 4
Insert Clip Art button (content placeholder), PPT 101
Insert Clip Art button (PowerPoint Drawing toolbar), PPT 100, PPT 104-105
Insert Columns button (Word Standard toolbar), WD 185
Insert command (Excel shortcut menu)
cells, EX 161
columns, EX 161
rows, EX 159, EX 160
Insert command (Word Table menu), INT 9-10, WD 184
Insert File button (Outlook Standard toolbar), OUT 28
Insert Function box (Formula bar), EX 84, EX 86
Insert Function button (Formula bar), EX 24
Insert Hyperlink button (PowerPoint Standard toolbar), INT 28
Insert Hyperlink button (Word Standard toolbar), INT 13
Insert Hyperlink feature, **INT 12**-14
INSERT key, AC 119
Insert menu (Access)
New Record command, AC 117
Query command, AC 36, AC 70
Report command, AC 47
Table command, AC 18

Insert menu (Excel)
  Cells command, EX 161
  Columns command, EX 161
  Function command, EX 24, EX 84, EX 86, EX 167
  Rows command, EX 159, EX 160
Insert menu (PowerPoint), New Slide command, PPT 31
Insert menu (Word)
  AutoText command, WD 179, WD 181
  Break command, WD 103
  Date and Time command, WD 177
  Hyperlink command, INT 13
  Page Numbers command, WD 84
  Picture command, clip art, WD 46
  Reference command, footnote, WD 94, WD 99
  Symbol command, WD 107
  Symbol command, nonbreaking space, WD 180
Insert mode, AC 119, EX 51, WD 57
Insert Options button, EX 161
Insert Page Number button (Word Header and Footer toolbar), WD 83
Insert Rows button (Word Standard toolbar), WD 184
Insert Table button (Word Standard toolbar), WD 182-183
Inserting
  AutoText entry, WD 179, WD 181
  cells, EX 159-161
  characters, EX 50
  clip art into document, WD 45-51
  clip art into content placeholder, PPT 100-103
  columns, EX 161, WD 185
  current date, WD 177
  field, AC 21
  graphic in letterhead, WD 162
  nonbreaking space, WD 180
  pictures, PPT 105
  range, EX 161
  rows in table, WD 184
  rows in worksheet, EX 159-161
  table in letter, WD 182-183
  text from Research task pane, WD 125
  text in an existing document, WD 57
Insertion point, EX 18, PPT 21, WD 11
  bulleted list, WD 188
  deleting text, WD 58
  Edit mode and, EX 50, EX 51
  inserting clip art and, WD 46
  inserting text, WD 57
  position displayed on status bar, WD 11
  status bar, WD 18
Inside address, **WD 175**, WD 178
Integration (Office 2003 applications), **INT 4**-40
Interactive Web page, *see* Dynamic Web page
Internet
  communicating over, OUT 6-59
  Excel 2003 and, WIN 78-79
  Microsoft Office 2003 and, WIN 76
  PowerPoint and, WIN 83-84
  Publisher 2003 and, WIN 86
  Word 2003 and, WIN 77-78
Internet service provider (ISP), **PPT 141**
IntelliMouse, Microsoft, WIN 8
Intranet, INT 31, **PPT 141**, WIN 76, 81-82
ISP, *see* Internet service provider
Italic, **EX 187**
Italic button (PowerPoint Formatting toolbar), PPT 24
Italic button (Word Formatting toolbar), WD 41
Italicized, **WD 41**

Join (tables), **AC 90-95**
  restricting records in, AC 95
Join line, **AC 91**
Join properties, **AC 93-94**
Jumping, **WD 107**
Junk E-mail Filter, OUT 29
Junk E-mail folder, **OUT 8**
  entering formulas using, EX 73-74
  scrolling using, WD 25
  selecting range using, EX 80
  shortcut keys, WD 85-87

Keyboard, using, WIN 34
Keyboard indicators, **EX 15**
Keychain drives, WIN 40

Labels
  chart, *see* Data labels
  data access page, INT 34-35
  mailing, *see* Mailing labels
Landscape orientation
  database, **AC 29**, AC 31
  document, WD 79
  presentation, **PPT 11, PPT 97**
  worksheet, **EX 113,** 114, EX 118
Language bar, AC 8, EX 8, OUT 7, PPT 8, WD 7
  closing, AC 9, EX 9, PPT 8, PPT 17, WD 8, WD 16
  displaying, EX 15
  states, AC 10, EX 15, PPT 16
Language bar command (Toolbars submenu), AC 9-10, PPT 16, WD 16
Language command (Word Tools menu), thesaurus, WD 118
Large Messages, **OUT 38**
Launching Microsoft Windows XP, WIN 7-8
Layout, **PPT 97.** *See also* Slide layout
Leader lines, with data labels, EX 197
Left Indent marker, **WD 87**
Left-aligned
  paragraph using shortcut keys, WD 86
  text in cell, **EX 18**
  text in document, **WD 36**, WD 37
Legal values, **AC 142-143**
Legend, **EX 41**
  3-D Pie chart, EX 190
Leland Mortgage Web site, INT 3-40
Letter, cover, *see* Cover letter
Letterhead, WD 160-175
Letters and Mailings command (Word Tools menu), WD 190-191
Level, **PPT 31,** PPT 36, PPT 39-40
  grouping, INT 32, INT 33
  number of, PPT 91
  outline, PPT 85, PPT 88-89
Line
  blank, *see* Blank lines
  border, *see* Border
  creating new using ENTER key, PPT 23
  formatting, WD 40
  join, AC 91
  selecting, WD 40
  separating Web page sections, WD 210
Line break, **WD 154**
Line break character, **WD 154**
Line number, displayed on status bar, WD 11
Line spacing, **WD 79**
  Biometrics research paper, WD 79-80
  double, WD 79-80
Line Spacing button arrow (Word Formatting toolbar), WD 80

Line wraps, **PPT 21**
Link, *see* Hyperlink
Linked Table Manager, **AC 180**
Linking, importing versus, AC 180
List styles, **WD 152**
Lists, **EX 4**
  bulleted, *see* Bulleted list
  contact, *see* Contact list
  database data stored as, **AC 174**
  distribution, *see* Distribution list
  numbered, WD 189
Live database, **AC 162**
Lock aspect ratio check box (PowerPoint Format Picture dialog box), **PPT 108**
Logical operators, in IF functions, EX 171
Logging on, off computer, WIN 9-10, WIN 72-75
Lookup field, **AC 146**-150
Lookup Wizard data type, AC 146-148
Loop, scrolling text, **INT 22**

Macro security, AC 5
Magnifying glass mouse pointer, AC 30
Mail, *see* E-mail; Mailing labels
Mail toolbar, **OUT 15**
Mailing labels, WD 190-191
Maintaining the database, **AC 114**-164
  datasheet appearance, AC 131-135
  filtering records, AC 120-125
  indexes and, AC 114, AC 157-162
  mass changes, AC 135-139
  ordering records, AC 155-156
  structure, AC 114, 126-130
  updating records, AC 116-120
Major key, *see* Primary sort key
Make-table query, AC 135
Manual page break, **WD 103**
Margins
  changing in Page Setup dialog box, WD 78
  changing in print layout view, WD 77, WD 79
  MLA style, WD 77-79
  printing and, AC 31
  See also Indentation
Marquee, EX 157
MAX function, **EX 82-84**
Maximizing
  Access window, AC 8
  Help window, WD 61
  PowerPoint window, PPT 8
  windows, WIN 21-23
Media Center PC, WIN 5
Media, removable, WIN 40-43
Memory, EX 42, EX 43, EX 157, PPT 29, WD 28
Menu, AC 12, EX 11, PPT 13, WD 12
  context-sensitive, WD 12
  displaying, WD 12-13
  full, AC 12, EX 12, PPT 14, WD 12-13
  popup, *see* Popup menu
  resetting, WD 15
  short, AC 12, EX 12, PPT 14, WD 12
  shortcut, AC 13-15, EX 49, PPT 16
  Start, WIN 11-14
  sub-, *see* Submenu
Menu bar, AC 12-13, EX 11, PPT 13, WD 12-13
Menu name, **EX 11-12, PPT 13**
Merge and Center button (Excel Formatting toolbar), EX 33, EX 93
Merged cell, splitting, EX 33
Merging cells, **EX 32,** EX 92-93
Merging table formats, EX 36

Message, business letter, **WD 175**, 180-189
Message Format box, OUT 15
Message header, **OUT 10**, OUT 11
Message importance, **OUT 34-38**
Message list icons, **OUT 10**
Message pane, **OUT 9-10**
Message sensitivity, **OUT 34-38**
Message window, OUT 11
.mht format, PPT 157
Microphone, AC 8, AC 9, EX 8, PPT 8, PPT 16, PPT 20, WD 7, WD 17
Microsoft Access 2003, *see* Access 2003
Microsoft Clip Organizer, **PPT 99**
Microsoft Excel 2003, *see* Excel 2003
Microsoft Internet Explorer, WIN 36
Microsoft Keyboards, WIN 34
Microsoft mice, WIN 8-9
Microsoft Office 2003, *see* Office 2003
Microsoft Office Access 2003 command (Microsoft Office submenu), AC 7-8
Microsoft Office Excel 2003 command (Microsoft Office submenu), EX 7
Microsoft Office Outlook 2003 command (Microsoft Office submenu), OUT 6
Microsoft Office PowerPoint 2003 command (Microsoft Office submenu), PPT 7
Microsoft Office Specialist Certification, AC 162, EX 53, EX 126, EX 209, EX 238, INT 38, OUT 58, PPT 56, WD 62, WD 121, WD 214
Microsoft Office submenu
  Microsoft Office Access 2003 command, AC 7-8
  Microsoft Office Excel 2003 command, EX 7
  Microsoft Office Outlook 2003 command, OUT 6
  Microsoft Office PowerPoint 2003 command, PPT 7
  Microsoft Office Word 2003 command, WD 6
Microsoft Office Word 2003 command (All Programs submenu), WD 6
Microsoft Outlook 2003, **OUT 4**, WIN 87-88
  contacts, OUT 38-58
  customizing, OUT 7
  e-mail, OUT 6-38
  new features, OUT 4
  starting, OUT 6
Microsoft PowerPoint 2003, *see* PowerPoint 2003
Microsoft Publisher 2003, WIN 85-86
Microsoft Web site, Getting Starting task pane and, AC 8
Microsoft Windows, *see* Windows
Microsoft Windows XP, *see* Windows XP
Microsoft Word, *see* Word 2003
MIN function, **EX 84-87**
Minimized (Language bar), **AC 9**, AC 10, **EX 15**, **PPT 16**, **WD 16**
Minimizing windows, WIN 19-21
Minor key, *see* Secondary sort key
Mixed cell reference, **EX 168**
MLA, *see* Modern Language Association of America
Mode indicator, **EX 14**
Modern Language Association of America (MLA), **WD 74**
  documentation style, WD 75, WD 76
Modify Style dialog box, WD 96-98
Month names, creating series of, using fill handle, EX 152-153
Mouse
  double-click, WIN 17-18
  Microsoft, WIN 8-9
  right-click, WIN 15
  right-dragging, WIN 32, WIN 55-56
  scrolling using, WD 24
  selecting items using, WD 113
Mouse pointer, EX 11, **PPT 12**, WIN 11
  note reference mark and, WD 99
  scrolling and, PPT 45
  text placeholder and, PPT 22
Move handle, **EX 13**, **WD 14**
Moving
  chart, EX 40-41
  clip art, PPT 108
  copy and paste used in, EX 157-158
  copying versus, EX 159
  cut and paste used in, EX 159
  drag and drop used in, EX 159
  field, AC 130
  files, folders, WIN 56
  sheet, EX 199
  tab stops, WD 177
  task pane title bar, WD 7
  text using drag-and-drop, WD 112-115
  toolbar, EX 13, EX 182, WD 82
  windows by dragging, WIN 26-27
MSN MoneyCentral Investor Stock Quotes, EX 122
Multi-level bulleted list slide, **PPT 34-42**
  creating on Outline tab, PPT 90-93
Multimedia, PPT 4
Multiple paragraphs, formatting, WD 33-35
Multiple-field indexes, **AC 160-161**
Multiplication (*), EX 74
My Computer window, WIN 18-19, WIN 41-43
My Documents window, WIN 25-26

Name
  document, on title bar, WD 30
  field, AC 15, AC 16, AC 18, AC 19
  files, folders, WIN 43, WIN 57-58
  form, AC 39
  menu, EX 11-12, PPT 13
  query, AC 36, AC 80
  sheet, EX 10, EX 197
  sheet tabs, EX 124
  table, AC 22, AC 33
  workbook, EX 43, EX 44
Name box, EX 16
  selecting cell using, EX 36-37
Navigating to hyperlink, WD 122-123
Navigation buttons, **AC 27**, AC 41
Navigation Pane (Outlook 2003), **OUT 8-9**, WIN 88
Navigation toolbar, **INT 38**, WIN 68
Negative numbers, formatting, EX 180
Nested IF function, **EX 176**
Network drives, WIN 40-41
New Blank Document button (Word Standard toolbar), WD 59, WD 160
New button (Database window toolbar), creating database using, AC 10, 17, AC 33
New command (Word File menu), Resume Wizard, WD 142
New Mail Message button (Outlook Standard toolbar), OUT 24
New Object button arrow (Database toolbar)
  creating form using, AC 38
  creating query using, AC 34, AC 68-69
  creating report using, AC 43
New Office Document command (All Programs submenu)
  starting Access, AC 8
  starting PowerPoint, PPT 8
New Query dialog box, AC 35
New Record button (Navigation bar), AC 28, AC 117
New Record command (Access Insert menu), AC 117
New Slide button (PowerPoint Formatting toolbar), PPT 30
New Slide command (PowerPoint Insert menu), PPT 31
New Table dialog box, AC 17
Next Record button (Navigation bar), AC 41, AC 119
Next Slide button, PPT 44
Nonbreaking hyphen, **WD 180**
Nonbreaking space, **WD 180**
Noninteractive Web page, *see* Static Web page
Nonprinting character, **WD 20**
Normal command (Word View menu), WD 77
Normal style
  document, **WD 95**
  worksheet, EX 52
Normal view (PowerPoint), **PPT 11**
  changing to, PPT 96
  moving to another slide in, PPT 44-46
Normal view (Word), WD 77
Note pane, WD 95
  closing, WD 99
Note reference mark, **WD 93**, WD 95
  mouse pointer on, WD 99
Note text, **WD 93**
Notepad, displaying contact list in, OUT 56-57
Notes and Handouts sheet (Header and Footer dialog box), PPT 112
Notes pane, **PPT 11**
  Outline tab, PPT 86
Notification area, desktop, WIN 11
NOW function, **EX 165-167**
Number (database), query criteria, AC 81-82
Number (document)
  alignment on decimal point, WD 165
  footnote format, WD 99
Number (worksheet), **EX 21**
  average of, EX 81-82
  changing formula to, EX 77
  entering, EX 21-23
  entering as text, EX 21
  entering in range, EX 72
  format symbols, EX 162-163
  formatting, EX 177
  formatting using Format Cells command, EX 100-102
  formatting using Formatting toolbar, EX 98-100
  highest, EX 82-84
  lowest, EX 84-87
  negative, *see* Negative numbers
  series of, creating using fill handle, EX 153
Number field, AC 16
Numbered list, WD 189
Nutrition and Fitness presentation, PPT 82-129

Object, PPT 10, PPT 12
  aspect ratio, PPT 108
  attributes, PPT 11
  embedded, INT 14-19
  formatting, INT 16-19
  list of, AC 34
  properties of, AC 87, WIN 11
  resizing, INT 16-19
  source, INT 14
  viewing in windows, WIN 27
Object command (Word Format menu), size, INT 17

Object Linking and Embedding (OLE), **INT 14**
Object menu, *see* Context-sensitive menu
Objective style, WD 151-152
Office 2003
  Help system, WIN 78-79
  introduction to, WIN 4, WIN 75-76
Office Assistant, hiding, WD 9
Office Clipboard, **EX 157, WD 165**-171
Office Clipboard command (Word Edit menu), WD 166-167
Office Clipboard gallery, WD 171
Office Speech Recognition software, AC 8, EX 8, **EX 15**-16, PPT 8, **PPT 16,** WD 7, **WD 16**
Offsetting, **EX 194**
OLE, *see* Object Linking and Embedding
One-to-many relationship, **AC 150**
Open button (Database toolbar), AC 26
Open command (Access File menu), database, AC 26
Open command (Access shortcut menu), table, AC 23, AC 34
Open command (PowerPoint File menu), PPT 52
Open documents
  multiple, WD 160
  switching between, WD 166
Open envelope icon, **OUT 10**
Opening
  database, AC 26-27, AC 68
  e-mail, OUT 11
  existing document, WD 55-56
  existing presentation, PPT 52
  existing workbook, EX 47-48
  form, AC 40
  query, AC 36, AC 37
  table, AC 23, AC 34
  task pane, EX 9
  windows, WIN 23
Operating systems, **WIN 4**
Option button, **AC 31**
Options buttons, EX 78-79
Options command (Excel Tools menu), formulas version, EX 119
Options command (Outlook Tools menu)
  e-mail signature, OUT 20-21
  message importance, OUT 36
Options command (PowerPoint Tools menu)
  black slide, PPT 42-43
  fast saves, PPT 111
Options command (Word Tools menu)
  dictionary, WD 121
  showing formatting marks, WD 21
OR criterion, **AC 83,** AC 84-85
Order of operations, **EX 74-75**
Ordering records, AC 155-156
Ordinal, making superscript, WD 156-157
Organize command (Outlook Tools menu), contacts, OUT 48
Organizing files, folders, WIN 39
Original size area (Format Object dialog box), **INT 19**
Other Layouts (Slide Layout task pane), PPT 97
Other Places area, desktop, WIN 25
Other Task Panes button (task pane title bar), EX 9
Outbox folder, **OUT 8-9**
Outline, PPT 82-95
  footer, PPT 112-113
  header, PPT 112-113
  hyperlinks, **INT 29**
  printing, PPT 122-125
Outline tab, **PPT 11, PPT 85-95**
  adding slide, PPT 89-90
  closing slide, PPT 93-94
  multi-level bulleted list text slides, PPT 90-93
  printing presentation, PPT 122-126
  title slide, PPT 88-89
Outline title, **PPT 84**
Outlining toolbar displaying, PPT 86-87
Outlining, PPT 4, **PPT 85-95**
Outlook 2003, introduction to, WIN 87-88
Outlook Calendar, smart tag to display, WD 192
Overhead transparency, *see* Transparency
OVR indicator, AC 119, WD 12, WD 57
Overtype mode, **AC 119,** WD 12, **WD 57**

Page breaks
  automatic, WD 101-102
  manual, WD 103
Page header, **AC 42**
Page numbers (document)
  displayed on status bar, WD 11
  in header, WD 81, WD 83-84
Page numbers (presentation)
  in outline, PPT 112
Page Numbers command (Word Insert menu), WD 84
Page preview
  integrated Web page, INT 23-24
  PowerPoint Web page, INT 28
Page Setup command (Excel File menu)
  black and white printing, EX 116
  print scaling, EX 120
Page Setup command (Word File menu)
  margins, WD 78
Page Setup dialog box (Excel)
  orientation, EX 114, EX 118
  print scaling, EX 120
  print settings, EX 114, EX 116
Page Setup dialog box (Word)
  margins, WD 78
  orientation, WD 79
Page tab (Page Setup dialog box), AC 31
Page totals, displayed on status bar, WD 11
Page Wizard, INT 32-34
Painting formats, EX 107
Pane (Access), **AC 18**
Pane (Excel)
  splitting window into, EX 202-204
Pane (PowerPoint)
  sizing, PPT 11
Panel names, **WD 141**
Paper clip icon, **OUT 10**
Paragraph (document)
  alignment, *see* Alignment
  bottom border, WD 172
  bulleted, *see* Bulleted list
  centering, WD 38, WD 45
  formatting, WD 31-45
  formatting multiple, WD 33-35
  indenting in MLA style, WD 87-89
  new, pressing ENTER key and, WD 18, WD 21
  selecting multiple, WD 33-34
  sorting, WD 109-110
  wordwrap, WD 22-23
Paragraph (presentation)
  level, *see* Level
  new, creating using ENTER key, PPT 33, PPT 34
  selecting, PPT 25
Paragraph command (Word Format menu)
  alignment, WD 37
  centering, WD 38
  indents, WD 89
  line spacing, WD 80
Paragraph dialog box, first-line indent, WD 98
Paragraph formatting, **WD 31**
  footnote, WD 96-98
  Grand Prix announcement document, WD 31-45
  shortcut keys for, WD 87
Paragraph mark (¶), displaying, WD 20-21
Paragraph styles, **WD 152**
Parameter query, **AC** 79-80
Parentheses
  arguments in, EX 82
  order of operations and, EX 75
Parenthetical citations, **WD 76**
Password, EX 44, PPT 30, WD 30, WIN 8, WIN 10
Paste area, *see* Destination area
Paste button (Excel Standard toolbar)
  advanced options, EX 159
  copy operations and, EX 157-158
  cut operations and, EX 159
  Office Clipboard, EX 157-158
Paste button (Word Standard toolbar), WD 114
Paste command (Excel Edit menu), EX 26
  functions, EX 88
  Office Clipboard, EX 157, EX 158
Paste command (Word Edit menu), WD 114
  Clipboard task pane, WD 171
Paste Options button, **WD 114-115,** WD 170-171
Paste Options menu (Excel), items on, EX 158
Paste Options menu (Word), WD 114-115
Paste Special, **INT 14,** INT 16
Paste Special command (Excel Edit menu), formats, EX 155
Paste Special command (Word Edit menu) Excel chart, INT 15-16
Pasting, WD 112, WD 165
  chart to Word document, INT 16
  text as hyperlink, INT 11
  undoing, EX 158
Paths, DOS, **WIN 40**
Percent, worksheet view, EX 201
Percent Style button (Excel Formatting toolbar), EX 103
Personal folder, contact list and, OUT 39-40
Personal information management (PIM), **WIN 87**
Photographs, WD 45
Phrase
  deleting, WD 58
  searching for files using, WIN 65-66
Picture command (PowerPoint Format menu), size, PPT 110
Picture command (Word Insert menu), clip art, WD 46
Picture toolbar, WD 49, WD 51
Pictures, inserting, PPT 105
Pie chart, **EX 187**
  color in slices, EX 193
  exploded, EX 187, EX 194
  3-D, EX 187-197
PIM, *see* Personal information management
Pixel, **EX 107**
Placeholder text, **WD 152**
  resume, WD 152-153
Placeholders, **PPT 12**
  changing slide layout and, PPT 97, PPT 99
  text, *see* Text placeholders
Plagiarism, WD 126
Plain Text message format, OUT 15, OUT 19
Point (font), **OUT 26, WD 16**
Point mode, entering formulas using, **EX 75-77**

Point size, **EX 28**
Popup Menu, PPT 121
  ending slide show using, PPT 49-50
  moving to specific slide using, PPT 48-49
Portrait orientation
  database, **AC 29,** AC 45
  document, WD 79
  presentation, **PPT 11, PPT 97**
  worksheet, **EX 113,** EX 116
Port, USB, and flash drive, WIN 40-43
Power failure, EX 42, PPT 43
PowerPoint 2003, INT 26, **PPT 4,** WIN 82-83
  customizing, PPT 8-10
  Help system, PPT 62-64
  new features, PPT 6
  quitting, PPT 50-51, PPT 64
  starting, PPT 7-8, PPT 51-52
PowerPoint Web pages, hyperlink to, INT 12-14
PowerPoint window, PPT 10-16
  maximizing, PPT 8
.ppt extension, **PPT 29**
Presentation, **PPT 4,** WIN 82-83
  displaying in black and white, PPT 56-59
  Nutrition and Fitness, 81-129
  opening existing, PPT 52
  outline, 82-95
  previewing as Web page, PPT 143-146
  printing, *see* Printing
  publishing, PPT 142, PPT 154-157
  saving as Web page, PPT 146-149
  saving with new file name, PPT 27-30
  saving with same file name, PPT 43-44
  Strategies for College Success, PPT 4-65
  title, PPT 20-21
  Web, PPT 141-157
  Web page, INT 26-30
Presentation graphics program. *See also* Microsoft PowerPoint 2003
Preset animation schemes, **PPT 114**
Preview
  contact list, OUT 49-50
  data to be deleted, AC 137
  report, AC 46
  table, AC 29-31
  Web page, EX 228-229
  worksheet, EX 113
  See also Print preview
Previewing the worksheet, **EX 113-115**
Previous Slide button, PPT 44
Primary key, **AC 6**
  choosing, AC 16, AC 19, AC 21
  importing worksheet and, AC 179
  index on, AC 158, AC 159
  ordering records and, AC 156
  referential integrity and, AC 150-153
Primary sort key, **AC 86**
Print area, **EX 45**
Print Area command (Excel File menu), EX 117
Print button (Excel Standard toolbar), EX 45
Print button (PowerPoint Standard toolbar), PPT 60
Print button (Word Standard toolbar), WD 53
Print command (Excel File menu), worksheet, EX 45
Print command (PowerPoint File menu)
  outlines, PPT 122
  slides, PPT 61
Print command (Word File menu), WD 13, WD 53
Print dialog box (Excel), Print what area, EX 116-117
Print dialog box (PowerPoint), outlines, PPT 122-123
Print layout view, **WD 82, WD 148**
  changing margins in, WD 77, WD 79
  header in, WD 82
  Text Width in, WD 170
Print Preview
  datasheet, AC 135
  document, **WD 158**
  table, AC 29, AC 30-31
Print Preview button (Excel Standard toolbar), EX 47, EX 114, EX 116
Print Preview button (Word Standard toolbar), WD 52, WD 158
Print Preview command (Excel File menu), EX 115
Print Preview command (PowerPoint File menu), outline, PPT 124
Print Preview command (Word File menu), WD 159
Print Scaling option, EX 120
Print what list (PowerPoint Print dialog box), PPT 122, **PPT 125**
Printing
  black and white, EX 116, EX 200, PPT 59
  Blue Chip Stock Club worksheet, EX 115-120
  contact list, OUT 49-50
  e-mail, OUT 12
  envelope, WD 191
  Extreme Blading Second Quarter Sales worksheet, EX 44-45
  formulas version, EX 119
  Grand Prix announcement, WD 53
  handout, PPT 125, PPT 156
  keyboard shortcuts, WD 87
  mailing label, WD 191
  margins and, AC 31
  orientation, EX 113, EX 114, EX 116, EX 118
  outline, PPT 122-25
  presentation created on Outline tab, PPT 122-126
  query results, AC 36, AC 72
  range, EX 45, EX 116-117
  relationships, AC 151
  report, AC 46-47
  section of worksheet, EX 116-117
  Strategies for College Success presentation, PPT 59-61
  table, AC 29, AC 31-32
Printout, EX 44, PPT 59, WD 53
Profile template, PPT 19
Programs
  application, **WIN 6,** WIN 34-36
  most frequently used, WIN 14
Projectors, portable, PPT 6
Promote button (Outlining toolbar), PPT 89
Proofreading, **WD 110-121,** WD 189
Properties
  changing, AC 156
  frame, WD 214
  join, AC 93-94
  object, WIN 11
  validation rules, AC 142-143
Properties command (Access View menu), Unique Properties value, AC 88
Properties command (Word File menu)
  document summary, WD 193
  statistics, WD 101
Property sheet, **AC 87**
Publish presentations, **PPT 142,** PPT 154-157
Publish workbooks, **EX 228,** EX 235
Publisher 2003, WIN 85-86
Publishing Web page, EX 228, EX 230, INT 29, INT 37
Pure Black and White command (Color/Grayscale button), PPT 57

QBE, *see* Query-by-Example
Queries (questions), AC 4, **AC 34, AC 66**
  action, AC 135
  append, AC 135, AC 139
  calculations used in, AC 96-103
  closing, AC 73
  comparison operators, AC 82-83
  compound criteria, AC 83-85
  creating, AC 68-70
  criteria, AC 75-80, AC 83-85
  crosstab, AC 104-106
  delete, AC 135, AC 137-138
  duplicate records, AC 154
  exporting to Word document using drag-and-drop, AC 175, AC 182-183
  filtering records, AC 120-125
  formatting, AC 98
  including all fields in, AC 74
  naming, AC 36
  opening, AC 36, AC 37
  parameter, AC 79-80
  printing results of, AC 36, AC 72
  running, AC 71
  saving, AC 80
  selecting fields for, AC 70-71
  Simple Query Wizard used to create, AC 34-36
  sorting data in, AC 85-89
  top-values, AC 89-90
  unmatched records, AC 154
  update, AC 135, AC 136-137
  using, AC 36-38
  using Select Query window, AC 66-107
  Web, EX 120-123
Query command (Access Insert menu), AC 36, AC 70
Query Datasheet toolbar, AC 72
Query Design toolbar, AC 71
Query languages, AC 68
Query menu (Access)
  Delete Query command, AC 139
  Run command, AC 71
  Show Table command, AC 93
  Update Query command, AC 137
Query object, AC 35
Query-by-Example (QBE), AC 70
Question mark (?) wildcard, **AC 76**
Quitting
  Access, AC 25-26, AC 49-50
  Excel, EX 46, EX 54-55
  PowerPoint, PPT 50-51, PPT 64
  Windows Explorer, WIN 61
  Word, WD 54, WD 62
Quoting source, WD 84

Range, **EX 23**
  AutoCalculate, EX 48
  AutoSum, EX 165
  average of, EX 81-82
  charting, EX 189
  clearing, EX 52
  copying, EX 26
  copying to nonadjacent destination area, EX 157-158
  deleting, EX 162
  dragging, EX 161

entering numbers in, EX 72
highest number in, EX 82-84
inserting, EX 161
lowest number in, EX 84-87
printing, EX 45, EX 116-117
selected, EX 26
selecting nonadjacent, EX 177
selecting using keyboard, EX 80
summing, EX 23-24
validation rules, AC 140-141
Range Finder, **EX 89-90**, EX 148
Range of values, **AC 139**
Reading e-mail, OUT 11
Reading Pane, **OUT 10**
Ready mode, **EX 14**, EX 44
Recalculation, automatic, EX 74
Record selector, **AC 23**, AC 41
Records, **AC 6**
adding, AC 116-117
adding to existing table, AC 27-29, AC 33-34
adding to new table, AC 22-25
changing contents of, AC 119
correcting errors, AC 25
deleting, AC 25, AC 41, AC 125-126
duplicate, AC 154
exporting, AC 181
filtering, AC 120-125
grouping, AC 102-103
grouping on data access page, INT 38
indexes, AC 157-162
Navigation buttons, AC 27
ordering, AC 155-156
ordering using index, AC 158
query, AC 36-37
report, AC 45
restricting in join, AC 95
saving, AC 24
searching for, AC 117-118
selecting, AC 23, AC 41
sorting, AC 155-156
sorting in query, AC 85-89
unmatched, AC 154
updating, AC 116-120, AC 135-139
Records menu (Access)
Filter command, AC 123, AC 124
Sort command, AC 155
Recover (database), **AC 162-163**
Recycle Bin, **WIN 32**
Redo button (Excel Standard toolbar), EX 52
Redo button (Word Standard toolbar), WD 39
Redo command (Excel Edit menu), EX 52
Redundancy, **AC 50-51**
#REF!, **EX 162**
Reference command (Word Insert menu), footnote, WD 94, WD 99
References
MLA style, WD 76
Research task pane and, WD 118, WD 124-126
on resume, WD 157
Referential integrity, **AC 150**-153
Refresh All button (External Data toolbar), EX 123
Relational operators, EX 104, EX 106
Relationship
index and, AC 159
printed copy of, AC 151
referential integrity and, AC 150-153
Relationship line, **AC 152**
Relationships button (Database toolbar), AC 151
Relationships command (Access Tools menu), AC 152
Relative addressing, absolute address versus, EX 168-170
Relative cell reference, **EX 168**
Relative reference, **EX 25, EX 78**
Removable media, WIN 40-43
Removing
hyperlink, WD 174
See also Deleting
Renaming files, folders, WIN 57-58
Repair (database), **AC 163-164**
Repeat command (Word Edit menu), **WD 39**
Replace command (Word Edit menu), WD 117
Replacing text, WD 116-117, WD 152
Reply button (Outlook Standard toolbar), OUT 14
Replying to e-mail, OUT 13-14
Report (database), AC 4
based on query, AC 81
creating, AC 42-46
e-mailing, AC 175, AC 184
fields for, AC 42, AC 44
grouping, AC 44-45
previewing, AC 46
printing, AC 31, AC 46-47
saving, AC 46
snapshot, AC 175, AC 184-185
Report (document), research, WD 73-126
Report command (Access Insert menu), AC 47
Report Wizard, AC 44
Requirements document, **EX 5-6**
Aquatics Wear worksheet, EX 148
Blue Chip Stock Club Investment Analysis worksheet, EX 67-68
Research command (Word Tools menu), WD 124
Research paper, WD 73-126
Research task pane, WD 118, WD 124-126
Resetting menus and toolbars, WD 15
Resizing
column, **AC 131**
embedded chart, INT 16-19
frames page, WD 211
graphic, **WD 49-51**
graphic in letterhead, WD 162-163
scrolling text, INT 22-23
table columns, WD 185-186
windows, WIN 31-32
Resolution, EX 6, EX 10, EX 11, EX 13, PPT 7, PPT 10
Restore Down button, WIN 21
Restored (Language bar), AC 9, EX 15, PPT 16, WD 16
Restoring windows, WIN 21-23
Restructure the database, **AC 114**, AC 126-130
Resume, **WD 138**-195
cover letter for, WD 138, WD 139, WD 175-189
envelopes for, WD 190-191
hyperlink in, WD 204, WD 206-207, WD 212
letterhead for cover letter, WD 160-175
personalizing, WD 150-159
references on, WD 157
saving as Web page, WD 203-206
wizard used to create, WD 141-148
Resume Wizard, **WD 141**-148
Rich Text Format (RTF)
message, OUT 15
presentation, PPT 87
Right-aligned, **WD 36-37**
Right-click, AC 14, PPT 16, WD 12, WIN 15, WIN 55-56
Rotating
cell entries, EX 98
text, EX 151-152
3-D Pie chart, EX 194-196
Rough draft, **PPT 59**
ROUND function, EX 100
Round tripping, **EX 232**
Row (database)
selecting, AC 18, AC 21
See also Records
Rows (Word table), INT 10, WD 182, 183
adding, WD 184
Row (worksheet)
bottom border, EX 100
deleting, EX 161-162
hidden, EX 111
inserting, EX 159-161
inserting multiple, EX 159, EX 161
number of, EX 10
summing, EX 27
titles, EX 16
Row boundary, **WD 186**
Row heading, **EX 10**
active cell, EX 16
Row height
best fit, EX 110
Blue Chip Stock Club worksheet, EX 107, 110
white space and, EX 72
Row selector, **AC 18**, AC 21
Row titles
Aquatics Wear worksheet, EX 156
Blue Chip Stock Club worksheet, EX 70-71
bold, EX 100
copying to nonadjacent destination area, EX 157-158
entering, EX 20-21
freezing, EX 163-164
indenting, EX 156
Row totals, nonadjacent cells, EX 175
Rows command (Excel Insert menu), EX 159, EX 160
RTF (Rich Text Format), **PPT 87**
Ruler, **WD 11**
horizontal, *see* Horizontal ruler
margins on, WD 79
table and, WD 151
Ruler command (Word View menu), WD 11, WD 87
Rules, e-mail, OUT 34
Run button (Query Design toolbar), AC 38, AC 71
Run command (Query menu), AC 71
Running animated slide show, PPT 120-121
Running query, AC 71

Salutation, **WD 175**, WD 178, WD 180
SAM hands-on assignments, WIN 90
Save As command (Excel File menu), EX 43
Save As command (PowerPoint File menu), PPT 29
Save As command (Word File menu), WD 30
Save As dialog box (Access)
form, AC 39
table, AC 33
Save As dialog box (Excel), EX 43
toolbar buttons, EX 44
Save As dialog box (PowerPoint), PPT 27-29
Save As dialog box (Word), WD 28-30
Save as Web Page command (Excel File menu), EX 231, EX 234-235
Save as Web Page command (PowerPoint File menu), PPT 147

Save as Web Page command (Word File menu), WD 205
Save button (Excel Standard toolbar), EX 42
Save button (PowerPoint Standard toolbar), PPT 27, PPT 44
Save button (Word Formatting toolbar), WD 28
Save command (Access File menu), AC 22, AC 80
Save copy, **AC 162**
Save in list (File New Database dialog box), AC 10
Save Options command (Word Tools submenu), WD 30
Saving
automatic, PPT 27, PPT 30
before printing, PPT 59-60
Biometrics research paper, WD 87
chart as dynamic Web page, EX 234-236
document as Web page, WD 203
document in new folder, WIN 51-54
existing document, WD 51-52
fast saves, PPT 111
form, AC 39
new document, WD 28-31
new workbook, EX 42-44
Outlook file formats and, OUT 56-58
presentation as Web page, PPT 146-149
presentation with new file name, PPT 27-30
presentation with same file name, PPT 43-44
query, AC 80
record, AC 24
report, AC 46
resume, WD 159
table, AC 22, AC 33
workbook as static Web page, EX 230-232
workbook using same file name, EX 88-89
Saving mode, EX 44
Scale area (Format Object dialog box), **INT 19**
Scanner, WD 45
Schema, **AC 185**
Screen
resolution, EX 6, EX 10, EX 11, EX 13
viewing area, EX 11
ScreenTip, AC 13, AC 19, EX 13, PPT 15, WD 13
Scroll arrows, **EX 11**, **PPT 11**
Scroll bars, **EX 11**, **PPT 11**, PPT 12, **WD 11**, WD 24, WD 43, WIN 27-29
horizontal, *see* Horizontal scroll bar
vertical, *see* Vertical scroll bar
Scroll boxes, **EX 11**, **PPT 11**, PPT 44-46, **WD 11**, WD 24
Scrolling, **INT 20**
text, **INT 19-23**
in windows, WIN 27-29
Scrolls, **WD 23-25**, WD 43
Search Companion balloon, WIN 63, WIN 65-66
Search Help topics, EX 53, EX 54
Search Folders folder, **OUT 9**, **OUT 38**
Search Results windows, WIN 64-65
Searching, **AC 117**
clip art, PPT 100, PPT 101, PPT 105, WD 47
for files, folders, WIN 61-66
for formatting, WD 117
help topics, WD 61
for record, AC 117-118
for special characters, WD 117
for synonym, WD 118-119
for text and replacing, WD 116-117
Secondary sort key, **AC 86**
Section number, displayed on status bar, WD 11
Security, macro, AC 5
Security settings, OUT 36
See-through view, **EX 26**
Select (text), **WD 33**
Select a cell, **EX 16**
methods, EX 37
using Name box, EX 36-37
Select All button
bolding entire worksheet, EX 150
clearing worksheet using, EX 53
Select Browse Object button (vertical scroll bar), WD 111, WD 117
Select Browse Object menu (Word), WD 110
Browse by Page icon, WD 111
Find icon, WD 117
Select Query window, AC 66, **AC 68**-107
Selected chart, EX 40
Selected text, **WD 33**
Selecting
cell, EX 16
cells for formula, EX 75
entire worksheet, EX 53
field, AC 18, AC 21
fields for query, AC 70-71
Forms object, AC 40
graphic, WD 49
group of words, WD 43-44
items using mouse, WD 113
line, WD 40
methods, EX 37
multiple paragraphs, WD 33-34
nonadjacent ranges, EX 177
nonadjacent text, WD 113
option button, AC 31
paragraph, PPT 25
range using keyboard, EX 80
range using mouse, EX 26
record, AC 23, AC 41
resume text, WD 152
row, AC 18, AC 21
sentence, WD 112
table items, WD 186
text placeholder, PPT 32
text to delete, WD 58
Selection,
clearing, EX 52
removing, WD 44
Selection rectangle, **PPT 21**, PPT 32, **WD 49**
Send button (Outlook Standard toolbar), OUT 14, OUT 16, OUT 29
Send To command (Excel File menu), e-mail, EX 125-126
Send To command (Word File menu), WD 123
Sending e-mail, OUT 29
Sensitivity analysis, **EX 204**
Sent Items folder, **OUT 9**, OUT 14
Sentence, selecting and moving, WD 112
Series of month names, creating using fill handle, EX 152-153
Series of numbers, creating using fill handle, EX 153
Setup button (Print Preview toolbar), AC 31
Servers, **WIN 5**
Service packs, WIN 6
7 x 7 rule, PPT 12
Shadow, drop, EX 183-184
Shadow Style button (Excel Drawing toolbar), EX 184
Shared Documents folder, WIN 19
Sheet
chart, EX 187, EX 188-192
moving, EX 199
renaming, EX 197
reordering, EX 197-198
Sheet name, EX 10
Sheet tab, **EX 10**
color, EX 198
renaming, EX 124, EX 197
Short menu, AC 12, EX 12, PPT 14, WD 12
Shortcut keys, **WD 85-87**, WIN 34
Shortcut menus, **AC 13-15**, EX 49, EX 52, **PPT 16**, WD 12, WIN 15-16
Show Buttons on Two Rows command (Toolbar Options list), EX 9, EX 14, WD 9
Show hidden icons button, WIN 11
Show Table command (Query menu), AC 93
Show/Hide ¶ button (Word Standard toolbar), WD 21
Shrink to fit, EX 157
Shrinking cell entries, EX 98
Signature
e-mail, OUT 19-23
letter, WD 175, WD 189
Signature block, **WD 175**, WD 189
Simple Query Wizard, AC 34-36
Single File Web Page format, **EX 230**, **PPT 146**, **WD 206**
Single-field index, **AC 159**-160
Size
aspect ratio, PPT 108
clip art, PPT 108-110
field, AC 20, AC 127-128
font, *see* Font size
graphic, WD 49-51
panes, PPT 11
toolbar buttons, EX 14
worksheet, EX 10
worksheet window, EX 11
zooming and, WD 21
See also Resizing
Size and rotate area (Format Object dialog box), **INT 19**
Size sheet (PowerPoint Format Picture dialog box), **PPT 108**
Sizing handles
chart, EX 40
document, **WD 49**-50
Sizing windows, WIN, 29-30
Slide, **PPT 10**
adding on Outline tab, PPT 89-90
adding to Strategies for College Success presentation, PPT 30-42
black, PPT 42-43
clip art, *see* Clip art
closing, *see* Closing slide
displaying, PPT 44
Microsoft Word and, PPT 87
scrolling text behavior, **INT 20**
7 x 7 rule, PPT 12
text, PPT 7
title, *see* Title slide
Slide behavior, scrolling text, **INT 22**
Slide Design – Animation Schemes task pane, **PPT 17**
Slide Design – Color Schemes task pane, **PPT 17**
Slide Design button (PowerPoint Formatting toolbar), PPT 18
Slide Design command (PowerPoint Format menu), PPT 20
Slide Design task pane, **PPT 17**-19
animation scheme, PPT 115
Slide indicator, **PPT 44**

Slide layout, **PPT 11**
changing, PPT 31, PPT 97-99
undoing, PPT 107
Slide Layout command (PowerPoint Format menu), PPT 31, PPT 98
Slide Layout task pane, **PPT 97,** PPT 98
Slide pane, **PPT 11**
Outline tab, PPT 86
Slide show, **PPT 4**
advancing manually through, PPT 47-48
animation, *see* Animation
custom, PPT 157
e-mailing, PPT 126-128
ending using Popup menu, PPT 49-50
ending with black slide, PPT 42-43
Slide Show button, PPT 46-47
Slide Show command (PowerPoint View menu), PPT 47
Slide Show menu (PowerPoint)
Animation Schemes command, PPT 114
Custom Animation command, PPT 119
View Show, PPT 121
Slide show view, **PPT 11, PPT 46**
Slide Sorter command (PowerPoint View menu), PPT 95
Slide sorter view, **PPT 11,** PPT 95-97
Slide Sorter View button, PPT 95-97
Slide title, PPT 31-32
Slides tab, **PPT 11**
Smart documents, EX 4
Smart tag, AC 5, **EX 78, PPT 106,** WD 85, WD 91, **WD 115-116, WD 191-**192
Smart Tag Actions menu, WD 116
Smart tag indicator, **EX 78, WD 116,** WD 191-192
Snaps, **EX 41**
Snapshot, report, **AC 175, AC 184-**185
Snapshot Viewer, **AC 184**
Soft page breaks, *see* Automatic page breaks
Sort (database), AC 5, **AC 86**
data in query, AC 85-89
duplicates and, AC 87-88
indexes and, AC 159
on multiple keys, AC 88-89
records, AC 155-156
Sorting (document), **WD 109**
Sorting (e-mail), OUT 10, OUT 31-32
Sort Ascending button (Table Datasheet toolbar), AC 155, AC 156
Sort command (Access Records menu), AC 155
Sort command (Word Table menu), WD 109
Sort Descending button (Table Datasheet toolbar), AC 155
Sort key, **AC 86**
multiple, AC 88-89
Sound clips, WD 45
Source area, **EX 25,** EX 88, EX 157
Source document, INT 17
Source file, folders, WIN 55
Source object, **INT 14**
Source program, **INT 14**
Space, nonbreaking, WD 180
spacebar
displaying formatting marks and, WD 20, WD 21
entering blank characters using, EX 52
Spacing, line, *see* Line spacing
Spam filters, OUT 15, OUT 29
Speakers, speech playback and, AC 10
Speaking commands, WD 7, WD 16
Special characters, file and folder names, WIN43
Speech playback, AC 10, **EX 16**
Speech recognition, AC 8, AC 9-10, EX 15-16, PPT 16-17, WD 7, WD 16
Speed, of scrolling text, **INT 22**
Spell checker, **EX 111**
Spell checking, PPT 53-55
AutoCorrect and, EX 18, WD 89-90
automatically, WD 27
dictionaries and, WD 121
grammar checking with, WD 119-120
multiple sheets, EX 199
using AutoCorrect button, EX 113
using Spelling and Grammar Status icon, WD 19, WD 25-27
using Spelling button, EX 111-112
Spelling and Grammar button (Word Standard toolbar), WD 119
Spelling and Grammar command (Word Tools menu), WD 120
Spelling and Grammar Status icon, **WD 19,** WD 25-27
Spelling button (Excel Standard toolbar), EX 112
Spelling button (PowerPoint Standard toolbar), PPT 54
Spelling command (Excel Tools menu), EX 112
Spelling command (PowerPoint Tools menu), PPT 55
Split command (Excel Window menu), EX 203
Splitter bar, **PPT 11**
Splitting a merged cell, **EX 33**
Spreadsheet program, *see* Excel 2003
SQL, AC 72
Standard toolbar
Excel, EX 13-14
My Computer window, WIN 18
Outlook Message window), OUT 11
PowerPoint, **PPT 15**
Word, **WD 14**
Start menu
displaying, WIN 11-14
opening windows using, WIN 25-26
starting applications using, WIN 35-36
Start menu (Windows taskbar)
All Programs, Microsoft Office, Microsoft Office Access 2003 command, AC 7-8
All Programs, Microsoft Office, Microsoft Office Excel 2003 command, EX 7
All Programs, Microsoft Office, Microsoft Office PowerPoint 2003 command, PPT 7
All Programs, Microsoft Office, Microsoft Office Word 2003 command, WD 6
Programs, Microsoft Office, Microsoft Office Outlook 2003 command, OUT 6
Start page, *see* Home page
Starting
Access, AC 7-8
application programs, WIN 34-36
Excel, EX 6-8, EX 47, EX 70
Help and Support Center services, WIN 66-67
Outlook, OUT 6
PowerPoint, PPT 7-8, PPT 51-52
Windows Explorer, WIN 37
Windows XP, WIN 7-8
Word, WD 6-7, WIN 49-50
Startup submenu (Excel), adding Excel to, EX 150
Static Web page, **EX 226,** EX 228-233
saving workbook as, EX 230-232
viewing in browser, EX 226, EX 232, EX 233
Statistical functions, EX 4
blank cell and, EX 81
Statistics, calculating, AC 99-103
Status bar, AC 13, EX 14-15, PPT 13, WD 11-12, WIN 38
insertion point position, WD 18
Status indicators, **WD 12**
Strategies for College Success presentation, PPT 4-65
Structure (database), **AC 126-**130
index and, AC 114, AC 157-162
Structure (table), AC 15
correcting errors in, AC 21
Style, WD 95, WD 151
applying, WD 98
base, WD 95
business letter, WD 175
character, WD 152
list, WD 152
modifying, WD 95-98
Normal, WD 95
paragraph, WD 152
table, WD 152
Style box arrow (Word Formatting toolbar), WD 95, WD 152
Styles and Formatting button (Word Formatting toolbar), WD 98, WD 173
Styles and Formatting task pane, **WD 152**
Subdatasheet, **AC 153-154**
Subject text box, OUT 14
Submenu, AC 12, EX 11, PPT 13, WD 13, WD 46
Subtitle
Blue Chip Stock Club worksheet, EX 91
Strategies for College Success presentation, PPT 22-23
Sum
calculating, EX 23-24
See also SUM function
SUM function, **EX 23**
copying using fill handle, EX 25
entering using AutoSum button, EX 23-24, EX 27
entering using Function command, EX 24
entering using Insert Function button, EX 24
Superscript, WD 93, WD 156-157
Support, *see* Help system
Symbol
AutoCorrect entries, WD 106-107
format, AC 143, EX 162-163
Symbol command (Word Insert menu), WD 107
nonbreaking space, WD 180
Synonym, **WD 118-119**
System date, EX 165-167
System menu, My Computer window, WIN 18

Tab character, **WD 165**
TAB key, WD 165
adding rows to table using, WD 184
completing field entry using, AC 24
indent using, WD 89
moving in table using, WD 183, WD 184
moving to next column using, AC 19
Tab marker, WD 163-165
moving, WD 177
Tab split box, **EX 11**
Tab stop, **WD 163-**165
cover letter, WD 176-177
custom, WD 164, WD 176-177
moving, WD 177
on ruler, WD 163-164, WD 176-177
setting using ruler, WD 176-177
setting using Tabs dialog box, WD 163-165

Table (database)
adding records to existing, AC 27-29, AC 33-34
adding records to new, AC 22-25
closing, AC 21-22, AC 25-26
creating, AC 10, AC 15-18, 17, AC 33
defining fields in, AC 18-20
joining for query, AC 90-95
linked, AC 180
make-table, AC 135
moving within, AC 27
name, AC 22, AC 33
opening, AC 23, AC 34
previewing, AC 29-31
printing, AC 29, AC 31-32
querying, *see* Queries
relationship between, AC 150
report, AC 42-47
saving, AC 22, AC 33
structure, AC 15
worksheet copied to, AC 173-182
Table (Word), **WD 150**
adding columns, WD 185
adding rows, WD 184
alignment, WD 186-187
AutoFormat, WD 187
border, INT 10-11 centering, WD 187
creating with Insert Table button, WD 182-183
entering data in, WD 183-185
inserting, INT 9-10
resume, WD 150-151
selecting items, WD 186
Table command (Access Insert menu), AC 18
Table formats, merging, EX 36
Table menu (Word)
AutoFit command, columns, WD 185
Insert command, INT 9-10
Insert command, rows, WD 184
Sort command, WD 109
Table Properties command, border, INT 11
Table move handle, WD 186
Table of Contents, Windows XP, WIN 68
Table Properties command (Word Table menu), border, INT 11
Table resize handle, **WD 186**
Table styles, **WD 152**
Tables and Borders button (Word Standard toolbar), drawing table, WD 183
Tablet PC, WD 4
Tabs command (Word Format menu), WD 164, WD 176
Tabs dialog box
displaying, WD 177
setting tab stops using, WD 163-165
Tabs pane, Outline tab, PPT 86
Tabular report, AC 45
Tags, *see* Smart tags
Task bar, **WIN 10**
Task pane, AC 8, EX 8, PPT 8, WD 7, **WIN 49**
Clip Art, WD 47-48
closing, EX 9
moving title bar, WD 7
opening, EX 9
Slide Design, PPT 17
switching among, WD 10
Task Pane command (Excel View menu), EX 9
Task Pane command (PowerPoint View menu), PPT 31
Task Pane command (Word View menu), WD 10, WD 148
Taskbar, **AC 13, PPT 7,** PPT 11
Template, PPT 17, **WD 138,** WD 141
design, *see* Design template
resume, WD 143
saving as, WD 175
Web presentation, PPT 142
Text, **EX 16**
Blue Chip Stock Club worksheet, EX 70-72
deleting from document, WD 56, WD 58-59
deleting, PPT 56
dictating, AC 8, AC 9, PPT 8, WD 7, WD 16
entering in worksheet, EX 16-21
entering numbers as, EX 21
entering in document, WD 16-27
entering using Click and Type, WD 82-83
finding and replacing, WD 116-117
formatting worksheet, EX 28-32
hidden, WD 20
highlighting, WD 213
hyperlinks, INT 11-12
inserting in existing document, WD 57
line wrap, PPT 21
moving using drag-and-drop, WD 112-115
note, WD 93
placeholder, *see* Placeholder text
replacing, PPT 56, WD 116-117
rotating, EX 151-152
scrolling, INT 19-23, WD 23-25, WD 43
selected, WD 33
selecting nonadjacent, WD 113
validation, AC 139
wordwrap, WD 22-23
wrapping, EX 71
Text and Content Layouts (Slide Layout task pane), PPT 97, PPT 98
Text areas, **PPT 12**
Text attribute, **PPT 23-27**
Outline tab, PPT 86
Text AutoFit, **PPT 21**
Text box, **WIN 10**
Text data
importing, AC 176
in query criteria, **AC 75-76**
Text field, AC 19
width, AC 16
Text Layouts (Slide Layout task pane), PPT 97
Text placeholders, **PPT 12**
selecting, PPT 32
subtitle, PPT 22-23
title, PPT 21
Text slide, **PPT 7**
bulleted list, PPT 30-42
multi-level bulleted list, PPT 34-42, PPT 90-93
single-level bulleted list, PPT 33-34
Text width, zooming, WD 169-170
Theme, Web page, **WD 207-208,** WD 211
Theme command (Word Format menu), WD 208, WD 211
Thesaurus, **WD 118**
3-D clustered column chart, EX 39
3-D Pie chart, EX 187-197
3-D View command (Excel Chart menu), EX 195
Thumbnail, PPT 11, PPT 96
Tilting 3-D Pie chart, EX 194-196
Time
current, AC 13
system, EX 165
Title
Blue Chip Stock Club worksheet, EX 70-72
chart, EX 189, 192
column, *see* Column titles
outline, PPT 84
report, AC 45
row, *see* Row titles
of works, WD 76, WD 104
worksheet, *see* Worksheet title
Title bar, AC 12
document name on, WD 30
Title slide, **PPT 10**
Outline tab, PPT 88-89
Strategies for College Success presentation, PPT 20-21
Toggle commands, EX 175
Toolbar, AC 13, EX 8, PPT 8, WD 7
button size, WD 15
customized, EX 181, EX 183
displaying, PPT 16
docked, EX 182-183, WD 14, WD 82
Drawing, *see* Drawing toolbar
floating, EX 182, WD 14, WD 82
Formatting, *see* Formatting toolbar
hiding, PPT 15
Help and Support Center, WIN 69-70
moving, EX 13, EX 182, WD 82
Picture, WD 49
Query Design, AC 71
removing button from, EX 91
resetting, EX 13, WD 15
Standard, *see* Standard toolbar
toggle buttons, WD 45
Web, WIN 84
Toolbar buttons
displaying on two rows, EX 9, EX 14, PPT 8, PPT 9, WD 9, WD 14
hidden, EX 13, WD 14
sizing, EX 14
Toolbar dock, **EX 182**
Toolbar Options button (PowerPoint Standard toolbar), PPT 9
Toolbar Options list (Excel), EX 9
Show Buttons on Two Rows command, EX 14
Toolbar Options list (Word), WD 9, WD 14
Toolbars command (PowerPoint View menu), Outlining, PPT 86
Tools button (Save As dialog box), PPT 30
Tools menu (Access)
Database Utilities command, Compact and Repair Database, AC 164
Relationships command, AC 152
Speech command, AC 10
Tools menu (Excel)
Auditing command, EX 148
AutoCorrect Options command, smart tags, EX 78
Error Checking command, EX 113, EX 148
Error Checking command, formulas, EX 90
Goal Seek command, EX 206-207
Options command, formulas version, EX 119
Spelling command, EX 112
Tools menu (Outlook)
Options command, e-mail signature, OUT 20-21
Options command, message importance, OUT 36
Organize command, contacts, OUT 48
Tools menu (PowerPoint)
Options command, black slide, PPT 42-43
Options command, fast saves, PPT 111
Spelling command, PPT 55
Tools menu (Save As dialog box), EX 44
Tools menu (Word)
AutoCorrect Options command, AutoFormat As You Type, WD 156

AutoCorrect Options command, smart tags, WD 115
AutoCorrect Options command, spell checking, WD 27
AutoCorrect Options command, WD 92
Language command, thesaurus, WD 118
Letters and Mailings command, WD 190-191
Options command, dictionary, WD 121
Options command, showing formatting marks, WD 21
Research command, WD 124
Spelling and Grammar command, WD 120
Word Count command, WD 100
Tools submenu, Save Options command, WD 30
ToolTips, WIN 21
Top-values query, **AC 89-90**
Totals
AutoCalculate, EX 48
AutoSum button and, EX 79-80
determining multiple, EX 26-27
summing, *see* SUM function
Totals button (Query Design toolbar), AC 100
Totals command (Access View menu), AC 101
Trace Error button, EX 79
Training, on-line, WIN 91
Transparency, PPT 61
Turning off computer, WIN 72-75
Type a question for help box (menu bar), AC 68, EX 9, EX 53-54, PPT 62-64, WD 60
Typography terms, PPT 23

Underline, **EX 187**
Underline button (Word Formatting toolbar), WD 42
Underlined titles of works, WD 76
Underlined, **WD 42**
Undo
AutoCorrect entries, WD 90, WD 106
deletions, EX 162
paste operation, EX 158
slide layout, PPT 107
sort, WD 110
what-if questions, EX 206
Undo button (Excel Standard toolbar), EX 51-52
Undo button (Word Standard toolbar), WD 39, WD 58
Undo command (Excel Edit menu), EX 51
Undo command (Word Edit menu), WD 39
Undo Paste command (Excel Edit menu), EX 158
Unfreeze Panes command (Excel Window menu), EX 176
Unfreezing worksheet titles, EX 175-176
Uniform Resource Locator (URL), **WIN 76**
Unique identifier, *see* Primary key
Unique Properties value, AC 88
Unmatched records, AC 154
Unread Mail, **OUT 38**
Update
cascade the, AC 151
date or time, WD 178
Update query, AC 135, **AC 136**-137
Update Query command (Query menu), AC 137
Updating, AC 4
records, AC 116-120
referential integrity and, AC 150-153
restructured database, AC 130
table that contains validation rules, AC 145-146
URL, *see* Uniform Resource Locator
USB flash drives, WIN 40-43
User interface, graphical, **WIN 6-7**
User names, WIN 8

Validation rules, **AC 139-146**
updating table that contains, AC 145-146
Validation text, **AC 139**
Value axis, *see* Y-axis
Values
assumptions, EX 146
default, AC 139, AC 141-142
legal, AC 142-143
formulas versus, EX 118
lookup field, AC 146-150
referential integrity and, AC 150-153
Values version, **EX 118**
Vertical alignment, EX 92, EX 96
Vertical ruler, **WD 11**
print layout view, WD 148
Vertical scroll bar, **PPT 12**, PPT 44-46, WD 24, WD 43
Vertical split bar, **EX 204**
Video clips, WD 45
View
presentation, **PPT 11**
worksheet, EX 201-204
View button (Form View toolbar), AC 42, AC 119, AC 120
View button arrow (Form View toolbar), AC 42
View button arrow (Query Datasheet toolbar), AC 72
View filter, e-mail, **OUT 32-34**
View menu (Access)
Datasheet View command, AC 120
Design View command, query, AC 73
Indexes command, AC 161
Properties command, Unique Properties value, AC 88
Totals command, AC 101
View menu (Excel)
Full Screen command, viewing area, EX 11
Task Pane command, EX 9
Zoom command, EX 202
View menu (Outlook), Arrange By command, OUT 31, OUT 32
View menu (PowerPoint)
Color/Grayscale command, black and white printing, PPT 59
Slide Show command, PPT 47
Slide Sorter command, PPT 95
Task Pane command, PPT 31
Toolbars command, Outlining, PPT 86
View menu (Word)
Header and Footer command, WD 102
Header and Footer command, WD 81-82
Normal command, WD 77
Ruler command, WD 11, WD 87
Task Pane command, WD 10
Task Pane command, Resume Wizard, WD 148
Zoom command, header, WD 82
Zoom command, text, WD 21
Viewing
e-mail attachment, OUT 18-19
header, WD 102
objects in windows, WIN 27
View-only Web page, *see* Static Web page
Viruses, e-mail format and, OUT 19

Web, *see* World Wide Web
Web address, removing hyperlink, WD 174
Web browser, WD 122
dynamic Web page in, EX 226, EX 236-237
editing Web page through, PPT 151-153
static Web page in, EX 226, EX 232, EX 233
viewing Web page in, WD 208-209
Web page preview and, EX 228-229
Web browser program. *See also* Internet Explorer
Web Discussions feature, INT 39
Web folders, EX 228, WD 204
Web layout view, WD 206
creating using Word, WD 203-215
dynamic, *see* Dynamic Web page
editing through browser, PPT 151-153
formats, EX 230, WD 206
formatting, WD 206-207
home page, INT 8
noninteractive, *see* Static Web page
PowerPoint presentation, INT 26-30
previewing presentation as, PPT 143-146
previewing, EX 228-229
publishing, EX 228, EX 230, INT 29, INT 37
remarks, INT 39
save formats, PPT 146
saving document as, WD 203
saving presentation as, PPT 146-149
scrolling text, INT 19-23
static, *see* Static Web page
tables in, INT 9-11
theme, WD 207-208, WD 211
viewing, INT 31, WD 208-209
viewing presentation, PPT 149-151
view-only, *see* Static Web page
Web page
authoring, WD 206
described, **WIN 76**
dynamic, **WIN 79**
Web Page format, EX 230, PPT 146, WD 206
Web Page Preview command (Excel File menu), EX 228-229
Web Page Preview command (PowerPoint File menu), INT 28, PPT 143, PPT 144
Web Page Preview command (Word File menu), INT 24, WD 209
Web presentation, PPT 141-157
Web programming languages, INT 25
Web query, importing data using, **EX 120**-123
Leland Mortgage, INT 3-40
testing, INT 38-39
Web site, **WIN 36**, WIN 44, **WIN 76**
Web source, importing external data from, using Web query, EX 120-123
Web support, AC 4, **EX 4**, PPT 6
Web toolbar, WIN 84
Web Tools toolbar, INT 19-20
Welcome to MSN.com window, WIN 36
What-if analysis, EX 148, **EX 204**-208
White space, EX 72
hiding, WD 149
Width
column, *see* Column width
text field, AC 16
Wildcards, **AC 76**-77
in validation rules, AC 142
Window
Database, AC 13
document, WD 10-12
minimizing, maximizing, WIN 19-24
moving by dragging, WIN 26
My Computer, *see* My Computer window
My Documents, *see* My Documents window
opening, WIN 17, WIN 25-26
resizing, WIN 31-32
scrolling in, WIN 27-29
sizing, WIN 29-30
splitting into panes, EX 202-204
Word, WD 8-15

Window menu (Excel
Freeze Panes command, EX 163-164
Split command, EX 203
Unfreeze Panes command, EX 176
Windows Clipboard, WD 165
Windows Explorer
described, using, WIN 37-40, WIN 61
file management in, WIN 55-61
tutorial, WIN 93-94
Windows SharePoint Services list, AC 5
Windows taskbar, *see* Taskbar
Windows Update, WIN 68
Windows XP
desktop, WIN 11
Help and Support feature, WIN 66-72
launching, WIN 7-8
operating systems, WIN 5-7
tutorial, WIN 92-93
Wizard, PPT 6, **WD 138**, WD 141
Word 2003, **WD 4**, WIN 76-78
creating Web pages using, WD 203-215
Help system, WD 14, **WD 60-62**
new features, WD 4
quitting, WD 54, WD 62
slides from, PPT 87
starting, WD 6-7
Word Count command (Word Tools menu), WD 100
Word Count toolbar, WD 100-101
Word document, *see* Document
Word processing, PPT 4
Word processing program. *See also* Word 2003
Word window
customizing, WD 8-10
elements of, WD 10-15
Words
antonyms for, WD 119
deleting, WD 58
flagged, WD 26, WD 27, WD 119
searching for files using, WIN 65-66
selecting group of, WD 43-44
synonyms for, WD 118-119
Wordwrap, **WD 22-23**
Workbook, **EX 9**
blank, EX 7
comparing, EX 4
copying cells from one to another, EX 157
e-mailing, EX 125-126
hyperlinks in, EX 237
name, EX 43, EX 44
opening existing, EX 47-48
publishing, EX 228, EX 235
saving as static Web page, EX 230-232
saving new, EX 42-44
saving using same file name, EX 88-89
Works cited, **WD 76**
Worksheet, **EX 4, EX 9**
Aquatics Wear, EX 145-208
Blue Chip Stock Club Investment Analysis, EX 65-128
clearing entire, EX 52-53
color in, EX 91
database conversion, AC 173-182
design, EX 68
development cycle, EX 5
errors in, *see* Correcting errors
Extreme Blading Second Quarter Sales, EX 3-55
formatting, EX 72
formatting using autoformat, EX 34-36
formatting using Formatting toolbar, EX 28-34
formulas version, EX 118
importing into database, AC 176-180
moving between, EX 124
numbers entered in, EX 21-23
organization of, EX 10-11
previewing, EX 113-115
printing Extreme Blading Second Quarter Sales, EX 44-45
printing section of, EX 116-117
requirements document, *see* Requirements document
selecting entire, EX 53
sheet name, EX 10
size of, EX 10
sketch of, EX 68-69
text entered in, EX 16-21
values version, EX 118
view of, EX 201-204
Worksheet name, changing, EX 124
Worksheet subtitle, formatting, EX 33-34
Worksheet title
Aquatics Wear, EX 150
Blue Chip Stock Club worksheet, EX 91-94
border, EX 95
centering, EX 32-33
entering, EX 17-18
formatting, EX 28-33, EX 180-181
freezing, EX 163-164
unfreezing, EX 175-176
Worksheet window, **EX 11**
elements of, EX 11-15
size, EX 11
Workstation, **WIN 5**
World Wide Web, **WIN 76**
clip art on, WD 48
works cited from, WD 108
Wrapping text, EX 71
Wrist injury, WD 25

X-axis (category axis), **EX 41**
.xls extension), **EX 43**
XML (Extensible Markup Language), AC 4, AC 5, AC 175, **AC 185**, EX 4, WD 4
XML data
exporting, AC 185-186
importing, AC 187-188

Y-axis (value axis), **EX 38**
chart scale and, EX 41
Years, two-digit, EX 72

Zero, displaying value of, EX 177
Zeros, trailing, EX 23
Zoom box (Excel Standard toolbar), EX 201
Zoom box arrow (PowerPoint Standard toolbar), **PPT 44**
Zoom command (Access shortcut menu), AC 97
Zoom command (Excel View menu), EX 202
Zoom command (Word View menu), header, WD 82
Zoom setting, **PPT 44**
Zooming
database, AC 97
document, WD 21
header, WD 82
presentation, PPT 44
text width, WD 169-170
worksheet, EX 201

Quick Reference Summary

In the Microsoft Office 2003 applications, you can accomplish a task in a number of ways. The following five tables (one each for Microsoft Office Word 2003, Microsoft Office Excel 2003, Microsoft Office Access 2003, Microsoft Office PowerPoint 2003, and Microsoft Office Outlook 2003,) provide a quick reference to each task presented in this textbook. The first column identifies the task. The second column indicates the page number on which the task is discussed in the book. The subsequent four columns list the different ways the task in column one can be carried out. You can invoke the commands listed in the MOUSE, MENU BAR, and SHORTCUT MENU columns using Voice commands.

Table 1 Microsoft Office Word 2003 Quick Reference Summary

TASK	PAGE NUMBER	MOUSE	MENU BAR	SHORTCUT MENU	KEYBOARD SHORTCUT
1.5 Line Spacing	WD 87	Line Spacing button arrow on Formatting toolbar	Format | Paragraph | Indents and Spacing tab	Paragraph | Indents and Spacing tab	CTRL+5
AutoCorrect Entry, Create	WD 91		Tools | AutoCorrect Options | AutoCorrect tab		
AutoCorrect Options	WD 90	AutoCorrect Options button			
AutoText Entry, Create	WD 179		Insert | AutoText | New		ALT+F3
AutoText Entry, Insert	WD 181		Insert | AutoText		Type entry, then F3
Blank Line Above Paragraph	WD 87		Format | Paragraph | Indents and Spacing tab	Paragraph | Indents and Spacing tab	CTRL+0 (zero)
Bold	WD 44	Bold button on Formatting toolbar	Format | Font | Font tab	Font | Font tab	CTRL+B
Border, Bottom	WD 172	Border button arrow on Formatting toolbar	Format | Borders and Shading | Borders tab		
Bulleted List	WD 187	Bullets button on Formatting toolbar	Format | Bullets and Numbering | Bulleted tab	Bullets and Numbering | Bulleted tab	* and then space, type text, ENTER
Capitalize Letters	WD 87		Format | Font | Font tab	Font | Font tab	CTRL+SHIFT+A
Case of Letters	WD 87				SHIFT+F3
Center	WD 38	Center button on Formatting toolbar	Format | Paragraph | Indents and Spacing tab	Paragraph | Indents and Spacing tab	CTRL+E
Center Vertically	WD 38		File | Page Setup | Layout tab		
Clip Art, Insert	WD 46		Insert | Picture | Clip Art		
Clipboard Task Pane, Display	WD 169	Double-click Office Clipboard icon in tray	Edit | Office Clipboard		
Close Document	WD 59	Close button on menu bar	File | Close		CTRL+W
Color Characters	WD 161	Font Color button arrow on Formatting toolbar	Format | Font | Font tab	Font | Font tab	
Copy (Collect Items)	WD 166	Copy button on Standard toolbar	Edit | Copy	Copy	CTRL+C
Count Words	WD 100	Recount button on Word Count toolbar	Tools | Word Count		
Custom Dictionary	WD 121		Tools | Options | Spelling and Grammar tab		
Date, Insert	WD 177		Insert | Date and Time		
Delete (Cut) Text	WD 59	Cut button on Standard toolbar	Edit | Cut	Cut	CTRL+X or DELETE
Demote List Item	WD 189	Decrease Indent button on Formatting toolbar			
Document Summary, Modify	WD 193		File | Properties | Summary tab		
Document Window, Open New	WD 160	New Blank Document button on Standard toolbar		File | New | Blank document	CTRL+N

Table 1 Microsoft Office Word 2003 Quick Reference Summary *(continued)*

TASK	PAGE NUMBER	MOUSE	MENU BAR	SHORTCUT MENU	KEYBOARD SHORTCUT
Double-Space Text	WD 80	Line Spacing button on Formatting toolbar	Format | Paragraph | Indents and Spacing tab	Paragraph | Indents and Spacing tab	CTRL+2
Double-Underline	WD 87		Format | Font | Font tab	Font | Font tab	CTRL+SHIFT+D
E-Mail Document	WD 123	E-mail button on Standard toolbar	File | Send To | Mail Recipient		
Envelope, Address	WD 190		Tools | Letters and Mailings | Envelopes and Labels		
Find	WD 117	Select Browse Object button on vertical scroll bar	Edit | Find		CTRL+F
Find and Replace	WD 116	Double-click left side of status bar	Edit | Replace		CTRL+H
File Properties, Display	WD 194	Views button arrow in Open dialog box			
First-Line Indent	WD 88	Drag First Line Indent marker on ruler	Format | Paragraph | Indents and Spacing tab	Paragraph | Indents and Spacing tab	
Font	WD 36	Font box arrow on Formatting toolbar	Format | Font | Font tab	Font | Font tab	CTRL+SHIFT+F
Font Size	WD 17	Font Size box arrow on Formatting toolbar	Format | Font | Font tab	Font | Font tab	CTRL+SHIFT+P
Footnote, Create	WD 94		Insert | Reference | Footnote		
Footnote, Delete	WD 99	Delete note reference mark			
Footnote, Edit	WD 99	Double-click note reference mark	View | Footnotes		
Footnotes to Endnotes, Convert	WD 99		Insert | Reference | Footnote		
Formatting Marks	WD 21	Show/Hide ¶ button on Standard toolbar	Tools | Options | View tab		CTRL+SHIFT+*
Formatting, Clear	WD 173	Style box arrow on Formatting toolbar			CTRL+SPACEBAR; CTRL+Q
Frame, New	WD 210	Desired button on Frames toolbar			
Frames Page, Create	WD 210		Format | Frames | New Frames Page		
Frame Properties, Modify	WD 214	Frame Properties button on Frames toolbar	Format | Frames | Frame Properties	Frame Properties	
Full Menu	WD 13	Double-click menu name	Click menu name and wait		
Go To	WD 111	Select Browse Object button on vertical scroll bar	Edit | Go To		CTRL+G
Hanging Indent, Create	WD 105	Drag Hanging Indent marker on ruler	Format | Paragraph | Indents and Spacing tab	Paragraph | Indents and Spacing tab	CTRL+T
Hanging Indent, Remove	WD 87	Drag Hanging Indent marker on ruler	Format | Paragraph | Indents and Spacing tab	Paragraph | Indents and Spacing tab	CTRL+SHIFT+T
Header, Display	WD 81		View | Header and Footer		
Help	WD 60 and Appendix A	Microsoft Office Word Help button on Standard toolbar	Help | Microsoft Office Word Help		F1
Highlight Text	WD 213	Highlight button arrow on Formatting toolbar			
HTML Source	WD 206		View | HTML Source		
Hyperlink, Convert to Regular Text	WD 174	AutoCorrect Options button | Undo Hyperlink		Remove Hyperlink	CTRL+Z
Hyperlink, Create	WD 108 and WD 212	Insert Hyperlink button on Standard toolbar		Hyperlink	Web address then ENTER or SPACEBAR
Hyperlink, Edit	WD 207	Insert Hyperlink button on Standard toolbar		Hyperlink	CTRL+K
Indent, Decrease	WD 87	Decrease Indent button on Formatting toolbar	Format | Paragraph | Indents and Spacing tab	Paragraph | Indents and Spacing tab	CTRL+SHIFT+M
Indent, Increase	WD 87	Increase Indent button on Formatting toolbar	Format | Paragraph | Indents and Spacing tab	Paragraph | Indents and Spacing tab	CTRL+M
Italicize	WD 41	Italic button on Formatting toolbar	Format | Font | Font tab	Font | Font tab	CTRL+I
Justify Paragraph	WD 87	Justify button on Formatting toolbar	Format | Paragraph | Indents and Spacing tab	Paragraph | Indents and Spacing tab	CTRL+J

Table 1 Microsoft Office Word 2003 Quick Reference Summary

TASK	PAGE NUMBER	MOUSE	MENU BAR	SHORTCUT MENU	KEYBOARD SHORTCUT
Leader Characters	WD 164		Format | Tabs		
Left-Align	WD 86	Align Left button on Formatting toolbar	Format | Paragraph | Indents and Spacing tab	Paragraph | Indents and Spacing tab	CTRL+L
Line Break, Enter	WD 154				SHIFT+ENTER
Mailing Label, Address	WD 191		Tools | Letters and Mailings | Envelopes and Labels		
Margins	WD 78	In print layout view, drag margin boundary on ruler	File | Page Setup | Margins tab		
Move Selected Text	WD 113	Drag and drop	Edit | Cut; Edit | Paste	Cut; Paste	CTRL+X; CTRL+V
Nonbreaking Hyphen	WD 180		Insert | Symbol | Special Characters tab		CTRL+SHIFT+HYPHEN
Nonbreaking Space	WD 180		Insert | Symbol | Special Characters tab		CTRL+SHIFT+SPACEBAR
Numbered List	WD 189	Numbering button on Formatting toolbar	Format | Bullets and Numbering | Numbered tab	Bullets and Numbering | Numbered tab	1. and then space, type text, ENTER
Open Document	WD 55	Open button on Standard toolbar	File | Open		CTRL+O
Outline Numbered List	WD 189		Format | Bullets and Numbering | Outline Numbered tab		
Page Break	WD 103		Insert | Break		CTRL+ENTER
Page Numbers, Insert	WD 83	Insert Page Number button on Header and Footer toolbar	Insert | Page Numbers		
Paste	WD 170	Paste button on Standard toolbar	Edit | Paste	Paste	CTRL+V
Paste Options, Menu	WD 115	Paste Options button			
Print Document	WD 53	Print button on Standard toolbar	File | Print		CTRL+P
Print Preview	WD 158	Print Preview button on Standard toolbar	File | Print Preview		CTRL+F2
Promote List Item	WD 189	Increase Indent button on Formatting toolbar			
Quit Word	WD 54	Close button on title bar	File | Exit		ALT+F4
Redo Action	WD 39	Redo button on Standard toolbar	Edit | Redo		
Repeat Command	WD 39		Edit | Repeat		
Research Task Pane	WD 124	ALT+click word in document	Tools | Research		
Research Task Pane, Insert text from	WD 125			Right-click selected text in task pane, click Copy; right-click document, click Paste	Select text in task pane, CTRL+C; click document, CTRL+V
Resize Graphic	WD 50	Drag sizing handle	Format | Picture | Size tab	Format Picture | Size tab	
Restore Graphic	WD 51	Format Picture button on Picture toolbar	Format | Picture | Size tab	Format Picture | Size tab	
Resume Wizard	WD 142		File | New | On my computer | Other Documents tab		
Right-Align	WD 37	Align Right button on Formatting toolbar	Format | Paragraph | Indents and Spacing tab	Paragraph | Indents and Spacing tab	CTRL+R
Ruler, Show or Hide	WD 11		View | Ruler		
Save as Web Page	WD 205		File | Save as Web Page		
Save Document - New Name or Format	WD 52		File | Save As		F12
Save Document - Same Name	WD 52	Save button on Standard toolbar	File | Save		CTRL+S
Save New Document	WD 28	Save button on Standard toolbar	File | Save		CTRL+S
Select Document	WD 113	Point to left and triple-click	Edit | Select All		CTRL+A
Select Graphic	WD 49	Click graphic			
Select Group of Words	WD 43	Drag through words			CTRL+SHIFT+ARROW
Select Line	WD 40	Point to left of line and click			SHIFT+DOWN ARROW
Select Multiple Paragraphs	WD 33	Point to left of first paragraph and drag down			CTRL+SHIFT+DOWN ARROW

Table 1 Microsoft Office Word 2003 Quick Reference Summary *(continued)*

TASK	PAGE NUMBER	MOUSE	MENU BAR	SHORTCUT MENU	KEYBOARD SHORTCUT
Select Paragraph	WD 113	Triple-click paragraph			
Select Sentence	WD 112	CTRL+click sentence			CTRL+SHIFT+ARROW
Select Word	WD 58	Double-click word			CTRL+SHIFT+ARROW
Single-Space Text	WD 87	Line Spacing button arrow on Formatting toolbar	Format | Paragraph | Indents and Spacing tab	Paragraph | Indents and Spacing tab	CTRL+1
Small Uppercase Letters	WD 87		Format | Font | Font tab	Font | Font tab	CTRL+SHIFT+K
Smart Tag Actions, Display Menu	WD 192	Point to smart tag indicator, click Smart Tag Actions button			
Sort Paragraphs	WD 109		Table | Sort		
Spelling and Grammar Check At Once	WD 119	Spelling and Grammar button on Standard toolbar	Tools | Spelling and Grammar	Spelling	F7
Spelling Check as You Type	WD 26	Double-click Spelling and Grammar Status icon on status bar		Right-click flagged word, click word on shortcut menu	
Style, Modify	WD 96	Styles and Formatting button on Formatting toolbar	Format | Styles and Formatting		
Styles and Formatting Task Pane, Display	WD 152	Styles and Formatting button on Formatting toolbar	View | Task Pane		
Subscript	WD 87		Format | Font | Font tab	Font | Font tab	CTRL+=
Superscript	WD 87		Format | Font | Font tab	Font | Font tab	CTRL+SHIFT+PLUS SIGN
Switch to Open Document	WD 166	Program button on taskbar	Window | document name		ALT+TAB
Synonym	WD 118		Tools | Language | Thesaurus	Synonyms | desired word	SHIFT+F7
Tab Stops, Set	WD 164	Click location on ruler	Format | Tabs		
Table AutoFormat	WD 187	AutoFormat button on Tables and Borders toolbar	Table | Table AutoFormat		
Table, Fit Columns to Table Contents	WD 185	Double-click column boundary	Table | AutoFit | AutoFit to Contents	AutoFit | AutoFit to Contents	
Table, Insert Empty	WD 183	Insert Table button on Standard toolbar	Table | Insert | Table		
Table, Insert Row	WD 184		Table | Insert | Rows Above/Below	Right-click selected row; Insert Rows	TAB from lower-right cell
Table, Resize Column	WD 186	Drag column boundary	Table | Table Properties | Column tab	Table Properties | Column tab	
Table, Select	WD 186	Click table move handle	Table | Select | Table		ALT+5 (on keypad)
Table, Select Cell	WD 186	Click left edge of cell			TAB
Table, Select Column	WD 186	Click top border of column			
Table, Select Cells	WD 186	Drag through cells			
Table, Select Row	WD 186	Click to left of row			
Task Pane, Display Different	WD 10	Other Task Panes button on task pane			
Template, Open	WD 175		File | New | On my computer		
Theme, Apply	WD 208		Format | Theme		
Toolbar, Dock	WD 82	Double-click toolbar title bar			
Toolbar, Float	WD 82	Drag toolbar move handle			
Toolbar, Show Entire	WD 14	Double-click toolbar move handle	Tools | Customize | Options tab		
Underline	WD 42	Underline button on Formatting toolbar	Format | Font | Font tab	Font | Font tab	CTRL+U
Underline Words	WD 87		Format | Font | Font tab	Font | Font tab	CTRL+SHIFT+W
Undo	WD 39	Undo button on Standard toolbar	Edit | Undo		CTRL+Z
User Information, Change	WD 194		Tools | Options | User Information tab		
Web Page Frame, Resize	WD 211	Drag frame border	Format | Frames | Frame Properties | Frame tab		
Web Page, Preview	WD 209		File | Web Page Preview		
White Space	WD 149	Hide or Show White Space button	Tools | Options | View tab		
Zoom	WD 21 and WD 169	Zoom box arrow on Formatting toolbar	View | Zoom		

Table 2 Microsoft Excel 2003 Quick Reference Summary

TASK	PAGE NUMBER	MOUSE	MENU BAR	SHORTCUT MENU	KEYBOARD SHORTCUT
AutoFormat	EX 34		Format | AutoFormat		ALT+O | A
AutoSum	EX 23	AutoSum button on Standard toolbar	Insert | Function		ALT+=
Bold	EX 30	Bold button on Formatting toolbar	Format | Cells | Font tab	Format Cells | Font tab	CTRL+B
Borders	EX 96	Borders button on Formatting toolbar	Format | Cells | Border tab	Format Cells | Border tab	CTRL+1 | B
Center	EX 97	Center button on Formatting toolbar	Format | Cells | Alignment tab	Format Cells | Alignment tab	CTRL+1 | A
Center Across Columns	EX 33	Merge and Center button on Formatting toolbar	Format | Cells | Alignment tab	Format Cells | Alignment tab	CTRL+1 | A
Chart	EX 39	Chart Wizard button on Standard toolbar	Insert | Chart		F11
Clear Cell	EX 52	Drag fill handle back	Edit | Clear | All	Clear Contents	DELETE
Close Workbook	EX 46	Close button on menu bar or workbook Control-menu icon	File | Close		CTRL+W
Color Background	EX 94	Fill Color button on Formatting toolbar	Format | Cells | Patterns tab	Format Cells | Patterns tab	CTRL+1 | P
Color Tab	EX 198			Tab Color	
Column Width	EX 107	Drag column heading boundary	Format | Column | Width	Column Width	ALT+O | C | W
Comma Style Format	EX 108	Comma Style button on Formatting toolbar	Format | Cells | Number tab | Accounting	Format Cells | Number tab | Accounting	CTRL+1 | N
Conditional Formatting	EX 104		Format | Conditional Formatting		ALT+O | D
Copy and Paste	EX 157	Copy button and Paste button on Standard toolbar	Edit | Copy; Edit | Paste	Copy to copy; Paste to paste	CTRL+C; CTRL+V
Currency Style Format	EX 98	Currency Style button on Formatting toolbar	Format | Cells | Number | Currency	Format Cells | Number | Currency	CTRL+1 | N
Cut	EX 159	Cut button on Standard toolbar	Edit | Cut	Cut	CTRL+X
Date	EX 166	Insert Function box in formula bar	Insert | Function		CTRL+SEMICOLON
Decimal Place, Decrease	EX 100	Decrease Decimal button on Formatting toolbar	Format | Cells | Number tab | Currency	Format Cells | Number tab | Currency	CTRL+1 | N
Decimal Place, Increase	EX 99	Increase Decimal button on Formatting toolbar	Format | Cells | Number tab | Currency	Format Cells | Number tab | Currency	CTRL+1 | N
Delete Rows or Columns	EX 161		Edit | Delete	Delete	
Drop Shadow	EX 184	Shadow Style button on Drawing toolbar			
E-Mail from Excel	EX 125	E-mail button on Standard toolbar	File | Send To | Mail Recipient		ALT+F | D | A
File Management	EX 232		File | Save As, right-click file name		ALT+F | A, right-click file name
Fit to Print	EX 118		File | Page Setup | Page tab		ALT+F | U | P
Folder, New	EX 230		File | Save As		ALT+F | A
Font Color	EX 32	Font Color button on Formatting toolbar	Format | Cells | Font tab	Format Cells | Font tab	CTRL+1 | F
Font Size	EX 31	Font Size box arrow on Formatting toolbar	Format | Cells | Font tab	Format Cells | Font tab	CTRL+1 | F
Font Type	EX 29	Font box arrow on Formatting toolbar	Format | Cells | Font tab	Format Cells | Font tab	CTRL+1 | F
Formula Assistance	EX 83	Insert Function box in formula bar	Insert | Function		CTRL+A after you type function name

Table 2 Microsoft Excel 2003 Quick Reference Summary *(continued)*

TASK	PAGE NUMBER	MOUSE	MENU BAR	SHORTCUT MENU	KEYBOARD SHORTCUT
Formulas Version	EX 118		Tools | Options | View tab | Formulas		CTRL+ACCENT MARK
Freeze Worksheet Titles	EX 163		Window | Freeze Panes		ALT+W | F
Full Screen	EX 11		View | Full Screen		ALT+V | U
Function	EX 81	Insert Function box in formula bar	Insert | Function		SHIFT+F3
Go To	EX 37	Click cell	Edit | Go To		F5
Goal Seek	EX 206		Tools | Goal Seek		ALT+T | G
Help	EX 53 and Appendix A	Microsoft Excel Help button on Standard toolbar	Help | Microsoft Excel Help		F1
Hide Column	EX 109	Drag column heading boundary	Format | Column | Hide	Hide	CTRL+0 (zero) to hide CTRL+SHIFT+) to display
Hide Row	EX 111	Drag row heading boundary	Format | Row | Hide	Hide	CTRL+9 to hide CTRL+SHIFT+(to display
In-Cell Editing	EX 50	Double-click cell			F2
Insert Rows or Columns	EX 160		Insert | Rows or Insert | Columns	Insert	ALT+I | R or C
Italicize	EX 186	Italic button on Formatting toolbar	Format | Cells | Font tab	Format Cells | Font tab	CTRL+I
Language Bar	EX 15 and Appendix B		Tools | Speech | Speech Recognition	Toolbars | Language bar	ALT+T | H | H
Merge Cells	EX 33	Merge and Center button on Formatting toolbar	Format | Cells | Alignment tab	Format Cells | Font tab | Alignment tab	ALT+O | E | A
Move Cells	EX 159	Point to border and drag	Edit | Cut; Edit | Paste	Cut; Paste	CTRL+X; CTRL+V
Name Cells	EX 37	Click Name box in formula bar, type name	Insert | Name | Define		ALT+I | N | D
New Workbook	EX 53	New button on Standard toolbar	File | New		CTRL+N
Open Workbook	EX 47	Open button on Standard toolbar	File | Open		CTRL+O
Percent Style Format	EX 103	Percent Style button on Formatting toolbar	Format | Cells | Number tab | Percentage	Format Cells | Number tab | Percentage	CTRL+1 | N
Preview Worksheet	EX 114	Print Preview button on Standard toolbar	File | Print Preview		ALT+F | V
Print Worksheet	EX 113	Print button on Standard toolbar	File | Print		CTRL+P
Quit Excel	EX 46	Close button on title bar	File | Exit		ALT+F4
Range Finder	EX 89	Double-click cell			
Redo	EX 52	Redo button on Standard toolbar	Edit | Redo		ALT+E | R
Remove Splits	EX 204	Double-click split bar	Window | Split		ALT+W | S
Rename Sheet Tab	EX 198	Double-click sheet tab		Rename	
Rotate Text	EX 151		Format | Cells | Alignment tab	Format Cells | Alignment tab	ALT+O | E | A
Row Height	EX 110	Drag row heading boundary	Format | Row | Height	Row Height	ALT+O | R | E
Save as Web Page	EX 230		File | Save as Web Page		ALT+F | G
Save Workbook, New Name	EX 42		File | Save As		ALT+F | A
Save Workbook, Same Name	EX 89	Save button on Standard toolbar	File | Save		CTRL+S
Select All of Worksheet	EX 53	Select All button on worksheet			CTRL+A
Select Cell	EX 16	Click cell			Use arrow keys

Table 2 Microsoft Excel 2003 Quick Reference Summary

TASK	PAGE NUMBER	MOUSE	MENU BAR	SHORTCUT MENU	KEYBOARD SHORTCUT
Select Multiple Sheets	EX 200	CTRL+click tab or SHIFT+click tab		Select All Sheets	
Series	EX 151	Drag fill handle	Edit | Fill | Series		ALT+E | I | S
Shortcut Menu	EX 92	Right-click object			SHIFT+F10
Spell Check	EX 112	Spelling button on Standard toolbar	Tools | Spelling		F7
Split Cell	EX 33	Merge and Center button on Formatting toolbar	Format | Cells | Alignment tab	Format Cells | Alignment tab	ALT+O | E | A
Split Window into Panes	EX 203	Drag vertical or horizontal split box	Window | Split		ALT+W | S
Stock Quotes	EX 121		Data | Import External Data | Import Data		ALT+D | D | D
Task Pane	EX 8		View | Task Pane		ALT+V | K
Toolbar, Dock	EX 182	Drag toolbar to dock			
Toolbar, Reset	Appendix D	Toolbar Options button on toolbar, Add or Remove Buttons, Customize, Toolbars tab		Customize | Toolbars	ALT+V | T | C | B
Toolbar, Show Entire	EX 13	Double-click move handle			
Toolbar, Show or Hide	EX 182	Right-click toolbar, click toolbar name	View | Toolbars		ALT+V | T
Underline	EX 187	Underline button on Formatting toolbar	Format | Cells | Font tab	Format Cells | Font tab	CTRL+U
Undo	EX 51	Undo button on Standard toolbar	Edit | Undo		CTRL+Z
Unfreeze Worksheet Titles	EX 176		Windows | Unfreeze Panes		ALT+W | F
Unhide Column	EX 109	Drag hidden column heading boundary to right	Format | Column | Unhide	Unhide	ALT+O | C | U
Unhide Row	EX 111	Drag hidden row heading boundary down	Format | Row | Unhide	Unhide	ALT+O | R | U
Web Page Preview	EX 228		File | Web Page Preview		ALT+F | B
Zoom	EX 201	Zoom box on Standard toolbar	View | Zoom		ALT+V | Z

Table 3 Microsoft Office Access 2003 Quick Reference Summary

TASK	PAGE NUMBER	MOUSE	MENU BAR	SHORTCUT MENU	KEYBOARD SHORTCUT
Add Field	AC 129	Insert Rows button	Insert | Rows	Insert Rows	INSERT
Add Group of Records	AC 139	Query Type button arrow | Append Query	Query | Append Query	Query Type | Append Query	
Add Record	AC 23, AC 116	New Record button	Insert | New Record		
Add Table to Query	AC 92	Show Table button	Query | Show Table	Show Table	
Advanced Filter/Sort	AC 124		Records | Filter | Advanced Filter Sort		
Apply Filter	AC 121, AC 123	Filter By Selection or Filter By Form button	Records | Filter		
Calculate Statistics	AC 100	Totals button	View | Totals	Totals	
Change Group of Records	AC 136	Query Type button arrow | Update Query	Query | Update Query	Query Type | Update Query	

Table 3 Microsoft Office Access 2003 Quick Reference Summary *(continued)*

TASK	PAGE NUMBER	MOUSE	MENU BAR	SHORTCUT MENU	KEYBOARD SHORTCUT
Clear Query	AC 75		Edit | Clear Grid		
Close Database	AC 26	Close Window button	File | Close		
Close Form	AC 39	Close Window button	File | Close		
Close Query	AC 73	Close Window button	File | Close		
Close Table	AC 21	Close Window button	File | Close		
Collapse Subdatasheet	AC 153	Expand indicator (-)			
Create Calculated Field	AC 96			Zoom	SHIFT+F2
Create Database	AC 10	New button	File | New		CTRL+N
Create Form	AC 38	New Object button arrow | AutoForm	Insert | AutoForm		
Create Index	AC 161	Indexes button	View | Indexes		
Create Query	AC 68	New Object button arrow | Query	Insert | Query		
Create Report	AC 43	New Object button arrow | Report	Insert | Report		
Create Snapshot	AC 184		File | Export, select SNP as file type	Export, select SNP as file type	
Create Table	AC 17	Tables object | Create table in Design view or Create table by using wizard	Insert | Table		
Crosstab Query	AC 104	New Object button arrow | Query	Insert | Query		
Default Value	AC 142	Default Value property box			
Delete Field	AC 130	Delete Rows button	Edit | Delete	Delete Rows	DELETE
Delete Group of Records	AC 138	Query Type button arrow | Delete Query	Query | Delete Query	Query Type | Delete Query	
Delete Record	AC 125	Delete Record button	Edit | Delete Record	Delete Record	DELETE
Exclude Duplicates	AC 87	Properties button	View | Properties | Unique Values Only	Properties | Unique Values Only	
Exclude Field from Query Results	AC 78	Show check box			
Expand Subdatasheet	AC 153	Expand indicator (+)			
Export Using Drag-and-Drop	AC 182	Drag object, then drop			
Export Using Export Command	AC 183		File | Export	Export	
Field Size	AC 19, AC 127	Field Size property box			
Field Type	AC 20	Data Type box arrow | appropriate type			Appropriate letter
Filter Records	AC 121, AC 123	Filter By Selection or Filter By Form button	Records | Filter		
Font in Datasheet	AC 133		Format | Font	Font	
Format	AC 144	Format property box			
Format a Calculated Field	AC 98	Properties button	View | Properties	Properties	
Format Datasheet	AC 134		Format | Datasheet	Datasheet	
Group in Query	AC 103	Totals button	View | Totals		

Table 3 Microsoft Office Access 2003 Quick Reference Summary

TASK	PAGE NUMBER	MOUSE	MENU BAR	SHORTCUT MENU	KEYBOARD SHORTCUT
Import	AC 177		File | Get External Data | Import	Import	
Include All Fields in Query	AC 74	Double-click asterisk in field list			
Include Field in Query	AC 71	Double-click field in field list			
Join Properties	AC 94		View | Join Properties	Join Properties	
Key Field	AC 19	Primary Key button	Edit | Primary Key	Primary Key	
Link	AC 180		File | Get External Data | Link Table	Link Tables	
Lookup Field	AC 147	Text box arrow | Lookup Wizard			
Move to First Record	AC 27	First Record button			CTRL+UP ARROW
Move to Last Record	AC 27	Last Record button			CTRL+DOWN ARROW
Move to Next Record	AC 27	Next Record button			DOWN ARROW
Move to Previous Record	AC 27	Previous Record button			UP ARROW
Open Database	AC 26	Open button	File | Open		CTRL+O
Open Form	AC 116	Forms object | Open button		Open	Use ARROW keys to move highlight to name, then press ENTER key
Open Table	AC 26	Tables object | Open button		Open	Use ARROW keys to move highlight to name, then press ENTER key
Preview Table	AC 30	Print Preview button	File | Print Preview	Print Preview	
Print Relationships	AC 151		File | Print Relationships		
Print Report	AC 47	Print button	File | Print	Print	CTRL+P
Print Results of Query	AC 72	Print button	File | Print	Print	CTRL+P
Print Table	AC 30	Print button	File | Print	Print	CTRL+P
Quit Access	AC 50	Close button	File | Exit		ALT+F4
Relationships (Referential Integrity)	AC 150	Relationships button	Tools | Relationships		
Remove Filter	AC 122	Remove Filter button	Records | Remove Filter/Sort		
Resize Column	AC 131	Drag right boundary of field selector	Format | Column Width	Column Width	
Restructure Table	AC 126	Tables object | Design button		Design View	
Return to Select Query Window	AC 72	View button arrow	View | Design View		
Run Query	AC 71	Run button	Query | Run		
Save Form	AC 39	Save button	File | Save		CTRL+S
Save Query	AC 80	Save button	File | Save		CTRL+S
Save Table	AC 21	Save button	File | Save		CTRL+S
Search for Record	AC 117	Find button	Edit | Find		CTRL+F
Select Fields for Report	AC 44	Add Field button or Add All Fields button			
Simple Query Wizard	AC 34	New Object button arrow | Query	Insert | Query		
Sort Data in Query	AC 86	Sort row | Sort row arrow | type of sort			
Sort Records	AC 155	Sort Ascending or Sort Descending button	Records | Sort | Sort Ascending or Sort Descending	Sort Ascending or Sort Descending	

Table 3 Microsoft Office Access 2003 Quick Reference Summary *(continued)*

TASK	PAGE NUMBER	MOUSE	MENU BAR	SHORTCUT MENU	KEYBOARD SHORTCUT
Switch Between Form and Datasheet Views	AC 41, AC 120	View button arrow	View | Datasheet View		
Top-Values Query	AC 89	Top Values button	View | Properties	Properties	
Use AND Criterion	AC 84				Place criteria on same line
Use OR Criterion	AC 85				Place criteria on separate lines
Validation Rule	AC 141	Validation Rule property box			
Validation Text	AC 141	Validation Text property box			

Table 4 Microsoft Office PowerPoint 2003 Quick Reference Summary

TASK	PAGE NUMBER	MOUSE	MENU BAR	SHORTCUT MENU	KEYBOARD SHORTCUT
Animate Text	PPT 114		Slide Show | Custom Animation | Add Effect button		ALT+D | M
Black Slide, End Show	PPT 42		Tools | Options | End with black slide		ALT+T | O | E
Check Spelling	PPT 54	Spelling button on Standard toolbar	Tools | Spelling		F7
Clip Art, Add Animation Effects	PPT 117		Slide Show | Custom Animation		ALT+D | M
Clip Art, Change Size	PPT 109	Format Picture button on Picture toolbar | Size tab	Format | Picture | Size tab	Format Picture | Size tab	ALT+O | I | Size tab
Clip Art, Insert	PPT 101, PPT 104	Insert Clip Art button on Drawing toolbar	Insert | Picture | Clip Art		ALT+I | P | C
Clip Art, Move	PPT 108	Drag			
Delete Text	PPT 56	Cut button on Standard toolbar	Edit | Cut	Cut	CTRL+X or BACKSPACE or DELETE
Demote a Paragraph on Outline tab	PPT 90	Demote button on Outlining toolbar			TAB or ALT+SHIFT+RIGHT ARROW
Design Template	PPT 18	Slide Design button on Formatting toolbar	Format | Slide Design	Slide Design	ALT+O | D
Display a Presentation in Black and White	PPT 57	Color/Grayscale button on Standard toolbar	View | Color/Grayscale | Pure Black and White		ALT+V | C | U
Edit Web Page through Browser	PPT 152	Edit button on Internet Explorer Standard Buttons toolbar	File on browser menu bar | Edit with Microsoft PowerPoint in browser window		ALT+F | D in browser window
E-Mail from PowerPoint	PPT 127	E-mail button on Standard toolbar	File | Send To | Mail Recipient		ALT+F | D | A
End Slide Show	PPT 50			End Show	ESC
Font	PPT 24	Font box arrow on Formatting toolbar	Format | Font	Font	ALT+O | F
Font Color	PPT 24	Font Color button arrow on Formatting toolbar, desired color	Format | Font	Font | Color	ALT+O | F | ALT+C | DOWN ARROW

Table 4 Microsoft Office PowerPoint 2003 Quick Reference Summary

TASK	PAGE NUMBER	MOUSE	MENU BAR	SHORTCUT MENU	KEYBOARD SHORTCUT
Font Size, Decrease	PPT 27	Decrease Font Size button on Formatting toolbar	Format | Font	Font | Size	CTRL+SHIFT+LEFT CARET (<)
Font Size, Increase	PPT 25	Increase Font Size button on Formatting toolbar	Format | Font	Font | Size	CTRL+SHIFT+RIGHT CARET (>)
Header and Footer, Add to Outline Page	PPT 112		View | Header and Footer | Notes and Handouts tab		ALT+V | H | Notes and Handouts tab
Help	PPT 62 and Appendix A	Microsoft PowerPoint Help button on Standard toolbar	Help | Microsoft PowerPoint Help		F1
Italicize	PPT 24	Italic button on Formatting toolbar	Format | Font | Font style	Font | Font style	CTRL+I
Language Bar	PPT 16 and Appendix B	Language Indicator button in tray	Tools | Speech | Speech Recognition		ALT+T | H | H
Move a Paragraph Down	PPT 87	Move Down button on Outlining toolbar			ALT+SHIFT+DOWN ARROW
Move a Paragraph Up	PPT 87	Move Up button on Outlining toolbar			ALT+SHIFT+UP ARROW
New Slide	PPT 30	New Slide button on Formatting toolbar	Insert | New Slide		CTRL+M
Next Slide	PPT 45	Next Slide button on vertical scroll bar			PAGE DOWN
Normal View	PPT 96	Normal View button at lower-left PowerPoint window	View | Normal		ALT+V | N
Open Presentation	PPT 52	Open button on Standard toolbar	File | Open		CTRL+O
Paragraph Indent, Decrease	PPT 37	Decrease Indent button on Formatting toolbar			SHIFT+TAB or ALT+SHIFT+LEFT ARROW
Paragraph Indent, Increase	PPT 36	Increase Indent button on Formatting toolbar			TAB or ALT+SHIFT+RIGHT ARROW
Preview Presentation as Web Page	PPT 144		File | Web Page Preview		ALT+F | B
Previous Slide	PPT 45	Previous Slide button on vertical scroll bar			PAGE UP
Print a Presentation	PPT 60	Print button on Standard toolbar	File | Print		CTRL+P
Print an Outline	PPT 122		File | Print | Print what box arrow | Outline View		CTRL+P | TAB | TAB | DOWN ARROW | Outline View
Promote a Paragraph on Outline tab	PPT 89	Promote button on Outlining toolbar			SHIFT+TAB or ALT+SHIFT+LEFT ARROW
Publish a Presentation	PPT 154		File | Save as Web Page | Publish | Publish		ALT+F | G | ALT+P | ALT+P
Quit PowerPoint	PPT 50	Close button on title bar or double-click control icon on title bar	File | Exit		ALT+F4 or CTRL+Q
Redo Action	PPT 22	Redo button on Standard toolbar	Edit | Redo		CTRL+Y or ALT+E | R
Save a Presentation	PPT 27	Save button on Standard toolbar	File | Save		CTRL+S
Save as Web Page	PPT 147		File | Save as Web Page		ALT+F | G
Slide Layout	PPT 98		Format | Slide Layout	Slide Layout	ALT+O | L
Slide Show View	PPT 47	Slide Show button at lower-left PowerPoint window	View | Slide Show		F5 or ALT+V | W

Table 4 Microsoft Office PowerPoint 2003 Quick Reference Summary *(continued)*

TASK	PAGE NUMBER	MOUSE	MENU BAR	SHORTCUT MENU	KEYBOARD SHORTCUT
Slide Sorter View	PPT 95	Slide Sorter View button at lower-left PowerPoint window	View | Slide Sorter		ALT+V | D
Spelling Check	PPT 54	Spelling button on Standard toolbar	Tools | Spelling	Spelling	F7
Task Pane	PPT 11		View | Task Pane		ALT+V | K
Toolbar, Reset	Appendix D	Toolbar Options button on toolbar, Add or Remove Buttons, Customize, Toolbars tab		Customize | Toolbars tab	ALT+V | T | C | B
Toolbar, Show Entire	PPT 9	Double-click move handle			
Undo Action	PPT 22	Undo button on Standard toolbar	Edit | Undo		CTRL+Z or ALT+E | U
Web Page, Preview	PPT 144		File | Web Page Preview		ALT+F | B
Zoom Percentage, Increase	PPT 44	Zoom Box arrow on Standard toolbar	View | Zoom		ALT+V | Z

Table 5 Microsoft Office Outlook 2003 Quick Reference Summary

TASK	PAGE NUMBER	MOUSE	MENU BAR	SHORTCUT MENU	KEYBOARD SHORTCUT
Address E-Mail Message	OUT 51	To button			CTRL+SHIFT+B
Attach File to E-Mail Message	OUT 28	Insert File button	Insert | File		ALT+I, L
Compose E-Mail Message	OUT 24	New button	File | New | Mail Message		CTRL+N
Create Contact List	OUT 42	New button	Actions | New Contact	New Contact	CTRL+N | ALT+A, N
Create Distribution List	OUT 54	New button	File | New | Distribution List		CTRL+SHIFT+L
Create E-Mail Signature	OUT 20		Tools | Options		ALT+T, O
Create Personal Folder	OUT 40		File | New | Folder	New Folder	CTRL+SHIFT+E
Create View Filter	OUT 32		View | Arrange By	Custom	ALT+V, A, M
Delete E-Mail Message	OUT 17	Delete button	Edit | Delete	Delete	CTRL+D
Display Contacts in a Category	OUT 49	Find button	Tools | Find		CTRL+E
Find a Contact	OUT 46	Find button	Tools | Find		CTRL+E
Flag E-Mail Messages	OUT 30		Actions | Follow Up	Follow Up	ALT+A, U
Forward E-Mail Message	OUT 16	Forward button	Actions | Forward	Forward	ALT+W
Open E-Mail Message	OUT 11		File | Open	Open	ALT+F, O
Organize Contacts	OUT 48	Organize button	Tools | Organize		ALT+T, Z
Print Contact List	OUT 50	Print button	File | Print		CTRL+P
Print E-Mail Message	OUT 12	Print button	File | Print		CTRL+P
Reply to E-Mail Message	OUT 13	Reply button	Actions | Reply	Reply	ALT+R
Save Contact List as Text File	OUT 56		File | Save As		ALT+F, A
Send E-Mail Message	OUT 29	Send button	File | Send To		ALT+S
Set Message Delivery Options	OUT 34	Options button			ALT+P
Set Message Importance and Sensitivity	OUT 34	Options button			ALT+P
Sort E-Mail Messages	OUT 31		View | Arrange By		ALT+V, A